Communications
in Computer and Information Science   299

Salvatore Greco   Bernadette Bouchon-Meunier
Giulianella Coletti   Mario Fedrizzi
Benedetto Matarazzo   Ronald R. Yager (Eds.)

Advances in Computational Intelligence

14th International Conference
on Information Processing and Management
of Uncertainty in Knowledge-Based Systems
IPMU 2012
Catania, Italy, July 9-13, 2012
Proceedings, Part III

 Springer

Volume Editors

Salvatore Greco
University of Catania, Italy
E-mail: salgreco@unict.it

Bernadette Bouchon-Meunier
University Pierre et Marie Curie, Paris, France
E-mail: bernadette.bouchon-meunier@lip6.fr

Giulianella Coletti
University of Perugia, Italy
E-mail: coletti@dmi.unipg.it

Mario Fedrizzi
University of Trento, Italy
E-mail: mario.fedrizzi@unitn.it

Benedetto Matarazzo
University of Catania, Italy
E-mail: matarazz@unict.it

Ronald R. Yager
IONA College, New Rochelle, NY, USA
E-mail: ryager@iona.edu

ISSN 1865-0929   e-ISSN 1865-0937
ISBN 978-3-642-31717-0   e-ISBN 978-3-642-31718-7
DOI 10.1007/978-3-642-31718-7
Springer Heidelberg Dordrecht London New York

Library of Congress Control Number: Applied for

CR Subject Classification (1998): I.2, H.3, F.1, H.4, I.5, I.4, C.2

Typesetting: Camera-ready by author, data conversion by Scientific Publishing Services, Chennai, India

Printed on acid-free paper

Springer is part of Springer Science+Business Media (www.springer.com)

Preface

We are glad to present the proceedings of the IPMU 2012 conference (International Conference on Information Processing and Management of Uncertainty in Knowledge-Based Systems) held in Catania, Italy, during July 9–13, 2012. The IPMU conference is organized every two years with the focus of bringing together scientists working on methods for the management of uncertainty and aggregation of information in intelligent systems. This conference provides a medium for the exchange of ideas between theoreticians and practitioners in these and related areas. This was the 14th edition of the IPMU conference, which started in 1986 and has been held every two years in the following locations in Europe: Paris (1986), Urbino (1988), Paris (1990), Palma de Mallorca (1992), Paris (1994), Granada (1996), Paris (1998), Madrid (2000), Annecy (2002), Perugia (2004), Paris (2006), Malaga (2008), Dortmund (2010). Among the plenary speakers of past IPMU conferences there are three Nobel Prize winners: Kenneth Arrow, Daniel Kahneman, Ilya Prigogine.

The program of IPMU 2012 consisted of six invited talks together with 258 contributed papers, authored by researchers from 36 countries, including the regular track and 35 special sessions. The invited talks were given by the following distinguished researchers: Kalyanmoy Deb (Indian Institute of Technology Kanpur, India), Antonio Di Nola (University of Salerno, Italy), Christophe Marsala (Université Pierre et Marie Curie, France), Roman Slowinski (Poznan University of Technology, Poland), Tomohiro Takagi (Meiji University, Japan), Peter Wakker (Erasmus University, The Netherlands). Michio Sugeno received the Kampé de Fériet Award, granted every two years on the occasion of the IPMU conference, in view of his eminent research contributions to the handling of uncertainty through fuzzy measures and fuzzy integrals, and fuzzy control using fuzzy systems.

The success of such an event is mainly due to the hard work and dedication of a number of people and the collaboration of several institutions. We want to acknowledge the help of the members of the International Program Committee, the additional reviewers, the organizers of special sessions, and the volunteer students. All of them deserve many thanks for having helped to attain the goal of providing a balanced event with a high level of scientific exchange and a pleasant environment. A special mention is deserved by Silvia Angilella, Salvatore Corrente, Fabio Rindone, and Giuseppe Vaccarella, who contributed greatly to the organization of the conference and especially to the review process.

We acknowledge the use of the EasyChair conference system for the paper submission and review. We would also like to thank Alfred Hofmann and Leonie Kunz, and Springer, for providing continuous assistance and ready advice whenever needed.

May 2012

Salvatore Greco
Bernadette Bouchon-Meunier
Giulianella Coletti
Mario Fedrizzi
Benedetto Matarazzo
Ronald R. Yager

Organization

Conference Committee

General Chair

Salvatore Greco — University of Catania, Italy

Co-chairs

Giulianella Coletti — University of Perugia, Italy
Mario Fedrizzi — University of Trento, Italy
Benedetto Matarazzo — University of Catania, Italy

Executive Directors

Bernadette Bouchon-Meunier — LIP6, Paris, France
Ronald R. Yager — Iona College, USA

Special Session Organizers

Alessandro Antonucci
Michal Baczynski
Edurne Barrenechea
Sebastiano Battiato
Jan Bazan
Abdelhamid Bouchachia
Humberto Bustine
David Carfi
Davide Ciucci
Jesus Chamorro
Giulianella Coletti
Didier Coquin
Alfredo Cuzzocrea
Giovanni Battista
    Dagnino
Didier Dubois
Fabrizio Durante
Zied Eloudi
Macarena Espinilla
Gisella Facchinetti
Javier Fernandez
Tommaso Flaminio
Giovanni Gallo

Roberto Ghiselli
    Ricci
Karina Gibert
Giovanni Giuffrida
Michel Grabisch
Przemyslaw
    Grzegorzewski
Maria Letizia Guerra
Francisco Herrera
Balasubramaniam
    Jayaram
Janusz Kacprzyk
Cengiz Kahraman
Cristophe Labreuche
Ioana Leustean
Edwin Lughofer
Enrico Marchioni
Nicolas Marin
Luis Martinez
Pedro Melo-Pinto
Radko Mesiar
Enrique Miranda
Antonio Moreno

Moamar Sayed
    Mouchaweh
Guillermo
    Navarro-Arribas
Vesa Niskanen
Miguel Pagola
Olga Pons
Ana Pradera
Anca Ralescu
Daniel Sanchez
Miquel Sanchez-Marré
Rudolf Seising
Andrzej Skowron
Dominik Slezak
Hung Son Nguyen
Carlo Sempi
Luciano Stefanini
Eulalia Szmidt
Marco Elio Tabacchi
Vicenc Torra
Gracian Trivino
Lionel Valet
Aida Valls

International Program Committee

J. Aczel (Canada)
J. Bezdek (USA)
P. Bonissone (USA)
G. Chen (China)
V. Cross (USA)
B. De Baets (Belgium)
T. Denoeux (France)
M. Detyniecki (France)
A. Di Nola (Italy)
D. Dubois (France)
F. Esteva (Spain)
J. Fodor (Hungary)
S. Galichet (France)
P. Gallinari (France)
M.A. Gil (Spain)
F. Gomide (Brazil)
M. Grabisch (France)
S. Grossberg (USA)
P. Hajek
    (Czech Republic)

L. Hall (USA)
F. Herrera (Spain)
K. Hirota (Japan)
F. Hoffmann (Germany)
J. Kacprzyk (Poland)
A. Kandel (USA)
J. Keller (USA)
F. Klawonn (Germany)
E.P. Klement (Austria)
L. Koczy (Hungary)
V. Kreinovich (USA)
R. Kruse (Germany)
H. Larsen (Denmark)
M.-J. Lesot (France)
T. Martin (UK)
J. Mendel (USA)
R. Mesiar (Slovakia)
S. Moral (Spain)
H.T. Nguyen (USA)
S. Ovchinnikov (USA)

G. Pasi (Italy)
W. Pedrycz (Canada)
V. Piuri (Italy)
O. Pivert (France)
H. Prade (France)
A. Ralescu (USA)
D. Ralescu (USA)
M. Ramdani (Maroc)
E. Ruspini (Spain)
S. Sandri (Brasil)
M. Sato (Japan)
G. Shafer (USA)
P. Shenoy (USA)
P. Sobrevilla (Spain)
M. Sugeno (Japan)
E. Szmidt (Poland)
S. Termini (Italy)
I.B. Turksen (Canada)
S. Zadrozny (Poland)

We thank the precious support of all the referees, which helped to improve the scientific quality of the papers submitted to the conference:

Daniel Abril
Tofigh Allahviranloo
Cecilio Angulo
Alessandro Antonucci
Luca Anzilli
Raouia Ayachi
Michal Baczynski
Valentina Emilia Balas
Rosangela Ballini
Adrian Ban
Mohua Banerjee
Carlos D. Barranco
Sebastiano Battiato
Jan Bazan
Benjamin Bedregal
Gleb Beliakov
Nahla Ben Amor
Sarah Ben Amor
Alessio Benavoli

Ilke Bereketli
Veronica Biazzo
Isabelle Bloch
Fernando Bobillo
Andrea Boccuto
Gloria Bordogna
Silvia Bortot
Imen Boukhris
Juergen Branke
Werner Brockmann
Antoon Bronselaer
Matteo Brunelli
Alberto Bugarín
Humberto Bustince
Tomasa Calvo
Domenico Candeloro
Andrea Capotorti
Marta Cardin
Fabrizio Caruso

Bice Cavallo
Nihan Çetin Demirel
Emre Cevikcan
Mihir Chakraborty
Davide Ciucci
Lavinia Corina Ciungu
Vincent Clivillé
Giulianella Coletti
Dante Conti
Didier Coquin
Giorgio Corani
Chris Cornelis
Miguel Couceiro
Pedro Couto
Alfredo Cuzzocrea
Nuzillard Danielle
Bernard De Baets
Gert De Cooman
Yves De Smet

Table of Contents – Part III

Fuzzy Numbers and Their Applications

Information Processing and Management of Uncertainty in Knowledge-Based Systems

Aggregation Functions

Imprecise Probabilities

Probabilistic Graphical Models with Imprecision: Theory and Applications

Belief Function Theory: Basics and/or Applications

Fuzzy Arithmetics for Fuzzy n-Poles: When Is Interactivity Irrelevant?

Andrea Sgarro and Laura Franzoi

Department of Mathematics and Geosciences
University of Trieste, Italy
sgarro@units.it, laura.franzoi@gmail.com

Abstract. We consider binary operations on fuzzy quantities whose interaction is specified by means of a joint possibility distribution. When and to what extent is this interaction relevant? We discuss the problem and tackle it in the case of fuzzy quantities with a finite support, called below fuzzy n-poles. We give a criterion for total irrelevance, once the two fuzzy operands are specified. We argue that fuzzy arithmetics should take inspiration from the arithmetics of random variables rather than crisp arithmetics, so as to get rid of notational inconsistencies.

Keywords: Fuzzy arithmetics, discrete fuzzy numbers, possibility theory, non-interactivity.

1 Introduction

In this paper we advocate an approach to fuzzy arithmetics which is directly inspired by what happens in the case of *random* numbers (random variables): as we argue below, this allows one to get rid of some notational inconsistencies, or at least notational weaknesses, found in fuzzy arithmetics. To achieve our point, we shall take the chance to discuss and solve (at least limited to a finite setting) a relevant problem: when is the result of a binary (algebraic) operation between two fuzzy quantities independent of the interaction between these quantities?

Let us start from probabilities and take the product of two equidistributed *random* numbers X and Y: of course the result depends on their joint probability distribution, which might range from probabilistic *independence* ($\text{Prob}\{X = x, Y = y\} = \text{Prob}\{X = x\} \times \text{Prob}\{Y = y\}$) to *deterministic equality* ($X = Y$ with probability 1). In the latter case $X \times Y$, X^2 and Y^2 would be equidistributed, while in general $X \times Y$ and X^2 (or Y^2) are genuinely *distinct* random numbers, each one with its own probability distribution. Just as in probability theory one specifies a random number or a random couple by assigning its respective probability distribution, in fuzzy arithmetics a *fuzzy* quantity X may be specified by giving a *possibility distribution* over the real line, and a fuzzy couple XY by giving a *joint* possibility distribution. Then notations as $\text{Poss}\{X = x\}$ or $\text{Poss}\{X = x, Y = y\}$ take the place of $\text{Prob}\{X = x\}$ and $\text{Prob}\{X = x, Y = y\}$ as found in probability theory. Actually, in the literature the "distribution" of

S. Greco et al. (Eds.): IPMU 2012, Part III, CCIS 299, pp. 1–8, 2012.

a fuzzy quantity is often specified by means of a normal[1] fuzzy set: we deem that using possibilities rather than degrees of membership $\mu_X(x)$ or $\mu_{XY}(x, y)$ is more convenient, since it makes it fairer to compare random numbers to fuzzy quantities; anyway, the rules one uses, based on maxima and minima as they are, are the same, and so this paper might be readily converted to the language of sets rather than logic. A consistent approach to fuzzy arithmetics based on joint interactive possibilities and on a generalized form of Zadeh's *extension principle* so as to perform binary operations (cf. (2) below) has been already advocated in the literature, e.g. in [1], [2].

To introduce our point, we take e.g. two fuzzy numbers X and Y with common triangular distribution (a, b, c), $a < b < c$:

$$\text{Poss}\{X = x\} = \text{Poss}\{Y = x\} = \frac{x - a}{b - a} \quad \text{for } a < x \leq b,$$

$$\text{Poss}\{X = x\} = \text{Poss}\{Y = x\} = \frac{c - x}{c - b} \quad \text{for } b \leq x < c, \text{ else } 0$$

(the support is here the open interval $]a, c[$) and consider the two limit cases of *deterministic equality*:

$$\text{Poss}\{X = x, Y = y\} = \text{Poss}\{X = x\} = \text{Poss}\{Y = y\} \quad \text{for } x = y,$$

$$\text{Poss}\{X = x, Y = y\} = 0 \quad \text{for } x \neq y$$

and *non-interactivity*, a notion which is deemed to be an adequate possibilistic analogue for probabilistic independence (cf. e.g. [3]):

$$\text{Poss}\{X = x, Y = y\} = \min\left[\text{Poss}\{X = x\}, \text{Poss}\{Y = y\}\right]$$

If X and Y are non-interactive, the distributions of $X \times Y$ and X^2 (or Y^2) are different if $a < 0$ and $c > 0$, but equal if a and c have the same sign, as shown by straightforward calculations performed according to Zadeh's *extension principle* in its standard form, cf. e.g. [4], [5]. Unfortunately, in fuzzy arithmetics one writes $X \times X$ even to cover the case when the two equidistributed factors are non-interactive, and so $X \times X$ might not be the same as X^2. This is confusing, but we shall show that this source of confusion, which never shows up in probability theory, can be totally removed.

Precisely as happens with random couples, the two *marginal* distributions of the fuzzy quantities X and Y are derivable from their joint distribution, cf. (1) below, but if only the marginal distributions $\text{Poss}\{X = x\}$ and $\text{Poss}\{Y = y\}$ are given, one *cannot* re-construct the joint distribution $\text{Poss}\{X = x, Y = y\}$, unless one has some further information, e.g. that the two fuzzy quantities are non-interactive. The problem we pose is: *when is interactivity irrelevant as to perform a binary operation, e.g. a product $X \times Y$, at least limited to the case of knowing that either deterministic equality or non-interactivity holds true, while*

---

[1] Normal means that at least one of the degrees of membership is equal to 1.

other forms of interactivity are ruled out a priori? Below we will cover in detail the case of "overall" irrelevance and fuzzy n-poles, i.e. fuzzy quantities with a finite support of size n. For a solution cf. below theorem 1 and corollary 1. In ongoing work we are investigating other cases, that cover the continuous case and "partial" irrelevance, i.e. when one knows a priori that there is either non-interactivity or deterministic equality. Actually, to aggregate two pre-assigned marginal distributions, one might resort to the pervasive notion of *copula* [6] in a fuzzy context, and so be able to discuss irrelevance under more flexible assumptions than ours.

Below we prefer to use the less committal terms fuzzy *quantity* or fuzzy n-pole rather than fuzzy *number* (continuous or finite), because in the literature one often demands that the distribution of a fuzzy number verifies certain convexity properties, cf. e.g. and [4], [5]; clearly the notions of irrelevance (complete or partial) as discussed here do have an obvious bearing also upon the arithmetics of fuzzy numbers *stricto sensu*. The present authors deem that one should feel free to speak about finite, countable or continuous fuzzy *numbers*, exactly as one speaks about finite, countable or continuous random numbers, however unruly their distribution might be. Actually, a general principle that we are defending below is that fuzzy arithmetics had be better developed so as to mimic *random* arithmetics rather than *crisp* arithmetics. In the latter an implication such as $x = y \Rightarrow x \times y = x^2$ is quite trivial, but, if one assumes that $X = Y$ simply means[2] that X and Y are equidistributed, whatever their interaction, the corresponding implication is in general *false* both in a random and in a fuzzy setting; cf. above and cf. also the final remark.

Some basic notions are quickly re-taken in the next section; the reader is referred to standard texts on fuzziness and possibilities, e.g. to [3], [5], [4].

2   Preliminaries: α-Slices and α-Chunks

Fuzzy quantities with a finite support are called below n-poles if n is the size of the support. The marginal possibility distributions $\Pi_X = [\mu_1 = 1 \geq \mu_2 \geq \ldots \geq \mu_n]$ and $\Pi_Y = [\nu_1 = 1 \geq \nu_2 \geq \ldots \geq \nu_m]$ are fixed, but the joint distribution $\Pi = \Pi_{XY}$ is not:

$$\pi_{i,j} = \text{Poss}\{X = x_i, Y = y_j\}, \ 1 \leq i \leq n, \ 1 \leq j \leq m \qquad (1)$$

$$\mu_i = \text{Poss}\{X = x_i\} = \max_{1 \leq j \leq m} \pi_{i,j}, \ \nu_j = \text{Poss}\{Y = y_j\} = \max_{1 \leq i \leq n} \pi_{i,j}$$

---

[2] Only a sophistic philosopher would ask whether the two crisp 7's in 7×7 are or are not the "same" 7 and how they "relate" to each other, even if the first is an abscissa, say, while the second is an ordinate, but the corresponding question is inescapable in a random or in a fuzzy setting, since "probably 7 $\times$ probably 7" or "vaguely 7 $\times$ vaguely 7" may yield different results depending on how the two equidistributed factors relate to each other. Probabilists have come to terms quite successfully with this fishy point, and write $X = Y$ only when the two factors are deterministically equal, being contented with something like $P_X = P_Y$ in the case when they are only equidistributed.

Ordering the two marginal distributions as we did entails no real restriction but is quite convenient. Without risk of confusion Π denotes both the joint distribution and the corresponding $n \times m$ matrix with possibility $\pi_{i,j}$ in position (i,j); we think of Π_X as a a column vector ordered bottom down and of Π_Y as row vector ordered left to right. We deal only with joint distributions Π that are *admissible*, i.e. compatible with the two pre-assigned marginal distributions Π_X and Π_Y.

A remarkable case of joint distribution is *non-interactivity* when $\pi_{i,j} = \min[\mu_i, \nu_j]$; observe that in this case all rows and columns in the matrix Π are monotone. One has *drastic* interactivity when the matrix Π is all-zero, save for its top row and its leftmost column which are equal to Π_Y and Π_X, respectively. If X and Y are equidistributed, $\Pi_X = \Pi_Y$, one has *deterministically equality* when the matrix Π is all-zero save for its main diagonal, where $\pi_{i,i} = \mu_i = \nu_i$.

To resume we give the following outline:

Synopsis 1. Admissible joint possibilities: $\mathrm{Poss}\{X = x_i, Y = y_j\} = \pi_{i,j}$ with *the prescribed marginal possibilities*
Marginal possibilities: $\mathrm{Poss}\{X = x_i\} = \max_{1 \le j \le m} \pi_{i,j}$, $\mathrm{Poss}\{Y = y_j\} = \max_{1 \le i \le n} \pi_{i,j}$
Non-interactivity: $\mathrm{Poss}\{X = x_i, Y = y_j\} = \min[\mathrm{Poss}\{X = x_i\}, \mathrm{Poss}\{Y = y_j\}]$
Drastic interactivity: $\pi_{i,j} = 0$ *unless* $i = 1$ *or* $j = 1$; *the top row and the leftmost column of the matrix* Π *are equal to* Π_Y *and* Π_X, *respectively*
Deterministic equality *(only for* $\Pi_X = \Pi_Y$*)*: $\pi_{i,j} = 0$ *unless* $i = j$; *the main diagonal of the matrix* Π *is equal to* $\Pi_Y = \Pi_X$

We shall deal with *binary*[3] operations $Z = X \circ Y$ which take on δ distinct values z, $\delta \le m \times n$:

$$\mathrm{Poss}\{Z = z\} = \max_{x,y:\, x \circ y = z} \mathrm{Poss}\{X = x, Y = y\} \tag{2}$$

Writing degrees of membership rather than possibilities and assuming non-interactivity, one re-finds the formula based on Zadeh's extension principle as usually stated in fuzzy arithmetics, cf. e.g. [4], [5].

As an example, let us have a look at dipoles, $n = m = 2$, assuming $\Pi_X = \Pi_Y$; with $0 < \xi \le 1$, a check shows that there are essentially two cases, i.e. case I:

	y_1	$y_2 = y_m$
x_1	1	ξ
$x_2 = x_n$	ξ	ζ

$0 \le \zeta \le \xi$, which gives non-interactivity for $\zeta = \xi$ and drastic interactivity for $\zeta = 0$, and case II:

	y_1	y_2
x_1	1	τ
x_2	η	ξ

---

[3] We think of the supports of X and Y as ordered according to their possibilities, and not the values they take on. Actually, we shall never explicitly use the fact that the three supports of X, Y and Z are made up of numbers, and so, in this sense, we are slightly generalising with respect to discrete fuzzy numbers as in [7].

$0 \leq \eta \leq \tau \leq \xi$, which gives deterministic equality for $\eta = \tau = 0$ and again non-interactivity for $\eta = \tau = \xi$ (case I and II overlap for $\xi = \zeta = \eta = \tau$).

Let us move to general $n \times m$ joint distributions $\Pi = \Pi_{XY}$. Let r be the number of distinct entries in the join of Π_X and Π_Y and let α be one of these entries: α might occur as a (possibly repeated) component only in Π_X, only in Π_Y or in both Π_X and Π_X. One has

$$r \leq n + m - 1 \tag{3}$$

since $\alpha = 1$ occurs at least once both in Π_X and in Π_Y. We are going to partition the matrix Π into r "slices", one for each α. Note that the following definition involves only Π_X and Π_Y but does *not* involve the joint distribution Π_{XY}. The "geometric" notions defined below serve only to be able to state the lemmas and the theorem of Section 3 in a compact way.

Definition 1. α-slices and α-chunks: *An α-slice is made up of all the positions (i, j) in the matrix Π such that either $[\mu_i = \alpha$ and $\nu_j \geq \alpha]$ or $[\mu_i \geq \alpha$ and $\nu_j = \alpha]$. If α occurs only in Π_X the α-slice is called* horizontal, *if it occurs only in Π_Y the α-slice is called* vertical, *else it is called* angular. *If α occurs in Π_X, a* horizontal α-chunk *is made up of all the positions (i, j) in the α-slice with a fixed i; if α occurs in Π_Y, a* vertical α-chunk *is made up of all the positions (i, j) in the α-slice with a fixed j.*

Only angular slices have both horizontal and vertical chunks, and then each horizontal chunk intersects each vertical one (when we say "intersects", we mean that the intersection is not void); if α has k occurrences in Π_X there are k horizontal α-chunks, if α has h occurrences in Π_Y there are h vertical α-chunks (an angular α-slice might be a rectangle, e.g. this always happens for $\alpha = 1$). As an example with marginal possibilities $1 > \xi > \zeta > \theta$ take:

$$
\begin{array}{c|cccc}
 & 1 & \xi & \xi & \zeta & \theta \\
\hline
1 & \star & \star & \bullet & \\
\zeta & \bullet & \bullet & \bullet & \bullet \\
\theta & & & & \\
\end{array}
\tag{4}
$$

where stars evidence the ξ-slice (a *vertical* slice, because ξ heads only columns, which is partitioned into two vertical chunks, one position each), while bullets evidence the ζ-slice (an angular one, as ζ heads both a column and a row); the latter slice has two chunks, one horizontal and one vertical, intersecting at position $(2, 4)$; the 1-chunk coincides with position $(1,1)$, the angular θ-chunk consists of the bottom row and the right-most column. As a further example let us go back to dipoles, $\xi < 1$: the 1-slice boils down to the single position $(1, 1)$, while the ξ-slice takes over the remaining three positions; in the latter slice there are two ξ-chunks intersecting at position $(2, 2)$, one horizontal and one vertical.

The following lemma, actually a characterization of admissible distributions, is quite obvious, since μ_i is the maximum over its row and ν_j is the maximum over its column:

Lemma 1. *In an admissible joint distribution Π the positions in an α-slice whose entries are equal to α appear in all the horizontal α-chunks if the slice is horizontal, in all the vertical α-chunks if the slice is vertical, and in all the horizontal plus all the vertical α-chunks if the slice is angular; all the remaining entries in the α-slice, if any, are $< \alpha$.*

3   Results and Examples

We come to the key notion in this paper:

Definition 2. Irrelevance: *Given Π_X and Π_Y, the admissible joint distribution Π is irrelevant for the binary operation $\circ$ when the distribution of $Z = X \circ Y$ is the same whatever the admissible Π.*

Definition 3. Stability: *A set of positions (i, j) in Π is called α-stable, if it has the same maximum joint possibility α whatever the admissible joint distribution Π with the pre-assigned marginal distributions Π_X and Π_Y. A partition into δ sets of the $n \times m$ positions (i, j) is called stable if each of its δ sets is α-stable for some of the α's.*

Such a partition will be also called a stable δ-*chotomy* of the matrix Π. From (2) one soon derives:

Lemma 2. *The admissible joint possibility distribution Π is irrelevant with respect to the binary operation $\circ$ if and only if the δ counterimages $\{(i, j) : x_i \circ y_j = z\}$ give back a stable δ-chotomy of the matrix Π.*

The structure of α-stable sets and so of stable δ-chotomies will be made clear by the following two results:

Lemma 3. *A set of positions is α-stable if and only if the following conditions are met: i) it does not intersect any β-slice with $\beta > \alpha$, ii) it includes at least an α-chunk.*

Proof. Sufficiency is obvious, just use lemma 1. We move to necessity. Observe that in the special case of admissible non-interactivity *all* the entries in the β-slices with $\beta > \alpha$ are $> \alpha$, and so i) has to hold. As for ii), assume that the α-slice is horizontal and no horizontal α-chunk is included. Then, if α occurs k times in Π_X there are k positions in distinct rows that are left out. Construct as follows a joint Π that is soon checked to be admissible: Π coincides with non-interactivity outside the α-slice, is all-zero inside the α-slice, save over those k positions where it is equal to α. Clearly, this admissible Π would violate stability. In the case when the α-slice is horizontal or angular one proceeds in a similar way.

Theorem 1. *A δ-chotomy of Π is stable iff each of its δ sets includes at least one α-chunk plus possibly some positions in β-slices with $\beta \leq \alpha$.*

The theorem is a straightforward consequence of Lemma 2 and 3. The corollary below gives a quick way to spot cases when there *cannot* be irrelevance.

Lemma 4. *There are at most* $\max[k,h]$ *disjoint α-stable sets with the same α, where $k = k(\alpha)$ is the number of occurrences of α in Π_X and $h = h(\alpha)$ is the number of its occurrences in Π_Y.*

Proof. Recall that any horizontal α-chunk intersects any vertical α-chunk, and so to have disjoint α-chunks they must be all horizontal or all vertical.

Because of the preceding lemma and of Theorem 1 stable partitions are necessarily δ-chotomies with $\delta \leq \rho$, where

$$\rho \doteq \sum_{1 \leq \iota \leq r} \max[k(\alpha_\iota), h(\alpha_\iota)] \tag{5}$$

Recall that r is the number of distinct components α_i in the join of Π_X ad Π_Y, cf (3), while k and h are defined in Lemma 4. So, one has:

Corollary 1. *A necessary condition for irrelevance is that the operation $\circ$ takes on at most ρ distinct values.*

Example 1. Let $\Pi_X = \Pi_Y = [1 > \mu_2 > \mu_3]$ be given with support $\{3, 2, 1\}$; in this case $\rho = r = 3$; the three slices are angular, each with one horizontal and one vertical chunk (for $\alpha = 1$ the two chunks coincide). We take into account the sum $X + Y$, the product XY, $X \circ Y \doteq X$, the maximum $X \vee Y$, the minimum $X \wedge Y$, $X * Y \doteq XY \wedge 3$, $X \diamond Y \doteq (X + Y) \wedge 3$. The question is: *when does one need to know also joint possibilities to perform the operation?* Sum and product take on too many distinct values, cf. the last corollary, and so the interaction is relevant. It is relevant also for $X * Y$, as the counterimage of 2 is $(3, 2)$ and $(2, 3)$ and so does not include any appropriate chunk, and also for $X \vee Y$, as the two counterimages of 2 and 1 do not include chunks, cf. Theorem 1. Instead, Theorem 1 implies that irrelevance holds for $X \circ Y$, $X \wedge Y$ and $X \diamond Y$. Let us go back to $Z = X \vee Y$; one has $\Pi_Z = [1, \mu_2, \mu_3]$ both for non-interactivity and deterministic equality, as soon checked; instead, if the admissible joint distribution Π is drastic, cf. Section 2, one has $\Pi_Z = [1, 0, 0]$: so, one has only "partial irrelevance", cf. the Introduction.

Final Remark. In fuzzy arithmetics one may come across claims as:

in general $X - X \neq 0$

which means that, when X and Y are equidistributed but non-interactive, in general their difference $X - Y$ is not crisp 0; of course, were they deterministically equal, their difference *would* be equal to crisp 0. We prefer to write

in general $\Pi_X = \Pi_Y$ does not imply $X - Y = $ crisp 0

while of course $X - X$ ($X - Y$ with X and Y deterministically equal) is always crisp 0, precisely as happens in probability. So, once more: to operate on random and fuzzy quantities one should specify quite clearly how they inter-relate. However, theorem 1 tells one that there are special cases when this piece of information is irrelevant; corollary 1 gives a simply way to check that irrelevancy cannot hold, because the binary operation takes on "too many" distinct values.

References

1. Fullér, R., Majlender, P.: On interactive fuzzy numbers. Fuzzy Sets and Systems 143(3), 355–369 (2004)
2. Fullér, R., Majlender, P.: On additions of interactive fuzzy numbers. Acta Polytechnica Hungarica (2), 59–73 (2005)
3. Klir, G.J., Folger, T.A.: Fuzzy sets, uncertainty and information. Prentice Hall (1988)
4. Dubois, D., Prade, H.: Fundamentals of fuzzy sets. Handbooks of fuzzy sets series. Kluwer Academic (2000)
5. Zimmermann, H.J.: Fuzzy set theory–and its applications. Springer (2001)
6. Nelsen, R.B.: An introduction to copulas. Springer (2006)
7. Voxman, W.: Canonical representations of discrete fuzzy numbers. Fuzzy Sets and Systems 118(3), 457–466 (2001)

Possibility and Gradual Number Approaches to Ranking Methods for Random Fuzzy Intervals

Farid Aiche[1] and Didier Dubois[2]

[1] Université Mouloud Mammeri de Tizi-Ouzou, Algeria
[2] IRIT, CNRS and Université de Toulouse, France

Abstract. This paper deals with methods for ranking fuzzy intervals in connection with probabilistic and interval orderings. According to the interpretation of a fuzzy interval, various such extensions can be laid bare. In this paper, we especially consider extensions of probabilistic orderings using possibilistic interpretations of fuzzy intervals, crisp substitutes thereof, and gradual numbers. This framework can encompass the comparison of fuzzy random variables: coupling one form of probabilistic comparison with one form of interval comparison induces a method for ranking random fuzzy intervals.

1 Introduction

The comparison of fuzzy intervals has generated a plethoric literature, unfortunately quite scattered and with many ad hoc proposals. Some authors such as Yuan [21], Wang and Kerre [19] tried to organize the set of existing methods, distinguishing the ones that change fuzzy intervals into precise numbers so as to get a ranking, from the ones that build fuzzy dominance relations. They also proposed some postulates any reasonable fuzzy interval comparison method should satisfy. Another possible guiding line for classifying comparison methods is to rely on the fact that fuzzy intervals generalize intervals, and represent a form of uncertainty. We can then propose a joint extension of interval and probability distribution comparison [8]. For classical intervals, the so-called interval ordering was proposed by Fishburn [12] and there also exists the canonical ordering induced by the interval extension of the maximum and the minimum. In probability theory, there exists stochastic dominance of the first order and statistical preference relations between random variables. Putting them together leads to recovering known fuzzy interval comparison methods. This point of view also naturally leads to handle the comparison of fuzzy random variables. In a previous article [1] a generalisation of stochastic dominance to random fuzzy intervals was proposed viewing fuzzy intervals as nested classical ones. In the present article, fuzzy intervals are viewed as possibility distributions or as classical intervals of gradual numbers [14]. Defuzzification methods for random fuzzy intervals are also exploited under this point of view.

The paper is organized as follows: in the next Section, we recall some definitions and properties useful for the rest of the paper, namely techniques for

S. Greco et al. (Eds.): IPMU 2012, Part III, CCIS 299, pp. 9–18, 2012.

comparing intervals, probabilistic variables and gradual numbers. In Section 3, we study ranking methods for fuzzy intervals interpreted as possibility distributions or standard intervals of gradual numbers. In Section 4, we define extensions of stochastic dominance and statistical preference to fuzzy random variables using their level cuts and possibility and necessity measures, as well as gradual numbers, and provide some of their properties. In Section 5 we briefly consider extensions of statistical preference. This paper complements another one [1] based on the random set interpretation.

2   Preliminaries

A fuzzy interval can be viewed as a generalized interval [9] and a relaxation of the notion of probability distribution [7]. More precisely there exist basically four interpretations of a fuzzy interval [8]:

1. An ordinal possibility distribution where possibility degrees reflect similarity to plausible values: probabilistic comparisons can be reformulated by changing probability into possibility and necessity [10].
2. A consonant random interval [11]: it is then natural to envisage probabilistic extensions of interval orders (see [3,5]).
3. A standard interval of gradual numbers [14]: then one must define methods for comparing gradual numbers and extend them to intervals thereof.
4. A probability family [7]: one may then consider interval extensions of probability distribution comparisons.

One then obtains an organized range of well-founded fuzzy interval comparison methods (to be compared with one another). This framework also lends itself to the comparison of random fuzzy intervals.

In this paper we focus on the first and the third points of view. The second point of view, in connection with first order stochastic dominance, was considered in [1]. Let us recall basic notions of comparison between intervals and random variables, as well as more recent gradual numbers.

2.1   Ranking Intervals

Let $A = [\underline{a}, \overline{a}]$ and $B = [\underline{b}, \overline{b}]$ be two intervals. Thus $\underline{a}, \overline{a}, \underline{b}$ and $\overline{b}$ are real numbers with $\underline{a} \leq \overline{a}$ and $\underline{b} \leq \overline{b}$. The ranking of intervals A and B relies on one of the four relations $>_i, i = 1, 2, 3, 4$, defined as follows:

$$[\underline{a}, \overline{a}] >_1 [\underline{b}, \overline{b}] \Leftrightarrow \underline{a} > \overline{b}; [\underline{a}, \overline{a}] >_2 [\underline{b}, \overline{b}] \Leftrightarrow \underline{a} > \underline{b} \tag{1}$$

$$[\underline{a}, \overline{a}] >_3 [\underline{b}, \overline{b}] \Leftrightarrow \overline{a} > \overline{b}; [\underline{a}, \overline{a}] >_4 [\underline{b}, \overline{b}] \Leftrightarrow \overline{a} > \underline{b}. \tag{2}$$

The relation $>_1$ is the strongest, $>_4$ is the weakest, $>_2$ and $>_3$ are of intermediary strength. Indeed the following properties hold:

- $A >_1 B \Rightarrow A >_2 B \Rightarrow A >_4 B$; $A >_1 B \Rightarrow A >_3 B \Rightarrow A >_4 B$.
- $A \geq_4 B$ if and only if $\neg(B >_1 A)$.

The following known interval comparison techniques can be retrieved:

- The relation $>_1$ is the interval order (Fishburn [12]).
- Interval extension of the usual ordering: $[\underline{a}, \overline{a}] \succeq [\underline{b}, \overline{b}]$ iff $\underline{a} \geq \underline{b}$ and $\overline{a} \geq \overline{b}$. Indeed $A \succeq B$ iff $\max([\underline{a}, \overline{a}], [\underline{b}, \overline{b}]) = [\underline{a}, \overline{a}]$ iff $\min([\underline{a}, \overline{a}], [\underline{b}, \overline{b}]) = [\underline{b}, \overline{b}]$.
- Subjective (pessimistic/optimistic) ordering à la Hurwicz:
  $[\underline{a}, \overline{a}] >_\lambda [\underline{b}, \overline{b}]$ iff $\lambda \underline{a} + (1 - \lambda)\overline{a} > \lambda \underline{b} + (1 - \lambda)\overline{b}$, $\lambda \in [0, 1]$.
  Moreover $A \succ B$ iff $[\underline{a}, \overline{a}] >_\lambda [\underline{b}, \overline{b}], \forall \lambda \in [0, 1]$.

2.2 Comparison of Random Variables

Let $(\Omega \times \Omega, \mathcal{F}, P)$ be a joint probability space. The statistical preference of a random variable $a^\#$ on Ω over another one $b^\#$ is: $P(a^\# > b^\#) = P(\{(\omega, \omega') : a^\#(\omega) > b^\#(\omega')\})$. One often chooses between two kinds of assumptions on random variables, with densities p_a and p_b respectively. They can be:

- Continuous and independent: $P(a^\# > b^\#) = \int_{x>y} p_a(x)p_b(y)dxdy$;
- Functionally related: $P(a^\# > b^\#) = P(\{\omega : a^\#(\omega) > b^\#(\omega)\})(\omega = \omega')$.

From such a valued relation, one may define, for each threshold $1 > \theta \geq 0.5$ relation $>_\theta^P$ between two random variables $a^\#$ and $b^\#$:

$$a^\# >_\theta^P b^\# \quad \Longleftrightarrow \quad P(a^\# > b^\#) > \theta.$$

For continuous random variables and $\theta = 0.5$ one may consider the relation:

$$a^\# >^P b^\# \quad \Longleftrightarrow \quad P(a^\# > b^\#) > P(b^\# > a^\#). \tag{3}$$

This relation $>^P$ may involve cycles (a Condorcet effect). Cycles with length 3 can be eliminated by choosing θ sufficiently high (as in De Baets et al.[7]).

There also exists 1rst order stochastic dominance: $a^\#$ is stochastically dominated by $b^\#$ if $\forall x \in \mathbb{R}$, $P(\{\omega : a^\#(\omega) > x\}) \leq P(\{\omega : b^\#(\omega) > x\})$, in other words, the inequality $F_a(x) \geq F_b(x), \forall x \in \mathbb{R}$ holds between cumulative distributions F_a and F_b of $a^\#$ and $b^\#$ respectively.

Finally, in many applications (e.g. decision theory) comparing random variables comes down to comparing the mean values of $a^\#$ and $b^\#$ (or their transforms by a monotonic function).

2.3 Comparison of Gradual Numbers

A gradual number [14] is a mapping $\widetilde{r} : (0, 1] \longrightarrow \mathbb{R}$ that assigns to any positive $\alpha \in (0, 1]$ a real number $\widetilde{r}(\alpha) = r_\alpha$. A typical example of gradual number is the converse of a cumulative probability distribution F^{-1} that is used in Monte-Carlo simulations, namely for any randomly chosen α a real value $F^{-1}(\alpha)$ is computed. However there is no monotonicity requirement for gradual numbers, which cannot be interpreted as membership functions.

Let $\widetilde{r}$ and $\widetilde{s}$ be two gradual numbers. The comparison between gradual numbers can be based on any of the following approaches:

– A partial ordering between $\tilde{r}$ and $\tilde{s}$ is naturally defined as

$$\tilde{r} \geq \tilde{s} \text{ iff } r_\alpha \geq s_\alpha, \forall \alpha \in (0, 1]. \tag{4}$$

In some way, it generalizes stochastic dominance of probability distributions to non-monotonic functions $]0, 1] \longrightarrow \mathbb{R}$.

– Comparing gradual numbers can also be achieved by evaluating the length of zones in $[0, 1]$ where $r_\alpha > s_\alpha$ and those where $r_\alpha < s_\alpha$:

$$\tilde{r} >^P \tilde{s} \text{ iff } \int_0^1 1_{r_\alpha \geq s_\alpha} d\alpha > \int_0^1 1_{r_\alpha \leq s_\alpha} d\alpha \tag{5}$$

Clearly, if $\tilde{r} = F_X^{-1}, \tilde{s} = F_Y^{-1}$ and variables X and Y are linked in the sense that $y = F_Y^{-1}(F_X(x))$, the statistical preference relation $>^P$ between such random variables is retrieved.

– Another method consists in exploiting the surfaces between gradual numbers:

$$\tilde{r} >^S \tilde{s} \text{ iff } \int_0^1 \max(0, r_\alpha - s_\alpha) d\alpha > \int_0^1 \max(0, s_\alpha - r_\alpha) d\alpha. \tag{6}$$

– Finally, it is natural to summarize a gradual number $\tilde{r}$ by the value $m(\tilde{r}) = \int_0^1 r_\alpha d\alpha$. This evaluation generalizes the mean value of a random variable to gradual numbers. It is easy to check that $\tilde{r} >^S \tilde{s}$ iff $m(\tilde{r}) > m(\tilde{s})$.

3   Ranking Fuzzy Intervals

Definition 1 (Fuzzy intervals [9]). *A fuzzy interval $\widetilde{A}$ is a fuzzy set of real numbers characterized by a membership function $\mu_{\widetilde{A}}$ taking its values on the unit interval such that:*

– $\exists \underline{a}, \overline{a} \geq \underline{a}, \forall x \in [\underline{a}, \overline{a}], \mu_A(x) = 1$.
– $\mu_{\widetilde{A}}(\lambda x_1 + (1 - \lambda)x_2) \geq \min(\mu_{\widetilde{A}}(x_1), \mu_{\widetilde{A}}(x_2)), \forall \lambda \in [0, 1]$ and $\forall x_1, x_2 \in \mathbb{R}$.

The $\alpha-cut$ $\widetilde{A}_\alpha$ of $\widetilde{A}$ is then an interval defined as follows: $\widetilde{A}_\alpha = \{x : \mu_{\widetilde{A}}(x) \geq \alpha\} = [\underline{a}_\alpha, \overline{a}_\alpha]$, where $\underline{a}_\alpha = \inf \widetilde{A}_\alpha$ and $\overline{a}_\alpha = \sup \widetilde{A}_\alpha$ In this Section, we consider fuzzy intervals as possibility distributions and classical intervals of gradual numbers and recall the corresponding ranking methods.

3.1   Ranking Ordinal Possibility Distributions

Consider $\widetilde{A}, \widetilde{B}$ two fuzzy intervals with membership functions $\mu_{\widetilde{A}}$ and $\mu_{\widetilde{B}}$ respectively. The possibility and necessity of $\widetilde{A} \leq \widetilde{B}$, denoted respectively by $pos(\widetilde{A} \leq \widetilde{B})$ and $nec(\widetilde{A} \leq \widetilde{B})$ are well-known [10] and defined as follows:

$$pos(\widetilde{A} \geq \widetilde{B}) = \sup_{x \geq y}(\min(\mu_{\widetilde{A}}(x), \mu_{\widetilde{B}}(y))); \tag{7}$$

$$nec(\widetilde{A} > \widetilde{B}) = 1 - pos(\widetilde{A} \leq \widetilde{B}) = 1 - \sup_{x \leq y}(\min(\mu_{\widetilde{A}}(x), \mu_{\widetilde{B}}(y)) \tag{8}$$

They are the possibilistic counterparts of statistical preference relations, and such that $nec(\tilde{A} > \tilde{B}) > 0 \implies pos(\tilde{A} > \tilde{B}) = 1$. It is obvious [6] that the following connections with interval order hold:

1. $pos(\tilde{A} \geq \tilde{B}) \geq \alpha$ iff $\tilde{A}_\alpha \geq_4 \tilde{B}_\alpha$ iff $\bar{a}_\alpha \geq \underline{b}_\alpha$
2. $nec(\tilde{A} \geq \tilde{B}) \geq \alpha$ iff $\tilde{A}_{1-\alpha} \geq_1 \tilde{B}_{1-\alpha}$ iff $\underline{a}_{1-\alpha} \geq \bar{b}_{1-\alpha}$

To retrieve other relations $>_2, >_3$ let us express them as follows on intervals: $A >_2 B$ if $\forall x \in A, \exists y \in B : x > y$ and $A >_3 B$ if $\exists x \in A, \forall y \in B : x > y$ (for $A >_1 B$ and $A >_4 B$, one must use $\forall$ twice and $\exists$ twice respectively).

The gradual extension of $>_2, >_3$ is then:

$$nec_2(\tilde{A} > \tilde{B}) = \inf_x \max(1 - A(x), \sup_{x>y} B(y)); \tag{9}$$

$$pos_3(\tilde{A} > \tilde{B}) = \sup_x \min(A(x), \inf_{x \leq y} 1 - B(y)). \tag{10}$$

Then, as expected: $nec_2(\tilde{A} > \tilde{B}) \geq \alpha$ iff $\tilde{A}_{1-\alpha} \geq_2 \tilde{B}_\alpha$ iff $\underline{a}_{1-\alpha} \geq \underline{b}_\alpha$ and $pos_3(\tilde{A} > \tilde{B}) \geq \alpha$ iff $\tilde{A}_\alpha \geq_3 \tilde{B}_{1-\alpha}$ iff $\bar{a}_\alpha \geq \bar{b}_{1-\alpha}$. Note that $\sup_{x>y} B(y) = pos_3(x > \tilde{B}) = pos(x > \tilde{B})$ and $\inf_{x \leq y} 1 - B(y) = nec_2(x > \tilde{B}) = nec(x > \tilde{B})$.

3.2   Ranking Fuzzy Intervals as Intervals of Gradual Numbers

A fuzzy interval $\tilde{A}$ can be viewed as an interval of gradual numbers obtained by picking a number in each α-cut of $\tilde{A}$. Mappings $\alpha \mapsto \underline{a}_\alpha$ and $\alpha \mapsto \bar{a}_\alpha$ define gradual numbers $\underline{\tilde{a}}$ and $\bar{\tilde{a}}$. A fuzzy interval can thus be viewed as a standard interval of gradual numbers, bounded by $\underline{\tilde{a}}$ and $\bar{\tilde{a}}$ [14]:

$$\tilde{A} = \{\tilde{r} : \underline{a}_\alpha \leq \tilde{r}(\alpha) \leq \bar{a}_\alpha, \forall \alpha \in (0,1]\} = \{\tilde{r} : \underline{\tilde{a}} \leq \tilde{r} \leq \bar{\tilde{a}}\} = \{\tilde{r} : \tilde{r} \in \tilde{A}\}.$$

Then we can retrieve a number of ranking methods as follows:

1. The fuzzy intervals can be compared using interval relations $>_i$ on gradual bounds of $\tilde{A}$ and $\tilde{B}$. Using the partial order $\tilde{r} \geq \tilde{s}$ we define $\tilde{A} \geq_1 \tilde{B}$ as $\underline{a}_\alpha \geq \bar{b}_\alpha, \forall \alpha \in [0,1]$, which enforces $nec(\tilde{A} \geq \tilde{B}) = 1$. Likewise, $\tilde{A} \geq_4 \tilde{B}$ comes down to $poss(\tilde{A} \geq \tilde{B}) = 1$. In contrast, $\tilde{A} \geq_2 \tilde{B}$ reads $\underline{a}_\alpha \geq \underline{b}_\alpha, \forall \alpha \in [0,1]$, i.e., $\underline{\tilde{a}} \geq \underline{\tilde{b}}$ and $\tilde{A} \geq_3 \tilde{B}$ reads $\bar{a}_\alpha \geq \bar{b}_\alpha, \forall \alpha \in [0,1]$, i.e., $\bar{\tilde{a}} \geq \bar{\tilde{b}}$.
   Joining these two relations, one retrieves $\tilde{A} \succeq \tilde{B}$ if and only if $\widetilde{\max}(\tilde{A}, \tilde{B}) = \tilde{A}$, where $\widetilde{\max}$ is the function max extended to fuzzy intervals. The Hurwicz criterion can also be extended to a partial order: $\tilde{A} \geq_\lambda \tilde{B}$ if $\forall \alpha \in (0,1] : \lambda \underline{a}_\alpha + (1-\lambda)\bar{a}_\alpha \geq \lambda \underline{b}_\alpha + (1-\lambda)\bar{b}_\alpha$. It can be read $\lambda \underline{\tilde{a}} + (1-\lambda)\bar{\tilde{a}} \geq \lambda \underline{\tilde{b}} + (1-\lambda)\bar{\tilde{b}}$.
2. Some defuzzification-based ranking methods can be interpreted in the gradual number setting. For instance, Yager index [20] replaces $\tilde{A}$ by the scalar value:

$$Y(\tilde{A}) = \int_0^1 \left(\frac{\bar{a}_\alpha + \underline{a}_\alpha}{2}\right) d\alpha. \tag{11}$$

It can be retrieved as the mean value $m(\frac{\underline{\tilde{a}} + \bar{\tilde{a}}}{2})$ of the gradual mid-point $\alpha \mapsto \frac{\bar{a}_\alpha + \underline{a}_\alpha}{2}$. The approach by L. Campos, A. Munoz [2] is also retrieved by computing the Hurwicz-like index, that takes the form $m(\lambda \underline{\tilde{a}} + (1-\lambda)\bar{\tilde{a}})$.

3. The order relation $>^S$ based on comparisons of surfaces between gradual numbers is used by Fortemps and Roubens [13] among many others. The method they propose comes down to separately comparing $\underline{\tilde{a}}$ and $\underline{\tilde{b}}$, then $\overline{\tilde{a}}$ and $\overline{\tilde{b}}$ by $>^S$ (by surfaces $\int_0^1 \max(0, \underline{a}_\alpha - \underline{b}_\alpha)d\alpha$, etc., as in (6)) and finally compare the sum of these contributions. It is equivalent to checking if $m(\frac{\underline{\tilde{a}}+\overline{\tilde{a}}}{2}) \geq m(\frac{\underline{\tilde{b}}+\overline{\tilde{b}}}{2})$.

4   Stochastic Dominance of Fuzzy Random Variables

Fuzzy random variables were first introduced by Kwakernaak [16] as follows:

Definition 2. *A fuzzy random variable $\widetilde{X}^\#$ is a function from a probability space (Ω, F, P) to a set of fuzzy intervals $FI(\mathbb{R})$ assigning to each $\omega \in \Omega$ a fuzzy interval $\widetilde{X}(\omega)$.*

Given the α-cut $\widetilde{X}_\alpha(\omega) = [\underline{\tilde{x}}_\alpha(\omega), \overline{\tilde{x}}_\alpha(\omega)]$, it holds $\underline{\tilde{x}}_\alpha(\omega) = \inf \{x/X(\omega)(x) \geq \alpha\}$, $\overline{\tilde{x}}_\alpha(\omega) = \sup \{x/X(\omega)(x) \geq \alpha\}$. They are dependent real random variables (via the choice of ω). In the following we generalize stochastic dominance to fuzzy random variables, using specific orderings of fuzzy intervals, based on possibility and necessity of dominance, and based on gradual numbers.

4.1   Stochastic Dominance of Fuzzy Random Variables Using Possibilty and Necessity

Let $\widetilde{A}^\#$ and $\widetilde{B}^\#$ be two fuzzy random variables and α-pos and β-nec denote respectively α-pos*sibly* and β-nec*essarily*.

1. $\widetilde{A}^\# \leq^{s.d}_{(\alpha\text{-pos},\beta\text{-nec})} \widetilde{B}^\#$ ($\widetilde{A}^\#$ is $(\alpha\text{-pos}, \beta\text{-nec})$-stochastically dominated by $\widetilde{B}^\#$)
   if: $P\left\{\omega : pos(\widetilde{A}(\omega) > x) \geq \alpha\right\} \leq P\left\{\omega : nec(\widetilde{B}(\omega) > x) \geq \beta\right\}, \forall x \in \mathbb{R}$

2. $\widetilde{A}^\# \leq^{s.d}_{(\alpha\text{-pos},\beta\text{-pos})} \widetilde{B}^\#$ ($\widetilde{A}^\#$ is $(\alpha\text{-pos}, \beta\text{-pos})$-stochastically dominated by $\widetilde{B}^\#$)
   if $P\left\{\omega : pos(\widetilde{A}(\omega) > x) \geq \alpha\right\} \leq P\left\{\omega : pos(\widetilde{B}(\omega) > x) \geq \beta\right\}, \forall x \in \mathbb{R}$

3. $\widetilde{A}^\# \leq^{s.d}_{(\alpha\text{-nec},\beta\text{-nec})} \widetilde{B}^\#$ ($\widetilde{A}^\#$ is $(\alpha\text{-nec}, \beta\text{-nec})$-stochastically dominated by $\widetilde{B}^\#$)
   if $P\left\{\omega : nec(\widetilde{A}(\omega) > x) \geq \alpha\right\} \leq P\left\{\omega : nec(\widetilde{B}(\omega) > x) \geq \beta\right\}, \forall x \in \mathbb{R}$

4. $\widetilde{A}^\# \leq^{s.d}_{(\alpha\text{-nec},\beta\text{-pos})} \widetilde{B}^\#$ ($\widetilde{A}^\#$ is $(\alpha\text{-nec}, \beta\text{-pos})$-stochastically dominated by $\widetilde{B}^\#$)
   if $P\left\{\omega : nec(\widetilde{A}(\omega) > x) \geq \alpha\right\} \leq P\left\{\omega : pos(\widetilde{B}(\omega) > x) \geq \beta\right\}, \forall x \in \mathbb{R}$

The form $\leq^{s.d}_{(\alpha\text{-pos},\beta\text{-nec})}$ is the strongest, $\leq^{s.d}_{(\alpha\text{-nec},\beta\text{-pos})}$ is the weakest and $\leq^{s.d}_{(\alpha\text{-pos},\beta\text{-pos})}$ and $\leq^{s.d}_{(\alpha\text{-nec},\beta\text{-nec})}$ are intermediary, due to the implications between them as follows:

Proposition 1. *Let $\widetilde{A}^\#$ and $\widetilde{B}^\#$ be two fuzzy random variables on a probability space (Ω, F, P) and α, β two real numbers in the interval $]0, 1]$. We have then:*

1. $\widetilde{A}^{\#} \leq^{s.d}_{(\alpha\text{-}pos,\beta\text{-}nec)} \widetilde{B}^{\#} \Rightarrow \widetilde{A}^{\#} \leq^{s.d}_{(\alpha\text{-}nec,\beta\text{-}nec)} \widetilde{B}^{\#} \Rightarrow \widetilde{A}^{\#} \leq^{s.d}_{(\alpha\text{-}nec,\beta\text{-}pos)} \widetilde{B}^{\#}.$

2. $\widetilde{A}^{\#} \leq^{s.d}_{(\alpha\text{-}pos,\beta\text{-}nec)} \widetilde{B}^{\#} \Rightarrow \widetilde{A}^{\#} \leq^{s.d}_{(\alpha\text{-}pos,\beta\text{-}pos)} \widetilde{B}^{\#} \Rightarrow \widetilde{A}^{\#} \leq^{s.d}_{(\alpha\text{-}nec,\beta\text{-}pos)} \widetilde{B}^{\#}.$

3. $\widetilde{A}^{\#} \leq^{s.d}_{(\alpha\text{-}q,\beta\text{-}nec)} \widetilde{B}^{\#} \Rightarrow \widetilde{A}^{\#} \leq^{s.d}_{(\alpha\text{-}q,\beta\text{-}pos)} \widetilde{B}^{\#},\ \forall q \in \{pos, nec\},\ \forall \alpha, \beta \in [0,1]$

4. $\widetilde{A}^{\#} \leq^{s.d}_{(\alpha\text{-}pos,\beta\text{-}r)} \widetilde{B}^{\#} \Rightarrow \widetilde{A}^{\#} \leq^{s.d}_{(\alpha\text{-}nec,\beta\text{-}r)} \widetilde{B}^{\#},\ \forall r \in \{pos, nec\},\ \forall \alpha, \beta \in [0,1]$

For given any $q \in \{pos, nec\}$ and $r \in \{pos, nec\}$, the relation $\leq^{s.d}_{(\alpha\text{-}q,\beta\text{-}r)}$ becomes stricter when α decreases and/or β increases.

Proposition 2. 1. $\widetilde{A}^{\#} \leq^{s.d}_{(\alpha\text{-}q,\beta\text{-}r)} \widetilde{B}^{\#} \Rightarrow \widetilde{A}^{\#} \leq^{s.d}_{(\gamma\text{-}q,\beta\text{-}r)} \widetilde{B}^{\#},\ \forall q, r \in \{pos, nec\}$
and $\forall \alpha, \beta, \gamma \in [0,1]$ such that $\gamma \geq \alpha$.

2. $\widetilde{A}^{\#} \leq^{s.d}_{(\alpha\text{-}q,\beta\text{-}r)} \widetilde{B}^{\#} \Rightarrow \widetilde{A}^{\#} \leq^{s.d}_{(\alpha\text{-}q,\delta\text{-}r)} \widetilde{B}^{\#},\ \forall q, r \in \{pos, nec\}$ and $\forall \alpha, \beta, \delta \in [0,1]$ such that $\delta \leq \beta$.

3. $\widetilde{A}^{\#} \leq^{s.d}_{(\alpha\text{-}q,\beta\text{-}r)} \widetilde{B}^{\#} \Rightarrow \widetilde{A}^{\#} \leq^{s.d}_{(\gamma\text{-}q,\delta\text{-}r)} \widetilde{B}^{\#},\ \forall \alpha, \beta, \gamma, \delta \in [0,1]$ such that $\gamma \geq \alpha$
and $\delta \leq \beta$.

Proposition 3. The relations $\leq^{s.d}_{(\alpha\text{-}p,\beta\text{-}q)}$, $p, q \in \{pos, nec\}$ are transitive under some assumptions:

1. $\widetilde{A}^{\#} \leq^{s.d}_{(\alpha\text{-}q,\beta\text{-}r)} \widetilde{B}^{\#}$ and $\widetilde{B}^{\#} \leq^{s.d}_{(\gamma\text{-}r,\delta\text{-}t)} \widetilde{C}^{\#}$ implies $\widetilde{A}^{\#} \leq^{s.d}_{(\alpha\text{-}q,\delta\text{-}t)} \widetilde{C}^{\#}$.
for all $q, r, t \in \{pos, nec\}$ and $\alpha, \beta, \gamma, \delta \in [0,1]$ such that $\gamma \leq \beta$.

2. $\widetilde{A}^{\#} \leq^{s.d}_{(\alpha\text{-}q,\beta\text{-}nec)} \widetilde{B}^{\#}$ and $\widetilde{B}^{\#} \leq^{s.d}_{(\gamma\text{-}pos,\delta\text{-}t)} \widetilde{C}^{\#}$ implies $\widetilde{A}^{\#} \leq^{s.d}_{(\alpha\text{-}q,\delta\text{-}t)} \widetilde{C}^{\#}$.
for all $q, t \in \{pos, nec\}$ and $\alpha, \beta, \gamma, \delta \in [0,1]$ such that $\gamma \leq \beta$.

Relations between stochastic dominance of fuzzy random variables using possibility and necessity and stochastic dominance of random intervals can be proved (note that $P(\widetilde{A}^{\#}_{\alpha} >_1 x) = P(\widetilde{A}^{\#}_{\alpha} >_2 x)$ and $P(\widetilde{A}^{\#}_{\alpha} >_3 x) = P(\widetilde{A}^{\#}_{\alpha} >_4 x)$):

Proposition 4. Let $\widetilde{A}^{\#}$ and $\widetilde{B}^{\#}$ be two fuzzy random variables. $\forall \alpha \in (0,1)$:

1. $\widetilde{A}^{\#} \leq^{s.d}_{(\alpha\text{-}pos,(1-\alpha)\text{-}nec)} \widetilde{B}^{\#}$ iff $P(\widetilde{A}_{\alpha} >_3 x) \leq P(\widetilde{B}_{\alpha} >_1 x), \forall x \in \mathbb{R}$

2. $\widetilde{A}^{\#} \leq^{s.d}_{(\alpha\text{-}pos,\alpha\text{-}pos)} \widetilde{B}^{\#}$ iff $P(\widetilde{A}_{\alpha} >_3 x) \leq P(\widetilde{B}_{\alpha} >_3 x), \forall x \in \mathbb{R}$

3. $\widetilde{A}^{\#} \leq^{s.d}_{((1-\alpha)\text{-}nec,(1-\alpha)\text{-}nec)} \widetilde{B}^{\#}$ iff $P(\widetilde{A}_{\alpha} >_1 x) \leq P(\widetilde{B}_{\alpha} >_1 x), \forall x \in \mathbb{R}$

4. $\widetilde{A}^{\#} \leq^{s.d}_{((1-\alpha)\text{-}nec,\alpha\text{-}pos)} \widetilde{B}^{\#}$ iff $P(\widetilde{A}_{\alpha} >_1 x) \leq P(\widetilde{B}_{\alpha} >_3 x), \forall x \in \mathbb{R}$

4.2 Stochastic Dominance of Fuzzy Random Variables Using Gradual Random Variables

As fuzzy random variables take values on fuzzy intervals, they are also random intervals of gradual numbers. We must study gradual random variables.

Definition 3. A gradual random variable $\widetilde{s}^{\#}$ is a function $\omega \mapsto \widetilde{s}(\omega)$ from a probability space (Ω, F, P) to a set of gradual numbers $GN(\mathbb{R})$.

Remark. For $\omega \in \Omega$, $\tilde{s}(\omega)$ is a gradual number, thus $\forall \alpha \in (0,1]$, $\tilde{s}(\omega)(\alpha)$ is a real number that we denote by $s_\alpha(\omega)$. Consequently $\forall \alpha \in (0,1]$, $\tilde{s}_\alpha^\#$ is a real random variable on (Ω, F, P).

Using definitions of stochastic dominance of real random variables and ranking methods for gradual numbers, we define stochastic dominance of gradual random variables as follows:

Definition 4. Let $\tilde{t}^\#$ and $\tilde{s}^\#$ be two gradual random variables. $\tilde{t}^\#$ is stochastically dominated by $\tilde{s}^\#$, denoted by $\tilde{t}^\# \leq_{s.d} \tilde{s}^\#$ if $\forall \alpha \in (0,1]$, $P\{\omega : t_\alpha(\omega) > x\} \leq P\{\omega : s_\alpha(\omega) > x\}$, $\forall x \in \mathbb{R}$.

In other words the stochastic dominance of a gradual random variable $\tilde{t}^\#$ by another one $\tilde{s}^\#$ is equivalent to the stochastic dominance of the real random variable t_α by s_α, $\forall \alpha \in (0,1]$

Using properties of possibility and necessity, we establish a connection between stochastic dominance of fuzzy random variables, using possibility and necessity and stochastic dominance of random gradual numbers.

Proposition 5. For any two fuzzy random variables $\tilde{A}^\#$ and $\tilde{B}^\#$, $\forall \alpha, \beta \in (0,1)$:

- $\tilde{A}^\# \leq_{(\alpha\text{-}pos,\beta\text{-}nec)}^{s.d} \tilde{B}^\#$ iff $(\overline{\tilde{a}}^\#)_\alpha \leq_{s.d} (\underline{\tilde{b}}^\#)_{1-\beta}$;
- $\tilde{A}^\# \leq_{(\alpha\text{-}pos,\beta\text{-}pos)}^{s.d} \tilde{B}^\#$ iff $(\overline{\tilde{a}}^\#)_\alpha \leq_{s.d} (\overline{\tilde{b}}^\#)_\beta$;
- $\tilde{A}^\# \leq_{(\alpha\text{-}nec,\beta\text{-}nec)}^{s.d} \tilde{B}^\#$ iff $(\underline{\tilde{a}}^\#)_{1-\alpha} \leq_{s.d} (\underline{\tilde{b}}^\#)_{1-\beta}$;
- $\tilde{A}^\# \leq_{(\alpha\text{-}nec,\beta\text{-}pos)}^{s.d} \tilde{B}^\#$ iff $(\underline{\tilde{a}}^\#)_{1-\alpha} \leq_{s.d} (\overline{\tilde{b}}^\#)_\beta$.

A form of stochastic dominance between fuzzy random variables can be obtained by stochastic dominance of fuzzy gradual numbers $\underline{\tilde{a}}^\#$ and $\overline{\tilde{a}}^\#$ bounding them. Four ordering relations $\tilde{A}^\# >_{s.d}^i \tilde{B}^\#$ are obtained, that extend relations $>_i, i = 1, 2, 3, 4$:

- $\tilde{A}^\# \geq_{s.d.}^1 \tilde{B}^\# \iff \forall \tilde{r}^\# \in \tilde{A}^\#, \forall \tilde{s}^\# \in \tilde{B}^\#, \tilde{r}^\# \geq_{s.d} \tilde{s}^\#$, i.e., $\underline{\tilde{a}}^\# \geq_{s.d} \overline{\tilde{b}}^\#$;
- $\tilde{A}^\# \geq_{s.d.}^2 \tilde{B}^\# \iff \forall \tilde{r}^\# \in \tilde{A}^\#, \exists \tilde{s}^\# \in \tilde{B}^\#, \tilde{r}^\# \geq_{s.d} \tilde{s}^\#$, i.e., $\underline{\tilde{a}}^\# \geq_{s.d} \underline{\tilde{b}}^\#$;
- $\tilde{A}^\# \geq_{s.d.}^3 \tilde{B}^\# \iff \exists \tilde{r}^\# \in \tilde{A}^\#, \forall \tilde{s}^\# \in \tilde{B}^\#, \tilde{r}^\# \geq_{s.d} \tilde{s}^\#$, i.e., $\overline{\tilde{a}}^\# \geq_{s.d} \overline{\tilde{b}}^\#$;
- $\tilde{A}^\# \geq_{s.d.}^4 \tilde{B}^\# \iff \exists \tilde{r}^\# \in \tilde{A}^\#, \exists \tilde{s}^\# \in \tilde{B}^\#, \tilde{r} \geq_{s.d} \tilde{s}^\#$, i.e., $\overline{\tilde{a}}^\# \geq_{s.d} \underline{\tilde{b}}^\#$.

Relations between stochastic dominance of gradual random variables and stochastic dominance of suitable real random variables are clear. For instance, $\tilde{A}^\# \geq_{s.d.}^1 \tilde{B}^\#$ iff $\forall \alpha \in (0,1]$, $(\underline{\tilde{a}}^\#)_\alpha \geq_{s.d} (\overline{\tilde{b}}^\#)_\alpha$. In fact, $\tilde{A}^\# >_{s.d.}^1 \tilde{B}^\#$ is very strong since it implies that $P(\tilde{A}^\# \cap \tilde{B}^\# = \emptyset) = 1$. Similar propositions could be written for the three other relations.

5   Statistical Preference between Fuzzy Random Variables

We only hint the extension of statistical preference to fuzzy random variables, using possibilistic, fuzzy average, and gradual number comparisons.

We can define $P(\tilde{A}^\# >_\theta^P \tilde{B}^\#)$ using possibilistic comparison relations between fuzzy realizations $\tilde{A}(\omega)$ and $\tilde{B}(\omega')$. For instance, a joint extension of $>_\theta^P$ and interval ordering is: $\tilde{A} >_\theta^{1P} \tilde{B}$ if $P(nec(\tilde{A}^\# > \tilde{B}^\#) > nec(\tilde{B}^\# > \tilde{A}^\#)) \geq \theta$, which is affected by the dependence structure between $\tilde{A}(\omega)$ and $\tilde{B}(\omega')$. But $nec(\tilde{A}(\omega) > \tilde{B}(\omega')) > 0$ implies $nec(\tilde{B}(\omega') > \tilde{A}(\omega)) = 0$ so this definition comes down to: $\tilde{A} >_\theta^{1P} \tilde{B} \iff P(nec(\tilde{A}^\# > \tilde{B}^\#) > 0) > \theta$.

Three other notions of statistical preference between fuzzy random variables can be defined, namely, $\tilde{A}^\# >_\theta^{2P} \tilde{B}^\#$ (with valued relation nec_2) $\tilde{A}^\# >_\theta^{3P} \tilde{B}^\#$ (with pos_3) and $\tilde{A}^\# >_\theta^{4P} \tilde{B}^\# \iff \tilde{B}^\# \geq_\theta^{1P} \tilde{A}^\#$ (with pos).

Besides, there are several ways to define an average statistical preference:

1. using the mean value interval $I_m(\tilde{A}) = [\int_0^1 \underline{a}_\alpha d\alpha, \int_0^1 \overline{a}_\alpha d\alpha][11,17]$, we can consider: $P(I_m(\tilde{A}^\#) >_i I_m(\tilde{B}^\#)) > \theta \geq 0.5$, applying any of the four basic interval comparison relations to $I_m(\tilde{A}(\omega))$ and $I_m(\tilde{B}(\omega))$;
2. using the random variable induced by the λ-pessimistic value: $m_\lambda(\tilde{A}^\#)(\omega)$: $P(m_\lambda(\tilde{A}^\#) > m_\lambda(\tilde{B}^\#)) > \theta$;
3. using the fuzzy mean value of the fuzzy random variable: $P(E(\tilde{A}^\#) >_i E(\tilde{B}^\#)) > \theta \geq 0.5, i = 1,2,3,4$, where $E(\tilde{A}^\#) = \int_\Omega \tilde{A}(\omega)dP(\omega)$ is a fuzzy Aumann integral [18].

Using gradual numbers, $P(\tilde{s}^\# > \tilde{r}^\#) \geq \theta$ must be defined first, and there are several possible choices such as:

- using stochastic dominance inside: $P(\{(\omega,\omega') : \forall \alpha, s_\alpha(\omega) > t_\alpha(\omega')\}) \geq \theta$ or yet $\forall \alpha \in (0,1], P(s^{\alpha\#} > r^{\alpha\#}) \geq \theta$, which is a weaker form;
- or with averages: $\int_0^1 P(s^{\alpha\#} > r^{\alpha\#})d\alpha \geq \theta$ or $P(m(\tilde{s})(\omega) >_\theta^P m(\tilde{r})(\omega')\}) > \rho$;
- finally, nesting stochastic prererences: $P(\{(\omega,\omega') : \tilde{s}(\omega) >_\theta^P \tilde{r}(\omega')\}) > \rho$.

On this basis, several statistical preference relations $P(\tilde{A}^\# >_i \tilde{B}^\#) \geq \theta$ between fuzzy random variables $\tilde{A}^\#$ and $\tilde{B}^\#$, based on the four relations $>_i$, can be defined as $P(\tilde{A}^\# >_i \tilde{B}^\#) = P(\tilde{s}^\# > \tilde{r}^\#)$ choosing suitable fuzzy bounds of $\tilde{A}^\#$ and $\tilde{B}^\#$ for $\tilde{s}^\#$ and $\tilde{r}^\#$: for $i = 1$: $\tilde{s}^\# = \underline{\tilde{a}}^\#$ and $\tilde{r}^\# = \overline{\tilde{b}}^\#$; for $i = 2$: $\tilde{s}^\# = \underline{\tilde{a}}^\#$ and $\tilde{r}^\# = \underline{\tilde{b}}^\#$; for $i = 3$: $\tilde{s}^\# = \overline{\tilde{a}}^\#$ and $\tilde{r}^\# = \overline{\tilde{b}}^\#$; for $i = 4$: $\tilde{s}^\# = \overline{\tilde{a}}^\#$ and $\tilde{r}^\# = \underline{\tilde{b}}^\#$.

Finally, the λ-pessimistic value can be used, deriving the gradual random variable $\tilde{m}_\lambda(\tilde{A}(\omega)) = \lambda\underline{\tilde{a}}(\omega) + (1-\lambda)\overline{\tilde{a}}(\omega)$, and computing statistical preference between fuzzy random variables using these random gradual number substitutes.

6   Conclusion

This paper pursues the study of fuzzy interval comparison methods from the point of view of their relations to the comparison of intervals and random variables. While in [1] , we have considered fuzzy intervals as special cases of random intervals, here we consider fuzzy intervals as possibility distributions and as intervals of gradual numbers. Remains to be studied the point of view of imprecise probability on this question. One possible application of this approach to ranking fuzzy intervals is to provide a systematic way of modelling fuzzy stochastic constraints in linear programming problems.

References

1. Aiche, F., Dubois, D.: An Extension of Stochastic Dominance to Fuzzy Random Variables. In: Hüllermeier, E., Kruse, R., Hoffmann, F. (eds.) IPMU 2010. LNCS (LNAI), vol. 6178, pp. 159–168. Springer, Heidelberg (2010)
2. Campos, L., Munoz, A.: A subjective approach for ranking fuzzy numbers. Fuzzy Sets and Systems 29, 145–153 (1989)
3. Chanas, S., Zielinski, P.: Ranking fuzzy intervals in the setting of random sets-further results. Inform. Sci. 117, 191–200 (1999)
4. De Baets, B., De Meyer, H.: On the cycle-transitive comparison of artificially coupled random variables. Int. J. Approximate Reasoning 47, 306–322 (2008)
5. Denoeux, T.: Extending stochastic order to belief functions on the real line. Information Sciences 179, 1362–1376 (2009)
6. Dubois, D.: Linear programming with fuzzy data. In: Bezdek, J.C. (ed.) Analysis of Fuzzy Information, vol. III, pp. 241–263. CRC Press (1987)
7. Dubois, D.: Possibility theory and statistical reasoning. Comput. Stat. & Data Anal. 51, 47–69 (2006)
8. Dubois, D.: The role of fuzzy sets in decision sciences: Old techniques and new directions. Fuzzy Sets and Systems 184(1), 3–28 (2011)
9. Dubois, D., Prade, H.: Operations on fuzzy numbers. Int. J. of Systems Science 30, 613–626 (1978)
10. Dubois, D., Prade, H.: Ranking fuzzy numbers in the setting of possibility theory. Information Sciences 30, 183–224 (2003)
11. Dubois, D., Prade, H.: The mean value of a fuzzy number. Fuzzy Sets and Systems 24, 279–300 (1987), 42, 87–101 (1991)
12. Fishburn, P.: Interval Orderings. Wiley, NewYork (1987)
13. Fortemps, P., Roubens, M.: Ranking and defuzzification methods based on area compensation. Fuzzy Sets and Systems 82, 319–330 (1996)
14. Fortin, J., Dubois, D., Fargier, H.: Gradual Numbers and Their Application to Fuzzy Interval Analysis. IEEE Trans. Fuzzy Systems 16, 388–402 (2008)
15. Kruse, R., Meyer, K.D.: Statistics with Vague Data. D. Reidel Publishing Company, Dordrecht (1987)
16. Kwakernaak, H.: Fuzzy random variables, II. Inform. Sci. 17, 253–278 (1979)
17. Ogura, Y., Li, S.-M., Ralescu, D.A.: Set Defuzzification and Choquet Integral. Int. J. of Uncertainty, Fuzziness and Knowledge-Based Systems 9, 1–12 (2001)
18. Puri, M.L., Ralescu, D.: Fuzzy random variables. J. Math. Anal. and Appl. 114, 409–420 (1986)
19. Wang, X., Kerre, E.E.: Reasonable properties for ordering of fuzzy quantities. Fuzzy Sets and Systems 118, 375–406 (2001)
20. Yager, R.R.: Ranking fuzzy subsets over the unit interval. In: Proc. IEEE Int. Conf. on Decision and Control, pp. 1435–1437 (1978)
21. Yuan, Y.: Criteria for evaluating fuzzy ranking methods of the unit interval. Fuzzy Sets and Systems 57, 295–311 (1991)

On Mean Value and Variance of Interval-Valued Fuzzy Numbers

Christer Carlsson[1], Robert Fullér[2,1], and József Mezei[1]

[1] IAMSR, Åbo Akademi University,
Joukahaisenkatu 3-5 A, FIN-20520 Turku
[2] Institute of Intelligent Engineering Systems, John von Neumann Faculty of Informatics
Óbuda University, Bécsi út 96/b, H-1034 Budapest, Hungary
{christer.carlsson,robert.fuller,jmezei}@abo.fi

Abstract. In this paper we introduce an interval-valued mean for interval-valued fuzzy numbers. We also define a variance for interval-valued fuzzy numbers. We discuss some basic properties of the new concepts. The mean value and variance can be utilized as a ranking method for interval-valued fuzzy numbers.

1 Introduction

The concepts of mean value and variance play a fundamental role in probability and possibility theory. In probability theory these basic characteristics of distributions can be defined as expected values of specific functions of the random variables. Dubois [8] showed that some concepts (e.g. mean value) in statistics can naturally be interpreted in the context of possibility theory. In possibility theory, there exist several ways to define mean value and variance of fuzzy numbers, for example, Dubois and Prade [5] defined an interval-valued expectation of fuzzy numbers, viewing them as consonant random sets; Yoshida et al. [22] introduced a possibility mean, a necessity mean and a credibility mean of fuzzy numbers; Liu [13] proposed a novel concept of expected value for normalized fuzzy variables motivated by the theory of Choquet integrals. Grzegorzewski [10] defined the mean value of intuitionistic fuzzy numbers. Dubois et al. [7] defined the potential variance of a symmetric fuzzy interval.

Carlsson and Fullér [3] defined the basic characteristics of fuzzy numbers based on Laplace's principle of Insufficient Reason: the possibilistic mean value (variance) of a fuzzy number is the weighted average of probabilistic mean values (variances) of the respective uniform distributions on the level sets of the fuzzy number. In this paper we extend the results of [4] and generalize the definitions of [3] to a wider class of fuzzy sets, namely interval-valued fuzzy numbers (IVFN's). In 2010 Zhang and Jiang [24] introduced the notations of weighted possibilistic mean and variance of IVFN's. The definitions introduced in [24] are significantly different from the results of this paper: we present a different approach to extend the mean value and variance using a different structure of level-sets.

IVFN's (and in general type-2 fuzzy sets) are extensively used in different problems of decision-making [21,15] and in financial modelling (stock index forecasting [11], time to market prediction [1]). On the other hand, there are only a few quantitative

S. Greco et al. (Eds.): IPMU 2012, Part III, CCIS 299, pp. 19–28, 2012.

methods to rank IVFN's [20] which makes the use of this type of modelling difficult in many situations. In this paper we show that the mean value and variance can be used to obtain a ranking method for IVNF's satisfying some reasonable properties.

This paper is organized as follows. After recalling some preliminary concepts in Sect. 2, the crisp and interval-valued mean value of an IVFN are defined in Sect. 3. In Sect. 4, we introduce the concept of variance for IVFN's as the generalization of the possibilistic variance. The new definitions are illustred in Sect. 5 where we employ them for a project selection problem. Finally, conclusions are presented in Sect. 6.

2   Interval-Valued Fuzzy Numbers

A *fuzzy number* A is a fuzzy set in $\mathbb{R}$ with a normal, fuzzy convex and continuous membership function of bounded support. The family of fuzzy numbers is denoted by $\mathcal{F}$. Fuzzy numbers can be considered as possibility distributions. An interval-valued fuzzy set is defined by a mapping A from the universe X to the set of closed intervals of $[0, 1]$ [6]. Let $A(u) = [A_*(u), A^*(u)]$, where A_* and A^* are called lower fuzzy set and upper fuzzy set of A, respectively. An interval-valued fuzzy set is said to be an *interval-valued fuzzy number*, if A^* and A_* are fuzzy numbers [16]. The family of interval-valued fuzzy numbers will be denoted by IVFN. An IVFN is also a special case of type-2 fuzzy sets introduced by Zadeh [23].

For the γ-level sets of A_* and A^* we will use the notations $[A_*]^\gamma = [a_1(\gamma), a_2(\gamma)]$, $[A^*]^\gamma = [A_1(\gamma), A_2(\gamma)]$ and $[A]^\gamma = ([A_*]^\gamma, [A^*]^\gamma)$. If $A, B \in$ IVFN, then their sum $A + B$ is defined by the max-min extension principle, with lower fuzzy set $A_* + B_*$ and upper fuzzy set $A^* + B^*$, that is,

$$[A + B]^\gamma = ([A_* + B_*]^\gamma, [A^* + B^*]^\gamma) = [A]^\gamma + [B]^\gamma$$

for all $\gamma \in [0, 1]$.

If $A \in$ IVFN, then $B \in \mathcal{F}$ is an embedded fuzzy number of A if

$$A_*(u) \le B(u) \le A^*(u),$$

for all $u \in \mathbb{R}$. The set of all the embedded fuzzy numbers of $A \in$ IVFN will be denoted by $\mathcal{F}(A)$.

The class of interval-valued fuzzy numbers can be characterized using a different concept of level-sets introduced in [16]: the $[\gamma_1, \gamma_2]$-level set of $A \in$ IVFN is defined as

$$A_{[\gamma_1,\gamma_2]} = \{x \in X : A_*(x) \ge \gamma_1, A^*(x) \ge \gamma_2\} = [A_L([\gamma_1, \gamma_2]), A_U([\gamma_1, \gamma_2])].$$

An interval-valued fuzzy set, A, is an interval-valued fuzzy number if

1. A is normal, i.e., there exists $x_0 \in \mathbb{R}$, such that $A(x_0) = [1, 1]$,
2. For arbitrary $[\gamma_1, \gamma_2] \in [I] - [0, 0]$, $A_{[\lambda_1, \lambda_2]}$ is a closed bounded interval.

We obtain the same class of IVFN's if we use this definition and if we require that A^* and A_* are fuzzy numbers.

Using the definition of $[\gamma_1, \gamma_2]$-level set, Zhang and Jiang [24] introduced the f-weighted interval-valued possibilistic mean of $A \in$ IVFN as

$$E_f(A) = [E_f^-(A), E_f^+(A)],$$

where

$$E_f^-(A) = \int_0^1 \int_{\gamma_1}^1 A_L([\gamma_1, \gamma_2]) f([\gamma_1, \gamma_2]) \mathrm{d}\gamma_2 \mathrm{d}\gamma_1$$

and

$$E_f^+(A) = \int_0^1 \int_{\gamma_1}^1 A_U([\gamma_1, \gamma_2]) f([\gamma_1, \gamma_2]) \mathrm{d}\gamma_2 \mathrm{d}\gamma_1.$$

In this definition $f : [I] \to \mathbb{R}$ is a non-negative, monotone increasing weighting function which satisfies the normalization condition

$$\int_0^1 \int_{\gamma_1}^1 f([\gamma_1, \gamma_2]) \mathrm{d}\gamma_2 \mathrm{d}\gamma_1 = 1.$$

The f-weighted possibilistic mean of A is the arithmetic mean of $E_f^-(A)$ and $E_f^+(A)$ ([24]):

$$\bar{E}_f(A) = \frac{E_f^-(A) + E_f^+(A)}{2}.$$

The authors showed that the f-weighted possibilistic mean is a linear operator.

Additionally, Zhang and Jiang [24] introduced the f-weighted variance of $A \in$ IVFN as

$$\mathrm{Var}_f(A) = \int_0^1 \int_{\gamma_1}^1 \left[\frac{A_U([\gamma_1, \gamma_2]) - A_L([\gamma_1, \gamma_2])}{2} \right]^2 f([\gamma_1, \gamma_2]) \mathrm{d}\gamma_2 \mathrm{d}\gamma_1.$$

3   Mean Value for Interval-Valued Fuzzy Numbers

Following Carlsson, Fullér and Mezei [4] we will introduce a mean value for interval-valued fuzzy numbers.

Definition 1 ([4]). *A mean (or expected) value of $A \in$ IVFN is defined as*

$$E(A) = \int_0^1 \gamma(M(U_\gamma) + M(L_\gamma)) \mathrm{d}\gamma, \tag{1}$$

where U_γ and L_γ are uniform probability distributions defined on $[A^*]^\gamma$ and $[A_*]^\gamma$, respectively, and M stands for the probabilistic mean operator.

It is easy to see that

$$E(A) = \int_0^1 \gamma \frac{A_1(\gamma) + A_2(\gamma) + a_1(\gamma) + a_2(\gamma)}{2} \mathrm{d}\gamma = \frac{E(A^*) + E(A_*)}{2},$$

where $E(A^*)$ and $E(A_*)$ denote the possibilistic mean value of A^* and A_*, respectively, as introduced by Carlsson and Fullér in 2001 [3]. *In other words, the possibilistic mean of an interval-valued fuzzy number is nothing else, but the arithmetic mean of the mean values of its upper and lower fuzzy numbers. If $A = A^* = A_* \in \mathcal{F}$ is an ordinary fuzzy number then this definition collapses into the possibilistic mean value introduced in [3].*

Note 1. Alternatively, we could use a different approach to define the mean value of $A \in$ IVFN by

$$E'(A) = \int_0^1 2\gamma \frac{E(U'_\gamma) + E(L'_\gamma)}{2} d\gamma = \int_0^1 \gamma (E(U'_\gamma) + E(L'_\gamma)) d\gamma,$$

where U'_γ and L'_γ are uniform probability distributions on the $[A_1(\gamma), a_1(\gamma)]$ and $[a_2(\gamma), A_2(\gamma)]$ (possibly degenerate) intervals, respectively. It is easy to see that $E(A) = E'(A)$.

The following lemma shows that the mean operator is linear in the sense of the max-min extended operations addition and multiplication by a scalar on IVFN.

Lemma 1. *If $A, B \in$ IVFN and $c \in \mathbb{R}$, then*

1. $E(cA) = cE(A)$,
2. $E(A + B) = E(A) + E(B)$.

Example 1. *We will calculate the possibilistic mean value of an interval-valued fuzzy number with triangular lower and upper membership functions. The membership function of a triangular fuzzy number A can be written as,*

$$A(x) = \begin{cases} 1 - \dfrac{a - x}{\alpha} & \text{if } a - \alpha \leq x \leq a \\ 1 - \dfrac{x - a}{\beta} & \text{if } a \leq x \leq a + \beta \\ 0 & \text{otherwise} \end{cases}$$

and we use the notation $A = (a, \alpha, \beta)$. An interval-valued fuzzy number $T = (T_*, T^*)$ of triangular form can be represented by six parameters $T = (a, \alpha, \beta; A, \theta, \tau)$ where $T_* = (a, \alpha, \beta)$ stands for its lower fuzzy number and $T^* = (A, \theta, \tau)$ denotes its upper fuzzy number. The γ-level sets of T_* and T^* are

$$[T_*]^\gamma = [a - (1 - \gamma)\alpha, a + (1 - \gamma)\beta]$$

and

$$[T^*]^\gamma = [A - (1 - \gamma)\theta, A + (1 - \gamma)\tau],$$

respectively. We can calculate the possibilistic mean value of T as,

$$E(T) = \frac{E(T^*) + E(T_*)}{2} = \frac{A + a}{2} + \frac{\beta - \alpha}{12} + \frac{\tau - \theta}{12}.$$

In order to define an inter-valued mean value (expectation) of $A \in$ IVFN, we need to consider the possibilistic mean values of all the embedded fuzzy numbers. It is easy to see that the set

$$\{u \in \mathbb{R} \mid \exists B \in \mathcal{F}(A) \text{ such that } E(B) = u\}$$

is an interval. We will use the notations $E^-(A)$ and $E^+(A)$ for the left and right endpoints of this interval, respectively.

Definition 2. *An interval-valued mean (or expected) value of $A \in$ IVFN is defined as*

$$E^I(A) = [E^-(A), E^+(A)].$$

It is easy to see that the embedded fuzzy number with the minimal (maximal) possibilistic mean value is defined by the γ-level sets $[A_1(\gamma), a_2(\gamma)]$ $([a_1(\gamma), A_2(\gamma)])$. Using this, the interval-valued possibilistic mean (or expected) value can be written as

$$E^I(A) = [E^-(A), E^+(A)] = \left[\int_0^1 \gamma(A_1(\gamma) + a_2(\gamma)) d\gamma, \int_0^1 \gamma(a_1(\gamma) + A_2(\gamma)) d\gamma \right].$$

$E^-(A)$ and $E^+(A)$ can be considered as the lower and upper possibilistic mean values of A, respectively. The possibilistic mean value of $A \in$ IVFN is nothing else but the arithmetic mean of the lower and upper mean values of A:

$$E(A) = \frac{E^-(A) + E^+(A)}{2}.$$

The following lemma is a direct consequence of the definition:

Lemma 2. *If $A, B \in$ IVFN and $c \in \mathbb{R}$, then*

1. $E^I(cA) = cE^I(A)$,
2. $E^I(A + B) = E^I(A) + E^I(B)$.

Example 2. *To illustrate the interval-valued expectation of an $A \in$ IVFN and to compare this new definition to the f-weighted interval-valued possibilistic mean, we will use the interval-valued fuzzy number of triangular form from Example 3.1 in [24]. The upper and lower fuzzy numbers of A are defined as*

$$A^*(x) = \begin{cases} 1 - \dfrac{0.3 - x}{0.2} & \text{if } 0.1 \leq x \leq 0.3 \\ 1 - \dfrac{x - 0.3}{2} & \text{if } 0.3 \leq x \leq 2.3 \\ 0 & \text{otherwise} \end{cases}$$

and

$$A_*(x) = \begin{cases} 1 - \dfrac{0.3 - x}{0.1} & \text{if } 0.2 \leq x \leq 0.3 \\ 1 - \dfrac{x - 0.3}{\beta} & \text{if } 0.3 \leq x \leq 0.8 \\ 0 & \text{otherwise} \end{cases}$$

The lower and upper mean values can be calculated as

$$E^-(A) = \int_0^1 \gamma(0.3 - 0.2(1-\gamma) + 0.3 + 0.5(1-\gamma))d\gamma = 0.35$$

and

$$E^+(A) = \int_0^1 \gamma(0.3 - 0.1(1-\gamma) + 0.3 + 2(1-\gamma))d\gamma = 0.617.$$

From this, we obtain that the interval-valued mean of A is $[0.35, 0.617]$ and the crisp mean value is

$$E(A) = \frac{E^-(A) + E^+(A)}{2} = 0.48,$$

while the f-weighted interval-valued possibilistic mean and f-weighted possibilistic mean calculated in [24] are $[0.402, 0.542]$ and 0.472, respectively.

4   Variance for Interval-Valued Fuzzy Numbers

Now we will introduce a variance for interval-valued fuzzy numbers.

Definition 3. *The possibilistic* variance *of $A \in$ IVFN is defined as*

$$\text{Var}(A) = \int_0^1 \gamma(\text{var}(U_\gamma) + \text{var}(L_\gamma))d\gamma, \tag{2}$$

where U_γ and L_γ are uniform probability distributions defined on $[A^*]^\gamma$ and $[A_*]^\gamma$, respectively, and var *stands for the probabilistic variance operator.*

It is easy to see that

$$\text{Var}(A) = \int_0^1 \gamma \frac{(A_1(\gamma) - A_2(\gamma))^2 + (a_1(\gamma) - a_2(\gamma))^2}{12} d\gamma = \frac{\text{Var}(A^*) + \text{Var}(A_*)}{2}$$

where $E(A^*)$ and $E(A_*)$ denote the possibilistic variance of A^* and A_*, respectively, as introduced by Fullér and Majlender in 2003 [9]. *In other words, the possibilistic variance of an interval-valued fuzzy number is nothing else, but the arithmetic mean of the variances of its upper and lower fuzzy numbers.* If $A = A^* = A_* \in \mathcal{F}$ is an ordinary fuzzy number then this definition collapses into the possibilistic variance introduced in [9].

Lemma 3. *If $A, B \in$ IVFN and $c, d \in \mathbb{R}$, then*

1. $\text{Var}(cA + d) = c^2\text{Var}(A)$.
2. *If $A^*(u) \leq B^*(u)$ and $A_*(u) \leq B_*(u)$ for every $u \in \mathbb{R}$, then $\text{Var}(A) \leq \text{Var}(B)$.*

Proof. The lemma follows from the properties of the possibilistic mean value [3]:

$$\text{Var}(cA + d) = \frac{\text{Var}(cA^* + d) + \text{Var}(cA_* + d)}{2}$$

$$= \frac{c^2\text{Var}(A^*) + c^2\text{Var}(A_*)}{2} = c^2\text{Var}(A).$$

The second part follows from the observations that $\text{Var}(A^*) \leq \text{Var}(B^*)$ and $\text{Var}(A_*) \leq \text{Var}(B_*)$.

Example 3. *We will calculate the variance of an interval-valued fuzzy number with tri-angular lower and upper membership functions. The interval-valued fuzzy number $T = (T_*, T^*)$ of triangular form is represented by six parameters $T = (a, \alpha, \beta; A, \theta, \tau)$. We can calculate the variance of T as,*

$$E(T) = \frac{\text{Var}(A^*) + \text{Var}(A_*)}{2} = \frac{(\beta + \alpha)^2 + (\tau + \theta)^2}{24}.$$

Note 2. Using the approach from Note 1, we can define a different concept of variance,

$$\text{Var}'(A) = \int_0^1 2\gamma \frac{\text{var}(U'_\gamma) + \text{var}(L'_\gamma)}{2} d\gamma = \int_0^1 \gamma(\text{var}(U'_\gamma) + \text{var}(L'_\gamma)) d\gamma,$$

where U'_γ and L'_γ are uniform probability distributions on the $[A_1(\gamma), a_1(\gamma)]$ and $[a_2(\gamma), A_2(\gamma)]$ (possibly degenerate) intervals, respectively. It is easy to see that in general, $\text{Var}(A) \neq \text{Var}'(A)$. If $A = A^* = A_* \in \mathcal{F}$, ($A$ is an ordinary fuzzy number), $\text{Var}'(A) = 0$.

5 New Ranking Method for Interval-Valued Fuzzy Numbers

There exist several methods for ranking fuzzy quantities, specifically fuzzy numbers. In [18,19], a set of ordering properties was introduced to analyze ranking methods for fuzzy sets (here we formulate them for interval-valued fuzzy numbers, $A, B, C \in$ IVFN [20]):

A1) For any $A \in$ IVFN : $A \succeq A$.
A2) If $A \succeq B$ and $B \succeq A$, then $A \sim B$.
A3) If $A \succeq B$ and $B \succeq C$, then $A \succeq C$.
A4) If $A \cap B = \emptyset$ and A is on the right of B, then $A \succeq B$.
A5) The order of A and B is not effected by the other $C \in$ IVFN under comparison.
A6) If $A \succeq B$, then $A + C \succeq B + C$.
A7) If $A \succeq B$ and $C \geq 0$, then $AC \succeq BC$.

Wu and Mendel [20] analyzed two ranking methods for interval-valued fuzzy sets. Namely,

1. Mitchell's method [14], which is based on the ranking of randomly chosen embed-ded type-1 fuzzy sets. This method satisfies [A1] and [A4].
2. A centroid-based ranking method, which uses the centroids of all the embedded type-1 fuzzy sets and satisfies the first 5 properties.

The mean value defined in (1) can be utilized as a ranking method for interval-valued fuzzy numbers: Let $A, B \in$ IVFN. Then,

$$A \succeq B \iff E(A) \geq E(B). \tag{3}$$

We can formulate the following proposition.

Proposition 1 ([4]). *Ranking method (3) satisfies the first six properties A1-A6.*

Let $A, B \in$ IVFN. Then,

$$E(A) > E(B) \Rightarrow A \succ B$$

and if

$$E(A) = E(B) \text{ and } \mathrm{Var}(A) < \mathrm{Var}(B) \Rightarrow A \succ B$$

This ranking method for interval-valued fuzzy numbers (considered as a refinement of the ranking method suggested in [4]) can be applied to capital budgeting decisions when the revenues from projects are represented by interval-valued trapezoidal fuzzy numbers (see [4]).

5.1 Project Selection with Interval-Valued Fuzzy Numbers

Many decision problems concern projects in which the cost and benefits accrue over a number of years. If costs and benefits are entirely monetary then we talk about capital budgeting or capital investment decisions. In most of the cases future cash flows (and interest rates) are not known exactly, and decision makers have to work with their estimations, such as 'around $10,000$ in the next few years' (or 'close to 4 %'). Fuzzy numbers appear to be an adequate tool to represent imprecisely given cash flows ([2,12,17]).

In many real-life decision making problems (e.g. portfolio selection), the decision makers have to face a situation when two or more alternatives (projects) offer the same estimated profit (net-present value). In this case the definition of variance can be used: using ranking method (3), we identify the investment opportunities with the highest estimated revenue and if there is more than with the same value, we choose the one with the smallest variance.

Suppose that revenues from projects are represented by interval-valued trapezoidal fuzzy numbers, that is, the lower and upper fuzzy numbers are of trapezoidal form. The membership function of a trapezoidal fuzzy number A can be written as,

$$A(x) = \begin{cases} 1 - \dfrac{a - x}{\alpha} & \text{if } a - \alpha \le x \le a \\ 1 & \text{if } a \le x \le b \\ 1 - \dfrac{x - b}{\beta} & \text{if } b \le x \le b + \beta \\ 0 & \text{otherwise} \end{cases}$$

and we use the notation $A = (a, b, \alpha, \beta)$. An interval-valued fuzzy number $R = (R_*, R^*)$ of trapezoidal form can be represented by eight parameters

$$R = (a, b, \alpha, \beta; A, B, \theta, \tau)$$

where $R_* = (a, b, \alpha, \beta)$ stands for its lower fuzzy number and $R^* = (A, B, \theta, \tau)$ denotes its upper fuzzy number.

Let $R_i = (a_i, b_i, \alpha_i, \beta_i; A_i, B_i, \theta_i, \tau_i)$ be a given net fuzzy cash flow of a project over n periods. We assume that the project starts with an initial investment (cost) X, where $X > 0$ is a crisp number. The fuzzy net present value (FNPV) of the project is computed by,

$$FNPV = \sum_{i=1}^{n} \frac{R_i}{(1+r)^i} - X, \tag{4}$$

where r is the (risk-adjusted) discount rate.

Example 4. *Consider a project with an initial cost of 20 and fuzzy cash flows for 3 periods,* $R_1 = (11, 12, 2, 2; 10, 13, 3, 4)$, $R_2 = (9, 10, 3, 2; 8, 11, 3, 4)$ *and* $R_3 = (3, 4, 3, 3; 2, 6, 4, 4)$. *If the discount rate is 5% then by substituting the discounted fuzzy returns into (4), we obtain the fuzzy net present value:*

$$FNPV = (1.23, 3.95, 7.22, 6.31; -1.49, 7.54, 9.03, 10.89).$$

From (1) it follows that the possibilistic mean value of a trapezoidal interval-valued fuzzy number $R = (a, b, \alpha, \beta; A, B, \theta, \tau)$ *is,*

$$E(A) = \frac{A + B + a + b}{4} + \frac{\beta - \alpha}{12} + \frac{\tau - \theta}{12}.$$

Using this equation, we can calculate the mean value of the fuzzy net present value as $E(FNPV) = 2.89$. *From (2) we can obtain the variance of the fuzzy net present value:* Var $= 13.76$.

Then we can rank projects according to the mean value of their fuzzy net present value and if we find two projects with maximal value, we choose the one with smaller variance.

6 Conclusions

We have introduced the interval-valued expectation for interval-valued fuzzy numbers. The crisp mean value is the arithmetic mean of the lower and upper mean values of the IVFN. We have shown that this mean operator is linear with respect to the extended addition and multiplication by a scalar of interval-valued fuzzy numbers. We also introduced the variance of IVFN's. A ranking method is proposed for interval-valued fuzzy numbers based on their mean value and variance and we showed an application to capital budgeting decisions when the revenues from projects are represented by interval-valued trapezoidal fuzzy numbers.

References

1. Baguley, P., Page, T., Koliza, V., Maropoulos, P.: Time to market prediction using type-2 fuzzy sets. J. Manuf. Tech. Manage. 17, 513–520 (2006)
2. Carlsson, C., Fullér, R.: Capital budgeting problems with fuzzy cash flows. Mathware Soft Comput. 6, 81–89 (1999)

3. Carlsson, C., Fullér, R.: On possibilistic mean value and variance of fuzzy numbers. Fuzzy Set. Syst. 122, 315–326 (2001)
4. Carlsson, C., Fullér, R., Mezei, J.: Project Selection with Interval-Valued Fuzzy Numbers. In: Twelfth IEEE International Symposium on Computational Intelligence and Informatics, CINTI 2011, Budapest, Hungary, pp. 23–26 (November 2011)
5. Dubois, D., Prade, H.: The mean value of a fuzzy number. Fuzzy Set. Syst. 24, 279–300 (1987)
6. Dubois, D., Prade, H.: Interval-valued fuzzy sets, possibility theory and imprecise probability. In: Proceedings of The International Conference in Fuzzy Logic and Technology, Barcelona, Spain, pp. 314–319 (November 2005)
7. Dubois, D., Fargier, H., Fortin, J.: The empirical variance of a set of fuzzy intervals. In: Proceedings of the 2005 IEEE International Conference on Fuzzy Systems, Reno, USA, pp. 885–890 (May 2005)
8. Dubois, D.: Possibility theory and statistical reasoning. Comput. Stat. Data An. 51, 47–69 (2006)
9. Fullér, R., Majlender, P.: On interactive fuzzy numbers. Fuzzy Set. Syst. 143, 355–369 (2003)
10. Grzegorzewski, P.: Distances and Orderings in a Family of Intuitionistic Fuzzy Numbers. In: Proceedings of the of the Third International Conference in Fuzzy Logic and Technology, Eusflat 2003, Zittau, Germany, pp. 223–227 (September 2003)
11. Huarng, K., Yu, H.-K.: A type-2 fuzzy time series model for stock index forecasting. Physica A 353, 445–462 (2005)
12. Kahraman, C., Ruan, D., Tolga, E.: Capital budgeting techniques using discounted fuzzy versus probabilistic cash flows. Inform. Sciences 142, 57–76 (2002)
13. Liu, B., Liu, Y.K.: Expected value of fuzzy variable and fuzzy expected value models. IEEE T. Fuzzy Syst. 10, 445–450 (2002)
14. Mitchell, H.B.: Ranking type-2 fuzzy numbers. IEEE T. Fuzzy Syst. 14, 287–294 (2006)
15. Ozen, T., Garibaldi, J.M.: Effect of type-2 fuzzy membership function shape on modelling variation in human decision making. In: Proceedings of Thee IEEE International Conference on Fuzzy Systems, Budapest, Hungary, pp. 971–976 (July 2004)
16. Wang, G., Li, X.: The applications of interval-valued fuzzy numbers and interval-distribution numbers. Fuzzy Set. Syst. 98, 331–335 (1998)
17. Wang, S.-Y., Lee, C.-F.: A Fuzzy Real Option Valuation Approach To Capital Budgeting Under Uncertainty Environment. Int. J. Inform. Technol. Decis. Mak. 9, 695–713 (2010)
18. Wang, X., Kerre, E.E.: Reasonable properties for the ordering of fuzzy quantities (I). Fuzzy Set. Syst. 118, 375–385 (2001)
19. Wang, X., Kerre, E.E.: Reasonable properties for the ordering of fuzzy quantities (II). Fuzzy Set. Syst. 118, 387–405 (2001)
20. Wu, D., Mendel, J.M.: A comparative study of ranking methods, similarity measures and uncertainty measures for interval type-2 fuzzy sets. Inform. Sciences 179, 1169–1192 (2009)
21. Yager, R.R.: Fuzzy subsets of type II in decisions. Cyber. Syst. 10, 137–159 (1980)
22. Yoshida, Y., Yasuda, M., Nakagami, J.-I., Kurano, M.: A new evaluation of mean value for fuzzy numbers and its application to American put option under uncertainty. Fuzzy Set. Syst. 157, 2614–2626 (2006)
23. Zadeh, L.A.: The concept of a linguistic variable and its application to approximate reasoning-I. Inform. Sciences 8, 199–249 (1975)
24. Zhang, Q.-S., Jiang, S.-Y.: On Weighted Possibilistic Mean, Variance and Correlation of Interval-valued Fuzzy Numbers. Comm. Math. Res. 26, 105–118 (2010)

Metric Properties of the Extended Weighted Semi-trapezoidal Approximations of Fuzzy Numbers and Their Applications

Adrian I. Ban, Alexandru A. Bica, and Lucian Coroianu

Department of Mathematics and Informatics, University of Oradea,
Universității 1, 410087 Oradea, Romania
{aiban,abica,lcoroianu}@uoradea.ro

Abstract. We compute the extended semi-trapezoidal approximation of a given fuzzy number, with respect to the weighted average Euclidean distance. The metric properties of the extended weighted semi-trapezoidal approximation of a fuzzy number, proved in the present article, help us to solve problems of weighted approximations (semi-trapezoidal and semi-triangular) under conditions and to obtain general results of aggregation of the weighted approximations.

Keywords: Fuzzy number, Semi-trapezoidal fuzzy number, Approximation.

1 Introduction

The extended trapezoidal fuzzy number of a fuzzy number was computed and the main properties were studied in [9], [10]. Fuzzy numbers with left-hand $\max\left(0, 1 - |x|^{s_L}\right)$ and right-hand $\max\left(0, 1 - |x|^{s_R}\right)$ type side functions ($s_L, s_R > 0$) were introduced in [8]. In [3], several aspects like computation, metric properties and applications of the extended semi-trapezoidal approximation (also called the extended parametric approximation) of a fuzzy number were discussed. In the present paper we compute the extended weighted semi-trapezoidal aproximation of a fuzzy number, that is the nearest extended semi-trapezoidal fuzzy number of a fuzzy number, with respect to the weighted average Euclidean distance, and we give some important metric properties of it. As possible applications, we point out the benefits in the calculus of the weighted semi-trapezoidal (symmetric semi-trapezoidal, triangular, symmetric triangular) approximations of a given fuzzy number, with additional requirements (see, e.g., [1], [2]). Moreover, we consider an important property of aggregation, as a generalization of some recent results (see [4]).

2 Preliminaries

We consider the α-cut representation of a fuzzy number A, that is

$$A_\alpha = [A_L(\alpha), A_U(\alpha)], \alpha \in [0, 1],$$

S. Greco et al. (Eds.): IPMU 2012, Part III, CCIS 299, pp. 29–38, 2012.

and we denote by $F(\mathbb{R})$ the set of all fuzzy numbers. For $A, B \in F(\mathbb{R}), A_\alpha = [A_L(\alpha), A_U(\alpha)]$ and $B_\alpha = [B_L(\alpha), B_U(\alpha)]$, the quantity $d_\lambda(A, B)$ given by

$$d_\lambda^2(A, B) = \int_0^1 \lambda_L(\alpha)(A_L(\alpha) - B_L(\alpha))^2 d\alpha \qquad (1)$$

$$+ \int_0^1 \lambda_U(\alpha)(A_U(\alpha) - B_U(\alpha))^2 d\alpha$$

where λ_L and λ_U are nonnegative weighted functions such that $\int_0^1 \lambda_L(\alpha) d\alpha > 0$ and $\int_0^1 \lambda_L(\alpha) d\alpha > 0$, defines a weighted distance between A and B (see, e. g., [11]). If $\lambda_L(\alpha) = \lambda_U(\alpha) = 1$, for every $\alpha \in [0, 1]$, then we get the well-known average Euclidean distance between A and B. Many other weighted functions λ_L, λ_U and hence different weighted distances are proposed in the literature (see [7], [13]).

An important subfamily of $F(\mathbb{R})$ is the set of trapezoidal fuzzy numbers. A trapezoidal fuzzy number is a fuzzy number A with linear sides, that is

$$A_L(\alpha) = a - \sigma(1 - \alpha), \qquad (2)$$
$$A_U(\alpha) = b + \beta(1 - \alpha), \alpha \in [0, 1], \qquad (3)$$

where $a, b, \sigma, \beta \in \mathbb{R}, a \leq b, \sigma \geq 0, \beta \geq 0$. In [9] (see also [10], [11]), the notion of extended trapezoidal fuzzy number was introduced to facilitate the calculus of the triangular and trapezoidal approximations of fuzzy numbers. According to [10], an ordered pair of polynomials of degree 0 or 1 is called an extended trapezoidal fuzzy number. In fact, an extended trapezoidal fuzzy number is a pair (A_L, A_U) as in (2), (3), without any additional conditions.

A (s_L, s_R) parametric fuzzy number (see [8]) is a fuzzy number A such that

$$A_L(\alpha) = a - \sigma(1 - \alpha)^{1/s_L} \qquad (4)$$

$$A_U(\alpha) = b + \beta(1 - \alpha)^{1/s_R}, \qquad (5)$$

where $a, b, \sigma, \beta, s_L, s_R \in \mathbb{R}, a \leq b, \sigma \geq 0, \beta \geq 0, s_L > 0, s_R > 0$. The notion of extended trapezoidal fuzzy number is generalized to parametric case in [3]. An extended (s_L, s_R) parametric fuzzy number A is an ordered pair of functions (A_L, A_U) as in (4)-(5), with $s_L > 0, s_R > 0$, but without any other condition on $a, b, \sigma, \beta \in \mathbb{R}$. Throughout this paper we use the more adequate terminology proposed in [12], that is (s_L, s_R) semi-trapezoidal fuzzy number instead of (s_L, s_R) parametric fuzzy number. We denote by $F_T^{s_L, s_R}(\mathbb{R})$ the set of (s_L, s_R) semi-trapezoidal fuzzy numbers, by $F_{s_L, s_R}^e(\mathbb{R})$ the set of extended (s_L, s_R) semi-trapezoidal fuzzy numbers and by $(a, b, \sigma, \beta)_{s_L, s_R}$ an element of $F_{s_L, s_R}^e(\mathbb{R})$. A (s_L, s_R) semi-trapezoidal fuzzy number with $\sigma = \beta$ is called a symmetric (s_L, s_R) semi-trapezoidal fuzzy number. A (s_L, s_R) semi-trapezoidal fuzzy number with $a = b$ is called an (s_L, s_R) semi-triangular fuzzy number. A (s_L, s_R) semi-trapezoidal fuzzy number with $a = b$ and $\sigma = \beta$ is called a symmetric (s_L, s_R) semi-triangular fuzzy number. We denote by $F_S^{s_L, s_R}(\mathbb{R}), F_t^{s_L, s_R}(\mathbb{R})$

and $F_s^{s_L, s_R}(\mathbb{R})$ the set of symmetric (s_L, s_R) semi-trapezoidal, (s_L, s_R) semi-triangular and symmetric (s_L, s_R) semi-triangular fuzzy numbers, respectively.

For the weighted functions λ_L and λ_U let us define the following integrals

$$l = \int_0^1 \lambda_L(\alpha)\, d\alpha \tag{6}$$

$$m = \int_0^1 \lambda_L(\alpha)(1-\alpha)^{1/s_L}\, d\alpha \tag{7}$$

$$n = \int_0^1 \lambda_L(\alpha)(1-\alpha)^{2/s_L}\, d\alpha \tag{8}$$

$$u = \int_0^1 \lambda_U(\alpha)\, d\alpha \tag{9}$$

$$v = \int_0^1 \lambda_U(\alpha)(1-\alpha)^{1/s_R}\, d\alpha \tag{10}$$

$$w = \int_0^1 \lambda_U(\alpha)(1-\alpha)^{2/s_R}\, d\alpha. \tag{11}$$

Because

$$a - \sigma(1-\alpha)^{1/s_L} = \frac{1}{\sqrt{l}}\left(\sqrt{l}a - \frac{m}{\sqrt{l}}\sigma\right) - \sigma\left((1-\alpha)^{1/s_L} - \frac{m}{l}\right)$$

$$b + \beta(1-\alpha)^{1/s_R} = \frac{1}{\sqrt{u}}\left(\sqrt{u}b + \frac{v}{\sqrt{u}}\beta\right) + \beta\left((1-\alpha)^{1/s_R} - \frac{v}{u}\right),$$

for every $\alpha \in [0,1]$, any $A = (a, b, \sigma, \beta)_{s_L, s_R} \in F_{s_L, s_R}^e(\mathbb{R})$ can be represented as

$$A_L(\alpha) = \frac{1}{\sqrt{l}}L - X\left((1-\alpha)^{1/s_L} - \frac{m}{l}\right) \tag{12}$$

$$A_U(\alpha) = \frac{1}{\sqrt{u}}U + Y\left((1-\alpha)^{1/s_R} - \frac{v}{u}\right), \tag{13}$$

where

$$L = a\sqrt{l} - \frac{m}{\sqrt{l}}\sigma \tag{14}$$

$$X = \sigma \tag{15}$$

$$U = b\sqrt{u} + \frac{v}{\sqrt{u}}\beta \tag{16}$$

$$Y = \beta \tag{17}$$

and l, m, u, v are given in (6), (7), (9), (10). Thus, an extended (s_L, s_R) semi-trapezoidal fuzzy number given by (12)-(13) will be denoted by $[L, U, X, Y]_{s_L, s_R}$.

3   Extended Weighted Semi-trapezoidal Approximation of a Fuzzy Number

The extended trapezoidal approximation of a fuzzy number was determined in [10]. The extended (s_L, s_R) semi-trapezoidal approximation of a fuzzy number (together the main metric properties) were studied in [3]. The formulas for calculating the extended weighted (s_L, s_R) semi-trapezoidal approximation of a fuzzy number are given in this section.

To find the extended weighted semi-trapezoidal approximation $A_{s_L,s_R}^{\lambda,e} = (a_e, b_e, \sigma_e, \beta_e)_{s_L,s_R}$ of a fuzzy number A, $A_\alpha = [A_L(\alpha), A_U(\alpha)], \alpha \in [0, 1]$, that is the nearest extended (s_L, s_R) semi-trapezoidal fuzzy number with respect to the metric (1) we must minimize

$$f(a, b, \sigma, \beta) = \int_0^1 \lambda_L(\alpha) \left(A_L(\alpha) - a + \sigma(1-\alpha)^{1/s_L} \right)^2 d\alpha$$
$$+ \int_0^1 \lambda_U(\alpha) \left(A_U(\alpha) - b - \beta(1-\alpha)^{1/s_R} \right)^2 d\alpha,$$

with respect to a, b, σ, β but without any condition on a, b, σ, β. We immediately have

$$f(a, b, \sigma, \beta) = la^2 + n\sigma^2 + ub^2 + w\beta^2 - 2ma\sigma + 2vb\beta$$
$$- 2a \int_0^1 \lambda_L(\alpha) A_L(\alpha) d\alpha + 2\sigma \int_0^1 \lambda_L(\alpha) A_L(\alpha)(1-\alpha)^{1/s_L} d\alpha$$
$$- 2b \int_0^1 \lambda_U(\alpha) A_U(\alpha) d\alpha - 2\beta \int_0^1 \lambda_U(\alpha) A_U(\alpha)(1-\alpha)^{1/s_R} d\alpha$$
$$+ \int_0^1 \lambda_L(\alpha) A_L^2(\alpha) d\alpha + \int_0^1 \lambda_U(\alpha) A_U^2(\alpha) d\alpha.$$

Theorem 1. $A_{s_L,s_R}^{\lambda,e} = (a_e, b_e, \sigma_e, \beta_e)_{s_L,s_R}$, where

$$a_e \doteq \frac{n \int_0^1 \lambda_L(\alpha) A_L(\alpha) d\alpha - m \int_0^1 \lambda_L(\alpha) A_L(\alpha)(1-\alpha)^{1/s_L} d\alpha}{nl - m^2} \tag{18}$$

$$b_e = \frac{w \int_0^1 \lambda_U(\alpha) A_U(\alpha) d\alpha - v \int_0^1 \lambda_U(\alpha) A_U(\alpha)(1-\alpha)^{1/s_R} d\alpha}{uw - v^2} \tag{19}$$

$$\sigma_e = \frac{m \int_0^1 \lambda_L(\alpha) A_L(\alpha) d\alpha - l \int_0^1 \lambda_L(\alpha) A_L(\alpha)(1-\alpha)^{1/s_L} d\alpha}{nl - m^2} \tag{20}$$

$$\beta_e = \frac{-v \int_0^1 \lambda_U(\alpha) A_U(\alpha) d\alpha + u \int_0^1 \lambda_U(\alpha) A_U(\alpha)(1-\alpha)^{1/s_R} d\alpha}{uw - v^2} \tag{21}$$

is the extended weighted (s_L, s_R) semi-trapezoidal approximation of A.

Proof. We obtain $\{a_e, b_e, \sigma_e, \beta_e\}$ given in (18)-(21) as a solution of the system

$$\frac{\partial f}{\partial a} = 2la - 2\int_0^1 \lambda_L(\alpha) A_L(\alpha)\, d\alpha - 2m\sigma = 0 \qquad (22)$$

$$\frac{\partial f}{\partial b} = 2ub - 2\int_0^1 \lambda_U(\alpha) A_U(\alpha)\, d\alpha + 2v\beta = 0 \qquad (23)$$

$$\frac{\partial f}{\partial \sigma} = 2n\sigma + 2\int_0^1 \lambda_L(\alpha) A_L(\alpha)(1-\alpha)^{1/s_L}\, d\alpha - 2ma = 0 \qquad (24)$$

$$\frac{\partial f}{\partial \beta} = 2w\beta - 2\int_0^1 \lambda_U(\alpha) A_U(\alpha)(1-\alpha)^{1/s_R}\, d\alpha + 2vb = 0. \qquad (25)$$

By the Schwarz inequality it follows that

$$\left(\int_0^1 \lambda_L(\alpha)(1-\alpha)^{1/s_L}\, d\alpha\right)^2 \le \int_0^1 \lambda_L(\alpha)\, d\alpha \int_0^1 \lambda_L(\alpha)(1-\alpha)^{2/s_L}\, d\alpha, \quad (26)$$

with equality if and only if $\lambda_L(\alpha) = \lambda_L(\alpha)(1-\alpha)^{2/s_L}$ almost everywhere $\alpha \in [0,1]$. With the notations in (6)-(11) we immediately obtain $nl > m^2$. We prove $uw > v^2$ in the same way. Because

$$\frac{\partial^2 f}{\partial a^2} = 2l > 0,$$

$$\begin{vmatrix} \frac{\partial^2 f}{\partial a^2} & \frac{\partial^2 f}{\partial a \partial b} \\ \frac{\partial^2 f}{\partial b \partial a} & \frac{\partial^2 f}{\partial b^2} \end{vmatrix} = \begin{vmatrix} 2l & 0 \\ 0 & 2u \end{vmatrix} = 4lu > 0$$

$$\begin{vmatrix} \frac{\partial^2 f}{\partial a^2} & \frac{\partial^2 f}{\partial a \partial b} & \frac{\partial^2 f}{\partial a \partial \sigma} \\ \frac{\partial^2 f}{\partial b \partial a} & \frac{\partial^2 f}{\partial b^2} & \frac{\partial^2 f}{\partial b \partial \sigma} \\ \frac{\partial^2 f}{\partial \sigma \partial a} & \frac{\partial^2 f}{\partial \sigma \partial b} & \frac{\partial^2 f}{\partial \sigma^2} \end{vmatrix} = \begin{vmatrix} 2l & 0 & -2m \\ 0 & 2u & 0 \\ -2m & 0 & 2n \end{vmatrix} = 8u\left(nl - m^2\right) > 0$$

$$\begin{vmatrix} \frac{\partial^2 f}{\partial a^2} & \frac{\partial^2 f}{\partial a \partial b} & \frac{\partial^2 f}{\partial a \partial \sigma} & \frac{\partial^2 f}{\partial a \partial \beta} \\ \frac{\partial^2 f}{\partial b \partial a} & \frac{\partial^2 f}{\partial b^2} & \frac{\partial^2 f}{\partial b \partial \sigma} & \frac{\partial^2 f}{\partial b \partial \beta} \\ \frac{\partial^2 f}{\partial \sigma \partial a} & \frac{\partial^2 f}{\partial \sigma \partial b} & \frac{\partial^2 f}{\partial \sigma^2} & \frac{\partial^2 f}{\partial \sigma \partial \beta} \\ \frac{\partial^2 f}{\partial \beta \partial a} & \frac{\partial^2 f}{\partial \beta \partial b} & \frac{\partial^2 f}{\partial \beta \partial \sigma} & \frac{\partial^2 f}{\partial \beta^2} \end{vmatrix} = \begin{vmatrix} 2l & 0 & -2m & 0 \\ 0 & 2u & 0 & 2v \\ -2m & 0 & 2n & 0 \\ 0 & 2v & 0 & 2w \end{vmatrix} = 16\left(nl - m^2\right)\left(uw - v^2\right) > 0.$$

we obtain that $(a_e, b_e, \sigma_e, \beta_e)$ given in (18)-(21) minimize the function f.

Remark 1. If $\lambda_L(\alpha) = \lambda_U(\alpha) = 1, \alpha \in [0,1]$ and $s_L = s_R = 1$ in (18)-(21) we obtain the extended trapezoidal approximation of A (see [10]). If $\lambda_L(\alpha) = \lambda_U(\alpha) = 1, \alpha \in [0,1]$ in (18)-(21) we obtain the extended (s_L, s_R) semi-trapezoidal approximation of A (see [3]).

4   Metric Properties of the Extended Weighted Semi-trapezoidal Approximation

In this section we give some essential metric properties of the extended weighted semi-trapezoidal approximation.

Due to (12)-(13) we have the possibility to write the distance between two extended (s_L, s_R) semi-trapezoidal fuzzy numbers almost like the Euclidean distance in $\mathbb{R}^4$. An application of this result is the proof, similarly with Theorem 8 in [3], of continuity of the weighted-semitrapezoidal approximation. The result was already obtained ([12], Proposition 7.2) by using notions of Convex Analysis.

Theorem 2. *If* $A, B \in F^e_{s_L, s_R}(\mathbb{R})$ *such that* $A = [L_1, U_1, X_1, Y_1]_{s_L, s_R}$ *and* $B = [L_2, U_2, X_2, Y_2]_{s_L, s_R}$ *then*

$$d_\lambda^2(A, B) = (L_1 - L_2)^2 + (U_1 - U_2)^2 \tag{27}$$
$$+ \frac{nl - m^2}{l}(X_1 - X_2)^2 + \frac{uw - v^2}{u}(Y_1 - Y_2)^2.$$

Proof. Because

$$\int_0^1 \lambda_L(\alpha)\left((1 - \alpha)^{1/s_L} - \frac{m}{l}\right) d\alpha = 0$$

and

$$\int_0^1 \lambda_U(\alpha)\left((1 - \alpha)^{1/s_R} - \frac{v}{u}\right) d\alpha = 0$$

we get

$$\int_0^1 \lambda_L(\alpha)(A_L(\alpha) - B_L(\alpha))^2 \, d\alpha$$

$$= \int_0^1 \lambda_L(\alpha)\left(\frac{1}{\sqrt{l}}(L_1 - L_2) + \left((1 - \alpha)^{1/s_L} - \frac{m}{l}\right)(X_1 - X_2)\right)^2 d\alpha$$

$$= \frac{1}{l}(L_1 - L_2)^2 \int_0^1 \lambda_L(\alpha) \, d\alpha$$

$$+ (X_1 - X_2)^2 \int_0^1 \lambda_L(\alpha)\left((1 - \alpha)^{1/s_L} - \frac{m}{l}\right)^2 d\alpha$$

$$+ 2(L_1 - L_2)(X_1 - X_2)\frac{1}{\sqrt{l}}\int_0^1 \lambda_L(\alpha)\left((1 - \alpha)^{1/s_L} - \frac{m}{l}\right) d\alpha$$

$$= (L_1 - L_2)^2 + \frac{nl - m^2}{l}(X_1 - X_2)^2$$

and analogously,

$$\int_0^1 \lambda_U(\alpha)(A_U(\alpha) - B_U(\alpha))^2 \, d\alpha = (U_1 - U_2)^2 + \frac{uw - v^2}{u}(Y_1 - Y_2)^2,$$

therefore (27) is immediate.

Theorem 3. *(i) If* $A \in F(\mathbb{R})$ *and* $A^{\lambda, e}_{s_L, s_R}$ *is the extended weighted semi-trapezoidal approximation of* A *then*

$$d_\lambda^2(A, B) = d_\lambda^2(A, A^{\lambda, e}_{s_L, s_R}) + d_\lambda^2(A^{\lambda, e}_{s_L, s_R}, B), \tag{28}$$

for every $B \in F^e_{s_L,s_R}(\mathbb{R})$.

(ii) If $A, B \in F(\mathbb{R})$ and $A^{\lambda,e}_{s_L,s_R}, B^{\lambda,e}_{s_L,s_R}$ are the extended weighted semi-trapezoidal approximations of A and B, respectively, then

$$d_\lambda(A^{\lambda,e}_{s_L,s_R}, B^{\lambda,e}_{s_L,s_R}) \leq d_\lambda(A, B). \tag{29}$$

Proof. The below equalities are proved as the corresponding equalities in the particular case $\lambda_L(\alpha) = \lambda_L(\alpha) = 1$ (see Appendix B and C in [3])

$$\int_0^1 \lambda_L(\alpha) \left(A_L(\alpha) - \left(A^{\lambda,e}_{s_L,s_R}\right)_L(\alpha) \right) \left(\left(A^{\lambda,e}_{s_L,s_R}\right)_L(\alpha) - B_L(\alpha) \right) d\alpha = 0 \tag{30}$$

$$\int_0^1 \lambda_U(\alpha) \left(A_U(\alpha) - \left(A^{\lambda,e}_{s_L,s_R}\right)_U(\alpha) \right) \left(\left(A^{\lambda,e}_{s_L,s_R}\right)_U(\alpha) - B_U(\alpha) \right) d\alpha = 0 \tag{31}$$

$$\int_0^1 \lambda_L(\alpha) \left(\left(A^{\lambda,e}_{s_L,s_R}\right)_L(\alpha) - \left(B^{\lambda,e}_{s_L,s_R}\right)_L(\alpha) \right) \tag{32}$$

$$\times \left(\left(\left(A^{\lambda,e}_{s_L,s_R}\right)_L(\alpha) - \left(B^{\lambda,e}_{s_L,s_R}\right)_L(\alpha) \right) - \left(A_L(\alpha) - B_L(\alpha)\right) \right) d\alpha = 0$$

$$\int_0^1 \lambda_U(\alpha) \left(\left(A^{\lambda,e}_{s_L,s_R}\right)_U(\alpha) - \left(B^{\lambda,e}_{s_L,s_R}\right)_U(\alpha) \right) \tag{33}$$

$$\times \left(\left(\left(A^{\lambda,e}_{s_L,s_R}\right)_U(\alpha) - \left(B^{\lambda,e}_{s_L,s_R}\right)_U(\alpha) \right) - \left(A_U(\alpha) - B_U(\alpha)\right) \right) d\alpha = 0.$$

(i) We have

$$d^2_\lambda(A, B) = \int_0^1 \lambda_L(\alpha) \left(A_L(\alpha) - \left(A^{\lambda,e}_{s_L,s_R}\right)_L(\alpha) \right)^2 d\alpha$$

$$+ \int_0^1 \lambda_L(\alpha) \left(\left(A^{\lambda,e}_{s_L,s_R}\right)_L(\alpha) - B_L(\alpha) \right)^2 d\alpha$$

$$+2 \int_0^1 \lambda_L(\alpha) \left(A_L(\alpha) - \left(A^{\lambda,e}_{s_L,s_R}\right)_L(\alpha) \right) \left(\left(A^{\lambda,e}_{s_L,s_R}\right)_L(\alpha) - B_L(\alpha) \right) d\alpha$$

$$+ \int_0^1 \lambda_U(\alpha) \left(A_U(\alpha) - \left(A^{\lambda,e}_{s_L,s_R}\right)_U(\alpha) \right)^2 d\alpha$$

$$+ \int_0^1 \lambda_U(\alpha) \left(\left(A^{\lambda,e}_{s_L,s_R}\right)_U(\alpha) - B_U(\alpha) \right)^2 d\alpha$$

$$+2 \int_0^1 \lambda_U(\alpha) \left(A_U(\alpha) - \left(A^{\lambda,e}_{s_L,s_R}\right)_U(\alpha) \right) \left(\left(A^{\lambda,e}_{s_L,s_R}\right)_U(\alpha) - B_U(\alpha) \right) d\alpha$$

and taking into account (1), (30) and (31) we obtain (28).

(ii) We get

$$d_\lambda^2(A,B) = \int_0^1 \lambda_L(\alpha) \left(\left(A_{s_L,s_R}^{\lambda,e}\right)_L(\alpha) - \left(B_{s_L,s_R}^{\lambda,e}\right)_L(\alpha) \right)^2 d\alpha$$

$$+ \int_0^1 \lambda_L(\alpha) \left(\left(\left(A_{s_L,s_R}^{\lambda,e}\right)_L(\alpha) - \left(B_{s_L,s_R}^{\lambda,e}\right)_L(\alpha) \right) - \left(A_L(\alpha) - B_L(\alpha)\right) \right)^2 d\alpha$$

$$- 2 \int_0^1 \lambda_L(\alpha) \left(\left(A_{s_L,s_R}^{\lambda,e}\right)_L(\alpha) - \left(B_{s_L,s_R}^{\lambda,e}\right)_L(\alpha) \right)$$

$$\times \left(\left(\left(A_{s_L,s_R}^{\lambda,e}\right)_L(\alpha) - \left(B_{s_L,s_R}^{\lambda,e}\right)_L(\alpha) \right) - \left(A_L(\alpha) - B_L(\alpha)\right) \right) d\alpha$$

$$+ \int_0^1 \lambda_U(\alpha) \left(\left(A_{s_L,s_R}^{\lambda,e}\right)_U(\alpha) - \left(B_{s_L,s_R}^{\lambda,e}\right)_U(\alpha) \right)^2 d\alpha$$

$$+ \int_0^1 \lambda_U(\alpha) \left(\left(\left(A_{s_L,s_R}^{\lambda,e}\right)_U(\alpha) - \left(B_{s_L,s_R}^{\lambda,e}\right)_U(\alpha) \right) - \left(A_U(\alpha) - B_U(\alpha)\right) \right)^2 d\alpha$$

$$- 2 \int_0^1 \lambda_U(\alpha) \left(\left(A_{s_L,s_R}^{\lambda,e}\right)_U(\alpha) - \left(B_{s_L,s_R}^{\lambda,e}\right)_U(\alpha) \right)$$

$$\times \left(\left(\left(A_{s_L,s_R}^{\lambda,e}\right)_U(\alpha) - \left(B_{s_L,s_R}^{\lambda,e}\right)_U(\alpha) \right) - \left(A_U(\alpha) - B_U(\alpha)\right) \right) d\alpha$$

and taking into account (1), (32) and (33) we immediately obtain (29).

5   Applications

5.1   Weighted Semi-trapezoidal and Semi-triangular Approximations Preserving Parameters

Let us assume that the parameters $P_k, k \in \{1,...,q\}$ are preserved by the extended weighted (s_L, s_R) semi-trapezoidal approximation of a fuzzy number A, that is

$$P_k\left(A_{s_L,s_R}^{\lambda,e}\right) = P_k(A), \forall k \in \{1,...,q\}. \tag{34}$$

Taking into account Theorem 3, (i) we obtain the equivalence of the problem of finding the weighted (s_L, s_R) semi-trapezoidal approximation of a given $A \in F(\mathbb{R})$, that is

$$\min_{B \in F_T^{s_L,s_R}(\mathbb{R})} d_\lambda(A,B)$$

$$P_k(A) = P_k(B), k \in \{1,...,q\}$$

with the following problem

$$\min_{B \in F_T^{s_L,s_R}(\mathbb{R})} d_\lambda\left(A_{s_L,s_R}^{\lambda,e},B\right)$$

$$P_k\left(A_{s_L,s_R}^{\lambda,e}\right) = P_k(B), k \in \{1,...,q\}.$$

In addition, it is easy to see that the optimization problem

$$\min_{B \in F_t^{s_L, s_R}(\mathbb{R})} d_\lambda(A, B)$$

$$P_k(A) = P_k(B), k \in \{1, ..., q\}$$

is equivalent to the following problem

$$\min_{B \in F_t^{s_L, s_R}(\mathbb{R})} d_\lambda(A_{s_L, s_R}^{\lambda, e}, B)$$

$$P_k(A_{s_L, s_R}^{\lambda, e}) = P_k(B), k \in \{1, ..., q\}$$

and similarly in the symmetric case for semi-trapezoidal and semi-triangular approximations. In this way, the computation of the (symmetric) semi-trapezoidal and (symmetric) semi-triangular approximations is simplified.

It is worth noticing here that the classical parameters associated with a fuzzy number (expected value, expected interval, value, ambiguity, etc.) can be easily extended to satisfy (34). As an example, let us consider the weighted value of a fuzzy number A, introduced by

$$Val_\lambda(A) = \int_0^1 \lambda_L(\alpha) \left(1 - (1 - \alpha)^{1/s_L}\right) A_L(\alpha) \, d\alpha$$

$$+ \int_0^1 \lambda_U(\alpha) \left(1 - (1 - \alpha)^{1/s_R}\right) A_U(\alpha) \, d\alpha.$$

If $s_L = s_R = 1$ and $\lambda_L(\alpha) = \lambda_U(\alpha) = 1$ then we get the classical formula of value of a fuzzy number (see [5] or [2]). In addition,

$$Val_\lambda(A_{s_L, s_R}^{\lambda, e}) = Val_\lambda(A),$$

therefore the method described above is applicable.

5.2 Weighted Semi-trapezoidal, Weighted Semi-triangular Approximations and Aggregation

In [4] the trapezoidal approximation of fuzzy numbers is discussed in relation to data aggregation. It is proved that if the average is chosen as the aggregation operator there is no difference whether the trapezoidal approximation is performed before or after aggregation. Among trapezoidal approximations, the nearest trapezoidal fuzzy number and the nearest trapezoidal fuzzy number preserving the expected interval, with respect to d_λ, are considered.

We define the weighted distance between $\{A_1, ..., A_p\} \subset F(\mathbb{R})$ and $B \in F_T^{s_L, s_R}(\mathbb{R})$ as

$$D_\lambda^2(\{A_1, ..., A_p\}, B) = \sum_{i=1}^p d_\lambda^2(A_i, B).$$

Because

$$\left(\frac{1}{p} \cdot (A_1 + ... + A_p)\right)_{s_L, s_R}^{\lambda, e} = \frac{1}{p} \cdot \left((A_1)_{s_L, s_R}^{\lambda, e} + ... + (A_p)_{s_L, s_R}^{\lambda, e}\right)$$

and taking into account (28) we obtain

$$D_\lambda^2 \left(\{A_1, ..., A_p\}, B_1 \right) - D_\lambda^2 \left(\{A_1, ..., A_p\}, B_2 \right)$$

$$= d_\lambda^2 \left(\frac{1}{p} \cdot (A_1 + ... + A_p), B_1 \right) - d_\lambda^2 \left(\frac{1}{p} \cdot (A_1 + ... + A_p), B_2 \right),$$

for every $B_1, B_2 \in F_T^{s_L, s_R}(\mathbb{R})$, as a first step towards a generalization of the result of aggregation in [4].

Acknowledgements. This work was supported by a grant of the Romanian National Authority for Scientific Research, CNCS-UEFISCDI, project number PN-II-ID-PCE-2011-3-0861. The contribution of the third author was possible with the financial support of the Sectoral Operational Programme for Human Resources Development 2007-2013, co-financed by the European Social Fund, under the project number POSDRU/107/1.5/S/76841 with the title "Modern Doctoral Studies: Internationalization and Interdisciplinarity."

References

1. Ban, A.I.: Approximation of fuzzy numbers preserving the expected interval. Fuzzy Sets and Systems 159, 1327–1344 (2008)
2. Ban, A.I., Brândaş, A., Coroianu, L., Negruţiu, C., Nica, O.: Approximations of fuzzy numbers by trapezoidal fuzzy numbers preserving the ambiguity and value. Computers and Mathematics with Applications 61, 1379–1401 (2011)
3. Ban, A.I., Coroianu, L.: Metric properties of the nearest extended parametric fuzzy number and applications. International Journal of Approximate Reasoning 52, 488–500 (2011)
4. Ban, A.I., Coroianu, L., Grzegorzewski, P.: Trapezoidal approximation and aggregation. Fuzzy Sets and Systems 177, 45–59 (2011)
5. Delgado, M., Vila, M.A., Voxman, W.: On a canonical representation of a fuzzy number. Fuzzy Sets and Systems 93, 125–135 (1998)
6. Grzegorzewski, P., Pasternak-Winiarska, K.: Bi-symmetrically weighted trapezoidal approximations of fuzzy numbers. In: 9th Int. Conf. on Intelligent Systems Design and Applications, pp. 318–323. IEEE Press, Washington (2009)
7. Grzegorzewski, P., Pasternak-Winiarska, K.: Weighted trapezoidal approximations of fuzzy numbers. In: Proc. of the Joint Int. Fuzzy Systems Assoc. World Congress and European Soc. of Fuzzy Logic and Techn. Conf., pp. 1531–1534 (2009)
8. Nasibov, E.N., Peker, S.: On the nearest parametric approximation of a fuzzy number. Fuzzy Sets and Systems 159, 1365–1375 (2008)
9. Yeh, C.-T.: A note on trapezoidal approximations of fuzzy numbers. Fuzzy Sets and Systems 158, 747–754 (2007)
10. Yeh, C.-T.: Trapezoidal and triangular approximations preserving the expected interval. Fuzzy Sets and Systems 159, 1345–1353 (2008)
11. Yeh, C.-T.: Weighted trapezoidal and triangular approximations of fuzzy numbers. Fuzzy Sets and Systems 160, 3059–3079 (2009)
12. Yeh, C.-T.: Weighted semi-trapezoidal approximations of fuzzy numbers. Fuzzy Sets and Systems 165, 61–80 (2011)
13. Zeng, W., Li, H.: Weighted triangular approximation of fuzzy numbers. International Journal of Approximate Reasoning 46, 137–150 (2007)

Uncertain Evidence in Bayesian Networks: Presentation and Comparison on a Simple Example

Ali Ben Mrad[1], Veronique Delcroix[2], Mohamed Amine Maalej[1], Sylvain Piechowiak[2], and Mohamed Abid[1]

[1] University of Sfax, Tunisia
ENIS, CES, Sfax, Tunisia
[2] Université Lille Nord de France, F-59000 Lille, France
UVHC, LAMIH UMR 8201, F-59313 Valenciennes, France

Abstract. We consider the problem of reasoning with *uncertain evidence* in Bayesian networks (BN). There are two main cases: the first one, known as *virtual evidence*, is evidence *with* uncertainty, the second, called *soft evidence*, is evidence *of* uncertainty. The initial inference algorithms in BNs are designed to deal with one or several hard evidence or virtual evidence. Several recent propositions about BN deal with soft evidence, but also with ambiguity and vagueness of the evidence. One of the proposals so far advanced is based on the fuzzy theory and called *fuzzy evidence*. The original contribution of this paper is to describe the different types of uncertain evidence with the help of a simple example, to explain the difference between them and to clarify the appropriate context of use.

Keywords: bayesian networks, uncertain evidence, virtual evidence, likelihood evidence, soft evidence, fuzzy evidence.

1 Introduction

Bayesian networks (BN) [Pe88, Je96] are powerful tools for knowledge representation and inference under uncertainty. They combine multiple sources of information to provide a formal framework within which complex systems can be represented and processed. The different sources of information are not always perfect, therefore, the observation can be uncertain and imprecise. For the purpose of this paper, we present five types of evidence: *hard evidence, virtual evidence* (VE), also called likelihood evidence, that is evidence *with* uncertainty [Pe88], *soft evidence* (SE) that is evidence *of* uncertainty [VK02], and two approaches of *fuzzy evidence* [MM11, TL07]. These methods are applied and presented on a simple example. A result of this work is to clarify the distinction between these different types of evidence. The presence of several soft evidences

S. Greco et al. (Eds.): IPMU 2012, Part III, CCIS 299, pp. 39–48, 2012.

has to be treated using specific algorithms. We detail the case of a single evidence and briefly explain the case of several evidences.

2 Different Types of Evidence in Bayesian Networks

2.1 Definitions and Vocabulary

Evidence in BN may be regular or uncertain. Regular evidence, called also hard evidence specifies which value a variable is in. This is the usual way to enter an observation to be propagated in a BN [Pe88, Je96]. Uncertain evidence specifies the probability distribution of a variable. We focus on two types of uncertain evidences. According to [VK02, PZ10], we use the terms *virtual evidence* and *soft evidence* as follows: *virtual evidence* [Pe88] can be interpreted as evidence *with* uncertainty, and can be represented as a likelihood ratio. This kind od evidence is also called *likelihood evidence*. *Soft evidence* [VK02], can be interpreted as evidence *of* uncertainty, and is represented as a probability distribution of one or more variables.

Many BN engines accept a probability distribution as input for the update. Most existing implementations of uncertain evidence are virtual evidence, but the literature is not consistent about naming uncertain evidence. The term *soft evidence* is used in many cases incorrectly as indicated in Table 1. In the cases listed in Table 1, the evidence is considered to be a virtual evidence and is propagated by adding a virtual node.

Table 1. Different Names of the Virtual Evidence (VE) in the BN Engines

BN engines	Names of the VE	Web Site
BNT	Soft evidence	http://www.cs.ubc.ca/~murphyk/ Software/BNT/bnt.html
Bayesialab	Likelihood distribution	http://www.bayesia.com
NETICA	Likelihood	http://www.norsys.com
HUGIN	Likelihood findings	http://www.hugin.com
GeNIe	Soft evidence	http://genie.sis.pitt.edu

2.2 Algorithms Dealing with Uncertain Evidence

The issue of how to deal with uncertain evidence in BN appears in [Pe88] and has recently been the subject of many algorithms developments as indicated in Table 2. To clarify the distinction between the different types of evidence in BN we present in the following sections an illustrative example and the modeling of the different types of evidence.

Table 2. Algorithms dealing with uncertain evidence (VE: virtual evidence, SE: soft evidence)

Algorithms	Type of evidence	References
VE method	VE	[Pe90]
Jeffrey's rule	VE and single SE	[Je83]
IPFP (Iterative Proportional Fitting Procedure)	SE	First appeared in [Kr37] Studied in [Cs75, Fi70, PD05] Extended in [Bo89, Cr00]
The big Clique algorithm and extension	SE	[VK02]
Derived Algorithm Combining VE method, Jeffrey's rule and IPFP	VE and SE	[PZ10]

3 Comparison of Different Types of Evidence with a Simple Example

3.1 Presentation of the "Snow Example"

Our example models the influence of the amount of snow on the congestion (Fig. 1). The variable S represents the "amount of snow in mm" with values in $[0, 120]$ and the variable C represents the "congestion" with values in $\{yes, no\}$.

Fig. 1. Bayesian network graph of the snow example

The conditional probability of C given S is defined by the equation:

$$P(C = yes \mid S) = e^{-\frac{1}{2} \times (\frac{S-60}{40})^2} \tag{1}$$

This probability function can be understood as follows: under the threshold of 60 mm of snow, the congestion is all the more probable that the amount of snow is important. Beyond this threshold, people leave their homes less and less and subsequently the probability of congestion decreases. Whereas some BN engines deal with continuous variables, or even mixted variables, the most common way is to use a discretization of the variable S (see Table 3). The BN engine Netica [Ne] offers the possibility to obtain the Conditional Probability Table (CPT) of the node S discretized from the equation (1). In the following cases, the CPT $P(C|S)$ is conformed to the equation (1), to ensure a proper comparison of results of the different methods. Our starting model is described by the graph presented in Fig. 1 and by the probabilities given in Tables 3 and 4 for the probabilities.

Table 3. $P(S)$

S_1	0	0.6
S_2	]0,40]	0.22
S_3	]40,80]	0.14
S_4	]80,120]	0.04

Table 4. $P(C \mid S)$

	S_1	S_2	S_3	S_4
yes	0.3247	0.6058	0.96	0.6058
no	0.6753	0.3942	0.04	0.3942

We propagate the same observation for the different types of evidence to ensure a good comparison. Assume that the amount of snow is effectively 80 mm. We are going to compute $P(C = yes|e)$, $P(C = yes|ve)$, $P(C = yes|se)$ where e represents an hard evidence, ve denotes a virtual evidence and se denotes a soft evidence. The last two parts concern the case of ambiguity.

3.2 Junction Tree Algorithm

We apply the junction tree inference algorithm [La88, Je90] to different types of evidence. We will trace the changes in calculation and graph during the successive stages of this algorithm. It can be summarized as follows:

- Construction process (or transformation of the graph): moralizing the graph, triangulating the graph, forming the junction tree.
- Initialization process: initializing the potential of cliques and separators.
- Propagation process: ordered series of local manipulations, called message passing, on the join-tree potentials. The result is a consistent join tree.
- Marginalization process: from the consistent join tree, compute the posterior probability $P(V)$ for each variable of interest V.

After construction of the junction tree, the network of our example is reduced to a single clique $\{SC\}$. The construction process is valid for all types of BN. However, the other three phases are different depending on the presence or absence of observations. In this paper, we study the case of presence of observation.

3.3 Hard Evidence

Hard evidence is an observation of a random variable having with certainty a particular value $V = v$. To encode observations on a variable V, we consider the notion of likelihood Λ_V as indicated in [HD96], which is encoded as follows: If V is observed, then $\Lambda_V(v) = 1$ when v is the observed value of V and $\Lambda_V(v) = 0$ otherwise. If V is not observed, then $\Lambda_V(v) = 1$ for each value v. The likelihood encoding of evidence is used in the initialization process to enter the observation in the junction tree. A hard evidence is represented by a likelihood where $\Lambda_V(v) = 1$ for exactly one value v. Assume that the amount of snow observed is 80 mm. This observation is interpreted as $S = S_3$ and illustrated in Table 5. The probability $P(C = yes \mid e)$ where e denotes the hard evidence $S = S_3$ is a part of the definition of the BN: $P(C = yes \mid e) = 0.96$ (see Table 4).

Table 5. Likelihood encoding an hard evidence

		S			C	
v	S_1	S_2	S_3	S_4	yes	no
$\Lambda_V(v)$	0	0	1	0	1	1

The drawback of discretization is that all values in the same interval are treated in the same way no matter their position in the interval. In our example, the observation of 41 mm or 79 mm provides the same results. Since the chosen discretization is coarse with only 4 states, the result may be not satisfying. The finer the discretization, the more relevant are the results, and the larger is the CPT. A discretization of S with 13 states provides $P(C = yes \mid e) = 0.93$ and with 60 states we obtain $P(C = yes \mid e) = 0.893$, where e represents the hard evidence $S = S_i$ and S_i is the interval containing 80 in the chosen discretization.

3.4   Virtual Evidence

Virtual Evidence (VE), proposed by Pearl in [Pe88], provides a convenient way of incorporating evidence *with* uncertainty. A VE on a variable V is represented by a likelihood Λ_V where each $\Lambda_V(v)$ is a real number in $[0, 1]$. Pearl's method extends the given BN by adding a binary virtual node which is a child of V. In our example, we add a node S_{obs} and a directed edge from S toward S_{obs} (see Fig. 2).

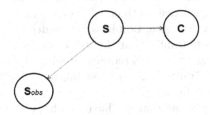

Fig. 2. Bayesian Network graph encoding a virtual evidence on S

In our example, we consider now the virtual evidence ve on S represented by the likelihood given in Table 7. This translates that the observed amount of snow is about 80 mm, and since the measure is rough, both intervals S_3 and S_4 must be considered. In the BN, the main value of S_{obs}, say yes, corresponds to the virtual evidence ve that is represented by the CPT of the virtual node S_{obs} (Table 6).

Table 6. CPT of $P(S_{obs} \mid S)$

	S_1	S_2	S_3	S_4
$S_{obs} = $ yes	0	0	0.5	0.5
$S_{obs} = $ no	1	1	0.5	0.5

Table 7. Likelihood encoding ve

		S			C	
v	S_1	S_2	S_3	S_4	yes	no
$\Lambda_V(v)$	0	0	0.5	0.5	1	1

The virtual evidence ve can be easily propagated by propagating the hard evidence $S_{obs} = yes$ in the augmented BN; we obtain $P(C = yes \mid ve) = P(C = yes \mid S_{obs} = yes) = 0.881$. This result can be obtained as follows:

$$P(C = yes \mid ve) = \frac{\sum_i P(C = yes \mid S_i) \times Q(S = S_i)}{\sum_{c,i} P(C = c \mid S_i) \times Q(S = S_i)} \tag{2}$$

where $Q(S = S_i) = P(S = S_i \mid S_{obs} = yes)$ represents the quantified values as indicated in [TA04]. In the VE method, the propagated value is the marginal on S, represented by the quantified values Q.

3.5   Soft Evidence

Soft evidence (SE), named by Valtorta in [VK02], can be interpreted as evidence of uncertainty. SE is given as a probability distribution of one or several variables $R(Y)$, $Y \subseteq X$, where X is the set of variables. Therefore, there is uncertainty about the specific state Y is in but we are sure of the probability distribution $R(Y)$. Since $R(Y)$ is a certain observation, this distribution should be preserved by updating belief. This is the main difference with virtual evidence for which this is not required.

In case of a single soft evidence, Chan and Darwiche [CD05] showed that a soft evidence can be converted into a virtual evidence and updating can be carried out by virtual evidence method as detailed in [PZ10]. This method is not directly applicable to the situation in which multiple soft evidences are presented since it does not guarantee that the soft evidence $R(Y)$ will be preserved after updating. Updating several SE requires specific algorithms to preserve the initial distribution (see Table 2). An interesting use of soft evidence regarding discretization is proposed in [DB08].

In our example, we assume that we have a soft evidence se on S, given by the distribution $R(S) = (0, 0, 0.5, 0.5)$. This means that we are sure that the amount of snow is in the interval $[40, 120]$. The likelihood ratio is $L(S) = \frac{R(S)}{P(S)}$ where $P(S)$ is the marginal probability of S given in Table 3. Thus, in our example, $L(S) = 0 : 0 : \frac{0.5}{0.14} : \frac{0.5}{0.04}$. After normalization, we obtain $(0 : 0 : 0.222 : 0.778)$. Eventually, these values of the likelihood ratio are considered as a virtual evidence; we obtain $P(C = yes \mid se) = 0.783$.

The comparison of the values of $P(C = yes \mid ve) = 0,881$ and $P(C = yes \mid se) = 0,783$ obtained in our example can be explained as follows. The soft evidence $(0, 0, 0.5, 0.5)$ has been converted into the virtual evidence $(0, 0, 0.222, 0.778)$ by using the likelihood ratio. Thus, the probability 0.222 associated to S_3 is less than the initial probability 0.5, in order to compensate the influence of the prior distribution over S, in which S_3 is more probable than S_4 (see table 1). Since S_3 leads to congestion with a higher probability than S_4, updating the VE $(0, 0, 0.5, 0.5)$ leads to a higher probability of congestion than updating the ve $(0, 0, 0.222, 0.778)$.

4 Fuzzy Evidence

In this section, we consider the proposition presented in [MM11] to model fuzzy evidence by using the fuzzy logic theory. In that aim, we consider the BN of the Fig. 1 in which the node S is replaced by the node S^f whose possible states are representing the amount of snow in natural language: $S_1^f = $ 'not at all', $S_2^f = $ 'a little', $S_3^f = $ 'some' and $S_4^f = $ 'a lot'. We substitute vagueness by a membership degree and we model the relationship between the amount of snow and the linguistics states of snowing by the fuzzy sets shown in Fig. 3. The CPT of $P(C \mid S^f)$ is given in Table 8. In order to be consistent with the previous example, it has been computed according to equation 1 and Fig. 3. The algorithm used to propagate ambiguous observations is based on the junction tree algorithm. Assume that the amount of snow is 80 mm. The fuzzy evidence fe can be expressed thanks to the following membership degrees:

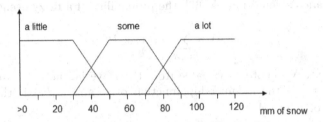

Fig. 3. Fuzzy sets of S^f

Table 8. $P(C \mid S^f)$

	S_1^f	S_2^f	S_3^f	S_4^f
$P(C = yes \mid S_i^f)$	0.3247	0.67	0.9137	0.6707

$$\mu_1(80) = 0, \ \mu_2(80) = 0, \ \mu_3(80) = 0.5, \ \mu_4(80) = 0.5.$$

Table 9 shows the likelihood encoding of the fuzzy evidence fe. It is used in the junction tree algorithm as in the previous section.

Table 9. Likelihood encoding fe

	S				C	
v	S_1^f	S_2^f	S_3^f	S_4^f	yes	no
$\Lambda_V(v)$	0	0	0.5	0.5	1	1

The result is obtained by:

$$P(C = yes \mid fe) = \frac{\sum_i P(C = yes \mid S_i^f) \times \mu_i(80)}{\sum_{c,i} P(C = c \mid S_i^f) \times \mu_i(80)} \tag{3}$$

This method applied to the snow example provides $P(C = yes \mid fe) = 0.792$.

The important distinction between uncertain evidence and fuzzy evidence is that with a fuzzy evidence, there is no uncertainty about the value 'not at all', 'a little', 'some' and 'a lot' of the snowfall but rather an ambiguity about the degree to which a value matches the category 'not at all', 'a little', 'some' and 'a lot'. This ambiguity is treated by fuzzy sets (Fig. 3).

5   Fuzzy Reasoning in Bayesian Networks

In this section, we introduce fuzzy Bayesian equations, as down in [TL07]. According to Zadeh's definition [Za68], the probability of a fuzzy event $\tilde{A}$ in X is given by

$$P(\tilde{A}) = \sum_{x \in X} \mu_{\tilde{A}}(x) \times P(x) \tag{4}$$

In our context, X denotes a variable from the Bayesian network and x is one of its value. $\mu_{\tilde{A}}$ is the membership function of $\tilde{A}$ and $\mu_{\tilde{A}}(x)$ is the grade of membership of x into $\tilde{A}$.

We present fuzzy Bayesian equations through our snow example. The Bayesian network considered is described by Fig. 1 and Tables 3 and 4. We are interested in fuzzy events consisted of S_i; for example the fuzzy event $\tilde{S} =$ 'some' (see Fig. 3) is described by the membership function: $\mu_{\tilde{S}}(S_1) = 0$, $\mu_{\tilde{S}}(S_2) = 0.0625$, $\mu_{\tilde{S}}(S_3) = 0.9375$, $\mu_{\tilde{S}}(S_4) = 0.0625$. In this case, following eq. 11 in [TL07], Bayesian equation is

$$P(C = yes \mid \tilde{S}) = \sum_{i \in I} \mu_{\tilde{S}}(S_i) \times P(S = S_i \mid C = yes) \times P(C = yes)/P(\tilde{S}) \tag{5}$$

The marginal fuzzy probability is $P(\tilde{S}) = \sum_{i \in I} \mu_{\tilde{S}}(S_i) \times P(S = S_i)$ (see eq. 12 in [TL07]) Thus we can figure out $P(C = yes \mid \tilde{S}) = 0.92$.

We may also be interested in fuzzy events of C_j, for example $\tilde{C} =$ 'little congestion'. Then, following eq. 10 in [TL07], Bayesian equation is

$$P(\tilde{C} \mid S = S_i) = \sum_j \mu_{\tilde{C}}(C_j) \times P(S = S_i \mid C = C_j) \times P(C = C_j)/P(S = S_i) \tag{6}$$

If $\tilde{S}$ and $\tilde{C}$ are both fuzzy events, then we have (see eq. 13 in [TL07])

$$P(C = \tilde{C} \mid S = \tilde{S}) = \sum_{j \in J} \sum_{i \in I} \mu_{\tilde{C}}(C_j) \times \mu_{\tilde{S}}(S_i) \times P(S = S_i \mid C = C_j)$$
$$\times P(C = C_j)/P(\tilde{S}) \tag{7}$$

The advantage of this method is threefold. First, we can insert fuzzy observation as shown in (5). Second, we can calculate the probability of a fuzzy event as shown in (6). Finally, we can calculate the probability of a fuzzy event conditional to another fuzzy event as shown in (7).

6   Conclusion

This paper considers the problem of reasoning with *uncertain evidence* in Bayesian Networks. The use of *uncertain evidence* significantly extends the power of Bayesian networks since it is needed in lots of real applications. A key contribution of our work is to describe and to explain the different ways of modeling and updating uncertain evidences. We also propose so-called *fuzzy evidence* which are pertinent for ambiguous observations. Our comparison between *hard evidence*, *virtual evidence*, *soft evidence* and *fuzzy evidence*, showed that each kind of evidence is adequate for a specific context.

Even if the term "soft evidence" has been used in a confusing way in the literature, it is clear that virtual evidence reflects an observation *with* uncertainty whereas soft evidence expresses an observation *of* uncertainty.

This throw light on the posterior probability of the observed node which not change in the case of soft evidence because we are certain about this probability distribution, but it changes in virtual evidence because we are uncertain of the probability distribution which is thus modified by the marginalization process. Concerning fuzzy evidence, the observation can belong in the same time to more than one class (80 mm is considered in the same time as 'some' and 'a lot' snowfall with membership degrees).

In the last section, we presented fuzzy reasoning in Bayesian network. This method allows to insert fuzzy evidence, to calculate the probability of fuzzy event, and to calculate the probability of fuzzy event conditional to a fuzzy observation.

References

[MM11]   Ben Mrad, A., Maalej, M.A., Delcroix, V., Piechowiak, S., Abid, M.: Fuzzy Evidence in Bayesian Networks. In: Proc. of Soft Computing and Pattern Recognition, Dalian, China (2011)

[Bo89]   Bock, H.H.: A conditional iterative proportional fitting (CIPF) algorithm with applications in the statistical analysis of discrete spatial data. Bull. ISI, Contributed Papers of 47th Session in Paris 1, 141–142 (1989)

[CD05]   Chan, H., Darwiche, A.: On the revision of probabilistic beliefs using uncertain evidence. Artificial Intelligence 163, 67–90 (2005)

[Cr00]   Cramer, E.: Probability measures with given marginals and conditionals: I-projections and conditional iterative proportional fitting. Statistics and Decisions 18, 311–329 (2000)

[Cs75]   Csiszar, I.: I-divergence geometry of probability distributions and minimization problems. The Annals of Probability 3(1), 146–158 (1975)

[DB08]   Di Tomaso, E., Baldwin, J.F.: An approach to hybrid probabilistic models. International Journal of Approximate Reasoning 47(2), 202–218 (2008)

[Fi70]   Fienberg, S.E.: An iterative procedure for estimation in contingency tables. Ann. Math. Statist. 41(3), 907–917 (1970)

[HD96]   Huang, C., Darwiche, A.: Inference in belief networks: A procedural guide. International Journal of Approximate Reasoning 15(3), 225–263 (1996)

[Je83]   Jeffrey, R.: The Logic of Decisions, 2nd edn. University of Chicago Press, Chicago (1983)

[Je96]   Jensen, F.: An Introduction to Bayesian Networks. Springer, New York (1996)

[Je90]   Jensen, F., Lauritzen, S., Olesen, K.: Bayesian updating in recursive graphical models by local computations. Computational Statistical Quaterly 4, 269–282 (1990)

[Kr37]   Kruithof, R.: Telefoonverkeer Rekening. De Ingenieur 52, 15–25 (1937)

[La88]   Lauritzen, S.: Local computation with probabilities on graphical structures and their application to expert systems. Journal of the Royal Statistical Society 50, 157 (1988)

[Ne]   http://www.norsys.com

[Pe88]   Pearl, J.: Probabilistic Reasoning in Intelligent Systems: Networks of Plausible Inference. Morgan Kaufman, San Mateo (1988)

[Pe90]   Pearl, J.: Jeffrey's rule, passage of experience, and neo-Bayesianism. In: Kyburg Jr., H.E., Loui, R.P., Carlson, G.N. (eds.) Knowledge Representation and Defeasible Reasoning, pp. 245–265. Kluwer Academic Publishers, Boston (1990)

[PD05]   Peng, Y., Ding, Z.: Modifying Bayesian networks by probability constraints. In: Proc. 21st Conf. Uncertainty in Artificial Intelligence, Edinburgh (2005)

[PZ10]   Peng, Y., Zhang, S., Pan, R.: Bayesian Network Reasoning with Uncertain Evidences. International Journal of Uncertainty, Fuzziness and Knowledge-Based Systems 18(5), 539–564 (2010)

[TL07]   Tang, H., Liu, S.: Basic Theory of Fuzzy Bayesian Networks and Its Application in Machinery Fault Diagnosis. In: Proc. of FSKD, vol. 4, pp. 132–137 (2007)

[TA04]   Tu, H., Allanach, J., Singh, S., Pattipati, K.R., Willett, P.: The adaptive safety analysis and monitoring system. In: Proc. SPIE 5403, p. 153 (2004)

[VK02]   Valtorta, M., Kim, Y., Vomlel, J.: Soft Evidential Update for Probabilistic Multiagent Systems. International Journal of Approximate Reasoning 29(1), 71–106 (2002)

[Za68]   Zadeh, L.A.: Probability measures of fuzzy events. Journal of Mathematical Analysis and Applications 23, 421–427 (1968)

Weighted Semi-trapezoidal Approximation of a Fuzzy Number Preserving the Weighted Ambiguity

Adrian I. Ban and Lucian Coroianu

Department of Mathematics and Informatics, University of Oradea,
Universităţii 1, 410087 Oradea, Romania
{aiban,lcoroianu}@uoradea.ro

Abstract. We use the metric properties of the nearest extended weighted semi-trapezoidal fuzzy number and the Karush-Kuhn-Tucker theorem to compute the weighted semi-trapezoidal approximation of a fuzzy number preserving the weighted ambiguity. The proposed approach is more general than existing methods and it can be applied to other approximations of fuzzy numbers under conditions.

Keywords: Fuzzy number, Ambiguity, Approximation, Semi-trapezoidal fuzzy number.

1 Introduction

Different kinds of approximations of fuzzy numbers (interval, triangular, trapezoidal, semi-triangular, semi-trapezoidal, with or without conditions) were proposed in many recent papers, to avoid the important difficulties in the data processing with fuzzy numbers. On the other hand, the ambiguity is an important characteristic which was introduced [7] to simplify the task of representing and handling of fuzzy numbers.

Formulas for computing the extended semi-trapezoidal approximation of a fuzzy number, with respect to average Euclidean distance and weighted average Euclidean distance were determined in [5] and [6], respectively. The properties already proved in [6], together the Karush-Kuhn-Tucker theorem, are used to find the nearest semi-trapezoidal fuzzy number of a given fuzzy number A, with respect to weighted average Euclidean distance (called weighted semi-trapezoidal approximation of A in the sequel), such that the ambiguity, in a generalized form, is preserved. As an important consequence, the trapezoidal approximation (with respect to average Euclidean distance) preserving ambiguity in its original form, is immediately obtained.

2 Preliminaries

We consider the α-cut representation of a fuzzy number A, that is $A_\alpha = [A_L(\alpha), A_U(\alpha)], \alpha \in [0,1]$, and we denote by $F(\mathbb{R})$ the set of all fuzzy

S. Greco et al. (Eds.): IPMU 2012, Part III, CCIS 299, pp. 49–58, 2012.

numbers. For $A, B \in F(\mathbb{R}), A_\alpha = [A_L(\alpha), A_U(\alpha)]$ and $B_\alpha = [B_L(\alpha), B_U(\alpha)]$, the quantity $d_\lambda(A, B)$ introduced by

$$d_\lambda^2(A, B) = \int_0^1 \lambda_L(\alpha)(A_L(\alpha) - B_L(\alpha))^2 \, d\alpha \qquad (1)$$

$$+ \int_0^1 \lambda_U(\alpha)(A_U(\alpha) - B_U(\alpha))^2 \, d\alpha$$

where λ_L and λ_U are nonnegative functions such that $\int_0^1 \lambda_L(\alpha) \, d\alpha > 0$ and $\int_0^1 \lambda_U(\alpha) \, d\alpha > 0$, defines a weighted distance between A and B (see, e. g., [8]). If $\lambda_L(\alpha) = \lambda_U(\alpha) = 1$, for every $\alpha \in [0, 1]$, we get the well-known average Euclidean distance between A and B, denoted by d. Many other weighted functions λ_L, λ_U and hence different weighted distances are proposed in the literature (see [10]).

The S-ambiguity $Amb_S(A)$ of $A \in F(\mathbb{R})$ with respect to a reducing function S (that is $S : [0, 1] \to [0, 1]$ is increasing, $S(0) = 0$ and $S(1) = 1$) is defined by

$$Amb_S(A) = \int_0^1 S(\alpha)(A_U(\alpha) - A_L(\alpha)) \, d\alpha. \qquad (2)$$

If $S(\alpha) = \alpha$ then we obtain the ambiguity $Amb(A)$ of a fuzzy number A (see [7]).

A trapezoidal fuzzy number is a fuzzy number A with linear sides, that is

$$A_L(\alpha) = a - \sigma(1 - \alpha), \qquad (3)$$
$$A_U(\alpha) = b + \beta(1 - \alpha), \alpha \in [0, 1], \qquad (4)$$

where $a, b, \sigma, \beta \in \mathbb{R}, a \leq b, \sigma \geq 0, \beta \geq 0$. In [12] (see also [13]), the notion of extended trapezoidal fuzzy number was introduced to facilitate the calculus of the nearest triangular and trapezoidal approximations of fuzzy numbers. According to [12], an ordered pair of polynomials of degree 0 or 1 is called an extended trapezoidal fuzzy number. In fact, an extended trapezoidal fuzzy number is a pair (A_L, A_U) as in (3), (4), without any additional conditions.

A (s_L, s_R) semi-trapezoidal fuzzy number (see [14]) is a fuzzy number $A, A_\alpha = [A_L(\alpha), A_U(\alpha)], \alpha \in [0, 1]$ given by

$$A_L(\alpha) = a - \sigma(1 - \alpha)^{1/s_L} \qquad (5)$$

$$A_U(\alpha) = b + \beta(1 - \alpha)^{1/s_R}, \qquad (6)$$

where $a, b, \sigma, \beta, s_L, s_R \in \mathbb{R}, a \leq b, \sigma \geq 0, \beta \geq 0, s_L > 0, s_R > 0$. The notion of extended trapezoidal fuzzy number is generalized to the semi-trapezoidal case in [5]. An extended (s_L, s_R) semi-trapezoidal fuzzy number A is an ordered pair of functions (A_L, A_U) as in (5)-(6), with $s_L > 0, s_R > 0$, but without any other condition on $a, b, \sigma, \beta \in \mathbb{R}$. We denote by $F_T^{s_L, s_R}(\mathbb{R})$ the set of (s_L, s_R) semi-trapezoidal fuzzy numbers and by $F_e^{s_L, s_R}(\mathbb{R})$ the set of extended (s_L, s_R) semi-trapezoidal fuzzy numbers.

Let us denote $l = \int_0^1 \lambda_L(\alpha)\, d\alpha, m = \int_0^1 \lambda_L(\alpha)(1-\alpha)^{1/s_L}\, d\alpha$, $n = \int_0^1 \lambda_L(\alpha)(1-\alpha)^{2/s_L}\, d\alpha, u = \int_0^1 \lambda_U(\alpha)\, d\alpha, v = \int_0^1 \lambda_U(\alpha)(1-\alpha)^{1/s_R}\, d\alpha$ and $w = \int_0^1 \lambda_L(\alpha)(1-\alpha)^{2/s_R}\, d\alpha$, for the weighted functions λ_L and λ_U.

Any extended (s_L, s_R) semi-trapezoidal fuzzy number $A = (a, b, \sigma, \beta)_{s_L, s_R}$ can be represented as (see [6])

$$A_L(\alpha) = \frac{1}{\sqrt{l}}L - X\left((1-\alpha)^{1/s_L} - \frac{m}{l}\right) \tag{7}$$

$$A_U(\alpha) = \frac{1}{\sqrt{u}}U + Y\left((1-\alpha)^{1/s_R} - \frac{v}{u}\right), \tag{8}$$

where

$$L = \sqrt{l}a - \frac{m}{\sqrt{l}}\sigma \tag{9}$$

$$X = \sigma \tag{10}$$

$$U = \sqrt{u}b + \frac{v}{\sqrt{u}}\beta \tag{11}$$

$$Y = \beta. \tag{12}$$

Thus, an extended (s_L, s_R) semi-trapezoidal fuzzy number given by (7)-(8) will be denoted by $[L, U, X, Y]_{s_L, s_R}$. We have $[L, U, X, Y]_{s_L, s_R} \in F^{s_L, s_R}(\mathbb{R})$ if and only if $X \geq 0, Y \geq 0$ and $\frac{1}{\sqrt{l}}L + \frac{m}{l}X \leq \frac{1}{\sqrt{u}}U - \frac{v}{u}Y$.

The below Karush-Kuhn-Tucker theorem (see [11], pp. 281-283) is an useful tool in the finding of the parametric or trapezoidal approximations of fuzzy numbers under conditions (see e.g. [9], [1]-[3]).

Theorem 1. *Let $f, g_1, ..., g_p : \mathbb{R}^n \to \mathbb{R}$ be convex and differentiable functions. Then $\overline{x}$ solves the convex programming problem*

$$\min f(x)$$
$$s.t. g_i(x) \leq h_i, i \in \{1, ..., p\}$$

if and only if there exists $\mu_i, i \in \{1, ..., p\}$, such that

(i) $\nabla f(\overline{x}) + \sum_{i=1}^{p} \mu_i \nabla g_i(\overline{x}) = 0$
(ii) $g_i(\overline{x}) - h_i \leq 0, \forall i \in \{1, ..., p\}$
(iii) $\mu_i \geq 0, \forall i \in \{1, ..., p\}$
(iv) $\mu_i(g_i(\overline{x}) - h_i) = 0, \forall i \in \{1, ..., p\}.$

3 Extended Weighted Semi-trapezoidal Approximation and Metric Properties

The extended trapezoidal approximation of a fuzzy number was determined in [12]. The extended (s_L, s_R) semi-trapezoidal approximation of a fuzzy number together the main metric properties were studied in [5]. The formulas of calculus of the extended weighted (s_L, s_R) semi-trapezoidal approximation of a fuzzy number and its metric properties were given in [6]. Namely, the extended weighted semi-trapezoidal approximation $A_{s_L,s_R}^{\lambda,e} = (a_e, b_e, \sigma_e, \beta_e)_{s_L,s_R}$ of $A \in F(\mathbb{R})$, $A_\alpha = [A_L(\alpha), A_U(\alpha)]$, $\alpha \in [0,1]$, is given by

$$a_e = \frac{n \int_0^1 \lambda_L(\alpha) A_L(\alpha)\, d\alpha - m \int_0^1 \lambda_L(\alpha) A_L(\alpha)(1-\alpha)^{1/s_L}\, d\alpha}{nl - m^2} \tag{13}$$

$$b_e = \frac{w \int_0^1 \lambda_U(\alpha) A_U(\alpha)\, d\alpha - v \int_0^1 \lambda_U(\alpha) A_U(\alpha)(1-\alpha)^{1/s_R}\, d\alpha}{uw - v^2} \tag{14}$$

$$\sigma_e = \frac{m \int_0^1 \lambda_L(\alpha) A_L(\alpha)\, d\alpha - l \int_0^1 \lambda_L(\alpha) A_L(\alpha)(1-\alpha)^{1/s_L}\, d\alpha}{nl - m^2} \tag{15}$$

$$\beta_e = \frac{-v \int_0^1 \lambda_U(\alpha) A_U(\alpha)\, d\alpha + u \int_0^1 \lambda_U(\alpha) A_U(\alpha)(1-\alpha)^{1/s_R}\, d\alpha}{uw - v^2}. \tag{16}$$

We obtain the extended weighted semi-trapezoidal approximation of $A \in F(\mathbb{R})$ in the representation $[L_e, U_e, X_e, Y_e]_{s_L,s_R}$ by using (9)-(12). Of course, if $\lambda_L(\alpha) = \lambda_U(\alpha) = 1, \alpha \in [0,1]$ and $s_L = s_R = 1$ in (13)-(16) we obtain the extended trapezoidal approximation of A (see [12]). If $\lambda_L(\alpha) = \lambda_U(\alpha) = 1, \alpha \in [0,1]$ in (13)-(16) we obtain the extended (s_L, s_R) semi-trapezoidal approximation of A (see [5]).

The distance between $A, B \in F_e^{s_L,s_R}(\mathbb{R})$, $A = [L_1, U_1, X_1, Y_1]_{s_L,s_R}$ and $B = [L_2, U_2, X_2, Y_2]_{s_L,s_R}$ can be represented almost like the Euclidean distance in $\mathbb{R}^4$ by (see [6])

$$d_\lambda^2(A, B) = (L_1 - L_2)^2 + (U_1 - U_2)^2 + \frac{nl - m^2}{l}(X_1 - X_2)^2 \tag{17}$$

$$+ \frac{uw - v^2}{u}(Y_1 - Y_2)^2.$$

The proof of the following result, already presented in [6], is similar with the proof in the weighted trapezoidal case (see [5]).

Proposition 1. *If $A \in F(\mathbb{R})$ and $A_{s_L,s_R}^{\lambda,e}$ is the extended weighted semi-trapezoidal approximation of A then*

$$d_\lambda^2(A, B) = d_\lambda^2(A, A_{s_L,s_R}^{\lambda,e}) + d_\lambda^2(A_{s_L,s_R}^{\lambda,e}, B), \tag{18}$$

for every $B \in F_e^{s_L,s_R}(\mathbb{R})$.

4   Weighted Semi-trapezoidal Approximation Preserving the Weighted Ambiguity

If the parameters $P_k, k \in \{1, ..., q\}$ are preserved by the extended weighted (s_L, s_R) semi-trapezoidal approximation of a fuzzy number A, that is

$$P_k\left(A_{s_L,s_R}^{\lambda,e}\right) = P_k(A), \forall k \in \{1, ..., q\},$$

then, taking into account Proposition 1, we obtain the equivalence of the problem of finding the weighted (s_L, s_R) semi-trapezoidal approximation of a given $A \in F(\mathbb{R})$, that is

$$\min_{B \in F_T^{s_L, s_R}(\mathbb{R})} d_\lambda(A, B)$$
$$P_k(A) = P_k(B), k \in \{1, ..., q\}$$

with the following problem

$$\min_{B \in F_T^{s_L, s_R}(\mathbb{R})} d_\lambda\left(A_{s_L, s_R}^{\lambda, e}, B\right)$$
$$P_k\left(A_{s_L, s_R}^{\lambda, e}\right) = P_k(B), k \in \{1, ..., q\}.$$

Below we consider the weighted ambiguity of a fuzzy number to illustrate the simplification of the problems passing to extended weighted (s_L, s_R) semi-trapezoidal approximation. We consider the following definition of the weighted ambiguity of a fuzzy number A, $A_\alpha = [A_L(\alpha), A_U(\alpha)], \alpha \in [0, 1]$:

$$Amb_\lambda(A) = \int_0^1 \lambda_U(\alpha)\left(1 - (1 - \alpha)^{1/s_R}\right) A_U(\alpha) d\alpha$$
$$- \int_0^1 \lambda_L(\alpha)\left(1 - (1 - \alpha)^{1/s_L}\right) A_L(\alpha) d\alpha.$$

If $s_L = s_R = 1$ and $\lambda_L(\alpha) = \lambda_U(\alpha) = 1$ then we get the classical formula of ambiguity of a fuzzy number (see [7] or [4]).

By a direct computation we obtain the following results.

Proposition 2.
$$Amb_\lambda\left(A_{s_L, s_R}^{\lambda, e}\right) = Amb_\lambda(A). \tag{19}$$

Proposition 3. Let $[L, U, X, Y]_{s_L, s_R} \in F_e^{s_L, s_R}(\mathbb{R})$. Then

$$Amb_\lambda\left([L, U, X, Y]_{s_L, s_R}\right) = \frac{m - l}{\sqrt{l}} L + \frac{u - v}{\sqrt{u}} U + \frac{m^2 - nl}{l} X + \frac{v^2 - uw}{u} Y. \tag{20}$$

Taking into account (17)-(20) we find the weighted (s_L, s_R) semi-trapezoidal approximation preserving the weighted ambiguity of a fuzzy number A,

$$[L_T(A), U_T(A), X_T(A), Y_T(A)]_{s_L, s_R} = [L_T, U_T, X_T, Y_T]_{s_L, s_R}$$

as a solution of the problem

$$\min_{L, U, X, Y \in \mathbb{R}} \left\{ (L - L_e)^2 + (U - U_e)^2 + \frac{nl - m^2}{l}(X - X_e)^2 \right. \tag{21}$$
$$\left. + \frac{uw - v^2}{u}(Y - Y_e)^2 \right\}$$

$$\frac{m-l}{\sqrt{l}}L + \frac{u-v}{\sqrt{u}}U + \frac{m^2-nl}{l}X + \frac{v^2-uw}{u}Y \qquad (22)$$

$$= \frac{m-l}{\sqrt{l}}L_e + \frac{u-v}{\sqrt{u}}U_e + \frac{m^2-nl}{l}X_e + \frac{v^2-uw}{u}Y_e$$

$$X \geq 0, Y \geq 0 \qquad (23)$$

$$\frac{1}{\sqrt{l}}L + \frac{m}{l}X \leq \frac{1}{\sqrt{u}}U - \frac{v}{u}Y. \qquad (24)$$

Because

$$L = L_e + \frac{\sqrt{l}\,(v-u)}{\sqrt{u}\,(m-l)}\,(U - U_e) - \frac{m^2-nl}{\sqrt{l}\,(m-l)}\,(X - X_e) \qquad (25)$$

$$- \frac{\sqrt{l}\,(v^2-uw)}{u\,(m-l)}\,(Y - Y_e),$$

we must solve

$$\min_{U,X,Y \in \mathbb{R}} \left\{ \left(\frac{\sqrt{l}\,(v-u)}{\sqrt{u}\,(m-l)}\,(U - U_e) - \frac{m^2-nl}{\sqrt{l}\,(m-l)}\,(X - X_e) \right. \right. \qquad (26)$$

$$\left. - \frac{\sqrt{l}\,(v^2-uw)}{u\,(m-l)}\,(Y - Y_e) \right)^2 + (U - U_e)^2$$

$$\left. + \frac{nl-m^2}{l}\,(X - X_e)^2 + \frac{uw-v^2}{u}\,(Y - Y_e)^2 \right\}$$

under conditions

$$X \geq 0, Y \geq 0 \qquad (27)$$

$$\left(\frac{v-u}{\sqrt{u}\,(m-l)} - \frac{1}{\sqrt{u}} \right)U + \left(\frac{m}{l} - \frac{m^2-nl}{l\,(m-l)} \right)X + \left(\frac{v}{u} - \frac{v^2-uw}{u\,(m-l)} \right)Y \qquad (28)$$

$$\leq -\frac{1}{\sqrt{l}}L_e + \frac{v-u}{\sqrt{u}\,(m-l)}U_e - \frac{m^2-nl}{l\,(m-l)}X_e - \frac{v^2-uw}{u\,(m-l)}Y_e.$$

Let us denote

$$a_1 = \frac{2l\,(v-u)^2}{u\,(m-l)^2} + 2, a_2 = -\frac{2\,(v-u)\,(m^2-nl)}{\sqrt{u}\,(m-l)^2}, \qquad (29)$$

$$a_3 = -\frac{2l\,(v-u)\,(v^2-uw)}{u\sqrt{u}\,(m-l)^2}, a_4 = -a_1 U_e - a_2 X_e - a_3 Y_e, \qquad (30)$$

$$a_5 = \frac{v-u-m+l}{\sqrt{u}\,(m-l)}, a_6 = -\frac{2\,(v-u)\,(m^2-nl)}{\sqrt{u}\,(m-l)^2}, \qquad (31)$$

$$a_7 = \frac{2\left(m^2 - nl\right)^2}{l\left(m - l\right)^2} + \frac{2\left(nl - m^2\right)}{l}, a_8 = \frac{2\left(v^2 - uw\right)\left(m^2 - nl\right)}{u\left(m - l\right)^2}, \qquad (32)$$

$$a_9 = -a_6 U_e - a_7 X_e - a_8 Y_e, a_{10} = \frac{m}{l} - \frac{m^2 - nl}{l\left(m - l\right)}, \qquad (33)$$

$$a_{11} = -\frac{2l\left(v - u\right)\left(v^2 - uw\right)}{u\sqrt{u}\left(m - l\right)^2}, a_{12} = \frac{2\left(v^2 - uw\right)\left(m^2 - nl\right)}{u\left(m - l\right)^2}, \qquad (34)$$

$$a_{13} = \frac{2l\left(v^2 - uw\right)^2}{u^2\left(m - l\right)^2} + \frac{2\left(uw - v^2\right)}{u}, a_{14} = -a_{11}U_e - a_{12}X_e - a_{13}Y_e \qquad (35)$$

$$a_{15} = \frac{v}{u} - \frac{v^2 - uw}{u\left(m - l\right)} \qquad (36)$$

$$a_{16} = -\frac{1}{\sqrt{l}}L_e + \frac{v - u}{\sqrt{u}\left(m - l\right)}U_e - \frac{m^2 - nl}{l\left(m - l\right)}X_e - \frac{v^2 - uw}{u\left(m - l\right)}Y_e. \qquad (37)$$

We get that $[L_T, U_T, X_T, Y_T]_{s_L, s_R}$ is the weighted (s_L, s_R) semi-trapezoidal approximation preserving the weighted ambiguity of a fuzzy number A if and only if (see (25))

$$L_T = L_e + \frac{\sqrt{l}\left(v - u\right)}{\sqrt{u}\left(m - l\right)}\left(U_T - U_e\right) - \frac{m^2 - nl}{\sqrt{l}\left(m - l\right)}\left(X_T - X_e\right)$$
$$- \frac{\sqrt{l}\left(v^2 - uw\right)}{u\left(m - l\right)}\left(Y_T - Y_e\right)$$

and (U_T, X_T, Y_T) is the solution of the system (the Karush-Kuhn-Tucker conditions, see Theorem 1, $(i) - (iv)$)

$$a_1 U + a_2 X + a_3 Y + a_4 + a_5 \mu_3 = 0 \qquad (38)$$
$$a_6 U + a_7 X + a_8 Y + a_9 - \mu_1 + a_{10}\mu_3 = 0 \qquad (39)$$
$$a_{11} U + a_{12} X + a_{13} Y + a_{14} - \mu_2 + a_{15}\mu_3 = 0 \qquad (40)$$
$$X \geq 0, Y \geq 0 \qquad (41)$$
$$a_5 U + a_{10} X + a_{15} Y \leq a_{16} \qquad (42)$$
$$\mu_1 \geq 0, \mu_2 \geq 0, \mu_3 \geq 0 \qquad (43)$$
$$\mu_1 X = 0 \qquad (44)$$
$$\mu_2 Y = 0 \qquad (45)$$
$$\mu_3 \left(a_5 U + a_{10} X + a_{15} Y - a_{16}\right) = 0. \qquad (46)$$

5   Trapezoidal Approximation Preserving Ambiguity

To obtain the trapezoidal approximation with respect to average Euclidean distance d we consider $\lambda_L(\alpha) = \lambda_U(\alpha) = 1$, for every $\alpha \in [0, 1]$ and $s_L = s_R = 1$ in the above section, that is $l = u = 1, m = v = \frac{1}{2}$ and $n = w = \frac{1}{3}$.

Because (see (29)-(37)) $a_1 = 4, a_2 = a_3 = a_6 = a_{11} = -\frac{1}{3}, a_4 = -4U_e + \frac{1}{3}X_e +$
$\frac{1}{3}Y_e, a_5 = 0, a_7 = \frac{2}{9}, a_8 = \frac{1}{18}, a_9 = \frac{1}{3}U_e - \frac{2}{9}X_e - \frac{1}{18}Y_e, a_{10} = a_{15} = \frac{1}{3}, a_{12} =$
$\frac{1}{18}, a_{13} = \frac{2}{9}, a_{14} = \frac{1}{3}U_e - \frac{1}{18}X_e - \frac{2}{9}Y_e$, from (38)-(46) we get

$$12U - 12U_e - X + X_e - Y + Y_e = 0 \tag{47}$$
$$-6U + 6U_e + 4X - 4X_e + Y - Y_e - 18\mu_1 + 6\mu_3 = 0 \tag{48}$$
$$-6U + 6U_e + X - X_e + 4Y - 4Y_e - 18\mu_2 + 6\mu_3 = 0 \tag{49}$$
$$X \geq 0, Y \geq 0 \tag{50}$$
$$X + Y \leq -3L_e + 3U_e - \frac{1}{2}X_e - \frac{1}{2}Y_e \tag{51}$$
$$\mu_1 \geq 0, \mu_2 \geq 0, \mu_3 \geq 0 \tag{52}$$
$$\mu_1 X = 0 \tag{53}$$
$$\mu_2 Y = 0 \tag{54}$$
$$\mu_3\left(X + Y + 3L_e - 3U_e + \frac{1}{2}X_e + \frac{1}{2}Y_e\right) = 0. \tag{55}$$

By solving the above system and taking into account (9)-(12) we obtain the trapezoidal approximation of a fuzzy number preserving the ambiguity (see [1]-[3], [9]). Let us denote

$$\Omega_1 = \left\{A \in F(\mathbb{R}) : \int_0^1 (1 - 3\alpha) A_L(\alpha)\, d\alpha + \int_0^1 (3\alpha - 1) A_U(\alpha)\, d\alpha \geq 0\right\}$$

$$\Omega_2 = \left\{A \in F(\mathbb{R}) : \int_0^1 (3\alpha - 1) A_L(\alpha)\, d\alpha + \int_0^1 (\alpha - 1) A_U(\alpha)\, d\alpha > 0\right\}$$

$$\Omega_3 = \left\{A \in F(\mathbb{R}) : \int_0^1 (\alpha - 1) A_L(\alpha)\, d\alpha + \int_0^1 (3\alpha - 1) A_U(\alpha)\, d\alpha < 0\right\}.$$

Theorem 2. Let $A, A_\alpha = [A_L(\alpha), A_U(\alpha)], \alpha \in [0,1]$ be a fuzzy number and $T(A) = (a, b, \sigma, \beta)$ the trapezoidal approximation (with respect to the metric d) of fuzzy number A, preserving the ambiguity of A.
(i) If $A \in \Omega_1$ then

$$a = \int_0^1 (6\alpha - 2) A_L(\alpha)\, d\alpha$$

$$b = \int_0^1 (6\alpha - 2) A_U(\alpha)\, d\alpha$$

$$\sigma = \int_0^1 (12\alpha - 6) A_L(\alpha)\, d\alpha$$

$$\beta = \int_0^1 (-12\alpha + 6) A_U(\alpha)\, d\alpha.$$

(ii) If $A \in \Omega_2$ then

$$a = b = \frac{1}{2} \int_0^1 (1 - 3\alpha) A_L(\alpha) \, d\alpha + \frac{1}{2} \int_0^1 (1 + 3\alpha) A_U(\alpha) \, d\alpha$$

$$\sigma = -6 \int_0^1 \alpha A_L(\alpha) \, d\alpha + 6 \int_0^1 \alpha A_U(\alpha) \, d\alpha$$

$$\beta = 0.$$

(iii) If $A \in \Omega_3$ then

$$a = b = \frac{1}{2} \int_0^1 (1 + 3\alpha) A_L(\alpha) \, d\alpha + \frac{1}{2} \int_0^1 (1 - 3\alpha) A_U(\alpha) \, d\alpha$$

$$\sigma = 0$$

$$\beta = -6 \int_0^1 \alpha A_L(\alpha) \, d\alpha + 6 \int_0^1 \alpha A_U(\alpha) \, d\alpha.$$

(iv) If $A \notin \Omega_1 \cup \Omega_2 \cup \Omega_3$ then

$$a = b = \int_0^1 (3\alpha - 1) A_L(\alpha) \, d\alpha + \int_0^1 (3\alpha - 1) A_U(\alpha) \, d\alpha$$

$$\sigma = 3 \int_0^1 (\alpha - 1) A_L(\alpha) \, d\alpha + 3 \int_0^1 (3\alpha - 1) A_U(\alpha) \, d\alpha$$

$$\beta = 3 \int_0^1 (1 - 3\alpha) A_L(\alpha) \, d\alpha + 3 \int_0^1 (1 - \alpha) A_U(\alpha) \, d\alpha.$$

6   Conclusion

The present paper together with [5] generalizes the problem of the approximation of fuzzy numbers with simpler form. More exactly, the approximation is searched in the space of semi-trapezoidal fuzzy numbers and the approximation is performed with respect to a general weighted L^2-type metric. A method to find the weighted semi-trapezoidal approximations preserving the weighted ambiguity (introduced in this paper) is proposed. The method can be easily adapted to other approximations problems such as weighted semi-trapezoidal approximations preserving (weighted) expected interval or the value. As in the case of the trapezoidal or semi-trapezoidal approximations, further studies concerning basic properties such as the additivity or continuity will be tackled in forthcoming papers.

Acknowledgements. This work was supported by a grant of the Romanian National Authority for Scientific Research, CNCS-UEFISCDI, project number PN-II-ID-PCE-2011-3-0861. The contribution of the second author was possible with the financial support of the Sectoral Operational Programme for Human Resources Development 2007-2013, co-financed by the European Social Fund, under the project number POSDRU/107/1.5/S/76841 with the title "Modern Doctoral Studies: Internationalization and Interdisciplinarity."

References

1. Ban, A.I.: Approximation of fuzzy numbers preserving the expected interval. Fuzzy Sets and Systems 159, 1327–1344 (2008)
2. Ban, A.I.: On the nearest parametric approximation of a fuzzy number-revisited. Fuzzy Sets and Systems 160, 3027–3047 (2009)
3. Ban, A.I.: Remarks and corrections to the triangular approximations of fuzzy numbers using α-weighted valuations. Soft Computing 15, 351–361 (2011)
4. Ban, A.I., Brândaş, A., Coroianu, L., Negruţiu, C., Nica, O.: Approximations of fuzzy numbers by trapezoidal fuzzy numbers preserving the ambiguity and value. Computers and Mathematics with Applications 61, 1379–1401 (2011)
5. Ban, A.I., Coroianu, L.: Metric properties of the nearest extended parametric fuzzy number and applications. Intern. J. of Approximate Reasoning 52, 488–500 (2011)
6. Ban, A.I., Bica, A.A., Coroianu, L.: Metric Properties of the Extended Weighted Semi-trapezoidal Approximations of Fuzzy Numbers and Their Applications. In: Greco, S., Corrente, S. (eds.) IPMU 2012, Part III. CCIS, vol. 299, pp. 29–38. Springer, Heidelberg (2012)
7. Delgado, M., Vila, M.A., Voxman, W.: On a canonical representation of a fuzzy number. Fuzzy Sets and Systems 93, 125–135 (1998)
8. Grzegorzewski, P.: Metrics and orders of fuzzy numbers. Fuzzy Sets and Systems 97, 83–94 (1998)
9. Grzegorzewski, P., Mrówka, E.: Trapezoidal approximations of fuzzy numbers-revisited. Fuzzy Sets and Systems 158, 757–768 (2007)
10. Grzegorzewski, P., Pasternak-Winiarska, K.: Weighted trapezoidal approximations of fuzzy numbers. In: Proc. of the Join Int. Fuzzy Systems Assoc. World Congress and European Soc. of Fuzzy Logic and Techn. Conf., pp. 1531–1534 (2009)
11. Rockafellar, R.T.: Convex Analysis. Princeton University Press, Princeton (1970)
12. Yeh, C.-T.: Trapezoidal and triangular approximations preserving the expected interval. Fuzzy Sets and Systems 159, 1345–1353 (2008)
13. Yeh, C.-T.: Weighted trapezoidal and triangular approximations of fuzzy numbers. Fuzzy Sets and Systems 160, 3059–3079 (2009)
14. Yeh, C.-T.: Weighted semi-trapezoidal approximations of fuzzy numbers. Fuzzy Sets and Systems 165, 61–80 (2011)

On the Interval Approximation of Fuzzy Numbers

Przemysław Grzegorzewski[1,2]

[1] Systems Research Institute, Polish Academy of Sciences
Newelska 6, 01-447 Warsaw, Poland
[2] Faculty of Mathematics and Information Science, Warsaw University of Technology
Plac Politechniki 1, 00-661 Warsaw, Poland
pgrzeg@ibspan.waw.pl, pgrzeg@mini.pw.edu.pl
http://www.ibspan.waw.pl/~pgrzeg

Abstract. The problem of the interval approximation of fuzzy numbers is discussed. A new family of interval approximation operators based on different distances between fuzzy numbers are considered.

Keywords: fuzzy number, interval approximation, distance between fuzzy numbers.

1   Introduction

Fuzzy set theory was recognized as an effective tool for modelling and processing imprecise information. However, sometimes membership functions representing fuzzy sets are too complicated for calculations and further decision making and hence some approximations are necessary. The biggest simplification is realized via defuzzification, where a fuzzy number is reduced to a single point on the real line. Unfortunately, although defuzzification leads to simple structures it results in overmuch loss of information. Therefore interval approximation of a fuzzy set is often advisable. In this approach we substitute a given fuzzy set by interval, which is - in some sense - close to the former one.

The most popular interval approximation operator is, so called, nearest ordinary set operator. However, this operator has a serious drawback - the lack of continuity. Thus some other operators were suggested in the literature (see, e.g. [2], [3], [8], [9]). In particular, Grzegorzewski [8] proposed the interval approximation leading to interval nearest to the original fuzzy number with respect to L_2-metric. In this paper we generalize results discussed in [8].

The paper is organized as follows. In Sec. 2 we recall basic notions related to fuzzy numbers. In Sec. 3 we discuss the problem of interval approximation of fuzzy numbers. Then, in Sec. 4, we propose the nearest interval approximation with respect to the generalized Trutschnig distance. Next, in Sec. 5, we explore the properties of the suggested approximation operator.

2   Fuzzy Numbers

Let A denote a fuzzy number, i.e. such fuzzy subset A of the real line $\mathbb{R}$ with membership function $\mu_A : \mathbb{R} \to [0,1]$ which is (see [5]): normal (i.e. there exist

S. Greco et al. (Eds.): IPMU 2012, Part III, CCIS 299, pp. 59–68, 2012.

an element x_0 such that $\mu_A(x_0) = 1$); fuzzy convex (i.e. $\mu_A(\lambda x_1 + (1 - \lambda)x_2) \geq \mu_A(x_1) \wedge \mu_A(x_2)$, $\forall x_1, x_2 \in \mathbb{R}$, $\forall \lambda \in [0, 1]$); whose μ_A is upper semicontinuous and $supp(A)$ is bounded (where $supp(A) = cl(\{x \in \mathbb{R} : \mu_A(x) > 0\})$, and cl is the closure operator). A space of all fuzzy numbers will be denoted by $\mathbb{F}(\mathbb{R})$.

It is known that for any fuzzy number A there exist four numbers $a_1, a_2, a_3, a_4 \in \mathbb{R}$ and two functions $l_A, r_A : \mathbb{R} \to [0, 1]$, where l_A is nondecreasing and r_A is nonincreasing, such that we can describe a membership function μ_A in a following manner

$$\mu_A(x) = \begin{cases} 0 & \text{if} \quad x < a_1 \\ l_A(x) & \text{if} \quad a_1 \leq x < a_2 \\ 1 & \text{if} \quad a_2 \leq x \leq a_3 \\ r_A(x) & \text{if} \quad a_3 < x \leq a_4 \\ 0 & \text{if} \quad a_4 < x. \end{cases} \tag{1}$$

Functions l_A and r_A are called the left side and the right side of a fuzzy number A, respectively.

Moreover, let $A_\alpha = \{x \in \mathbb{R} : \mu_A(x) \geq \alpha\}$, $\alpha \in (0, 1]$, and $A_0 = supp(A)$, denote an α-cut of a fuzzy number A. As it is known, every α-cut of a fuzzy number is a closed interval, i.e. $A_\alpha = [A_L(\alpha), A_U(\alpha)]$, where $A_L(\alpha) = \inf\{x \in \mathbb{R} : \mu_A(x) \geq \alpha\}$ and $A_U(\alpha) = \sup\{x \in \mathbb{R} : \mu_A(x) \geq \alpha\}$.

The core of a fuzzy number A is the set of all points that surely belong to A, i.e. $core(A) = \{x \in \mathbb{R} : \mu_A(x) = 1\} = A_{\alpha=1}$.

One of the most important aspects of fuzzy data analysis is the usage of a suitable distance on the family $\mathbb{F}(\mathbb{R})$, a distance that is both not too hard to calculate and which reflects the intuitive meaning of fuzzy sets. The most popular one is the distance $d_2 : \mathbb{F}(\mathbb{R}) \times \mathbb{F}(\mathbb{R}) \to [0, +\infty)$ which is actually the L_2-distance in $\mathbb{F}(\mathbb{R})$ defined for two arbitrary fuzzy numbers A and B as follows (see, e.g. [7])

$$d_2(A, B) = \sqrt{\int_0^1 (A_L(\alpha) - B_L(\alpha))^2 d\alpha + \int_0^1 (A_U(\alpha) - B_U(\alpha))^2 d\alpha}, \tag{2}$$

where $[A_L(\alpha), A_U(\alpha)]$ and $[B_L(\alpha), B_U(\alpha)]$ are the α-cuts of A and B, respectively. Distance (2) is a particular case of the weighted distance

$$d_{ZL}(A, B) = \sqrt{\int_0^1 (A_L(\alpha) - B_L(\alpha))^2 \lambda(\alpha) d\alpha + \int_0^1 (A_U(\alpha) - B_U(\alpha))^2 \lambda(\alpha) d\alpha}$$

where λ is an integrable and nonnegative weighting function. Some authors assume that a weighting function λ is increasing on $[0, 1]$ and such that $\lambda(0) = 0$. These properties mean that higher weight and thus greater importance is attributed to higher α-cuts. Such typical weighted function applied by many authors is simply $\lambda(\alpha) = \alpha$ (e.g. [16]). However, non-monotonic weighting function may be also of interest like bi-symmetrical weighting functions (see [11], [12]).

Another interesting distance was proposed by Bertoluzza et al. [1] and generalized by Trutschnig et al. [14] which can be expressed in terms of the squared

Euclidean distance between the mids and spreads of the interval level sets of the two fuzzy numbers involved. For each fuzzy number $A \in \mathbb{F}(\mathbb{R})$ we define the following two functions: its mid

$$mid(A(\alpha)) = \frac{1}{2}(A_L(\alpha) + A_U(\alpha)) \tag{3}$$

and spread

$$spr(A(\alpha)) = \frac{1}{2}(A_U(\alpha) - A_L(\alpha)), \tag{4}$$

which attribute to each α-cut A_α the center and the half of the length of that α-cut, respectively. Then for two arbitrary fuzzy numbers A and B we get the distance $\delta_\theta : \mathbb{F}(\mathbb{R}) \times \mathbb{F}(\mathbb{R}) \to [0, +\infty)$ as follows

$$\delta_\theta^2(A, B) = \int_0^1 \left([mid(A(\alpha)) - mid(B(\alpha))]^2 + \theta \, [spr(A(\alpha)) - spr(B(\alpha))]^2 \right) d\alpha, \tag{5}$$

where $\theta \in (0, 1]$ is a parameter indicating the relative importance of the spreads against the mids.

One can easily check that for $\theta = 1$ the Trutschnig distance (5) is equivalent to the most widespread distance (2), i.e. $\delta_{\theta=1}^2(A, B) = \frac{1}{2}d_2^2(A, B)$ for any $A, B \in \mathbb{F}(\mathbb{R})$. It means that (2) attaches the same importance to mids and spreads. However, it seems that the distance between mids is often more important than that of the spreads because especially mids determine the position of the set. Hence distances $A \in \mathbb{F}(\mathbb{R})$ with $\theta < 1$ should be rather of interest.

We may also consider the generalized Trutschnig distance $\delta_{\theta,\lambda} : \mathbb{F}(\mathbb{R}) \times \mathbb{F}(\mathbb{R}) \to [0, +\infty)$ such that

$$\delta_{\theta,\lambda}^2(A, B) = \int_0^1 \left([mid(A(\alpha)) - mid(B(\alpha))]^2 + \theta \, [spr(A(\alpha)) - spr(B(\alpha))]^2 \right) \lambda(\alpha) d\alpha, \tag{6}$$

where $\lambda : [0, 1] \to [0, 1]$ is a weighting function. Of course, if $\lambda = 1$ then $\delta_{\theta,\lambda} = \delta_\theta$.

To represent a fuzzy number in a concise way some characteristics of fuzzy numbers are commonly applied. Probably the most important one is the *expected interval* $EI(A)$ of a fuzzy number A, introduced independently by Dubois and Prade [6] and Heilpern [13]. It is given by

$$EI(A) = [EI_L(A), EI_U(A)] = \left[\int_0^1 A_L(\alpha) d\alpha, \int_0^1 A_U(\alpha) d\alpha \right]. \tag{7}$$

Carlson and Fuller [2] proposed the so-called *interval-valued possibilistic mean*:

$$M(A) = [M_*(A), M^*(A)] = \left[2 \int_0^1 A_L(\alpha) \alpha d\alpha, 2 \int_0^1 A_U(\alpha) \alpha d\alpha \right]. \tag{8}$$

The middle point of the expected interval given by

$$EV(A) = \frac{1}{2} \left(\int_0^1 A_L(\alpha) d\alpha + \int_0^1 A_U(\alpha) d\alpha \right) \tag{9}$$

is called the *expected value* of a fuzzy number and it represents the typical value of the fuzzy number A (see [6], [13]). The middle point of the interval-valued possibilistic mean, i.e.

$$\overline{M}(A) = \int_0^1 (A_L(\alpha) + A_U(\alpha))\alpha d\alpha \tag{10}$$

is called the *crisp possibilistic mean value* of A and serves also as a natural location parameter of a fuzzy number. Another parameter characterizing the typical value of the magnitude that the fuzzy number A represents is called the *value* of fuzzy number A and is defined by (see [4])

$$Val(A) = \int_0^1 (A_L(\alpha) + A_U(\alpha))\lambda(\alpha)d\alpha, \tag{11}$$

where λ denotes, as before, the weighting function. One can easily see that $\overline{M}(A)$ is a particular case of $Val(A)$ for the linear weighting function $\lambda(\alpha) = \alpha$.

To describe the nonspecifity of a fuzzy number we usually use so-called *width* of a fuzzy number (see [3]) defined by

$$w(A) = \int_{-\infty}^{\infty} \mu_A(x)dx = \int_0^1 (A_U(\alpha) - A_L(\alpha))d\alpha. \tag{12}$$

Another index characterizing the vagueness of fuzzy number A, called the *ambiguity*, is given by (see [4])

$$Amb(A) = \int_0^1 (A_U(\alpha) - A_L(\alpha))\lambda(\alpha)d\alpha. \tag{13}$$

3   Interval Approximation of a Fuzzy Number

Suppose we want to approximate a fuzzy number by a crisp interval. Thus we have to use an operator $C : \mathbb{F}(\mathbb{R}) \to \mathbb{I}(\mathbb{R})$ which transforms fuzzy numbers into family of closed intervals $\mathbb{I}(\mathbb{R})$ on the real line (of course, $\mathbb{I}(\mathbb{R}) \subset \mathbb{F}(\mathbb{R})$). Different methods for finding interval approximations of fuzzy sets are used. The easiest way is to substitute a fuzzy number either by its support

$$C_0(A) = supp(A) \tag{14}$$

or by its core

$$C_1(A) = core(A), \tag{15}$$

but using this methods all information due to fuzziness of the notion under discussion is neglected. Hence probably the best known and the most popular in practice operator is

$$C_{0.5}(A) = \{x \in \mathbb{R} : \mu_A(x) \geq 0.5\}. \tag{16}$$

This operator seems to be a compromise between two extremes C_0 and C_1. Moreover, it has a quite natural interpretation: any $x \in \mathbb{R}$ belongs to the approximation interval $C_{0.5}(A)$ of a fuzzy number A if and only if its degree of belongingness to A is not smaller than its degree of belongingness to the complement of A (i.e. $\neg A$). $C_{0.5}(A)$ is sometimes called in literature the *nearest ordinary set of a fuzzy set A*. However, this simple and natural operator has a very unpleasant drawback – the lack of continuity (see, e.g. [8]).

Last three methods, i.e. (14), (15) and (16) are particular cases of the general $\alpha-$cut method for obtaining interval approximations of fuzzy numbers

$$C_\alpha(A) = \{x \in \mathbb{R} : \mu_A(x) \geq \alpha\} = A_\alpha, \quad \alpha \in (0, 1], \qquad (17)$$

i.e. we substitute given fuzzy number by its $\alpha-$cut, where α may be interpreted as a degree of conviction or acceptability of the imprecise information. Actually, $C_0(A) = A_{\alpha=0}$, $C_{0.5}(A) = A_{\alpha=0.5}$ and $C_1(A) = A_{\alpha=1}$. Unfortunately all C_α operators reveal the lack of continuity.

Although one can try to approximate a fuzzy number in many ways, an interval approximation of a fuzzy number should fulfil at least two natural requirements, comprised in a following definition:

Definition 1. *An operator $C : \mathbb{F}(\mathbb{R}) \rightarrow \mathbb{I}(\mathbb{R})$ is called an interval approximation operator if for any $A \in \mathbb{F}(\mathbb{R})$*
(1) $C(A) \subseteq supp(A)$
(2) $core(A) \subseteq C(A)$.

The definition given above leads to very broad family of operators including, of course, all C_α operators. However it seems desirable to apply approximation operators which satisfy some additional requirements, like continuity, invariance to translation and scale, monotonicity, identity, preservation of some important characteristics, etc. The broad list of requirements for trapezoidal approximation operators that might be useful also there is given in [10].

Hence looking for the interval approximation having some desired properties Grzegorzewski [8] tried to find the operator $C_G : \mathbb{F}(\mathbb{R}) \rightarrow \mathbb{I}(\mathbb{R})$ which for any $A \in \mathbb{F}(\mathbb{R})$ produces the interval nearest to A with respect to metric (2). The solution is

$$C_G(A) = \left[\int_0^1 A_L(\alpha)d\alpha, \int_0^1 A_U(\alpha)d\alpha \right]. \qquad (18)$$

which is actually equivalent to the expected interval, i.e. $C_G(A) = EI(A)$. Operator C_G is continuous, invariant to translation and scale. It is worth noting that the interval approximation operator (18) is also the nearest to A with respect to the Hamming distance among all the intervals of the same width (see [3]).

4   Interval Approximation with Respect to $\delta_{\theta,\lambda}$ Distance

In this section we will consider the interval approximation operator which produces outputs nearest to inputs with respect to the generalized Trutschnig distance (6). Given $A \in \mathbb{F}(\mathbb{R})$ with α-cuts $[A_L(\alpha), A_U(\alpha)]$ we'll try to find a closed interval $C_{T,\theta,\lambda}(A) = [c_L, c_U]$ which is nearest to A with respect to metric $\delta_{\theta,\lambda}$. We can apply $\delta_{\theta,\lambda}$ since each interval is also a fuzzy number with constant α−cuts for all $\alpha \in (0, 1]$. Hence $(C_{T,\theta,\lambda}(A))_\alpha = [c_L, c_U]$ for each $\alpha \in (0, 1]$. Therefore, we have to minimize $\delta_{\theta,\lambda}(A, C_{T,\theta,\lambda}(A))$ with respect to c_L and c_U, where

$$\delta^2_{\theta,\lambda}(A, C_{T,\theta,\lambda}(A)) = \int_0^1 \left[(mid(A_\alpha) - mid(C_\alpha))^2 + \theta \left(spr(A_\alpha) - spr(C_\alpha) \right)^2 \right] \lambda(\alpha)d\alpha.$$

In order to minimize $\delta_{\theta,\lambda}(A, C_{T,\theta,\lambda}(A))$ it suffices to minimize function $D(c_L, c_U) = \delta^2_{\theta,\lambda}(A, C_{T,\theta,\lambda}(A))$. By (3) and (4) we get

$$D(c_L, c_U) = \frac{1}{4} \int_0^1 \Big[(A_L(\alpha) + A_U(\alpha) - c_L - c_U)^2$$
$$+ \theta \left(A_U(\alpha) - A_L(\alpha) - c_U + c_L \right)^2 \Big] \lambda(\alpha)d\alpha.$$

Thus we have to find partial derivatives

$$\frac{\partial D(c_L, c_U)}{\partial c_L} = -\frac{1}{2} \int_0^1 (A_L(\alpha) + A_U(\alpha) - c_L - c_U) \lambda(\alpha)d\alpha$$
$$+ \frac{\theta}{2} \int_0^1 (A_U(\alpha) - A_L(\alpha) - c_U + c_L) \lambda(\alpha)d\alpha$$

$$\frac{\partial D(c_L, c_U)}{\partial c_U} = -\frac{1}{2} \int_0^1 (A_L(\alpha) + A_U(\alpha) - c_L - c_U) \lambda(\alpha)d\alpha$$
$$- \frac{\theta}{2} \int_0^1 (A_U(\alpha) - A_L(\alpha) - c_U + c_L) \lambda(\alpha)d\alpha$$

and then solving $\frac{\partial D(c_L, c_U)}{\partial c_L} = 0$ and $\frac{\partial D(c_L, c_U)}{\partial c_U} = 0$ we get

$$(c_L + c_U) \int_0^1 \lambda(\alpha)d\alpha = \int_0^1 (A_L(\alpha) + A_U(\alpha)) \lambda(\alpha)d\alpha$$

$$(c_U - c_L) \int_0^1 \lambda(\alpha)d\alpha = \int_0^1 (A_U(\alpha) - A_L(\alpha)) \lambda(\alpha)d\alpha.$$

The solution is

$$c_L = \frac{\int_0^1 A_L(\alpha)\lambda(\alpha)d\alpha}{\int_0^1 \lambda(\alpha)d\alpha} \qquad (19)$$

$$c_U = \frac{\int_0^1 A_U(\alpha)\lambda(\alpha)d\alpha}{\int_0^1 \lambda(\alpha)d\alpha}. \qquad (20)$$

Moreover, since $\frac{\partial D^2(c_L, c_U)}{\partial c_L^2} = \frac{\partial D^2(c_L, c_U)}{\partial c_U^2} = \frac{1}{2}(1+\theta) \int_0^1 \lambda(\alpha)d\alpha > 0$ and $\frac{\partial D^2(c_L, c_U)}{\partial c_U \partial c_L}$
$= \frac{\partial D^2(c_L, c_U)}{\partial c_L \partial c_U} = \frac{1}{2}(1 - \theta) \int_0^1 \lambda(\alpha)d\alpha$ hence

$$\det \begin{bmatrix} \frac{\partial D^2(c_L, c_U)}{\partial c_L^2} & \frac{\partial D^2(c_L, c_U)}{\partial c_U \partial c_L} \\ \frac{\partial D^2(c_L, c_U)}{\partial c_L \partial c_U} & \frac{\partial D^2(c_L, c_U)}{\partial c_U^2} \end{bmatrix} = \theta \left(\int_0^1 \lambda(\alpha)d\alpha \right)^2 > 0$$

so c_L and c_U given by (19) and (20), respectively, minimize $D(c_L, c_U)$ and - simultaneously - minimize $\delta_{\theta,\lambda}(A, C_{T,\theta,\lambda}(A))$. Therefore, $C_{T,\theta,\lambda}(A) = [c_L, c_U]$ is the interval nearest to A with respect to the generalized Trutschnig distance (6).

Looking on our results we obtain immediately an interesting conclusions.

Remark 1. For any parameter $\theta \in (0,1]$ the interval approximation operator $C_{T,\theta,\lambda} : \mathbb{F}(\mathbb{R}) \to \mathbb{I}(\mathbb{R})$ producing intervals nearest to the input with respect to metric $\delta_{\theta,\lambda}$ does not depend on θ.

Hence, further on our interval approximation operator will be no longer denoted as $C_{T,\theta,\lambda}$ but by $C_{T,\lambda}$, i.e. we have

$$C_{T,\lambda}(A) = \left[\frac{\int_0^1 A_L(\alpha)\lambda(\alpha)d\alpha}{\int_0^1 \lambda(\alpha)d\alpha}, \frac{\int_0^1 A_U(\alpha)\lambda(\alpha)d\alpha}{\int_0^1 \lambda(\alpha)d\alpha} \right]. \tag{21}$$

5 Properties

In this section we consider some properties of the interval approximation operators $C_{T,\lambda}$ suggested in Sec. 3.

Proposition 1. *The interval approximation operator $C_{T,\lambda}$ is invariant to translations, i.e. $C_{T,\lambda}(A + z) = C_{T,\lambda}(A) + z$ for any $A \in \mathbb{F}(\mathbb{R})$ and for any $z \in \mathbb{R}$.*

Proposition 2. *The interval approximation operator $C_{T,\lambda}$ is scale invariant, i.e. $C_{T,\lambda}(\gamma \cdot A) = \gamma \cdot C_{T,\lambda}(A)$ for any $A \in \mathbb{F}(\mathbb{R})$ and for any $\gamma \in \mathbb{R} \setminus \{0\}$.*

Proposition 3. *The interval approximation operator $C_{T,\lambda}$ fulfills the identity criterion, i.e. if $A \in \mathbb{I}(\mathbb{R})$ then $C_{T,\lambda}(A) = A$.*

The proofs of the above three propositions are standard.

Proposition 4. *The interval approximation operator $C_{T,\lambda}$ is monotonic, i.e. for any $A, B \in \mathbb{F}(\mathbb{R})$ if $A \subseteq B$ then $C_{T,\lambda}(A) \subseteq C_{T,\lambda}(B)$.*

Proof: Since $A \subseteq B$ there exist a nonnegative function $h(\alpha) \geq 0$ such that $A_L(\alpha) = B_L(\alpha) + h(\alpha)$ for all $\alpha \in (0,1]$. Hence for $C_{T,\lambda}(A) = [c_L(A), c_U(A)]$ we get $c_L(A) \int_0^1 \lambda(\alpha)d\alpha = \int_0^1 A_L(\alpha)\lambda(\alpha)d\alpha = \int_0^1 (B_L(\alpha) + h(\alpha))\lambda(\alpha)d\alpha$
$= \int_0^1 B_L(\alpha)\lambda(\alpha)d\alpha + \int_0^1 h(\alpha)\lambda(\alpha)d\alpha$. By the theorem on mean value for integrals there exist such constant $\xi \in (0,1)$ that $\int_0^1 h(\alpha)\lambda(\alpha)d\alpha = h(\xi)\int_0^1 \lambda(\alpha)d\alpha$ so $c_L(A) = c_L(B) + h(\xi) \geq c_L(B)$.

Similarly, if $A \subseteq B$ then there exist a function $k(\alpha) \geq 0$ such that $A_U(\alpha) = B_U(\alpha) - h(\alpha)$ for all $\alpha \in [0,1]$. In the same manner we can see that there exist a constant $\zeta \in (0,1)$ such that $c_U(A) = c_U(B) - k(\zeta) \leq c_U(B)$. Thus finally $C_{T,\lambda}(A) = [c_L(A), c_U(A)] \subseteq [c_L(B), c_U(B)] = C_{T,\lambda}(B)$ and the criterion of monotony holds. $\square$

It would be also desirable that if two fuzzy numbers A and B are close – in some sense – then their interval approximations are also close. One can also prove that

Proposition 5. *If the weighting function λ is continuous then the interval approximation operator $C_{T,\lambda}$ is continuous, i.e.*

$$\forall (\varepsilon > 0)\ \exists (\sigma > 0)\quad d(A, B) < \sigma \Rightarrow d(C_{T,\lambda}(A), C_{T,\lambda}(B)) < \varepsilon,$$

where $d : \mathbb{F}(\mathbb{R}) \times \mathbb{F}(\mathbb{R}) \to [0, +\infty)$ denotes a metric defined in the family of all fuzzy numbers.

It can be shown that our interval approximation operator $C_{T,\lambda}$ is preserves some indices characterizing fuzzy numbers mentioned in Sec. 2.

Proposition 6. *If A is a symmetrical fuzzy number then the interval approximation operator $C_{T,\lambda}$ preserves the expected value, i.e. $EV(C_{T,\lambda}(A)) = EV(A)$.*

Proof: By (9) and (21)

$$EV(C_{T,\lambda}(A)) = \frac{c_L + c_U}{2} = \frac{\int_0^1 (A_L(\alpha) + A_U(\alpha))\lambda(\alpha)d\alpha}{2\int_0^1 \lambda(\alpha)d\alpha}. \tag{22}$$

However, if $A \in \mathbb{F}(\mathbb{R})$ is symmetrical then its α-cuts satisfy the relation: $A_U(\alpha) = 2q - A_L(\alpha)$ for each $\alpha \in (0,1]$, where $q = \frac{1}{2}(A_L(0) + A_U(0))$. Substituting $A_U(\alpha) = 2q - A_L(\alpha)$ into (22) we get $EV(C_{T,\lambda}(A)) = q$. By (9) we obtain that for a symmetrical fuzzy number $EV(A) = q$. So the theorem holds.   □

Proposition 7. *The interval approximation operator $C_{T,\lambda}$ preserves the value of a fuzzy number, i.e. $Val(C_{T,\lambda}(A)) = Val(A)$.*

Proposition 8. *The interval approximation operator $C_{T,\lambda}$ preserves the ambiguity of a fuzzy number, i.e. $Amb(C_{T,\lambda}(A)) = Amb(A)$.*

The proofs of the last two propositions are straightforward.

Proposition 9. *Let $C_{T,\alpha}$ denote the interval approximation operator for the linear weighting function $\lambda(\alpha) = \alpha$. Then $EV(C_{T,\alpha}(A)) = \overline{M}(A) = Val(A)$ and $w(C_{T,\alpha}(A)) = 2Amb(A)$.*

Proof: By (9) and (10) we get

$$EV(C_{T,\alpha}(A)) = \frac{\int_0^1 (A_L(\alpha) + A_U(\alpha))\alpha d\alpha}{2\int_0^1 \alpha d\alpha} = \int_0^1 (A_L(\alpha) + A_U(\alpha))\alpha d\alpha = \overline{M}(A)$$

which is also equivalent to $Val(A)$ for $\lambda(\alpha) = \alpha$. Similarly, we obtain

$$w(C_{T,\alpha}(A)) = \frac{\int_0^1 (A_U(\alpha) - A_L(\alpha))\alpha d\alpha}{\int_0^1 \alpha d\alpha} = 2\int_0^1 (A_U(\alpha) - A_L(\alpha))\alpha d\alpha = 2Amb(A)$$

□

Now we will compare the interval approximation operator $C_{T,\lambda}$ with the approximation operators discussed in Sec. 3. Let us firstly consider a situation with equally weighting for all α-cuts. Thus putting $\lambda(\alpha) = 1$ into (21) and comparing the output with (18) we get another intriguing result that the interval approximation with respect to metric δ_θ coincide with the interval approximation with respect to L_2-metric d_2.

Theorem 1. *Let $C_{T,1} : \mathbb{F}(\mathbb{R}) \to \mathbb{I}(\mathbb{R})$ denote an interval approximating operator producing intervals nearest to the input with respect to metric δ_θ with equally weighted α-cuts, i.e. $\lambda(\alpha) = 1$ for each $\alpha \in (0,1]$. Then the interval approximation operator $C_{T,1}$ is equivalent with the Grzegorzewski operator (18), i.e. $C_{T,1} = C_G$.*

Comparing (8) with (21) one can easily prove

Theorem 2. *Let $C_{T,\alpha}$ denote the interval approximation operator for the linear weighting function $\lambda(\alpha) = \alpha$. Then the interval approximation operator $C_{T,\alpha}$ producing intervals nearest to the input with respect to $\delta_{\theta,\alpha}$ is the interval-valued possibilistic mean, i.e. $C_{T,\alpha}(A) = M(A)$.*

Taking into account last remark one may be interested in the comparison of the interval approximation interval obtained using the Grzegorzewski operator (18) and the approximation interval (21) nearest to the input with respect to metric $\delta_{\theta,\lambda}$ with the linear weighting function $\lambda(\alpha) = \alpha$. The following lemma holds.

Lemma 1. *For any fuzzy number A its interval approximation $C_G(A)$ contains $C_{T,\alpha}(A)$, i.e. $C_{T,\alpha}(A) \subseteq C_G(A)$.*

The most important subfamily of fuzzy numbers are trapezoidal fuzzy numbers $\mathbb{F}^T(\mathbb{R}) \subset \mathbb{F}(\mathbb{R})$. A membership function of any trapezoidal fuzzy number A can be described in a following manner

$$\mu_A(x) = \begin{cases} 0 & \text{if } x < a_1 \\ \frac{x-a_1}{a_2-a_1} & \text{if } a_1 \le x < a_2 \\ 1 & \text{if } a_2 \le x \le a_3 \\ \frac{a_4-x}{a_4-a_3} & \text{if } a_3 < x \le a_4 \\ 0 & \text{if } a_4 < x, \end{cases}$$

where $a_1 \le a_2 \le a_3 \le a_4$. In [8] it was shown that in the subfamily of trapezoidal fuzzy numbers the interval approximation operators C_G and (16) are equivalent, i.e. $C_G(A) = C_{0.5}(A) \quad \forall A \in \mathbb{F}^T(\mathbb{R})$. Now let us consider the interval approximation operator $C_{T,\alpha}$ corresponding to metric $\delta_{\theta,\lambda}$ with the linear weighting function $\lambda(\alpha) = \alpha$ for the subfamily of trapezoidal fuzzy numbers.

Theorem 3. *In the subfamily of trapezoidal fuzzy numbers the interval approximation operators $C_{T,\alpha}$ is equivalent to the interval approximation operator (17) for $\alpha = \frac{2}{3}$, i.e.*

$$C_{T,\alpha}(A) = C_{2/3}(A) \quad \forall A \in \mathbb{F}^T(\mathbb{R}). \tag{23}$$

Proof: The α−cuts of the trapezoidal fuzzy numbers are given by $A_\alpha = [A_L(\alpha), A_U(\alpha)] = [a_1 + (a_2 - a_1)\alpha, a_4 - (a_4 - a_3)\alpha]$. Hence $C_{T,\alpha}(A) = \left[2\int_0^1 (a_1 + (a_2 - a_1)\alpha)\,\alpha d\alpha, 2\int_0^1 (a_4 - (a_4 - a_3)\alpha)\,\alpha d\alpha \right] = [\frac{1}{3}a_1 + \frac{2}{3}a_2, \frac{2}{3}a_3 + \frac{1}{3}a_4]$. Since $A_{2/3} = [\frac{1}{3}a_1 + \frac{2}{3}a_2, \frac{2}{3}a_3 + \frac{1}{3}a_4] = C_{2/3}$ thus we get the desired conclusion. $\square$

6   Conclusions

In the paper we have considered the interval approximation operator of fuzzy numbers leading to intervals nearest to the original fuzzy number with respect to the generalized Trutschnig distance. We have shown that this operator has not only many interesting properties but it also generalizes some other approximation operators like suggested in [8] and others.

References

1. Bertoluzza, C., Corral, N., Salas, A.: On a new class of distances between fuzzy numbers. Mathware and Soft Computing 2, 71–84 (1995)
2. Carlsson, C., Fuller, R.: On possibilistic mean value and variance of fuzzy numbers. Fuzzy Sets and Systems 122, 315–326 (2001)
3. Chanas, S.: On the interval approximation of a fuzzy number. Fuzzy Sets and Systems 122, 353–356 (2001)
4. Delgado, M., Vila, M.A., Voxman, W.: On a canonical representation of a fuzzy number. Fuzzy Sets and Systems 93, 125–135 (1998)
5. Dubois, D., Prade, H.: Operations on fuzzy numbers. Int. J. Syst. Sci. 9, 613–626 (1978)
6. Dubois, D., Prade, H.: The mean value of a fuzzy number. Fuzzy Sets and Systems 24, 279–300 (1987)
7. Grzegorzewski, P.: Metrics and orders in space of fuzzy numbers. Fuzzy Sets and Systems 97, 83–94 (1998)
8. Grzegorzewski, P.: Nearest interval approximation of a fuzzy number. Fuzzy Sets and Systems 130, 321–330 (2002)
9. Grzegorzewski, P.: Approximation of a fuzzy number preserving entropy-like non-specifity. Operations Research and Decisions 4, 49–59 (2003)
10. Grzegorzewski, P., Mrówka, E.: Trapezoidal approximations of fuzzy numbers. Fuzzy Sets and Systems 153, 115–135 (2005)
11. Grzegorzewski, P., Pasternak-Winiarska, K.: Weighted trapezoidal approximations of fuzzy numbers. In: Carvalho, J.P., Dubois, D., Kaymak, U., Sousa, J.M.C. (eds.) Proceedings of the Joint 2009 International Fuzzy Systems Association World Congress and 2009 European Society of Fuzzy Logic and Technology Conference, Lisbon, pp. 1531–1534 (2009)
12. Grzegorzewski, P., Pasternak-Winiarska, K.: Bi-symmetrically weighted trapezoidal approximations of fuzzy numbers. In: Abraham, A., Benitez Sanchez, J.M., Herrera, F., Loia, V., Marcelloni, F., Senatore, S. (eds.) Proceedings of Ninth International Conference on Intelligent Systems Design and Applications, Pisa, pp. 318–323 (2009)
13. Heilpern, S.: The expected value of a fuzzy number. Fuzzy Sets and Systems 47, 81–86 (1992)
14. Trutschnig, W., González-Rodríguez, G., Colubi, A., Gil, M.A.: A new family of metrics for compact, convex (fuzzy) sets based on a generalized concept of mid and spread. Information Sciences 179, 3964–3972 (2009)
15. Yeh, C.-T.: Weighted trapezoidal and triangular approximations of fuzzy numbers. Fuzzy Sets and Systems 160, 3059–3079 (2009)
16. Zeng, W., Li, H.: Weighted triangular approximation of fuzzy numbers. International Journal of Approximate Reasoning 46, 137–150 (2007)

Approximation of Fuzzy Numbers
by F-Transform

Luciano Stefanini and Laerte Sorini

DESP - Department of Economics, Society and Politics
University of Urbino "Carlo Bo", Italy
{lucste,laerte.sorini}@uniurb.it

Abstract. The fuzzy transform setting (F-transform) is proposed as a tool for representation and approximation of type-1 and type-2 fuzzy numbers; the inverse F-transform on appropriate fuzzy partition of the membership interval [0,1] is used to characterize spaces of fuzzy numbers in such a way that arithmetic operations are defined and expressed in terms of the F-transform of the results. A type-2 fuzzy number is represented as a particular fuzzy-valued function and it is expressed in terms of a two-dimensional F-transform where the first dimension represents the universe domain and the second dimension represents the membership domain. Operators on two dimensional F-transform are then proposed to approximate arithmetic operations with type 2 fuzzy numbers.

Keywords: Fuzzy Transform, Fuzzy Numbers, Fuzzy Arithmetic, Type-2 Fuzzy Numbers.

1 Introduction

The fuzzy transform (F-transform) has recently been introduced by I. Perfilieva in [3] and [4]. Several connections between theory (with extensions to the multidimensional case in [14]) and applications are covered e.g. in [1], [2], [5], [6], [7], [8], [13] and [15]. A special issue of *Fuzzy Sets and Systems* (Vol. 180, 2011, pages 1-184) has been devoted to recent results on F-transform, its properties and its applications.

The F-transform offers a new setting to obtain good approximations (including interpolation) of functions of single and multiple variables and is proposed here as a tool to approximate and to represent fuzzy numbers (or intervals) of type-1 and type-2. A type-1 fuzzy number u is represented in terms of its level cuts $[u]_\alpha = [u_\alpha^-, u_\alpha^+]$ for all $\alpha \in [0,1]$; the two functions $u^- : \alpha \longrightarrow u_\alpha^-$ and $u^+ : \alpha \longrightarrow u_\alpha^+$ are usually called the *lower* and the *upper* branches of the LU-representation (L=lower, U=upper). The two branch functions u^- and u^+ are approximated by the F-transform on appropriate fuzzy partitions of the membership interval $[0,1]$.

A similar construction can be proposed to approximate and represent a type-2 fuzzy number, by the use of a two-dimensional F-transform where the first

S. Greco et al. (Eds.): IPMU 2012, Part III, CCIS 299, pp. 69–78, 2012.

dimension represents the universe (or primary) domain and the second dimension represents the membership interval $[0, 1]$.

The F-transform setting is finally used to obtain good approximations of the arithmetic operations with type-1 and type-2 fuzzy numbers; in fact, using the F-transform approximation, we are able to obtain the F-transform of the standard arithmetic for fuzzy numbers as expressed in terms of the α-cuts of the operands in addition, scalar multiplication, difference, product, division, maximum, minimum, including the application of the Zadeh's extension principle to extend real-valued functions to fuzzy arguments.

The organization of the paper is as follows. In section 2 we begin with the basic definitions and properties of type-1 fuzzy numbers and we describe the unidimensional F-transform and its basic properties. In section 3 we use F-transform to represents type-1 fuzzy numbers and we illustrate the corresponding arithmetic operators. In section 4 we extend the use of F-transform to approximate type-2 fuzzy numbers.

2   F-Transform and Its Basic Properties

We briefly recall the basic definitions and properties of the F-transform (see [3]).

Definition 1. *A fuzzy partition for a given real compact interval* $[a, b]$ *is constructed by a decomposition* $\mathbb{P} = \{a = x_1 < x_2 < ... < x_n = b\}$ *of* $[a, b]$ *into* $n - 1$ *subintervals* $[x_{k-1}, x_k]$, $k = 2, ..., n$ *and by a family* $\mathbb{A} = \{A_1, A_2, ..., A_n\}$ *of* n *fuzzy numbers (the basic functions) identified by the membership values* $A_1(x), A_2(x), ..., A_n(x)$ *for* $x \in [a, b]$; *the required properties (to complete this notation, we set* $x_0 = a$ *and* $x_{n+1} = b$*) are as follows:*

1. *each* $A_k : [a, b] \longrightarrow [0, 1]$ *is continuous with* $A_k(x_k) = 1$, $A_k(x) = 0$ *for* $x \notin [x_{k-1}, x_{k+1}]$;
2. *for* $k = 2, 3, ..., n - 1$, A_k *is increasing on* $[x_{k-1}, x_k]$ *and decreasing on* $[x_k, x_{k+1}]$; A_1 *is decreasing on* $[a, x_2]$; A_n *is increasing on* $[x_{n-1}, b]$;
3. *for all* $x \in [a, b]$ *the following holds* $\sum_{k=1}^{n} A_k(x) = 1$.

We denote a fuzzy partition by the pair $(\mathbb{P}, \mathbb{A})$. On each subinterval $]x_{k-1}, x_k[$ of the decomposition $\mathbb{P}$, only two basic functions $A_{k-1}(x)$ and $A_k(x)$ are non zero for $k = 2, ..., n$.

We consider the direct and inverse F-transform defined in [3]; a compact interval $[a, b]$ is given, and a fuzzy partition $(\mathbb{P}, \mathbb{A})$ of $[a, b]$ is selected. Given m distinct points $t_j \in [a, b]$, $j = 1, ..., m$, such that each set $T_k = \{t_j | A_k(t_j) > 0\}$, $k = 1, ..., n$, is nonempty (assuming $t_1 < t_2 < ... < t_m$), we say that $\mathbb{T} = \{t_1, t_2, ..., t_m\}$ is *sufficiently* dense with respect to $(\mathbb{P}, \mathbb{A})$.

Definition 2. *(from [3]) The (direct) F-transform of an integrable function* $f :$ $[a, b] \longrightarrow \mathbb{R}$ *on partition* $(\mathbb{P}, \mathbb{A})$ *is the* n-*tuple of real numbers* $\boldsymbol{F} = (F_1, F_2, ..., F_n)$ *given by*

$$F_k = \int_a^b f(x) A_k(x) dx \Big/ \int_a^b A_k(x) dx \ \ for \ k = 1, ..., n.$$

If f is known at m sufficiently dense points $t_1, t_2, ..., t_m \in \mathbb{T}$ with respect to $(\mathbb{P}, \mathbb{A})$, the discrete direct F-transform is

$$F_k = \sum_{j=1}^m f(t_j) A_k(t_j) \Big/ \sum_{j=1}^m A_k(t_j) \ \ for \ k = 1, ..., n.$$

Definition 3. (from [3]) Given the fuzzy transform $\mathbf{F} = (F_1, F_2, ..., F_n)$ of a function $f : [a, b] \longrightarrow \mathbb{R}$ on a fuzzy partition $(\mathbb{P}, \mathbb{A})$, the inverse F-transform (iF-transform) is the function $\widehat{f}_{\mathbf{F}} : [a, b] \longrightarrow \mathbb{R}$ given by

$$\widehat{f}_{\mathbf{F}}(x) = \sum_{k=1}^n F_k A_k(x) \ \ for \ x \in [a, b]. \tag{1}$$

Note the important property that $\widehat{f}_{\mathbf{F}}(x)$ is monotonic on each subinterval $[x_{k-1}, x_k]$, and it is increasing if $F_{k-1} > F_k$, decreasing if $F_{k-1} < F_k$ or constant if $F_{k-1} = F_k$. The F-transform of monotone functions is analyzed in [7].

The following approximation property ([3]) is one of the fundamentals of the F-transform setting.

Theorem 1. ([3]) If $f : [a, b] \longrightarrow \mathbb{R}$ is a continuous function then, for any positive real ε, there exists a fuzzy partition $(\mathbb{P}_\varepsilon, \mathbb{A}_\varepsilon)$ such that the associated F-transform $\mathbf{F}_\varepsilon = (F_{1,\varepsilon}, F_{2,\varepsilon}, ..., F_{n_\varepsilon,\varepsilon})^T$ and the corresponding iF-transform $\widehat{f}_{\mathbf{F}_\varepsilon} : [a, b] \longrightarrow \mathbb{R}$ satisfy

$$\left| f(x) - \widehat{f}_{\mathbf{F}_\varepsilon}(x) \right| < \varepsilon \ for \ all \ x \in [a, b].$$

The basic properties of the F-transform are described in [3] (see also [12]):

Theorem 2. Let $f : [a, b] \longrightarrow \mathbb{R}$ be continuous and let $\mathbf{F} = (F_1, F_2, ..., F_n)^T$ be its F-transform with respect to a given partition $(\mathbb{P}, \mathbb{A})$. Then

(i) each F_k is a minimizer of the function $\phi_k(y) = \int_a^b (f(x) - y)^2 A_k(x) dx$;

(ii) the iF-transform satisfies

$$\int_a^b \widehat{f}_{\mathbf{F}}(x) dx = \int_a^b f(x) dx \ \ or \ (discrete \ case) \sum_{j=1}^m \widehat{f}_{\mathbf{F}}(t_j) = \sum_{j=1}^m f(t_j). \tag{2}$$

and, for all $k = 1, ..., n$,

$$F_k = \widehat{f}_{\mathbf{F}}(x_k). \tag{3}$$

The F-transform and the iF-transform are additive and homogeneous, hence linear ([3]):

Theorem 3. *Let* $f, g : [a, b] \longrightarrow \mathbb{R}$ *be two continuous functions and let* $\boldsymbol{F} = (F_1, F_2, ..., F_n)^T$ *and* $\boldsymbol{G} = (G_1, G_2, ..., G_n)^T$ *be the corresponding F-transform with respect to a given partition* $(\mathbb{P}, \mathbb{A})$. *Then*

(1) the F-transform of $f + g$ *is* $\boldsymbol{F} + \boldsymbol{G}$;
(2) the F-transform of λf *is* $\lambda \boldsymbol{F}$ *for all* $\lambda \in \mathbb{R}$.
Consequently, $\widehat{(f + g)}_{\boldsymbol{F}+\boldsymbol{G}} = \widehat{f}_{\boldsymbol{F}} + \widehat{g}_{\boldsymbol{G}}$ *and* $\widehat{(\lambda f)}_{\lambda \boldsymbol{F}} = \lambda \widehat{f}_{\boldsymbol{F}}$.

3   F-Transform Approximation of Fuzzy Numbers

We will denote by $\mathbb{R}_{\mathcal{F}}$ the set of fuzzy numbers or intervals, i.e. normal, fuzzy convex, upper semicontinuous and compactly supported fuzzy sets defined over the real line.

Let $u \in \mathbb{R}_{\mathcal{F}}$ be a fuzzy number. For $\alpha \in]0, 1]$, the α-level set of u (or simply the $\alpha-$cut) is defined by $[u]_\alpha = \{x | x \in \mathbb{R}, u(x) \geq \alpha\}$ and for $\alpha = 0$ by the closure of the support $[u]_0 = cl\{x | x \in \mathbb{R}, u(x) > 0\}$. The *core* of u is the set of elements of $\mathbb{R}$ having membership grade 1, i.e., $[u]_1 = \{x | x \in \mathbb{R}, u(x) = 1\}$.

It is well-known that the $level - cuts$ are "nested", i.e. $[u]_\alpha \subseteq [u]_\beta$ for $\alpha > \beta$. A fuzzy set u is a fuzzy number if and only if the $\alpha - cuts$ are nonempty compact intervals of the form $[u]_\alpha = [u_\alpha^-, u_\alpha^+] \subset \mathbb{R}$. The "nested" property is the basis for the LU representation (L for lower, U for upper). We refer to the functions $u_{(.)}^-$ and $u_{(.)}^+$ as the *lower* and *upper* branches on u, respectively; a fuzzy number is then defined, equivalently, by the pair (u^-, u^+) of functions $u^- : \alpha \longrightarrow u_\alpha^-$ and $u^+ : \alpha \longrightarrow u_\alpha^+$ representing its lower and upper branches.

If $u = (u^-, u^+)$ and $v = (v^-, v^+)$ are two given fuzzy intervals, the addition $u + v$ and the scalar multiplication ku are defined as having α-cuts, for $\alpha \in [0, 1]$

$$[u + v]_\alpha = [u]_\alpha + [v]_\alpha = \{x + y | x \in [u]_\alpha, \ y \in [v]_\alpha\}$$
$$[ku]_\alpha = k[u]_\alpha = \{kx | x \in [u]_\alpha\}, \ [0]_\alpha = \{0\}.$$

The subtraction $u - v$ is defined as the addition $u + (-v)$ where $-v = (-1)v$ and the standard multiplication uv and division $\frac{u}{v}$ (if $0 \notin [v_0^-, v_0^+]$) have α-cuts, for $\alpha \in [0, 1]$

$$[uv]_\alpha = [(uv)_\alpha^-, (uv)_\alpha^+] \tag{4}$$
$$(uv)_\alpha^- = \min\left\{u_\alpha^- v_\alpha^-, u_\alpha^- v_\alpha^+, u_\alpha^+ v_\alpha^-, u_\alpha^+ v_\alpha^+\right\}$$
$$(uv)_\alpha^+ = \max\left\{u_\alpha^- v_\alpha^-, u_\alpha^- v_\alpha^+, u_\alpha^+ v_\alpha^-, u_\alpha^+ v_\alpha^+\right\}$$

and

$$[\frac{u}{v}]_\alpha = [\left(\frac{u}{v}\right)_\alpha^-, \left(\frac{u}{v}\right)_\alpha^+]$$

(5)

$$\left(\frac{u}{v}\right)_\alpha^- = \min\left\{\frac{u_\alpha^-}{v_\alpha^-}, \frac{u_\alpha^-}{v_\alpha^+}, \frac{u_\alpha^+}{v_\alpha^-}, \frac{u_\alpha^+}{v_\alpha^+}\right\}$$

$$\left(\frac{u}{v}\right)_\alpha^+ = \max\left\{\frac{u_\alpha^-}{v_\alpha^-}, \frac{u_\alpha^-}{v_\alpha^+}, \frac{u_\alpha^+}{v_\alpha^-}, \frac{u_\alpha^+}{v_\alpha^+}\right\}.$$

The F-transform can be used to approximate any fuzzy number $u \in \mathbb{R}_\mathcal{F}$, by approximating its α-cuts $[u]_\alpha = [u_\alpha^-, u_\alpha^+]$ with the F-transform of the two monotonic functions u_α^-, u_α^+ as functions of $\alpha \in [0,1]$.

Let $(\mathbb{P}, \mathbb{A})$ be a fuzzy partition of interval $[0,1]$ with $\mathbb{P} = \{0 = \alpha_1 < \alpha_2 < ... < \alpha_n = 1\}$ and $\mathbb{A} = \{A_1, A_2, ..., A_n\}$, the basic functions, identified by the membership values $A_1(\alpha), A_2(\alpha), ..., A_n(\alpha)$ for $\alpha \in [0,1]$, i.e. $A_k \in [0,1]_\mathcal{F}$.

Let U_k^- and U_k^+, $k = 1, 2, ..., n$, be the F-transforms of functions u_α^- and u_α^+; then their iF-transforms $\widehat{u}_\alpha^-$ and $\widehat{u}_\alpha^+$ are given by

$$\widehat{u}_\alpha^- = \sum_{k=1}^{n} U_k^- A_k(\alpha) \text{ for } \alpha \in [0,1]$$

$$\widehat{u}_\alpha^+ = \sum_{k=1}^{n} U_k^+ A_k(\alpha) \text{ for } \alpha \in [0,1].$$

It is well known (see [7]) that $\widehat{u}_\alpha^-$ and $\widehat{u}_\alpha^+$ are monotone functions and it is immediate to see that $\widehat{u}_1^- \leq \widehat{u}_1^+$ because $u_\alpha^- \leq u_\alpha^+$ for all $\alpha \in [0,1]$. It follows that $\{[\widehat{u}_\alpha^-, \widehat{u}_\alpha^+]; \alpha \in [0,1]\}$ define the α-cuts of fuzzy number $\widehat{u} \in \mathbb{R}_\mathcal{F}$.

In the discrete F-transform setting, U_k^- and U_k^+, $k = 1, 2, ..., n$, can be obtained from m level-cuts $[u_{\alpha_i'}^-, u_{\alpha_i'}^+]$ such that $0 \leq \alpha_1' < \alpha_2' < ... < \alpha_m' \leq 1$ is sufficiently dense with the fuzzy partition $(\mathbb{P}, \mathbb{A})$.

It is immediate to verify that the F-transform approximation $\widehat{u} \in \mathbb{R}_\mathcal{F}$ of $u \in \mathbb{R}_\mathcal{F}$ preserves the mean interval

$$\left[\int_0^1 u_\alpha^- d\alpha, \int_0^1 u_\alpha^+ d\alpha\right] = \left[\int_0^1 \widehat{u}_\alpha^- d\alpha, \int_0^1 \widehat{u}_\alpha^+ d\alpha\right].$$

Furthermore, the fuzziness $Fuz(u) = \int_0^{0.5} (u_\alpha^+ - u_\alpha^-) d\alpha - \int_{0.5}^1 (u_\alpha^+ - u_\alpha^-) d\alpha$ can be forced to be preserved, i.e., $Fuz(u) = Fuz(\widehat{u})$, by choosing a decomposition $\mathbb{P}$ with $\alpha = 0.5$ as a point; indeed, if the fuzzy partition of $[0,1]$ has the point $\alpha_k = 0.5$, it is possible to obtain two separate fuzzy partitions of $[0, 0.5]$ and $[0.5, 1]$ with nodes $\{0 = \alpha_1 < \alpha_2 < ... < \alpha_k = 0.5\}$ and $\{0.5 = \alpha_k < \alpha_{k+1} < ... < \alpha_n = 1\}$ and basic functions $\{A_1, A_2, ..., A_k\}$ and $A = \{A_k, A_{k+1}, ..., A_n\}$ such that they are disjoint and their union is the partition $(\mathbb{P}, \mathbb{A})$ of $[0,1]$.

3.1   Spaces of Functions Generated by F-Transform

Let $[a, b]$ be a given interval and consider a fuzzy partition $(\mathbb{P}, \mathbb{A})$ of $[a, b]$, with $\mathbb{P} = \{a = x_1 < x_2 < ... < x_n = b\}$ and $\mathbb{A} = \{A_1, A_2, ..., A_n\}$. A particular case of discrete F-transform is when we take the points $t_1, t_2, ..., t_m$ to be coincident with the basic points $x_1 < x_2 < ... < x_n$ of $\mathbb{P}$.

Definition: A function $\varphi : [a, b] \longrightarrow \mathbb{R}$ such that the following equality holds

$$\varphi(x) = \sum_{k=1}^{n} \varphi(x_k) A_k(x), \quad \forall x \in [a, b] \tag{6}$$

is said to be *generated* by the F-transform with the fuzzy partition $(\mathbb{P}, \mathbb{A})$.

We denote by $\mathbb{F}(\mathbb{P}, \mathbb{A})$ the space of functions $\varphi : [a, b] \longrightarrow \mathbb{R}$ of the form (6) and we say that $\mathbb{F}(\mathbb{P}, \mathbb{A})$ is the space *reproduced* by the fuzzy partition $(\mathbb{P}, \mathbb{A})$. If $\varphi \in \mathbb{F}(\mathbb{P}, \mathbb{A})$ it is immediate to see that $\{\varphi(x_k), \ k = 1, 2, ..., n\}$ is its discrete F-transform at points $x_1, x_2, ..., x_n$; in fact, for $k = 1, ..., n$ we have $\sum_{j=1}^{n} \varphi(x_j) A_k(x_j) = \varphi(x_k)$ and $\sum_{j=1}^{n} A_k(x_j) = 1$, because $A_k(x_j) = 0$ if $k \neq j$ and $A_k(x_k) = 1$. It follows that the iF-transform of $\varphi \in \mathbb{F}(\mathbb{P}, \mathbb{A})$ with respect to $(\mathbb{P}, \mathbb{A})$ is φ itself and the space $\mathbb{F}(\mathbb{P}, \mathbb{A})$ contains exactly the functions having themselves as iF-transform.

Remark 1. Consider that, in general, it is not true that φ coincides with its iF-transform $\widehat{\varphi}_{\Phi}(x) = \sum_{k=1}^{n} \Phi_k A_k(x)$.

The space $\mathbb{F}(\mathbb{P}, \mathbb{A})$ is in one-to-one correspondence with $\mathbb{R}^n$ by the following bijection $j_{(\mathbb{P}, \mathbb{A})} : \mathbb{R}^n \longleftrightarrow \mathbb{F}(\mathbb{P}, \mathbb{A})$

$$j_{(\mathbb{P}, \mathbb{A})}(\varphi_1, ..., \varphi_n) = \sum_{k=1}^{n} \varphi_k A_k$$

and the inverse of the bijection $j_{(\mathbb{P}, \mathbb{A})}$ is obtained by the F-transform with respect to $(\mathbb{P}, \mathbb{A})$.

Examples of basic functions $\mathbb{A} = \{A_1, A_2, ..., A_n\}$ to construct fuzzy partitions $(\mathbb{P}, \mathbb{A})$ are given in [12].

3.2   Fuzzy Numbers Generated by F-Transform

We can construct a space of fuzzy numbers generated by F-transform with a given partition $(\mathbb{P}, \mathbb{A})$ of $[0, 1]$.

Let $\mathbb{P} = \{0 = \alpha_1 < \alpha_2 < ... < \alpha_n = 1\}$ be given; a fuzzy number $u \in \mathbb{R}_{\mathcal{F}}$ with α-cuts $[u_\alpha^-, u_\alpha^+]$ $\alpha \in [0, 1]$ such that the following equalities hold

$$u_\alpha^- = \sum_{k=1}^{n} u_{\alpha_k}^- A_k(\alpha), \quad \forall \alpha \in [0, 1] \tag{7}$$

$$u_\alpha^+ = \sum_{k=1}^{n} u_{\alpha_k}^+ A_k(\alpha), \quad \forall \alpha \in [0, 1] \tag{8}$$

is said *generated* by the F-transform with the fuzzy partition $(\mathbb{P}, \mathbb{A})$.

The space $\mathcal{F}(\mathbb{P}, \mathbb{A})$ is in one-to-one correspondence with

$$\mathbb{V}_{2n} = \{(\boldsymbol{u}^-, \boldsymbol{u}^+) \mid \boldsymbol{u}^-, \boldsymbol{u}^+ \in \mathbb{R}^n \text{ with } u_1^- \leq \ldots \leq u_n^- \leq u_n^+ \leq \ldots \leq u_1^+\}.$$

Consider the bijection $j_{\mathcal{F}(\mathbb{P}, \mathbb{A})} : \mathbb{V}_{2n} \longleftrightarrow \mathcal{F}(\mathbb{P}, \mathbb{A})$

$$[j_{\mathcal{F}(\mathbb{P}, \mathbb{A})}(\boldsymbol{u}^-, \boldsymbol{u}^+)]_\alpha = \left[\sum_{k=1}^n u_k^- A_k(\alpha), \sum_{k=1}^n u_k^+ A_k(\alpha) \right];$$

the inverse of the bijection $j_{\mathcal{F}(\mathbb{P}, \mathbb{A})}$ is obtained by the F-transform.

A representation of $u \in \mathcal{F}(\mathbb{P}, \mathbb{A})$ in terms of its α-cuts is the following

$$u = \left\{ [u_k^-, u_k^+] \, ; k = 1, \ldots, n \right\} \text{ and}$$

$$[u]_\alpha = \left[\sum_{k=1}^n u_k^- A_k(\alpha), \sum_{k=1}^n u_k^+ A_k(\alpha) \right]$$

3.3 Fuzzy Arithmetic with F-Transform

From the linearity of the F-transform, it follows that $\mathcal{F}(\mathbb{P}, \mathbb{A})$ is a linear space. The standard arithmetic operations, including the application of Zadeh's extension principle (for extension of a continuous function), are immediate to obtain in terms of F-transform representation.

Let $u, v \in \mathcal{F}(\mathbb{P}, \mathbb{A})$

$$u = \left\{ [u_k^-, u_k^+] \, ; k = 1, \ldots, n \right\},$$

$$[u]_\alpha = \left[\sum_{k=1}^n u_k^- A_k(\alpha), \sum_{k=1}^n u_k^+ A_k(\alpha) \right],$$

$$v = \left\{ [v_k^-, v_k^+] \, ; k = 1, \ldots, n \right\},$$

$$[v]_\alpha = \left[\sum_{k=1}^n v_k^- A_k(\alpha), \sum_{k=1}^n v_k^+ A_k(\alpha) \right].$$

We have

$$u + v = \left\{ [u_k^- + v_k^-, u_k^+ + v_k^+] \, ; k = 1, \ldots, n \right\}$$

$$\lambda u = \left\{ [\lambda u_k^-, \lambda u_k^+] \, ; k = 1, \ldots, n \right\}, \text{ if } \lambda \geq 0$$
$$\lambda u = \left\{ [\lambda u_k^+, \lambda u_k^-] \, ; k = 1, \ldots, n \right\}, \text{ if } \lambda < 0$$

$$uv = \left\{ [(uv)_k^-, (uv)_k^+] \, ; k = 1, \ldots, n \right\},$$
$$(uv)_k^- = \min \left\{ u_k^- v_k^-, u_k^- v_k^+, u_k^+ v_k^-, u_k^+ v_k^+ \right\}$$
$$(uv)_k^+ = \max \left\{ u_k^- v_k^-, u_k^- v_k^+, u_k^+ v_k^-, u_k^+ v_k^+ \right\}$$

$$u/v = \left\{ \left[(u/v)_k^-, (u/v)_k^+ \right]; k = 1, ..., n \right\},$$
$$(u/v)_k^- = \min \left\{ u_k^-/v_k^-, u_k^-/v_k^+, u_k^+/v_k^-, u_k^+/v_k^+ \right\}$$
$$(u/v)_k^+ = \max \left\{ u_k^-/v_k^-, u_k^-/v_k^+, u_k^+/v_k^-, u_k^+/v_k^+ \right\}.$$

Consider finally a given continuous function $y = f(x^1, ..., x^d)$ of d real variables $x^1, ..., x^d$ and d fuzzy numbers $u^j = \{[u_k^{j-}, u_k^{j+}]; k = 1, ..., n\}$, $j = 1, ..., d$, corresponding to the partition $(\mathbb{P}, \mathbb{A})$ and $\alpha_k \in [0, 1]$, $k = 1, ..., n$. Let $v = f(u^1, ..., u^d)$ denote the fuzzy extension of f. The resulting intervals $[v_k^-, v_k^+]$ are obtained by solving the box-constrained optimization problems

$$(EP)_k : \begin{cases} v_k^- = \min \left\{ f(x^1, ..., x^d) | x_j \in [u_k^{j-}, u_k^{j+}], \ j = 1, ..., d \right\} \\ v_k^+ = \max \left\{ f(x^1, ..., x^d) | x_j \in [u_k^{j-}, u_k^{j+}], \ j = 1, ..., d \right\} \end{cases} \tag{9}$$

and the α-cuts of v are approximated on $(\mathbb{P}, \mathbb{A})$ by

$$[v]_\alpha = \left[\sum_{k=1}^n v_k^- A_k(\alpha), \sum_{k=1}^n v_k^+ A_k(\alpha) \right].$$

Two important characteristics of the optimization problems (9), to be solved for each $\alpha_k \in \mathbb{P}$, are that a) for given $k = 1, ..., n$, function $f(x^1, ..., x^d)$ is to be minimized and maximized for values of the variables on the same intervals $x_j \in [u_k^{j-}, u_k^{j+}]$, $j = 1, ..., d$, and b) all the intervals are nested, i.e., $[u_{k+1}^{j-}, u_{k+1}^{j+}] \subseteq [u_k^{j-}, u_k^{j+}]$ for $j = 1, ..., d$. To solve the $2n$ problems (9) we use an ad-hoc implementation of the multiple population differential evolution (DE) algorithm, described and analyzed in [9], where the two properties a) and b) above are taken into accout by solving the $2n$ min and max optimization problems simultaneously, so reducing the number of evaluations of function $f(x^1, ..., x^d)$.

4   F-Transform and Type-2 Fuzzy Numbers

Consider a fuzzy valued function $f : [a, b] \longrightarrow \mathbb{R}_{\mathcal{F}}$ with $[f(x)]_\alpha = [f_\alpha^-(x), f_\alpha^+(x)]$, $\alpha \in [0, 1]$. For all $x \in [a, b]$, the level cuts of the fuzzy number $f(x)$ can be approximated in terms of the 2-dimensional F-transform defined by a fuzzy partition $(\mathbb{P}, \mathbb{A})$ of $[0, 1]$ and a fuzzy partition $(\mathbb{Q}, \mathbb{B})$ of $[a, b]$. Let $\mathbb{P} = \{0 = \alpha_1 < \alpha_2 < ... < \alpha_p = 1\}$ be a decomposition of $[0, 1]$ with basic functions $\mathbb{A} = \{A_1, A_2, ..., A_p\}$ and let $\mathbb{Q} = \{a = x_1 < x_2 < ... < x_q = b\}$ be a decomposition of $[a, b]$ with basic functions $\mathbb{B} = \{B_1, B_2, ..., B_q\}$. Then, the approximation $\widehat{f}(x)$, for all $x \in [a, b]$, has α-cuts $[\widehat{f}_\alpha^-(x), \widehat{f}_\alpha^+(x)]$ with

$$\widehat{f}_\alpha^-(x) = \sum_{i=1}^p \sum_{j=1}^q F_{i,j}^- B_j(x) A_i(\alpha)$$

$$\widehat{f}_\alpha^+(x) = \sum_{i=1}^p \sum_{j=1}^q F_{i,j}^+ B_j(x) A_i(\alpha)$$

where $F_{i,j}^-$ and $F_{i,j}^+$ are obtained by a 2-dimensional F-transform, i.e. by minimizing the functionals

$$F_{i,j}^- = \arg\min_{y_{i,j}} \int\limits_0^1 \int\limits_a^b \left(f_\alpha^-(x) - y_{i,j}\right)^2 B_j(x)A_i(\alpha)dxd\alpha$$

$$F_{i,j}^+ = \arg\min_{y_{i,j}} \int\limits_0^1 \int\limits_a^b \left(f_\alpha^+(x) - y_{i,j}\right)^2 B_j(x)A_i(\alpha)dxd\alpha$$

It is easy to see that $\Phi_i^-(x) = \sum\limits_{j=1}^q F_{i,j}^- B_j(x)$ and $\Phi_i^+(x) = \sum\limits_{j=1}^q F_{i,j}^+ B_j(x)$ are the unidimensional F-transforms of $f_\alpha^-(x)$ and $f_\alpha^+(x)$, for fixed x, with respect to the fuzzy partition $(\mathbb{P}, \mathbb{A})$ of $[0,1]$; and that $\Psi_j^-(\alpha) = \sum\limits_{i=1}^p F_{i,j}^- A_i(\alpha)$ and $\Psi_j^+(\alpha) = \sum\limits_{i=1}^p F_{i,j}^+ A_i(\alpha)$ are the unidimensional F-transforms of $f_\alpha^-(x)$ and $f_\alpha^+(x)$, for fixed α, with respect to the fuzzy partition $(\mathbb{Q}, \mathbb{B})$ of $[a,b]$. It follows that $F_{i,j}^-$ and $F_{i,j}^+$ can be viewed either in terms of the F-transform of $\Phi_i^-(x)$ and $\Phi_i^+(x)$ with respect to the fuzzy partition $(\mathbb{Q}, \mathbb{B})$ of $[a,b]$ or in terms of the F-transform of $\Psi_j^-(\alpha)$ and $\Psi_j^+(\alpha)$ with respect to the fuzzy partition $(\mathbb{P}, \mathbb{A})$ of $[0,1]$.

As a type-2 fuzzy number is essentially a fuzzy-valued function, we can approximate it by using a two-dimensional F-transforms. Analogously to type-1 fuzzy numbers , type-2 fuzzy numbers on $[a,b]$ can be generated in way similar to the space $\mathcal{F}(\mathbb{P}, \mathbb{A})$, by choosing matrices $\boldsymbol{\Phi}^-, \boldsymbol{\Phi}^+$ of order $q \times p$ and

$$u_\alpha^-(x) = \sum_{i=1}^p \sum_{j=1}^q \Phi_{i,j}^- B_j(x)A_i(\alpha)$$

$$u_\alpha^+(x) = \sum_{i=1}^p \sum_{j=1}^q \Phi_{i,j}^+ B_j(x)A_i(\alpha)$$

where $u(x) \in \mathcal{F}(\mathbb{P}, \mathbb{A})$ is the fuzzy membership value of $x \in [a,b]$ and $(\mathbb{Q}, \mathbb{B})$ is a fuzzy partition of $[a,b]$.

We require $\Phi_{1,j}^- \leq \ldots \leq \Phi_{p,j}^- \leq \Phi_{p,j}^+ \leq \ldots \leq \Phi_{1,j}^+$ for all j, because the secondary membership functions are read on the columns of the matrices. The nodes of the two partitions define a grid on $[a,b] \times [0,1]$ and the secondary membership functions are "vertical" for each x.

The space of type-2 fuzzy numbers generated by the fuzzy partitions $(\mathbb{P}, \mathbb{A})$ and $(\mathbb{Q}, \mathbb{B})$ can be embedded into $\mathbb{R}^{2(p \times q)}$ using two matrices $\boldsymbol{\Phi}^-, \boldsymbol{\Phi}^+$ of order $q \times p$.

5   Concluding Remarks

We suggest the use os the F-transform setting to obtain good approximations of fuzzy numbers and fuzzy-valued functions.

Two properties of the F-transform seem to be of particular interest in our case: the F-transform has a monotonicity property useful to well approximate the monotonic branches of the membership function of a fuzzy numbers, and F-transform preserve the integral of the approximated function, which translated to the invariance of the so called fuzziness of a fuzzy number.

Further work is planned to improve the approximation of type-1 and type-2 fuzzy numbers and to extend operators based on F-transform for operations with type-2 fuzzy numbers.

Acknowledgement. Our research has been partially supported by the national project PRIN 2008JNWWBP_004 (Models and Fuzzy Calculus for Economic and Financial Decisions), which is financed by the Italian Ministry of University.

References

1. Di Martino, F., Loia, V., Sessa, S.: Fuzzy transforms method and attribute dependency in data analysis. Information Sciences 180, 493–505 (2010)
2. Di Martino, F., Loia, V., Sessa, S.: Fuzzy transforms for compression and decompression of color videos. Information Sciences 180, 3914–3931 (2010)
3. Perfilieva, I.: Fuzzy Transforms: Theory and Applications. Fuzzy Sets and Systems 157, 993–1023 (2006)
4. Perfilieva, I.: Fuzzy Transforms: A Challenge to conventional transforms. In: Hawkes, P.W. (ed.) Advances in Images and Electron Physics, vol. 147, pp. 137–196. Elsevier Academic Press (2007)
5. Perfilieva, I.: Fuzzy Transforms and Their Applications to Image Compression. In: Bloch, I., Petrosino, A., Tettamanzi, A.G.B. (eds.) WILF 2005. LNCS (LNAI), vol. 3849, pp. 19–31. Springer, Heidelberg (2006)
6. Perfilieva, I., Dankova, M.: Image fusion on the basis of fuzzy transform. In: Ruan, D., et al. (eds.) Computational Intelligence in Decision and Control, pp. 471–476. World Scientific (2008)
7. Perfilieva, I., De Baets, B.: Fuzzy transforms of monotone functions with applications to image compression. Information Sciences 180, 3304–3315 (2010)
8. Perfilieva, I., Novak, V., Dvorak, A.: Fuzzy transform in the analysis of data. International Journal of Approximate Reasoning 48, 36–46 (2008)
9. Stefanini, L.: Differential Evolution methods for LU-fuzzy Arithmetic. In: Proceedings EUSFLAT 2007, Ostrawa (September 2007)
10. Stefanini, L.: Fuzzy Transform with Parametric LU-Fuzzy Partitions. In: Ruan, D., et al. (eds.) Computational Intelligence in Decision and Control, pp. 399–404. World Scientific (2008)
11. Stefanini, L.: Fuzzy Transform and Smooth Functions. In: Carvalho, J.P., Dubois, D., Kaymak, U., Sousa, J.M.C. (eds.) Proceeding of the IFSA-EUSFLAT 2009 Conference, Lisbon, pp. 579–584 (2009)
12. Stefanini, L.: F-Transform with Parametric Generalized Fuzzy Partitions. Fuzzy Sets and Systems 180, 98–120 (2011), doi:10.1016/j.fss.2011.01.017
13. Stepnicka, M., Polakovic, O.: A neural network approach to the fuzzy transform. Fuzzy Sets and Systems 160, 1037–1047 (2009)
14. Stepnicka, M., Valasek, R.: Fuzzy Transforms for functions of two variables. In: Ramik, J., Novak, V. (eds.) Methods for Decision Support in Environment with Uncertainty, University of Ostrava, IRAFM, pp. 96–102 (2003)
15. Stepnicka, M., Valasek, R.: Numerical solution of partial differential equations with help of fuzzy transforms. In: Proceedings of the FUZZ-IEE 2005 Conference, Reno, Nevada (2005)

Numerical Solution of Linear Fuzzy Fredholm Integral Equations of the Second Kind Using Fuzzy Haar Wavelet

Shokrollah Ziari[1,*], Reza Ezzati[2], and Saeid Abbasbandy[3]

[1] Department of Mathematics, Firuozkooh Branch, Islamic Azad University,
Firuozkooh, Iran
[2] Department of Mathematics, Karaj Branch, Islamic Azad University, Karaj, Iran
[3] Department of Mathematics, Science and Research Branch,
Islamic Azad University, Tehran, 14778, Iran
shok _ ziari@yahoo.com

Abstract. In this paper, a new approach based on fuzzy Haar wavelet is proposed to solve linear fuzzy Fredholm integral equations of the second kind (FFIE-2). Moreover, the error estimate of the proposed method is given. Finally, illustrative examples are included to show the accuracy and efficiency of the proposed method.

Keywords: Fuzzy Fredholm Integral Equation, Fuzzy Haar Wavelet, Error estimation.

1 Introduction

Wavelet theory is relatively new and an emerging area in mathematical research. Wavelet permits the accurate representation of a variety of functions and operators. Also, wavelets are the suitable and powerful tool for approximating functions based on wavelet basis functions.

Fuzzy integral equations arise in many applications such as physics, geographic, medical, biology, social sciences, etc. Many practical problems in science and engineering can be transformed into Fuzzy Fredholm integral equations of the second kind, thus their solution is one of the main goals in various areas of applied sciences and engineering. Many authors, such as [5,22,23,29] used the Haar wavelet for numerical solution of differential, integral and integro-differential equations in the crisp case. The simplest wavelets are based on the Haar functions, which they are piecewise constant functions on real line.

Systems of linear and nonlinear equations arise from various areas of science and engineering. Since many real world systems are too complex to be defined in precise terms, imprecision is often involved. Analyzing such systems requires the use of fuzzy information. Therefore, the fuzzy concept proposed by Zadeh, [28,29] is deemed to be quite useful in many applications. Thus, the need for

---

* Corresponding author.

S. Greco et al. (Eds.): IPMU 2012, Part III, CCIS 299, pp. 79–89, 2012.

solving linear systems whose parameters are all of partially represented fuzzy numbers, is apparent.

The concept of fuzzy integral was initiated by Dubois and Prade [11] and then investigated by Kaleva [20], Goetschel and Voxman [17], Nanda [24] and others. Also, the subject of fuzzy integration is used for solving fuzzy integral equations. In [20], Kaleva defined the integral of fuzzy function using the Lebesque type concept for integration. The fuzzy Riemann integral and its numerical integration was investigated by Wu in [19]. In [6], the authors introduced some quadrature rules for solving the integral of fuzzy-number-valued mappings. In [12], the authors gave one of the applications of fuzzy integral for solving FFIE-2. Friedman et al. [14] presented a numerical algorithm for solving FFIE-2 with arbitrary kernel. Also, they investigated numerical procedures for solving FFIE-2 by using the embedding method [15]. Babolian et al. [4] used the Adomian decomposition method (ADM) to solve FFIE-2. Abbssbandy et al. [1] obtained solution of FFIE-2 by using Nystrom method.

Here, by using fuzzy Haar wavelet, we propose a numerical approach for solving FFIE-2

$$\tilde{u}(x) = \tilde{f}(x) \oplus \lambda \odot (FR) \int_a^b k(x,t) \odot \tilde{u}(t)dt, \quad \lambda > 0,$$

where $k(x,t)$ is an arbitrary kernel function over the square $a \leq x, t \leq b$, and $\tilde{u}(x)$ is a fuzzy real valued function. Also, we present the error estimation for approximating the solution of FFIE-2.

This paper is organized as follows: In Section 2, we review some elementary concepts of the fuzzy set theory and brief of Haar wavelets. In Section 3, we drive the proposed method to obtain numerical solution of FFIE-2 based on fuzzy Haar wavelet. Error estimation of the proposed method is given in Section 4. Section 5 presents some numerical examples for proposed method. Finally, Section 6 gives our concluding remarks.

2   Preliminaries

Definition 1 [2]. A fuzzy number is a function $\tilde{u} : R \to [0,1]$ having the properties:

(1) $\tilde{u}$ is normal, that is $\exists\, x_0 \in R$ such that $\tilde{u}(x_0) = 1$,
(2) $\tilde{u}$ is fuzzy convex set

$$(i.e.\ \tilde{u}(\lambda x + (1-\lambda)y) \geq \min\{\tilde{u}(x), \tilde{u}(y)\} \quad \forall x, y \in R, \lambda \in [0,1]),$$

(3) $\tilde{u}$ is upper semi-continuous on R,
(4) the $\overline{\{x \in R : \tilde{u}(x) > 0\}}$ is compact set, where $\overline{A}$ denotes the closure of A.

The set of all fuzzy numbers is denoted by R_F.

An alternative definition which yields the same R_F is given by Kaleva [20].

Definition 2 [20]. An arbitrary fuzzy number is represented, in parametric form, by an ordered pair of functions $(\underline{\tilde{u}}(r), \overline{\tilde{u}}(r)), 0 \leq r \leq 1$, which satisfy the following requirements:

(1) $\underline{\tilde{u}}(r)$ is a bounded left continuous non-decreasing function over $[0,1]$,

(2) $\overline{\tilde{u}}(r)$ is a bounded left continuous non-increasing function over $[0,1]$,

(3) $\underline{\tilde{u}}(r) \leq \overline{\tilde{u}}(r)$, $0 \leq r \leq 1$.

The addition and scaler multiplication of fuzzy numbers in R_F are defined as follows:

(1) $\tilde{u} \oplus \tilde{v} = (\underline{\tilde{u}}(r) + \underline{\tilde{v}}(r), \overline{\tilde{u}}(r) + \overline{\tilde{v}})$,

(2) $(\lambda \odot \tilde{u}) = \begin{cases} (\lambda\underline{\tilde{u}}(r), \lambda\overline{\tilde{u}}(r)) & \lambda \geq 0, \\ (\lambda\overline{\tilde{u}}(r), \lambda\underline{\tilde{u}}(r)) & \lambda < 0. \end{cases}$

Definition 3 [3]. For arbitrary fuzzy numbers $\tilde{u} = (\underline{\tilde{u}}(r), \overline{\tilde{u}}(r))$, $\tilde{v} = (\underline{\tilde{v}}(r), \overline{\tilde{v}}(r))$ the quantity $D(\tilde{u}, \tilde{v}) = \sup_{r \in [0,1]} \max\{|\underline{\tilde{u}}(r) - \underline{\tilde{v}}(r)|, |\overline{\tilde{u}}(r) - \overline{\tilde{v}}(r)|\}$ is the distance between $\tilde{u}$ and $\tilde{v}$.

The following properties hold [6]:

(1) (R_F, D) is a complete metric space,

(2) $D(\tilde{u} \oplus \tilde{w}, \tilde{v} \oplus \tilde{w}) = D(\tilde{u}, \tilde{v})$ $\forall \tilde{u}, \tilde{v}, \tilde{w} \in R_F$,

(3) $D(k \odot \tilde{u}, k \odot \tilde{v}) = |k| D(\tilde{u}, \tilde{v})$ $\forall \tilde{u}, \tilde{v} \in R_F$ $\forall k \in R$,

(4) $D(\tilde{u} \oplus \tilde{v}, \tilde{w} \oplus \tilde{e}) \leq D(\tilde{u}, \tilde{w}) + D(\tilde{v}, \tilde{e})$ $\forall \tilde{u}, \tilde{v}, \tilde{w}, \tilde{e} \in R_F$.

Definition 4 [3]. Let $\tilde{f}, \tilde{g} : [a, b] \rightarrow R_F$ be fuzzy real number valued functions. The uniform distance between $\tilde{f}, \tilde{g}$ is defined by

$$D^*(\tilde{f}, \tilde{g}) = \sup\left\{ D(\tilde{f}(x), \tilde{g}(x)) \,|\, x \in [a, b] \right\}. \tag{1}$$

Definition 5 [3]. A fuzzy real number valued function $\tilde{f} : [a, b] \rightarrow R_F$ is said to be continuous in $x_0 \in [a, b]$, if for each $\varepsilon > 0$ there is $\delta > 0$ such that $D(\tilde{f}(x), \tilde{f}(x_0)) < \varepsilon$, whenever $x \in [a, b]$ and $|x - x_0| < \delta$. We say that $\tilde{f}$ is fuzzy continuous on $[a, b]$ if $\tilde{f}$ is continuous at each $x_0 \in [a, b]$, and denotes the space of all such functions by $C_F[a, b]$.

Definition 6 [19]. Let $\tilde{f} : [a, b] \rightarrow R_F$. $\tilde{f}$ is fuzzy-Riemann integrable to $I \in R_F$ if for any $\varepsilon > 0$, there exists $\delta > 0$ such that for any division $P = \{[u, v]; \xi\}$ of $[a, b]$ with the norms $\Delta(p) < \delta$, we have,

$$D\left(\sum_{P}{}^{*}(v - u) \odot \tilde{f}(\xi), I \right) < \varepsilon, \tag{2}$$

where $\sum^*$ denotes the fuzzy summation. In this case, it is denoted by $I = (FR)\int_a^b \tilde{f}(x)dx$.

In [17], the authors proved that if $C_F[a, b]$, its definite integral exists, and also,

$$\underline{(FR)\int_a^b \tilde{f}(t; r)dt} = \int_a^b \underline{\tilde{f}}(t, r)dt,$$

$$\overline{(FR)\int_a^b \tilde{f}(t; r)dt} = \int_a^b \overline{\tilde{f}}(t, r)dt. \tag{3}$$

Lemma 1 [3]. If $\tilde{f}, \tilde{g} : [a, b] \subseteq R \to R_F$ are fuzzy continuous functions, then the function $F : [a, b] \to R_+$ by $F(x) = D(\tilde{f}(x), \tilde{g}(x))$ is continuous on $[a, b]$, and

$$D\left((FR)\int_a^b \tilde{f}(x)dx, (FR)\int_a^b \tilde{g}(x)dx\right) \leq \int_a^b D(\tilde{f}(x), \tilde{g}(x))dx. \qquad (4)$$

Definition 7 [23]. The Haar wavelet is the family of functions as follows:

$$h_n(t) = H(2^j t - k) = \begin{cases} 1 & t \in [\frac{k}{p}, \frac{k+0.5}{p}), \\ -1 & t \in [\frac{k+0.5}{p}, \frac{k+1}{p}), \\ 0 & otherwise, \end{cases} \qquad (5)$$

where $j = 0, 1, ..., J$ indicates the level of the wavelet, and $k = 0, 1, ..., p-1$ is the translation parameter, $p = 2^j$. The integer number J determines the maximal level of resolution and the index of n is calculated from the relation $n = m+k+1$. Also, define $h_1(t) = 1$ for all t. The orthogonality property of Haar wavelet is given by

$$< h_i(t), h_l(t) >= \int_0^1 h_i(t)h_l(t)dt = \begin{cases} 2^{-j} & i = l, \\ 0 & i \neq l, \end{cases} \qquad (6)$$

where $< ., . >$ denotes the inner product form.

Here, we define the fuzzy wavelet function as follows:

Definition 8 [16]. For $f \in C_F([0, 1])$ and Haar wavelet function $H(t)$ a real valued bounded function with support of $H(t) \subset [0, 1]$, the fuzzy wavelet function defined by

$$(W_j f)(t) = \sum_{k=1}^{2^{j+1}} {}^* \tilde{f}\left(\frac{k}{2^j}\right) \odot H(2^j t - k) \qquad t \in [0, 1], \qquad (7)$$

where $H(2^j t - k)$ is as the same in Definition 7, and $\sum^*$ means addition with respect to $\oplus$ in R_F.

Definition 9 [21]. The fuzzy linear system

$$A \odot \tilde{x} = B \odot \tilde{x} \oplus \tilde{y}, \qquad (8)$$

where $A = (a_{ij}), B = (b_{ij})$, $1 \leq i, j \leq n$ are crisp coefficient matrices and $\tilde{y}$ a fuzzy number vector, is called dual fuzzy linear system.

Definition 10 [26]. A fuzzy number vector $(\tilde{x}_1, \tilde{x}_2, ..., \tilde{x}_n)$ given by $\tilde{x}_i = (\underline{x}_i(r), \overline{x}_i(r))$, $i = 1, ..., n$, $0 \leq r \leq 1$, is called a solution of (8) if

$$\begin{cases} \sum_{j=1}^{*n} a_{ij} \odot \tilde{x}_j = \sum_{j=1}^{n} \underline{a_{ij} \odot \tilde{x}_j} = \sum_{j=1}^{n} \underline{b_{ij} \odot \tilde{x}_j} + \underline{\tilde{y}_i}, \quad i = 1, ..., n, \\ \\ \overline{\sum_{j=1}^{*n} a_{ij} \odot \tilde{x}_j} = \sum_{j=1}^{n} \overline{a_{ij} \odot \tilde{x}_j} = \sum_{j=1}^{n} \overline{b_{ij} \odot \tilde{x}_j} + \overline{\tilde{y}_i}, \quad i = 1, ..., n. \end{cases} \tag{9}$$

To solve dual fuzzy linear systems, one can refer to [13, 26].

3   Proposed Method for Solving Linear FFIE-2

The FFIE-2 is as follows:

$$\tilde{u}(x) = \tilde{f}(x) \oplus \lambda \odot (FR) \int_a^b k(x,t) \odot \tilde{u}(t)dt, \quad \lambda > 0 \tag{10}$$

where $k(x,t)$ is an arbitrary kernel function over the square $0 \leq x, t \leq 1$, and $\tilde{u}(x)$ is a fuzzy real valued function. In [8], the authors presented sufficient conditions for the existence and unique solution of (10) as following theorem:

Theorem 3 [8]. Let $k(x,t)$ be continuous for $a \leq x, t \leq b, \lambda > 0$, and $\tilde{f}(x)$ a fuzzy continuous of $x, a \leq x \leq b$. If

$$\lambda < \frac{1}{M(b-a)},$$

where

$$M = \max_{a \leq x, t \leq b} |k(x,t)|,$$

then the iterative procedure

$$\tilde{u}_0(x) = \tilde{f}(x),$$

$$\tilde{u}_k(x) = \tilde{f}(x) \oplus \lambda \odot (FR) \int_a^b k(x,t) \odot \tilde{u}_{k-1}(t)dt, \quad k \geq 1$$

converges to the unique solution of (10). Specially,

$$\sup_{a \leq x \leq b} D(\tilde{u}(x), \tilde{u}_k(x)) \leq \frac{L^k}{1-L} \sup_{a \leq x \leq b} D(\tilde{u}_0(x), \tilde{u}_1(x)),$$

where $L = \lambda M(b-a)$.

Throughout this paper, we consider fuzzy Fredholm integral equation (10) with $a = 0, b = 1$ and $\lambda = 1$, thus FFIE-2 defined in (10) converts to the following equation

$$\tilde{u}(x) = \tilde{f}(x) \oplus (FR) \int_0^1 k(x,t) \odot \tilde{u}(t)dt. \tag{11}$$

Now, we use fuzzy wavelet like operator due to approximate solution of equation (11). Thus, we consider:

$$\tilde{u}(x) \cong \sum_{j=1}^{m} {}^{*} \, \tilde{a}_j \odot h_j(x) = \tilde{A}_m^T \odot H_m(x), \qquad (12)$$

where $m = 2^{J+1}$, the J indicates maximal level of resolution. The fuzzy Haar coefficient vector $\tilde{A}_m$ and Haar function vector $H_m(x)$ are defined as:

$$\tilde{A}_m = [\tilde{a}_1, \tilde{a}_2, ..., \tilde{a}_m]^T, \qquad (13)$$

$$H_m(x) = [h_1(x), h_2(x), ..., h_m(x)]^T. \qquad (14)$$

By substituting (12) into (11), we obtain the following system of equations

$$\sum_{j=1}^{m} {}^{*} \, \tilde{a}_j \odot h_j(x) = \tilde{f}(x) \oplus (FR) \int_0^1 k(x,t) \sum_{j=1}^{m} {}^{*} \tilde{a}_j \odot h_j(t) dt. \qquad (15)$$

Suppose that $k(x,t) \cong \sum_{i=1}^{m} \sum_{j=1}^{m} k_{ij} h_i(x) h_j(t)$ in matrix form

$$k(x,t) \cong H_m^T(x) K H_m(t), \qquad (16)$$

where $K = [k_{ij}], 1 \le i, j \le m$, and $k_{ij} = < h_i(x), < k(x,t), h_j(x) >>$.

We define the $m-$square Haar matrix $\hat{H}_{m\times m}$ as follows:

$$\hat{H}_{m\times m} = [H_m(\frac{1}{2m}), H_m(\frac{3}{2m}), ..., H_m(\frac{2m-1}{2m})]^T. \qquad (17)$$

Thus, we have

$$K \cong (\hat{H}^{-1})^T \hat{K}(\hat{H}^{-1}),$$

where $\hat{K} = [\hat{k}_{ij}]_{m\times m}$, $\hat{k}_{ij} = k(\frac{2i-1}{2m}, \frac{2j-1}{2m})$.

Using relation (12), (13) and (17) we obtain

$$[\tilde{u}(\frac{1}{2m}), \tilde{u}(\frac{3}{2m}), ..., \tilde{u}(\frac{2m-1}{2m})] = \tilde{A}_m^T \odot \hat{H}_{m\times m}. \qquad (18)$$

Correspondingly, we have

$$[\tilde{f}(\frac{1}{2m}), \tilde{f}(\frac{3}{2m}), ..., \tilde{f}(\frac{2m-1}{2m})] = \tilde{C}_m^T \odot \hat{H}_{m\times m}. \qquad (19)$$

The fuzzy Haar coefficient vector $\tilde{C}_m^T$ can be obtained by solving fuzzy linear system (19).

By approximating functions $\tilde{f}(x)$, $\tilde{u}(x)$ and $k(x,t)$ in the matrix form with the help of (12), (16), and substituting in FFIE-2 (11) we get:

$$H_m^T(x) \odot \tilde{A}_m = H_m^T(x) \odot \tilde{C}_m \oplus (FR) \int_0^1 H_m^T(x) K h(t) H_m^T(t) \odot \tilde{A}_m dt. \quad (20)$$

This gives

$$H_m^T(x) \odot \tilde{A}_m = H_m^T(x) \odot \tilde{C}_m \oplus H_m^T(x) K \odot \int_0^1 H_m(t) H_m^T(t) dt \odot \tilde{A}_m. \quad (21)$$

The orthogonality of the sequence $\{h_n\}$ on $[0, 1)$ implies that

$$\int_0^1 H_m(t) H_m^T(t) dt = D_{m \times m}, \quad (22)$$

where $m-$square matrix D is diagonal matrix given by $D = [d_{ij}]_{m \times m}$,

$$d_{ij} = \begin{cases} 2^{-j} & i = j, \\ 0 & i \neq j. \end{cases} \quad (23)$$

So, we obtain the following system of equations

$$\tilde{A}_m = \tilde{C}_m \oplus (KD \odot \tilde{A}_m). \quad (24)$$

The above system is a dual fuzzy linear system. Clearly, after solving above system, the coefficients of $\tilde{A}_m$ will be obtained.

4   Error Estimation

Now, we obtain error estimation for given FFIE-2 as (11). Suppose that

$$\tilde{u}_n(x) = \sum_{k=1}^{2^{n+1}} {}^*\tilde{u}\left(\frac{k}{2^n}\right) \odot H(z),$$

is approximate solution of $\tilde{u}(x)$, where $z = 2^n t - k$.
Therefore, we get:

$$D\left(\tilde{u}(x), \tilde{u}_n(x)\right) =$$

$$= D\left((FR) \int_0^1 k(x,t) \odot \tilde{u}(t) dt, (FR) \int_0^1 k(x,t) \sum_{k=1}^{2^{n+1}} {}^*\tilde{u}\left(\frac{k}{2^n}\right) \odot H(z) dt\right)$$

$$\leq M \int_0^1 D\left(\tilde{u}(t), \sum_{k=1}^{2^{n+1}} {}^*\tilde{u}\left(\frac{k}{2^n}\right) \odot H(z)\right) dt,$$

where $M = max_{\,0 \leq x,t \leq 1} |k(x,t)|$. Therefore, we have:

$$D\left(\tilde{u}(x), \tilde{u}_n(x)\right) \leq M \int_0^1 D\left(\tilde{u}(t), \tilde{u}_n(t)\right) dt,$$

$$\sup_{x \in [0,1]} D\left(\tilde{u}(x), \tilde{u}_n(x)\right) \leq M \sup_{x \in [0,1]} D\left(\tilde{u}(x), \tilde{u}_n(x)\right)$$

Therefore, if $M < 1$, we will have:

$$\lim_{n \to \infty} \sup_{x \in [0,1]} D\left(\tilde{u}(x), \tilde{u}_n(x)\right) = 0.$$

5   Numerical Examples

In this section, we present two examples. Also, we compare obtained solution by using proposed method with exact solution.

For following examples, since the FFIE-2 as (11) is defined only for $t \in [0,1]$, the transformation $z = (b - a)x + a, \quad s = (b - a)t + a$ must be done.

Example 1.[19] Consider the following FFIE-2:

$$\underline{f}(x,r) = (\frac{-2}{\pi})cos(x)(r^2 + r),$$

$$\overline{f}(x,r) = (\frac{-2}{\pi})cos(x)(3 - r),$$

$$k(x,t) = cos(x - t), \quad 0 \leq x, t \leq \frac{\pi}{2}, \quad \lambda = \frac{4}{\pi},$$

and $a = 0, b = \frac{\pi}{2}$.

The exact solution of this example is as follows:

$$\underline{u}(x,r) = sin(x)(r^2 + r),$$

$$\overline{u}(x,r) = sin(x)(3 - r).$$

Example 2 .[18] Consider the following FFIE-2:

$$\underline{f}(x,r) = rx + \frac{3}{26} - \frac{3}{26}r - \frac{1}{13}x^2 - \frac{1}{13}x^2 r,$$

$$\overline{f}(x,r) = 2x - rx + \frac{3}{26}r + \frac{1}{13}x^2 r - \frac{3}{26} - \frac{3}{13}x^2,$$

$$k(x,t) = \frac{(x^2 + t^2 - 2)}{13}, \quad 0 \leq x, t \leq 2,$$

and $a = 0, b = 2$.

The exact solution of this example is as follows:

$$\underline{u}(x,r) = rx,$$

$$\overline{u}(x,r) = (2 - r)x.$$

We can compare the numerical solution obtained by proposed method with $J = 5$, $x = 0.6$ and the exact solution in Table 1 and Table 2.

Table 1. Numerical results for Example 1

r − level	$\underline{u}(x,r)$	$\overline{u}(x,r)$	$\underline{u}_5(x,r)$	$\overline{u}_5(x,r)$	$|\underline{u} - \underline{u}_5|$	$|\overline{u} - \overline{u}_5|$
0.0000	0.0000	2.4271	0.0000	2.4311	0.0000	0.0041
0.1000	0.0890	2.3461	0.0891	2.3501	0.0001	0.0038
0.2000	0.1942	2.2652	0.1945	2.2691	0.0003	0.0037
0.3000	0.3155	2.1843	0.3160	2.1880	0.0005	0.0035
0.4000	0.4530	2.1034	0.4538	2.1070	0.0008	0.0034
0.5000	0.6068	2.0225	0.6078	2.0259	0.0010	0.0033
0.6000	0.7767	1.9416	0.7780	1.9449	0.0013	0.0031
0.7000	0.9627	1.8607	0.9643	1.8639	0.0016	0.0030
0.8000	1.1650	1.7798	1.1669	1.7828	0.0020	0.0029
0.9000	1.3834	1.6989	1.3857	1.7018	0.0023	0.0027
1.0000	1.6180	1.6180	1.6208	1.6208	0.0027	0.0165

Table 2. Numerical results for Example 2

r − level	$\underline{u}(x,r)$	$\overline{u}(x,r)$	$\underline{u}_5(x,r)$	$\overline{u}_5(x,r)$	$|\underline{u} - \underline{u}_5|$	$|\overline{u} - \overline{u}_5|$
0.0000	0.0000	2.4000	-0.0135	2.4197	0.0135	0.0197
0.1000	0.1200	2.2800	0.1062	2.2980	0.0118	0.0180
0.2000	0.2400	2.1600	0.2298	2.1763	0.0102	0.0163
0.3000	0.3600	2.0400	0.3515	2.0547	0.0085	0.0147
0.4000	0.4800	1.9200	0.4731	1.9330	0.0069	0.0130
0.5000	0.6000	1.8000	0.5948	1.8114	0.0052	0.0114
0.6000	0.7200	1.6800	0.7164	1.6897	0.0036	0.0097
0.7000	0.8400	1.5600	0.8381	1.5681	0.0019	0.0081
0.8000	0.9600	1.4400	0.9598	1.4464	0.0002	0.0064
0.9000	1.0800	1.3200	1.0814	1.3247	0.0014	0.0047
1.0000	1.2000	1.2000	1.2031	1.2031	0.0031	0.0031

6   Conclusions

In this paper, we presented a new approach to solve linear FFIE-2 using fuzzy Haar wavelet like operator. Also, we proved the error estimation for approximated solution of FFIE-2.

References

1. Abbasbandy, S., Babolian, E., Alavi, M.: Numerical method for solving linear fredholm fuzzy integral equations of the second kind. Chaos Solutions an Fractals 31, 138–146 (2007)
2. Anastassiou, G.A., Gal, S.G.: On a fuzzy trigonometric approximation theorem of Weirstrass-type. Jornal of Fuzzy Mathematics 9(3), 701–708 (2001)

3. Anastassiou, G.A.: Fuzzy mathematics: Approximation theory. Springer, Heidelberg (2010)
4. Babolian, E., Sadeghi Goghary, H., Abbasbandy, S.: Numerical solution of linear Fredholm fuzzy integral equations of the second kind. Appl. Math. Comput. 182, 791–796 (2006)
5. Babolian, E., Shahsavaran, A.: Numerical solution of nonlinear Fredholm integral equations of the second kind using Haar wavelets. Jornal of Computational and Applied Mathematics 225, 87–95 (2009)
6. Bede, B., Gal, S.G.: Quadrature rules for integrals of fuzzy-number-valued functions. Fuzzy Sets and Systems 145, 359–380 (2004)
7. Chen, C.F., Hsiao, C.H.: Haar wavelet method for solving lumped and distributed-parameter systems. IEE Proc.-Control Theory Appl. 144(1), 87–94 (1996)
8. Congxin, W., Ming, M.: On the integrals, series and integral equations of fuzzy set-valued functions. J. of Harbin Inst. of Technology 21, 11–19 (1990)
9. Congxin, W., Zengtai, G.: On Henstock integral of fuzzy-number-valued functions. Fuzzy Sets and Systems 120, 523–532 (2001)
10. Chui, C.K.: Wavelets, A mathematical tool for signal analysis. SIAM, Philadelphia (1997)
11. Dobois, D., Prade, H.: Towards fuzzy differential caculus. Fuzzy Sets and Systems 8, 1–7, 105–116, 225–233 (1982)
12. Friedman, M., Ma, M., Kandel, A.: Numerical methods for calculating the fuzzy integral. Fuzzy Sets and Systems 83, 57–62 (1996)
13. Friedman, M., Ma, M., Kandel, A.: Fuzzy linear systems. Fuzzy Sets and Systems 96, 201–209 (1998)
14. Friedman, M., Ma, M., Kandel, A.: Solutions to fuzzy integral equations with arbitrary kernels. International Jornal of Approximate Reasoning 20, 249–262 (1999)
15. Friedman, M., Ma, M., Kandel, A.: Numerical solutions of fuzzy differential and integral equations. Fuzzy Sets and Systems 106, 35–48 (1999)
16. Gal, S.: Handbook of analytic-computational methods in applied mathematics. In: Anastassiou (ed.) Approximation Theory in Fuzzy Setting, ch. 13, pp. 617–666. G. Chapman & CRC Boca Raton, New York (2000)
17. Goetschel, R., Voxman, W.: Elementary fuzzy calculus. Fuzzy Sets and Sys. 18, 31–43 (1986)
18. Hsiao, C.H., Wu, S.P.: Numerical solution of time-varying functional differential equations via Haar wavelets. Appl. Math. Comput. 188, 1049–1058 (2007)
19. Wu, H.-C.: The fuzzy Riemann integral and its numerical integration. Fuzzy Sets and Systems 110, 1–25 (2000)
20. Kaleva, O.: Fuzzy differential equations. Fuzzy Sets and Systems 24, 301–317 (1987)
21. Ma, M., Friedman, M., Kandel, A.: Duality in fuzzy linear systems. Fuzzy Sets and Systems 109, 55–58 (2000)
22. Maleknejad, K., Mirzaee, F.: Solving linear integro-differential equations system by Using rationalized Haar functions method. Appl. Math. Comput. 155, 317–328 (2004)
23. Maleknejad, K., Mirzaee, F.: Using rationalized Haar wavelet for solving linear integral equations. Appl. Math. Comput. 160, 579–587 (2005)
24. Nanda, S.: On integration of fuzzy mappings. Fuzzy Sets and Systems 32, 95–101 (1989)
25. Puri, M., Ralescu, D.: Fuzzy random variables. J. Math. Anal. Appl. 114, 409–422 (1986)

26. Ezzati, R.: A method for solving dual fuzzy general linear systems. Appl. Comput. Math. 7, 241–235 (2008)
27. Ezzati, R.: Solving fuzzy linear systems. Soft Computing (2007), doi:10.1007/s00500-009-0537
28. Zadeh, L.A.: A fuzzy-set-theoric interpretation of linguistic hedages. Journal of Cybernetics 2, 4–34 (1972)
29. Zadeh, L.A.: The concept of the linguistic variable and its application to approximation reasoning. Informatin Sciences 8, 199–249 (1975)

On a View of Zadeh's Z-Numbers

Ronald R. Yager

Machine Intelligence Institute, Iona College New Rochelle, NY 10801
yager@panix.com

Abstract. We first recall the concept of Z-numbers introduced by Zadeh. These objects consist of an ordered pair (A, B) of fuzzy numbers. We then use these Z-numbers to provide information about an uncertain variable V in the form of a Z-valuation, which expresses the knowledge that the probability that V is A is equal to B. We show that these Z-valuations essentially induce a possibility distribution over probability distributions associated with V. We provide a simple illustration of a Z-valuation. We show how we can use this representation to make decisions and answer questions. We show how to manipulate and combine multiple Z-valuations. We show the relationship between Z-numbers and linguistic summaries. Finally we provide for a representation of Z-valuations in terms of Dempster-Shafer belief structures, which makes use of type-2 fuzzy sets.

1   Introduction

Zadeh [1] defined a Z-number associated with an uncertain variable V as an ordered pair of fuzzy numbers, (A, B) where A is a fuzzy subset of the domain X of the variable V and B is a fuzzy subset of the unit interval. A Z-number can be used to represent the information about an uncertain variable of the type where A represents a value of the variable and B represents an idea of certainty or probability. A Z-number is closely related to the idea of linguistic summary [2, 3]. Zadeh [1] refers to the ordered triple, (V, A, B) as a Z-valuation and indicates this is equal to the assignment statement V is (A, B. Generally this Z-valuation is indicating that V takes the value A with probability equal B. Some examples of these Z-valuations are

(Age Mary, Young, likely)
(Income Bill, about 200K, not likely)
(Enemy number of soldiers, about 300, pretty sure)
(Weight Bill, heavy, confident)

Thus Z-valuations are providing some information about the value of the associated variable. A number of issues arise regarding these objects such as the representation of the information contained in a Z-valuation, the manner in which we can manipulate this information and our ability to combine or fuse multiple pieces of information of this type. Many of the answers are dependent upon the nature of the underling uncertainty associated with the variable.

S. Greco et al. (Eds.): IPMU 2012, Part III, CCIS 299, pp. 90–101, 2012.

2   Modeling Z-Valuations

Consider now we have the information V is (A, B) where (A, B) is a Z-number and it is assumed the V is a random variable. This Z-valuation can be viewed as a restriction on V interpreted as

$$\text{Prob(V is A) is B.}$$

While we don't know the underlying probability distribution (density), from this information we can obtain a possibility distribution G, fuzzy subset, over the space $\mathcal{P}$ of all probability distributions on X. Assume p is some probability distribution (or density function) over X. Using Zadeh's definition of the probability of a fuzzy subset [4] we express the probability that V is A, $\text{Prob}_p(\text{V is A)})$ as $\int_X A(x)p(x)dx$.

Using this we can get G(p), the degree to which p satisfies our Z–valuation, $\text{Prob}_p(\text{V is A)}$ is B, as

$$G(p) = B(\text{Prob}_p(\text{V is A)}) = B(\int_X A(x)p(x)dx)$$

In this way, we can represent the information contained in V *is* (A, B), under the assumption that V is a random variable, as a possibility distribution over the space $\mathcal{P}$ of probability distributions.

While the space $\mathcal{P}$ is a large space, simplifying assumptions, such as assuming the underlying distribution is a particular class of parameterized distributions, such as a normal or uniform, can be used to simplify the space and allow use of the information.

Here we shall provide an example that will help illustrate the usefulness of the preceding approach. Assume V is a variable corresponding to the "waiting time" for a bus to come. The exponential distribution provides a useful formulation for modeling random variables corresponding to waiting times of the type described above [5]. We recall the density function of an exponential distribution is

$$f_V(x) = \lambda e^{-\lambda x} \text{ for x} \geq 0 \text{ and } \lambda \geq 0.$$

We also recall for this type of distribution that

$$\text{Prob}(a \leq V \leq b) = \int_a^b f_v(x)dx = \int_a^b \lambda e^{-\lambda x} dx = e^{-a\lambda} - e^{-b\lambda}$$

$$\text{Prob(V} \leq b) = \text{Prob}(0 \leq V \leq b) = 1 - b^{-b\lambda}$$

Consider now we have the information *the waiting time for a bus is almost certainly no greater than 10 minutes*.

Here we have information about the waiting time for the bus, V, expressed as a Z-valuation, V *is* (A, B). Here V is a random variable whose probability density function is expressible in terms of an exponential distribution. In addition, A is the linguistic value "less than 10 minutes" and B is the linguistic value "almost certainly".

In this illustration A is simply an interval type fuzzy subset;

$$A(x) = 1 \text{ for x} \leq 10 \text{ and } A(x) = 0 \text{ for x} > 10$$

In this situation for any λ we have

$$\text{Prob}_\lambda \ (\text{V } is \text{ A}) = \int_0^\infty A(x)f_\lambda(x)dx = \int_0^{10} e^{-\lambda x}dx = 1 - e^{-10\lambda}$$

In this example our underlying space $\mathcal{P}$ of probability distribution is the class of all exponential distributions. Each distribution of the type is uniquely defined by its parameter $\lambda \geq 0$. Hence we see our space $\mathcal{P}$ can be simply represented by the space $\{\lambda \geq 0\}$ with the understanding that each λ corresponds to an exponential distribution.

Consider now the linguistic value B, which is "almost certainly". For simplicity we shall define this using a crisp interval fuzzy subset

$$B(y) = 1 \text{ if } 0.9 \leq y \leq 1 \text{ and } B(y) = 0 \text{ if } 0 \leq x < 0.9$$

We obtain the membership function G over the space $\lambda \in [0, \infty]$, corresponding to the family of exponential distribution functions, as $G(\lambda) = B(1 - e^{-10\lambda})$. With our definition for B we get

$$G(\lambda) = 1 \text{ if } 1 - e^{-10\lambda} \geq 0.9 \text{ and } G(\lambda) = 0 \text{ if } 1 - e^{-10\lambda} < 0.9$$

Solving this we get $G(\lambda) = 1$ if $\lambda \geq 0.23$. Thus here then we have a possibility distribution G over exponential distributions with parameter λ such that $G(\lambda) = 0$ if $\lambda < 0.23$ and $G(\lambda) = 1$ if $\lambda \geq 0.23$

We can use the information contained in G to answer various questions. Let us find out what is the expected waiting time, E(V). Recalling that the expected value of a random variable with an exponential distribution is $1/\lambda$ we have EV $= \bigcup\limits_{\lambda \in [0, \infty]} \{\dfrac{G(\lambda)}{\dfrac{1}{\lambda}}\}$. Here the membership grades are EV(t) = 0 if t > 4.35 and EV(t) = 1 if t $\leq$ 4.35. Thus the expected waiting time is the linguistic value *less the 4.35 minutes*.

Another question we can ask is what is the probability that the waiting time will be greater than fifteen minutes. Here we see that for an exponential distribution with parameter λ we have

$$\text{Prob}_\lambda(\text{V} \geq 1.5) = \int_{15}^\infty \lambda e^{-\lambda x}dx = e^{-15\lambda} - e^{-\infty\lambda} = e^{-15\lambda}.$$

Denoting $\text{Prob}_G(\text{V} \geq 15)$ as the probability of waiting more than 15 minutes we see using Zadeh's extension principle that

$$\text{Prob}_G(\text{V} \geq 15) = \bigcup\limits_{\lambda \in [0, \infty]} \left\{\frac{G(\lambda)}{e^{-15\lambda}}\right\} = \bigcup\limits_{\lambda \geq 0.23} \left\{\frac{G(\lambda)}{e^{-15\lambda}}\right\}$$

Since $e^{-(15)(0.23)} = 0.03$ and $e^{-(15)\lambda}$ decreases as λ increases with $e^{-(15)\lambda} \to 0$ as $\lambda \to \infty$ we get that $\text{Prob}_G(\text{V} \geq 15) \leq 0.03$. Thus the $\text{Prob}_G(\text{V} \geq 15)$ has the linguistic value of "*not more then 0.03*"

Other more sophisticated questions can be answered. One question is what is the probability that the waiting will be *short*. Assume we represent *short* as a fuzzy set S.

Here if f_λ is an exponential distribution with parameter λ then $\text{Prob}_\lambda(V \text{ is short}) = \int_0^\infty S(x)\lambda e^{-\lambda x}dx$. Using this we can obtain

$$\text{Prob}_G(V \text{ is short}) = \bigcup_{\lambda \geq 023}\left\{\frac{G(\lambda)}{\text{Prob}_\lambda(V \text{ is short})}\right\}.$$

We can use this information to help make a decision. Consider the following decision rule

*If the probability that the waiting time is short is **High** then take a bus.*

*If the probability that the waiting is short is **not High** then walk.*

We now can express **High** as a fuzzy subset H of the unit interval. Using this we need to determine the degree to which concept HIGH is satisfied by the value $\text{Prob}_G(V \text{ is short})$. In this case because of the simple nature of $\text{Prob}_G(V \text{ is short})$ as

"at least $\int_0^\infty S(x)(0.23)e^{-.23x}dx$" we can use this value to obtain a measure of the satisfaction of the concept High. Thus we let

$$\alpha = \text{High}\left(\int_0^\infty S(x)(0.23)e^{-.23x}\right)dx)$$

indicate the degree to which the value of V satisfies the condition that the waiting time is short is High. Here then we see if $\alpha \geq 0.5$ we take a bus and if $\alpha < 0.5$ we walk.

3   Operations on Z-Valuations

Let us now return to the more general situation where V is a general random variable. As we have previously indicated a Z-valuation, V *is* (A, B) induces a possibility distribution G over the space $\mathcal{P}$ of all probability distributions where

$$G(p) = B\left(\int_{-\infty}^\infty A(x)p(x)dx\right).$$

Having our information in this format allows us to perform many operations with this information. These operations are greatly added by the extension principle of Zadeh [6]. Let us look at some of these.

Assume we have q Z-valuations on the variable V each on the form V *is* (A_j, B_j) for $j = 1$ to q. Each of these induces a possibility distribution G_j over the space of all probability distributions $\mathcal{P}$. For $p \in \mathcal{P}$ we have $G_j(p) = B\left(\int_{-\infty}^\infty A_j(x) \cdot p(x)dx\right)$. Now the overall information about the underlying probability distribution is obtained by combining these q possible distributions into a fused possibility distribution G on $\mathcal{P}$. Various methods can be used to combine these q distributions, the choice depends on the semantics associated with the relationships between the pieces of information, the multiple Z–valuations. In the following we briefly describe some of these.

One approach to combine these is to take the conjunction of the q possibility distributions, here we get $G(p) = \text{Min}_j [G_j(p)]$. In this situation we are indicating that we must simultaneously accommodate all of the sources of information.

Another possible aggregation of these individual possibility distributions can be made using the OWA operator [7, 8]. In the case of aggregating q objects we have a collection of q weights, w_j for $j = 1$ to q such that $w_j \in [0, 1]$ and their sum is one. If we let ind_p be an index function such the $\text{ind}_p(j)$ is the index of the jth largest of the $G_i(p)$ then we obtain $G(p) = \sum_{j=1}^{q} w_j G_{\text{ind}(j)}(p)$. The OWA operator allows us to implement quantifier-guided aggregation. Here we have a quantifier Q such as *most* or *almost all* and need only satisfy Q of the Z-valuations.

Let us look at the pure conjunction aggregation in the situation in which we are interested in the waiting time for the bus. In the preceding we had a person express their perception of the waiting time. Consider now we have a second person whose experience with respect bus the waiting time is summarized as follow:

Most often I have to wait about five minutes for the bus.

Here again we have the information about the value of V expressed as a Z-valuation, V *is* (A_2, B_2). In this case A_2 is the linguistic value " about 5 minutes" and B_2 would be value "most often." In a manner analogous to the preceding we obtain for this Z-valuation a possibility distribution G_2 over the domain $\lambda \geq 0$. Once having obtained G_2 can then combine it with our original distribution to obtain a combined distribution.

In the preceding in the face of multiple Z-valuation on some variable we tried to find a solution to simultaneously satisfy all of these. In essence we looked at these as q observations of the same phenomena. Another possible view of the situation is that the q Z-valuations where made on different sets of observation. For example in the case of the bus the different observations where based on the experience of different people who use the bus at different times of the day. In this case we consider each of these perceptions based on different sample of observations. Let us step outside our current problem and consider how to combine this type of information.

Assume we have an experiment with possible outcomes $Y = \{y_1, ..., y_r\}$. Assume we perform the experiment n times and obtain n_i as the number of times outcome y_i occurs, our estimate of the probability of y_i is n_i/n. Assume we have an additional set of observations consisting of m experiments in which m_i is the number of times y_i occurs. In this case our estimate of the probability of y_i is m_i/m. We now can combine these two to obtain a situation in which we have performed m + n experiments in which $m_i + n_i$ is the number of times y_i has occurred. In this case the combined estimated probability of y_i is $p_i = \dfrac{m_i + n_i}{m + n}$. We note that we can express this as

$$p_i = \frac{m_i}{m+n} + \frac{n_i}{m+n} = \frac{m}{m+n} \frac{m_i}{m} + \frac{n}{m+n} \frac{n_i}{n}$$

If $\frac{m}{m+n} = \alpha$ then $p_i = \alpha \frac{m_i}{m} + (1 - \alpha) \frac{n_i}{n}$. This is simply a weighted sum of the two estimates. If $m = n$ then $\alpha = 0.5$. It is interesting to observe that the term α can be seen as capturing the relative experience or expertise associated with each observer.

We can now use this to motivate an alternate way to combine multiple Z-valuation perceptions of the value of V. For simplicity we shall initially assume only two observations expressed as Z-valuations: V is (A_1, B_1) and V is (A_2, B_2). Each of these generates a possibility distribution G_i over the space $\mathcal{P}$,

$$G_i(p) = B_i\left(\int_X p(x)A_i(x)\, dx \right).$$

Assume we assign a reliability (expertise or credibility) of w_i to each of these and require that $w_1 + w_2 = 1$. Using this we define the combined possibility distribution $G = w_1 G_1 \oplus w_2 G_2$. Using the extension principle and the rules of fuzzy arithmetic we then calculate $G(p)$ such that $G(P) \quad \underset{p=w_1p_1 \oplus w_2p_2}{\text{Max}} [G_1(p_1) \wedge G_2(p_2)]$ where $p = w_1 p_1 \oplus w_2 p_2$ in defined such that $p(x) = w_1 p_1(x) + w_2 p_2(x)$.

Assume now V and U are two independent random variables. Let us now assume we have Z-valuations about each of these

$$V \ is \ (A_1, B_1) \text{ and } U \ is \ (A_2, B_2).$$

As described in the preceding the information contained in each of these can be expressed as a possibility distribution over the space of probability distributions $\mathcal{P}$. Here then we obtain G_U and G_V. Consider now a random variable W = U + V. Using Zadeh's extension principle and the fact that the sum of random variables involves the convolution of the respective density functions [9] we can obtain the possibility distribution over $\mathcal{P}$, G_W, associated with the random variable W. We recall that if p_1 and p_2 are two density functions their convolution is defined as the density function $p = p_1 \ o \ p_2$ such that

$$p(z) = \int_{-\infty}^{\infty} p_1(z-y)p_2(y)\,dy = \int_{-\infty}^{\infty} p_1(x)p_2(z-x)\,dx$$

Using these we can now find the possibility distribution G_W associated with W = U + V. In particular for any $p_w \in \mathcal{P}$ we obtain

$$G_W(p_w) = \text{Max}_{p_u, p_v} [G_U(p_u) \wedge G_V(p_v)]$$

Subject to $p_w = p_u \ o \ p_v$ that is $p_w(w) = \int_{-\infty}^{\infty} p_u(w-y)p_v(y)\,dy$.

If $W = aU + bV$ we can also obtain G_W [9]. In this case for any $p_w \in \mathcal{P}$ we obtain

$$G_W(p_w) \quad = \quad Max_{p_u, p_v}[G_U(p_u) \wedge G_V(p_v)] \qquad \text{subject to} \qquad p_w(w) \quad =$$

$$\frac{b}{|ab|}\int_{-\infty}^{\infty} p_u(\frac{w-by}{a}) \cdot p_v(y)dy$$

We provide an illustration of this in the case of our example of waiting for a bus. Assume we must take two buses and we are interested in the total waiting time. Assume the information about the waiting time of the first bus is expressed as V *is* (A_1, B_1) and that of the second bus is expressed as U *is* (A_2, B_2). Our interest here is in the sum of the two waiting times, $W = V + U$. First we see that for V *is* (A_1, B_1) we can generate a possibility distribution G_V over the space of exponential distributions such that $G_V(\lambda)$ is possibility of an exponential distribution for V with parameter λ. Here $G_V(\lambda) = B_1(\int_0^{\infty} A_1(x)\lambda e^{-\lambda x} dx)$. Similarly for the waiting time of the second bus we have $G_U(\delta) = B_2(\int_0^{\infty} A_2(x)\delta e^{-\delta x}dx)$. We now can find the knowledge G_W. Here for each λ and δ we get $p_W = p_\lambda \circ p_\delta$ where

$$p_w(w) = \int_0^{\infty} \lambda e^{-(w-y)\lambda}\delta e^{-\delta y}dv = \lambda\delta e^{-w\lambda}\int_0^{\infty} e^{-(\delta-\lambda)y}dy$$

Let us recall [9] that if V and U are two random variables with respective probability distribution functions p_V and p_V then if W is the random variable defined as $W = Max[V, U]$ then the probability density p_W associated with W is obtained as

$$p_W(z) = p_V(z) \cdot Prob(U \le z) + p_U(z) Prob(V \le z)$$

where $Prob(U \le z) = \int_{-\infty}^{z} p_u(x)dx$ and $Prob(V \le z) = \int_{-\infty}^{z} p_v(x)dx$

In the case where $R = Min[U, V]$ then p_R is obtained as

$$p_R(z) = p_u(z)(1 - Prob(V \le z)) + p_V(z)(1 - Prob(U \le z))$$

Assume the information we have about the values of the variables U and V are expressed via Z-valuations, V *is* (A_1, B_1) and U *is* (A_2, B_2). Using our previous approach we can obtain for each of these a possibility distribution over the space of probability distributions such that $G_U(p_u)$ is the possibility that p_u is the underlying probability distribution associated with U and similarly $G_V(p_v)$ is the possibility that p_v is the underlying probability distribution associated with V. From this we can obtain the respective possibility distributions associated with W and R. In particular for any $p_w \in \mathcal{P}$ we have

$$G_W(p_w) = Max_{p_u, p_v}[G_U(p_u) \wedge G_V(p_v)]$$

Sub to

$$p_W(z) = p_v(z)\text{Prob}(U \le z) + p_u(z)\text{Prob}(V \le z)$$

and

$$G_R(p_w) = \text{Max}_{p_u, p_v} [G_U(p_u) \wedge G_V(p_v)]$$

Sub to

$$p_R(z) = p_v(z)(1 - \text{Prob}(U \le z)) + P_u(z)(1 - \text{Prob}(V \le z))$$

We consider the following illustration. At a bus stop there are two different buses a person can take to get their destination. The waiting time for each of the buses as expressed in terms of Z-valuation, U *is* (A_1, B_1) and V *is* (A_2, B_2), U being the wait time for one bus and V being the wait time for the other bus. Here then we can assume the underlying distribution for these variables are exponential. Thus here letting λ and δ be the associated parameters we get

$$G_u(\lambda) = B_1 \left(\int_0^\infty A_1(x)\lambda e^{-\lambda x}dx \right) \text{ and } G_v(\delta) = B_2 \left(\int_0^\infty A_2(x)\delta e^{-\delta x}dx \right)$$

Here then for any pair λ and δ

$$p_W(z) = \lambda e^{-\lambda z}(e^{-\delta z}) + (\delta e^{-\delta z})(e^{-\lambda z}) \tag{I}$$

$$p_R(z) \lambda e^{-\lambda z}(1 - e^{-\delta z}) + \delta e^{-\delta z}(1 - e^{-\lambda z}) \tag{II}$$

Finally we obtain

$$G_W(p_w) = \text{Max}_{\lambda, \delta}[G_U(\lambda) \wedge G_V(\delta)] \quad \text{Subject to (I)}$$
$$G_R(p_R) = \text{Max}_{\delta, \lambda}[G_U(\lambda) \wedge G_V(\delta)] \quad \text{Subject to (II)}$$

4   Reasoning with Z-Valuations

In some cases it may be possible to infer one Z-valuation from another Z-valuation. Consider the Z-valuation V *is* (A, B), from this we obtain a possibility distribution G over $\mathcal{P}$ such that for $p \in \mathcal{P}$ we have $G(p) = B(\text{Prob}_p(V \text{ } is \text{ } A)) = B(\int A(x)p(x)dx)$.

Using Zadeh's entailment principle [6] we can infer any G^* where $G^*(P) \ge G(p)$.

Consider now another Z-valuation V *is* (A_1, B_1) where $A \supseteq A_1$ and B_1 is "at least" B. Here B_1 has $B_1(z) = \text{Max}_y[B(y) \wedge H(y, z)]$ where $H(y, z)$ is a crisp relationship such that $H(y, z) = 1$ if $z \ge y$ and $H(x, z) = 0$ if $y > z$. We see here that for any z, $B_1(z) \ge B(z)$. More interestingly assume $z_1 > z$. Consider now $B_1(z_1) = \text{Max}_x[B(x) \wedge H(x, z_1)]$. Since $z_1 > z$ then $H(z, z_1) = 1$ from this we see that $B_1(z_1) \ge B(z)$.

Consider now the possibility distribution G_1 generated from the Z-valuation, V *is* (A_1, B_1). For any p we have $G_1(p) = B_1(\int A_1(x)p(x)dx)$. Since $A \subseteq A_1$ then $A(y) \leq A_1(y)$ for any y. Hence for any p we have $\int_X A_1(x)p(x)dx \geq \int_X A(x)p(x)dx$.

Furthermore since $B_1(z_1) \geq B(z)$ for $z_1 \geq z$ then we see that $G_1(p) \geq G(p)$. The implication here is that from a Z-valuation V *is* (A, B) we can always infer the Z-valuation V *is* $(A_1,$ at least B) where $A \subseteq A_1$.

An example of this in the context of our waiting time for a bus would be the following. From the original perception, *a waiting time of about three minutes is likely* we can infer *a waiting time of over two minutes is more than likely.*

If B is such that $B(0) = 0$, $B(1) = 1$ and $B(x) \geq B(y)$ if $x \geq y$ we shall say B is an *affirmative type* confidence value. Assume B_1 and B_2 are affirmative type confidences such that $B_1 \subseteq B_2$. We shall say B_1 is a more strongly affirmative confidence. Consider now the valuation V *is* (A, B_1) where B_1 is an affirmative type confidence. We see the associated G is $G_1(p) = B_1(\int_X A(x)p(x)dx)$. We also observe that if B_2 is also affirmative where $B_1 \subseteq B_2$ then $G_2(p) = B_2(\int_X A(x)p(x)dx) \geq G_1(P)$. Using the entailment principle we can then infer V *is* (A, B_2) from V *is* (A, B_1). Thus we infer a less strongly affirmative Z-valuation.

Assume A_1 and A_2 are values such that $A_1 \subseteq A_2$ we say that A_2 is less precise than A_1. We see that if we have the Z-valuation V *is* (A_1, B_1) we can infer the valuation V *is* (A_2, B_2) since $G_1(p) = B_1(\int_X A_1(x)p(x)dx) \leq B_2(\int_X A_2(x)p(x)dx)$. Thus we always infer a more imprecise less strongly affirmative valuation from a given valuation.

Let B be a confidence value such that $B(1) = 0$, $B(0) = 1$ and $B(x) \geq B(y)$ if $x \leq y$. We shall refer to B as a *refuting type* confidence. Assume B_3 and B_4 are two refuting type confidence such that $B_3 \subseteq B_4$ we shall say that B_3 is more strongly refuting. Consider now the Z-valuation V *is* (A, B_3) where B_3 is a refuting type confidence, in this case $G_3(p) = B_3(\int_X A(x)p(x)dx)$. We see if B_4 is a less strongly refuting confidence, $B_3 \subseteq B_4$ then $G_4(p) = B_4(\int_X A(x)p(x)dx \geq G_3(p)$. We see that we can infer V *is* (A, B_4) from V *is* (A, B_3). In addition if A_4 is less precise then A_3, $A_3 \subseteq A_4$ we easily can show that from V is (A_3, B_3) we infer V *is* (A_4, B_4).

Assume B is a fuzzy subset of the unit interval corresponding to a degree of confidence. We define its antonym $\hat{B}$ as a fuzzy of the unit interval such that $\hat{B}(x) = B(1 - x)$. We see for example if B is very big then $\hat{B}$ is very small. If B is near 0.7 then $\hat{B}$ near 0.3. We also note if B is a supporting type confidence, $B(x) = 1$ and

$B(x) \geq B(y)$ if $x \geq y$, then $\hat{B}(x) = B(1 - x)$ is a refuting type confidence. Assume A is a value we define its negation, $\bar{A}$ as a fuzzy subset such that $\bar{A}(x) = 1 - A(x)$.

Consider now the Z-valuation, V *is* (A, B). This induces the knowledge G where $G(p) = B(\int_X A(x)p(x)dx)$. Consider now the Z-valuation, V *is* ($\bar{A}$, $\hat{B}$). This induces the knowledge $\tilde{G}$ where

$$\tilde{G}(p) = \hat{B}(\int_X \bar{A}(x)p(x)dx) = \hat{B} (\int_X ((1-A(x))p(x)dx$$

$$\tilde{G}(p) = \hat{B}(1- \int_X A(x)p(x)) = B(\int A(x)p(x)) = G(p)$$

Thus we see that the valuation V is (A, B) and V is ($\bar{A}$, $\hat{B}$) provide the same information.

A more general situation is the following. Assume V is a variable taking its value in X. Consider the statement (Prob V *is* A) *is* B. This then can be seen as a Z-valuation V *is* (A, B). Consider now the question what is the probability that V *is* D. Let us see what we can say here. We see that V *is* (A, B) indices the possibility distribution G over the space probability distributions $\mathcal{P}$ where

$$G(P) = \bigcup_p \left\{ \frac{B(\int_X A(x)p(x)dx)}{p} \right\}$$

We observe that for any probability distribution p we have $\text{Prob}_p(V \ is \ D) = \int D(x)p(x)dx$. From this we see that Prob(V is D) given V is (A, B) is a fuzzy subset H over [0, 1] such that for each $y \in [0, 1]$ we have $H(y) = \text{Max}_{P \in R_y} [G(p)] = \text{Max}_{P \in R_y} [B(\int_X A(x)p(x)dx)]$ where $R_y = \{p/ \int_X D(x)p(x)dx = y\}$. Essentially this is fuzzy probability

$$H = \bigcup_p \left\{ \frac{G(p)}{\int_X D(x)p(x)dx} \right\} = \bigcup_p \left\{ \frac{B(\int_X A(x)p(x)dx)}{\int_X D(x)p(x)dx} \right\}$$

5   Linguistic Summaries and Z-Valuations

In [2, 3] we introduced the idea of linguistic summaries here we show the strong connection between the idea of Z-valuations and linguistic summaries. We first review the idea of a linguistic summary. Assume $Y = \{y_1, \ldots y_n\}$ are a set of objects that manifest some feature V that takes its value in the space X. Here for simplicity we shall assume X is discrete, $X = \{x_1, \ldots x_q\}$. Furthermore we let $V(y_j)$ indicate the value of this feature for object y_j. Here then our data D consists of the bag $<V(y_1), \ldots V(y_n)>$. We note that we can associate with this data D a probability distribution P over the space X such that for each $x_j \in X$

$$p_j = \frac{Card(D_j)}{n}$$

where $D_j = \{y_k / V(y_k) = x_j \}$. Thus p_j is the proportion of elements in Y that have for V the value of x_j.

As described in [2, 3] a linguistic summary provides a way to express the information contained in D in a linguistic fashion. In particular a linguistic summary consists of three items:

>   1. A summarizer, S
>   2. A quantity in agreement, Q
>   3. A measure of validated or truth of this summary, T.

A linguistic summary provides a human friendly way of expressing the information in the data set D.

Here we note that a summarizer S is a fuzzy subset of the domain of V, X, corresponding to some linguistic concept. A quantity in agreement is formally a fuzzy subset of the unit interval corresponding to some idea of proportion. Typically it is a representation of some linguistic expression of proportion such as most, "about half", "almost all", "most".

The truth or validity of the linguistic summary (S, Q) with respect to the data D can be obtained as follows: [2, 3]

1. For each $d_i = V(y_i)$ calculate the degree to which d_j satisfies the summarizer S, $S(d_i)$

2. Let $r = \frac{1}{n} \sum_{i=1}^{n} S(d_i)$, the proportion of D that satisfy S.

3. Then $T = Q(r)$, the membership great of r is the proposed quantity in agreement.

We note that for any summarizer S_K and quantity in agreement Q_K we can calculate T_K, its validity as providing an appropriate summary of the data D. Now one can consider the space R of all pairs (S_K, Q_K) and for each of these T_K indicates the possible membership of (S_K, Q_K) in the set of valid summaries of the data D.

In a more abstract view, T_K is a representation of the validity of the linguistic summary (S_K, Q_K) for a probability distribution P over the space X. In this case the probability distribution is such that $p_j = Prob(x_j) = \frac{Card(D_j)}{n}$

We now can view Zadeh's concept of a Z-valuation in this light. Essentially we can view the Z-valuation, V *is* (A, B), as a linguistic summary. Here A is the summarizer and B is the quantity in agreement. Furthermore in this perspective the linguistic summary (A, B) is assumed to be a valid summary of the underlying probability distribution. Here the problem now becomes that of determining which underlying probability distributions are compatible with the expression Z-valuation, linguistic summary. Thus in the fuzzy subset G earlier introduced, G(P) is the possibility that P is the underling probability distribution. On the other in the case of linguistic summarization we start with a known probability distribution P and we are interested in providing a valid linguistic summary of the information contained in P.

Acknowledgement. This work supported by Multidisciplinary University Research Initiative (MURI) grant (Number W911NF-09-1-0392) for "Unified Research on Network-based Hard/Soft Information Fusion", issued by the US Army Research Office (ARO) under the program management of Dr. John Lavery. Also supported by an ONR grant for "Human Behavior Modeling Using Fuzzy and Soft Technologies", award number N000141010121.

References

1. Zadeh, L.A.: A note on Z-numbers. Information Science 181, 2923–2932 (2011)
2. Yager, R.R.: A new approach to the summarization of data. Information Sciences 28, 69–86 (1982)
3. Yager, R.R.: On linguistic summaries of data. In: Piatetsky-Shapiro, G., Frawley, B. (eds.) Knowledge Discovery in Databases, pp. 347–363. MIT Press, Cambridge (1991)
4. Zadeh, L.A.: Probability measures of fuzzy events. Journal of Mathematical Analysis and Applications 10, 421–427 (1968)
5. Ross, S.M.: Introduction to Probability and Statistics for Engineers and Scientists. Harcourt, San Diego (2000)
6. Zadeh, L.A.: Computing with Words-Principal Concepts and Idea. Springer, Berlin (to appear)
7. Yager, R.R.: On ordered weighted averaging aggregation operators in multi-criteria decision making. IEEE Transactions on Systems, Man and Cybernetics 18, 183–190 (1988)
8. Yager, R.R., Kacprzyk, J., Beliakov, G.: Recent Developments in the Ordered Weighted Averaging Operators: Theory and Practice. Springer, Berlin (2011)
9. Papoulis, A.: Probability, Random Variables and Stochastic Processes. McGraw-Hill, New York (1965)

Solving Real-World Fuzzy Quadratic Programming Problems by a Parametric Method

Carlos Cruz[1], Ricardo C. Silva[2], and José Luis Verdegay[1]

[1] Department of Computer Science and Artificial Intelligence,
CITIC–University of Granada, E-18071, Granada, Spain
{carloscruz,verdegay}@decsai.ugr.es
[2] Institute of Science and Technology, Federal University of São Paulo,
rua Talim, 330, Vila Nair, 12231-280, São José dos Campos, SP, Brazil
ricardo.coelho@unifesp.br

Abstract. Although fuzzy quadratic programming problems are of the utmost importance in an increasing variety of practical fields, there are remaining technological areas in which has not been tested their applicability or, if tried, have been little studied possibilities. This may be the case of Renewable Energy Assessment, Service Quality, Technology Foresight, Logistics, Systems Biology, etc. With this in mind, the goal of this paper is to apply a parametric approach previously developed by authors to solve some of these problems, specifically the portfolio selection problem by using BM&FBOVESPA data of some Brazilian securities and the economic dispatch problem, which schedules a power generation in an appropriate manner in order to satisfy the load demand.

Keywords: fuzzy mathematical optimization, quadratic programming, soft computing, fuzzy sets and systems.

1 Introduction

Soft Computing methodologies have repeatedly proven their efficiency and effectiveness in modeling situations and solving complex problems on a wide variety of scenarios. In the case of the formulation of real world problems their parameters are seldom known exactly and therefore they have to be estimated by the decision maker.

Thus, problems as energy management [20], portfolio selection and investment risk [1,8], control systems [12], production problem and scheduling [19], among others, can be formulated as a fuzzy quadratic programming problem [6]:

$$\min \tilde{\mathbf{c}}^t \mathbf{x} + \frac{1}{2} \mathbf{x}^t \tilde{\mathbf{Q}} \mathbf{x}$$

$$\text{s.t. } \tilde{\mathbf{A}} \mathbf{x} \leq^f \tilde{\mathbf{b}} \tag{1}$$

$$\mathbf{x} \geq \mathbf{0},$$

S. Greco et al. (Eds.): IPMU 2012, Part III, CCIS 299, pp. 102–111, 2012.

where $\mathbf{x} \in \mathbb{R}^n$, $\tilde{\mathbf{c}} \in \mathbb{F}(\mathbb{R})^n$, $\tilde{\mathbf{b}} \in \mathbb{F}(\mathbb{R})^m$, $\tilde{\mathbf{A}} \in \mathbb{F}(\mathbb{R})^{n \times m}$ is an $m \times n$ matrix with fuzzy entries, and $\tilde{\mathbf{Q}} \in \mathbb{F}(\mathbb{R})^{n \times n}$ is an $n \times n$ symmetric matrix with fuzzy entries, and the symbol "$\leq^f$" represents the fuzzy order relation. $\mathbb{F}(\mathbb{R})$ defines the set of fuzzy numbers $\tilde{a} = (a^L, a^U, \alpha, \beta)_{LR}$, where $a^L \leq a^U$, $\alpha > 0$, $\beta > 0$, and $a^L, a^U, \alpha, \beta \in \mathbb{R}$. Each fuzzy number is represented by a membership functions $\mu : \mathbb{R} \to [0,1]$, where each $\mathbf{a} \in \mathbb{R}^n$ provide the decision maker's satisfaction degree.

But there are still technological environments in which their applicability has not yet been tested, or if it has tested, their possibilities have not been investigated deep enough. This may be the case of Renewable Energies, Service Quality Evaluation, Technological Foresight, Logistics or Systems Biology. They are advanced technological areas of vital importance to our society that, due to the great relevance of the solutions given to the problems that may rise in them, they can affect our way of living and interacting.

With this in mind, the goal of this paper is to apply a parametric approach [16,14] developed by authors to solve two real-world problems with an imprecise order relation in the set of constraints.

The paper is organized as follows: Section 2 describes the parametric approach that solve quadratic programming problems with an imprecise order relation in the set of constraints. In Section 3 two problems are modeled and solved by the proposal method: the portfolio selection problem using historical data took by BM&FBOVESPA, Brazil; and the economic dispatch problem, which schedules a power generation in an appropriate manner in order to satisfy the load demand. Finally, conclusions are presented in Section 4.

2   Using a Parametric Approach to Solve Quadratic Programming Problems with Fuzzy Constraints

There are some approaches that solve quadratic programming problems with uncertainty of the order relation in the set of constraints, such as the extension of Zimmermann's original approach [23,24] described in [2], and other based on Werners's work [22] and also extended in [2]. They require that a decision maker choose an acceptable satisfaction level.

We are going to apply a parametric approach developed and tested by authors in last works [16,5,7] which provides a fuzzy solution (not a point -singleton like-solution). This method finds the curve that generates all optimal solutions to each different satisfaction level and moreover it does not depend on defining this level. The uncertanties can be presented in other parts of the mathematical formulation such as costs of the objective function. To solve this kind of problem, we can apply the approaches described in [17,15].

As in [16], the constraints of a quadratic problem are defined as having a fuzzy nature, that is, some violations in the accomplishment of such restrictions are permitted. Therefore, if we denote each constraint $\sum_{j=1}^n a_{ij}x_j$, by $(Ax)_i$ and $i = 1, \ldots, m$, the problem can be addressed as follows

$$\min \mathbf{c^t x} + \frac{1}{2}\mathbf{x^t Q x}$$
$$\text{s.t. } (Ax)_i \leq^f b_i, i = 1, \ldots, m \qquad (2)$$
$$x_j \geq 0, j = 1, \ldots, n$$

where the membership functions

$$\mu_i : \mathbb{R}^n \to (0, 1], \quad i = 1, \ldots, m$$

on the fuzzy constraints are to be determined by the decision maker. It is clear that each membership function will give the membership (satisfaction) degree such that any $x \in \mathbb{R}^n$ accomplishes the corresponding fuzzy constraint upon which it is defined. This degree is equal to 1 when the constraint is perfectly accomplished (no violation), and decreases to zero for greater violations. For non-admissible violations the accomplishment degree will equal zero in all cases. In the linear case (and formally also in the non linear one), these membership functions can be formulated as follows

$$\mu_i(\mathbf{x}) = \begin{cases} 1 & (Ax)_i \leq b_i \\ 1 - \dfrac{(Ax)_i - b_i}{d_i} & b_i \leq (Ax)_i \leq b_i + d_i \\ 0 & (Ax)_i > b_i + d_i \end{cases}$$

where d_i is the maximum permited violation for ith constraint function, with $i = 1, \ldots, m$. In order to solve this problem, first let us define for each fuzzy constraint,

$$X_i = \left\{ \mathbf{x} \in \mathbb{R}^n \mid (Ax)_i \leq^f b_i, \mathbf{x} \geq 0 \right\}.$$

If $\mathbf{X} = \bigcap X_i (i = 1, \ldots, m)$ then the former fuzzy quadratic problem can be addressed in a compact form as

$$\min \left\{ \mathbf{c^t x} + \frac{1}{2}\mathbf{x^t Q x} \mid \mathbf{x} \in \mathbf{X} \right\}.$$

It is clear that $\forall \alpha \in (0, 1]$, an α-cut of the fuzzy constraint set will be the classical set

$$X(\alpha) = \{ \mathbf{x} \in \mathbb{R}^n \mid \mu_X(\mathbf{x}) \geq \alpha \}$$

where $\forall \mathbf{x} \in \mathbb{R}^n$,

$$\mu_X(\mathbf{x}) = \min \mu_i(\mathbf{x}(\alpha)), i = 1, \ldots, m$$

Hence an α-cut of the i-th constraint will be denoted by $X_i(\alpha)$. Therefore, if $\forall \alpha \in (0, 1]$,

$$S(\alpha) = \left\{ \mathbf{x} \in \mathbb{R}^n \mid \mathbf{c^t x} + \frac{1}{2}\mathbf{x^t Q x} = \min \mathbf{c^t y} + \frac{1}{2}\mathbf{y^t Q y}, \ \mathbf{y} \in X(\alpha) \right\}$$

the fuzzy solution to the problem will therefore be the fuzzy set defined by the following membership function

$$S(\mathbf{x}) = \begin{cases} \sup\{\alpha : \mathbf{x} \in S(\alpha)\} & \mathbf{x} \in \bigcup_{\alpha} S(\alpha) \\ 0 & \text{otherwise.} \end{cases}$$

Provided that $\forall \alpha \in (0,1]$,

$$X(\alpha) = \bigcap_{i=1,\ldots,m} \{\mathbf{x} \in \mathbb{R}^n \mid (Ax)_i \leq r_i(\alpha), \mathbf{x} \geq 0, \mathbf{x} \in \mathbb{R}^n\}$$

with $r_i(\alpha) = b_i + d_i(1-\alpha)$. The operative solution to the former problem can be found, α-cut by α-cut, by means of the following auxiliary parametric quadratic programming model,

$$\min \mathbf{c}^t\mathbf{x} + \tfrac{1}{2}\mathbf{x}^t\mathbf{Q}\mathbf{x}$$
$$\text{s.t. } (Ax)_i \leq b_i + d_i(1-\alpha), i = 1,\ldots,m \tag{3}$$
$$x_j \geq 0, j = 1,\ldots,n, \alpha \in [0,1].$$

Thus, the fuzzy quadratic programming problem was parameterized at the end of the first phase. In the second phase the parametric quadratic programming problem is solved for each of the different α values using conventional quadratic programming techniques.

The results obtained for each α value generate a set of solutions and then the Representation Theorem can be used to integrate all these specific alpha-solutions.

3   Numerical Experiments

In order to illustrate the above described parametric method to solve quadratic programming problems under fuzzy environment, we are going to focus on two practical problems. The first problem is based on a general portfolio selection problem, while the other is focused on solving an economic dispatch problem.

The tests were all performed on a PC with 2.7GHZ Intel® Core™ i7, 4GB RAM running Mac OSX Lion operational system. All the problems presented in this work were resolved using **fmincon** function to solve constraint programming problems of *ToolBox Optimization* of MATLAB® 7.11 program.

3.1   Portfolio Selection Problem

The general portfolio selection problem was described by Markowitz [11] to analyze the risk investments. This analysis is an important research field in the modern finance, that vagueness, approximate values and lack of precision are very frequent in that context, and that quadratic programming problems have shown to be extremely useful to solve a variety of portfolio models, in the following we will present a general solution approach for fuzzy quadratic programming problems that, if needed, can be easily particularized to solve more specific portfolio models [9,18,3]. It is important to emphasize that, at the present time, we do not try to improve other solution methods for this kind of important problems, but only to show how our solution approach performs.

In order to show the performance of our method, we used the set of historical data shown in Table 1 took by BM&FBOVESPA that is the most important Brazilian institution to intermediate equity market transactions and the only securities, commodities and futures exchange in Brazil. It was chosen ten Brazilian securities and the columns 2-11 represent Celesc, Cemip, Coelce, CPFL, Copel, Eletrobras, EDP, AES Tiete, Light, and Tractebel securities data, respectively. These securities form the Electric Power index in this market. The returns on the ten securities, during the period of March 2006 up to December 2011, are presented in Table 1.

Table 1. Fuzzy portfolio selection problem

	#1	#2	#3	#4	#5	#6	#7	#8	#9	#10
Periods	Celesc	Cemig	Coelce	CPFL	Copel	Eletrobras	EDP	AES Tiete	Light	Tractebel
2006 Mar	0.0289	-0.1038	-0.0455	-0.0526	-0.0742	0.0771	-0.0762	0.0752	-0.3400	0.0516
2006 Jun	-0.0701	-0.0755	-0.0784	-0.1489	-0.0632	-0.0372	-0.1181	-0.1538	-0.0283	-0.0698
2006 Set	0.0427	-0.0764	0.0286	0.0482	0.1673	0.0208	0.0288	0.0957	0.0823	0.0227
2006 Dez	0.9521	0.1875	0.0830	0.0733	0.0200	0.0605	0.1576	0.0770	0.3133	0.0222
2007 Mar	0.0740	0.0001	0.0481	0.0275	-0.0250	0.0196	-0.1060	-0.0077	0.0347	0.0057
2007 Jun	0.1648	-1.4610	0.4623	0.2505	0.2793	0.2086	0.2374	0.1333	0.2045	0.1838
2007 Set	-0.0220	-0.0523	0.0365	-0.0903	-0.1365	-1.1561	-0.2988	-0.1755	-0.0033	-0.0161
2007 Dez	0.0682	-0.2000	-0.1581	-0.0558	-0.0933	-0.1241	-0.0550	0.5383	-0.0716	0.0517
2008 Mar	0.0454	-0.0222	0.0413	-0.0479	0.0885	-0.5263	0.0339	0.0595	0.1100	-0.0537
2008 Jun	0.0886	0.1898	-0.1980	0.0273	-0.0167	0.4872	0.0067	0.0876	-0.0475	-0.3558
2008 Set	-0.0700	-0.0340	-0.0919	-0.0225	-0.7341	-0.6659	-0.1480	-0.0613	-0.1800	0.8236
2008 Dez	-0.2693	-0.1835	0.1770	-0.1774	0.4233	0.2037	0.0524	-0.0228	-0.5528	-2.6951
2009 Mar	-0.0364	0.0360	0.0132	0.0016	0.0747	-0.0108	0.0351	-0.1343	-0.0028	-0.1524
2009 Jun	0.0176	-0.3089	0.0582	0.0104	0.1172	0.0953	0.1035	0.2673	0.1373	0.1770
2009 Set	0.0670	0.0241	0.2049	0.0034	0.1292	-0.0380	0.0736	0.1000	-0.0210	-0.0911
2009 Dez	0.0268	0.1456	0.0130	0.0954	0.1536	0.2405	0.1297	0.0331	0.0010	0.0493
2010 Mar	0.0201	-0.0064	0.0007	-0.0503	-0.0107	0.1069	-0.0344	-0.0482	0.0501	0.0250
2010 Jun	-0.0742	-0.1284	-0.1467	0.1028	0.0212	-0.0981	-0.0087	-0.0560	0.0010	-0.2713
2010 Set	0.0256	0.0470	0.0184	-0.0183	0.0013	-0.1067	0.0598	-0.5072	0.0868	0.0798
2010 Dez	0.1212	-0.0277	0.0559	0.0607	0.1024	0.0306	-0.0030	0.1093	0.0437	0.0376
2011 Mar	0.0493	0.1135	0.0902	0.0673	0.0596	0.0474	0.1108	0.0617	0.0300	0.0726
2011 Jun	-0.0511	0.0152	-0.0435	-1.0803	-0.0711	-0.1809	-0.0662	-0.0559	-0.0681	0.0190
2011 Set	-0.1089	-0.1421	0.0126	-0.0810	-0.2242	-0.2895	-0.1897	0.0105	-0.0259	-0.0757
2011 Dez	-0.0185	0.1665	0.0534	0.2071	0.1285	0.0919	0.2203	0.0843	0.0845	0.1257

This example will consider performance of portfolios with respect to "return" and "risk". This assumes that a Real, which is the Brazilian currency, of realized or unrealized capital gains is exactly equivalent to a Real of dividends, no better and no worse. This assumption is appropriate for certain investors, for example, some types of tax-free institutions. Other ways of handling capital gains and dividends, which are appropriate for other investors, can be viewed in [11].

Here we show the results obtained for the problems by the fuzzy quadratic programming methods introduced in Section 2. In Tables 1 were presented the solution of the real-world portfolio selection problem.

Table 2. Fuzzy portfolio selection problem

α	#1	#2	#3	#4	#5	#6	#7	#8	#9	#10	**FunObj**
0.0	0.1759	0.0593	0.5523	0.0000	0.0000	0.0000	0.0000	0.2124	0.0000	0.0000	0.0083
0.1	0.1989	0.0421	0.5468	0.0000	0.0000	0.0000	0.0000	0.2122	0.0000	0.0000	0.0091
0.2	0.2200	0.0247	0.5430	0.0000	0.0000	0.0000	0.0000	0.2122	0.0000	0.0000	0.0101
0.3	0.2443	0.0077	0.5363	0.0000	0.0000	0.0000	0.0000	0.2117	0.0000	0.0000	0.0111
0.4	0.3114	0.0000	0.5140	0.0000	0.0000	0.0000	0.0000	0.1746	0.0000	0.0000	0.0124
0.5	0.4151	0.0000	0.4759	0.0000	0.0000	0.0000	0.0000	0.1090	0.0000	0.0000	0.0147
0.6	0.5189	0.0000	0.4378	0.0000	0.0000	0.0000	0.0000	0.0433	0.0000	0.0000	0.0180
0.7	0.6290	0.0000	0.3710	0.0000	0.0000	0.0000	0.0000	0.0000	0.0000	0.0000	0.0224
0.8	0.7516	0.0000	0.2484	0.0000	0.0000	0.0000	0.0000	0.0000	0.0000	0.0000	0.0282
0.9	0.8741	0.0000	0.1259	0.0000	0.0000	0.0000	0.0000	0.0000	0.0000	0.0000	0.0357
1.0	0.9967	0.0000	0.0033	0.0000	0.0000	0.0000	0.0000	0.0000	0.0000	0.0000	0.0448

3.2   Economic Dispatch Problem

The second problem is focused on solving an economic dispatch problem, which schedules a power generation in an appropriate manner in order to satisfy the load demand while minimizing the total operational cost, i.e, this problem allocates the load demand to the committed generating units in the most economical or profitable way, while respecting security and reliability constraints. In recent years, environmental factors such as global warming and pollution have increased to critical levels in some places. In this context, renewable energy resources like wind power have shown a wide potential to reduce pollutant emissions, which were also formed by fuel consumption for thermal power plants. Nevertheless, the expected generation output from a wind farm is difficult to predict accurately because of the intermittent natural variability of the wind. New challenges arise with regard to the integration of large amounts of wind generation into the traditional power system.

The electrical power system from some countries are interconnected that involves several generations areas with different power plants such as thermal, hydro, wind, and solar. The objective is to reach the most economical generation policy that could supply the load demand without violating constraints, such as power balance, security, transmission line and generation limits, power system spinning reserve requirement. In this work, the system under study is composed by thermal power plants and a wind energy system. Thus, the goal of this problem is to determine the optimal amounts of generation power over the study period so that the the total thermal unit fuel cost is minimized subject to different constraints [10,13,4,20].

Without loss of generality, a economic dispatch problem with wind penetration consideration can be formulated by a quadratic programming problem. The objective function represents the cost curves of differential generators and the total fuel cost $FC(P_G)$ can be represented on the following way:

$$\min FC(P_G) = \sum_{i=1}^{M} a_i + b_i P_{Gi} + c_i P_{Gi}^2 \tag{4}$$

where M is the number of generators committed to the operating system, a_i, b_i, c_i are the cost coefficients of the i-th generator, and P_{Gi} is the real power output of the i-th generator.

Because of the physical or operational limits in practical systems, there is a set of constraints that should be satisfied throughout the system operations for a feasible solution. The first constraint is called power balance and satisfies the total demand, which has to be covered by the total thermal power generation and the wind power. This relation can be represented by

$$\sum_{i=1}^{M} P_{Gi} + W_{av} \geq_f P_D \tag{5}$$

where W_{av} is the available wind power and $\geq_f$ represents the uncertainties from the wind farm generation and the transmission loss. This loss can be computed based on Kron's loss formula but it is not the focus in this work. So, we assume this transmission loss

The second constraint is the generation capacity for each thermal power unit. For normal system operations, real power output of each generator is restricted by lower and upper bounds as follows:

$$P_{Gi}^{min} \leq P_{Gi} \leq P_{Gi}^{max} \tag{6}$$

where P_{Gi}^{min} and P_{Gi}^{max} are the minimum and maximum power from generator i.

There are many other mathematical formulations more complex but the aim of this work is not to solve economic dispatch models, that here are soly considered for the sake of illustrating the fuzzy quadractic programming problems solution approach presented, which in fact is the goal and main aim of this contribution.

In this paper, we apply the fuzzy quadratic programming approach, described in [5], to solve a economic dispatch problem based on a typical IEEE 30-bus test system with six generators [21]. The system parameters including fuel cost coefficients and generator capacities are listed in Table 3. The load demand used in the simulations is 2,834GW and the available wind power is 0,5668GW.

Here we show the results obtained for the problems by the fuzzy quadratic programming methods introduced in Section 2. The unit committed problem

Table 3. Fuel cost coefficients and generator capacities

Generator i	a_i	b_i	c_i	P_{Gi}^{min}	P_{Gi}^{min}
G_1	10	200	100	0.05	0.50
G_2	10	150	120	0.05	0.60
G_3	20	180	40	0.05	1.00
G_4	10	100	60	0.05	1.20
G_5	20	180	40	0.05	1.00
G_6	10	150	100	0.05	0.60

described in this work were solved by using the linear approach of the ϕ_i function as presented by Problem (3). In Tables 4 were presented the solution of the real-world economy dispatch problem.

Table 4. Fuzzy energy generation

α	Decision Variables						FunObj
0.0	0.0501	0.2501	0.3751	0.9167	0.3751	0.3001	477.6953
0.1	0.0530	0.2525	0.3826	0.9217	0.3826	0.3030	484.2223
0.2	0.0560	0.2550	0.3901	0.9267	0.3901	0.3060	490.7662
0.3	0.0590	0.2575	0.3975	0.9317	0.3975	0.3090	497.3270
0.4	0.0620	0.2600	0.4050	0.9366	0.4050	0.3120	503.9047
0.5	0.0650	0.2625	0.4124	0.9416	0.4124	0.3150	510.4993
0.6	0.0680	0.2650	0.4199	0.9466	0.4199	0.3180	517.1108
0.7	0.0709	0.2675	0.4273	0.9516	0.4273	0.3209	523.7392
0.8	0.0739	0.2699	0.4348	0.9565	0.4348	0.3239	530.3846
0.9	0.0769	0.2724	0.4423	0.9615	0.4423	0.3269	537.0468
1.0	0.0799	0.2749	0.4497	0.9665	0.4497	0.3299	543.7259

4   Conclusions

Fuzzy quadratic programming problems are of utmost importance in an increasing variety of practical fields because real-world applications inevitably involve some degree of uncertainty or imprecision. In contrast with to what happens in fuzzy linear programming problems, unfortunately to date, not much research has been done in this important class of problems.

Some of these problems are the portfolio selection problem aand the the economic dispatch problem. In these context this paper has applied an operative and novel method for solving Fuzzy Quadratic Programming problems which is carried out by performing two phases where a set of optimal solutions is obtained to each $\alpha, \beta, \gamma \in [0, 1]$ that finally provide to the user with a fuzzy solution.

The authors aim to extend the line of investigation involving Fuzzy Quadratic Programming problems in order to try to solve practical real-life problems by facilitating the building of Decision Support Systems.

Acknowledgments. The authors want to thank the financial support from the agency FAPESP (project number 2010/51069-2) and the Spanish projects CEI BioTic GENIL from the MICINN, as well as TIN2011-27696-C02-01, P11-TIC-8001, TIN2008-06872-C04-04, and TIN2008-01948.

References

1. Appadoo, S., Bhatt, S., Bector, C.R.: Application of possibility theory to investment decisions. Fuzzy Optimization and Decision Making 7, 35–57 (2008)
2. Bector, C.R., Chandra, S.: Fuzzy mathematical programming and fuzzy matrix games. STUDFUZZ, vol. 169. Springer, Berlin (2005)
3. Carlsson, C., Fullér, R., Majlender, P.: A possibilistic approach to selecting portfolio with highest utility score. Fuzzy Sets and Systems 131, 13–21 (2002)
4. Ciornei, I., Kyriakides, E.: Heuristic solution for the nonconvex dispatch of generation in power systems with high wind power share. In: PES 2009. IEEE Power & Energy Society General Meeting, pp. 1–7 (2009)
5. Cruz, C., Silva, R.C., Verdegay, J.L.: Extending and relating different approaches for solving fuzzy quadratic problems. Fuzzy Optimization and Decision Making 10(3), 193–210 (2011)
6. Cruz, C., Silva, R.C., Verdegay, J.L., Yamakami, A.: A survey of fuzzy quadratic programming. Recent Patents on Computer Science 1(3), 182–1930 (2008)
7. Cruz, C., Silva, R.C., Verdegay, J.L., Yamakami, A.: A parametric approach to solve quadratic programming problems with fuzzy environment in the set of constraints. In: IFSA/EUSFLAT Conf. 2009, pp. 1158–1163 (2009)
8. Ida, M.: Portfolio selection problem with interval coefficients. Applied Mathematics Letters 16, 709–713 (2003)
9. León, T., Liern, V., Vercher, E.: Viability of infeasible portfolio selection problems: A fuzzy approach. European Journal of Operational Research 139, 178–189 (2002)
10. Liang, R.H., Liao, J.H.: A fuzzy-optimization approach for generation scheduling with wind and solar energy systems. IEEE Transactions on Power Systems 22(4), 1665–1674 (2007)
11. Markowitz, H.M.: Portfolio Selection: Efficient Diversification of Investments, 2nd edn. Blackwell Publisher, Massachusetts (1991)
12. Mollov, S., Babuska, R., Abonyi, J., Verbruggen, H.B.: Effective optimization for fuzzy model predictive control. IEEE Transactions on Fuzzy Systems 12(5), 661–675 (2004)
13. Padhy, N.P.: Unit commitment - a bibliographical survey. IEEE Transactions on Power Systems 19(2), 1196–1205 (2004)
14. Silva, R.C., Cruz, C., Verdegay, J.L., Yamakami, A.: A Survey of Fuzzy Convex Programming Models. In: Lodwick, W.A., Kacprzyk, J. (eds.) Fuzzy Optimization. STUDFUZZ, vol. 254, pp. 127–143. Springer, Heidelberg (2010)
15. Silva, R.C., Cruz, C., Yamakami, A.: A parametric method to solve quadratic programming problems with fuzzy costs. In: IFSA/EUSFLAT Conf. 2009, pp. 1398–1403 (2009)
16. Silva, R.C., Verdegay, J.L., Yamakami, A.: Two-phase method to solve fuzzy quadratic programming problems. In: IEEE International Conference on Fuzzy Systems, pp. 1–6 (2007)

17. Silva, R.C., Verdegay, J.L., Yamakami, A.: A parametric convex programming approach applied to portfolio pelection problems with fuzzy costs. In: Proceedings IEEE International Conference on Fuzzy Systems, FUZZ-IEEE 2010, pp. 1–63 (2010)
18. Tanaka, H., Guo, P., Türksen, B.T.: Portfolio selection based on fuzzy probabilities and possibility distributions. Fuzzy Sets and Systems 111, 387–397 (2000)
19. Tang, J., Wang, D.: An interactive approach based on a genetic algorithm for a type of quadratic programming problems with fuzzy objective and resources. Computers and Operations Research 24(5), 413–422 (1997)
20. Wang, L., Singh, C.: Balancing risk ad cost in fuzzy economic dispatch including wind power netration based on particle swarm optimization. Electric Power Systems Research 78, 1361–1368 (2008)
21. Wang, L.F., Singh, C.: Environmental/economic power dispatch usng a fuzzified multi-objective particle swarm optimization algorithm. Electrical Power System Resource 77, 1654–1664 (2007)
22. Werners, B.: Interative multiple objective programming suject to flexible constraints. European Journal of Operational Research 31, 342–349 (1987)
23. Zimmermann, H.J.: Fuzzy programming and linear programming with several objective functions. Fuzzy Sets and Systems 1, 45–55 (1978)
24. Zimmermann, H.J.: Fuzzy mathematical programming. Computers & Operations Research 10(4), 291–298 (1983)

Naive Bayesian Classifier
Based on Neighborhood Probability

Jame N.K. Liu[1], Yulin He[2], Xizhao Wang[2], and Yanxing Hu[1]

[1] Department of Computing, The Hong Kong Polytechnic University,
Hung Hom, Kowloon, Hong Kong
[2] College of Mathematics and Computer Science, Hebei University,
Baoding 071002, China
csnkliu@inet.polyu.edu.hk, csylhe@gmail.com, xizhaowang@ieee.org

Abstract. When calculating the class-conditional probability of continuous attributes with naive Bayesian classifier (NBC) algorithm, the existing methods usually make use of the superposition of many normal distribution probability density functions to fit the true probability density function. Accordingly, the value of the class-conditional probability is equal to the sum of values of normal distribution probability density functions. In this paper, we propose a NPNBC model, i.e. the naive Bayesian classifier based on the neighborhood probability. In NPNBC, when calculating the class-conditional probability for a continuous attribute value in the given unknown example, a small neighborhood is created for the continuous attribute value in every normal distribution probability density function. So, the neighborhood probabilities for each normal distribution probability density function can be obtained. The sum of these neighborhood probabilities is the class-conditional probability for the continuous attribute value in NPNBC. Our experimental results demonstrate that NPNBC can obtain the remarkable performance in classification accuracy when compared with the normal method and the kernel method. In addition, we also investigate the relationship between the classification accuracy of NPNBC and the value of neighborhood.

Keywords: naive Bayesian classifier, neighborhood probability, NPNBC, normal method, kernel method.

1 Introduction

In the supervised classification problems, NBC [4] is a simple and efficiently probabilistic model based on Bayesian theory. NBC performs well over a wide range of practical applications, including medical diagnosis [7], text categorization [12], email filtering [11] and information retrieval [8]. Compared with more sophisticated classification algorithms, such as decision tree and neural network, NBC can offer very good classification accuracy [2]. And, NBC can deal with the classification problems with a large number of variables and large data sets.

According to the prior probability and the class-conditional probability of the unknown sample, NBC calculates the posterior probability and determine

S. Greco et al. (Eds.): IPMU 2012, Part III, CCIS 299, pp. 112–121, 2012.

the class for the unknown sample. NBC assumes that all attributes of a sample are independent. This means that each attribute is conditionally independent of every other attribute. In the learning problems, the attributes may be continuous and nominal. The continuous or normal attributes refer to attributes taking on numerical values (integer or real) or categorical values respectively. In NBC model, for the nominal-valued attributes, the class-conditional probability is equal to the frequency (the number of times the value was observed divided by the total number of observations) [4]. However, for the continuous-valued attributes, the case is more complex. One must estimate the class-conditional probability function from a given set of training data with class information. There are mainly two methods for estimating the class-conditional probability function: the normal method [9] and the kernel method [6]. In the normal method, NBC assumes that the continuous-valued attributes are generated by a single Gaussian distribution. The mean and standard deviation can be straightly calculated from the training dataset. The normal method is a simple and common technique. It is fast in training and testing and requires little memory. But when the continuous-valued attributes do not hold for Gaussian distribution, the normal method can not perform well. To deal with this case, John and Langley [6] propose to use Parzen windows method [10] to estimate the underling class-conditional probability function. It used the superposition of many normal distribution probability density functions to fit the true probability density function of the continuous-valued attributes. The means of Gaussian distributions are the given attribute values and standard deviation is the windows width [9]. This method is called kernel method because every Gaussian distribution is seen as a kernel [6].

In this paper, we propose the naive Bayesian classifier based on the neighborhood probability-NPNBC. In NPNBC, when we calculate the class-conditional probability for a continuous attribute value in the given unknown example, a small neighborhood is created for the continuous attribute value in every kernel. So, the neighborhood probabilities for each kernel can be obtained. The summation of these neighborhood probabilities is the class-conditional probability for the continuous attribute value in NPNBC. Our experimental comparisons demonstrate that NPNBC can obtain the remarkable performance in classification accuracy compared with the normal method [9] and the kernel method [6]. In addition, we also investigate the relationship between the classification accuracy of NPNBC and the value of neighborhood. The rest of the paper is organized as follows: In section 2, we summarize the two exiting methods for dealing with the continuous-valued attributes. NPNBC is proposed in section 3. In section 4, we describe our experimental setup and results. Finally, we make a conclusion and outline the main directions for future research.

2   The Related Works

NBC algorithm [4] works as follows: Assume A_1, A_2, $\cdots$, A_d are d attributes. A sample X is represented by a vector $\{x_1, x_2, \cdots, x_d\}$, where x_i is the value of attribute $A_i(1 \leq i \leq d)$. According to the Bayesian theory, NBC calculates the probability $p(C|\boldsymbol{X})$ that a given sample $\boldsymbol{X}$ belongs to a given class C:

$$p(C|\boldsymbol{X}) = \frac{p(\boldsymbol{X}|C)p(C)}{p(\boldsymbol{X})} \propto p(\boldsymbol{X}|C)p(C) = p(x_1, x_2, \cdots, x_d|C)p(C)$$

$$= p(x_1|C)p(x_2|C)\cdots p(x_d|C)p(C) = \left[\prod_{i=1}^{d} p(x_i|C)\right]p(C).$$

The value of $p(C)$ can be easily estimated from the training data set. $p(x_i|C)$ is the class-conditional probability of the attribute-value $x_i(1 \leq i \leq d)$. If x_i is continuous, there are mainly two methods to calculate the value of $p(x_i|C)$: the normal method [9] and the kernel method [6]. In the following, we review these methods respectively.

2.1   The Normal Method

Let $x_i^{(j)}(1 \leq j \leq N_C, 1 \leq i \leq d)$ be the value of attribute A_i in the ith sample of class C, where N_C is the number of samples in the class C. The normal method [9] assumes that the distribution of attribute A_i follows the Gaussian normal distribution. For the continuous attribute value $x_i(1 \leq i \leq d)$ in the unknown sample $\{x_1, x_2, \cdots, x_d\}$, we calculate the value of $p(x_i|C)$ according to the following formulation:

$$p(x_i|C) = g(x_i; \mu_C, \sigma_C) = \frac{1}{\sqrt{2\pi}\sigma_C}exp[-\frac{(x_i-\mu_C)^2}{2\sigma_C^2}],$$

$$\text{where } \mu_C = \frac{\sum_{j=1}^{N_C} x_i^{(j)}}{N_C}, \text{ and } \sigma_C^2 = \frac{\sum_{j=1}^{N_C}\left(x_i^{(j)}-\mu_C\right)^2}{N_C-1}.$$

The mean μ_C and variance σ_C are estimated from the values of attribute $A_i(1 \leq i \leq d)$ in the training dataset with class C. The benefit of the normal method [9] is that if the true distribution of attribute A_i follows the normal distribution the performance of NBC is very well. However, in fact, the assumption of the normal distribution may not hold for all domains. This suggests that we should explore other methods to estimate the distribution of attribute A_i.

2.2   The Kernel Method

John and Langley [6] use the average of a large set of Gaussian kernels to estimate the distribution of attribute $A_i(1 \leq i \leq d)$. In the kernel method, we calculate the value of $p(x_i|C)$ as follows:

$$p(x_i|C) = \frac{1}{\sqrt{2\pi}N_C h}\sum_{j=1}^{N_C}\exp\left\{-\frac{\left[x_i-x_i^{(j)}\right]^2}{2h^2}\right\}, \tag{1}$$

where, the parameter h is the width of the window. In this paper, we set $h = \frac{1}{\sqrt{N_C}}$.

By transforming the form of formulation (1), we can see that

$$p(x_i|C) = \frac{1}{N_C}\sum_{j=1}^{N_C}\left\{\frac{1}{\sqrt{2\pi}h}\exp\left\{-\frac{\left[x_i-x_i^{(j)}\right]^2}{2h^2}\right\}\right\} = \frac{1}{N_C}\sum_{j=1}^{N_C}\left\{g\left[x_i; x_i^{(j)}, h\right]\right\}.$$

3   NBC Based on Neighborhood Probability-NPNBC

In this section, we will introduce a novel naive Bayesian model: the naive Bayesian classifier based on neighborhood probability (simply NPNBC). We first depict the basic idea of NPNBC. Then, the principle of NPNBC is given. Finally, we verify the feasibility of NPNBC.

3.1   The Basic Idea of NPNBC

As discussed in previous sections, the kernel method used the average value of many normal kernels to estimate the value of $p(x_i|C)$ [6]. From formulation (1) we can see that the value of $p(x_i|C)$ is relevant to the length between x_i and $x_i^{(j)}$ ($1 \leq j \leq N_C, 1 \leq i \leq d$). For the given h, if the length between x_i and a certain data point $x_i^{(j)}$ is larger, i.e. $\left|x_i - x_i^{(j)}\right| > 3.5$, the value of $\frac{1}{\sqrt{2\pi}h} \exp\left\{-\frac{\left[x_i-x_i^{(1)}\right]^2}{2h^2}\right\}$ is smaller. We call $\frac{1}{\sqrt{2\pi}h} \exp\left\{-\frac{\left[x_i-x_i^{(1)}\right]^2}{2h^2}\right\}$ as the probability density unit (PDU) of $x_i^{(j)}$. For example, let $h = 1$, if $\left|x_i - x_i^{(j)}\right| = 4.15$, then the PDU of $x_i^{(j)}$ is 0.000073. When we compute the class-conditional probability $p(x_i|C)$, because the value of the PDU of $x_i^{(j)}$ is very small, the class information that x_i gains from $x_i^{(j)}$ is little and $x_i^{(j)}$ exerts very weak influence to the classification determination of x_i. In this case, we can consider that the information of $x_i^{(j)}$ is lost while determining the class for x_i.

The basic idea of NPNBC is that when the value of $\left|x_i - x_i^{(j)}\right|$ is very small, x_i can still obtain more information about classification from $x_i^{(j)}$ rather than lose the information of $x_i^{(j)}$. In NPNBC, we extend the neighborhood definite integral to the PDU of $x_i^{(j)}$ and calculate the neighborhood probability of x_i lying within a small interval $[x_i - \vartheta, x_i + \vartheta]$, where ϑ is a small value. In other words, NPNBC uses the value $\int_{x_k-\vartheta}^{x_k+\vartheta} \left\{\frac{1}{\sqrt{2\pi}h} \exp\left\{-\frac{\left[x_i-x_i^{(j)}\right]^2}{2h^2}\right\}\right\} dx$ to replace the PDU of $x_i^{(j)}$. In NPNBC we call $\int_{x_k-\vartheta}^{x_k+\vartheta} \left\{\frac{1}{\sqrt{2\pi}h} \exp\left\{-\frac{\left[x_i-x_i^{(j)}\right]^2}{2h^2}\right\}\right\} dx$ as the neighborhood probability unit (NPU) of $x_i^{(j)}$. By introducing the NPU of $x_i^{(j)}$, the value of class-conditional probability $p(x_i|C)$ can be computed according to the following formulation:

$$p(x_i|C) = \frac{1}{N_C} \sum_{j=1}^{N_C} \left\{\int_{x_i-\vartheta}^{x_i+\vartheta} \left\{\frac{1}{\sqrt{2\pi}h} \exp\left\{-\frac{\left[x-x_i^{(j)}\right]^2}{2h^2}\right\}\right\} dx\right\}. \tag{2}$$

Referring to Fig.1, we give an example to depict NPNBC in detail. Also, we assume that there are three values $x_i^{(1)}, x_i^{(2)}, x_i^{(3)}$ of continuous attribute A_i with

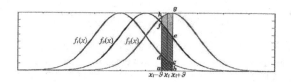

Fig. 1. The example of NPNBC

class C, we calculate the value of $p(x_i|C)$ for the unknown attribute value x_i according to the following expression:

$$p(x_i|C) = \tfrac{1}{3}(S_{abcd} + S_{abef} + S_{abgh})$$

$$= \tfrac{1}{3}\sum_{j=1}^{3}\left\{\int_{x_k-\vartheta}^{x_k+\vartheta}\left\{\frac{1}{\sqrt{2\pi}h}\exp\left\{-\frac{\left[x_i-x_i^{(j)}\right]^2}{2h^2}\right\}\right\}dx\right\},$$

where, S_{abcd} is the area of region $abcd$, S_{abef} the area of region $abef$, and S_{abgh} the area of region $abgh$.

3.2   The Principle of NPNBC

For a given sample $\boldsymbol{X} = \{x_1, x_2, \cdots, x_d\}$, where $x_1, x_2, \cdots, x_d$ are all continuous values of attributes $A_1, A_2, \cdots, A_d$. NPNBC calculates the probability $\hat{p}(C|\boldsymbol{X})$ that a given sample $\boldsymbol{X}$ belongs to a given class C:

$$\hat{p}(C|\boldsymbol{X}) = \int\int\cdots\int_{\Omega} p(C|\boldsymbol{X})\,d\Omega \propto \int\int\cdots\int_{\Omega} p(\boldsymbol{X}|C)\,p(C)\,d\Omega$$

$$= p(C)\int_{x_1-\vartheta}^{x_1+\vartheta} p(x_1|C)\,dx_1\int_{x_2-\vartheta}^{x_2+\vartheta} p(x_2|C)\,dx_2\cdots\cdot\int_{x_d-\vartheta}^{x_d+\vartheta} p(x_d|C)\,dx_d$$

$$= \frac{p(C)}{N_C}\prod_{i=1}^{d}\left\{\sum_{j=1}^{N_C}\left\{\int_{x_i-\vartheta}^{x_i+\vartheta}\frac{1}{\sqrt{2\pi}h}\left\{\exp\left\{-\frac{\left[x_i-x_i^{(j)}\right]^2}{2h^2}\right\}\right\}dx_i\right\}\right\},$$

where, $p(C) = \frac{N_C}{N}$, N_C is the number of samples in the class C, N is the total number of samples in the training data set. In conclusion, the probability $p(C|\boldsymbol{X})$ can be calculated in NPNBC with the following expression:

$$\hat{p}(C|\boldsymbol{X}) = \frac{1}{N}\prod_{i=1}^{d}\left\{\sum_{j=1}^{N_C}\left\{\int_{x_i-\vartheta}^{x_i+\vartheta}\frac{1}{\sqrt{2\pi}h}\left\{\exp\left\{-\frac{\left[x_i-x_i^{(j)}\right]^2}{2h^2}\right\}\right\}dx_i\right\}\right\}. \tag{3}$$

3.3   The Feasibility of NPNBC

According to the conclusion of the kernel method [6], for a given sample $\boldsymbol{X} = \{x_1, x_2, \cdots, x_d\}$, we can compute the value of $p(C|\boldsymbol{X})$ as follows:

$$p(C|\boldsymbol{X}) = \frac{1}{N}\prod_{i=1}^{d}\left\{\sum_{j=1}^{N_C}\frac{1}{\sqrt{2\pi}h}\left\{\exp\left\{-\frac{\left[x_i-x_i^{(j)}\right]^2}{2h^2}\right\}\right\}\right\}. \tag{4}$$

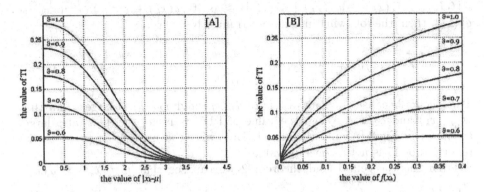

Fig. 2. [A] The relationship between $|x_k - \mu|$ and TI and [B] the relationship between $f(x_k)$ and TI

To verify the feasibility of NPNBC, we need to compare formulation (3) with (4) and find the difference and relation between (3) and (4). So, we first introduce the definition of transformation increment (TI).

Definition 1. Assume $f(x) = \frac{1}{\sqrt{2\pi}\sigma} \exp\left[-\frac{(x-\mu)^2}{2\sigma^2}\right]$, let $\int_{x_k-\vartheta}^{x_k+\vartheta} f(x)\,dx = f(x_k) + \Delta E(x_k, \mu)$, then we call $\Delta E(x_k, \mu)$ as the transformation increment of x_k with regard to μ.

TI establishes the relation between $\int_{x_k-\vartheta}^{x_k+\vartheta} f(x)\,dx$ and $f(x_k)$. Now, we observe the following two relationships: (1) between $|x_k - \mu|$ and TI; (2) between $f(x_k)$ and TI according to the Fig.2. Let $\sigma = 1.0$.

For the given ϑ, from Fig.2-[A], we can see that as the values of $|x_k - \mu|$ are reduced, the TI increases; in Fig.2-[B], we can see that as the values of $f(x_k)$ increase, the TI also increases. It offers the possibility for the realization of NPNBC. By introducing the following theorems and deductions, we give an in-depth understanding of TI and depict the feasibility of NPNBC.

Theorem 1. Let $f(x) = \frac{1}{\sqrt{2\pi}\sigma} \exp\left[-\frac{(x-\mu_f)^2}{2\sigma^2}\right]$ and $g(x) = \frac{1}{\sqrt{2\pi}\sigma} \exp\left[-\frac{(x-\mu_g)^2}{2\sigma^2}\right]$. For a given x_k, if $f(x_k) \succ g(x_k)$, then, $\int_{x_k-\vartheta}^{x_k+\vartheta} f(x)\,dx \succ \int_{x_k-\vartheta}^{x_k+\vartheta} g(x)\,dx$.

Theorem 2. Let $f_1(x) = \frac{1}{\sqrt{2\pi}\sigma} \exp\left[-\frac{(x-\mu_{f_1})^2}{2\sigma^2}\right]$, $f_2(x) = \frac{1}{\sqrt{2\pi}\sigma} \exp\left[-\frac{(x-\mu_{f_2})^2}{2\sigma^2}\right]$, $g_1(x) = \frac{1}{\sqrt{2\pi}\sigma} \exp\left[-\frac{(x-\mu_{g_1})^2}{2\sigma^2}\right]$, and $g_2(x) = \frac{1}{\sqrt{2\pi}\sigma} \exp\left[-\frac{(x-\mu_{g_2})^2}{2\sigma^2}\right]$. For a given x_k, when $\{[\Delta E(x_k, \mu_{g_1}) + \Delta E(x_k, \mu_{g_2})] - [\Delta E(x_k, \mu_{f_1}) + \Delta E(x_k, \mu_{f_2})]\}$

$-\{[f_1(x_k) + f_2(x_k)] - [g_1(x_k) + g_2(x_k)]\} > 0$, if $f_1(x_k) + f_2(x_k) > g_1(x_k) + g_2(x_k)$, then, the following inequality (5) must be true:

$$\int_{x_k-\vartheta}^{x_k+\vartheta} f_1(x)\,dx + \int_{x_k-\vartheta}^{x_k+\vartheta} f_2(x)\,dx \prec \int_{x_k-\vartheta}^{x_k+\vartheta} g_1(x)\,dx + \int_{x_k-\vartheta}^{x_k+\vartheta} g_2(x)\,dx. \qquad (5)$$

This occurs because the sum of TIs of $f_1(x_k)$ and $f_2(x_k)$ is larger than that of $g_1(x_k)$ and $g_2(x_k)$. When the value of PDU is large, the TI is also large, as shown in Fig.2-[A] and theorem 1. But, with the increase of $|x_k - \mu|$, the reduction of TI is not a constant value.

From the theorem 1 and theorem 2 we can see that if $f(x_k) > g(x_k)$, $\int_{x_k-\vartheta}^{x_k+\vartheta} f(x)\,dx > \int_{x_k-\vartheta}^{x_k+\vartheta} g(x)\,dx$ must be true; However, if $f_1(x_k) + f_2(x_k) > g_1(x_k) + g_2(x_k)$, $\int_{x_k-\vartheta}^{x_k+\vartheta} f_1(x)\,dx + \int_{x_k-\vartheta}^{x_k+\vartheta} f_2(x)\,dx > \int_{x_k-\vartheta}^{x_k+\vartheta} g_1(x)\,dx + \int_{x_k-\vartheta}^{x_k+\vartheta} g_2(x)\,dx$ may be not true.

Deduction 1. Let

$$f_i(x) = \frac{1}{\sqrt{2\pi}\sigma} \exp\left[-\frac{(x-\mu_{f_i})^2}{2\sigma^2}\right], \quad g_j(x) = \frac{1}{\sqrt{2\pi}\sigma} \exp\left[-\frac{(x-\mu_{g_j})^2}{2\sigma^2}\right],$$

where $i = 1, 2, \cdots, N_i$, $j = 1, 2, \cdots, N_j$. For a given x_k, when

$$\left\{\sum_{j=1}^{N_j} \Delta E(x_k, \mu_{g_j}) - \sum_{i=1}^{N_i} \Delta E(x_k, \mu_{f_i})\right\} - \left\{\sum_{i=1}^{N_i} f_i(x_k) - \sum_{j=1}^{N_j} g_j(x_k)\right\} > 0, \qquad (6)$$

if $\sum_{i=1}^{N_i} f_i(x) > \sum_{j=1}^{N_j} g_j(x)$, then, the inequality (7) must be true:

$$\sum_{i=1}^{N_i}\left[\int_{x_k-\vartheta}^{x_k+\vartheta} f_i(x)\,dx\right] < \sum_{j=1}^{N_j}\left[\int_{x_k-\vartheta}^{x_k+\vartheta} g_j(x)\,dx\right]. \qquad (7)$$

Deduction 2. Let

$$f_p^{(i)}(x) = \frac{1}{\sqrt{2\pi}\sigma} \exp\left[-\frac{(x-\mu_{f_{ip}})^2}{2\sigma^2}\right], \quad g_q^{(j)}(x) = \frac{1}{\sqrt{2\pi}\sigma} \exp\left[-\frac{(x-\mu_{g_{jp}})^2}{2\sigma^2}\right],$$

where $p = 1, 2, \cdots, N_p$, $q = 1, 2, \cdots, N_q$. For a given x_k, if $\prod_{i=1}^{d}\left[\sum_{p=1}^{N_p} f_p^{(i)}(x)\right] > \prod_{i=1}^{d}\left[\sum_{q=1}^{N_q} g_q^{(j)}(x)\right]$, then, the following inequality

Table 1. The comparison of classification accuracy (%)

Dataset	Number of attributes	Number of classes	Number of instances	NPNBC	Kernel method	Normal method
Glass	9	7	214	54.29	51.40	50.47
Ionosphere	34	2	351	92.78	91.74	82.62
Iris	4	3	150	96.00	96.00	95.33
Parkinson	22	2	195	79.00	70.77	69.23

$$\prod_{i=1}^{d} \left\{ \sum_{p=1}^{N_p} \left[\int_{x_k-\vartheta}^{x_k+\vartheta} f_p^{(i)}(x)\, dx \right] \right\} > \prod_{i=1}^{d} \left\{ \sum_{q=1}^{N_q} \left[\int_{x_k-\vartheta}^{x_k+\vartheta} g_q^{(j)}(x)\, dx \right] \right\} \qquad (8)$$

may be not true.

Ultimately, the deduction 2 guarantees that when we determine the class label for new sample X , NPNBC may obtain the conclusion which is different from the kernel method [6]. It offers the possibility for the realization of NPNBC.

4   Experiments and Results

In this section, we validate and analyze the performance of NPNBC by comparing NPNBC with the normal method [9] and the kernel method [6] on 4 UCI standard datasets [13]: Glass Identification, Iris, Ionosphere and Parkinson. The description of data sets and experimental results can be seen from Table 1. The results are obtained via 10 runs of 10-folds cross validation [1] on each data set.

In the experiment, we use the standard tools in Weka 3.7 [18]-*NativeBayes-K* and *NativeBayesSimple*-to implement kernel method and Normal method. We discuss the relationship between the parameter ϑ in equation (3) and the classification accuracy of NPNBC. Fig.3 summarizes the learning curves of NPNBC on these four UCI datasets. Let ϑ range from 0.1 to 2 in step of 0.1. From Fig.3 we know that with the values of the small neighborhood being increased, the classification accuracy of NPNBC will increase. In Glass, when $\vartheta=0.16$, the classification accuracy of NPNBC is 0.5429. In Ionosphere, when $\vartheta=0.1$, the classification accuracy of NPNBC is 0.9278. In Iris, when $\vartheta=0.14$, the classification accuracy of NPNBC is 0.9600. In Parkinson, when $\vartheta=0.14$, the classification accuracy of NPNBC is 0.7900. Through this experiment, we validate that the classification accuracy of NPNBC is sensitive to the change of the value of neighborhood. In addition, the comparative results are listed in Table 1. From Table 1 we can see that the proper selection of parameter ϑ can guarantee NPNBC significantly outperforms the kernel method and the normal method in the classification accuracy. We also give the comparison of time complexity between NPNBC and two other previous methods of naive Bayesian classifier in Talbe 2 where n is the number of training samples, m is the number of testing samples, k is the number of attributes of in the sample.

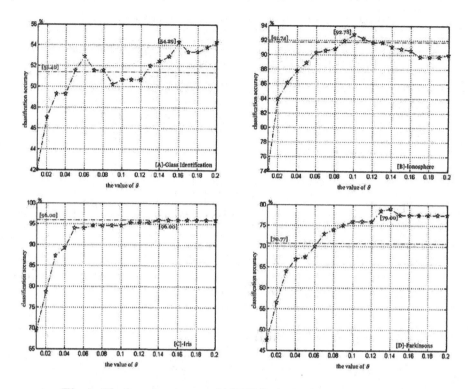

Fig. 3. The learning curves of NPNBC on the four UCI datasets

5   Conclusion

In this paper, we propose the naive Bayesian classifier based on the neighborhood probability (NPNBC). In NPNBC, when calculating the class-conditional probability for a continuous attribute value in the given unknown example, a small neighborhood is created for the continuous attribute value in every kernel. The summation of these neighborhood probabilities is the class-conditional probability for the continuous attribute value in NPNBC. The experimental results show that NPNBC demonstrates remarkable performance in classification accuracy compared to previous methods. Our scheduled further development in this research topic includes: (1) determine the optimal neighborhood for NPNBC

Table 2. The comparison of time complexity

	Training time complexity	Testing time complexity
NPNBC	$O(nk)$	$O(mnk)$
Normal method	$O(nk)$	$O(mk)$
Kernel method	$O(nk)$	$O(mnk)$

based on fuzzy integral [14] and fuzzy measure [15]; and (2) Compare the classification performance of NPNBC with fuzzy decision tree [16], [17], support vector machine [3], extreme learning machine [5], and other techniques.

Acknowledgments. The authors would like to thank three anonymous reviewers for their constructive comments on the earlier version of this manuscript. This work is in part supported by GRF grant 5237/08E, CRG grant G-U756 of The Hong Kong Polytechnic University, The National Natural Science Foundation of China 61170040.

References

1. Demšar, J.: Statistical Comparisons of Classifiers over Multiple Data Sets. Mach. Learn. J. Mach. Learn. Res. 7, 1–30 (2006)
2. Domingos, P., Pazzani, M.: On the Optimality of the Simple Bayesian Classifier under Zero-One Loss. Mach. Learn. 29, 103–130 (1997)
3. He, Q., Wu, C.X.: Separating Theorem of Samples in Banach Space for Support Vector Machine Learning. Int. J. Mach. Learn. Cyber. 1, 49–54 (2011)
4. Howson, C., Urbach, P.: Scientific Reasoning: The Bayesian Approach, 3rd edn. Open Court Publishing Company (2005)
5. Huang, G.B., Wang, D.H., Lan, Y.: Separating Theorem of Samples in Banach Space for Support Vector Machine Learning. Int. J. Mach. Learn. Cyber. 2, 107–122 (2011)
6. John, G.H., Langley, P.: Estimating Continuous Distributions in Bayesian Classifiers. In: 11th Conference on Uncertainty in Artificial Intelligence, pp. 338–345 (1995)
7. Kononenko, I.: Inductive and Bayesian Learning in Medical Diagnosis. Appl. Artificial Intelligence 7, 317–337 (1993)
8. Lewis, D.D.: Naive (Bayes) at Forty: The Independence Assumption in Information Retrieval. In: Nédellec, C., Rouveirol, C. (eds.) ECML 1998. LNCS, vol. 1398, pp. 4–15. Springer, Heidelberg (1998)
9. Mitchell, T.: Machine Learning. McGraw Hill (1997)
10. Parzen, E.: On Estimation of a Probability Density Function and Mode. Ann. Math. Statist. 33, 1065–1076 (1962)
11. Schneider, K.M.: A Comparision of Event Models for Naive Bayes Anti-Spam E-Mail Filtering. In: 10th Conference on European Chapter of the Association for Computational Linguistics, pp. 307–314 (2003)
12. Sebastiani, F.: Machine Learning in Automated Text Categorization. ACM Comput. Surv. 34, 1–47 (2002)
13. UCI Machine Learning Repository, http://archive.ics.uci.edu/ml/
14. Wang, L.J.: An Improved Multiple Fuzzy NNC System Based on Mutual Information and Fuzzy Integral. Int. J. Mach. Learn. Cyber. 1, 25–36 (2011)
15. Wang, X.Z., He, Y.L., Dong, L.C., Zhao, H.Y.: Particle Swarm Optimization for Determining Fuzzy Measures from Data. Inf. Sci. 181, 4230–4252 (2011)
16. Wang, X.Z., Dong, C.R.: Improving Generalization of Fuzzy If-Then Rules by Maximizing Fuzzy Entropy. IEEE Trans. Fuzzy Syst. 17, 556–567 (2009)
17. Wang, X.Z., Dong, L.C., Yan, J.H.: Maximum Ambiguity Based Sample Selection in Fuzzy Decision Tree Induction. IEEE Trans. Knowl. Data Eng. (2011), doi:10.1109/ TKDE.2011.67
18. Witten, I.H., Frank, E.: Data Mining: Practical Machine Learning Tools and Techniques. Morgan Kaufmann (2005)

Five Weaknesses of ASPIC$^+$

Leila Amgoud

IRIT – CNRS
amgoud@irit.fr

Abstract. This paper analyzes the ASPIC+ argumentation system. It shows that it is grounded on two monotonic logics which are not Tarskian ones. Moreover, the system suffers from four main problems: i) it is built on a poor notion of contrariness, ii) it uses a very restricted notion of consistency, iii) it builds on some counter-intuitive assumptions, and iv) it may return undesirable results.

1 Introduction

An *argumentation system* consists of a set of *arguments* and an *attack relation* among them. A *semantics* is applied for evaluating the arguments. It computes one (or more) set(s) of acceptable arguments, called *extension*(s). One of the most abstract systems is that proposed by Dung in [7]. It leaves the definition of the notion of argument and that of attack relation completely unspecified. Thus, the system can be instantiated in different ways for reasoning about defeasible information stored in a knowledge base. An instantiation starts with an underlying *logic* which is a pair $(\mathcal{L}, \mathtt{CN})$. The part $\mathcal{L}$ represents the logical language in which the information of the knowledge base are encoded. It is thus, a set of well-formed formulas. The second component of a logic is its consequence operator $\mathtt{CN}$. It represents the reasoning patterns that are used. In an argumentation system, $\mathtt{CN}$ is used for generating arguments from a knowledge base and also for defining attacks among arguments. It is worth mentioning that in almost all existing argumentation systems, the underlying logic $(\mathcal{L}, \mathtt{CN})$ is monotonic (see [8]). This makes the construction of arguments monotonic, that is an argument remains an argument even when arbitrary information is received. However, the status of an argument may change. Consequently, the logic produced by the argumentation system is nonmonotonic. In sum, an argumentation system is grounded on a monotonic logic and produces a nonmonotonic one.

Recently, Prakken proposed an instantiation of Dung's system [11], called ASPIC$^+$. It is an extended version of ASPIC system which was developed in [2]. ASPIC$^+$ takes as input an unspecified set of formulas, a contrariness function between formulas and two sets of rules: strict rules and defeasible ones. From these sets, arguments are built and attacks between arguments are specified. Thus, the only parameter which is somehow left unspecified is the underlying logic. In [11], it was claimed that this system satisfies the rationality postulates defined in [6] and in [10] it is argued that the logic underlying ASPIC$^+$ is too general that it captures even Tarskian monotonic logics [12].

Our aim in this paper is to investigate the properties of this system, especially since some of the claims in [10,11] contradict those made in [1]. We start by showing that

S. Greco et al. (Eds.): IPMU 2012, Part III, CCIS 299, pp. 122–131, 2012.

ASPIC+ builds on strong assumptions, and on too restrictive notions of contrariness and consistency. These poor notions may lead to the violation of the rationality postulates of [6], namely the one on consistency. In a second part of the paper, we investigate the monotonic logic underlying ASPIC+. Prakken claims that strict and defeasible rules may play two roles: either they encode information of the knowledge base, in which case they are part of the language $\mathcal{L}$, or they represent inference rules, in which case they are part of the consequence operator CN. In this paper, we define precisely the two corresponding logics, and show that they are monotonic but are not among the Tarskian ones. Moreover, we show that when rules encode information, then the system is fully instantiated apart from the kind of formulas that may be stored in $\mathcal{L}$. This unique generality is fatal for the system since it may lead to the violation of the rationality postulates defined in [6], namely consistency. When the rules are part of the consequence operator, the logic is far from capturing Tarski's logics [12], contrarily to what is claimed in [10]. Indeed, not only it is unable to capture the monotonic logics that do not allow negation, but it is also unable to capture even those which have negation in their logical language. The main problem comes from the definition of consistency which is too poor.

The paper is structured as follows: In section 2, we recall ASPIC$^+$ and show its limits. Section 3 recalls the monotonic logics of Tarski. In section 4, we discuss deeply the case where rules encode knowledge, while in section 5 we study the case where they encode inference rules. The last section is devoted to some concluding remarks.

2   APIC$^+$ Argumentation Framework

In [11], Prakken has proposed an instantiation of Dung's framework, called ASPIC$^+$. It considers an abstract logical language L, that is a language which may be instantiated in different ways. It may for instance contain propositional formulas, etc. The only requirement on L is that it is equipped with a notion of *contrariness*, denoted by $^-$.

Definition 1 (Contrariness). *Let* L *be a logical language and* $^-$ *is a* contrariness *function from* L *to* 2^L. *For* $x, y \in$ L, *if* $x \in \bar{y}$, *then if* $y \notin \bar{x}$ *then* x *is called a* contrary *of* y, *otherwise* x *and* y *are called* contradictory.

Remark 1. *It is worth mentioning that the above definition of contrariness does not capture the real intuition of contrary as discussed by several philosophers and logicians (e.g. [5]). Indeed, a formula x is a contrary of y iff they cannot be both true but they can both be false. They are contradictory if the truth of one implies the falsity of the other and vise versa. Let us consider the following simple example:*

Example 1. *Assume that* L $= \{>, \geq, <, \leq, =, \neq\}$. *For instance,* $\bar{>} = \{<, \leq, =\}$ *and* $\bar{<} = \{>, \geq, =\}$. *Note that* $>$ *is the contrary of* $<$ *and vise versa and* $< \in \bar{>}$ *and* $> \in \bar{<}$. *According to Def. 1, $>$ and $<$ are contradictory while this is not the case.*

In addition to the language L, two kinds of rules are assumed: *strict* rules and *defeasible* ones.

Definition 2 (Rules). *Let* $x_1, \ldots, x_n, x$ *be elements of* L. *A strict rule* is of the form $x_1, \ldots, x_n \rightarrow x$ *meaning that if* $x_1, \ldots, x_n$ *hold then without exception x holds. A* defeasible rule *is of the form* $x_1, \ldots, x_n \Rightarrow x$ *meaning that if* $x_1, \ldots, x_n$ *hold then presumably* x *holds.* $\mathcal{R}_s$ *(resp.* $\mathcal{R}_d$*) stands for the set of all strict (resp. defeasible) rules with* $\mathcal{R}_s \cap \mathcal{R}_d = \emptyset$.

A notion of consistency is associated to this logical formalism as follows.

Definition 3 (Consistency). *A set* $X \subseteq \mathsf{L}$ *is* consistent *iff* $\nexists\ x, y \in X$ *such that* $x \in \bar{y}$, *otherwise it is* inconsistent.

Remark 2. *Note that the above notion of consistency only captures* binary *conflicts between formulas. That is, it does not capture ternary or more conflicts. Let us consider the following example:*

Example 2. *Assume that* L *contains propositional formulas and that* $X = \{x, x \rightarrow y, \neg y\}$. *It is clear that* $\bar{x} = \{\neg x, \neg\neg\neg x, \ldots\}$, $\neg\bar{y} = \{y, \neg\neg y, \ldots\}$ *and* $x \rightarrow y = \{x \wedge \neg y, \neg\neg(x \wedge \neg y), \ldots\}$. *From Definition 3, the set* X *is consistent whereas it is not!*

In [11], arguments are built from a knowledge base $\mathcal{K}$. It may contain four categories of information: *axioms* (which are certain information) $(\mathcal{K}_n)$, *ordinary* premises $(\mathcal{K}_p)$, *assumptions* $(\mathcal{K}_a)$ and *issues* $(\mathcal{K}_i)$. The set $\mathcal{K}_n$ is assumed to be consistent. These subbases are disjoint and $\mathcal{K} = \mathcal{K}_n \cup \mathcal{K}_p \cup \mathcal{K}_a \cup \mathcal{K}_i$. In what follows, for a given argument, the function Prem (resp. Conc, Sub, DefRules, TopRule) returns all the formulas of $\mathcal{K}$ which are involved in the argument (resp. the conclusion of the argument, its sub-arguments, the defeasible rules that are used, and the last rule used in the argument).

Definition 4 (Argument). *An* argument A *is:*

- x *if* $x \in \mathcal{K}$ *with* Prem$(A) = \{x\}$, Conc$(A) = x$, Sub$(A) = \{A\}$, DefRules$(A) = \emptyset$, TopRule$(A) =$ *undefined.*
- $A_1, \ldots, A_n \longrightarrow x^1$ *(resp.* $A_1, \ldots, A_n \Longrightarrow x$*) if* $A_1, \ldots, A_n$, *with* $n \geq 0$, *are arguments such that there exists a strict rule* Conc$(A_1), \ldots,$ Conc$(A_n) \rightarrow x$ *(resp. a defeasible rule* Conc$(A_1), \ldots,$ Conc$(A_n) \Rightarrow x$*).*
  Prem$(A) =$ Prem$(A_1) \cup \ldots \cup$ Prem(A_n),
  Conc$(A) = x$,
  Sub$(A) =$ Sub$(A_1) \cup \ldots \cup$ Sub$(A_n) \cup \{A\}$,
  DefRules$(A) =$ DefRules$(A_1) \cup \ldots \cup$ DefRules(A_n) *(resp.* DefRules$(A) =$ DefRules$(A_1) \cup \ldots \cup$ DefRules$(A_n) \cup \{$Conc$(A_1), \ldots$ Conc$(A_n) \Rightarrow x\}$*),*
  TopRule$(A) =$ Conc$(A_1), \ldots,$ Conc$(A_n) \rightarrow x$ *(resp.* TopRule$(A) =$ Conc$(A_1),$ $\ldots,$ Conc$(A_n) \Rightarrow x$*).*

An argument A *is* strict *if* DefRules$(A) = \emptyset$, defeasible *if* DefRules$(A) \neq \emptyset$, firm *if* Prem$(A) \subseteq \mathcal{K}_n$, *and* plausible *if* Prem$(A) \not\subseteq \mathcal{K}_n$.

Arguments may not have equal strengths in [11]. Thus, a partial preorder denoted by $\succeq$ is available. For two arguments, A and B, the notation $A \succeq B$ means that A is at least as good as B. The strict version of $\succeq$ is denoted by $\succ$. This preorder should satisfy

---

[1] The symbols $\longrightarrow$ and $\Longrightarrow$ are used to denote arguments. In [11], arguments are denoted by $\rightarrow$ and $\Rightarrow$ while these latter are used for defining rules.

two basic requirements: The first one ensures that firm and strict arguments are stronger than all the other arguments, while the second condition says that a strict rule cannot make an argument weaker or stronger.

Definition 5 (Admissible argument ordering). *Let A be a set of arguments. A partial preorder $\succeq$ on A is an* admissible argument ordering *iff for any pair $A, B \in A$:*

R_1: *if A is firm and strict and B is defeasible or plausible, then $A \succ B$.*
R_2: *if $A = A_1, \ldots, A_n \to x$, then $\forall i = 1, n, A_i \succeq A$ and for some $i = 1, n, A \succeq A_i$.*

Remark 3. *The previous requirements reduce the generality of the preference relation. For instance, requirement R_1 is violated by the preference relation proposed in [4]. In that paper, each argument promotes a value and the best argument is the one which promotes the most important value. Assume that there are two arguments A and B which promote respectively values v_1 and v_2 with v_1 being more important than v_2. If we assume that A is defeasible and B is both strict and firm, then from requirement R_1, B should be preferred to A. However, in [4], A is strictly preferred to B.*

Since information in a knowledge base K may be inconsistent, arguments may be conflicting too. In [11], Prakken has modeled three ways of attacking an argument: undermining its conclusion, or one of its premises or one of its defeasible rules.

Definition 6 (Attacks). *Let A and B be two arguments.*

- *A undercuts B (on C) iff $\mathrm{Conc}(A) \in \bar{C}$ with $C \in \mathrm{Sub}(B)$ and of the form $C_1, \ldots, C_n \Longrightarrow x$.*
- *A rebuts B (on C) iff $\mathrm{Conc}(A) \in \bar{x}$ for some $C \in \mathrm{Sub}(B)$ of the form $C_1, \ldots, C_n \Longrightarrow x$. A contrary-rebuts B iff $\mathrm{Conc}(A)$ is a contrary of x.*
- *A undermines B iff $\mathrm{Conc}(A) \in \bar{x}$ for some $x \in \mathrm{Prem}(B) \setminus K_n$. A contrary-undermines B iff $\mathrm{Conc}(A)$ is a contrary of x or if $x \in K_a$.*

Remark 4. *Note that the first relation (undercut) applies the notion of contrariness on an argument. This is technically wrong since contrariness $^-$ is a function defined for formulas of the language L. Neither arguments nor defeasible rules are elements of the set L. Moreover, due to the incorrect definition of the notion of contrariness, the notions of 'contrary-rebut' and 'contrary-undermine' do not make sense since they are assumed to be non symmetric while this is not always the case. Besides, in [11], the author claims that these three relations are syntactic and do not reflect any preference between arguments. However, in the definition of rebut, it is clear that an argument whose top rule is strict cannot be attacked by an argument with a defeasible top rule. Thus, the former is preferred to the latter. Moreover, this preference is not intuitive as shown by the following example.*

Example 3. *Assume an argumentation system with the two following arguments:*
$A :\Rightarrow p, p \Rightarrow q, q \Rightarrow r, r \to x$
$B :\to d, d \to e, e \to f, f \Rightarrow \neg x.$
According to the above definition, A rebuts B but B does not rebut A. Thus, $\{A\}$ is an admissible set and consequently x is concluded from the corresponding knowledge base. This is not intuitive since there is a lot of uncertainty on r. Works on non-monotonic reasoning would rather prefer B to A since defeasible rules violate transitivity and thus, p may not be r.

As in any preference-based argumentation system, in [11] preferences between arguments are used in order to decide which attacks result in defeats.

Definition 7 (Defeat). *Let A and B be two arguments.*

- *A successfully rebuts B if A rebuts B on C and either A contrary-rebuts C or not(C ≻ A).*
- *A successfully undermines B if A undermines B on x and either A contrary-undermines B or not(x ≻ A).*
- *A defeats B iff no premise of A is an issue and A undercuts or successfully rebuts or successfully undermines B.*

Remark 5. *Note that the previous definition uses preferences only when the attack relation is symmetric. While this avoids the problem of conflicting extensions described in [3], it greatly restricts the use of preferences.*

The instantiation of Dung's system is thus the pair $(\mathcal{A}_s, \text{defeat})$ where $\mathcal{A}_s$ is the set of all arguments built using Definition 4 from $(\mathcal{K}, \text{Cl}(\mathcal{R}_s), \mathcal{R}_d)$. $\text{Cl}(\mathcal{R}_s)$ is the closure of strict rules under contraposition, that is $\text{Cl}(\mathcal{R}_s)$ contains all strict rules and all their contrapositions. A contraposition of a strict rule $x_1, \ldots, x_n \to x$ is, for instance, the strict rule $x_2, \ldots, x_n, \bar{x} \to \bar{x}_1$, where $\bar{x}$ and x are contradictory. Recall that in [6], contraposition was proposed for ensuring the rationality postulate on consistency.

Dung's acceptability semantics are applied for evaluating the arguments.

Definition 8 (Acceptability semantics). *Let $\mathcal{B} \subseteq \mathcal{A}_s$, $A \in \mathcal{A}_s$. $\mathcal{B}$ is* conflict-free *iff $\nexists A, B \in \mathcal{B}$ s.t. A defeats B. $\mathcal{B}$ defends A iff $\forall B \in \mathcal{A}_s$ if B defeats A, then $\exists C \in \mathcal{B}$ s.t. C defeats B. $\mathcal{B}$ is* admissible *iff it is conflict-free and defends all its elements. $\mathcal{B}$ is a preferred* extension *iff it is a maximal (for set inclusion) admissible set.*

In [11], it was shown that under several conditions, each extension $\mathcal{B}$ of the argumentation system $(\mathcal{A}_s, \text{defeat})$, the set $\{\text{Conc}(A) \mid A \in \mathcal{B}\}$ is consistent. This result is surprising especially since there are notions that are ill-defined like undercutting. Moreover, due to the limits of the notions of contrariness and consistency, the result produced in [11] is incorrect. Let us consider the following example.

Example 2 (Continued): Assume again that L contains propositional formulas, and that $\mathcal{K}_n = \{x, x \to y, \neg y\}$ and all the other sets are empty. From Definition 3, the set $\mathcal{K}_n$ is consistent, thus it satisfies the requirement of [11]. Consequently, the following arguments are built: $A_1 : x$, $A_2 : x \to y$, $A_3 : \neg y$. Note that the three arguments are not attacking each others. Thus, the set $\{A_1, A_2, A_3\}$ is an admissible/preferred set. This set supports three conclusions which are inconsistent. Another source of problems for ASPIC$^+$ is the abstract aspect of the language L. Indeed, it is argued that it can be instantiated in any way. The following example shows that some instantiations may lead to undesirable results, namely inconsistent ones.

Example 4. *Assume that L contains propositional formulas, that all the sets are empty except $\mathcal{R}_d = \{\Rightarrow x, \Rightarrow \neg x \lor y, \Rightarrow \neg y\}$. Only the following three arguments can be* *built:* $A_1 :\Rightarrow x$, $A_2 :\Rightarrow \neg x \lor y$, $A_3 :\Rightarrow \neg y$. *Note that the three arguments are not attacking each others. Thus, the set* $\{A_1, A_2, A_3\}$ *is an admissible/preferred set. This set supports three conclusions which are inconsistent contrarily to what is claimed in [11]. Note that this example would return this undesirable result even if the definition of consistency was more general than the one given in Definition 3.*

The previous example reveals another problem with ASPIC⁺ system. Its result is not closed under defeasible rules. Indeed, the three conclusions x, $\neg x \lor y$, and $\neg y$ are inferred while y which follows from the two first ones is not deduced. In works on non-monotonic reasoning, namely the seminal paper [9], it is argued that one should accept as plausible consequences all that is logically implied by other plausible consequences. This property is known as *right weakening*.

Finally, in [10] it was argued that the underlying logic of ASPIC+ captures classical logics, namely propositional and first order logics. It is sufficient to assume that the sets $\mathcal{R}_d$, $\mathcal{K}_n$, $\mathcal{K}_a$ and $\mathcal{K}_i$ are empty, and that strict rules are the reasoning patterns of propositional or first order logics. The authors claim that ASPIC⁺ still satisfies the rationality postulate in this case. The following example shows that this claim is incorrect.

Example 4 (Continued): Assume that L contains propositional formulas, $\mathcal{K}_p = \{x, \neg x \lor y, \neg y\}$ and that $\mathcal{R}_s$ contains all the reasoning patterns of propositional logic. Thus, the following arguments can be built: $A_1 : x$, $A_2 : \neg y$, $A_3 : \neg x \lor y$, $A_4 : A_2, A_3 \to \neg x$, $A_5 : A_1, A_3 \to y$, $A_6 : A_1, A_2 \to \neg(\neg x \lor y)$. It is easy to check that A_1 rebuts A_4, A_4 rebuts A_1, A_2 rebuts A_5, A_5 rebuts A_2, A_3 rebuts A_6, A_6 rebuts A_3, A_4 undermines A_5 and A_6 on x, A_5 undermines A_4 and A_6 on $\neg y$, and A_6 undermines A_4 and A_5 on $\neg x \lor y$. Consequently, the set $\{A_1, A_2, A_3\}$ is admissible/preferred which violates consistency. Note that this example would return this undesirable result even if the definition of consistency was more general than the one given in Def. 3 (see [1]).

3   Tarski's Monotonic Logics

Before studying the underlying logic of ASPIC+, let us first recall the abstract logic $(\mathcal{L}, \mathrm{CN})$ as defined by Tarski [12]. While there is no requirement on the language $\mathcal{L}$, the consequence operator CN should satisfy the following basic axioms.

1. $X \subseteq \mathrm{CN}(X)$ **(Expansion)**
2. $\mathrm{CN}(\mathrm{CN}(X)) = \mathrm{CN}(X)$ **(Idempotence)**
3. $\mathrm{CN}(X) = \bigcup_{Y \subseteq_f X} \mathrm{CN}(Y)^2$ **(Finiteness)**
4. $\mathrm{CN}(\{x\}) = \mathcal{L}$ for some $x \in \mathrm{L}$ **(Absurdity)**
5. $\mathrm{CN}(\emptyset) \neq \mathcal{L}$ **(Coherence)**

Once $(\mathcal{L}, \mathrm{CN})$ is fixed, a notion of *consistency* arises as follows:

Definition 9 (Consistency). *Let* $X \subseteq \mathcal{L}$. X *is* consistent *w.r.t. the logic* $(\mathrm{L}, \mathrm{CN})$ *iff* $\mathrm{CN}(X) \neq \mathcal{L}$. *It is* inconsistent *otherwise.*

---

² $Y \subseteq_f X$ means that Y is a finite subset of X.

Almost all well-known monotonic logics (classical logic, intuitionistic logic, modal logic, etc.) are special cases of the above notion of an abstract logic. The following logic for representing the color and the size of objects is another Tarskian logic.

Example 5. *Let $\mathcal{L} = \mathcal{L}_{col} \cup \mathcal{L}_{size} \cup \mathcal{L}_{err}$ with $\mathcal{L}_{col} = \{white, yellow, red, orange, blue, black\}$, $\mathcal{L}_{size} = \{tiny, small, big, huge\}$, and $\mathcal{L}_{err} = \{\bot\}$. The consequence operator captures the fact that if two different colours or two different sizes are present in the description of an object, then information concerning that object is inconsistent. We define CN as follows: for all $X \subseteq \mathcal{L}$,*

$$\text{CN}(X) = \begin{cases} \mathcal{L} & \textit{if } (\exists x, y \in X \textit{ s.t. } x \neq y \\ & \quad \textit{and } (\{x, y\} \subseteq \mathcal{L}_{col} \textit{ or } \{x, y\} \subseteq \mathcal{L}_{size})) \\ & \quad \textit{or if } (\bot \in X) \\ X & \textit{else} \end{cases} \quad \textit{For example, } \text{CN}(\emptyset) = \emptyset,$$

$\text{CN}(\{red, big\}) = \{red, big\}$, $\text{CN}(\{red, blue, big\}) = \text{CN}(\{\bot\}) = \mathcal{L}$. *The set $\{red, big\}$ is consistent, while $\{red, blue, big\}$ is inconsistent. Note that this logic does not need any connector of negation.*

4   Rules as Object Level Language

As said before, the (strict and defeasible) rules in ASPIC+ may either encocde information or reasoning patterns. In this section, we investigate the first case. Our aim is to study the properties of the corresponding logic, denoted by $(\mathcal{L}_o, \text{CN}_o)$.

The language $\mathcal{L}_o$ is composed of the logical formulas of the set L. Note that in [11] no particular requirement is made on L, neither on the kind of connectors that are used nor on the way of defining the formulas. However, as said before, L is equipped with the contrariness function $\bar{}$. The language $\mathcal{L}_o$ contains also two kinds of information: strict rules (elements of $\mathcal{R}_s$) encoding *certain knowledge* like 'penguins do not fly' and defeasible rules (elements of $\mathcal{R}_d$) encoding defeasible information like 'generally birds fly'. Note that in ASPIC system [2], the same language is considered with the difference that L contains only literals. Thus, $\mathcal{L}_o = L \cup \mathcal{R}_s \cup \mathcal{R}_d$ with $L \cap (\mathcal{R}_s \cup \mathcal{R}_d) = \emptyset$.

An important question now is what are the contents of the bases $\mathcal{K}_n$, $\mathcal{K}_p$, $\mathcal{K}_a$ and $\mathcal{K}_i$ in this case. Since $\mathcal{K}_n$ contains axioms, or undefeasible information, this may be represented by strict rules since these latter encode certain information. Similarly, since ordinary premises are defeasible, then they should be represented by defeasible rules. Otherwise, the language would be redundant and ambiguous. In sum, $\mathcal{K} = \mathcal{K}_a \cup \mathcal{K}_i$.

When strict and defeasible rules encode knowledge, the consequence operator of the logic used in ASPIC$^+$ is not specified. The only indication can be found in Definition 4 of the notion of argument. A *possible* CN_o would be the following:

Definition 10 (Consequence operator). CN_o *is a function from $2^{\mathcal{L}_o}$ to $2^{\mathcal{L}_o}$ s.t. for all $X \subseteq \mathcal{L}_o$, $x \in \text{CN}_o(X)$ iff there exists a sequence $x_1, \ldots, x_n$ s.t.*

1. x is x_n, and
2. for each $x_i \in \{x_1, \ldots, x_n\}$,

- $\exists y_1, \ldots, y_j \rightarrow x_i \in X \cap \mathcal{R}_s$ (resp. $\exists y_1, \ldots, y_j \Rightarrow x_i \in X \cap \mathcal{R}_d$) s.t. $\{y_1, \ldots, y_j\} \subseteq \{x_1, \ldots, x_{i-1}\}$, or
- $x_i \in X \cap \mathrm{L}$

Example 6. Let $X = \{x, x \rightarrow y, t \Rightarrow z\}$, $\mathrm{CN}_o(X) = \{x, y, z\}$.

Property 1. Let $X \subseteq \mathcal{L}_o$.

- $\mathrm{CN}_o(X) \subseteq \mathrm{L}$
- If $X \subseteq \mathrm{L}$, then $\mathrm{CN}_o(X) = X$
- $\mathrm{CN}_o(\emptyset) = \emptyset$

Now that the logic $(\mathcal{L}_o, \mathrm{CN}_o)$ is defined, let us see whether it is a Tarskian one.

Proposition 1. Let $(\mathcal{L}_o, \mathrm{CN}_o)$ be as defined above. CN_o is monotonic, satisfies idempotence, coherence and finiteness axioms.

The next result shows that CN_o violates expansion and absurdity axioms.

Proposition 2. Let $(\mathcal{L}_o, \mathrm{CN}_o)$ be as defined above.

- For all $X \subseteq \mathcal{L}_o$ s.t. either $X \cap \mathcal{R}_s \neq \emptyset$ or $X \cap \mathcal{R}_d \neq \emptyset$, it holds that $X \not\subseteq \mathrm{CN}_o(X)$.
- There is no $x \in \mathcal{L}_o$ s.t. $\mathrm{CN}_o(\{x\}) = \mathcal{L}_o$.

The previous result shows that the logic $(\mathcal{L}_o, \mathrm{CN}_o)$ is not a Tarskian one since CN_o violates the key axioms proposed in [12]. Moreover, the notion of consistency given in Definition 3 is weaker than that proposed in [12]. According to Tarski, a set $X \subseteq \mathcal{L}$ is consistent iff $\mathrm{CN}(X) \neq \mathcal{L}$. Thus, this notion captures not only binary minimal conflicts (as with Definition 3), but also ternary or more ones.

5   Rules as Reasoning Patterns

In the previous section, we have seen how strict and defeasible rules are used for encoding certain and defeasible information. The second way of using these rules is as *inference* rules. In [11], it is argued that strict rules may represent classical reasoning patterns, like modus ponens whereas defeasible rules may capture argument schemes. In this section, we study the resulting logic denoted by $(\mathcal{L}_i, \mathrm{CN}_i)$.

Let us start by defining the logical language $\mathcal{L}_i$. In this case, it is exactly the set L, that is $\mathcal{L}_i = \mathrm{L}$. Thus, the only requirement on $\mathcal{L}_i$ is that it has a contrariness function $^-$. It is worth mentioning that the distinction made in [11] between the four bases $\mathcal{K}_n, \mathcal{K}_p, \mathcal{K}_i, \mathcal{K}_a$ is meaningful. Thus, arguments are built from these bases.

Let us now define the consequence operator CN_i. It is similar to CN_o, except that strict and defeasible rules express inference schemas.

Definition 11 (Consequence operator). CN_i is a function from $2^{\mathcal{L}_i}$ to $2^{\mathcal{L}_i}$ s.t. for all $X \subseteq \mathcal{L}_i$, $x \in \mathrm{CN}_i(X)$ iff there exists a sequence $x_1, \ldots, x_n$ s.t.

1. x is x_n, and
2. for each $x_i \in \{x_1, \ldots, x_n\}$,

- $\exists y_1, \ldots, y_j \to x_i \in \mathcal{R}_s$ *(resp.* $\exists y_1, \ldots, y_j \Rightarrow x_i \in \mathcal{R}_d$*) s.t.* $\{y_1, \ldots, y_j\} \subseteq \{x_1, \ldots, x_{i-1}\}$, or
- $x_i \in X$

Proposition 3. *The logic* $(\mathcal{L}_i, \mathrm{CN}_i)$ *is monotonic. It satisfies expansion, idempotence, coherence, and finiteness.*

Property 2
- $\mathrm{CN}_i(\emptyset) = \mathrm{cl}(\mathcal{R}_s \cup \mathcal{R}_d)$ *where* $\mathrm{cl}(\mathcal{R}_s \cup \mathcal{R}_d)$ *is the smallest set such that:*
  - *if* $\to x \in \mathcal{R}_s$ *(resp.* $\Rightarrow x \in \mathcal{R}_d$*), then* $x \in \mathrm{cl}(\mathcal{R}_s \cup \mathcal{R}_d)$
  - *if* $x_1, \ldots, x_n \to x \in \mathcal{R}_s$ *(resp.* $x_1, \ldots, x_n \Rightarrow x \in \mathcal{R}_d$*) and* $\{x_1, \ldots, x_n\} \subseteq \mathrm{cl}(\mathcal{R}_s \cup \mathcal{R}_d)$, *then* $x \in \mathrm{cl}(\mathcal{R}_s \cup \mathcal{R}_d)$
- $\mathrm{CN}_i(\emptyset) = \emptyset$ *iff* $\nexists \to x \in \mathcal{R}_s$ *and* $\nexists \Rightarrow x \in \mathcal{R}_d$ *for any* $x \in \mathsf{L}$

Example 7. *Let* $\mathcal{R}_s = \{x, y \to z; \to x\}$ *and* $\mathcal{R}_d = \{\Rightarrow y\}$. $\mathrm{cl}(\mathcal{R}_s \cup \mathcal{R}_d) = \{x, y, z\}$.

The previous property shows that the coherence axiom of Tarski may be violated by CN_i. It is namely the case when $\mathrm{cl}(\mathcal{R}_s \cup \mathcal{R}_d) = \mathsf{L}$. CN_i does not guarantee neither the absurdity axiom. Indeed, there is no $x \in \mathcal{L}_i$ such that $\mathrm{CN}_i(\{x\}) = \mathcal{L}_i$. In case strict rules encode propositional logic, then such formula exists. However, we can build other logics which do not offer such possibility. Let us consider the following logic which expresses the links between the six symbols of comparisons described in Example 1.

Example 1 (Continued): Assume that $\mathcal{L}_i = \{>, \geq, <, \leq, =, \neq, \geq \wedge \leq, > \vee <\}$, $\mathcal{R}_d = \emptyset$, and $\mathcal{R}_s = \{> \to \geq, < \to \leq, = \to \geq \wedge \leq, \neq \to > \vee <\}$. Note that there is no element in $\mathcal{L}_i$ that has the whole set $\mathcal{L}_i$ as a set of consequences.

As a consequence, the logic $(\mathcal{L}_i, \mathrm{CN}_i)$ is not a Tarskian one since it violates the coherence and absurdity axioms. Note that this result holds even when CN_i encodes exactly the classical inference $\vdash$. The reason in this case is due to the poor definition of consistency. As shown is Example 2, in propositional logic the set $\{x, x \to y, \neg y\}$ is inconsistent while it is consistent according to Definition 3.

It is also worth mentioning that there is another family of Tarskian logics that cannot be captured by the monotonic logic $(\mathcal{L}_i, \mathrm{CN}_i)$. It is the family of logics whose language does not allow negation or contrariness like the one given in Example 5.

6 Conclusion

This paper investigated ASPIC+ argumentation system. It shows that this system suffers from the following drawbacks: i) The system is grounded on several assumptions which may appear either counter-intuitive like the one on rebut, or restrictive like the one on the preference relation between arguments. ii) The system uses a too restrictive notion of consistency. This not only reduces the generality of the system, but also leads to undesirable results. iii) The system returns results which may not be closed under defeasible rules. Thus, it violates the right weakening axiom [9]. iv) The system violates the rationality postulate on consistency. There are different sources of this problem: the notion of consistency which does not capture ternary or more conflicts between formulas, the abstract nature of the elements of the language L, and finally the use of rebut relation. In [1], it was shown that symmetric relations lead to the violation of consistency. v) Contrarily to what is claimed in [11,10], the underlying logics of AS-PIC+ cannot encode the Tarskian ones: neither the ones which make use of a notion of negation nor the ones which do not.

References

1. Amgoud, L., Besnard, P.: Bridging the Gap between Abstract Argumentation Systems and Logic. In: Godo, L., Pugliese, A. (eds.) SUM 2009. LNCS, vol. 5785, pp. 12–27. Springer, Heidelberg (2009)
2. Amgoud, L., Caminada, M., Cayrol, C., Lagasquie, M., Prakken, H.: Towards a consensual formal model: inference part. Deliverable D2.2 of ASPIC project (2004)
3. Amgoud, L., Vesic, S.: A new approach for preference-based argumentation frameworks. Ann. Math. Artif. Intell. 63(2), 149–183 (2011)
4. Bench-Capon, T.J.M.: Persuasion in practical argument using value-based argumentation frameworks. J. of Logic and Computation 13(3), 429–448 (2003)
5. Béziau, J.-Y.: New light on the square of oppositions and its nameless corner. Logical Investigations 10, 218–233 (2003)
6. Caminada, M., Amgoud, L.: On the evaluation of argumentation formalisms. AIJ 171(5-6), 286–310 (2007)
7. Dung, P.: On the acceptability of arguments and its fundamental role in nonmonotonic reasoning, logic programming and n-person games. AIJ 77, 321–357 (1995)
8. Hunter, A.: Base logics in argumentation. In: Proceedings of COMMA 2010, pp. 275–286 (2010)
9. Kraus, S., Lehmann, S., Magidor, D.: Nonmonotonic reasoning, preferential models and cumulative logics. AIJ 44, 167–207 (1990)
10. Modgil, S., Prakken, H.: Revisiting preferences and argumentation. In: Proceedings of IJCAI 2011, pp. 1021–1026 (2011)
11. Prakken, H.: An abstract framework for argumentation with structured arguments. Argument and Computation, 1–31 (2010)
12. Tarski, A.: On Some Fundamental Concepts of Metamathematics. In: Woodger, E.H. (ed.) Logic, Semantics, Metamathematics. Oxford Uni. Press (1956)

A Feature Reduction Strategy for the Analysis of Voluminous Biomedical Patterns

Nick J. Pizzi

Department of Computer Science
University of Manitoba
Winnipeg, Canada
pizzi@cs.umanitoba.ca

Abstract. The analysis of voluminous patterns is often problematic due to the confounding effect of features that are not relevant to the problem at hand. For instance, the classification of biomedical spectra is often best achieved through the identification of a subset of highly discriminatory features while ignoring the non-relevant ones. With respect to pattern classification, we present a feature reduction strategy, which begins with the instantiation of many classifiers operating on different subsets of features, employing a feature sampling method to identify discriminatory feature subsets. These subsets are further aggregated to improve the overall performance of the underlying classifiers. We empirically demonstrate, using a voluminous biomedical dataset, that this strategy produces superior classification accuracies compared against a set of benchmarks.

Keywords: feature aggregation, magnetic resonance spectra, feature selection, pattern classification, biomedical informatics, biomedical data analysis.

1   Introduction

The complexity of biomedical spectra is often due to their voluminous nature and requires the latest pattern analysis methods for their successful classification [1–7]. Biomedical spectral classification involves constructing a predictive mapping between the spectra (patterns) and their respective disease states (classes). Formally, a pattern classifier is a computational system that constructs a mapping, $f:X \rightarrow \Omega$, where $X=\{(x_k,w_k), k=1,2,\ldots,N\}$, $x_k \in \Re^n$, $w_k \in \Omega=\{1,2,\ldots,c\}$, N is the number of spectra, n is the number of spectral features; and c is the number of disease states. A correct classification occurs when the classifier maps spectrum, x_i, to disease state, w_p, and $w_p=w_i$.

While many pattern classifiers exist [8–13], effective classification normally requires a complementary pre-processing strategy. In this regard, the classification of biomedical spectra often requires only a subset of spectral features, those possessing significant discriminatory power, while the remaining features have a tendency to confound the effectiveness of the underlying classifier [14]. In such cases, a sensible pre-processing strategy is to select the discriminatory features and prune the confounding ones. To this end, we present a classification system, *fuzzy feature sampling*

S. Greco et al. (Eds.): IPMU 2012, Part III, CCIS 299, pp. 132–141, 2012.

and aggregation (FSA), that identifies discriminatory feature subsets using a fuzzy logic based sampling rule and feature aggregator. We empirically evaluate this pre-processing strategy using magnetic resonance spectra and compare the performance against a set of benchmarks. Section 2 provides details on this strategy and Section 3 describes the experiment design including the benchmark classifiers and dataset. Section 4 is a presentation of the results followed by concluding remarks in Section 5.

2   Dimensionality Reduction Using Feature Sampling

The pseudo code for the FSA algorithm is listed below. FSA is a variation of the classification algorithm based on a stochastic feature selection architecture developed by the author [15–16]. The two principle differences are the use of the fuzzy sampling method (line 2.b) and the fuzzy feature aggregation method (line 2.c.ii). We now present the FSA classification architecture and motivation in more detail.

```
FSA Algorithm
1. Initialize classification parameters
2. Iterate: until accuracy/iteration thresholds are met
       a. Instantiate a classifier
       b. Select feature subsets using frequency histogram
          and fuzzy sampling method
       c. Iterate: t-fold validation for classifier
              i. Allocate spectra to design or test sets
             ii. Mix subsets using fuzzy aggregation
            iii. Train classifier using design spectra
             iv. Assess performance using test spectra
       d. Update feature frequency histogram, if necessary
       e. Update current best classifier, if necessary
3. Return best classifier and feature subset pair
```

The motivation for pre-processing strategies using feature selection is to simplify the determination and construction of optimal class boundaries that delineate patterns (spectra) belonging to one class (disease state) from those belonging to other classes [15], [17–18]. Formally, feature selection involves finding a mapping $g':X \rightarrow X'$, where $X' \subseteq \Re^m$ $(m<<n)$ is the reduced spectral feature space. Pattern classification involves constructing a mapping from the reduced spectral feature space to the space of class labels (disease states), $g:X' \rightarrow \Omega$. FSA is a dimensionality reduction technique that may be used with any homogeneous or heterogeneous set of classifiers. Essentially, FSA iteratively presents, in a highly parallelized fashion, many feature regions (contiguous feature subsets) to the set of classifiers, and retains the best classifier/region pair. FSA randomly allocates the original spectra into design or test sets. Once the design phase is complete, the test set is used to validate the classification performance. Coupled with internal t-fold validation, this provides a reliable measure of the effectiveness of the underlying classification system.

The first step (line 1 above) involves parameter initialization. One selects the minimum and maximum number of feature regions and the minimum, a, and maximum, b, sizes for a feature region. For a spectrum, $x=[x_1...x_n]$, a feature region is defined to be a contiguous subset of its features, $x^{\alpha\beta}=[x_\alpha...x_\beta]$ ($1 \leq a \leq \alpha \leq \beta \leq b \leq n$). Other parameters include: those specific to each type of pattern classifier; sampling rate for each classifier type; fitness function used to evaluate performance; and stopping criteria (accuracy threshold, P_ε, and maximum number of iterations, η). The second step involves: the instantiation of a pattern classifier; the selection of a candidate set of feature regions from the dataset's original spectral features; and the aggregation of the selected feature regions. The feature regions are randomly selected (satisfying the above mentioned criteria) and all other features are pruned.

In this investigation, we use one classifier type within FSA, linear discriminant analysis (LDA) [19]. LDA computes linear boundaries between c classes while taking into account between-class and within-class variances. LDA allocates a spectrum, x, to disease state w for which the probability distribution, $p_w(x)$, is greatest. That is, x is allocated to w, if $q_w p_w(x) \geq q_v p_v(x)$ ($\forall v=1,2,...,c$ [$v \neq w$]), where q_w is the proportional probability of the disease state. The discriminant function, D_w, for disease state w (where μ_w is the mean for w and W is the covariance matrix of X) is

$$D_w(x) = \log q_w + \mu_w^T W^{-1}(x - \tfrac{1}{2}\mu_w) \tag{1}$$

However, FSA is not restricted to this classifier. One may use any homogeneous or heterogeneous set of classifiers such as neural networks, Bayesian classifiers, evolutionary approaches, or support vector machines [9–10], [20–24].

FSA assesses the performance of each specific classifier instance. First, the feature region subset is randomly allocated to either a design set or a test set. Second, the classifier instance is trained using the design set regions to produce prediction coefficients. Accuracy is measured using the coefficients with the test set feature regions. This is repeated several times (t-fold validation) with different design and test sets allocations. If the performance (accuracy), P, of the current classifier instance exceeds the histogram fitness threshold then the frequency histogram (see below) is updated to reflect the fact that the feature regions contributed to a "successful" classification. The above steps are repeated until: (*i*) $P > P_\varepsilon$; or (*ii*) the number of iterations exceeds η.

P is measured using a $c \times c$ confusion matrix, R, of actual versus predicted disease states. Several fitness functions may be used such as: $P_o = N^{-1} \sum_i R_{ii}$, the ratio of correctly classified spectra to total spectra ($i,j=1...c$); $P_A = c^{-1} \sum_i (R_{ii}/\sum_j R_{ij})$ the average accuracy for each state; or a chance-corrected measure of agreement such as the κ-score, $P_\kappa = (P_o - P_L)/(1 - P_L)$ ($P_L = N^{-2} \sum_i (\sum_j R_{ij} \sum_j R_{ji})$ is the agreement due to chance) [25].

2.1   Feature Performance Histogram

An important constituent of FSA is the feature performance histogram, $e=[e_1...e_n]$ ($e_i \in [0,1]$), which is used to generate an ad hoc cumulative distribution function that is subsequently used to randomly sample new subsets of features regions. The histogram reflects the current classification "performance" of each individual feature. That is, if a feature, x_i, is regularly present in feature regions that contribute to high (low) values of P, then e_i will also be high (low). Instead of uniformly sampling from the set of original features when selecting feature regions, feature sampling is based on past "success" (large components of e). The fuzzy logic update rule uses e and the classification accuracy for the current classifier iteration, P_C. The updated histogram, e', is computed as

$$e_i' = \begin{cases} h_1(P_C) \vee e_i & \text{if} \quad P_C \geq e_i, P_C > \varepsilon \\ h_2(P_C) \wedge e_i & \text{if} \quad P_C < e_i, P_C > \varepsilon \quad (i=1...n) \\ e_i & \text{if} \quad P \leq \varepsilon \end{cases} \tag{2}$$

where $\wedge$ is a t-norm (in this study, we use the product operator), $\vee$ is an s-norm (we use the probabilistic), $h_1(x)=x^2$ is the concentration operator, $h_2(x)=x^{1/2}$ is the dilation operator, and $\varepsilon=0.5$ is a threshold below which no adjustment is made to the corresponding histogram element. The rationale behind (2) is that an update should only occur when the current classification accuracy is greater than chance and P_C should have an attenuated effect on e_i. Before FSA begins, e must be initialized to a reasonable set of values; we use $e_i=0.05$ ($\forall i=1...n$). Intuitively, the initial values need to be the same, as there is no prior information about performance, so all features should have equal likelihood of being selected. Also, the initial values should be small, but not 0, so that any spectral feature has some likelihood, however small, to be selected during an iteration.

2.2   Aggregating Feature Regions

Another important constituent of FSA is the fuzzy logic based aggregation of spectral feature regions to produce new feature combinations. In terms of classification mappings, we are moving from determining class boundaries within the original feature space to determining class boundaries within a new parameterized (feature region combinations) space. As a pre-processing strategy, the intent here is that if the original spectral feature space had non-linear class boundaries (such as piece-wise linear discontinuities, convex hulls, and so on), the new parameter space, in which the parameters themselves are "non-linear", may have simpler (for instance, near-linear) class boundaries [26–28]. Given two feature regions (as previously defined), $z^1=[z_\alpha...z_\beta]$ and $z^2=[z_\delta...z_\gamma]$ ($1 \leq a \leq \alpha \leq \beta \leq b \leq n$ and $1 \leq a \leq \delta \leq \gamma \leq b \leq n$), we may define a new fuzzy aggregation of spectral features, z, as

$$z = \begin{cases} \{z_i^1 \circ z_j^2\} & i=\alpha...\beta, j=\delta...\gamma \\ \{z_i^1 \circ z_j^1\} & i,j=\alpha...\beta(i<j) \\ \{z_i^2 \circ z_j^2\} & i,j=\delta...\gamma(i<j) \\ z^k & k=1 \text{ or } k=2 \end{cases} \tag{3}$$

where $\circ$ is either the t-norm or s-norm. We use the product and probabilistic sum operators for the respective t-norm and s-norm because of their properties of smoothly combining operands. Using (3), z has equal likelihood of being assigned one of the following: (*i*) the pair-wise aggregation (conjunction or disjunction, depending on $\circ$) of each z^1 feature with each z^2 feature (first case in (3)); (*ii*) the pair-wise aggregation (conjunction or disjunction, depending on $\circ$) of all features in either z^1 or z^2 (second or third case in (3), respectively); or (*iii*) one of the original feature regions, z^1 or z^2 (last case in (3)). As biomedical spectra are typically scaled to the unit interval, (3) can be easily applied.

3   Experiment Design

The latest biomedical spectroscopic modalities produce information rich but complex and voluminous data [29]. For instance, magnetic resonance spectroscopy, which exploits the interaction between an external homogenous magnetic field and a nucleus that possesses spin, is a reliable and versatile spectroscopic modality [30]. Coupled with robust multivariate methods, it is especially useful in the classification and inter-pretation of high-dimensional biomedical spectra of tissues and biofluids [31]. Typically, the curse of dimensionality, a low spectrum to feature ratio, is a serious classification challenge with biomedical spectra: the excess degrees of freedom tend to cause overfitting, which affects the reliability of the chosen classifier. We will use a dataset with this characteristic to assess the classification performance of FSA.

We obtained a biomedical dataset of tissue spectra acquired from a magnetic re-sonance spectrometer. There are $N=150$ spectra composed of $n=3860$ spectral features (metabolite concentrations). The spectra are divided into a "normal" class ($N_n=86$) and an "abnormal" class ($N_a=64$). These data were normalized to the unit interval. Figure 1 plots the minimum, maximum, and median feature values for the normal (i) and abnormal (ii) tissue spectra.

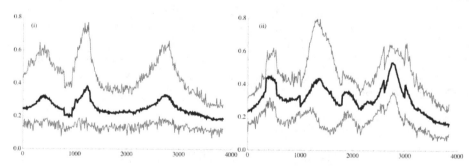

Fig. 1. Magnetic resonance spectral plot of minimum, maximum (gray), and median (black) feature values for the (i) normal, $N_n=86$, and (ii) abnormal, $N_a=64$, classes

3.1   Validation Protocol

Pattern classification studies are biased when they use the entire dataset to determine the predictive mapping. This approach leads to implausible prediction outcomes that do not take into account the possibility of overfitting, wherein the mapping possesses no generalized predictive power for new patterns. Therefore, it is important to perform some type of results validation. For instance, patterns in X may be randomly allocated to a design set, X^D, containing N^D patterns or a test set, X^T, containing N^T patterns ($N^D + N^T = N$). Now, a classification mapping is produced using only design patterns, $f':X^D \rightarrow \Omega$, while accuracy is measured using f' with the validation patterns. We use this validation approach in this investigation: $N^D = 86$, with 43 normal and 40 abnormal spectra; and $N^T = 64$, with 43 normal and 21 abnormal spectra. We also use internal t-fold cross validation (t=9); for each experiment, we randomly build t different test and design set pairs and, in turn, present the pairs to the current classifier instance being tested. In this study, FSA performance is measured using κ (see Section 2); however, we present the final classification results using P_O. In all cases described in Section 4, we report the median confusion matrix as well as the mean and standard deviation of P_O. Finally, all performance results using P_O are based on the disease state predictions using test set patterns.

3.2   Experiment Parameters

We use two standard classification approaches as benchmarks against which to measure the effectiveness of FSA. The first benchmark is LDA, as described in Section 2, using all spectral features. We also use LDA with ten different averages of the features, using window sizes of 2, 4, 5, 10, 20, 193, 386, 772, 965, and 1930. The second benchmark is a support vector machine (SVM) [21], [32] again using all spectral features and averaged features as previously described. We also use a several kernel functions, $K(x_1, x_2)$, to effect non-linear projections of the features [22]: polynomial, $(a_1 x_1 \cdot x_2 + a_2)^d$; sigmoid, $\tanh(a_1 x_1 \cdot x_2 + a_2)$; and Gaussian, $\exp(-\frac{1}{2}|x_1 - x_2|^2/\sigma)$. In the interest of brevity, we only report the best LDA and SVM classification results. The FSA parameters include: minimum and maximum number of feature regions, $a=2$, $b=5$, respectively; feature region cardinality range, 5–50; classifier type, LDA; fuzzy feature aggregation rule, equal likelihood of cases in (3); stopping criteria, maximum number of iterations, $\eta = 100000$, and accuracy threshold, $P\varepsilon = 0.99$ (note that in no experiment was the accuracy threshold exceeded); and t=9. All results presented in the next section are only for test set spectra ($N^T = 64$).

4   Results and Discussion

Table 1 lists the average FSA classification results using the test set spectra. The confusion matrix of actual versus predicted disease states listed in this table is the median matrix of the t=9 classification runs. The overall classification accuracy, P_O, is the mean value over the runs. The results from FSA and three variants are presented in a quadrant fashion: the original spectral feature regions ("Original") versus the fuzzy aggregation rule to combine regions ("Aggregate"); and random sampling ("Random") of the features versus fuzzy feature sampling of the performance histogram ("Histogram"). Aggregate and Histogram comprise the FSA strategy.

We see that FSA, the fuzzy feature sampling rule coupled with the fuzzy feature region aggregation method, produced the best overall result, $P_O=0.94\pm0.02$, while the lowest value, $P_O=0.84\pm0.03$, occurred using a random sampling of the original features. From the point of view of feature regions, we also observe that fuzzy feature aggregation produced superior classification results compared to using the original feature regions. This may be due to inherent non-linearities in the class boundaries that can be delineated in the parameterized space but cannot be delineated in the original feature space. From the point of view of the feature performance histogram, it is clear that fuzzy feature sampling produced superior classification results compared to the purely random sampling approach. In biomedical applications, it is important to minimize the number of false positives that the prediction method generates (a false positive causes needless patient anxiety and needless healthcare expenditures). In our case, this means having as few normal spectra being erroneously predicted to fall into the abnormal disease state. Again, we observe that the fuzzy feature sampling coupled with fuzzy feature aggregation generated only two false positives; as percentages, 10% versus 19% and 24%. Table 2 lists the average classification results using the benchmarks. With LDA, the best result, $P_O=0.81\pm0.03$, was achieved using feature averaging with a window size of 20 (193 averaged features). This result is statistically comparable to using random sampling of the original features. With SVM, the best result, $P_O=0.88\pm0.02$, was achieved using a Gaussian kernel and feature averaging with a window size of 20. This result is statistically comparable to both random sampling with feature aggregation and fuzzy sampling of the original features. However, SVM produced statistically poorer classification results than FSA.

Table 1. Average FSA Classification Results (Test Set)

| Sampling | Actual versus Predicted | Feature Regions | | | | | |
| | | Original | | | Aggregate | | |
		Normal	Abnormal	Accuracy	Normal	Abnormal	Accuracy
Random	Normal	38	5	0.88	39	4	0.91
	Abnormal	5	16	0.76	4	17	0.81
	P_O		0.84±0.03			0.88±0.02	
Histogram	Normal	40	3	0.93	41	2	0.95
	Abnormal	4	17	0.81	2	19	0.90
	P_O		0.89±0.03			0.94±0.02	

Table 2. Average Benchmark Classification Results (Test Set)

| Actual vs. Predicted | LDA | | | SVM | | |
	Normal	Abnormal	Accuracy	Normal	Abnormal	Accuracy
Normal	37	6	0.86	40	3	0.93
Abnormal	6	15	0.71	5	16	0.76
P_O		0.81±0.03			0.88±0.02	

Table 3 lists the spectral feature regions that were selected using FSA and the three variants. Three variants identified two discriminatory features, while the fourth, using random sampling and the original features, identified three regions. Interestingly, while the latter variant produced the poorest classification results of the four, it also required far more of the original features to achieve this inferior result: 131 versus 23 (original with histogram), 19 (aggregate with random), and 39 (FSA). The two aggregation cases improved the performance of the respective random and histogram counterparts through the use of aggregation of regions. In the former case, one feature region, $[x_{397}...x_{404}]$, was aggregated (see Histogram Region 1 in Table 3). In the latter case, three feature regions were aggregated, $[x_{1989}...x_{1996}]$ (Region 1), $[x_{3001}...x_{3012}]$, and $[x_{3474}...x_{3492}]$ (Region 2) (see Histogram in Table 3). An interesting biomedical observation relates to the feature regions identified using the histogram sampling and region aggregation. These variants identified four discriminatory regions, roughly around indices 400, 1900, 3000, and 3500. The first three regions correspond to concentrations of biological metabolites that were previously identified by the biomedical expert to have significance in the discrimination between normal and abnormal disease states. While the final region does not have any known biological significance, it is numerically essential to the strong classification performance of FSA.

Table 3. Spectral Feature Regions Selected Using FSA and Variants

Sampling		Feature Regions	
		Original	Aggregate
Random	Region 1	$[x_{221}...x_{255}]$	$[x_{397}...x_{404}] \wedge [x_{397}...x_{404}]$
	Region 2	$[x_{395}...x_{441}]$	$[x_{2987}...x_{2997}]$
	Region 3	$[x_{415}...x_{463}]$	$\varnothing$
Histogram	Region 1	$[x_{407}...x_{417}]$	$[x_{1889}...x_{1896}] \wedge [x_{1889}...x_{1896}]$
	Region 2	$[x_{2981}...x_{2992}]$	$[x_{3001}...x_{3012}] \wedge [x_{3474}...x_{3492}]$

5   Conclusion

Via empirical evaluation using a voluminous biomedical dataset of magnetic resonance spectra, we have demonstrated the effectiveness of the fuzzy feature sampling and aggregation classification system that identifies discriminatory feature subsets using a fuzzy logic based sampling rule and feature aggregator. Figure 2 is a summary plot of the mean classification results (including their standard deviations) of this approach, including three variants, compared to the benchmark classifier results. It is clear that feature aggregation coupled with fuzzy feature sampling produced the best overall classification result; a 6% improvement over the best of the variants and a 7% improvement over the best benchmark. Moreover, this result was achieved using only 1% of the original spectral features. Future research activities will revolve around the fuzzy aggregation rule (for instance, examining other candidate operators for the parameterized feature space) and the feature update rule (for instance, examining the effects of a simulated annealing operation on the histogram sampling).

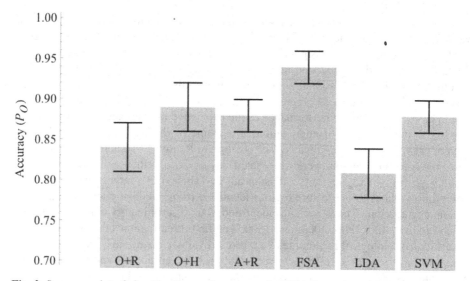

Fig. 2. Summary plot of classification performance using FSA, its variants (O+R, random sampling of original features, O+H, histogram sampling using the original features, and A+R, random sampling of the aggregated features), and benchmarks.

Acknowledgements. We gratefully acknowledge the support of the Natural Sciences and Engineering Research Council for this investigation.

References

1. Dreiseitla, S., Ohno-Machadob, L.: Logistic Regression and Artificial Neural Network Classification Models: A Methodology Review. J. Biomed. Inform. 35, 352–359 (2002)
2. Bishop, C.M.: Pattern Recognition and Machine Learning. Springer, Dodrecht (2006)
3. El-Deredy, W.: Pattern Recognition Approaches in Biomedical and Clinical Magnetic Resonance Spectroscopy: A Review. NMR Biomed. 10, 99–124 (1997)
4. Rokach, L.: Pattern Classification Using Ensemble Methods. World Scientific, Singapore (2010)
5. Jin, Y., Wang, L.: Fuzzy Systems in Bioinformatics and Computational Biology. Springer, Heidelberg (2009)
6. Hastie, T., Tibshirani, R., Friedman, J.: The Elements of Statistical Learning: Data Mining, Inference, and Prediction. Springer, New York (2009)
7. Belkić, D., Belkić, K.: Signal Processing in Magnetic Resonance Spectroscopy with Biomedical Applications. CRC Press, Boca Raton (2010)
8. Bouchon-Meunier, B., Coletti, G., Yager, R.R.: Modern Information Processing: From Theory to Applications. Elsevier, Amsterdam (2006)
9. Witten, I.H., Frank, E.: Data Mining: Practical Machine Learning Tools and Techniques. Morgan Kaufmann, San Francisco (2005)
10. Maimon, O., Rokach, L.: Data Mining and Knowledge Discovery Handbook. Springer, Dodrecht (2005)
11. Ripley, B.D.: Neural Networks and Related Methods for Classification. J. Roy. Stat. Soc. B 56, 409–456 (1994)

12. Bargiela, A., Pedrycz, W.: Human-Centric Information Processing Through Granular Modelling. Springer, Heidelberg (2009)
13. Hair, J.F., Black, W.C., Babin, B.J., Anderson, R.E.: Multivariate Data Analysis. Prentice-Hall, Hoboken (2009)
14. Pizzi, N.J., Pedrycz, W.: Aggregating Multiple Classification Results Using Fuzzy Integration and Stochastic Feature Selection. Intl. J. Approx. Reason. 51, 883–894 (2010)
15. Pizzi, N.J.: Classification of Biomedical Spectra Using Stochastic Feature Selection. Neural Network World 15, 257–268 (2005)
16. Pizzi, N.J., Pedrycz, W.: Randomized Feature Selection Using Scopira. In: Proceedings of the Annual Meeting of the North American Fuzzy Information Processing Society, Banff, Canada, June 27–30, pp. 669–674 (2004)
17. Liu, Q., Sung, A., Chen, Z., Xu, J.: Feature Mining and Pattern Classification for LSB Matching Steganography in Grayscale Images. Patt. Recogn. 41, 56–66 (2008)
18. Kasabov, N., Song, Q.: DENFIS: Dynamic Evolving Neural-Fuzzy Inference System and its Application for Time-Series Prediction. IEEE Trans. Fuzzy Syst. 10, 144–154 (2002)
19. Seber, G.A.F.: Multivariate Observations. Wiley, Hoboken (2004)
20. Jain, A.K., Duin, R.P.W., Mao, J.: Statistical Pattern Recognition: A Review. IEEE Trans. Patt. Anal. Mach. Intell. 22, 4–37 (2000)
21. Schölkopf, B., Smola, A.J.: Learning with Kernels: Support Vector Machines, Regularization, Optimization, and Beyond. MIT Press, Cambridge (2002)
22. Wang, L.: Support Vector Machines: Theory and Applications. Springer, Berlin (2005)
23. De Jong, K.A.: Evolutionary Computation: A Unified Approach. MIT Press, Cambridge (2006)
24. Press, W.H., Teukolsky, S.A., Vetterling, W.T., Flannery, B.P.: Numerical Recipes: The Art of Scientific Computing. Cambridge University Press, Cambridge (2007)
25. Everitt, B.S.: Moments of the Statistics Kappa and Weighted Kappa. British J. Math. Stat. Psych. 21, 97–103 (1968)
26. Pedrycz, W., Breuer, A., Pizzi, N.J.: Genetic Design of Feature Spaces for Pattern Classifiers. Artif. Intell. Med. 32, 115–125 (2004)
27. Pizzi, N.J., Pedrycz, W.: A Fuzzy Logic Network for Pattern Classification. In: Proceedings of the Annual Meeting of the North American Fuzzy Information Processing Society, Cincinnati, USA, June 14–17, pp. 53–58 (2009)
28. Krzanowski, W.: Principles of Multivariate Analysis. Oxford University Press, New York (1988)
29. Pavia, D.L., Lampman, G.M., Kriz, G.S.: Introduction to Spectroscopy. Harcourt Brace College, Fort Worth (1996)
30. Friebolin, H.: Basic One- and Two-Dimensional NMR Spectroscopy. Wiley, New York (2005)
31. Pizzi, N.J.: Fuzzy Quartile Encoding as a Preprocessing Method for Biomedical Pattern Classification. Theoretical Comp. Sci. 412, 5909–5929 (2011)
32. Vapnik, V.: Statistical Learning Theory. Wiley, New York (1998)

Discovering the Preferences of Physicians with Regards to Rank-Ordered Medical Documents

Dympna O'Sullivan[1], Szymon Wilk[2], Wojtek Michalowski[3],
Roman Słowiński[2], Roland Thomas[4], and Ken Farion[5,6]

[1] Department of Computer Science, Aston University, Birmingham, UK
d.m.osullivan@aston.ac.uk
[2] Institute of Computing Science, Poznan University of Technology, Poznan, Poland
{szymon.wilk,roman.slowinski}@cs.put.poznan.pl
[3] Telfer School of Management, University of Ottawa, Ottawa, Canada
wojtek@telfer.uottawa.ca
[4] Sprott School of Business, Carleton University, Ottawa, Canada
roland_thomas@carleton.ca
[5] Departments of Pediatrics and Emergency Medicine, University of Ottawa, Ottawa, Canada
[6] Children's Hospital of Eastern Ontario, Ottawa, Canada
farion@cheo.on.ca

Abstract. The practice of evidence-based medicine involves consulting documents from repositories such as Scopus, PubMed, or the Cochrane Library. The most common approach for presenting retrieved documents is in the form of a list, with the assumption that the higher a document is on a list, the more relevant it is. Despite this list-based presentation, it is seldom studied how physicians perceive the importance of the order of documents presented in a list. This paper describes an empirical study that elicited and modeled physicians' preferences with regard to list-based results. Preferences were analyzed using a GRIP method that relies on pairwise comparisons of selected subsets of possible rank-ordered lists composed of 3 documents. The results allow us to draw conclusions regarding physicians' attitudes towards the importance of having documents ranked correctly on a result list, versus the importance of retrieving relevant but misplaced documents. Our findings should help developers of clinical information retrieval applications when deciding how retrieved documents should be presented and how performance of the application should be assessed.

Keywords: Physician preferences, Evidence-Based Medicine, Document Retrieval, Rank-ordered Lists, Information Retrieval.

1   Introduction

As part of our research on clinical decision support systems, we have developed a method for automatically retrieving documents from the Cochrane Library that are relevant in the context of a patient-physician encounter [1]. An evaluation of our method's performance prompted us to reflect on the following question: "*What are*

S. Greco et al. (Eds.): IPMU 2012, Part III, CCIS 299, pp. 142–150, 2012.
© Springer-Verlag Berlin Heidelberg 2012

physician's expectations and preferences with regards to the rank-ordered presentation of retrieved documents?" Specifically, how do physicians rate the importance of being presented with relevant document on a particular position in a list? Alternatively, how do they value documents that are relevant but misplaced on a list (for example, presented in 2nd instead of 1st place)?

Information retrieval applications that are currently in use return lists of ranked documents where document features are used to estimate a document's relevance for a given query and to compute positions in a ranked list. The established method of evaluating the relevance of documents is to compare retrieved documents with a gold standard for retrieval, which is usually provided by an expert. The effectiveness of the automatic application is then measured in terms of precision – the number of relevant documents a query retrieves divided by the total number of documents retrieved, and recall – the number of relevant documents retrieved divided by the total number of relevant documents that should have been retrieved for the query. However, these metrics do not take into account the position of a document on a rank-ordered list and how physicians perceive mistakes with regard to relevant but misplaced documents. Other measurements such as mean average precision that averages precision over a number of queries has the effect of promoting relevant results closer to the top of a list, however it cannot capture preferences with regard to relevant documents that are out of position on a list. In order to illustrate such an occurrence, assume that for a given query, the gold standard indicates that the correct triple of documents should be [*a*, *b*, *c*], while the information retrieval application retrieved a triple [*b*, *k*, *c*]. Comparing these two triples it can be observed that the retrieval application did not retrieve the most relevant document *a*, it did retrieve a relevant document *b* but placed it in the wrong position (1st instead of 2nd), retrieved an irrelevant document *k*, and retrieved and presented a document *c* in the correct position. All measures of the effectiveness of a retrieval application would focus on the fact that two out of three documents were correctly retrieved while ignoring the order in which they are presented. Such a view would be correct if physicians do not differentiate in terms of the position on which a given document is presented. However, it is not clear if this assumption is correct. Therefore, we studied the following question: *is it correct when evaluating the performance of an information retrieval application to ignore physicians' preferences associated with the order (position) in which documents are presented?* The search for the answer to this question forms the basis of the paper.

The paper is organized as follows. In the next section we briefly discuss research on list-based presentation of search results. In section 3 we describe a study that gathered physician preferences with regard to rank-ordered lists of 3 documents (prior consultations with physicians confirmed that a list with maximum length of 3 documents should be used to present evidence at the point-of-care). Physicians were asked to provide preference information through pairwise comparisons of subsets of rank-ordered lists and these comparisons were analyzed using a GRIP method, which is outlined in the same section. The results of the experiment are presented in Section 4 and the paper concludes with a discussion in Section 5.

2   Background Research

Presenting information as a list is widely used but also widely criticized, because ranked presentation style coupled with the low precision of search engines make it hard for users to find the information they are looking for [2]. In spite of such criticism and subsequent attempts to introduce other methods such as clustering for organizing search results, list-based presentation continues to be the dominant way for organizing information presentation.

Other researchers have studied whether users evaluating list-based presentation follow a depth-first strategy (the user examines each entry in the list in turn starting from the top, and decides immediately whether to open the document in question), or a breadth-first strategy (the user looks ahead at a number of list entries and then revisits the most promising ones) [3]. The results showed that a significant majority (85%), of users relies on a depth-first strategy. Another study used eye tracking (measuring spatially stable gaze during which visual attention was directed to a specific area of the display), to estimate how users process list-based information [4]. The results indicated that users tended to view the first and second-ranked entries right away, and then there is a large gap before viewing the third-ranked entry. A study by Keane et al. [5], also confirmed the inclination of users to access items at the beginning of list. The authors showed that high position on a list often trumpets document's relevance. Considering the potential impact of this inherent user behavior on search results, a school of research is actively devising solutions to overcome the effect of falsely over-promoting web pages by placing them at the top of results list where they will be selected preferentially by users [6, 7].

All these findings have strong implications for the presentation of evidence-based documents to physicians. We hypothesize that if documents presented close to the top of a list have little relevance or are irrelevant, it is likely the entire list will be discarded. While the above statement is confirmed by the research quoted earlier, there is no evidence of how strong physician's preferences are with regards to ordering and positions on rank-ordered lists. Specifically, little is known about how much value they place on receiving relevant documents in the correct order on a list versus how they assess being presented with relevant documents but not necessarily in the right order.

3   Experimental Design

The problem of assessing rank-ordered documents by a physician can be seen as a multiple criteria evaluation problem, where each criterion represents physician's preferences with regards to the relevance of a document presented at a given position on a list. In other words, the value function is a preference model of a specific physician or a group of physicians, which serves to rank a set of rank-ordered lists of documents, taking into account preferences concerning relevance and position of documents on a list. As a preference model, an additive value function can be used, which is a sum of marginal value functions that represent preferences of a physician on specific criteria.There are many theoretical approaches to estimating an additive value function, including those that rely on the ordinal regression model. In these approaches, preferential information is captured first through the pairwise comparisons of a subset of alternatives (i.e. lists of documents), and then a value function compatible with this information is built [8, 9]. Such a value function represents preferences of a specific user and it can be applied to assess other alternatives that have not been evaluated before.

In our study we used the Generalized Regression with Intensities of Preference (GRIP) method (see [10] for detailed discussion), that derives an additive value function using partial preferential information given by a user in the form of pairwise comparisons of selected alternatives (so-called *reference alternatives*), and ordinal intensities of preference among some of them. It constructs not only the preference relation in the considered set of alternatives, but it also gives information about intensities of preference for pairs of alternatives from this set for a given decision maker. After obtaining results of pairwise comparisons, GRIP checks if any additive value function compatible with the provided preferential information exists. If such a function cannot be found, the method is able to identify pairwise comparisons that prevent representation by an additive value function. Such pairwise comparisons are called *inconsistent* and need to be revised (modified or removed), before proceeding further. Once inconsistencies have been addressed, GRIP constructs marginal value functions for all considered criteria and derives from them an additive value function. This function has to satisfy certain mathematical properties, and because it is computed on a basis of all possible marginal value functions that are consistent with provided preferential information, it is often called a *representative additive value function*. In the analysis presented in the paper we focus only on the marginal value functions associated with the representative function as they provide required insight into physicians' preferences with regards to the retrieved documents.

The experimental design of our study is illustrated in Figure 1. The study consisted of three phases. The first phase started with devising a set of coded triples that represented all feasible combinations of retrieved documents. Each position in a triple, which was considered by GRIP as criterion to be evaluated, was coded as X, N or Y, where X indicates an irrelevant document at a given position, N indicates that a retrieved document is relevant but is placed in an incorrect position on a rank-ordered list, and Y indicates that a relevant document was retrieved and ranked correctly. Thus, for example the triple [b, k, c] mentioned in Section 1 was coded as NXY given [a, b, c] as a gold standard. The coding scheme produced 24 feasible triples out of 27 possible combinations (the smaller number of considered triples is due to some triples being infeasible – i.e. a triple YYN is not feasible because it has two documents that are in the correct position and are relevant, thus the third document cannot be misplaced but can be either irrelevant (X) or correct (Y)).

From the set of 24 triples, a subset of 10 reference triples was selected for 10 pairwise comparisons that corresponded to less obvious evaluations. For example, YYX is intuitively preferred over XYX (retrieving two relevant documents placed correctly on first two positions is preferred over retrieving just one relevant document that is correctly placed); while comparing NNN with YYX is more difficult (is it preferred that all retrieved documents are relevant but misplaced as opposed to retrieving two documents that are relevant and positioned correctly and a third one that is irrelevant?). Using coded triples for pairwise comparisons allowed us to avoid bias associated with such factors as graphic presentation, or trust in a particular author or publisher.

In the second phase, 6 experienced physicians, all from Ottawa area teaching hospitals, evaluated pairs of reference triples. Study participants represented a range of clinical specialties – emergency medicine, community medicine, internal medicine, intensive care medicine and anesthesiology. All were experienced with using electronic repositories of clinical documents. Prior to the experiment they were informed about the purpose of the study, the experimental design, and how they should conduct pairwise comparisons. Examples of comparisons using triples that were not evaluated in the study were presented and explained. Each physician was asked to independently assess each pair and to state if one triple was preferred over the other, or if they were equally preferred.

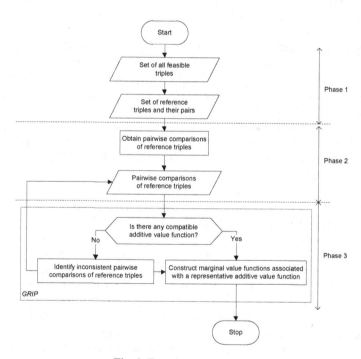

Fig. 1. Experimental design

In the third phase, results of Phase 2 evaluations were used by GRIP to derive three marginal value functions that measure physician preferences regarding the specific position of a document in a triple (1st, 2nd and 3rd).

4   Results

Coded reference triples were presented to the physicians for pairwise evaluation. Table 1 presents the results of the pairwise comparisons of these triples. Each of the physicians (denoted as P1, P2, ... P6) was asked to express her/his preferences for one triple (T1) over another (T2) as: T1 preferred over T2 (denoted by symbol "≻"), T2 preferred over T1 (denoted by symbol "≺"), and T1 equally preferred to T2 (denoted by symbol "~"). Responses of physicians P2 and P3 as well as P5 and P6 were identical and therefore are grouped together as (P2_3) and (P5_6), respectively.

Table 1. Physician's pairwise comparisons of triples

T1	T2	P1	P2_3	P 4	P5_6
NNN	YYX	≺	≻	≻	≺
NNX	YXY	≺	≺	≺	≺
NXN	XYY	≺	≻	~	~
NXX	XYX	≺	≺	≺	≺
XNX	XXY	≺	≻	~	≻
XNN	YXX	≺	≻	≺	≺
NNN	YXY	≻	≻	≺	≺
NNX	XYY	≺	≻	~	≻
XNN	XYX	≻	≻	≺	≻
NXX	XXY	≻	≻	≺	≻

The responses presented in Table 1 formed an input for GRIP. The method was applied iteratively to preferential information provided by each physician. First, GRIP identified those responses that no additive value function was able to represent. Such inconsistent responses were removed manually, and then a representative value function able to reconstruct the remaining responses was found. GRIP identified inconsistent pairwise comparisons in responses given by all physicians, except P1; they are marked with grey background in Table 1.

Considering that value domains for each position are discrete (codes X, N and Y), the resulting marginal value function derived as described above becomes a set of the breakpoints. These breakpoints (codes Y and N) are represented in Table 2 for each physician and for each position. The marginal value of code X on any position is equal to 0; therefore it has been excluded from the table.

The analysis of the values in Table 2 provides insights into physician preferences with regards to the presentation of documents. Starting with position 1, all physicians place a high importance on having a relevant document on the 1st position of a list. A correct document (Y) on position 1 receives the highest marginal value across all

Table 2. Breakpoint marginal values at positions 1, 2, and 3 in a triple

	Position 1					Position 2					Position 3			
	P1	P2_3	P4	P5_6		P1	P2_3	P4	P5_6		P1	P2_3	P4	P5_6
N	0.31	0.31	0.1	0.26	N	0.19	0.31	0.2	0.26	N	0.19	0.19	0.1	0.11
Y	0.42	0.42	0.4	0.53	Y	0.35	0.35	0.4	0.32	Y	0.23	0.23	0.2	0.16

participants. However physicians are less uniform while placing value on having a misplaced but relevant document (N) on this position. Some are willing to accept misplacement – for example, the analysis of responses provided by P1 and P2_3 for position 1, indicates a smaller drop in marginal values. However, for P4 and P5_6, the difference in marginal values is much more pronounced, indicating that these physicians are less willing to accept on the top position, a document that is relevant but should be ranked lower. Thus, the general conclusion that can be drawn for position 1 is that all physicians want to have the most relevant document in the 1st position on a rank-ordered list.

Moving to positions 2 and 3, physicians are less definitive in their preferences. While all of them value a relevant document (Y) on position 2 higher than on position 3, their preferences are not so definitive with regards to a misplaced document (N) on these two positions. While for P1 there is no difference if a misplaced document is placed on position 2 or 3; however this is not the case for P2_3 and P5_6 who clearly take position into account by assigning higher value to misplaced document (N) if it is on position 2 rather than 3. Responses of P4 fall somewhere in-between – while there is a preference for position 2 over 3, the difference is not that pronounced. In summary, it is possible to conclude that when moving to lower positions, rank order is still important but with diminishing magnitude in the difference between values for correct (Y) and misplaced (N) documents.

The overall conclusion that we draw from the GRIP analysis is that rank order is important for physicians when viewing a list of documents. In particular, it is important that they are presented with a correct document on the 1st position of a rank-ordered list. After position 1, their attitude varies, for some it is still very important that the second most relevant document is correctly placed in position 2, while for others relevance of the documents dominates over ranking for positions 2 and 3 (a document needs to be relevant but can be misplaced). This is coupled with a general reduction in the value of retrieved documents if they are placed on lower positions in a rank-ordered list.

5   Discussion

This paper presented the results of an empirical experiment to model physician preferences with regard to the presentation of rank-ordered list of documents. In particular we wanted to learn if *"it is correct when evaluating the performance of an information retrieval application to ignore physicians' preferences associated with the order (position) in which documents are presented?* ''Physicians were asked to do pairwise comparisons of rank-ordered triples of documents, and their responses were analyzed using the GRIP method. The results of the experiment show that there is no definitive method of presenting rank-ordered medical documents, however, these general conclusions can be drawn:

- Physicians pay significant attention to the 1st position on a rank-ordered list and they expect that the most relevant document is presented first,
- From a physician's perspective, the importance of presented documents diminishes the lower it is positioned on a rank-ordered list.

These conclusions indicate that the answer to our research question is negative, meaning that it is not correct to ignore order in which documents are presented while evaluating a performance of an information retrieval application.

The obtained results correlate with research on general user searches on the Web (e.g. [4, 5]). They also indicate that when measuring the performance of information retrieval applications it is not sufficient to evaluate only retrieval of correct documents, because physicians clearly put value on the position on a list where a document is presented.

The findings of our study are useful when developing clinical information retrieval applications. They indicate that rank-ordered lists should be short (participating physicians were willing to evaluate lists composed of maximum 3 documents), and that it is imperative to place the most relevant document in the 1st position on a rank-ordered list. However, physicians differ in how they assess subsequent positions – for some having a correctly positioned relevant document in position 2 on a list is very important, while for others, after the first position the relevance of a document gains over its correct positioning.

In future work we intend to use the results of this study in developing a method for more accurately evaluating medical document retrieval. This will translate into revising traditional evaluation metrics such as precision and recall so, for example, a precision value calculated for a document triple YNX will be higher than for a triple NYX (this is not captured when using existing document retrieval performance measures).

Acknowledgment. The authors would like to thank all the physicians who participated in the study. The support of the NSERC-CHRP Program and the Polish National Science Centre (grant no. N N519 441939) are gratefully acknowledged.

References

1. O'Sullivan, D.M., Wilk, S., Michalowski, W.J., Farion, K.J.: Automatic indexing and retrieval of encounter-specific evidence for point-of-care support. Journal of Biomedical Informatics 43(4), 623–631 (2010)

2. Zamir, O., Etzioni, O.: Grouper: A dynamic clustering interface to Web search results. In: 8th International Conference on World Wide Web (WWW 2009), pp. 1361–1374 (1999)
3. Klöckner, K., Wirschum, N., Jameson, A.: Depth- and breadth-first processing of search result lists. In: 22nd SIGCHI Conference on Human Factors in Computing Systems (CHI 2004) (2004)
4. Joachims, T., Granka, L., Pang, B., Hembrooke, H., Gay, G.: Accurately interpreting click-through data as implicit feedback. In: ACM SIGIR Conference on Research and Development in Information Retrieval (SIGIR 2005), pp. 154–161 (2005)
5. Keane, M.T., O'Brien, M., Smyth, B.: Are people biased in their use of search engines? Communications of ACM 51(2), 49–52 (2008)
6. Cho, J., Roy, S.: Impact of search engines on page popularity. In: 13th International World Wide Web Conference (WWW 2004) (2004)
7. Pandey, S., Roy, S., Olston, C., Cho, J., Chakrabarti, S.: Shuffling a stacked deck: The case for partially randomized ranking of search engine results. In: 31st international Conference on Very Large Data Bases (VLDB 2005) (2005)
8. Greco, S., Slowinski, R., Figueira, J.R., Mousseau, V.: Robust ordinal regression. In: Ehrgott, M., Figueira, J., Greco, S. (eds.) Trends in Multiple Criteria Decision Analysis, ch. 9, pp. 241–283. Springer Science + Business Media Inc., New York (2010)
9. Siskos, Y., Grigoroudis, V., Matsatsinis, N.: UTA methods. In: Figueira, J., Greco, S., Ehrgott, M. (eds.) Multiple Criteria Decision Analysis: State of the Art Surveys, ch. 8, pp. 297–343. Springer Science + Business Media Inc., New York (2005)
10. Figueira, J.R., Greco, S., Slowinski, R.: Building a set of additive value functions representing a reference preorder and intensities of preference: GRIP method. European Journal of Operational Research 195, 460–486 (2009)

Experiences with Eliciting Probabilities from Multiple Experts

Linda C. van der Gaag[1], Silja Renooij[1], Hermi J.M. Schijf[1],
Armin R. Elbers[2], and Willie L. Loeffen[2]

[1] Department of Information and Computing Sciences, Utrecht University, NL
[2] Department of Virology, Central Veterinary Institute of Wageningen UR, NL

Abstract. Bayesian networks are typically designed in collaboration with a single domain expert from a single institute. Since a network is often intended for wider use, its engineering involves verifying whether it appropriately reflects expert knowledge from other institutes. Upon engineering a network intended for use across Europe, we compared the original probability assessments obtained from our Dutch expert with assessments from 38 experts in six countries. While we found large variances among the assessments per probability, very high consistency was found for the qualitative properties embedded in the series of assessments per assessor. The apparent robustness of these properties suggests the importance of enforcing them in a Bayesian network under construction.

1 Introduction

Bayesian networks are rapidly becoming the models of choice for reasoning with uncertainty in decision-support systems, most notably in domains governed by biological processes. While much attention has focused on algorithms for learning Bayesian networks from data, our experiences with designing networks for the biomedical field show that systematically collected data are often wanting, or are not amenable to automated model construction. Often therefore, expert knowledge constitutes the only source of information for a network's design. Since the construction of a high-quality Bayesian network is a difficult and time-consuming creative process, for both the engineers involved and the consulted experts, common engineering practice is to closely collaborate with just a single, or a very small number of experts, even if the network is intended for wider use.

In collaboration with two experts from the Central Veterinary Institute in the Netherlands, we are in the process of developing a decision-support system to supply veterinary practitioners with an independent tool for the early detection of Classical Swine Fever (CSF) in pigs. At the core of the system lies a Bayesian network for computing the posterior probability of a CSF infection being present, given the clinical signs observed at a pig farm by an attending veterinarian. For its design, in-depth interviews were held with the two participating experts and case reviews were conducted with eight Dutch swine practitioners. The conditional probabilities required for the network were mostly not available from the literature, nor were sufficiently rich data available for their estimation. As a consequence, all required probabilities were assessed by a single CSF expert.

S. Greco et al. (Eds.): IPMU 2012, Part III, CCIS 299, pp. 151–160, 2012.

While being built with Dutch experts, our Bayesian network for the early detection of Classical Swine Fever is intended for use across the European Union. Bayesian networks in fact are often intended for wider use than just by the experts with whom they are being constructed. Engineering a network then involves verifying whether it appropriately reflects practices and insights from other experts as well. Upon engineering our CSF network, we had the opportunity of attending project meetings with pig experts and veterinary practitioners in six European countries outside the Netherlands. During these meetings, we were granted time with the experts to discuss some details of the current network. Among other information, we gathered assessments for a limited number of conditional probabilities for our network. Our intention was not to elicit assessments from multiple experts in order to aggregate these for use in our network. Rather, we were interested in whether or not experts from different countries would provide similar assessments for relations between diseases and clinical signs that are supposed to hold universally across countries. We thus mimicked a realistic elicitation setting and compared the obtained assessments with each other and with the original assessments provided by our Dutch expert.

During the project meetings, we obtained a total of 58 series of probability assessments from 38 experts in six countries. We investigated the assessments obtained for the separate probabilities by establishing summary statistics, both per country and across countries. We further studied the series of assessments obtained and the qualitative properties of dominance embedded in them. We found large variances among the numerical assessments per probability, both within and between countries. Much higher consistency was found for the embedded dominance properties, however. Apparently, this type of qualitative information is more robust than numerical information. This robustness suggests the importance of explicitly eliciting qualitative properties of probability and ensuring that these are properly captured in a Bayesian network under construction.

The present paper reports our findings and experiences from the project meetings. In Sect. 2, we briefly introduce the background of our application. Sect. 3 describes the set-up of the meetings and the elicitation method used. Sect. 4 summarises the assessments obtained. In Sect. 5, we analyse our findings from a qualitative perspective. The paper ends with our reflections in Sect. 6.

2   The Context

In a European project involving seven countries, a decision-support system is being developed for the early detection of Classical Swine Fever in pigs. CSF is an infectious viral disease with a potential for rapid spread through contact between infected and non-infected susceptible pigs. When a pig is first infected, it will show an increased body temperature and a sense of malaise. Later in the infection, the animal is likely to develop an inflammation of the intestinal tract; also problems with the respiratory tract are beginning to reveal themselves through such signs as a conjunctivitis, snivelling, and coughing. The final stages of the disease are associated with an accumulating failure of body systems, which will

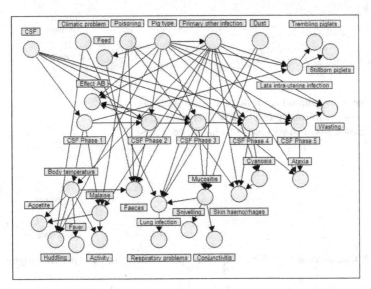

Fig. 1. The graphical structure of the Bayesian network for the early detection of CSF

ultimately cause the pig to die. The longer a CSF infection remains undetected, the longer the virus can circulate without hindrance, not just within a herd but also between herds, with major socio-economic consequences. Yet, the aspecificity of the early signs of the disease causes the clinical diagnosis of CSF to be highly uncertain for a relatively long period after the infection has occurred.

Within the CSF project, we are developing a decision-support system to supply veterinary practitioners with an independent tool to identify CSF-suspect situations as early on in an outbreak as possible. The system takes for its input the clinical signs seen at a pig farm by an attending veterinarian and computes the probability of a CSF infection being present; based upon the computed probability, a recommendation for further proceedings is given. For computing the posterior probability of CSF given the observed clinical signs, the system builds upon a Bayesian network which models the pathogenesis of the disease. Fig. 1 shows the network's graphical structure; it currently includes 32 stochastic variables, for which over 1100 (conditional) probabilities are specified.

3   Set-Up of the Project Meetings

Between December 2006 and May 2007, project meetings were held at renowned veterinary institutes in Belgium, Denmark, Germany, Great-Britain, Italy, and Poland. For each meeting, a small number of experts were invited from all over the host country; the invitees ranged from veterinary pig practitioners to researchers conducting experimental CSF infection studies. During the meetings, we were granted some time to discuss details of the CSF network. Within the allotted time, the experts were presented with a lecture about the working of the network; in addition, the assessment task to be performed was introduced.

Consider a pig *without an infection of the mucous* in the upper respiratory tract. How likely is it that this pig shows tear marks as a result of a *conjunctivitis* ?

certain (almost)	— 100
probable	— 85
	— 75
expected	
fifty-fifty	— 50
uncertain	
	— 25
improbable	— 15
(almost) impossible	— 0

Fig. 2. A fragment of text for a requested probability, and the accompanying scale

For the assessment task, a tailored elicitation method was used, in which a requested probability was presented to the assessor as a fragment of text stated in veterinary terms and accompanied by a vertical scale with numerical and verbal anchors as illustrated in Fig. 2; for further details of the elicitation method, we refer to [1]. The assessor was asked to carefully consider the fragment of text and to indicate his assessment by marking the scale. The use of the probability scale was demonstrated during the plenary introduction of the task.

For our investigations, we selected twelve probabilities. In the present paper, we focus on the six probabilities summarised in Table 1; for the other six probabilities similar results were found. The six probabilities from the table were elicited from the experts in the displayed order. The probabilities p_1 through p_4 denote the probabilities of finding the tear marks associated with a conjunctivitis (abbreviated to 'conjunct') in an animal in the early stages of a CSF infection ('csf') and, respectively, no further primary infections ('no-other'), a respiratory infection ('resp'), a gastro-intestinal infection ('intest'), and both types of primary infection ('resp+intest'); note that in the current version of the network the variable *Conjunctivitis* is related indirectly to both *CSF* and *Primary other infection*. The probabilities p_5 and p_6 denote the probabilities of finding the clinical sign of snivelling ('sniv') in an animal with or without a mucous infection

Table 1. The six probabilities discussed in this paper, with the original assessments

Probability	Original assessment
$p_1 = \Pr(\text{conjunct} \mid \text{csf, no-other})$	0.29
$p_2 = \Pr(\text{conjunct} \mid \text{csf, resp})$	0.66
$p_3 = \Pr(\text{conjunct} \mid \text{csf, intest})$	0.29
$p_4 = \Pr(\text{conjunct} \mid \text{csf, resp+intest})$	0.66
$p_5 = \Pr(\text{sniv} \mid \text{muco})$	0.20
$p_6 = \Pr(\text{sniv} \mid \text{no-muco})$	0.01

in the upper respiratory tract, respectively; these two probabilities define the conditional probability table for the variable *Snivelling* in the network. For comparison purposes, Table 1 further includes the original assessments provided by our Dutch expert during the elicitations for the network's construction.

With the set-up outlined above, we obtained assessments for the probabilities p_1 through p_6 from a total of 38 experts in six countries. In the sequel, we will refer to these countries by the letters $\mathcal{A}$ through $\mathcal{F}$, for reasons of anonymity.

4   Taking a Quantitative Perspective: Summary Statistics

We investigated the separate assessments obtained from the veterinary experts by establishing various summary statistics, both per country and across countries. In this section, we report these standard statistics and review our findings.

4.1   The Data Obtained, the Analyses and the Results

Upon studying the responses obtained from our elicitation efforts, we found that the experts had used different methods for indicating their assessments on the probability scale. Most experts had put an explicit mark on the vertical line of the scale, as was demonstrated during the plenary instruction. The positions of these marks were measured and translated into numerical assessments for further analysis. Some experts, however, had encircled one of the verbal anchors positioned beside the scale. Since the anchors indicate a fuzzy probability range [2], these circles were not used for numerical analysis. We obtained 58 complete series of assessments from our 38 experts: 29 series for the probabilities p_1 through p_4, and 29 series for the probabilities p_5 and p_6. In incomplete series, another 10 assessments were given, providing us with a total of 184 numerical assessments.

For each probability under study, we computed standard statistics over the assessments obtained, which included the range, mean and standard deviation of the assessments per country; we further determined the mean and standard deviation of the six country means. Table 2 shows the resulting statistics for the probability p_1 in some detail; the statistics for the remaining five probabilities are provided in Table 3. We further computed some statistics per probability

Table 2. Ranges, means $\bar{x}$ and standard deviations s of the assessments for the probability p_1 per country; assessments and means in bold lie in the modal interval $[0.7, 0.8)$

Country	n	Assessments	Range	$\bar{x}$ (s)
$\mathcal{A}$	5	0.60 **0.75 0.75 0.75** 0.80	[0.60, 0.80]	**0.73** (0.08)
$\mathcal{B}$	6	0.30 0.40 0.50 **0.71 0.75** 0.85	[0.30, 0.85]	0.59 (0.22)
$\mathcal{C}$	5	0.15 0.15 0.20 0.25 0.30	[0.15, 0.30]	0.21 (0.07)
$\mathcal{D}$	5	0.40 0.50 **0.75** 0.90 0.95	[0.40, 0.95]	**0.70** (0.24)
$\mathcal{E}$	3	**0.70 0.75 0.79**	[0.70, 0.79]	**0.75** (0.05)
$\mathcal{F}$	7	0.15 0.34 0.50 0.64 **0.75 0.75 0.79**	[0.15, 0.79]	0.56 (0.24)
All means			[0.21, 0.75]	0.59 (0.20)

Table 3. Means $\bar{x}$ and standard deviations s of the assessments for the probabilities $p_2, \ldots, p_6$ per country; means in bold lie within the relevant modal interval

Country	p_2 n	$\bar{x}$ (s)	p_3 n	$\bar{x}$ (s)	p_4 n	$\bar{x}$ (s)	p_5 n	$\bar{x}$ (s)	p_6 n	$\bar{x}$ (s)
$\mathcal{A}$	5	**0.80** (0.08)	5	**0.70** (0.09)	5	**0.81** (0.08)	5	0.58 (0.22)	5	**0.15** (0.06)
$\mathcal{B}$	6	0.77 (0.18)	6	0.58 (0.21)	6	**0.82** (0.11)	7	**0.78** (0.20)	6	0.47 (0.28)
$\mathcal{C}$	6	0.27 (0.31)	5	0.24 (0.08)	6	0.43 (0.25)	6	0.68 (0.19)	5	**0.13** (0.06)
$\mathcal{D}$	5	0.70 (0.22)	4	0.46 (0.30)	4	0.78 (0.21)	3	0.82 (0.06)	3	0.50 (0.35)
$\mathcal{E}$	3	0.78 (0.08)	3	**0.74** (0.06)	2	**0.82** (0.04)	3	0.83 (0.20)	4	0.46 (0.38)
$\mathcal{F}$	7	0.75 (0.15)	7	0.65 (0.17)	7	0.75 (0.15)	7	**0.78** (0.05)	7	**0.19** (0.06)
All means	6	0.68 (0.21)	6	0.56 (0.19)	6	0.73 (0.15)	6	**0.75** (0.10)	6	0.32 (0.18)

over all countries, which are summarised in Table 4. Note that the overall mean per probability may differ from the mean of the country means as a result of unequal sizes of the groups of assessors per country.

To conclude, we tested the null hypothesis of equal country means for each probability under study. For this purpose, we performed an analysis of variance using a significance level of 0.05. For all probabilities except p_5, the null hypothesis of equal means across countries was rejected. For the probabilities $p_1, \ldots, p_4$ and p_6, we further performed post-hoc testing of pairwise equality under the assumption of equal variances. Post-hoc testing for p_6 did not reveal any significant pairwise differences of the means per country. For the probabilities $p_1, \ldots, p_4$, however, post-hoc testing showed significant pairwise differences involving country $\mathcal{C}$. More specifically, for the probability p_1, $\mathcal{C}$'s country mean was found to differ from the country means of both country $\mathcal{A}$ and country $\mathcal{E}$. For the probability p_2, $\mathcal{C}$'s country mean differed from the country means of each of the other countries. $\mathcal{C}$'s country mean for p_3 differed from those of countries $\mathcal{A}$, $\mathcal{E}$ and $\mathcal{F}$. For probability p_4, to conclude, $\mathcal{C}$'s country mean was different from the country means of both $\mathcal{A}$ and $\mathcal{B}$. No further significant differences were found.

4.2   Discussion

The results of the numerical analyses per probability show very little consensus in the assessments obtained per country and across countries. Since the elicitation efforts in the six countries were not conducted in a controlled laboratory setting, numerous factors may have influenced the assessments, ranging from the way the task was introduced to the atmosphere in the group. Among these factors, a likely explanation for the large differences in numerical assessments obtained is found in the varying levels and expertise of the assessors, even within the focused area of Classical Swine Fever: it is well known from the theory of naive probability [3], that probability estimates are influenced by the assessor's experience. An interesting finding in this respect is that in some countries the assessments for the first probability p_1 were rather close to one another, while in other countries larger ranges were found; this closeness of assessments may point to similarities in background and experience, yet may also be explained from a

Table 4. Ranges, modal intervals *mod* with frequencies # and means $\bar{x}$ with standard deviations s of all assessments per probability; means in bold lie in the modal interval

	n	*range*	*mod* (#)	$\bar{x}$ (s)
p_1	31	[0.15, 0.95]	[0.7, 0.8) (12)	0.58 (0.25)
p_2	32	[0.10, 1.00]	[0.8, 0.9) (10)	0.67 (0.27)
p_3	30	[0.15, 0.85]	[0.7, 0.8) (8)	0.56 (0.23)
p_4	30	[0.20, 1.00]	[0.8, 0.9) (10)	0.72 (0.21)
p_5	31	[0.26, 1.00]	[0.7, 0.8) (12)	**0.74** (0.18)
p_6	30	[0.05, 0.96]	[0.1, 0.2) (14)	0.30 (0.25)

bias introduced by someone remarking out loud that some scenario, for example, is quite likely. Another explanation for the observed differences lies in the commonly used *anchoring-and-adjustment* heuristic: using this heuristic, people choose a relevant known probability as an anchor to tie their assessment to by adjustment. From cognitive-science studies, it is well known that even for self-generated anchors, the adjustments made are typically insufficient [4,5]. Since our assessors generated the first assessment in each series by consulting their memory, variations in these first assessments inevitably caused variations in the subsequent related assessments by the anchoring-and-adjustment heuristic.

While the above observations can explain the variation among assessors, they do not explain the observed differences between countries. Remarkable differences were found, for example, for the means for each of the probabilities $p_1, \ldots, p_4$ from country C, compared to the means from the other countries. A possible explanation is that the experts from country C found the four probabilities very hard to assess, because these were conditioned on the presence of a CSF infection and, as they stated, "CSF doesn't exist in our country". Another possible explanation, supported by the sound recording of the elicitation, is that the experts actually assessed the complements of the requested probabilities: during the meeting a moderator had translated the fragments of text into the experts' mother tongue and we got strong indications from an independent native speaker who afterwards listened to the recording, that the translations were not always to the point. A third, less likely, explanation is that the experts from country C showed other biases than the assessors from the other countries.

Differences were also found between the assessments provided by our Dutch expert and the assessments obtained from the experts from the other countries: the Dutch assessments all lie in lower-ordered intervals than the modal intervals found in the other countries. A likely explanation for this finding may be that our expert provided his assessments from an entirely different background: the Dutch expert had been closely involved in the construction of the network for more than two years and had provided all probabilities required for its quantification, while the other assessors did not have intimate knowledge of the network and were confronted with a few probabilities in a single day's meeting. Moreover, as a result of the one-on-one elicitation sessions with our Dutch expert, any questions regarding a requested probability could be answered on the spot and obvious errors or inconsistencies could thus be prevented. In addition, our expert was explicitly trained in treating any variable not mentioned in a requested probability, as an unknown. Although this issue was elaborated upon in the plenary instruction for the other experts, it is not unlikely that probabilities were assessed in the context of a default value for unmentioned variables.

To conclude we would like to mention that without tailored experimentation in a more controlled elicitation setting, no definite conclusions can be drawn about the origins of the observed differences in the probability assessments.

5 Taking a Qualitative Perspective: Stochastic Dominance

In the previous section, we reviewed numerical properties of the probability assessments obtained from the veterinary experts in the six visited countries. From our investigations, we concluded that the assessments showed little consensus. We now address the qualitative properties embedded in the series of assessments.

5.1 The Data Obtained, the Analyses and the Results

For our qualitative analysis, we had available the same 58 series of numerical assessments from which we established standard statistics in the previous section. In addition to these numerical series, we had also available 10 complete sets of verbal assessments, that is, assessments composed of encircled verbal anchors from the probability scale. We observe that while we could not use these assessments in our quantitative analysis, the stability of the rank order of the verbal anchors does allow studying their qualitative properties [2].

For the qualitative analysis, we observe that although the six probabilities under study are probabilistically independent, they are not so from a domain point of view. Based upon common knowledge, for example, we can state that a pig with a mucositis in the upper respiratory tract is more likely to snivel than a pig without a mucositis. The statement essentially expresses that more severe clinical signs are more likely given more severe values on a disease scale. Properties stating that one conditional probability distribution is ranked as superior to another, are called properties of dominance [6]. In this section, we investigate the dominance properties embedded in the series of assessments obtained.

For studying dominance properties, a total ordering of the conditioning contexts in the series of probabilities under study is required. For the probabilities $p_1, \ldots, p_4$ therefore a total ordering of the other primary infections is needed; based upon domain knowledge, we decided to use the ordering 'no-other' < 'intest' < 'resp' < 'resp+intest'. For the probabilities p_5 and p_6, we chose 'no-muco' < 'muco' for the conditioning contexts. In addition, a total ordering of the probabilities themselves is required. For the numerical assessments, the standard numerical ordering is used. For the verbal assessments, we took the ordering on the verbal anchors from the probability scale, that is, we assumed 'impossible' < 'improbable' < ... < 'probable' < 'certain'. Based upon common knowledge, we should now find the following dominance properties in the series of assessments:

- $p_1 \leq p_3 \leq p_2 \leq p_4$;
- $p_6 \leq p_5$.

We note that the assessments from our Dutch expert exhibit these properties.

For the probabilities $p_1, \ldots, p_4$, the assessments of 18 of the 29 experts (62%) who gave a complete numerical series, were found to obey the expected dominance property. In seven series, a violation was caused by the assessment for the probability p_1 being too high compared to that for either p_2, p_3 or p_4; in the four remaining violating series, the assessment for the probability p_4 was too low compared to that for p_2. The assessments of three of the five experts (60%) who gave a complete set of verbal assessments for $p_1, \ldots, p_4$, also obeyed the expected dominance property. For the probabilities p_5 and p_6, we found that the assessments of 28 of the 29 experts (97%) who gave a complete numerical series, exhibited the expected property of dominance. The only violation was caused by the assessments $p_5 = 0.40$ and $p_6 = 0.50$, given by an expert from country B. The assessments of all five experts (100%) who gave a complete set of verbal assessments for p_5 and p_6, embedded the expected dominance property.

5.2   Discussion

The results of our qualitative analysis show that the dominance properties embedded in the obtained series of assessments are far more consistent among the individual experts and across countries, than the statistics studied in Sect. 4. For the probabilities $p_1, \ldots, p_4$ for example, a relatively large number of experts (62%) matched the expected property of dominance by providing assessments with $p_1 \leq p_3 \leq p_2 \leq p_4$. This finding is of interest since the probabilities were presented to the experts for assessment in a different order: the assessors thus did not simply provide increasingly higher, or lower, values. Assuming that they employed an anchoring-and-adjustment heuristic, this finding means that after providing an assessment for p_1, an assessor adjusted towards a higher value for p_2; for the probability p_3, he subsequently adjusted to a lower value, yet not below his earlier assessment for p_1; for the final probability in the series, again an adjustment towards a higher value was performed, to beyond the assessment for p_2. Also of interest is the finding that six violations of the property of dominance among the probabilities $p_1, \ldots, p_4$ were caused not by an adjustment in the wrong direction but by a wrong amount. More specifically, after having provided an assessment for p_2, the adjustment to a lower value for p_3 was too large, with p_3 ending up smaller than p_1; alternatively, after having provided an assessment for p_3, the adjustment to a higher value for p_4 was not large enough, with p_4 ending up smaller than p_2. For the probabilities p_5 and p_6, the direction of adjustment was (presumably) incorrect for a single pair of assessments.

6   Conclusions

As part of engineering a Bayesian network for the early detection of Classical Swine Fever in pigs, we elicited a limited number of conditional probabilities from

38 pig experts and veterinary practitioners from six European countries outside the Netherlands. The goal of the elicitation was to gain insight in the extent to which our Dutch expert-based network reflected the practices and insights of veterinary experts across Europe. All in all, we obtained 58 series of probability assessments, pertaining to two groups of related conditional probabilities. In this paper, we investigated summary statistics over the separate assessments and studied properties of stochastic dominance embedded in the assessment series. While the statistics showed only limited consensus, the dominance properties proved to be far more consistent among assessors and across countries. This finding suggests that at least the properties of stochastic dominance captured in our network have sufficient support in other European countries.

To our best knowledge, anchoring and adjusting has not been studied in tasks where a series of more than two related probabilities is assessed. It is unknown therefore, whether people would typically use the first anchor for all subsequent assessments, or tie each assessment to the previous one. Insights in the strategies which are commonly used by assessors can come only from carefully controlled experiments. Based upon our experiences and pending experimental evidence, we propose that assessors first establish a stable ordering on a series of related probabilities; the probabilities subsequently are presented in the ordering agreed upon. By thus prefixing the ordering of the probabilities, order violations ensuing from incorrect amounts of adjustment are forestalled. If at all possible, moreover, the assessors had best be provided with at least one reliable anchor, for example based upon literature or estimated from a rich enough data collection. Variation in individual assessments from multiple experts nonetheless is bound to occur because of differences in background and experience.

Acknowledgement. We would like to thank the Classical Swine Fever experts participating in the EPIZONE project meetings for their willingness to partake in the probability assessment task.

References

1. van der Gaag, L.C., Renooij, S., Witteman, C.L.M., Aleman, B., Taal, B.G.: How to elicit many probabilities. In: Laskey, K.B., Prade, H. (eds.) Proceedings of the Fifteenth Conference on Uncertainty in Artificial Intelligence, pp. 647–654. Morgan Kaufmann Publishers, San Francisco (1999)
2. Renooij, S., Witteman, C.L.M.: Talking probabilities: communicating probabilistic information with words and numbers. International Journal of Approximate Reasoning 22, 169–194 (1999)
3. Johnson-Laird, P.N., Legrenzi, P., Girotto, V., Legrenzi, M.S., Caverni, J.-P.: Naive probability: A mental model theory of extensional reasoning. Psychological Review 106, 62–88 (1999)
4. Epley, N.: A tale of Tuned Decks? Anchoring as accessibility and anchoring as adjustment. In: Koehler, D.J., Harvey, N. (eds.) The Blackwell Handbook of Judgment and Decision Making, pp. 240–256. Blackwell Publisher, Oxford (2004)
5. Jacowitz, K.E., Kahneman, D.: Measures of anchoring in estimation tasks. Personality and Social Psychology Bulletin 21, 1161–1166 (1995)
6. Levy, H.: Stochastic Dominance. Investment Decision Making under Uncertainty. Studies in Risk and Uncertainty, vol. 12. Springer, New York (2006)

Discretisation Effects
in Naive Bayesian Networks

Roel Bertens, Linda C. van der Gaag, and Silja Renooij

Department of Information and Computing Sciences, Utrecht University
P.O. Box 80.089, 3508 TB, The Netherlands
{R.Bertens,L.C.vanderGaag,S.Renooij}@uu.nl

Abstract. Naive Bayesian networks are often used for classification problems that involve variables of a continuous nature. Upon capturing such variables, their value ranges are modelled as finite sets of discrete values. While the output probabilities and conclusions established from a Bayesian network are dependent of the actual discretisations used for its variables, the effects of choosing alternative discretisations are largely unknown as yet. In this paper, we study the effects of changing discretisations on the probability distributions computed from a naive Bayesian network. We demonstrate how recent insights from the research area of sensitivity analysis can be exploited for this purpose.

1 Introduction

Naive Bayesian networks are being used for a large range of classification problems. These networks in essence are probabilistic graphical models of restricted topology, describing a joint probability distribution over a set of stochastic variables. Efficient algorithms are available for computing any prior or posterior probability of interest over the variables of a network, and over its main output variable more specifically. Most of these algorithms assume all variables to be discrete. A classification problem under study however, may involve variables which are of a continuous nature. For capturing such variables, their value ranges should be modelled as finite sets of discrete values. Several different methods are available for automated discretisation of continuous-valued variables in general; for an overview of such methods, we refer to [1]. For Bayesian-network modelling, these general methods unfortunately tend to yield unsatisfactory results [2]. Yet, while the output probabilities established from a Bayesian network are dependent of the actual ways in which its variables are discretised [3], the effects of choosing alternative discretisations are largely unknown.

In this paper, we study the effects of changing the discretisations of continuous-valued feature variables on the posterior probability distributions computed from a naive Bayesian network. We note that discretising a continuous variable amounts to setting one or more threshold values to split its value range into intervals. Choosing an alternative discretisation thus amounts to changing one or more of these threshold values. From the conditional probability table for the variable at hand it is now readily seen that changing even a single threshold

S. Greco et al. (Eds.): IPMU 2012, Part III, CCIS 299, pp. 161–170, 2012.

value will result in changes in the values of many of the parameter probabilities involved. These parameter values do not change independently: their changes are functionally related through the change in threshold value. We will demonstrate how this functional dependency allows exploiting recent insights from the research area of sensitivity analysis of Bayesian networks in general [4], to efficiently study the effects of changing discretisations. Throughout the paper, we will illustrate our findings using real-world breast-cancer screening data.

The paper is organised as follows. In Sect. 2, we introduce our notations and briefly review sensitivity analysis of Bayesian networks in general. In Sect. 3, we establish functions that describe the effects of changing the discretisation of a feature variable on the probability distributions computed from a naive Bayesian network. The paper ends with our concluding observations in Sect. 4.

2   Preliminaries

We introduce our notational conventions and review recent insights from the field of sensitivity analysis of Bayesian networks in general.

2.1   Naive Bayesian Networks

We consider joint probability distributions $\Pr(\mathbf{V})$ over sets $\mathbf{V}$ of discrete stochastic variables. For our notations, we will use (possibly indexed) upper-case letters V to denote single variables, and bold-faced upper-case letters $\mathbf{V}$ to indicate sets of variables. The possible values of a variable V are denoted by (indexed or primed) small letters v_i; we will write v and $\bar{v}$ more specifically, for the two values of a binary variable V. Bold-faced small letters $\mathbf{v}$ are used to denote joint value combinations for the variables from a set $\mathbf{V}$.

A Bayesian network in general is a probabilistic graphical model describing a joint probability distribution $\Pr(\mathbf{V})$ over the set of variables $\mathbf{V}$. The variables from $\mathbf{V}$ are modelled as nodes in a directed acyclic graph, and the (in)dependency relation among them is captured by arcs. Associated with each variable V in the graph are parameter probabilities $p(V \mid \pi(V))$ from the distribution Pr which jointly describe the influence of the possible values of the parents $\pi(V)$ of V on the probabilities over V itself; these parameter probabilities constitute the conditional probability table of the variable V. A naive Bayesian network now is a Bayesian network of highly restricted topology, consisting of a single class variable C and one or more feature variables E_i. In its graphical structure, all feature variables are connected directly with the class variable, and are unconnected otherwise; the feature variables are thereby modelled as mutually independent given the class variable. Naive Bayesian networks are commonly used for computing posterior probability distributions $\Pr(C \mid \mathbf{e})$ over the possible values of the class variable, given a joint value combination $\mathbf{e}$ for the set $\mathbf{E}$ of feature variables.

2.2   Sensitivity Analysis

Sensitivity analysis is a general technique for studying the effects of parameter variation on the output of a mathematical model. For Bayesian networks more specifically, sensitivity analysis amounts to investigating the effects of varying the values of one or more parameter probabilities on an output probability of interest; to this end, tailored algorithms have been developed [5,6].

In a one-way sensitivity analysis of a Bayesian network, a single parameter probability p is being varied as x and the other parameter probabilities p' from the same conditional probability distribution are co-varied as $\frac{(1-x)}{(1-p)} \cdot p'$. The effects of this variation are described by a mathematical function $f(x)$ which expresses the output probability of interest in terms of the parameter under study. For a marginal probability of interest, this sensitivity function $f(x)$ is linear in the parameter being varied. For a conditional probability of interest, the effects of parameter variation are described by a fraction of two linear functions. The function $f(x)$ then essentially is a fragment of one of the branches of a rectangular hyperbola [5]. Since both the parameter under study and the probability of interest are restricted to values from $[0, 1]$, the range of points is effectively constrained to just a fragment of the hyperbola; the two-dimensional space of feasible points in general is termed the unit window.

In the sequel, we will use higher-order sensitivity analyses in which multiple parameter probabilities are being varied simultaneously. In general, in an n-way sensitivity analysis in which n parameters are being varied, a marginal probability of interest is described by a multi-linear function in these parameters. For a conditional probability of interest, the sensitivity function again is a fraction of two such functions. For example, a two-way sensitivity function that expresses a posterior probability of interest $\Pr(c \mid e)$ in terms of two parameter probabilities which are being varied as x and y, has the following form:

$$f_{\Pr(c|e)}(x, y) = \frac{f_{\Pr(c, e)}(x, y)}{f_{\Pr(e)}(x, y)} = \frac{a_1 \cdot x \cdot y + a_2 \cdot x + a_3 \cdot y + a_4}{b_1 \cdot x \cdot y + b_2 \cdot x + b_3 \cdot y + b_4}$$

where the constants $a_i, b_i, i = 1, \ldots, 4$, are built from the non-varied parameters of the network under study. The two parameter probabilities and the output probability of interest again are restricted to the $[0, 1]$-range, which defines a three-dimensional space of feasible points called the unit cube.

3   Studying the Effects of Discretisation

The basic formalism of naive Bayesian networks requires all included variables to be discrete. Upon modelling domain knowledge, variables which take their value from an intrinsically continuous value range will therefore have to be discretised. Such a discretisation amounts to splitting the variable's value range into two or more disjoint intervals and associating each such interval with a value of a (newly defined) discrete variable. In Sect. 3.1, we will study binary discretisations in view of a binary class variable; in Sect. 3.2, we extend our results to naive Bayesian networks including non-binary variables in general.

3.1   Binary Discretisation in Two-Class Naive Bayesian Networks

We consider a continuous feature variable E and address its binary discretisation, that is, we assume that the value range of E is split into two intervals by means of a threshold value t. Slightly abusing notation, we will write $E < t$ and $E \geq t$ for the two values of the (now discretised) variable E, and use e' to indicate either of these values. Upon including the discretised variable E as a feature variable in a naive Bayesian network with the binary class variable C, a conditional probability table is constructed for E with the parameter probabilities $p(E < t \mid c)$ and $p(E \geq t \mid c)$, and the probabilities $p(E < t \mid \bar{c})$ and $p(E \geq t \mid \bar{c})$. It is now readily seen that changing the discretisation of E by choosing a different threshold value t, will affect *all* parameters from this table. Since these parameter probabilities do not stem all from the same conditional distribution, we must conclude that we cannot study the effects of changing E's discretisation by conducting a one-way sensitivity analysis. It is not necessary however, to use a full four-way sensitivity analysis in all parameters involved either. We observe that by varying the parameter probability $p(E < t \mid c)$, the variation of $p(E \geq t \mid c)$ is covered by standard co-variation; similarly, variation of $p(E \geq t \mid \bar{c})$ is handled by varying $p(E < t \mid \bar{c})$. A two-way sensitivity analysis thus should suffice for studying the effects of changing the discretisation of E on the output probabilities computed from a naive Bayesian network.

In Sect. 2, we reviewed the general form of a two-way sensitivity function expressing an output probability $\Pr(c \mid \mathbf{e})$ computed from a Bayesian network in terms of two parameter probabilities being varied as x and y:

$$f_{\Pr(c|\mathbf{e})}(x,y) = \frac{f_{\Pr(c,\,\mathbf{e})}(x,y)}{f_{\Pr(\mathbf{e})}(x,y)} = \frac{a_1 \cdot x \cdot y + a_2 \cdot x + a_3 \cdot y + a_4}{b_1 \cdot x \cdot y + b_2 \cdot x + b_3 \cdot y + b_4}$$

For studying the effects of changing the discretisation of our feature variable E, the two parameter probabilities to be varied are $p(E < t \mid c)$ and $p(E < t \mid \bar{c})$ (or their complements). We note that these parameter probabilities stem from different conditional distributions, that is, they are conditioned on different values of the class variable. As a consequence, the two parameters have no interaction effects and the constants a_1 and b_1 are equal to zero. The independency properties of a naive Bayesian network even further constrain the general form of the function, as is shown in the following proposition.

Proposition 1. *Let C be the binary class variable of a naive Bayesian network which further includes the set $\mathbf{E}$ of feature variables. Let $\Pr(c \mid \mathbf{e})$ be the network's probability of interest, for a joint combination of observed values $\mathbf{e}$ for $\mathbf{E}$. Now, let $x = p(e' \mid c)$ and $y = p(e' \mid \bar{c})$ be the parameter probabilities for the observed value e' of the binary feature variable E. Then, the two-way sensitivity function expressing $\Pr(c \mid \mathbf{e})$ in x and y is of the form*

$$f_{\Pr(c|\mathbf{e})}(x,y) = \frac{a \cdot \Pr(c) \cdot x}{a \cdot \Pr(c) \cdot x + a' \cdot \Pr(\bar{c}) \cdot y}$$

where a and a' are constants.

Proof. Using Bayes' theorem and exploiting the independency properties of a naive Bayesian network, we find for our probability of interest $\Pr(c \mid \mathbf{e})$ that

$$\Pr(c \mid \mathbf{e}) = \frac{\Pr(\mathbf{e} \mid c) \cdot \Pr(c)}{\Pr(\mathbf{e} \mid c) \cdot \Pr(c) + \Pr(\mathbf{e} \mid \bar{c}) \cdot \Pr(\bar{c})}$$

$$= \frac{\prod_{e'_k \in \mathbf{e}} \Pr(e'_k \mid c) \cdot \Pr(c)}{\prod_{e'_k \in \mathbf{e}} \Pr(e'_k \mid c) \cdot \Pr(c) + \prod_{e'_k \in \mathbf{e}} \Pr(e'_k \mid \bar{c}) \cdot \Pr(\bar{c})}$$

The result follows with $a = \prod_{e'_k \in \mathbf{e} \setminus e'} \Pr(e'_k \mid c)$ and $a' = \prod_{e'_k \in \mathbf{e} \setminus e'} \Pr(e'_k \mid \bar{c})$. $\square$

We note that the constants a and a' in the sensitivity function stated above are readily computed from the parameter probabilities of the feature variables in the naive Bayesian network; the two-way sensitivity function can in fact be established without the need of any propagation, as a result of the conditional independencies holding among the feature variables. We further note that if the probability of interest pertains to the value c of the class variable C, then the numerator of the sensitivity function does not include the parameter probability being varied as y; similarly, for a probability of interest involving $\bar{c}$, the numerator does not include x. We observe that if the value e' specified in the parameters x and y for E differs from the actually observed value, then both the numerator and the denominator of the sensitivity function include an additional constant. Alternatively, we can choose the complements of x and y as the parameters to be varied, which will again result in a function of the above form. We illustrate the form of the two-way sensitivity function derived above by means of a simple naive Bayesian network for classifying mammographic images.

Example 1. To distinguish between benign and malignant mass lesions, a simple naive Bayesian network was constructed from breast-cancer screening data from the UCI Data Repository [7]. The available data involved several discrete variables modelling properties of the mass lesions seen in mammographic images, and a continuous variable describing the age of a patient. The naive Bayesian network was constructed with the class variable *Severity*, with the values *benign* and *malignant*; the continuous variable *Age* and the five-valued variable *Shape* were selected for its feature variables. We now suppose that we are interested in the output probability $\Pr(Severity = benign \mid Age < t, Shape = 4)$ for the class variable. In our analysis, we further focus on the effects of varying the two parameter probabilities $x = p(Age < t \mid Severity = benign)$ and $y = p(Age < t \mid Severity = malignant)$ associated with the feature variable *Age*.

To establish the two-way sensitivity function which describes our output probability of interest in terms of the two parameter probabilities being varied, we need to determine the prior probability of a mass lesion being benign and the conditional probabilities of a shape-4 mass for benign lesions and for malignant lesions respectively. We computed these probabilities from the data collection after removal of the five cases for which no value for the variable *Age* was available. The prior probability of a benign lesion was found to be $\Pr(Severity = benign) =$

0.54. For the variable *Shape*, we found $p(Shape = 4 \mid Severity = benign) = 0.16$ and $p(Shape = 4 \mid Severity = malignant) = 0.71$. With these probabilities, we determined the two-way sensitivity function $f_{benign}(x, y)$ for the output probability of interest to be

$$f_{benign}(x, y) = \frac{0.54 \cdot 0.16 \cdot x}{0.54 \cdot 0.16 \cdot x + 0.46 \cdot 0.71 \cdot y}$$

Figure 1(a) shows the fragment of the function $f_{benign}(x, y)$ that lies within the unit cube; the function $f_{malignant}(x, y)$ describing the effects of varying the same parameter probabilities x and y on the complementary output probability $\Pr(Severity = malignant \mid Age < t, Shape = 4)$ is shown in Fig. 1(b). From Fig. 1(a), we can read for example that a relatively small probability $\Pr(Severity = benign \mid Age < t, Shape = 4)$ of a shape-4 mass lesion being benign in younger patients will be found for small values of the parameter x.   □

In Proposition 1, we stated the general form of a two-way sensitivity function which expresses an output probability computed from a two-class naive Bayesian network in terms of two parameter probabilities of a binary feature variable. This two-way function specifies a value for the output probability for each combination of values for the two parameters. We now recall that our aim is to use sensitivity analysis as a means for studying the effects of changing the binary discretisation of a continuous-valued feature variable. In view of such a discretisation, the two parameters under study are not unrelated, as is assumed in a two-way sensitivity analysis in general. We observe that since varying the threshold value t in a binary discretisation affects all parameter probabilities of its feature variable, the two parameters under study are dependent of t, and are in fact varied as $x(t)$ and $y(t)$. As a result of this dependency, their variation is related through a function $h(t) = (x(t), y(t))$. From the way in which discretisations are formalised, we have that this function $h(t)$ cannot be any arbitrary function. The following lemma in fact shows that the function is either monotonically non-decreasing or monotonically non-increasing in each of the dimensions of its co-domain.

Lemma 1. *Let C be a binary class variable, let E be a continuous-valued feature variable, and let t be a threshold value for binary discretisation of E. Let $x(t) = p(E < t \mid c)$ and $y(t) = p(E < t \mid \bar{c})$ be parameter probabilities of E, and let h be the function with $h(t) = (x(t), y(t))$. Then, h is monotonically non-decreasing in both dimensions of its co-domain.*

Proof. The property stated in the lemma derives from the interdependency of test characteristics in epidemiology [8], and is easily verified by observing that as the threshold t is shifted to larger values of the continuous variable E, then the probability $p(E < t \mid C)$ cannot decrease, regardless of the value of C.   □

From the lemma, we have that the function $h(t)$ is monotonically non-decreasing in any output dimension pertaining to the value $E < t$ of the feature variable E; it is monotonically non-increasing in a dimension pertaining to $E \geq t$.

For studying the overall effect of changing a binary discretisation, we must now explicitly take the induced relation between the two parameter probabilities

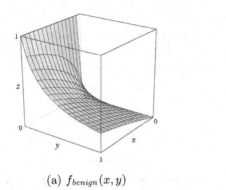
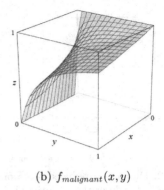

(a) $f_{benign}(x,y)$ (b) $f_{malignant}(x,y)$

Fig. 1. Two-way sensitivity functions for the class variable *Severity* given *Age* < *t* and *Shape* = 4, with the parameters $x = p(Age < t \mid Severity = benign)$ and $y = p(Age < t \mid Severity = malignant)$, assuming independent variation

into account in the sensitivity function under study. Based upon considerations of practicability, we propose to approximate this relation by $y(t) = g(x(t))$ for some function g. Note that by doing so, the dimensionality of the sensitivity function is reduced and its ease of interpretation is enhanced. Studying the effects of changing a discretisation then requires the function

$$f_{\Pr(c|e)}(x(t), g(x(t))) = \frac{a_1 \cdot x(t) + a_2 \cdot g(x(t)) + a_3}{b_1 \cdot x(t) + b_2 \cdot g(x(t)) + b_3}$$

where the constants involved are again built from the non-varied parameters of the network under study. We note that this function is a function in a single parameter probability, but not a one-way sensitivity function; to simplify our notations, we will again omit the explicit dependency of the parameter probabilities $x(t)$ and $y(t)$ on t and write x and y for short. We note in addition that the function g that is chosen to approximate the induced relation between the parameter probabilities x and y cannot be arbitrarily shaped, but should preserve the monotonicity properties of its underlying function h; g is further defined by knowledge of the problem at hand, as is shown in the following example.

Example 2. We consider again, from Example 1, the problem of establishing the severity of mass lesions from mammographic images. From the available data, we approximated the true relation between the parameter probabilities $x = p(Age < t \mid Severity = benign)$ and $y = p(Age < t \mid Severity = malignant)$ by a linear function: by means of linear regression of y on x, we constructed the function $y = 1.00 \cdot x - 0.21$; note that this function preserves the property of non-decreasing values of y for increasing values of x. We now recall that the surface $f_{benign}(x,y)$ from Fig. 1(a) described the probability of interest $\Pr(Severity = benign \mid Age < t, Shape = 4)$ in terms of the two parameters x and y under the assumption of independent variation. By intersecting this surface with the plane $y = 1.00 \cdot x - 0.21$, we therefore find the function that expresses the probability of interest in terms of x taking its actual, albeit approximated, variation effect

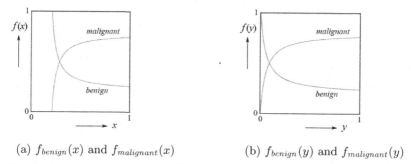

(a) $f_{benign}(x)$ and $f_{malignant}(x)$ (b) $f_{benign}(y)$ and $f_{malignant}(y)$

Fig. 2. Dimension-reduced functions for the class variable *Severity* given *Age* < *t* and *Shape* = 4, taking the variational dependency of x and y into account

with y into consideration. The intersection curve thus describes the sensitivity of the output probability to changes occasioned in x as a result of varying the discretisation threshold t. The function capturing the intersection curve is

$$f_{benign}(x) = \frac{0.09 \cdot x}{0.09 \cdot x + 0.33 \cdot (1.00 \cdot x - 0.21)}$$

Figure 2(a) displays this function, along with the function for the complement of the probability of interest. We observe that the depicted functions do not specify a value for the probability of interest for the smaller values of the parameter x. This finding originates from the approximated variational dependency of x and y: for small values of x, there are no matching values $g(x)$ for y within the feasible range $[0, 1]$. Note that the finding underlines our earlier observation that the depicted functions are no one-way sensitivity functions, but dimension-reduced two-way sensitivity functions instead. Figure 2(b) again shows the two intersection functions, this time from the perspective of the parameter y; the variational dependency of x and y was now approximated by linear regression of x on y, which resulted in $x = 0.90 \cdot y + 0.25$.   □

3.2   Discretisation in Naive Bayesian Networks in General

Thus far, we assumed the class variable of a naive Bayesian network to be binary and considered binary discretisations only. We will now argue that our results are readily generalised to naive Bayesian networks in general, that is, to naive Bayesian networks which include an n-ary class variable and in which the value range of a continuous variable is split into multiple disjoint intervals.

Non-binary Class Variables. We consider an n-ary class variable C with the possible values c_j, $j = 1, \ldots, n$, $n \geq 2$, and assume that we construct a binary discretisation for our continuous-valued feature variable E through a threshold value t as before. Changing the discretisation of E by choosing a different threshold value will again affect all parameter probabilities specified for E. These parameter probabilities now pertain to n different conditional probability distributions, that is, to n distributions over E conditioned on all possible class values.

To study the effects of changing E's discretisation therefore, we have to vary as x_j the parameter probabilities $p(E < t \mid c_j)$ for all $j = 1, \ldots, n$. The sensitivity function describing the effects of this variation on an output probability of interest thus is an n-way sensitivity function. Despite its higher dimensionality, this sensitivity function again is highly constrained by the independency properties of a naive Bayesian network. For an output probability $\Pr(c_k \mid \mathbf{e})$ for some value c_k, $1 \le k \le n$, of the class variable C, the sensitivity function in $x_1, \ldots, x_n$ more specifically has the following form:

$$f_{\Pr(c_k|\mathbf{e})}(x_1, \ldots, x_n) = \frac{a_k \cdot \Pr(c_k) \cdot x_k}{a_1 \cdot \Pr(c_1) \cdot x_1 + \ldots + a_n \cdot \Pr(c_n) \cdot x_n}$$

where a_j, $j = 1, \ldots, n$, again are constants; the proof and conditions of this property are analogous to those of Proposition 1. The sensitivity function stated above again assumes independent variation of its parameters $x_1, \ldots, x_n$, as with n-way analyses in general. As before however, these parameters are mutually related through a function $h(t) = (x_1(t), \ldots, x_n(t))$ which is either monotonically non-decreasing or monotonically non-increasing in each of the dimensions of its co-domain. To take the variational relation among the parameters into account, we propose again to approximate this relation by choosing a single focal parameter x_i and to functionally relate each other parameter x_j, $j = 1, \ldots, n, j \ne i$, to x_i by constructing a function g_j with $x_j = g_j(x_i)$ which preserves the monotonicity properties of the underlying function h. A dimension-reduced sensitivity function then results, showing the overall effects of changing a discretisation on a computed class probability.

Non-binary Discretisations. We address a continuous-valued feature variable E for which we construct an m-ary discretisation, that is, whose value range is split into $m \ge 3$ disjoint intervals; for ease of exposition, we assume the class variable again to be binary. We observe that constructing an m-ary discretisation amounts to setting threshold values t_j, $j = 1, \ldots, m - 1$, with $t_j < t_{j+1}$. For such a discretisation, we consider changing just a single threshold value t_k, $1 \le k \le m - 1$, keeping all other thresholds at their original values. We feel that changing multiple threshold values simultaneously would not just complicate the details of our analysis, but would also yield impractical results. Now, changing the threshold value t_k of the discretisation of our feature variable E will again affect its conditional probability table. Not all parameter probabilities will be influenced by the change, however: only the parameter probabilities $p(t_{k-1} \le E < t_k \mid C)$ and $p(t_k \le E < t_{k+1} \mid C)$ will be affected, for each possible value of the class variable. We recall that with binary discretisations we could handle the relation between the affected parameter probabilities from the same conditional distribution by standard co-variation, which allowed us to reduce the dimensionality of the sensitivity function. For m-ary discretisations, the commonly assumed co-variation scheme no longer applies, however: if the parameter probability $p(t_{k-1} \le E_i < t_k \mid c)$ is varied as x, then the parameter $p(t_k \le E_i < t_{k+1} \mid c)$ is varied as $1 - x - \sum_{j=1,\ldots,k-2,k+1,\ldots,m-2} p(t_j \le E_i < t_{j+1} \mid c)$ and all other parameters $p(t_j \le E_i < t_{j+1} \mid c)$, $j = 1, \ldots, m - 1$,

$j \neq k - 1, k$, from the same distribution are kept constant. It is readily seen however, that this scheme of variation will again result in a two-way sensitivity function of the form stated in Proposition 1. By taking the variational relation between the two parameter probabilities into account as before therefore, again a dimension-reduced sensitivity function results that allows studying the overall effects of the change in discretisation on a class probability of interest.

4 Conclusions and Further Research

Focusing on naive Bayesian networks, we studied the effects of changing the discretisation of a network's continuous feature variable on the posterior probabilities computed for its class variable. We showed that recent insights from sensitivity analysis of Bayesian networks in general serve to analytically describe these effects. We argued more specifically that changing the discretisation of a feature variable affects multiple parameter probabilities, and showed how the relation that is thus induced among these parameters can be explicitly taken into account for establishing a dimension-reduced sensitivity function that shows the overall effects of the change of discretisation on a class probability of interest. We currently are extending our results to Bayesian network classifiers in general and are studying changes in discretisation that induce a change of the most likely class value. We hope to be able to report our further insights in the discretisation effects in Bayesian network classifiers in the near future.

References

1. Dougherty, J., Kohavi, R., Sahami, M.: Supervised and unsupervised discretization of continuous features. In: Russel, S.J. (ed.) Proceedings of the 12th International Conference on Machine Learning, pp. 194–202. Morgan Kaufmann, CA (1995)
2. Uusitalo, L.: Advantages and challenges of Bayesian networks in environmental modelling. Ecological Modelling 203, 312–318 (2007)
3. Myllymäki, P., Silander, T., Tirri, H., Uronen, P.: B-Course: a web-based tool for Bayesian and causal data analysis. International Journal of Artificial Intelligence Tools 11, 369–387 (2002)
4. Coupé, V.M.H., van der Gaag, L.C.: Properties of sensitivity analysis of Bayesian belief networks. Annals of Mathematics and Artificial Intelligence 36, 323–356 (2002)
5. van der Gaag, L.C., Renooij, S., Coupé, V.M.H.: Sensitivity analysis of probabilistic networks. In: Lucas, P., Gámez, J., Salmerón, A. (eds.) Advances in Probabilistic Graphical Models. STUDFUZZ, vol. 214, pp. 103–124. Springer, NY (2007)
6. Kjærulff, U., van der Gaag, L.C.: Making sensitivity analysis computationally efficient. In: Boutilier, C., Goldszmidt, M. (eds.) Proceedings of the 16th Conference on Uncertainty in Artificial Intelligence, pp. 317–325. Morgan Kaufmann, CA (2000)
7. http://archive.ics.uci.edu/ml/datasets/Mammographic+Mass
8. Dawson-Saunders, B., Trapp, R.G.: Basic & Clinical Biostatistics. McGraw-Hill, NY (2001)

Fuzzy Concept Lattices with Incomplete Knowledge

Michal Krupka* and Jan Laštovička

Department of Computer Science
Palacký University in Olomouc
17. listopadu 12, CZ-77146 Olomouc
Czech Republic
{michal.krupka,jan.lastovicka}@upol.cz

Abstract. We study the problem of incomplete data in Formal Concept Analysis in fuzzy setting, namely the problem of constructing a concept lattice of incomplete data. We develop a simple general framework for dealing with unknown values in fuzzy logic, define incomplete fuzzy formal contexts, and present a method of constructing concept lattices of such contexts.

Keywords: Incomplete Data, Concept Lattice, Fuzzy Logic.

1 Introduction

Formal Concept Analysis (FCA) [16,8] is an exploratory method of analysis of binary tabular data. The method identifies some important clusters (formal concepts) in the data and organizes them into a structure called concept lattice. FCA has found various interesting applications in several areas (see [7] and the references therein). Formal Concept Analysis in fuzzy setting [2] allows the data to contain not only binary values, but values from the unit interval $[0, 1]$, or, more generally, from arbitrary residuated lattice. The values are interpreted, as usual in fuzzy logic, as degrees to which some information is true.

Incomplete data in FCA has been studied by several authors [6,11,12,14], who focused namely on attribute implications in incomplete data. The problem of finding a concept lattice of incomplete data has not been studied up to now. In [13], we offer first results in this area for classical (crisp) FCA. The present paper contains a generalization of the results from [13] to the fuzzy setting from [1,2].

In this paper, we develop a method of constructing a fuzzy concept lattice of incomplete data. Our main motivation is that the user might be interested in studying the structure of data even in situations when the data are not complete. As it turns out, the concept lattice can be constructed and its size is usually reasonable small (in situations when there is not a large amount of incompleteness

---

* The first author acknowledges the support by project reg. no. CZ.1.07/2.3.00/ 20.0059 of the European Social Fund in the Czech Republic.

S. Greco et al. (Eds.): IPMU 2012, Part III, CCIS 299, pp. 171–180, 2012.

in the data). It also contains the information on all concept lattices which can be obtained by possible completions of the data.

The organization of the paper is as follows. Section 2 contains basic definitions from residuated lattices, fuzzy sets, and fuzzy FCA used in the paper. In Sec. 3 we develop a simple general framework for working with unknown values in fuzzy logic. Section 4 contains our main results and in Sec. 5 we present an illustrative example.

Due to the limited space, we omit proofs.

2   Preliminaries

2.1   Residuated Lattices and Fuzzy Sets

We use complete residuated lattices as structures of truth values of fuzzy logic. We recall basic definitions here, see [2] for details.

A *complete residuated lattice* [2] is an algebra $\langle L, \wedge, \vee, \otimes, \rightarrow, 0, 1 \rangle$, where $\langle L, \wedge, \vee, 0, 1 \rangle$ is a complete lattice with the least element 0 and the greatest element 1; $\langle L, \otimes, 1 \rangle$ is a commutative monoid (i.e., $\otimes$ is commutative, associative, and $a \otimes 1 = 1 \otimes a = a$ for each $a \in L$); $\otimes$ *(product)* and $\rightarrow$ *(residuum)* satisfy the so-called *adjointness property*: $a \otimes b \leq c$ iff $a \leq b \rightarrow c$ for each $a, b, c \in L$ (the order $\leq$ on L is defined as usual by $a \leq b$ iff $a \wedge b = a$).

Elements a of L are called *truth degrees*, $\otimes$ and $\rightarrow$ (truth functions of) "fuzzy conjunction" and "fuzzy implication".

A subset $L' \subseteq L$ is called a *complete residuated sublattice* of **L**, if it contains the elements 0 and 1 and is closed with respect to arbitrary products, residua, and (possibly infinite) infima and suprema. L' together with appropriate restrictions of the operations of **L** is a complete residuated lattice. A complete residuated sublattice $L' \subseteq \mathbf{L}$ is *generated* by a subset $P \subseteq L'$, if it is the smallest complete residuated sublattice of **L** (w.r.t. set inclusion) containing P.

The set L^V of all mappings from V to L with operations defined elementwise forms a complete residuated lattice denoted $\mathbf{L}^V$.

A homomorphism of complete residuated lattices $h : \mathbf{L} \rightarrow \mathbf{L}'$ is called *complete*, if it preserves arbitrary suprema and infima: $\bigvee_{j \in J} h(a_j) = h(\bigvee_{j \in J} a_j)$, $\bigwedge_{j \in J} h(a_j) = h(\bigwedge_{j \in J} a_j)$.

For $a, b \in L$ we set $\neg a = a \rightarrow 0$ and $a \leftrightarrow b = (a \rightarrow b) \wedge (b \rightarrow a)$. The operations $\neg$ and $\leftrightarrow$ are called *negation* and *biresiduum*, respectively. For a non-negative integer n, the *n-th power of* $a \in L$ is defined inductively by $a^0 = 1$, $a^{n+1} = a \otimes a^n$.

Common examples of complete residuated lattices include those defined on the unit interval $[0, 1]$, (i.e. $L = [0, 1]$), $\wedge$ and $\vee$ being minimum and maximum, $\otimes$ being a left-continuous t-norm with the corresponding $\rightarrow$. The three most important pairs of adjoint operations on the unit interval are

$$\text{Łukasiewicz:} \quad \begin{aligned} a \otimes b &= \max(a + b - 1, 0), \\ a \rightarrow b &= \min(1 - a + b, 1), \end{aligned} \tag{1}$$

$$a \otimes b = \min(a, b),$$

Gödel:
$$a \to b = \begin{cases} 1 \text{ if } a \leq b, \\ b \text{ otherwise,} \end{cases} \tag{2}$$

$$a \otimes b = a \cdot b,$$

Goguen:
$$a \to b = \begin{cases} 1 \text{ if } a \leq b, \\ \frac{b}{a} \text{ otherwise.} \end{cases} \tag{3}$$

Complete residuated lattices on $[0, 1]$ given by (1), (2), and (3) are called *standard Łukasiewicz, Gödel, and Goguen (product) algebras*, respectively.

The Łukasiewicz operations can be restricted to any equidistant finite chain $L = \{0, \frac{1}{n}, \ldots, \frac{n-1}{n}, 1\}$, the Gödel operations can be restricted to any subset L of $[0, 1]$, containing 0 and 1. The residuated lattices obtained by these restrictions are called a *finite Łukasiewicz chain* and a *Gödel chain*, respectively.

A residuated lattice **L** is *simple*, if for each $a \in L$, $a < 1$, there exists an integer $n > 0$ such that $a^n = 0$. This property can be weakened for complete residuated lattices: **L** is *weakly simple* if for each $a \in L$, $a < 1$ it holds $\bigwedge_{n \in \{1,2,\ldots\}} a^n = 0$.

Standard Łukasiewicz algebra is simple, standard Goguen algebra is weakly simple. Standard Gödel algebra is not weakly simple.

A *truth stressing hedge* (or simply a *hedge*) [9,10] on a residuated lattice **L** is a unary operation $*$ satisfying (i) $1^* = 1$, (ii) $a^* \leq a$, (iii) $(a \to b)^* \leq a^* \to b^*$, (iv) $a^{**} = a^*$, for all $a, b \in L$. The condition (iii) has the following equivalent form: (iii)' $a^* \otimes b^* \leq (a \otimes b)^*$. A hedge $*$ is (a truth function of) the logical connective "very true" [10].

Among all hedges, the greatest one is given by $a^* = a$ and is called *identity*. The smallest hedge is called the *globalization* and is given by $1^* = 1$ and $a^* = 0$ for $a < 1$.

An element $a \in L$ is said to be a *fixpoint* of a hedge $*$, if $a^* = a$. The set of all fixpoints of $*$ is denoted by $*(L)$. We have the following simple characterization of $*(L)$.

Lemma 1. *A subset $H \subseteq \mathbf{L}$ is a set of all fixpoints of some hedge $*_H$ on $\mathbf{L}$, if and only if the following conditions are satisfied:*

1. $1 \in H$,
2. *H is closed w.r.t. $\otimes$,*
3. *H is closed w.r.t. arbitrary suprema.*

For each $a \in L$ it holds

$$a^{*_H} = \bigvee \{h \in H \mid h \leq a\}. \tag{4}$$

An **L**-*set* (or *fuzzy set*) A *in universe* X is a mapping $A\colon X \to L$, where values $A(x)$, $x \in X$, are interpreted as degrees to which x is an element of A. The set of all **L**-sets in universe X is denoted by L^X. A *binary* **L**-*relation between sets* X *and* Y is an **L**-set $I \in L^{X \times Y}$.

An **L**-set $A \in L^X$ is also denoted $\{^{A(x)}/x \mid x \in X\}$. If for all $x \in X$ distinct from $x_1, x_2, \ldots, x_n$ we have $A(x) = 0$, we also write $\{^{A(x_1)}/x_1, ^{A(x_2)}/x_1, \ldots, ^{A(x_n)}/x_n\}$. We usually write x instead of $^1/x$.

Mappings $h : L_1 \to L_2$ of two residuated lattices $\mathbf{L}_1$ and $\mathbf{L}_2$ can transform $\mathbf{L}_1$-sets to $\mathbf{L}_2$-sets: for an $\mathbf{L}_1$-set $A \in (L_1)^X$ the composition $h \circ A$ is an $\mathbf{L}_2$-set, $h \circ A \in (L_2)^X$.

2.2 Formal Concept Analysis in Fuzzy Setting

Formal Concept Analysis has been introduced by Wille [16] (see also [8]). The fuzzy version of FCA we use in this paper has been developed by Belohlavek [1], and, independently, by Pollandt [15]. Our standard reference is [2]. The extension to hedges is given in [4,3,5].

Let $\mathbf{L}$ be a complete residuated lattice. By a *formal* $\mathbf{L}$-*context* we understand a triple $\langle X, Y, I \rangle$, where X and Y are sets and I is an $\mathbf{L}$-relation between X and Y, $I : X \times Y \to L$. The sets X and Y are interpreted as a set of objects, resp. attributes, and for any $x \in X$, $y \in Y$ the value $I(x, y) \in L$ is interpreted as the degree to which the object x has the attribute y.

For any $\mathbf{L}$-set $A \in L^X$ of objects we define an $\mathbf{L}$-set $A^{\uparrow_I} \in L^Y$ of attributes by

$$A^{\uparrow_I}(y) = \bigwedge_{x \in X} A(x) \to I(x, y). \tag{5}$$

Similarly, for any $\mathbf{L}$-set $B \in L^Y$ of attributes we define an $\mathbf{L}$-set $B^{\downarrow_I}$ of objects by

$$B^{\downarrow_I}(x) = \bigwedge_{y \in Y} B(y) \to I(x, y). \tag{6}$$

The $\mathbf{L}$-set $A^{\uparrow_I}$ is interpreted as the $\mathbf{L}$-set of all attributes shared by objects from A. Similarly, the $\mathbf{L}$-set $B^{\downarrow_I}$ is interpreted as the $\mathbf{L}$-set of all objects having the attributes from B in common. If there is no danger of confusion, we write simply $^{\uparrow}$ and $^{\downarrow}$ instead of $^{\uparrow_I}$ and $^{\downarrow_I}$.

An $\mathbf{L}$-*formal concept* of a formal $\mathbf{L}$-context $\langle X, Y, I \rangle$ is a pair $\langle A, B \rangle \in L^X \times L^Y$ such that $A^{\uparrow} = B$ and $B^{\downarrow} = A$. A is called *the extent*, B *the intent* of $\langle A, B \rangle$. The set of all formal concepts of $\langle X, Y, I \rangle$ is denoted $\mathcal{B}(X, Y, I)$ and called the $\mathbf{L}$-*concept lattice of* $\langle X, Y, I \rangle$.

The condition

$$\langle A_1, B_1 \rangle \le \langle A_2, B_2 \rangle \quad \text{iff} \quad A_1 \subseteq A_2 \quad (\text{iff} \quad B_2 \subseteq B_1), \tag{7}$$

defines a partial ordering on $\mathcal{B}(X, Y, I)$. Together with this ordering, $\mathcal{B}(X, Y, I)$ is a complete lattice with infima and suprema given by

$$\bigwedge_{j \in J} \langle A_j, B_j \rangle = \left\langle \bigcap_{j \in J} A_j, \left(\bigcup_{j \in J} B_j \right)^{\downarrow\uparrow} \right\rangle, \tag{8}$$

$$\bigvee_{j \in J} \langle A_j, B_j \rangle = \left\langle \left(\bigcup_{j \in J} A_j \right)^{\uparrow\downarrow}, \bigcap_{j \in J} B_j \right\rangle, \tag{9}$$

and is called *the* $\mathbf{L}$-*concept lattice of* $\langle X, Y, I \rangle$.

The following is a generalization of the notion of **L**-concept lattices to **L**-concept lattices with hedges. Let $*_X$, $*_Y$ be two hedges on **L**. Set for each $A \in L^X$, $B \in L^Y$,

$$A^{\uparrow_I^{*_X}}(y) = \bigwedge_{x \in X} A(x)^{*_X} \to I(x,y), \quad B^{\downarrow_I^{*_Y}}(x) = \bigwedge_{y \in Y} B(y)^{*_Y} \to I(x,y), \quad (10)$$

and let

$$\mathcal{B}(X^{*_X}, Y^{*_Y}, I) = \{\langle A, B \rangle \in L^X \times L^Y \mid A^{\uparrow_I^{*_X}} = B, B^{\downarrow_I^{*_Y}} = A\}. \quad (11)$$

The set $\mathcal{B}(X^{*_X}, Y^{*_Y}, I)$ with a partial ordering, defined by (7), is again a complete lattice, and is called the **L**-*concept lattice of* $\langle X, Y, I \rangle$ *with hedges* $*_X$, $*_Y$.

If $*_X$ is the identity, then we denote $\mathcal{B}(X^{*_X}, Y^{*_Y}, I)$ by $\mathcal{B}(X, Y^{*_Y}, I)$. Each element of $\mathcal{B}(X, Y^{*_Y}, I)$ is also a formal concept of $\mathcal{B}(X, Y, I)$: $\mathcal{B}(X, Y^{*_Y}, I) \subseteq \mathcal{B}(X, Y, I)$. The main properties of $\mathcal{B}(X, Y^{*_Y}, I)$ are summarized in the following theorem.

Theorem 1. *(1) It holds* $\mathcal{B}(X, Y^{*_Y}, I) = \{\langle A, B \rangle \in \mathcal{B}(X, Y, I) \mid A = D^{\downarrow_I}$ *for some* $D \in (*_Y(L))^Y\}$.
(2) $\mathcal{B}(X, Y^{*_Y}, I)$ *is a* $\bigwedge$-*sublattice of* $\mathcal{B}(X, Y, I)$.

The main idea of adding hedges to fuzzy concept lattices is that it allows us affect the size of concept lattices. In many applications it is not necessary to work with all formal **L**-concepts from $\mathcal{B}(X, Y, I)$. The restriction to **L**-concepts from $\mathcal{B}(X, Y^{*_Y}, I)$ has the advantage that the lattice $\mathcal{B}(X, Y^{*_Y}, I)$ is much smaller than the whole concept lattice $\mathcal{B}(X, Y, I)$. We shall use this advantage later in the paper.

Below are some simple results on a correspondence between homomorphisms of residuated lattices and homomorphisms of concept lattices [2,13].

Lemma 2. *Let* $h: \mathbf{L} \to \mathbf{L}'$ *be a complete homomorphism of complete residuated lattices,* $\langle X, Y, I \rangle$ *a formal* **L**-*context. Then for each* $A \in \mathbf{L}^X$ *and* $B \in \mathbf{L}^Y$ *it holds*

$$(h \circ A)^{\uparrow_{h \circ I}} = h \circ A^{\uparrow_I}, \quad (h \circ B)^{\downarrow_{h \circ I}} = h \circ B^{\downarrow_I}. \quad (12)$$

Lemma 3. *Let* $h: \mathbf{L} \to \mathbf{L}'$ *be a complete homomorphism of complete residuated lattices,* $\langle X, Y, I \rangle$ *a formal* **L**-*context. Then for each formal concept* $\langle A, B \rangle \in \mathcal{B}(X, Y, I)$ *it holds* $\langle h \circ A, h \circ B \rangle \in \mathcal{B}(X, Y, h \circ I)$.

We denote the induced mapping $\mathcal{B}(X, Y, I) \to \mathcal{B}(X, Y, h \circ I)$ by $h^{\mathcal{B}(X,Y,I)}$.

Theorem 2. *Let* $h: \mathbf{L} \to \mathbf{L}'$ *be a complete homomorphism of complete residuated lattices,* $\langle X, Y, I \rangle$ *a formal* **L**-*context. Then the mapping* $h^{\mathcal{B}(X,Y,I)}$ *is a complete homomorphism. If* h *is injective, then so is* $h^{\mathcal{B}(X,Y,I)}$, *if* h *is surjective, then so is* $h^{\mathcal{B}(X,Y,I)}$.

Theorem 3. *Let* **L** *be isomorphic to the direct product* $\mathbf{L}_1 \times \mathbf{L}_2$, $p_1: L \to L_1$ *and* $p_2: L \to L_2$ *are the respective projections. Then* $\mathcal{B}(X, Y, I)$ *is isomorphic to the direct product* $\mathcal{B}(X, Y, p_1 \circ I) \times \mathcal{B}(X, Y, p_2 \circ I)$ *and the mappings* $p_1^{\mathcal{B}(X,Y,I)}$ *and* $p_2^{\mathcal{B}(X,Y,I)}$ *correspond to the respective Cartesian projections.*

3   Residuated Lattices with Variables

In this section, we develop a simple general framework for working with unknown values in fuzzy logic. Our assumptions are the following. We have a complete residuated lattice $\mathbf{L}$ which serves as a structure of truth values. In addition, we have a finite set $U = \{u_1, \ldots, u_n\}$, whose elements represent distinct unknown values from $\mathbf{L}$. Elements of U are called *variables*.

To enable the possibility of applying operations of a complete residuated lattice (i.e., arbitrary products, residua, and infinite infima and suprema) to truth degrees from $\mathbf{L}$ and variables, we assume another complete residuated lattice $\mathbf{K}$, together with a mapping $\iota_U : U \to \mathbf{K}$ and an injective complete homomorphism $\iota_{\mathbf{L}} : \mathbf{L} \to \mathbf{K}$. The mappings ι_U, resp. $\iota_{\mathbf{L}}$ are used to identify elements of U, resp. $\mathbf{L}$, with some elements of $\mathbf{K}$. For brevity, we often suppose that $U \subseteq \mathbf{K}$ and $\mathbf{L} \subseteq \mathbf{K}$, and ι_U and $\iota_{\mathbf{L}}$ are the respective canonical inclusions.

To make sure that each element of $\mathbf{K}$ can be computed from truth degrees from $\mathbf{L}$ and variables, we assume that $\mathbf{K}$ is generated by the set $\iota_U(U) \cup \iota_{\mathbf{L}}(L) \subseteq \mathbf{K}$.

Elements of $\mathbf{K}$ can be viewed as terms, constructed from elements of $\mathbf{L}$ and variables by means of operations of a complete residuated lattice (including arbitrary infima and suprema). In this interpretation, different terms can denote the same element (for example, the terms "$u_1 \otimes u_2$" and "$1 \otimes u_1 \otimes u_2$" denote the same element of $\mathbf{K}$, namely $\iota_U(u_1) \otimes \iota_U(u_2)$).

Mappings $v : U \to \mathbf{L}$ are called *assignments*. They model situations when we assign values to the variables. Since $\mathbf{K}$ is generated by $\iota_U(U) \cup \iota_{\mathbf{L}}(L) \subseteq \mathbf{K}$, then for each assignment v there exists at most one complete homomorphism $\bar{v} : \mathbf{K} \to \mathbf{L}$, such that $\bar{v} \circ \iota_U = v$ and $\bar{v} \circ \iota_{\mathbf{L}} = \mathrm{id}_{\mathbf{L}}$ (i.e., $\bar{v}$ is uniquely determined by its values from $\iota_U(U) \cup \iota_{\mathbf{L}}(L) \subseteq \mathbf{K}$: for $u \in U$, $\bar{v}(\iota_U(u)) = v(u)$ and for $a \in L$, $\bar{v}(\iota_{\mathbf{L}}(a)) = a$). If $\bar{v}$ exists, then we say that it is the complete homomorphism that *extends the assignment v to $\mathbf{K}$*.

If the homomorphism $\bar{v}$ exists, then the assignment v is called *admissible*. The set of all admissible assignments is denoted by V. The variables $u_1, \ldots, u_k$ are called *independent*, if each assignment is admissible (i.e., $V = \mathbf{L}^U$). The other cases model situations when there are some known dependencies between the unknown values. For example, if $\iota_U(u_1) \leq \iota_U(u_2)$, then there is no admissible assignment v such that $v(u_1) > v(u_2)$.

Note that each complete homomorphism $\bar{v} : \mathbf{K} \to \mathbf{L}$ induces the admissible assignment $v = \bar{v} \circ \iota_U$. Thus, we have a bijective correspondence between V and the set of all complete homomorphisms from $\mathbf{K}$ to $\mathbf{L}$.

The following theorem shows two fundamental properties of our framework:

1. Generality: for every possible dependency between variables there exists a suitable residuated lattice $\mathbf{K}$.
2. Efficiency: this residuated lattice is (up to isomorphism) the smallest element of the class of residuated lattices satisfying the generality requirement 1.

Theorem 4. *The following hold for each subset $V \subseteq \mathbf{L}^U$.*

(1) Let $\mathbf{K} \subseteq \mathbf{L}^V$ *be the residuated lattice, generated by the subset* $\iota_U(U) \cup \iota_L(L) \subseteq \mathbf{L}^V$, *where the mappings* ι_U *and* ι_L *are defined by* $(\iota_U(u))(v) = v(u)$ *and* $(\iota_L(a))(v) = a$. *Then for each* $v \in V$ *there is exactly one complete homomorphism* $\bar{v} \colon \mathbf{K} \to \mathbf{L}$, *extending* v *to* $\mathbf{K}$.

(2) Let $\mathbf{K}'$ *be a complete residuated lattice with a mapping and* $\iota'_U \colon U \to K'$ *and a complete homomorphism* $\iota'_L \colon \mathbf{L} \to \mathbf{K}'$, *such that for each* $v \in V$ *there is a complete homomorphism* $\bar{v}' \colon \mathbf{K}' \to \mathbf{L}$, *extending* v *to* $\mathbf{K}'$. *Then there exists a surjective complete homomorphism* $s \colon \mathbf{K}' \to \mathbf{K}$ *such that for each* $v \in V$ *it holds* $\bar{v}' = \bar{v} \circ s$.

The following theorem gives a sufficient condition for $\mathbf{K} = \mathbf{L}^V$.

Theorem 5. *If* $\mathbf{L}$ *is weakly simple, then for the residuated lattice* $\mathbf{K}$ *from the previous theorem it holds* $\mathbf{K} = \mathbf{L}^V$.

4 Incomplete Contexts and Their Concept Lattices

Let $U = \{u_1, \ldots, u_k\}$ be a set of variables, $\mathbf{L}$ a residuated lattice, $V \subseteq L^U$ a set of assignments, representing known dependencies between the variables. Using Theorem 4, we construct the minimal residuated lattice $\mathbf{K}$ such that V is the set of admissible assignments.

We use this framework throughout the rest of this paper. For brevity, we suppose that $U \cup L \subseteq K$ and the mappings ι_U, ι_L are the respective canonical inclusions.

An *incomplete context with variables* $u_1, \ldots, u_k$ is a formal $\mathbf{K}$-context $\langle X, Y, I \rangle$, where I takes values only from L and $U \colon I(X \times Y) \subseteq U \cup L$ (i.e., the table, representing the formal context, contains only elements of $\mathbf{L}$ and variables).

For an admissible assignment $v \colon U \to \mathbf{L}$, the formal $\mathbf{L}$-context $\langle X, Y, \bar{v} \circ I \rangle$ is called the *v-completion* of $\langle X, Y, I \rangle$.

Elements of the $\mathbf{K}$-concept lattice $\mathcal{B}(X, Y, I)$ are called *incomplete concepts*. If for an incomplete concept $\langle A, B \rangle \in \mathcal{B}(X, Y, I)$ it holds $A(X) \not\subseteq L$ or $B(Y) \not\subseteq L$, then $\langle A, B \rangle$ is called *strictly incomplete*.

For $\langle A, B \rangle \in \mathcal{B}(X, Y, I)$ and an admissible assignment $v \in V$, the pair $\langle \bar{v} \circ A, \bar{v} \circ B \rangle$ is called the *v-completion* of $\langle A, B \rangle$. By Lemma 3, $\langle \bar{v} \circ A, \bar{v} \circ B \rangle \in \mathcal{B}(X, Y, \bar{v} \circ I)$.

In the next theorem, we investigate the structure of the $\mathbf{K}$-concept lattice $\mathcal{B}(X, Y, I)$. The proof follows easily from Theorems 4, 2, 3.

Theorem 6. $\mathcal{B}(X, Y, I)$ *is isomorphic to a complete sublattice of the direct product* $\prod_{v \in V} \mathcal{B}(X, Y, \bar{v} \circ I)$. *The mappings* $\bar{v}^{\mathcal{B}(X,Y,I)} \colon \mathcal{B}(X, Y, I) \to \mathcal{B}(X, Y, \bar{v} \circ I)$ *correspond to the respective Cartesian projections.*

If $\mathbf{L}$ *is weakly simple, then* $\mathcal{B}(X, Y, I)$ *is isomorphic to* $\prod_{v \in V} \mathcal{B}(X, Y, \bar{v} \circ I)$.

The above theorem has two principal consequences. First, the lattice $\mathcal{B}(X, Y, I)$ can be quite large; in cases when $\mathbf{L}$ is weakly simple, the size of $\mathcal{B}(X, Y, I)$ depends exponentially on the number of admissible assignments, which again depends exponentially on the number of variables (Theorem 4). Second, the mappings $\bar{v}^{\mathcal{B}(X,Y,I)}$ are surjective. Thus, each formal concept of the **L**-concept lattice $\mathcal{B}(X,Y,\bar{v} \circ I)$ is a v-completion of some formal concept of $\mathcal{B}(X,Y,I)$.

The second consequence means that the incomplete concept lattice $\mathcal{B}(X,Y,I)$ contains the information on formal concepts of all v-completions of the incomplete context $\langle X,Y,I \rangle$. The first consequence represents the major obstacle to using the incomplete concept lattice $\mathcal{B}(X,Y,I)$ in practice.

The problem of the size of the incomplete concept lattice $\mathcal{B}(X,Y,I)$ can be dealt with using hedges. Since **L** is a complete sublattice of **K**, it satisfies the requirements of Lemma 1. Thus, we can use the hedge $*_L$ and construct the concept lattice $\mathcal{B}(X,Y^{*_L},I) \subseteq \mathcal{B}(X,Y,I)$ (see Theorem 1). The following theorem shows that this concept lattice retains the property that for each admissible assignment $v \in V$, each formal concept from $\mathcal{B}(X,Y,v \circ I)$ is a v-completion of some formal concept from $\mathcal{B}(X,Y^{*_L},I)$.

Theorem 7. *For each $v \in V$, the restriction $\bar{v}^{\mathcal{B}(X,Y^{*_L},I)} : \mathcal{B}(X,Y^{*_L},I) \to \mathcal{B}(X,Y,v \circ I)$ of $\bar{v}^{\mathcal{B}(X,Y,I)}$ is surjective.*

5   Illustrative Example

Let **L** be the finite Gödel chain with $L = \{0,0.5,1\}$. **L** is not weakly simple (it holds $0.5^2 = 0.5$ in **L**). Further let $U = \{u_1, u_2\}$, and V be the set of all assignments v such that $v(u_1) \le v(u_2)$. V has 6 elements.

The residuated lattice **K** from Theorem 4 has 135 elements out of $3^6 = 729$ elements of $\mathbf{L}^V$ (see Theorem 5). Elements of **K** can be viewed as terms build up from variables u_1, u_2 and constants 0, 0.5, 1 (or, more exactly, as classes of undistinguishable terms; see the previous section).

Consider an incomplete formal context $\langle X,Y,I \rangle$, where $X = \{x_1, x_2, x_3, x_4\}$, $Y = \{y_1, y_2, y_3\}$, and a **K**-relation $I \in K^{X \times Y}$ is given by the table in Fig. 1 (left). The concept lattice $\mathcal{B}(X,Y,I)$ has 5120 elements. However, the concept lattice $\mathcal{B}(X,Y^{*_L},I)$ is much smaller. It consists of the following 15 formal concepts: $c_1 = \langle \{x_1,x_2,x_3,x_4\}, \emptyset \rangle$, $c_2 = \langle \{x_1,x_3,x_4\}, \{^{0.5}/y_3\} \rangle$, $c_3 = \langle \{x_1, {}^{0.5 \to u_1}/x_2\}, \{^{0.5}/y_1, {}^{0.5 \wedge \neg u_1}/y_3\} \rangle$, $c_4 = \langle \{x_2, {}^{0.5 \to u_2}/x_3, x_4\}, \{^{u_2 \vee \neg u_2}/y_2\} \rangle$, $c_5 = \langle \{^{0.5 \to u_2}/x_3, x_4\}, \{^{u_2 \vee \neg u_2}/y_2, {}^{0.5 \vee \neg u_2}/y_3\} \rangle$, $c_6 = \langle \{^{0.5}/x_1, {}^{u_1}/x_2\}, \{y_1, {}^{\neg u_1}/y_3\} \rangle$, $c_7 = \langle \{x_2, {}^{u_2}/x_3, x_4\}, \{y_2\} \rangle$, $c_8 = \langle \{x_1\}, \{^{0.5}/y_1, {}^{0.5}/y_3\} \rangle$, $c_9 = \langle \{^{u_2}/x_3, x_4\}, \{y_2, {}^{u_2 \to 0.5}/y_3\} \rangle$, $c_{10} = \langle \{^{0.5}/x_1, {}^{0.5}/x_3, x_4\}, \{y_3\} \rangle$, $c_{11} = \langle \{^{0.5 \to u_1}/x_2\}, \{^{u_1 \vee \neg u_1}/y_1, y_2, {}^{\neg u_1}/y_3\} \rangle$, $c_{12} = \langle \{^{u_2 \wedge 0.5}/x_3, x_4\}, \{y_2, y_3\} \rangle$, $c_{13} = \langle \{^{0.5}/x_1\}, \{y_1, y_3\} \rangle$, $c_{14} = \langle \{^{u_1}/x_2\}, \{y_1, y_2, {}^{\neg u_1}/y_3\} \rangle$, $c_{15} = \langle \emptyset, \{y_1, y_2, y_3\} \rangle$. The concept lattice $\mathcal{B}(X,Y^{*_L},I)$ is depicted in Fig. 1 (right).

Consider now admissible assignments v_1, v_2, v_3, such that $v_1(u_1) = v_1(u_2) = 0$, $v_2(u_1) = v_2(u_2) = 0.5$, $v_3(u_1) = 0$, $v_3(u_2) = 1$. In Fig. 2 (top) there are depicted the completions $\langle X,Y,\bar{v}_1 \circ I \rangle$, $\langle X,Y,\bar{v}_2 \circ I \rangle$, $\langle X,Y,\bar{v}_3 \circ I \rangle$ and their respective concept lattices $\mathcal{B}(X,Y,\bar{v}_1 \circ I)$, $\mathcal{B}(X,Y,\bar{v}_2 \circ I)$, $\mathcal{B}(X,Y,\bar{v}_3 \circ I)$ (bottom). The concepts in the figure are labeled as follows: if the label is c, then the labeled concept is equal to $\bar{v}^{\mathcal{B}(X,Y,I)}(c)$ for the appropriate $v \in \{v_1, v_2, v_3\}$.

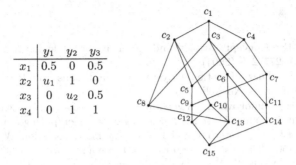

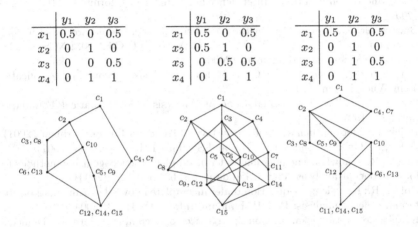

Fig. 1. An incomplete context $\langle X, Y, I \rangle$ (left) and its concept lattice $\mathcal{B}(X, Y^{*L}, I)$ (right)

Fig. 2. The completions $\langle X, Y, \bar{v}_1 \circ I \rangle$, $\langle X, Y, \bar{v}_2 \circ I \rangle$, $\langle X, Y, \bar{v}_3 \circ I \rangle$ of the formal context from Sec. 5 (top, from left to right) and the respective concept lattices (bottom)

6   Conclusion

The incomplete concept lattice $\mathcal{B}(X, Y^{*L}, I)$ introduced in this paper provides users the possibility to view conceptual hierarchies of incomplete data in fuzzy formal contexts. This concept lattice contains the information on the completed concept lattice for all possible completions. The main question remaining to be answered is that on the size of the incomplete concept lattice. Here, the critical factor is the number of variables in the table. In the above example, the size of the incomplete lattice is not substantially larger than the size of the concept lattice of a corresponding completed formal context (in the case of the lattice $\mathcal{B}(X, Y, \bar{v}_2 \circ I)$, it is nearly the same); our preliminary experiments indicate that we can expect similar results in many real-world situations the number of variables is not large.

References

1. Belohlavek, R.: Concept lattices and order in fuzzy logic. Ann. Pure Appl. Log. 128(1-3), 277–298 (2004)
2. Belohlavek, R.: Fuzzy Relational Systems: Foundations and Principles. Kluwer Academic Publishers, Norwell (2002)
3. Belohlavek, R., Funiokova, T., Vychodil, V.: Galois connections with hedges. In: Liu, Y., Chen, G., Ying, M. (eds.) Fuzzy Logic, Soft Computing & Computational Intelligence: Eleventh International Fuzzy Systems Association World Congress, vol. II, pp. 1250–1255. Tsinghua University Press and Springer (2005)
4. Belohlavek, R., Vychodil, V.: Reducing the size of fuzzy concept lattices by hedges. In: Proceedings of FUZZ-IEEE 2005: The 14th IEEE International Conference on Fuzzy Systems, pp. 663–668 (2005)
5. Belohlavek, R., Vychodil, V.: Fuzzy concept lattices constrained by hedges. Journal of Advanced Computational Intelligence and Intelligent Informatics 11(6), 536–545 (2007)
6. Burmeister, P., Holzer, R.: On the treatment of incomplete knowledge in formal concept analysis. In: Ganter, B., Mineau, G.W. (eds.) ICCS 2000. LNCS, vol. 1867, pp. 385–398. Springer, Heidelberg (2000)
7. Carpineto, C., Romano, G.: Concept Data Analysis: Theory and Applications. John Wiley & Sons (2004)
8. Ganter, B., Wille, R.: Formal Concept Analysis – Mathematical Foundations. Springer (1999)
9. Hájek, P.: Metamathematics of Fuzzy Logic (Trends in Logic). Springer (2001)
10. Hájek, P.: On very true. Fuzzy Sets and Systems 124(3), 329–333 (2001)
11. Holzer, R.: Knowledge acquisition under incomplete knowledge using methods from formal concept analysis: Part I. Fundam. Inf. 63(1), 17–39 (2004)
12. Holzer, R.: Knowledge acquisition under incomplete knowledge using methods from formal concept analysis: Part II. Fundam. Inf. 63(1), 41–63 (2004)
13. Krupka, M., Lastovicka, J.: Concept Lattices of Incomplete Data. In: Domenach, F., Ignatov, D., Poelmans, J. (eds.) ICFCA 2012. LNCS, vol. 7278, pp. 180–194. Springer, Heidelberg (2012)
14. Obiedkov, S.: Modal logic for evaluating formulas in incomplete contexts. In: Priss, U., Corbett, D.R., Angelova, G. (eds.) ICCS 2002. LNCS (LNAI), vol. 2393, pp. 314–325. Springer, Heidelberg (2002)
15. Pollandt, S.: Fuzzy Begriffe: Formale Begriffsanalyse von unscharfen Daten. Springer, Heidelberg (1997)
16. Wille, R.: Restructuring lattice theory: an approach based on hierarchies of concepts. In: Rival, I. (ed.) Ordered Sets, Boston, pp. 445–470 (1982)

Imperfect Information Fusion Using Rules with Bilattice Based Fixpoint Semantics

Daniel Stamate and Ida Pu

Department of Computing, Goldsmiths College, University of London, London, UK

Abstract. We present an approach to reasoning non-uniformly by default with uncertain, incomplete and inconsistent information using sets of rules/extended logic programs in the context of multivalued logics with a bilattice structure. A fixpoint semantics for extended logic programs used in the process of inference is described, along with its computational approach. We show how this theoretic approach is applicable to the problem of integration of imperfect information coming from multiple sources.

1 Introduction

Information integration has received much attention for a number of years now in Database, Artificial Intelligence, Logic Programming, Multimedia Information Systems, World Wide Web and other research communities. Various approaches to information fusion have been proposed, adapted to the particular research areas, as the integration of data in a distributed database or from different databases, or the integration of information collected by an agent from other sources, or merging belief bases represented via logic programs, or integrating information coming from different sources as text, sound or image, or from Web sources.

In order to propose an approach to information integration, two main questions may arise: (1) how is information coming from multiple sources combined?; (2) given the problems of possible conflicting information coming from mutually contradictory sources, of missing information coming from incomplete sources, or of uncertain information coming from sources of limited reliability, what meaning can one assign to the fused information? That is, what is the result of the integration? The information that is incomplete, or totally or partially inconsistent, or uncertain will be called *imperfect information* in what follows.

Let us consider the following simple example of medical diagnosing in which information from medical doctors and test results is integrated. It is not uncommon in the case of a suspected potential serious condition (C) of a patient (P) to run and combine results of alternative tests (Test1 and Test2), and the medical doctor (MD1) to ask for another colleague's (MD2) opinion in order to establish a diagnosis. The following rules illustrate this process:

$$Diagnosis(P,C) \leftarrow Tests(P,C) \land MDsSuspect(P,C)$$
$$Tests(P,C) \leftarrow Test1(P,C) \oplus Test2(P,C)$$
$$MDsSuspect(P,C) \leftarrow MD1Suspects(P,C) \otimes MD2Sustects(P,C)$$

S. Greco et al. (Eds.): IPMU 2012, Part III, CCIS 299, pp. 181–190, 2012.

With respect to the question (1) above, the approach to the information integration that we propose in this paper is based on the logic programming paradigm, as it uses inference rules to integrate information in a logic based context. The logic rules we use, however, form extended logic programs as there is a need to employ, apart operations extending the conventional connectives as the conjunction $\wedge$, the disjunction $\vee$ and the negation $\neg$, two more operations $\otimes$ and $\oplus$ called the *consensus* and the *collecting together* (or *gullibility*) operations, to be formally and most generally defined in the next section. In the above example, we are looking for what is the consensus between the two MDs regarding a suspected condition, and this will be combined with the results of the two tests, collected together.

Note that medical tests are not 100% reliable so it makes sense to use confidence degrees as logical values for atoms as $Test1(P, C)$. On the other hand one may get contradictory test results in which case it makes sense to use "inconsistent" as a logical value for $Tests(P, C)$. Or the tests may fail so it makes sense to use "unknown" as a logical value for $Tests(P, C)$. Therefore with respect to the question (2), we choose an appropriate formalism based on multivalued logics expressed by the concept of *bilattice* introduced in [4], that constitutes a powerful tool in expressing the three aspects of imperfect information, namely the uncertainty, the incompleteness and the inconsistency.

In order to illustrate the concept of bilattice, assume first that we want to express the truthness of an information A. In the ideal case we may employ the logical values true or false, but in reality this approach may often be too simplistic. If we use a degree between 0 and 1 instead of a classical logical value, the approach is more appropriate in expressing uncertainty but less helpful in expressing lack of information, or the presence of contradictions in information. Indeed, no value from [0,1] can express, alone, incompleteness or inconsistency.

A natural idea would then be to use a pair $\langle c, d \rangle$ instead of one value as above, that would consist in a degree of confidence c and a degree of doubt d, both numbers in [0,1], which do not necessarily add up to 1 (otherwise the single value c would suffice and we would be again in the previous case). $\langle c, d \rangle$ can be regarded as a logical value. In this setting $\langle 0, 1 \rangle$ and $\langle 1, 0 \rangle$, represent no confidence, full doubt, and full confidence, no doubt, so they would correspond to the classical logical values *false* and *true*, respectively. On the other hand $\langle 0, 0 \rangle$ and $\langle 1, 1 \rangle$, represent no confidence, no doubt, and full confidence, full doubt, respectively, and express a total lack of information or a total inconsistency, respectively. Let us call these values *unknown* and *inconsistent*.

Two orders, namely the *truth* and the *information* (or *knowledge*) orders, denoted $\leq_t$ and $\leq_i$, can naturally be defined on the set of confidence-doubt pairs, denoted $\mathcal{L}^{\mathcal{CD}}$ and called the confidence-doubt logic [10], as follows: $\langle x, y \rangle \leq_t \langle z, w \rangle$ iff $x \leq z$ and $w \leq y$, and $\langle x, y \rangle \leq_i \langle z, w \rangle$ iff $x \leq z$ and $y \leq w$, where $\leq$ is the usual order between reals. The meet and join operations w.r.t. $\leq_t$ and $\leq_i$ are denoted $\wedge$, $\vee$ for the former order, and $\otimes$ and $\oplus$ for the latter order, respectively. They are explicitly expressed below:

$$\langle x, y \rangle \wedge \langle z, w \rangle = \langle min(x, z), max(y, w) \rangle; \langle x, y \rangle \vee \langle z, w \rangle = \langle max(x, z), min(y, w) \rangle$$
$$\langle x, y \rangle \otimes \langle z, w \rangle = \langle min(x, z), min(y, w) \rangle; \langle x, y \rangle \oplus \langle z, w \rangle = \langle max(x, z), max(y, w) \rangle$$

Note that $\wedge$ and $\vee$ can be naturally interpreted as extensions of the classical conjunction and disjunction. Moreover, $\otimes$ and $\oplus$ are two new operations whose definitions are naturally consistent with the meaning of the words *consensus* and *gullibility*, respectively. An extension of the classical negation for confidence-doubt pairs is naturally defined by $\neg \langle x, y \rangle = \langle y, x \rangle$.

We conclude this section by noting that $\mathcal{L}^{\mathcal{CD}}$ illustrates the concept of *bilattice* that is formally presented below.

2   Extended Logic Programs on Bilattices

Bilattices, which were introduced by Ginsberg in [4], offer one of the most capable frameworks to express, in the same time, the characteristics of the information to be incomplete, totally or partially inconsistent, or uncertain. In addition, bilattices have an algebraic structure that allows to express approaches built on this concept in an elegant manner, and to facilitate elegant and often shorter proofs of results. Due to their powerful capability in expressing and reasoning with imperfect information, and/or to serve as multivalued logics, they have found numerous applications in various areas of Computer Science including Artificial Intelligence and extended Logic Programming [4,2,3,6,7,9,1,10].

Definition 1. *A bilattice is a triple $\langle \mathcal{B}, \leq_t, \leq_i \rangle$, where $\mathcal{B}$ is a nonempty set, and $\leq_t$ and $\leq_i$ are partial orders each giving $\mathcal{B}$ the structure of a complete lattice.*

Given the bilattice $\mathcal{B}$, join and meet operations under $\leq_t$, called the *truth order*, are denoted $\vee$ and $\wedge$, called *extended disjunction* and *extended conjunction*, and join and meet operations under $\leq_i$, called the *information* (or *knowledge*) order, are denoted $\oplus$ and $\otimes$, called *collecting together* (or *gullibility*) and *consensus*, respectively. The greatest and least elements under $\leq_t$ are denoted by *true* and *false*, which correspond to and extends the classical logical values. The greatest and least elements under $\leq_i$ are denoted $\top$ and $\bot$, called *inconsistent* and *unknown*, respectively. $\mathcal{B}$ has a negation, denoted $\neg$, if $\neg$ is a unary operation on $\mathcal{B}$ that is antimonotone w.r.t. the truth order and monotone w.r.t. the information order. In addition $\neg true = false$, $\neg false = true$, $\neg \bot = \bot$ and $\neg \top = \top$. A bilattice is *infinitely distributive* if all infinitary as well as finitary distributive laws hold. An example of such a bilattice is provided by $\mathcal{L}^{\mathcal{CD}}$.

From now on the bilattices we consider in this paper are assumed to be infinitely distributive bilattices with negation. Fitting [2,3] extended the notion of logic program, that we will call *extended program*, to bilattices as follows. Let $\mathcal{B}$ be a bilattice, whose elements will be referred to as logical values.

Definition 2. *(1) A formula is an expression built up from literals and elements of $\mathcal{B}$, using $\wedge$, $\vee$, $\otimes$, $\oplus$, $\neg$, $\exists$, $\forall$. (2) A rule r is of the form $H(v_1, ..., v_n) \leftarrow F(v'_1, ..., v'_m)$ where the atomic formula $H(v_1, ..., v_n)$ is the head, and the formula*

$F(v'_1, ..., v'_m)$ *is the body. It is assumed that the free variables of the body are among* $v_1, ..., v_n$. *(3) An extended program is a finite set of rules, assuming that no predicate letter appears in the head of more than one rule.*

Note that the restrictions from (2) and (3) in the above definition cause no loss of generality, since any program as above but without these restrictions, can be rewritten into a program as defined above, as shown by [2,3]. On the other hand, any conventional logic program with negation can be written as in Definition 2, if one employs $\wedge$, $\vee$ and *true* only, from the operations and elements of the bilattice $\mathcal{B}$. For technical reasons, from now on, we consider any extended program to be instantiated s.t. all the free variables are replaced by ground terms (i.e. terms without variables). Note that, due to the way extended programs have been defined, their instantiated versions have no more than one rule with the same atom in the head.

Example 1. Consider the following extended program on the bilattice $\mathcal{L}^{CD}$:

$$A \leftarrow B \oplus F; \quad B \leftarrow \neg E; \quad D \leftarrow B \vee C; \quad E \leftarrow \langle 0.7, 0.3 \rangle; \quad C \leftarrow C \otimes E.$$

Roughly speaking, by using the rules, E is assigned a confidence of 0.7 and a doubt of 0.3, or the logical value $\langle 0.7, 0.3 \rangle$; also B is assigned the logical value $\langle 0.3, 0.7 \rangle$. Note that the confidence and doubt for F cannot be directly derived from the extended program as there is no rule defining F. In such a case in which the extended program does not provide any evidence that permits to infer a degree of confidence and doubt for F, we can assign F a confidence and doubt by default. Possible default values can be suggested for instance by the reliability of the source providing the information F, or by the frequency of cases when the information provided by the source was true in the past, or simply we can consider the logical value $\langle 0, 0 \rangle$ if nothing is known about the source, or $\langle 0, 1 \rangle$ if a pessimistic approach is preferred w.r.t. the source, and so on.

The process of deriving information from an extended program will be formally introduced in the next section. The main idea implemented by this process is that the information is derived by firing the program rules, and by employing the default logical values associated with the sources, provided that the default information that is used is consistent with the program rules.

Given an extended program P and a bilattice $\mathcal{B}$, an *interpretation* is a mapping that assigns a logical value from $\mathcal{B}$ to each atom from the Herbrand base (called also *ground atom*). Its role in this framework is to formally express information. Note that an interpretation can be intuitively represented as a (finite or infinite) table composed of two rows: the ground atoms are placed in the first row, and their corresponding logical values are placed in the second row, as illustrated by the interpretation I below, based on $\mathcal{L}^{CD}$:

$$I = \begin{bmatrix} A & B & C & D & E & F \\ \langle 1,0 \rangle & \langle 0,0 \rangle & \langle 0,1 \rangle & \langle 1,1 \rangle & \langle 0.4, 0.8 \rangle & \langle 0,1 \rangle \end{bmatrix}.$$

Note that the default values corresponding to the sources in Example 1 can be formally provided as an interpretation too, that we call *default interpretation*. We introduced a similar concept called *hypothesis* in [7] whose role was to compensate incomplete information.

3   Bilattice Based Fixpoint Semantics

The following naturally extends the truth and information orders to the set of interpretations denoted by Int_P. Moreover we define the order $\leq_p$ between two interpretations I and J to express the fact that the "known information" from I (that is, the set of atoms from the Herbrand base associated to logical values not equal to $\perp$) is a part of the "known information" from J. In this case we simply say that J extends I, or I is a part of J.

Definition 3. *If I and J are interpretations then:*
(1) $I \leq_t J$ if $I(A) \leq_t J(A)$ (2) $I \leq_i J$ if $I(A) \leq_i J(A)$
(3) $I \leq_p J$ if $I(A) \neq \perp$ implies $I(A) = J(A)$
for any ground atom A.

The interpretations can be extended to closed formulae (i.e. formulae not containing free variables) as follows: $I(X \wedge Y) = I(X) \wedge I(Y)$, and similarly for the other operations of the bilattice, $I((\exists x)F(x)) = \bigvee_{s \in GT} I(F(s))$, and $I((\forall x)F(x)) = \bigwedge_{s \in GT} I(F(s))$, where GT stands for the set of all ground terms.

Definition 4. *The ultimate evaluation $\mathcal{U}(I, C)$ of a closed formula C w.r.t. interpretation I is a logical value α defines by: if $J(C) = I(C)$ for any interpretation J s.t. $I \leq_p J$ then $\alpha = I(C)$, else $\alpha = \perp$.*

Roughly speaking, the ultimate evaluation of a formula C w.r.t. an interpretation I captures the logical value of C that is invariant to any extension of information beyond I. For instance if $I(A_1) = true$ for a ground atom A_1 and $I(A) = \perp$ for any other ground atom A then $\mathcal{U}(I, A_1 \vee A_2) = true$ and $\mathcal{U}(I, A_1 \oplus A_2) = \perp$, where A_2 is a ground atom s.t. $A_1 \neq A_2$. This is due to the fact that $A_1 \oplus A_2$ changes its value when extending I, while $A_1 \vee A_2$ does not. Informally speaking, the information in I is sufficient to establish the final logical value of the latter formula, but not of the former.

The value $\mathcal{U}(I, C)$ can be efficiently computed as shown by the following:

Proposition 1. *Let $I_\top$ be the interpretation obtained from I by assigning the value $\top$ to any atom A s.t. $I(A) = \perp$, and C a closed formula. If $I(C) = I_\top(C)$ then $\mathcal{U}(I, B) = I(B)$, else $\mathcal{U}(I, C) = \perp$.*

The first inference operator Φ_P associated with an extended program P, called the *production operator*, transforms an interpretation I into the interpretation $\Phi_P(I)$ that intuitively corresponds to the information generated through the activation of the program rules. Formally, for any ground atom A:

if there is $A \leftarrow C \in P$ then $\Phi_P(I)(A) = \mathcal{U}(I, C)$, else $\Phi_P(I)(A) = \perp$ (E1)

We show that the production operator has the following interesting properties:

Proposition 2. Φ_P *is monotone w.r.t.* $\leq_i$ *and* $\leq_p$ *orders.*

The second type of inference assumes the use of a fixed *default interpretation* $\mathcal{D}$. The question that arises is: for which ground atoms precisely can one use the default logical values assigned to them by $\mathcal{D}$? The answer will be given by the definition of the so called *default operator* that we provide below.

First we introduce two intermediary operators called the *revision operator*, denoted Rev, and the *refining operator*, denoted Ψ_P, whose roles are to revise and refine an arbitrary interpretation X. The revision of X w.r.t. the interpretation J is the interpretation $Rev(X, J) = X'$ s.t. $X'(A) = X(A)$ for any ground atom A for which either $J(A) = \bot$ or $X(A) = J(A)$, and $X'(A) = \bot$ for any other ground atom A. Roughly speaking, Rev transforms in $\bot$ any logical value $X(A)$ not matching $J(A)$, when $J(A) \neq \bot$ (that is, the revision of X is "compatible" with J). The refinement of X w.r.t. the interpretation I is the interpretation

$$\Psi_P(X, I) = Rev(X, \Phi_P(Rev(X, I) \oplus I)). \tag{E2}$$

Roughly speaking, X is first revised to be "compatible" with the information from I, then I is added obtaining an interpretation that will be used to activate the program rules and to derive a new interpretation I', with respect to which X will be revised to be "compatible" with I' (and thus to be "compatible" with the program rules also).

By making use of the refining operator Ψ_P, we wish to obtain the default information X (that is, $X \leq_p \mathcal{D}$) that can complete the interpretation I which represents the sure information derived from the extended program so far. Formally, we have the following requirements/conditions:

(1) $X \leq_p \mathcal{D}$ (2) $X = \Psi_P(X, I)$ and
(3) under the previous two conditions X is maximal w.r.t. $\leq_p$.

Roughly speaking, X is to be a part of the default interpretation $\mathcal{D}$ (condition (1)), that is stable when refined w.r.t. I (condition (2)). In addition X is supposed to complete as much as possible the information in I (condition (3)). That is, we are interested in the maximal fixpoints of the operator $\lambda X \Psi_P(X, I)$ that are parts of $\mathcal{D}$, which we call *actual default interpretations* w.r.t. I and $\mathcal{D}$. We show below that there exists a unique actual default interpretation w.r.t. I and $\mathcal{D}$.

Proposition 3. *Let I be an interpretation and $\mathcal{D}$ be a default interpretation. The following hold: (1) The $(\lambda X)\Psi_P(X, I)$ operator has a greatest fixpoint below $\mathcal{D}$ w.r.t. $\leq_p$, denoted by $Def_P^{\mathcal{D}}(I)$. 2) $Def_P^{\mathcal{D}}(I)$ is the limit of the following sequence of interpretations that is decreasing w.r.t. $\leq_p$, which is defined by: $X_0 = \mathcal{D}$; $X_n = \Psi_P(X_{n-1}, I)$ if n is a successor ordinal; and $X_n = inf_{\leq_p, m<n} X_m$ if n is a limit ordinal.*

Note that the first part of Proposition 3 involves that $Def_P^{\mathcal{D}}(I)$ is the unique actual default interpretation, while the second part provides a means of computation for $Def_P^{\mathcal{D}}(I)$. This computation consists of starting with the default interpretation $\mathcal{D}$ and iterating the operator $(\lambda X)\Psi_P(X, I)$ until a fixpoint is reached. We call $Def_P^{\mathcal{D}}$ the *default operator*, as it is obvious that it reflects the application of the inference by default.

The two types of inference described above are now combined via a new operator, denoted Γ_P and called the *integrating operator*, defined by:

$$\Gamma_P(I) = \Phi_P(I) \oplus Def_P^{\mathcal{D}}(I). \tag{E3}$$

Roughly speaking, in order to generate the total information that can be derived from the extended program P, we start with the least degree of information characterized by an interpretation I_0 in which all the ground atoms are unknown, denoted by $Const_\perp$ (i.e. $Const_\perp(A) = \perp$ for any ground atom A). We apply the two types of inference to the current information, which corresponds to one application of the Γ_P operator, and we get a new interpretation I_1. This iterative process continues until nothing changes, that is, until a fixpoint is reached. Formally we define the sequence $\mathcal{S}$ of interpretations as follows, and study its properties:

$$I_0 = Const_\perp; \quad I_n = \Gamma_P(I_{n-1}) \text{ for a successor ordinal } n;$$
$$I_n = sup_{\leq_p, m < n} I_m \text{ for a limit ordinal } n.$$

Theorem 1. *The following hold: (1) $\mathcal{S}$ is increasing w.r.t. $\leq_p$ (and thus w.r.t. $\leq_i$) and reaches a limit denoted by s; (2) $\Gamma_P(s) = s$ and (3) for any x s.t. $\Gamma_P(x) = x$ we have $s \leq_i x$.*

Thus s is the least fixpoint of Γ_P w.r.t. $\leq_i$, and represents the total information that can be inferred from the extended program P completed with the default information $\mathcal{D}$. We choose s to designate the semantics of P w.r.t. the default interpretation $\mathcal{D}$, and we refer to it as the *fixpoint semantics* of P w.r.t. $\mathcal{D}$. We omit to refer to $\mathcal{D}$ when this is not essential or is understood from the context.

We conclude this section by a result that shows that the fixpoint semantics of the extended program P is closed to the application of the program rules, or in other words, is a fixpoint of the production operator.

Theorem 2. *If s is the fixpoint semantics of P then $\Phi_P(s) = s$.*

4   Computational Results

Proposition 4. *If $Values(P)$ is the set of logical values appearing in the extended program P, and $Closure(H)$ is the closure of the set of logical values from a subset H of the bilattice $\mathcal{B}$, to which one adds true, false, $\top$, and $\perp$, w.r.t. the finite and infinite applications of the negation, join and meet operations, then $\langle Closure(Values(P)), \leq_t, \leq_i \rangle$ is a finite bilattice.*

Computationally speaking, even if the bilattice $\mathcal{B}$ is infinite, and the closure ordinals corresponding to the calculations of the fixpoints of the refining operator Ψ_P and the integrating operator Γ_P may be at least ω (i.e. the first infinite ordinal), only a finite number of logical values from $\mathcal{B}$ are used in the calculation of the fixpoint semantics of P. More precisely, these logical values belong to the finite bilattice $Closure(Values(P))$. Moreover, if P is a function free extended program, then the effective calculation of the fixpoint semantics of P is feasible as shown by the following:

Theorem 3. *If the extended program P is function free then, for any interpretations I and X, the following hold: (1) the calculation of $\Phi_P(I)$ according to equation $(E1)$ terminates; (2) the calculation of $\Psi_P(X, I)$ according to equation $(E2)$ terminates; (3) the calculation of $Def_P^{\mathcal{D}}$ by a finite number of iterations of $(\lambda Y)\Psi_P(Y, I)$ starting with $\mathcal{D}$, terminates; (4) the calculation of $\Gamma_P(I)$ according to equation $(E3)$ terminates; (5) the fixpoint semantics of P can be computed in a finite number of steps by iterative application of $(\lambda Y)\Gamma_P(Y)$ and starting with the interpretation $Const_\perp$.*

Along the lines of Theorem 3, we propose now an algorithm for the computation of the fixpoint semantics of a function free extended program P w.r.t. the default interpretation $\mathcal{D}$. In the pseudo-code below the interpretations are represented as finite sets of pairs of atoms and logical values of the form (A, v).

```
1.   function Rev(Y, Z)
2.   W := Y;
3.   for every pair (A, v1) ∈ W
4.       if v1 ≠ ⊥ and (A, v2) ∈ Z and v2 ≠ ⊥ and
5.       v2 ≠ v1
6.           then replace (A, v1) with (A, ⊥) in W;
7.   return W;

8.   function Phi(P, I)
9.   I⊤ := I;
10.  J = ∅;
11.  for any pair (A, v) ∈ I⊤
12.      if v = ⊥ then
13.          replace (A, v) with (A, ⊤) in I⊤;
14.  for any rule A ← B in P
15.      if I(B) = I⊤(B) then insert (A, I(B)) in J
16.          else insert (A, ⊥) in J;
17.  for any atom A not appearing in J insert (A, ⊥) in J;
18.  return J;

19.  function FixpointSemantics(P, D)
20.  I2 := Const⊥;
21.  repeat
22.      I1 := I2;
23.      J₂ := D;
24.      repeat
```

```
25.          J1 := J2;
26.            J2 := Rev(J1, Phi(P, Rev(J1, I1) ⊕ I1))
27.       until J1 = J2;
28.        I2 := Phi(P, I1) ⊕ J1
29.    until I1 = I2;
30.    return I1.
```

The code lines 1-7 implement the revision operator Rev. The code lines 8-18 implement the production operator Φ_P. In particular the lines 11-13 prepare the ultimate evaluation of formulae in rule bodies (according to Definition 4 and Proposition 1) which is performed in the lines 14-16. The main function provided in the lines 19-30 performs the actual computation of the fixpoint semantics (according to the construction of the sequence $\mathcal{S}$ in Theorem 1 and Theorem 3). In particular the lines 23-27 evaluate the default operator $Def_P^{\mathcal{D}}$, and the line 28 evaluates the integrating operator Γ_P.

Example 2. If we consider the extended program from Example 1 with the default interpretation $\mathcal{D}$ that assigns $\langle 0, 1 \rangle$ to each ground atom, and apply the above algorithm, we obtain the fixpoint semantics of P represented by the following interpretation:

$$I = \left[\begin{array}{cccccc} A & B & C & D & E & F \\ \langle 0.3, 1 \rangle & \langle 0.3, 0.7 \rangle & \langle 0, 0 \rangle & \langle 0.3, 0 \rangle & \langle 0.7, 0.3 \rangle & \langle 0, 1 \rangle \end{array} \right].$$

5   Further Results and Ongoing Work

Our approach can be related to Fitting's work regarding the reasoning under uncertainty based on bilattices and extended logic programs. In particular [2,3] present the multivalued stable models for extended programs in the context of bilattices, in particular of Belnap's four valued logic, that generalize the concept of stable models in the conventional bivalued logic. We have:

Theorem 4. *Let P be an extended program considered on the bilattice $\mathcal{B}$, and $mstable(P)$ be its multivalued stable model, as defined in [2,3], which is the smallest w.r.t. the information/knowledge order. Then the fixpoint semantics of P w.r.t. the default interpretation $\mathcal{D}$ assigning the value false to any ground atom, as defined in this work, coincides with $mstable(P)$.*

We show also that our semantics captures the α-fixed models of extended programs on bilattices, introduced by us in [6]. For different logical values α, in particular *false*, *true* and $\perp$, the α-models provide various meanings to the same extended program P, depending on how one chooses to complete the missing information by adopting a pessimistic, optimistic, or skeptical approach, respectively. It was proven in [6] that α-fixed models capture conventional semantics as the Kripke-Kleene semantics [3] and the well-founded semantics, which in turns coincides with Przymusinski's three-valued stable semantics [8]. Thus the fixpoint semantics presented in this work is a natural extension of the above well-known three-valued semantics of conventional logic programs.

Theorem 5. *Given an extended program P considered on the bilattice $\mathcal{B}$, for any logical value α from $\mathcal{B}$, the α-fixed model of P as defined in [6], coincides with the fixpoint semantics of P w.r.t. the default interpretation that uniformly assigns the value α to any ground atom.*

Corollary 1. *Let P be a conventional logic program with negation considered in the context of the bilattice $\mathcal{L}^{\mathcal{CD}}$. The following hold: (1) The fixpoint semantics of P w.r.t. the default interpretation $\mathcal{D}$ assigning the value false to any ground atom, coincides with the well-founded semantics of P, and with Przymusinski's three-valued stable semantics of P; (2) The fixpoint semantics of P w.r.t. the default interpretation $\mathcal{D}$ assigning the value $\bot$ to any ground atom, coincides with the Kripke-Kleene semantics of P.*

We currently investigate how the semantics defined for information integration in this approach can be related to a recent work presented in [5], which provides a logic programming based approach making use of a program semantics based on conventional stable models, for merging belief bases. It would be interesting to understand more precisely how the two approaches integrating information/beliefs and their corresponding program semantics relate to each other, although the present framework is more general as based on multivalued logics.

Moreover we intend to explore the possibility of extending this approach by considering imprecise degrees of confidence and doubt (i.e. confidence and doubt intervals) instead of punctual values, and we are looking for corresponding appropriate algebraic structures to use in this context instead of bilattices.

References

1. Deschrijver, G., Arieli, O., Cornelis, C., Kerre, E.: A bilattice-based framework for handling graded truth and imprecision. J. Uncertainty, Fuzziness and Knowledge-Based Systems 15(1) (2007)
2. Fitting, M.C.: The family of stable models. J. Logic Programming 17 (1993)
3. Fitting, M.C.: Fixpoint semantics for logic programming - a survey. Theoretical Computer Science 278 (2002)
4. Ginsberg, M.L.: Multivalued logics: a uniform approach to reasonning in artificial intelligence. Computationnal Intelligence 4 (1988)
5. Hué, J., Papini, O., Würbel, E.: Merging Belief Bases Represented by Logic Programs. In: Sossai, C., Chemello, G. (eds.) ECSQARU 2009. LNCS, vol. 5590, pp. 371–382. Springer, Heidelberg (2009)
6. Loyer, Y., Spyratos, N., Stamate, D.: Parameterised semantics for logic programs - a unifying framework. Theoretical Computer Science 308(1-3) (2003)
7. Loyer, Y., Spyratos, N., Stamate, D.: Hypothesis-based semantics of logic programs in multivalued logics. ACM Trans. Comput. Logic 15(3) (2004)
8. Przymusinski, T.C.: The well-founded semantics coincides with the three-valued stable semantics. Fundamenta Informaticae 13(4) (1990)
9. Shet, V.D., Neumann, J., Ramesh, V., Davis, L.S.: Bilattice-based logical reasoning for human detection. In: Proc. of 2007 IEEE Conference on Computer Vision and Pattern Recognition (2007)
10. Stamate, D.: Default reasoning with imperfect information in multivalued logics. In: Proc. of 38th IEEE International Symposium on Multiple-Valued Logic (2008)

Assimilation of Information
in RDF-Based Knowledge Base

Marek Z. Reformat and Parisa D. Hossein Zadeh

University of Alberta,
Edmonton, AB T6G 2V4, Canada
{Marek.Reformat,dehlehho}@ualberta.ca

Abstract. The Resource Description Framework (RDF) defines an interesting way of representing data based on a simple principle of expressing any piece of information as a triple: subject-property-object. This notion gains a lot of interest as a promising form of representing any type of data and facts on the Web.

This paper is about automatic assimilation of information.

We propose two procedures: one for assessing relevance between two pieces of information, another for information integration. Both of them can be executed by an agent on the behalf of the user. In a nutshell, the idea is as follows: an agent browses the web and finds some facts, determines their relevance to the facts already known to the user, and integrates them. The proposed procedures are based on compatibility of user's information with the web contents, and on the level of user's confidence in the information already known to the user.

1 Introduction

In 2001, the concept of Semantic Web has been introduced [1] as a new paradigm of storing and utilizing data on the Web. The primary data representation format used by the Semantic Web is ontology [2]. Ontology is a set of concepts in a specific domain, together with their detailed definitions, ordered in a hierarchical way. A fundamental building block of any ontology-based representation is Resource Description Framework – RDF. At the same time, RDF becomes a basic element of *Linked Data* (*LD*) paradigm [3]. In *LD*, all information is represented as a vast network of interconnected RDF triples.

An RDF triple contains three elements: subject-property-object. A *subject* is an element that a particular piece of information is about, an *object* is an element that describes the subject, and a *property* indicates relationship between the subject and the object of a given triple. There is no restrictions on the type of items that can be used as subjects, objects, and properties. In general, a subject in one triple can be an object in another triple, as well as the whole triple can be either object or subject.

A very important feature of RDF is related to identification of triples' elements. The Uniform Reference Identifiers – URIs – are used here [3]. An element of a triple represented by an URI points to a place on the web – a web page or a

S. Greco et al. (Eds.): IPMU 2012, Part III, CCIS 299, pp. 191–200, 2012.

location on the page. All subjects and properties of RDF triples are identified by URIs. Only objects can be represented by URIs or any numerical or character literals. An example of a simple network of triples – called RDF graph – with URIs is shown in Figure 1. It represents information about the resource *JS*. This resource is of a type *person*, has a given name *John*, and a family name *Smith*. It is a creator of a *www.ualberta.ca* with a title *university_of_alberta*.

In this paper we treat an RDF graph (Figure 1) as a definition of a item, i.e., the central resource is defined by all resources to which the central resource is connected. These defining resource are called features.

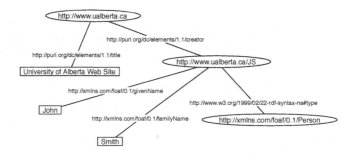

Fig. 1. RDF graph: example

The application of URIs to identify elements of RDF triples means that there is no need to "have" pieces of information stored locally, only the addresses of their locations are required.

The introduction of RDF-based information representation creates the opportunity to treat the use's knowledge base as an "extension" of the web. This idea is based on the fact that the information known to the user is stored as her "private" RDFs. The private triples are still connected to elements on the web via URIs, and they represent the information experienced by the user.

Such a concept allows for a new way of searching for information and its assimilation. The search process means releasing of software agents that work on the behalf of the user. They crawl the web for new information, compare it with the information known to the user – her private RDF triples – and depending of its novelty, integrate this information with the user's knowledge.

In this paper, that indirectly introduces the concept of agent-based search, we focus on a number of procedures required for: determining a novelty of information; integrating a new information with the user's knowledge; assessing levels of compatibility between the user's information and the web contents; and estimating confidence in the user's information after the integration process. As a result, we are introducing and showing how to build/maintain the user's knowledge base containing information and facts experienced by the user – her agents – on the web, together with experience-based compatibility of this information, and confidence in it.

2   Repository of User's Experience and Knowledge

An automatic process of collecting new information on the user's behalf means
that the information currently known to the user has to be clearly identified
and stored. The experience in searching the web for information – experience in
browsing the web, looking for data at different locations, gaining information and
learning new things, all this need to be captured in a local repository representing
the user's current state of knowledge. Such repository in not isolated but fully
"integrated" with the web – it is an extension of the web.

2.1   Personal Linked Data and Special Properties

The increasing popularity of LD has triggered an idea of using RDF triples as
the fundamental components of the user's personal repository. Hence, we will
call this repository a "personal LD" or pLD for short.

Similarly as in the case of LD, the pLD is a mesh of triples. However, all
triples in the pLD represent information the user knows, i.e., information that
the user (her software agents) has already "seen and experienced". The fact that
each element of a triple can be an URI, means that the pLD does not need to
store all pieces of information. What is stored in the pLD are URIs pointing to
places on the web that contain information the user is aware of.

In order to represent user's processes of searching and collecting information
in a more realistic manner, we need the ability to express experience-based compatibility [1] of information, and levels of confidence in this information. Thus, we
introduce three special RDF properties to represent this information:

- individual relevance (REL) to store values of relevance between two pieces
  of information being compared;
- information compatibility (IC) to store experience-based compatibility of the
  information expressed by a triple with the web contents;
- confidence level (CL) to bind a given triple to a value representing confidence
  in the stored information.

The first property (REL) is added to a given triple (already known) every time
a new piece of information is being compared with the triple, and the level of
relevance exceeds a threshold value set up by the user. This threshold value represents the user's minimum level of relevance between two pieces of information
which the user is willing to accept. Eventually, the triple has a number of REL
properties that are used to calculate values of IC and CL.

The fragment of the pLD is presented in Figure 2. There are four REL properties created for the triple $< r_i; p_x; r_a >$, three for the triple $< r_i; p_y; r_b >$,
and two for $< r_i; p_x; r_c >$. This means the resource r_a was a part of four different comparisons of r_i with some other resources, r_b with three, and r_c with two

---

[1] The compatibility we consider here is the result of encountering variety of pieces of
information on the web, and comparing them with the already known information.

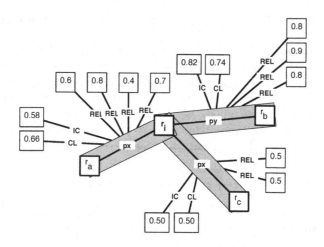

Fig. 2. A snippet of *pLD* with new RDF triples: *REL*, *IC*, and *CL*

comparisons. Based on these *REL*s, the values of properties *IC* and *CL* – for each triple individually – are calculated (Section 3).

2.2 Personal Linked Data as User's Knowledge Base

The proposed *pLD*, equipped with three special RDF triples, is the user's knowledge base. It is suitable for: 1) *representing user's state of knowledge* – via keeping references to all pieces of information the user (her agents) encountered and assimilated during the previous browsing activities; 2) *representing degrees of compatibility of stored pieces of information* – determined based on the relevance between known pieces of information and pieces experienced by the user (her agents) during the information collection processes; 3) *representing confidence levels in pieces of information stored in the base* – determined as a combination of information compatibility and frequency of exposure to related information.

The compatibility property can be interpreted as an assurance that RDF triples stored in the *pLD* "agree" with the information on the web, while the confidence property can be interpreted as the user's belief in these RDF triples. If we take a resource and look at its connections with other resources (features), some of these connections are correct and have a high value of confidence – indicators that these pieces of information are in the agreement with information available on the web, and they have been encountered by the user (her agents) multiple times. It should be noted that a single triple can have a high compatibility value but a low confidence level (information known to the user is in "sync" with the web, but it has been encountered just a very few times). However, if a triple is "seen" multiple times but its compatibility value is low the value of confidence in that triple is also low.

3   Information Assimilation Mechanism

A process of assimilation of information is conducted in two stages [5]: determining relevance of new information when compared with the information already known to the user[2]; and its integration with the already known information.

3.1   Relevance Determination

The first phase of the assimilation process is determining a level of relevancy of the *new information* when compared with the *known information*. It is done via assessment of similarity between a new piece of information – *new resource* – and the contents of the *pLD*. The similarity assessment means comparison of features of resources. This approach seems natural – a set of resources that are features of the *new resource* are compared with the features of *known resources* stored in the *pLD*. It is done on the one-by-one basis, i.e., the *new resource* and its features are compared with the resources and their features that already exist in the *pLD*.

In general, the comparison of triples can take place in four different scenarios, defined by all possible combination of resources' features – shared or unique, and properties – common or unique. A thorough analysis of the process of determining similarity between resources in *LD* has been preformed in [6].

For the purpose of our ultimate goal – assimilation of information – we consider only one of these scenarios. This scenario takes into consideration only the resources that are connected to both *new* and *known resources* via the same properties. We will call them *bilateral features*. The features that are connected to both resources via different connections (properties) will be called here *unilateral features*. The bilateral features contribute directly to the relevance of two resources according to the formula:

$$relevance(r_i, r_j) = \frac{\sum\limits_{r_k \in R_{i,j}^b} CL(< r_i; p_*; r_k >) * IC(< r_i; p_*; r_k >)}{\sum\limits_{r_l \in R_i} CL(< r_i; p_*; r_l >) * IC(< r_i; p_*; r_l >)} \tag{1}$$

where R_i represents the set of all features of the *known resource* r_i, $R_{i,j}^b$ the set of bilateral features between r_i and the *new resource* r_j. P_* indicates that any common property is acceptable, as long as it connects r_i with a bilateral feature. The $IC(< r_i; p_*; r_k >)$ represents compatibility of information, i.e., a degree of compatibility of the triple $< r_i; p_*; r_k >$, while $CL(< r_i; p_*; r_k >)$ represents a level of confidence in this triple. The numerator represents a sum of products $IC * CL$ for the bilateral features, while the denominator represents a sum of the products for all features of the resource r_i. This means that a relevance value is calculated in the reference to the *known resource*.

---

[2] We will use the term "new information" or "new resource" to describe the information to be assimilated, and the term "known information" or "known resource(s)" to indicate the information already known to the user.

Example I. Let us take a look at Figure 3. It represents two resources – the *known resource* r_i, and the *new resource* r_j. As we can see on the *pLD* side, each connection is marked by its type (numerical value in bold), as well as the values of IC and CL associated with it.

The first step in determining the level of relevance between the resources r_i and r_j is to identify shared features (resources) and common properties. The sets are: $R_{i,j}^{sh} = \{r_A, r_B, r_C, r_D\}$, and $P_{i,j} = \{1, 2, 3, 4\}$. Based on these sets we can determine bilateral features: $R_{i,j}^b = \{r_A, r_B, r_C\}$, and a set of connections linking them to r_i: $P_{i,j}^b = \{1, 2, 4\}$. The level of relevance of r_i and r_j can be determined as:

$$relevance(r_i, r_j)$$

$$= \frac{.7*.6 + .6*.8 + .9*.5}{.7*.6 + .6*.8 + .9*.5 + .2*.4 + .5*.7 + .9*.6 + .6*.7 + .8*.7 + .1*.5}$$

$$= \frac{1.35}{3.35} = 0.403$$

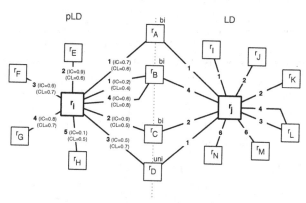

Fig. 3. Determining relevance between two resources r_i and r_j

3.2   Knowledge Integration

Once the level of relevance is determined, the process of integration means adding the *new resource* and its features to the *pLD*. This process takes three steps:

- adding a triple *SameAs* between *known* and *new* resources, and adding triples *REL*, *CL* and *IC* to it;
- modifying triples *REL*, *CL* and *IC* of bilateral and unilateral features;
- adding triples *REL*, *CL* and *IC* to connections between *new* resource and its features.

Adding the *New Resource*. The *new resource* is being added if the determined level of relevance exceeds the threshold value identified by the user. The triple

$$< known\_resource; SameAs; new\_resource >$$

is created. The value of REL added to it is obtained via aggregation, for example using min function, of the determined level of relevance and the trust value[3] associated with the source of the information. The value of IC is calculated based on it (for the case of a single REL, the value of IC is equal to REL). The value of CL is calculated using Equation 3.

Modifying Connections to Bilateral Features. This modification means adding another REL and updating ICs and CLs of the connections between r_i (*known resource*) and each bilateral feature. At first, the determined relevance value is assigned as REL to each connection. The IC value for each such connection is re-calculated based on all relevance values (REL) associated with it:

$$IC(< r_i; p_*; r_a >) = REL_{avg} - \alpha * REL_{std} \qquad (2)$$

where r_a is a bilateral feature, and p_* a property of the connection. The REL_{avg} and REL_{std} are average and standard deviation calculated over all RELs of a given connection. The value of α (in the range from 0.0 to 0.5) represents user's disbelief in treating an average value as a good representative of set of values. Large value means large disbelief. Our interaction with a number of individuals has led to $\alpha = 0.25$.

The CL values are calculated according to:

$$CL(< r_i; p_*; r_a >) = LapR(< r_i; p_*; r_a >) - \beta * REL_{std}(< r_i; p_*; r_a >) \quad (3)$$

where

$$LapR(< r_i; p_*; r_a >) = \frac{N+1}{N+2} \qquad (4)$$

is called a Laplace ratio, and N represents a number of REL properties assigned to $< r_i; p_*; r_a >$. The value of β represents user's belief that standard deviation should be included in the determination of confidence values. Higher values of β means the user wants to include the influence of variability of the relevance values. Once again, our interaction with users had led to $\beta = 1.0$.

Modifying Connections to Unilateral Features. Based on the definition of the unilateral features it is known that the connection from r_i to the unilateral feature and the connection from r_j to the same unilateral feature are different.

---

[3] The trust value can be obtained as the result of other calculations, or some default value can be assumed. The process of determining the trust in an information source is beyond the scope of this paper.

Therefore, we do not modify the connection between r_i and the feature, but we add a new connection between r_i and the feature – this connection has the property of the connection between the *new* resource r_j and the feature. The values of REL, IC, and CL are the same as calculated for **Adding the *new* resource** above.

Modifying Connections of the *New Resource*. Each connection between the *new resource* and all its features is also labeled with properties REL, IC, and CL calculated as for **Adding the *new resource*** above.

Example II. Both resources r_i and r_j from *Example I* need to be integrated. The process of integration requires one more value – user's trust in the source of information, i.e., in the origin of resource r_j. For the purpose of this example we assume the value of trust is equal to 0.7.

There are two new connections: between r_i and r_j with the property *SameAs*, and between r_i and r_D with the property **1**. The first one is due to the relevance between r_i and r_j calculated in *Example I*, while the second is due to the fact that the resource r_D is a unilateral feature.

The modification of connections occurs for the connections from r_i to bilateral features. It means the addition of the determined relevance value as another REL. The IC is re-calculated using this updated set of REL, while CL is re-calculated using the Laplace Ratio.

Figure 4 shows the integrated information together with all obtained levels of IC and CL. The connections in bold represent new or modified connections of the resource r_i.

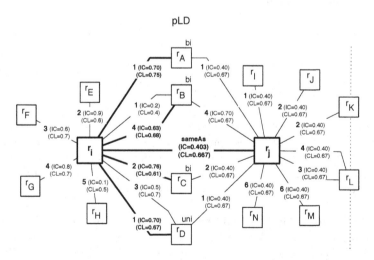

Fig. 4. Assimilation of a resource r_j to pLD

4   Case Study

A very simple case study is included to illustrate the proposed process of information assimilation. The example shows how an existing knowledge base (containing a few triples) is expended by integrating two sets of triples found by a software agent.

4.1   Experimental Setup

Three resources, together with their features, have been taken from *dbpedia.org*. They represent three resources: Georges Braque, Pablo Picasso, and Braque, Figure 5. As it can be seen, the connections are labeled with acronyms of properties: SUB – subject, MOV – movement, INDby – influenced by, IND – influenced.

It is assumed that the information about the resource Georges Braque **GBrq** is a part of the user's *pLD*. The initial values of *REL* and *IC* are set to 0.5, and *CL* to 0.67 (Laplace Ratio in the case of a single connection). The user's threshold for acceptance of the new information is 0.5. The trust in the source of information is 0.7.

4.2   Integration Process

At first, the resource Pablo Picasso **PPic** is being integrated with *pLD* (step marked with *int-1*). Secondly, Braque **Brq** is added (marked as *int-2*), Figure 5.

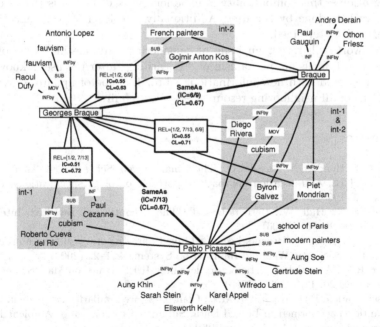

Fig. 5. *pLD* after integrating Georges Braque (**GBrq**) with Pablo Picasso (**PPic**), and Braque (**Brq**)

The relevance value between **GBrq** and **PPic** has been determined to be $7/13$, and it exceeds the threshold. The triple with the property *SameAs* (bold line) has been added. It is equipped with $REL = [min(7/10, 7/13) = 7/13]$, $IC = 7/13 = 0.54$ and $CL = 2/3 = 0.67$. All bilateral features are affected: their values of IC and CL are equal to 0.51 and 0.72 respectively.

The relevance value between **GBrq** and **Brq** has been determined to be $6/9$. The value is the IC associated with *SameAs* property (bold line) is $6/9 = 0.67$, and of CL is 0.67.

Now, the connections of the resource **GBrq** to the features common with **PPic** and **Brq** have three different set of IC and CL values: one due to integration of **PPic** only (*int-1*): *Paul Cezanne, cubism, Roberto Cueva del Rio*, due to assimilation of **Brq** (*int-2*): *French painters, Gojmir Anton Kos*, and due to both **GBrq** and **PPic** (*int-1 & int-2*): *Byron Galvez, cubism, Diego Rivera, Piet Mondrian*. For values of IC and CL see Figure 5.

5   Conclusion

The paper presents the results of initial research activities focused on assimilation of new information by the user (her software agents) browsing the web. The approach uses a data representation format called RDF. The novel method allows for assessing relevance of new information, and integrating it with already known information. The important aspect of this approach is its ability to assess compatibility of the information with the web contents at the time of its integration – this compatibility is experience-based, i.e., it is the "sum" of all observations done by the user. Additionally, the level of confidence in the information is determined.

Future work will target an issue of considering only specific types of connections, it will focus on mechanism of "re-learning" after the user's knowledge base is integrated with new information, a broader type of update – involving connections of all neighboring resources – is also required.

References

[1] Lee, T.B., Hendler, J., Lassila, O.: The semantic web. Sci. Am. 284, 34–43 (2001)
[2] Gruber, T.R.: A translation approach to portable ontology specifications. Knowl. Acquis. 5, 199–220 (1993)
[3] Shadbolt, N., Hall, W., Berners-Lee, T.: The semantic web revisited. Intelligent Systems 21, 96–101 (2006)
[4] Bizer, C., Heath, T., Berners-Lee, T.: Linked data-the story so far. International Journal on Semantic Web and Information Systems 4, 1–22 (2009)
[5] Yager, R.R.: A model of participatory learning. IEEE Trans. on Man, Systems and Cybernetics 20, 1229–1234 (1990)
[6] Hossein Zadeh, P.D., Reformat, M.Z.: Context-aware Similarity Assessment within Semantic Space formed in Linked Data. Submitted to Journal of Ambient Intelligence, and Humanized Computing (2011)

Quantitative Semantics for Uncertain Knowledge Bases

Daniel Stamate

Department of Computing, Goldsmiths College, University of London, London, UK

Abstract. The paper presents a quantitative approach for handling uncertain information in knowledge bases using multivalued logics with an intuitive double algebraic structure of lattice and semilattice. The logical values, seen as quantities, represent various degrees of truth associated to the base facts, which may be combined and propagated by applying inference rules forming an extended logic program. A corresponding quantitative semantics is defined for uncertain knowledge bases, that extends successful conventional semantics as the well-founded semantics.

1 Introduction

Real world information is not always exact, but mostly imperfect, in the sense that we handle estimated values, probabilistic measures, degrees of uncertainty, etc, rather than exact values and information which is certainly true or false.

In the conventional database or knowledge base systems the information handled is assumed to be rather exact, as a fact either is in the base (so it is true) or is not (so it is false). That is, in such a context we use quite simplified models of the "real" world.

This paper presents an approach for querying and updating knowledge bases with uncertain information. In our approach, a knowledge base can be defined in a quantitative declarative language, and is seen as a pair $\Delta = (P, F)$, where P is essentially a function free, extended logic program with negation and F is a set of facts.

In order to model such knowledge bases, we extend Kleene's three-valued logic (*true*, *false* and *unknown*) by adding new values representing quantities seen as various degrees of truth. We structure these values by defining two orders, the truth order and the knowledge order. We then extend Przymusinski's three-valued stable semantics [10] to a multivalued/quantitative one, along the lines of Fitting [9]. We use these extensions for describing the quantitative semantics of knowledge bases with uncertain information and their updates.

Let us illustrate our approach using a simple example. Consider we want to produce a list of albums by Leonard Bernstein, sorted according to their jazziness. To do this we use:

- a relation $A(AlbumNo, Artist)$ and
- the estimates of an expert as to the music type (baroque, classic romantic, jazzy, etc). Let us think of these estimates as of a relation $E(AlbumNo, Type)$.

S. Greco et al. (Eds.): IPMU 2012, Part III, CCIS 299, pp. 201–210, 2012.
© Springer-Verlag Berlin Heidelberg 2012

Each tuple in the relation E is associated with a number/quantity, say a real between -1 and 1, indicating the expert's opinion as to whether the album is of the type: 1 (or -1) indicates that the expert thinks the music of the album is certainly (or is not at all, respectively) of the type; 0 expresses that the expert has no particular opinion (so no information available); 0.9 (or -0.9) means that the expert is highly confident that the music is (or is not, respectively) of the type, etc.

The query Q that we want to answer is defined by the simple logic program formed of one rule whose body is a conjunct of two atoms as follows:

$$Q(X) \leftarrow A(X, leonardBernstein) \& E(X, jazz)$$

The question arising here is how we combine the uncertain information provided by relation E with the certain information from the relation A. A natural solution would be to assign the value 1 to all the tuples in the relation A and -1 to all the tuples in the complementary relation (i.e. not stored in A), and to combine a tuple value with an estimate of the expert by using *min* operation. Various functions that may be used to define logical operations for combining uncertain information are discussed in [8].

In the light of our discussion, there are applications where we need *(a)* more than two logical values and *(b)* more that one order over these values (i.e. more than one way of structuring the set of logical values). Indeed, the values can be ordered w.r.t. their degree of truth as for instance -1 and 1, being seen as *false* and *true*, are the least and the greatest values, respectively. The values can be ordered also w.r.t. their degree of information or knowledge as for instance 0, -1, and 1, being seen as *unknown*, *false* and *true*, are the least, one maximal and another maximal values, respectively. Therefore we will introduce and use a multivalued logic with two orders, a truth order and a knowledge order.

Let us mention that there exist several formalisms on which various approaches tackling the matter of uncertain, incomplete and inconsistent information in logic programs, databases and knowledge bases, are based. Some of the most used formalisms include the probability theory [13,11,3], the theory of fuzzy logic/sets [5], the multivalued logics [9,6,12], and the possibilistic logic [5,4,7]. [2] provides interesting unified views of various approaches treating the problem of uncertainty, vagueness and probabilistic reasoning in logic programs.

In the following Section 2 we formally introduce the multivalued logic that we use, while in Section 3 we define programs on such a logic, and their quantitative semantics. In Section 4 we study uncertain knowledge bases and their updating based on the quantitative semantics we introduce. Finally we provide some concluding remarks and research directions in Section 5.

2   The Logic L_m

The multivalued logic that we introduce and use in this paper comprises the usual values of the three-valued logic, i.e. *true*, *false* and *unknown*, as well as additional values expressing various degrees of truth. As illustrated in the example provided in the introduction, we use numbers/quantities to represent these logical values, as follows: 1 for *true*, -1 for *false*, 0 for *unknown*, and $\pm 1/m, \ldots, \pm (m-1)/m$ for different degrees of truthness or falseness, where m is a positive integer. The values 1 and -1 express *exact* information while the values $0, \pm 1/m, \ldots, \pm (m-1)/m$ express partial or *uncertain* information; particularly, the value 0 expresses the lack of information. We denote by L_m the set of these $2m+1$ logical values, that is,

$$L_m = \{\pm (n/m) \mid n = 0, \ldots, m\}.$$

As mentioned in the introduction, we consider two orders on the set L_m, the truth order that we denote by $\leq_t$, and the knowledge order that we denote by $\leq_k$. The truth order shows the degree of truth, and the knowledge order shows the degree of knowledge (or of information). The logical values of L_m are thus ordered as follows:

- truth order: $-1 \leq_t -n_1/m \leq_t -n_2/m \leq_t 0 \leq_t n_2/m \leq_t n_1/m \leq_t 1$
- knowledge order: $0 \leq_k -n_2/m \leq_k -n_1/m \leq_k -1$ and $0 \leq_k n_2/m \leq_k n_1/m \leq_k 1$,

for all the integers n_1 and n_2 between 0 and m s.t. $n_1 \geq n_2$.

Note that L_1 is isomorphic with the well known Kleene's three-valued logic that comprises the values *true*, *false* and *unknown*. On the other hand L_2 is a five-valued logic having two new values w.r.t. L_1, namely $1/2$ and $-1/2$, which, in the context of the logic L_2, will be interpreted qualitatively as *possibly true* and *possibly false*, respectively.

Motivation for possible uses of the logics L_m, with various values for m, can be found in various applications relevant to the area of knowledge based systems. For instance, in [1], in order to express degrees of belief in the handled knowledge, one uses linguistic labels like *null evidence*, *negligible evidence*, *small evidence*, *some evidence*, *half likely*, *likely*, *most likely*, *extremely likely*, and *certain*. These labels, seen as qualitative representations of belief degrees, may be mapped into the non negative part of L_8, corresponding to the quantities $0, 1/8, 2/8, 3/8, 4/8, 5/8, 6/8, 7/8$, and 1, respectively. Obviously the opposite labels correspond in the same way to the non positive part of L_8. The advantage in using numbers for belief degrees instead of labels is the possibility of flexibly defining operators that combine these degrees, using different mathematical functions (see [8]). In our framework, this reduces to defining the logical connectives. However linguistic labels are more appropriate to use when dealing for instance with knowledge based systems, in particular during the process of knowledge acquisition from human experts, before converting these labels into quantities.

We shall use the logic L_2 as a context for our examples, for illustrative purposes. However all our results are valid for the logic L_m for an arbitrary m. Unless mentioned otherwise, from now on we refer to the general logic L_m.

In the truth order, we shall use the logical connectives $\wedge, \vee$ and $\neg$ that we define as follows (see [8] for various functions that may be adapted and used to define logical connectives):

$l_1 \wedge l_2 = \min(l_1, l_2)$, $l_1 \vee l_2 = \max(l_1, l_2)$ and $\neg l = -l$

for any l, l_1 and l_2 in L_m. The connectives $\wedge$ and $\vee$ are in fact the meet and join operations in the truth order. It is not difficult to see that $(L_m, \wedge, \vee)$ is a complete lattice w.r.t. this order. In the knowledge order, L_m is a complete semilattice.

3   Logic Programs and Their Quantitative Semantics

The programs that we use in this paper are essentially conventional logic programs with negation, adapted to the context of the logic L_m, in the sense that the logical values of L_m can appear as 0-arity predicate symbols in the bodies of the rules. Another difference from the conventional logic programs lies in the semantics defined here, which is a quantitative one in order to express uncertainty. We consider function free logic programs that are to be used, in our approach, as inference mechanisms in the knowledge bases we introduce.

3.1   Programs

The programs that we consider are built from *atoms*, which are predicate symbols with a list of arguments, for example $Q(a_1, .., a_n)$, where Q is the predicate symbol. An argument can be either a variable or a constant, and we assume that each predicate symbol is associated with a nonnegative integer called its arity. A *literal* is an atom A, or a negated atom of the form $\neg A$. Atoms are called also positive literals, and negated atoms are called also negative literals. A *rule* is a statement of the form $A \leftarrow B_1, B_2, ..., B_n$, where A is an atom and each B_i $(i = 1, ..., n)$ is either a literal or a value from L_m, seen in this case as a 0-arity predicate. The atom A is called the *head* of the rule and $B_1, B_2, ..., B_n$ is called the *body* of the rule. A *program* is a finite set of rules. Such a program consisting of five rules is illustrated below.

P : $A \leftarrow \neg B$; $B \leftarrow \neg C$; $C \leftarrow \neg A$; $D \leftarrow 1/2$; $E \leftarrow A, \neg D$.

A *positive* program is a program in which the negation symbol $\neg$ does not appear.

The *Herbrand universe* of a program P is the set of all constants that appear in P (and if no constant appears in P then the Herbrand universe is assumed to be a fixed singleton). By *instantiation* of a variable x we mean the replacement of x by a constant from the Herbrand universe. If we instantiate all the variables of an atom or of a rule, then we obtain an instantiated atom or rule. The *Herbrand base* of a program P is the set of all possible instantiations of the atoms appearing in P. The Herbrand base of a program P is denoted by HB_P .

3.2   Valuations and Models

Given a program P, we define a *valuation* to be any function that assigns a logical value from L_m to every atom of the Herbrand base. We shall make use of two special valuations that we denote by $\mathbf{0}$ and $-\mathbf{1}$. The valuation $\mathbf{0}$ assigns the value 0 to every atom in the Herbrand base; it is the "nothing known" valuation. The valuation $-\mathbf{1}$ assigns the value -1 to every atom in the Herbrand base; it is the "all false" valuation.

Given a valuation v, we extend it to elements of L_m (seen here as predicates of arity 0), to literals and to conjunctions of literals and 0-arity predicates from L_m as follows:

$v(l) = l$, where l is any element of L_m,
$v(\neg A) = \neg v(A)$, where A is any instantiated atom,
$v(B_1 \wedge B_2 \wedge ... \wedge B_n) = v(B_1) \wedge v(B_2) \wedge ... \wedge v(B_n)$, for $n \geq 0$,

where the B_i's are instantiated literals or elements from L_m.

We can extend the two orders $\leq_t$ and $\leq_k$ to the set V of all valuations in a natural way: for any valuations u and v, we say that

$u \leq_t v$ if $u(A) \leq_t v(A)$ for all A in HB_P and
$u \leq_k v$ if $u(A) \leq_k v(A)$ for all A in HB_P.

It is then not difficult to see that, in the truth order, V becomes a complete lattice while, in the knowledge order, V becomes a complete semilattice.

In the truth order, we say that a valuation v *satisfies* an instantiated rule $A \leftarrow B_1, B_2, ..., B_n$ if $v(A) \geq_t v(B_1 \wedge B_2 \wedge ... \wedge B_n)$. This definition is natural, as it expresses the fact that if A is deduced from $B_1, B_2, ..., B_n$ then A must be assigned a logical value greater than or equal to the value assigned to $B_1 \wedge B_2 \wedge ... \wedge B_n$. Now, if a valuation v satisfies all possible instantiations of the rules of a program P, then v is called a *model* of P. Given a program P, we shall denote by P^* the set of all possible instantiations of the rules of P. Note that P^* is also a program, possibly much larger, in general, than P, but finite.

Given a program P, we define the *immediate consequence operator* of P to be a mapping $\Phi_P : V \to V$ defined as follows: for every valuation u in V, $\Phi_P(u)$ is a valuation s.t. for every atom A of the Herbrand base,

$$\Phi_P(u)(A) = lub_t\{u(C) \mid A \leftarrow C \text{ in } P^*\}.$$

Here lub_t denotes the least upper bound in the truth order.

3.3   Quantitative Semantics of Positive Programs

We can show easily that if P is a positive program then its immediate consequence operator Φ_P is monotone in the truth order. Now, as the set V of all valuations is a complete lattice, Φ_P has a least fixpoint w.r.t. $\leq_t$, denoted by $lfp_t\ \Phi_P$. We can show that this least fixpoint is, in fact, the least model of P w.r.t. $\leq_t$. So we call $lfp_t\ \Phi_P$ the *quantitative semantics* of P, or simply the semantics of P. It follows that the semantics of P can be computed as the limit of the following sequence of iterations of Φ_P:

$$u_0 = -1 \quad \text{and} \quad u_{n+1} = \Phi_P(u_n) \text{ for } n \geq 0.$$

Here, -1 is the valuation that assigns the value -1 to every atom of the Herbrand base. Note that since the programs contain no function symbols the computation of the semantics $lfp_t\Phi_P$ terminates in a finite number of steps. Note also that, due to the way the semantics is computed, i.e. by iterating the immediate consequence operator to reach its fixpoint or, equivalently, by repeatedly applying the rules until nothing new is obtained, the semantics can be intuitively interpreted as the total knowledge that can be extracted/inferred from the program.

3.4   Quantitative Semantics of Programs with Negation

If the program P contains negative literals then the immediate consequence operator Φ_P is no more monotone. As a consequence we can no more define the semantics of P as the least model of P w.r.t. the truth order, since such a model may not exist. So we have to look for a new definition of semantics for P extending the semantics of positive programs. The idea, explained intuitively through the following example, is, again, to try to deduce all the possible knowledge from a program with negation.

Example 1. Consider the logic L_2 and the following program P, where A, B, C and D are predicates of arity 0:

$$A \leftarrow \neg B; \quad B \leftarrow \neg C; \quad C \leftarrow \neg A; \quad D \leftarrow 1/2; \quad E \leftarrow A, \neg D.$$

Note that P is already instantiated, that is $P^* = P$. We begin by assuming "nothing known" about the negative literals of the program i.e., we begin with the valuation $v_0 = \mathbf{0}$ for the negative literals. Now, if we replace all the negative literals of P^* by their values under v_0 (i.e. by 0), then we obtain the following positive program denoted by P/v_0:

$$A \leftarrow 0; \quad B \leftarrow 0; \quad C \leftarrow 0; \quad D \leftarrow 1/2; \quad E \leftarrow A, 0.$$

The semantics of P/v_0 is:

$$lfp_t\,\Phi_{P/v_0} = \begin{bmatrix} A & B & C & D & E \\ 0 & 0 & 0 & 1/2 & 0 \end{bmatrix}.$$

As a result, we have increased our knowledge, since we now know that D is associated with $1/2$ (as opposed to 0 that we had assumed initially). This increased knowledge is represented by the valuation $v_1 = lfp_t\Phi_{P/v_0}$.

The next step is to use v_1 instead of v_0. That is, we can now replace all the negative literals of P^* by their new values under v_1, and infer more knowledge from the new positive program P/v_1 we thus obtain. This knowledge is given by the semantics $lfp_t\Phi_{P/v_1}$ of the program P/v_1, that we denote by v_2. The process continues with generating new positive programs and computing their semantics until no new knowledge can be inferred. Although we do not illustrate the complete process here, in our example the total knowledge inferred from the positive programs we build (and hence from the original program P), is given by the valuation:

$$v_2 = lfp_t\ \Phi_{P/v_2} = \begin{bmatrix} A & B & C & D & E \\ 0 & 0 & 0 & 1/2 & -1/2 \end{bmatrix}$$

Intuitively speaking, the total knowledge inferred from the program, i.e. the valuation v_2 above, naturally represents the semantics of the program.

We formally define the semantics of a program P with negation as follows.

Definition 1. *The mapping $GL_P : V \to V$ defined by $GL_P(v) = lfp_t\Phi_{P/v}$, for all v in V, is called the extended Gelfond-Lifschitz transformation of P.*

Using the algebraic properties of complete lattice and complete semilattice of L_m w.r.t. $\leq_t$ and $\leq_k$ respectively, we can show the following:

Theorem 1. *The operator GL_P is monotone in the knowledge order.*

Now, as the set V of all valuations is a complete semilattice in the knowledge order, GL_P has a least fixpoint w.r.t. $\leq_k$, denoted by $lfp_k GL_P$. In the previous example, this least fixpoint is the valuation v_2. We can show that the fixpoints of GL_P are models of P, and we call them *multivalued models* of P. The $lfp_k GL_P$ is the multivalued model of P that has the least degree of information. In fact, $lfp_k GL_P$ represents all the information/knowledge that one can extract from P, as we have seen in the previous example. So we choose $lfp_k GL_P$ to represent the semantics of P and we call it the *quantitative semantics* of P. It follows that the quantitative semantics of P can be computed as the limit of the following sequence of iterations of GL_P:

$$v_0 = \mathbf{0} \quad \text{and} \quad v_{n+1} = GL_P(v_n) \text{ for any } n \geq 0.$$

The limit can be reached in a finite number of iterations due to the function free programs we consider. We note that, if we use the three-valued logic L_1 then the quantitative semantics described here coincides with Przymusinski's three-valued stable semantics [10] that, in turn, coincides with the well-founded semantics.

4 Knowledge Bases with Uncertain Information

4.1 Quantitative Semantics for Knowledge Bases

The rules of a program represent our general perception or knowledge of a part of the "real" world. Our general perception represented by the rules, is then confronted to the observation of "real" world facts. Informally, a fact is a statement such as "an ostrich possibly cannot fly", describing the results of our observation. More formally, a fact is an instantiated atom along with the logical value that observation assigns to it. As a consequence, we shall represent facts as pairs of the form $\langle A, l \rangle$, where A is an instantiated atom and l is any value from L_m. For instance, in logic L_2, the fact above will be represented as $\langle\ Flies(ostrich), -1/2 \rangle$. We have the following

Definition 2. *An uncertain knowledge base is a pair* $\Delta = (P, F)$*, where* P *is a program and* F *is a set of facts in the context of the logic* L_m*.*

Now, when we observe a fact $\langle A, l \rangle$ and we place it in the knowledge base, we certainly intend to assign the logical value l to A, *no matter* what value is assigned to A by the quantitative semantics of P. In other words, the semantics of the knowledge base will be that of P modified so that A is assigned the value l. More formally, in order to define the semantics of a knowledge base $\Delta = (P, F)$, we first transform P^*, using F, as follows:

- Step 1: Delete from P^* every rule whose head appears in a fact of F
- Step 2: Add a rule $A \leftarrow l$ for every fact $\langle A, l \rangle$ in F.

Let us denote by $P \diamond F$ the program obtained by applying the above steps 1 and 2 to P^*. Note that Step 1 removes every rule of P^* that can possibly influence the value assigned to A in the semantics of Δ; and Step 2 guarantees that A will actually be assigned the value l. Informally speaking, the two steps above resolve any potential inconsistency between rules and facts in the knowledge base by giving priority to facts[1]. However, inconsistency may be generated by contradictory facts alone, hence the following definitions:

Definition 3. *A knowledge base* $\Delta = (P, F)$ *is called consistent if* F *does not contain two facts of the form* $\langle A, l \rangle$ *and* $\langle A, l' \rangle$ *with* $l \neq l'$.

Definition 4. *The quantitative semantics of a consistent knowledge base* $\Delta = (P, F)$ *is defined to be the quantitative semantics of the program* $P \diamond F$.

The following proposition shows that facts are trivially contained in the semantics of the knowledge base.

Proposition 1. *Let* $\Delta = (P, F)$ *be a knowledge base and let* v *be its semantics. Then, for every fact* $\langle A, l \rangle$ *in* F*, we have* $v(A) = l$.

Given a knowledge base Δ whose semantics is v, we call a *knowledge base fact* any pair $\langle A, v(A) \rangle$, where A is an instantiated atom.

4.2   Knowledge Base Updating

Informally, by updating a knowledge base $\Delta = (P, F)$ we mean adding a fact $\langle A, l \rangle$ in the set F. Of course, the intention is that the atom A must be assigned the value l in the semantics of the updated knowledge base.

The knowledge base updating is formally defined as follows:

Definition 5. *Let* $\Delta = (P, F)$ *be a consistent knowledge base. The update of* Δ *by a fact* $\langle A, l \rangle$*, denoted by* $upd(\Delta, A, l)$*, is a new consistent knowledge base* $\Delta' = (P, F')$*, where* F' *is defined by:*
(1) remove from F *every fact* $\langle A, l' \rangle$ *such that* $l' \neq l$ *and*
(2) to the result thus obtained, add $\langle A, l \rangle$.

---

[1] Note that inconsistency cannot appear due to rules alone.

4.3   Properties of Updates

The updating operation, as defined here, enjoys certain properties that correspond to intuition. In order to state these properties, let us call two knowledge bases Δ and Δ' (with the same Herbrand base) *equivalent* if they have the same semantics. We shall denote this by $\Delta \equiv \Delta'$. The first property of updating is idempotence, as expressed by the following:

Proposition 2. *For any knowledge base Δ, and for any instantiated atom A and logical value l, we have: $upd(upd(\Delta, A, l), A, l) \equiv upd(\Delta, A, l)$.*

The following property says that, under certain conditions, the order in which updates are performed is not important:

Proposition 3. *For any knowledge base Δ, and for any instantiated atoms A and A' and logical values l and l' we have:*
$upd(upd(\Delta, A, l), A', l) \equiv upd(upd(\Delta, A', l), A, l)$, and if A and A' are distinct atoms then $upd(upd(\Delta, A, l), A', l') \equiv upd(upd(\Delta, A', l'), A, l)$.

The following proposition states a property of "reversibility" for updates. Roughly speaking, this property means that if we modify the value of a knowledge base fact $\langle A, l \rangle$ from l to l', and from l' back to l, then we recover the original knowledge base facts (that is, the original and the final knowledge bases are equivalent).

Proposition 4. *Let Δ be a knowledge base and let $\langle A, l \rangle$ be a knowledge base fact in Δ. Then $upd(upd(\Delta, A, l'), A, l) \equiv \Delta$.*

Another property of updates is monotonicity. Roughly speaking, this property means that if the value of a knowledge base fact increases then so does the knowledge base semantics. In the knowledge order, this property holds for any knowledge base:

Proposition 5. *Let $\Delta = (P, F)$ be a knowledge base with semantics v, let $\langle A, l \rangle$ be any fact, and let v' be the semantics of the knowledge base $\Delta' = upd(\Delta, A, l)$. Then the following statements hold:*
    (1) if $l \geq_k v(A)$ then $v' \geq_k v$ and   (2) if $l \leq_k v(A)$ then $v' \leq_k v$.

In the truth order, however, monotonicity holds only for knowledge bases with positive programs:

Proposition 6. *Let $\Delta = (P, F)$ be a knowledge base with semantics v, let $\langle A, l \rangle$ be any fact, and let v' be the semantics of the knowledge base $\Delta' = upd(\Delta, A, l)$. If P is a positive program, then the following statements hold:*
    (1) if $l \geq_t v(A)$ then $v' \geq_t v$ and   (2) if $l \leq_t v(A)$ then $v' \leq_t v$.

5   Conclusion

In order to express uncertainty in knowledge bases we have introduced a multivalued logic called L_m, with a double algebraic structure of lattice and semilattice w.r.t. two orders - the truth order and the knowledge order, respectively. We have defined a quantitative semantics for logic programs and knowledge bases in the context of the logic L_m, which extends successful conventional semantics as the three-valued stable semantics and the well-founded semantics.

We note that the logic L_m may be used to express various degrees of uncertainty but not inconsistency. That is, the problem of dealing with constraints and/or inconsistent data has not been tackled here. Moreover, in our approach a consistent knowledge base remains so after performing any update operation on it.

Future work concerns the extension of the approach presented here such that the knowledge base facts have imprecise degrees of uncertainty as intervals of punctual values.

References

1. Baroni, P., Giacomin, M., Guida, G.: A- and V-uncertainty: an exploration about uncertainty modeling from a knowledge engineering perspective. International Journal on Artificial Intelligence Tools 16(2) (2007)
2. Baral, C.: Logic Programming and Uncertainty. In: Benferhat, S., Grant, J. (eds.) SUM 2011. LNCS, vol. 6929, pp. 22–37. Springer, Heidelberg (2011)
3. Baral, C., Gelfond, M., Rushton, N.: Probabilistic reasoning with answer sets. Theory and Practice of Logic Programming 9(1) (2009)
4. Benferhat, S., Prade, H.: Compiling possibilistic knowledge bases. In: Proc. of the 17th European Conference on Artificial Intelligence (2006)
5. Bosc, P., Prade, H.: An Introduction to the Fuzzy Set and Possibility Theory-Based Treatment of Flexible Queries and Uncertain or Imprecise Databases. Uncertainty Management in Information Systems. Kluwer Academic Publishers (1996)
6. Deschrijver, G., Arieli, O., Cornelis, C., Kerre, E.: A bilattice-based framework for handling graded truth and imprecision. J. Uncertainty, Fuzziness and Knowledge-Based Systems 15(1) (2007)
7. Dubois, D., Prade, H.: Possibilistic logic: a retrospective and prospective view. Fuzzy Sets and Systems 144, 3–23 (2004)
8. Fagin, R.: Combining fuzzy information from multiple systems. J. Computer and System Sciences 58, 1 (1999)
9. Fitting, M.: Fixpoint semantics for logic programming - a survey. Theoretical Computer Science 278(1-2) (2002)
10. Przymusinski, T.C.: Extended Stable Semantics for Normal and Disjunctive Programs. In: Proc. of the Seventh Intl. Conference on Logic Programming (1990)
11. Ross, R., Subrahmanian, V.S., Grant, J.: Aggregate Operators in Probabilistic Databases. Journal of the ACM 52(1) (2005)
12. Stamate, D.: Queries with multivalued logic based semantics for imperfect information fusion. In: Proc. of 40th IEEE International Symposium on Multiple-Valued Logic (2010)
13. Subrahmanian, V.S.: Probabilistic Databases and Logic Programming. In: Codognet, P. (ed.) ICLP 2001. LNCS, vol. 2237, p. 10. Springer, Heidelberg (2001)

Weighted Attribute Combinations
Based Similarity Measures

Marco Baioletti, Giulianella Coletti, and Davide Petturiti

Dip. Matematica e Informatica, Università di Perugia,
via Vanvitelli 1, 06123 Perugia, Italy
{baioletti,coletti,davide.petturiti}@dmi.unipg.it

Abstract. In this paper we introduce three parameterized similarity measures which take into account not only the single features of two objects under comparison, but also all the significant combinations of attributes. In this way a great expressive power can be achieved and field expert knowledge about relations among features can be encoded in the weights assigned to each combination. Here we consider only binary attributes and, in order to face the difficulty of weights' elicitation, we propose some effective techniques to learn weights from an already labelled dataset. Finally, a comparative study of classification power with respect to other largely used similarity indices is presented.

Keywords: weighted attribute combination, similarity measure, binary data, classification.

1 Introduction

An important task in many fields, such as artificial intelligence, statistics and information retrieval, is to quantify how two given objects O_1 and O_2 are "similar". Usually this is done by means of a *similarity measure*, i.e., a function which given the descriptions of O_1 and O_2 returns a real number, generally in $[0, 1]$.

While a similarity measure is based on the concept of *proximity* between objects, it is also possible to quantify how much they differ each other, obtaining a corresponding *dissimilarity measure*.

The most naive approach to model dissimilarity between objects is to map them in a metric space and use the ensuing distance function to express dissimilarity. Of course, the metric assumption is quite strong and deeply tied to the nature of the available data nevertheless it is often inconsistent with human reasoning. Indeed Tversky, in his seminal work [15], showed that human assessed similarity violates "naturally" two metric conditions such as *symmetry* and the *triangular inequality*.

In this paper we focus on similarity measures for *binary data*, i.e., for objects described in terms of presence/absence attributes. Following Tversky's proposal, in the relevant literature (see, e.g., [12,7]) a plethora of different similarity indices have been proposed in the case of binary data and these, in turn, have been extended to fuzzy data [3]. Given the considerable number of existing measures,

S. Greco et al. (Eds.): IPMU 2012, Part III, CCIS 299, pp. 211–220, 2012.
© Springer-Verlag Berlin Heidelberg 2012

in [1,2] a qualitative study of similarity relation is carried on while in [11] a comparison between largely used measures is provided.

The most famous similarity measure for binary data used in computer science is certainly the *Jaccard index*. In this case, let A and B denote the sets of positive attributes in objects O_1 and O_2, then the similarity is given by

$$J(A, B) = \frac{|A \cap B|}{|A \cup B|} \tag{1}$$

where $|\cdot|$ denotes the set cardinality. Other well-known similarity measures are, for example, the *Dice index* and the *Ochiai index*, but there exist many others.

All the cited measures are essentially based on the cardinality of a description A, meaning that only the single features are taken into account and all are given the same "importance".

A first generalization of this approach is to diversify the relevance of each attribute x_i assigning it a non-negative real weight w_i. This is the case, for example, of the following weighted version of Jaccard index

$$J_w(A, B) = \frac{\sum_{x_i \in A \cap B} w_i}{\sum_{x_i \in A \cup B} w_i}. \tag{2}$$

However, also this generalization does not take into account the possible *interactions* among attributes. Indeed the simultaneous presence of two or more attributes in two objects O_1 and O_2 can make them more similar, while if this combination appears only in one of them, they should be less similar.

This way of reasoning is quite common in human behaviour. For instance, suppose that we are comparing two cars. If we know both cars are red, then we are willing to say that they are relatively similar and the same holds true if we know that both cars are expensive. Nevertheless, if we know that both are red *and* expensive, we consider them much more similar to each other. In fact, this combination of two attributes lead us to think both cars are Ferrari. Surely, this is not enough to reach such a conclusion: other combinations of attributes are needed. On the other hand, if we know that the first car has *also* a little horse sign, while the second car has not, then their degree of similarity should be less.

Following this line, we propose a generalization of Jaccard measure which takes into account, at least in theory, all the possible subsets of attributes, giving to each of them a non-negative weight.

In this way we obtain a family of similarity measure with a high expressive power and in which it is possible to convey background knowledge about the application domain, through the weights.

This expressiveness is due to the great freedom in assessing a large number of parameters, but then this could cause a difficulty in eliciting the weights. To face this problem it is necessary to put some constraints on the weight function in order to reduce the number of parameters to be specified.

Here we propose a method to automatically learn the weights from a classified dataset: this can be used also to help an expert in the eliciting process. We finally compare the similarities learned with this method to other well-known similarity measures, in a classification task.

2   Preliminaries

We assume that objects are described by means of a set $X = \{x_1, x_2, \ldots, x_n\}$ of binary features whose *presence* or *absence* is "significant" for the particular application. In this way the *description* of an object O consists essentially of a binary random vector $(a_1, a_2, \ldots, a_n) \in \{0,1\}^n$ or, equivalently, a subset $A \in \mathcal{P}(X)$ where $x_i \in A$ if and only if $a_i = 1$.

In this setting a *similarity measure* is generally defined as a function $S : \mathcal{P}(X) \times \mathcal{P}(X) \to [0,1]$. There is no universal consensus about the properties a similarity measure should satisfy: commonly required properties are *reflexivity*, *symmetry*, some kinds of *monotonicity* and *T-transitivity*, where T is a *t*-norm.

Recall that a *t-norm* T is a commutative, associative, monotonic, binary operation on $[0,1]$ having 1 as neutral element [10]. In particular, we denote with T_M, T_P, T_L and T_D the minimum, the algebraic product, the Łukasiewicz and the drastic *t*-norm, respectively, observing that $T_D < T_L < T_P < T_M$.

Notice that T-transitivity requires $S(A,B) \geq T(S(A,C), S(C,B))$ for every $A, B, C \in \mathcal{P}(X)$ and it is especially meaningful for T equal to T_P or T_L since, in this case the functions $\delta(A,B) = -\log S(A,B)$ and $\delta'(A,B) = 1 - S(A,B)$ satisfy the triangle inequality [4], respectively.

3   Weighted Attribute Combinations Based Similarities

We call *significance assessment* a function $\sigma : \mathcal{P}(X) \to [0, +\infty)$ satisfying the following conditions:

(S1) $\sigma(\emptyset) = 0$;
(S2) $\sigma(\{x_i\}) > 0$ for every $x_i \in X$.

The function σ assigns a non-negative real weight to each combination of attributes quantifying its "significance" in evaluating the similarity between two objects. Notice that requirement **(S2)** imposes to assign a positive weight to singletons. This restriction has a clear semantic interpretation: since choosing the description of objects, only those attributes which the expert considers "significant" are taken into account, then it is quite natural to require for them a positive significance weight.

The function σ is then used to compute another function $\varphi : \mathcal{P}(X) \to [0, +\infty)$ defined for every $A \in \mathcal{P}(X)$ as:

$$\varphi(A) = \sum_{B \subseteq A} \sigma(B). \tag{3}$$

It is possible to verify that φ satisfies the following properties:

(P1) $\varphi(A) = 0$ if and only if $A = \emptyset$;
(P2) φ is monotonic w.r.t. set inclusion;
(P3) $\varphi\left(\bigcup_{i=1}^{k} A_i\right) \geq \sum_{\emptyset \neq I \subseteq \{1,\ldots,k\}} (-1)^{|I|+1} \varphi\left(\bigcap_{i \in I} A_i\right)$ for $k \in \mathbb{N}$ and $A_i \in \mathcal{P}(X)$.

We stress that in the case the significance assessment σ fulfils the further normalization condition $\sum\limits_{A \in \mathcal{P}(X)} \sigma(A) = 1$, then φ is a *belief function* in the context of the Dempster-Shafer theory of evidence [14].

Now we introduce three classes of similarity measures ranging in $[0, 1]$, each parameterized by a significance assessment σ:

$$S_1(A, B) = \frac{\varphi(A \cap B)}{\varphi(A \setminus B) + \varphi(B \setminus A) + \varphi(A \cap B)}, \tag{4}$$

$$S_2(A, B) = \frac{\varphi(A \cap B)}{\varphi(A \Delta B) + \varphi(A \cap B)}, \tag{5}$$

$$S_3(A, B) = \frac{\varphi(A \cap B)}{\varphi(A \cup B)}. \tag{6}$$

Notice that for $i = 1, 2, 3$, in the case $A = B = \emptyset$, then a $\frac{0}{0}$ form is achieved. In this circumstance, in order to guarantee reflexivity, we set

$$S_i(\emptyset, \emptyset) = 1. \tag{7}$$

It is easily seen that measures S_i, $i = 1, 2, 3$, are a generalization of the weighted Jaccard index (2), indeed in the case $\sigma(A) = 0$ for all $A \in \mathcal{P}(X)$ s.t. $|A| > 1$ we obtain the same measure. Moreover, for every σ, **(P3)** implies

$$S_1(A, B) \geq S_2(A, B) \geq S_3(A, B). \tag{8}$$

In fact, the three generalizations have the role to stress in a different way the weight of the aggregation of the features present in both objects or in only one of them.

By the definition of similarities S_i, $i = 1, 2, 3$, and properties **(P1)**–**(P3)** the following proposition easily follows.

Proposition 1. *For $i = 1, 2, 3$ and for every significance assessment σ it holds:*

(strict reflexivity) $S_i(A, B) = 1$ *if and only if $A = B$, for $A, B \in \mathcal{P}(X)$;*
(symmetry) $S_i(A, B) = S_i(B, A)$ *for every $A, B \in \mathcal{P}(X)$;*
(exclusiveness) $S_i(A, B) = 0$ *if and only if $A \cap B = \emptyset \neq B$, for $A, B \in \mathcal{P}(X)$.*

The following proposition shows two forms of monotonicity [3,5] of the introduced similarity measures.

Proposition 2. *For $i = 1, 2, 3$ and for every significance assessment σ it holds:*

(monotonicity) *if $A \cap B \supseteq A \cap B'$ and $B \setminus A \subseteq B' \setminus A$ and $A \setminus B \subseteq A \setminus B'$,*
then $S_i(A, B) \geq S_i(A, B')$, for every $A, B, B' \in \mathcal{P}(X)$;
(chain monotonicity) *if $A \subseteq B \subseteq C$, then $S_i(A, B) \geq S_i(A, C)$ and $S_i(B, C) \geq S_i(A, C)$, for every $A, B, C \in \mathcal{P}(X)$.*

Proof. Both properties follow from the monotonicity of φ and the strict monotonicity of the function $f(x, y) = \frac{x}{y+x}$ with respect to both variables. $\square$

We note that the role of σ is crucial in measuring similarity, in fact for different choices of σ we can have different orders in similarity for every S_i, $i = 1, 2, 3$, as Example 1 shows.

Example 1. Consider the feature set $X = \{x_1, x_2\}$ and the following significance assessment: $\sigma(\emptyset) = 0$, $\sigma(\{x_1\}) = \sigma(X) = 1$ and $\sigma(\{x_2\}) = 2$. If we take $A = \{x_1\}$, $B = D = X$ and $C = \{x_2\}$, then straightforward computations show that $S_i(A, B) < S_i(C, D)$ for $i = 1, 2, 3$.

On the other hand if we consider the significance assessment $\sigma'(\emptyset) = 0$, $\sigma'(\{x_2\}) = \sigma'(X) = 1$ and $\sigma'(\{x_1\}) = 2$ then we have $S_i(A, B) > S_i(C, D)$ for $i = 1, 2, 3$.

We investigate now the T-transitivity of similarity measures S_i, $i = 1, 2, 3$, focusing on T_D, T_L, T_P and T_M t-norms.

First of all we notice that due to exclusiveness property, none of the three families of similarity measures can be T_P-transitive or T_M-transitive as proved in [6]. Nevertheless, due to the great freedom of the significance assessment σ, it holds that generally all the three similarity measures are not T-transitive with T a Frank t-norm [10], as shown by the next example.

Example 2. Consider the feature set $X = \{x_1, x_2, x_3\}$ together with the significance assessment $\sigma(\emptyset) = 0$, $\sigma(\{x_2\}) = \sigma(\{x_3\}) = \sigma(\{x_1, x_2\}) = \sigma(\{x_1, x_3\}) = \sigma(\{x_2, x_3\}) = 1$, $\sigma(\{x_1\}) = 20$ and $\sigma(X) = 75$;

For $A = \{x_1\}$, $B = X$ and $C = \{x_1, x_2\}$ it results $S_i(A, B) = \frac{20}{23}$, $S_i(A, C) = \frac{20}{21}$ and $S_i(C, B) = \frac{22}{23}$, for $i = 1, 2$. Moreover, for $A' = \{x_1, x_2\}$, $B' = \{x_1, x_3\}$ and $C' = \{x_1\}$ we have $S_3(A', B') = \frac{1}{5}$ and $S_3(A', C') = S_3(C', B') = \frac{10}{11}$.

It is easily checked that for the given A, B, C, A', B' and C' it holds

$$S_i(A, B) < T(S_i(A, C), S_i(C, B)), \ i = 1, 2, \text{ and}$$

$$S_3(A', B') < T(S_3(A', C'), S_3(C', B')),$$

with T equal to T_M, T_P, T_L. In particular, since for every Frank t-norm T, it holds $T_L < T < T_M$ [10], then the conclusion follows for every t-norm of the Frank's class.

The following example shows the lack of T-transitivity is due to a particular choice of σ. Indeed, a different assessment of σ leads to T-transitivity for some t-norms.

Example 3. Consider the feature set of Example 2 on which the following significance assessment is given: $\sigma(\emptyset) = \sigma(\{x_1, x_2\}) = \sigma(\{x_1, x_3\}) = \sigma(\{x_2, x_3\}) = 0$, $\sigma(X) = 1$, $\sigma(\{x_2\}) = 6$ and $\sigma(\{x_1\}) = \sigma(\{x_3\}) = 26$.

For every $A, B, C \in \mathcal{P}(X)$ one can check that

$$S_i(A, B) \geq T_L(S_i(A, C), S_i(C, B)),$$

for $i = 1, 2, 3$, implying each similarity S_i (with the given σ) is T_L-transitive. Notice that T_L-transitivity implies, for example, also $T_{-0.5}^{SW}$-transitivity, where $T_{-0.5}^{SW}(x, y) = \max(2x + 2y - 2 - xy, 0)$ is the Sugeno-Weber t-norm with parameter -0.5. Previous statement directly follows from $T_{-0.5}^{SW} < T_L$.

For what concerns T_D-transitivity, the following result holds.

Proposition 3. *For $i = 1, 2, 3$ and for every significance assessment σ it holds:*

(T_D-transitivity) $S_i(A, B) \geq T_D(S_i(A, C), S_i(C, B))$, *for $A, B, C \in \mathcal{P}(X)$.*

Proof. If $S_i(A, C) \neq 1 \neq S_i(C, B)$ the conclusion is trivial. On the contrary, by the strict reflexivity property, $S_i(A, C) = 1$ only in the case $A = C$, and analogously $S_i(C, B) = 1$ only in the case $C = B$. In both cases the conclusion follows. $\square$

4   Learning the Significance Assessment

In the previous section we have seen some examples with a small number of attributes, in which it was possible to reason about all the existing subsets and to assign to each of them a meaningful weight.

In real applications this is scarcely possible: the number of attributes can be much larger, making infeasible for an expert even to consider all the possible subsets. Moreover, since there is an almost complete freedom on the values of σ, an operative criterion to elicit it does not exist: the significance assessment can only reflect a subjective judgement.

Therefore it is necessary to find a procedure which allows to find in a mechanical way the weights for all the subsets (or for a part of them) in a way to have "good results" with the corresponding similarity measures. A possible solution for these problems is to learn the similarity function from some available already classified data.

Suppose we have a set $\mathcal{D} = \{(\mathbf{x}_1, y_1), \ldots, (\mathbf{x}_N, y_N)\}$ of N labelled data, called *training set*. Each $\mathbf{x}_i$ is a n-tuple and y_i is its corresponding class label, belonging to a finite set $\mathcal{C}$. The principle is that objects assigned to the same class should be as similar as possible, while objects in different classes should be dissimilar.

This approach is strictly related to metric function learning (see, e.g., [16,8,17]), where the goal is to learn a Mahalanobis metric function from data. In particular, we adapt the technique of Neighbourhood Component Analysis, used in [8], to our problem.

A similarity function and the classified data $\mathcal{D}$ can indeed be used to define a nearest-neighbourhood classifier: given any object O, assign to O the class which corresponds to the nearest object $O' \in \mathcal{D}$ to O.

As done in [8], for a fixed similarity S_i, the problem is to find the value of σ which maximizes $N_{LOO}(\sigma)$, the number of correctly classified objects in $\mathcal{D}$ by means of *leave-one-out* (LOO) technique. Namely, for each $O \in \mathcal{D}$, we compute the nearest-neighbour $O' \in \mathcal{D} \setminus \{O\}$ and see whether the class of O' is the same as the class of O. The affirmative case is considered a success, while the negative case is a failure: $N_{LOO}(\sigma)$ is therefore the number of successes.

This is a continuous optimization problem, in which the objective function, however, is not continuous. Therefore the standard techniques for optimization problems (such as gradient-descent) cannot be used. Indeed in [8], they replace the objective function with a differentiable one, obtained by using a *soft max* to compute the nearest-neighbour $O' \in \mathcal{D} \setminus \{O\}$.

We have decided to use two different stochastic incomplete methods to face this optimization problem: Particle Swarm Optimization (PSO) and Differential Evolution (DE).

Both these algorithms operate on a population of a fixed number of candidate solutions, i.e., possible values for σ. The population is subject to an evolution phase for K epochs. At the end the best candidate found in all the epochs is returned as a solution for the optimization problem. The algorithms differ in the way the population evolves. For a comprehensive description of both algorithms, refer to [13] for Differential Evolution and to [9] for Particle Swarm Optimization.

Although there is no guarantee that PSO and DE produce optimal solutions, these algorithms often provide very good or near optimal solutions, in a reasonable computational time.

However, the number of possible components of σ is too large, therefore we propose two different limitations on the number of considered subsets. These limitations reduce the search space and provide a compact form for σ, so they produce a great reduction in computation time. Even though this affects the completeness (only some of the possible candidate solutions will ever be taken into account), it is possible however to obtain good non-optimal solutions.

A first bound is L, the maximum acceptable cardinality of the subsets: $\sigma(A)$ is forced to 0 for those subsets such that $|A| > L$. In this way σ is sparse and has $O(n^L)$ non-zero elements.

Another possible bound is M, the maximum number of non-zero elements in σ, which has no relation with the cardinality but preserves the property **(S2)**.

The two bounds can be combined together, in this way there are only up to M non-zero values of σ, corresponding to subsets with at most L elements.

It is easy to see that L and M can be used to have a trade off between completeness and computation time: smaller values make the search procedure faster, while higher values could produce a higher value for the objective function.

5 Experimental Results

We have implemented in C two procedures which learn σ from labelled data using, respectively, PSO and DE, to optimize the objective function $N_{LOO}(\sigma)$.

To test the efficiency of our proposal we have performed a series of experiments in which we compared the accuracy of a NN-classifier based on the learned similarity functions S_1, S_2, S_3, with respect to the same classifier based on three classical similarity measures: Jaccard (J), Dice (D) and a similarity based on the Euclidean distance d_2: $E(A, B) = 1 - \frac{d_2(A,B)^2}{n}$. The classifiers are compared by computing their *accuracy* on a different dataset $\mathcal{T}$, called *test data*, in which all the data are already classified.

We generated random datasets with m instances of n binary attributes and c possible classes, using Weka's package `weka.datagenerators.classifiers.cl-assification.RDG1` which creates a set of randomly generated rules and assigns a class to each instance according to this rule set. The dataset is divided in a training set and a test set, with a classical 4-fold cross-validation scheme. For each triple (m, n, c) we performed $t = 50$ experiments and reported the accuracy of S_1, S_2, S_3, J, E, D. The number of attributes n has been varied from 8 to 12, the number of classes from 3 to 5, while for each value of n we have used a suitable value for m, which provides training sets of roughly the 35% of all the possible combinations of values.

After some preliminary tests, we decided to set $L = 3$ and $M = 2n$, which is a good compromise between completeness and computation time.

Notice that a search procedure, like PSO or DE, in a high dimensional space often produces solutions with the same quality or even worse than a search in a restricted subspace (like imposing the constraints on L and M) because the algorithm could be not able to explore all the possible dimensions. A preliminary test we have performed justified this fact.

In Table 1 we show the results obtained with the DE algorithm, while in Table 2 are presented the analogous data obtained with the PSO.

Table 1. Mean percentage classification error obtained with DE

n	m	c	S_1	S_2	S_3	J	E	D
8	120	3	16.7%	16.9%	18.7%	21.8%	22.0%	21.8%
8	120	4	17.6%	16.9%	20.3%	24.8%	24.4%	24.8%
8	120	5	19.4%	19.5%	21.4%	26.4%	26.7%	26.4%
9	240	3	12.9%	13.0%	14.9%	19.0%	19.4%	19.0%
9	240	4	13.2%	13.6%	15.5%	21.6%	21.9%	21.6%
9	240	5	15.1%	14.9%	17.0%	23.1%	23.1%	23.1%
10	480	3	9.6%	10.0%	11.6%	17.7%	17.4%	17.7%
10	480	4	9.9%	10.2%	12.6%	19.8%	19.5%	19.8%
10	480	5	9.8%	9.8%	12.2%	19.4%	19.5%	19.4%
11	960	3	7.7%	7.8%	9.4%	16.1%	16.2%	16.1%
11	960	4	8.0%	8.1%	10.5%	17.5%	17.4%	17.5%
11	960	5	9.8%	9.8%	11.8%	19.5%	19.5%	19.5%
12	1920	3	5.2%	5.3%	7.1%	14.6%	14.5%	14.6%
12	1920	4	7.0%	7.0%	9.0%	16.5%	16.4%	16.5%
12	1920	5	8.1%	8.1%	10.4%	18.2%	18.0%	18.2%

First of all, notice that the accuracy results obtained with all the similarities S_i are systematically better than those obtained with all the classical measures. Note that as n increases, the accuracy should increase because with a higher number of attributes it should be easier to determine the correct class. Anyway, the accuracy of classical measures shows a much slower growth with respect to our measures, thus the difference among the latter and the former tends to increase as well.

As expected, for a fixed combination of n and m, as c increases the accuracy of all the similarities tends to decrease.

Table 2. Mean percentage classification error obtained with PSO

n	m	c	S_1	S_2	S_3	J	E	D
8	120	3	17.3%	16.7%	18.6%	21.8%	22.0%	21.8%
8	120	4	17.9%	17.7%	19.3%	24.8%	24.4%	24.8%
8	120	5	20.0%	20.1%	22.6%	26.4%	26.7%	26.4%
9	240	3	13.3%	12.8%	15.0%	19.0%	19.4%	19.0%
9	240	4	13.6%	13.8%	16.3%	21.6%	21.9%	21.6%
9	240	5	14.6%	14.6%	18.4%	23.1%	23.1%	23.1%
10	480	3	9.7%	9.8%	12.1%	17.7%	17.4%	17.7%
10	480	4	9.8%	10.3%	12.4%	19.8%	19.5%	19.8%
10	480	5	9.6%	9.7%	13.1%	19.4%	19.5%	19.4%
11	960	3	8.0%	8.1%	10.3%	16.1%	16.2%	16.1%
11	960	4	8.4%	8.6%	10.8%	17.5%	17.4%	17.5%
11	960	5	10.3%	10.1%	12.6%	19.5%	19.5%	19.5%
12	1920	3	5.5%	5.7%	8.0%	14.6%	14.5%	14.6%
12	1920	4	7.4%	7.4%	9.4%	16.5%	16.4%	16.5%
12	1920	5	8.5%	8.6%	10.9%	18.2%	18.0%	18.2%

Although S_3 is the more immediate generalization of Jaccard index, the experimental results show that among our measures S_3 always produces worst results, while S_1 appears to be slightly better than S_2. A possible explanation for this behaviour is that S_1 handles separately common feature combinations and those which belong to only one object, providing a more precise similarity measure.

Finally, the results obtained with PSO and those obtained with DE are comparable, none of them appears to be better, possibly there is a slight dominance of the DE results on PSO.

6   Conclusions and Future Works

In this paper we have presented three generalizations of Jaccard measure which take into account the simultaneous presence of two or more attributes. We have also described a method for learning the parameter σ of each measure (the significance assessment) and proved that our measures always perform better than classical similarity measures in a classification task.

A first line of future investigation is to characterize the significance assessments which give rise to a T_L-transitive similarity measures, because of its theoretical importance. Such a characterization could provide a "natural" constraint on σ, making it easier to be elicited and learned.

The choice of learning σ by optimizing N_{LOO} function is somehow arbitrary and it would be worth to see if other techniques are more suitable for this aim. Moreover, the bound on M can change the nature of the optimization problem to be solved: a mixed combinatorial-continuous formulation is possible, thus making other resolving technique, like genetic algorithms, more apt.

Finally, since similarity measures are also used in clustering, it would be interesting to compare the behaviour of a clustering algorithm with all the similarity measures here proposed and the classical ones.

References

1. Bouchon-Meunier, B., Coletti, G., Lesot, M.J., Rifqi, M.: Towards a Conscious Choice of a Similarity Measure: A Qualitative Point of View. In: Sossai, C., Chemello, G. (eds.) ECSQARU 2009. LNCS (LNAI), vol. 5590, pp. 542–553. Springer, Heidelberg (2009)
2. Bouchon-Meunier, B., Coletti, G., Lesot, M.J., Rifqi, M.: Towards a Conscious Choice of a Fuzzy Similarity Measure: A Qualitative Point of View. In: Hüllermeier, E., Kruse, R., Hoffmann, F. (eds.) IPMU 2010. LNCS (LNAI), vol. 6178, pp. 1–10. Springer, Heidelberg (2010)
3. Bouchon-Meunier, B., Rifqi, M., Bothorel, S.: Towards general measures of comparison of objects. Fuzzy Sets and Systems 84, 143–153 (1996)
4. De Baets, B., Janssens, S., De Meyer, H.: On the transitivity of a parametric family of cardinality-based similarity measures. Int. J. of Approximate Reasoning 50, 104–116 (2009)
5. De Baets, B., De Meyer, H., Naessens, H.: A class of rational cardinality-based similarity measures. J. of Computational and Applied Mathematics 132, 51–69 (2001)
6. De Baets, B., De Meyer, H., Naessens, H.: On rational cardinality-based inclusion measures. Fuzzy Sets and Systems 128, 169–183 (2002)
7. Choi, S.S., Cha, S.H., Tappert, C.: A Survey of Binary Similarity and Distance Measures. J. on Systemics, Cybernetics and Informatics 1, 43–48 (2010)
8. Goldberger, J., Roweis, S., Salakhutdinov, R., Hinton, G.E.: Neighborhood Components Analysis. In: NIPS 17, pp. 513–520. MIT Press, Cambridge (2005)
9. Kennedy, J., Eberhart, R.C.: Swarm Intelligence. Morgan Kaufmann (2001)
10. Klement, E.P., Mesiar, R., Pap, E.: Triangular Norms. In: Trends in Logic, vol. 8, Kluwer Academic Publishers, Dordrecht (2000)
11. Lesot, M.J., Rifqi, M.: Order-Based Equivalence Degrees for Similarity and Distance Measures. In: Hüllermeier, E., Kruse, R., Hoffmann, F. (eds.) IPMU 2010. LNCS (LNAI), vol. 6178, pp. 19–28. Springer, Heidelberg (2010)
12. Lesot, M.J., Rifqi, M., Benhadda, H.: Similarity measures for binary and numerical data: a survey. Int. J. of Knowledge Engineering and Soft Data Paradigms 1, 63–84 (2009)
13. Price, K., Storn, R., Lampinen, J.: Differential Evolution - A Practical Approach to Global Optimization. Springer (2005)
14. Shafer, G.: A Mathematical Theory of Evidence. Princeton University Press (1976)
15. Tversky, A.: Features of similarity. Psychological Review 84, 327–352 (1977)
16. Xing, E., Ng, A.Y., Jordan, M., Russell, S.: Distance metric learning, with application to clustering with side-information. In: NIPS 15, pp. 505–512. MIT Press, Cambridge (2003)
17. Weinberger, K.Q., Blitzer, J., Saul, L.K.: Distance metric learning for large margin nearest neighbor classification. In: NIPS 18, pp. 1473–1480. MIT Press, Cambridge (2006)

Algorithms for Computation of Concept Trilattice of Triadic Fuzzy Context

Petr Osicka*

DAMOL (Data Analysis and Modeling Laboratory),
Department of Computer Science,
Palacký University, Olomouc, Czech Republic
osicka@acm.org

Abstract. Triadic concept analysis (TCA) is a method of relational data analysis whose aim is to extract a hierarchically structured set of particular clusters from a three-way data describing objects, attributes, and conditions. We present two algorithms for the problem of computing all such clusters from a data describing degrees to which objects have attributes under conditions.

1 Introduction

Various methods of analysis of three-way (or in general multi-way) data proved to be applicable in many areas including psychometrics, chemometrics, signal processing, computer vision, neuroscience, and data mining, [15], [16], [19]. In this paper, we focus on triadic concept analysis (TCA), a particular method of analysis of three-way relational data. The input to TCA consists of a three-dimensional table that captures a relationship between objects, attributes, and conditions. We assume that the relationship is a matter of degree rather than a yes-no relationship, that is an object has an attribute under a condition to a degree. Common examples of such data include results of querying a database at different points in time, folksonomies, and the like. The degrees in which objects, attributes and conditions are related are assumed to form a residuated lattice, an ordered scale of degrees equipped with truth functions of logical connectives [20].

The output of TCA is a hierarchically ordered set of clusters, called triadic fuzzy concepts. Triadic fuzzy concepts are triplets $\langle A, B, C \rangle$, where A is a fuzzy set of objects, B is a fuzzy set of attributes and, C is a fuzzy set of conditions, such that A, B, C are maximal in the sense that all objects of A have all attributes of B under all conditions of C. The set of all triadic fuzzy concepts, called concept trilattice, can be ordered by three quasiorders induced by componentwise subsethood relations and forms a complete trilattice, for details see [8].

* This work was supported by project reg. no. CZ.1.07/2.3.00/20.0059 of the European Social Fund in the Czech Republic.

S. Greco et al. (Eds.): IPMU 2012, Part III, CCIS 299, pp. 221–230, 2012.

TCA was first proposed in [22] as a method of analysis of three-dimensional Boolean matrices and generalized to the case of matrices with grades in [8]. TCA extends formal concept analysis (FCA), a method of analysis of two-dimensional Boolean matrices developed in [21]. Since then several extensions to the case of matrices with grades was proposed [5]. The output of FCA is a set of clusters, called formal (or dyadic) concepts. Since the inception of TCA and FCA, a strong mathematical background for both methods was developed, [10], [11] ,[12], [3]; and many applications were proposed, most notably decompositions of both Boolean matrices and matrices with grades, [7], [9] .

The aim of this paper is to develop algorithms for computation of the set of triadic fuzzy concepts present in the input table. For boolean matrices, one can compute triadic conceps using TRIAS algorithm proposed in [14]. However, for matrices with grades no such algoritm exists. We present two ways to compute all triadic concept of such inputs. The first approach consist in trasformation of the matrix with grades into ordinary matrix, computation of the set of ordinary triadic concepts using the TRIAS algoritm, and transformation of the result back into fuzzy setting. The second algorithm is an extension of the TRIAS algorithm to the case of graded data in a way that allows for a direct computation of triadic fuzzy concepts. We prove correctness of the presented algorithms and discuss their computational complexity.

The paper is organized as follows. In Section 2 we recall basic notions from fuzzy logic, formal concept analysis and triadic concept analysis. In Section 3 and Section 4 we cover the two approaches to computation of triadic concepts. We conclude the paper with some ideas for further research in Section 5.

2   Preliminaries

2.1   Fuzzy Logic and Fuzzy Sets

In this section we recall the fundamental notions from fuzzy logic and fuzzy sets theory. For a more detailed treatment on the material contained in this section we refer the reader to [3],[13].

A concept central to fuzzy logic is the concept of *graded truth*. In fuzzy setting, we allow logical propositions to not only be fully true or fully false, but also partially true. We assume that truth degrees form a *complete residuated lattice*, [20]. A complete residuated lattice $\mathbf{L}$ is a tuple $\langle L, \wedge, \vee, \otimes, \rightarrow, 1, 0 \rangle$ such that

- $\langle L, \wedge, \vee, 1, 0 \rangle$ is a complete lattice with the greatest element 1 and the least element 0, i.e. a partially ordered set, where infima ($\wedge$) and suprema ($\vee$) of arbitrary subset of L exist,
- $\langle L, \otimes \rangle$ is a commutative monoid with the neutral element 1, i.e. $\otimes$ is associative and commutative, and $a \otimes 1 = a$ holds for all $a \in L$,
- the *adjointnes property* $a \otimes b \leq c$ iff $b \leq a \rightarrow c$ holds for all $a, b, c \in L$.

The operations $\otimes$ and $\rightarrow$ are taken as truth functions of conjunction and implication, respectively, $\wedge$ and $\vee$ are semantical counterparts of universal and existencial quantifiers, respectively. Complete residuated lattices cover wide range of structures of truth degrees, including all of the most widely used ones. Perhaps the most common example is a unit interval $L = [0, 1]$ with $\wedge, \vee$ being maximum and minimum, respectively, $\otimes$ being a (left-continuous) t-norm, and $\rightarrow$ given by $a \rightarrow b = \vee\{c \mid a \otimes c \leq b\}$. Particular cases (and in a sense the important ones [3],[13]) are standard Łukasiewicz, Gödel, and product algebras where $\otimes$ is defined by

$$a \otimes b = \begin{cases} \max(0, a + b - 1) & \text{(Łukasiewicz algebra)} \\ \min(a, b) & \text{(Gödel algebra)} \\ a \cdot b & \text{(product algebra)} \end{cases}$$

In applications, another common choice of **L** is a finite chain equipped with a restriction of a t-norm. For example, $L = \{a_1 = 0, \ldots, a_n = 1\} \subseteq [0, 1]$ with $\otimes$ defined either by $a_i \otimes a_j = a_{\max(i+j-n,0)}$ (Łukasiwicz chain) or as a restriction of Gödel t-norm to L. Residuated lattices are used in several areas of mathematics, most notably in mathematical fuzzy logic [13].

Now we recall the notions of fuzzy sets and fuzzy relations. An **L**-set (fuzzy set) A in a universal set X is a map $A : X \rightarrow L$. For $x \in X$, $A(x)$ is the degree to which x belongs to A. The set of all **L**-sets over X is denoted by L^X. A fuzzy set A is also denoted by $\{A(x)/x \mid x \in X\}$, we do not enumerate elements $x \in X$ such that $A(x) = 0$. An n-ary **L**-relation (fuzzy relation) R between sets $U_1, \ldots, U_n$ is an **L**-set over $U_1 \times \ldots U_n$.

The operations with **L**-sets are defined componentwise. For example, the union of **L**-sets $A, B \in L^X$ is defined as **L**-set $(A \cup B) \in L^X$ such that

$$(A \cup B)(x) = A(x) \vee B(x)$$

for all $x \in X$. An **L**-set A is a subset of an **L**-set B if $A(x) \leq B(x)$ for all $x \in X$, denoted by $A \subseteq B$.

Carthesian product of fuzzy sets $A_1, \ldots, A_n$ in $X_1, \ldots, X_n$, respectively, is the n-ary fuzzy relation $A_1 \otimes \cdots \otimes A_n \in L^{X_1 \times \cdots \times X_n}$ defined by

$$(A_1 \otimes \cdots \otimes A_n)(x_1, \ldots, x_n) = A_1(x_1) \otimes \cdots \otimes A_n(x_n)$$

For example, the Carthesian product of fuzzy sets $A \in L^X$ and $B \in L^Y$ is the binary relation $A \otimes B$ on $X \times Y$ given by $(A \otimes B)(x, y) = A(x) \otimes B(y)$.

2.2   Formal Concept Analysis, Triadic Concept Analysis

A *formal context* (or *dyadic context*) is a triplet $\langle X, Y, I \rangle$ where X and Y are non-empty sets and I is a fuzzy relation between X and Y, i.e. $I \subseteq L^{X \times Y}$. X and Y are interpreted as the sets of objects and attributes, respectively; I is interpreted as the incidence relation ("to have relation"). That is, $\langle x, y \rangle \in I$ is interpreted as the degree to which object x has attribute y. A formal context

$\mathbf{K} = \langle X, Y, I \rangle$ induces a pair of operators $^\uparrow : L^X \to L^Y$ and $^\downarrow : L^Y \to L^X$ defined for $C \subseteq L^X$ and $D \subseteq L^Y$ by

$$C^\uparrow(y) = \bigwedge_{x \in X} C(x) \to I(x, y),$$

$$D^\downarrow(x) = \bigwedge_{y \in Y} D(y) \to I(x, y).$$

These operators, called *concept-forming operators*, form a fuzzy Galois connection [1] between X and Y. A *formal concept* (or *dyadic concept*) of $\langle X, Y, I \rangle$ is a pair $\langle C, D \rangle$ consisting of sets $C \subseteq L^X$ and $D \subseteq L^Y$ such that $C^\uparrow = D$ and $D^\downarrow = C$; C and D are then called the *extent* and *intent* of $\langle C, D \rangle$. The set of all formal concepts of $\langle X, Y, I \rangle$ is denoted by $\mathcal{B}(X, Y, I)$ (or just $\mathcal{B}(I)$) and is called the *concept lattice* of $\langle X, Y, I \rangle$.

A *triadic fuzzy context* is a quadruple $\langle X_1, X_2, X_3, I \rangle$ where X_1, X_2, and X_3 are the set of objects, attributes, and conditions, respectively; I is a ternary fuzzy relation between X_1, X_2, and X_3, with $I(x_1, x_2, x_3)$ being interpreted as the truth degree of "object x_1 has attribute x_2 under condition x_3". When it is convenient we take $\{i, j, k\} = \{1, 2, 3\}$ and denote the degree $I(x_1, x_2, x_3)$ also by $I\{x_i, x_j, x_k\}$. From $\mathbf{K}$ a number of dyadic fuzzy contexts can be induced. For a fuzzy set $C_k : X_k \to L$, we define a dyadic fuzzy context $\langle X_i, X_j, I^{ij}_{C_k} \rangle$ by

$$I^{ij}_{C_k}(x_i, x_j) = \bigwedge_{x_k \in X_k} (C_k(x_x) \to I\{x_i, x_j, x_k\}).$$

The concept-forming operators induced by $\langle X_i, X_j, I^{ij}_{C_k} \rangle$ are denoted by $^{(i,j,C_k)}$. Therefore, for fuzzy sets $C_i \in L^{X_i}$ and $C_j \in L^{X_j}$, $x_j \in X_j$, and $x_k \in X_k$, we put

$$C_i^{(i,j,C_k)}(x_j) = \bigwedge_{x_i \in X_i} C_i(x_i) \to I^{ij}_{C_k}(x_i, x_j),$$

$$C_j^{(i,j,C_k)}(x_i) = \bigwedge_{x_j \in X_j} C_j(x_j) \to I^{ij}_{C_k}(x_i, x_j).$$

A *triadic fuzzy concept* of $\langle X_1, X_2, X_3, I \rangle$ is a triplet $\langle A_1, A_2, A_3 \rangle$ of fuzzy sets $A_i \in L^{X_i}$ such that $A_1 = A_2^{(1,2,A_3)}$, $A_2 = A_3^{(2,3,A_1)}$, and $A_3 = A_1^{(3,1,A_2)}$. A_1, A_2, and A_3 are called the *extent*, *intent*, and *modus* of $\langle A_1, A_2, A_3 \rangle$. We denote the set of all triadic fuzzy concepts of $\mathbf{K} = \langle X_1, X_2, X_3, I \rangle$ by $\mathcal{T}(X_1, X_2, X_3, I)$ (or just $\mathcal{T}(\mathbf{K})$), and call it the *concept trilattice* of $\langle X_1, X_2, X_3, I \rangle$. By the basic theorem of triadic concept analysis [8] $\mathcal{T}(X_1, X_2, X_3, I)$ equipped with quasiorders $\lesssim_i$, $i = 1, 2, 3$, defined by $\langle A_1, A_2, A_3 \rangle \lesssim_i \langle B_1, B_2, B_3 \rangle$ iff $A_i \subseteq B_i$ is indeed a trilattice [22].

We need the following theorem.

Theorem 1 ([8], Geometrical interpretation of triadic concepts). *For every triadic fuzzy context $\mathbf{K} = \langle X_1, X_2, X_3, I \rangle$:*

(a) *If $\langle A_1, A_2, A_3 \rangle \in \mathcal{T}(\mathbf{K})$ then $A_1 \otimes A_2 \otimes A_3 \subseteq I$. Moreover, $\langle A_1, A_2, A_3 \rangle$ is maximal with respect to pointwise set inclusion, i.e. there does not exist $\langle B_1, B_2, B_3 \rangle \in \langle \mathbf{L}^{X_1}, \mathbf{L}^{X_2}, \mathbf{L}^{X_3} \rangle$ other than $\langle A_1, A_2, A_3 \rangle$ such that $A_i \subseteq B_i$ for every $i = 1, 2, 3$.*

(b) *If $A_1 \otimes A_2 \otimes A_3 \subseteq I$ then there exists $\langle B_1, B_2, B_3 \rangle \in \mathcal{T}(\mathbf{K})$ such that $A_i \subseteq B_i$ for every $i = 1, 2, 3$.*

3   Reduction to the Ordinary Case

In this section we describe the first approach to computation of a concept trillattice. The approach relies on a connection between concept trillatices of graded data and concept trilattices of Boolean data. The idea inspired by [2] and [18] is the following: first, we transform a triadic fuzzy context into an ordinary triadic context, then we carry out the computation using some algorithm for the ordinary case, and finally we transform the obtained concept trilattice back to the fuzzy setting. The needed connection between the fuzzy and ordinary setting is established in the following theorem.

Theorem 2. (Boolean representation) *Let $\mathbf{K} = \langle X_1, X_2, X_3, I \rangle$ be a fuzzy triadic context and $\mathbf{K}_{crisp} = \langle X_1 \times L, X_2 \times L, X_3 \times L, I_{crisp} \rangle$ with I_{crisp} defined by $((x_1, a), (x_2, b), (x_3, c)) \in I_{crisp}$ iff $a \otimes b \otimes c \leq I(x_1, x_2, x_3)$ be a triadic context. Then $\mathcal{T}(\mathbf{K})$ is isomorphic to $\mathcal{T}(\mathbf{K}_{crisp})$.*

Proof. Recall that for a fuzzy set $A \in L^X$, we define an ordinary set $\lfloor A \rfloor \subseteq X \times L$ by

$$\lfloor A \rfloor = \{(x, a) \mid x \in X, a \in L, A(x) \geq a\}$$

In the opposite direction, given an ordinary set $B \subseteq X \times L$ such that $(x, a) \in B$ implies $(x, b) \in B$ for all $b \leq a$, and the set $\{a \mid (x, a) \in B\}$ has the greatest element, the fuzzy set $\lceil B \rceil$ is defined by

$$\lceil B \rceil(x) = \bigvee \{a \mid (x, a) \in B\}$$

For more details, see [3].

Now, consider mappings $\varphi : \mathcal{T}(\mathbf{K}) \to \mathcal{T}(\mathbf{K}_{crisp})$ defined by

$$\varphi(\langle A_1, A_2, A_3 \rangle) = \langle \lfloor A_1 \rfloor, \lfloor A_2 \rfloor, \lfloor A_3 \rfloor \rangle, \tag{1}$$

and $\psi : \mathcal{T}(\mathbf{K}_{crisp}) \to \mathcal{T}(\mathbf{K})$ defined by

$$\psi(\langle B_1, B_2, B_3 \rangle) = \langle \lceil B_1 \rceil, \lceil B_2 \rceil, \lceil B_3 \rceil \rangle. \tag{2}$$

Theorem 1 implies that $\langle \lfloor A_1 \rfloor, \lfloor A_2 \rfloor, \lfloor A_3 \rfloor \rangle \in \mathcal{T}(\mathbf{K}_{crisp})$ for all $\langle A_1, A_2, A_3 \rangle \in \mathcal{T}(\mathbf{K})$, and $\psi(\langle B_1, B_2, B_3 \rangle) \in \mathcal{T}(\mathbf{K})$ for all $\langle B_1, B_2, B_3 \rangle \in \mathcal{T}(\mathbf{K}_{crisp})$.

Namely, let $\langle A_1, A_2, A_3 \rangle \in \mathcal{T}(\mathbf{K})$. Then

$$(x_i, b) \in (\lfloor A_j \rfloor^{(i,j, \lfloor A_k \rfloor)} \text{ iff}$$
$$\text{for all } ((x_j, a), (x_k, c)) \in \lfloor A_j \rfloor \times \lfloor A_k \rfloor$$
$$\{(x_i, b), (x_j, a), (x_k, c)\} \in I_{crisp} \text{ iff}$$
$$\text{for all } x_j \in X_j, x_k \in X_k, a \leq A_j(x_j), b \leq A_k(x_k)$$
$$a \otimes b \otimes c \leq I\{x_i, x_j, x_k\} \text{ iff}$$
$$\text{for all } x_j \in X_j, x_k \in X_k$$
$$A_j(x_j) \otimes A_k(x_k) \otimes b \leq I\{x_i, x_j, x_k\} \text{ iff}$$
$$b \leq A_i(x_i).$$

Algorithm 1. COMPUTECONCEPTS($\mathbf{K} = \langle X_1, X_2, X_3, I \rangle$)

1. $I_{crisp} \leftarrow \emptyset$
2. **foreach** $(x_1, x_2, x_3) \in X_1 \times X_2 \times X_3$:
3.   **foreach** $(a, b, c) \in L \times L \times L$ **such that** $a \otimes b \otimes c \leq I(x_1, x_2, x_3)$:
4. $I_{crisp} \leftarrow I_{crisp} \cup \{((x_1, a), (x_2, b), (x_3, c))\}$
5. $\mathcal{F}_{crisp} \leftarrow$ COMPUTEORDINARYCONCEPTS($\langle X_1 \times L, X_2 \times L, X_3 \times L, I_{crisp} \rangle$)
6. $\mathcal{F} \leftarrow \emptyset$
7. **foreach** $\langle A_1, A_2, A_3 \rangle \in \mathcal{F}_{crisp}$:
8. $\mathcal{F} \leftarrow \mathcal{F} \cup \{\langle \lceil A_1 \rceil, \lceil A_2 \rceil, \lceil A_3 \rceil \rangle\}$
9. **return** $\mathcal{F}$

This proves $\langle \lfloor A_1 \rfloor, \lfloor A_2 \rfloor, \lfloor A_3 \rfloor \rangle \in \mathcal{T}(\mathbf{K}_{crisp})$.

For the opposite direction, let $\langle B_1, B_2, B_3 \rangle \in \mathcal{T}(\mathbf{K}_{crisp})$. Then

$$(\lceil A_j \rceil^{(i,j,\lceil A_k \rceil)})(x_i) = b \text{ iff}$$

$$b = \bigvee \{a \mid \lceil A_j \rceil(x_j) \otimes \lceil A_k \rceil(x_j) \otimes a \leq I(x_i, x_j, x_k), x_j \in X_j, x_k \in X_k\} \text{ iff}$$

$$b = \bigvee \{a \mid ((x_i, a), (x_j, c), (x_k, d)) \in I_{crisp}, ((x_j, c), (x_k, d)) \in A_j \times A_k\} \text{ iff}$$

$$b = \bigvee \{a \mid (x_i, a) \in A_j^{(i,j,A_k)}\} = \lceil A_i \rceil(x_i)$$

Therefore $\psi(\langle B_1, B_2, B_3 \rangle) \in \mathcal{T}(\mathbf{K})$.

Since $\lceil \lfloor A \rfloor \rceil = A$ for each fuzzy set A, the mappings φ and ψ are mutually inverse and φ is a bijection. Moreover, $\lfloor A \rfloor \subseteq \lfloor B \rfloor$ iff $A \subseteq B$ for all fuzzy sets A and B and thus φ preserves $\lesssim_1, \lesssim_2, \lesssim_3$. $\square$

The previous theorem immediately gives the algorithm listed as Algorithm 1. On lines 1-4, the transformation of the input triadic fuzzy context $\mathbf{K}$ to an ordinary context is carried on. The next step, on line 5, is the computation of concept trilattice using some algorithm for the ordinary case. Finally, on lines 7-8, the ordinary triadic concepts are trasformed back into fuzzy triadic concepts (see the map ψ in the proof of the previous theorem).

Complexity Since the complexity of the whole algorithm depends on the choice of COMPUTEORDINARYCONCEPTS, we discuss only the complexity of transformations from and to ordinary setting. The cycle on line 2 lasts $|X_1| \cdot |X_2| \cdot |X_3|$ iterations, while the cycle on line 3 lasts $|L|^3$ iterations. The backwards transformation on lines 7-8 takes $|\mathcal{T}(\mathbf{K})| \cdot |L| \cdot (|X_1| + |X_2| + |X_3|)$ operations. Since in the worst case the number of triadic concepts is exponential in the size of its context, the later term dominates the time complexity. Therefore the complexity of the transformations is $O(|\mathcal{T}(\mathbf{K})| \cdot |L| \cdot (|X_1| + |X_2| + |X_3|))$.

4   TRIAS **in Fuzzy Setting**

In this section we show that by a direct fuzzification of TRIAS algorithm [14] we obtain a direct algorithm for computation of the set of triadic fuzzy concepts

---

Algorithm 2. FUZZYTRIAS($\mathbf{K} = \langle X_1, X_2, X_3, I \rangle$)

---

1.   **foreach** $(x_1, x_2, x_3 \in X_1 \times X_2 \times X_3)$:
2. $I^{(1)}(x_1, (x_2, x_3)) \leftarrow I(x_1, x_2, x_3)$
3. $\mathcal{T} \leftarrow \emptyset$
4. $\langle A, B \rangle \leftarrow$ FIRSTCONCEPT($\langle X_1, X_2 \times X_3, I^{(1)} \rangle$)
5.   **do**
6. $\langle C, D \rangle \leftarrow$ FIRSTCONCEPT($\langle X_2, X_3, B \rangle$)
7.   **do**
8.   **if** $A = C^{(1,2,D)}$
9.   **then** $\mathcal{T} \leftarrow \mathcal{T} \cup \{\langle A, C, D \rangle\}$
10.   **while** $\langle C, D \rangle \leftarrow$ NEXTCONCEPT($\langle X_2, X_3, B \rangle, \langle C, D \rangle$)
11.   **while** $\langle A, B \rangle \leftarrow$ NEXTCONCEPT($\langle X_1, X_2 \times X_3, I^{(1)} \rangle, \langle A, B \rangle$)
12.   **return** $\mathcal{T}$

---

present in the input data. We call the algorithm FUZZYTRIAS and list it as Algorithm 2.

For an input triadic fuzzy context $\mathbf{K} = \langle X_1, X_2, X_3, I \rangle)$, FUZZYTRIAS first on lines 2-3 constructs a dyadic fuzzy context $\mathbf{K}^{(1)} = \langle X_1, X_2 \times X_3, I^{(1)} \rangle$ where the binary fuzzy relation $I^{(1)}$ is defined by $I^{(1)}(x_1, (x_2, x_3)) = I(x_1, x_2, x_3)$. Then it calls subroutines FIRSTCONCEPT and NEXTCONCEPT to compute and iterate through the set of formal concepts of $\mathbf{K}^{(1)}$. These subroutines form an interface to some algorithm for computation of concept lattice of dyadic fuzzy context, such as NextClosure [4] or Lindig algoritm [6]. FIRSTCONCEPT returns the first generated concept, NEXTCONCEPT returns the concept generated after the one passed to it as an argument. In the pseudocode we use a convention that NEXTCONCEPT returns *false* if its argument is the last generated concept. Any other returned value is, when interpreted as logical value, considered *true*. It does not matter whether the algorithm first generates all formal concepts and then iterates through them, or it computes formal concepts on demand. On lines 4-11 FUZZYTRIAS iterates through all concepts $\langle A, B \rangle$ of $\mathbf{K}^{(1)}$. The extent A is considered a candidate for an extent of some triconcepts of $\mathcal{T}(\mathbf{K})$, the intent B is in fact a binary fuzzy relation between X_2 and X_3 and thus can be understood as dyadic fuzzy context $\langle X_2, X_3, B \rangle$. On lines 7-10 the algoritm iterates through all formal concepts $\langle C, D \rangle$ of this context. For each $\langle C, D \rangle$ it checks if $A = C^{(1,2,D)}$ (which is in fact a check whether $\langle A, C, D \rangle$ is a triadic concept; see the proof of correctness that follows). If so, $\langle A, C, D \rangle$ is added to the set of triadic fuzzy concepts. At the end, the set of all triadic concepts is returned.

Correctness We need the following lemmas.

Lemma 1. *If* $\langle A_1, A_2, A_3 \rangle \in \mathcal{T}(\mathbf{K})$, *then* $\langle A_i, A_j \rangle \in \mathcal{B}(I_{A_k}^{ij})$ *for all* $\{i, j, k\} \in \{1, 2, 3\}$

Proof. Easy to observe from the definition of a triadic fuzzy concept.   □

Lemma 2. *Let* $\mathbf{K} = \langle X_1, X_2, X_3, I \rangle$ *be fuzzy triadic context and* $\mathbf{K}^{(1)} = \langle X_1, X_2 \times X_3, I^{(1)} \rangle$ *a fuzzy dyadic context with* $I^{(1)}(x_1, (x_2, x_3)) = I(x_1, x_2, x_3)$. *Then*

(i) $A_1^{\downarrow_{I^{(1)}}} = I_{A_1}^{23}$ *for all* $A_1 \in L^{X_1}$

(ii) *if* $\langle A_1, A_2, A_3 \rangle \in \mathcal{T}(\mathbf{K})$ *then* A_1 *is an extent of some concept in* $\mathcal{B}(\mathbf{K}^{(1)})$

Proof. (i) By an easy computation.

(ii) It suffices to prove $A_1^{\downarrow_{I^{(1)}}\uparrow_{I^{(1)}}} \subseteq A_1$. Since for every fuzzy binary relation I it holds $I(x,y) = \bigvee_{\langle A,B \rangle \in \mathcal{B}(I)} A(x) \otimes B(y)$, we have

$$
A_1^{\downarrow_{I^{(1)}}\uparrow_{I^{(1)}}}(x_1) = I_{A_1}^{23}{}^{\uparrow_{I^{(1)}}}(x_1) =
$$

$$
= \bigwedge_{(x_2,x_3)\in X_2\times X_3} I_{A_1}^{23}(x_2,x_3) \rightarrow I^{(1)}(x1,(x_2,x_3)) =
$$

$$
= \bigwedge_{(x_2,x_3)\in X_2\times X_3} (\bigvee_{\langle B_2,B_3 \rangle \in \mathcal{B}(I^{(1)})} B_2(x_2) \otimes B_3(x_3)) \rightarrow I^{(1)}(x1,(x_2,x_3)) =
$$

$$
= \bigwedge_{(x_2,x_3)\in X_2\times X_3} \bigwedge_{\langle B_2,B_3 \rangle \in \mathcal{B}(I^{(1)})} B_2(x_2) \otimes B_3(x_3) \rightarrow I^{(1)}(x1,(x_2,x_3)) \leq
$$

$$
\leq \bigwedge_{(x_2,x_3)\in X_2\times X_3} A_2(x_2) \otimes A_3(x_3) \rightarrow I(x_1,x_2,x_3) = A_1(x_1)
$$

$\square$

Remark 1. The opposite direction of Lemma 2 (ii) does not hold in general. Indeed, there is a fuzzy triadic context $\mathbf{K}$ such that there is an extent A of $\mathbf{K}^{(1)}$ that is not an extent of any triconcept of $\mathcal{T}(\mathbf{K})$. As an example, let $\mathbf{L}$ be a three-element Łukasiewicz chain and $\mathbf{K} = \langle X, Y, Z, I \rangle$ be given by the following table.

	z_1			z_2		
	y_1	y_2	y_3	y_1	y_2	y_3
x_1	0.5	1	0	0	0.5	1
x_2	0	1	0	1	1	1
x_3	0	0	0.5	1	0	1

Then $\{0/x_1, 0.5/x_2, 1/x_3\}$ is an extent of some concept of $\mathbf{K}^{(1)}$, but at the same time it is not an extent of any triconcept of $\mathbf{K}$. $\square$

The desired correctness of FUZZYTRIAS is given in the following theorem.

Theorem 3. *Given a triadic fuzzy context* $\mathbf{K} = \langle X_1, X_2, X_3, I \rangle$, FUZZYTRIAS *outputs* $\mathcal{T}(\mathbf{K})$.

Proof. First, observe that the following claims hold.

- Claim 1: For every triadic concept $\langle A_1, A_2, A_3 \rangle \in \mathcal{T}(\mathbf{K})$ there is $B \in L^{X_2 \times X_3}$ such that $\langle A_1, B \rangle \in \mathcal{B}(X_1, X_2 \times X_3, I^{(1)})$ and $\langle A_2, A_3 \rangle \in \mathcal{B}(X_2, X_3, B)$.
- Claim 2: For every dyadic concept $\langle A, B \rangle \in \mathcal{B}(X_1, X_2 \times X_3, I^{(1)})$ and every $\langle C, D \rangle \in \mathcal{B}(X_2, X_3, B)$ it holds that if $A = C^{(1,2,D)}$ then $\langle A, C, D \rangle$ is a triadic fuzzy concept.

From Claim 2 it follows that each tripple $\langle A, C, D \rangle$ that passes the test on line 8 is a triadic concept of $\mathbf{K}$. Claim 1 then implies that every triadic concept of $\mathbf{K}$ is generated on lines 4-11.

Complexity. The time complexity of FuzzyTrias depends on the time complexity of underlying algorithm for computation of dyadic fuzzy concepts. It is well known, that in the worst case the number of dyadic fuzzy concepts is exponential in the size of input data and in the number of degrees in the residuated lattice, and that the computation of one dyadic fuzzy concept takes polynomial time. The sizes of $\mathbf{K}^{(1)}$ and I_A^{23} (for any $A \in L^{X_1}$) are linear in the size of $\mathbf{K}$. Since FuzzyTrias contains two nested cycles that iterate through all the dyadic fuzzy concepts of $\mathbf{K}^{(1)}$ and I_A^{23} (lines 5-11) we can conclude that the number of iteration the algorithm goes throught is exponential in the size of input. Since the complexity of operations done for each iteration of the inner cycle (lines 7-10) and the complexity of the creation of $\mathbf{K}^{(1)}$ (lines 1-2) are polynomial, the complexity of the whole algorithm is dominated by the number of dyadic fuzzy concepts. Therefore, we can conclude that the time complexity of FuzzyTrias is $O(p_1(|X_1|, |X_2|, |X_3|, |L|) \cdot |\mathcal{B}(\mathbf{K}^{(1)})| \cdot p_2(|X_1|, |X_2|, |X_3|, |L|) \cdot \max_{\langle A, B \rangle \in \mathcal{B}(\mathbf{K}^{(1)})} \{|\mathbf{B}(X_2, X_3, B)|\})$, where p_1 and p_2 are polynomials that capture the time of computation of a dyadic concept and their exact form depends on the algorithm we choose for this task.

5   Conclusions

We have presented two algorithms for computation of the set of all triadic fuzzy concepts of a triadic fuzzy context. First algorithm consist in transformation of the graded input data to the Boolean data and carring out the computation using some already existing algorithm for the ordinary setting. The second algorithm is a fuzzified version of Trias algorithm. We proved correctness of both algorithms and discussed their time complexity. Future research shall include the following.

- Efficient implementation and experimental comparison of both presented algorithms. The motivation lies in the fact that experiments conducted with algorithms for dyadic concept analysis of graded data [6] revealed that in practice the direct algorithm is more effective than the algorithm based on transformation to the ordinary case. Intuitively, one expects similar situation in the case of algorithms for triadic concept analysis.
- Further development of FuzzyTrias algorithm. The presented algorithm has exponential time delay, that is the computation of one triadic concept may take exponential time. We will study the possibilities to overcome this and develop an algorithm with polynomial time delay.

References

1. Belohlavek, R.: Fuzzy Galois connections. Math. Logic Quarterly 45(4), 497–504 (1999) ISSN 0942-5616
2. Belohlavek, R.: Reduction and a simple proof of characterization of fuzzy concept lattices. Fundamenta Informaticae 46(4), 277–285 (2001) ISSN 0169-2968
3. Belohlavek, R.: Fuzzy Relational Systems: Foundations and Principles. Kluwer, Academic/Plenum Publishers, New York (2002)
4. Belohlavek, R.: Algorithms for fuzzy concept lattices. In: Proc. Fourth Int. Conf. on Recent Advances in Soft Computing, RASC 2002, Nottingham, United Kingdom, December 12-13, pp. 200–205 (2002)
5. Belohlavek, R., Vychodil, V.: What is a fuzzy concept lattice? In: Proc. CLA 2005, 3rd Int. Conference on Concept Lattices and Their Applications, September 7-9, pp. 34–45. Czech Republic, Olomouc (2005) ISBN 80-248-0863-3
6. Belohlavek, R., De Baets, B., Outrata, J., Vychodil, V.: Computing the lattice of all fixpoints of a fuzzy closure operator. IEEE Transactions on Fuzzy Systems 18(3), 546–557 (2010)
7. Belohlavek, R.: Optimal decompositions of matrices with entries from residuated lattices. J. Logic and Computation (September 7, 2011), doi:10.1093/logcom/exr023
8. Belohlavek, R., Osicka, P.: Triadic concept lattices of data with graded attributes. International Journal of General Systems (December 12, 2011), doi:10.1080/03081079.2011.643548
9. Belohlavek, R., Osička, P., Vychodil, V.: Factorizing Three-Way Ordinal Data Using Triadic Formal Concepts. In: Christiansen, H., De Tré, G., Yazici, A., Zadrozny, S., Andreasen, T., Larsen, H.L. (eds.) FQAS 2011. LNCS, vol. 7022, pp. 400–411. Springer, Heidelberg (2011), doi:10.1007/978-3-642-24764-4_35
10. Biedermann, K.: An equational theory for trilattices. In: Algebra Universalis, vol. 42. Birkhäuser, Basel (1999)
11. Biedermann, K.: Triadic Galois Connections Triadic Galois connections. In: Denecke, K., Lüders, O. (eds.) General Algebra and Applications in Discrete Mathematics, pp. 23–33. Shaker, Aachen (1997)
12. Ganter, B., Wille, R.: Formal Concept Analysis. Mathematical Foundations. Springer, Berlin (1999)
13. Hájek, P.: Metamathematics of Fuzzy Logic. Kluwer, Dordrecht (1998)
14. Jäschke, R., Hotho, A., Schmitz, C., Ganter, B., Stumme, G.: TRIAS – An Algorithm for Mining Iceberg Tri-Lattices. In: ICDM 2006, pp. 907–911 (2006)
15. Kolda, T.G., Bader, B.W.: Tensor decompositions and applications. SIAM Review 51(3), 455–500 (2009)
16. Kroonenberg, P.M.: Applied Multiway Data Analysis. J. Wiley (2008)
17. Lehmann, F., Wille, R.: A Triadic Approach to Formal Concept Analysis. In: Ellis, G., Rich, W., Levinson, R., Sowa, J.F. (eds.) ICCS 1995. LNCS, vol. 954, pp. 32–43. Springer, Heidelberg (1995)
18. Pollandt, S.: Fuzzy Begriffe. Springer, Berlin (1997)
19. Smilde, A., Bro, R., Geladi, P.: Multi-way Analysis: Applications in the Chemical Sciences. J. Wiley (2004)
20. Ward, M., Dilworth, R.P.: Residuated lattices. Trans. Amer. Math. Soc. 45, 335–354 (1939)
21. Wille, R.: Restructuring lattice theory: an approach based on hierarchies of concepts. In: Rival, I. (ed.) Ordered Sets, pp. 445–470. Reidel, Dordrecht (1982)
22. Wille, R.: The basic theorem of triadic concept analysis. Order 12, 149–158 (1995)

Classification of Uncertain Data: An Application in Nondestructive Testing

Jens Hülsmann and Werner Brockmann

Universität Osnabrück,
Albrechstr. 28, 49069 Osnabrück, Germany
{jens.huelsmann,werner.brockamnn}@uos.de
http://www.informatik.uni-osnabrueck.de/techinf/

Abstract. The classification of data with dynamically changing uncertainty characteristics is a problem for many practical applications. As an example in the field of nondestructive testing (NDT), magnetic flux leakage (MFL) measurements are used to inspect pipelines. The data is analyzed manually afterwards. In this paper we use a framework for handling uncertainties called Trust Management and a extended fuzzy rule based classifier to identify different installations within pipelines by MFL-data. The results show a classification performance of over 90% with an additional, reliable measure for the trustworthiness of every single classification result.

Keywords: Classification, Uncertainty, Trust Management, Nondestructive Testing, Magnetic Flux Leakage.

1 Motivation and Background

Worldwide there are about two million kilometers of pipelines for substances like water, gas, oil and other refined products [4]. This network is a main backbone of today's resource distribution. To maintain a safe operation of this infrastructure, these pipelines have to be inspected regularly. As most parts of the pipes are not accessible, the inspection is mostly done by so called in-line inspection. Special machines, called pipeline inspection gauge (PIG), with sensors for nondestructive testing (NDT) are pumped through the pipelines and collect data about its state. This technology is essential to ensure a fully operable infrastructure and to avoid damage caused to the environment as a result of leaking substances. As most of the pipelines are made of steel, a magnetic inspection is adequate. A well-established technique is the magnetic flux leakage testing (MFL). The steel pipe is magnetized and the flux leakage field is measured [13]. These data collected in the pipelines have to be analyzed afterwards for locations with flaws and potentially critical inhomogeneities. Due to the length of the pipelines, some are several hundred kilometer long, an enormous amount of intensive data analysis is required. All data have to be inspected closely by a human data analyst. These analysts are highly trained specialists for finding corrosion, cracks, dents and other critical things in the pipelines. As this analysis is safety critical, the

S. Greco et al. (Eds.): IPMU 2012, Part III, CCIS 299, pp. 231–240, 2012.

results have to meet strict requirements [14]. The autonomous operation of the inspection tool has several consequences: There is no human intervention or observation during the measurement process. A repetition is near to impossible; one has to take the data as they come. But when a particular structure occurs in the data, what is it? Is it critical or not? To take this decision, the analyst has to understand the specifics of magnetic measurement data and the measurement process. Additionally the data are biased with a lot of unforeseeable effects (see [15]) that can be seen as introducing uncertainty to the data. These uncertainties go far beyond the classical measurement error of the sensors as there are many interacting physical effects and unsupervised circumstances. The localization of the tool in the pipeline is not always measured accurately, the magnetic flux sensors can get dirty or loose contact to the pipe body due to jerking and vibration. Also measurement conditions like the tools speed or the pipe wall thickness can change. All these effects are indeterministic and effect local properties of the measurement data. The analyst thus has to look at them as being affected by dynamically changing uncertainty. Our goal is to improve the data analysis within this task by providing a pre-classified dataset which considers these uncertainties explicitly. Basically, a good classification performance, with a focus on minimizing false negatives, is designated. False negatives are the most serious mistake, as they correspond to a missed region, which is potentially critical. But the illustrated purpose also yields some tough additional requirements for the software used. The whole workflow has to be transparent, so that the calculated results are comprehensible and interpretable. If misclassification occurs, one must be able to know exactly what happened in the whole data processing chain. As this holds for both directions, from the raw-data to the classification result and the other way round, we call it *bidirectional traceability*. Another key feature is that all parameters of the whole data analysis workflow should be as clear and intuitive as possible and free of random initialization. In this paper we propose such a workflow for classifying particular common non-defects such as installations and welds in the pipeline data.

2   State of the Art

2.1   Classification of MFL Data

For a MFL measurement in pipelines, the pipe wall is magnetized to saturation with permanent magnets near to the wall. The principle is to measure the components of the leakage field between the poles of the magnets by a three dimensional hall-sensor. The structure of the steel pipe is reflected in this field, although one cannot recalculate the geometrical structure of the material directly [9]. The measurement thus needs to be calibrated and interpreted afterwards. For an introduction to the theoretical background see [13]. A detailed description of the application for in-line inspection can be found in [17]. The work of [15] gives exemplary data of defect measurements. For the investigation in the paper we use real pipeline data from a leading company for pipeline inspection services. In Fig. 1 the axial component of a MFL measurement is shown for illustration. The "ring" around the pipeline is a signal caused by a girth weld. An automation of the analysis of MFL data has been widely discussed. An example of dimension reduction and feature extraction respectively is given in [16]. They use a nine dimensional feature vector, extracted from the three components of the magnetic field. The axial component is the main source of information for the feature vector, five features are exclusively calculated from this component. In [3] and [7] artificial neural networks are used to classify defects in MFL data. However neither of them works on real data from operational pipelines. The work of [3] only use simulated defects. For more realistic measurements, artificial defects like special shallow wells are used [7].

Fig. 1. Axial channel of the MFL signal for a girth weld

2.2 Classification under Uncertainty

For the classification of MFL data, one source of uncertainty arises during the measurement process and another comes into play during the operation phase of the classifier. Uncertainty here means a low trustworthiness of a measurement or a result. In detail, the source of uncertainty can be an external one, i.e. the feature vector or a part of it is uncertain, or an internal one, i.e. the classifier itself is uncertain, e.g. due to poor training data. As the feature vector is the input of the classifier, the external and the internal uncertainties superpose when data are analyzed. To cope with these uncertainties, a discriminant value of the class assignment at the output can be obtained. It is derived in all major classification algorithms, e.g. based on internal distance measures. A classifier is then less certain the larger the distance or the less the discriminance is in the operation phase. An approach to get a more significant discriminance measures is the concept of conflict and ignorance [6]. For an application in fuzzy rule based classification see [10]. For a given feature vector, the ignorance is a measure for the distance to any class, the conflict is a measure for the degree of overlap between classes at the feature vector. This measures at the classifiers output are much more comprehensible than the common discriminance measures, but only address the internal uncertainty, i.e. the class structure. In [2] we extended a SVM classifier in order to increase the robustness by explicitly modeling the external uncertainty of the input data at runtime, i.e., dynamically during the operation phase. In [11] we made a similar extension to a fuzzy rule based classifier, called *CLARISSA* (CLAssification by a Robust, Intelligent State Space Analysis). Both extensions fuse the information of the inputs uncertainties with the internal uncertainties of the class structure to provide a reliable measure for the output uncertainty. The classification performance of this algorithms is successfully tested on results on acknowledged benchmark datasets like IRIS, WINE and WBCD [8]. Within the Trust Management framework [1](see below), the fuzzy rule based classifier of [11] is used in a special mode, where the classifier can reject the feature vector due to a lack of knowledge about the corresponding position in the feature space, i.e. in case of ignorance. For a safety critical but supervised classification task like the one in this paper, this is an appropriate if not even mandatory way. The basic idea of a rejecting classifier was proposed in [5]. For an example in dealing with the needed thresholds see [12]. If such a classifier rejects a feature vector or its classification, respectively, instead of a class the reason for the reject gets obvious. In union with the above-mentioned concepts of conflict and ignorance, there are two possible reasons: The allocation to a class is ambiguous, i.e. more than one class would fit the feature vector, or the feature vector is too far away from learned classes. This way, the reason for a low output certainty can be tracked down to the level of single training examples or overlaps between classes if the CLARISSA-approach is used. Besides this, a proper classifier can serve as a drain for uncertainties in the feature vector. If a feature is uncertain, but not needed for the non-ambiguous allocation to a class, this feature is not taken into account. In this case the result is certain despite of an input uncertainty. The results in [11] hence showed a better classification performance for noisy data and a strong correlation of the output uncertainty and the probability of misclassification.

3   Modeling Uncertainties with Trust Management

In this NDT application, we extended the workflow with a framework which explicitly processes uncertainties, called *Trust Management* [1]. The information about the trustworthiness respectively uncertainties of a part or data in a technical system can be determined in different ways. For sensors often a sensor model or additional information from other sensors is used. For example, a sensor reading near to the end of a measurement range often is not very trustworthy due to non-linear sensor effects. In the further processing steps, the trustworthiness results can hence not be better then that of the data they rely on, except there was redundancy in the source data or additional information is provided e.g. by a system model. In the framework of Trust Management, the trustworthiness is reflected by a *Trust Signal* which is a meta-information to a normal signal, e.g. a sensor-reading, or to an internally generated signal, which depends on uncertain information. Also system components or functional modules can be attributed with a Trust Signal. In our case, all sources of uncertainty are reflected by Trust Signals. A Trust Signal has a scalar value from the interval $[0, 1]$, called the *Trust Level*, and indicates the trustworthiness of the signal/component it is associated with. Two rules generally apply here: If it is 1.0 the data can be fully trusted, hence it can be handled as normal. If the Trust Level is 0.0, the value has not to influence the output. It is important to note that the Trust Signal is not a probabilistic representation, because it does not depend on or declare anything about the statistical properties of the data it is assigned to. The module, which receives the Trust Signal enhanced data, has to decide in which way it incorporates the regular and the Trust Level data into the processing of its output. If the input data are not trustworthy enough, it can switch to a fall back strategy or gradually fade out the influence of the affected input(s). As the modules are normally part of a data processing chain, the module should again make a statement about the trustworthiness of its output, according to its specific data processing and the trustworthiness of its inputs.

4   Concept and Realization

For the classification of MFL-data, we realized a multi-staged data processing workflow shown in Fig. 2. It mainly divides into five parts:

- the searching for regions that contain installations, called Regions Of Interest (ROI),
- the evaluation of the uncertainties of the raw data in the particular ROI,
- the calculation of the feature vector for the ROI,
- the evaluation of the uncertainties of every single feature in the vector,
- the classification of the feature vector with the CLARISSA-classifier.

In the first step, the parts of the pipeline which have to be classified are determined by a ROI algorithm. After that, the raw-data in the ROI are closely inspected for defect or disturbed sensors, noise, and other common data flaws. Models for the calculation of particular Trust Levels are designed based on background knowledge provided by experts and statistical evaluation. Thereafter a 12-dimensional feature vector, similar to the one in [16] is computed. The Trust Level for each feature is again calculated with a manually designed model, following the approach in [1]: Typical and well known values of the features are initially trustworthy. If there are special properties of the feature, like the sensitivity to noise or nonlinear effects near the end of the measurement range, they may lower the certainty of the raw data and the features which are based on them. The final step is to use the features with their according Trust Level as

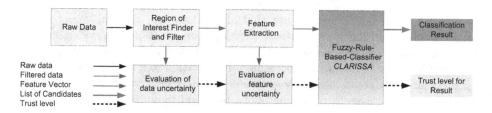

Fig. 2. General overview of the workflow components

the input for the CLARISSA-classifier. It gradually fades the uncertain features out of the classification depending on the particular Trust Level, i.e. due to the external information about the uncertainty. Additionally it implicitly fuses the input Trust Levels with the uncertainty of the internal structure of the trained classifier and provides an output Trust Level for any assigned class. A high Trust Level refers to a certain decision about a class label.

5 Investigation and Results

This section is divided into three parts. First we will have a look on the raw performance in classification; second we will assess the reliable of the results. Then the consequences will be discussed.

5.1 Investigation Set-Up

For the investigation, we trained the classifier with about 1000 hand-picked examples from a database of real data. The examples were taken from different pipelines with a diameter from 6" to 48" to get a robust classifier for a broad spectrum of signal characteristics and pipelines. The concrete performance is examined for data from a real 50 km long, 16"-diameter pipeline. It contains over 6500 marked installations from all different classes.

5.2 Pure Classification Performance

The general performance of a classifier for pipeline inspection has two aspects: the part of detected ROIs, which cover the installations, called the probability of detection (POD), and the performance of a correct classification of a ROI, called the probability of identification (POI). The POD is a performance measure for the actual ROI-algorithm and its data preprocessing. A not-found ROI cannot be classified. The POI is a performance measure for the classifier itself. Hence, the classical performance measures for classification tasks can be applied in a given set of ROIs. To give a significant performance measure for the overall workflow, we use the correct classifications against the ground truth given by experienced human analysts, counting not-found ROIs as false negatives, which is a more pessimistic performance measure. The overall performance of the workflow is rated in finding an installation and assigning the right label to it. Here 90,8% of right labels are obtained. The remaining 9.2% split into 4.1% false negatives (not found by the ROI-finder, thus not a mistake of the classifier), 3.0% of rejects and 2.1% wrong class labels. Half of the rejects are due to ambiguity, the rest due to a lack of knowledge. In a practical scenario, where the ground truth is not available, the 3.0% of the ROIs which are rejected by the classifier can be classified manually and thus improve the performance up to 93.8%. For the pure classification performance is already improved by the CLARISSA-approach. If an uncertain feature causes an ambiguous class label, the classification is rejected. This effect raises the amount of rejects and lowers the amount of wrong class labels by each 0.1% (To measure this effect, all feature Trust Levels are set to 1.0). Despite this does no seem a great gain, with the lowering of wrong class label assignments it optimizes the most critical part of the results. In further investigations, we found this mechanism much more important for raw-data which is seriously disturbed. As the ROI-algorithm is not perfect, it produces negative reports. I.e., a ROI is indicated, but no installation is localized there. For the investigated pipeline the amount of negative reports is 3.2% compared to the number of installations in the ground truth. In this set about 8 of 10 ROIs are rejected due to ignorance and thus are predestined for further manual inspection. This investigation stands for a variety of pipelines with different diameters and measurement conditions where we get similar results. The trained classifiers as well as the other workflow parameters do not need to be adapted or retrained for different pipelines and PIGs.

5.3   Assessment of the Results with Trust Management

To investigate the benefits of having the opportunity of assessing the reliability of the workflows results, we need to have a closer look on the particular results it produces within the Trust Management framework. After analyzing a pipeline automatically, a list of ROIs is produced. Each of them contains

- its location and orientation along the pipeline,
- measures for the trustworthiness of the raw data and the deduced features, called data Trust Levels,
- a class label or a reason for the reject from the classifier,
- a measure for the trustworthiness of the classification result, calculated by CLARISSA, called classification Trust Level,
- a measure for the overall trustworthiness of the regions of interest, called total Trust Level, which is in this case the minimum of the data- and classification Trust Level. It hence reflects the trustworthiness of a final classification result.

For the above mentioned pipeline the distribution of correct classifications and negative reports is shown in Fig. 3 by a histogram over 10 equally spaced bins of the total trust level. It shows that 67% of the classified ROIs have a trust level higher than 0.7. In this set all classifications are correct. The other way

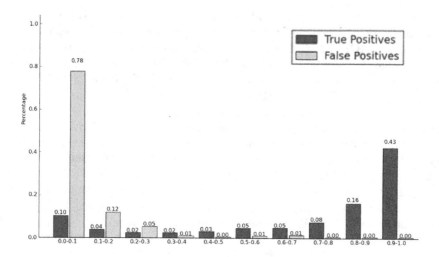

Fig. 3. Classification results and their total Trust Levels. On the x-axis the $[0, 1]$-interval is split up into 10 bins with a width of 0.1. The y-axis show the relative amount of right and wrong classifications in the respective interval.

round, 95% of the negative reports get a trust level smaller than 0.3. This U-Shape is a very characteristic. And this concrete distribution is also similar for a broad spectrum of inspected pipelines. As the trust levels are hierarchically built upon the measurement data and some general and abstract expert knowledge, they offer the opportunity to trace back the reason for an uncertain result. It is possible to differentiate between a lack of knowledge in the classifier and insufficient trustworthiness of the raw data and the features deduced from them. In a scenario like this, it helps to improve the specific part of the workflow, e.g. to get more or better training data if the classifier cannot produce trustworthy results from trustworthy raw-data or to spend more manual efforts.

5.4   Discussion

The usage of trust management and the CLARISSA-classifier for the classification of MFL data leads to two major results. First of all, we can classify installations in pipelines with a high performance, despite the varying data quality and all above-mentioned dynamic uncertainties in the raw data. Second, with the Trust Level of a result we provide a reliable additional measure to rate the trustworthiness of the result for a concrete pipeline under inspection. They serve as a detailed source of information about potentially occurring uncertainties of the results and also assist in engineering and parameterization of the workflow. For a safety critical NDT task like pipeline inspection this ensures a high quality of the results which are automatically classified with a high trust level. This example further shows that the method of Trust Management is suited more generally for data analysis tasks with varying degrees of uncertainty in the underlying raw-data and classifiers. By modeling the expert knowledge about the possible flaws in the data at a general level, a good measure for the data quality is achieved. By the use of the CLARISSA-classifier, we can provide detailed information about the reason for a possible reject and the trustworthiness of a result.

6   Conclusion and Outlook

In this paper we showed an application of an extended fuzzy rule based classifier to automatically analyze magnetic flux leakage data from in-line pipeline inspection. To deal with the dynamic uncertainties in the raw data we apply Trust Management to model them explicitly. The classification workflow uses the information about the individual uncertainties to weight a certain feature higher compared to an uncertain one and thus achieves better results in terms of classification performance. As the whole processing workflow is closely monitored by Trust Management and no black-box algorithms are used, it offers bidirectional traceability, which is a key feature needed for safety critical classification tasks.

Acknowledgment. The work has been partly supported by the German Federal Ministry of Economics and Technology, support code KF2312001ED9.

References

1. Brockmann, W., Buschermöhle, A., Hülsmann, J.: A Generic Concept to Increase the Robustness of Embedded Systems by Trust Management. In: Proc. Int. Conf. Systems, Man, and Cybernetics, pp. 2037–2044. IEEE (2010)
2. Buschermöhle, A., Rosemann, N., Brockmann, W.: Stable Classification in Environments with Varying Degrees of Uncertainty. In: Proc. Int. Conf. on Computational Intelligence for Modelling, Control & Automation, pp. 441–446. IEEE Computer Society (2008)
3. Carvalho, A., Rebello, J., Sagrilo, L., Camerini, C., Miranda, I.: MFL Signals and Artificial Neural Networks Applied to Detection and Classification of Pipe Weld Defects. NDT & E International 39(8), 661–667 (2006)
4. Central Intelligence Agency: The world factbook (November 2011),
   http://www.cia.gov/library/publications/the-world-factbook/
5. Chow, C.: On Optimum Recognition Error and Reject Tradeoff. IEEE Trans. Information Theory 16(1), 41–46 (1970)
6. Dubuisson, B., Masson, M.: A Statistical Decision Rule with Incomplete Knowledge about Classes. Pattern Recognition 26(1), 155–165 (1993)
7. Ehteram, S., Moussavi, S., Sadeghi, M., Mahdavi, S., Kazemi, A.: Intelligent Monitoring Approach for Pipeline Defect Detection from MFL Inspection. Journal of Convergence Information Technology 5(2), 43–49 (2010)
8. Frank, A., Asuncion, A.: UCI Machine Learning Repository (2010),
   http://archive.ics.uci.edu/ml
9. Haueisen, J., Unger, R., Beuker, T., Bellemann, M.: Evaluation of Inverse Algorithms in the Analysis of Magnetic Flux Leakage Data. IEEE Trans. Magnetics 38(3), 1481–1488 (2002)

10. Hühn, J., Hüllermeier, E.: FR3: A Fuzzy Rule Learner for Inducing Reliable Classifiers. IEEE Trans. on Fuzzy Systems 17(1), 138–149 (2009)
11. Hülsmann, J., Buschermöhle, A., Brockmann, W.: Incorporating Dynamic Uncertainties into a Fuzzy Classifier. In: Proc. 7th Conf. of the European Society for Fuzzy Logic and Technology, EUSFLAT, vol. 1, pp. 388–395. Atlantis Press (2011)
12. Landgrebe, T., Tax, D., Paclík, P., Duin, R.: The Interaction between Classification and Reject Performance for Distance-Based Reject-Option Classifiers. Pattern Recognition Letters 27(8), 908–917 (2006)
13. Mix, P.: Introduction to Nondestructive Testing: A Training Guide, pp. 73–77. Wiley Interscience (2005)
14. Pipeline Operators Forum: Specifications and Requirements for Intelligent PIG Inspection of Pipelines (2009),
    http://www.pipelineoperators.org/publicdocs/POF_specs_2009.pdf
15. Slessarev, D., Sukhorukov, V., Belitsky, S., Vasin, E., Stepanov, N.: Magnetic In-Line Inspection of Pipelines: Some Problems of Defect Detection, Identification and Measurement. In: Proc. 9th European NDT Conf. ECNDT (2006),
    http://www.ndt.net
16. Song, Q.: Data Fusion for MFL Signal Characterization. Applied Mechanics and Materials 44, 3519–3523 (2011)
17. US National Energy Technology Laboratory, PHMSA. Pipeline Inspection Technologies Demonstration Report. Tech. rep. (2006)

Ant Based Clustering of Two-Class Sets with Well Categorized Objects

Krzysztof Pancerz[1], Arkadiusz Lewicki[1], and Ryszard Tadeusiewicz[2]

[1] Institute of Biomedical Informatics
University of Information Technology and Management in Rzeszów, Poland
{kpancerz,alewicki}@wsiz.rzeszow.pl
[2] AGH University of Science and Technology, Kraków, Poland
rtad@agh.edu.pl

Abstract. In the paper, a new ant based algorithm for clustering a set of well categorized objects is shown. A set of well categorized objects is characterized by high similarity of the objects within classes and relatively high dissimilarity of the objects between different classes. The algorithm is based on versions of ant based clustering algorithms proposed earlier by Deneubourg, Lumer and Faieta as well as Handl et al. In our approach, a new local function, formulas for picking and dropping decisions, as well as some additional operations are proposed to adjust the clustering process to specific data.

Keywords: ant based clustering, well categorized objects.

1 Preliminaries

In data mining, we encounter a diversity of methods supporting data analysis which can be generally classified into two groups, called supervised and unsupervised learning, respectively (cf. [1]). One of unsupervised approaches investigated by us is clustering of data. In the paper, we consider the ant based clustering algorithm based mainly on versions proposed by Deneubourg [2], Lumer and Faieta [8] as well as Handl et al. [7]. The last algorithm is called ATTA. Clustering algorithms examine data to find groups (clusters) of items (objects, cases) which are similar to each other and dissimilar to the items belonging to other groups.

In some cases, the use of algorithms proposed earlier in the literature leads to a number of resulting groups smaller than the real one. At the beginning of our research, we take into consideration a set of objects clustered into two disjoint classes. After an ant based clustering process, we need to obtain two coherent clusters on a grid on which objects were initially scattered. To satisfy this requirement, after empirical studies, a new local function, formulas for picking and dropping decisions as well as some additional operations are proposed to adjust the clustering process to specific data.

In making picking and dropping decisions, we propose to use some threshold similarity which is adjusted to data (objects) to be clustered. Such an adjustment

S. Greco et al. (Eds.): IPMU 2012, Part III, CCIS 299, pp. 241–250, 2012.

is based on the fact that, in a set of well categorized objects, the objects belonging to different classes are significantly dissimilar whereas the objects belonging to the same class are strongly similar. Our proposition is also characterized by more deterministic picking and dropping decisions than in algorithms presented earlier in the literature. If some conditions are satisfied, picking and dropping operations are made deterministically, i.e., with the probability equal to 1. Moreover, some additional operations should prevent, first of all, unwanted situation, namely, forming more smaller clusters of very similar objects which should belong to one bigger cluster and making all ants busy by carrying objects for which there are no proper clusters to drop them into. The current paper should be treated as the first stage of improving ant based clustering algorithms for well categorized objects.

In this paper, for simplicity, we assume that objects to be clustered belong to two disjoint classes. However, the presented approach can be extended, in the future, to many-class categorizations of objects (cases). Let $U = \{u_1, u_2, \ldots, u_n\}$ be a set of all objects. We take into consideration the situation in which objects are described in the attribute space enabling us to determine some numerical similarity measure $d(u_i, u_j)$ between any two objects $u_i, u_j \in U$, where $i, j = 1, 2, \ldots, n$. In the clustering area, a variety of similarity measures can be applied (see, for example, [6]). After a clustering process, we obtain two disjoint sets of objects: C_{k_1} (a set of objects clustered in class k_1) and C_{k_2} (a set of objects clustered in class k_2), where $C_{k_1} \subseteq U, C_{k_2} \subseteq U, C_{k_1} \cap C_{k_2} = \emptyset$, and $C_{k_1} \cup C_{k_2} = U$. In our case, a set U of objects described above is well categorized if and only if:

- $diam(C_{k_1}) << single\_link(C_{k_1}, C_{k_2})$,
- $diam(C_{k_2}) << single\_link(C_{k_1}, C_{k_2})$,

where:

- $diam(C_{k_j}) = \max_{u,v \in C_{k_j}} d(u, v), \ j = 1, 2,$
- $single\_link(C_{k_1}, C_{k_2}) = \min_{u \in C_{k_1}, v \in C_{k_2}} d(u, v).$

The rest of the paper is organized as follows. Section 2 presents more exactly our new algorithm. Section 3 delivers results of experiments performed on real life data using the algorithm proposed in Section 2. Finally, Section 4 provides conclusions.

2   Algorithm

The ant based clustering algorithm proposed in this paper is mainly based on algorithms proposed earlier by Deneubourg [2], Lumer and Faieta [8] as well as Handl et al. [7]. A number of modifications have been implemented, that adjust the algorithm to the problem of clustering well categorized data. In such data, objects belonging to the same class are highly similar, whereas objects belonging to different classes are relatively highly dissimilar.

A set of steps is formally listed in Algorithm 1. In this algorithm: U is a set of labeled objects (cases) being clustered (the size of U is n), N is a number of iterations performed for the clustering process, $Ants$ is a set of ants used in the clustering process, $p_{pick}(u)$ and $p_{drop}(u)$ are probabilities of the picking and dropping operations made for a given object u, respectively (see Formulas 3 and 4).

A local function, in our approach, is not directly calculated on the basis of dissimilarity measures of objects, but on the basis of a content of a given neighborhood. For the neighborhood to be checked, a relative number of similar objects to a given one is determined. This relative number constitutes a local function. Let P be a set of all places of the square grid G on which objects are scattered. Let the size of G be $M \times M$. Each place p of G is described by two coordinates, that will be written as $p(i, j)$, where $i, j = 1, \ldots, M$. Let $\pi(p)$ be a neighborhood of the place $p(i, j)$ where the object u is foreseen to be dropped or where the object u is foreseen to be picked up. This neighborhood $\pi(p)$ is defined as a square surrounding $p(i, j)$, i.e.:

$$\pi(p) = \{p^*(i^*, j^*) \in P : abs(i^* - i) <= r \text{ and } abs(j^* - j) <= r\},$$

where r is a radius of perception of ants and abs denotes the absolute value.

Let $U(p)$ denote the set of objects occupying a given place p because, in our approach, a given place p can be occupied by more than one object, i.e., some heaps can be created. A local function $f_{loc}(u)$ for the object u designated to pick up from or to drop at the place p is calculated as:

$$f_{loc}(u) = \frac{N_{sim}^{\pi(p)}}{N_{all}^{\pi(p)}}, \tag{1}$$

where:

- $N_{sim}^{\pi(p)}$ is a number of all objects u^* in the neighborhood $\pi(p)$ similar to u, i.e.:

$$d(u^*, u) <= \vartheta_{sim},$$

  where d is a given dissimilarity measure normalized to the interval $[0, 1]$, and ϑ_{sim} is a similarity threshold,
- $N_{all}^{\pi(p)}$ is a number of all objects placed in the neighborhood $\pi(p)$.

If some conditions are satisfied, picking and dropping operations are made deterministically, i.e., with the probability equal to 1. The decision to pick up a given object u is always made if:

- density of a neighborhood of u is less than threshold density $minDens$ - this helps us to avoid forming more smaller clusters of very similar objects which should belong to one bigger cluster,
- a local function $f_{loc}(u)$ calculated for u (according to Formula 2) is less than or equal to ϑ_{sim}^{pick}, where ϑ_{sim}^{pick} is a similarity threshold for picking objects up.

Density of a neighborhood $\pi(p)$ for the object u, designated to pick up from or to drop at the place p, is calculated as:

$$dens(u) = \frac{N_{all}^{\pi(p)}}{(r+1)^2},\tag{2}$$

where:

- $N_{all}^{\pi(p)}$ is a number of all objects placed in the neighborhood $\pi(p)$,
- $(r+1)^2$ - is a number of all places in the neighborhood $\pi(p)$.

Density is incremented during a clustering process.

The decision to drop a given object u is always made if:

- u is carried by the same ant for a long time, i.e., the ant cannot find a proper cluster for u (for this reason, a special counter $workTime$ for each ant is set, this counter determines how long, i.e., how many iterations, the ant carries the same object; if a given threshold is exceeded, the ant is released) - this prevents making all ants busy by carrying objects for which there are no proper clusters to drop them into,
- a local function $f_{loc}(u)$ calculated for u (according to Formula 2) is greater than or equal to ϑ_{sim}^{drop}, where ϑ_{sim}^{drop} is a similarity threshold for dropping objects.

Picking and dropping decisions for the object u can be formally expressed by the following threshold formulas:

$$p_{pick}(u) = \begin{cases} 1 & \text{if } f_{loc}(u) <= \vartheta_{sim}^{pick} \\ \frac{1}{(1-\vartheta_{sim}^{pick})^2}(f_{loc}(u)-1)^2 & \text{otherwise} \end{cases}\tag{3}$$

and

$$p_{drop}(u) = \begin{cases} 1 & \text{if } f >= \vartheta_{sim}^{drop} \\ \frac{1}{(\vartheta_{sim}^{drop})^2}f_{loc}^2 & \text{otherwise} \end{cases}\tag{4}$$

An example of a threshold function for the picking operation if $\vartheta_{sim}^{pick} = 0.8$ is shown in Figure 1 whereas an example of the threshold function for the dropping operation if $\vartheta_{sim}^{drop} = 0.6$ is depicted in Figure 2.

Thresholds ϑ_{sim}^{pick} and ϑ_{sim}^{drop} for picking and dropping operations, respectively, are automatically adjusted to data according to the definition of well categorized data given in Section 1. We assume that $\vartheta_{sim}^{pick} = \vartheta_{sim}^{drop} = \vartheta_{sim}$. ϑ_{sim} is set between the largest diameter and the smallest single link. Searching for threshold is performed according to Algorithm 2.

3   Experiments

Our experiments were carried out on real MMPI data. The data were collected and examined by a team of researchers consisting of W. Duch, T. Kucharski,

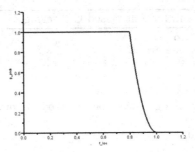

Fig. 1. An exemplary threshold function for the picking operation

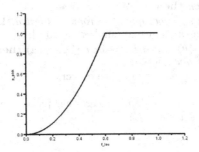

Fig. 2. An exemplary threshold function for the dropping operation

J. Gomuła, R. Adamczak [3]. In our earlier paper [10], using the same data, we have examined different similarity measures used in the ant based clustering process. The data are categorized into nineteen nosological classes and the reference class (*norm*). Each class corresponds to one of psychiatric nosological types: neurosis (*neur*), psychopathy (*psych*), organic (*org*), schizophrenia (*schiz*), delusion syndrome (*del.s*), reactive psychosis (*re.psy*), paranoia (*paran*), sub-manic state (*man.st*), criminality (*crim*), alcoholism (*alcoh*), drug addiction (*drug*), simulation (*simu*), dissimulation (*dissimu*), and six deviational answering styles (*dev1, dev2, dev3, dev4, dev5, dev6*). Each object (patient) is described by a data vector consisting of thirteen descriptive attributes. Values of attributes are expressed by the so-called T-scores. The T-scores scale, which is traditionally attributed to MMPI, represents the following parameters: offset ranging from 0 to 100 T-scores, average equal to 50 T-scores, standard deviation equal to 10 T-scores.

Below, we present results obtained for four data sets. The first data set ($MMPI_1$) consists of objects categorized by experts into two classes: the reference class (*norm*) and the 6th deviational answering style (*dev6*). The second data set ($MMPI_2$) consists of objects categorized by experts into two classes: alcoholism (*alcoh*) and the 2nd deviational answering style (*dev2*). The third data set ($MMPI_3$) consists of objects categorized by experts into two classes: psychopathy (*psych*) and the 4th deviational answering style (*dev4*). The last

Algorithm 1. Algorithm for Ant Based Clustering

---

for *each object $u_i \in U$* **do**
  Place u_i randomly on a grid G;
  Set o as dropped;
end
for *each ant $a_j \in Ants$* **do**
  Place a_j randomly on a grid place occupied by one of objects from U;
  Set a_j as unladen;
  $workTime(a_j) \leftarrow 0$;
end
for $k \leftarrow 1$ **to** N **do**
  for *each ant $a_j \in Ants$* **do**
    if a_j *is unladen* **then**
      if *place of a_j is occupied by dropped object u* **then**
        Draw a random real number $r \in [0, 1]$;
        if $dens(u) < minDens$ *or* $r \leq p_{pick}(u)$ **then**
          set o as picked;
          set a_j as carrying the object;
        else
          move a_j randomly to another place occupied by one of
          objects from U;
        end
      else
        move a_j randomly to another place occupied by one of objects
        from U;
      end
    else
      Draw a random real number $r \in [0, 1]$;
      if $r \leq p_{drop}(u)$ **then**
        move u randomly to a new place on a grid;
        set u as dropped;
        set a_j as unladen;
        $workTime(a_j) \leftarrow 0$;
      else
        $workTime(a_j) \leftarrow workTime(a_j) + 1$;
      end
    end
    if $workTime(a_j) > maxWorkTime$ **then**
      set u as dropped;
      set a_j as unladen;
      move a_j randomly to another place occupied by one of objects from
      U;
      $workTime(a_j) \leftarrow 0$;
    end
  end
  increase $minDens$;
end

Algorithm 2. Algorithm for searching for the threshold for picking and dropping operations

---

Input   : $U = \{u_1, u_2, \ldots, u_n\}$ - a set of objects to be clustered.
Output: ϑ_{sim} - threshold for picking and dropping operations.
$D \leftarrow \emptyset$;
for *each object* $u_i \in U$, $i = 1, \ldots n$ **do**
$\quad$ **for** *each object* $u_j \in U$, $j = i+1, \ldots n$ **do**
$\quad\quad |\quad D \leftarrow d(u_i, u_j)$;
$\quad$ **end**
end
Sort D in non-descending order;
Find a maximal difference $(d_{m+1} - d_m)$ between two consecutive distances in D,
where $m = 1, \ldots, card(D) - 1$;
$\vartheta_{sim} \leftarrow \frac{d_m + d_{m+1}}{2}$;

---

data set ($MMPI_4$) consists of objects categorized by experts into two classes: dissimulation (*dissimu*) and the 5th deviational answering style (*dev5*).

The results of an ant based clustering process performed by means of our algorithm have been compared (see Table 1), in terms of properly formed clusters for categorized objects, with results obtained using the well known k-means algorithm [9]. For comparison, results of three popular analytical evaluation measures have been used:

- F-measure [11],
- the Dunn index [4], [5],
- the intra-cluster variance.

Experiments for the ant based clustering have been performed with the following parameters:

- *dissimilarity measure*: Euclidean,
- *grid size*: 100×100,
- *no. of ants*: 40,
- *radius of perception*: 3,
- *no. of iterations*: from 50000 to 100000.

Experiments for the k-means clustering have been performed with the following parameters:

- *dissimilarity measure*: Euclidean,
- *maximal no. of iterations*: 400000.

Exemplary Figures 3 and 4 show that clusters have been properly formed. All objects belonging to the same class have been concentrated in one region on the grid. This was the main goal in our research to obtain objects belonging to the same class collected in one cluster as well as to have clusters sharply distinguished, i.e., placed in discernible places on the grid. However, it is easy to see in figures that for sets with imbalanced distribution of objects among classes

Table 1. Results of experiments

Data Set	F-measure	Dunn index	Intra-cluster variance
The proposed algorithm			
$MMPI_1$ (norm - dev6)	**1.00**	**1.42**	**12 121 347.00**
$MMPI_2$ (alcoh - dev2)	1.00	1.79	940 343.15
$MMPI_3$ (psych - dev4)	1.00	1.34	2 873 406.20
$MMPI_4$ (dissimu - dev5)	**1.00**	0.66	1 921 829.7
The k-means algorithm			
$MMPI_1$ (norm - dev6)	0.85	0.09	12 126 835.00
$MMPI_2$ (alcoh - dev2)	1.00	1.79	940 343.15
$MMPI_3$ (psych - dev4)	1.00	1.34	2 873 406.20
$MMPI_4$ (dissimu - dev5)	0.98	1.01	1 847 465.60

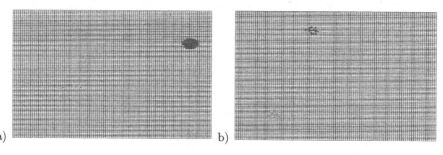

a)   b)

Fig. 3. Exemplary spatial distribution on the grid after performing Algorithm 1 for sets $MMPI_1$ (a) and $MMPI_2$ (b)

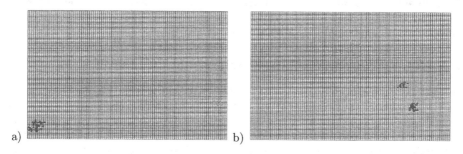

a)   b)

Fig. 4. Exemplary spatial distribution on the grid after performing Algorithm 1 for sets $MMPI_3$ (a) and $MMPI_4$ (b)

(i.e., a significantly different number of objects in particular classes), a cluster for a minority class consists of more scattered objects. This is one of problems of our proposition which needs to be solved in the future. Another problem is to determine a way to adjust changes of a minimum density parameter during a clustering process.

It is worth noting that, for sets $MMPI_1$ and $MMPI_4$, clusters have been properly formed in accordance with classes to which objects were classified by the experts. The k-means algorithm made some mistakes for these sets in spite of well categorized objects. It can follow from imbalanced distribution of objects among classes. In this case, the proposed method works better.

4   Conclusions

In the paper, we have examined a problem of clustering sets of well categorized objects. Due to definitions of a new local function, formulas for picking and dropping decisions as well as some additional operations, we have obtained the algorithm building singular distinguishable clusters for objects belonging to the same class. Experiments have been performed for two-class sets of objects. In the future, we plan to evaluate, and alternatively modify, our approach for sets of objects with more than two classes or with classes with less sharp boundaries. Moreover, there is a need to propose the ant based algorithm with a hierarchical process of clustering to form as few clusters as possible with internal homogeneous structures. In this case, the second stage should consist of ants moving not singular objects but the whole groups of them.

Acknowledgments. This paper has been partially supported by the grant No. N N519 654540 from the National Science Centre in Poland.

References

1. Cios, K., Pedrycz, W., Swiniarski, R., Kurgan, L.: Data mining. Knowledge Discovery Approach. Springer, New York (2007)
2. Deneubourg, J., Goss, S., Franks, N., Sendova-Franks, A., Detrain, C., Chrétien, L.: The dynamics of collective sorting: Robot-like ants and ant-like robots. In: Proceedings of the First International Conference on Simulation of Adaptive Behaviour: From Animals to Animats 1, pp. 356–365. MIT Press, Cambridge (1991)
3. Duch, W., Kucharski, T., Gomuła, J., Adamczak, R.: Machine learning methods in analysis of psychometric data. In: Application to Multiphasic Personality Inventory MMPI-WISKAD, Toruń (1999) (in Polish)
4. Dunn, J.: A fuzzy relative of the isodata process and its use in detecting compact well-separated clusters. Journal of Cybernetics 3(3), 32–57 (1973)
5. Dunn, J.: Well-separated clusters and optimal fuzzy partitions. Journal of Cybernetics 4(1), 95–104 (1974)
6. Gan, G., Ma, C., Wu, J.: Data Clustering. Theory, Algorithms, and Applications. SIAM, Philadelphia (2007)
7. Handl, J., Knowles, J., Dorigo, M.: Ant-based clustering and topographic mapping. Artificial Life 12(1), 35–62 (2006)
8. Lumer, E., Faieta, B.: Diversity and adaptation in populations of clustering ants. In: Proceedings of the Third International Conference on Simulation of Adaptive Behaviour: From Animals to Animats 3, pp. 501–508. MIT Press, Cambridge (1994)

9. MacQueen, J.: Some methods for classification and analysis of multivariate observations. In: Proceedings of the Fifth Berkeley Symposium on Mathematical Statistics and Probability, vol. 1, pp. 281–297. University of California Press (1967)
10. Pancerz, K., Lewicki, A., Tadeusiewicz, R., Gomuła, J.: Ant Based Clustering of MMPI Data - An Experimental Study. In: Yao, J., Ramanna, S., Wang, G., Suraj, Z. (eds.) RSKT 2011. LNCS, vol. 6954, pp. 366–375. Springer, Heidelberg (2011)
11. van Rijsbergen, C.J.: Information Retrieval. Butterworth, London (1979)

Construction Methods for Uninorms
via Rotation, Rotation-Annihilation,
and Twin Rotation

Sándor Jenei[1,2,*]

[1] Institute of Mathematics and Informatics, University of Pécs, Pécs, Ifjúság u. 6.,
H-7624 Pécs, Hungary
`jenei@ttk.pte.hu`
[2] Department of Knowledge-Based Mathematical Systems, Johannes Kepler
University, Altenbergerstrasse 69, Johannes Kepler University, Linz, Austria
`sandor.jenei@jku.at`

Abstract. Uninorms are known to have a kind of partial compensatory
behaviour, which makes them useful for decision theory and related fields.
Residuated uninorms play a prominent role in the theory of substructural
logics and, in particular, in mathematical fuzzy logic. We shall present
here some construction methods that result in residuated uninorms along
with some recent classification theorems which show the limitation of
the constructions. Among them is a very recent Mostert-Shields style
classification theorem on SIU-algebras.

Keywords: Uninorm, aggregation operator, associativity, compensation,
rotation, rotation-annihilation, triple rotation, twin rotation.

1 Introduction and Preliminaries

Aggregation operators (that is, $[0,1]^2 \to [0,1]$ mappings M that are increasing
and satisfy $M(0,0) = 0$ and $M(1,1) = 1$) play an important role in several
fields of applied mathematics such as fuzzy modelling/control and fuzzy decision
making. In these fields, it is very important to have a large spectrum of such
operations at hand so that the practitioner can find the aggregation operator
that best fits to the application in question.

Uninorms are commutative, isotone monoids on $[0,1]$. They were introduced
in [30] to generalize the notion of t-norms and t-conorms by allowing the neutral
element t to belong to the open unit interval $]0,1[$. T-norms (resp. t-conorms)
are uninorms with neutral element 1 (resp. 0). Uninorms can be considered associative, partially compensative aggregation operators: Indeed, denoting the unit
element of the uninorm by t, its value is in between the minimum and the maximum functions on its subdomain $[0,t] \times [t,1]$. The first paper about associative

* Supported by the OTKA-76811 grant, the SROP-4.2.1.B-10/2/KONV-2010-0002
grant, and the MC ERG grant 267589.

S. Greco et al. (Eds.): IPMU 2012, Part III, CCIS 299, pp. 251–260, 2012.
© Springer-Verlag Berlin Heidelberg 2012

aggregation operations is [3] where the author, using the name "aggregative operator" has introduced a special class of uninorms. This class coincides with what we recently call representable uninorm class, and contains, for instance the "Three Pi" operator of Yager (see Fig. 1)

$$M(x, y) = \frac{xy}{xy + (1 - x)(1 - y)}. \tag{1}$$

Representable uninorms are those ones, which have a representation by means of a one-place function, similar to continuous Archimedean t-norms and t-conorms; as said above, this class coincides with Dombi's class of aggregative operators.

Residuated lattices have been introduced in the 30s of the last century by Ward and Dilworth [29] to investigate ideal theory of commutative rings with unit. Examples of residuated lattices include Boolean algebras, Heyting algebras [7], MV-algebras [1], basic logic algebras, [9] and lattice-ordered groups; a variety of other algebraic structures can be rendered as residuated lattices. Residuated lattices turned out to be algebraic counterparts of substructural logics [26,25,8]. Applications of substructural logics and residuated lattices span across proof theory, algebra, and computer science.

FL_e-algebras are particular residuated lattices (see Definition 1). They can be considered generalizations of residuated uninorms for lattices. On $[0, 1]$, monoidal operations of FL_e-algebras and integral FL_e-algebras are referred to as left-continuous uninorms and left-continuous t-norms, respectively. Those uninorms and t-norms are left-continuous, as two-place functions, because they are residuated.

The first observations on the structure of uninorms were presented in [6]: Any uninorm U has an underlying t-norm T and t-conorm S acting on the subdomains $[0, t] \times [0, t]$ and $[t, 1] \times [t, 1]$ of $[0, 1]^2$, respectively. Keeping in mind that any uninorm (in either the narrow or the broad sense) has its underlying t-norm and t-conorm, in order to construct uninorms the following two questions emerge:

Q1: Given a pair of a t-norm and a t-conorm (acting on the subdomains $[0, t] \times [0, t]$ and $[t, 1] \times [t, 1]$, respectively) how can we extend the operation on the remaining parts (that is, on $[0, t] \times [t, 1]$ and $[t, 1] \times [0, t]$) in such a way that the resulted operation becomes a uninorm?

As one may guess, the investigation of this amounts to checking the associativity of the resulted operation.

Q2: If there exists an associative extension for a given pair of t-norm and t-conorm, how many such extension does there exist? Provide a list.

The first question may be referred to as the construction problem, whereas the second may be referred to as the classification problem.

As for the *construction problem*, it is easy to see that the minimum and the maximum operations both work, that is, for any pair T and S, evaluating the rest of the domain by either of them, one always obtains an associative operation; that is, a uninorm. Both for left-continuous t-norms and for left-continuous uninorms, those with an involutive negation are of special interest. For t-norms negation is defined by $\neg x = x \to 0$, while for uninorms negation is defined as $\neg x = x \to f$, where f is a fixed, but arbitrary element of $[0,1]$, and stands for falsum just like 0 does in case of a t-norm. Involutive t-norms and uninorms have very interesting symmetry properties [11,14,10,23] and, as a consequence, for involutive t-norms and uninorms we have beautiful geometric constructions which are lacking for general left-continuous t-norms and uninorms [12,19,22].

As for the *classification* *problem* of residuated lattices, this task seems to be possible only by posing additional conditions. A first result in this direction is due to Mostert and Shields who investigated certain topological semigroups on compact manifolds with connected, regular boundary in [27]. Being topological means that the monoidal operation of the residuated lattice is continuous with respect to the underlying topology. They proved that such semigroups are ordinal sums in the sense of Clifford [2] of product, Boolean, and Łukasiewicz summands. Next, the dropping of the topologically connected property of the underlying chain can successfully be compensated by assuming the divisibility condition (which is, in fact, the dual notion of the well-known naturally ordered property). Under the assumption of divisibility, residuated chains, that is BL-chains, have been classified, again, as ordinal sums of product, Boolean, and Łukasiewicz summands. The divisibility condition proved to be strong enough for the classification of residuated lattices over arbitrary lattices too [20]. Fodor at al. have classified those uninorms which have continuous underlying t-norm and t-conorm [5,4]. Here we classify strongly involutive uninorms algebras (SIU-algebras), that is bounded, representable, sharp, involutive FL_e-algebras over arbitrary lattices for which their cone operations are dually isomorphic. Let us remark that assuming the duality condition proved to be equivalent to assuming the divisibility condition *only* for the positive and negative cones of such algebras.

2   Preliminaries

As said in the introduction, uninorms are commutative, isotone monoids on $[0,1]$. On general universe, however, we shall refer to *residuated* uninorms as monoidal operations of FL_e-algebras:

Definition 1. Call $\mathcal{U} = \langle X, \circledast, \leq, t, f \rangle$ an *FL_e-algebra* if $\mathcal{C} = \langle X, \leq \rangle$ is a poset and $\circledast$ is a commutative, residuated monoid over $\mathcal{C}$ with neutral element t. Define the positive and the negative cone of $\mathcal{U}$ by $X^+ = \{x \in X \mid x \geq t\}$ and $X^- = \{x \in X \mid x \leq t\}$, respectively. Call an FL_e-algebra $\mathcal{U}$ *involutive*, if for $x \in X$, $(x')' = x$ holds, where $x' = x \to_\circledast f$. Call an involutive FL_e-algebra $\mathcal{U}$ *sharp*, if $t = f$. Call a sharp, involutive FL_e-algebra a *SIU-algebra*, if for $x, y \in X^-$, $x' \circledast y' = (x \circledast y)'$ holds.

The defining condition for SIU-algebras is equivalent to the requirement that the negative and the positive cone operations are BL-algebras [14,10]. On $[0,1]$ this means that the underlying t-norm and t-conorm are assumed to be continuous.

A *negation* N on $[a, b] \subset \mathbf{R}$ is a decreasing unary operation on $[a, b]$ satisfying $N(a) = b$ and $N(b) = a$. A negation is called *strong* (or an involution) if it is involutive, i.e. if $N(N(x)) = x$ for any $x \in [a, b]$. Consider a left-continuous binary operation M on $[a, b] \subset \mathbf{R}$ which is commutative, associative, and isotone: The *residual implication* I_M corresponding to M is the binary operation I_M on $[a, b]$ defined by $I_M(x, y) = \max\{t \in [a, b] \mid M(x, t) \le y\}$. The *residual negation* N_M corresponding to M is the negation N_M on $[a, b]$ defined by $N_M(x) = I_M(x, a)$. We say that M has a strong residual negation if N_M is a strong negation on $[a, b]$. M is *called rotation-invariant w.r.t. a strong negation* N on $[a, b]$ if the following equivalence holds for any $x, y, z \in [a, b]$: $M(x, y) \le z \Leftrightarrow M(N(z), x) \le N(y)$.

Let $\mathcal{U}$ be an FL_e-algebra. The algebra $\mathcal{U}$ is called *conic* if every element of X is comparable with t, that is, if $X = X^+ \cup X^-$. $\mathcal{U}$ is called *bounded* if X has top $\top$ and bottom $\bot$ element. If X is linearly ordered, we speak about FL_e-*chains*. Since $\circledast$ is residuated, it is as well partially-ordered (isotone), and therefore, $' : X \to X$ is an order-reversing involution. A partially-ordered monoid is called integral (resp. dually integral) if the underlying poset has its greatest (resp. least) element and it coincides with the neutral element of the monoid. It is not difficult to see that $\circledast$ restricted to X^- (resp. X^+) is integral (resp. dually integral).

3   Rotation of Uninorms

Proposition 1. [13] *Consider a strong negation N with unique fixpoint c and a left-continuous binary operation M on $[0, 1]$ which is commutative, associative, and isotone. Let M_1 be the linear transformation of M into $[c, 1]$, $I^- = [0, c]$ and $I^+ =]c, 1]$. Then the binary operation $M_{\mathbf{rot}}$ on $[0, 1]$ defined by*

$$M_{\mathbf{rot}}(x, y) = \begin{cases} M_1(x, y) & , \textit{if } x, y \in I^+ \\ N(I_{M_1}(x, N(y))) & , \textit{if } x \in I^+ \textit{ and } y \in I^- \\ N(I_{M_1}(y, N(x))) & , \textit{if } x \in I^- \textit{ and } y \in I^+ \\ 0 & , \textit{if } x, y \in I^- \end{cases} \tag{2}$$

is a left-continuous rotation-invariant operation which is commutative, associative, and isotone if and only if either

(C1) $M(x, y) = 0$ *implies* $\min(x, y) = 0$ *or*
(C2) *there exists* $c \in]0, 1]$ *such that* $M(x, y) = 0$ *if and only if* $x, y \le c$.

Moreover, it holds that $M_{\mathbf{rot}} \le \min$ if and only if $M \le \min$. $M_{\mathbf{rot}}$ is called the rotation of M (with respect to N).

Proposition 1 reveals that exactly those uninorms are suitable for playing the role of M, for which their underlying t-norm satisfies condition (C1) or condition (C2):

Theorem 1. *Consider a strong negation N with unique fixpoint c and a left-continuous uninorm U with neutral element t. Let U_1 be the linear transformation of U into $[t, 1]$ and denote the image of e under this linear transformation by c^*. Then the rotation U_{rot} is a left-continuous uninorm with neutral element c^*.*

Example 1. The rotation of the "Three Pi" operator defined in (1) and the rotation of the uninorm U, which is defined by

$$U(x, y) = \begin{cases} \min(x, y) \text{ , if } \max(x, y) \leq \tfrac{1}{2}, \\ \max(x, y) \text{ , otherwise.} \end{cases} \tag{3}$$

with respect to $N(x) = 1 - x$ are depicted in Figure 1.

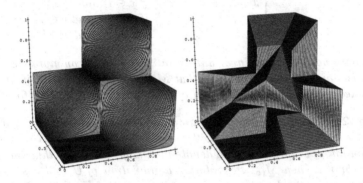

Fig. 1. The rotation of "Three Pi" (left) and the rotation of U, see Example 1

4   Rotation-Annihilation with Uninorms

Proposition 2. [13] *Consider a strong negation N with unique fixpoint c, $d \in$ $]c, 1[$ and define a strong negation N_d by*

$$N_d(x) = \frac{N(x \cdot (d - N(d)) + N(d)) - N(d)}{d - N(d)}.$$

Consider a left-continuous binary operation M on $[0, 1]$ which is commutative, associative, and isotone and let M_1 be the linear transformation of M into $[d, 1]$.

(D1) *If $x, y > 0$ implies $M(x, y) > 0$, then let M^* be a left-continuous t-subnorm that is rotation-invariant w.r.t. N_d. Further, let $I^- = [0, N(d)[$, $I^0 = [N(d), d]$ and $I^+ =]d, 1]$.*

(D2) *If there exist $x, y > 0$ such that $M(x, y) = 0$, then let M^* be a left-continuous t-norm that is rotation-invariant w.r.t. N_d (or equivalently, let M^* be a left-continuous t-norm with residual negation N_d). Further, let $I^- = [0, N(d)]$, $I^0 =]N(d), d[$ and $I^+ = [d, 1]$.*

Let M_1 be the linear transformation of M into $[d, 1]$, M_2 be the linear transformation of M^* into $[N(d), d]$ and M_3 be the annihilation of M_2 defined by

$$M_3(x, y) = \begin{cases} 0 & , \text{ if } x, y \in [N(d), d] \text{ and } x \leq N(y) \\ M_2(x, y) & , \text{ if } x, y \in [N(d), d] \text{ and } x > N(y). \end{cases}$$

Then the binary operation $M_{\mathbf{ra}}$ on $[0, 1]$ defined by

$$M_{\mathbf{ra}}(x, y) = \begin{cases} M_1(x, y) & , \text{ if } x, y \in I^+ \\ N(I_{M_1}(x, N(y))) & , \text{ if } x \in I^+, y \in I^- \\ N(I_{M_1}(y, N(x))) & , \text{ if } x \in I^-, y \in I^+ \\ 0 & , \text{ if } x, y \in I^- \\ M_3(x, y) & , \text{ if } x, y \in I^0 \\ y & , \text{ if } x \in I^+ \text{ and } y \in I^0 \\ x & , \text{ if } x \in I^0 \text{ and } y \in I^+ \\ 0 & , \text{ if } x \in I^- \text{ and } y \in I^0 \\ 0 & , \text{ if } x \in I^0 \text{ and } y \in I^- \end{cases} \tag{4}$$

is a left-continuous rotation-invariant operation which is commutative, associative, and isotone. Moreover, it holds that $M_{\mathbf{ra}} \leq \min$ if and only if $M \leq \min$. $M_{\mathbf{ra}}$ is called the rotation-annihilation of M and M^* (with respect to N).

Theorem 2. *Consider a strong negation N with unique fixpoint c, $d \in]c, 1[$ and a left-continuous uninorm U with neutral element t. Let U_1 be the linear transformation of U into $[d, 1]$ and denote the image of t under this linear transformation by t^*. Then $M_{\mathbf{ra}}$, the rotation-annihilation of U and a suitable M^* (as in Proposition 2, depending on the zero values of U) is a left-continuous uninorm with neutral element t^*.*

Example 2. Consider $N(x) = 1 - x$ and $d = 2/3$. For $\varepsilon \in [0, 1]$, the rotation-invariant t-subnorm, which is dual to $S_{\mathbf{L}}^\varepsilon$, is given by $T_{\mathbf{L}}^\varepsilon = \max(0, x + y - 1 - \varepsilon)$. In Figure 2, two rotation-annihilations are presented.

5   Twin Rotation of Semigroups

Since the related recent classification theorem is about the general lattice-ordered case, we change our universe of discourse from the unit interval to lattices here. In [19] the authors gave a structural description of conic, involutive FL_e-algebras by proving that the cone operations of any involutive, conic FL_e-algebra uniquely determine the FL_e-algebra via (5):

Theorem 3. [19] **(Conic Representation Theorem)** *For any conic, involutive FL_e-algebra it holds true that*

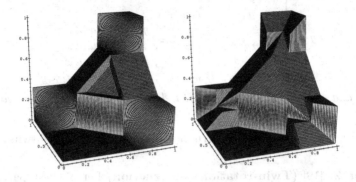

Fig. 2. Rotation-annihilation of "Three Pi" and $T_L^{0.3}$ (left), and of U (defined in (3)) and T_L (right), see Example 2

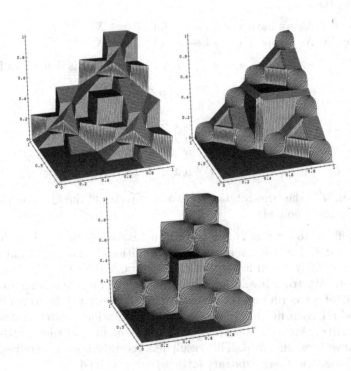

Fig. 3. Some uninorms that were constructed by iteratively applying some of the presented methods

$$x * y = \begin{cases} x \oplus y & \text{if } x, y \in X^+ \\ x \otimes y & \text{if } x, y \in X^- \\ (x \to_\oplus y')' & \text{if } x \in X^+, y \in X^-, \text{ and } x \leq y' \\ (y \to_\otimes x')' & \text{if } x \in X^+, y \in X^-, \text{ and } x \not\leq y' \\ (y \to_\oplus x')' & \text{if } x \in X^-, y \in X^+, \text{ and } x \leq y' \\ (x \to_\otimes y')' & \text{if } x \in X^-, y \in X^+, \text{ and } x \not\leq y' \end{cases} \tag{5}$$

where $\otimes$ and $\oplus$ denote the negative and the positive cone operation of $*$, respectively.

Theorem 3 gives rise to a new construction method, the so-called twin-rotation.

Definition 2. [19] **(Twin-rotation construction)** Let X_1 be a partially ordered set with top element t, and and X_2 be a partially ordered set with bottom element t such that the connected ordinal sum $os_c\langle X_1, X_2\rangle$ of X_1 and X_2 (that is putting X_1 under X_2, and identifying the top of X_1 with the bottom of X_2) has an order reversing involution $'$. Let $\otimes$ and $\oplus$ be commutative, residuated semigroups on X_1 and X_2, respectively, both with neutral element t. Assume, in addition, that

1. in case $t' \in X_1$ we have $x \to_\otimes t' = x'$ for all $x \in X_1$, $x \geq t'$, and
2. in case $t' \in X_2$ we have $x \to_\oplus t' = x'$ for all $x \in X_2$, $x \leq t'$.

Denote $\mathcal{U}_\otimes^\oplus = \langle os_c\langle X_1, X_2\rangle, *, \leq, t, f\rangle$ where $f = t'$ and $*$ is defined as follows:

$$x * y = \begin{cases} x \otimes y & \text{if } x, y \in X_1 \\ x \oplus y & \text{if } x, y \in X_2 \\ (x \to_\oplus y')' & \text{if } x \in X_2, y \in X_1, \text{ and } x \leq y' \\ (y \to_\oplus x')' & \text{if } x \in X_1, y \in X_2, \text{ and } x \leq y' \\ (y \to_\otimes (x' \wedge t))' & \text{if } x \in X_2, y \in X_1, \text{ and } x \not\leq y' \\ (x \to_\otimes (y' \wedge t))' & \text{if } x \in X_1, y \in X_2, \text{ and } x \not\leq y' \end{cases} \tag{6}$$

Call $*$ (resp. $\mathcal{U}_\otimes^\oplus$) the twin-rotation of $\otimes$ and $\oplus$ (resp. of the first and the second partially ordered monoid).

It is not difficult to see that $\mathcal{U}_\otimes^\oplus$ in Definition 2 is well-defined, it is an involutive FL_e-algebra if and only if $*$ is associative, Conditions 1 and 2 of Definition 2 are necessary for $\mathcal{U}_\otimes^\oplus$ to be an involutive FL_e-algebra, and that $\mathcal{U}_\otimes^\oplus$ is conic.

Willing to construct involutive FL_e-algebras, the only remaining question is which pairs of a t-norm and a t-conorm work? In other words, which pairs of a t-norm and a t-conorm can be used in the twin-rotation construction such that $*$ is associative? A partial answer to this was given in [15], where SIU-algebras on $[0, 1]$ have been classified. This result has recently been generalized in [18], where SIU-algebras (over arbitrary lattices) are classified:

Theorem 4. [18] $\mathcal{U} = \langle X, *, \leq, t, f\rangle$ *is a SIU-algebra if and only if its negative cone is a BL-algebra with components which are either product or minimum components, $\oplus$ is the dual of $\otimes$, and $*$ is given by (5).*

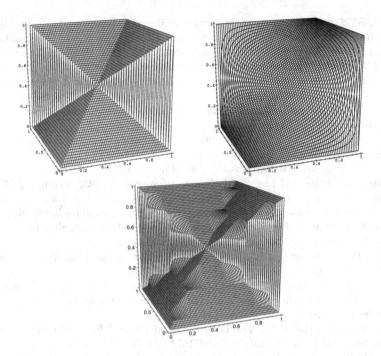

Fig. 4. Illustration for the classification of SIU-algebras, see Theorem 4

References

1. Cignoli, R., D'Ottaviano, I.M.L., Mundici, D.: Algebraic Foundations of Many-Valued Reasoning. Kluwer, Dordrecht (2000)
2. Clifford, A.H.: Naturally totally ordered commutative semigroups. Amer. J. Math. 76, 631–646 (1954)
3. Dombi, J.: Basic concepts for a theory of evaluation: The aggregative operator. European J. Oper. Res. 10, 282–293 (1982)
4. Fodor, J.: Personal communication
5. J. Fodor and B. De Baets, A single-point characterization of representable uninorms, Fuzzy Sets and Systems (to appear, 2012), doi:10.1016/j.fss.2011.12.001
6. Fodor, J., Yager, R., Rybalov, A.: Structure of uninorms. Int. J. Uncertainty, Fuzziness and Knowledge-Based Systems 5, 411–427 (1997)
7. Johnstone, P.T.: Stone spaces. Cambridge University Press, Cambridge (1982)
8. Galatos, N., Jipsen, P., Kowalski, T., Ono, H.: Residuated Lattices: An Algebraic Glimpse at Substructural Logics. Studies in Logic and the Foundations of Mathematics, vol. 151, p. 532 (2007)
9. Hájek, P.: Metamathematics of Fuzzy Logic. Kluwer Academic Publishers, Dordrecht (1998)
10. Jenei, S.: Erratum On the reflection invariance of residuated chains. Annals of Pure and Applied Logic 161, 220–227 (2009); Annals of Pure and Applied Logic 161, 1603-1604 (2010)
11. Jenei, S.: On the geometry of associativity. Semigroup Forum 74(3), 439–466 (2007)

12. Jenei, S.: Structure of Girard Monoids on [0,1]. In: Klement, E.P., Rodabaugh, S.E. (eds.) Topological and Algebraic Structures in Fuzzy Sets, A Handbook of Recent Developments in the Mathematics of Fuzzy Sets. Trends in Logic, vol. 20, pp. 277–308. Kluwer Academic Publishers, Dordrecht (2003)
13. Jenei, S.: On the structure of rotation-invariant semigroups. Archive for Mathematical Logic 42, 489–514 (2003)
14. Jenei, S.: On the reflection invariance of residuated chains. Annals of Pure and Applied Logic 161, 220–227 (2009)
15. Jenei, S.: On the relationship between the rotation construction and ordered Abelian groups. Fuzzy Sets and Systems 161(2), 277–284 (2010)
16. Jenei, S.: Structural description of a class of involutive FL_e-algebras via skew symmetrization. Journal of Logic and Computation, doi:10.1093/logcom/exp060
17. Jenei, S., De Baets, B.: Partially compensative associative operators by rotation and rotation-annihilation. IEEE Transactions on Fuzzy Systems 5, 606–614 (2004)
18. Jenei, S., Montagna, F.: Strongly involutive FL_e-algebras (submitted)
19. Jenei, S., Ono, H.: On involutive FL_e-algebras (submitted)
20. Jipsen, P., Montagna, F.: Embedding theorems for normal GBL-algebras. Journal of Pure and Applied Algebra 214, 1559–1575 (2010)
21. Klement, E.P., Mesiar, R., Pap, E.: On the relationship of associative compensatory operators to triangular norms and conorms. Int. J. Uncertainty, Fuzziness and Knowledge-Based Systems 4, 129–144 (1996)
22. Maes, K.C., De Baets, B.: The triple rotation method for constructing t-norms. Fuzzy Sets and Systems 158(15), 1652–1674 (2007)
23. Maes, K.C., De Baets, B.: On the structure of left-continuous t-norms that have a continuous contour line. Fuzzy Sets and Systems 158(8), 843–860 (2007)
24. Maes, K.C., De Baets, B.: Rotation-invariant t-norms: where triple rotation and rotation-annihilation meet. Fuzzy Sets and Systems 160, 1998–2016 (2009)
25. Ono, H.: Structural rules and a logical hierarchy. In: Petrov, P.P. (ed.) Proceedings of the Summer School and Conference on Mathematical Logic, Heyting 1988, pp. 95–104. Plenum Press (1990)
26. Ono, H.: Logics without the contraction rule. Journal of Symbolic Logic 50, 169–201 (1985)
27. Mostert, P.S., Shields, A.L.: On the structure of semigroups on a compact manifold with boundary. Ann. Math. 65, 117–143 (1957)
28. Yager, R., Rybalov, A.: Uninorm aggregation operators. Fuzzy Sets and Systems 80, 111–120 (1996)
29. Ward, M., Dilworth, R.P.: Residuated lattices. Transactions of the American Mathematical Society 45, 335–354 (1939)
30. Yager, R., Rybalov, A.: Uninorm aggregation operators. Fuzzy Sets and Systems 80, 111–120 (1996)

Natural Means of Indistinguishability Operators

Gabriel Mattioli and Jordi Recasens

Sec. Matemàtiques i Informàtica
ETS Arquitectura del Vallès
Universitat Politècnica de Catalunya
C. Pere Serra 1-15
Sant Cugat del Vallès 08190
Spain
{gabriel.mattioli,j.recasens}@upc.edu

Abstract. It has been shown that the lattice $\mathcal{E}$ of indistinguishability operators, the lattice $\mathcal{H}$ of sets of extensional sets and the lattices $\mathcal{U}$ and $\mathcal{L}$ of upper and lower approximations respectively are isomorphic. This paper will study the relation between $\mathcal{E}$, $\mathcal{H}$, $\mathcal{U}$ and $\mathcal{L}$ under the effect of the natural mean aggregation, i.e. the quasi arithmetic mean, associated to the t-norm.

Keywords: Indistinguishability operator, Extensional set, Upper Approximation, Lower Approximation, Aggregation Operator, Natural Mean Operator, Quasi-arithmetic Mean.

1 Introduction

The concept of indistinguishability operator has been defined as the natural fuzzification of the classical mathematical concept of equivalence relation, and these operators give a way to tackle Poincaré's Paradox and relax Leibniz's Law of Identity [10].

Whereas classical equivalence relations can be very rigid and therefore define a tight relation in the universe of discourse, their fuzzy version relaxes this tightness and several interesting properties emerge. Probably one of the most relevant is the duality between indistinguishability operators and metric spaces.

In the classical context equivalence relations lead to the definition of equivalence classes. These classes are crisp sets and only sets that are union of equivalence classes become observable under the effect of this equivalence relation. Their fuzzy version, named extensional sets, are softer and present several results which allow us to have a much deeper comprehension of the corresponding indistinguishability operator.

In [9] it is shown that the lattice of indistinguishability operators $\mathcal{E}$, sets of extensional sets $\mathcal{H}$ and upper and lower approximations, $\mathcal{U}$ and $\mathcal{L}$ respectively, are isomorphic. These isomorphisms consider only the intersection and union of indistinguishability operators. Other kind of operators have to be considered in order to take into account the semantic information of these concepts. For

S. Greco et al. (Eds.): IPMU 2012, Part III, CCIS 299, pp. 261–270, 2012.

instance, a very interesting field is how several indistinguishability operators can be aggregated. This problem is of great importance in practical contexts, where several attributes have to be considered at the same time [7].

This paper will study the relation between $\mathcal{E}$, $\mathcal{H}$, $\mathcal{U}$ and $\mathcal{L}$ when we consider the aggregation of indistinguishability operators by means of the natural mean operator. The results will show that at this level these concepts are not isomorphic. While some implications are preserved, there are some that fail, so the results in [9] are not extendable to this context. It will be shown which ones are preserved and counterexamples of the other ones will be given.

Although the results obtained do not provide isomorphisms between $\mathcal{E}$, $\mathcal{H}$, $\mathcal{U}$ and $\mathcal{L}$, from a practical point of view the inequalities obtained are still of great use. As it will be shown, we can provide bounds that can be effectively calculated with very low computational cost; while in some contexts, for instance when the data set is very large, the precise calculation may be very costly.

This work is structured as follows: The main concepts and results used and involved in the work will be given in Section 2. In Section 3 it is shown how $\mathcal{E}$, $\mathcal{H}$, $\mathcal{U}$ and $\mathcal{L}$ can be given a lattice structure and it is proved that they are all isomorphic. Section 4 contains the main core of the work. This section will deal with the aggregation of indistinguishability operators by means of the quasi-arithmetic mean defined by the generator of the t-norm, and it will be proved how the mean of extensional sets, upper and lower approximations do not coincide in general with the extensional set, upper and lower approximation respectively of means since only one inequality remains true. A very simple counterexample will illustrate the inequality that fails. Finally Section 5 will deal with the conclusions of the work, where the main results of this paper will be summarized and possible future lines of research will be outlined.

2   Preliminaries

In this section the main concepts and results related to Indistinguishability operators used in this work will be recalled. In this paper we will assume that the t-norm is always continuous and Archimedean, this way it will be possible to operate in terms of the additive generator t of the t-norm. [8]

Definition 1. *Let T be a t-norm.*

- *The residuation $\overrightarrow{T}$ of T is defined for all $x, y \in [0, 1]$ by*

$$\overrightarrow{T}(x|y) = \sup\{\alpha \in [0, 1] | T(\alpha, x) \leq y\}.$$

- *The birresiduation $\overleftrightarrow{T}$ of T is defined for all $x, y \in [0, 1]$ by*

$$\overleftrightarrow{T}(x, y) = \min\{\overrightarrow{T}(x|y), \overrightarrow{T}(y|x)\} = T(\overrightarrow{T}(x|y), \overrightarrow{T}(y|x)).$$

It is straightforward from the definition to see that these definitions can be rewritten in terms of the additive generator t of the t-norm. This will prove to be very useful along the paper to simplify some calculus.

Proposition 1. *Let T be a t-norm generated by an additive generator t. Then:*

- $T(x,y) = t^{[-1]}(t(x) + t(y))$
- $\overrightarrow{T}(x|y) = t^{[-1]}(t(y) - t(x))$

Definition 2. *Let T be a t-norm. A fuzzy relation E on a set X is a T-indistinguishability operator if and only if for all $x, y, z \in X$*

a) $E(x,x) = 1$ *(Reflexivity)*
b) $E(x,y) = E(y,x)$ *(Symmetry)*
c) $T(E(x,y), E(y,z)) \leq E(x,z)$ *(T-transitivity).*

Following we recall the definition of extensional sets. While indistinguishability operators fuzzify equivalence relations, extensional sets represent the fuzzification of equivalence classes together with their unions and intersections [3].

Definition 3. *Let X be a set and E a T-indistinguishability operator on X. A fuzzy subset μ of X is called extensional if and only if:*

$$\forall x, y \in X \quad T(E(x,y), \mu(y)) \leq \mu(x).$$

We will denote H_E the set of all extensional fuzzy subsets of X with respect to E.

Proposition 2. *Let X be a set, E a T-indistinguishability operator on X and μ a fuzzy subset of X. Then:*

$$\mu \in H_E \Leftrightarrow E_\mu \geq E$$

The set of extensional fuzzy subsets can be characterized as follows.

Proposition 3. *[2] Let E be a T-indistinguishability operator and H_E its set of extensional fuzzy sets. Then, $\forall \mu \in H_E, (\mu_i)_{i \in I}$ a family of extensional sets and $\forall \alpha \in [0,1]$ the following properties hold:*

1. $\bigvee_{i \in I} \mu_i \in H_E$
2. $\bigwedge_{i \in I} \mu_i \in H_E$
3. $T(\alpha, \mu) \in H_E$
4. $\overrightarrow{T}(\mu|\alpha) \in H_E$
5. $\overrightarrow{T}(\alpha|\mu) \in H_E$

Theorem 1. *[2] Let H be a subset of $[0,1]^X$ satisfying the properties of Proposition 3. Then there exists a unique T-indistinguishability operator E such that $H = H_E$.*

The set of all sets of extensional sets on X will be denoted by $\mathcal{H}$.

Following we define two operators ϕ_E and ψ_E that, given a fuzzy subset μ, provide its best upper and lower approximation by extensional sets of E respectively.

Definition 4. *Let X be a set and E a T-indistinguishability operator on X. The maps $\phi_E \colon [0,1]^X \to [0,1]^X$ and $\psi_E \colon [0,1]^X \to [0,1]^X$ are defined $\forall x \in X$ by:*

$$\phi_E(\mu)(x) = \sup_{y \in X} T(E(x,y), \mu(y))$$

$$\psi_E(\mu)(x) = \inf_{y \in X} \overrightarrow{T}(E(x,y)|\mu(y)).$$

$\phi_E(\mu)$ is the smallest extensional fuzzy subset greater than or equal to μ; hence it is its best upper approximation by extensional sets. Analogously, $\psi_E(\mu)$ provide the best approximation by extensional fuzzy subsets less than or equal to μ. From a topological viewpoint these operators can be seen as closure and interior operators on the set $[0,1]^X$ [3]. It is remarkable that these operators also appear in a natural way in the field of fuzzy rough sets [4],[5] and fuzzy modal logic [1] where they stand for a fuzzy possibility and necessity respectively.

In [4] it is proved that these operators can be characterized by the following families of properties.

Theorem 2. *Given a set X and an operator $\phi \colon [0,1]^X \to [0,1]^X$, ϕ is the upper approximation of a certain indistinguishability operator if and only if the following properties are fulfilled.*

1. $\mu \le \mu' \Rightarrow \phi_E(\mu) \le \phi_E(\mu')$
2. $\mu \le \phi_E(\mu)$
3. $\phi_E(\mu \vee \mu') = \phi_E(\mu) \vee \phi_E(\mu')$
4. $\phi_E(\phi_E(\mu)) = \phi_E(\mu)$
5. $\phi_E(\{x\})(y) = \phi_E(\{y\})(x)$
6. $\phi_E(T(\alpha, \mu)) = T(\alpha, \phi_E(\mu))$

Theorem 3. *Given a set X and an operator $\phi \colon [0,1]^X \to [0,1]^X$, ϕ is the upper approximation of a certain indistinguishability operator if and only if the following properties are fulfilled.*

1. $\mu \le \mu' \Rightarrow \psi_E(\mu) \le \psi_E(\mu')$
2. $\psi_E(\mu) \le \mu$
3. $\psi_E(\mu \wedge \mu') = \psi_E(\mu) \wedge \psi_E(\mu')$
4. $\psi_E(\psi_E(\mu)) = \psi_E(\mu)$
5. $\psi_E(\overrightarrow{T}(x|\alpha)(y)) = \psi_E(\overrightarrow{T}(y|\alpha)(x)$
6. $\psi_E(\overrightarrow{T}(\alpha|\mu)) = \overrightarrow{T}(\alpha, \psi_E(\mu))$

The set of all upper (lower) approximations, i.e. the set of all operators verifying the properties of Theorem 2 (Theorem 3), will be denoted $\mathcal{U}$ ($\mathcal{L}$).

3   The Lattices of Indistinguishability Operators, Sets of Extensional Fuzzy Subsets, Upper and Lower Approximations

In this section, operations on $\mathcal{E}$, $\mathcal{H}$, $\mathcal{U}$ and $\mathcal{L}$ will be defined that give these sets a lattice structure. The last result states that these lattices are isomorphic.

It is well known that given two indistinguishability operators E, F, its intersection $E \cap F$ is also an indistinguishability operator. However the union $E \cup F$ does not preserve transitivity and hence is not in general an indistinguishability operator. This fact motivates the following definition.

Definition 5. *Let T be a t-norm and R a fuzzy proximity (a reflexive and symmetric fuzzy relation) on a set X. The transitive closure $\overline{R}$ of R is the T-indistinguishability operator defined by*

$$\overline{R} = \bigcap_{E \in A} E$$

where A is the set of T-indistinguishability operators on X greater than or equal to R.

This way, the union operator can be closed under transitivity and hence become an internal operation in $\mathcal{E}$. It is then straightforward to see that $\mathcal{E}$ has a lattice structure with the natural ordering given by $\leq$ and the operations $E \cap F$ and $\overline{E \cup F}$.

A similar situation appears in $\mathcal{H}$. Given $H_E, H_F \in \mathcal{H}$ two sets of extensional fuzzy subsets, the intersection of them is the set of extensional fuzzy subsets of a certain indistinguishability operator, but not its union. We have to define then the concept of extensional closure.

Definition 6. *Let $J \subseteq [0,1]^X$. Its extensional closure $\overline{J}$ is defined by:*

$$\overline{J} := \bigcap_{H \in [0,1]^X, J \subseteq H} H$$

where H is a set of fuzzy subsets of X satisfying the properties of Proposition 3:

Now $\mathcal{H}$ becomes a lattice considering the ordering given by $\subseteq$ and the operations $H_E \cap H_F$ and $\overline{H_E \cup H_F}$.

The situation is analogous in the case of upper and lower approximations. $\phi_E \wedge \phi_F$ is still an upper approximation but not $\phi_E \vee \phi_F$, and a dual result happens in $\mathcal{L}$. We have to define again closure and interior operators in order to close these operations.

Definition 7. *Let f be a map defined on $[0,1]^X \to [0,1]^X$. The ϕ-closure $\overline{f}$ of f is defined as:*

$$\overline{f} = \bigwedge_{f \leq \phi, \phi \in U} \phi$$

where U is the set of maps $\phi : [0,1]^X \to [0,1]^X$ satisfying the properties of Theorem 2.

Definition 8. *Let f be a map defined on $[0,1]^X \to [0,1]^X$. The ψ-closure $\widetilde{f}$ of f is defined as:*

$$\underline{f} = \bigvee_{\psi \in L, f \leq \psi} \psi$$

where L is the set of maps $\psi : [0,1]^X \to [0,1]^X$ *satisfying the properties of Theorem 3.*

It can be proved that the set of all upper approximations by extensional sets on a universe X is a lattice $\mathcal{U}$ with the ordering $\leq$ and the operations $\wedge$ and $\overline{\vee}$. Analogously, $\mathcal{L}$ will be the lattice $(\mathcal{L}, \leq, \vee, \underline{\wedge})$ of lower approximations.

Finally, it is interesting to ask whether it is possible to rewrite the set of extensional fuzzy subsets, upper approximation and lower approximation of the intersection $E \cap F$ and closed union $\overline{E \cup F}$ of indistinguishability operators in terms of the initial sets of extensional fuzzy subsets and approximations of the indistinguishability operators. This problem has been solved with the following result. As an interesting corollary we will have that $\mathcal{E}, \mathcal{H}, \mathcal{U}$ and $\mathcal{L}$ are isomorphic lattices.

Theorem 4. *[9] Let E,F be two T-indistinguishability operators on a set X. Then:*

- $H_{E \cap F} = \overline{H_E \cup H_F}$
- $H_{\overline{E \cup F}} = H_E \cap H_F$
- $\phi_{E \wedge F} = \overline{\phi_E \wedge \phi_F}$
- $\phi_{\overline{E \cup F}} = \phi_E \vee \phi_F$
- $\psi_{E \wedge F} = \psi_E \wedge \psi_F$
- $\psi_{\overline{E \cup F}} = \psi_E \vee \psi_F$

Corollary 1. $\mathcal{E} \cong \mathcal{H} \cong \mathcal{U} \cong \mathcal{L}$

4 Natural Means Operating on Indistinguishability Operators, Sets of Extensional Fuzzy Subsets, Upper and Lower Approximations

This section will try to extend the isomorphism given in Theorem 4 to the field of natural means. In Theorem 4 it was possible, for instance, to rewrite the set of extensional subsets associated to the intersection of two indistinguishability operators as the closed union of the initial sets of extensional subsets of the indistinguishability operators. The problem this section will face is the same one applied to quasi-arithmetic means. The result will be that some implications are preserved but the whole result of Theorem 4 cannot be transfered to natural mean aggregations of indistinguishability operators. The results that are preserved will be proved and counterexamples will be given to illustrate the parts that fail.

First of all, let us recall the definition of quasi-arithmetic mean.

Definition 9. *Let* $t : [0,1] \to [0, \infty)$ *be a continous strict monotonic map and* $x, y \in [0,1]$. *The quasi-arithmetic mean* m_t *of x and y is defined as:*
$$m_t(x, y) = t^{-1}\left(\frac{t(x) + t(y)}{2}\right)$$

The next result proves that continuous quasi-arithmetic means are in bijection with t-norms.

Proposition 4. *[7] The map assigning every continuous Archimedean t-norm with additive generator t the quasi-arithmetic mean m_t is a bijection.*

In this paper we will call quasi-arithmetic means simply means or natural means. The term natural comes from the fact that the same additive generator t of the t-norm T is used to define the mean of T-indistinguishability operators. In practical contexts this means that after all the only choice that has to be made is the t-norm or equivalently its additive generator t.

It is well known that the natural mean of two indistinguishability operators is an indistinguishability operator too.

Proposition 5. *Let T be a t-norm and E, F two T-indistinguishability operators. Then the mean of E and F defined as:*
$$m_t(E,F)(x,y) = t^{-1}\left(\frac{t(E(x,y))+t(F(x,y))}{2}\right)$$
is a T indistinguishability operator on X.

Lemma 1. *Let E be a T-indistinguishability operator on a set X. $\mu \in H_E$ if and only if $\forall x, y \in X$:*
$$t(E(x,y)) + t(\mu(y)) \geq t(\mu(x))$$

Proof. $\mu \in H_E \Leftrightarrow T(E(x,y), \mu(y)) \leq \mu(x) \Leftrightarrow t^{-1}(t(E(x,y)) + t(\mu(y))) \leq \mu(x)$. And as t is a monotone decreasing function this is equivalent to $t(E(x,y)) + t(\mu(y)) \geq t(\mu(x))$

First of all lets analyze the mean of extensional sets.

Proposition 6. *Let t be the additive generator of a t-norm T and E, F two T-indistinguishability operators with associated sets of extensional sets H_E and H_F respectively. Then:*
$$m_t(H_E, H_F) \leq H_{m_t(E,F)}$$

Proof. Let $\mu \in H_E$ and $\nu \in H_F$. We have to see that

$$T(m_t(E,F)(x,y), m_t(\mu(y),\nu(y))) \leq m_t(\mu(x),\nu(x)).$$

Expanding, this is analogous to prove that

$$t^{-1}(t(t^{-1}(\frac{t(E(x,y)) + t(F(x,y))}{2})) + t(t^{-1}(\frac{t(\mu(y)) + t(\nu(y))}{2})))$$
$$\leq t^{-1}(\frac{t(\mu(x)) + t(\nu(x))}{2}).$$

Simplifying,

$$t^{-1}(\frac{t(E(x,y)) + t(F(x,y))}{2}) + \frac{t(\mu(y)) + t(\nu(y))}{2})) \leq t^{-1}(\frac{t(\mu(x)) + t(\nu(x))}{2}).$$

Which is equivalent to: $t(E(x,y)) + t(F(x,y)) + t(\mu(y)) + t(\nu(y)) \geq t(\mu(x)) + t(\nu(x))$.
And this is true because $\mu \in H_E$ and $\nu \in H_F$.

Lets show in a counterexample that equality is not reached in general.

Example 1. Let X be a finite set of cardinality 3. Let us consider the following T-indistinguishability operators with T the Lukasiewicz t-norm.

$$E = \begin{pmatrix} 1 & 0.6 & 0.7 \\ 0.6 & 1 & 0.8 \\ 0.7 & 0.8 & 1 \end{pmatrix} \quad F = \begin{pmatrix} 1 & 0.8 & 0.7 \\ 0.8 & 1 & 0.6 \\ 0.7 & 0.6 & 1 \end{pmatrix}$$

The natural mean $m_t(E, F)$ of E and F is:

$$m_t(E, F) = \begin{pmatrix} 1 & 0.7 & 0.7 \\ 0.7 & 1 & 0.7 \\ 0.7 & 0.7 & 1 \end{pmatrix}$$

Let us consider the fuzzy subset $\mu = \begin{pmatrix} 1 & 1 & 0.7 \end{pmatrix}$.

$\mu \in H_{m_t(E,F)}$ since $E_\mu \geq m_t(E, F)$ (Proposition 2).

But the extensional fuzzy subsets of E must have the third component ≥ 0.8 and the ones of F must have it ≥ 0.7. Hence it is not possible to find $\alpha \in H_E$ and $\beta \in H_F$ such that $\mu = m_t(\alpha, \beta)$.

The situation is very similar when we study what happens with the natural mean of upper approximations.

Proposition 7. *Let t be the additive generator of a t-norm T and E, F two T-indistinguishability operators with associated upper approximations ϕ_E and ϕ_F respectively. Then:*

$m_t(\phi_E, \phi_F) \geq \phi_{m_t(E,F)}$

Proof. Let $\mu \in [0,1]^X$ be a fuzzy subset and $x \in X$. We have to see that $m_t(\phi_E, \phi_F)(\mu(x)) \geq \phi_{m_t(E,F)(\mu(x))}$.

Expanding the expression we have to see

$$t^{-1}\left(\frac{t(\sup_{y\in X} t^{-1}(t(E(x,y)) + t(\mu(y)))) + t(\sup_{y\in X} t^{-1}(t(F(x,y)) + t((\mu(y))))}{2}\right)$$

$$\geq \sup_{y\in X} t^{-1}(t(t^{-1}(\frac{t(E(x,y)) + t(F(x,y))}{2} + t(\mu(y)))).$$

This is equivalent to

$$t^{-1}\left(\frac{\inf_{y\in X}(t(E(x,y)) + t(\mu(y))) + \inf_{y\in X}(t(F(x,y)) + t(\mu(y)))}{2}\right)$$

$$\geq t^{-1}(\in f_{y\in X}(\frac{t(E(x,y)) + t(F(x,y))}{2} + t(\mu(y)))).$$

Equivalently,

$$\inf_{y\in X}(t(E(x,y)) + t(\mu(y))) + \inf_{y\in X}(t(F(x,y)) + t(\mu(y)))$$

$$\leq \inf_{y\in X}(t(E(x,y)) + t(F(x,y)) + 2t(\mu(y))).$$

Which is true because the addition of infima is smaller than or equal to the infimum of the addition.

Equality is not reached in general either. Further we illustrate it with the same indistinguishability operators E, F as in Counterexample 1.

Again, in the case of lower approximations only an inequality is true.

Proposition 8. *Let t be the additive generator of a t-norm T and E, F two T-indistinguishability operators with associated lower approximations ψ_E and ψ_F respectively. Then:*

$$m_t(\psi_E, \psi_F) \le \psi_{m_t(E,F)}$$

Proof. Let $\mu \in [0,1]^X$ be a fuzzy subset and $x \in X$.
Rewriting this inequality terms of t, it has to be proved

$$t^{-1}\left(\frac{t(\inf_{y\in X}(t^{-1}(t(\mu(y)) - t(E(x,y)))) + t(\inf_{y\in X}(t^{-1}(t(\mu(y)) - t(F(x,y))))}{2}\right)$$
$$\le \inf_{y\in X} t^{-1}(t(\mu(y)) - t(t^{-1}(\frac{t(E(x,y)) + t(F(x,y))}{2})))$$

Simplifying we have the equivalent expression

$$t^{-1}\left(\frac{\sup_{y\in X}(t(\mu(y)) - t((E(x,y)))) + \sup_{y\in X}(t(\mu(y)) - t((F(x,y))))}{2}\right)$$
$$\le \inf_{y\in X} t^{-1}(t(\mu(y)) - \frac{t(E(x,y)) + t(F(x,y))}{2})$$

Which is equivalent to

$$\sup_{y\in X}(t(\mu(y)) - t(E(x,y))) + \sup_{y\in X}(t(\mu(y)) - t(F(x,y)))$$
$$\ge \sup_{y\in X}(2t(\mu(y)) - t(E(x,y)) - t(F(x,y))).$$

And this is true because the addition of suprema is greater than or equal to the supremum of the addition.

Equality is not true in general as it is shown with the following counterexample.

Example 2. Let us consider the same T-indistinguishability operators and the same fuzzy subset of Example 1.

$\mu \in H_{m_t(E,F)}$ and $\mu \in H_F$ but $\mu \notin H_E$.

Upper and lower approximations are fixed points on the set of extensional fuzzy subsets, so:

$\phi_{m_t(E,F)}(\mu) = \phi_F(\mu) = \mu$, $\psi_{m_t(E,F)}(\mu) = \psi_F(\mu) = \mu$.

But $\mu \notin H_E \Rightarrow \phi_E(\mu) > \mu$ and $\psi_E(\mu) < \mu$.

So $\phi_{m_t(E,F)}(\mu) < m_t(\phi_E, \phi_F)$ and $\psi_{m_t(E,F)}(\mu) > m_t(\psi_E, \psi_F)$, and hence equality is not reached.

5   Concluding Remarks

This work has studied if it was possible to extend the set-theoretical isomorphism between $\mathcal{E}$, $\mathcal{H}$, $\mathcal{U}$ and $\mathcal{L}$ to the application of the natural mean operator. Counterintuitively, the result has been that this is not possible. It has been proved, however that some inequalities actually hold and how in general equality is not reached has been shown with a simple counterexample.

As future work it would be interesting to study how much does the mean of the operators differ from the operator of the means. This means to study how far is the bound found from the real value. Another possible line of research to find under which weaker hypothesis it is possible to find equality, and therefore have a proper extension of the isomorphism found in Theorem 4. The authors expect to present results on these topics in forthcoming works.

Acknowledgment. Research partially supported by project number TIN2009-07235.

The first author is supported by the Universitat Politècnica de Catalunya (UPC).

References

1. Bou, F., Esteva, F., Godo, L., Rodríguez, R.: On the Minimum Many-Valued Modal Logic over a Finite Residuated Lattice. Journal of Logic and Computation (2010), doi:10.1093/logcom/exp062
2. Castro, J.L., Klawonn, F.: Similarity in Fuzzy Reasoning. Mathware & Soft Computing 2, 197–228 (1996)
3. Jacas, J., Recasens, J.: Fixed points and generators of fuzzy relations. J. Math. Anal. Appl 186, 21–29 (1994)
4. Morsi, N.N., Yakout, M.M.: Axiomatics for fuzzy rough sets. Fuzzy Sets and Systems 100, 327–342 (1998)
5. Boixader, D., Jacas, J., Recasens, J.: Upper and lower approximation of fuzzy sets. Int. J. of General Systems 29, 555–568 (2000)
6. Bělohlavek, R.: Fuzzy Relational Systems: Foundations and Principles. Kluwer Academic Publishers, New York (2002)
7. Jacas, J., Recasens, J.: Aggregation of T-Transitive Relations. Int J. of Intelligent Systems 18, 1193–1214 (2003)
8. Klement, E.P., Mesiar, R., Pap, E.: Triangular norms. Kluwer Academic Publishers, Dordrecht (2000)
9. Mattioli, G., Recasens, J.: Dualities and Isomorphisms between Indistinguishabilities and Related Concepts. In: FUZZ IEEE, Taiwan (2011)
10. Recasens, J.: Indistinguishability Operators. Modelling Fuzzy Equalities and Fuzzy Equivalence Relations Series: STUDFUZZ, vol. 260 (2011)
11. Valverde, L.: On the Structure of F-indistinguishability Operators. Fuzzy Sets and Systems 17, 313–328 (1985)
12. Zadeh, L.A.: Similarity relations and fuzzy orderings. Inform. Sci. 3, 177–200 (1971)

Aggregation Operators for Awareness of General Information

Doretta Vivona[1] and Maria Divari[2]

[1] Sapienza Universitá di Roma, Dip.SBAI, v.A.Scarpa n.16, 00161 Roma, Italy
doretta.vivona@uniroma1.it
[2] Sapienza Universitá di Roma, v.Borgorose n.15, 00189 Roma, Italy
maria.divari@alice.it

Abstract. The aim of this paper is to present a definition of awareness of information and some aggregation operators of this quantity.

1 Introduction

The inspiration of this paper was born by discussion of a second degree level dissertation in Nursering Science at "'Sapienza" University of Rome (February 2010). In this dissertation, was discussed the possibility that the patient was able to have more awareness about received diagnosis.

In general, the information of an event (crisp or fuzzy) is not linked with awareness of the same event.

For example: we cannot have an information about an illness, but at the same time, we cannot know all its implications.

It could be very usefull to have awareness of the information, as it occcurs in medicine. In fact, we can know the diagnosis (information about a diagnosis), but we are not able to take into account all implications of the given information.

As a consequence, the introduction of parameters which help to reach more awareness, reduces the possibility that information is fuzzy [7, 8].

The aggregation operators are a instrument usefull to collect dates of any phenomenon. Many authors have studied these operators [2, 3, 6].

In this paper, first, we shall introduce a definition and some properties of the measures of *awareness* of information. Second, we shall propose a class of the measures of awareness, solving a system of functional conditions.

Finally, we shall consider a particular aggregation operators applied to this awareness.

2 Preliminaries

Let Ω be an abstract space and $\mathcal{F}$ the σ-algebra of all not empty fuzzy sets F [9, 7], such that $(\Omega, \mathcal{F})$ is a measurable space.

Our setting is the information theory without probability or fuzzy measure, called general information in the sense of Kampé De Feriét-Forte-Benvenuti [4, 5].

S. Greco et al. (Eds.): IPMU 2012, Part III, CCIS 299, pp. 271–275, 2012.

We recall that the *measure of general information* [1] is a map

$$J(\cdot) : \mathcal{F} \to [0, +\infty]$$

such that:

(i) $F' \supset F \Rightarrow J(F') \leq J(F)$,

(ii) $J(\emptyset) = +\infty$, $J(\Omega) = 0$.

3   Statment of the Problem: Awareness AW_J

Fixed an information J, we consider three increasing functions:

$$\mu_J, \lambda_J, \nu_J : \mathcal{F} \to [0, 1]$$

called *quality of information, ability of learning and availability of understanding*, (shortly information, learning and understanding, respectively).

We think that the fuzziness AW_J of the information J is a function Ψ which depends only on μ_J, λ_J and ν_J i.e. $AW_J : \mathcal{F} \to [0, 1]$ and

$$AW_J(F) = \Psi\left(\mu_J(F), \lambda_J(F), \nu_J(F)\right).$$

We describe the natural properties of AW_J from the natural properties of μ_J, λ_J, ν_J.

Fixed F, we think that if the quality of information is max $(\mu_J(F) = 1)$, the learning is max $(\lambda_J(F) = 1)$ and the understanding is max $(\nu_J(F) = 1)$, then awareness is max: $AW_J(E) = 1$.

On the other hand, if the information, learning and understanding are all null $\mu_J(F) = \lambda_J(F) = \nu_J(F) = 0$, we impose that awareness is min: $AW_J(F) = 0$.

Moreover, we think that awareness $AW_J(F)$ is increasing with respect to the three variables because μ_J, λ_J, ν_J are themselves monotone.

The properties of the function Ψ are the following:

1) $\Psi(1, 1, 1) = 1$,

2) $\Psi(0, 0, 0) = 0$,

3) $\Psi\left(\mu_J(F'), \lambda_J(F'), \nu_J(F')\right) \leq \Psi\left(\mu_J(F), \lambda_J(F), \nu_J(F)\right)$,
$\forall\ F', F \in \mathcal{F}$, $F' \supset F$.

Putting $\mu_J(F) = x, \lambda_J(F) = y, \nu_J(F) = z, \mu_J(F') = x', \lambda_J(F') = y', \nu_J(F') = z', x' \leq x, y' \leq y, z' \leq z$, we obtain the following system of functional conditions:

$$\begin{cases} (1')\ \Psi(1, 1, 1) = 1 \\[2mm] (2')\ \Psi(0, 0, 0) = 0 \\[2mm] (3')\ \Psi(x', y', z') \leq \Psi(x, y, z),\ x' \leq x, y' \leq y, z' \leq z. \end{cases}$$

First, we give the following:

Proposition 1. *A class of solution of the system* $[(1') - (3')]$ *is*

$$\Psi_h(x, y, z) = h^{-1}\left(h(x) \cdot h(y) \cdot h(z)\right),\tag{1}$$

where $h : [0, 1] \to [0, 1]$ *is any increasing function with* $h(0) = 0$ *and* $h(1) = 1$.

Proof. Our proof starts with the observation that from the values of the function h it is:

1') $\Psi_h(1, 1, 1) = h^{-1}\left(h(1) \cdot h(1) \cdot h(1)\right) = 1$;

2') $\Psi_h(0, 0, 0) = h^{-1}\left(h(0) \cdot h(0) \cdot h(0)\right) = 0$.

Moreover, as h and h^{-1} are increasing, for $x' \leq x, y' \leq y, z' \leq z$ it results:

3') $\Psi_h(x', y', z') = h^{-1}\left(h(x') \cdot h(y') \cdot h(z')\right) \leq h^{-1}\left(h(x) \cdot h(y) \cdot h(z)\right) = \Psi_h(x, y, z)$. $\qquad\square$

Second, we prove:

Proposition 2. *If* $k : [0, 1] \to [0, 1]$ *is any increasing function with* $k(0) = 0$, $k(1) = 1$ *and* $\theta : [0, 1] \times [0, 1] \to [0, 1]$ *is any increasing function with respect to both variables and* $\theta(0, 0) = 0$, $\theta(1, 1) = 1$, *then a class of solution of the system* $[(1') - (3')]$ *is*

$$\Psi_k(x, y, z) = k^{-1}\left(k(x) \cdot \theta\big[k(y), k(z)\big]\right).\tag{2}$$

Proof. Our proof is similar to the one in the previous Proposition: from the values of the functions k and θ,

1') $\Psi_k(1, 1, 1) = k^{-1}\left(k(1) \cdot \theta\big[k(1), k(1)\big]\right) = 1$;

2') $\Psi_h(0, 0, 0) = k^{-1}\left(k(0) \cdot \theta\big[k(0), k(0)\big]\right) = 0$.

Moreover, as k, k^{-1} and θ are increasing, for $x' \leq x, y' \leq y, z' \leq z$:

3') $\Psi_k(x', y', z') = k^{-1}\left(k(x') \cdot \theta\big[k(y'), k(z')\big]\right) \leq k^{-1}\left(k(x) \cdot \theta\big[k(y), k(z)\big]\right) = \Psi_k(x, y, z)$. $\qquad\square$

Remark 1. For example we can choose $\theta(u, v) = u \cdot v$, or $\theta(u, v) = u \wedge v$, or $\theta(u, v) = u \vee v$: they are increasing functions.

4   Some Aggregation Operators for AW_J

An aggregation operator [3, 6] is a procedure by which a unique value can be associated to the results obtained through different tests or different values of a data base.

The unique value is a kind of mean or average.

In this paragraph this paper we shall characterize some classes of aggregation operators for awareness.

We propose an approach based on the axioms of the paper [2]: for the aggregation operator we request only the natural properties of idempotence, monotonicity and continuity from below.

Given an information measure J, let $\mathcal{AW}_J$ the family of the $AW_J(\cdot)$. We characterize the aggregation operator

$$L : \mathcal{AW}_J \to [0, K],$$

$0 < K < +\infty$ of $n \in [0, +\infty]$ awarenesses $AW_J(F_1), AW_J(F_2), ..., AW_J(F_n)$, with $AW_J \in \mathcal{AW}_J$, $F_i \in \mathcal{F}, \forall\, i = 1, ..., n$.

We recall that L has the following properties:

(I) $AW_J(F_i) = c, \forall i = 1, ..., n \Longrightarrow L(\underbrace{c, c, ..., c}_{n}) = c$ idempotence,

(II) $AW_J(F_1) \le AW_J(F_1') \Longrightarrow$
$L(AW_J(F_1), ..., AW_J(F_n)) \le L(AW_J(F_1), ..., AW_J(F_n))$ monotonicity,

(III) $AW_J(F_{1m}) \nearrow AW_J(F_1) \Longrightarrow$
$L(AW_J(F_{1m}), ..., AW_J(F_n)) \nearrow L(AW_J(F_1), ..., AW_J(F_n))$ continuity from below.

From [(I)-(III)], putting $AW_J(F_i) = x_i \in [(0, +\infty), i = 1, ..., n$, we have the following system of conditions:

$$\begin{cases} (I') \ L(\underbrace{c, c, ..., c}_{n}) = c \\ (II') \ x_1' \le x_1 \Longrightarrow L(x_1', ..., x_n) \le L(x_1, ..., x_n) \\ (III') \ x_{1m} \nearrow x_1 \Longrightarrow L(x_{1m}, ..., x_n) \nearrow L(x_1, ..., x_n). \end{cases}$$

4.1   Solution of the Problem

In this paragraph, we get three classes of solutions of the system [(I')-(III')].

Proposition 3. *Two solutions of the system* [(I')-(III')] *are:*

$$L(x_1, x_2, ..., x_n) = \wedge_{i=1}^{n} x_i \ ,$$

and

$$L(x_1, x_2, ..., x_n) = \vee_{i=1}^{n} x_i \ .$$

Proof. It is immediate the check.   □

Proposition 4. *If* $l : [0, +\infty] \to [0, +\infty]$ *is any continuous, increasing function with respect to the first variable, then a class of solution of the system* [(I')-(III')] *is:*

$$L(x_1, x_2, ..., x_n) = l^{-1} \left(\frac{l(x_1) + l(x_2) + ... + l(x_n)}{n} \right)$$

where

Proof. The proof is easy:

$$(I') \; L(\underbrace{c, c, ..., c}_{n}) = l^{-1} \left(\frac{l(c) + l(c) + ... + l(c)}{n} \right) = l^{-1} \left(\frac{n \; l(c)}{n} \right) = c;$$

(II') derives from the monotonicity of the function l;

(III') is a consequence of the continuity of l. $\square$

Remark 2. If the function h is linear, then the aggregation operator L is the aritmetic average.

5 Conclusion

In this paper, we have introduced awareness of a given information AW_J, which depend on the so-called quality of information μ_J, ability of learning λ_J, and availability of understanding ν_J.

Then, we have considered some agggregation operarors of awareness and we have given some forms of these operators.

It could be interesting an application to general conditional information, because many diagnosises can be conditioned by contigent aspects as tests.

References

[1] Benvenuti, P., Vivona, D., Divari, M.: A General Information for Fuzzy Sets. In: Bouchon-Meunier, B., Zadeh, L.A., Yager, R.R. (eds.) IPMU 1990. LNCS, vol. 521, pp. 307–316. Springer, Heidelberg (1991)

[2] Benvenuti, P., Vivona, D., Divari, M.: Aggregation operators and associated fuzzy measures. Int. Journal of Uncertainty, Fuzziness and Knowledge-Based Systems 2, 197–204 (2001)

[3] Calvo, T., Mayor, G., Mesiar, R.: Aggregation operator. New Trend and Applications. Physica-Verlag, Heidelberg (2002)

[4] Kampé De Fériet, J., Forte, B.: Information et Probabilité. C. R. Acad. Sc. Paris 265, 110–114, 142–146, 350–353 (1967)

[5] Kampé De Fériet, J., Benvenuti, P.: Sur une classe d'informations. C. R. Acad. Sc. Paris, Serie A 269, 97–101 (1969)

[6] Klement, E.P.: Binary aggregation operators which are bounded by the minimum (a mathematical overview). In: Proc. of the Conf. AGOP 2005, Lugano, Svizzera, pp. 13–16 (2005)

[7] Klir, G.J., Folger, T.A.: Fuzzy sets, Uncertainty, and Information. Prentice-Hall International editions (1988)

[8] Kosko, B.: Fuzzy Thinking: The New Science of Fuzzy Logic. Hyperion Eds. (1993)

[9] Zadeh, L.A.: Fuzzy sets. Inf. and Control 8, 338–353 (1965)

On the Relation between Effort-Dominating and Symmetric Minitive Aggregation Operators

Marek Gagolewski[1,2]

[1] Systems Research Institute, Polish Academy of Sciences
ul. Newelska 6, 01-447 Warsaw, Poland
[2] Faculty of Mathematics and Information Science, Warsaw University of Technology
pl. Politechniki 1, 00-661 Warsaw, Poland
`gagolews@ibspan.waw.pl`

Abstract. In this paper the recently introduced class of effort-dominating impact functions is examined. It turns out that each effort-dominating aggregation operator not only has a very intuitive interpretation, but also is symmetric minitive, and therefore may be expressed as a so-called quasi-I-statistic, which generalizes the well-know OWMin operator.

These aggregation operators may be used e.g. in the Producer Assessment Problem whose most important instance is the scientometric/bibliometric issue of fair scientists' ranking by means of the number of citations received by their papers.

Keywords: Aggregation operators, impact functions, arity-monotonic, OWMax, OWMin, OMA, OWA, Hirsch's h-index, scientometrics.

1 Preliminaries

Information aggregation is a process that plays a very important role in many human activities, e.g. in statistics, engineering, and scientometrics. For example, in the Producers Assessment Problem [5,7] we are interested in the construction of a class of mappings that project the space of arbitrary-sized real vectors of individual goods' quality measures into a single number that reflects both (a) general quality of goods, and (b) the producer's overall productivity.

Nondecreasing, symmetric, and arity-monotonic aggregation operators useful in the PAP are called *impact functions*. For example, in [6] the most fundamental properties of L-, S-, quasi-L-, and quasi-S-statistics, which generalize OWA [13], OWMax [2], OMA [10], and symmetric maxitive aggregation operators, respectively, were analyzed.

In [7] the class of effort-dominating operators was introduced. It was used to construct possibility distributions of impact functions' output values under — but not limited to — right-censored input data. As this very appealing class of aggregation operators has not been thoroughly examined yet, in this paper we are interested in finding how they are related to other functions known from the aggregation theory [cf. 8].

S. Greco et al. (Eds.): IPMU 2012, Part III, CCIS 299, pp. 276–285, 2012.

1.1 Notational Convention

From now on let $\mathbb{I} = [a, b]$ denote any closed interval of the extended real line, $\bar{\mathbb{R}} = [-\infty, \infty]$. The set of all arbitrary-length vectors with elements in $\mathbb{I}$, i.e. $\bigcup_{n=1}^{\infty} \mathbb{I}^n$, is denoted by $\mathbb{I}^{1,2,\cdots}$. If not stated otherwise explicitly, we assume that $n, m \in \mathbb{N} = \{1, 2, \dots\}$. Moreover, let $[n] = \{1, 2, \dots, n\}$.

For any $\mathbf{x} = (x_1, \dots, x_n)$, $\mathbf{y} = (y_1, \dots, y_n) \in \mathbb{I}^n$, we write $\mathbf{x} \leq \mathbf{y}$ if and only if $(\forall i \in [n])\ x_i \leq y_i$. Let $x_{(i)}$ denote the ith order statistic of $\mathbf{x} = (x_1, \dots, x_n)$. For $\mathbf{x}, \mathbf{y} \in \mathbb{I}^n$, we write $\mathbf{x} \cong \mathbf{y}$ if and only if there exists a permutation σ of the set $[n]$ such that $\mathbf{x} = (y_{\sigma(1)}, \dots, y_{\sigma(n)})$. A vector $(x, x, \dots, x) \in \mathbb{I}^n$ is denoted briefly by $(n * x)$. For each $\mathbf{x} \in \mathbb{I}^n$ and $\mathbf{y} \in \mathbb{I}^m$, $(\mathbf{x}, \mathbf{y})$ denotes the concatenation of the vectors, i.e. $(x_1, \dots, x_n, y_1, \dots, y_m) \in \mathbb{I}^{n+m}$.

If $\mathsf{f}, \mathsf{g} : \mathbb{I} \to \bar{\mathbb{R}}$ then $\mathsf{f} \preceq \mathsf{g}$ (g dominates f) if and only if $(\forall x \in \mathbb{I})\ \mathsf{f}(x) \leq \mathsf{g}(x)$. The image of f is denoted by $\operatorname{img} \mathsf{f}$.

1.2 Aggregation Operators

Let $\mathcal{E}(\mathbb{I})$ denote the set of all **aggregation operators** in $\mathbb{I}^{1,2,\cdots}$, i.e. $\mathcal{E}(\mathbb{I}) = \{\mathsf{F} : \mathbb{I}^{1,2,\cdots} \to \mathbb{I}\}$. The class of aggregation operators reflects the very general idea of combining multiple numeric values into a single one, in some way representative of the whole input. Note that the aggregation (averaging) functions [cf. 8,11] form a particular subclass of aggregation operators.

In this paper we focus our attention on nondecreasing, arity-monotonic, and symmetric aggregation operators. Such operators are called **impact functions**[1].

Definition 1. *We say that* $\mathsf{F} \in \mathcal{E}(\mathbb{I})$ *is* **nondecreasing**, *denoted* $\mathsf{F} \in \mathcal{P}_{(\text{nd})}$, *if*

$$(\forall n)\ (\forall \mathbf{x}, \mathbf{y} \in \mathbb{I}^n)\ \mathbf{x} \leq \mathbf{y} \Longrightarrow \mathsf{F}(\mathbf{x}) \leq \mathsf{F}(\mathbf{y}).$$

Definition 2. *We call* $\mathsf{F} \in \mathcal{E}(\mathbb{I})$ **arity-monotonic**, *denoted* $\mathsf{F} \in \mathcal{P}_{(\text{am})}$, *if*

$$(\forall n, m)\ (\forall \mathbf{x} \in \mathbb{I}^n)\ (\forall \mathbf{y} \in \mathbb{I}^m)\ \ \mathsf{F}(\mathbf{x}) \leq \mathsf{F}(\mathbf{x}, \mathbf{y}).$$

Definition 3. *We say that* $\mathsf{F} \in \mathcal{E}(\mathbb{I})$ *is* **symmetric**, *denoted* $\mathsf{F} \in \mathcal{P}_{(\text{sym})}$, *if*

$$(\forall n)\ (\forall \mathbf{x}, \mathbf{y} \in \mathbb{I}^n)\ \mathbf{x} \cong \mathbf{y} \Longrightarrow \mathsf{F}(\mathbf{x}) = \mathsf{F}(\mathbf{y}).$$

Moreover, let us consider the following pre-order[2] on $\mathbb{I}^{1,2,\cdots}$. For any $\mathbf{x} \in \mathbb{I}^n$ and $\mathbf{y} \in \mathbb{I}^m$ we write $\mathbf{x} \trianglelefteq \mathbf{y}$ if and only if $n \leq m$ and $x_{(n-i+1)} \leq y_{(m-i+1)}$ for all $i \in [n]$. Recall that $x_{(n-i+1)}$ denotes the ith largest element of $\mathbf{x}$.

We have recently shown (see [7] for the proof) that an aggregation operator F satisfies the three above properties if and only if F is a morphism (order-preserving mapping) between the pre-ordered set $(\mathbb{I}^{1,2,\cdots}, \trianglelefteq)$ and $(\bar{\mathbb{R}}, \leq)$.

---

[1] Originally, in [5,7] we have required impact functions to fulfill some additional boundary conditions, which are not needed in this context.

[2] Formally, it is easily seen that $\trianglelefteq$ is not anti-symmetric (and hence is not a partial order, contrary to our statement in [7]) unless it is defined on the set of equivalence classes of $\cong$. Thanks to Prof. Michał Baczyński for pointing out this error.

Theorem 1. *Let* $F \in \mathcal{E}(\mathbb{I})$. *Then* $F \in \mathcal{P}_{(nd)} \cap \mathcal{P}_{(am)} \cap \mathcal{P}_{(sym)}$ *if and only if*

$$(\forall \mathbf{x}, \mathbf{y} \in \mathbb{I}^{1,2,\cdots}) \quad \mathbf{x} \trianglelefteq \mathbf{y} \implies F(\mathbf{x}) \le F(\mathbf{y}). \tag{1}$$

2   Effort-Dominating Impact Functions

Given an aggregation operator $F \in \mathcal{E}(\mathbb{I})$ and a constant $v \in \text{img } F$, let $F^{-1}[v] := \{\mathbf{x} \in \mathbb{I}^{1,2,\cdots} : F(\mathbf{x}) = v\}$ denote the *v-level set* of F. Additionally, if $F \in \mathcal{P}_{(sym)}$ then, to avoid ambiguity, we assume that $F^{-1}[v]$ consists only of vectors in $\mathbb{I}^{1,2,\cdots}$ that are unique w.r.t. to the relation $\cong$ (e.g. their terms are sorted nonincreasingly).

Let us recall the notion of an effort-measurable aggregation operator [7].

Definition 4. *We say that* $F \in \mathcal{P}_{(nd)} \cap \mathcal{P}_{(am)} \cap \mathcal{P}_{(sym)}$ *is **effort-measurable**, denoted* $F \in \mathcal{P}_{(em)}$, *if* $\left(F^{-1}[v], \trianglelefteq\right)$ *is a partially ordered set with a unique least element for any* $v \in \text{img } F$.

In other words, $F \in \mathcal{P}_{(em)}$ if and only if for any $v \in \text{img } F$, $\left(F^{-1}[v], \trianglelefteq\right)$ is a lower semilattice (a meet- or $\wedge$-semilattice).

Example 1. Not every $F \in \mathcal{P}_{(nd)} \cap \mathcal{P}_{(am)} \cap \mathcal{P}_{(sym)}$ is effort-measurable. E.g. for a quasi-L-statistic [cf. 6] $L_\triangle$ such that $L_\triangle(x_1, \ldots, x_n) = \sum_{i=1}^{n} (n-i+1) \, x_{(n-i+1)}$, we have $L_\triangle^{-1}[3] = \{(3), (1,1), (1.5,0), (1,0,0), \ldots\}$, which has no least element w.r.t. $\trianglelefteq$. Moreover, the l_p-indices proposed in [4; cf. also 3] also are not effort-measurable. □

For any given $F \in \mathcal{P}_{(em)}$ and $v \in \text{img } F$, let μ^v denote the least element of $F^{-1}[v]$, i.e. $\mu^v := \min\{F^{-1}[v]\}$. Clearly, for $w = \min\{\text{img } F\}$ we have $\mu^w = (a)$. Additionally, from now on $M(F) := \{\mu^v : v \in \text{img } F\}$.

Example 2. Consider the aggregation operator $\text{Max} \in \mathcal{P}_{(em)}$, defined as $\text{Max}(x_1, \ldots, x_n) = x_{(n)}$ for $(x_1, \ldots, x_n) \in \mathbb{I}^{1,2,\cdots}$. We have $\text{img } \text{Max} = \mathbb{I}$, $\text{Max}^{-1}[v] = \{(x_1, \ldots, x_n) \in \mathbb{I}^{1,2,\cdots} : x_{(n)} = v\}$, $\mu^v = (v) \in \mathbb{I}^1$, and $M(\text{Max}) = \mathbb{I}^1$. □

From the class of effort-measurable aggregation operators let us distinguish the set of *effort-dominating* operators.

Definition 5. *We say that* $F \in \mathcal{P}_{(em)}$ *is **effort-dominating**, denoted* $F \in \mathcal{P}_{(ed)}$, *if* $(M(F), \trianglelefteq)$ *is a chain.*

We see that in case of effort-dominating aggregation operators we have $\mu_v \vartriangleleft \mu_{v'} \iff v < v'$ for all $v, v' \in \text{img } F$. It is very important to note that each $F \in \mathcal{P}_{(ed)}$ may be defined in the following, highly intuitive manner. For any $\mathbf{x} \in \mathbb{I}^{1,2,\cdots}$ it holds

$$F(\mathbf{x}) = \underset{v \in \text{img } F}{\arg\max} \{\mu^v \in M(F) : \mu^v \trianglelefteq \mathbf{x}\}. \tag{2}$$

We therefore look for the greatest v such that μ^v is still dominated by the input vector (cf. Fig. 1).

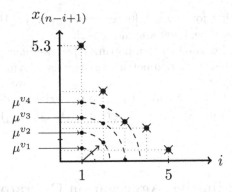

Fig. 1. $x_{(n-i+1)}$ as a function of i for $\mathbf{x} = (5.3, 3.2, 1.8, 1.5, 0.5)$ and the process of determining $\mathsf{F}(\mathbf{x})$

Example 3. Let $\mathbb{I} = [0, \infty]$. The widely-known Hirsch's h index [9], introduced in 2005 in the field of bibliometrics, is an impact function H such that for $(x_1, \ldots, x_n) \in \mathbb{I}^{1,2,\cdots}$ we have $\mathsf{H}(x_1, \ldots, x_n) = \max\{i = 0, 1, \ldots, n : x_{(n-i+1)} \geq i\}$ under the convention $x_{(n+1)} = x_{(n)}$. We have $\mu^0 = (0)$, and $\mu^n = (n * n)$ for $n \in \mathbb{N}$, therefore $\mathsf{H} \in \mathcal{P}_{(ed)}$. $\qquad\square$

Example 4. Let $\mathbb{I} = [0, \infty]$. The r_p-index [3,4] for $p \geq 1$ is an impact function

$$\mathsf{r_p}(x_1, \ldots, x_n) := \sup\{r \geq 0 : \mathbf{s}^{p,r} \trianglelefteq \mathbf{x}\},$$

where $(x_1, \ldots, x_n) \in [0, \infty]^{1,2,\cdots}$ and $\mathbf{s}^{p,r} \in \mathbb{I}^{\lceil r \rceil}$, $r > 0$, denotes a sequence

$$\mathbf{s}^{p,r} = \begin{cases} \left(\sqrt[p]{r^p - 0^p}, \sqrt[p]{r^p - 1^p}, \ldots, \sqrt[p]{r^p - \lceil r-1 \rceil^p} \right) & \text{if } p < \infty, \\ (r, r, \ldots, r) & \text{if } p = \infty, \end{cases}$$

under the assumption $\mathbf{s}^{p,0} = (0)$, see Fig. 2.

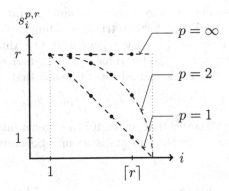

Fig. 2. $s_i^{p,r}$ as a function of i for $p = 1, 2, \infty$

It may be shown that for any $\mathbf{x} \in [0, \infty]^{1,2,\cdots}$, $r_\infty(\lfloor \mathbf{x} \rfloor) = H(\mathbf{x})$, and $r_1(\lfloor \mathbf{x} \rfloor) = W(\mathbf{x})$, where W is the Woeginger's w-index [12].

Clearly, each r_p-index is effort-dominating [7] — we have $\mu^v = \mathbf{s}^{v,r}$. The r_∞-index may be expressed as a symmetric maxitive or a symmetric modular aggregation operator [6]. However, for $x_{(2)} \geq x_{(1)} \geq 0$, e.g. we have $r_1(x_{(2)}, x_{(1)}) = (x_{(2)} \wedge 2) \wedge (1 + (x_{(1)} \wedge 1))$, for which there do not exist nondecreasing functions $f_{1,2}, f_{2,2} : \mathbb{I} \to \mathbb{R}$, such that $r_1(x_{(2)}, x_{(1)}) = f_{1,2}(x_{(2)}) \vee f_{2,2}(x_{(1)})$, or $r_1(x_{(2)}, x_{(1)}) = f_{1,2}(x_{(2)}) + f_{2,2}(x_{(1)})$. $\qquad\square$

3 Symmetric Minitive Aggregation Operators

Let us first recall the notion of a triangle of functions [cf. 6]:

Definition 6. *A **triangle of functions** is a sequence*

$$\triangle = (f_{i,n})_{i \in [n], n \in \mathbb{N}},$$

where $(\forall n)$ $(\forall i \in [n])$ $f_{i,n} : \mathbb{I} \to \mathbb{I}$.

Such objects may be used to generate interesting classes of aggregation operators, e.g. quasi-S- (consising of — but not limited to — all symmetric maxitive operators), and quasi-L-statistics (symmetric modular operators [cf. 10]). Here we introduce another one.

Definition 7. *A **quasi-I-statistic** generated by* $\triangle = (f_{i,n})_{i \in [n], n \in \mathbb{N}}$ *is a function* $\mathsf{ql}_\triangle \in \mathcal{E}(\mathbb{I})$ *defined for any* $(x_1, \ldots, x_n) \in \mathbb{I}^{1,2,\cdots}$ *as*

$$\mathsf{ql}_\triangle(\mathbf{x}) = \bigwedge_{i=1}^{n} f_{i,n}(x_{(n-i+1)}). \tag{3}$$

Please note that $\wedge$ denotes the minimum (*I*nfimum) operator, hence the name. We obviously have $\mathsf{ql}_\triangle \in \mathcal{P}_{(sym)}$ for any triangle of functions $\triangle$.

It is easily seen that quasi-I-statistics generalize OWMin operators [1], for which we have $f_{i,n}(x) = c_{i,n} \vee x$ for some $c_{i,n} \in \mathbb{I}$, and symmetric minitive aggregation operators, i.e. the set of all $F \in \mathcal{E}(\mathbb{I})$ such that $(\forall n)$ $(\forall \mathbf{x}, \mathbf{y} \in \mathbb{I}^n)$ it holds $F(\mathbf{x} \overset{S}{\wedge} \mathbf{y}) = F(\mathbf{x}) \wedge F(\mathbf{y})$, where $\mathbf{x} \overset{S}{\wedge} \mathbf{y} = (x_{(n)} \wedge y_{(n)}, \ldots, x_{(1)} \wedge y_{(1)})$.

The following theorem states that, without loss of generality, triangles of functions generating nondecreasing quasi-I-statistics may be assumed to be of a particular form.

Theorem 2. *Let* $\mathbb{I} = [a, b]$ *and* $\triangle = (f_{i,n})_{i \in [n], n \in \mathbb{N}}$. *Then* $\mathsf{ql}_\triangle \in \mathcal{P}_{(nd)}$ *if and only if there exists* $\nabla = (g_{i,n})_{i \in [n], n \in \mathbb{N}}$ *satisfying the following conditions:*

(i) $(\forall n)$ $(\forall i \in [n])$ $g_{i,n}$ *is nondecreasing,*
(ii) $(\forall n)$ $(\forall i \in [n])$ $g_{i,n}(b) = g_{1,n}(b)$,
(iii) $(\forall n)$ $g_{1,n} \preceq \cdots \preceq g_{n,n}$,

such that $\mathsf{ql}_\triangle = \mathsf{ql}_\triangledown$.

Proof. ($\Longrightarrow$) Let us fix n. Let $e_n = \mathsf{qS}_\triangle(n * b) = \bigwedge_{i=1}^{n} f_{i,n}(b)$. Therefore, as $\mathsf{ql}_\triangle \in \mathcal{P}_{(\mathrm{nd})}$, for all $\mathbf{x} \in \mathbb{I}^n$ it holds $\mathsf{ql}_\triangle(\mathbf{x}) \le e_n$. As a consequence,

$$\mathsf{ql}_\triangle(\mathbf{x}) = \bigwedge_{i=1}^{n} f_{i,n}(x_{(n-i+1)}) = \bigwedge_{i=1}^{n} \left(f_{i,n}(x_{(n-i+1)}) \wedge e_n \right).$$

Please note that, as $\mathsf{ql}_\triangle$ is nondecreasing, we have $(\forall \mathbf{x} \in \mathbb{I}^n)$ $(\forall i \in [n])$ $\mathsf{ql}_\triangle(\mathbf{x}) \le \mathsf{ql}_\triangle((n-i)*b, i*x_{(i)})$, because $(x_{(n)}, \ldots, x_{(1)}) \le ((n-i)*b, i*x_{(i)})$. We therefore have $\mathsf{ql}_\triangle(\mathbf{x}) \ge f_{j,n}(x_{(n-i+1)})$, where $1 \le i \le j \le n$. However, by definition, for each $\mathbf{x}$ there exists $k \in [n]$ for which $\mathsf{ql}_\triangle(\mathbf{x}) = f_{k,n}(x_{(n-k+1)})$. Thus,

$$\mathsf{ql}_\triangle(\mathbf{x}) = \mathsf{ql}_\triangle((n-1)*b, 1*x_{(1)})$$
$$\wedge\ \mathsf{ql}_\triangle((n-2)*b, 2*x_{(2)})$$
$$\vdots$$
$$\wedge\ \mathsf{ql}_\triangle((n-n)*b, n*x_{(n)}).$$

Consequently,

$$\mathsf{ql}_\triangle(\mathbf{x}) = \bigwedge_{i=1}^{n} \left(\bigwedge_{j=i}^{n} f_{j,n}(x_{(n-i+1)}) \wedge e_n \right).$$

We may thus set $g_{i,n}(x) := \bigwedge_{j=i}^{n} f_{j,n}(x) \wedge e_n$ for all $i \in [n]$. We see that $g_{1,n} \preceq \cdots \preceq g_{n,n}$, and $g_{1,n}(b) = \cdots = g_{n,n}(b) = e_n$.

We will show that each $g_{i,n}$ is nondecreasing. Assume otherwise. Let there exist i and $a \le x < y \le b$ such that $g_{i,n}(x) > g_{i,n}(y)$. We have $\mathsf{qS}_\triangledown((n-i)*b, i* x) = g_{i,n}(x) > \mathsf{qS}_\triangledown((n-i)*b, i*y) = g_{i,n}(y)$, a contradiction.

($\Longleftarrow$) Trivial. $\square$

Please note that, clearly, whenever $\triangledown$ fulfills all the above conditions then it holds $\operatorname{img}\mathsf{ql}_\triangledown = \bigcup_{n=1}^{\infty} \left(\bigcup_{i=1}^{n} \operatorname{img} g_{i,n} \right)$.

Now let us find out when a nondecreasing quasi-I-statistic is arity-monotonic.

Theorem 3. *Let* $\mathbb{I} = [a,b]$ *and* $\triangle = (f_{i,n})_{i\in[n], n\in\mathbb{N}}$ *be such that* $(\forall n)$ $(\forall i \in [n])$ $f_{i,n}$ *is nondecreasing,* $f_{i,n}(b) = f_{1,n}(b)$, *and* $f_{1,n} \preceq \cdots \preceq f_{n,n}$. *Then* $\mathsf{ql}_\triangle \in \mathcal{P}_{(\mathrm{am})}$ *if and only if* $(\forall n)$ $(\forall i \in [n])$ $f_{i,n} \preceq f_{i,n+1}$, *and* $f_{n+1,n+1}(a) \ge f_{1,n}(b)$.

Proof. ($\Longrightarrow$) We have $(\forall x \in \mathbb{I})$ $\mathsf{ql}_\triangle(x) = f_{1,1}(x)$. Moreover, $\mathsf{ql}_\triangle(x, a) = f_{1,2}(x) \wedge f_{2,2}(a)$. Therefore, $\mathsf{ql}_\triangle(x) \le \mathsf{ql}_\triangle(x, a)$ if $f_{2,2}(a) \ge f_{1,1}(b)$ (when $x = b$) and $f_{1,2} \succeq f_{1,1}$.

Fix n. $\mathsf{ql}_\triangle(n * b) \le \mathsf{ql}_\triangle(n * b, a)$ implies that $f_{n+1,n+1}(a) \ge f_{1,n}(b) = \cdots = f_{n,n}(b)$. Now take arbitrary $\mathbf{x} \in \mathbb{I}^n$. $\mathsf{ql}_\triangle(x_{(n)}, (n-1)*a) \le \mathsf{ql}_\triangle(x_{(n)}, (n)*a)$, implies that $f_{1,n} \preceq f_{1,n+1}$ (note that, according to the assumption, $f_{1,n+1}(a) \leq \cdots \leq f_{n+1,n+1}(a)$). For $\mathsf{ql}_\triangle(x_{(n)}, x_{(n-1)}, (n-2)*a) \leq \mathsf{ql}_\triangle(x_{(n)}, x_{(n-1)}, (n-1)*a)$ to hold for any $b \geq x_{(n)} \geq x_{(n-1)} \geq a$, we must have additionally $f_{2,n} \preceq f_{2,n+1}$. By considering the remaining $n-2$ terms of $\mathbf{x}$ we approach the condition $(\forall i \in [n])$ $f_{i,n} \preceq f_{i,n+1}$.

($\Longleftarrow$) Trivial. $\qquad\qquad\qquad\qquad\qquad\qquad\qquad\qquad\qquad\qquad\qquad$ □

4 The Relationship between the Two Classes

We are obviously interested in the relationship between the nondecreasing, arity-monotonic quasi-I-statistics and effort-dominating aggregation operators. It turns out that all effort-dominating aggregation operators belong to the class of quasi-I-statistics.

Theorem 4. *Let* $\mathsf{F} \in \mathcal{P}_{(ed)}$ *and* $\mathbb{I} = [a, b]$. *Then there exists* $\triangle = (f_{i,n})_{i \in [n], n \in \mathbb{N}}$ *such that* $\mathsf{ql}_\triangle = \mathsf{F}$.

Proof. Take any $\mathsf{F} \in \mathcal{P}_{(ed)}$. For any n and $i \in [n]$, let $l_{i,n} := \min\{\mu^v_{(n-i+1)} : |\mu^v| = n\}$, and $u_{i,n} := \max\{\mu^v_{(n-i+1)} : |\mu^v| = n\}$. As $M(\mathsf{F})$ is a chain w.r.t. $\lhd$ and $\mathsf{F} \in \mathcal{P}_{(nd)} \cap \mathcal{P}_{(am)} \cap \mathcal{P}_{(sym)}$, we have $l_{i,n} \leq u_{i,n} \leq l_{i,n+1}$.

Let us first consider restriction of F to $\mathbb{I}^1$. For any $x_{(1)} \in \mathbb{I}$ we have:

$$F(x_{(1)}) = \max\{v : \mu^v_{(1)} \leq x_{(1)}, |\mu^v| = 1\}$$
$$:= f_{1,1}(x_{(1)}).$$

Note that $f_{1,1}$ is nondecreasing.

Furthermore, for $b \geq x_{(2)} \geq x_{(1)} \geq a$ it holds:

$$F(x_{(2)}, x_{(1)}) = \begin{cases} \big(\max\{v : \mu^v_{(2)} \leq x_{(2)}, |\mu^v| = 2\} & \text{for} \quad x_{(2)} \geq l_{1,2}, \\ \wedge \ \max\{v : \mu^v_{(1)} \leq x_{(1)}, |\mu^v| = 2\}\big) & \text{and } x_{(1)} \geq l_{2,2}, \\ f_{1,1}(x_{(2)}) & \text{otherwise,} \end{cases}$$

which may be written as:

$$F(x_{(2)}, x_{(1)}) = f_{1,2}(x_{(2)}) \wedge f_{2,2}(x_{(1)}),$$

where:

$$f_{1,2}(x_{(2)}) = \begin{cases} f_{1,1}(x_{(2)}) & \text{for } x_{(2)} < l_{1,2}, \\ \max\{v : \mu^v_{(2)} \leq x_{(2)}, |\mu^v| = 2\} & \text{otherwise,} \end{cases}$$

$$f_{2,2}(x_{(1)}) = \begin{cases} f_{1,1}(u_{1,1}) & \text{for } x_{(1)} < l_{2,2}, \\ \max\{v : \mu^v_{(1)} \leq x_{(1)}, |\mu^v| = 2\} & \text{otherwise.} \end{cases}$$

Note that both $f_{1,2}$ and $f_{2,2}$ are nondecreasing, $f_{1,1} \preceq f_{1,2} \preceq f_{2,2}$, $f_{1,2}(b) = f_{2,2}(b)$, and $f_{2,2}(a) \geq f_{1,1}(b) = f_{1,1}(u_{1,1})$.

Now for $n = 3$, let $b \geq x_{(3)} \geq x_{(2)} \geq x_{(1)} \geq a$. It holds:

$$F(x_{(3)}, x_{(2)}, x_{(1)}) = \begin{cases} (\max\{v : \mu^v_{(3)} \leq x_{(3)}, |\mu^v| = 3\} & \text{for} \quad x_{(3)} \geq l_{1,3} \\ \quad \wedge \; \max\{v : \mu^v_{(2)} \leq x_{(2)}, |\mu^v| = 3\}) & \text{and } x_{(2)} \geq l_{2,3}, \\ \quad \wedge \; \max\{v : \mu^v_{(1)} \leq x_{(1)}, |\mu^v| = 3\}) & \text{and } x_{(1)} \geq l_{3,3}, \\ f_{1,2}(x_{(3)}) \wedge f_{2,2}(x_{(2)}) & \text{otherwise,} \end{cases}$$

which is equivalent to:

$$F(x_{(3)}, x_{(2)}, x_{(1)}) = f_{1,3}(x_{(3)}) \wedge f_{2,3}(x_{(2)}) \wedge f_{3,3}(x_{(1)}),$$

where

$$f_{1,3}(x_{(3)}) = \begin{cases} f_{1,2}(x_{(3)}) & \text{for } x_{(3)} < l_{1,3}, \\ \max\{v : \mu^v_{(3)} \leq x_{(3)}, |\mu^v| = 3\} & \text{otherwise,} \end{cases}$$

$$f_{2,3}(x_{(2)}) = \begin{cases} f_{2,2}(x_{(2)}) & \text{for } x_{(2)} < l_{2,3}, \\ \max\{v : \mu^v_{(2)} \leq x_{(2)}, |\mu^v| = 3\} & \text{otherwise,} \end{cases}$$

$$f_{3,3}(x_{(1)}) = \begin{cases} f_{1,2}(u_{1,2}) & \text{for } x_{(1)} < l_{3,3}, \\ \max\{v : \mu^v_{(1)} \leq x_{(1)}, |\mu^v| = 3\} & \text{otherwise.} \end{cases}$$

By applying similar reasoning for any $n > 3$, we approach the equation

$$F(x_{(n)}, \ldots, x_{(1)}) = \bigwedge_{i=1}^{n} f_{i,n}(x_{(n-i+1)}),$$

where for $i < n$ we have

$$f_{i,n}(x_{(n-i+1)}) = \begin{cases} f_{i,n-1}(x_{(n-i+1)}) & \text{for } x_{(n-i+1)} < l_{i,n}, \\ \max\{v : \mu^v_{(n-i+1)} \leq x_{(n-i+1)}, |\mu^v| = n\} & \text{otherwise,} \end{cases}$$

and

$$f_{n,n}(x_{(1)}) = \begin{cases} f_{1,n-1}(u_{1,n-1}) & \text{for } x_{(1)} < l_{n,n}, \\ \max\{v : \mu^v_{(1)} \leq x_{(1)}, |\mu^v| = n\} & \text{otherwise.} \end{cases}$$

This formula generates each $f_{i,n}$ being nondecreasing, $f_{1,n} \preceq \cdots \preceq f_{n,n}$, $f_{i,n-1} \preceq f_{i,n}$, $f_{i,n}(b) = f_{1,n}(b)$, and $f_{n,n}(a) \geq f_{1,n-1}(b)$, thus F is a nondecreasing, arity-monotonic quasi-I-statistic, which completes the proof. □

Example 5. By the construction above, we have:

$$r_p(x_1, \ldots, x_n) = \begin{cases} \bigwedge_{i=1}^{n} \left((n \wedge x_{(n-i+1)}) \vee (i-1) \right) & \text{if } p = \infty, \\ \bigwedge_{i=1}^{n} \left(\left(n \wedge \sqrt[p]{x^p_{(n-i+1)} + (i-1)^p} \right) \vee (i-1) \right) & \text{if } p \in [1, \infty). \end{cases}$$

□

Interestingly, if we are given an already nondecreasingly-sorted input vector $\mathbf{x} \in \mathbb{I}^n$ and an effort-dominating impact function F for which the value $\max\{v : \mu^v_{(n-i+1)} \leq x_{(n-i+1)}, |\mu^v| = n\}$ may be computed in $O(1)$-time for all i, n (just as in Example 5) then $\mathsf{F}(\mathbf{x})$ may be computed in $O(n)$-time.

On the other hand, not each $\mathsf{ql}_\triangle \in \mathcal{P}_{(\mathrm{nd})} \cap \mathcal{P}_{(\mathrm{am})}$ belongs to $\mathcal{P}_{(\mathrm{ed})}$.

Example 6. Let $\mathbb{I} = [0,2]$ and $\triangle = (\mathsf{f}_{i,n})_{i \in [n], n \in \mathbb{N}}$ be such that $\mathsf{f}_{1,1} = \lfloor x \rfloor$, $\mathsf{f}_{1,2}(x) = x$, $\mathsf{f}_{2,2}(x) = 2$, and $(\forall n \geq 3)$ $(\forall i \in [n])$ $\mathsf{f}_{i,n}(x) = 2$. We see that $\mathsf{ql}_\triangle \in \mathcal{P}_{(\mathrm{em})} \cap \mathcal{P}_{(\mathrm{nd})} \cap \mathcal{P}_{(\mathrm{am})}$. However, e.g. $\mu^0 = (0) \trianglelefteq \mu^{0.5} = (0.5, 0) \ntrianglelefteq \mu^1 = (1)$. Therefore, $M(\mathsf{ql}_\triangle)$ is not a chain w.r.t. $\trianglelefteq$, and hence $\mathsf{ql}_\triangle \notin \mathcal{P}_{(\mathrm{ed})}$. $\square$

For the sake of completeness, we shall show which triangles of functions generate effort-dominating quasi-I-statistics.

Theorem 5. *Let $\mathbb{I} = [a,b]$ and $\triangle = (\mathsf{f}_{i,n})_{i \in [n], n \in \mathbb{N}}$ be such that $(\forall n)$ $(\forall i \in [n])$ $\mathsf{f}_{i,n}$ is nondecreasing, $\mathsf{f}_{i,n}(b) = \mathsf{f}_{1,n}(b)$, $\mathsf{f}_{1,n} \preceq \cdots \preceq \mathsf{f}_{n,n}$, and $\mathsf{ql}_\triangle \in \mathcal{P}_{(\mathrm{am})}$. Then $\mathsf{ql}_\triangle \in \mathcal{P}_{(\mathrm{ed})}$ if and only if*

$$(\forall n)\ (\forall i \in [n])\ (\forall x < u_{i,n})\ \mathsf{f}_{i,n+1}(x) = \mathsf{f}_{i,n}(x),$$

where $u_{i,n} = \min\{y : \mathsf{f}_{i,n}(y) = \mathsf{f}_{i,n}(b)\}$.

Proof. ($\Longrightarrow$) Assume the opposite. Take the smallest n and the smallest $i \in [n]$ for which there exists $x < u_{i,n}$ such that $\mathsf{f}_{i,n}(x) < \mathsf{f}_{i,n+1}(x)$. We have 2 cases.

(i) Let $(\exists y)$ such that $\mathsf{f}_{i,n}(y) = \mathsf{f}_{i,n+1}(x)$. As each function is nondecreasing, $y > x$ holds. But in this case the least element (w.r.t. $\trianglelefteq$) of $\{\mathbf{x} : \mathsf{ql}_\triangle(\mathbf{x}) = \mathsf{f}_{i,n+1}(x)\}$ does not exist and hence $\mathsf{ql}_\triangle$ is not even effort-measurable.

(ii) Otherwise, we have $\mu^{\mathsf{f}_{i,n}(x)} \ntrianglelefteq \mu^{\mathsf{f}_{i,n+1}(x)}$ (note that $\mathsf{f}_{i,n}(x), \mathsf{f}_{i,n+1}(x) \in \mathrm{img}\, \mathsf{ql}_\triangle$), and therefore $M(\mathsf{ql}_\triangle)$ is not a chain, a contradiction.

($\Longleftarrow$) By arity-monotonicity, we have $(\forall n)$ $(\forall i \in [n])$ $\mathsf{f}_{i,n} \preceq \mathsf{f}_{i,n+1}$, and $\mathsf{f}_{n+1,n+1}(a) \geq \mathsf{f}_{1,n}(b)$. Take any $v, v' \in \mathrm{img}\, \mathsf{ql}_\triangle$ such that $v < v'$. Let us take the smallest m such that $(\exists x)$ $\mathsf{f}_{1,m}(x) = v$ and the smallest m' such that $(\exists y)$ $\mathsf{f}_{1,m}(y) = v'$. Note that, by the assumptions taken, $(\forall n < m)$ $(\forall \mathbf{x} \in \mathbb{I}^n)$ $\mathsf{ql}_\triangle(\mathbf{x}) < v$, and the same holds for m' and v'. Additionally, we have $m \leq m'$.

It holds $\mu^v_{(m-i+1)} = \min\{x : \mathsf{f}_{i,m}(x) \geq v\}$ for $i \in [m]$, and $\mu^{v'}_{(m'-j+1)} = \min\{x : \mathsf{f}_{j,m'}(x) \geq v'\}$ for $j \in [m']$. But $(\forall i \in [m])$ $\mu^v_{(m-i+1)} \leq \mu^{v'}_{(m'-i+1)}$, because $\mathsf{f}_{i,m}(\mu^v_{(m-i+1)}) = \mathsf{f}_{i,m'}(\mu^v_{(m-i+1)})$ and each function is nondecreasing. Therefore, $\mu^v \trianglelefteq \mu^{v'}$, QED. $\square$

5   Conclusions

In this paper we have shown that all effort-dominating aggregation operators, among which we may find Gagolewski-Grzegorzewski's r_p-indices [3,4], Hirsch's h-index $= r_\infty(\lfloor \mathbf{x} \rfloor)$ [9], and Woeginger's w-index $= r_1(\lfloor \mathbf{x} \rfloor)$ [12], are symmetric-minitive.

Effort-dominating aggregation operators, proposed in [7], have a very intuitive interpretation: their value may be determined by comparing an input vector with elements of a set of "minimal quality requirements" needed to reach a particular "quality level".

Such aggregation operators may be used e.g. in the Producer Assessment Problem [see 5,7], whose most important instance is the issue of fair ranking of scientists by means of the number of citations received by their papers.

Acknowledgments. The author would like to thank Prof. Michał Baczyński, Prof. Przemysław Grzegorzewski, and Prof. Radko Mesiar for stimulating discussion. Also, the author would like to express his gratitude to K. Fokow for proof-reading of the manuscript.

References

1. Dubois, D., Prade, H.: Semantics of quotient operators in fuzzy relational databases. Fuzzy Sets and Systems 78(1), 89–93 (1996)
2. Dubois, D., Prade, H., Testemale, C.: Weighted fuzzy pattern matching. Fuzzy Sets and Systems 28, 313–331 (1988)
3. Gagolewski, M.: Bibliometric impact assessment with R and the CITAN package. Journal of Informetrics 5(4), 678–692 (2011)
4. Gagolewski, M., Grzegorzewski, P.: A geometric approach to the construction of scientific impact indices. Scientometrics 81(3), 617–634 (2009)
5. Gągolewski, M., Grzegorzewski, P.: Arity-Monotonic Extended Aggregation Operators. In: Hüllermeier, E., Kruse, R., Hoffmann, F. (eds.) IPMU 2010. CCIS, vol. 80, pp. 693–702. Springer, Heidelberg (2010)
6. Gagolewski, M., Grzegorzewski, P.: Axiomatic characterizations of (quasi-) L-statistics and S-statistics and the Producer Assessment Problem. In: Galichet, S., Montero, J., Mauris, G. (eds.) Proc. Eusflat/LFA 2011, pp. 53–58 (2011)
7. Gagolewski, M., Grzegorzewski, P.: Possibilistic analysis of arity-monotonic aggregation operators and its relation to bibliometric impact assessment of individuals. International Journal of Approximate Reasoning 52(9), 1312–1324 (2011)
8. Grabisch, M., Pap, E., Marichal, J.L., Mesiar, R.: Aggregation functions, Cambridge (2009)
9. Hirsch, J.E.: An index to quantify individual's scientific research output. Proceedings of the National Academy of Sciences 102(46), 16569–16572 (2005)
10. Mesiar, R., Mesiarová-Zemánková, A.: The ordered modular averages. IEEE Transactions on Fuzzy Systems 19(1), 42–50 (2011)
11. Ricci, R.G., Mesiar, R.: Multi-attribute aggregation operators. Fuzzy Sets and Systems 181(1), 1–13 (2011)
12. Woeginger, G.J.: An axiomatic characterization of the Hirsch-index. Mathematical Social Sciences 56(2), 224–232 (2008)
13. Yager, R.R.: On ordered weighted averaging aggregation operators in multicriteria decision making. IEEE Transactions on Systems, Man, and Cybernetics 18(1), 183–190 (1988)

On Migrative t-Conorms and Uninorms

M. Mas, M. Monserrat, Daniel Ruiz-Aguilera, and Joan Torrens

Universitat de les Illes Balears
Carretera de Valldemossa, km 7.5
07122 Palma - Spain
{dmimmg0,dmimma0,daniel.ruiz,dmijts0}@uib.es

Abstract. In this paper the notions of α-migrative t-conorms over a fixed t-conorm S_0, and α-migrative uninorms over another fixed uninorm U_0 with the same neutral element are introduced. All continuous t-conorms that are α-migrative over the maximum, the probabilistic sum and the Lukasiewicz t-conorm are characterized. Uninorms belonging to one of the classes $\mathcal{U}_{\min}$, $\mathcal{U}_{\max}$, idempotent or representable that are α-migrative over a uninorm U_0 in $\mathcal{U}_{\min}$ or $\mathcal{U}_{\max}$ are also characterized.

Keywords: Aggregation function, migrativity, t-norm, t-conorm, uninorm.

1 Introduction

Aggregation functions have experienced a great development in recent years due to its many applications in various fields, both scientific and social (see for example [4,8,16]). In particular, various kinds of aggregation functions are particularly important for its role in the theory of fuzzy sets and their applications (see [18]). This is the case of t-norms, t-conorms and, more generally, conjunctions and disjunctions that intend to generalize the logical connectives "AND", "OR" of classical logic. Often the study of these connectives is directed toward the characterization of those that verify certain properties that may be useful in each context. The study of these properties for certain aggregation functions usually involves the resolution of functional equations. Examples for both, t-norms and t-conorms, as for uninorms, can be found in [7,12,13,14,18,19].

One of this properties is α-*migrativity*, introduced in [11]. For any $\alpha \in [0,1]$ and a mapping $F : [0,1]^2 \to [0,1]$, this property is described as

$$F(\alpha x, y) = F(x, \alpha y) \quad \text{for all } x,y \in [0,1]. \tag{1}$$

The migrativity property (and its generalizations) has been studied for t-norms in [12,13], for semicopulas, quasi-copulas and copulas in [10,20,3] and for aggregation functions in general in [6,15,5]. The interest of this property comes from its applications, for example in decision making processes ([6]), when a repeated, partial information needs to be fusioned in a global result, or in image processing ([20]).

S. Greco et al. (Eds.): IPMU 2012, Part III, CCIS 299, pp. 286–295, 2012.

Note that in the equation (1) the product αx can be replaced by any t-norm T_0 obtaining the property for t-norms called (α, T_0)-migrativity, that can be written as

$$T(T_0(\alpha, x), y) = T(x, T_0(\alpha, y)) \quad \text{for all } x, y \in [0, 1] \tag{2}$$

being T_0 a t-norm and $\alpha \in [0, 1]$. This generalization of the migrativity for t-norms has been recently studied in [13].

In this paper we conduct a similar study for other generalizations, based on the same idea of the equation (2), but for t-conorms and for uninorms. Thus, we define the analougus concepts (α, S_0)-migrative t-conorm, where S_0 is a t-conorm, and (α, U_0)-migrative uninorm, where U_0 is also a uninorm. Our study is similar to the one presented in [13] for these new properties, characterizing the (α, S_0)-migrative t-conorms and, in the case of uninorms, we begin the study with some of the possible cases to consider depending on the previously fixed uninorm.

This article is organized into different sections. After this introduction, we include a preliminary section to establish the necessary notation and recall some basic definitions. Next, two main sections are devoted to the continuous t-conorms and uninorms cases where the underlying operations being continuous. We end with a section of conclusions and future work.

2   Preliminaries

We will assume the basic theory of t-norms and t-conorms, see [1,18]. We will just give in this section initial definitions, all the notations and results required can be found in [18].

Definition 1. *A binary application $T : [0, 1]^2 \to [0, 1]$ is called a* t-norm *if it is associative, commutative, non-decreasing in each place and such that $T(1, x) = x$ for all $x \in [0, 1]$.*

Definition 2. *A binary application $S : [0, 1]^2 \to [0, 1]$ is called a* t-conorm *if it is associative, commutative, non-decreasing in each place and such that $S(0, x) = x$ for all $x \in [0, 1]$.*

Definition 3. *A function $N : [0, 1] \to [0, 1]$ is called a* negation *if it is non-increasing with $N(0) = 1$ and $N(1) = 0$. If a negation N is continuous and strictly decreasing, then it is called* strict negation. *If a negation N is involutive, i.e. $N(N(x)) = x$ for all $x \in [0, 1]$, then N is called a* strong negation.

Definition 4. *Given a binary application $F : [0, 1]^2 \to [0, 1]$ and a strict negation N, its N-dual is defined as the application $F_N^* : [0, 1]^2 \to [0, 1]$ given by*

$$F_N^*(x, y) = N^{-1}(F(N(x), N(y))) \quad \text{for all } x, y \in [0, 1].$$

In the case of $N(x) = 1 - x$, we will denote the N-dual as F^*.

It is well known that, when N is a strong negation, the dualization operation is involutive, that is, for any binary application F it is verified $(F_N^*)_N^* = F$. Moreover, the next proposition is satisfied.

Proposition 1. *Let N be a strong negation. A binary application $F : [0,1]^2 \to [0,1]$ is a t-norm if and only if its dual application F_N^* is a t-conorm.*

Definition 5. *Given a t-norm T_0 and $\alpha \in [0,1]$, a t-norm T is said to be (α, T_0)-migrative or α-migrative over T_0 if*

$$T(T_0(\alpha, x), y) = T(x, T_0(\alpha, y)) \quad \text{for all } x, y \in [0,1]. \tag{3}$$

A detailed study of continuous t-norms that are α-migrative over the minimum, the product and the Lukasiewicz t-norms can be found in [13]. An extension of this work has been made in [21] where continous t-norms α-migrative over any continous t-norm T_0 are characterized.

2.1   Uninorms

Definition 6. *A binary application $U : [0,1]^2 \to [0,1]$ is called a* uninorm *if it is associatve, commutative, non-decreasing in each place and has a neutral element $e \in [0,1]$.*

Evidently, a uninorm with neutral element $e = 1$ is a t-norm and a uninorm with neutral element $e = 0$ is a t-conorm. For any other value $e \in]0, 1[$ the operation works as a t-norm in the $[0, e]^2$ square, as a t-conorm in $[e, 1]^2$ and its values are between minimum and maximum in the set of points $A(e)$ given by

$$A(e) = [0, e[\times]e, 1] \cup]e, 1] \times [0, e[.$$

We will usually denote a uninorm with neutral element e and underlying t-norm and t-conorm, T and S, by $U \equiv \langle T, e, S \rangle$. For any uninorm it is satisfied that $U(0,1) \in \{0,1\}$ and a uninorm U is called *conjunctive* if $U(1,0) = 0$ and *disjunctive* when $U(1,0) = 1$. On the other hand, the most studied classes of uninorms are:

- Uninorms in $\mathcal{U}_{\min}$ (respectively $\mathcal{U}_{\max}$), those given by minimum (respectively maximum) in $A(e)$.
- *Idempotent* uninorms, those that satisfy $U(x,x) = x$ for all $x \in [0,1]$.
- *Representable* uninorms, those that are continuous in $[0,1]^2 \setminus \{(1,0),(0,1)\}$.

In what follows we give a characterization of the uninorms in $\mathcal{U}_{\min}$ and $\mathcal{U}_{\max}$ that will be mainly used in the paper. Characterization of idempotent and representable uninorms can be found in [2] and [14], respectively.

Theorem 1. *([14]) Let $U : [0,1]^2 \to [0,1]$ be a uninorm with neutral element $e \in]0,1[$. Then, the sections $x \mapsto U(x,1)$ and $x \mapsto U(x,0)$ are continuous except perhaps in $x = e$ if and only if U is given by one of the following formulas.*

(a) If $U(0,1) = 0$, then

$$U(x,y) = \begin{cases} eT_U\left(\frac{x}{e}, \frac{y}{e}\right) & \text{if } (x,y) \in [0,e]^2 \\ e + (1-e)S_U\left(\frac{x-e}{1-e}, \frac{y-e}{1-e}\right) & \text{if } (x,y) \in [e,1]^2 \\ \min(x,y) & \text{otherwise,} \end{cases} \tag{4}$$

where T_U is a t-norm, and S_U is a t-conorm.

(b) If $U(0,1) = 1$, then the same structure holds, changing minimum by maximum in $A(e)$.

Uninorms as in case a) will be denoted by $\mathcal{U}_{\min}$ and those as in case b) by $\mathcal{U}_{\max}$.

3 (α, S_0)-Migrative t-Conorms

In this section we will study the case of continuous t-conorms. Note that if we require equation (1) to be a t-conorm and we take the value $x = 0$, we obtain $y = \alpha y$ for all $y \in [0,1]$. That is, no α-migrative t-conorms exist for $\alpha \neq 1$, while for $\alpha = 1$ all t-conorms satisfy (1).

The same applies if we look for t-conorms that satisfy (3) for given t-norm T_0. It is clear from this that we need to adapt the migrativity equation to the case of t-conorms requiring migrativity over a fixed t-conorm S_0.

Definition 7. *Let α be in $[0,1]$ and S_0 any t-conorm. We will say that a t-conorm S is (α, S_0)-migrative or that S is α-migrative over S_0, if for all $x, y \in [0,1]$ it is verified*

$$S(S_0(\alpha, x), y) = S(x, S_0(\alpha, y)). \tag{5}$$

Note that from the previous definition any t-conorm S is always $(0, S_0)$-migrative and also $(1, S_0)$-migrative for any t-conorm S_0. Thus, in what follows we will focus on the case $\alpha \in \,]0,1[$.

Another immediate consideration is that, due to associativity and commutativity, S_0 is always (α, S_0)-migrative for all α. In addition, by duality we obtain the next result.

Proposition 2. *Consider $\alpha \in \,]0,1[$ and S_0 a t-conorm. A t-conorm S is (α, S_0)-migrative if and only if its dual t-norm S^* is $(1 - \alpha, T_0)$-migrative, where T_0 is the dual t-norm of S_0.*

Proof. We have that the formula of (α, S_0)-migrativity for S

$$S(S_0(\alpha, x), y) = S(x, S_0(\alpha, y))$$

is equivalent to

$$1 - S(1 - (1 - S_0(\alpha, x)), y) = 1 - S(1 - (1 - x), 1 - (1 - S_0(\alpha, y))).$$

And thus, taking into account that $S^*(x,y) = 1 - S(1-x, 1-y)$, we obtain:

$$S^*(1 - S_0(\alpha, x), 1 - y) = S^*(1 - x, 1 - S_0(\alpha, y)),$$

and now, replacing $S_0^*(x, y) = 1 - S_0(1 - x, 1 - y)$

$$S^*(S_0^*(1 - \alpha, 1 - x), 1 - y) = S^*(1 - x, S_0^*(1 - \alpha, 1 - y)),$$

and changing $T_0 = S_0^*$, $z = 1 - x$, $t = 1 - y$ we obtain

$$S^*(T_0(1 - \alpha, z), t) = S^*(z, T_0(1 - \alpha, t)),$$

and the result is satisfied.   □

Thus, next results can be derived for t-conorms from known results for t-norms, see [12] and [13]. First, directly from Theorem 3 in [13] we obtain the next result.

Proposition 3. *Consider $\alpha \in {]0, 1[}$ and S_0 a t-conorm. The next statements are equivalent for any t-conorm S:*

i) S is (α, S_0)-migrative.
ii) S_0 is (α, S)-migrative.
iii) α-sections of S and S_0 coincide. That is, $S(\alpha, x) = S_0(\alpha, x)$ for all $x \in [0, 1]$.

Next three theorems characterize (α, S_0)-migrative continuous t-conorms depending on the t-conorm S_0: maximum, probabilistic sum and Łukasiewicz t-conorm.

Theorem 2. *Consider $\alpha \in {]0, 1[}$ and $S_0 = \max$ the maximum t-conorm. Any t-conorm S is $(\alpha, \max)$-migrative if and only if S is an ordinal sum of two t-conorms S_1, S_2 of the form*

$$S = \langle (0, \alpha, S_1), (\alpha, 1, S_2) \rangle. \tag{6}$$

Proof. Just note that S is $(\alpha, \max)$-migrative if and only if S^* is $(1 - \alpha, \min)$-migrative and then we can apply Theorem 4 in [13].   □

Note that the previous characterization is true for any t-conorm not necessarily continuous. In next cases we do restrict to the continuous case. Both results can be easily derived from duality like in Theorem 2. We only prove the first one since the other is quite similar.

Theorem 3. *Consider $\alpha \in {]0, 1[}$ and $S_0 = S_{\mathbf{P}}$ the probabilistic sum t-conorm. Given a continuous t-conorm S, the next statements are equivalent.*

i) S is $(\alpha, S_{\mathbf{P}})$-migrative.
ii) S is a strict t-conorm with additive generator s verifying

$$s(\alpha + x - \alpha x) = s(\alpha) + s(x) \quad \text{for all } x \in [0, 1]. \tag{7}$$

iii) S is a strict t-conorm with additive generator s and there exists a continuous, strictly increasing function $s_0 : [0, \alpha] \to [0, s_0(\alpha)]$ with $s_0(0) = 0$ and $s_0(\alpha) < +\infty$ such that s is given by

$$s(x) = k s_0(\alpha) + s_0 \left(1 - \frac{1 - x}{(1 - \alpha)^k} \right)$$

if $1 - (1 - \alpha)^k \leq x < 1 - (1 - \alpha)^{k+1}$, for all $k \geq 0$.

Proof. i) $\Leftrightarrow$ ii) S is $(\alpha, S_{\mathbf{P}})$-migrative, if and only if S^* is $(1-\alpha, T_{\mathbf{P}})$-migrative, and by the results for t-norms ([12], Theorem 2), if and only if S^* is strict and the additive generator t of S^* satisfies

$$t((1-\alpha)x) = t(1-\alpha) + t(x) \quad \text{for all } x \in [0,1]. \tag{8}$$

As we know that the relation between the additive generator t of S^* and the additive generator s of S is $s(1-x) = t(x)$ then, changing $x = 1-z$, and using (8), we obtain

$$s(\alpha + x - \alpha x) = s(1 - z + \alpha z) = s(1 - (1-\alpha)z) = t((1-\alpha)z) =$$
$$= t(1-\alpha) + t(z) = s(\alpha) + s(1-z) = s(\alpha) + s(x).$$

ii)$\Leftrightarrow$ iii) The additive generator s of S satisfies (7), if and only if the additive generator t of S^* satisfies (8).

Translating the result for t-norms ([12], Theorem 3), we have that t satisfies (8) if and only if there exists a continuous, strictly decreasing function t_0 : $[1-\alpha, 1] \to [0, t_0(1-\alpha)[$ with $t_0(1-\alpha) < +\infty$ and $t_0(1) = 0$ such that

$$t(x) = kt_0(1-\alpha) + t_0\left(\frac{x}{(1-\alpha)^k}\right) \quad \text{if } x \in](1-\alpha)^{k+1}, (1-\alpha)^k],$$

where k is any non-negative integer.

Again, taking into account that $s(x) = t(1-x)$, there exists a continuous, strictly increasing function s_0 such that $s_0(x) = t_0(1-x)$, $s_0 : [0, \alpha] \to [0, s_0(\alpha)[$ with $s_0(\alpha) < +\infty$ and $s_0(0) = 0$ such that

$$s(x) = t(1-x) = ks_0(\alpha) + s_0\left(1 - \frac{1-x}{(1-\alpha)^k}\right)$$

if $x \in [1 - (1-\alpha)^k, 1 - (1-\alpha)^{k+1}[$, and then the theorem is proved. $\square$

Definition 8. *Given $a \in [0,1]$, we define recursively $a_{\mathbf{L}}^{(n)}$ by $a_{\mathbf{L}}^{(0)} = 1$, $a_{\mathbf{L}}^{(1)} = a$ and*

$$a_{\mathbf{L}}^{(k)} = T_{\mathbf{L}}(a_{\mathbf{L}}^{(k)}, a) \quad \text{for all } k \geq 2.$$

With this notation, we can state the result for $(\alpha, S_{\mathbf{L}})$-migrative t-conorms.

Theorem 4. *Consider $\alpha \in]0, 1[$ and $S_0 = S_{\mathbf{L}}$ the Łukasiewicz t-conorm. Given a continuous t-conorm S, the next statements are equivalent.*

i) S is $(\alpha, S_{\mathbf{L}})$-migrative.

ii) S is a nilpotent t-conorm with normalized additive generator s (such that $s(1) = 1$) verifying

$$s(\alpha + x) = s(\alpha) + s(x) \quad \text{for all } x \in [0, 1 - \alpha].$$

iii) S *is a nilpotent t-conorm with normalized additive generator* s *and there exists an automorphism* φ_0 *of the interval* $[0,1]$ *and a real number* a *with* $\frac{n-1}{n} \le a \le \frac{n}{n+1}$ *where* $n = \max\{k \mid 1 - \alpha \ge \frac{k-1}{k}\}$, *such that*

$$\varphi_0\left(\frac{\alpha - (1-\alpha)_{\mathbf{L}}^{(n)}}{\alpha}\right) = \frac{1 - a - a_{\mathbf{L}}^{(n)}}{1-a}$$

and s *is given by*

$$s(x) = 1 - a_{\mathbf{L}}^{(k)} - (1-a)\varphi_0\left(\frac{1 - x - (1-\alpha)_{\mathbf{L}}^{(k)}}{\alpha}\right)$$

if $1 - (1-\alpha)_{\mathbf{L}}^{(k-1)} \le x < 1 - (1-\alpha)_{\mathbf{L}}^{(k)}$, *when* $1 \le k \le n$ *and, however*

$$s(x) = 1 - (a_{\mathbf{L}}^{(n)} + a - 1) - (1-a)\varphi_0\left(\frac{1 - x - (1-\alpha)_{\mathbf{L}}^{(n)} + \alpha}{\alpha}\right)$$

if $1 - (1-\alpha)_{\mathbf{L}}^{(n)} \le x \le 1$.

4 (α, U_0)-Migrative Uninorms

In this section we start the study for the case of uninorms. In a similar way to the cases for t-norms and t-conorms, we can give the next definition.

Definition 9. *Consider* $\alpha \in [0,1]$ *and* U_0 *a uninorm with neutral element* $e \in$ $]0,1[$. *We will say that a uninorm* U *with neutral element* e *is* (α, U_0)-*migrative or that* U *is* α-*migrative over* U_0, *if, for all* $x, y \in [0,1]$

$$U(U_0(\alpha, x), y) = U(x, U_0(\alpha, y)). \tag{9}$$

From now on we will suppose that $e \in]0,1[$ is fixed and that all uninorms U_0, U used have the same neutral element e. Note that therefore a first obvious result is that any uninorm U is (e, U_0)-migrative for any uninorm U_0.

Proposition 4. *Consider* $\alpha \in [0,1]$ *and* U_0 *any uninorm with neutral element* e. *The next statements are equivalent for a uninorm* U *with neutral element* e:

i) U *is* (α, U_0)-*migrative.*
ii) U_0 *is* (α, U)-*migrative.*
iii) $U(\alpha, x) = U_0(\alpha, x)$ *for all* $x \in [0,1]$.

Proof. It is similar to Theorem 3 in [13].

Now we will distinguish the cases considering U_0 in $\mathcal{U}_{\min}$ and $\mathcal{U}_{\max}$. In all cases we will also suppose that $\alpha \ne e$ and that underlying t-norms and t-conorms are continuous.

4.1   When U_0 is in $\mathcal{U}_{\min}$

In this section we will deal with uninorms U_0 in $\mathcal{U}_{\min}$. Following Proposition 4, to find which uninorms are (α, U_0)-migrative, we have to find out which uninorms have their α-section equal to the α-section of U_0. We will do it by considering the most common classes of uninorms (see the Preliminaries).

Proposition 5. *Consider* $\alpha \in [0, 1]$, $U_0 \equiv \langle T_0, e, S_0 \rangle_{\min}$ *and* $U \equiv \langle T, e, S \rangle_{\min}$. *Then,*

i) If $\alpha < e$, U is (α, U_0)-migrative if and only if T is $(\frac{\alpha}{e}, T_0)$-migrative.
ii) If $\alpha > e$, U is (α, U_0)-migrative if and only if S is $(\frac{\alpha - e}{1 - e}, S_0)$-migrative.

Proof. i) Consider $\alpha < e$.

If U is (α, U_0)-migrative, then, by Proposition 4, we have that $U(\alpha, x) = U_0(\alpha, x)$ for all $x \in [0, 1]$.

If $x \leq e$, then $U_0(x, \alpha) = eT_0(\frac{x}{e}, \frac{\alpha}{e})$ and $U(x, \alpha) = eT(\frac{x}{e}, \frac{\alpha}{e})$ and therefore $T(z, \frac{\alpha}{e}) = T_0(z, \frac{\alpha}{e})$, for all $z \in [0, 1]$, that means that T is $(\frac{\alpha}{e}, T_0)$-migrative.

On the reverse, if T is $(\frac{\alpha}{e}, T_0)$-migrative, we have $T(z, \frac{\alpha}{e}) = T_0(z, \frac{\alpha}{e})$ for all $z \in [0, 1]$, and then $U(x, \alpha) = U_0(x, \alpha)$ for all $x \in [0, e]$. Also, as $U, U_0 \in \mathcal{U}_{\min}$, $U(x, \alpha) = U_0(x, \alpha) = x$ for all $x \in [e, 1]$. Therefore, U is (α, U)-migrative.

ii) If $\alpha > e$, the proof is similar to the previous case.   □

Proposition 6. *Consider* $\alpha \in [0, 1]$ *and* $U_0 \equiv \langle T_0, e, S_0 \rangle_{\min}$. *If U is in $U_{\max}$ or it is a representable uninorm, then U is not (α, U_0)-migrative.*

Proof. Consider $\alpha < e$ (the case $\alpha > e$ is similar), then as $U_0 \equiv \langle T_0, e, S_0 \rangle_{\min}$, $U_0(\alpha, x) = \min(\alpha, x)$ for all $x > e$. We distinguish two cases:

- If $U \in U_{\max}$, then for all $x > e$, $U(\alpha, x) = \max(\alpha, x) = x$, and so $U(\alpha, x) \neq U_0(\alpha, x)$.
- If U is representable, we have that all sections are strictly increasing and again that for all $x > e$, $U(\alpha, x) \neq U_0(\alpha, x)$.

Therefore, in both cases, α-sections of U and U_0 does not coincide, and so U is not (α, U_0)-migrative.   □

Proposition 7. *Consider* $\alpha \in [0, 1]$ *and* $U_0 \equiv \langle T_0, e, S_0 \rangle_{\min}$. *If U is an idempotent uninorm with associated function g, then*

i) If $\alpha < e$, U is (α, U_0)-migrative if and only if $g(\alpha) = 1$, $U(\alpha, 1) = \alpha$ and T_0 is an ordinal sum of the form

$$T_0 = \left\langle \left(0, \frac{\alpha}{e}, T_1\right), \left(\frac{\alpha}{e}, 1, T_2\right) \right\rangle. \tag{10}$$

ii) If $\alpha > e$, U is (α, U_0)-migrative if and only if $g(\alpha) = e$ and S_0 is an ordinal sum of the form

$$S_0 = \left\langle \left(0, \frac{\alpha - e}{1 - e}, S_1\right), \left(\frac{\alpha - e}{1 - e}, 1, S_2\right) \right\rangle.$$

Proof. i) If $\alpha < e$ and U is (α, U_0)-migrative, then by Proposition 4, $U(\alpha, x) = \min(\alpha, x) = \alpha$ and then for all $x > e$, $U(\alpha, x) = \min(x, y) = U_0(\alpha, x)$, and as U is idempotent, this means that $g(\alpha) = 1$ and $U(\alpha, 1) = \min(\alpha, 1) = \alpha$. For $x < e$, migrativity of U over U_0 means that T_0 is migrative over min, and taking into account the same result for t-norms, we have that there exist two t-norms T_1 and T_2 such that T_0 is given by (10).

ii) Is similar to the previous case.   □

4.2   When U_0 is in $\mathcal{U}_{\max}$

All results in this section can be obtained similarly to the previous ones.

Proposition 8. *Consider* $\alpha \in [0,1]$, $U_0 \equiv \langle T_0, e, S_0 \rangle_{\max}$ *and* $U \equiv \langle T, e, S \rangle_{\max}$. *Then,*

i) *If* $\alpha < e$, U *is* (α, U_0)-*migrative if and only if* T *is* $(\frac{\alpha}{e}, T_0)$-*migrative.*
ii) *If* $\alpha > e$, U *is* (α, U_0)-*migrative if and only if* S *is* $(\frac{f-\alpha}{1-e}, S_0)$-*migrative.*

Proposition 9. *Consider* $\alpha \in [0,1]$ *and* $U_0 \equiv \langle T_0, e, S_0 \rangle_{\max}$. *If* U *is in* $\mathcal{U}_{\mathrm{rep}} \cup \mathcal{U}_{\min}$, *then* U *is not* (α, U_0)-*migrative.*

Proposition 10. *Consider* $\alpha \in [0,1]$ *and* $U_0 \equiv \langle T_0, e, S_0 \rangle_{\max}$. *If* U *is an idempotent uninorm with associated function* g, *then*

i) *If* $\alpha < e$, U *is* (α, U_0)-*migrative if and only if* $g(\alpha) = e$ *and* T_0 *is an ordinal sum of the form* $T_0 = \left\langle \left(0, \frac{\alpha}{e}, T_1\right), \left(\frac{\alpha}{e}, 1, T_2\right) \right\rangle$.
ii) *If* $\alpha > e$, U *is* (α, U_0)-*migrative if and only if* $g(\alpha) = 0$, $U(\alpha, 0) = \alpha$ *and* S_0 *is an ordinal sum of the form* $S_0 = \left\langle \left(0, \frac{\alpha-e}{1-e}, S_1\right), \left(\frac{\alpha-e}{1-e}, 1, S_2\right) \right\rangle$.

5   Conclusions and Future Work

In this article we have introduced and studied an extension of the migrativity property for t-conorms and uninorms. In the first case we have characterized all continuous t-conorms α-migrative over the maximum, probabilistic sum and Łukasiewicz t-conorms. We have made a similar characterization for uninorms in classes $\mathcal{U}_{\min}$ and $\mathcal{U}_{\max}$. This study may be extended to α-migrativity for:

- t-conorms over any continuous t-conorm (the case of t-norms has been solved in a paper in press, [21]).
- idempotent and representable uninorms (when U and U_0 are both representable, the migrativity property will be equivalent to solve a restricted Cauchy equation similarly to the case of Archimedean t-norms and t-conorms, see [5,12,21]), continuous uninorms in $]0,1[^2$ (see [17]) or the locally internal ones ($U(x,y) \in \{x,y\}$) in the region $A(e)$ (see [9]).

Acknowledgments. This work has been supported by the Spanish grant MTM-2009-10320 (with FEDER support).

References

1. Alsina, C., Frank, M.J., Schweizer, B.: Associative Functions. Triangular Norms and Copulas. World Scientific, New Jersey (2006)
2. De Baets, B.: Idempotent uninorms. European Journal of Operational Research 118, 631–642 (1999)
3. Beliakov, G., Calvo, T.: On migrative means and copulas. In: Proceedings of the AGOP 2009, pp. 107–110. Palma de Mallorca (2009)
4. Beliakov, G., Pradera, A., Calvo, T.: Aggregation Functions: A Guide for Practicioners. Springer, Heidelberg (2007)
5. Bustince, H., De Baets, B., Fernandez, J., Mesiar, R., Montero, J.: A generalization of the migrativity property of aggregation functions. Infromation Sciences 191, 76–85 (2012)
6. Bustince, H., Montero, J., Mesiar, R.: Migrativity of aggregation functions. Fuzzy Sets and Systems 160, 766–777 (2009)
7. Calvo, T., De Baets, B., Fodor, J.: The functional equations of Frank and Alsina for uninorms and nullnorms. Fuzzy Sets and Systems 120, 385–394 (2001)
8. Calvo, T., Mayor, G., Mesiar, R. (eds.): Aggregation operators. New trends and applications. STUDFUZZ, vol. 97. Physica-Verlag, Heidelberg (2002)
9. Drygaś, P.: On properties of uninorms with underlying t-norm and t-conorms given as ordinal sums. Fuzzy Sets and Systems 161, 149–157 (2010)
10. Durante, F., Ghiselli Ricci, R.: Supermigrative semi-copulas and triangular norms. Information Sciences 179, 2689–2694 (2009)
11. Durante, F., Sarkoci, P.: A note on the convex combination of triangular norms. Fuzzy Sets and Systems 159, 77–80 (2008)
12. Fodor, J., Rudas, I.J.: On continuous triangular norms that are migrative. Fuzzy Sets and Systems 158, 1692–1697 (2007)
13. Fodor, J., Rudas, I.J.: An extension of the migrative property for triangular norms. Fuzzy Sets and Systems 168, 70–80 (2011)
14. Fodor, J., Yager, R.R., Rybalov, A.: Structure of uninorms. International Journal of Uncertainty, Fuzziness and Knowledge-Based Systems 5, 411–427 (1997)
15. Ghiselli Ricci, R.: Supermigrative aggregation functions. In: Proceedings of the 6th International Summer School on Aggregation Operators, AGOP 2011, Benevento (Italy), pp. 145–150 (July 2011)
16. Grabisch, M., Marichal, J.L., Mesiar, R., Pap, E.: Aggregation functions. In: Encyclopedia of Mathematics and its Applications, vol. 127, Cambridge University Press (2009)
17. Hu, S.K., Li, Z.F.: The structure of continuous uninorms. Fuzzy Sets and Systems 124, 43–52 (2001)
18. Klement, E.P., Mesiar, R., Pap, E.: Triangular norms. Kluwer Academic Publishers, Dordrecht (2000)
19. Mas, M., Mayor, G., Torrens, J.: The distributivity condition for uninorms and t-operators. Fuzzy Sets and Systems 128, 209–225 (2002)
20. Mesiar, R., Bustince, H., Fernandez, J.: On the α-migrativity of semicopulas, quasi-copulas and copulas. Information Sciences 180, 1967–1976 (2010)
21. Xie, A., Liu, H.: Solutions to the extended migrative functional equation based on continuous triangular norms (2011) (preprint)

Fuzzy Relations between Two Universes: Soft Assessments of R-neighborhoods

Slavka Bodjanova[1] and Martin Kalina[2]

[1] Department of Mathematics, Texas A&M University-Kingsville,
Kingsville, TX 78363, USA
`kfsb000@tamuk.edu`
[2] Department of Mathematics,
Slovak Technical University, Sk-813 68 Bratislava, Slovakia
`kalina@math.sk`

Abstract. A fuzzy relation R between two finite universes is considered. A uniform theoretical characterization of lower and upper assessments of subsets and partitions of R by pairs of fuzzy sets, pairs of real numbers and pairs of fuzzy relations is proposed. The notions of LU-fuzzy sets, LU-coefficients and LU-fuzzy relations are introduced and their properties are discussed. Some assessments based on aggregation functions are presented.

Keywords: fuzzy relations, aggregation functions, rough sets, rough fuzzy sets, soft evaluations, approximation.

1 Introduction

Soft assessments based on various generalizations of the notion of a set, e.g., fuzzy sets [3], rough sets [9], rough fuzzy sets and fuzzy rough sets [4], shadowed sets [10] or near sets [11] have been successfully applied in various areas of engineering, natural sciences and social sciences. Contrary to a crisp assessment (usually a real number), a soft assessment allows some degree of ambiguity.

In our study we assume a fuzzy relation R describing the degrees of relationship of elements from a finite universe V to another finite universe W. Throughout this paper we will use the notations $\tilde{2}^V$ and $\mathcal{F}(V)$ for the family of all non-empty subsets from V and the family of all fuzzy sets defined on V, respectively. Given $x \in V$, the set of all elements from W which are related to x is called the R-neighborhood of x. More accurately, the R-neighborhood of x is characterized by a fuzzy set $r_x \in \mathcal{F}(W)$ defined for all $y \in W$ by $r_x(y) = R(x, y)$. When $A \in \tilde{2}^V$ and the cardinality of A is at least 2, the R-neighborhood of A is created by the R-neighborhoods of elements included in A. Hence

$$r_A = \{r_x : x \in A\} = R/A, \tag{1}$$

which is the granule (subset) of R induced by A. In [1] we investigated real-valued evaluations of granules of a fuzzy relation with the aim to assess the

S. Greco et al. (Eds.): IPMU 2012, Part III, CCIS 299, pp. 296–305, 2012.

relationship between sets of elements from two related universes. In this paper we explore which pair of fuzzy sets $(\underline{r}_A, \overline{r}_A) \in \mathcal{F}(W) \times \mathcal{F}(W)$ can be considered as a soft assessment of R/A. Recall that the inverse relation of R is the relation $R^{-1} \in \mathcal{F}(W \times V)$ such that for all $(y, x) \in W \times V: R^{-1}(y, x) = R(x, y)$. Then the R^{-1}-neighborhood of a set $Z \in \tilde{2}^W$ is given by

$$r_Z^{-1} = \{r_y^{-1} : y \in Z\} = R^{-1}/Z. \tag{2}$$

Evaluations of R-neighborhoods (or R^{-1}-neighborhoods) of subsets from a finite universe by pairs of fuzzy sets from another related universe will be studied in Section 2.

Soft assessments $(\underline{r}_A, \overline{r}_A)$ and $(\underline{r}_Z^{-1}, \overline{r}_Z^{-1})$ can be combined and used in an interval-valued assessment of the R-neighborhood of the set $A \times Z \in \tilde{2}^{V \times W}$ (or R^{-1}-neighborhood of the set $Z \times A \in \tilde{2}^{W \times V}$). Evaluations of R-neighborhoods of subsets from the Cartesian product of two related universes will be explored in Section 3.

It is well known that the relationship between a fuzzy set and its partition into crisp clusters can be described by a pair of coarser fuzzy sets called rough fuzzy sets [4]. A relation $R \in \mathcal{F}(V \times W)$ may be partitioned according to a partition P of elements from V, W or $V \times W$. Soft evaluations of R-neighborhoods of clusters from P can be used in a soft evaluation of the granulation of R induced by P by a pair of coarser fuzzy relations. An extension of rough fuzzy sets to rough fuzzy relations and then to the generalized rough fuzzy relations will be discussed in Section 4.

Note that assessments associated with a fuzzy relation between two universes have been studied, e.g., in [5,7,8] with the aim to provide various generalizations of rough sets. Our focus is on upper and lower assessments of subsets and partitions of a fuzzy relation from a more general point of view. We introduce the notion of LU-assessments and we derive LU-assessments based on a pair of fuzzy sets, a pair of real numbers or a pair of fuzzy relations. An assessment by rough sets is a particular case of an LU-assessment based on a pair of sets.

2   Assessments by Pairs of Fuzzy Sets

Let $R \in \mathcal{F}(V \times W)$. Lower and upper assessments of R-neighborhoods of subsets from $\tilde{2}^V$ by pairs of fuzzy sets $(\underline{r}_A, \overline{r}_A) \in \mathcal{F}(W) \times \mathcal{F}(W)$ can be used, e.g., in the following applications:

Case 1: Approximation of individual R-neighborhoods of elements from $A \in \tilde{2}^V$. In this case we expect that for all $(x, y) \in A \times W$

$$\underline{r}_A(y) \leq r_x(y) \leq \overline{r}_A(y). \tag{3}$$

Case 2: Assessment of A in a family of sets $\Omega = \{\Omega_y \in 2^V, y \in W\}$. If $\bigcup_{y \in W} \Omega_y$ covers V and we expect that

$$\bigcup \{\Omega_y : \underline{r}_A(y) = 1\} \subset A \subset \bigcup \{\Omega_y : \overline{r}_A(y) = 1\}, \tag{4}$$

we obtain a rough set approximation of A in the knowledge base Ω.

Case 3: Sharpening (pessimistic or optimistic partial defuzzification) of a soft evaluation of R/A by an evaluation function $h : \bigcup_{n \in N}[0,1]^n \to [0,1]$, where N is the set of all positive integers. Then for $y \in W$ we obtain the membership grade $h(R/A)(y) = h(r_y^{-1}(x) : x \in A)$ and we expect that

$$\underline{r}_A(y) \le h(R/A)(y) \le \overline{r}_A(y). \tag{5}$$

In all applications, fuzzy sets $\underline{r}$ and $\overline{r}$ should satisfy some common properties.

Definition 1. *A mapping $\varphi : \tilde{2}^V \times \mathcal{F}(V \times W) \to \mathcal{F}(W)^2$ is called an LU-assessment of granules of fuzzy relations on $V \times W$ induced by non-empty subsets from V if for an arbitrary $A \in \tilde{2}^V$ and $R \in \mathcal{F}(V \times W)$*

$$\varphi(A, R) = (\underline{r}_A, \overline{r}_A) \tag{6}$$

such that for all $y \in W$ the following hold:

P1) $\underline{r}_A(y) \le \overline{r}_A(y)$,
P2) if $R(x,y) = 0$ for all $x \in A$ then $\underline{r}_A(y) = \overline{r}_A(y) = 0$,
P3) if $R(x,y) = 1$ for all $x \in A$ then $\overline{r}_A(y) = 1$,
P4) if for $S \in \mathcal{F}(V \times W)$ we have that $S(x,y) \le R(x,y)$ for all $x \in A$ then $\underline{s}_A(y) \le \underline{r}_A(y)$ and $\overline{s}_A(y) \le \overline{r}_A(y)$.

The pair of fuzzy sets $(\underline{r}_A, \overline{r}_A)$ is called an LU-fuzzy set associated with the granule R/A.

Property $P2$ guarantees that each assessment of the empty set of R is the empty set. On the other hand, property $P3$ requires that only the upper assessment of a non-empty crisp subset of R is a nonempty crisp subset of W. According to the property $P4$, any increase in the strength of the relationship between V and W results in an increase of membership coefficients in both assessments $\underline{r}$ and $\overline{r}$.

Remark 1. Note that fuzzy set $\tilde{\varphi}_{R/A} \in \mathcal{F}(W)$ defined for all $y \in W$ by $\tilde{\varphi}_{R/A}(y) = \overline{r}_A(y) - \underline{r}_A(y)$ describes ambiguity of assessment of R/A by $(\underline{r}_A, \overline{r}_A)$.

We recognize two types of duality between the lower and the upper fuzzy sets in LU-assessments.

Definition 2. *An LU-assessment $\varphi : \tilde{2}^V \times \mathcal{F}(V \times W) \to \mathcal{F}(W)^2$ is dual with respect to complementary relations on $V \times W$ if for all $A \in \tilde{2}^V$, $R \in \mathcal{F}(V \times W)$ and $y \in W$*

$$\underline{r}_A(y) = 1 - \overline{r^c}_A(y), \tag{7}$$

where $R^c(x,y) = 1 - R(x,y)$ for all $(x,y) \in V \times W$, and it is dual with respect to complementary subsets on V if for all $A \in \tilde{2}^V$, $R \in \mathcal{F}(V \times W)$ and $y \in W$

$$\underline{r}_A(y) = 1 - \overline{r}_{A^c}(y), \tag{8}$$

where $A^c = V \setminus A$.

Analogously, we recognize two types of monotonicity of LU-assessments. Monotonicity with respect to the inclusion of fuzzy relations is characterized by property $P4$ in Definition 1. Monotonicity with respect to the inclusion of subsets from V may vary from application to application. We will discuss the three cases mentioned at the beginning of this section.

Case 1: When the cardinality of $A \in \tilde{2}^V$ increases, there is more ambiguity in an assessment of an individual R-neighborhood r_x, $x \in A$ by $(\underline{r}_A, \overline{r}_A)$. Therefore, for $A, B \in \tilde{2}^V$, $A \subset B$ we expect that $\underline{r}_B \subset \underline{r}_A$ and $\overline{r}_A \subset \overline{r}_B$, and therefore $\tilde{\varphi}_{R/A} \subset \tilde{\varphi}_{R/B}$.

Case 2: When the cardinality of $A \in \tilde{2}^V$ increases, the cardinality of its approximate representation in the knowledge base Ω also increases. Hence, for $A, B \in \tilde{2}^V$, $A \subset B$ we expect that $\underline{r}_A \subset \underline{r}_B$ and $\overline{r}_A \subset \overline{r}_B$.

Case 3: Monotonicity of $(\underline{r}, \overline{r})$ depends on the properties of the evaluation function h. Obviously, there are also LU-assessments which are not monotonic with respect to the inclusion of subsets from V.

Comparing the properties from Definition 1 with the properties of aggregation functions [2], we easily conclude that LU-assessments can be based on aggregation functions, especially triangular norms (t-norms) [6] and triangular conorms (t-conorms).

Proposition 1. *Let T be a t-norm and S a t-conorm. Then a mapping φ^{TS} : $\tilde{2}^V \times \mathcal{F}(V \times W) \to \mathcal{F}(W)^2$ defined for all $(A, R) \in \tilde{2}^V \times \mathcal{F}(V \times W)$ by*

$$\varphi^{TS}(A, R) = (\underline{r}_A^T, \overline{r}_A^S) \tag{9}$$

such that for all $y \in W$

$$\underline{r}_A^T(y) = T(r_y^{-1}(x), x \in A), \tag{10}$$
$$\overline{r}_A^S(y) = S(r_y^{-1}(x), x \in A), \tag{11}$$

is an LU-assessment of granules of fuzzy relations on $V \times W$ induced by nonempty subsets from V.

Lemma 1. *LU-assessment φ^{TS} satisfies the following properties:*

i) $\underline{r}_A^T \subset r_x \subset \overline{r}_A^S$ *for all $x \in A$,*
ii) *if $A = \{x\}$, $x \in V$ then $\underline{r}_A^T = r_x = \overline{r}_A^S$,*
iii) *if for $y \in W : R(x, y) = 1$ for all $x \in A$ then $\underline{r}_A^T(y) = \overline{r}_A^S(y) = 1$,*
iv) *if $A, B \in \tilde{2}^V$, $A \subset B$ then $\underline{r}_B^T \subset \underline{r}_A^T$ and $\overline{r}_A^S \subset \overline{r}_B^S$,*
v) *if S is the dual t-conorm to T then for all $y \in W : \underline{r}_A^T(y) = 1 - \overline{r^c}_A^S(y)$.*

The assessment φ^{TS} can be used in applications described by *Case 1*.

Fuzzy sets are often approximated by crisp sets. For $\alpha \in (0, 1]$, the α-cut of a fuzzy set $f \in \mathcal{F}(W)$ is the crisp subset of W

$$f_\alpha = \{y \in W : f(y) \geq \alpha\}. \tag{12}$$

Proposition 2. *Assume* $\alpha \in (0,1]$. *Then a mapping* $\varphi^\alpha : \tilde{2}^V \times \mathcal{F}(V \times W) \to \mathcal{F}(W)^2$ *defined for all* $(A,R) \in \tilde{2}^V \times \mathcal{F}(V \times W)$ *by*

$$\varphi^\alpha(A,R) = (\underline{r}_A^\alpha, \overline{r}_A^\alpha) \tag{13}$$

such that for all $y \in W$

$$\underline{r}_A^\alpha(y) = \begin{cases} 1 & \text{if } (r_y^{-1})_\alpha \subset A, \\ 0 & \text{otherwise,} \end{cases} \tag{14}$$

and

$$\overline{r}_A^\alpha(y) = \begin{cases} 1 & \text{if } (r_y^{-1})_\alpha \cap A \neq \emptyset, \\ 0 & \text{otherwise,} \end{cases} \tag{15}$$

is an LU-assessment of granules of fuzzy relations on $V \times W$ *induced by non-empty subsets from* V.

Lemma 2. *LU-assessment* φ^α *satisfies the following properties:*

i) if $\bigcup_{y \in W}(r_y^{-1})_\alpha \supset V$ *then*
   $\bigcup\{(r_y^{-1})_\alpha : \underline{r}_A^\alpha(y) = 1\} \subset A \subset \bigcup\{(r_y^{-1})_\alpha : \overline{r}_A^\alpha(y) = 1\}$,
ii) if $A, B \in \tilde{2}^V$, $A \subset B$ *then* $\underline{r}_A^\alpha \subset \underline{r}_B^\alpha$ *and* $\overline{r}_A^\alpha \subset \overline{r}_B^\alpha$,
iii) if $(r_y^{-1})_\alpha \neq \emptyset$ *then* $\underline{r}_A^\alpha(y) = 1 - \overline{r}_{A^c}^\alpha(y)$,
iv) if $\alpha_1, \alpha_2 \in (0,1]$, $\alpha_1 \leq \alpha_2$ *then* $\underline{r}_A^{\alpha_2} \subset \underline{r}_A^{\alpha_1}$ *and* $\overline{r}_A^{\alpha_2} \subset \overline{r}_A^{\alpha_1}$.

The assessment φ^α can be used in applications described by *Case 2.* The pair of sets $(\bigcup\{(r_y^{-1})_\alpha : \underline{r}_A^\alpha(y) = 1\}, \bigcup\{(r_y^{-1})_\alpha : \overline{r}_A^\alpha(y) = 1\})$ is a generalized rough set [12]. It represents a lower and an upper approximation of A in the knowledge base created by the α-cuts of R^{-1}-neighborhoods of elements from W. Contrary to the φ^{TS} assessment, when $r_y^{-1}(x) = 1$ for all $x \in A$, we may still obtain $\underline{r}^\alpha(y) = 0$. This will happen when $r_y^{-1}(x) = 1$ for some $x \in A^c$. The assessment φ^α classifies elements $y \in W$ as strongly related to A (which means that $\underline{r}^\alpha(y) = 1$), related to A (i.e., $\overline{r}_A^\alpha(y) = 1$) and not related to A (elements with $\overline{r}_A^\alpha(y) = 0$) at level α.

Proposition 3. *Let* h *be an aggregation function and* $\alpha, \beta \in (0,1]$, $\beta < \alpha$. *Then a mapping* $\varphi^{h,\beta,\alpha} : \tilde{2}^V \times \mathcal{F}(V \times W) \to \mathcal{F}(W)^2$ *defined for all* $(A,R) \in \tilde{2}^V \times \mathcal{F}(V \times W)$ *by*

$$\varphi^{h,\beta,\alpha}(A,R) = (\underline{r}_A^{h,\beta}, \overline{r}_A^{h,\alpha}) \tag{16}$$

such that for all $y \in W$

$$\underline{r}_A^{h,\beta}(y) = \begin{cases} 0 & \text{if } h(r_y^{-1}(x), x \in A) \leq \beta, \\ h(r_y^{-1}(x), x \in A) & \text{otherwise,} \end{cases} \tag{17}$$

and

$$\overline{r}_A^{h,\alpha}(y) = \begin{cases} 1 & \text{if } h(r_y^{-1}(x), x \in A) \geq \alpha, \\ h(r_y^{-1}(x), x \in A) & \text{otherwise,} \end{cases} \tag{18}$$

is an LU-assessment of granules of fuzzy relations on $V \times W$ *induced by non-empty subsets from* V.

Lemma 3. *LU-assessment* $\varphi^{h,\beta,\alpha}$ *satisfies the following properties:*

i) *for* $A, B \in \tilde{2}^V$, $A \subset B$, *if* $h(r_y^{-1}(x), x \in A) \leq h(r_y^{-1}(x), x \in B)$ *then* $\underline{r}_A^{h,\beta} \subset \underline{r}_B^{h,\beta}$ *and* $\overline{r}_A^{h,\alpha} \subset \overline{r}_B^{h,\alpha}$;
if $h(r_y^{-1}(x), x \in A) \geq h(r_y^{-1}(x), x \in B)$ *then* $\underline{r}_A^{h,\beta} \supset \underline{r}_B^{h,\beta}$ *and* $\overline{r}_A^{h,\alpha} \supset \overline{r}_B^{h,\alpha}$,

ii) *if* $r_y^{-1}(x) = 1$ *for all* $x \in A$ *then* $\underline{r}_A^{h,\beta}(y) = \overline{r}_A^{h,\alpha}(y) = 1$,

iii) *if* $\alpha_1, \beta_1, \alpha_2, \beta_2 \in (0,1]$; $\beta_2 \leq \beta_1 < \alpha_1 \leq \alpha_2$ *then* $\underline{r}_A^{h,\beta_1} \subset \underline{r}_A^{h,\beta_2}$
and $\overline{r}_A^{h,\alpha_2} \subset \overline{r}_B^{h,\alpha_1}$,

iv) *if* $\alpha \in (0.5, 1]$ *and* $\beta = 1 - \alpha$, *then for all* $y \in W$: $\underline{r}_A^{h,\beta}(y) = 1 - \overline{r^c}_A^{h,\alpha}(y)$.

Fuzzy sets $\underline{r}_A^{h,\beta}$ and $\overline{r}_A^{h,\alpha}$ represent a pessimistic and an optimistic partial defuzzification of a fuzzy set $h(R/A)$ given for all $y \in W$ by

$$h(R/A)(y) = h(r_y^{-1}(x), x \in A).$$

The membership grades of elements from W with low contributions to $h(R/A)$ are sharpened in the fuzzy set $\underline{r}_A^{h,\beta}$ to 0. On the other hand, the membership grades with high contributions are sharpened in the fuzzy set $\overline{r}_A^{h,\alpha}$ to 1. Vague concepts "low" and "high" are specified by the thresholds β and α, respectively.

All definitions, propositions and lemmas in this section can be easily modified and used for characterization of LU-assessments of granules of the inverse fuzzy relation $R^{-1} \in \mathcal{F}(W \times V)$ induced by subsets from $\tilde{2}^W$ by pairs of fuzzy sets $(\underline{r}^{-1}, \overline{r}^{-1})$ defined on V.

3   Interval-Valued Assessments

In this section we focus on interval-valued assessments of granules of a fuzzy relation $R \in \mathcal{F}(V \times W)$ created by subsets of elements from $\tilde{2}^{V \times W}$. For an arbitrary pair of sets $(A, Z) \in \tilde{2}^V \times \tilde{2}^W$, the R-neighborhood of $A \times Z$ is a subset of R given by

$$R/(A \times Z) = (R/A) \cap (R^{-1}/Z). \tag{19}$$

We are interested in an evaluation of $R/(A \times Z)$ by a pair of coefficients from the unit interval. Analogously as an LU-assessment by a pair of fuzzy sets, a proper lower and upper evaluation by a pair of real numbers should satisfy some general properties similar to the properties listed in Definition 1.

Definition 3. *A mapping* $\rho : \tilde{2}^{V \times W} \times \mathcal{F}(V \times W) \to [0,1]^2$ *is called a proper interval-valued assessment of granules of fuzzy relations on* $V \times W$ *induced by non-empty subsets from* $V \times W$ *if for an arbitrary pair of sets* $(A, Z) \in \tilde{2}^V \times \tilde{2}^W$ *and* $R \in \mathcal{F}(V \times W)$

$$\rho(A \times Z, R) = (\underline{R}(A, Z), \overline{R}(A, Z)) \tag{20}$$

such that

P1) $\underline{R}(A, Z) \leq \overline{R}(A, Z)$,

P2) if $R(x, y) = 0$ for all $(x, y) \in A \times Z$ then $\underline{R}(A, Z) = \overline{R}(A, Z) = 0$,

P3) if $R(x, y) = 1$ for all $(x, y) \in A \times Z$ then $\overline{\overline{R}}(A, Z) = 1$,

P4) if for $S \in \mathcal{F}(V \times W)$ we have that $S(x, y) \leq R(x, y)$ for all $(x, y) \in A \times Z$ then $\underline{S}(A, Z) \leq \underline{R}(A, Z)$ and $\overline{S}(A, Z) \leq \overline{R}(A, Z)$.

The pair of coefficients $(\underline{R}(A, Z), \overline{R}(A, Z))$ is called an LU-coefficient associated with the granule $R/(A \times Z)$.

Coefficients $\underline{R}(A, Z)$ and $\overline{R}(A, Z)$ can be interpreted as a lower and an upper degree of the relationship of a set $A \in \tilde{2}^V$ to a set $Z \in \tilde{2}^W$, respectively.

Proposition 4. Consider $R \in \mathcal{F}(V \times W)$, $(A, Z) \in \tilde{2}^V \times \tilde{2}^W$ and aggregation functions h_1, h_2, g_1, g_2. Let the pair of fuzzy sets defined for all $y \in W$ by $(\underline{r}_A(y), \overline{r}_A(y)) = (h_1(r_y^{-1}(x), x \in A), h_2(r_y^{-1}(x), x \in A))$ be an LU-assessment of R/A and the pair of fuzzy sets defined for all $x \in V$ by $(\underline{r}_Z^{-1}(x), \overline{r}_Z^{-1}(x)) = (g_1(r_x(y), y \in Z), g_2(r_x(y), y \in Z))$ be an LU-assessment of R^{-1}/Z. Then the pair of coefficients $(\underline{R}(A, Z), \overline{R}(A, Z))$ such that

$$\underline{R}(A, Z) = g_1(\underline{r}_A(y), y \in Z), \tag{21}$$

$$\overline{R}(A, Z) = g_2(\overline{r}_A(y), y \in Z) \tag{22}$$

is a proper interval-valued assessment of $R/(A \times Z)$. The pair of coefficients $(\underline{R}^{-1}(Z, A), \overline{R}^{-1}(Z, A))$ where

$$\underline{R}^{-1}(Z, A) = h_1(\underline{r}_Z^{-1}(x), x \in A), \tag{23}$$

$$\overline{R}^{-1}(Z, A) = h_2(\overline{r}_Z^{-1}(x), x \in A) \tag{24}$$

is a proper interval-valued assessment of $R^{-1}/(Z \times A)$.

Remark 2. In general, $\underline{R}(A, Z) \neq \underline{R}^{-1}(Z, A)$ and $\underline{R}(A, Z) \neq \underline{R}^{-1}(Z, A)$. Therefore, the relationship of A to Z is different from the relationship of Z to A. However, if in Proposition 4 we use $h_1 = g_1 = G_1$ and $h_2 = g_2 = G_2$, where G_1 and G_2 are associative aggregation functions, then $\underline{R}(A, Z) = \underline{R}^{-1}(Z, A)$ and $\overline{R}(A, Z) = \overline{R}^{-1}(Z, A)$.

Because $R/A = R/(A \times W)$ and $R^{-1}/Z = R^{-1}(Z \times V)$, granules R/A and R^{-1}/Z evaluated in Section 1 by LU-fuzzy sets can be also evaluated by LU-coefficients proposed in Definition 3.

Lemma 4. Let $R \in \mathcal{F}(V \times W)$, $A \in \tilde{2}^V$ and $\varphi(A, R) = (\underline{r}_A, \overline{r}_A)$ be a proper LU-assessment of R/A. Assume an aggregation function G. Then for all $Z \in \tilde{2}^W$, the coefficient $\rho(A \times Z, R) = (\underline{R}(A, Z), \overline{R}(A, Z))$ given by

$$\underline{R}(A, Z) = G(\underline{r}_A(y), y \in Z), \tag{25}$$

$$\overline{R}(A, Z) = G(\overline{r}_A(y), y \in Z) \tag{26}$$

is a proper interval-valued assessment of $R/(A \times Z)$.

Remark 3. When $(\underline{r}_A, \overline{r}_A) = (\underline{r}_A^\alpha, \overline{r}_A^\alpha)$, where $\underline{r}_A^\alpha, \overline{r}_A^\alpha$ are described in Proposition 2, and G is the arithmetic mean, then the coefficients $\underline{R}(A, Z), \overline{R}(A, Z)$ from Lemma 4 can be interpreted as the proportions of elements from Z which are strongly related and which are related to A at level α, respectively.

4   Assessments by Pairs of Fuzzy Relations

Let $\mathcal{P}(V)$ denote the family of all partitions of elements from V. Consider a partition $P = \{P_1, \ldots, P_k\} \in \mathcal{P}(V)$ and a partition $Q = \{Q_1, \ldots, Q_m\} \in \mathcal{P}(W)$, $k, m \in N$. Then the partition $P \times Q \in \mathcal{P}(V \times W)$ is created by clusters $P_i \times Q_j$, $i = 1, \ldots, k$, $j = 1, \ldots, m$ and the R-neighborhood of $P \times Q$ can be described by the granulation of R created by granules $R/(P_i \times Q_j)$. Hence

$$R\{P \times Q\} = \{R/(P_i \times Q_j) : P_i \in P, Q_j \in Q\}. \tag{27}$$

In this section we explore an evaluation of $R\{P \times Q\}$ by a pair of coarser fuzzy relations $(\underline{R}\{P \times Q\}, \overline{R}\{P \times Q\}) \in \mathcal{F}(U \times W)$. Proper lower and upper evaluations should satisfy some common properties similar to the properties listed in Definition 1 and Definition 3.

Definition 4. *A mapping* $\xi : \mathcal{P}(V \times W) \times \mathcal{F}(V \times W) \to \mathcal{F}(V \times W)$ *is called a proper LU-assessment of granulations of fuzzy relations on* $V \times W$ *induced by partitions of elements from* $V \times W$ *if for an arbitrary pair of partitions* $(P, Q) \in \mathcal{P}(V) \times \mathcal{P}(W)$, $P = \{P_1, \ldots, P_k\}, Q = \{Q_1, \ldots, Q_m\}, k, m \in N$ *and* $R \in \mathcal{F}$ $(V \times W)$

$$\xi(P \times Q, R) = (\underline{R}\{P \times Q\}, \overline{R}\{P \times Q\}) \tag{28}$$

such that for all $(x, y) \in V \times W, i = 1, \ldots, k, j = 1, \ldots, m$

P1) if $(x, y) \in P_i \times Q_j$ *then* $\underline{R}\{P \times Q\}(x, y) = \underline{R}_{ij} \le \overline{R}\{P \times Q\}(x, y) = \overline{R}_{ij}$,
P2) if $R(x, y) = 0$ *for all* $(x, y) \in P_i \times Q_j$ *then* $\underline{R}_{ij} = \overline{R}_{ij} = 0$,
P3) if $R(x, y) = 1$ *for all* $(x, y) \in P_i \times Q_j$ *then* $\overline{R}_{ij} = 1$,
P4) if for $S \in \mathcal{F}(V \times W)$ *we have that* $S(x, y) \le R(x, y)$ *for all* $(x, y) \in P_i \times Q_j$ *then* $\underline{S}_{ij} \le \underline{R}_{ij}$ *and* $\overline{S}_{ij} \le \overline{R}_{ij}$.

The pair of fuzzy relations $(\underline{R}\{P \times Q\}, \overline{R}\{P \times Q\})$ *is called an LU-fuzzy relation associated with the granulation* $R\{P \times Q\}$.

Proposition 5. *Assume* $R \in \mathcal{F}(V \times W)$. *Let* $\rho = (\underline{R}, \overline{R})$ *be a proper interval-valued assessment of granules of* R *created by subsets from* $V \times W$. *Then for* $P = \{P_1, \ldots, P_k\} \in \mathcal{P}(V)$ *and* $Q = \{Q_1, \ldots, Q_m\} \in \mathcal{P}(W), k, m \in N$ *the pair of fuzzy relations on* $V \times W$

$$\xi(P \times Q, R) = (\underline{R}\{P \times Q\}, \overline{R}\{P \times Q\})$$

defined for all $(x, y) \in P_i \times Q_j, i = 1, \ldots, k, j = 1, \ldots, m$ *by*

$$\underline{R}\{P \times Q\}(x, y) = \underline{R}(P_i, Q_j), \tag{29}$$
$$\overline{R}\{P \times Q\}(x, y) = \overline{R}(P_i, Q_j), \tag{30}$$

is an LU-fuzzy relation associated with the granulation $R\{P \times Q\}$.

Dubois and Prade defined in [4] rough fuzzy set associated with a partition $P \in \mathcal{P}(V)$ and a fuzzy set $f \in \mathcal{F}(V)$ as the pair $(\underline{f}, \overline{f})$ of fuzzy sets in the quotient space U/P such that for each $P_i \in P$

$$\underline{f}(P_i) = \min_{x \in P_i} f(x) \text{ and } \overline{f}(P_i) = \max_{x \in P_i} f(x). \tag{31}$$

Note that P induces a granulation (partition) of f. Fuzzy sets $f_*, f^* \in \mathcal{F}(V)$ defined for all $x \in V$ by

$$f_*(x) = \underline{f}(P_i) \text{ and } f^*(x) = \overline{f}(P_i) \text{ if } x \in P_i \tag{32}$$

are coarser versions of f. We say that f_* and f^* are lower and upper approximations of f with respect to P, respectively. Now we will extend the notion of a rough fuzzy set to the notion of a rough fuzzy relation.

Definition 5. *Let R be a fuzzy relation from U to W. Consider a partition $P = \{P_1, \ldots, P_k\}$ of U and a partition $Q = \{Q_1, \ldots, Q_m\}$ of W. Then the rough fuzzy relation associated with $P \times Q$ and R is defined as the pair $(R\underline{R}, R\overline{R})$ of fuzzy relations from U/P to W/Q such that for all $(P_i, Q_j) \in P \times Q$*

$$R\underline{R}(P_i, Q_j) = \min_{(x,y) \in P_i \times Q_j} R(x,y) \text{ and } R\overline{R}(P_i, Q_j) = \max_{(x,y) \in P_i \times Q_j} R(x,y). \tag{33}$$

Fuzzy relations $R_*, R^* \in \mathcal{F}(U \times W)$ defined for all $(x,y) \in U \times W$ by

$$R_*(x,y) = R\underline{R}(P_i, Q_j) \text{ if } (x,y) \in P_i \times Q_j \tag{34}$$

and

$$R^*(x,y) = R\overline{R}(P_i, Q_j) \text{ if } (x,y) \in P_i \times Q_j \tag{35}$$

are coarser versions of R. We say that R_* and R^* are the lower and the upper approximations of R with respect to $P \times Q$. Clearly, the pair of fuzzy relations (R_*, R^*) is an LU-fuzzy relation associated with granulation $R\{P \times Q\}$. Using LU-fuzzy relations, we can generalize rough fuzzy relations as follows.

Definition 6. *Let R be a fuzzy relation from U to W. Consider a partition $P = \{P_1, \ldots, P_k\}$ of U, a partition $Q = \{Q_1, \ldots, Q_m\}$ of W and an LU-fuzzy relation $\xi = (\underline{R}\{P \times Q\}, \overline{R}\{P \times Q\})$ such that for all $i = 1, \ldots k$ and $j = 1, \ldots, m$: if $(x,y) \in P_i \times Q_j$ then $\underline{R}\{P \times Q\}(x,y) = \underline{R}_{ij}$ and $\overline{R}\{P \times Q\}(x,y) = \overline{R}_{ij}$. Then the generalized rough fuzzy relation associated with $P \times Q$, R and ξ is defined as the pair $(R\underline{R}, R\overline{R})$ of fuzzy relations from U/P to W/Q such that for all $(P_i, Q_j) \in P \times Q$*

$$R\underline{R}(P_i, Q_j) = \underline{R}_{ij} \text{ and } R\overline{R}(P_i, Q_j) = \overline{R}_{ij}. \tag{36}$$

Remark 4. When for all $(x,y) \in P_i \times Q_j$, $i = 1, \ldots k$ and $j = 1, \ldots, m$

$$R\underline{R}(P_i, Q_j) \leq R(x,y) \leq R\overline{R}(P_i, Q_j),$$

the generalized rough fuzzy relation from Definition 6 can be used as a coarser approximation of the granulation of R created by $P \times Q$.

5 Conclusion

We provided a theoretical background and some examples of soft evaluations of granules and granulations of fuzzy relations between two universes by lower and upper assessments (LU-assessments). When the goal of an evaluation is an approximation, various LU- assessments based on rough set theory can be used. More about the relationship between rough sets and LU-fuzzy sets and some applications of LU-assessments in decision making under uncertainty will be presented in our future work.

Acknowledgments. The work of Martin Kalina was supported by the Science and Technology Assistance Agency under the contract No. APVV-0073-10 and by the grant agency VEGA, grant number 1/0143/11.

References

1. Bodjanova, S., Kalina, M.: Gradual Evaluation of Granules of a Fuzzy Relation: R-related Sets. In: Hüllermeier, E., Kruse, R., Hoffmann, F. (eds.) IPMU 2010. CCIS, vol. 80, pp. 268–277. Springer, Heidelberg (2010)
2. Calvo, T., Kolesarova, A., Komornikova, M., Mesiar, R.: Aggregation Operators: Properties, Classes and Construction Methods. In: Calvo, T., Mayor, G., Mesiar, R. (eds.) Aggregation Operators. New Trends and Applications, pp. 3–104. Physica-Verlag, Heidelberg (2002)
3. Dubois, D., Prade, H. (eds.): Fundamentals of Fuzzy Sets. Kluwer, Dordrecht (2000)
4. Dubois, D., Prade, H.: Rough Fuzzy Sets and Fuzzy Rough Sets. International Journal of Generalized System 17, 191–209 (1990)
5. Dubois, D., Prade, H.: Upper and Lower Images of a Fuzzy Set Induced by a Fuzzy Relation: Applications to Fuzzy Inference and Diagnosis. Information Sciences 64, 203–232 (1992)
6. Klement, E.P., Mesiar, R., Pap, E.: Triangular Norms. Kluwer Academic Publishers, Dordrech (2000)
7. Li, T.-J., Zhang, W.-X.: Rough-Fuzzy Approximations on Two Universes of Discourse. Information Sciences 178, 892–906 (2008)
8. Li, T.-J.: Rough Approximation Operators on Two Universes of Discourse and Their Fuzzy Extensions. Fuzzy Sets and Systems 159, 3033–3050 (2008)
9. Pawlak, Z.: Rough Sets. International Journal of Computer and Information Sciences 11, 341–356 (1982)
10. Pedrycz, W.: Shadowed Sets: Representing and Processing Fuzzy Sets. IEEE Transactions on Systems, Man, and Cybernetics–Part B: Cybernetics 28, 103–109 (1998)
11. Peters, J.F.: Near Sets. General Theory about Nearness of Objects. Applied Mathematical Sciences 1(53), 2609–2629 (2007)
12. Yao, Y.Y., Wong, S.K.M., Lin, T.Y.: A Review of Rough Sets Models. In: Lin, T.Y., Cercone, N. (eds.) Rough Sets in Data Mining: Analysis for Imprecise Data, pp. 47–75. Kluwer, Boston (1997)

Qualitative Integrals and Desintegrals: How to Handle Positive and Negative Scales in Evaluation

Didier Dubois[1], Henri Prade[1], and Agnès Rico[2]

[1] IRIT, CNRS and Université de Toulouse, France
{dubois,prade}@irit.fr
[2] ERIC, Université de Lyon, France
agnes.rico@univ-lyon1.fr

Abstract. Integrals are currently used in multiple criteria analysis for synthesizing into a global evaluation the *advantages* possessed by a potential choice. As such, integrals are operators that increase with the criteria evaluations. However, an item may be also evaluated in terms of its *defects*. Then the more and the greater the defects, the smaller the evaluation should be. An operator that can provide a synthesis of the defects of an item in this sense is called a *desintegral*. Desintegrals are maximal when *no* defects at all are present, while integrals are maximal when *all* advantages are sufficiently present. So, the greater the value of an integral, or a desintegral, the better the corresponding item since advantages are greater, or defects are smaller respectively. Desintegrals implicitly refer to a negative scale, since an order-reversing mapping of the scale used for evaluating each criterion transforms the degree to which the value is advantageous into a degree to which it is disadvantageous, and conversely. In this paper, we provide an organised description of counterparts to Sugeno integrals that synthesize positive or negative evaluations in the qualitative framework of a totally ordered residuated lattice equipped with an involutive negation. We exploit three kinds of criteria weighting schemes that are allowed by this algebraic structure.

1 Introduction

Choquet integrals and Sugeno integrals are widely used in multiple criteria aggregation, respectively in quantitative and in qualitative settings [9]. Roughly speaking, quantitative integration amounts to cumulate elementary evaluations in order to build a global one, and any strict increase of these evaluations lead to a cumulative effect as expected. In the qualitative setting, Sugeno integrals rather provide a synthesis of the elementary evaluations, and are only increasing in a broad sense. Thus, using integrals, we start from the bottom / minimal value of any evaluation, say 0, and cumulate or synthesize elementary evaluations, which have thus a positive flavor, as contributions to the global evaluation.

Desintegration is the converse. We start with the top/ maximal evaluation, say 1, and each time a negative feature is reported, it contributes to diminish

S. Greco et al. (Eds.): IPMU 2012, Part III, CCIS 299, pp. 306–316, 2012.

the global evaluation. In the negative evaluation framework, we call the counter-part of a Sugeno integral a *desintegral*. With the idea of desintegrals, we try to model evaluations such that if an object has some properties, then its evaluation becomes worse. More generally, the better a feature is satisfied, the worse the global evaluation. So the features, properties or criteria have a negative flavor.

Moreover, the form of the aggregation operation is affected by the way the criteria weights modify the local evaluations, and the pessimistic or optimistic nature of the evaluation. So there may exist variants of qualitative aggregation techniques that differ from Sugeno integrals not only due the polarity of the involved scales, but also in the handling of the importance weights.

The paper is structured as follows. The next section is devoted to the descrip-tion of the considered landscape of aggregation operations, and their motivations. Section 3 focuses on the properties of one example of residuated implication-based counterpart of Sugeno integrals, that combines qualitative ratings in neg-ative scales and construct a gobal rating on a positive scale. In the conclusion we mention some open problems and briefly discuss the joint use of Sugeno integrals and the Sugeno desintegrals when some criteria have a positive flavor and others have a negative flavor.

2   General Setting and Motivation

In a bipolar evaluation framework one may handle reasons in favor of an alterna-tive and reasons against it. In most situations, criteria are evaluated on positive scales and the resulting aggregation is also valued on a positive scale. Namely assuming this scale is the unit interval, the bottom 0 is viewed as worse than the top 1 and the aggregation is monotonically increasing. However one may consider aggregating negative criteria, that is, features that are to be explicitly avoided. In that case the local evaluation scales are negative (0 is better than 1), and if the global scale is a positive one, the aggregation operation needs to be monotonically decreasing. The more fulfilled are the negative features, the smaller is the global evaluation.

2.1   Algebraic Framework

Let us consider a set of criteria $C = \{C_1, \ldots, C_n\}$. Some objects or acts are evaluated according to the criteria. The evaluation scale associated to each cri-terion is a totally ordered scale L, for instance a finite one or $[0, 1]$. In such a context an object is viewed as a function f from C to L, encoded as a vector $(f_1, \ldots, f_n) \in [0, 1]^n$. f_i is the evaluation of f according to the criterion C_i.

We consider L as a Heyting algebra, i.e., a complete residuated lattice with top 1 and bottom 0. More precisely, $< L, \wedge, \vee, \rightarrow, 0, 1 >$ is a complete lattice. Of course, $< L, \wedge, 1 >$ is a commutative monoid (i.e $\wedge$ is associative, commutative and for all $a \in L$ $a \wedge 1 = a$). The operator $\rightarrow$ called the residuum is such that $(a \rightarrow b) \wedge a \leq b$, and moreover $a \rightarrow b = \sup\{c : a \wedge c \leq b\}$. In such a case $\rightarrow$ is Gödel implication. Let us present some basic properties of residuated lattices useful in the sequel: For all $a, b, c \in L$,

- $a \leq b$ if and only if $a \rightarrow b = 1$;
- $a \rightarrow a = 1$, $a \rightarrow 1 = 1$, $0 \rightarrow a = 1$, $1 \rightarrow a = a$;
- $a \leq b$ entails $c \rightarrow a \leq c \rightarrow b$ and $b \rightarrow c \leq a \rightarrow c$.

The adjointness property reads: $a \leq b \rightarrow c$ if and only if $a \wedge b \leq c$. Moreover as L is a totally ordered set the prelinearity property: for all a, b, $(a \rightarrow b) \vee (b \rightarrow a) = 1$ is always satisfied.

In order to handle the polarity of the evaluation scale, we also need an order-reversing operation on L, denoted by $1 - \cdot$, that is decreasing and involutive (a Kleene negation). If L is a positive scale (1 means good, 0 means bad), then $\{1 - a : a \in L\}$ is a negative scale (1 means bad, 0 means good). On a complete residuated lattice, a negation is defined by $\neg a = a \rightarrow 0$ such that $\neg a = 1$ if $a = 0$ and 0 otherwise, hence not involutive. This intuitionistic negation clearly differs from the Kleene negation.

Overall the structure $< L, \wedge, \vee, \rightarrow, 1 - \cdot, 0, 1 >$ is a complete De Morgan residuated lattice, since $< L, \wedge, \vee, 1 - \cdot, 0, 1 >$ is a De Morgan algebra. We consider such a framework because of its qualitative nature that fits the requirements of Sugeno integral.

2.2   Aggregation and Scale Polarity

Due to the polarity of the evaluation scales, there are 4 cases to be considered for an aggregation operation $L_1 \times ... \times L_n \mapsto L$:

1. Scales L_i and L are positive (satisfaction).
2. Scales L_i are negative (dissatisfaction) and L is positive (satisfaction).
3. Scales L_i are positive (satisfaction) and L is negative (dissatisfaction).
4. Scales L_i and L are negative (dissatisfaction).

In the first case of positive scales, there are two elementary qualitative aggregation schemes that make sense: $\wedge_{i=1}^n f_i$ if one is very demanding, and $\vee_{i=1}^n f_i$ if one fulfilled criterion is enough.

In the second case where negative ratings are merged on a positive scale, the value x_i is all the greater as the evaluation is bad, and the global score is all the greater as the resulting evaluation is better. The counterpart of these two elementary aggregations can be handled by first reversing the negative scales and then aggregating the results as previously, or on the contrary aggregating the negative scores and reversing the global result:

- The demanding case reads: $\wedge_{i=1}^n (1 - f_i) = 1 - \vee_{i=1}^n f_i$
- The loose global evaluation reads $\vee_{i=1}^n (1 - f_i) = 1 - \wedge_{i=1}^n f_i$

Note that when aggregating negative scores $\vee$ is demanding while $\wedge$ is loose. Then, the aggregation operation is monotonically decreasing. The two other cases can be discussed likewise. We now successively examine qualitative weighted aggregations in cases 1 and 2, with positive and then negative input scales. In both cases, the global evaluation lies in a positive scale.

2.3   Three Qualitative Weighted Aggregations for Positive Scales

Let π_i be the importance level of criterion i, valued on a positive scale. Namely, π_i is all the greater as criterion i is important. These levels are not used in the same way in a loose or a demanding aggregation. Moreover they may alter the local evaluations f_i in at least three manners.

Saturation Levels. The most well-known cases for positive criteria are when the importance weights act as saturation levels. The corresponding prioritized aggregation schemes are of the form $SLMAX_\pi(f) = \vee_{i=1}^n \pi_i \wedge f_i$ (prioritized maximum) and $SLMIN_\pi(f) = \wedge_{i=1}^n (1-\pi_i) \vee f_i$ (prioritized minimum). They are special cases of Sugeno integral, where the weights $\mu(A)$ generalize importance weights π_i to groups of criteria $A \subseteq C$. The fuzzy measure $\mu : 2^C \to [0,1]$ is an increasing set function such that $\mu(\emptyset) = 0$ and $\mu(C) = 1$, as larger groups of criteria are more important than smaller ones. The Sugeno integral of f with respect to μ is denoted by $\smallint_\mu (f) = \vee_{A \subseteq C} \mu(A) \wedge \wedge_{i \in A} f_i$ [1] If all local evaluations f_i equal a constant a then $\smallint_\mu (f) = a$. The prioritized maximum and prioritised minimum are recovered if μ is a possibility or a necessity measure respectively.

Softening Thresholds. Another approach to the weights π_i is to consider them as softeners that make local evaluations less demanding. One may for instance, consider that $f_i \geq \pi_i$ is enough to reach full satisfaction. Otherwise one sticks to evaluation f_i. More precisely, such a modified satisfaction is computed with the Gödel implication: $\pi_i \to f_i$ where $x \to y = \begin{cases} 1 \text{ if } x \leq y \\ y \text{ otherwise} \end{cases}$. Note that $\pi_i = 0$ represents such a high tolerance as to consider the criterion to be ever fulfilled. This thresholding scheme is easily applied to the demanding aggregation in the form $STMIN_\pi(f) = \wedge_{i=1}^n \pi_i \to f_i$. Note that in the previous prioritization scheme $SLMAX_\pi(f) = 1 - SLMIN_\pi(1 - f)$. Preserving this connection leads to define the loose counterpart of the $STMIN_\pi$ connective as

$STMAX_\pi(f) = \vee_{i=1}^n \pi_i \star f_i$ where $x \star y = 1 - x \to (1 - y) = \begin{cases} 0 \text{ if } x \leq 1 - y \\ y \text{ otherwise} \end{cases}$.

This non commutative conjunction was introduced in [4]. In the more general case of weighting groups of criteria by means of a monotonic increasing set-function μ, a residuated implication-based counterpart of a Sugeno integral is of the form

$$\oint_\mu^\uparrow (f) = \wedge_{A \subseteq C} \mu(A) \to \vee_{i \in A} f_i.$$

Proposition 1. *If μ is a possibility measure, then $\oint_\mu^\uparrow (f) = STMIN_\pi(f)$.*

---

[1] This notation whereby the capacity appears as a subscript is unusual for integrals. It is conveniently concise for this paper where the domain plays no particular role.

Proof. Suppose $\mu = \Pi$ based on the possibility degrees π_i. It is obvious that $\oint_{\Pi}^{\uparrow}(f) \leq STMIN_\pi(f)$ as the former considers the infimum over many more situations. Now let A be a set such that $\oint_{\Pi}^{\uparrow}(f) = \max_{j \in A} \pi_j \rightarrow \vee_{i \in A} f_i$. Let k, ℓ such that $\oint_{\Pi}^{\uparrow}(f) = \pi_k \rightarrow f_\ell$. If $\pi_k \rightarrow f_\ell = 1$, then $\oint_{\Pi}^{\uparrow}(f) \geq STMIN_\pi(f)$ is obvious. Otherwise $\pi_k \rightarrow f_\ell < 1$. But by construction $f_\ell \geq f_k$. Hence $\oint_{\Pi}^{\uparrow}(f) = f_\ell \geq \pi_k \rightarrow f_k \geq STMIN_\pi(f)$. QED.

The extension of the $STMAX_\pi$ aggregation is $\oint_{\mu}^{r\star}(f) = \vee_{A \subseteq \mathcal{C}} \mu(A) \star \wedge_{i \in A} f_i$.

Drastic Thresholdings. Note that $STMIN_\pi(f)$ cannot be considered as a proper generalization to fuzzy events of a necessity measure, since when the f_i's belong to $\{0, 1\}$, we do not get $STMIN_\pi(f) = N(A) = \min_{i \notin A}(1 - \pi_i)$ for $A = \{i | f_i = 1\}$. It is known [5] that the natural extension of necessity measures to fuzzy events based on Gödel implication is $DTMIN_\pi(f) = \min_i(1 - f_i) \rightarrow (1 - \pi_i)$. The effect of the weight π_i on the rating f_i is as follows: if $f_i \geq \pi_i$, the rating becomes maximal, i.e. 1, otherwise it is always turned into $1 - \pi_i$. Two remarks are worth stating. First, the local rating scale reduces to the binary scale $\{1 - \pi_i, 1\}$. Second, if π_i is high, the local rating is drastically downgraded to $1 - \pi_i$. The loose counterpart of the $DTMIN_\pi$ connective is $DTMAX_\pi(f) = \vee_{i=1}^{n} f_i \star \pi_i$ where $\star$ is the same non-commutative conjunction as above. The extension of the $DTMIN_\pi$ aggregation to weighting groups of criteria is of the form (where $\overline{A}$ is the complement of A)

$$\oint_{\mu}^{\Uparrow}(f) = \wedge_{A \subseteq \mathcal{C}}\left(\wedge_{i \in A}(1 - f_i) \rightarrow \mu(\overline{A})\right).$$

Proposition 2. *if μ is a necessity measure based on π, then $\oint_{\mu}^{\Uparrow}(f) = DTMIN_\pi(f)$.*

The extension of the $DTMAX_\pi$ aggregation is $\oint_{\mu}^{l\star}(f) = \vee_{A \subseteq \mathcal{C}} \wedge_{i \in A} f_i \star \mu(A)$.

2.4   Three Qualitative Weighting Methods for Negative Scales

Let us turn to the case where we rate local features on negative scales and get a global evaluation on a positive scale. Under this convention, a value t_i acts as a tolerance or permissiveness level on a negative scale: the higher t_i, the less important criterion i. Then the threshold scheme for negative criteria goes as follows: the tolerance level t_i now serves to turn negative flexible ratings (f_i now represents a degree of defect or violation, where the greater f_i, the worse the rating) into positive ones that are further aggregated on a positive scale. There are again three qualitative aggregation schemes that reflect the three cases encountered in the positive case. They are called *desintegrals* since they will involve decreasing set functions ν, called a fuzzy *antimeasure*: It is a decreasing set function $\nu : 2^{\mathcal{C}} \rightarrow [0, 1]$ such that $\nu(\emptyset) = 1$ and $\nu(\mathcal{C}) = 0$.

Saturation Levels. The result of applying tolerance t_i to the negative rating f_i results in a positive rating that cannot be below t_i. Moreover the local rating scale is reversed, which leads to a local positive rating $(1-f_i) \vee t_i$. The corresponding demanding aggregation scheme is $SLMIN_t^{neg}(f) = \wedge_{i=1}^{n}(1 - f_i) \vee t_i$, while the loose one is of the form $SLMAX_t^{neg}(f) = \vee_{i=1}^{n}(1 - t_i) \wedge (1 - f_i)$. Note that $SLMIN_t^{neg}(f) = SLMIN_{1-\pi}(1-f)$ and $SLMAX_t^{neg}(f) = SLMAX_{1-\pi}(1-f)$. The corresponding extension of $SLMAX_t^{neg}$ based on a monotonically decreasing function ν to the weighting of groups of defects is given by the expression

$$\oint_{\nu}^{\downarrow}(f) = \vee_{A \subseteq C}(\nu(\overline{A}) \wedge \wedge_{i \in A}(1 - f_i))$$

where we recognize the formal Sugeno integral $\oint_{\nu(\cdot)}(1 - f)$. Morover $\oint_{\nu}^{\downarrow}(f) = SLMAX_t^{neg}(f)$ if $\nu(A) = \max_{i \in \overline{A}}(1 - t_i)$.

Softening Thresholds. Here t_i is viewed as a tolerance threshold such that it is enough to have $f_i \leq t_i$ (i.e. the defect rating remains smaller than the threshold) for the requirement to be totally fulfilled. Recall that now the requirement is to avoid defects. If the object possesses the defect to an extent higher than t_i, then the rating value is reversed, leading to a poor positive local rating. This weighting scheme is captured by the formula $(1 - t_i) \rightarrow (1 - f_i)$ where $\rightarrow$ is Gödel implication. This thresholding scheme is easily applied to the demanding aggregation in the form $STMIN_t^{neg}(f) = \wedge_{i=1}^{n}(1 - t_i) \rightarrow (1 - f_i)$. We can define the loose counterpart of the $STMIN_t^{neg}$ connective as $STMAX_t^{neg}(f) = \vee_{i=1}^{n}(1 - t_i) \star (1 - f_i)$ using the non commutative conjunction introduced before. In the more general case of weighting groups of defects by means of a monotonic decreasing set-function ν, a residuated implication-based desintegral that generalizes $STMIN_t^{neg}$ is of the form

$$\oint_{\nu}^{\downarrow}(f) = \wedge_{A \subseteq C}((1 - \nu(A)) \rightarrow \vee_{i \in A}(1 - f_i)).$$

It is easy to check that $\oint_{\nu}^{\downarrow}(f) = \oint_{1-\nu}^{\uparrow}(1 - f)$.

Proposition 3. If $\nu(A) = \Delta(A) = \wedge_{i \in A} t_i$, then $\oint_{\nu}^{\downarrow}(f) = STMIN_t^{neg}(f)$.

The antimeasure Δ is known as a guaranteed possibility measure [5]. Moreover, the corresponding extension of $STMAX_t^{neg}$ is the desintegral
$$\oint_{1-\nu}^{r\star}(1 - f) = \vee_{A \subseteq C}((1 - \nu(A)) \star \wedge_{i \in A}(1 - f_i)).$$

Drastic Thresholdings. The last weighting scheme can be described as follows. If $f_i > t_i$ then the local rating is considered bad and the (positive) result is downgraded to t_i. If $f_i \leq t_i$ then the local rating is fine and the (positive) result is 1. It corresponds again to using Gödel implication and now computing $f_i \rightarrow t_i$. Note that $t_i = 0$ means complete intolerance with respect to the slightest possession of defect i. Demanding that no bad feature be satisfied leads to a demanding aggregation of positive ratings $f_i \leq t_i$. This is $DTMIN_t^{neg}(f) = \wedge_{i=1}^n f_i \rightarrow t_i$, that is a guaranteed possibility function Δ applied to fuzzy event f [5]. Note that the local negative rating scale is changed into a binary positive scale $\{t_i, 1\}$. The loose counterpart of $DTMIN_t^{neg}$ is $DTMAX_t^{neg} = \vee_{i=1}^n (1 - f_i) \star (1 - t_i)$. The extension of the $DTMIN_t^{neg}$ aggregation to tolerance levels attached to groups of defects corresponds to the following desintegral with respect to antimeasure ν is given by

$$\oint_\nu^\Downarrow (f) = \wedge_{A \subseteq C} \wedge_{i \in A} f_i \rightarrow \nu(A),$$

with the following convention: $\wedge_{i \in \emptyset} f_i = 0$ (otherwise, one must restrict the above expression to non-empty sets).

Proposition 4. If $\nu(A) = \Delta(A) = \wedge_{i \in A} t_i$, then $\oint_\nu^\Downarrow (f) = DTMIN_t^{neg}(f)$.

Proof. According to the definitions we have $\oint_\nu^\Downarrow (f) \leq DTMIN_t^{neg}(f)$, so let us prove that $DTMIN_t^{neg}(f) \leq \oint_\nu^\Downarrow (f)$. Let A^* be the set associated to the minimum in the definition of $\oint_\nu^\Downarrow (f)$, i.e., $\oint_\nu^\Downarrow (f) = \wedge_{i \in A^*} f_i \rightarrow \wedge_{i \in A^*} t_i$. The only possible values are 1 and $\wedge_{i \in A^*} t_i$. On both sides, we can have different criteria associated to the minimum. We denote them by j and k, i.e., $\oint_\nu^\Downarrow (f) = f_j \rightarrow t_k$. If $\oint_\nu^\Downarrow (f) = 1$, there is no difficulty. If $\oint_\nu^\Downarrow (f) < 1$, then $f_j > t_k$. As $f_j = \wedge_{x \in A^*} f_i$ we have $f_k \geq f_j > t_k$. So $f_j \rightarrow t_k = f_k \rightarrow t_k \geq \inf_{i \in C} (f_i \rightarrow t_i)$. So $\oint_\nu^\Downarrow (f) \geq DTMIN_t^{neg}(f)$.

The extension of $DTMAX_t^{neg}$ is $\oint_\nu^{l\star}(1 - f) = \vee_{A \subseteq C} \wedge_{i \in A} (1 - f_i) \star \nu(A)$.

The above survey can be summarized using the following terminology: we call (qualitative) *integral* (resp. *desintegral*) a weighted aggregation operation that is *increasing* (resp. *decreasing*) with respect to the local ratings. We call an integral or a desintegral *conjunction-based* (resp. *implication-based*) when it takes the form of a maximum (resp. minimum) of the conjunction of (resp. implication between) weights and ratings. We call an integral or a desintegral *drastic* (resp. *soft*) when the result can only belong to the set of weights, making the local rating scale binary (resp. when the result belongs to the original rating scale or its reverse). In the following we more particularly study drastic desintegrals with respect to general set-functions. Indeed, one may find situations where the weighting function is nonmonotonic. For instance, if good objects are those that possess exactly k properties out of $n > k$.

3   Properties of the Drastic Desintegrals

In this section, we consider, as an example, the properties of drastic desintegrals $\oint_\sigma^\Downarrow (f)$, where $\sigma : 2^C \rightarrow [0, 1]$ is a general set-function. The name desintegral is justified by the following

Proposition 5. If $f \leq g$ then $\oint_\sigma^\Downarrow (g) \leq \oint_\sigma^\Downarrow (f)$.

The Sugeno integral $\oint_\mu$ with respect to a fuzzy measure μ is an aggregation function satisfying the following properties.

Proposition 6. *For all functions f, g and for all a in $[0, 1]$,*
$$\oint_\mu(f \wedge g) \leq \oint_\mu(f) \wedge \oint_\mu(g), \quad \oint_\mu(f \vee g) \geq \oint_\mu(f) \vee \oint_\mu(g)$$
$$\oint_\mu(a \wedge f) = a \wedge \oint_\mu(f), \quad \oint_\mu(a \rightarrow f) \leq a \rightarrow \oint_\mu(f).$$

As may be expected the drastic desintegrals satisfy similar but opposite properties. More precisely the following result, proved in [6] for an MV-algebra with an antimeasure, is still satisfied in our context.

Proposition 7. *For all functions f, g and for all a in $[0, 1]$,*
$$\oint_\sigma^\Downarrow(f \wedge g) \geq \oint_\sigma^\Downarrow(f) \vee \oint_\sigma^\Downarrow(g), \quad \oint_\sigma^\Downarrow(f \vee g) \leq \oint_\sigma^\Downarrow(f) \wedge \oint_\sigma^\Downarrow(g)$$
$$\oint_\sigma^\Downarrow(a \wedge f) \leq a \rightarrow \oint_\sigma^\Downarrow(f), \quad \oint_\sigma^\Downarrow(a \rightarrow f) \geq a \wedge \oint_\sigma^\Downarrow(f).$$

In order to use the drastic desintegrals we need to understand how the set functions used can be interpreted.

Proposition 8. *For all $A \subseteq \mathcal{A}$, $\sigma(A)$ represents an upper bound of the global satisfaction rating that an object can receive with a drastic desintegral if it satisfies all properties in the group A to a degree higher than $\sigma(A)$.*

Proof. Since the hypothesis implies $\wedge_{C_i \in A} f_i > \sigma(A)$, $\wedge_{C_i \in A} f_i \rightarrow \sigma(A) = \sigma(A)$, which entails $\oint_\sigma^\Downarrow(f) \leq \wedge_{C_i \in A} f_i \rightarrow \sigma(A)$.

Example 1. We consider three criteria C_1, C_2, C_3. We want to select objects that satisfy only C_1, only C_2 or only C_3. We consider σ defined as follows $\sigma(C_1) = \sigma(C_2) = \sigma(C_3) = 1$; σ is 0 otherwise.

Let us compute $\oint_\sigma^\Downarrow(1, 0, 0)$: If $A \neq \{C_1\}$ then $\wedge_{C_i \in A} f_i = 0$ and $\wedge_{C_i \in A} f_i \rightarrow \sigma(A) = 1$. If $A = \{C_1\}$ then $\wedge_{C_i \in A} f_i \rightarrow \sigma(A) = 1 \rightarrow 1 = 1$. So we have $\oint_\sigma^\Downarrow(1, 0, 0) = 1$. Similarly we have $\oint_\sigma^\Downarrow(0, 1, 0) = \oint_\sigma^\Downarrow(0, 0, 1) = 1$.

Let us compute $\oint_\sigma^\Downarrow(1, 1, 0)$: If $A = \{C_1, C_2\}$ then $\wedge_{C_i \in A} f_i = 1$ and $\wedge_{C_i \in A} f_i \rightarrow \sigma(A) = 1 \rightarrow 0 = 0$. So we have $\oint_\sigma^\Downarrow(1, 1, 0) = 0$. Similarly we have $\oint_\sigma^\Downarrow(1, 0, 1) = \oint_\sigma^\Downarrow(0, 1, 1) = \oint_\sigma^\Downarrow(0, 1, 1) = 0$.

In the above example, if we consider σ such that $\sigma(C_1) = \sigma(C_2) = \sigma(C_3) = 0.5$ and σ is 0 otherwise then $\oint_\sigma^\Downarrow(1, 0, 0) = \oint_\sigma^\Downarrow(0, 1, 0) = \oint_\sigma^\Downarrow(0, 0, 1) = 0.5$. Also we have $\oint_\sigma^\Downarrow(1, 1, 0) = \oint_\sigma^\Downarrow(1, 0, 1) = \oint_\sigma^\Downarrow(0, 1, 1) = 0$.

The global evaluation of an object calculated with a drastic desintegral, belongs to the interval $[0, 1]$. In order to interpret the obtained result, for example in order to select objects, we need to identify the objects that obtain the best evaluation and those that receive the worst one.

Proposition 9. $\oint_\sigma^\Downarrow(f) = 1$ *if and only if $\forall A$, $\exists C_i \in A$ such that $f_i \leq \sigma(A)$.*
$\oint_\sigma^\Downarrow(f) = 0$ *if and only if $\exists A$ such that $\sigma(A) = 0$ and $\forall C_i \in A$, $f_i > 0$.*

Proof. $\oint_\sigma^\Downarrow(f) = 1$ if and only if $\forall A$, $\wedge_{C_i \in A} f_i \to \sigma(A) = 1$ i.e. $\forall A$, $\wedge_{C_i \in A} f_i \leq \sigma(A)$, which is equivalent to $\exists C_i \in A$ such that $f_i \leq \sigma(A)$. $\oint_\sigma^\Downarrow(f) = 0$ if and only if $\exists A$ such that $\wedge_{C_i \in A} f_i \to \sigma(A) = 0$, i.e, $\sigma(A) = 0$ and $\wedge_{C_i \in A} f_i > 0$.

We conclude this section with mathematical properties classically studied for aggregation functions.

Proposition 10. $\oint_\sigma^\Downarrow(0,\ldots,0) = 1$, $\oint_\sigma^\Downarrow(1,\ldots,1) = \wedge_{A \subseteq C} \sigma(A)$,
$\oint_\sigma^\Downarrow(c,\ldots,c) = \wedge_{\{A|\sigma(A)<c\}} \sigma(A)$, *(with convention* $\wedge_{A \in \emptyset} \sigma(A) = 1$*)*.
$\oint_\sigma^\Downarrow(1_A) = \wedge_{B \subseteq A} \sigma(B)$ *(we denote the characteristic function of A by 1_A).*

Proof. $\oint_\sigma^\Downarrow(0,\ldots,0) = \wedge_{A \subseteq C} 0 \to \sigma(A) = 1$, $\oint_\sigma^\Downarrow(1,\ldots,1) = \wedge_{A \subseteq C} 1 \to \sigma(A) = \wedge_{A \subseteq C} \sigma(A)$. $\oint_\sigma^\Downarrow(c,\ldots,c) = \wedge_{A \subseteq C} c \to \sigma(A)$ where $c \to \sigma(A)$ is 1 if $c \leq \sigma(A)$ and is $\sigma(A)$ otherwise.
   If $B \nsubseteq A$ then $\wedge_{C_i \in B} 1_A \to \sigma(A) = 0 \to \sigma(A) = 1$.
   If $B \subseteq A$, then $\wedge_{C_i \in B} 1_A \to \sigma(B) = 1 \to \sigma(B) = \sigma(B)$.

If there exists A such that $\sigma(A) = 0$ then $\oint_\sigma^\Downarrow(1,\ldots,1) = \oint_\sigma^\Downarrow(c,\ldots,c) = 0$. More generally, if σ is a fuzzy antimeasure then $\oint_\sigma^\Downarrow(0,\ldots,0) = 1$, $\oint_\sigma^\Downarrow(1,\ldots,1) = \oint_\sigma^\Downarrow(c,\ldots,c) = 0$ and $\oint_\sigma^\Downarrow(1_A) = \sigma(A)$. Note that this particular case can be also proved using the results presented in [6].

4   Concluding Remarks

This paper outlines a framework for a class of general aggregation functions on a complete residuated, totally ordered set with an order-reversing negation. As some of them use residuated implications, they cannot be generated from standard Sugeno integrals and negation. A number of questions remain pending. For instance, Sugeno integral can be written in two equivalent ways as

$$\oint_\mu (x) = \vee_{A \subseteq C} \mu(A) \wedge \wedge_{i \in A} f_i = \wedge_{A \subseteq C} \mu(\overline{A}) \vee \vee_{i \in A} f_i.$$

In the right-hand side expression we can recognise a Kleene-Dienes implication-based qualitative integral ($a \rightarrowtail b = (1-a) \vee b$) with respect to the conjugate set-function $\overline{\mu}(A) = 1 - \mu(\overline{A})$. Hence the natural question is whether this type of identity remains valid on our qualitative structure, for Gödel implication, and the corresponding non-commutative conjunction. Besides, other algebraic frameworks are worth studying from this perspective, like MV-algebras [6].
   Another question is the simultaneous handling of positive and negative criteria for decision evaluation. Suppose the set of the criteria is divided into two parts: the set of positive criteria denoted $\mathcal{C}^+$ and the set of negative criteria denoted $\mathcal{C}^-$ where $\mathcal{C}^+ \cup \mathcal{C}^- = \mathcal{C}$ and $\mathcal{C}^+ \cap \mathcal{C}^- = \emptyset$. On $\mathcal{C}^+$, a fuzzy measure μ represents the satisfactory level needed to have a good evaluation. Hence the global evaluation with respect to the positive criteria can be calculated using for example the

Sugeno integral with respect to μ: $\oint_{\mu}$. On $\mathcal{C}^-$ an antimeasure ν, represents an upper bound of the global satisfaction level an object can receive if it satisfies all the properties with a level bigger than ν. Hence the global evaluation with respect to the negative criteria can be computed using for example the drastic desintegral with respect to ν: $\oint_{\nu}^{\Downarrow}$.

One may try to merge the positive evaluations obtained from a integral over positive criteria and a desintegral with respect to negative ones, or on the contrary handle them separately for making a final comparison of objects. We tend to favor a separate handling of positive and negative aspects, in contrast with other approaches like Cumulative Prospect Theory that are numerical, or the ones of Grabisch [8,7] that try to work with a single qualitative bipolar scale where available combination of positive and negative values look debatable. See also [10]. On the contrary, we are more in the spirit of bivariate bipolar approaches to evaluation such as the ones proposed by Bonnefon and colleagues [2,3]. However, their approach is restricted to Boolean valuation scales (all-or-nothing positive or negative criteria) and importance levels bear on single criteria. The framework presented in this paper opens the way to a generalization of qualitative bipolar decision evaluation to criteria with more refined value scales and generalized weightings of groups of criteria. Our bipolar approach is also somewhat similar to Atanassov "Intuitionistic Fuzzy Set" (AIFS) aggregation function theory[1], since it also handles pairs of positive and negative values. However, in the AIFS approach, a pair (μ, ν) of membership and non-membership values is such that $\mu + \nu \leq 1$ and is interpreted as an uncertainty gap of the form $[\mu, 1 - \nu]$, while in our view the positive and negative evaluations are to be considered as two independent precise evaluations to be used conjointly.

References

1. Beliakov, G., Bustince, H., Goswami, D.P., Mukherjee, U.K., Pal, N.R.: On averaging operators for Atanassov's intuitionistic fuzzy sets. Inf. Sci. 181(6), 1116–1124 (2011)
2. Bonnefon, J.-F., Dubois, D., Fargier, H., Leblois, S.: Qualitative heuristics for balancing the pros and the cons. Theory and Decision 65, 71–95 (2008)
3. Dubois, D., Fargier, H., Bonnefon, J.-F.: On the qualitative comparison of decisions having positive and negative features. J. of Artif. Intellig. Res. 32, 385–417 (2008)
4. Dubois, D., Prade, H.: A theorem on implication functions defined from triangular norms. Stochastica 8, 267–279 (1984)
5. Dubois, D., Prade, H.: Fuzzy rules in knowledge-based systems Modelling gradedness, uncertainty and preference. In: Yager, R.R., Zadeh, L.A. (eds.) An Introduction to Fuzzy Logic Applications in Intelligent Systems, pp. 45–68. Kluwer Acad. (1992)
6. Dvořák, A., Holčapek, M.: Fuzzy integrals over complete residuated lattices. In: Carvalho, J.P., Dubois, D., Kaymak, U., da Costa Sousa, J.M. (eds.) Proc. Joint 2009 Inter. Fuzzy Systems Association World Congress and 2009 Europ. Society of Fuzzy Logic and Technology Conf (ISFA-EUSFLAT), Lisbon, July 20-24, pp. 357–362 (2009)

7. Grabisch, M.: The Möbius transform on symmetric ordered structures and its application to capacities on finite sets. Discrete Mathematics 287(1-3), 17–34 (2004)
8. Grabisch, M.: The symmetric Sugeno integral. Fuzzy Sets Syst. 139, 473–490 (2003)
9. Grabisch, M., Labreuche, C.: A decade of application of the Choquet and Sugeno integrals in multi-criteria decision aid. Ann. Oper. Res. 175, 247–286 (2010)
10. Greco, S., Matarazzo, B., Slowinski, R.: Bipolar Sugeno and Choquet integrals. In: Proc. EUROFUSE Workshop on Informations Systems, Varenna, Italy, pp. 191–196 (September 2002)

Stability in Aggregation Operators

Daniel Gómez[1], Javier Montero[2], J. Tinguaro Rodríguez[2], and Karina Rojas[2]

[1] Escuela de Estadística. Complutense University, Madrid,
Av. Puerta de Hierro s/n 28050, Madrid, Spain
dagomez@estad.ucm.es
[2] Facultad de Ciencias Matematicas. Complutense University, Madrid,
Plz. Ciencias s/n 28050, Madrid, Spain
{monty,jtrodrig}@mat.ucm.es, krpatuelli@yahoo.com

Abstract. Aggregation functions have been widely studied in literature. Nevertheless, few efforts have been dedicated to analyze those properties related with the family of operators in a global way. In this work, we analyze the stability in a family of aggregation operators The stability property for a family of aggregation operators tries to force a family to have a stable/continuous definition in the sense that the aggregation of $n-1$ items should be similar to the aggregation of n items if the last item is the aggregation of the previous $n-1$ items. Following this idea some definitions and results are given.

1   Introduction

Many properties have been studied in relation with the aggregation operator functions such as continuity, commutativity, monotonicity, associativity (and a large etcetera) (see for example [1,4,5,6,7,8], among others). But in contrast, few efforts have been dedicated to research the relations among the members of a family of aggregation operators. As has been pointed recently [15], these common properties (as for example continuity) show us some desirable characteristics related with each aggregation function A_n, but do not give us any information about the consistency of the family of aggregation operators in the sense of the relations that should exist among its members.

In the context of aggregation operators, it is usually assumed that the information that has to be aggregated is given in terms of a vector of elements in the unit interval, assigning to each vector another number in the unit interval, which constitutes the aggregated value of the original information. Taking into account that, in practice, most of the time one cannot guarantee that the cardinal of the information is going to be fixed (some information can get lost or deleted due to errors in observation or transmission, or because sometimes one gets some additional information not previously taken into account), we need to be able to solve each aggregation problem without knowing a priori the cardinal of data.

Trying to eliminate the classical assumption that considers the aggregations functions as independent pieces of the aggregation process, we will define here the idea of stability in a family of aggregation functions $\{A_n\}$ (from now on

S. Greco et al. (Eds.): IPMU 2012, Part III, CCIS 299, pp. 317–325, 2012.
© Springer-Verlag Berlin Heidelberg 2012

FAO) breaking this idea of independence that usually is assumed. This is, the operators that compose a FAO have to be somehow related so the aggregation process remains *the same* throughout the dimension n of the data. For example, it would seem quite strange to propose an FAO using the minimum for $n = 2$, the arithmetic mean for $n = 3$, the geometric mean for $n = 4$ and the median for $n = 5$ (and though it could seem that a formal approach could solve this problem by demanding a conceptual unity through a mathematical formula, it should be noted that the last example allows a trivial compact mathematical formulation). Therefore, it seems logical to study properties giving sense to the sequences $A(2)$, $A(3)$, $A(4)$, ..., . Otherwise we may have only a bunch of disconnected operators.

2   Stability of a Family of Aggregation Operators

Aggregation implies not only the ability to aggregate an arbitrary finite number of information units, but also to make it following some general instruction. Such a general instruction can not be simply a formula depending on the number of items to be aggregated. With this aim, we have considered a property close to the continuity of functions in order to assure some robustness in the result of the aggregation process. Let $A_n(x_1, \ldots, x_n)$ be the aggregated value for the n-dimensional data $x_1, \ldots, x_n$. Now, let us suppose that a new element x_{n+1} has to be aggregated. If x_{n+1} is close to the aggregation result $A_n(x_1, \ldots, x_n)$ given by the n-dimensional data $x_1, \ldots, x_n$, then the result of aggregating the $n + 1$ elements should not differ too much with the result of aggregation of n items. Following the idea of stability for any mathematical tool, if $|x_{n+1} - A_n(x_1, \ldots, x_n)|$ is small, then $|A_{n+1}(x_1, \ldots, x_n, x_{n+1}) - A_n(x_1, \ldots, x_n)|$ should be also small. This idea is partially gathered in the $self - identity$ definition given in [17].

Definition 1. *(Yager 1997). Let $\{A_n : [0,1]^n \to [0,1], n \in N\}$ be a family of aggregation operators. Then, it is said that the family $\{A_n\}$ satisfies the self-identity property if, $\forall n \in N$ and $\forall x_1, \ldots x_n \in [0,1]$, the following holds:*

$$A_n(x_1, x_2, \ldots x_{n-1}, A_{n-1}(x_1, x_2 \ldots, x_{n-1})) = A_{n-1}(x_1, x_2, \ldots, x_{n-1}) \qquad (1)$$

Let us observe that self-identity is close to the stability idea in the sense that if the new item that has to be aggregated coincides with the aggregation value of the previous data, then the new result should not change. Nevertheless, in the self-identity definition it is implicitly imposed the fact that the information has to be aggregated in some order, specifically from left to right, so we have to put the last data in the $n - th$ position of the aggregation function.

Let us remark that if the aggregation operator is not symmetric (i.e. there exist a n for which the aggregation operator A_n is not symmetric), then the position of the new data is relevant in the final output of the aggregation process. For example, in the *backward inductive extension* $\{A_n^b, n \in N\}$ and *forward inductive extension* $\{A_n^f, n \in N\}$ (see [3] for more details) of any binary aggregation operator, defined for $n > 2$ as $A_n^b = L_2(x_1, L_2(\ldots, L_2(x_{n-1}, x_n)\ldots))$ for $n > 2$, and $A_n^f = L_2(\ldots, (L_2(L_2(x_1, x_2), x_3)), \ldots, x_n)$ *for* $n > 2$, where L_2 is a binary aggregation operator, i.e. $L_2 : [0,1]^2 \to [0,1]$.

It can be proved that the family of aggregation functions $\{A_n^f, n \in N\}$ satisfies the self identity property if L_2 is idempotent. But, the family $\{A_n^b, n \in N\}$ does not satisfy the self identity property since the order in which this family aggregate the information is inverse (i.e. from right to left). In our opinion, the family $A_n^b = L_2(x_1, L_2(\ldots, L_2(x_{n-1}, x_n)\ldots)$ *for* $n > 2$ should be consistent in the sense of stability when the information is aggregated from right to left . Taking into account this, we present the following definitions of stability, that extend the notion of self-identity both in the direction of allowing its application to non-symmetric operators.

Definition 2. *Let* $\{A_n : [0,1]^n \to [0,1], n \in N\}$ *be a family of aggregation operators. Then, it is said that* $\forall n \geq 3$ *and* $\forall \{x_n\}_{n \in N}$ *in* $[0,1]$:

1. *It fulfills the property of R-strict stability, if the following holds:*

$$A_n(x_1, x_2, \ldots x_{n-1}, A_{n-1}(x_1, x_2 \ldots, x_{n-1})) = A_{n-1}(x_1, x_2, \ldots, x_{n-1}) \qquad (2)$$

   A_n *will be called R-strictly stable family.*

2. *It fulfills the property of L-strict stability, if the following holds:*

$$A_n(A_{n-1}(x_1, x_2, \ldots, x_{n-1}), x_1, x_2, \ldots x_{n-1}) = A_{n-1}(x_1, x_2, \ldots, x_{n-1}) \qquad (3)$$

   A_n *will be called L-strictly stable family.*

3. *It fulfills the property of L-R strict stability if* A_n *satisfies the two points above, and it will be called L-R strict stable family.*

Let us observe that if A_n is symmetric, then the three previous definitions are equivalent and coincide with the self-identity property defined by Yager. Now, it is very easy to check that with any binary idempotent operator the inductive extension forward (A^f) satisfies the property of *R-strict stability*, and the inductive extension backward (A^b) satisfies the property of *L-strict stability*.

Although the previous definition presents a reasonable approach to the idea of consistency of a FAO (i.e., from the point of view of its stability), it is important to note that not all consistent families are included in this definition. Let us consider the example of the productory family of aggregation operators, defined as $\left\{ P_n(x_1, \ldots, x_n) = \prod_{i=1}^{n} (x_i), n \in N \right\}$. In our opinion, this family defines an aggregation process that can be considered as consistent, because the set of successions $\{x_n\}_{n \in N}$ in which the productory FAO fails to be stable has probability zero. But it does not satisfy any of the three previous definitions.

Therefore, in order to extend the proposed approach to other consistent $FAOs$, we propose the following two definitions, that express a relaxed version of the same stability concept: in the first one, stability is fulfilled in the limit, while in the second one, a weaker concept of stability is reached by demanding the operators to be, in the limit, almost sure stable.

Definition 3. *Let $\{A_n : [0,1]^n \to [0,1], n \in N\}$ be a family of aggregation operators. Then, it is said that $\forall n \geq 3$ and $\forall \{x_n\}_{n \in N}$ in $[0,1]$:*

1. *It fulfills the property of R-stability, if the following holds:*

$$\lim_{n \to +\infty} \left| A_n(x_1, ...x_{n-1}, A_{n-1}(x_1, ..., x_{n-1})) - A_{n-1}(x_1, ..., x_{n-1}) \right| = 0 \quad (4)$$

A_n will be called R-stable family.

2. *It fulfills the property of L-stability, if for all succession $\{x_n\}_{n \in N}$ in $[0,1]$, the following holds:*

$$\lim_{n \to +\infty} \left| A_n(A_{n-1}(x_1, ..., x_{n-1}), x_1, ...x_{n-1}) - A_{n-1}(x_1, ..., x_{n-1}) \right| = 0 \quad (5)$$

A_n will be called L-stable family.

3. *It fulfills the property of L-R stability if A_n satisfies the above two points, and it will be called L-R stable family.*

3   Weak Stability of a Family of Aggregation Operators

In the previous section, we have defined the concept of strict stability and stability (in a weakly version). Therefore, this last definition (stability in the limit) properly extends the application range of the stability notion proposed in this paper to some consistent, non-strictly stable $FAOs$, as some of the most used weighted mean operators. However, again the productory FAO Pn fails to fulfil this notion of consistency. For example, if $(x_1, x_2,) = (1/2, 1, 1,)$, then $P_{n-1} = 1/2$, but $P_n(x_1, , x_{n-1}, P_{n-1}) = (P_{n-1})^2 = 1/4$, $\forall\, n > 2$, so the productory family is neither strictly stable nor stable. Nevertheless, since:

$$P_n(x_1, ...x_{n-1}, P_{n-1}(x_1, ..., x_{n-1})) - P_{n-1}(x_1, ..., x_{n-1})$$

is equal to

$$\prod_{i=1}^{n-1} x_i \cdot \prod_{i=1}^{n-1} x_i - \prod_{i=1}^{n-1} x_i = \prod_{i=1}^{n-1} x_i \cdot \left(\prod_{i=1}^{n-1} x_i - 1 \right).$$

The productory is not stable only because of those successions $\{x_n\}_{n \in N}$ such that $\prod_{i=1}^{n} x_n \xrightarrow{n \to \infty} c \in (0,1)$, which entails that $x_n \xrightarrow{n \to 1} 1$ (but notice that the opposite is not true, since if $\exists k \,/\, x_k = 0$ then $\prod_{n=1}^{\infty} x_n = 0$.

This leads to guess that these successions that makes the product FAO to not fulfil stability actually constitute a very reduced subset SP of the set S of all successions in $[0, 1]$, or in other words, the probability of gathering a collection of data which potentially leads to a non-stable behavior is small enough or even zero.

It is possible to formalize these ideas by means of the probability concept. Let $S = \{\{x_n\}_{n \in N} : x_i \in [0, 1]\ \forall i\}$ be the set of successions in $[0, 1]$, and let $\{A_n\}$ be a FAO involved in the aggregation process of a succession $s_{n-1} = (x_1, , x_{n-1}) \in S$. Consider an experiment given by "observe the stability of $\{A_n(s_n)\}$", or in other words, "observe the distance between $A_n(s_{n-1}, A_{n-1}(s_{n-1}))$ and $A_{n-1}(s_{n-1})$" (for the case of the stability from the right). The sample space E associated is given by the set of the possible stability levels of $\{A_n(s_n)\}$. Thus, if the cardinality of S tends to infinite, it is possible to obtain the probability of the event given by "gathering a succession s_n which leads to a stable behavior of $\{A_n\}$ FAO ", ie, $P[\lim_{n \to +\infty} |A_n(s_{n-1}, A_{n-1}(s_{n-1})) - A_{n-1}(s_{n-1})| = 0]$.

This way, if the value of the data items $(X_1, ..., X_n, ...)$ are assumed to be $U([0, 1])$ independent variables, then it is possible to introduce a probability measure over the set of successions S through the conjoint probability distribution function.

$$P(a_1 \leq X_1 \leq b_1, ..., a_n \leq X_n \leq b_n, ...) = \prod_{i=1}^{\infty} P(a_i \leq X_i \leq b_i) = \prod_{i=1}^{\infty} (b_i - a_i) \quad (6)$$

Where $a_i, b_i \in [0, 1]\ \forall i$. Thus, for example, the probability of a given succession $\{x_n\}_{n \in N}$ is clearly zero, and the probability of the set of all successions such that $x_i \in [0, 1/2]\ \forall i \leq N$ and $x_i \in [0, 1]\ \forall i > N$, for a given N, is $(1/2)^N$. Then, it is possible to see that $SP = \left\{\{x_n\}_{n \in N} / \prod_{n=1}^{\infty} x_n \xrightarrow{n \to \infty} c \in (0, 1)\right\}$ in which the productory FAO fails to be stable has probability zero.

Effectively, as pointed above, $SP \subset S1 = \{(x_n)_{n \in N} / x_n \to 1\}$. And notice that, for each $\varepsilon > 0$, $S1$ can be partitioned into the sets

$$C_n = \{\{x_k\}_{k \in N} / |x_k - 1| < \varepsilon,\ \forall k \geq n\},$$

$n \in N$. Since $C_n \cap C_m = \emptyset$ if $n \cong m$, it then holds that:

$$P(SP) \leq P(\{\{x_n\}_{n \in N} / x_n \to 1\}) = P\left(\bigcup_{n \in N} C_n\right) = \sum_{n=1}^{\infty} P(C_n) \leq \sum_{n=1}^{\infty} \prod_{k=n}^{\infty} \varepsilon^k = 0 \quad (7)$$

And thus it can be said that the probability of the productory FAO not being stable is zero.

Therefore, the productory FAO verifies the notion of stability in a weaker version, that can be characterized in terms of almost sure convergence to a strictly stable FAO. This leads to introduce the concept of almost sure stability, or weak stability, as follows:

Definition 4. Let $\{A_n : [0,1]^n \to [0,1], n \in N\}$ be a family of aggregation operators. Then, we will say that $\forall n \geq 3$ and $\forall \{x_n\}_{n \in N}$ in $[0,1]$:

1. It fulfills the property of R-weak stability, if the following holds:

$$P[(x_n) \,/ \lim_{n \to +\infty} |A_n(x_1, ...x_{n-1}, A_{n-1}(x_1, ..., x_{n-1})) - A_{n-1}(x_1, ..., x_{n-1})| = 0] = 1,$$
(8)

   A_n will be called R-weakly stable family.

2. It fulfills the property of L-weak stability, if the following holds:

$$P[(x_n) \,/ \lim_{n \to +\infty} |A_n(A_{n-1}(x_1, ..., x_{n-1}), x_1, ...x_{n-1}) - A_{n-1}(x_1, ..., x_{n-1})| = 0] = 1,$$
(9)

   A_n will be called L-weak stable family

3. It fulfills the property of L-R weak stability if A_n satisfies the above two points, and it will be called L-R weakly stable family.

Now, it is possible to look for the relationships between these three different levels of stability. Since the stable and weakly stable $FAOs$ converge to strictly stable $FAOs$, and the stable $FAOs$ are a special case of weakly stable $FAOs$, it is easy to see that the following results hold:

Proposition 1. Let $\{A_n : [0,1]^n \to [0,1], n \in N\}$ be a family of aggregation operators. Then the following holds:

1. If the family $\{A_n\}_n$ satisfies the property of strict stability then it also satisfies the property of stability.
2. If the family $\{A_n\}_n$ satisfies the property of stability then it satisfies the property of weak stability.

Therefore, if a FAO is not weakly stable, then it does not verify any of the three levels of stability. We will call such a FAO instable.

Definition 5. Let $\{A_n : [0,1]^n \to [0,1], n \in N\}$ be a family of aggregation operators. Then, we will say that:

1. It fulfills the property of R-instability, if the family is not R-weakly stable, and it will be called R-unstable family.
2. It fulfills the property of L-instability, if the family is not L-weakly stable, and it will be called L-unstable family.
3. It fulfills the property of L-R instability if A_n satisfies the above two points, and it will be called L-R unstable family.

4   Stability Levels of Some Well-Known Families of Aggregation Operators

In this section, the stability level some of the most frequently used aggregation operators is analyzed, looking at these operators in a global way (as families) in order to know in advance the level of robustness of the aggregation process involved in them.

In *Table 1* we show the stability level of the most used families of aggregation operators. As can be seen in this table, the OWA, and the weighted mean operators, in general, are families unstable (as we show in the following proposition), since their stability will be strictly dependent on the way in which the weights are defined Let us observe, for example, that if any condition is imposed to the weights we could have OWA or weighted mean families unnatural as an operator that for $n = 2$ is the maximum, for $n = 3$ is the minimum, for $n = 4$ is the mean, and so on.

Table 1. Level of stability of some families of aggregation operators

Family of aggregation operators $\{A_n\}_{n \in N}$	Strict stability	Stability	Weak stability	Instability
$Min_n = Min(x_1, \ldots, x_n)$	R, L	R, L	R, L	–
$Max_n = Max(x_1, \ldots, x_n)$	R, L	R, L	R, L	–
$Md_n = Md(x_1, \ldots, x_n)$	R, L	R, L	R, L	–
$M_n = \sum_{i=1}^{n} \frac{x_i}{n}$	R, L	R, L	R, L	–
$G_n = (\prod_{i=1}^{n} x_i)^{1/n}$	R, L	R, L	R, L	–
$H_n = \frac{n}{\sum_{i=1}^{n} 1/x_i}$	R, L	R, L	R, L	–
$Q_n = \prod_{i=1}^{n} x^i$	–	–	R, L	–
$P_n = \prod_{i=1}^{n} x_i$	–	–	R, L	–
$A_n^f = A_n^f(x_1, \ldots, x_n)$	R	R	R	L
$A_n^b = A_n^b(x_1, \ldots, x_n)$	L	L	L	R
$W_n = \sum_{i=1}^{n} x_i \cdot w_i$	–	–	–	R, L
$O_n = \sum_{i=1}^{n} x_{(i)} \cdot w_i$	–	–	–	R, L

Note: R and L indicate level of stability from the right and from the left respectively.
Note: The weights of the weighted families of aggregation operator do not have additional restrictions.

Recall that, for any data cardinality n, the weights are usually assumed to form a vector $w^n = (w_1^n, \ldots, w_n^n) \in [0,1]^n$, such that $\sum_{i=1}^{n} w_i^n = 1$. The corresponding weighted mean operator is then given by $W_n(x_1, \ldots, x_n) = \sum_{i=1}^{n} x_i \cdot w_i$.

It is important to stress that our aim is not to propose a new method to determine these weights (as it would depend on the problem being considered), but simply to specify the relationships that should exist between two weights vectors of different dimension in order to produce a consistent aggregation process.

Proposition 2. $\forall x_1, \ldots x_n \in [0, 1]$, *the weighted mean operator family given by* $\{W_n : [0,1]^n \to [0,1], n \in N\}$ *and the OWA operators family given by*

$\{O_n : [0,1]^n \rightarrow [0,1], n \in N\}$ *are unstable FAOs if their weights do not have any additional restriction.*

Proof. If any constraint is imposed to the weights in a OWA family, the family denoted as $\{IA_n\}$ and defined as

$$IA_n(x_1,\ldots,x_n) = \begin{cases} Max(x_1,\ldots,x_n) & \text{if } n \text{ odd} \\ Min(x_1,\ldots,x_n) & \text{if } n \text{ even} \end{cases}$$

can be viewed as a particular case of OWA.

Since the OWA aggregation function is symmetric, the three definitions of weak stability are equivalent (L weak, R weak and LR weak). To prove that $\{IA_n\}$ is unstable, since the definition of L weak stability is

$$P\left[(x_n) / \lim_{n \to +\infty} |A_n(x_1,\ldots x_{n-1}, A_{n-1}(x_1,\ldots,x_{n-1})) - A_{n-1}(x_1,\ldots,x_{n-1})| = 0\right] = 1$$

It is enough to find a family R of successions with $P(R) > 0$ and satisfying also that $\forall (x_n) \in R$, $\lim_{n \to +\infty} |A_n(x_1,\ldots x_{n-1}, A_{n-1}(x_1,\ldots,x_{n-1})) - A_{n-1}(x_1,\ldots,x_{n-1})|$ $\neq 0$ which trivially can be founded.

5   Conclusions and Final Remarks

In our opinion an aggregation family should never be understood just as a family of n-ary operators. Rather, all these aggregation operators must be deeply related following some building procedure throughout the aggregation process. To this aim, we have presented here two properties that follows such an objective. It is clear that we should not define a family of aggregation operators $\{A_n\}$ in which A_2 is the mean, A_3 geometric mean, A_4 is the minimum. Thus, in our opinion the aggregation process demands a conceptual unit idea rather than a mathematical formula.

The stability notion proposed in this paper makes emphasize in the idea of robustness-stability-continuity of the family in the sense that the operator defined for n data items should not differ too much of the operator defined for $n-1$ elements.

Another aspect that should be considered in the aggregation process is related with the structure of the data. The notion of consistency in the relation among the aggregation functions is not trivial and could depend on the structure of the data. In [1] a possible definition of consistency in the framework of recursive rules is done. For more general situations, we present a mechanism that permits us to build the aggregation function taking into account the structure of the data that has to be aggregated. Nevertheless, the definition proposed here is just a seminal effort and possible modifications coming from a further analysis (we think) merit to be carried out.

Acknowledgment. This research has been partially supported by the Government of Spain, grant TIN2009-07901.

References

1. Amo, A., Montero, J., Molina, E.: Representation of consistent recursive rules. European Journal of Operational Research 130, 29–53 (2001)
2. Beliakov, G., Pradera, A., Calvo, T.: Aggregation Functions, a Guide to Practitioners. Springer, Berlin (2007)
3. Calvo, T., Kolesarova, A., Komornikova, M., Mesiar, R.: Aggregation operators, properties, classes and construction methods. In: Calvo, T., et al. (eds.) Aggregation Operators New trends ans Aplications, pp. 3–104. Physica-Verlag, Heidelberg (2002)
4. Calvo, T., Mayor, G., Torrens, J., Suer, J., Mas, M., Carbonell, M.: Generation of weighting triangles associated with aggregation fuctions. International Journal of Uncertainty, Fuzziness and Knowledge-Based Systems 8(4), 417–451 (2000)
5. Cutello, V., Montero, J.: Hierarchical aggregation of OWA operators: basic measures and related computational problems. Uncertainty, Fuzzinesss and Knowledge-Based Systems 3, 17–26 (1995)
6. Cutello, V., Montero, J.: Recursive families of OWA operators. In: Proceedings FUZZ-IEEE Conference, pp. 1137–1141. IEEE Press, Piscataway (1994)
7. Cutello, V., Montero, J.: Recursive connective rules. International Journal of Intelligent Systems 14, 3–20 (1999)
8. Gómez, D., Montero, J.: A discussion of aggregation functions. Kybernetika 40, 107–120 (2004)
9. Gómez, D., Montero, J., Yáñez, J., Poidomani, C.: A graph coloring algorithm approach for image segmentation. Omega 35, 173–183 (2007)
10. Gómez, D., Montero, J., Yánez, J.: A coloring algorithm for image classification. Information Sciences 176, 3645–3657 (2006)
11. Grabisch, M., Marichal, J., Mesiar, R., Pap, E.: Aggregation Functions. Encyclopedia of Mathematics and its Applications (2009)
12. Kolesárová, A.: Sequential aggregation. In: González, M., et al. (eds.) Proceedings of the Fifth International Summer School on Aggregation Operators, AGOP, pp. 183–187. Universitat de les Illes Balears, Palma de Mallorca (2009)
13. Montero, J., Gómez, D., Bustince, H.: On the relevance of some families of fuzzy sets. Fuzzy Sets and Systems 158, 2429–2442 (2007)
14. Montero, J., López, V., Gómez, D.: The Role of Fuzziness in Decision Making. STUDFUZZ, vol. 215, pp. 337–349. Springer, Heidelberg (2007)
15. Rojas, K., Gómez, D., Rodríguez, J.T., Montero, J.: Some Properties of Consistency in the Families of Aggregation Operators. In: Melo-Pinto, P., Couto, P., Serôdio, C., Fodor, J., De Baets, B. (eds.) Eurofuse 2011. AISC, vol. 107, pp. 169–176. Springer, Heidelberg (2011)
16. Yager, R.R.: On ordered weighted averaging aggregation operators in multi-criteria decision making. IEEE Transactions on Systems, Man and Cybernetics 18, 183–190 (1988)
17. Yager, R.R., Rybalov, A.: Nonconmutative self-identity aggregation. Fuzzy Sets and Systems 85, 73–82 (1997)

Negations Generated by Bounded Lattices t-Norms

Benjamín Bedregal[1], Gleb Beliakov[2], Humberto Bustince[3], Javier Fernandez[3], Ana Pradera[4], and Renata Hax Sander Reiser[5]

[1] Universidade Federal do Rio Grande do Norte
Departamento de Informática e Matemática Aplicada
Campus Universitário s/n, Lagoa Nova, 59072-970 Natal-RN, Brazil
bedregal@dimap.ufrn.br
[2] Deakin University, School of Information Technology
Burwood, Australia
gleb.beliakov@deakin.edu.au
[3] Universidad Publica de Navarra
Departamento de Automática y Computación
Campus Arrosadia Campus s/n, 31006 Pamplona, Spain
{bustince,fcojavier.fernandez}@unavarra.es
[4] Universidad Rey Juan Carlos
Departamento de Ciencias de la Computación
28933 Móstole, Madrid, Spain
ana.pradera@urjc.es
[5] Universidade Federal de Pelotas
Centro de Desenvolvimento Tecnológico
Campus Capão do Leão, s/n 96010-000 Pelotas, Brazil
reiser@inf.ufpel.edu.br

Abstract. From the birth of fuzzy sets theory, several extensions have been proposed changing the possible membership values. Since fuzzy connectives such as t-norms and negations have an important role in theoretical as well as applied fuzzy logics, these connectives have been adapted for these generalized frameworks. Perhaps, an extension of fuzzy logic which generalizes the remaining extensions, proposed by Joseph Goguen in 1967, is to consider arbitrary bounded lattices for the values of the membership degrees. In this paper we extend the usual way of constructing fuzzy negations from t-norms for the bounded lattice t-norms and prove some properties of this construction.

Keywords: L-Fuzzy logics, bounded lattices, t-norms, L-negations, L-automorphisms.

1 Introduction

The necessity of considering truth values beyond the classical "true" and "false" was manifested a very long time back. For example, Plato claimed that between true and false there is a third alternative and Eubulides of Miletus, alerted us with sorites paradox, on the difficulty of determining a threshold for vague properties (sets), and so, of saying when an object satisfies or not some property. In modern times, the Polish and American logicians Jan Łukasiewicz and Emil Post, respectively, introduce the idea of

S. Greco et al. (Eds.): IPMU 2012, Part III, CCIS 299, pp. 326–335, 2012.

3-valued logics. Later, Kurt Gödel extended it by considering n possible truth values and Lotfi Zadeh in [26] introduced the theory of fuzzy sets, where the membership degrees can take values in $[0, 1]$ and so, in their logical counterpart, the truth values of propositions are real numbers in $[0, 1]$. From then, several extensions of fuzzy set theory have been proposed; for example, Interval-valued fuzzy sets, Atanassov's intuitionistic fuzzy sets, interval-valued intuitionistic fuzzy sets, n-dimensional fuzzy sets and some others which can be considered as a special case of lattice-valued fuzzy sets introduced by Joseph Goguen in [12]. For the latter, given a lattice, the membership degree of an element is a value of that lattice.

An important question in fuzzy logic is the way of extending the classical propositional connectives for the fuzzy framework. In the beginning of the fuzzy logics, several particular functions or a family of such functions were proposed to represent the conjunction, disjunction, negation and implication. But, most of these proposals have some common properties, which led Claudi Alsina, Enric Trillas and Llorenç Valverde in [2] to use the notion of triangular norm (t-norm in short)[1] and its dual notion (t-conorms) to model conjunction and disjunction in fuzzy logics. For the case of negations, Enric Trillas in [25] proposed the axiomatic that is accepted nowadays. There are some relations among the connectives. For example it is well known that each t-norm can be obtained from a t-conorm and the standard negation ($N(x) = 1 - x$) and conversely, each t-conorm can be obtained from a t-norm and the standard negation, i.e. t-norm and t-conorms are dual connectives. An interesting question, is whether from t-norms, t-conorms and fuzzy implications it is possible to obtain, in a canonical way, a negation.

Since fuzzy connectives, i.e. t-norms, t-conorms, negations and implications, play an important role in fuzzy logics, theoretically as well as in applications, several works have been made to introduce connectives in each one of the extensions of fuzzy logic (see for example [5,10]). In the case of lattice-valued fuzzy set theory, basically, there are two directions to include lattice-valued logical connectives:

1. Add connectives to the lattice structures beyond of the infimum and supremum operators, i.e. to consider enriched lattices with some extra operators, and in general, to consider properties which relate different connectives. For example, BL-algebras [15] and MV-algebras [8] which provides the algebraic setting for the basic logic[2] and for Łukasiewicz's infinite-valued propositional logic, respectively.

2. Generalize the notion of fuzzy connective for lattice-valued fuzzy logics by considering the same (or analogous) axioms (conditions) as those required for such connectives. This have been made, mainly, with the aggregation operators (t-norms and t-conorms) and negations (see for example [6,4,9,17,20,22]).

In this paper we follow this second direction to study the way of constructing bounded lattice negations from bounded lattice t-norms and how these constructions are preserved when a bounded lattice automorphism is applied to the negation and the t-norm.

---

[1] T-norm was introduced by Karl Menger in [19] to model distance in probabilistic metric spaces. But Berthold Schweizer and Abe Sklar in [24] were who gave the axiomatic form as it is known today. A deep study on t-norms can be found in the books [1,18].

[2] Basic Logic in [15] is a positive propositional logic with two connectives: an implication and a strong conjunction.

The paper is organized as follows. In section 2 we provide a background on bounded lattices. In sections 3 and 4 we provide the notions of negation and t-norm on bounded lattices and some properties of these connectives. The section 5 is the main one of this paper, and provides the way of obtaining negations from t-norms on bounded lattices, as well as some properties. Finally, in section 6 some final remarks on the paper are stated.

2 Bounded Lattices

In this subsection we define some useful concepts on bounded lattices which are based in the papers [6,22]. If the reader needs a deeper text on lattice theory we suggest the books [7,11,13].

Definition 1. *Let $\leq$ be a partial order on a set L. The partial order set $\langle L, \leq \rangle$ is a lattice if for all $a, b \in L$ the set $\{a, b\}$ has a supremum and infimum (in L). If there are two elements, 1 and 0, in L such that $0 \leq x \leq 1$ for each $x \in L$, then $\langle L, \leq, 0, 1 \rangle$ is called a bounded lattice.*

Definition 2. *Let $\wedge$ and $\vee$ be two binary operations on a nonempty set L. Then the algebraic structure $\langle L, \vee, \wedge \rangle$ is a lattice if for each $x, y, z \in L$, the following properties hold:*

1. $x \wedge y = y \wedge x$ and $x \vee y = y \vee x$;
2. $(x \wedge y) \wedge z = x \wedge (y \wedge z)$ and $(x \vee y) \vee z = x \vee (y \wedge z)$;
3. $x \wedge (x \vee y) = x$ and $x \vee (x \wedge y) = x$.

If there are elements 1 and 0 in L such that, for all $x \in L$, $x \wedge 1 = x$ and $x \vee 0 = x$, then $\langle L, \vee, \wedge, 0, 1 \rangle$ is a bounded lattice.

Remark 1. It is well known that definitions 1 and 2 are equivalent. This allows us to use both definitions indiscriminately. Therefore, according to necessity, we shall use one or another. Indeed, if we consider a bounded lattice $\langle L, \leq, 0, 1 \rangle$ as a partially ordered set, then the following binary operations: $\forall\, x, y \in L$, $x \wedge y = \inf\{x, y\}$ and $x \vee y = \sup\{x, y\}$ are such that $\langle L, \vee, \wedge, 0, 1 \rangle$ is a bounded lattice in algebraic sense. Conversely, from a bounded lattice $\langle L, \vee, \wedge, 0, 1 \rangle$ in the algebraic sense, the partial order $\leq$ on L defined by $x \leq y$ iff $x \vee y = y$ or, equivalently, $x \leq y$ iff $x \wedge y = x$, is such that $\langle L, \leq, 0, 1 \rangle$ is a bounded lattice.

Definition 3. *Let $\langle L, \leq_L \rangle$ be a lattice. L is said to be complete if any $X \subseteq L$ has an infimum and a supremum (in L).*

Each complete lattice L is a bounded lattice, in fact $0_L = \inf L$ (or $\sup \emptyset$) and $1_L = \sup L$ (or $\inf \emptyset$).

Definition 4. *Let $\langle L, \leq_L, 0_L, 1_L \rangle$ and $\langle M, \leq_M, 0_M, 1_M \rangle$ be bounded lattices. A mapping $f : L \to M$ is said to be a lattice order-homomorphism, or just an ord-homomorphism, if, for all $x, y \in L$, it follows that*

1. *If $x \leq_L y$ then $f(x) \leq_M f(y)$;*
2. *$f(0_L) = 0_M$ and $f(1_L) = 1_M$.*

Remark 2. From now on, we assume that L and M are bounded lattices with the following structure: $\langle L, \leq_L, 0_L, 1_L \rangle$ and $\langle M, \leq_M, 0_M, 1_M \rangle$, respectively.

Let $f, g : L^n \to L$. If $f(x_1, \ldots, x_n) \leq_L g(x_1, \ldots, x_n)$ for each $x_1, \ldots, x_n \in L$ then we write $f \leq_L g$.

Definition 5. *A mapping $f : L \longrightarrow M$ is a lattice algebraic-homomorphism, or just an alg-homomorphism, if, for all $x, y \in L$, we have*

1. *$f(x \wedge_L y) = f(x) \wedge_M f(y)$;*
2. *$f(x \vee_L y) = f(x) \vee_M f(y)$;*
3. *$f(0_L) = 0_M$ and $f(1_L) = 1_M$.*

Proposition 1. *Every alg-homomorphism is an ord-homomorphism, but not every ord-homomorphism is an alg-homomorphism.*

Proof. See page 30 in [14]. □

Definition 6. *An ord-homomorphism (alg-homomorphism) $f : L \to M$ is an ord-isomorphism (alg-isomorphism) if there exists an ord-homomorphism (alg-homomorphism) $f^{-1} : M \to L$ such that $f \circ f^{-1} = Id_M$ and $f^{-1} \circ f = Id_L$, where Id_M (Id_L) is the identity function on M (L). f^{-1} is called the inverse of f.*

Contrary to the case of ord-homomorphism and alg-homomorphism, both notions of isomorphism agree, in the sense that f is an ord-isomorphism if and only if (iff) f is an alg-isomorphism. Therefore, we will call simply isomorphism to both ord-isomorphisms and alg-isomorphisms. The next proposition presents a well known characterization of isomorphisms on bounded lattices.

Proposition 2. *A function $f : L \to M$ is an isomorphism iff f is bijective and for each $x, y \in L$, we have that*

$$x \leq_L y \text{ iff } f(x) \leq_M f(y) \tag{1}$$

When L and M are the same lattice, we call isomorphisms of *automorphisms*, or *L-automorphisms* when it is important to remark the lattice. Thus, the Proposition 2 guarantee that our notion of automorphism on a bounded lattice is equivalent with the usual notion of automorphism, as for example in [4]. We will denote the set of all automorphisms on a bounded lattice L by $Aut(L)$. Since, clearly, Id_L is an automorphism and automorphisms are closed under composition and inversion, then the algebra $\langle Aut(L), \circ \rangle$ is a group. In algebra, an important tool is the action of the groups on sets [16]. In our case the action of the automorphism group transforms lattice functions in other lattice functions.

Definition 7. *Given a function $f : L^n \to L$, the action of an L-autormorphism ρ over f is the function $f^\rho : L^n \to L$ defined as in equation (2).*

$$f^\rho(x_1, \ldots, x_n) = \rho^{-1}(f(\rho(x_1), \ldots, \rho(x_n))) \tag{2}$$

f^ρ is said to be conjugate of f.

Notice that if $f : L^n \to L$ is conjugate of $g : L^n \to L$ and g of $h : L^n \to L$ then, as automorphisms are closed under composition, f is conjugate of h; and if f is conjugate of g then, because the inverse of an automorphism is also an automorphism, g is also conjugate of f. Thus, the automorphism action on the set of n-ary functions on L (L^{L^n}) determines an equivalence relation on L^{L^n}.

3 Negations on L

Fuzzy negations are generalizations of the classical negation $\neg$ and, as in classical logics, they have been used to define other connectives from binary connectives. In this subsection we present a natural extension of fuzzy negations by considering arbitrary bounded lattices as possible truth values.

Definition 8. *A mapping $N : L \to L$ is a negation on L or just an L-negation, if the following properties are satisfied for each $x, y \in L$:*

(N1) $N(0_L) = 1_L$ *and* $N(1_L) = 0_L$ *and;*
(N2) *If $x \leq_L y$ then $N(y) \leq_L N(x)$.*

Moreover, the L-negation N is strong if it also satisfies the involutive property, i.e.

(N3) $N(N(x)) = x$ *for each $x \in L$.*

The L-negation N is called frontier if it satisfies the property:

(N4) $N(x) \in \{0_L, 1_L\}$ *iff $x = 0_L$ or $x = 1_L$.*

Observe that each strong L-negation is a frontier L-negation and that an L- negation is a frontier L-negation iff it is both non-filling ($N(x) = 1_L$ iff $x = 0_L$) and non-vanishing ($N(x) = 0_L$ iff $x = 1_L$) (see [3], pg. 14).

Proposition 3. *Let N be a strong L-negation. Then*

1. *N is strict;*
2. *If $N(x) \leq_L N(y)$ then $y \leq_L x$;*
3. *N is bijective.*

Proof. 1. If $y <_L x$ then by **(N2)**, $N(x) \leq_L N(y)$. Suppose that $N(x) = N(y)$ then $N(N(x)) = N(N(y))$ and so $x = y$, which is in contradiction with the premise. Therefore, $N(x) <_L N(y)$.
    2. If $N(x) \leq_L N(y)$ then, by **(N2)**, $N(N(y)) \leq_L N(N(x))$ and so $y \leq_L x$.
    3. Because N is strict then N is trivially injective. As for any $y \in L$, $N(N(y)) = y$, then N is also surjective. So, N is bijective.   □
    From this proposition, it follows that for each strong L-negation, $x \parallel_L y$ iff $N(x) \parallel_L N(y)$.

Proposition 4. *The functions* $N_\perp, N_\top : L \to L$ *defined by*

$$N_\perp(x) = \begin{cases} 1_L & \text{if } x = 0_L \\ 0_L & \text{otherwise} \end{cases}$$

and

$$N_\top(x) = \begin{cases} 0_L & \text{if } x = 1_L \\ 1_L & \text{otherwise} \end{cases}$$

are L-negations, such that for any L-negation N, *we have that* $N_\perp \leq_L N \leq_L N_\top$.

Proof. Straightforward. □

Proposition 5. *Let* $N : L \to L$, ρ *be an L-automorphism. For each* $i = 1, \ldots, 4$, N *satisfies the property* (**Ni**) *iff* N^ρ *satisfies* (**Ni**).

Proof. ($\Rightarrow$)

(**N1**) $N^\rho(0_L) = \rho^{-1}(N(\rho(0_L))) = \rho^{-1}(N(0_L)) = \rho^{-1}(1_L) = 1_L$. Analogously, $N^\rho(1_L) = 0_L$;

(**N2**) If $x \leq_L y$ then $\rho(x) \leq_L \rho(y)$ and so $N(\rho(y)) \leq_L N(\rho(x))$. Therefore, by isotonicity of ρ^{-1}, $\rho^{-1}(N(\rho(y))) \leq_l \rho^{-1}(N(\rho(x)))$;

(**N3**) $N^\rho(N^\rho(x)) = \rho^{-1}(N(\rho(\rho^{-1}(N(\rho(x)))))) = \rho^{-1}(N(N(\rho(x)))) = \rho^{-1}(\rho(x)) = x$; and

(**N4**) If $N^\rho(x) = 0_L$ then, by eq. (2) and because $\rho(0_L) = 0_L$, $N(\rho(x)) = 0_L$. So, since N satisfies (**N4**), $\rho(x) \in \{0_L, 1_L\}$ and therefore $x = 0_L$ or $x = 1_L$.

($\Leftarrow$) Straightforward from the previous item and the fact that for any function $f : L \to L$, $(f^\rho)^{\rho^{-1}} = f$. □

Corollary 1. *Let* $N : L \to L$ *be a mapping and* ρ *be an L-automorphism.* N *is an (strong, frontier) L-negation iff* N^ρ *is an (strong, frontier) L-negation.*

Proof. Straightforward from Proposition 5. □

4 T-norms on L

Classical conjunctions have been modeled in fuzzy logics via functions called t-norms. In this subsection we present the natural generalization to consider arbitrary bounded lattices as possible truth values.

Definition 9. *(see [9]) A mapping* $T : L \times L \to L$ *is a t-norm on* L *if the following properties are satisfied for each* $x, y, z \in L$:

(**T1**) $T(x, y) = T(y, x)$;

(**T2**) $T(x, T(y, z)) = T(T(x, y), z)$;

(**T3**) *if* $y \leq_L z$ *then* $T(x, y) \leq_L T(x, z)$; *and*

(**T4**) $T(x, 1_L) = x$.

T *is positive if for each* $x, y \in L$ *it satisfies the property*

(T5) $T(x, y) = 0_L$ iff $x = 0_L$ or $y = 0_L$.

An $x \in L$ is an idempotent element of T if $T(x, x) = x$.

An element $x \in L - \{0_L\}$ such that $T(x, y) = 0_L$ for some $y \in L - \{0_L\}$ is called a zero divisor of T. Clearly, T is positive iff T has no zero divisors.

The next lemma and proposition were stated in [4], but the paper not includes the proof, perhaps because their simplicity.

Lemma 1. *Let T be a t-norm on L. Then for each $x, y \in L$, $T(x, y) \leq_L x \wedge_L y$.*

Proof. By **(T3)** and **(T4)**, $T(x, y) \leq_L T(x, 1_L) = x$ and $T(x, y) \leq_L T(1_L, y) = y$. Therefore, $T(x, y) \leq_L x \wedge_L y$.   □

Proposition 6. *Let T be a t-norm on L. Then $T_\perp \leq_L T \leq_L T_\top$, where*

$$T_\top(x, y) = x \wedge_L y \text{ and } T_\perp(x, y) = \begin{cases} x \wedge_L y & \text{if } x = 1_L \text{ or } y = 1_L \\ 0_L & \text{otherwise} \end{cases}. \tag{3}$$

Proof. Clearly, $T_\perp$ and $T_\top$ are t-norms on L. By Lemma 1, $T \leq_L T_\top$ and trivially, $T_\perp \leq_L T$.   □

Proposition 7. *Let T be a t-norm on L. Each $x \in L$ is an idempotent element of T iff $T = T_\top$.*

Proof. ($\Rightarrow$) Let $x, y \in L$. Then by Lemma 1, $T(x, y) \leq_l x \wedge_L y$ and since each element of L is idempotent for T, then (*) $T(x, y) \leq_L T(x \wedge_L y, x \wedge_L y)$. On the other hand, since $x \wedge_L y \leq_L x$ and $x \wedge_L y \leq_L y$, then by **(T3)**, $T(x \wedge_L y, x \wedge_L y) \leq_L T(x, y)$. So, by (*), $T(x, y) = T(x \wedge_L y, x \wedge_L y) = x \wedge_L y$, i.e. $T = T_\top$.

($\Leftarrow$) Straightforward from equation (3).   □

Proposition 8. *Let $T : L \times L \to L$, ρ be an L-automorphism. For each $i = 1, \ldots, 5$, T satisfies the property (Ti) iff T^ρ satisfies (Ti).*

Proof. ($\Rightarrow$) Let $x, y, z \in L$, then

(T1) Straightforward;

(T2) $T^\rho(x, T^\rho(y, z)) = \rho^{-1}(T(\rho(x), \rho(\rho^{-1}(T(\rho(y), \rho(z))))))$ by eq. (2)
$= \rho^{-1}(T(\rho(x), T(\rho(y), \rho(z))))$
$= \rho^{-1}(T(T(\rho(x), \rho(y)), \rho(z)))$ by **(T2)**
$= \rho^{-1}(T(\rho(\rho^{-1}(T(\rho(x), \rho(y)))), \rho(z)))$
$= T^\rho(, T^\rho(x, y), z)$ by eq. (2)

(T3) If $y \leq_L z$ then $\rho(y) \leq_L \rho(z)$ and so, by **(T3)**, $T(\rho(x), \rho(y)) \leq_L T(\rho(x), \rho(z))$. Therefore, $\rho^{-1}(T(\rho(x), \rho(y))) \leq_L \rho^{-1}(T(\rho(x), \rho(z)))$, i.e. $T^\rho(x, y) \leq_L T^\rho(x, z)$;

(T4) $T^\rho(x, 1_L) = \rho^{-1}(T(\rho(x), \rho(1_L))) = \rho^{-1}(T(\rho(x), 1_L)) = \rho^{-1}(\rho(x)) = x$; and

(T5) $T^\rho(x, y) = 0_L$ iff $\rho^{-1}(T(\rho(x), \rho(y))) = 0_L$ iff $T(\rho(x), \rho(y)) = 0_L$ iff, by **(T5)**, $\rho(x) = 0_L$ or $\rho(y) = 0_L$ iff $x = 0_L$ or $y = 0_L$.

($\Leftarrow$) Straightforward from the previous item and the fact that for any function $f : L^n \to L$, $(f^\rho)^{\rho^{-1}} = f$.   □

Corollary 2. *Let $T : L \times L \to L$ be a mapping and ρ be an L-automorphism. T is a t-norm on L iff T^ρ is a t-norm on L.*

Proof. Straightforward from Proposition 8.   □

5   Negation on L Obtained from t-norms on L

In [18,21] it was observed that it is possible to obtain, in a canonical way, a fuzzy nega-tion N_T from a t-conorm T. This negation is called natural negation of T or negation induced by T. In the most general case, where we have a t-conorm on a bounded lattice L, it is not always possible to obtain a fuzzy negation, because the construction of N_T is based in the supremum of, possibly, infinite sets.

Proposition 9. *Let L be a complete lattice and T be a t-norm on L. Then the function $N_T : L \to L$ defined by*

$$N_T(x) = \sup\{z \in L : T(x,z) = 0_L\} \tag{4}$$

is an L-negation.

Proof. **(N1)** $N_T(1_L) = \sup\{z \in L : T(1_L,z) = 0_L\} = \sup\{0_L\} = 0_L$ and
$N_T(0_L) = \sup\{z \in L : T(0_L,z) = 1_L\} = \sup L = 1_L$;
(N2) If $x \leq_L y$ then for any $z \in L, T(x,z) \leq_L T(y,z)$ and therefore, if $T(y,z) = 0_L$
then $T(x,z) = 0_L$. So, $\{z \in L : T(y,z) = 0_L\} \subseteq \{z \in L : T(x,z) = 0_L\}$.
Hence, $N_T(y) = \sup\{z \in L : T(y,z) = 0_L\} \leq_L \sup\{z \in L : T(x,z) = 0_L\} = N_T(x)$. □

Theorem 1. *Let T be a t-norm on L. If T is positive then $N_T = N_\perp$.*

Proof. If $x \neq 0_L$ and $z \in L$ then, by **(T5)**, $T(x,z) = 0_L$ iff $z = 0_L$. So, by eq. (4), $N_T(x) = \sup\{0_L\} = 0_L$. Therefore, $N_T = N_\perp$. □

Theorem 2. *Let T be a t-norm on L. If N_T is a frontier negation then each $x \in L-\{0_L\}$ is a zero divisor of T.*

Proof. If $x \neq 1_L$, then, as N_T is frontier, $N_T(x) \neq 0_L$ and so $\sup\{z \in L : T(x,z) = 0_L\} \neq 0_L$. So, $\{z \in L : T(x,z) = 0_L\} \neq \{0_L\}$. Thus, since $T(x,0_L) = 0_L$, $\{0_L\} \subset \{z \in L : T(x,z) = 0_L\}$. Therefore, there exists $z \in L-\{0_L\}$ such that $T(x,z) = 0_L$. Hence, x is a zero divisor of T. □

Theorem 3. *Let T be a t-norm on L and ρ be an L-automorphism. Then $N_T^\rho = N_{T^\rho}$.*

Proof. Let $x \in L$, then $N_T^\rho(x) = \rho^{-1}(N_T(\rho(x))) = \rho^{-1}(\sup\{z \in L : T(\rho(x),z) = 0_L\}) = \rho^{-1}(\sup\{z \in L : T^\rho(x,\rho^{-1}(z)) = 0_L\}) = \sup\{\rho^{-1}(z) \in L : T^\rho(x,\rho^{-1}(z)) = 0_L\} = \sup\{z \in L : T^\rho(x,z) = 0_L\} = N_{T^\rho}(x).$ □

6   Final Remarks

In this paper, we have generalized the notions and some properties of fuzzy negations and t-norms for negations and t-norms valued in arbitrary bounded lattices, as well as actions of automorphisms on the same lattice. In particular, we have extended the way of constructing fuzzy negations from t-norms for this case and we have proved that these constructions are preserved under the action of L-automorphisms. Finally, we have also introduced the new class of frontier L-negations and proved that if an L-negation obtained from a t-norm is frontier then each element in the lattice is a zero divisor of the t-norm.

Each one of the other extensions of fuzzy logics (e.g Interval-valued, Atanassov Intuitionistic, fuzzy multisets, etc.), can also be naturally generalized by considering an arbitrary lattice instead of $\langle [0, 1], \leq \rangle$. For example, as made in [6,23] with the interval-valued extension. Thus, as a future work we intend to explore how the negation obtained from a t-norm is related with these constructions.

Acknowledgement.   B. Bedregal was supported by projects 308256/2009-3, 201118/2010-6 and 480832/2011-0 of the Brazilian research council CNPq. H. Bustince was supported by project TIN 2010-15055 of the Spanish Ministry of Science. A. Pradera was supported by projects TIN2009-07901 y TEC2009-14587-C03-03 from the Spanish Government. R. Reiser was supported by FAPERGS-Brazil (under the process number 11/1520-1 of Edital PqG 02/2011). We are grateful to the referees for their valuable suggestions.

References

1. Alsina, C., Frank, M.J., Schweizer, B.: Associative Functions: Triangular Norms And Copulas. World Scientific Publishing Company (2006)
2. Alsina, C., Trillas, E., Valverde, L.: On non-distributive logical connectives for fuzzy set theory. Busefal 3, 18–29 (1980)
3. Baczyński, M., Jayaram, B.: Fuzzy Implications. Springer, Heidelberg (2008)
4. De Baets, B., Mesiar, R.: Triangular norms on product lattices. Fuzzy Sets and Systems 104(1), 61–75 (1999)
5. Bedregal, B.C.: On interval fuzzy negations. Fuzzy Sets and Systems 161, 2290–2313 (2010)
6. Bedregal, B.C., Santos, H.S., Callejas-Bedregal, R.: T-norms on bounded lattices: t-norm morphisms and operators. In: Proceedings of 2006 IEEE International Conference on Fuzzy Systems, Vancouver, Canada, pp. 22–28 (2006)
7. Birkhoff, G.: Lattice Theory. American Mathematical Society, Providence (1973)
8. Chang, C.C.: Algebraic analisys of many valued logics. Trans. of the American Mathematical Society 88, 467–490 (1958)
9. De Cooman, G., Kerre, E.E.: Order norms on bounded partially ordered sets. Fuzzy Methematics 2, 281–310 (1994)
10. Da Costa, C.G., Bedregal, B.C., Doria Neto, A.D.: Relating De Morgan triples with Atanassov's intuitionistic De Morgan triples via automorphisms. Int. J. Approximate Reasoning 52(4), 473–487 (2010)
11. Davey, B.A., Priestley, H.A.: Introduction to Lattices and Order, 2nd edn. Cambridge University Press, Cambridge (2002)
12. Goguen, J.: L-fuzzy sets. Journal of Mathematical Analysis and Applications 18(1), 145–174 (1967)
13. Grätzer, G.: Lattice Theory: First Concepts and Distributive Lattices. Dover Publications (2009)
14. Grätzer, G.: Lattice Theory: Foundation. Birkhäuser (2011)
15. Hájek, P.: Metamathematics of Fuzzy Logic. Springer, Heildelberg (2001)
16. Hungerford, T.W.: Algebra. Springer, New York (1974)

17. Karaçal, F.: On the directed decomposability of strong negations and S-implications operators on product lattices. Information Sciences 176(20) (2006)
18. Klement, E.P., Mesiar, R., Pap, E.: Triangular Norms. Kluwer, Dordrecht (2000)
19. Menger, K.: Statistical metrics. Proc. Nat. Academic Science 28(12), 535–537 (1942)
20. Mesiar, R., Komorníková, M.: Aggregation Functions on Bounded Posets. In: 35 Years of Fuzzy Sets Theory: Celebratory volume Dedicated to the Retirement of Etiene E. Kerre, pp. 3–17. Springer (2010)
21. Nguyen, H.T., Walker, E.A.: A First Course in Fuzzy Logics, 2nd edn. CRC Press, Boca Raton (2000)
22. Palmeira, E.S., Bedregal, B.: Extension of fuzzy logic operators defined on bounded lattices via retractions. Computers and Mathematics with Applications 63, 1026–1038 (2012)
23. Reiser, R.H.S., Dimuro, G.P., Bedregal, B., Santos, H.S., Callejas-Bedregal, R.: S-implications on complete lattice and the interval constructor. Tendências em Matemática Aplicada e Computacional – TEMA 9(1), 143–154 (2008)
24. Schweizer, B., Sklar, A.: Associative functions and abstract semigroups. Publ. Math. Dedrecen 10, 69–81 (1963)
25. Trillas, E.: Sobre funciones de negación en la teoria de los conjuntos difusos. Stochastica 3(1), 47–59 (1979)
26. Zadeh, L.A.: Fuzzy sets. Information and Control 8, 338–353 (1965)

The Problem of Missing Data in LSP Aggregation

Jozo Dujmović

Department of Computer Science
San Francisco State University
1600 Holloway Ave, San Francisco, CA 94132, USA
jozo@sfsu.edu

Abstract. Aggregation of continuous logic variables or degrees of fuzzy membership using soft computing aggregation models assumes the availability of all input data. Unfortunately, in many applications some inputs are missing. In this paper we propose an aggregation process that tolerates missing data. The aggregation process is implemented in the context of LSP evaluation criteria. Using the proposed method the aggregators automatically reconfigure themselves so that only the available data are aggregated. The corresponding evaluation decisions can be based on incomplete data.

Keywords: Aggregation, LSP method, missing data, missingness-tolerant aggregation, null values, penalty functions.

1   Introduction

Flexible query answering systems increasingly use soft computing evaluation criteria for comparison and ranking of alternatives. Each alternative is described by n attributes that are used as inputs for various user evaluation criteria. Users specify their requirements either by creating a specific criterion function, or by editing parameters of a predefined criterion function. When the evaluation criterion is defined, the next step in the evaluation process consists of collecting input data from various databases accessible over the Internet. The collected data are then used to evaluate and compare all available alternatives, and to generate a sorted list according to decreasing level of satisfaction of user requirements.

Traditional soft computing criterion functions can be used only if all input attributes are available. Unfortunately, the process of collecting data from various Internet sources frequently yields incomplete data where one or more attributes are missing. In such cases, incomplete alternatives must be omitted even in cases where those attributes that are available look very attractive.

A typical example of this process is encountered in flexible query answering systems used in on-line real estate. Such systems provide information about homes that are offered for sale. The user specifies a criterion for home evaluation and expects to get a list of suitable homes starting with the best alternative. In a typical case, the real estate web site is providing up to 30 individual home attributes [1]. These attributes

S. Greco et al. (Eds.): IPMU 2012, Part III, CCIS 299, pp. 336–346, 2012.

describe the internal properties of home. However, homebuyers are also interested in knowing the quality of neighborhood surrounding the home location, and these data must come from sources different from the real estate companies. Consequently, the attributes collected from various sources, and that increases the probability of incomplete data. If a very attractive home, located in a very attractive location, misses a single attribute (e.g. information about the availability of public paid parking in a relative vicinity of home), such a home cannot be directly evaluated using a soft computing criterion function and offered to the user. Consequently, there is clear practical interest to develop soft computing criteria that can tolerate missing data.

The problem of missing data is ubiquitous in statistical analysis [2-5]. Statisticians usually differentiate three types of "missingness." If the attributes $a_1,...,a_n$ are used to compute an indicator $x = G(a_1,...,a_n)$ then the probability p_i that an attribute a_i is missing can be constant and independent of the values of $a_1,...,a_n$. Such an attribute is *missing completely at random* (denoted MCAR). If p_i does not depend on a_i but it can depend on $a_k, k \neq i$, then this form of missingness is *missing at random* (denoted MAR). If p_i is a function of a_i, then this case is classified as *missing not at random* (MNAR). The MNAR cases usually occur when data are intentionally omitted (in self-administered surveys these are regularly inconvenient values that respondents refuse to disclose). For example, instead of disclosing that a home does not have a breakfast room/area, or a laundry, a home seller may decide to leave those attributes unknown (without a value). An example of MAR is the case where the probability of missing data about the type of floor is value-independent, i.e. the same for all types of floor, but it depends on the type of home, and can be different for a condo, townhouse, duplex, or a single family house.

In statistical analysis the treatments of missing data include the deletion of all incomplete data sets, or substitution of missing data with some appropriate substitutes (e.g. mean substitution, regression substitution, and other techniques [2,3]). The goal of statistical techniques is to provide best estimates of statistical parameters of the population based on incomplete sample data. The goal of suitability aggregation is different and consists of evaluating an incompletely specified object of MNAR type generating a realistic estimate of its overall suitability.

The problem of missing data is also present in database systems [6,7] and in related fuzzy decision models [8,9]. In database systems missing (or unknown) data are classified as missing and applicable (A), and missing and inapplicable (I) [6,9]. So, each atomic relation of a tuple can have four distinct values: known (true or false) and unknown (A, or I). Then, a four-valued logic can be used to manipulate missing information in a way that enables search and processing of incomplete tuples. If the cases A and I are not differentiated, then they are considered a null value and a three-valued logic is used to deal with incomplete tuples.

In this paper we propose a missingness-tolerant aggregation that is applicable to soft computing criteria based on evaluation logic [10], and the LSP evaluation method [11]. In the context of the LSP method we investigate a process of evaluation of `attributes and aggregation of suitability in cases where some of input attributes are missing (they are unknown, but applicable, and MNAR). Such context is different from similar problems in statistical analysis or in the search of a relational database. The corresponding methodology is presented in subsequent sections.

2   The Structure of LSP Criterion Functions

LSP criterion functions are mappings of the form $R^n \rightarrow I = [0,1]$ that have a standardized structure shown in Fig. 1. The criterion function is organized in a way that permits systematic expression of user requirements. Input attributes $a_1,...,a_n$ are either numerical values (e.g. the area of home) or numerically coded discrete values of attributes (e.g. numerical codes for various types of roof or floor). Each attribute is separately evaluated using an elementary criterion function that maps the values of attribute to the degree of truth (or, alternatively, the degree of fuzzy membership) $g_i : R \rightarrow I$, $i = 1,...,n$. Elementary criteria reflect user needs regarding each individual attribute. In the evaluation logic interpretation, the degrees of truth $x_1,...,x_n$ are called elementary preferences and they denote the degrees of suitability of attributes $a_1,...,a_n$ from the standpoint of satisfying user requirements.

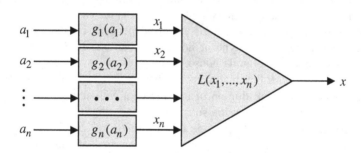

Fig. 1. A general LSP model of evaluation criterion

The final phase of the LSP method is a logic aggregation of the degrees of truth $x_1,...,x_n$ to generate the overall preference x that reflects the overall suitability of an evaluated object [11]. The logic aggregation function $L : I^n \rightarrow I$ is organized as a tree-like structure based on superposition of basic evaluation logic aggregators: partial conjunction, partial disjunction, neutrality, partial absorption, etc. [10-13]. Therefore, the LSP criterion determines the overall suitability $x = G(a_1,...,a_n)$ and for this calculation it is necessary to know the values of all attributes. If some of the attributes are missing, then there are only two options: either we exclude the incomplete object, or (as shown below) we substitute null values with appropriate substitutes.

3   Penalty-Controlled Numerical Coding of Missing Data

Let us first note that in almost all cases the values of attributes are nonnegative. In very rare cases (e.g. if evaluation includes temperatures or elevation with respect to the see level) the values of attributes can be negative. However, we can claim with certainty that the values of attributes are never less than some large negative threshold value T (e.g. $T = -10^{30}$). Therefore, in regular cases $a_i > T$, $i = 1, ..., n$. For incomplete sets of attributes the values $a_i \leq T$, $i \in \{1, ..., n\}$ can be used for numerical coding of missing input data.

Elementary criteria $g_i(a_i)$, $i = 1, ..., n$ can be arbitrary functions. The most frequent canonical forms are the following:

- Preferred large values (unacceptable if $a_i \leq A$, and perfect if $A < B \leq a_i$):
$$\lambda(a_i) = \max(0, \min(1, (a_i - A)/(B - A))), \ i \in \{1, ..., n\}$$
- Preferred small values (perfect if $a_i \leq C$, and unacceptable if $C < D \leq a_i$):
$$\sigma(a_i) = \max(0, \min(1, (D - a_i)/(D - C))), \ i \in \{1, ..., n\}$$
- Preferred range of values (assuming $A < B < C < D$, perfect if $a_i \in [B, C]$, and unacceptable if $a_i \leq A$ or $a_i \geq D$):
$$\rho(a_i) = \lambda(a_i) + \sigma(a_i) - 1, \ i \in \{1, ..., n\}$$

For simplicity, let us assume that the elementary criteria are based on one of these functions: $g_i(a_i) = \varphi(a_i) \in \{\lambda(a_i), \sigma(a_i), \rho(a_i)\}$ (generally, $\varphi : R \rightarrow I$).

If a_i, $i \in \{1, ..., n\}$ is missing, we can differentiate two cases: the case where there is no reason for penalty, and the case where there is a reason for penalty. The cases where it is justifiable to apply a penalty for missing data are those where we have reasons to believe that if a_i were known, the overall suitability would be less than the suitability computed using reduced criterion that excludes a_i. In other words, these are cases where a_i is intentionally missing because it has an inconvenient value. Let $P_i \in I$ denote a desired penalty for this specific attribute (frequently, it is possible to use the same penalty for all attributes). Cases without penalty are characterized using $P_i = 0$. The effect of maximum penalty $P_i = 1$ should be the same as the effect of $g_i(a_i) = 0$. Consequently, the elementary criteria can express missing data as follows:

$$x_i = g_i(a_i) = \begin{cases} -1 + P_i, & a_i \leq T \text{ (missing data)} \\ \varphi(a_i), & a_i > T \text{ (regular data)} \end{cases} ; \quad \text{now, } g_i : R \rightarrow [-1, 1].$$

This definition generates the following characteristic values of preference/suitability:

$x_i = -1$ Missing data without penalty ($P_i = 0$)

$-1 < x_i < 0$ Missing data with a degree of penalty $P_i = 1 + x_i$; $(0 < P_i < 1)$

$x_i = 0$ Missing data with max. penalty ($P_i = 1$), or no satisfaction

$0 < x_i < 1$ Partial satisfaction of user requirements

$x_i = 1$ Total (perfect) satisfaction of user requirements

Therefore, elementary attribute criteria transmit information about missing data as negative or zero values of preference/suitability. The next step is to organize the aggregation process so that it tolerates negative data (data in the range [-1,1]).

4   Missingness-Tolerant Aggregation

Aggregation of preference can be based on a variety or aggregators. In this paper we assume that the essential aggregator (the generalized conjunction/disjunction [12]) is based on quasi-arithmetic means [14-19]. Let a preference aggregation function of m variables be $z = A_m(x_1,...,x_k,...,x_m)$, and let x_k be an attribute whose value is $x_k = e$, $e \in I$, yielding the aggregated preference $z_e = A_m(x_1,...,e,...,x_m)$. If x_k is missing then we must use the reduced criterion $A_{m-1}(x_1,...,x_{k-1},x_{k+1},...,x_m)$ and for some values of e we can get the unchanged result:

$$A_{m-1}(x_1,...,x_{k-1},x_{k+1},...,x_m) = A_m(x_1,...,e,...,x_m) = z_e$$

If a unique constant value of e satisfies the above relation for any $k \in \{1,...,n\}$ and for any input values, then it is called the *extended neutral element* [17]. Such element should substitute all missing data.

Unfortunately, in evaluation logic the extended neutral element does not exist. However, for all aggregators based on quasi-arithmetic means we can select $e = A_{m-1}(x_1,...,x_{k-1},x_{k+1},...,x_m)$ and the following holds:

$$A_{m-1}(x_1,...,x_{k-1},x_{k+1},...,x_n) =$$
$$A_m(x_1,...,x_{k-1},A_{m-1}(x_1,...,x_{k-1},x_{k+1},...,x_m),x_{k+1},...,x_m)$$

This relationship has the following intuitive interpretation: if an input is missing then the most reasonable assumption is that its value (in the sense of preference or suitability) is in concordance with the values of remaining attributes in the group. This property can be called *the concordance principle*. In other words, if an attribute has a value that is in concordance with the aggregated value of remaining attributes in a group, then such an attribute is redundant, it does not affect the aggregated preference, and it can be omitted without consequences.

The concordance principle shows that if x_k is missing then there are two options. The first option is to use the original aggregator $A_m(x_1,...,x_k,...,x_m)$ where the missing value is substituted by the concordance value $x_k = C_k = A_{m-1}(x_1,...,x_{k-1},x_{k+1},...,x_m)$ and the result of aggregation will again be $A_{m-1}(x_1,...,x_{k-1},x_{k+1},...,x_m)$. Clearly, the second option, which is simpler and more natural, is the "use what you have" option which omits the missing attribute and uses directly the reduced aggregator $A_{m-1}(x_1,...,x_{k-1},x_{k+1},...,x_m)$.

The concordance principle is related to associativity properties studied in [15,17-19]. In the case of aggregation based on quasi-arithmetic means with a strictly monotonic generator function $F: I \rightarrow R \cup \{\pm\infty\}$ a simple proof of the concordance principle is the following:

$$A_m(x_1,...,x_k,...,x_m) = F^{-1}\left(\sum_{i=1}^{m} W_i F(x_i)\right), \quad 0 < W_i < 1, \quad i=1,...,m, \quad \sum_{i=1}^{m} W_i = 1$$

Then, we insert in this aggregator the following value of x_k:

$$x_k = A_{m-1}(x_1,...,x_{k-1},x_{k+1},...,x_m) = F^{-1}\left(\frac{1}{1-W_k}\sum_{\substack{i=1 \\ i\neq k}}^{m} W_i F(x_i)\right), \quad 1-W_k = \sum_{\substack{i=1 \\ i\neq k}}^{m} W_i$$

The proof can be completed as follows:

$$A_m(x_1,...,x_{k-1}, A_{m-1}(x_1,...,x_{k-1},x_{k+1},...,x_m), x_{k+1},...,x_m) = F^{-1}\left(\sum_{i=1}^{m} W_i F(x_i)\right)$$

$$= F^{-1}\left(\sum_{i=1}^{k-1} W_i F(x_i) + \frac{W_k}{1-W_k}\sum_{\substack{i=1 \\ i\neq k}}^{m} W_i F(x_i) + \sum_{i=k+1}^{m} W_i F(x_i)\right)$$

$$= F^{-1}\left(\left(1+\frac{W_k}{1-W_k}\right)\sum_{\substack{i=1 \\ i\neq k}}^{m} W_i F(x_i)\right) = F^{-1}\left(\frac{1}{1-W_k}\sum_{\substack{i=1 \\ i\neq k}}^{m} W_i F(x_i)\right)$$

$$= A_{m-1}(x_1,...,x_{k-1},x_{k+1},...,x_m)$$

For example, if we have a simple arithmetic mean $z = 0.5x_1 + 0.3x_2 + 0.2x_3$ and if x_1 is missing, then we should use the reduced aggregator $z = 0.6x_2 + 0.4x_3$, or the original aggregator where we insert the concordance value $x_1 = 0.6x_2 + 0.4x_3$ to obtain the same result of aggregation: $z = 0.5(0.6x_2 + 0.4x_3) + 0.3x_2 + 0.2x_3 = 0.6x_2 + 0.4x_3$.

The concordance principle in the simplest case of two variables $A_2(x_1,x_2)$ means that if one variable is missing (e.g. x_2) then the preference is computed as

$A_2(x_1, x_1) = x_1$, i.e. the resulting value is the value of the remaining variable. In the case of three variables, $A_3(x_1, x_2, x_3)$, the missing variable (e.g. x_3) should be substituted by the concordance value $A_2(x_1, x_2)$ yielding $A_3(x_1, x_2, A_2(x_1, x_2)) = A_2(x_1, x_2)$, and so forth.

In the case where two variables (x_j and x_k) are missing the presented technique can be expanded in an analogous way, as follows:

$$x_j = x_k = A_{m-2}(x_1, ..., x_{j-1}, x_{j+1}, ..., x_{k-1}, x_{k+1}, ..., x_m)$$

$$= F^{-1}\left(\frac{1}{1-W_j-W_k} \sum_{\substack{i=1 \\ i \notin \{j,k\}}}^{m} W_i F(x_i)\right), \quad 1-W_j-W_k = \sum_{\substack{i=1 \\ i \notin \{j,k\}}}^{m} W_i$$

Then,

$$A_m(x_1, ..., x_{j-1}, A_{m-2}(x_1, ..., x_{j-1}, x_{j+1}, ..., x_{k-1}, x_{k+1}, ..., x_m), x_{j+1}, ...$$
$$..., x_{k-1}, A_{m-2}(x_1, ..., x_{j-1}, x_{j+1}, ..., x_{k-1}, x_{k+1}, ..., x_m), x_{k+1}, ..., x_m)$$

$$= F^{-1}\left(\sum_{i=1}^{m} W_i F(x_i)\right)$$

$$= F^{-1}\left(\sum_{\substack{i=1 \\ i \notin \{j,k\}}}^{m} W_i F(x_i) + \frac{W_j}{1-W_j-W_k} \sum_{\substack{i=1 \\ i \notin \{j,k\}}}^{m} W_i F(x_i) + \frac{W_k}{1-W_j-W_k} \sum_{\substack{i=1 \\ i \notin \{j,k\}}}^{m} W_i F(x_i)\right)$$

$$= F^{-1}\left(\left(1+\frac{W_j+W_k}{1-W_j-W_k}\right) \sum_{\substack{i=1 \\ i \notin \{j,k\}}}^{m} W_i F(x_i)\right) = F^{-1}\left(\frac{1}{1-W_j-W_k} \sum_{\substack{i=1 \\ i \notin \{j,k\}}}^{m} W_i F(x_i)\right)$$

$$= A_{m-2}(x_1, ..., x_{j-1}, x_{j+1}, ..., x_{k-1}, x_{k+1}, ..., x_m)$$

In a general case we can have a set of μ missing inputs $\{x_i\}$, $i \in \theta \subset \{1, ..., m\}$, $\mu = |\theta| \in \{1, ..., m-1\}$. In such a case we first compute the aggregate of existing (known) inputs (this is a direct generalization of the previous cases $\mu = 1$ and $\mu = 2$):

$$x_k|_{k \in \theta} = A_{m-\mu}(...x_i|_{i \notin \theta}...) = F^{-1}\left(\frac{1}{1-\sum_{i \in \theta} W_i} \sum_{i \notin \theta}^{m} W_i F(x_i)\right), \quad 1-\sum_{i \in \theta} W_i = \sum_{i \notin \theta}^{m} W_i$$

Then, this value can be inserted as a substitute for all missing inputs using a general substitution relation for $0 < \mu < m$, as follows:

$$A_m(...x_i|_{i \notin \theta}...x_k|_{k \in \theta}...) = A_m(...x_i|_{i \notin \theta}...A_{m-\mu}(...x_i|_{i \notin \theta}...)...) = A_{m-\mu}(...x_i|_{i \notin \theta}...)$$

The presented technique as applicable in all cases where we use the zero penalty. In cases where we want to have nonzero penalty, we have

$$A_m(...x_i|_{i \notin \theta}...x_k|_{k \in \theta}...)$$

$$= A_m(...x_i|_{i \notin \theta}...[(1-P_k)A_{m-\mu}(...x_i|_{i \notin \theta}...)]|_{k \in \theta}...) \le A_{m-\mu}(...x_i|_{i \notin \theta}...),$$

$$0 \le P_k \le 1, \quad k \in \theta, \quad 0 < \mu < m.$$

In the case of partial conjunction, partial disjunction, and neutrality, if $0 < \mu < m$ then we have $x_i = P_i - 1 \le 0$, $i \in \theta \ne \varnothing$ and $x_i \ge 0$, $i \notin \theta$; note that the cases of maximum penalty $(P_i = 1)$ and no value $(x_i = 0)$ are equivalent. Thus, the penalty-controlled missingness-tolerant aggregator is defined as follows:

$$z = \begin{cases} A_m(x_1,...,x_m), & 0 \le x_i \le 1, \quad i = 1,...,m, & \mu = 0, \ \theta = \varnothing \\ A_m(...x_i|_{i \notin \theta}...[|x_k| A_{m-\mu}(...x_i|_{i \notin \theta}...)]|_{k \in \theta}...), & 0 < \mu < m \\ -A_m(|x_1|,...,|x_m|), & -1 \le x_i < 0, \quad i = 1,...,m, & \mu = m \end{cases}$$

Using the quasi-arithmetic mean $z = F^{-1}(W_1 F(x_1) + ... + W_m F(x_m))$ we can now perform missingness-tolerant aggregation based on the following algorithm:

1. Using preferences $x_1,...,x_m$, $x_i \in [-1,1]$, $i = 1,...,m$ generated by penalty-controlled elementary criteria compute the sum of weights of known attributes:
$$W_{sum} = \sum_{x_i \ge 0} W_i, \quad 0 \le W_{sum} \le 1$$

2. If $W_{sum} = 1$, return $z = F^{-1}(W_1 F(x_1) + ... + W_m F(x_m))$ (no missing data).

3. If $W_{sum} = 0$, return $z = -F^{-1}\left(\sum_{i=1}^{m} W_i F(|x_i|)\right)$, i.e. a negative average negated penalty $(|x_i| = 1 - P_x = \neg P_x)$, which is a non-positive value that will propagate in the subsequent stage of aggregation.

4. Compute the reduced aggregated preference $\bar{x} = F^{-1}\left(W_{sum}^{-1} \sum_{x_i \ge 0} W_i F(x_i)\right)$

5. If all penalties of missing data are zero, then return the aggregated preference
$$z = \bar{x}. \text{ Otherwise return } z = F^{-1}\left(\sum_{x_i \ge 0} W_i F(x_i) + \sum_{x_i < 0} W_i F(|x_i| | \bar{x})\right).$$

Generally, the value of penalty can be different for each input attribute. More often than not, it is convenient to use a fixed penalty $P_i = P$, $\forall i$. Penalties propagate (coded as negative preferences) through the aggregation structure and disappear when combined with regular positive preference scores.

Let us now investigate the missingness-tolerant aggregation in the case of conjunctive ($\unrhd$) and disjunctive ($\unrhd$) partial absorption functions [13,10]. The conjunctive partial absorption (CPA) is a combination of a mandatory input x and a desired/optional input y. The mandatory input x must be (at least partially) satisfied. Assuming $x > 0$, the optional input (y) can partially compensate an insufficient level of x:

$x \unrhd y = x \overline{\overline{\Delta}}(x\tilde{\nabla}y)$ ($\overline{\overline{\Delta}}$ denotes a full conjunction or a hard partial conjunction and $\tilde{\nabla}$ denotes the total disjunction, i.e. any form of disjunction or the arithmetic mean; we assume that $\overline{\overline{\Delta}}$ and $\tilde{\nabla}$ are modeled using quasi-arithmetic means). Applying strictly the missingness-tolerant algorithm to the CPA aggregator we have:

$$x \unrhd y = \begin{cases} x\overline{\overline{\Delta}}(x\tilde{\nabla}y), & x \geq 0,\ y \geq 0 \\ x\overline{\overline{\Delta}}[x\tilde{\nabla} \mid y \mid x], & x \geq 0,\ y < 0 \\ [\mid x \mid (\mid x \mid y\tilde{\nabla}y)]\overline{\overline{\Delta}}(\mid x \mid y\tilde{\nabla}y), & x < 0,\ y \geq 0 \\ -\mid x \mid \overline{\overline{\Delta}}(\mid x \mid \tilde{\nabla} \mid y \mid), & x < 0,\ y < 0 \end{cases}$$

If the optional input y is missing ($x \geq 0$, $y < 0$) the nonexistent value is substituted by $\mid y \mid x = (1 - P_y)x$, where P_y denotes the desired y-penalty. In the case of maximum penalty ($P_y = 1$) the aggregation is equivalent to zero optional input, and in the case without penalty we have $x \unrhd y = x$. If the mandatory input x is missing ($x < 0$, $y \geq 0$) then in the case of maximum penalty we have $x \unrhd y = 0$. In the case of zero penalty, however, we have $x \unrhd y = y$, which may sometimes be a questionable result. If we use penalty $P_x > 0$ then $x \unrhd y < y$. If both inputs are missing, the output is a partial absorption of negated input penalties. E.g., for partial absorption based on the arithmetic and harmonic means, if $P_x = 1 - \mid x \mid = P_y = 1 - \mid y \mid = 1/2$, $x\tilde{\nabla}y = (x + y)/2$ and $x\overline{\overline{\Delta}}y = 2xy/(x + y)$, then we have the following CPA:

$$x \unrhd y = \begin{cases} 2x(x + y)/(3x + y), & x \geq 0,\ y \geq 0 \\ 2x(1 + \mid y \mid)/(3 + \mid y \mid) = 6x/7, & x \geq 0,\ y = -\tfrac{1}{2} \\ \mid x \mid y = 0.5y, & x = -\tfrac{1}{2},\ y \geq 0 \\ 2x(x + y)/(3x + y) = -0.5, & x = -\tfrac{1}{2},\ y = -\tfrac{1}{2} \end{cases}$$

The disjunctive partial absorption is a combination of a sufficient input x and a desired/optional input y. The sufficient input x can fully compensate the lack of optional input y. The desired input can partially (and frequently significantly) compensate the lack of sufficient input: $x \rhd y = x\overline{\overline{\nabla}}(x\tilde{\Delta}y)$ ($\overline{\overline{\nabla}}$ denotes a full disjunction or a hard partial disjunction and $\tilde{\Delta}$ denotes the total conjunction, i.e. any form of conjunction or the arithmetic mean). The missingness-tolerant disjunctive partial absorption aggregator can be organized in the same way as in the case of conjunctive partial absorption.

5   Conclusions

In many LSP evaluation problems input data can be missing, and it is necessary to perform evaluation with incomplete input data. In such cases we must perform evaluation using the reduced set containing only the available input attributes. However, if incomplete input data reflect an intention to hide inconvenient inputs, it is appropriate to use penalty to discourage the practice of hiding disadvantages, and to compute overall suitability that is more realistic than the result obtained without penalty.

References

1. Zillow, Inc., Real Estate and Mortgage Data for Your Site (November 2011), http://zillow.com/howto/api/APIOverview.htm
2. Allison, P.D.: Missing Data. Sage Publications, Thousand Oaks (2001)
3. Little, R.J.A., Rubin, D.B.: Statistical analysis with missing data. Wiley, New York (1987)
4. Howell, D.C.: The analysis of missing data. In: Outhwaite, W., Turner, S. (eds.) Handbook of Social Science Methodology. Sage Publications, London (2007)
5. Howell, D.C.: Treatment of missing data (2009), http://www.uvm.edu/~dhowell/StatPages/More_Stuff/Missing_Data/Missing.html
6. Codd, E.F.: Missing Information (Applicable and Inapplicable) in Relational Databases. ACM SIGMOD Record 15(4), 53–78 (1986)
7. Reiter, R.: A sound and sometimes complete query evaluation algorithm for relational databases with null values. J. Assoc. Comput. Mach (ACM) 33(2), 349–370 (1986)
8. Liao, S.Y., Wang, H.Q., Liu, W.Y.: Functional Dependencies with Null Values, Fuzzy Values, and Crisp Values. IEEE TFS 7(1), 97–103 (1999)
9. De Tré, G., De Caluwe, R., Prade, H.: Null Values in Fuzzy Databases. Journal of Intelligent Information Systems 30(2), 93–114 (2008)
10. Dujmović, J.J.: Preference Logic for System Evaluation. IEEE Transactions on Fuzzy Systems 15(6), 1082–1099 (2007)
11. Dujmović, J., Nagashima, H.: LSP Method and its Use for Evaluation of Java IDE's. International Journal of Approximate Reasoning 41(1), 3–22 (2006)
12. Dujmović, J.J., Larsen, H.L.: Generalized Conjunction/Disjunction. International Journal of Approximate Reasoning 46, 423–446 (2007)
13. Dujmović, J.J.: Partial Absorption Function. Journal of the University of Belgrade, EE Dept., Series Mathematics and Physics (659), 156–163 (1979)
14. Gini, C., et al.: Means. Italian Original, Le Medie, Milano (1958)

15. Mitrinović, D.S., Bullen, P.S., Vasić, P.M.: Means and Related Inequalities (In Serbo-Croatian), Publications of the University of Belgrade EE Dept., No. 600, Belgrade (1977)
16. Bullen, P.S.: Handbook of Means and Their Inequalities. Kluwer (2003 and 2010)
17. Grabisch, M., Marichal, J.-L., Mesiar, R., Pap, E.: Aggregation Functions. Cambridge University Press, Cambridge (2009)
18. Torra, V., Narukawa, Y.: Modeling Decisions. Springer (2007)
19. Beliakov, G., Pradera, A., Calvo, T.: Aggregation Functions: A Guide for Practitioners. Springer (2007)

General Interpolation by Polynomial Functions of Distributive Lattices

Miguel Couceiro[1], Didier Dubois[2], Henri Prade[2], Agnès Rico[3],
and Tamás Waldhauser[4,1]

[1] FSTC, University of Luxembourg, Luxembourg
miguel.couceiro@uni.lu
[2] IRIT, CNRS and Université de Toulouse, France
{dubois,prade}@irit.fr
[3] ERIC, Université de Lyon, France
agnes.rico@univ-lyon1.fr
[4] Bolyai Institute, University of Szeged, Aradi vértanúk tere 1,
H-6720 Szeged, Hungary
twaldha@math.u-szeged.hu

Abstract. For a distributive lattice L, we consider the problem of interpolating functions $f : D \to L$ defined on a finite set $D \subseteq L^n$, by means of lattice polynomial functions of L. Two instances of this problem have already been solved.

In the case when L is a distributive lattice with least and greatest elements 0 and 1, Goodstein proved that a function $f : \{0,1\}^n \to L$ can be interpolated by a lattice polynomial function $p : L^n \to L$ if and only if f is monotone; in this case, the interpolating polynomial p was shown to be unique.

The interpolation problem was also considered in the more general setting where L is a distributive lattice, not necessarily bounded, and where $D \subseteq L^n$ is allowed to range over cuboids $D = \{a_1, b_1\} \times \cdots \times \{a_n, b_n\}$ with $a_i, b_i \in L$ and $a_i < b_i$. In this case, the class of such partial functions that can be interpolated by lattice polynomial functions was completely described.

In this paper, we extend these results by completely characterizing the class of lattice functions that can be interpolated by polynomial functions on arbitrary finite subsets $D \subseteq L^n$. As in the latter setting, interpolating polynomials are not necessarily unique. We provide explicit descriptions of all possible lattice polynomial functions that interpolate these lattice functions, when such an interpolation is available.

1 Introduction and Motivation

The importance of aggregation functions is made apparent by their wide use, not only in pure mathematics (e.g., in the theory of functional equations, measure and integration theory), but also in several applied fields such as operations research, computer and information sciences, economics and social sciences, as well as in other experimental areas of physics and natural sciences. In particular,

S. Greco et al. (Eds.): IPMU 2012, Part III, CCIS 299, pp. 347–355, 2012.

the use of aggregation functions has attracted much attention in decision theory for it provides an elegant and powerful formalism to model preference [1,6] (for general background on aggregation functions, see [7]).

In the qualitative approach to decision making, Sugeno integral [14,15] remains one of the most noteworthy aggregation functions, and this is partially due to the fact that it provides a meaningful way to fuse or merge criteria within universes where essentially no structure, other than order, is assumed (unlike other classical aggregation functions, such as weighted arithmetic means, which require a rich arithmetical structure).

Even though primarily defined over real intervals, Sugeno integrals can be extended to wider domains (not only to arbitrary linearly ordered sets or chains, but also to bounded distributive lattices with bottom and top elements 0 and 1, respectively) via the notion of lattice polynomial function. Essentially, a lattice polynomial function is a combination of variables and constants using the lattice operations $\wedge$ and $\vee$. As it turned out (see e.g. [2,9]), Sugeno integrals coincide exactly with those lattice polynomial functions that are idempotent (that is, which preserve constant tuples); in fact, it can be shown that the preservation of 0 and 1 suffices.

Apart from their theoretical interest, the consideration of Sugeno integrals on distributive lattices (rather than simply on scales or linearly ordered sets) or on finite Boolean algebras [10] is both useful and natural since scores for different criteria may be incomparable (for instance, when "ignorance" and "indifference" are possible scores).

Now in many real-life situations, we are faced with the problem of finding an aggregation operation based on scarce data that are not sufficient to determine a unique function. This fact gives rise to an interesting problem that appears in complete analogy with the classical theory of real polynomial functions, namely, that of interpolation. In this paper we are interested on aggregation functions defined over lattices and thus we consider the problem of interpolating lattice functions $f \colon L^n \to L$ on finite sets $D \subseteq L^n$ by means of Sugeno integrals or, more generally, by lattice polynomial functions.

The interpolation problem also has a learning flavor. The problem of covering a set of data by a set of Sugeno integrals, has been considered in the linearly ordered case [11,13]. More precisely, the condition of existence of a Sugeno integral interpolating a set of data has been laid bare, and the set of solutions (when non-empty) has been characterized as being upper and lower bounded by particular Sugeno integrals (easy to build from data). This process has been shown to be closely related to the version space approach in learning [12]. The theorems presented in this paper generalize these results to the more general case of partially ordered scales, and also open the possibility of the elicitation of families of generalized Sugeno integrals from, e.g., pieces of data where local and global evaluations may be imprecisely known.

The paper is organized as follows. In Section 2 we recall basic notions and terminology, provide the preliminary results needed throughout the paper, and address the interpolation problem we shall be dealing with. As it will become clear, a solution to this problem (when it exists) is not necessarily unique. Thus we present in Section 3 necessary and sufficient conditions for the existence of such a solution and, as a by-product, describe all possible solutions. Moreover, by confining ourselves to linearly ordered sets, we derive previous results obtained in this restricted setting. In Section 4 we address problems left open, and in Section 5 we discuss possible applications of our results.

2   Preliminaries

Throughout this paper let L be a distributive lattice. Recall that a *polynomial function over* L is a mapping $p\colon L^n \to L$ that can be expressed as a combination of the lattice operations $\wedge$ and $\vee$, projections and constants.

In the case when L is bounded, i.e., with a least and a greatest element (which we denote by 0 and 1, respectively), Goodstein [5] showed that polynomial functions $p\colon L^n \to L$ coincide exactly with those lattice functions that can be represented in *disjunctive normal form* (DNF for short) by

$$p(\mathbf{x}) = \bigvee_{I \subseteq [n]} \left(c_I \wedge \bigwedge_{i \in I} x_i \right), \quad \text{where } \mathbf{x} = (x_1, \ldots, x_n) \in L^n. \,^1 \tag{1}$$

Furthermore, by taking $c_I^* := \bigvee_{J \subseteq I} c_J$, we also have

$$p(\mathbf{x}) = \bigvee_{I \subseteq [n]} \left(c_I^* \wedge \bigwedge_{i \in I} x_i \right),$$

and thus we can assume that the coefficients c_I are monotone in the sense that $c_I \leq c_J$ whenever $I \subseteq J$. Under this monotonicity assumption we can recover the coefficients of the DNF from certain values of the polynomial function p. To this extent, for each $I \subseteq [n]$, let $\mathbf{1}_I$ be the tuple in L^n whose i-th component is 1 if $i \in I$ and 0 if $i \notin I$. In this way, $p(\mathbf{1}_I) = c_I$.

These facts are reassembled in the following theorem, which asserts in particular that polynomial functions are uniquely determined by their restrictions to the hypercube $\{0, 1\}^n$.

Theorem 1 (Goodstein [5]). *Let L be a bounded distributive lattice, and let f be a function $f\colon \{0, 1\}^n \to L$. There exists a polynomial function p over L such that $p|_{\{0,1\}^n} = f$ if and only if f is monotone. In this case p is uniquely determined, and can be represented by the DNF*

$$p(\mathbf{x}) = \bigvee_{I \subseteq [n]} \left(f(\mathbf{1}_I) \wedge \bigwedge_{i \in I} x_i \right).$$

Goodstein's theorem can be seen as a solution to an instance of the Interpolation Problem (see below), namely, interpolation on the hypercube $D = \{0, 1\}^n$: a

---

[1] As usual, the empty meet has value 1 and, dually, the empty join has value 0.

function $f\colon \{0,1\}^n \to L$ can be interpolated by a polynomial function $p\colon L^n \to L$ if and only if f is monotone, and in this case p is unique.

This result was generalized in [3] by allowing L to be an arbitrary (possibly unbounded) distributive lattice and by considering functions $f\colon D \to L$, where $D = \{a_1, b_1\} \times \cdots \times \{a_n, b_n\}$ with $a_i, b_i \in L$ and $a_i < b_i$, for each $i \in [n]$. Let $\widehat{\mathbf{e}}_I$ be the "characteristic vector" of $I \subseteq [n]$ (i.e., the tuple $\widehat{\mathbf{e}}_I \in L^n$ whose i-th component is b_i if $i \in I$ and a_i if $i \notin I$). The task of finding a polynomial function (or rather all polynomial functions) that takes prescribed values on the tuples $\widehat{\mathbf{e}}_I$ can be regarded as yet another instance of the Interpolation Problem.

Restricted Interpolation Problem. *Given $D := \{\mathbf{e}_I^D : I \subseteq [n]\}$ and a function $f\colon D \to L$, find all polynomial functions $p\colon L^n \to L$ such that $p|_D = f$.*

In [3], necessary and sufficient conditions were established for the existence of an interpolating polynomial function. Moreover, it was shown that in this more general setting, uniqueness is not guaranteed, and all possible interpolating polynomial functions were provided, thus settling the Restricted Interpolation Problem.

In this paper we extend these results by solving the following general interpolation problem.

Interpolation Problem. *Let L be a distributive lattice. Given an arbitrary finite set $D \subseteq L^n$ and $f\colon D \to L$, find all polynomial functions $p\colon L^n \to L$ such that $p|_D = f$.*

3   Main Results

Let $D \subseteq L^n$ be a finite set, and consider a partial function $f\colon D \to L$. In this section we provide necessary and sufficient conditions that guarantee the existence of a polynomial function $p\colon L^n \to L$ that interpolates f, that is, $p|_D = f$. As a by-product, we will determine all possible interpolating polynomial functions over a natural extension of the distributive lattice L which we now describe.

By the Birkhoff-Priestley representation theorem, we can embed L into a Boolean algebra B; see, e.g., [4]. For the sake of canonicity, we assume that L generates B; under this assumption B is uniquely determined up to isomorphism. The boundary elements of B will be denoted by 0 and 1. This notation will not lead to ambiguity since if L has a least (resp. greatest) element, then it must coincide with 0 (resp. 1). The complement of an element $a \in B$ is denoted by $a'\colon a \vee a' = 1$ and $a \wedge a' = 0$.

Given a function $f\colon D \to L$, we define the following two elements in B for each $I \subseteq [n]$:

$$c_I^- := \bigvee_{\mathbf{a} \in D} \left(f(\mathbf{a}) \wedge \bigwedge_{i \notin I} a_i' \right) \quad \text{and} \quad c_I^+ := \bigwedge_{\mathbf{a} \in D} \left(f(\mathbf{a}) \vee \bigvee_{i \in I} a_i' \right).$$

Observe that $I \subseteq J$ implies $c_I^- \leq c_J^-$ and $c_I^+ \leq c_J^+$. Let p^- and p^+ be the polynomial functions over B given by these two systems of coefficients:

$$p^-(\mathbf{x}) := \bigvee_{I \subseteq [n]} \left(c_I^- \wedge \bigwedge_{i \in I} x_i \right) \quad \text{and} \quad p^+(\mathbf{x}) := \bigvee_{I \subseteq [n]} \left(c_I^+ \wedge \bigwedge_{i \in I} x_i \right).$$

As it will become clear, p^- and p^+ are the least and greatest polynomial functions over B whose restriction to D coincides with f (whenever such a polynomial function exists). First, we need to establish a few auxiliary results.

Given $I \subseteq [n]$ and $\mathbf{a} = (a_1, \ldots, a_n), \mathbf{x} = (x_1, \ldots, x_n) \in B^n$, let $\mathbf{x}_I^{\mathbf{a}}$ be the n-tuple whose i-th component is a_i if $i \in I$, and x_i otherwise. If $I = \{i\}$, then we write $\mathbf{x}_i^{a_i}$ instead of $\mathbf{x}_I^{\mathbf{a}}$.

Lemma 1. *Let $p \colon B^n \to B$ be a polynomial function over B. For $I \subseteq [n]$ and $\mathbf{x} \in B^n$, the polynomial functions q_I^- and q_I^+ given by*

$$q_I^-(\mathbf{a}) := p(\mathbf{x}_I^{\mathbf{a}}) \wedge \bigwedge_{i \in I} a_i' \quad \text{and} \quad q_I^+(\mathbf{a}) := p(\mathbf{x}_I^{\mathbf{a}}) \vee \bigvee_{i \in I} a_i',$$

are nonincreasing.

Proof. Since monotonicity is defined componentwise, to show that q_I^- is nonincreasing it suffices to consider the case when I is a singleton.

So let $I = \{i\}$ and $\mathbf{a} \in B^n$. In this case, $p(\mathbf{x}_i^{\mathbf{a}})$ can be regarded as a unary polynomial function and thus, by (1), it is of the form $s \vee (a_i \wedge t)$, for some $s \leq t$. Hence, q_I^- can be expressed as

$$q_I^-(\mathbf{a}) = \left(s \vee (a_i \wedge t) \right) \wedge a_i'.$$

By distributivity, we get $q_I^-(\mathbf{a}) = s \wedge a_i'$, which shows that the first claim holds. The second claim follows dually, and the proof of the lemma is complete. $\quad\square$

Corollary 1. *Let $p \colon B^n \to B$ be a polynomial function over B. For every $I \subseteq [n]$ and $\mathbf{a} \in B^n$,*

$$p(\mathbf{1}_I) \leq p(\mathbf{a}) \vee \bigvee_{i \in I} a_i' \quad \text{and} \quad p(\mathbf{1}_I) \geq p(\mathbf{a}) \wedge \bigwedge_{i \notin I} a_i'.$$

Proof. Let $\mathbf{b} = \mathbf{a}_{[n] \setminus I}^0$; clearly, $\mathbf{a}, \mathbf{1}_I \geq \mathbf{b}$. Since p is nondecreasing, we have $p(\mathbf{1}_I) \geq p(\mathbf{b})$, and since $b_i' = 1$ for every $i \in [n] \setminus I$, it follows from Lemma 1 that

$$p(\mathbf{1}_I) \geq p(\mathbf{b}) \wedge \bigwedge_{i \notin I} b_i' \geq p(\mathbf{a}) \wedge \bigwedge_{i \notin I} a_i'.$$

This shows that the second claim holds; the first follows similarly. $\quad\square$

Using Corollary 1, we can now provide necessary conditions on the coefficients of interpolating polynomials.

Lemma 2. *Let $f\colon D \to L$ be a function defined on a finite set $D \subseteq L^n$, and let $p\colon B^n \to B$ be a polynomial function over B given by (1). If $p|_D = f$, then $c_I^- \leq c_I \leq c_I^+$.*

Proof. Suppose $p|_D = f$. By Corollary 1, for every $I \subseteq [n]$ and $\mathbf{a} \in D$,

$$p(\mathbf{a}) \wedge \bigwedge_{i \notin I} a_i' \leq p(\mathbf{1}_I) \leq p(\mathbf{a}) \vee \bigvee_{i \in I} a_i'.$$

Since $p(\mathbf{a}) = f(\mathbf{a})$, for every $\mathbf{a} \in D$, it follows that

$$\bigvee_{\mathbf{a} \in D} \left(f(\mathbf{a}) \wedge \bigwedge_{i \notin I} a_i' \right) \leq p(\mathbf{1}_I) \leq \bigwedge_{\mathbf{a} \in D} \left(f(\mathbf{a}) \vee \bigvee_{i \in I} a_i' \right),$$

and hence $c_I^- \leq c_I \leq c_I^+$ as desired. $\square$

To show that this condition is also sufficient, we make use of the following lemma.

Lemma 3. *Let $f\colon D \to L$ be a function defined on a finite set $D \subseteq L^n$. Then $p^-(\mathbf{b}) \geq f(\mathbf{b}) \geq p^+(\mathbf{b})$, for every $\mathbf{b} \in D$.*

Proof. By definition of p^- and using the fact that for each $I \subseteq [n]$,

$$c_I^- = \bigvee_{\mathbf{a} \in D} \left(f(\mathbf{a}) \wedge \bigwedge_{i \notin I} a_i' \right) \geq f(\mathbf{b}) \wedge \bigwedge_{i \notin I} b_i',$$

we have

$$p^-(\mathbf{b}) = \bigvee_{I \subseteq [n]} \left(c_I^- \wedge \bigwedge_{i \in I} b_i \right) \geq \bigvee_{I \subseteq [n]} \left(f(\mathbf{b}) \wedge \bigwedge_{i \notin I} b_i' \wedge \bigwedge_{i \in I} b_i \right)$$

$$= f(\mathbf{b}) \wedge \bigvee_{I \subseteq [n]} \left(\bigwedge_{i \notin I} b_i' \wedge \bigwedge_{i \in I} b_i \right).$$

By repeated application of distributivity, it is not difficult to verify that

$$\bigvee_{I \subseteq [n]} \left(\bigwedge_{i \notin I} b_i' \wedge \bigwedge_{i \in I} b_i \right) = 1,$$

and thus $p^-(\mathbf{b}) \geq f(\mathbf{b})$. Dually, we can also verify that $f(\mathbf{b}) \geq p^+(\mathbf{b})$, which completes the proof. $\square$

We can now characterize the class of functions over a distributive lattice L that can be interpolated on finite domains by polynomial functions over the Boolean algebra generated by L. In fact, the following theorem explicitly determines all possible interpolating polynomial functions, whenever such polynomial functions exist.

Theorem 2. *Let $f\colon D \to L$ be a function defined on a finite set $D \subseteq L^n$, and let $p\colon B^n \to B$ be a polynomial function over B given by (1). Then the following conditions are equivalent:*

1. p interpolates f, i.e., $p|_D = f$;
2. $c_I^- \leq c_I \leq c_I^+$;
3. $p^- \leq p \leq p^+$.

Proof. Clearly, $(2) \Longleftrightarrow (3)$. By Lemma 2, $(1) \Longrightarrow (2)$. Moreover, if (3) holds, then using Lemma 3 we conclude that for every $\mathbf{b} \in D$,

$$f(\mathbf{b}) \leq p^-(\mathbf{b}) \leq p(\mathbf{b}) \leq p^+(\mathbf{b}) \leq f(\mathbf{b}).$$

Hence, $p|_D = f$. □

From Theorem 2 it follows that a necessary and sufficient condition for the existence of a polynomial function $p : B^n \to B$ such that $p|_D = f$ is $c_I^- \leq c_I^+$, for every $I \subseteq [n]$.

Moreover, if for every $I \subseteq [n]$, there is $c_I \in L$ such that $c_I^- \leq c_I \leq c_I^+$, then and only then there is a polynomial function $p : L^n \to L$ such that $p|_D = f$.

The latter condition leads us to considering the case when L is a complete lattice (i.e., for which arbitrary joins and meets exist), and to defining two operators cl and int as follows: For $b \in B$, let

$$cl\,(b) := \bigwedge_{x \in L, x \geq b} x \quad \text{and} \quad int\,(b) := \bigvee_{x \in L, x \leq b} x.$$

It is not difficult to see that for any $b_1, b_2 \in B$, we have

$$cl\,(b_1 \vee b_2) = cl\,(b_1) \vee cl\,(b_2) \quad \text{and} \quad int\,(b_1 \wedge b_2) = int\,(b_1) \wedge int\,(b_2).$$

Using this fact, the necessary and sufficient condition given above for the existence of an interpolating polynomial function over L can be translated into the following system of inequalities.

Corollary 2. *If L is complete, then there is a polynomial function $p : L^n \to L$ such that $p|_D = f$ if and only if for every $I \subseteq [n]$ there is $c_I \in L$ such that $c_I^- \leq c_I \leq c_I^+$ or, equivalently,*

$$cl(c_I^-) = \bigvee_{\mathbf{a} \in D} cl(f(\mathbf{a}) \wedge \bigwedge_{i \notin I} a_i') \leq \bigwedge_{\mathbf{a} \in D} int(f(\mathbf{a}) \vee \bigvee_{i \in I} a_i') = int(c_I^+),$$

for every $I \subseteq [n]$.

Remark 1. Corollary 2 generalizes Theorem 10 in [3] which established necessary and sufficient conditions for the existence of a solution of the Restricted Interpolation Problem.

In the case when L is a finite chain, a solution to the Interpolation Problem was given in [11] and where, rather than polynomial functions, the interpolating functions were assumed to be Sugeno integrals, i.e., idempotent polynomial functions; see [8,9].

Now if L is a finite chain, then

$$cl(c_I^-) = \bigvee\{f(\mathbf{a}) : \mathbf{a} \in D, \quad \forall i \notin I, \quad a_i < f(\mathbf{a})\}, \quad \text{and}$$
$$int(c_I^+) = \bigwedge\{f(\mathbf{a}) : \mathbf{a} \in D, \quad \forall i \in I, \quad a_i > f(\mathbf{a})\}.$$

Hence, $cl(c_I^-) \leq int(c_I^+)$ if and only if for every $\mathbf{a}, \mathbf{b} \in D$,

$$f(\mathbf{a}) > f(\mathbf{b}) \Rightarrow \exists i \notin I : a_i \geq f(\mathbf{a}) \quad \text{or} \quad \exists i \in I : b_i \leq f(\mathbf{b}). \tag{2}$$

It is not difficult to see that condition (2) holds for every $I \subseteq [n]$ if and only if condition (3) (see theorem below) also holds. The following result basically reformulates Theorem 3 of [11] in the language of lattice theory.

Theorem 3 ([11]). *Let L be a finite chain, and let $f : D \to L$ be a function defined on a finite subset $D \subseteq L^n$. Then there exists a polynomial function $p : L^n \to L$ such that $p|_D = f$ if and only if*

$$\forall \mathbf{a}, \mathbf{b} \in D : \ f(\mathbf{a}) > f(\mathbf{b}) \Rightarrow \exists i \in [n] : b_i \leq f(\mathbf{b}) < f(\mathbf{a}) \leq a_i. \tag{3}$$

4   Further Work

When we consider a function $f : D \to L$, a polynomial function can be indentified if and only if for every $I \subseteq [n]$ there exists $c_I \in L$ such that $c_I^- \leq c_I \leq c_I^+$. In some practical cases this condition would be not satisfied, i.e., the data would be inconsistent with respect to a polynomial function. In such a case one issue can be to build a family of polynomial functions as it is done in the totally ordered context in [13]. More precisely, a partition of the dataset can be built in which each set of the partition is compatible with a family of polynomial functions. In general, many partitions are possible since their definition without other conditions depends on the order in which the data are considered. We can add a condition to choose one partition. For example, we can decide to look for the smallest partition in terms of number of subsets.

The complexity to check the conditions $c_I^- \leq c_I^+$ for all $I \subseteq [n]$ is at least 2^n, so these conditions become costly when n increases. In the totally ordered context presented in [11] the complexity can be reduced since the check only needs p^2 comparisons of compatibility where p is the cardinality of D. This raises the question of finding a similar result in our context.

5   Applications and Concluding Remarks

To replace missing data is a common problem for the statistical treatment of data. There are many methods to give a value to the missing data. On the other hand, Sugeno integral is classically used in decision theory to represent the behavior of a decision-maker. Since polynomials functions are a generalization of Sugeno integrals, it seems natural to make use of these polynomial functions to replace the missing data.

Acknowledgments. The first named author is supported by the internal research project F1R-MTH-PUL-09MRDO of the University of Luxembourg. The fifth named author acknowledges that the present project is supported by the TÁMOP-4.2.1/B-09/1/KONV-2010-0005 program of the National Development Agency of Hungary, by the Hungarian National Foundation for Scientific Research under grants no. K77409 and K83219, by the National Research Fund of Luxembourg, and cofunded under the Marie Curie Actions of the European Commission (FP7-COFUND).

References

1. Bouyssou, D., Dubois, D., Prade, H., Pirlot, M. (eds.): Decision-Making Process – Concepts and Methods. ISTE/John Wiley (2009)
2. Couceiro, M., Marichal, J.-L.: Characterizations of discrete Sugeno integrals as polynomial functions over distributive lattices. Fuzzy Sets and Systems 161(5), 694–707 (2010)
3. Couceiro, M., Waldhauser, T.: A generalization of Goodstein's theorem: interpolation by polynomial functions of distributive lattices, http://arxiv.org/abs/1110.0321
4. Davey, B.A., Priestley, H.A.: Introduction to Lattices and Order. Cambridge University Press, New York (2002)
5. Goodstein, R.L.: The Solution of Equations in a Lattice. Proc. Roy. Soc. Edinburgh Section A 67, 231–242 (1965/1967)
6. Grabisch, M.: The application of fuzzy integrals in multicriteria decision making. Eur. J. Oper. Res. 89(3), 445–456 (1996)
7. Grabisch, M., Marichal, J.-L., Mesiar, R., Pap, E.: Aggregation Functions. Encyclopedia of Mathematics and its Applications. Cambridge University Press, Cambridge (2009)
8. Marichal, J.-L.: On Sugeno integral as an aggregation function. Fuzzy Sets and Systems 114, 347–365 (2000)
9. Marichal, J.-L.: Weighted lattice polynomials. Discrete Mathematics 309(4), 814–820 (2009)
10. Rico, A.: Sugeno integral in a finite Boolean algebra. Fuzzy Sets and Systems 159, 1709–1718 (2008)
11. Rico, A., Grabisch, M., Labreuche, C., Chateauneuf, A.: Preference modeling on totally ordered sets by the Sugeno integral. Discrete Applied Math. 147(1), 113–124 (2005)
12. Prade, H., Rico, A., Serrurier, M.: Elicitation of Sugeno Integrals: A version space learning perspective. In: Rauch, J., Raś, Z.W., Berka, P., Elomaa, T. (eds.) ISMIS 2009. LNCS, vol. 5722, pp. 392–401. Springer, Heidelberg (2009)
13. Prade, H., Rico, A., Serrurier, M., Raufaste, E.: Elicitating Sugeno Integrals: Methodology and a Case Study. In: Sossai, C., Chemello, G. (eds.) ECSQARU 2009. LNCS, vol. 5590, pp. 712–723. Springer, Heidelberg (2009)
14. Sugeno, M.: Theory of Fuzzy Integrals and its Applications. PhD thesis. Tokyo Institute of Technology, Tokyo (1974)
15. Sugeno, M.: Fuzzy measures and fuzzy integrals – a survey. In: Gupta, M.M., Saridis, G.N., Gaines, B.R. (eds.) Fuzzy Automata and Decision Processes, pp. 89–102. North-Holland, New York (1977)

Aggregation of Weakly Quasi-convex Fuzzy Sets

Vladimir Janiš[1], Susana Montes[2], and Tania Iglesias[2]

[1] Matej Bel University, Slovak Republic
vladimir.janis@umb.sk
[2] University of Oviedo, Spain
{montes,iglesiasctania}@uniovi.es

Abstract. Weakly quasi-convex fuzzy sets have been defined as an extension of the class of quasi-convex fuzzy sets. We study the binary commutative aggregation operators which preserve weak quasi-convexity. It is shown, that there is only one such aggregation operator and it is the trivial (the largest) one. As a corollary we obtain that in general the intersection of weakly quasi-convex fuzzy sets is not weakly quasi-convex.

1 Introduction

Convexity plays a prominent role in various applications, most of all perhaps in the optimization theory. When working with fuzzy sets and fuzzy optimization (see [1]), it is necessary to specify the notion of convexity for fuzzy sets.

A very common definition of a convex fuzzy set is the following:

Definition 1. *A fuzzy set μ of a linear space is said to be convex, if for all $x, y \in \operatorname{supp} \mu$ and $\lambda \in [0, 1]$ there is*

$$\mu(\lambda x + (1 - \lambda)y) \geq \lambda\mu(x) + (1 - \lambda)\mu(y).$$

However, this definition is in many cases not very convenient. First, it cannot be used for more general fuzzy sets, like lattice-valued ones. The second and more important reason is, that convexity of a fuzzy set in this sence is not equivalent with the convexity of its cuts. (An α-cut of a fuzzy set μ will be denoted by $(\mu)_\alpha$.) Therefore the quasi-convex fuzzy sets are defined as follows:

Definition 2. *A fuzzy subset μ of a linear space is quasi-convex, if for all $x, y \in \operatorname{supp} \mu$ and $\lambda \in [0, 1]$ there is*

$$\mu(\lambda x + (1 - \lambda)y) \geq \min\{\mu(x), \mu(y)\}.$$

It is easy to show that a fuzzy set is quasi-convex if and only if all its cuts are convex.

In [4] the concept of quasi-convexity is slightly weakened, where just existence of a value above the minimum of the endpoints is required:

Definition 3. *([4]) A fuzzy subset μ of a linear space is weakly quasi-convex if for all $x, y \in \operatorname{supp} \mu$ there exists $\lambda \in (0, 1)$ such that*

$$\mu(\lambda x + (1 - \lambda)y) \geq \min\{\mu(x), \mu(y)\}.$$

S. Greco et al. (Eds.): IPMU 2012, Part III, CCIS 299, pp. 356–359, 2012.

Clearly every quasi-convex fuzzy set is also weakly quasi-convex while the opposite is not true, as it can be seen from the proofs later.

In a similar way to the case of quasi-convexity we can show that a fuzzy set is weakly quasi-convex if and only if for each $\alpha \in (0, 1]$ the set $\{\lambda x + (1 - \lambda)y; 0 < \lambda < 1\} \cap (\mu)_\alpha$ is nonempty, whenever $x, y \in (\mu)_\alpha$ and $(\mu)_\alpha \neq \emptyset$ (for details see [4]).

Preservation of convexity under intersection is one of the basic properties of convex sets. There is a natural question about the preservation of the above mentioned generalizations of convexity. Moreover, we will not restrict ourselves to the intersection, but we will consider an arbitrary binary commutative aggregation operator.

By a binary aggregation operator on the unit interval we understand a mapping $A : [0, 1]^2 \to [0, 1]$ that is non-decreasing in both variables and fulfills $A(0, 0) = 0, A(1, 1) = 1$. For more details see [2]

2 Case of Quasi-convex Fuzzy Sets

Considering intersections of fuzzy sets we come to the notion of a triangular norm. However, triangular norms are special cases of aggregation operators and therefore we formulate our question in the following way: Suppose μ and ν are quasi-convex fuzzy sets. Under which aggregation of their values is the result again a quasi-convex fuzzy set? For fuzzy sets μ, ν and an aggregation operator A by their aggregation we mean the fuzzy set $A(\mu, \nu)(t) = A(\mu(t), \nu(t))$.

This problem has been solved in [3] for lattice valued aggregation operators with the following result:

Proposition 1. *Let $A : L^2 \to L$ be an aggregation operator on a bounded lattice L, let $\mu, \nu : R^n \to L$ be quasi-convex fuzzy sets. Then the following are equivalent:*

1. *The lattice-valued fuzzy set $A(\mu, \nu)$ is quasi-convex,*
2. *$A(\alpha \wedge \gamma, \beta \wedge \delta) = A(\alpha, \beta) \wedge A(\gamma, \delta)$ for each $\alpha, \beta, \gamma, \delta \in L$.*

For real valued symmetric (commutative) aggregation operators the following result was obtained in [3]:

Proposition 2. *Let $A : [0, 1]^2 \to [0, 1]$ be a symmetric aggregation operator, let μ, ν be quasi-convex fuzzy sets on the real line. Then the following are equivalent:*

1. *The fuzzy set $A(\mu, \nu)$ is quasi-convex,*
2. *$A(\alpha, \alpha) = A(\alpha, 1)$ for each $\alpha \in [0, 1]$.*

Our aim is to provide a similar description of suitable aggregation operators for weakly quasi-convex fuzzy sets.

3 Main Results

We will consider an arbitrary symmetric binary aggregation operator on a unit interval. First we will formulate some necessary conditions for A to preserve weak quasi-convexity.

Proposition 3. *Let A be a symmetric binary aggregation operator such that for each weakly quasi-convex fuzzy sets μ and ν the fuzzy set $A(\mu, \nu)$ is weakly quasi-convex. If $\alpha \in (0, 1]$, then $A(\alpha, 1) = 1$.*

Proof. Suppose that A preserves weak quasi-convexity. Denote by Q the set of all rational numbers and let $\alpha \in (0, 1]$. Take $\mu, \nu : [0, 1] \to [0, 1]$ such that

$$\mu(t) = \begin{cases} 1, & t \in Q, \\ \alpha, & t \in R \setminus Q, \end{cases} \qquad \nu(t) = \begin{cases} 1, & t \in (R \setminus Q) \cup \{0, 1\}, \\ \alpha, & t \in (0, 1) \cap Q. \end{cases}$$

Clearly both μ, ν are weakly quasi-convex. For their aggregation we have

$$A(\mu, \nu)(0) = A(\mu, \nu)(1) = A(1, 1) = 1.$$

As we assume that $A(\mu, \nu)$ is weakly quasi-convex there has to be at least one $t \in (0, 1)$ for which $A(\mu, \nu)(t) \geq 1$. Accounting the symmetry of A this implies that $A(\alpha, 1) = 1$. $\qquad\square$

Both fuzzy sets in the proof were examples of weakly quasi-convex fuzzy sets that are not quasi-convex.

The second necessary condition deals with the diagonal elements of A.

Proposition 4. *Let A be a symmetric binary aggregation operator such that for each weakly quasi-convex fuzzy sets μ and ν the fuzzy set $A(\mu, \nu)$ is weakly quasi-convex. If $\alpha \in (0, 1]$, then $A(\alpha, \alpha) = 1$.*

Proof. Suppose that A preserves weak quasi-convexity. Take $\mu, \nu : [0, 1] \to [0, 1]$ such that

$$\mu(t) = \begin{cases} 1, & t = 0, \\ \alpha, & t \in (0, 1], \end{cases} \qquad \nu(t) = \begin{cases} \alpha, & t \in [0, 1), \\ 1, & t = 1. \end{cases}$$

These fuzzy sets are again weakly quasi-convex. Using the result of Proposition 3 we see that their aggregation is the fuzzy set with the boundary values $A(\mu, \nu)(0) = A(\mu, \nu)(1) = A(\alpha, 1) = 1$.

As A preserves weak quasi-convexity, there has to be some $t \in (0, 1)$ such that $A(\mu, \nu)(t) = 1$. From this we obtain $A(\alpha, \alpha) = 1$ for each $\alpha \in (0, 1]$. $\qquad\square$

So we see that for suitable aggregation operators the values of the aggregation in the semi-open square $(0, 1]^2$ have to be 1. The value $A(0, 0)$ is equal to 0 by the definition of an aggregation operator and the remaining values are shown in the following proposition.

Proposition 5. *Let A be a symmetric binary aggregation operator such that for each weakly quasi-convex fuzzy sets μ and ν the fuzzy set $A(\mu, \nu)$ is weakly quasi-convex. If $\alpha \in (0, 1]$, then $A(\alpha, 0) = 1$.*

Proof. Suppose that A preserves weak quasi-convexity. Take $\mu, \nu : [0, 1] \to [0, 1]$ such that

$$\mu(t) = \begin{cases} \alpha, & t \in Q, \\ 0, & t \in R \setminus Q, \end{cases} \qquad \nu(t) = \begin{cases} \alpha, & t \in (R \setminus Q) \cup \{0, 1\}, \\ 0, & t \in (0, 1) \cap Q. \end{cases}$$

These are weakly quasi-convex fuzzy sets and by the consideration similar to the previous ones we come to the conclusion $A(\alpha, 0) = A(\alpha, \alpha) = 1$.   □

As a consequence we get that if a symmetric aggregation operator preserves weak quasi-convexity, it has to be the operator for which $A(0, 0) = 0$ and $A(\alpha, \beta) = 1$ in all other cases, i.e. the largest possible aggregation operator. Conversely, it is trivial to see that such aggregation operator preserves weak quasi-convexity.

We can therefore summarize the following:

Proposition 6. *The only symmetric aggregation operator A such that for any weakly quasi-convex fuzzy sets μ, ν the fuzzy set $A(\mu, \nu)$ is weakly quasi-convex is the mapping $A(0, 0) = 0$ and $A(\alpha, \beta) = 1$ otherwise.*

4   Conclusion

We have shown that the only symmetric aggregation operator preserving weak quasi-convexity is the largest one. Hence for any non-trivial symmetric aggregation there exist weakly quasi-convex fuzzy sets μ, ν such that $A(\mu, \nu)$ is not weakly quasi-convex. As any triangular norm that is used to represent intersections of fuzzy sets is a special case of a symmetric aggregation operator (and the maximal aggregation operator is not a triangular norm), we can state, that in general any intersection of weakly quasi-convex fuzzy sets does not preserve weak quasi-convexity.

Acknowledgements. The research in this paper is supported by the Agency of the Slovak Ministry of Education for the Structural Funds of the EU, under project ITMS:26220120007 and grant 1/0297/11 provided by Slovak grant agency VEGA and the Spanish Ministry of Science and Innovation grant MTM2010-17844.

References

1. Ammar, E., Metz, J.: On fuzzy convexity and parametric fuzzy optimization. Fuzzy Sets and Systems (49), 135–141 (1992)
2. Calvo, T., Mayor, G., Mesiar, R. (eds.): Aggregation operators. STUDFUZZ, vol. 97. Physica Verlag, Heidelberg (2002)
3. Janiš, V., Kráľ, P., Renčová, M.: Aggregation operators preserving quasiconvexity. Information Science (submitted)
4. Syau, Y.R.: Some properties of weakly convex fuzzy mappings. Fuzzy Sets and Systems (123), 203–207 (2001)

The Bipolar Universal Integral

*Salvatore Greco[1], Radko Mesiar[2], and Fabio Rindone[1]

[1] Department of Economics and Business,
University of Catania, Corso Italia 55, 95129 Catania, Italy
{salgreco,frindone}@unict.it
[2] Department of Mathematics and Descriptive Geometry,
Faculty of Civil Engineering, Slovak University of Technology, Bratislava, Slovakia
and Institute of Theory of Information and Automation,
Czech Academy of Sciences, Prague, Czech Republic
radko.mesiar@stuba.sk

Abstract. The concept of universal integral, recently proposed, generalizes the Choquet, Shilkret and Sugeno integrals. Those integrals admit a bipolar formulation, useful in those situations where the underlying scale is bipolar. In this paper we propose the bipolar universal integral generalizing the Choquet, Shilkret and Sugeno bipolar integrals. To complete the generalization we also provide the characterization of the bipolar universal integral with respect to a level dependent bi-capacity.

Keywords: Choquet, Sugeno and Shilkret integrals, universal integral, bipolar integrals.

1 Introduction

Recently a concept of universal integral has been proposed [14]. The universal integral generalizes the Choquet integral [2], the Sugeno integral [18] and the Shilkret integral [17]. Moreover, in [12], [13] a formulation of the universal integral with respect to a level dependent capacity has been proposed, in order to generalize the level-dependent Choquet integral [9], the level-dependent Shilkret integral [1] and the level-dependent Sugeno integral [15]. The Choquet, Shilkret and Sugeno integrals admit a bipolar formulation, useful in those situations where the underlying scale is bipolar ([5], [6], [10], [8]). In this paper we introduce and characterize the bipolar universal integral, which generalizes the Choquet, Shilkret and Sugeno bipolar integrals. We introduce and characterize also the bipolar universal integral with respect to a level dependent capacity, which generalizes the level-dependent bipolar Choquet, Shilkret and Sugeno integrals proposed in [9], [8].

The paper is organized as follows. In section 2 we introduce the basic concepts. In section 3 we define and characterize the bipolar universal integral. In section 4 we give an illustrative example of a bipolar universal integral which is neither the Choquet nor Sugeno or Shilkret type. In section 5 we define and characterize the bipolar universal integral with respect to a level dependent bi-capacity. Finally, in section 6, we present conclusions.

S. Greco et al. (Eds.): IPMU 2012, Part III, CCIS 299, pp. 360–369, 2012.
© Springer-Verlag Berlin Heidelberg 2012

2 Basic Concepts

Given a set of criteria $N = \{1, \ldots, n\}$, an *alternative* x can be identified with a score vector $x = (x_1, \ldots, x_n) \in [-\infty, +\infty]^n$, being x_i the evaluation of x with respect to the ith criterion. For the sake of simplicity, without loss of generality, in the following we consider the bipolar scale $[-1, 1]$ to expose our results, so that $x \in [-1, 1]^n$. Let us consider the set of all disjoint pairs of subsets of N, i.e. $\mathcal{Q} = \{(A, B) \in 2^N \times 2^N : A \cap B = \emptyset\}$. With respect to the binary relation $\precsim$ on $\mathcal{Q}$ defined as $(A, B) \precsim (C, D)$ iff $A \subseteq C$ and $B \supseteq D$, $\mathcal{Q}$ is a lattice, i.e. a partial ordered set in which any two elements have a unique supremum $(A, B) \vee (C, D) = (A \cup C, B \cap D)$ and a unique infimum $(A, B) \wedge (C, D) = (A \cap C, B \cup D)$. For all $(A, B) \in \mathcal{Q}$ the indicator function $1_{(A,B)} : N \to \{-1, 0, 1\}$ is the function which attains 1 on A, -1 on B and 0 on $(A \cup B)^c$.

Definition 1. *A function $\mu_b : \mathcal{Q} \to [-1, 1]$ is a normalized bi-capacity ([5], [6], [10]) on N if*

- $\mu_b(\emptyset, \emptyset) = 0$, $\mu_b(N, \emptyset) = 1$ and $\mu_b(\emptyset, N) = -1$;
- $\mu_b(A, B) \leq \mu_b(C, D) \ \forall \ (A, B), (C, D) \in \mathcal{Q} : (A, B) \precsim (C, D)$.

Definition 2. *The bipolar Choquet integral of $x = (x_1, \ldots, x_n) \in [-1, 1]^n$ with respect to a bi-capacity μ_b is given by ([5], [6], [10], [9]):*

$$Ch_b(x, \mu_b) = \int_0^\infty \mu_b(\{i \in N : x_i > t\}, \{i \in N : x_i < -t\})dt. \tag{1}$$

The bipolar Choquet integral of $x = (x_1, \ldots, x_n) \in [-1, 1]^n$ with respect to the bi-capacity μ_b can be rewritten as

$$Ch_b(x, \mu_b) = \sum_{i=1}^n \left(|x_{(i)}| - |x_{(i-1)}|\right) \mu_b(\{j \in N : x_j \geq |x_{(i)}|\}, \{j \in N : x_j \leq -|x_{(i)}|\}), \tag{2}$$

being $() : N \to N$ any permutation of index such that $0 = |x_{(0)}| \leq |x_{(1)}| \leq \ldots \leq |x_{(n)}|$. Let us note that to ensure that $(\{j \in N : x_j \geq |t|\}, \{j \in N : x_j \leq -|t|\}) \in \mathcal{Q}$ for all $t \in \mathbb{R}$, we adopt the convention - which will be maintained trough all the paper - that in the case of $t = 0$ the inequality $x_j \leq -|t| = 0$ must be intended as $x_j < -|t| = 0$.

In this paper we use the symbol $\bigvee$ to indicate the maximum and $\bigwedge$ to indicate the minimum. The *symmetric maximum* of two elements - introduced and discussed in [3], [4] - is defined by the following binary operation:

$$a \otimes b = \begin{cases} -(|a| \vee |b|) & \text{if } b \neq -a \text{ and either } |a| \vee |b| = -a \text{ or } = -b \\ 0 & \text{if } b = -a \\ |a| \vee |b| & \text{else.} \end{cases}$$

In [16] it has been showed as on the domain $[-1, 1]$ the symmetric maximum coincides with two recent symmetric extensions of the Choquet integral, the balancing Choquet integral and the fusion Choquet integral, when they are computed with respect to the strongest capacity (i.e. the capacity which attains zero on the empty set and one elsewhere). However, the symmetric maximum of a set X cannot be defined, being $\oslash$ non associative. Suppose that $X = \{3, -3, 2\}$, then $(3 \oslash -3) \oslash 2 = 2$ or $3 \oslash (-3 \oslash 2) = 0$, depending on the order. Several possible extensions of the symmetric maximum for dimension $n, n > 2$ have been proposed (see [4], [7] and also the relative discussion in [16]). One of these extensions is based on the splitting rule applied to the maximum and to the minimum as described in the following. Let $X = \{x_1, \ldots, x_m\} \subseteq \mathbb{R}$, the *bipolar maximum* of X, shortly $\bigvee^b X$, is defined as follow: if there exists an element $x_k \in X$ such that $|x_k| > |x_j| \; \forall j : x_j \neq x_k$ then $\bigvee^b X = x_k$; otherwise $\bigvee^b X = 0$. Clearly, the bipolar maximum of a set X is related to the symmetric maximum of two elements by means of

$$\bigvee^b X = \left(\bigvee X\right) \oslash \left(\bigwedge X\right). \qquad (3)$$

In the same way and for an infinite set X, it is possible to define the concept of $\sup^{bip} X$ as the symmetric maximum applied to the supremum and the infimum of X.

Definition 3. *The bipolar Shilkret integral of $x = (x_1, \ldots, x_n) \in [-1, 1]^n$ with respect to a bi-capacity μ_b is given by [8]:*

$$Sh_b(x, \mu_b) = \bigvee_{i \in N}^b \{|x_i| \cdot \mu_b(\{j \in N : x_j \geq |x_i|\}, \{j \in N : x_j \leq -|x_i|\})\}. \qquad (4)$$

Definition 4. *A bipolar measure on N with a scale $(-\alpha, \alpha)$, $\alpha > 0$, is any function $\nu_b : Q \to (-\alpha, \alpha)$ satisfying the following properties:*

1. $\nu_b(\emptyset, \emptyset) = 0$;
2. $\nu_b(N, \emptyset) = \alpha$, $\nu_b(\emptyset, N) = -\alpha$;
3. $\nu_b(A, B) \leq \nu_b(C, D) \; \forall \; (A, B), (C, D) \in \mathcal{Q} \; : \; (A, B) \precsim (C, D)$.

Definition 5. *The bipolar Sugeno integral of $x = (x_1, \ldots, x_n) \in (-\alpha, \alpha)^n$ with respect to the bipolar measure ν_b on N with scale $(-\alpha, \alpha)$ is given by [8]:*

$$Su_b(x, \nu_b) = \bigvee_{i \in N}^b \Big\{ \text{sign}\left(\nu_b\left(\{j \in N : x_j \geq |x_i|\}, \{j \in N : x_j \leq -|x_i|\}\right)\right) \cdot$$

$$\cdot \bigwedge \{|\nu_b(\{j \in N : x_j \geq |x_i|\}, \{j \in N : x_j \leq -|x_i|\})|, |x_i|\} \Big\}. \qquad (5)$$

3   The Universal Integral and the Bipolar Universal Integral

In order to define the universal integral it is necessary to introduce the concept of pseudomultiplication. This is a function $\otimes : [0, 1] \times [0, 1] \to [0, 1]$, which is nondecreasing in each component (i.e. for all a_1, a_2, b_1, $b_2 \in [0,1]$ with $a_1 \leq a_2$ and $b_1 \leq b_2$, $a_1 \otimes b_1 \leq a_2 \otimes b_2$), has 0 as annihilator (i.e. for all $a \in [0,1]$, $a \otimes 0 = 0 \otimes a = 0$) and has a neutral element $e \in]0,1]$ (i.e. for all $a \in [0,1]$, $a \otimes e = e \otimes a = a$). If $e = 1$ then $\otimes$ is a *semicopula*, i.e. a binary operation $\otimes : [0,1]^2 \to [0,1]$ that is nondecreasing in both components and has 1 as neutral element. Observe that in the definition of semicopula it is not necessary to state that 0 is a annihilator, because this can be elicited. A semicopula satisfies $a \otimes b \leq \min\{a,b\}$ for all $(a,b) \in [0,1]^2$, indeed, suppose that $a = \min\{a,b\}$ then $a \otimes b \leq a \otimes 1 = a$. It follows that for all $a \in [0,1]$, $0 \leq 0 \otimes a \leq 0$ and $0 \leq a \otimes 0 \leq 0$, i.e. $a \otimes 0 = 0 \otimes a = 0$ and, then, 0 is a annihilator. A semicopula $\otimes : [0,1]^2 \to [0,1]$ which is associative and commutative is called a *triangular norm*.

A capacity [2] or fuzzy measure [18] on N is a non decreasing set function $m : 2^N \to [0,1]$ such that $m(\emptyset) = 0$ and $m(N) = 1$.

Definition 6. *[14] Let F be the set of functions $f : N \to [0,1]$ and M the set of capacities on N. A function $I : M \times F \to [0,1]$ is a universal integral on the scale $[0,1]$ (or fuzzy integral) if the following axioms hold:*

(I1) $I(m,f)$ is nondecreasing with respect to m and with respect to f;
(I2) there exists a semicopula $\otimes$ such that for any $m \in M$, $c \in [0,1]$ and $A \subseteq N$,
  $I(m, c \cdot 1_A) = c \otimes m(A)$;
(I3) for all pairs $(m_1, f_1), (m_2, f_2) \in M \times F$, such that for all $t \in [0,1]$,
  $m_1 \{i \in N : f_1(i) \geq t\} = m_2 \{i \in N : f_2(i) \geq t\}$, $I(m_1, f_1) = I(m_2, f_2)$.

We can generalize the concept of universal integral from the scale $[0,1]$ to the symmetric scale $[-1,1]$ by extending definition 6.

Definition 7. *Let F_b be the set of functions $f : N \to [-1,1]$ and M_b the set of bi-capacities on Q. A function $I_b : M_b \times F_b \to [-1,1]$ is a bipolar universal integral on the scale $[-1,1]$ (or bipolar fuzzy integral) if the following axioms hold:*

(I1) $I_b(m_b, f)$ is nondecreasing with respect to m_b and with respect to f;
(I2) there exists a semicopula $\otimes$ such that for any $m_b \in M_b$, $c \in [0,1]$ and $(A,B) \in Q$, $I(m_b, c \cdot 1_{(A,B)}) = sign(m_b(A,B)) \; (c \otimes |m_b(A,B)|)$;
(I3) for all pairs $(m_{b_1}, f_1), (m_{b_2}, f_2) \in M_b \times F_b$, such that for all $t \in [0,1]$,
  $m_{b_1} (\{i \in N : f_1(i) \geq t\}, \{i \in N : f_1(i) \leq -t\}) =$
  $= m_{b_2} (\{i \in N : f_2(i) \geq t\}, \{i \in N : f_2(i) \leq -t\})$, $I(m_{b_1}, f_1) = I(m_{b_2}, f_2)$.

Clearly, in definition 6, F can be identified with $[0,1]^n$ and in definition 7, F_b can be identified with $[-1,1]^n$, such that a function $f : N \to [-1,1]$ can be regarded as a vector $\boldsymbol{x} \in [-1,1]^n$. Note that the bipolar Choquet, Shilkret and Sugeno integrals are bipolar universal integrals in the sense of Definition 7. Observe that the underlying semicopula $\otimes$ is the standard product in the case of the bipolar Choquet and Shilkret integrals, while $\otimes$ is the minimum (with neutral element $\beta = 1$) for the Sugeno integral.

Now we turn our attention to the characterization of the bipolar universal integral. Due to axiom $(I3)$ for each universal integral I_b and for each pair $(m_b, \boldsymbol{x}) \in M_b \times F_b$, the value $I_b(m_b, \boldsymbol{x})$ depends only on the function $h^{(m_b, \boldsymbol{x})}$: $[0,1] \to [-1,1]$, defined for all $t \in [0,1]$ by

$$h^{(m,\boldsymbol{x})}(t) = m_b\left(\{i \in N : x_i \geq t\}, \{i \in N : x_i \leq -t\}\right). \tag{6}$$

Note that for each $(m_b, \boldsymbol{x}) \in M_b \times F_b$ such a function is not in general monotone but it is Borel measurable, since it is a step function, i.e. a finite linear combination of indicator functions of intervals. To see this, suppose that $() : N \to N$ is a permutation of criteria such that $|x_{(1)}| \leq \ldots \leq |x_{(n)}|$ and let us consider the following intervals decomposition of $[0,1]$: $A_1 = [0, |x_{(1)}|]$, $A_j =]|x_{(j)}|, |x_{(j+1)}|]$ for all $j = 1, \ldots, n-1$ and $A_{n+1} =]|x_{(n)}|, 1]$. Thus, we can rewrite the function h as

$$h^{(m,\boldsymbol{x})}(t) = \sum_{j=1}^{n} m_b\left(\{i \in N : x_i \geq |x_{(j)}|\}, \{i \in N : x_i \leq -|x_{(j)}|\}\right) \cdot 1_{A_j}(t). \tag{7}$$

Let $\mathcal{H}_n$ be the subset of all step functions with no more than n-values in $\mathcal{F}_{[-1,1]}^{([0,1], \mathcal{B}([0,1]))}$, the set of all Borel measurable functions from $[0,1]$ to $[-1,1]$.

Proposition 1. *A function $I_b : M_b \times F_b \to [-1,1]$ is a bipolar universal integral on the scale $[-1,1]$ related to some semicopula $\otimes$ if and only if there is a function $J : \mathcal{H}_n \to \mathbb{R}$ satisfying the following conditions:*

(J1) J is nondecreasing;
(J2) $J(d \cdot 1_{[x, x+c]}) = sign(d)(c \otimes |d|)$ for all $[x, x+c] \subseteq [0,1]$ and for all $d \in [-1,1]$;
(J3) $I(m_b, f) = J\left(h^{(m_b, f)}\right)$ for all $(m_b, f) \in M_b \times F_b$.

4   An Illustrative Example

The following is an example of a bipolar universal integral (which is neither the Choquet nor Sugeno or Shilkret type), and illustrates the interrelationship between the functions I, J and the semicopula $\otimes$. Let $I_b : M_b \times F_b \to \mathbb{R}$ be given by

$$I(m_b, f) = \sup^{bip}\left\{\frac{t \cdot m_b(\{f \geq t\}, \{f \leq -t\})}{1 - (1-t)(1 - |m_b(\{f \geq t\}, \{f \leq -t\})|)} \mid t \in]0,1]\right\}. \tag{8}$$

Note that (8) defines a bipolar universal integral, indeed if $m_b \geq m_b'$ and $f \geq f'$ then $h^{(m_b, f)} \geq h^{(m_b', f')}$ and being the function $t \cdot h/[1 - (1-t)(1 - |h|)]$ non decreasing in $h \in \mathbb{R}$, we conclude that $I(m_b, f) \geq I(m_b', f')$ using the monotonicity of the bipolar supremum. Moreover

$$I(m_b, c \cdot 1_{(A,B)}) = sign(m_b(A,B))\frac{t \cdot |m_b(\{f \geq t\}, \{f \leq -t\})|}{1 - (1-t)(1 - |m_b(\{f \geq t\}, \{f \leq -t\})|)} =$$
$$= sign(m_b(A,B))(c \otimes |m_b(A,B)|). \tag{9}$$

This means that the semicopula underlying the bipolar universal integral (9) is the Hamacher product

$$a \otimes b = \begin{cases} 0 & \text{if } a = b = 0 \\ \frac{a \cdot b}{1-(1-a)(1-b)} & \text{if } |a| + |b| \neq 0. \end{cases}$$

Now let us compute this integral in the simple situation of $N = \{1,2\}$. In this case the functions we have to integrate can be identified with two dimensional vectors $x = (x_1, x_2) \in [-1,1]^2$ and we should define a bi-capacity on Q. For example

$$m_b(\{1\}, \emptyset) = 0.6, \quad m_b(\{2\}, \emptyset) = 0.2, \quad m_b(\{1\}, \{2\}) = 0.1,$$

$$m_b(\{2\}, \{1\}) = -0.3, \quad m_b(\emptyset, \{1\}) = -0.1 \quad \text{and} \quad m_b(\emptyset, \{2\}) = -0.5.$$

First let us consider the four cases $|x_1| = |x_2|$. If $x \geq 0$:

$$I(m_b, (x, x)) = x, \quad I(m_b, (x, -x)) = \frac{0.1x}{0.1 + 0.9x},$$

$$I(m_b, (-x, x)) = \frac{-0.3x}{0.3 + 0.7x} \quad \text{and} \quad I(m_b, (-x, -x)) = -x.$$

For all the other possible cases, we have the following formula

$$I(m_b, (x, y)) = \begin{cases} V^b\left\{y, \frac{0.6x}{0.6+0.4x}\right\} & x > y \geq 0 \\[2mm] V^b\left\{\frac{0.1|y|}{0.1+0.9|y|}, \frac{0.6x}{0.6+0.4x}\right\} & x \geq 0 > y > -x \\[2mm] V^b\left\{\frac{0.1x}{0.1+0.9x}, \frac{-0.5|y|}{0.5+0.5|y|}\right\} & x \geq 0 \geq -x > y \\[2mm] V^b\left\{x, \frac{-0.5|y|}{0.5+0.5|y|}\right\} & 0 > x > y \\[2mm] V^b\left\{x, \frac{0.2y}{0.2+0.8y}\right\} & y > x \geq 0 \\[2mm] V^b\left\{\frac{-0.3|x|}{0.3+0.7|x|}, \frac{0.2y}{0.2+0.8y}\right\} & y \geq 0 > x > -y \\[2mm] V^b\left\{\frac{-0.3y}{0.3+0.7y}, \frac{-0.1|x|}{0.1+0.9|x|}\right\} & y \geq 0 \geq -y > x \\[2mm] V^b\left\{y, \frac{-0.1|x|}{0.1+0.9|x|}\right\} & 0 > y > x. \end{cases} \tag{10}$$

5   The Bipolar Universal Integral with Respect to a Level Dependent Bi-capacity

All the bipolar fuzzy integrals (1), (4) and (5) as well as the universal integral, admit a further generalization with respect to a *level dependent capacity* ([9],

[8], [13]). Next, after remembering previous definitions, we will give the concept of *bipolar universal integral with respect to a level dependent capacity.*

Definition 8. *[9] A bipolar level dependent bi-capacity is a function* μ_{bLD} : $\mathcal{Q} \times [0,1] \to [-1,1]$ *satisfying the following properties:*

1. *for all* $t \in [0,1]$, $\mu_{bLD}(\emptyset, \emptyset, t) = 0$, $\mu_{bLD}(N, \emptyset, t) = 1$, $\mu_{bLD}(\emptyset, N, t) = -1$;
2. *for all* $(A, B, t), (C, D, t) \in \mathcal{Q} \times [0,1]$ *such that* $(A, B) \precsim (C, D)$, $\mu_{bLD}(A, B, t) \le \mu_{bLD}(C, D, t)$;
3. *for all* $(A, B) \in \mathcal{Q}$, $\mu_{bLD}(A, B, t)$ *considered as a function with respect to* t *is Borel measurable.*

Definition 9. *[9] The bipolar Choquet integral of a vector* $\boldsymbol{x} = (x_1, \dots, x_n) \in [-1,1]^n$ *with respect to the level dependent bi-capacity* μ_{bLD} *is given by*

$$Ch_{bLD}(\boldsymbol{x}) = \int_0^{max_i|x_i|} \mu_{bLD}(\{i \in N : x_i \ge t\}, \{i \in N : x_i \le -t\}, t) dt. \quad (11)$$

A level dependent bi-capacity μ_{bLD} is said Shilkret compatible if for for all $t, r \in [-1,1]$ such that $t \le r$, and $(A, B), (C, D) \in \mathcal{Q}$ with $(A, B) \precsim (C, D)$, $t\mu_{bLD}((A, B), t) \le r\mu_{bLD}((C, D), r)$.

Definition 10. *[8] The bipolar level dependent Shilkret integral of* $\boldsymbol{x} = (x_1, \dots, x_n) \in [-1,1]^n$ *with respect to a Shilkret compatible bi-capacity level dependent,* μ_{bLD}, *is given by*

$$Sh_{bLD}(\boldsymbol{x}, \mu_{bLD}) = \bigvee_{i \in N}^b \left\{ \sup_{t \in]0, |x_i|]} \{t \cdot \mu_{bLD}(\{j \in N : x_j \ge t\}, \{j \in N : x_j \le -t\}, t)\} \right\}. \quad (12)$$

Definition 11. *[8] A bipolar level dependent measure on* N *with a scale* $[-\alpha, \alpha]$ *with* $\alpha > 0$, *is any function* $\nu_{bLD} : \mathcal{Q} \times [-\alpha, \alpha] \to [-\alpha, \alpha]$ *satisfying the following properties:*

1. $\nu_{bLD}(\emptyset, \emptyset, t) = 0$ *for all* $t \in [-\alpha, \alpha]$;
2. $\nu_{bLD}(N, \emptyset, t) = \alpha$, $\nu_{bLD}(\emptyset, N, t) = -\alpha$ *for all* $t \in (\alpha, \beta)$;
3. *for all* $(A, B), (C, D) \in \mathcal{Q}$ *such that* $(A, B) \precsim (C, D)$, *and for all* $t \in [-\alpha, \alpha]$, $\nu_{bLD}(A, B, t) \le \nu_{bLD}(C, D, t)$.

Definition 12. *[8] The bipolar level dependent Sugeno integral of* $\boldsymbol{x} = (x_1, \dots, x_n) \in [-\alpha, \alpha]^n$ *with respect to the bipolar measure* ν_{bLD} *is given by*

$$\bigvee_{i \in N}^b \left\{ \sup_{t \in]0, |x_i|]}^{bip} \{ \text{sign} [\nu_{bLD}(\{j \in N : x_j \ge t\}, \{j \in N : x_j \le -t\}, t)] \right.$$
$$\left. \cdot \min \{ |\nu_{bLD}(\{j \in N : x_j \ge t\}, \{j \in N : x_j \le -t\}, t)|, t\} \} \right\} = Su_{bLD}(\boldsymbol{x}, \nu_{bLD}). (13)$$

A level dependent bi-capacity can be, also, indicated as $M_b^t = (m_{b,t})_{t \in]0,1]}$ where $m_{b,t}$ is a bi-capacity. Given a level dependent bi-capacity $M_b^t = (m_{b,t})_{t \in]0,1]}$ for each alternative $\boldsymbol{x} \in [-1,1]^n$ we can define the function $h_{M_b^t,f} : [0,1] \to [-1,1]$, which accumulates all the information contained in M_b^t and f, by:

$$h_{M_b^t,f}(t) = m_{b,t}(\{j \in N : x_j \geq t\}, \{j \in N : x_j \leq -t\}) \qquad (14)$$

In general, the function $h_{M_b^t,f}$ is neither monotone nor Borel measurable. Following the ideas of inner and outer measures in Caratheodory's approach [11], we introduce the two functions $\left(h_{M_b^t,f}\right)^* : [0,1] \to [-1,1]$ and $\left(h_{M_b^t,f}\right)_* : [0,1] \to [-1,1]$ defined by

$$\left(h_{M_b^t,f}\right)^* = \inf\left\{h \in \mathcal{H} \mid h \geq h_{M_b^t,f}\right\},$$
$$\left(h_{M_b^t,f}\right)_* = \sup\left\{h \in \mathcal{H} \mid h \geq h_{M_b^t,f}\right\}. \qquad (15)$$

Clearly, both functions (15) are non increasing and, therefore, belong to $\mathcal{H}$. If the level dependent bi-capacity M_b^t is constant, then the three functions considered in (14), (15) coincide.

Let $\mathcal{M}_b$ the set of all level dependent bi-capacities on Q, for a fixed $M_b^t \in \mathcal{M}_b$ a function $f : N \to [-1,1]$ is M_b^t-measurable if the function $h_{M_b^t,f}$ is Borel measurable. Let $F_{[-1,1]}^{M_b^t}$ be the set of all M_b^t measurable functions. Let us consider

$$\mathcal{L}_{[-1,1]} = \bigcup_{M_b^t \in \mathcal{M}_b} M_b^t \times F_{[-1,1]}^{M_b^t}$$

Definition 13. *A function $L_b : \mathcal{L}_{[-1,1]} \to [-1,1]$ is a level-dependent bipolar universal integral on the scale $[-1,1]$ if the following axioms hold:*

(I1) $I_b(m,f)$ is nondecreasing in each component;

(I2) there is a bipolar universal integral $I_b : M_b \times F_b \to \mathbb{R}$ such that for each bipolar capacity $m_b \in M_b$, for each $\boldsymbol{x} \in [-1,1]^n$ and for each level dependent bipolar capacity $M_b^t \in \mathcal{M}_b$, satisfying $m_{b,t} = m_b$ for all $t \in]0,1]$, we have

$$L_b\left(M_b^t, \boldsymbol{x}\right) = I_b\left(m_b, \boldsymbol{x}\right);$$

(I3) for all pairs $(M_{b_1}, f_1), (M_{b_2}, f_2) \in \mathcal{L}_{[-1,1]}$ with $h_{M_{b_1},f_1} = h_{M_{b_2},f_2}$ we have

$$L_b\left(M_{b_1}, f_1\right) = L_b\left(M_{b_2}, f_2\right).$$

Obviously the bipolar Choquet, Shilkret and Sugeno integrals with respect to a level dependent capacity are level-dependent bipolar universal integrals in the sense of Definition 13.

Finally, we present the representation theorem which gives necessary and sufficient conditions to be a function $L_b : \mathcal{L}_{[-1,1]} \to [-1,1]$ a level-dependent bipolar universal integral.

Proposition 2. *A function $L_b : \mathcal{L}_{[-1,1]} \to [-1,1]$ is a level-dependent bipolar universal integral related to some semicopula $\otimes$ if and only if there is a semicopula $\otimes : [0,1]^2 \to [0,1]$ and a function $J : \mathcal{H} \to \mathbb{R}$ satisfying the following conditions:*

(J1) J is nondecreasing;
(J2) $J(d \cdot 1_{]0,c]}) = sign(d)(c \otimes |d|)$ for all $[x, x+c] \subseteq [0,1]$ and for all $d \in [-1,1]$;
(J3) $L_b(M_b, f) = J(h_{M_b,f})$ for all $(M_b^t, f) \in \mathcal{L}_{[-1,1]}$.

6   Conclusions

The concept of universal integral generalizes, over all, the Choquet, Shilkret and Sugeno integrals. Those integrals admit a bipolar formulation, helpful for the case in which the underlying scale is bipolar. In this paper we have defined and characterized the bipolar universal integral, thus providing a common frame including the bipolar Choquet, Shilkret and Sugeno integrals. Moreover, we have also defined and characterized the bipolar universal integral with respect to a level dependent bi-capacity, which includes, as notable examples, the bipolar level dependent Choquet, Shilkret and Sugeno integrals.

Acknowledgment. This work was supported by grants GACRP 402/11/0378 and VEGA 1/0171/12.

References

[1] Bodjanova, S., Kalina, M.: Sugeno and Shilkret integrals, and T-and S-evaluators. In: SISY 2009 - 7th International Symposium on Intelligent Systems and Informatics, pp. 109–114 (2009)

[2] Choquet, G.: Theory of Capacities. Annales de l'Institute Fourier (Grenoble) 5, 131–295 (1953/1954)

[3] Grabisch, M.: The symmetric Sugeno integral. Fuzzy Sets and Systems 139(3), 473–490 (2003)

[4] Grabisch, M.: The Möbius transform on symmetric ordered structures and its application to capacities on finite sets. Discrete Mathematics 287(1-3), 17–34 (2004)

[5] Grabisch, M., Labreuche, C.: Bi-capacities–I: definition, Möbius transform and interaction. Fuzzy Sets and Systems 151(2), 211–236 (2005)

[6] Grabisch, M., Labreuche, C.: Bi-capacities–II: the Choquet integral. Fuzzy Sets and Systems 151(2), 237–259 (2005)

[7] Grabisch, M., Marichal, J.L., Mesiar, R., Pap, E.: Aggregation Functions (Encyclopedia of Mathematics and its Applications). Cambridge University Press (2009)

[8] Greco, S.: Generalizing again the Choquet integral: the profile dependent Choquet integral. In: Mesiar, R., Klement, E.P., Dubois, D., Grabisch, M. (eds.) Decision Theory: Qualitative and Quantitative Approaches. Linz Seminar on Fuzzy Set and System, pp. 66–79 (2011)

[9] Greco, S., Matarazzo, B., Giove, S.: The Choquet integral with respect to a level dependent capacity. Fuzzy Sets and Systems 175(1), 1–35 (2011)

[10] Greco, S., Matarazzo, B., Slowinski, R.: Bipolar Sugeno and Choquet integrals. In: De Baets, B., Fodor, J., Pasi, G. (eds.) EUROWorking Group on Fuzzy Sets, Workshop on Informations Systems (EUROFUSE 2002), pp. 191–196 (2002)

[11] Halmos, P.R.: Measure theory, vol. 18. Springer (1974)

[12] Klement, E.P., Kolesárová, A., Mesiar, R., Stupňanová, A.: Universal Integrals Based on Level Dependent Capacities. In: IFSA-EUSFLAT. Citeseer (2009)

[13] Klement, E.P., Kolesárová, A., Mesiar, R., Stupňanová, A.: A generalization of universal integrals by means of level dependent capacities (Preprint submitted to Knowledge-Based Systems) (2011)

[14] Klement, E.P., Mesiar, R., Pap, E.: A universal integral as common frame for Choquet and Sugeno integral. IEEE Transactions on Fuzzy Systems 18(1), 178–187 (2010)

[15] Mesiar, R., Mesiarová-Zemánková, A., Ahmad, K.: Level-dependent Sugeno integral. IEEE Transactions on Fuzzy Systems 17(1), 167–172 (2009)

[16] Mesiar, R., Mesiarová-Zemánková, A., Ahmad, K.: Discrete Choquet integral and some of its symmetric extensions. Fuzzy Sets and Systems 184(1), 148–155 (2011)

[17] Shilkret, N.: Maxitive measure and integration. In: Indagationes Mathematicae (Proceedings), vol. 74, pp. 109–116. Elsevier (1971)

[18] Sugeno, M.: Theory of fuzzy integrals and its applications. Ph.D. Thesis. Tokyo Institute of Technology (1974)

Web-Geometric View on Uninorms and Structure of Some Special Classes

Milan Petrík[1] and Radko Mesiar[2]

[1] Institute of Computer Science,
Academy of Sciences of the Czech Republic,
Prague, Czech Republic
Department of Mathematics and Statistics,
Faculty of Science, Masaryk University,
Brno, Czech Republic
petrik@cs.cas.cz

[2] Department of Mathematics and Descriptive Geometry,
FCE, Slovak University of Technology,
Bratislava, Slovakia
Centre of Excellence IT4Innovations,
Division of the University of Ostrava, IRAFM,
Ostrava, Czech Republic
mesiar@math.sk

Abstract. This paper studies the relation between associativity of uninorms and geometry of their level sets which is enabled by adopting the concepts of web geometry, a branch of differential geometry, and the Reidemeister closure condition. Based on this result, the structure of some special classes of uninorms is described. Namely, it is the class of uninorms with involutive underlying t-norms and t-conorms and the class of uninorms with involutive underlying t-norms and idempotent underlying t-conorm (as well as the corresponding dual cases).

Keywords: associativity, contour, level set, Reidemeister closure condition, structural characterization, underlying triangular norm, underlying triangular conorm, uninorm, web geometry.

1   Introduction

The notion of *uninorm* has been introduced by Yager and Rybalov [12] as a generalization of the notions of *triangular norm* (*t-norm* for short) and *triangular conorm* (*t-conorm* for short). It is a commutative, associative, non-decreasing binary operation $*: [0,1]^2 \to [0,1]$ with a neutral (unit) element $e \in [0,1]$. A t-norm is exactly a uninorm with a neutral element $e = 1$ while a t-conorm is exactly a uninorm with a neutral element $e = 0$. For an overview and the basic results on uninorms, see the related papers [4,5].

In inspiration by the previous results [10,9], this paper intents to show a relation between associativity of uninorms and geometry of their level sets. This task is done by adopting the concepts of *web geometry* [1,2], a branch of differential

S. Greco et al. (Eds.): IPMU 2012, Part III, CCIS 299, pp. 370–378, 2012.
© Springer-Verlag Berlin Heidelberg 2012

geometry, and the *Reidemeister closure condition* [11]. We focus here only on the uninorms with a neutral element $e \in {]}0,1{[}$; the definition of a uninorm with $e = 1$ resp. $e = 0$ coincide with the definition of a t-norm resp. t-conorm and such cases have been treated already elsewhere [10]. Concerning another results dealing with the associativity of uninorms in a geometric way, we refer to the work by Jenei [6] and Maes and De Baets [7].

2   Preliminaries

Having a t-norm $\circ\colon [0,1]^2 \to [0,1]$ resp. a t-conorm $\bullet\colon [0,1]^2 \to [0,1]$ their *induced negators* are defined as functions $\underset{\circ}{\neg}\colon [0,e] \to [0,e]$ resp. $\underset{\bullet}{\neg}\colon [0,e] \to [0,e]$ given by

$$\underset{\circ}{\neg}x = \sup\{y \in [0,1] \mid x \circ y = 0\},$$

$$\underset{\bullet}{\neg}x = \inf\{y \in [0,1] \mid x \bullet y = 1\}.$$

A t-norm resp. a t-conorm is called *involutive* if its corresponding negator is *involutive*, i.e., if $\underset{\circ}{\neg}\underset{\circ}{\neg}x = x$ resp. $\underset{\bullet}{\neg}\underset{\bullet}{\neg}x = x$ for all $x \in [0,1]$. In such cases $\underset{\circ}{\neg}$ resp. $\underset{\bullet}{\neg}$ is a decreasing bijection of $[0,1]$.

A uninorm $*\colon [0,1]^2 \to [0,1]$ (can be a t-norm or a t-conorm) is called *idempotent* if $x * x = x$ for all $x \in [0,1]$. While the only idempotent t-norm resp. t-conorm is the minimum resp. the maximum, the class of idempotent uninorms is richer [3,8].

The next definion and theorem describe how a uninorm is given by a t-norm and a t-conorm.

Definition 1. *Let* $*\colon [0,1]^2 \to [0,1]$ *be a commutative, non-decreasing binary operation with a neutral element* $e \in {]}0,1{[}$. *We define the binary operations* $\underset{*}{\wedge}\colon [0,1]^2 \to [0,1]$ *and* $\overset{*}{\vee}\colon [0,1]^2 \to [0,1]$ *by:*

$$x \underset{*}{\wedge} y = \frac{(e \cdot x) * (e \cdot y)}{e}, \tag{1}$$

$$x \overset{*}{\vee} y = \frac{((e + (1-e) \cdot x) * (e + (1-e) \cdot x)) - e}{1 - e} \tag{2}$$

where $+$ *resp.* $\cdot$ *denotes usual addition resp. multiplication of real numbers. It can be trivially observed that*

$$x * y = e \cdot \left(\tfrac{x}{e} \underset{*}{\wedge} \tfrac{y}{e}\right) \qquad \textit{for } (x,y) \in [0,e]^2,$$

$$x * y = e + (1-e) \cdot \left(\tfrac{x-e}{1-e} \overset{*}{\vee} \tfrac{y-e}{1-e}\right) \textit{ for } (x,y) \in [e,1]^2.$$

Theorem 1. *[5] Let* $*\colon [0,1]^2 \to [0,1]$ *be a uninorm with a neutral element* $e \in {]}0,1{[}$. *Then* $\underset{*}{\wedge}$ *and* $\overset{*}{\vee}$ *is a t-norm and a t-conorm, respectively.*

Due to this fact, in the case of a uninorm $*\colon [0,1]^2 \to [0,1]$ the operation $\underset{*}{\wedge}$ resp. $\overset{*}{\vee}$ is called *underlying t-norm* resp. *underlying t-conorm* of $*$.

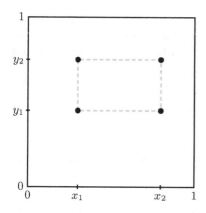 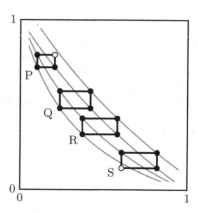

Fig. 1. Left: Four points, (x_1, y_1), (x_1, y_2), (x_2, y_1), and (x_2, y_2), forming the rectangle $P = \langle x_1, x_2 \rangle \times \langle y_1, y_2 \rangle$. Right: Illustration of the equivalence relation $\approx$ defined on the set of rectangles. The gray curves represent level sets of a uninorm. Observe that $Q \approx R$ which does not hold for any other pair.

3   Web-Geometric View on Uninorms

Let $\diamond\colon [0,1]^2 \to [0,1]$ be a binary operation. Its *a-level set*, for some $a \in [0,1]$, is the set

$$\{(x, y) \in [0,1]^2 \mid x \diamond y = a\}. \tag{3}$$

Further, we say that $(a, b), (c, d) \in [0, 1]^2$ are *equivalent*, and we write $(a, b) \approx (c, d)$, if $a \diamond b = c \diamond d$. Notice that the relation $\approx$ is an equivalence induced by $\diamond$ and, immediately, the equivalence classes of $\approx$ are exactly the level sets of $\diamond$ as introduced in (3).

By a *rectangle* P in $[0,1]^2$ we mean a set of points (called *vertices*) of the type

$$P = \{(x_1, y_1), (x_1, y_2), (x_2, y_1), (x_2, y_2)\}.$$

where $x_1, x_2, y_1, y_2 \in [0, 1]$ are called the *coordinates* of the rectangle P. We denote the fact, that the rectangle P is uniquely given by the coordinates x_1, x_2, y_1, y_2, by

$$P = \langle x_1, x_2 \rangle \times \langle y_1, y_2 \rangle,$$

Note that if we interchange the two x-coordinates or interchange the two y-coordinates in the above notation we obtain an equivalent rectangle as the notation, actually, denotes again the same set of vertices. Thus

$$\langle x_1, x_2 \rangle \times \langle y_1, y_2 \rangle = \langle x_2, x_1 \rangle \times \langle y_1, y_2 \rangle = \langle x_1, x_2 \rangle \times \langle y_2, y_1 \rangle = \langle x_2, x_1 \rangle \times \langle y_2, y_1 \rangle.$$

Clearly, every rectangle is a proper subset of $[0, 1]^2$ and it is a set of either four vertices, two vetices, or one vertex. An example of a rectangle is illustrated in Figure 1-left; note that, although a rectangle is a set of points, we will connect them, for better visibility, by lines and thus depict our rectangle as a real rectangle.

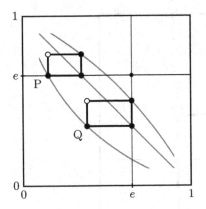 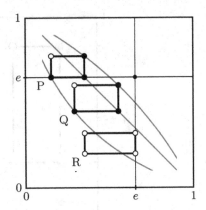

Fig. 2. Left: Example of a pair of rectangles P, Q that are (e, e)-aligned, i.e., $P \simeq_{e,e} Q$. Indeed, this pair is (e, e)-local since the neutral element e is a coordinate of both of the rectangles. Moreover, the pairs of vertices where e is a coordinate lay on the same level set. Right: Example of rectangles that are not (e, e)-aligned, i.e., $P \not\simeq_{e,e} Q \not\simeq_{e,e} R$. The pair P, Q is not (e, e)-aligned as e is not a coordinate of Q. The pair P, R is not (e, e)-aligned as the pairs of vertices where e is a coordinate do not lay on the same level set.

Now, we are going to define some relations on the set of rectangles; see Figure 1-right and Figure 2 for an illustration.

Definition 2. *We say that two rectangles, P and R, are* equivalent *according to $\diamond$ (denoted by $P \cong Q$) if there exist $a, b, c, d, m, n, o, p \in [0, 1]$ such that $P = \langle a, b \rangle \times \langle c, d \rangle$, $R = \langle m, n \rangle \times \langle o, p \rangle$, and*

$$(a, c) \cong (m, o),$$
$$(a, d) \cong (m, p),$$
$$(b, c) \cong (n, o),$$
$$(b, d) \cong (n, p).$$

Definition 3. *Let $e \in [0, 1]$ be a neutral element of $\diamond$, i.e., $x \diamond e = e \diamond x = x$ for all $x \in [0, 1]$. e say that two rectangles, P and R, are (e, e)-local if there exist $b, c, d, m, n, p \in [0, 1]$ such that $P = \langle e, b \rangle \times \langle c, d \rangle$, $R = \langle m, n \rangle \times \langle e, p \rangle$. If, moreover,*

$$(e, c) \cong (m, e), \qquad (4)$$
$$(e, d) \cong (m, p), \qquad (5)$$
$$(b, c) \cong (n, e) \qquad (6)$$

then we say that P and R are (e, e)-aligned according to $\diamond$ (denoted by $P \simeq_{e,e} Q$).

Remark 1. Less precisely, two rectangles, P and R, are (e, e)-local if e is an x-coordinate of one and a y-coordinate of the other. Further, they are (e, e)-aligned

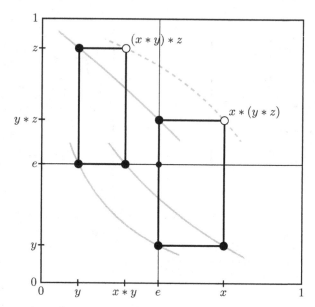

Fig. 3. Correspondence between associativity of a general uninorm and equivalence of (e, e)-aligned rectangles

if they are (e, e)-local and if those pairs of vertices where e appears lay on same level sets (see Figure 2). Notice that the equations (4), (5), and (6), according to the definition of the neutral element, can be written also as

$$c = m, \tag{7}$$
$$d = m \diamond p, \tag{8}$$
$$b \diamond c = n. \tag{9}$$

Observe that, on the set of (e, e)-local rectangles, $\cong$ is a subrelation of $\simeq_{e,e}$. Moreover, both $\cong$ and $\simeq_{e,e}$ are equivalences.

The following theorem gives a characterization of the associativity of general uninorms. The whole idea of the proof is illustrated in Figure 3.

Theorem 2. *Let* $*: [0,1]^2 \to [0,1]$ *be a commutative non-decreasing binary operation with a neutral element* $e \in [0,1]$. *Then the following two statements are equivalent:*

(i) $*$ *is associative (and hence a uninorm),*
(ii) P $\simeq_{e,e}$ R *implies* P $\cong$ R *for every pair of* (e, e)-*local rectangles* P, R $\subset$ $[0,1]^2$.

Proof. First, we prove the implication i $\Rightarrow$ ii. Let $*$ be a uninorm and $b, c, d, m, n, p \in [0,1]$ such that P $= \langle e, b \rangle \times \langle c, d \rangle$ and R $= \langle m, n \rangle \times \langle e, p \rangle$ are (e, e)-local and (e, e)-aligned rectangles. Thus (7), (8), and (9) hold and, in order to prove P $\cong$ R, we have to show $b * d = n * p$. The proof is concluded by establishing the equalities

$$b * d = (b * m) * p = (b * c) * p = b * (c * p) = n * p$$

which follow by consecutive invocation of (8), (7), the associativity of $*$, and, finally, (9) from the left to the right in this order.

Now, we proceed with proving the implication ii $\Rightarrow$ i. We are going to show that the equality $x * (y * z) = (x * y) * z$ will be satisfied for any $x, y, z \in [0, 1]$. Let us consider the following (e, e)-local rectangles (see Figure 3)

$$P = \langle e, x \rangle \times \langle y, y * z \rangle,$$
$$R = \langle y, x * y \rangle \times \langle e, z \rangle.$$

The rectangles are (e, e)-aligned; indeed, the equivalences

$$(e, y) \cong (y, e),$$
$$(e, y * z) \cong (y, z),$$
$$(x, y) \cong (x * y, e),$$

thanks to the definition of the neutral element, hold (consult with Figure 3). Whence, by the assumption, the rectangles are also equivalent and the equivalence

$$(x, y * z) \cong (x * y, z),$$

which is just another way of representing the promised associativity equation, holds too.

4   Structure of Uninorms Given by Idempotent and Involutive t-Norms and t-Conorms

This section introduces a result describing the structure of uninorms with idempotent or involutive underlying t-norms and t-conorms. We are going to describe which functional values in the area $[0, e[\times]e, 1]$ can a uninorm $*$ achieve if $\underset{*}{\wedge}$ and $\overset{*}{\vee}$ (see (1) and (2), respectively) are given. The proof has been achieved with a help of the web-geometric approach described above. However, as the proof is rather long and technical, we present here only the results. Recall that the case when both the underlying t-norm and the t-conorm are idempotent has been described already [3,8].

The first theorem describes the situation when both the underlying t-norm and the underlying t-conorm are involutive. See Figure 4 for an illustration.

Theorem 3. *Let* $*\colon [0, 1]^2 \to [0, 1]$ *be a commutative, non-decreasing binary operation with a neutral element* $e \in]0, 1[$ *such that* $\underset{*}{\wedge}$ *resp.* $\overset{*}{\vee}$, *defined as in* (1) *resp.* (2), *is an involutive t-norm resp. an involutive t-conorm. Then the following two statements are equivalent:*

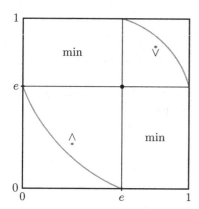
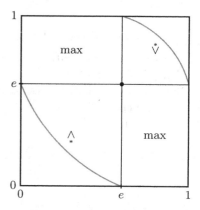

Fig. 4. A uninorm with involutive underlying t-norm and t-conorm. According to Theorem 3, the only possible functional values on the sub-domain $[0, e[\, \times\,]e, 1] \cup\,]e, 1] \times [0, e[$ are given either as the minimum (left part) or as the maximum (right part) of the arguments.

1. *The operation* $*$ *is associative and thus an uninorm.*
2. *The operation* $*$ *satisfies*

$$\text{either } x * y = \min\{x, y\} \text{ for all } (x, y) \in [0, e[\, \times\,]e, 1] \cup\,]e, 1] \times [0, e[\, ,$$
$$\text{or } x * y = \max\{x, y\} \text{ for all } (x, y) \in [0, e[\, \times\,]e, 1] \cup\,]e, 1] \times [0, e[\, .$$

The second theorem describes the uninorms with an involutive underlying t-norm and an idempotent underlying t-conorm (which is always the maximum operation). Notice that the situation with an idempotent underlying t-norm and an involutive underlying t-conorm is just the dual case. See Figure 5 for an illustration.

Theorem 4. *Let* $*\colon [0, 1]^2 \to [0, 1]$ *be a commutative, non-decreasing binary operation with a neutral element* $e \in\,]0, 1[$ *such that* $\underset{*}{\wedge}$ *resp.* $\underset{*}{\vee}$, *defined as in* (1) *resp.* (2), *is an involutive t-norm resp. the maximum t-conorm. Then the following two statements are equivalent:*

1. *The operation* $*$ *is associative and thus an uninorm.*
2. *There exist a value* $b \in [e, 1]$ *such that*

$$x * y = \begin{cases} \min\{x, y\} & \text{if } (x, y) \in [0, e[\, \times\,]e, b[\, \cup\,]e, b[\, \times [0, e[\, , \\ \max\{x, y\} & \text{if } (x, y) \in [0, e[\, \times\,]b, 1] \cup\,]b, 1] \times [0, e[\end{cases}$$

and such that

$$\text{either } x * y = \min\{x, y\} \quad \text{for all } (x, y) \in [0, e[\, \times \{b\} \cup \{b\} \times [0, e[\, ,$$
$$\text{or } \quad x * y = \max\{x, y\} \quad \text{for all } (x, y) \in [0, e[\, \times \{b\} \cup \{b\} \times [0, e[\, .$$

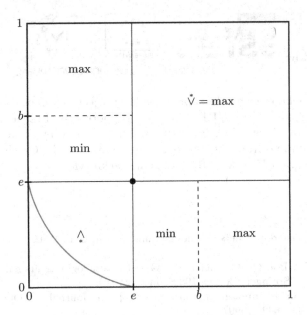

Fig. 5. A uninorm with involutive underlying t-norm and idempotent (i.e. the maximum) underlying t-conorm. According to Theorem 4, there is a boundary $b \in [e, 1]$ separating the sub-domain $[0, e[\times]e, 1] \cup]e, 1] \times [0, e[$ into two sub-areas; in one the functional values are given as the minimum and in the second the functional values are given as the minimum of the arguments.

5   Concluding Remarks

The class of uninorms with involutive underlying t-norms and t-conorms and the class of uninorms with involutive underlying t-norms and idempotent underlying t-conorm (as well as the corresponding dual cases) have been investigated and their structure has been described with a help of the web-geometric view on uninorms, especially by means of the Reidemeister closure condition. More precisely speaking, for a uninorm of such a kind with a neutral element $e \in]0, 1[$, possible functional values have been described for the points in the area $[0, e[\times]e, 1]$. As mentioned before, we have not dealt with the case when the underlying t-norm and the t-conorm are both idempotent as this case has already been solved elsewhere [3,8]. Let us remark, however, that even this result can be derived easily using the same approach.

Acknowledgements. Milan Petrík was supported by the Czech Science Foundation under Project P201/12/P055 and acknowledges the support by ESF Project CZ.1.07/2.3.00/20.0051 Algebraic methods in Quantum Logic of the Masaryk University.

Supported by

INVESTMENTS IN EDUCATION DEVELOPMENT

Radko Mesiar acknowledges the support by the project IT4Innovations Centre of Excellence, reg. no. CZ.1.05/1.1.00/02.0070 supported by Research and Development for Innovations Operational Programme financed by Structural Founds of Europe Union and from the means of state budget of the Czech Republic. A support of the grant VEGA 1/0171/12 is also acknowledged.

References

1. Aczél, J.: Quasigroups, nets and nomograms. Advances in Mathematics 1, 383–450 (1965)
2. Blaschke, W., Bol, G.: Geometrie der Gewebe, topologische Fragen der Differentialgeometrie. Springer, Berlin (1939) (in German)
3. De Baets, B.: Idempotent uninorms. European Journal of Operational Research 118, 631–642 (1999)
4. Fodor, J., De Baets, B.: Uninorm Basics. STUDFUZZ, vol. 215, pp. 49–64. Springer, Heidelberg (2007)
5. Fodor, J., Yager, R.R., Rybalov, A.: Structure of uninorms. Internat. J. Uncertain. Fuzziness Knowledge-Based Systems 5, 411–427 (1997)
6. Jenei, S.: Structural description of involutive uninorms and finite uninorm chains via skew symmetrization. In: Journal of Logic and Computation (to appear)
7. Maes, K.C., De Baets, B.: A contour view on uninorm properties. Kybernetika 42, 303–318 (2006)
8. Martín, J., Mayor, G., Torrens, J.: On locally internal monotonic operations. Fuzzy Sets and Systems 137(1), 27–42 (2003)
9. Petrík, M., Sarkoci, P.: Convex combinations of nilpotent triangular norms. Journal of Mathematical Analysis and Applications 350, 271–275 (2009), doi:10.1016/j.jmaa.2008.09.060
10. Petrík, M., Sarkoci, P.: Associativity of triangular norms characterized by the geometry of their level sets (submitted)
11. Reidemeister, K.: Topologische Fragen der Differentialgeometrie. V. Gewebe und Gruppen. Mathematische Zeitschrift 29(1), 427–435 (1929) (in German)
12. Yager, R., Rybalov, A.: Uninorm aggregation operators. Fuzzy Sets and Systems 80, 111–120 (1996)

Multi-polar Aggregation

Andrea Mesiarová-Zemánková[1,2] and Khurshid Ahmad[1]

[1] Department of Computer Science, Trinity College, Dublin, Ireland
[2] Mathematical Institute, Slovak Academy of Sciences, Bratislava, Slovakia
zemankova@mat.savba.sk, {zemankoa,kahmad}@scss.tcd.ie

Abstract. In this contribution we introduce a notion of an m-polar aggregation operator as a generalization of aggregation operators and bipolar aggregation operators, and we introduce the main properties of these aggregation operators. Extensions of some (bipolar) aggregation operators to m-polar aggregation operators are also introduced, as well as metrics on the category space $K \times [0,1]$ related to m-polar aggregation.

Keywords: aggregation operator, bipolar aggregation operator, Choquet integral, bi-capacity.

1 Introduction

Aggregation operators has become an indispensable tool in many domains and the field of aggregation theory is widely growing in the past years [1,2]. An aggregation operator is a function working on an arbitrary number of inputs from unit interval $[0,1]$, i.e., $A \colon \bigcup_{n \in \mathbb{N}} [0,1]^n \longrightarrow [0,1]$. The bipolar aggregation started to be interesting in seventies [12,17] and the need for bipolar aggregation operators is still growing. Among several bipolar aggregation operators recall symmetric and asymmetric Choquet integral [3,4,18,19], their generalization used in cumulative prospect theory [22], symmetric maximum and minimum [5]. However, definition of a bipolar aggregation operator was introduced for the first time in [14]. The bipolar scale allows to deal with positive, supporting information as well as negative, excluding one. Several bipolar concepts have been developed recently, among others recall bipolar fuzzy logic and bipolar fuzzy set theory [24].

Our work in the field of the automatic text analysis for affect or other qualitative indicators brought us to the need of further extension of bipolar aggregation. Namely, instead of two categories positive/negative our approach requires more categories. Therefore the aim of this contribution is the introduction of m-polar aggregation operators and their basic properties.

As an example assume the classification of text documents into m different categories $1, \ldots, m$ based on the words (phrases) contained in the document. In this example we focus just to a specific collection of important words (phrases) that are contained in some dictionary D. Each word (phrase) $w \in D$ is assumed to be important for exactly one of the given categories. We focus to such extremal words simply because it makes a good distinction between categories and it

S. Greco et al. (Eds.): IPMU 2012, Part III, CCIS 299, pp. 379–387, 2012.

keeps the dictionary D short enough. To each $w \in D$ we assign two values: $k_w \in \{1, \ldots, m\}$ denotes the category for which w is important and $x_w \in [0,1]$ denotes a degree how much is the word central for the category k_w. The degree x_w is usually high enough, for example $x_w = 1$ means that word(phrase) w appears only in text documents from category k_w.

Each text document d can be expressed as a collection of words(phrases) contained in it, i.e., $d = (w_1, \ldots, w_n)$. Since we are interested only in words from the dictionary D we transform the vector $(w_1, \ldots, w_n)$ into the vector $(v_1, \ldots, v_n)$, where

$$v_i = \begin{cases} (k_{w_i}, x_{w_i}) & \text{if } w_i \in D \\ 0 & \text{else.} \end{cases}$$

Now we want to aggregate pairs v_i together in order to produce one overall score pair (k, x) which will show us that document d belongs to category k with centrality x. This is where the aggregation on m-polar inputs take place.

Note that related concepts to m-polar aggregation are the Choquet integral with respect to a k-ary capacity [9,10], multiple-output Choquet integral models and Choquet-integral-based evaluations by fuzzy rules [20,21]. It appears that there is a need for general theory of m-polar aggregation operators.

2 m-Polar Aggregation Operators

We will start with definitions of an aggregation operator and a bipolar aggregation operator [2,14].

Definition 1. *(i) A mapping $A \colon \bigcup_{n \in \mathbb{N}} [0,1]^n \longrightarrow [0,1]$ is called an aggregation operator if*

(A1) A is non-decreasing, i.e., for any $n \in \mathbb{N}$, $\mathbf{x}, \mathbf{y} \in [0,1]^n$, $\mathbf{x} \le \mathbf{y}$ it holds $A(\mathbf{x}) \le A(\mathbf{y})$;

(A2) $0, 1$ are idempotent elements of A, i.e., for any $n \in \mathbb{N}$, $A(\underbrace{0, \ldots, 0}_{n\text{-}times}) = 0$ and $A(\underbrace{1, \ldots, 1}_{n\text{-}times}) = 1$;

(A3) for $n = 1$, $A(x) = x$ for all $x \in [0,1]$.

(ii) A mapping $B \colon \bigcup_{n \in \mathbb{N}} [-1,1]^n \longrightarrow [-1,1]$ is called a bipolar aggregation operator if

(B1) B is non-decreasing, i.e., for any $n \in \mathbb{N}$, $\mathbf{x}, \mathbf{y} \in [-1,1]^n$, $\mathbf{x} \le \mathbf{y}$ it holds $B(\mathbf{x}) \le B(\mathbf{y})$;

(B2) $0, 1, -1$ are idempotent elements of B, i.e., for any $n \in \mathbb{N}$, $B(\underbrace{0, \ldots, 0}_{n\text{-}times}) = 0$, $B(\underbrace{1, \ldots, 1}_{n\text{-}times}) = 1$ and $B(\underbrace{-1, \ldots, -1}_{n\text{-}times}) = -1$;

(B3) for $n = 1$, $B(x) = x$ for all $x \in [-1,1]$.

In the case of an aggregation operator, i.e., without polarity, all inputs belong just to one category, i.e., all inputs are non-negative. In the bipolar case, the inputs already belong to two categories: non-negative and non-positive, while 0 is something in between, i.e., it belongs to both categories. Bipolar inputs can be taken in the following way: positive input, for example 0.3, is in fact input composed of two parts $(+, 0.3)$, negative input, for example -0.5 can be similarly represented as $(-, 0.5)$. In the following we will extend the number of categories to any natural number m and we will deal with the set of input categories $K = \{1, \ldots, m\}$.

Definition 2. *Let $m \in \mathbb{N}$ and let $K = \{1, \ldots, m\}$ be the set of m categories. Assume the input pairs of the form (k, x), with $k \in K$, $x \in\,]0, 1]$ and a neutral input $0 \in \mathbb{R}$ (which belongs to each category), with convention $0 = (k, 0)$ for all $k \in K$. A mapping $M: \bigcup_{n \in \mathbb{N}} (K \times [0, 1])^n \longrightarrow K \times [0, 1]$, will be called an m-polar aggregation operator if*

(M1) M is non-decreasing, i.e, if $x_i \leq y_i$ then for

$$M((k_1, x_1), \ldots, (k_{i-1}, x_{i-1}), (k_i, x_i), (k_{i+1}, x_{i+1}), \ldots, (k_n, x_n)) = (k, x)$$
$$M((k_1, x_1), \ldots, (k_{i-1}, x_{i-1}), (k_i, y_i), (k_{i+1}, x_{i+1}), \ldots, (k_n, x_n)) = (p, y)$$

we have one of the following cases: $(k = p = k_i) \wedge (x \leq y)$, or $(k = p \neq k_i) \wedge (x \geq y)$, or $(k \neq p \wedge k \neq k_i) \wedge (p = k_i)$. Note that in the case when $\min(x, y) = 0$ we assume the representation where $k = p$.

(M2) $M(\underbrace{0, \ldots, 0}_{n\text{-times}}) = 0$ and $M((k, 1), \ldots, (k, 1)) = (k, 1)$ for all $k \in K$;

(M3) for $n = 1$, $M((k, x)) = (k, x)$ for all $(k, x) \in K \times [0, 1]$.

The space $K \times [0, 1]$ will be called a category space. For standard aggregation operators we get $K = \{1\}$ and therefore the category specification can be omitted. In a bipolar case $K = \{1, 2\}$ and we can identify for example positive inputs with the first category and negative inputs with the second category, i.e., for 0.3 and -0.5 we have $0.3 \sim (1, 0.3)$ and $-0.5 \sim (2, 0.5)$. After some computations, the following proposition can be proved.

Proposition 1. *For $m = 1$ m-polar aggregation operator is an aggregation operator. For $n = 2$ m-polar aggregation operator is a bipolar aggregation operator.*

In the following we will assume $K = \{1, \ldots, m\}$.

Example 1. (i) The basic example of an m-polar aggregation operator is the oriented maximum operator which is for $\mathbf{x} = ((k_1, x_1), \ldots, (k_n, x_n))$ with $k_i \in K$, $x_i \in [0, 1]$ given by

$$\mathrm{omax}((k_1, x_1), \ldots, (k_n, x_n)) = (\mathrm{clx}(k_1, \ldots, k_n), \max(x_1, \ldots, x_n))$$

if $\{k_i \mid x_i = \max(x_1, \ldots, x_n)\} = \{k\}$ for some $k \in K$ (which means that all maximal inputs are from the same category) with $\mathrm{clx}(k_1, \ldots, k_n) = k_i$ if $x_i = \max(x_1, \ldots, x_n)$, in all other cases $\mathrm{omax}((k_1, x_1), \ldots, (k_n, x_n)) = 0$.

Note that in the bipolar case for two inputs the oriented maximum coincide with the symmetric maximum defined by Grabisch [7]. For more inputs it coincides with the splitting rule (see [8,11]) defined on the bipolar scale by

$$SPL(x_1, \ldots, x_n) = (\bigvee_{i=1}^{n} x_i^+) \diamond (\bigvee_{i=1}^{n} x_i^-),$$

where $\diamond$ stands for the bipolar symmetric maximum and there is $\mathbf{x}^+ = (\max(0, x_1), \ldots, \max(0, x_n))$ and $\mathbf{x}^- = (\max(0, -x_1), \ldots, \max(0, -x_n))$;

(ii) Projection to i-th coordinate is an m-polar aggregation operator.

(iii) For $\mathbf{x} = ((k_1, x_1), \ldots, (k_n, x_n))$ with $k_i \in K$, $x_i \in [0, 1]$ let

$$\mathbf{x}^i = ((i, d_1), \ldots, (i, d_n))$$

for $i = 1, \ldots, m$, where $d_j = x_j$ if j-th input belong to i-th category and $d_j = 0$ otherwise. Then the above is a decomposition of $\mathbf{x}$ to m parts according to categories (which in the bipolar case corresponds to positive $\mathbf{x}^+$ and negative $\mathbf{x}^-$ part of the input).

Generalizing the bipolar case [13,14], an ordinal sum construction for m-polar aggregation operators can be introduced as follows: let A^k be an aggregation operator for all $k \in K$ and let $*: \bigcup_{n \in \mathbb{N}} (K \times [0, 1])^n \longrightarrow K \times [0, 1]$ be an m-polar aggregation operator. Then the operator $M^*: \bigcup_{n \in \mathbb{N}} (K \times [0, 1])^n \longrightarrow K \times [0, 1]$, given by

$$M^*((k_1, x_1), \ldots, (k_m, x_m)) = \begin{cases} (k, A^k(\mathbf{x})) & \text{if } k_i = k \text{ for all } i \\ *(A^1(\mathbf{x}^1), \ldots, A^m(\mathbf{x}^m)) & \text{else,} \end{cases}$$

is an m-polar aggregation operator, which will be called m-polar $*$-ordinal sum of aggregation operators.

(iv) In the case that the set K is ordered the m-polar aggregation operator called the ordered category projection can be assumed. In such a case, without any loss of generality, assume that category 1 is the most important, category 2 is the second most important and so on. Let A^k be an aggregation operator for all $k \in K$. Then the m-polar aggregation operator $OP: \bigcup_{n \in \mathbb{N}} (K \times [0, 1])^n \longrightarrow K \times [0, 1]$ given by

$$OP((k_1, x_1), \ldots, (k_n, x_n)) = (k, A^k(\mathbf{x}^k)),$$

where $k = \min(k_1, \ldots, k_n)$, with convention $0 = (m, 0)$, will be called an ordered category projection.

3   Properties of Multi-polar Aggregation Operators

In this section we will discuss the basic properties of m-polar aggregation operators. First we will start with the introduction of a metric on the category space $K \times [0,1]$.

3.1   Metric on $K \times [0,1]$

Definition of a metric on $K \times [0,1]$ is important for several properties, for example for definition of continuity.

Definition 3. *Let $d \colon (K \times [0,1])^2 \longrightarrow \mathbb{R}_0^+$ be given by*

$$d((k_1, x), (k_2, y)) = \begin{cases} |x - y| & \text{if } k_1 = k_2 \\ x + y & \text{else.} \end{cases}$$

Then d will be called an oriented distance on $K \times [0,1]$.

Proposition 2. *Let $d \colon (K \times [0,1])^2 \longrightarrow \mathbb{R}_0^+$ be an oriented distance on $K \times [0,1]$. Then d is a distance, i.e.,*

(i) $d((k_1, x), (k_2, y)) \geq 0$ for all $(k_1, x), (k_2, y) \in K \times [0,1]$;

(ii) $d((k_1, x), (k_2, y)) = 0$ if and only if $k_1 = k_2$ and $x = y$;

(iii) $d((k_1, x), (k_2, y)) = d((k_2, y), (k_1, x))$ for all $(k_1, x), (k_2, y) \in K \times [0,1]$;

(iv) $d((k_1, x), (k_3, z)) \leq d((k_1, x), (k_2, y)) + d((k_2, y), (k_3, z))$ for all $(k_1, x), (k_2, y), (k_3, z) \in K \times [0,1]$.

One can imagine the domain $K \times [0,1]$ and the above defined distance on it as m paths with the common origin, where no shortcuts outside paths are allowed. Then distance between two points is the distance one should walk to get from the first point to the second point.

3.2   Properties of m-Polar Aggregation Operators

Among the most important properties of aggregation operators we will begin with positive homogeneity and continuity. These two properties are important in investigation of fuzzy m-polar integrals, especially for the m-polar Choquet integral.

Definition 4. *Let $M \colon \bigcup_{n \in \mathbb{N}} (K \times [0,1])^n \longrightarrow K \times [0,1]$ be an m-polar aggregation operator. Then*

(i) M is positive homogenous if for all $c \in [0,1]$ there is $M((k_1, c \cdot x_1), \ldots, (k_n, c \cdot x_n)) = (k, c \cdot x)$, where $M((k_1, x_1), \ldots, (k_n, x_n)) = (k, x)$.

(ii) M *is continuous if for all* $i \in \{1, \ldots, n\}$ *and for all* $\varepsilon > 0$ *there exists a* $\delta > 0$ *such that if* $d((k_i, x_i), (q_i, y_i)) < \delta$ *then for*

$$\mathbf{x} = ((k_1, x_1), \ldots, (k_{i-1}, x_{i-1}), (k_i, x_i), (k_{i+1}, x_{i+1}) \ldots, (k_n, x_n))$$

and

$$\mathbf{y} = ((k_1, x_1), \ldots, (k_{i-1}, x_{i-1}), (q_i, y_i), (k_{i+1}, x_{i+1}) \ldots, (k_n, x_n))$$

we have

$$d(M(\mathbf{x}), M(\mathbf{y})) < \varepsilon.$$

(iii) M *is associative if for all* $i \in \{1, \ldots, n\}$ *there is* $M((k_1, x_1), \ldots, (k_n, x_n)) = M((k, y), (q, z))$, *where* $(k, y) = M((k_1, x_1), \ldots, (k_i, x_i))$ *and* $(q, z) = M((k_{i+1}, x_{i+1}), \ldots, (k_n, x_n))$.

(iv) M *is commutative (symmetric) if the value of* $M((k_1, x_1), \ldots, (k_n, x_n))$ *does not depend on the order of inputs.*

Definition 5. *Let* $M \colon \bigcup_{n \in \mathbb{N}} (K \times [0, 1])^n \longrightarrow K \times [0, 1]$ *be an m-polar aggregation operator. Then the element* $(k, x) \in K \times [0, 1]$ *is called*

(i) a k-category neutral element of M *if* x *is a neutral element of an aggregation operator* A *given by*

$$A(x_1, \ldots, x_n) = M((k, x_1), \ldots, (k, x_n)).$$

(ii) a neutral element of M *if*

$$M((k_1, x_1), \ldots, (k, x), \ldots, (k_n, x_n)) = M((k_1, x_1), \ldots, (k_n, x_n))$$

for all $k_i \in K$, $x_i \in [0, 1]$.

After introducing associativity, commutativity and neutral element of an m-polar aggregation operator we are able to define an m-polar t-norm. Natural requirement is that if all inputs belong just to one category then the m-polar t-norm is just an ordinary t-norm. However, monotonicity connected with above mentioned property imply the following lemma.

Lemma 1. *Let* $M \colon \bigcup_{n \in \mathbb{N}} (K \times [0, 1])^n \longrightarrow K \times [0, 1]$ *be an m-polar aggregation operator such that* $M((k, x), 0) = 0 = M(0, (k, x))$ *for all* $k \in K$, $x \in [0, 1]$. *Then* $M((k_1, x_1), (k_2, x_2)) = 0$ *for all* $k_1, k_2 \in K$, $x_1, x_2 \in [0, 1]$, $k_1 \neq k_2$.

Therefore we are able to give the following definition.

Definition 6. *A mapping* $T \colon \bigcup_{n \in \mathbb{N}} (K \times [0, 1])^n \longrightarrow K \times [0, 1]$ *is an n-ary m-polar t-norm if it is given by*

$$T((k_1, x_1), \ldots, (k_n, x_n)) = \begin{cases} T_k(x_1, \ldots, x_n) & \text{if } k_i = k \text{ for all } i \\ 0 & \text{else,} \end{cases}$$

where T_k *is a standard t-norm.*

Recall that YinYang bipolar t-norms were defined in [24], however, in our case bipolar t-norm refer to a t-norm defined on a different domain than in [24].

In the bipolar case, bipolar t-norms are just linear transformations of null-norms on $[0, 1]$. Similarly, m-polar t-conorms can be defined as commutative, associative, m-polar aggregation operators with neutral element 0 such that

$$C((k, x_1), \ldots, (k, x_n)) = (k, C_k(x_1, \ldots, x_n)),$$

where C_k is an ordinary t-conorm for $k \in K$. In the bipolar case, bipolar t-conorms are just linear transformations of uninorms on $[0, 1]$ which confirms the connection between uninorms and bipolar aggregation (see for example [23]). Assume a $*$-ordinal sum from Example 1, where $*$ is an ordered category projection from the same example, and A^k is a t-conorm for all $k \in K$. In the bipolar case $\{1, 2\}$- and $\{2, 1\}$-ordered category projections corresponds to maximal and minimal uninorms, i.e. such that $U(x, y) = \max(x, y)$ $(U(x, y) = \min(x, y))$ for all $x, y \in [0, 1], x \leq e \leq y$, where e is a neutral element of the uninorm U. Here $\{1, 2\}$ $(\{2, 1\})$ denotes the order of importance of categories. Similarly, in m-polar case such an ordinal sum yield an m-polar t-conorm.

4   Conclusions

In this contribution we have defined m-polar aggregation operators and their basic properties. We expect application of our results in all domains where (bipolar) aggregation in applied and where more category classification is needed.

Our future work [16] is dedicated to definition of several m-polar Choquet integrals (extending bipolar Choquet integrals [3,4,19,22]), m-polar balancing Choquet integral (extending balancing Choquet integral [15]), Choquet integral with respect to a multi-capacity (extending the concept of bi-capacity [6]) and study of their properties. Note that the multi-capacity is defined as follows:

Let $Q = \{(E_1, \ldots, E_m) \mid E_i \cap E_j = \emptyset, \bigcup_{i=1}^m E_i \subseteq X\}$. Then the function $v \colon Q \longrightarrow K \times [0, 1]$ is a normed multi-capacity if

(i) $v(\emptyset, \ldots, \emptyset) = 0$, $v(\emptyset, \ldots, \underbrace{X}_{i\text{-th}}, \ldots, \emptyset) = (i, 1)$;

(ii) if $E_i \subseteq F_i$ then for
$v(E_1, \ldots, E_i, \ldots, E_m) = (k, x)$ and $v(E_1, \ldots, F_i, \ldots, E_m) = (q, y)$ we have one of the following options: $k = q = i \wedge x \leq y$ or $k \neq i = q$ or $k = q \neq i \wedge x \geq y$.

We will explore related concepts of Choquet integrals defined in [9,10,20,21]: the Choquet integral with respect to a k-ary capacity, multiple-output Choquet integral models and Choquet-integral-based evaluations by fuzzy rules.

Acknowledgement. This work was supported by AXA Research Fund and partially by grants VEGA 2/0059/12 and APVV-0178-11. Authors are grateful to anonymous referees for valuable comments.

References

1. Beliakov, G., Pradera, A., Calvo, T.: Aggregation Functions: A Guide for Practitioners. Springer, New York (2007)
2. Calvo, T., Kolesárová, A., Komorníková, M., Mesiar, R.: Aggregation Operators: Properties, Classes and Construction Methods. In: Calvo, T., Mayor, G., Mesiar, R. (eds.) Aggregation Operators, pp. 3–107. Physica-Verlag, Heidelberg (2002)
3. Choquet, G.: Theory of capacities. Ann. Inst. Fourier 5, 131–295 (1953-1954)
4. Denneberg, D.: Non-additive Measure and Integral. Kluwer Academic Publishers, Dordrecht (1994)
5. Grabisch, M., De Baets, B., Fodor, J.: On symmetric pseudo-additions. In: Proc. IPMU 2002, Annecy, pp. 1349–1355 (2002)
6. Grabisch, M., Labreuche, C.: Bi-capacities for decision making on bipolar scales. In: Proc. EUROFUSE Workshop on Information Systems, Varenna, pp. 185–190 (2002)
7. Grabisch, M.: The symmetric Sugeno integral. Fuzzy Sets and Systems 139, 473–490 (2003)
8. Grabisch, M.: The Möbius function on symmetric ordered structures and its application to capacities on finite sets. Discrete Math 287(1-3), 17–34 (2004)
9. Grabisch, M., Labreuche, C.: Capacities on lattices and k-ary capacities. In: Proc. EUSFLAT 2003, Zittau, Germany, pp. 304–307 (2003)
10. Grabisch, M., Labreuche, C.: Bipolarization of posets and natural interpolation. Journal of Mathematical Analysis and Application 343, 1080–1097 (2008)
11. Grabisch, M., Marichal, J.-L., Mesiar, R., Pap, E.: Aggregation Functions. Cambridge Univ. Press, Cambridge (2009)
12. Hájek, P., Havránek, T., Jiroušek, R.: Uncertain Information Processing in Expert Systems. CRC Press, Boca Raton (1992)
13. Mesiar, R., De Baets, B.: New Construction Methods for Aggregation operators. In: Proc. IPMU 2000, Madrid, pp. 701–707 (2000)
14. Mesiarová, A., Lazaro, J.: Bipolar Aggregation operators. In: Proc. AGOP 2003, pp. 119–123. Alcalá de Henares (2003)
15. Mesiarová-Zemánková, A., Mesiar, R., Ahmad, K.: The balancing Choquet integral. Fuzzy Sets and Systems 161(17), 2243–2255 (2010)
16. Mesiarová-Zemánková, A., Ahmad, K.: Multi-polar Choquet integral. Fuzzy Sets and Systems (submitted)
17. Shortliffe, E.H.: Computer-Based Medical Consultations: MYCIN. Elsevier/North-Holland, Amsterdam (1976)
18. Pap, E.: Null-Additive Set Functions. Kluwer Academic Publishers, Dordrecht (1995)
19. Šipoš, J.: Integral with respect to a premeasure. Math. Slovaca 29, 141–145 (1979)
20. Takahagi, E.: Choquet-Integral-Based Evaluations by Fuzzy Rules: Methods for Developing Fuzzy Rule Tables on the Basis of Weights and Interaction Degrees. In: Hüllermeier, E., Kruse, R., Hoffmann, F. (eds.) IPMU 2010. CCIS, vol. 80, pp. 515–524. Springer, Heidelberg (2010)
21. Takahagi, E.: Multiple-output Choquet integral models and their applications in classification methods. International Journal of Intelligent Technologies and Applied Statistics 4(4), 519–530 (2011)

22. Tversky, A., Kahneman, D.: Advances in prospect theory: cumulative representation of uncertainty. J. of Risk and Uncertainty (1992)
23. Yager, R., Rybalov, A.: Bipolar aggregation using the Uninorms. Fuzzy Optimization and Decision Making 10(1), 59–70 (2011)
24. Zhang, W.-R.: YinYang Bipolar T-norms and T-conorms as granular neurological operators. In: Proc. IEEE International Conference on Granular Computing, Atlanta, pp. 91–96 (2006)

An Imprecise Probability Approach to Joint Extensions of Stochastic and Interval Orderings

Inés Couso[1] and Didier Dubois[2]

[1] Universidad Oviedo, Gijon, Spain
[2] IRIT-CNRS, Toulouse, France

Abstract. This paper deals with methods for ranking uncertain quantities in the setting of imprecise probabilities. It is shown that many techniques for comparing random variables or intervals can be generalized by means of upper and lower expectations of sets of gambles, so as to compare more general kinds of uncertain quantities. We show that many comparison criteria proposed so far can be cast in a general form.

1 Introduction and Motivation

In decision-making, one is interested by two, not necessarily related questions: on the one hand, one may wish to know if a decision is better than another; on the other hand it is also important to determine whether a decision is good or not, per se. So given a set of potential actions $\mathcal{A}$, a preference relation $\succeq$ on $\mathcal{A}$ and a set $\mathcal{D}$ of desirable actions must be obtained. An action is to be viewed as a mapping from a state space Ω to a set of consequences C, equipped with a complete preordering relation $\geq$ expressing that one consequence is better than another. This can be done by a utility mapping $u : C \to L$, where L is a totally ordered value scale. Then, the basic comparison between actions is the Pareto ordering, whereby $a \geq_P b$ is defined as usual: $u(a(\omega)) \geq u(b(\omega)), \forall \omega \in \Omega$ and $u(a(\omega)) > u(b(\omega))$ for at least one state. In contrast, desirability underlies a bipolar view of the value scale L, that is, there exists $0 \in L$ where $\lambda > 0$ is a rating with a positive flavor. An example of neutral action is then precisely such that $u(a_0(\omega)) = 0, \forall \omega \in \Omega$. Clearly, one should have that $\{a, a >_P 0\} \subset \mathcal{D}$ while $\{a, 0 >_P a\} \cap \mathcal{D} = \emptyset$. Additional conditions may be required, depending on the nature of the scale L. In order to define a more refined preference ordering of actions than the Pareto-ordering, one needs to express whether the benefits and inconvenients of one action can be counterbalanced or not by the benefits and inconvenients of another action. In this view, we may retain in favor of a its positive sides that are not counterbalanced by similar assets of b and negative sides of b that are not present with a. This can take the form of a difference-like internal operation between two actions a and b yielding a third action $a \ominus b$, such that $a \ominus b(\omega) > 0$ if and only if $a(\omega) > b(\omega)$. Then, the preference relation of a over b is defined by the desirability of $a \ominus b$:

$$a \succ b \iff a \ominus b \in \mathcal{D}.$$

S. Greco et al. (Eds.): IPMU 2012, Part III, CCIS 299, pp. 388–399, 2012.

In other words, a is preferred to b if the losses that a may cause are not worse than those caused by b and a has more assets than b.

Walley [20] follows this approach: he defines the desirable set $\mathcal{D}$ from first principles and actions are directly understood as *gambles* $X : \Omega \to \mathbb{R}$ the latter corresponding to earning (if $X(\omega) > 0$) or losing (if $X(\omega) < 0$) a certain amount of money, and there is no utility function per se. The gamble is thus assumed to be a primitive object whose desirability is stable under sums and positive scalar multiplication. There is no distortion of the scale by a utility function. Uncertainty units are measured on the bipolar value scale $\mathbb{R}$, when restricting to Boolean gambles (that are all desirable since provoking no loss) encoding events: $A : \Omega \to \{0, 1\} \subseteq \mathbb{R}$. The lower probability $\underline{P}(A)$ is defined as the least value $r \in \mathbb{R}$ such that A outperforms the constant act $\tilde{r}(r) = r$, that is $\underline{P}(A) = \sup\{r : A - r \in \mathcal{D}\}$.

The issue of comparing uncertain variables is at the heart of choice under uncertainty. In this paper we consider various comparison criteria in the settings of Savage, Walley and related authors [2]. We show that all of them take the form of checking whether $X \ominus Y$ is desirable. We show it takes the form of some function of the lower expectation of a quantity $g(X, Y)$ being positive, where $g : \mathbb{R}^2 \to \mathbb{R}$ can be written as $g(x, y) = f(x, y) - f(y, x)$, with f increasing in the first component and decreasing in the second one. The paper is organised as follows.

In Section 2, we review known notions of dominance in the (classical) probabilistic setting. We show that all of these orderings can be expressed by means of the formula $E_P[g(X, Y)] \geq 0$. Then we consider the case where uncertainty is modelled by mere intervals. In Section 3, we show that some orderings from the imprecise probability literature can be seen as extensions of the previous ones. In particular, Denoeux [7] extends first stochastic dominance to the context of random sets and Troffaes [19] surveys several extensions of the expectation dominance in the context of credal sets. We also recall extensions of statistical dominance to the general context of upper and lower probabilities [15] and also to the general context of imprecise probabilities [4]. In Section 4, we propose a general formula that encompasses the above criteria. It is closely related to the formula $E_P[g(X, Y)] \geq 0$ proposed in Section 2. Finally, we provide some specific comments about the special cases of closed intervals and fuzzy intervals, respectively. Many interval and fuzzy ranking methods can be seen as special cases of preference relations between gambles.

2   Comparing Random Variables v.s. Ill-Known Quantities

The most elementary forms of uncertainty for gambles is when the state of the world is known probabilistically (for instance there is some statistical evidence on the variability of $X(\omega)$) or when the information is incomplete (if ω occurs we only know that $X(\omega) \in E \subset \mathbf{R}$.) This section reviews different stochastic orderings in the literature, contrasts them with interval orderings, and puts them in a single format.

2.1   Stochastic Orderings

Consider two random variables $X : \Omega \to \mathbb{R}$ and $Y : \Omega \to \mathbb{R}$ defined on the same probability space $(\Omega, \mathcal{F}, P)$.

There are three main kinds of stochastic orderings in the literature:

1. *First order stochastic dominance* [12]: X dominates Y if $P(X > x) \geq P(Y > x), \forall x \in \mathbb{R}$, or equivalently, when $P_1(x, \infty) \geq P_2(x, \infty), \forall x \in \mathbb{R}$, where P_1 and P_2 respectively denote the probability measures induced by each variable. We will denote it $X \geq_{1st} Y$.
2. *Dominance in the sense of expected utility* [18]: Given an increasing function $u : \mathbb{R} \to \mathbb{R}$, X dominates Y wrt u if $E_P(u(X)) \geq E_P(u(Y))$. We will denote it $X \geq_u Y$. It is well known that $X \geq_{1st} Y$ if and only if $X \geq_u Y$, for all increasing utility functions $u : \mathbb{R} \to \mathbb{R}$. A special case is *Dominance in Expectation*: X dominates Y if $E_P(X) \geq E_P(Y)$. This relation represents the particular case of the previous one, when the utility function u is the identity function $u(x) = x, \forall x \in \mathbb{R}$.
3. *Statistical preference* [5]: X is statistically preferred to Y if $P(X > Y) + 0.5P(X = Y) \geq 0.5$. It is clear that the above inequality is equivalent to $P(X > Y) \geq P(Y > X)$. It is also related to the sign of the median of the difference $X - Y$. In fact, in [4] the following sequence of implications is established:

$$\text{Me}(X-Y) > 0 \Rightarrow P(X > Y) > P(Y > X) \Rightarrow P(X > Y) \geq P(X > Y) \Rightarrow \text{Me}(X-Y) \geq 0.$$

2.2   A Common Formulation

All the above stochastic orderings can be put into a common formulation. Consider a function $g : \mathbb{R}^2 \to \mathbb{R}$ increasing (not necessarily strictly increasing) in the first component and decreasing (again, non necessarily strict) in the second one. All the above orderings can be expressed as follows[1]:

$$X \text{ is preferred to } Y \text{ if } E_P[g(X, Y)] \geq 0, \tag{1}$$

Furthermore, we will observe that, in all the cases, the function g can be expressed as a difference: $g(x, y) = f(x, y) - f(y, x)$, where f is increasing in the first component and decreasing in the second one. Let us also consider the "swap mapping" sw:$\mathbb{R}^2 \to \mathbb{R}^2$ defined as sw$(x, y) = (y, x), \forall (x, y) \in \mathbb{R}^2$. Then $g : \mathbb{R}^2 \to \mathbb{R}$ is the mapping $g = f - f \circ \text{sw}$. Therefore, all these criteria can be equivalently written (due to the linearity of the expectation) as:

$$X \text{ is preferred to } Y \text{ if } E_P[f(X, Y)] \geq E_P[f(Y, X)]. \tag{2}$$

Below, we provide the specific expression for the function $g(x, y) = f(x, y) - f(y, x)$ for each of the above orderings. Notice that f is constant in the second

---

[1] Capital letters are used for random variables and lower-case letters are used for numbers in the real line.

component for the first three preference relations (first stochastic dominance, dominance wrt a utility function and dominance of expectation). So, in those cases, it can be identified with an increasing utility function $u : \mathbb{R} \to \mathbb{R}$, such that $u(x) = f(x, y)$, $\forall y \in \mathbb{R}, x \in \mathbb{R}$.

1. *First order stochastic dominance*: Consider the function $g_{x_0} : \mathbb{R}^2 \to \mathbb{R}$ defined as

$$g_{x_0}(x, y) = u_{x_0}(x) - u_{x_0}(y), \text{ where } u_{x_0}(x) = 1_{x > x_0} = \begin{cases} 1 & \text{if } x > x_0 \\ 0 & \text{otherwise.} \end{cases} \quad (3)$$

The mapping $f_{x_0}(x, y) = u_{x_0}(x)$ is increasing in the first component and it is constant in the second one. Therefore, $g_{x_0}(x, y) = f_{x_0}(x, y) - f_{x_0}(y, x)$ is increasing in the first component and decreasing in the second one. Furthermore, we can easily check that X stochastically dominates Y (first order) if and only if

$$E_P[g_{x_0}(X, Y)] \geq 0, \ \forall x_0 \in \mathbb{R}.$$

2. *Dominance wrt an increasing utility function*: For each specific utility function $u : \mathbb{R} \to \mathbb{R}$, we will consider the functions $f_u : \mathbb{R}^2 \to \mathbb{R}$ and $g_u : \mathbb{R}^2 \to \mathbb{R}$ respectively defined as $f_u(x, y) = u(x)$ and $g_u(x, y) = f_u(x, y) - f_u(y, x) = u(x) - u(y)$, $\forall (x, y) \in \mathbb{R}^2$. Then, we can easily check that X dominates Y wrt u when $E_P(g_u(X, Y)) \geq 0$. Dominance of expectation is retrieved using $u(x) = x$ in the above expressions.

3. *Statistical preference*: Consider the function $f : \mathbb{R}^2 \to \mathbb{R}$ defined as

$$f(x, y) = 1_{x > y} = \begin{cases} 1 & \text{if } x > y \\ 0 & \text{otherwise.} \end{cases} \quad (4)$$

Now, let us define g as the difference $g(x, y) = f(x, y) - f(y, x)$. We easily observe that $E_P[f(X, Y)] = P(X > Y)$. Therefore, X is statistically preferred to Y if and only if $E_P[g(X, Y)] = E_P[f(X, Y) - f(Y, X)] \geq 0$.

2.3 Comparing Ill-Known Quantities Modeled by Real Intervals

Let $\omega \in \Omega$ be the state of the world and let us consider the respective outcomes of the gambles X and Y, $X(\omega) = x$ and $Y(\omega) = y$, in this case. Suppose that both of them are ill-perceived. The available incomplete information about them is respectively represented by the disjunctive intervals $[a, b]$ and $[c, d]$. Various modes of comparison of intervals were reviewed in Aiche and Dubois [1]. These comparisons rely in the comparison of the endpoints:

- $[a, b] \leq_{+}^{-} [c, d]$ if $a \leq d$; $[a, b] \leq_{-}^{-} [c, d]$ if $a \leq c$.
- $[a, b] \leq_{+}^{+} [c, d]$ if $b \leq d$; $[a, b] \leq_{-}^{+} [c, d]$ if $b \leq c$.

The following implications are obvious:

$$[a, b] \leq_{-}^{+} [c, d] \Rightarrow [a, b] \leq_{-}^{-} [c, d] \Rightarrow [a, b] \leq_{+}^{-} [c, d]; \quad (5)$$

$$[a, b] \leq_-^+ [c, d] \Rightarrow [a, b] \leq_+^+ [c, d] \Rightarrow [a, b] \leq_+^- [c, d]; \tag{6}$$

$$[a, b] \leq_-^+ [c, d] \Rightarrow \neg([a, b] <_+^- [a, b]). \tag{7}$$

These relations are known in the literature:

- The relation $\leq_-^+$ is an interval order (Fishburn [10]). In the case of independent random variables X and Y, $P(X > Y) = 1$ is generally equivalent to $Support(Y) <_-^+ Support(X)$.
- $\leq_-^-$ is the maximin criterion; $\leq_+^+$ is the maximax criterion
- The simultaneous use of $\leq_-^-$ and $\leq_+^+$: $[a, b] \leq_{lat} [c, d]$ if and only if $[a, b] \leq_-^-$ $[c, d]$ and $[a, b] \leq_+^+ [c, d]$. This is the canonical order induced by the lattice structure of intervals, equipped with the operations max and min extended to intervals:
  $[a, b] \leq_{lat} [c, d] \Leftrightarrow \max([a, b], [c, d]) = [c, d] \iff \min([a, b], [c, d]) = [a, b]$ (we call it *lattice interval* order).

Finally, one way of comparing intervals consists in choosing a number in each interval and to compare these numbers. The selection of representatives of the intervals can be based on some pessimism index $\alpha \in [0, 1]$ reflecting the attitude of a decision-maker. This is the well-known Hurwicz criterion, such that if $[a, b] \leq_\alpha [c, d]$ means $\alpha a + (1 - \alpha)b \leq \alpha c + (1 - \alpha)d$. It is obvious that $[a, b] \leq_{lat} [c, d] \iff [a, b] \leq_\alpha [c, d], \forall \alpha \in [0, 1]$. Note that the Hurwicz order of intervals plays the same role with respect to the lattice interval order as the ranking of random variables by their expected utility with respect to stochastic dominance.

These orderings again take the form $g(X, Y) \leq 0$ for one or several functions g.

- For the interval ordering, just let $g_-^+(X, Y) = \inf[a_X, b_X] \ominus [a_Y, b_Y] = a_X - b_Y$ where $\ominus$ is the interval difference. For its dual $\leq_+^-$, then $g_+^-(X, Y) = \sup[a_X, b_X] \ominus [a_Y, b_Y] = b_X - a_Y$
- For the maximin and maximax, just let $g(X, Y) = \inf[a_X, b_X] - \inf[a_Y, b_Y]$ and $\bar{g}(X, Y) = \sup[a_X, b_X] - \sup[a_Y, b_Y]$, respectively
- For the lattice ordering, the two above conditions must be met.
- For the Hurwicz criterion: $g_\alpha(X, Y) = \alpha \underline{g}(X, Y) + (1 - \alpha)\bar{g}(X, Y)$.

The latter is not equivalent to the Hurwicz-like comparison of $[a_X, b_X] \ominus [a_Y, b_Y]$ to 0. Indeed, since $[a_X, b_X] \ominus [a_Y, b_Y] = [a_X - b_Y, b_X - a_Y]$, the latter reads:

$$g_\alpha^\ominus(X, Y) = \alpha g_-^+(X, Y) - (1 - \alpha)g_+^-(X, Y) = \alpha(a_X - b_Y) + (1 - \alpha)(b_X - a_Y) \leq 0$$

instead of $\alpha(a_X - a_Y) + (1 - \alpha)(b_X - b_Y) \leq 0$. In fact $g_\alpha^\ominus(X, Y) \geq 0$ reads $\alpha a_X + (1 - \alpha)b_X \geq (1 - \alpha)a_Y + \alpha b_Y$. So, if $\alpha < 1/2$, this is a weakening of the interval ordering, while if $\alpha > 1/2$, this is a strengthening of its negation. Note that $g_\alpha^\ominus(X, Y) - g_\alpha(X, Y) = (b_Y - a_Y)(1 - 2\alpha)$ so that the relative strength of these criteria depends on the degree of pessimism α and the two criteria coincide for a neutral attitude ($\alpha = 1/2$).

3   Preference Relations within Imprecise Probability Theory

In the imprecise probabilities setting, a preference relation for pairs of variables (or *gambles*) can be understood in two different ways:

W1. The expert initial information is assessed by means of comparative preference statements between gambles and, afterwards, a set of joint feasible linear previsions or, equivalently, a pair of lower and upper previsions on the set of gambles is derived from it. This is the approach followed in the general theory of imprecise probabilities (see [3,4,20]).

W2. A pair of lower and upper previsions is considered on the class of gambles. A preference relation based on it is considered. Such relation is closely related to the notion of "almost preference" in Walley's framework. This is the approach considered in [7,15,16,19], for instance.

Here, we will consider the second approach.

3.1   Generalizations of First Stochastic Dominance

Denoeux [7] has generalized the notion of first stochastic dominance to the case of random intervals. Let m_1 and m_2 respectively denote the (generalized) basic mass assignments whose focal elements are closed intervals of the real line, corresponding to sets $\mathcal{F}_j, j = 1, 2$. Denote their belief functions by Bel_1 and Bel_2, respectively, and their (dual) plausibility functions by Pl_1 and Pl_2:

$$Bel_j(A) = \sum_{[a,b] \in \mathcal{F}_j, [a,b] \subseteq A} m_j([a,b]) \text{ and } Pl_j(A) = \sum_{[a,b] \in \mathcal{F}_j, [a,b] \cap A \neq \emptyset} m_j([a,b]), j = 1, 2$$

Four generalizations of first stochastic dominance are provided in [7]:

- $m_1 \leq_{1st}^{(-,+)} m_2$ if $Bel_1(x, \infty) \leq Pl_2(x, \infty), \forall x \in \mathbb{R}$.
- $m_1 \leq_{1st}^{(-,-)} m_2$ if $Bel_1(x, \infty) \leq Bel_2(x, \infty), \forall x \in \mathbb{R}$.
- $m_1 \leq_{1st}^{(+,+)} m_2$ if $Pl_1(x, \infty) \leq Pl_2(x, \infty), \forall x \in \mathbb{R}$.
- $m_1 \leq_{1st}^{(+,-)} m_2$ if if $Pl_1(x, \infty) \leq Bel_2(x, \infty), \forall x \in \mathbb{R}$.

When, in particular, both families of focal elements are singletons ($n = m = 1$), we easily observe that each of the four above relations reduces to each of the interval comparisons considered in Subsection 2.3. In contrast, when the endpoints of every focal interval coincide, all the four above criteria coincide with the criterion of first stochastic dominance considered in Subsection 2.1.

3.2   Generalizations of Expectation Dominance

In [14,19], several strategies to find optimal decisions within the imprecise probabilities setting are surveyed. When the underlying preference criterion induces a total ordering, the optimal decision is unique. Otherwise, it may induce a set

of optimal decisions. In this subsection, we will list the preference criteria associated to those optimal decision strategies. So, for each particular criterion, we
refer to the preference criterion itself instead of referring to the optimal decision
associated to it (as it is done in [14,19]). All the criteria listed in this subsection
extend the dominance of expectation. Let us first introduce some notation. Con-
sider a set of gambles $\mathcal{K}$ (bounded mappings from Ω to $\mathbb{R}$.) In agreement with
[19], we will assume that all the gambles in $\mathcal{K}$ are measurable wrt the field $\mathcal{F}$
and a pair of dual coherent lower and upper previsions $\underline{P}$ and $\overline{P}$ defined on $\mathcal{K}$.
They represent a credal set $\mathcal{P}$ (a closed convex set of probability measures) on
$\mathcal{F}$, in the sense that:

$$\mathcal{P} = \{P \text{ additive probability } : P \geq \underline{P}\} = \{P \text{ additive probability } : P \leq \overline{P}\}$$

and $\underline{P} = \inf \mathcal{P}$ and $\overline{P} = \sup \mathcal{P}$. Let us denote by $E_{\underline{P}}$ and $E_{\overline{P}}$ the natural
extensions of $\underline{P}$ and $\overline{P}$, respectively, to the class of all $\mathcal{F}$-measurable gambles,
i.e.:

$$E_{\underline{P}}(Z) = \inf\{E_P(Z) : P \in \mathcal{P}\}, \text{ and } E_{\overline{P}}(Z) = \sup\{E_P(Z) : P \in \mathcal{P}\}.$$

Consider now a pair of $\mathcal{F}$-measurable gambles (or random variables) $X : \Omega \to \mathbb{R}$
and $Y : \Omega \to \mathbb{R}$.

1. *Maximin criterion* ([11]): it consists in replacing the expectation with the
   lower expectation. X is preferred to Y if $E_{\underline{P}}(X) \geq E_{\underline{P}}(Y)$. It is a total
   ordering.
2. *Maximax criterion* ([17]): it consists in replacing the expectation with the
   upper expectation. X is preferred to Y if $E_{\overline{P}}(X) \geq E_{\overline{P}}(Y)$. It is also a total
   ordering.
3. *Hurwicz criterion* ([13]): it considers a pessimistic index $\alpha \in [0,1]$. According
   to it, X is preferred to Y if $\alpha E_{\underline{P}}(X) + (1 - \alpha)E_{\overline{P}}(X) \geq \alpha E_{\underline{P}}(Y) + (1 -
   \alpha)E_{\overline{P}}(Y)$. It is also a total ordering.
4. *Interval dominance* ([21]): X is said to be preferred to Y if $E_{\underline{P}}(X) \geq E_{\overline{P}}(Y)$.
   (It does not induce a total ordering.)
5. *Maximality*: $E_{\underline{P}}(X - Y) \geq 0$. It coincides with the almost preference relation
   considered by Walley [20]. (It does not induce a total ordering.)
6. *E-admissibility*: X is preferred to Y if there exists at least one probability
   $P \in \mathcal{P}$ such that $E_P(X) \geq E_P(Y)$. (It does not induce a total ordering.)
7. *Interval extension of expectation preference*: X is preferred to Y if $E_{\underline{P}}(X) \geq
   E_{\underline{P}}(Y)$ and $E_{\overline{P}}(X) \geq E_{\overline{P}}(Y)$. In other words, if the maximum of the in-
   tervals $[E_{\underline{P}}(X), E_{\overline{P}}(X)]$ and $[E_{\underline{P}}(Y), E_{\overline{P}}(Y)]$ (wrt interval-arithmetics) coincides with $[E_{\underline{P}}(X), E_{\overline{P}}(X)]$. (It does not induce a total ordering.)

Implication Relations. We can straightforward obtain that:

– [1 and 2] $\Leftrightarrow$ 7 $\Leftrightarrow$ [3 is fulfilled for every $\alpha \in [0,1]$].
– 4 $\Rightarrow$ 1, 2, 3, and 7.
– 5 $\Rightarrow$ 6.

Furthermore, given two arbitrary gambles, the following inequality can be easily checked [20]:

$$E_{\underline{P}}(X) - E_{\overline{P}}(Y) \leq E_{\underline{P}}(X - Y)$$

Therefore, the implication 4 ⇒ 5 also holds. However, under several different independence assumptions $E_{\underline{P}}(X - Y)$ coincides with $E_{\underline{P}}(X) - E_{\overline{P}}(Y)$ (see [6] for a detailed list). Therefore, under such assumptions, interval dominance is equivalent to maximality dominance.

3.3   Generalizations of Statistical Preference

Two different generalizations of the notion of statistical preference to convex probability sets $\mathcal{P}$ were introduced in some previous works:

- *Combining statistical preference and interval ordering* [15,16]: X is said to dominate Y when [2]
$$\underline{P}(X > Y) \geq \overline{P}(Y \geq X). \tag{8}$$

- *Signed-preference* [4]. The approach followed there to introduce signed-preference is W1. Thus, to relate that generalization with the present one, we will refer here to the notion of *almost- signed-preference*. X is said to be almost-signed-preferred to Y when $E_{\underline{P}}(1_{X>Y} - 1_{Y>X}) \geq 0$.

In the special case where $\mathcal{P}$ defines mere intervals for X and Y, Eq. (8) reduces to interval ordering $\geq_{+}^{-}$. A different approach considers intervals as uniform distributions over them. The statistical preference criterion has been particularized to this case, in order to define a total ordering over the family of closed intervals in several works (see [15,16], for instance).

4   A General Common Expression of Preference between Gambles

Most of the preference relations reviewed in Subsections 3.2 and 3.3 can be expressed as particular cases of one of the following preference relations, which respectively generalize Eqs (1) and (2):

$$E_\mu[g(X,Y)] \geq 0, \text{ with } \mu \in \{\underline{P}, \overline{P}\} \tag{9}$$

$$E_{\mu_1}[f(X,Y)] \geq E_{\mu_2}[f(Y,X)], \text{ with } \mu_1, \mu_2 \in \{\underline{P}, \overline{P}\} \tag{10}$$

In fact, using the mappings $f(x,y) = x$ and $g = f - f \circ \text{sw}$ defined in Subsection 2.2 for comparing expectations, if we choose:

- the set function $\mu = \underline{P}$ and Eq. (9), we get the maximality criterion.
- the set functions $\mu_1 = \mu_2 = \underline{P}$, and Eq. (10), we get the maximin criterion.

---

[2] In this expression, $X > Y$ represents the subset $\{\omega \in \Omega : X(\omega) > Y(\omega)\}$.

- the set functions $\mu_1 = \mu_2 = \overline{P}$, and Eq. (10), we get the maximax criterion.
- the set functions $\mu_1 = \underline{P}$ and $\mu_2 = \overline{P}$, and Eq. (10), we get the interval-dominance criterion.

Considering the mappings $f(x, y) = 1_{x>y}$ and $g = f - f \circ \mathrm{sw}$ defined in Eq. (4), if we choose:

- the set function $\mu = \underline{P}$ and Eq. (9), we get the almost-signed preference relation.
- the set functions $\mu_1 = \underline{P}$ and $\mu_2 = \overline{P}$, and Eq. (10), we get the criterion introduced in [15,16].

In this section, we try to encompass generalizations of the notion of first stochastic dominance (Subsection 3.1) as well.

4.1   General Formulation

Eqs (9) and (10) generalize most of the preference methods reviewed in Subsection 3.2 and the two methods considered in Subsection 3.3. But they do not generalize the criteria reviewed in Subsection 3.1. This is due to the fact that the formulation followed in Subsection 3.1 (taken from [7]) is a bit different. There, a family of probability measures on $\mathbb{R}^2$ is considered. On the contrary, a family of probability measures $\mathcal{P}$ on Ω and a random vector $(X, Y) : \Omega \to \mathbb{R}^2$ is considered in Subsections 3.2 and 3.3, following the nomenclature of [4,15,16,19].

As we will clarify below, most of those preference criteria reviewed in Sections 2 and 3 can be encompassed into one of the two following forms of dominance criteria. Let us consider a set of probability measures $\mathcal{Q}$ on a field $\mathcal{G} \subseteq \wp(\mathbb{R}^2)$ and the mapping $g = f - f \circ \mathrm{sw}$, where $f : \mathbb{R}^2 \to \mathbb{R}$ is increasing in the first component and decreasing in the second one, and sw is the swap mapping.

1. *First form*: The first component is said to dominate the second one when:

$$E_\mu(g) \geq 0, \text{ where } \mu \in \{\underline{Q}, \overline{Q}\} \tag{11}$$

2. *Second form*: The first component is said to dominate the second one when:

$$E_{\mu_1}(f) \geq E_{\mu_2}(f \circ \mathrm{sw}), \text{ where } \mu_1, \mu_2 \in \{\underline{Q}, \overline{Q}, \} \tag{12}$$

where $\underline{Q}$ and $\overline{Q}$ respectively denote the lower and upper envelopes of the set $\mathcal{Q}$, $\underline{Q} = \inf \mathcal{Q}$ and $\overline{Q} = \sup \mathcal{Q}$.

These two criteria generalize the majority[3] of the preference relations considered in Section 3:

---

[3] We generalize all of them, except for the E-admissibility and the Hurwicz criterion. A more general formula encompassing all criteria could be written, but we avoid it for the sake of simplicity.

– *Generalization of stochastic orderings* -Subsections 2.1 and 2.2 - In order to generalize those notions, we just have to consider the singleton $\mathcal{Q} = \{P_{(X,Y)}\}$, where $P_{(X,Y)}$ represents the joint probability measure induced by (X, Y) on $\mathcal{G}$, i.e., the probability measure defined as follows:

$$P_{(X,Y)}(C) = P((X, Y)^{-1}(C)) = P(\{\omega \in \Omega : (X, Y)(\omega) \in C\}), \ C \in \mathcal{G}.$$

Thus, any of the above equations (Eq. (11) or (12)) applied to this family $\mathcal{Q}$ coincides with Eq. (1).

– *Generalization of first stochastic dominance* - Subsection 3.1 - Given two (generalized) plausibility measures Pl_1 and Pl_2, consider the family of probability measures:

$$\mathcal{Q} = \{Q \text{ prob.} : Q_1 \leq Pl_1, Q_2 \leq Pl_2\}$$

where Q_1 and Q_2 are the marginals of Q for X and Y respectively. Using the family of functions $\{f_{x_0} = 1_{x > x_0} : x_0 \in \mathbb{R}\}$ of Eq. (3), and the second form above, we generalize the four Denoeux criteria for comparing random intervals considered in Subsection 3.1:

- For $\mu_1 = \underline{Q}$ and $\mu_2 = \overline{Q}$, we generalize the criterion $\leq_{1st}^{(-+)}$.
- For $\mu_1 = \mu_2 = \underline{Q}$, we generalize the criterion $\leq_{1st}^{(--)}$.
- For $\mu_1 = \mu_2 = \overline{Q}$, we generalize the criterion $\leq_{1st}^{(++)}$.
- For $\mu_1 = \overline{Q}$ and $\mu_2 = \underline{Q}$, we generalize the criterion $\leq_{1st}^{(+,-)}$.

In particular, when both families of focal sets are singletons, or, equivalently, when the family $\mathcal{Q}$ can be written as:

$$\mathcal{Q} = \{Q : Q([a, b] \times [c, d]) = 1\},$$

the above criteria are reduced to the corresponding criteria of comparison between intervals (Subsection 2.3).

– *Generalization of expectation dominance* Using the mapping $f(x, y) = x$, $\forall x \in \mathbb{R}$, we generalize some of the criteria of Subsection 3.2. Consider the set of probability measures $\mathcal{P}$ on $\mathcal{F} \subseteq \wp(\Omega)$ and the pair of random variables X and Y defined on Ω, and let $\underline{P_{(X,Y)}}$ and $\overline{P_{(X,Y)}}$ respectively denote the lower and upper probabilities associated to the family: $\mathcal{P}_{(X,Y)} = \{P_{(X,Y)} : P \in \mathcal{P}\}$, where, for each probability measure $P \in \mathcal{P}$, $P_{(X,Y)}$ denotes the probability measure induced by (X, Y) as we have considered above.

- For $\mu_1 = \underline{P_{X,Y}}$ and $\mu_2 = \overline{P_{X,Y}}$, in Eq. (12), we get the interval dominance criterion.
- For $\mu_1 = \mu_2 = \underline{P_{X,Y}}$, in Eq. (12), we get the maximin criterion.
- For $\mu_1 = \mu_2 = \overline{P_{X,Y}}$, in Eq. (12), we get the maximax criterion.
- For $\mu = P_{X,Y}$, in Eq. (11), we get the maximality criterion.

– *Generalization of statistical preference* Now consider $f(x, y) = 1_{x > y}$ defined in Eq. (4). Then we can generalize the statistical preference relations considered in Subsection 3.3. In particular:

- For $\mu_1 = \underline{P_{X,Y}}$ and $\mu_2 = \overline{P_{X,Y}}$ in Eq. (12), we get the criterion considered in Eq. (8).
- For μ, in Eq. (11), we get almost signed-preference.

4.2   The Special Case of Fuzzy Intervals

A fuzzy interval $\tilde{A}$ (usually called a fuzzy number in the literature) can be interpreted (among other many interpretations) as a possibility distribution on the real line, such that the α-cuts of $\tilde{A}$, i.e. $(\tilde{A})_\alpha = \{a : \tilde{A}(a) \geq \alpha\}$, are convex (fuzzy interval). Let a_α and b_α be the infimum and the supremum of each cut, respectively. The possibility distribution $\tilde{A} : \mathbb{R} \to [0,1]$ is associated to a possibility measure $\Pi_{\tilde{A}}(B) = \sup_{b \in B} \tilde{A}(b)$. It is the upper bound of the convex set of probability measures $\mathcal{P}(\tilde{A})$ satisfying the following restrictions:

$$P(A_\alpha) \geq 1 - \alpha, \ \forall \alpha \in [0,1], \tag{13}$$

where $A_\alpha = [a_\alpha, b_\alpha]$, $\alpha \in (0,1]$ is the α-cut of $\tilde{A}$. According to this view, fuzzy ranking methods can be defined using imprecise probability criteria listed above. Many such methods are based on comparison of the end-points of the α-cuts. In particular, under the random interval interpretation of fuzzy sets, they are related to the comparison of percentiles. This mode of comparison is very closely related to first stochastic dominance and Denoeux definitions (reviewed in Subsection 3.1) directly apply (see [1]).

Some other methods are related to the comparison of expected intervals [8], $[\int_0^1 a_\alpha d\alpha, \int_0^1 b_\alpha d\alpha]$ bounded by upper and lower expectations induced by $\mathcal{P}(\tilde{A})$. So they can be seen as expectation-dominance methods, in fact particular cases in the family of methods reviewed in Subsection 3.2. Usually absent from fuzzy ranking methods is the Walley style maximality criterion. If X and Y are ill-known quantities induced by $\tilde{A}_1$ and $\tilde{A}_2$ respectively, we must check if $E_{\underline{P}}(X - Y) = \int_0^1 (a_{1\alpha} - b_{2\alpha}) d\alpha > 0$, assuming a dependence structure between X and Y allowing the use of fuzzy interval subtraction [9]. It clearly comes down to comparing $\int_0^1 a_{1\alpha} d\alpha$ to $\int_0^1 b_{2\alpha} d\alpha$, and then reduces to an extension of interval ordering $\geq_+^-$. This would not be true with other kinds of dependence structures. Therefore, many fuzzy ranking methods can be viewed as special cases of preference relations between gambles, and they are closely related to Eq.s (11) and (12). This point deserves a special study of its own.

Acknowledgements. Supported by the Spanish Ministry of Sciences and Innovation, Research Project TIN2011-24302.

References

1. Aiche, F., Dubois, D.: An Extension of Stochastic Dominance to Fuzzy Random Variables. In: Hüllermeier, E., Kruse, R., Hoffmann, F. (eds.) IPMU 2010. LNCS, vol. 6178, pp. 159–168. Springer, Heidelberg (2010)
2. Chateauneuf, A., Cohen, M.: Cardinal extensions of the EU model based on Choquet integral. In: Bouyssou, D., Dubois, D., Pirlot, M., Prade, H. (eds.) Decision-Making Process Concepts and Methods, ch. 3. ISTE & Wiley, London (2009)
3. Couso, I., Moral, S.: Sets of Desirable Gambles and Credal Sets. In: 6th International Symposium on Imprecise Probability: Theories and Applications, Durham, United Kingdom (2009)

4. Couso, I., Sánchez, L.: The Behavioral Meaning of the Median. In: Borgelt, C., González-Rodríguez, G., Trutschnig, W., Lubiano, M.A., Gil, M.Á., Grzegorzewski, P., Hryniewicz, O. (eds.) Combining Soft Computing and Statistical Methods in Data Analysis. AISC, vol. 77, pp. 115–122. Springer, Heidelberg (2010)
5. David, H.: The method of paired comparisons. In: Griffin's Statistical Monographs & Courses, vol. 12. Charles Griffin & D. Ltd., London (1963)
6. De Cooman, G.: Further thoughts on possibilistic previsions: A rejoinder. Fuzzy Sets and Systems 153, 375–385 (2005)
7. Denoeux, T.: Extending stochastic ordering to belief functions on the real line. Information Sciences 179, 1362–1376 (2009)
8. Dubois, D., Prade, H.: The mean value of a fuzzy number. Fuzzy Sets and Systems 24, 279–300 (1987)
9. Dubois, D., Prade, H.: Random sets and fuzzy interval analysis. Fuzzy Sets and Systems 42, 87–101 (1991)
10. Fishburn, P.: Interval Orderings. Wiley, New-York (1987)
11. Gilboa, I., Schmeidler, D.: Maxmin expected utility with non-unique prior. Journal of Mathematical Economics 181, 41–153 (1989)
12. Hadar, J., Russell, W.: Rules for Ordering Uncertain Prospects. American Economic Review 59, 25–34 (1969)
13. Jaffray, J.Y., Jeleva, M.: Information processing under imprecise risk with the Hurwicz criterion. In: Proc. of the Fifth Int. Symposium on Imprecise Probabilities and Their Applications, ISIPTA 2007 (2007)
14. Kikuti, D., Cozman, F.G., De Campos, C.P.: Partially ordered preferences in decision trees: computing strategies with imprecision in probabilities. In: Brafman, R., Junker, U. (eds.) Multidisciplinary IJCAI 2005 Workshop on Advances in Preference Handling, pp. 118–123 (2005)
15. Sánchez, L., Couso, I., Casillas, J.: Modeling Vague Data with Genetic Fuzzy Systems under a Combination of Crisp and Imprecise Criteria. In: Proceedings of the 2007 IEEE Symposium on Computational Intelligence in Multicriteria Decision Making, MCDM 2007 (2007)
16. Sánchez, L., Couso, I., Casillas, J.: Genetic Learning of Fuzzy Rules based on Low Quality Data. Fuzzy Sets and Systems 160, 2524–2552 (2009)
17. Satia, J.K., Roy, J., Lave, E.: Markovian decision processes with uncertain transition probabilities. Operations Research 21(3), 728–740 (1973)
18. Savage, L.J.: The Foundations of Statistics. Wiley (1954); 2nd edn. Dover Publications Inc., New York (1972)
19. Troffaes, M.C.W.: Decision making under uncertainty using imprecise probabilities. International Journal of Approximate Reasoning 45, 17–19 (2007)
20. Walley, P.: Statistical Reasoning with Imprecise Probabilities. Chapman and Hall (1991)
21. Zaffalon, M., Wesnes, K., Petrini, O.: Reliable diagnoses of dementia by the naive credal classifier inferred from incomplete cognitive data. Artificial Intelligence in Medicine 29, 61–79 (2003)

Imprecise Bernoulli Processes

Jasper De Bock and Gert de Cooman

Ghent University, SYSTeMS Research Group
Technologiepark–Zwijnaarde 914, 9052 Zwijnaarde, Belgium
{jasper.debock,gert.decooman}@UGent.be

Abstract. In classical Bernoulli processes, it is assumed that a single Bernoulli experiment can be described by a precise and precisely known probability distribution. However, both of these assumptions can be relaxed. A first approach, often used in sensitivity analysis, is to drop only the second assumption: one assumes the existence of a precise distribution, but has insufficient resources to determine it precisely. The resulting imprecise Bernoulli process is the lower envelope of a set of precise Bernoulli processes. An alternative approach is to drop both assumptions, meaning that we don't assume the existence of a precise probability distribution and regard the experiment as inherently imprecise. In that case, a single imprecise Bernoulli experiment can be described by a set of desirable gambles. We show how this set can be extended to describe an imprecise Bernoulli process, by imposing the behavioral assessments of epistemic independence and exchangeability. The resulting analysis leads to surprisingly simple mathematical expressions characterizing this process, which turn out to be the same as the ones obtained through the straightforward sensitivity analysis approach.

Keywords: imprecise Bernoulli processes, sets of desirable gambles, epistemic independence, exchangeability, sensitivity analysis, Bernstein polynomials, IID processes, exchangeably independent natural extension.

1 Introduction

In classical probability theory, a Bernoulli process is defined as an infinite sequence of binary variables $X_1, \ldots, X_n, \ldots$ that are independent and identically distributed (IID). In this definition, a single Bernoulli experiment is implicitly assumed to have a precise and precisely known probability distribution. However this assumption can be relaxed. A first approach, used in sensitivity analysis, is to assume the existence of a precise probability distribution, but allowing it to be imprecisely known, for example due to limited resources. The resulting imprecise Bernoulli process is then the lower envelope of a set of precise Bernoulli processes. A second approach is to regard a single Bernoulli experiment as inherently imprecise, thereby dropping the assumption an underlying precise probability distribution. In such cases, using sensitivity analysis can no longer be justified and their is no known alternative method that is computationally tractable. In this paper, we offer a solution to this problem by introducing

S. Greco et al. (Eds.): IPMU 2012, Part III, CCIS 299, pp. 400–409, 2012.
© Springer-Verlag Berlin Heidelberg 2012

our notion of an *imprecise Bernoulli process*, defining it by imposing the behavioral assessments of *exchangeability* and *epistemic independence*. This is a generalisation of the precise-probabilistic definition, since applying our definition to precise distributions, is equivalent with imposing the IID property. We describe our imprecise Bernoulli process using the language of coherent sets of desirable gambles [3,4,7], because these constitute the most general and powerful imprecise probability models we know of. We give a short introduction to the relevant theory in Section 2. In Section 3, we look at how the marginal model for one variable, describing a single Bernoulli experiment, can be represented as a coherent set of desirable gambles. Section 4 recalls how the assessment of exchangeability can be mathematically formulated in the theory of coherent sets of desirable gambles. In Section 5, we add the assessment of epistemic independence to that of exchangeability and extend the marginal model for a single variable to the smallest (most conservative) imprecise Bernoulli process satisfying those two requirements. We call this the exchangeably independent natural extension of the marginal model. We end by showing in Section 6 that the resulting imprecise Bernoulli process is identical to the one obtained by applying the sensitivity analysis approach mentioned above. This leads us to conclude that an assessment of exchangeability and epistemic independence serves as a behavioural justification for the rather strong assumptions associated with sensitivity analysis.

2 Desirability and Coherence

Let us begin by giving a short introduction to the theory of coherent sets of *desirable gambles*, as it will be an important tool for our analysis. We refer to Refs. [3,4,7] for more details and further discussion. Consider a finite, non-empty set Ω, called the possibility space, which describes the possible and mutually exclusive outcomes of some experiment.

Sets of Desirable Gambles: A gamble f is a real-valued map on Ω which is interpreted as an uncertain reward. If the outcome of the experiment turns out to be ω, the (possibly negative) reward is $f(\omega)$. A non-zero gamble is called desirable if we accept the transaction in which (i) the actual outcome ω of the experiment is determined, and (ii) we receive the reward $f(\omega)$. The zero gamble is not considered to be desirable, mainly because we want desirability to represent a strict preference to the zero gamble.

We will model a subject's beliefs regarding the possible outcomes Ω of an experiment by means of a set $\mathcal{D}$ of desirable gambles, which will be a subset of the set $\mathcal{G}(\Omega)$ of all gambles on Ω. For any two gambles f and g in $\mathcal{G}(\Omega)$, we say that $f \geq g$ if $f(\omega) \geq g(\omega)$ for all ω in Ω and $f > g$ if $f \geq g$ and $f \neq g$.

Coherence: In order to represent a rational subject's beliefs regarding the outcome of an experiment, a set $\mathcal{D} \subseteq \mathcal{G}(\Omega)$ of desirable gambles should satisfy some rationality requirements. If these requirements are met, we call the set $\mathcal{D}$ *coherent*.

Definition 1 (Coherence). *A set of desirable gambles $\mathcal{D} \subseteq \mathcal{G}(\Omega)$ is called coherent if it satisfies the following requirements, for all gambles f, f_1, and f_2 in $\mathcal{G}(\Omega)$ and all real $\lambda > 0$:*

C1. *if $f = 0$ then $f \notin \mathcal{D}$;*
C2. *if $f > 0$ then $f \in \mathcal{D}$;*
C3. *if $f \in \mathcal{D}$ then $\lambda f \in \mathcal{D}$ [scaling];*
C4. *if $f_1, f_2 \in \mathcal{D}$ then $f_1 + f_2 \in \mathcal{D}$ [combination].*

Requirements C3 and C4 make $\mathcal{D}$ a convex cone: $\text{posi}(\mathcal{D}) = \mathcal{D}$, where we have used the positive hull operator posi which generates the set of finite strictly positive linear combinations of elements of its argument set:

$$\text{posi}(\mathcal{D}) := \left\{ \sum_{k=1}^{n} \lambda_k f_k : f_k \in \mathcal{D}, \lambda_k \in \mathbb{R}_0^+, n \in \mathbb{N}_0 \right\}.$$

Here $\mathbb{R}_0^+$ is the set of all positive real numbers, and $\mathbb{N}_0$ the set of all natural numbers (positive integers). The axioms also guarantee that if $f < 0$ then $f \notin \mathcal{D}$.

Weakly Desirable Gambles: We now define *weak desirability*, a concept that will lie at the basis of our discussion of exchangeability. Loosely speaking, a gamble is weakly desirable if adding anything desirable to it renders the result desirable.

Definition 2 (Weak desirability). *Consider a coherent set $\mathcal{D}$ of desirable gambles. Then a gamble f is called weakly desirable if $f + f'$ is desirable for all desirable f': $f + f' \in \mathcal{D}$ for all f' in $\mathcal{D}$. We use $\mathcal{W}_{\mathcal{D}}$ to denote the set of all weakly desirable gambles associated with $\mathcal{D}$.*

Coherent Lower and Upper Previsions: With a set of gambles $\mathcal{D}$, we can associate a *lower prevision* $\underline{P}_{\mathcal{D}}$ and an *upper prevision* $\overline{P}_{\mathcal{D}}$, which can respectively be interpreted as a lower and upper expectation. For any gambles f we define:

$$\underline{P}_{\mathcal{D}}(f) := \sup\{\mu \in \mathbb{R} : f - \mu \in \mathcal{D}\} \text{ and } \overline{P}_{\mathcal{D}}(f) := \inf\{\mu \in \mathbb{R} : \mu - f \in \mathcal{D}\}. \quad (1)$$

$\underline{P}_{\mathcal{D}}(f)$ is the subject's supremum acceptable price for buying the uncertain reward f, and $\overline{P}_{\mathcal{D}}(f)$ his infimum acceptable price for selling f. Observe that the so-called *conjugacy relation* $\underline{P}_{\mathcal{D}}(-f) = -\overline{P}_{\mathcal{D}}(f)$ is always satisfied. We call a real functional $\underline{P}$ on $\mathcal{G}(\Omega)$ a *coherent lower prevision* if there is some coherent set of desirable gambles $\mathcal{D}$ on $\mathcal{G}(\Omega)$ such that $\underline{P} = \underline{P}_{\mathcal{D}}$.

3   Imprecise Bernoulli Experiments

In order for the infinite sequence X_1, ..., X_n, ... of variables to represent an imprecise Bernoulli process, a necessary requirement is that all individual variables have the same marginal model, describing our subject's uncertainty about a single Bernoulli experiment. In our framework, this is a coherent set of desirable gambles $\mathcal{D}_1$. Let us take a closer look at what this model looks like.

Consider a binary variable X taking values in the set $\mathcal{X} = \{a, b\}$. A gamble f on $\mathcal{X}$ can be identified with a point $(f(a), f(b))$ in two-dimensional Euclidean space. A coherent set of desirable gambles $\mathcal{D}_1$ is a convex cone in this space (the grey area in the figure below), which has to include all gambles $f > 0$ (the dark grey area) but cannot include the zero gamble (the white dot).

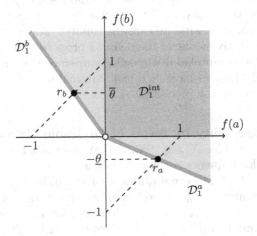

Such a cone can be characterised using its extreme rays $\mathcal{D}_1^a$ and $\mathcal{D}_1^b$ (the thick, gray lines in the figure above), which in turn are characterised by the gambles $r_a = (1 - \underline{\theta}, -\underline{\theta})$ and $r_b = (\overline{\theta} - 1, \overline{\theta})$ (the black dots):

$$\mathcal{D}_1^a := \{\lambda_a r_a : \lambda_a > 0\} \text{ and } \mathcal{D}_1^b := \{\lambda_b r_b : \lambda_b > 0\}.$$

It follows from coherence that $0 \leq \underline{\theta} \leq \overline{\theta} \leq 1$.

Since the cone $\mathcal{D}_1$ need not be closed, each of its extreme rays might be included or not. We use δ_a (δ_b) to indicate wether $\mathcal{D}_1^a$ ($\mathcal{D}_1^b$) is included in $\mathcal{D}_1$ or not, by setting it equal to 1 or 0 respectively. Coherence imposes some restrictions on the possible values of δ_a and δ_b. For instance, δ_a must equal 1 if $\underline{\theta} = 0$ and 0 if $\underline{\theta} = 1$. Similarly, δ_b has to be 1 if $\overline{\theta} = 1$ and 0 if $\overline{\theta} = 0$. Finally, δ_a and δ_b cannot both equal 1 if $\underline{\theta} = \overline{\theta}$.

Define $\delta\mathcal{D}_1^a$ to be $\mathcal{D}_1^a$ if $\delta_a = 1$ and to be the empty set $\emptyset$ if $\delta_a = 0$. Analogous definitions hold for $\delta\mathcal{D}_1^b$ and for other sets defined further on. We use $\mathcal{D}_1^{int}$ to denote the set of all gambles $f \in \mathcal{D}_1$ that are not part of one of the extreme rays $\mathcal{D}_1^a$ or $\mathcal{D}_1^b$ and thus lie in the interior of $\mathcal{D}_1$:

$$\mathcal{D}_1^{int} := \{\lambda + \lambda_a r_a + \lambda_b r_b : \lambda > 0, \lambda_a \geq 0, \lambda_b \geq 0\}.$$

We can now generally define an arbitrary coherent set of desirable gambles describing our subject's beliefs about a single binary variable as follows:

$$\mathcal{D}_1 := \mathcal{D}_1^{int} \cup \delta\mathcal{D}_1^a \cup \delta\mathcal{D}_1^b. \tag{2}$$

All that is needed to uniquely determine a set of desirable gambles described by this equation, is the values of $\underline{\theta}$, $\overline{\theta}$, δ_a and δ_b.

4   Exchangeability

A sequence of variables is called *exchangeable* if, simply put, the order of the variables is irrelevant. In classical Bernoulli processes, exchangeability is a direct consequence of the IID property. In an imprecise-probabilistic context, it turns out that this is not necessarily the case (see, for instance, [1,2] for an approach to IID processes without exchangeability), and we therefore impose exchangeability explicitly as one of the defining properties. This leads to a generalisation of the precise-probabilistic definition, since exchangeability implies that the individual variables have identical marginal models (and are therefore identically distributed in the precise case).

Defining Exchangeability in Terms of Desirable Gambles: Consider a finite sequence of variables X_1, ..., X_n and an associated set $\mathcal{D}_n$ of desirable gambles on $\mathcal{X}^n$. This sequence assumes values $x = (x_1, \ldots, x_n)$ in $\mathcal{X}^n$. We use $\mathcal{P}_n$ to denote the set of all permutations π of the index set $\{1, \ldots, n\}$. With any such permutation $\pi \in \mathcal{P}_n$, we associate a permutation of $\mathcal{X}^n$, defined by $\pi x = \pi(x_1, \ldots, x_n) := (x_{\pi(1)}, \ldots, x_{\pi(n)})$. Similarly, for any gamble f in $\mathcal{G}(\mathcal{X}^n)$, we define the permuted gamble $\pi^t f = f \circ \pi$, so $(\pi^t f)(x) = f(\pi x)$.

If a subject assessess the sequence X_1, ..., X_n to be exchangeable, this means that for any gamble $f \in \mathcal{G}(\mathcal{X}^n)$ and any permutation $\pi \in \mathcal{P}_n$, he is indifferent between the gambles $\pi^t f$ and f, which we translate by saying that he regards exchanging $\pi^t f$ for f as weakly desirable, see [6, Section 4.1.1] and [3] for more motivation and extensive discussion. Equivalently, we require that the gamble $f - \pi^t f$ is weakly desirable.[1] We define $\mathcal{W}_{\mathcal{P}_n} := \{f - \pi^t f : f \in \mathcal{G}(\mathcal{X}^n) \text{ and } \pi \in \mathcal{P}_n\}$.

Definition 3 (Exchangeability). *A coherent set $\mathcal{D}_n$ of desirable gambles on $\mathcal{X}^n$ is called exchangeable if all gambles in $\mathcal{W}_{\mathcal{P}_n}$ are weakly desirable:* $\mathcal{W}_{\mathcal{P}_n} \subseteq \mathcal{W}_{\mathcal{D}_n}$.

An infinite sequence of variables X_1, ..., X_n, ... is called exchangeable if each of its finite subsequences is, or equivalently, if for all $n \in \mathbb{N}_0$ the variables X_1, ..., X_n are exchangeable. This is modelled as follows: the subject has an exchangeable coherent set of desirable gambles on $\mathcal{X}^n$, for all $n \in \mathbb{N}_0$.

For such a family of sets $\mathcal{D}_n$ of desirable gambles to consistently represent beliefs about an infinite sequence of variables, it should also be *time consistent*. This means that, with $n_1 \leq n_2$, if we consider a gamble h on $\mathcal{X}^{n_2}$ that really only depends on the first n_1 variables, it should not matter, as far as its desirability is concerned, whether we consider it to be a gamble on $\mathcal{X}^{n_1}$ or a gamble on $\mathcal{X}^{n_2}$: $h \in \mathcal{D}_{n_2} \Leftrightarrow h \in \mathcal{D}_{n_1}$. See Ref. [3] for a formal definition of this intuitive property.

---

[1] We do not require it to be actually desirable, as it can be zero, and the zero gamble is not regarded as desirable.

As a direct consequence of exchangeability, for any gamble $f \in \mathcal{G}(\mathcal{X}^n)$ and any permutation $\pi \in \mathcal{P}_n$, the gamble $\pi^t f$ is desirable if and only if f is. Limiting ourselves to those permutations in which only the indexes 1 and n are switched, and gambles f that only depend on X_1 or X_n, we see that exchangeability implies that the marginal modal describing X_n is essentially identical to the one describing X_1, and therefore equal to $\mathcal{D}_1$, for all $n \in \mathbb{N}_0$.

Representation in Terms of Polynomials: Consider the set $\mathcal{V}$ of all polynomial functions on $[0,1]$. Subscripting this set with an integer $n \in \mathbb{N}$ means that we limit ourselves to the set of polynomials of degree up to n. The *Bernstein basis polynomials* $B_{k,n}(\theta) := \binom{n}{k}\theta^k(1-\theta)^{n-k}$ form a basis for the linear space $\mathcal{V}_n$ [5]: for each polynomial p whose degree $\deg(p)$ does not exceed n, there is a unique n-tuple $b_p^n = (b_0, b_1, \ldots, b_n)$ such that $p = \sum_{k=0}^n b_k B_{k,n}(\theta)$. We call a polynomial p *Bernstein positive* if there is some $n \geq \deg(p)$ such that $b_p^n > 0$, meaning that $b_i \geq 0$ for all $i \in \{0, \ldots, n\}$ and $b_i > 0$ for at least one $i \in \{0, \ldots, n\}$. The set of all Bernstein positive polynomials is denoted by $\mathcal{V}^+$. We are now ready to introduce the concept of *Bernstein coherence* for polynomials:

Definition 4 (Bernstein coherence). *We call a set $\mathcal{H}$ of polynomials in $\mathcal{V}$ Bernstein coherent if for all p, p_1, and p_2 in $\mathcal{V}$ and all real $\lambda > 0$:*

B1. *if $p = 0$ then $p \notin \mathcal{H}$;*
B2. *if $p \in \mathcal{V}^+$, then $p \in \mathcal{H}$;*
B3. *if $p \in \mathcal{H}$ then $\lambda p \in \mathcal{H}$;*
B4. *if $p_1, p_2 \in \mathcal{H}$ then $p_1 + p_2 \in \mathcal{H}$.*

With any $\theta \in [0,1]$, we can associate a binary probability mass function on $\mathcal{X} = \{a, b\}$ by letting $\theta_a := \theta$ and $\theta_b := 1 - \theta$. Such a mass function uniquely determines a binomial distribution on $\mathcal{X}^n$. For every sequence of observations $x \in \mathcal{X}^n$, its probability of occurrence is given by $P_\theta(x) := \theta^{C_a(x)}(1-\theta)^{C_b(x)}$, where $C_a(x)$ and $C_b(x)$ respectively denote the number of occurrences of a and b in the sequence x. The expectation associated with the binomial distribution with parameters n and θ is then given by $\mathrm{Mn}_n(f|\theta) := \sum_{x \in \mathcal{X}^n} P_\theta(x)f(x)$, for all gambles f on $\mathcal{X}^n$.

We can now define a linear map Mn_n from $\mathcal{G}(\mathcal{X}^n)$ to $\mathcal{V}$, defining it by $\mathrm{Mn}_n(f) = \mathrm{Mn}_n(f|\cdot)$. In other words, if we let $p = \mathrm{Mn}_n(f)$, then $p(\theta) = \mathrm{Mn}_n(f|\theta)$ for all $\theta \in [0,1]$. To conclude, we let $\mathrm{Mn}_n(\mathcal{D}) := \{\mathrm{Mn}_n(f) : f \in \mathcal{D}\}$ for all $\mathcal{D} \subseteq \mathcal{G}(\mathcal{X}^n)$ and $(\mathrm{Mn}_n)^{-1}(\mathcal{H}) := \{f \in \mathcal{G}(\mathcal{X}^n) : \mathrm{Mn}_n(f) \in \mathcal{H}\}$ for all $\mathcal{H} \subseteq \mathcal{V}$.

Recent work [3] has shown that de Finetti's famous representation result for exchangeable events (binary variables) can be significantly generalised as follows:

Theorem 1 (Infinite Representation). *A family $\mathcal{D}_n$, $n \in \mathbb{N}_0$ of sets of desirable gambles on $\mathcal{X}^n$ is time consistent, coherent and exchangeable if and only if there is some Bernstein coherent set $\mathcal{H}_\infty$ of polynomials in $\mathcal{V}$ such that $\mathcal{D}_n = (\mathrm{Mn}_n)^{-1}(\mathcal{H}_\infty)$ for all $n \in \mathbb{N}_0$. In that case this $\mathcal{H}_\infty$ is uniquely given by $\mathcal{H}_\infty = \bigcup_{n \in \mathbb{N}_0} \mathrm{Mn}_n(\mathcal{D}_n)$.*

We call $\mathcal{H}_\infty$ the *frequency representation* of the coherent, exchangeable and time consistent family of sets of desirable gambles $\mathcal{D}_n$, $n \in \mathbb{N}_0$.

5   Imprecise Bernoulli Processes

We now have a way of representing our uncertainty regarding an infinite sequence of variables $X_1, \ldots, X_n, \ldots$ that we assess to be exchangeable, by means of a frequency representation $\mathcal{H}_\infty$. The only remaining property we have to impose in order to arrive at an imprecise Bernoulli process, is epistemic independence. We call an infinite sequence of variables epistemically independent if learning the value of any finite number of variables does not change our beliefs about any finite subset of the remaining, unobserved ones. It is proven in Ref. [3] that imposing this type of independence on an exchangeable sequence of variables becomes really easy if we use its frequency representation.

Theorem 2 (Independence). *Consider an exchangeable sequence of binary variables* $X_1, \ldots, X_n, \ldots$, *with frequency representation* $\mathcal{H}_\infty$. *These variables are epistemically independent if and only if*

$$(\forall k, n \in \mathbb{N}_0 \colon k \le n)(\forall p \in \mathcal{V}) \; (p \in \mathcal{H}_\infty \Leftrightarrow B_{k,n}p \in \mathcal{H}_\infty). \tag{3}$$

We shall call such models exchangeably independent.

It follows that an imprecise Bernoulli process, defined by the properties of exchangeability and epistemic independence, can be described mathematically using a Bernstein coherent set $\mathcal{H}_\infty$ of polynomials that satisfies Eq. (3). By Theorem 1, $\mathcal{H}_\infty$ is equivalent with a time consistent and exchangeable family of coherent sets of desirable gambles $\mathcal{D}_n = (\mathrm{Mn}_n)^{-1}(\mathcal{H}_\infty)$, $n \in \mathbb{N}_0$. In order for this imprecise Bernoulli process to marginalise to a given set of desirable gambles $\mathcal{D}_1$, representing the marginal model we want to extend, we should have that $\mathcal{D}_1 = (\mathrm{Mn}_1)^{-1}(\mathcal{H}_\infty)$, or equivalently that $\mathcal{H}_1 := \mathrm{Mn}_1(\mathcal{D}_1) = \mathcal{H}_\infty \cap \mathcal{V}_1$. We start by investigating what the set of polynomials $\mathcal{H}_1$ looks like.

Polynomial Representation of the Marginal Model: For a given marginal model $\mathcal{D}_1$, the corresponding set of polynomials is given by

$$\mathcal{H}_1 := \mathrm{Mn}_1(\mathcal{D}_1) = \{\mathrm{Mn}_1(f) : f \in \mathcal{D}_1\}, \tag{4}$$

where $\mathrm{Mn}_1(f) = \theta f(a) + (1 - \theta)f(b)$. Due to the linearity of the transformation Mn_1, and considering that $\mathrm{Mn}_1(r_a) = \theta - \underline{\theta}$ and $\mathrm{Mn}_1(r_b) = \overline{\theta} - \theta$, it follows from Eqs. (2) and (4) that

$$\mathcal{H}_1 = \mathcal{H}_1^{\mathrm{int}} \cup \delta\mathcal{H}_1^a \cup \delta\mathcal{H}_1^b, \tag{5}$$

where we defined

$$\mathcal{H}_1^{\mathrm{int}} := \{\lambda + \lambda_a(\theta - \underline{\theta}) + \lambda_b(\overline{\theta} - \theta) : \lambda > 0, \lambda_a \ge 0, \lambda_b \ge 0\};$$
$$\mathcal{H}_1^a := \{\lambda_a(\theta - \underline{\theta}) : \lambda_a > 0\}; \tag{6}$$
$$\mathcal{H}_1^b := \{\lambda_b(\overline{\theta} - \theta) : \lambda_b > 0\}. \tag{7}$$

Proposition 1. $\mathcal{H}_1^{\mathrm{int}}$ *is the set of all linear polynomials h in θ that are strictly positive over $[\underline{\theta}, \overline{\theta}]$:* $h \in \mathcal{H}_1^{\mathrm{int}} \Leftrightarrow h \in \mathcal{V}_1$ *and $h(\theta) > 0$ for all $\theta \in [\underline{\theta}, \overline{\theta}]$.*

The next task is now to find the smallest Bernstein coherent set of polynomials that satisfies Eq. (3) and contains the representation $\mathcal{H}_1$ of a given marginal model $\mathcal{D}_1$. We will call this set the *exchangeably independent natural extension* of $\mathcal{H}_1$.

Polynomial Representation of the Global Model: We start by defining the following set of polynomials:

$$\mathcal{H}_\infty := \mathrm{posi}\{hp : h \in \mathcal{H}_1 \text{ and } p \in \mathcal{V}^+\}, \tag{8}$$

which will be closely related to the sets

$$\mathcal{H}_\infty^{\mathrm{int}} := \mathrm{posi}\{hp : h \in \mathcal{H}_1^{\mathrm{int}} \text{ and } p \in \mathcal{V}^+\};$$

$$\mathcal{H}_\infty^a := \mathrm{posi}\{hp : h \in \mathcal{H}_1^a \text{ and } p \in \mathcal{V}^+\} = \{(\theta - \underline{\theta})p : p \in \mathcal{V}^+\}; \tag{9}$$

$$\mathcal{H}_\infty^b := \mathrm{posi}\{hp : h \in \mathcal{H}_1^b \text{ and } p \in \mathcal{V}^+\} = \{(\overline{\theta} - \theta)p : p \in \mathcal{V}^+\}. \tag{10}$$

For $\mathcal{H}_1^a$ and $\mathcal{H}_1^b$, the alternative characterisations that are given above are easy to prove. For $\mathcal{H}_\infty^{\mathrm{int}}$, finding an alternative characterisation turns out to be more involved.

Theorem 3. *The following statements are equivalent:*

  (i) $h \in \mathcal{H}_\infty^{\mathrm{int}}$;
  (ii) $(\exists \epsilon > 0)(\forall \theta \in [\underline{\theta} - \epsilon, \overline{\theta} + \epsilon] \cap (0,1))\ h(\theta) > 0$;
  (iii) $h = ph'$ *for some* $p \in \mathcal{V}^+$ *and* h' *such that* $(\forall \theta \in [\underline{\theta}, \overline{\theta}])\ h'(\theta) > 0$.

When both $\underline{\theta} \neq 1$ *and* $\overline{\theta} \neq 0$, *these tree statements are also equivalent with:*

  (iv) $(\forall \theta \in [\underline{\theta}, \overline{\theta}] \setminus \{0,1\})\ h(\theta) > 0$.

It turns out that the set of polynomials $\mathcal{H}_\infty$ is indeed very closely related to the sets $\mathcal{H}_\infty^{\mathrm{int}}$, $\mathcal{H}_\infty^a$ and $\mathcal{H}_\infty^b$, since instead of using Eq. (8), $\mathcal{H}_\infty$ can be equivalently characterised by

$$\mathcal{H}_\infty = \mathcal{H}_\infty^{\mathrm{int}} \cup \delta \mathcal{H}_\infty^a \cup \delta \mathcal{H}_\infty^b. \tag{11}$$

We are now ready to formulate the most important result of this paper, which says that a set $\mathcal{H}_\infty$, given by Eq. (8), represents an imprecise Bernoulli process.

Theorem 4. $\mathcal{H}_\infty$ *is the smallest Bernstein coherent superset of* $\mathcal{H}_1$ *that satisfies the epistemic independence condition* (3).

This means that the set $\mathcal{H}_\infty$ given by Eq. (8) is the exchangeably independent natural extension of $\mathcal{H}_1$. It follows from Theorem 1 that $\mathcal{H}_\infty$ represents an imprecise Bernoulli proces that marginalises to $\mathcal{D}_1$ if $\mathcal{D}_1 = (\mathrm{Mn}_1)^{-1}(\mathcal{H}_\infty)$. This is equivalent to demanding that $\mathcal{H}_\infty$ should contain no other polynomials in $\mathcal{V}_1$ than those in $\mathcal{H}_1$. Due to Eq. (11), it suffices to check this property separately for each of the three subsets of $\mathcal{H}_\infty$. For $\mathcal{H}_\infty^a$ and $\mathcal{H}_\infty^b$ this property follows from Eqs. (5)–(7) and (9)–(10). For $\mathcal{H}_\infty^{\mathrm{int}}$, it follows from Proposition 1, Theorem 3 and Eqs. (5)–(7). We conclude that $\mathcal{H}_\infty$ is the smallest (most conservative) representation of an imprecise Bernoulli process that marginalises to a set of desirable gambles $\mathcal{D}_1$ that is given by Eq. (2).

6 Justifying a Sensitivity Analysis Approach

It now only remains to explain how the results obtained above relate to our previous statement that a sensitivity analysis approach to dealing with imprecise Bernoulli processes can be justified using an assessment of epistemic independence and exchangeability.

Consider an arbitrary gamble $f \in \mathcal{G}(\mathcal{X}^n)$, $n \in \mathbb{N}_0$ and a probability $\theta \in [0,1]$ that characterises a probability mass function on $\mathcal{X} = \{a, b\}$. As is shown in Section 4, $\mathrm{Mn}_n(f|\theta)$ is the expectation of f, associated with the binomial distribution with parameters n and θ. If one defines an imprecise Bernoulli process using the sensitivity analysis approach, this results in letting θ vary over an interval $[\underline{\theta}, \overline{\theta}]$ and the lower (upper) expectation of f associated with such an imprecise Bernoulli process is then the minimum (maximum) of $\mathrm{Mn}_n(f|\theta)$ as θ ranges over this interval. We will now show that this intuitive result is also obtained using the type of imprecise Bernoulli process we considered in the previous sections.

Theorem 5. *Consider the set of polynomials $\mathcal{H}_\infty$ defined by Eq. (8). Then for any polynomial function p on $[0,1]$:*

$$\underline{P}_{\mathcal{H}_\infty}(p) := \sup\{\mu \in \mathbb{R} : p - \mu \in \mathcal{H}_\infty\} = \min\{p(\theta) : \theta \in [\underline{\theta}, \overline{\theta}]\}. \tag{12}$$

By Theorem 1 and Eq. (1), the lower prevision (or minimum expected value) of a gamble $f \in \mathcal{G}(\mathcal{X}^n)$, $n \in \mathbb{N}_0$, corresponding with an imprecise Bernoulli process represented by a Bernstein coherent set $\mathcal{H}_\infty$ of polynomials, is given by

$$\begin{aligned}
\underline{E}(f) := \underline{P}_{\mathcal{D}_n}(f) &= \underline{P}_{(\mathrm{Mn}_n)^{-1}(\mathcal{H}_\infty)}(f) \\
&= \sup\{\mu \in \mathbb{R} : f - \mu \in (\mathrm{Mn}_n)^{-1}(\mathcal{H}_\infty)\} \\
&= \sup\{\mu \in \mathbb{R} : \mathrm{Mn}_n(f) - \mu \in \mathcal{H}_\infty\} = \underline{P}_{\mathcal{H}_\infty}(\mathrm{Mn}_n(f)),
\end{aligned}$$

thereby implying the following de Finetti-like representation result for lower previsions: $\underline{P}_{\mathcal{D}_n} = \underline{P}_{\mathcal{H}_\infty} \circ \mathrm{Mn}_n$. Using Theorem 5, we find that

$$\underline{E}(f) = \min\{\mathrm{Mn}_n(f|\theta) : \theta \in [\underline{\theta}, \overline{\theta}]\},$$

which is exactly what we would get using the sensitivity analysis approach. Notice also that $\overline{E}(f) := \overline{P}_{(\mathrm{Mn}_n)^{-1}(\mathcal{H}_\infty)}(f) = -\underline{E}(-f)$ because of the conjugacy relation between lower and upper previsions. As a direct consequence, we find that, similarly:

$$\overline{E}(f) = \max\{\mathrm{Mn}_n(f|\theta) : \theta \in [\underline{\theta}, \overline{\theta}]\}.$$

7 Conclusions

The existence of a precise probability distribution describing the outcomes of a single Bernoulli experiment is not crucial to the definition of a Bernoulli process. It can be relaxed by replacing it with an assessment of exchangeability, which means that we consider the order of the different Bernoulli experiments to be irrelevant. Taken together with epistemic independence, exchangeability then becomes a defining property for an imprecise Bernoulli process. Using this approach, we have derived an expression for the most conservative imprecise Bernoulli process, corresponding with a given marginal model. The resulting imprecise Bernoulli process is exactly the same as the one obtained using a sensitivity analysis approach. An assessment of exchangeability and epistemic independence can therefore be used as a behavioural justification for the strong assumptions associated with the latter approach.

Although we have not discussed this here, we have also looked at how to make multinomial processes imprecise, and we are confident that our results for binomial processes can be generalised. We will report these results elsewhere, together with proofs for (generalisations of) the theorems mentioned above.

We have used the very general theory of sets of desirable gambles to develop our notion of an imprecise Bernoulli process. The important sensitivity analysis result at the end, however, is stated purely in terms of lower and upper previsions, which constitute a less general model than sets of desirable gambles. It would be interesting to see if and how this result can be obtained directly using the language of previsions, without using sets of desirable gambles.

Given the importance of binomial (and multinomial) processes in practical statistics, we hope that our results can lead to a better understanding, and perhaps to much needed practical applications, of imprecise probability theory in statistics.

Acknowledgments. Jasper De Bock is a Ph.D. Fellow of the Fund for Scientific Research – Flanders (FWO) and wishes to acknowledge the financial support of the FWO. Research for this paper was also partially funded by the IWT SBO project 60043, and by FWO project G.0125.12.

References

1. De Cooman, G., Miranda, E.: Weak and strong laws of large numbers for coherent lower previsions. Journal of Statistical Planning and Inference 138(8), 2409–2432 (2008)
2. De Cooman, G., Miranda, E.: Forward irrelevance. Journal of Statistical Planning and Inference 139(2), 256–276 (2009)
3. De Cooman, G., Quaeghebeur, E.: Exchangeability and sets of desirable gambles. International Journal of Approximate Reasoning (2010) (in print); Special issue in honour of Kyburg, Jr., H.E.
4. Couso, I., Moral, S.: Sets of desirable gambles: conditioning, representation, and precise probabilities. International Journal of Approximate Reasoning 52(7), 1034–1055 (2011)
5. Prautzsch, H., Boehm, W., Paluszny, M.: Bézier and B-Spline Techniques. Springer, Berlin (2002)
6. Walley, P.: Statistical Reasoning with Imprecise Probabilities. Monographs on Statistics and Applied Probability, vol. 42. Chapman and Hall, London (1991)
7. Walley, P.: Towards a unified theory of imprecise probability. International Journal of Approximate Reasoning 24, 125–148 (2000)

Possibilistic KNN Regression
Using Tolerance Intervals

Mohammad Ghasemi Hamed[1,2], Mathieu Serrurier[1], and Nicolas Durand[1,2]

[1] IRIT - Université Paul Sabatier
118 route de Narbonne 31062, Toulouse Cedex 9, France
[2] ENAC/MAIAA - 7 avenue Edouard Belin 31055 Toulouse, France

Abstract. By employing regression methods minimizing predictive risk, we are usually looking for precise values which tends to their true response value. However, in some situations, it may be more reasonable to predict intervals rather than precise values. In this paper, we focus to find such intervals for the K-nearest neighbors (KNN) method with precise values for inputs and output. In KNN, the prediction intervals are usually built by considering the local probability distribution of the neighborhood. In situations where we do not dispose of enough data in the neighborhood to obtain statistically significant distributions, we would rather wish to build intervals which takes into account such distribution uncertainties. For this latter we suggest to use tolerance intervals to build the maximal specific possibility distribution that bounds each population quantiles of the true distribution (with a fixed confidence level) that might have generated our sample set. Next we propose a new interval regression method based on KNN which take advantage of our possibility distribution in order to choose, for each instance, the value of K which will be a good trade-off between precision and uncertainty due to the limited sample size. Finally we apply our method on an aircraft trajectory prediction problem.

Keywords: Possibilistic regression, tolerance interval, K-nearest neighbors.

1 Introduction

When dealing with regression problems, it may be risky to predict a point which may be illusionary precise. In these cases, predicting an interval that contains the true value with a desired confidence level is more reasonable. In this scope, one can employ different statistical methods to find a response value prediction interval. These intervals can be estimated once for the whole dataset based on residuals. However, the disadvantage of this approach is to assume that prediction interval sizes are independent of test instances. On the other hand, local estimation methods, such as KNN regression, can be used to find an interval that is more likely to reflect the instance neighborhood. In order to calculate such local intervals we have to estimate the probability distribution of the neighborhood. But, Even if we know the family of the probability distribution, the

S. Greco et al. (Eds.): IPMU 2012, Part III, CCIS 299, pp. 410–419, 2012.

estimated local interval does not reflect the uncertainty on the estimated distribution which is caused by the limited size of the sample set. The goal of this paper is to find such interval for KNN.

One interpretation of the possibility theory is in term of families of probability distributions [3]. For a given sample set, there exists already different methods for building possibility distribution which encodes the family of probability distribution that may have generated the sample set[1,11]. The mentioned methods are based on confidence bands. In this paper we suggest to use tolerance intervals to build the maximal specific possibility distribution that bounds each population quantile of the true distribution (with a fixed confidence level) that might have generated our sample set. The obtained possibility distribution will bound each confidence interval independently with a desired confidence level. On the contrary, a possibility distribution encoding confidence band will bound all the confidence intervals simultaneously with a desired confidence level. This is why our proposed possibility distribution has always smaller α-cuts than the other ones and it still guarantee to obtain intervals which contains the true value with a desired confidence level. This is particularly critical in domains imposing some security constraints. We embed this approach into KNN regression in order to obtain statistically significant intervals. We also propose to take into account the tolerance interval calculus while choosing the parameter K. The obtained interval, will be a good trade-off between precision and uncertainty with respect to the sample size.

This paper is structured as follows: we begin with a background on the possibility and probabilistic interpretation of the possibility theory. We will then look at the different possibility distribution inferred from the same sample set. In the fourth section we will see different KNN interval regression algorithm and finally we compare the mentioned approaches on the prediction of aircraft altitude.

2   Possibility Theory

Possibility theory, introduced by Zadeh [14,5], was initially created in order to deal with imprecisions and uncertainties due to incomplete information which may not be handled by a single probability distribution. In the possibility theory, we use a membership function π to associate a distribution over the universe of discourse Ω. In this paper, we only consider the case of $\Omega = \mathbb{R}$.

Definition 1. *A possibility distribution π is a function from Ω to $(\mathbf{R} \to [0,1])$.*

Definition 2. *The α-cut A_α of a possibility distribution $\pi(\cdot)$ is the interval for which all the point located inside have a possibility degree $\pi(x)$ greater or equal than α :$A_\alpha = \{x|\pi(x) \geq \alpha, x \in \Omega\}$*

The definition of the possibility measure Π is based on the possibility distribution π such as $\Pi(A) = sup(\pi(x), \forall x \in A)$. One interpretation of possibility theory is to consider a possibility distribution as a family of probability distributions (see [3]). Thus, a possibility distribution π will represent the family of the probability distributions Θ for which the measure of each subset of Ω will be bounded by its possibility measures :

Definition 3. *A possibility measure Π is equivalent to the family Θ of probability measures such that*

$$\Theta = \{P|\forall A \in \Omega, P(A) \leq \Pi(A)\}. \tag{1}$$

In many cases it is desirable to move from the probability framework to the possibility framework. Dubois et al.[6] suggest that when moving from probability to possibility framework we should use the "maximum specificity" principle which aims at finding the most informative possibility distribution. The "most specific" possibility distribution for a finite mode probability distribution has the following formula [4] :

$$\pi^*(x) = sup(1 - P(I_\beta^*), x \in I_\beta^*)$$

where π^* is the "most specific" possibility distribution, I_β^* is the smallest β-content interval [4]. Therefore, given f and its transformation π^* we have : $A_{1-\beta}^* = I_\beta^*$. The equation (1) states that a possibility transformation using [6] encodes a family of probability distributions for which each quantile is bounded by a possibility α-cut.

Note that for every unimodal symmetric probability density function $f(\cdot)$, the smallest β-content interval I_β^* of f is also its inter-quantile by taking lower and upper quantiles respectively at $\frac{1-\beta}{2}$ and $1 - \frac{1-\beta}{2}$. Thus, the maximum specified possibility distribution $\pi^*(\cdot)$ of $f(\cdot)$ can be built just by calculating the β-content inter-quantile I_β of $f(\cdot)$ for all the values of β, where $\beta \in [0,1]$.

3   Inferring Possibility Distribution from Data

Having a sample set drawn from a probability distribution function, one can use different statistical equations in order to express different kinds of uncertainty related to the probability distribution that underlies the sample set. Thus, it can be valuable to take benefit of possibility distributions to encode such uncertainties in a more global manner. Given the properties expected, we can describe two different types of possibility distribution : possibility distribution encoding confidence band and possibility transformation encoding tolerance interval. After a brief description of the first one, we will focus more deeply on the last one which is the most suitable for regression.

In frequentist statistics, a confidence band is an interval defined for each value x of the random variable X such that for a repeated sampling, the frequency of $F(x)$ located inside the interval $[L(x), U(x)]$ for all the values of X tends to the confidence coefficient γ. The confidence band of a parametric probability distribution can be constructed using confidence region of parameters of the underlying probability distribution [2]. In this case the confidence band or its maximum specified possibility transformation represents a family of probability distribution that may has been generated by all the parameters included in the confidence region used to build the confidence band (see Aregui and Denoeux [1] and Masson and Denoeux [11]).

A tolerance interval is an interval which guarantee with a specified confidence level γ, to contain a specified $\alpha\%$ proportion of the population. As the sample set grows, confidence intervals downsize towards zero, however, increasing the sample sample size leads the tolerance intervals to converge towards fixed values which are the quantiles. We will call an α tolerance interval(tolerance region) with confidence level γ, an α-content γ-coverage tolerance interval we represent it by $I_{\gamma,\alpha}^T$. Each α-content γ-coverage tolerance, by definition contains at least $\alpha\%$ proportion of the true unknown distribution, hence it can be encoded by the $(1-\alpha)$-cut of a possibility distribution. So for a given γ we represent α-content γ-coverage tolerance intervals, $\alpha \in (0,1)$ of a sample set by $(1-\alpha)$-cuts of a possibility distribution which we name as γ-confidence tolerance possibility distribution (γ-CTP distribution π_γ^{CTP}).

Possibility Transformation Encoding Tolerance Interval : Normal Case.
When our sample set comes from a univariate normal distribution, the lower and upper tolerance bounds (X_L and X_U, respectively) are calculated by the equation (2) in which $\bar{X}$ is the sample mean, S the sample standard deviation, $\chi_{1-\gamma,n-1}^2$ represents the p-value of the chi-square distribution with $n-1$ degree of freedom and $Z_{1-\frac{1-\alpha}{2}}$ is the critical value of the standard normal distribution with probability $(1-\frac{1-\alpha}{2})$ [7]. The boundaries of the α-cut $A_\alpha = [X_L, X_U]$ of the built possibility distribution is defined as follows:

$$X_L = \bar{X} - \mathbf{k}S, \ X_U = \bar{X} - \mathbf{k}S \ where \ \mathbf{k} = \sqrt{\frac{(n-1)(1+\frac{1}{n})Z_{1-\frac{1-\alpha}{2}}^2}{\chi_{1-\gamma,n-1}^2}} \quad (2)$$

We obtain the following possibility distribution π_γ^{CTP}:

$$\pi_\gamma^{CTP}(x) = 1 - max\{\alpha, x \in A_\alpha\} \ where \ A_\alpha = I_{\gamma,1-\alpha}^T \quad (3)$$

For more detail on the different tolerance intervals see [7]. In the figure (3) we represented the 0.95 CTP distribution ($\pi_{0.95}^{CTP}$ using equation (2)) for different sample set drawn from the normal distribution (all having $(\bar{X}, S) = (0,1)$). The green distribution represents the probability-possibility transformation of $\mathcal{N}(0,1)$. Note that for $n \geq 100$ the tolerance interval is approximately the same as the estimated distribution.

Possibility Transformation Encoding Tolerance Interval : Distribution Free Case. The problem of non-parametric tolerance interval was first treated by Wilks [13]. Wald [12] generalized the method to the multivariate case. The principle for finding a distribution free α-content γ-coverage tolerance interval or region of continuous random variable X is based on order statistics. For more information on finding **k** in (2) values for distribution free tolerance intervals and regions see [13,12,7]. Note that when constructing possibility distributions encoding tolerance intervals based on Wilks method which requires finding symmetrical head and tail order statistics (Wald definition does not have the symmetry constraint), we obtain possibility distributions which do not guarantee that our α-cuts include the mode and they are not also the smallest possible α-cuts. In fact, for any symmetric unimodal distribution, if we choose the Wilks method, we will have tolerance intervals which are also the smallest possible ones and include the mode of the distribution. For the calculation of the sample size requirement for tolerance intervals see [7]. In figure 1, we have the blue curves which represent the distribution-free 0.95-confidence tolerance possibility distribution for a sample set of size 450 (0.95 DFCTP distribution) drawn from $\mathcal{N}(0,1)$ and the green distribution which represent the possibility transformation for $\mathcal{N}(0,1)$. In figure (2), we used two different sample set with $n = 194$ to build two different 0.9 DFCTP distributions. In this example, in order to reduce the required sample size, we restricted the biggest α to 0.98.

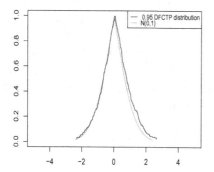
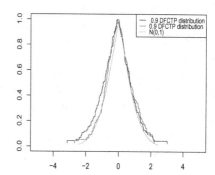

Fig. 1. Distribution free 0.95-confidence tolerance possibility distribution for a sample set with size 450 drawn from $\mathcal{N}(0,1)$

Fig. 2. Distribution free 0.9-confidence tolerance possibility distributions for a sample set with size 194 drawn from $\mathcal{N}(0,1)$

4   Interval Prediction with K-Nearest Neighbors

4.1   K-Nearest Neighbors (KNN)

Smoothing is the process of creating an approximating function that looks for capturing relevant patterns in the data, while filtering noise. In a classical regression problem, we have m pairs $(\overrightarrow{x}_i, y_i)$ of data where $\overrightarrow{x}_i$ is a vector of input variables and y_i is the response value. These data follows an unknown mean function r with a random error term ϵ defined as:

$$y_i = r(\overrightarrow{x}_i) + \epsilon_i, \ where \ E(\epsilon_i) = 0. \tag{4}$$

A KNN estimator is a local estimator of the function r based on the neighborhood of the considered instance. A KNN is defined as follows :

$$\hat{r}(\overrightarrow{x}) = (\sum_{i=1}^{n} K_b(\overrightarrow{x} - \overrightarrow{x}_i))^{-1} \sum_{i=1}^{n} K_b(\overrightarrow{x} - \overrightarrow{x}_i)y_i \tag{5}$$

where $K_b(u) = \frac{1}{2b}I(|u| \le b)$ ($I(\cdot)$ is the indicator function) is an uniform kernel with a variable bandwidth $b = d(k)$, where $d(k)$ is the distance between $\overrightarrow{x}$ and its furthest K-nearest neighbors. Mack [10] considered the KNN estimator in a general case with kernels other than the uniform kernel. In the same work, he studied the bias and variance of this more general KNN estimator.

4.2 Possibilistic KNN with Fixed K

In some problems, we are not only interested in obtaining the most probable regression response value, but we would rather look for intervals which for all input instances simultaneously contain their corresponding response values with a desired probability. It means that the frequency of all the response variables which are contained in their corresponding prediction intervals is at least the prefixed given value. As we saw in the definition of smoothing, equation (4), we suppose that the error is a random variable. Based on our *a priori* knowledge about the distribution of the error we can use different statistical methods to predict a such intervals.

In machine learning problems, it is common to suppose that the response variable y_i in regression is a random variable distributed with $\mathcal{N}(f(x_i), \sigma_i^2)$ where $\sigma_i^2 = Var(\epsilon_i)$ and estimate y_i by its maximum likelihood estimation $\hat{y}_i = \mathcal{N}(\hat{f}(x_i), \hat{\sigma}^2{}_i)$. Based on the normality assumption of the errors, there are two methods used in order to estimate $\mathcal{N}(f(x_i), \sigma_i^2)$. In the case of homoscedasticity (the variance of the distribution is constant) for all error terms, the sample variance of the residuals will be used as the estimation of the variance of error. This method is usually used for global approaches like ordinary least square estimation, SVM or neural networks in which the model is assumed to be homoscedastic, or with negligible heteroscedasticity. The heteroscedasticity (the variance depends on the input vector) may also be ignored when we do not dispose of enough data in order to perform significant evaluations. In the other hand, if we assume that our model is heteroscedastick, one can estimate the distribution of the error by a normal distribution which its mean is still estimated by the KNN estimated value and its variance is estimated by the variance of the sample set in the neighborhood of x_i. Since KNN is a local estimation method used for situations where it is less efficient to use a global model than a local one, exploiting the neighborhood of the input data to estimate the local distribution of error may be justified.

However, if the distribution of the error is estimated locally, it does not take into account the sample size, therefore the estimated quantiles of the error or the response variable may not contain the desired proportion of data. In order to have a more cautious approach, we propose to build a possibility distribution with α-cuts which guarantee to contain, with a confidence level γ, the $(1 - \alpha)\%$ proportion of the true unknown distribution. Possibility distributions for the neighborhood of $\overrightarrow{x}_i$ built by γ confidence bands guarantee with confidence level γ, that all its α-cuts simultaneously contains at least $(1 - \alpha)\%$ proportion of true unknown distribution that may have generated the neighborhood of $\overrightarrow{x}_i$ (the simultaneous condition holds for one input instance). If we consider a γ-CTP distribution π_γ^{CTP}, it guarantee that each α-cut, independently, will contain $(1 - \alpha)\%$ proportion of the true unknown distribution that may have generated the data. Of course, this property is weaker, but it is sufficient in the case of interval prediction and it leads to more specific possibility distributions. Thus, given a input vector $\overrightarrow{x}$ we will take the mean $\bar{X} = \hat{r}(\overrightarrow{x})$ and the standard deviation S as the standard deviation of the y_i of the K nearest instances. After choosing a value for the confidence level γ (usually 0.95) we build π_γ^{CTP} using Equation 3. Now we will use the π_γ^{CTP} distribution for each instance to obtains intervals which ensure us to have simultaneously $(1-\alpha)\%$ of the response variable for all input instances. It means that for all input vector $\overrightarrow{x}_i$ the percentage of α-cuts which contains the corresponding y_i will be at least γ (for ex: 0.95).

4.3   KNN Interval Regression with Variable K Using 0.95 CTP Distribution

It is common to fix K and use a weighted KNN estimator, we will call this combination as "KNN regression" or "KNN regression with fixed K". The fixed K idea in KNN regression comes from the homoscedasticity assumption. In this section we propose to use the tolerance interval to find the "best" K for each x_i. Let the sample set containing the K-nearest neighbors of x_i be $Kset_i$. For each x_i, we begin by a initial value of K and we build the 0.95 CTP distribution of $Kset_i$. Now taking the K which yields the most specific 0.95 CTP distribution means that for each x_i, we choose the value of K that has the best trade off between the precision and the uncertainty to contain the response value. Indeed, when K decreases the neighborhood considered is more faithful but uncertainty increases. On the contrary, when K increases, the neighborhood becomes less faithful but the size of the tolerance intervals decrease. In fact the mentioned possibility distribution takes into account the sample size, so its α-cuts will reflect the density of neighborhood. Thus, by choosing the K that minimizes a fixed α-cut (the 0.05-cut in our case) ensures to have the best trade off between the faithfulness of the neighborhood and the uncertainty of the prediction due to the sample size.

The idea is to use prediction intervals which are the most reasonable. For instance, for each given $\overrightarrow{x}_i$ and k, the 0.05-cut of the π_γ^{CTP} contains at least, with a prefixed γ confidence level, 95% of the true distribution that may have generated y_i, because it contains at least 0.95% of the population of the true unknown normal distributions that may have generated the $Kset_i$. This approach explores the neighborhood for the value of k that is the most statistically significant. The MIN_K and MAX_K in the algorithm 1 are global limits which stop the search if we did not found the best K. This may occurs when we have some area of

---

Algorithm 1. Possibilistic local KNN

1: $MIN_K \leftarrow K$
2: $IntervalSize_{min} \leftarrow Inf$
3: **for all** $i \in 5, \ldots, MAX_K$ **do**
4:     $Kset_i \leftarrow$ Find the K nearest neighbors of x_i
5:     $IntervalSize \leftarrow$ 0.05-cut of 0.95 CTP distribution of $Kset_i$
6:     **if** $IntervalSize \leq IntervalSize_{min}$ **then**
7:         $MIN_K \leftarrow i$
8:         $IntervalSize_{min} \leftarrow IntervalSize$
9:     **end if**
10: **end for**

---

the dataset where the response variable is relatively dense. In practice, we know that this kind of local density is not always a sign of similarity, therefore we put these two bounds to restrict our search in the region where we think to be the most likely to contain the best neighborhood of x_i.

5   Application to Aircraft Trajectory Prediction

In this section, we compare the effectiveness of the regression approaches mentioned previously with respect to an aircraft prediction problem. Our data set is composed of 8 continuous precise regression variables and one precise response variable. The predictors are selected among more than 30 features obtained by a principal component analysis on a variables set giving informations about the aircraft trajectory, the aircraft type, its last positions and etc. Our goal is to compare these methods when predicting the altitude of a climbing aircraft 10 minutes ahead. Because the trajectory prediction is a critical task, we are interested in predicting intervals which contains 95% of the time the real aircraft position, thus we mainly use the inclusion percentage to compare method results. The database contains up to 1500 trajectories and all the results mentioned in the following are computed from a 10-cross validation schema. In a first attempt we will use $\frac{2}{3}$ of instances will to tune the hyper-parameters. Then all of instances will serve to validate the results using a 10-cross validation schema. In the hyper-parameters tuning we used the Root Mean Squared Error (RMSE) of response variable (trajectory altitude) to find the best fixed K and local K. The final result for the fixed K was $K = 11$ with $RMSE = 1197$ and $(MIN_K, MAX_k) = (7, 30)$ with $RMSE = 1177$ for KNN regression with variable K. The kernel function used in our methods was the Tricube kernel $K_b(u) = \frac{70}{81b}(1 - |u|^3)^3 \mathbf{I}_{\{|u| \leq b\}}$. The RMSE found by the two approaches demonstrate that, for this data set, the variable K selection method is as efficient as the conventional fixed K method. We used the following methods to estimate a prediction interval for our response variable : "KNN Interval regression with variable K using 0.95 CTP distribution" (VKNN-CTP), "KNN interval regression using 0.95 CTP distribution" (KNN-CTP), "KNN Interval regression with global normal quantile" (KNN) and "KNN Interval regression with local normal quantile" (LKNN). The table

Table 1. Inclusion percentage compared to the interval size

	KNN	LKNN	KNN-CTP	VKNN-CTP
Inclusion percentage	0.933	0.93	0.992	0.976
0.95 Interval size $(A_{0.05})$	4664 (0)	4694 (1397)	7865 (2341)	5966 (1407)

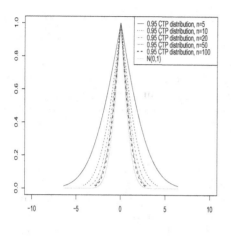

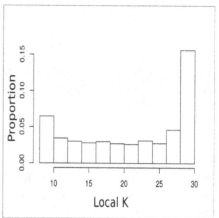

Fig. 3. 0.95-confidence tolerance possibility distributions for a sample set with sizes 5 to 100 and $(\overline{X}, S) = (0, 1)$ in green

Fig. 4. Histogram of K found by using 0.95 CTP distribution

below contains the mean interval size together with their standard deviation in parenthesis and the inclusion percentage of the compared methods. We can notice that the conventional fixed K KNN approaches (KNN-normal global and local) are not enough underestimate the confidence interval size. As expected, the KNN approaches based on the 0.95 CTP distribution, always over estimate these intervals. The most specific estimation is made with the VKNN-CTP algorithm. Figure 4 shows the histogram of different values of K found by using the 0.95 CTP distribution. We can observe that the values of K are uniformly distributed along the range with a maximum reached for $K = 25$. It suggest, as expected, that the dataset is not homoscedastic.

6   Conclusion

In this work, we propose a method for building a possibility distribution encoding tolerance intervals of a sample set drawn from a normal distribution with unknown parameters. The α-cuts of the π_γ^{CTP} distribution bound the $(1 - \alpha)\%$

proportions the true unknown normal distribution with the confidence level γ, regardless of the size of the sample set. Then, we embed these new kind of possibility distributions into a KNN regression algorithm. The suggested method is valuable to be employed for heteroscedastick data. This approach exploits the neighborhood in order to find an "optimal" K for each input instance. The possibility distribution allows us to choose intervals for the prediction that are guaranteed to contain a chosen amount of possible response values. We compared our approach with classical ones on an aircraft trajectory prediction problem. We show that classical KNN provide smaller confidence intervals which fail to guarantee the required level of inclusion percentage. For future works, we propose to build in the same way the possibility distributions encoding prediction intervals [8][9]. We will also extend this approach to normal mixtures and distribution free sample sets.

References

1. Aregui, A., Denœux, T.: Constructing predictive belief functions from continuous sample data using confidence bands. In: ISIPTA, pp. 11–20 (July 2007)
2. Cheng, R.C.H., Iles, T.C.: Confidence bands for cumulative distribution functions of continuous random variables. Technometrics 25(1), 77–86 (1983)
3. Didier, D.: Possibility theory and statistical reasoning. Compu. Stat. Data An. 51, 47–69 (2006)
4. Dubois, D., Foulloy, L., Mauris, G., Prade, H.: Probability-possibility transformations, triangular fuzzy sets and probabilistic inequalities. In: Rel. Comp. (2004)
5. Dubois, D., Prade, H.: Fuzzy sets and systems - Theory and applications. Academic press, New York (1980)
6. Dubois, D., Prade, H., Sandri, S.: On possibility/probability transformations. In: IFSA, pp. 103–112 (1993)
7. Hahn, G.J., Meeker, W.Q.: Statistical Intervals: A Guide for Practitioners. John Wiley and Sons (1991)
8. Hahn, G.J.: Factors for calculating two-sided prediction intervals for samples from a normal distribution. JASA 64(327), 878–888 (1969)
9. Konijn, H.S.: Distribution-free and other prediction intervals. Am. Stat. 41(1), 11–15 (1987)
10. Mack, Y.P.: Local properties of k-nn regression estimates 2(3), 311–323 (1981)
11. Masson, M., Denoeux, T.: Inferring a possibility distribution from empirical data. Fuzzy Sets Syst. 157, 319–340 (2006)
12. Wald, A.: An extension of wilks' method for setting tolerance limits. Ann. of Math. Stat. 14(1), 45–55 (1943)
13. Wilks, S.S.: Determination of sample sizes for setting tolerance limits. Ann. of Math. Stat. 12(1), 91–96 (1941)
14. Zadeh, L.A.: Fuzzy sets as a basis for a theory of possibility. Fuzzy Set. Syst. 1(1), 3–28 (1978)

Classification Based on Possibilistic Likelihood

Mathieu Serrurier and Henri Prade

IRIT - Université Paul Sabatier
118 route de Narbonne 31062, Toulouse Cedex 9, France

Abstract. Classification models usually associate one class for each new instance. This kind of prediction doesn't reflect the uncertainty that is inherent in any machine learning algorithm. Probabilistic approaches rather focus on computing a probability distribution over the classes. However, making such a computation may be tricky and requires a large amount of data. In this paper, we propose a method based on the notion of possibilistic likelihood in order to learn a model that associates a possibility distribution over the classes to a new instance. Possibility distributions are here viewed as an upper bound of a family of probability distributions. This allows us to capture the epistemic uncertainty associated with the model in a faithful way. The model is based on a set of kernel functions and is obtained through an optimization process performed by a particle swarm algorithm. We experiment our method on benchmark dataset and compares it with a naive Bayes classifier.

1 Introduction

It is well known that machine learning algorithms are constrained by some learning bias (language bias, hypothesis bias, algorithm bias, etc ...). In that respect, learning a precise model may be illusionary. Moreover, in cases where security issues are critical for instance, predicting only one class, without describing the uncertainty about this prediction, may be unsatisfactory. Some algorithms such as naive Bayes classifiers [12], Bayesian networks [14] or K-nearest-neighbor methods [3] learn a probability distribution over classes rather than a precise class. However, learning faithful probability distributions require a lot of data. It is also sometimes needed to have some prior knowledge about the type of the probability distribution that underlies the data (or to assume a particular type by default).

Quantitative possibility measures can be viewed as upper bounds of probabilities. Then, a possibility distribution represents a family of probability distributions [7]. This view was first implicitly suggested by Zadeh [17] when emphasizing the idea that what is probable must be possible. Following this intuition a probability-possibility transformation has been proposed [9]. This transformation associates a probability distribution with the maximally specific possibility distribution which is such that the possibility of any event is indeed an upper bound of the corresponding probability. Possibility distributions are then able to describe epistemic uncertainty and to describe knowledge states such

S. Greco et al. (Eds.): IPMU 2012, Part III, CCIS 299, pp. 420–429, 2012.
© Springer-Verlag Berlin Heidelberg 2012

as total ignorance, partial ignorance or complete knowledge. There exist some machine learning algorithms that are based on possibility theory (see [2,10,1] for instance), but in most of the cases they consider imprecise data and are based on qualitative possibility theory which encodes orderings rather than a family of probability distributions.

In this paper, we propose a new classification algorithm which learns a possibility distribution over classes from precise data. This approach is similar to the imprecise regression recently proposed in[15]. It is based on the notion of possibilistic likelihood [16]. The proposed likelihood function is in agreement with the view of possibility distribution as representing a family of probability distributions and with the probability-possibility transformation. A possibilistic classifier will be a set of kernel functions. The goal of our approach is to find the possibilistic classifier that maximizes the possibilistic likelihood. Since finding this maximum is not tractable in general, we use a meta-heuristics for the optimization process. According to the properties of possibilistic likelihood, the distribution learned encodes an upper bound of the possible probability distributions over the classes. The interest of using possibility distributions is manyfold. First, it encodes epistemic uncertainty, which cannot be described by a single probability distribution [5]. Second, possibility distributions are less precise and informative than probability distributions, then they require less data to be faithful and no prior knowledge. Third, possibility distributions are not constrained by having its degrees summing to 1. This latter point makes this kind of distribution easier to approximate and to embed in an optimization process.

The paper is structured as follows. Section 2 provides some background about possibility distributions and their interpretation in terms of a family of probabilities. In section 3, we define the notion of possibilistic likelihood. Section 4 describes the framework of possibilistic classification based on possibilistic likelihood. Lastly, we compare our approach with naive Bayes classifier on benchmark datasets.

2   Background

2.1   Possibility Distribution

Possibility theory, introduced by Zadeh [17], was initially proposed in order to deal with imprecision and uncertainty due to incomplete information as the one provided by linguistic statements. This kind of epistemic uncertainty cannot be handled by a single probability distribution, especially when a priori knowledge about the nature of the probability distribution is lacking. A possibility distribution π is a mapping from Ω to $[0,1]$. In this paper we will only consider the case where $\Omega = \{C_1, \ldots, C_q\}$ is a discrete universe (of classes in this paper). The value $\pi(x)$ is named possibility degree of x. For any subset of Ω, the possibility measure is defined as follows :

$$\forall A \in 2^{\Omega}, \Pi(A) = max\{\pi(x), x \in A\}.$$

If it exists at least one singleton $x \in \Omega$ for which we have $\pi(x) = 1$, the distribution is normalized. We can distinguish two extreme cases of knowledge situation:

- complete knowledge: $\exists x \in \Omega$ such as $\pi(x) = 1$ and $\forall y \in \Omega, y \neq x, \pi(y) = 0$;
- total ignorance: $\forall x \in \Omega, \pi(x) = 1$.

The necessity is the dual measure of the possibility measure. We have:

$$\forall A \in 2^{\Omega}, N(A) = 1 - \Pi(\overline{A}).$$

The α-level cuts of the distribution π are defined by:

$$D_{\alpha} = \{x \in \Omega, \pi(x) \geq \alpha\}.$$

2.2   A Possibility Distribution as a Family of Probability Distributions

One view of possibility theory is to consider a possibility distribution as a family of probability distributions (see [4] for an overview). Thus, a possibility distribution π will represent the family of the probability distributions for which the measure of each subset of Ω will be respectively lower and upper bounded by its necessity and its possibility measures. More formally, if $\mathcal{P}$ is the set of all probability distributions defined on Ω, the family of probability distributions $\mathcal{P}_{\pi}$ associated with π is defined as follows:

$$\mathcal{P}_{\pi} = \{p \in \mathcal{P}, \forall A \in \Omega, N(A) \leq P(A) \leq \Pi(A)\}. \tag{1}$$

where P is the probability measure associated with p. In this scope, the situation of total ignorance corresponds to the case where all probability distributions are possible. This type of ignorance cannot be described by a single probability distribution.

According to this probabilistic interpretation, a method for transforming probability distributions into possibility distributions has been proposed in [9]. The idea behind this is to choose the most informative possibility measure that upper bounds the considered probability measure. This possibility measure corresponds to the tightest possibility distribution. Let us consider a set of data $X = \{x_1, \ldots, x_n\}$ that are realizations of a random variable on Ω. Let $\alpha_1, \ldots, \alpha_q$ be the frequency of the elements of X that belong respectively to $\{C_1, \ldots, C_q\}$.

Let us also assume that the frequencies of examples in class C_i are put in decreasing order, i.e. $\alpha_1 \geq \ldots \geq \alpha_q$. In the following, given a possibility distribution π, we note π_i the value $\pi(x \in C_i)$. It has been shown in [6] that the transformation of p^* (which is derived from the frequencies) into a possibility distribution π^* (see Equation (3)), is:

$$\forall i \in \{1, \ldots, q\}, \pi_i^* = \sum_{j=i}^{q} \alpha_j. \tag{2}$$

This possibility distribution is one of the cumulated functions of p^*. It is worth noticing that it is the tightest one.

Example 1. For instance, we consider X that leads to the frequency $\alpha_1 = 0.5, \alpha_2 = 0.3, \alpha_3 = 0.2$. We obtain $\pi_1^* = 0.5 + 0.3 + 0.2 = 1$, $\pi_2^* = 0.3 + 0.2 = 0.5$ and $\pi_3^* = 0.2$.

3   Possibilistic Likelihood

There exist different kinds of methods for eliciting possibility distributions from data. For instance, some approaches directly build the possibility distribution on the basis of a proximity relation defined on the universe of the data [8]. G. Mauris proposes a method for constructing a possibility distribution when only very few pieces of data are available (even only one or two) based on probability inequalities [13]. This latter method is justified in the probabilistic view of possibility theory. These methods, how different they are, have in common to build the distributions directly. Formally a likelihood coincides to a probability value. However, it is commonly used for evaluating the adequateness of a probability distribution with respect to a set of data. In the following, likelihood functions will be always viewed as adequateness functions. In this section we define a likelihood function for a possibility distribution which supports the interpretation of a possibility distribution in terms of a family of probability distributions (see [16] for details), and which then measures the adequateness of a possibility distribution with respect to a set of data.

We only consider the case of a discrete universe, i.e. $\Omega = \{C_1, \ldots, C_q\}$. In order to define such a function we will propose an alternative to the logarithmic-based likelihood function in the probabilistic case. The logarithmic-based likelihood defined as follows (under the strict constraint $\sum_i^q p_i = 1$):

$$\mathcal{L}_{log}(p|x_1, \ldots, x_n) = -\sum_{i=1}^{n} log(p(x_i))$$

or, when considering frequency directly

$$\mathcal{L}_{log}(p|x_1, \ldots, x_n) = -\sum_{i=1}^{q} \alpha_i log(p_i).$$

It is equivalent to compute the joint probability of the elements of x with respect to p. This definition of the likelihood has a strong limitation, since it gives a very high weight to the error when probability is very low. This is especially true when Ω is continuous. Since $\mathcal{L}_{log}$ is not defined when $p(x_i) = 0$, an unbounded density cannot be approximated by a bounded one by optimization of $\mathcal{L}_{log}$. We propose another likelihood function that overcomes these limitations:

$$\mathcal{L}_{surf}(p|x_1, \ldots, x_n) = (\sum_{i=1}^{n} p(x_i)) - \frac{1}{2} * \sum_{i=1}^{q} p_i^2$$

or, when considering frequency directly

$$\mathcal{L}_{surf}(p|x_1, \ldots, x_n) = (\sum_{i=1}^{q} \alpha_i * p_i) - \frac{1}{2} * \sum_{i=1}^{p} p_i^2.$$

Roughly speaking, L_{surf} favors the probability distributions that are close to the optimal one in terms of surface. Thus, when, Ω is continuous, it allows for the approximation of unbounded densities by bounded ones. It has been shown in [16] that, given X, the probability distribution that maximizes L_{log} is the same that the one that maximizes L_{surf}.

We use the L_{surf} for defining a possibilistic counterpart to the likelihood. What we want to obtain is a function that is maximized for the possibility distribution π with the following properties:

- π is a cumulated function of p
- $\forall i, j, \pi_i \geq \pi_j \equiv p_i \geq p_j$.

In the following we consider that the ordering of subsets, frequencies and possibility degrees reflect the possibility order, i.e. $\pi_1 \geq \ldots \geq \pi_q$. We propose the following function:

$$\mathcal{L}_{pos}(\pi|x_1,\ldots,x_n) = \sum_{i=1}^{q}(-\alpha_i * \sum_{j=1}^{i}(1-\pi_j)) - \sum_{i=1}^{q}\frac{(1-\pi_i)^2}{2} + \sum_{i=1}^{q}(1-\pi_i) \quad (3)$$

The rationale behind this is to evaluate the cumulated distribution in the spirit of $\mathcal{L}_{surf}$. Thus, the terms $((1-\pi_i) * (1 - (\sum_{j=i}^{q}\alpha_i))) - \frac{(1-\pi_i)^2}{2}$ correspond to the evaluation of $\mathcal{L}_{surf}$ for the set $\overline{C_i} \cup \ldots \cup \overline{C_q}$. Note that, if you consider $C_i \cup \ldots \cup C_q$ instead of $\overline{C_i} \cup \ldots \cup \overline{C_q}$, what is obtained is the largest cumulative distribution instead of the tightest one. In order to have a cleaner interpretation of this likelihood function, we rewrite it again as follows :

$$\mathcal{L}_{pos}(\pi|x_1,\ldots,x_n) = \sum_{i=1}^{q}\pi_i * (\sum_{j=i}^{q}\alpha_j) - \frac{1}{2}\sum_{i=1}^{q}\pi_i^2 + \frac{q}{2} - \sum_{i=1}^{q}\alpha_i * i \quad (4)$$

The first term $\sum_{i=1}^{q}\pi_i * (\sum_{j=i}^{q}\alpha_j) - \frac{1}{2}\sum_{i=1}^{q}\pi_i^2$ corresponds to the $\mathcal{L}_{surf}$ applied to the cumulated probability distribution conditioned by the order induced by the possibility degrees. If the α_i's and the π_i's are in the same ordering, we can show that this part of the formulas is equivalent to the squared of the distance between the optimal distribution (the most specific cumulated distribution) and the current one. Thus, the terms $\frac{q}{2} - \sum_{i=1}^{q}\alpha_i * i$ tends to favor the possibility distributions that respect the frequency ordering.

Proposition 1. *Given a set of data $X = \{x_1,\ldots,x_n\}$ belonging to a discrete universe $\Omega = \{C_1,\ldots,C_q\}$, the possibility distribution π^* that maximizes the function $\mathcal{L}_{pos}$ is the probability-possibility transformation of the optimal probability distribution p^* (i.e. $\forall i \in \{1,\ldots,q\}, p_i^* = \alpha_i$), according to equation (2).*

Proof. We look for the probability distribution π^* that maximizes $\mathcal{L}_{pos}$.
We have:
$$\forall i = 1\ldots q, \frac{\delta\mathcal{L}_{pos}(\pi|x_1,\ldots,x_n)}{\delta\pi_i} = \sum_{j=i}^{q}\alpha_i - \pi_i$$

thus

$$\forall i = 1 \ldots q, \frac{\delta \mathcal{L}_{pos}(\pi | x_1, \ldots, x_n)}{\delta \pi_i} = 0 \Leftrightarrow p_i = \sum_{j=i}^{q} \alpha_i.$$

Since the derivative of $\mathcal{L}_{pos}(\pi | x_1, \ldots, x_n)$ with respect to π_i (the parameters of π) does not depend on the other variable π_j, $j \neq i$, we obtain $\pi_i^* = p_i = \sum_{j=i}^{q} \alpha_i$ which corresponds to a cumulated distribution of the α_i's. Since the part $\sum_{i=1}^{q} \alpha_i * i$ is maximized when $\alpha_1 \geq \ldots \geq \alpha_q$, the distribution π^* corresponds exactly to Equation (2).   ∎

This proposition shows that $\mathcal{L}_{pos}$ is an acceptable likelihood function for possibility distributions viewed as families of probabilities. As for $\mathcal{L}_{surf}$ the likelihood depends on the surface shared between the considered possibility distribution and the optimal one. If we only consider one piece of data x such that $x \in C_j$ we obtain :

$$\mathcal{L}_{pos}(\pi | x) = \frac{1}{n} \left(\sum_{i=1}^{j} \pi_i - \frac{1}{2} \sum_{i=1}^{q} \pi_i^2 + \frac{q}{2} - j \right) \tag{5}$$

It is worth noticing that, when optimal distributions can only be approximated, finding the best approximation with respect to $\mathcal{L}_{pos}$ is not equivalent to finding the best probability approximation with respect to probabilistic likelihood and then turning it into a possibility distribution.

Example 2. For instance, we consider X that leads to the frequency $\alpha_1 = 0.5$, $\alpha_2 = 0.3$, $\alpha_3 = 0.2$. We know require that $p_3 = 0$ and $\pi_3 = 0$. In this context, the optimal p with respect to $\mathcal{L}_{surf}$ ($\mathcal{L}_{log}$ is not applicable here) is $p_1 = 0.6$, $p_2 = 0.4$, $p_3 = 0$. The optimal π with respect to $\mathcal{L}_{poss}$ is $\pi_1 = 1$, $\pi_2 = 0.5$, $\pi_3 = 0$. The transformation π' of p is $\pi_1' = 1$, $\pi_2' = 0.4$, $\pi_3' = 0$. We observe that π' is different than π and that π is a better approximation of the optimal possibility distribution given is Example 1.

This result is fundamental since it illustrates that using a probabilistic likelihood and then the probability-possibility transformation is not an effective approach for constructing a possibility distribution from data. The maximization of $\mathcal{L}_{pos}$ is more adapted in this scope.

4   A Possibilistic Likelihood-Based Classifier

4.1   Principle

Since the representation of the examples corresponds necessarily to an incomplete view of the world, the goal of a possibilistic likelihood-based classification is to look for imprecise hypotheses that take into account this incompleteness. Thus, given a set of crisp data, we will search for a model that is as precise as possible and which provides a faithful description of the data. When the imprecision tends to 0, we obtain a crisp hypothesis that describes the concept exactly. Then, what we obtain is a function that associates to each input example a possibility distribution over that classes. Since it is based on the possibilistic likelihood, the resulting distribution can be viewed as the upper bound of the family of probability distributions that represents the imprecision about the classes that may be associated to the example. The advantage of using possibility distributions rather than probability distributions in this scope is twofold. First, having a faithful representation in terms of a probability distribution requires a large amount of data. Indeed, computing the probability of a class is more demanding than only finding the most probable class. Since a possibility distribution provides an upper bound, it is not as precise as a probability distribution, and then requires less data for being learned. Second, a possibility distribution hasn't the constraint to have the sum of its degrees equal to 1, and then it is more easy to approximate by optimization.

A classification database is a set of m pairs $(\overrightarrow{x}_i, c_i)$, $1 \le i \le m$, where $\overrightarrow{x}_i \in \mathbb{R}^n$ is a vector of n input variables and $c_i \in \{C_1, \ldots, C_q\}$ is the class variable. A possibilistic classifier Pcl is a function that associates to an input vector a possibility distribution over the classes. The goal of Possibilistic-likelihood based classifier is to find a possibilistic classifier Pcl that maximizes the possibilistic likelihood for each piece of data :

$$\mathcal{L}_{pos}(Pcl) = \frac{\sum_{i=1}^{m} \mathcal{L}_{pos}(\pi_i | c_i)}{m * (q-1)} \tag{6}$$

where $\pi_i = Pcl(\overrightarrow{x}_i)$. The maximum is reached when the $\pi_i(c_i) = 1$ and 0 for the other class (totally precise prediction). The division by $m * (q-1)$ ensures that $\mathcal{L}_{pos}(Pcl)$ is in $[-1, 1]$. Since the learning bias may prevent reaching this maximum, we will obtain a possibility distribution that describes both the most possible class and the plausibility of the other ones.

4.2   Construction and Learning of a Possibilistic Classifier

Let us consider a classification problem with q classes $(C_1 \ldots C_q)$. We define a possibilistic likelihood classifier like a family of q independent kernel functions (e.g. Gaussian kernels in our application) $Pcl = \{kf_1 \ldots kf_q\}$. We have

$$kf_i(\overrightarrow{x}) = a_{i,0} + a_{i,1} * K(s_1, \overrightarrow{x}) + \ldots + a_{i,r} * K(s_r, \overrightarrow{x}),$$

where $s_1, \ldots, s_k$ are support vectors which are computed previously by using a k-means algorithm. The possibility distribution is obtained by normalizing and bounding the results of the kernel functions i.e.

$$\pi(c_i) = [Pcl(\overrightarrow{x})](c_i) = \begin{cases} 1 & \text{if } i = argmax_{j=1 \ldots q}(kf_j(\overrightarrow{x})) \\ 1 & \text{if } kf_j(\overrightarrow{x}) > 1 \\ 0 & \text{if } kf_j(\overrightarrow{x}) < 0 \\ kf_j(\overrightarrow{x}) & \text{otherwise} \end{cases}$$

Finding the optimal functions $kf_1 \ldots kf_q$ constitutes an hard problem which is not solvable by classical optimization methods. We propose to solve the problem by using a particle swarm optimization algorithm [11]. The goal of the particle swarm method is to determine the Pcl that maximizes the possibilistic likelihood. One of the advantages of the particle swarm optimization with respect to the other meta-heuristics is that it is particularly suitable for continuous problems. Here, one particle represents the parameters of the kernel functions (the parameters $a_{i,1}, \ldots, a_{i,r}$ for each $kf_1 \ldots kf_q$). At each step the algorithm, each particle is moved along its velocity vector (randomly fixed at the beginning). For each particle, the velocity vector is updated at each step by considering the current vector, the vector from the current particle position to its best known position and the vector from the current particle position to the global swarm's best known position. The second advantage of the algorithm is that it is easy to tune. The three parameters for the updating of the velocity ω, ϕ_p and ϕ_g correspond respectively to the coefficient for the current velocity, the velocity to the particle best known position and the velocity to the global swarm's best known position. The number of particles and the number of iterations depend on the problem, but there are generic values that perform well in most of the cases. We use these default values in the experimentations reported below.

5   Experimentations

In this section, we present some experiments with the algorithm described in the previous section. In order to check the effectiveness of the algorithm, we used five benchmarks from UCI[1]. All the dataset used have numerical attributes. The Diabetes database describes 2 classes with 768 examples. The Ecoli database contains 336 examples that describe 8 classes. The Ionosphere database describes 2 classes with 351 examples. The Magic telescope database contains 19020 examples that describe 2 classes. The Segment database describes 7 classes with 2310 examples. We compare our results with the naive Bayes classifier. For each algorithm, we measure the accuracy but also the possibilistic likelihood. For the naive Bayes classifier, we obtain the possibility distribution by applying the probability-possibility transformation to the probability distribution obtained. The results presented in the following table are for 10-cross validation. * indicates that the result is significantly better than for the other method (paired two-sided t-test, p = 0.05). Results are provided in the following table. Possibilistic likelihood-based classifier is denoted as PLBC and naive Bayes classifier as NBC.

database	accuracy		Poss. likelihood	
	PLBC	NBC	PLBC	NBC
Diabetes	76.4[8.0]	75.7[5.1]	79.8[6.1]	79.0[4.7]
Ecoli	84.9[4.6]	86.9[2.5]	94.4[3.5]	96.8[1.4]
Ionosphere	93.7*[3.4]	84.9[6.2]	93.8*[3.4]	85.8[5.7]
Magic Telescope	81.3*[0.6]	72.7[0.8]	83.3*[0.8]	74.6[0.8]
Segment	87.4*[1.8]	79.8[3.5]	97*[0.6]	95.8[0.7]

---

[1] http://www.ics.uci.edu/ mlearn/MLRepository.html

The table shows that the PLBC approach outperforms NBC on 3 of the 5 databases with a statistically significant difference both for the accuracy and the possibilistic likelihood. On the two remaining databases, there is no statistically significant differences. Since the methods are clearly different in the theoretical and the algorithmic points of view, it may be debatable to conclude that the good performance is due to the use of the possibilistic setting. However, these clearly results show that this approach competes with the probabilistic ones.

6   Conclusions and Further Works

In this paper we have proposed a classification method based on the possibilistic likelihood. This approach allows us to predict a possibility distribution over classes rather than a unique class. To the best of our knowledge, the algorithm proposed is the first one that learns a possibility distribution understood as family of probability distributions from precise data. The flexibility of possibility distributions allows us to embed possibilistic likelihood into a complex optimization process that learns directly the set of kernel functions that are the core of the possibilistic classifier. Since possibility distributions are less precise that probability distributions, it requires less data for learning. Thus, our possibility classification algorithm can be used when we do not have a very large dataset at our disposal, or when prior knowledge is not available. In this context, the model found will faithfully describes the most plausible class and the imprecision around it. The experiments on benchmark datasets exhibits good performance and suggests that the approach is promising.

One other advantage of possibility distributions it that we can easily introduce some security margins. Then, we also plan to take into consideration the quantity of data that are used for determining the possibility distribution at each point in order to re-inject the uncertainty due the estimation based on a sample. In the future, it will be also interesting to consider the decision process when considering such kind of distribution. Indeed, we could make the distinction between the case of complete knowledge, partial ignorance and total ignorance. Lastly, we have to compare our algorithm more deeply with the other probabilistic approaches.

References

1. Benferhat, S., Tabia, K.: An Efficient Algorithm for Naive Possibilistic Classifiers with Uncertain Inputs. In: Greco, S., Lukasiewicz, T. (eds.) SUM 2008. LNCS (LNAI), vol. 5291, pp. 63–77. Springer, Heidelberg (2008)
2. Borgelt, C., Kruse, R.: Efficient maximum projection of database-induced multivariate possibility distributions. In: Proc. 7th IEEE Int. Conf. on Fuzzy Systems, pp. 663–668 (1998)
3. Cover, T.M., Hart, P.E.: Nearest neighbour pattern classification. IEEE Transactions on Information Theory 13, 21–27 (1967)
4. Dubois, D.: Possibility theory and statistical reasoning. Computational Statistics and Data Analysis 51, 47–69 (2006)

5. Dubois, D.: The Role of Epistemic Uncertainty in Risk Analysis. In: Deshpande, A., Hunter, A. (eds.) SUM 2010. LNCS, vol. 6379, pp. 11–15. Springer, Heidelberg (2010)

6. Dubois, D., Foulloy, L., Mauris, G., Prade, H.: Probability-possibility transformations, triangular fuzzy sets, and probabilistic inequalities. Reliable Computing 10, 273–297 (2004)

7. Dubois, D., Prade, H.: When upper probabilities are possibility measures. Fuzzy Sets and Systems 49, 65–74 (1992)

8. Dubois, D., Prade, H.: On data summarization with fuzzy sets. In: Proc. of the 5th Inter. Fuzzy Systems Assoc. World Congress (IFSA 1993), Seoul, pp. 465–468 (1993)

9. Dubois, D., Prade, H., Sandri, S.: On possibility/probability transformations. In: Proceedings of Fourth IFSA Conference, pp. 103–112. Kluwer Academic Publ. (1993)

10. Jenhani, I., Ben Amor, N., Elouedi, Z.: Decision trees as possibilistic classifiers. Inter. J. of Approximate Reasoning 48(3), 784–807 (2008)

11. Kennedy, J., Eberhart, R.: Particle swarm optimization. In: Proceedings of IEEE International Conference on Neural Networks, pp. 1942–1948 (1995)

12. Langley, P., Iba, W., Thompson, K.: An analysis of bayesian classifiers. In: Proceedings of AAAI 1992, vol. 7, pp. 223–228 (1992)

13. Mauris, G.: Inferring a possibility distribution from very few measurements. In: Soft Methods for Handling Variability and Imprecision. Advances in Soft Computing, vol. 48, pp. 92–99. Springer, Heidelberg (2008)

14. Pearl, J.: Probabilistic Reasoning in Intelligent Systems: Networks of Plausible Inference. Morgan Kaufmman, San Francisco (1988)

15. Serrurier, M., Prade, H.: Imprecise Regression Based on Possibilistic Likelihood. In: Benferhat, S., Grant, J. (eds.) SUM 2011. LNCS, vol. 6929, pp. 447–459. Springer, Heidelberg (2011)

16. Serrurier, M., Prade, H.: Maximum-likelihood principle for possibility distributions viewed as families of probabilities (regular paper). In: IEEE International Conference on Fuzzy Systems (FUZZ-IEEE), Taipei, Taiwan, pp. 2987–2993 (2011)

17. Zadeh, L.A.: Fuzzy sets as a basis for a theory of possibility. Fuzzy sets and systems 1, 3–25 (1978)

Maximin and Maximal Solutions for Linear Programming Problems with Possibilistic Uncertainty

Erik Quaeghebeur, Nathan Huntley, Keivan Shariatmadar,
and Gert de Cooman

Ghent University, SYSTeMS Research Group
Technologiepark–Zwijnaarde 914, 9052 Zwijnaarde, Belgium

Abstract. We consider linear programming problems with uncertain constraint coefficients described by intervals or, more generally, possibility distributions. The uncertainty is given a behavioral interpretation using coherent lower previsions from the theory of imprecise probabilities. We give a meaning to the linear programming problems by reformulating them as decision problems under such imprecise-probabilistic uncertainty. We provide expressions for and illustrations of the maximin and maximal solutions of these decision problems and present computational approaches for dealing with them.

Keywords: linear program, interval uncertainty, vacuous lower prevision, possibility distribution, coherent lower prevision, imprecise probabilities, decision making, maximinity, maximality.

1 Introduction

Linear programming problems thank their importance both to the great variety of optimization questions that can be modeled by them and to the existence of computationally efficient algorithms for solving them [2]. A linear programming problem can be expressed in the following full (left) and compact (right) forms:

$$
\begin{array}{llcll}
\text{maximize} & \sum_{k=1}^{n} c_k x_k & & \text{maximize} & c^T x \\
\text{subject to} & \forall_{\ell=1}^{m} (\sum_{k=1}^{n} a_{\ell k} x_k \leq b_\ell), & \equiv & \text{subject to} & ax \leq b, \\
& \forall_{k=1}^{n} (x_k \geq 0) & & & x \geq 0
\end{array}
$$

where x in $\mathbb{R}^n$ is the optimization vector of dimension $n \in \mathbb{N}$, a in $\mathbb{R}^{m \times n}$ and b in $\mathbb{R}^m$ are the constraint coefficient matrix and (column) vector with $m \in \mathbb{N}$ the number of nontrivial constraints, and c in $\mathbb{R}^n$ is the objective function coefficient vector—c^T is its transpose. (The lower case matrix notation is justified below.)

We are interested in linear programming problems in which there is uncertainty in some or all of the constraints. Being able to treat them allows us to more realistically deal with real-life operations research problems [8, Section 5].

If we are uncertain about the value of a particular constraint coefficient, we represent it by an upper case letter, e.g., $A_{\ell k}$ or B_ℓ, and similarly A and B if this

S. Greco et al. (Eds.): IPMU 2012, Part III, CCIS 299, pp. 430–439, 2012.

matrix and vector have one or more uncertain components. To these (matrices or vectors of) uncertain coefficients we must associate a model to formalize the uncertainty. These problems can then be expressed as

$$\text{maximize} \quad c^T x$$
$$\text{subject to} \quad Ax \leq B, \, x \geq 0$$
$$\text{with} \quad \text{given uncertainty model for } (A, B)$$

This uncertainty means that, for a given choice of x, it may be uncertain whether x satisfies the constraints or not, and therefore it is not clear what it means to 'maximize' $c^T x$ in such a problem.

Our approach is to transform the problem into a decision problem (Section 2) in which a fixed penalty is received if any of the constraints are broken [7]. Since this is a reformulation as a decision problem, it can then in principle be solved using a suitable optimality criterion for the uncertainty models being used, for instance maximizing expected utility when probability distributions are used, as we do in Section 3 to introduce the basic ideas. In Section 4, we show how these ideas are generalized to all uncertainty models that can be seen as *coherent lower or upper previsions* [11] and introduce *maximinity* and *maximality*, the two chosen amongst many compatible optimality criteria. We focus on two specific types of uncertainty models: intervals—vacuous lower probabilities—in Section 5, and, more generally, possibility distributions—maxitive upper probabilities—in Section 6. A simplifying assumption we make in this paper is that the uncertainty models for the various uncertain constraint coefficients are *independent*, the formal meaning of which we will make precise for each type.

We were surprised at how different this approach is from those usually found in the literature—we only have space for a fleeting overview. First the probabilistic case: Dantzig [4] looked at the problem as a staged one: first choose x, observe (A, B), and then 'repair' broken constraints. Charnes & Cooper [3] proposed to solve the problem under the added 'chance constraint' that the probability of failing a constraint is below some level. Our solution for the interval case with maximinity, although arrived at differently, essentially reduces to the approach of Soyster [9]; further results in this vein can be found in the domains of inexact and robust optimization [5,1]. The possibility distribution case has been analyzed from a very wide range of angles by the fuzzy sets community—all nevertheless differing from ours; the approach of Jamison & Lodwick [6] is one to mention, because they also pursue a penalty idea, but use a different optimality criterion.

To illustrate our methods, we introduce a running example, in which only one constraint coefficient is uncertain (left: full form, right: shorthand form):

$$\begin{array}{ll} \text{maximize} & 2x_1 + 3x_2 \\ \text{subject to} & 1x_1 + 3x_2 \leq 2, \\ & 1x_1 + 1x_2 \leq B_2, \\ & -3x_1 - 3x_2 \leq -1, \\ & x_1 \geq 0, \, x_2 \geq 0 \end{array} \quad \equiv \quad \begin{array}{ll} \text{maximize} & c^T x := 2x_1 + 3x_2 \\ \text{subject to} & x \lhd B_2 \end{array}$$

For reference, we first show, in Figure 1, the usual linear programming problem, i.e., for some particular precisely known B_2, and its solution.

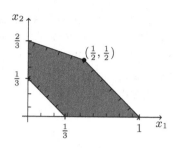

$$\text{maximize} \quad c^T x := 2x_1 + 3x_2$$
$$\text{subject to} \quad x \lhd 1$$

Fig. 1. Example linear programming problem: the constraints are drawn using hairy lines; the feasible set is shaded dark gray; the convex solution set of optimization vectors attaining the maximal value $5/2$ is a singleton in this case, represented as a black dot

2   Reformulation as a Decision Problem

Now we describe the decision problem that we use in the case of uncertainty. For each optimization vector x and each possible realization (a, b) of (A, B), we associate a utility $c^T x$, unless x fails a constraint, in which case the utility becomes a *penalty value* L. This value L should be chosen so it is strictly worse to fail the constraints than to satisfy them, and so L should be strictly less than $c^T x$ for any x that is feasible for some possible realization (a, b).

We use $Ax \leq B$ as a shorthand for the event $\{(a, b) \in \mathbb{R}^{m \times n} \times \mathbb{R}^m : ax \leq b\}$ and so the corresponding *indicator function* $I_{Ax \leq B}$ is 1 on this event and 0 elsewhere; idem for $Ax \not\leq B$. Then the gain or *utility function* associated to x is

$$G_x := c^T x I_{Ax \leq B} + L I_{Ax \not\leq B} = L + (c^T x - L) I_{Ax \leq B}. \tag{1}$$

Given such a utility function and an uncertainty model for (A, B), we can use a suitable optimality criterion to determine the optimal choices of x.

As can be gleaned from the formulation of our running example and Figure 1, independent of the uncertainty about B_2, any feasible optimization vector x will have a value of at least $2/3$, as achieved in $(1/3, 0)$. Therefore we are allowed the choice $L = 0$, which simplifies our discussion of the running example.

3   Probability Mass Functions

A simple probabilistic case serves as a good introduction to the main ideas of our method. Assume the uncertainty about the independent scalar uncertain variables is expressed using probability mass functions and let p be the corresponding product probability mass function for (A, B) with Cartesian product support $\mathcal{A} \times \mathcal{B}$. Let P denote both the associated probability measure for subsets of $\mathcal{A} \times \mathcal{B}$ and *linear prevision* (expectation operator) for *gambles* (real-valued functions) on $\mathcal{A} \times \mathcal{B}$.

Utility functions are gambles. The expected utility of choosing an optimization vector $x \geq 0$ is

$$P(G_x) = P(L + (c^T x - L) I_{Ax \leq B}) = L + (c^T x - L) P(Ax \leq B). \tag{2}$$

We give meaning to the linear program with uncertain constraints thus defined by saying that the solution must *maximize expected utility*:

$$\begin{array}{ll} \text{maximize} & c^T x \\ \text{subject to} & Ax \le B,\, x \ge 0 \\ \text{with} & \text{given } p \end{array} \quad \rightarrow \quad \begin{array}{ll} \text{maximize} & L + (c^T x - L)P(Ax \le B) \\ \text{subject to} & x \ge 0 \end{array}$$

As the objective function is in general not affine in x, the resulting optimization problem is in general no longer a linear program. In general, it is also difficult to compute the probabilistic factor $P(Ax \le B)$, let alone find an expression for it. In Figure 2, we give a simple example that can nevertheless be solved by hand.

We use a conceptually useful generalization of the feasibility concept: an optimization vector x is $P(Ax \le B)$-feasible; for correspondence with the standard case, 0-feasible vectors are called infeasible and 1-feasible vectors feasible.

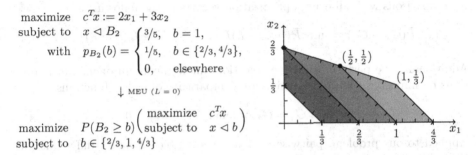

$$\begin{array}{ll} \text{maximize} & c^T x := 2x_1 + 3x_2 \\ \text{subject to} & x \lhd B_2 \\ \text{with} & p_{B_2}(b) = \begin{cases} {}^3/_5, & b = 1, \\ {}^1/_5, & b \in \{{}^2/_3, {}^4/_3\}, \\ 0, & \text{elsewhere} \end{cases} \end{array}$$

$$\downarrow \text{MEU } (L = 0)$$

$$\begin{array}{ll} \text{maximize} & P(B_2 \ge b)\begin{pmatrix} \text{maximize} & c^T x \\ \text{subject to} & x \lhd b \end{pmatrix} \\ \text{subject to} & b \in \{{}^2/_3, 1, {}^4/_3\} \end{array}$$

Fig. 2. Example linear programming problem with probabilistic uncertainty: the feasible set is shaded dark gray, the $^4/_5$-feasible set gray, and the $^1/_5$-feasible set light gray; because the set of optimization vectors is partitioned according to probability value, the maximization can be done in a nested manner; the solution set of optimization vectors attaining the maximal *expected* value 2 is given using black dots

4   Generalizing the Probabilistic Case

Coherent Lower and Upper Previsions. A wide range of uncertainty models can be represented using coherent lower and upper previsions from the theory of imprecise probabilities [11]. Like linear previsions, these are expectation operators, but whereas linear previsions can be interpreted as specifying fair prices for buying and selling gambles, coherent lower and upper previsions can be respectively interpreted as specifying supremum acceptable buying prices and infimum acceptable selling prices. They are conjugate operators; given a coherent lower prevision $\underline{P}$, the conjugate coherent upper prevision is given by $\overline{P}(f) = -\underline{P}(-f)$ for every gamble f.

Coherent lower and upper probabilities are derived concepts for which we use the same symbol: given an event $\mathcal{E}$, we have $\underline{P}(\mathcal{E}) = \underline{P}(I_\mathcal{E})$ and $\overline{P}(\mathcal{E}) = \overline{P}(I_\mathcal{E})$. As before, we generalize the feasibility concept: an optimization vector x is called *inner* $\underline{P}(Ax \leq B)$-feasible and *outer* $\overline{P}(Ax \leq B)$-feasible; for correspondence with the standard case, outer 0-feasible vectors are called infeasible and inner 1-feasible points feasible.

Optimality Criteria. When using coherent lower and upper previsions it is no longer possible to maximize expected utility. Several generalizations have been proposed, of which we consider maximinity and maximality. Troffaes [10] gives a more detailed discussion of these and other optimality criteria.

Under the *maximinity* criterion, applied to our problem, those optimization vectors $x \geq 0$ are optimal that *maximize the lower expected utility*

$$\underline{P}(G_x) = \underline{P}(L + (c^T x - L)I_{Ax \leq B}) = L + (c^T x - L)\underline{P}(Ax \leq B). \tag{3}$$

Under the *maximality* criterion, those $x \geq 0$ are optimal that are *undominated* in comparisons with all other optimization vectors in the following sense:

$$\inf_{z \in \mathbb{R}^n} \overline{P}(G_x - G_z) = \inf_{z \in \mathbb{R}^n} \overline{P}((c^T x - L)I_{Ax \leq B} - (c^T z - L)I_{Az \leq B}) \geq 0. \tag{4}$$

Additionally, we perform a further selection among maximin or maximal solutions by imposing *dominance*, pointwise comparisons of utility functions:

$$\forall z \in \mathbb{R}^n : G_z = G_x \text{ or } \max(G_x - G_z) > 0. \tag{5}$$

Applied to our problem, pairwise comparisons between x and z differ qualitatively based on where G_x and G_z take a value larger than L:

(i) If $Ax \leq B \not\subseteq Az \leq B$, then z does not dominate x because G_x and G_z are incomparable.
(ii) If $Ax \leq B = Az \leq B$, then z dominates x if $c^T x < c^T z$ and therefore x must satisfy $c^T x \geq \max_{(Ax \leq B)=(Az \leq B)} c^T z$; in particular, if $Az \leq B$ is empty for all z, no selection is made—we do not consider this trivial case further on.
(iii) If $Ax \leq B \subset Az \leq B$, then z dominates x if $c^T x \leq c^T z$ and therefore x must satisfy $c^T x > \max_{(Ax \leq B) \subset (Az \leq B)} c^T z$; in particular, if $Az \leq B$ is nonempty, all those x for which $Ax \leq B$ is empty are weeded out.

In general, and also for the problems we consider in this paper, checking dominance in a computationally efficient way remains an open problem.

5   Intervals

Assume the uncertainty about the $A_{\ell k}$ and B_ℓ is expressed using real intervals $[\underline{a_{\ell k}}, \overline{a_{\ell k}}]$ and $[\underline{b_\ell}, \overline{b_\ell}]$. Independence is implemented by taking Cartesian products such as $\mathcal{A} := [\underline{a}, \overline{a}] := \times_{1 \leq k \leq n, 1 \leq \ell \leq m}[\underline{a_{\ell k}}, \overline{a_{\ell k}}]$ and $\mathcal{B} := [\underline{b}, \overline{b}] := \times_{1 \leq \ell \leq m}[\underline{b_\ell}, \overline{b_\ell}]$. Then we can model the uncertainty using joint vacuous coherent lower and upper previsions $\underline{P}$ and $\overline{P}$ defined for every gamble f on $\mathcal{A} \times \mathcal{B}$ by

$$\underline{P}(f) := \min_{(a,b) \in \mathcal{A} \times \mathcal{B}} f(a,b) \quad \text{and} \quad \overline{P}(f) := \max_{(a,b) \in \mathcal{A} \times \mathcal{B}} f(a,b). \tag{6}$$

Intervals and Maximinity. In case the maximinity criterion is used, Equation (3) shows the quantity $\underline{P}(Ax \leq B)$ is important. By Definition (6), it is 1— and x is feasible—if and only if x satisfies the constraints $ax \leq b$ for all $\underline{a} \leq a \leq \overline{a}$ and $\underline{b} \leq b \leq \overline{b}$; otherwise it is 0. Because we may assume $x \geq 0$, componentwise, the inequality's left-hand side will be maximal and the right-hand side minimal for $a = \overline{a}$ and $b = \underline{b}$; so if the constraints are satisfied for these values, they are also satisfied for all the others: the feasible set is $\overline{a}X \leq \underline{b} := \{x \geq 0 : \overline{a}x \leq \underline{b}\}$.

For feasible x, Equation (3) shows that the lower prevision is equal to c^Tx— the penalty L falls out of the equation. So if the feasible set is nonempty, the maximin solutions are the those that maximize this quantity:

$$
\begin{array}{ll}
\text{maximize} & c^Tx \\
\text{subject to} & Ax \leq B,\ x \geq 0 \\
\text{with} & \underline{a} \leq A \leq \overline{a},\ \underline{b} \leq B \leq \overline{b}
\end{array}
\qquad \rightarrow \qquad
\begin{array}{ll}
\text{maximize} & c^Tx \\
\text{subject to} & \overline{a}x \leq \underline{b}, \\
& x \geq 0
\end{array}
$$

The resulting optimization problem is then again a linear program. This is illustrated in Figure 3. Dominance is automatically satisfied, because $Ax \leq B$ is equal (to $\mathcal{A} \times \mathcal{B}$) for all feasible x.

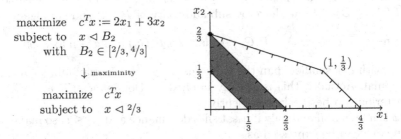

Fig. 3. Example linear programming problem with interval uncertainty and maximinity: the feasible set is shaded dark gray; the convex solution set of optimization vectors attaining the maximal *lower expected*—i.e., maximin—value 2 is a singleton in this case, represented as a black dot

If the feasible set is empty, all $x \geq 0$ are maximin solutions. But now dominance does come into play; e.g., Dominance (iii) weeds out everything outside of $\underline{a}X \leq \overline{b}$, which is the outer feasible set.

Intervals and Maximality. In case the maximality criterion is used, Equation (4) shows the quantity $\overline{P}(G_x - G_z)$ is important. Definition (6) tells us that for optimization vectors x and z we have $\overline{P}(G_x - G_z) \geq 0$ if and only if there is a pair (a, b) in $\mathcal{A} \times \mathcal{B}$ such that $G_x(a, b) \geq G_z(a, b)$.

In Dominance (ii), we stated that we only considered problems for which the outer feasible set $\underline{a}X \leq \overline{b}$ is nonempty. As seen above, Dominance (iii) tells us we can restrict attention to the outer feasible set when looking for maximal solutions. Now, outer feasible x that satisfy dominance (5) also satisfy Equation (4), because the latter here reduces to $\min_{\underline{a}z \leq \overline{b}} \max(G_x - G_z) \geq 0$.

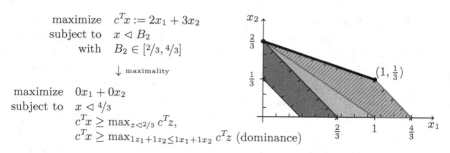

Fig. 4. Example linear programming problem with interval uncertainty and maximality: the feasible set is shaded dark gray and the 1-outer feasible set light gray; the maximin solution corresponds to the leftmost black dot; the convex solution set of outer
feasible points with an *upper* expected value greater than or equal to the maximin
value is given by the hatched area; the maximal solutions satisfying dominance—given
by the thick black line—are the optimization vectors x corresponding to the gam-
bles $(2x_1 + 3x_2)I_{x \lhd B_2} = (2x_1 + 3x_2)I_{1x_1 + 1x_2 \leq B_2}$ undominated within this hatched set

If moreover the feasible set $\overline{a}Z \leq \underline{b}$ is nonempty, then for outer feasible x—
with $\overline{P}(Ax \leq B) = 1$—we have by sub-additivity of $\overline{P}$ [11] and conjugacy that

$$\min\nolimits_{\overline{a}z \leq \underline{b}} \overline{P}(G_x - G_z) \leq \overline{P}(G_x) - \max\nolimits_{\overline{a}z \leq \underline{b}} \underline{P}(G_z) = c^T x - \max\nolimits_{\overline{a}z \leq \underline{b}} c^T z.$$

So no x with $c^T x$ smaller than the value $\max_{\overline{a}z \leq \underline{b}} c^T z$ of a maximin solution can
be maximal. Actually, this is already implied by Dominance (ii) and (iii), but
this criterion can be checked efficiently.

So x is maximal if and only if it satisfies dominance and $\underline{a}x \leq \overline{b}$, so maximality
for intervals can be expressed as

maximize $c^T x$	maximize $0^T x$
subject to $Ax \leq B, x \geq 0$	subject to $\underline{a}x \leq \overline{b}, x \geq 0,$
with $\underline{a} \leq A \leq \overline{a},$ $\quad\rightarrow$	$c^T x \geq \max_{\overline{a}z \leq \underline{b}} c^T z,$
$\underline{b} \leq B \leq \overline{b}$	dominance

The resulting optimization problem is a classical feasibility problem compounded
with a dominance problem. This case is illustrated in Figure 4.

6 Possibility Distributions

Assume that the uncertainty models for the $A_{\ell k}$ and B_ℓ are unimodal possibility distributions $\pi_{\ell k}$ and π_ℓ. Independence is implemented with the usual—
least complex—definition of joint possibility: $\pi_A(a) := \min_{1 \leq k \leq n, 1 \leq \ell \leq m} \pi_{\ell k}(a_{\ell k})$,
$\pi_B(b) := \min_{1 \leq \ell \leq m} \pi_\ell(b_\ell)$, and $\pi(a, b) := \min\{\pi_A(a), \pi_B(b)\}$. For any D among
the $A_{\ell k}$ and B_ℓ, and $0 \leq t < 1$, we define bounds $\underline{d}_t := \inf\{d \in \mathbb{R} : \pi(d) > t\}$ and
$\overline{d}_t := \sup\{d \in \mathbb{R} : \pi(d) > t\}$. We write $\underline{a}_t, \overline{a}_t, \underline{b}_t,$ and $\overline{b}_t$ for the matrices and vectors
with respective components $\underline{a_{\ell k_t}}, \overline{a_{\ell k_t}}, \underline{b_{\ell_t}},$ and $\overline{b_{\ell_t}}$. Then $\mathcal{A} \times \mathcal{B} := [\underline{a}_0, \overline{a}_0] \times [\underline{b}_0, \overline{b}_0]$
is (the closure of) the set of possible realizations of (A, B).

We can model the uncertainty using a joint upper probability $\overline{P}$ defined for every subset $\mathcal{E}$ of $\mathcal{A} \times \mathcal{B}$ by $\overline{P}(\mathcal{E}) := \sup_{(a,b)\in\mathcal{E}} \pi(a,b)$—lower probabilities follow by conjugacy and lower and upper previsions by Choquet integration [7].

Possibility Distributions and Maximinity. By Equation (3), we seek to maximize $\underline{P}(G_x) = L + (c^T x - L)\underline{P}(Ax \le B) = L + (c^T x - L)\big(1 - \overline{P}(Ax \not\le B)\big)$. With every x there corresponds a unique value for $\overline{P}(Ax \not\le B)$, so this maximization can be done in a nested manner:

$$\max_{x\ge 0} \underline{P}(G_x) = L + \max_{t\in[0,1]}(1-t)\max_{x\ge 0}\{c^T x - L : \overline{P}(Ax \not\le B) = t\}$$
$$= L + \max_{t\in[0,1]}(1-t)\max_{x\ge 0}\{c^T x - L : \overline{P}(Ax \not\le B) \le t\},$$

where the second equality follows from the fact that for $\overline{P}(Ax \not\le B) = s < t$ with fixed x and t it holds that $(1-s)(c^T x - L) \ge (1-t)(c^T x - L)$.

Next we show that $\overline{P}(Ax \not\le B) = r := \inf\{0 \le \tau < 1 : \overline{a}_\tau x \le \underline{b}_\tau\}$: We have $ax \le b$ for a and b such that $\pi(a,b) > r$, hence $\overline{P}(Ax \not\le B) \le r$. For any $s < r$ we have $\overline{a}_s x \not\le \underline{b}_s$, hence $\overline{P}(Ax \not\le B) = \sup_{(a,b)\in\mathcal{A}\times\mathcal{B}}\{\pi(a,b) : ax \not\le b\} \ge r$. It follows that $\overline{P}(Ax \not\le B) \le t$ if and only if $\overline{a}_t x \le \underline{b}_t$.

Hence the problem becomes

$$
\begin{array}{l}
\text{maximize} \quad c^T x \\
\text{subject to} \quad Ax \le B, \\
\qquad\qquad\quad x \ge 0 \\
\text{with} \quad \text{given } \pi
\end{array}
\rightarrow
\begin{array}{l}
\text{maximize} \quad L + (1-t)\left(\begin{array}{l}\text{maximize} \quad c^T x - L \\ \text{subject to} \quad \overline{a}_t x \le \underline{b}_t, \\ \qquad\qquad\quad x \ge 0\end{array}\right) \\
\text{subject to} \quad 0 \le t < 1
\end{array}
$$

So we maximize over all $0 \le t \le 1$, where for any particular $t < 1$, we just need to solve a single linear program. This maximization over t can be done using, e.g., a bisection algorithm. Dominance is again automatically satisfied, now because $Ax \le B$ is equal (to $\overline{a}_t x \le \underline{b}_t$) for all $(1-t)$-inner feasible x. This case is illustrated in Figure 5.

$$
\begin{array}{l}
\text{maximize} \quad c^T x := 2x_1 + 3x_2 \\
\text{subject to} \quad x \lhd B_2 \\
\text{with} \quad \pi_2(b) = \begin{cases} 1, & b = 1, \\ 1/5, & b \in [2/3, 4/3] \setminus \{1\}, \\ 0, & \text{elsewhere} \end{cases}
\end{array}
$$

$\downarrow$ maximinity $(L = 0)$

$$
\begin{array}{l}
\text{maximize} \quad (1-t)\left(\begin{array}{l}\text{maximize} \quad c^T x \\ \text{subject to} \quad x \lhd \underline{b_{2}}_t\end{array}\right) \\
\text{subject to} \quad t \in \{0, 1/5\}
\end{array}
$$

Fig. 5. Example linear programming problem with possibilistic uncertainty and maximinity: the feasible set is shaded dark gray and the $2/3$-inner feasible set gray; the solution set of optimization vectors attaining the maximin value 2 is given using black dots

Possibility Distributions and Maximality. We again start by focusing on the core of Equation (4), which can be written as [7]:

$$\overline{P}(G_x - G_z) = \begin{cases} -(c^Tz - L) + (c^Tx - c^Tz)\overline{P}(Ax \le B) \\ \quad + (c^Tz - L)\overline{P}(Ax \le B \vee Az \not\le B) \\ \quad + (c^Tz - L)\overline{P}(Ax \le B \wedge Az \not\le B), \quad c^Tx \ge c^Tz, \\ -(c^Tz - L) - (c^Tx - c^Tz)\overline{P}(Az \not\le B) \\ \quad + (c^Tx - L)\overline{P}(Ax \le B \vee Az \not\le B) \\ \quad + (c^Tx - L)\overline{P}(Ax \le B \wedge Az \not\le B), \quad c^Tx \le c^Tz. \end{cases}$$

In this expression, only the factor $\overline{P}(Ax \le B \wedge Az \not\le B)$ is hard to compute for given x and z. However, to determine whether or not z dominates x, we only need to find out whether $\overline{P}(G_x - G_z) < 0$ or not, so we do not need to compute the factor's value, but only whether it is larger than some critical value that is a function of the (easily computable) rest of the expression. At the current state of our investigations, this comparison requires us to solve at most m linear programs per (x, z)-pair.

We have not yet found a way to exploit this result to derive an explicit optimization problem—such as the feasibility problem for the interval case—that has the undominated elements as its solution. So currently we use an approximation approach for dealing with this kind of problem: we discretize the space of optimization vectors and perform pairwise comparisons between points in this grid; this approach is infeasible for problems with non-small n.

This case is illustrated in Figure 6 with an example we can solve exactly.

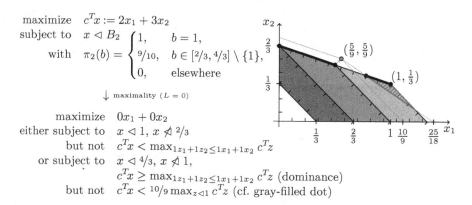

Fig. 6. Example linear programming problem with possibilistic uncertainty and maximality—note the modified possibility distribution: the inner feasible set is shaded dark gray, (the infeasible part of) the 1-outer feasible set is shaded gray, the $9/10$-outer feasible set is shaded light gray; the solution set of is drawn using thick black lines and the hatched area again consists of optimization vectors that are nonmaximal because they are dominated (cf. Figure 4); the solution set consists of a union of intersections of convex sets of optimization vectors

7   Conclusions

We have used simple two-valued utility functions. Our approach is in principle compatible with more complex utility functions. For example, in this paper, we only deal with uncertainty in the constraints. Uncertainty in the objective function could in principle be taken into account directly in the utility function of the decision problem. To keep the computational complexity of the problems we study still somewhat manageable, we have refrained from considering more complex utility functions—but it is an obvious avenue for further research.

Currently, the two main new contributions of our research, as presented in this paper, are the formulation of the feasibility problem for the interval-maximality case and the formulation of the efficiently solvable nested optimization problem for the possibility-maximinity case. We have bumped our head discovering that finding an efficient approach for determining dominance is a worthy goal. But this should not divert all our attention away from adding other types of uncertainty models—such as linear-vacuous previsions, the next step up in complexity—to the list of those we can efficiently find maximin solutions for.

Acknowledgments. This research was supported by the IWT SBO project 60043, "Fuzzy Finite Element Method". We thank the reviewers for comments that were useful and to the point.

References

1. Ben-Tal, A., Nemirovski, A.: Robust optimization – methodology and applications. Mathematical Programming 92(3), 453–480 (2002)
2. Bertsimas, D., Tsitsiklis, J.N.: Introduction to linear optimization. Athena Scientific (1997)
3. Charnes, A., Cooper, W.W.: Chance-constrained programming. Management Science 6(1), 73–79 (1959)
4. Dantzig, G.B.: Linear programming under uncertainty. Management Science 1(3/4), 197–206 (1955)
5. Fiedler, M., Nedoma, J., Ramík, J., Rohn, J., Zimmermann, K.: Linear Optimization Problems with Inexact Data. Springer (2006)
6. Jamison, K.D., Lodwick, W.A.: Fuzzy linear programming using a penalty method. Fuzzy Sets and Systems 119(1), 97–110 (2001)
7. Quaeghebeur, E., Shariatmadar, K., De Cooman, G.: Constrained optimization problems under uncertainty with coherent lower previsions. Fuzzy Sets and Systems (in press)
8. Sahinidis, N.V.: Optimization under uncertainty: state-of-the-art and opportunities. Computers & Chemical Engineering 28(6–7), 971–983 (2004)
9. Soyster, A.L.: Convex programming with set-inclusive constraints and applications to inexact linear programming. Operations Research 21(5), 1154–1157 (1973)
10. Troffaes, M.C.M.: Decision making under uncertainty using imprecise probabilities. International Journal of Approximate Reasoning 45(1), 17–29 (2007)
11. Walley, P.: Statistical Reasoning with Imprecise Probabilities. In: Monographs on Statistics and Applied Probability, vol. 42. Chapman & Hall, London (1991)

Lower Previsions Induced by Filter Maps

Gert de Cooman[1] and Enrique Miranda[2]

[1] Ghent University, SYSTeMS, Technologiepark–Zwijnaarde 914, 9052 Zwijnaarde, Belgium
gert.decooman@UGent.be
[2] University of Oviedo, Dept. of Statistics and O.R.–C-Calvo Sotelo, s/n 33007 Oviedo, Spain
mirandaenrique@uniovi.es

Abstract. Coherent lower previsions are amongst the most prominent uncertainty models within imprecise probability theory. We show how they can model information about the joint behaviour of two variables, when these are related by means of a *filter map*: a model for the imprecise observation of a random variable by means of a class of filters. Our construction preserves a number of interesting properties, such as n-monotonicity, and it generalises a number of existing results for multi-valued mappings.

Keywords: Coherent lower previsions, set filters, natural extension, n-monotonicity, lower inverses.

1 Introduction and Motivation

This paper deals with a specific class of coherent lower previsions, and discusses some of their properties. Before we explain why this class is interesting, let us mention a few basic facts about coherent lower previsions, a quite general uncertainty model used in the theory of imprecise probabilities. This should allow the reader to understand the motivation in this introductory section, and to follow the basic arguments in the rest of the paper. For a more thorough understanding, and for following the proofs, a more involved knowledge of lower prevision theory is necessary; due to limitations of space, we must point to Refs. [12,2] for the necessary details, and for a detailed discussion of the interpretation of lower previsions and why they are useful uncertainty models.

1.1 Basic Notions

Consider a variable X assuming values in a non-empty set $\mathscr{X}$. A subject is uncertain about the actual value that X assumes in $\mathscr{X}$. A *gamble* f on $\mathscr{X}$ is any bounded real-valued variable $f\colon \mathscr{X} \to \mathbb{R}$, interpreted as an uncertain reward $f(X)$. The set of all gambles on $\mathscr{X}$ is denoted by $\mathscr{G}(\mathscr{X})$. It is a linear space, closed under point-wise addition and multiplication by real numbers.

A *lower prevision* is a real-valued functional $\underline{P}$ defined on some subset of $\mathscr{G}(\mathscr{X})$, called its *domain* and denoted by $\mathrm{dom}\,\underline{P}$. $\underline{P}$ is said to *avoid sure loss* when $\sum_{k=1}^{n} \underline{P}(f_k) \leq \sup[\sum_{k=1}^{n} f_k]$ for all $n \in \mathbb{N}_0$ and all $f_1, \ldots, f_n \in \mathrm{dom}\,\underline{P}$, where $\mathbb{N}_0$ is the set of all non-negative integers (zero included). $\underline{P}$ is called *coherent* if [12, Section 2.5.3]:

$$\sum_{k=1}^{n} \underline{P}(f_k) - m\underline{P}(f_0) \leq \sup\left[\sum_{k=1}^{n} f_k - mf_0\right] \text{ for all } n, m \in \mathbb{N}_0 \text{ and } f_0, f_1, \ldots, f_n \in \mathrm{dom}\,\underline{P}.$$

$$(1)$$

S. Greco et al. (Eds.): IPMU 2012, Part III, CCIS 299, pp. 440–449, 2012.
© Springer-Verlag Berlin Heidelberg 2012

A lower prevision $\underline{P}$ defined on all gambles is coherent if and only if [12, Section 2.3.3] for all non-negative real λ and any pair f, g of gambles on $\mathscr{X}$:

C1. $\underline{P}(f) \geq \inf f$;
C2. $\underline{P}(\lambda f) = \lambda \underline{P}(f)$;
C3. $\underline{P}(f+g) \geq \underline{P}(f) + \underline{P}(g)$.

Avoiding sure loss is a weaker condition than coherence. If a lower prevision $\underline{P}$ avoids sure loss, then we can correct it into a coherent lower prevision that is as small as possible. This is done by means of the *natural extension* $\underline{E}_P$, whose main properties are summarised in the following theorem:

Theorem 1. *[12, Theorem 3.1.2] Let $\underline{P}$ be a lower prevision that avoids sure loss. Let $\underline{E}_P$ be the lower prevision on the set $\mathscr{G}(\mathscr{X})$ of all gambles f given by*

$$\underline{E}_P(f) := \sup \left\{ \mu : f - \mu \geq \sum_{k=1}^{n} \lambda_k [f_k - \underline{P}(f_k)] \text{ for some } n \in \mathbb{N}_0, \lambda_k > 0, f_k \in \mathrm{dom}\underline{P} \right\}.$$
(2)

Then:

(i) *$\underline{E}_P$ is a coherent lower prevision;*
(ii) *$\underline{E}_P$ is the point-wise smallest coherent lower prevision that satisfies $\underline{E}_P(f) \geq \underline{P}(f)$ for all $f \in \mathrm{dom}\underline{P}$;*
(iii) *$\underline{P}$ is coherent if and only if $\underline{E}_P(f) = \underline{P}(f)$ for all $f \in \mathrm{dom}\underline{P}$.*

One particular example of coherent lower previsions are the so-called *vacuous* lower previsions. For any subset A of $\mathscr{X}$—also called an event—the vacuous lower prevision relative to A is defined on $\mathscr{G}(\mathscr{X})$ by

$$\underline{P}_A(f) = \inf_{x \in A} f(x) \text{ for all gambles } f \text{ on } \mathscr{X}.$$

This lower prevision is used to model the information that $X \in A$ (and nothing else).

A coherent lower prevision defined on indicators I_A of events A only is called a *coherent lower probability*. To simplify notation, we will sometimes use the same symbol to denote a set A and its indicator function I_A, so we will write $\underline{P}(A)$ instead of $\underline{P}(I_A)$.

Besides coherence, there are other mathematical properties that can be imposed on lower previsions. For instance:

Definition 1. *Let $n \geq 1$. A lower prevision defined on the set $\mathscr{G}(\mathscr{X})$ of all gambles is called n-monotone if for all $p \in \mathbb{N}_0$, $p \leq n$, and all $f, f_1, \ldots, f_p$ in $\mathscr{G}(\mathscr{X})$:*

$$\sum_{I \subseteq \{1,\ldots,p\}} (-1)^{|I|} \underline{P}\left(f \wedge \bigwedge_{i \in I} f_i \right) \geq 0,$$

where $\wedge$ is used to denote the point-wise minimum.

n-monotone lower previsions have been studied in detail in [2,11]. Any n-monotone lower prevision on $\mathscr{G}(\mathscr{X})$ that satisfies $\underline{P}(\mathscr{X}) = 1$ and $\underline{P}(\emptyset) = 0$ is in particular coherent, and it corresponds to the Choquet integral with respect to its (coherent) restriction to events, which is called an *n*-monotone lower probability. A lower prevision that is *n*-monotone for all $n \geq 1$ is called *completely monotone*. Such is for instance the case for the vacuous lower previsions $\underline{P}_A$ considered above.

Another important class of completely monotone lower previsions are the linear previsions.

Definition 2. *A lower prevision P defined on the set $\mathscr{G}(\mathscr{X})$ of all gambles is called a* linear prevision *when it satisfies $P(f+g) = P(f) + P(g)$ for every pair of gambles f, g on $\mathscr{X}$, and moreover $P(f) \geq \inf f$ for every gamble f on $\mathscr{X}$.*

Any linear prevision corresponds to the expectation (Choquet or Dunford integral) with respect to its restriction to events, which is a finitely additive probability.

Linear previsions can be used to characterise avoiding sure loss, coherence and natural extension. Consider, for any lower prevision $\underline{P}$, the set

$$\mathscr{M}(\underline{P}) := \{P \text{ linear prevision}: (\forall f \in \operatorname{dom}\underline{P})P(f) \geq \underline{P}(f)\}$$

of all linear previsions that dominate it on its domain. Then $\underline{P}$ avoids sure loss if and only if $\mathscr{M}(\underline{P}) \neq \emptyset$, and $\underline{P}$ is coherent if and only if

$$\underline{P}(f) = \min\{P(f): P \in \mathscr{M}(\underline{P})\} \text{ for all } f \in \operatorname{dom}\underline{P}. \tag{3}$$

In other words, a coherent lower prevision $\underline{P}$ is always the lower envelope of the set $\mathscr{M}(\underline{P})$ of linear previsions that dominate it. Moreover, if $\underline{P}$ avoids sure loss, then its natural extension $\underline{E}_P$ can be calculated by taking the lower envelope of the set $\mathscr{M}(\underline{P})$:

$$\underline{E}_P(f) = \min\{P(f): P \in \mathscr{M}(\underline{P})\} \text{ for all } f \in \mathscr{G}(\mathscr{X}), \tag{4}$$

and $\mathscr{M}(\underline{P}) = \mathscr{M}(\underline{E}_P)$.

In particular, the vacuous lower prevision on a set A is the lower envelope of the set of linear previsions P satisfying $P(A) = 1$: $\mathscr{M}(\underline{P}_A) = \{P \text{ linear prevision}: P(A) = 1\}$.

Of particular interest in the context of this paper are the coherent lower probabilities that assume only the values 0 and 1 on the set $\mathscr{P}(\mathscr{X})$ of all events: $(\forall A \in \mathscr{P}(\mathscr{X}))\underline{P}(A) \in \{0,1\}$.

Proposition 1. *[12, Section 2.9.8] A lower probability $\underline{P}$ on $\mathscr{P}(\mathscr{X})$ assuming only the values 0 and 1 is coherent if and only if the set $\{A \in \mathscr{P}(\mathscr{X}): \underline{P}(A) = 1\}$ is a proper (set) filter.*

A (set) *filter* on $\mathscr{X}$ is a non-empty collection $\mathscr{F}$ of subsets of $\mathscr{X}$ that is *increasing* (if $A \in \mathscr{F}$ and $A \subseteq B$ then also $B \in \mathscr{F}$) and *closed under finite intersections* (if $A, B \in \mathscr{F}$ then also $A \cap B \in \mathscr{F}$). A *proper* filter does not contain $\emptyset$. The set of all proper filters on $\mathscr{X}$ is denoted by $\mathbb{F}(\mathscr{X})$.

Interestingly, coherent zero-one-valued lower probabilities have a unique coherent extension from events to all gambles (see also Note 4 in [12, Section 3.2.6]):

Proposition 2. *Consider any coherent lower probability $\underline{P}$ on $\mathscr{P}(\mathscr{X})$ assuming only the values 0 and 1, implying that $\mathscr{F} := \{A: \underline{P}(A) = 1\}$ is a proper filter. Then the only coherent extension of $\underline{P}$ to the set $\mathscr{G}(\mathscr{X})$ is the lower prevision $\underline{P}_\mathscr{F}$ given by*

$$\underline{P}_\mathscr{F}(f) := \sup_{F \in \mathscr{F}} \underline{P}_F(f) = \sup_{F \in \mathscr{F}} \inf_{x \in F} f(x) \text{ for all gambles } f \text{ on } \mathscr{X}.$$

The coherent lower previsions $\underline{P}_{\mathscr{F}}$ are completely monotone. In fact, they are the extreme points of the convex set of all completely monotone coherent lower previsions on $\mathscr{G}(\mathscr{X})$ [1, Chapter VII]. It is the essence of Choquet's Theorem [1] that any completely monotone coherent lower prevision is a countably additive convex combination of such $\underline{P}_{\mathscr{F}}$.

We will also consider lower previsions in a conditional context, and consider two random variables X and Y assuming values in $\mathscr{X}$ and $\mathscr{Y}$, respectively. A *conditional lower prevision* $\underline{P}(\cdot|Y)$ on $\mathscr{G}(\mathscr{X} \times \mathscr{Y})$ is a two-place real-valued function, defined on $\mathscr{G}(\mathscr{X} \times \mathscr{Y}) \times \mathscr{Y}$ that to any (f, y) assigns the lower prevision $\underline{P}(f|y)$ of f, conditional on $Y = y$. For fixed f, $\underline{P}(f|Y)$ is a gamble on $\mathscr{Y}$ that assumes the value $\underline{P}(f|y)$ in $y \in \mathscr{Y}$. For fixed $y \in \mathscr{Y}$, $\underline{P}(\cdot|y)$ is a lower prevision on $\mathscr{G}(\mathscr{X} \times \mathscr{Y})$. A basic requirement for a conditional lower prevision is that it should be separately coherent:

Definition 3. *A conditional lower prevision* $\underline{P}(\cdot|Y)$ *on* $\mathscr{G}(\mathscr{X} \times \mathscr{Y})$ *is called* separately coherent *when it satisfies the following conditions, for all gambles* $f, g \in \mathscr{G}(\mathscr{X} \times \mathscr{Y})$, *all real* $\lambda > 0$ *and all* $y \in \mathscr{Y}$:

SC1. $\underline{P}(f|y) \geq \inf_{x \in \mathscr{X}} f(x, y)$,
SC2. $\underline{P}(\lambda f|y) = \lambda \underline{P}(f|y)$,
SC3. $\underline{P}(f + g|y) \geq \underline{P}(f|y) + \underline{P}(g|y)$,

In that case, each $\underline{P}(\cdot|y)$ is a coherent lower prevision on $\mathscr{G}(\mathscr{X} \times \mathscr{Y})$ that is completely determined by its behaviour on $\mathscr{G}(\mathscr{X})$, for $\underline{P}(f|y) = \underline{P}(f(\cdot, y)|y)$ [12, Lemma 6.2.4]. For this reason, we will also say that $\underline{P}(\cdot|Y)$ is a conditional lower prevision on $\mathscr{G}(\mathscr{X})$.

1.2 Motivation

Consider two variables X and Y assuming values in the non-empty (but not necessarily finite) sets $\mathscr{X}$ and $\mathscr{Y}$.

Let us first look at a single-valued map γ between the spaces $\mathscr{Y}$ and $\mathscr{X}$. Given a linear prevision P on $\mathscr{G}(\mathscr{Y})$, such a map induces a linear prevision P_γ on $\mathscr{G}(\mathscr{X})$ by $P_\gamma(A) := P(\gamma^{-1}(A)) = P(\{y \in \mathscr{Y} : \gamma(y) \in A\})$ for all $A \subseteq \mathscr{X}$, or equivalently

$$P_\gamma(f) := P(f \circ \gamma) \text{ for all gambles } f \text{ on } \mathscr{X}, \tag{5}$$

which is a well-known 'change of variables result' for previsions (or expectations). If we have a variable Y, and the variable X is given by $X := \gamma(Y)$, then any gamble $f(X)$ on the value of X can be translated back to a gamble $f(\gamma(Y)) = (f \circ \gamma)(Y)$ on the value of Y, which explains where Eq. (5) comes from: *If the uncertainty about Y is represented by the model P, then the uncertainty about $X = \gamma(Y)$ is represented by P_γ.*

There is another way of motivating the same formula, which lends itself more readily to generalisation. We can interpret the map γ as conditional information: *if we know that $Y = y$, then we know that $X = \gamma(y)$.* This conditional information can be represented by a so-called conditional linear prevision $P(\cdot|Y)$ on $\mathscr{G}(\mathscr{X})$, defined by

$$P(f|y) := f(\gamma(y)) = (f \circ \gamma)(y) \text{ for all gambles } f \text{ on } \mathscr{X}. \tag{6}$$

It states that conditional on $Y = y$, all probability mass for X is located in the single point $\gamma(y)$. Clearly $P(f|Y) = (f \circ \gamma)(Y)$, which allows us to rewrite Eq. (5) as:

$$P_\gamma(f) = P(P(f|Y)) \text{ for all gambles } f \text{ on } \mathscr{X}, \tag{7}$$

which shows that Eq. (5) is actually a special case of the Law of Iterated Expectations, the expectation form of the Law of Total Probability, in classical probability (see, for instance, [3, Theorem 4.7.1]).

Assume now that, more generally, the relation between X and Y is determined as follows. There is a so-called *multi-valued map* $\Gamma\colon \mathscr{Y} \to \mathscr{P}(\mathscr{X})$ that associates with any $y \in \mathscr{Y}$ a non-empty subset $\Gamma(y)$ of $\mathscr{X}$, and *if we know that $Y = y$, then all we know about X is that it can assume any value in $\Gamma(y)$.* There is no immediately obvious way of representing this conditional information using a precise probability model. If we want to remain within the framework of precise probability theory, we must abandon the simple and powerful device of interpreting the multi-valued map Γ as conditional information. But if we work with the theory of coherent lower previsions, as we are doing here, it is still perfectly possible to interpret Γ as conditional information that can be represented by a special conditional *lower* prevision $\underline{P}(\cdot|Y)$ on $\mathscr{G}(\mathscr{X})$, where

$$\underline{P}(f|y) = \underline{P}_{\Gamma(y)}(f) = \inf_{x \in \Gamma(y)} f(x) \text{ for all gambles } f \text{ on } \mathscr{X} \tag{8}$$

is the vacuous lower prevision associated with the event $\Gamma(y)$. Given information about Y in the form of a coherent lower prevision $\underline{P}$ on $\mathscr{G}(\mathscr{Y})$, it follows from Walley's Marginal Extension Theorem (see [12, Section 6.7]) that the corresponding information about X is the lower prevision $\underline{P}_\Gamma$ on $\mathscr{G}(\mathscr{X})$ defined by

$$\underline{P}_\Gamma(f) = \underline{P}(\underline{P}(f|Y)) \text{ for all gambles } f \text{ on } \mathscr{X}, \tag{9}$$

which is an immediate generalisation of Eq. (7). This formula provides a well-justified method for using the conditional information embodied in the multi-valued map Γ to turn the uncertainty model $\underline{P}$ about Y into an uncertainty model $\underline{P}_\Gamma$ about X. This approach has been introduced and explored in great detail by Miranda et al. [8].

What we intend to do here, is take this idea of conditional information one useful step further. To motivate going even further than multi-valued maps, we look at an interesting example, where we assume that the information about the relation between X and Y is the following: *If we know that $Y = y$, then all we know about X is that it lies arbitrarily close to $\gamma(y)$, in the sense that X lies inside any neighbourhood of $\gamma(y)$.* We are assuming that, in order to capture what 'arbitrarily close' means, we have provided $\mathscr{X}$ with a topology $\mathscr{T}$ of open sets. We can model this type of conditional information using the conditional *lower* prevision $\underline{P}(\cdot|Y)$ on $\mathscr{G}(\mathscr{X})$, where

$$\underline{P}(f|y) = \underline{P}_{\mathscr{N}_{\gamma(y)}}(f) = \sup_{N \in \mathscr{N}_{\gamma(y)}} \inf_{x \in N} f(x) \text{ for all gambles } f \text{ on } \mathscr{X} \tag{10}$$

is the smallest coherent lower prevision that gives lower probability one to any element of the *neighbourhood filter* $\mathscr{N}_{\gamma(y)} := \{N \subseteq \mathscr{X} : (\exists O \in \mathscr{T})\gamma(y) \in O \subseteq N\}$ of $\gamma(y)$. Information about Y in the form of a coherent lower prevision $\underline{P}$ on $\mathscr{G}(\mathscr{Y})$ can now be turned into information $\underline{P}(\underline{P}(\cdot|Y))$ about X, via this conditional model, using Eq. (9).

2   Induced Lower Previsions

So, given this motivation, let us try and capture these ideas in an abstract model. All the special cases mentioned above can be captured by considering a so-called *filter map* Φ from $\mathscr{Y}$ to $\mathscr{X}$, i.e. a map $\Phi: \mathscr{Y} \to \mathbb{F}(\mathscr{X})$ that associates a proper filter $\Phi(y)$ with each element y of $\mathscr{Y}$.[1] The simple idea underlying the arguments in the previous section, is that this filter map represents some type of conditional information, and that this information can be represented by a (specific) conditional lower prevision.

Using this filter map Φ, we associate with any gamble f on $\mathscr{X} \times \mathscr{Y}$ a *lower inverse* $f_\circ$ (under Φ), which is the gamble on $\mathscr{Y}$ defined by

$$f_\circ(y) := \underline{P}_{\Phi(y)}(f(\cdot, y)) = \sup_{F \in \Phi(y)} \inf_{x \in F} f(x, y) \text{ for all } y \text{ in } \mathscr{Y}, \tag{11}$$

where $\underline{P}_{\Phi(y)}$ is the coherent lower prevision on $\mathscr{G}(\mathscr{X})$ associated with the filter $\Phi(y)$.

Similarly, we define for any gamble g on $\mathscr{X}$ its *lower inverse* $g_\bullet$ (under Φ) as the gamble on $\mathscr{Y}$ defined by

$$g_\bullet(y) := \underline{P}_{\Phi(y)}(g) = \sup_{F \in \Phi(y)} \inf_{x \in F} g(x) \text{ for all } y \text{ in } \mathscr{Y}. \tag{12}$$

Eqs. (11) and (12) are obviously very closely related to, and inspired by, the expressions (6), (8) and (10). In particular, we find for any $A \subseteq \mathscr{X} \times \mathscr{Y}$ that $(I_A)_\circ = I_{A_\circ}$, where we let

$$A_\circ := \{y \in \mathscr{Y} : (\exists F \in \Phi(y)) F \times \{y\} \subseteq A\}$$

denote the so-called *lower inverse* of A (under Φ). And if $B \subseteq \mathscr{X}$, then

$$(B \times \mathscr{Y})_\circ = B_\bullet := \{y \in \mathscr{Y} : (\exists F \in \Phi(y)) F \subseteq B\},$$

is the set of all y for which B occurs eventually with respect to the filter $\Phi(y)$.

Now consider any lower prevision $\underline{P}$ on $\mathrm{dom}\,\underline{P} \subseteq \mathscr{G}(\mathscr{Y})$ that avoids sure loss. Then we can consider its natural extension $\underline{E}_P$, and use it together with the filter map Φ to construct an *induced lower prevision* $\underline{P}_\circ$ on $\mathscr{G}(\mathscr{X} \times \mathscr{Y})$:

$$\underline{P}_\circ(f) = \underline{E}_P(f_\circ) \text{ for all gambles } f \text{ on } \mathscr{X} \times \mathscr{Y}. \tag{13}$$

The so-called $\mathscr{X}$-marginal $\underline{P}_\bullet$ of this lower prevision is the lower prevision on $\mathscr{G}(\mathscr{X})$ given by

$$\underline{P}_\bullet(g) = \underline{E}_P(g_\bullet) \text{ for all gambles } g \text{ on } \mathscr{X}. \tag{14}$$

Eqs. (13) and (14) are very closely related to, and inspired by, the expressions (5), (7), and (9). Induced lower previsions result if we use the conditional information embodied in a filter map to turn an uncertainty model about Y into an uncertainty model about X.

---

[1] We assume that the filter $\Phi(y)$ is proper [$\emptyset \notin \Phi(y)$] mainly to make things as simple as possible. For details about how to manage without this and similar assumptions, see for instance [8, Technical Remarks 1 and 2].

3   Properties of Induced Lower Previsions

Let us define a *prevision kernel from $\mathscr{Y}$ to $\mathscr{X}$* as any map K from $\mathscr{Y} \times \mathscr{G}(\mathscr{X})$ to $\mathbb{R}$ such that $K(y, \cdot)$ is a linear prevision on $\mathscr{G}(\mathscr{X})$ for all y in $\mathscr{Y}$. Prevision kernels are clear generalisations of probability or Markov kernels [7, p. 20], but without the measurability conditions.

We can extend $K(y, \cdot)$ to a linear prevision on $\mathscr{G}(\mathscr{X} \times \mathscr{Y})$ by letting $K(y, f) = K(y, f(\cdot, y))$ for all gambles f on $\mathscr{X} \times \mathscr{Y}$. For any lower prevision $\underline{P}$ on Y that avoids sure loss, we denote by $\underline{P}K$ the lower prevision on $\mathscr{G}(\mathscr{X} \times \mathscr{Y})$ defined by

$$\underline{P}K(f) = \underline{E}_P(K(\cdot, f)) \text{ for all gambles } f \text{ on } \mathscr{X} \times \mathscr{Y}.$$

If $\underline{P}$ is a linear prevision on $\mathscr{G}(\mathscr{Y})$, then $\underline{P}K$ is a linear prevision on $\mathscr{G}(\mathscr{X} \times \mathscr{Y})$. As an immediate consequence, $\underline{P}K$ is always a coherent lower prevision on $\mathscr{G}(\mathscr{X} \times \mathscr{Y})$, as a lower envelope of linear previsions [see Eq. (3)]. We also use the following notation:

$$\mathscr{K}(\Phi) = \left\{ K \text{ prevision kernel} \colon (\forall y \in \mathscr{Y}) K(y, \cdot) \in \mathscr{M}(\underline{P}_{\Phi(y)}) \right\} \tag{15}$$
$$= \{ K \text{ prevision kernel} \colon (\forall y \in \mathscr{Y})(\forall A \in \Phi(y)) K(y, A) = 1 \}.$$

The next proposition can be seen as a special case of Walley's lower envelope theorem for marginal extension [12, Theorem 6.7.4]. We closely follow his original proof.

Proposition 3. *Let $n \in \mathbb{N}$, the set of natural numbers without zero, and let $\underline{P}$ be a lower prevision that avoids sure loss, and is defined on a subset of $\mathscr{G}(\mathscr{Y})$. Then:*

(i) *$\underline{P}_\circ$ is a coherent lower prevision.*
(ii) *For all $K \in \mathscr{K}(\Phi)$ and $P \in \mathscr{M}(\underline{P})$, $PK \in \mathscr{M}(\underline{P}_\circ)$; and for all gambles f on $\mathscr{X} \times \mathscr{Y}$ there are $K \in \mathscr{K}(\Phi)$ and $P \in \mathscr{M}(\underline{P})$ such that $\underline{P}_\circ(f) = PK(f)$.*
(iii) *If $\underline{E}_P$ is n-monotone, then so is $\underline{P}_\circ$.*

Proof. We begin with the proof of (i). We use coherence condition (1). For arbitrary m in $\mathbb{N}_0$, n in $\mathbb{N}_0$, and gambles $f_0, f_1, \ldots, f_m$ in $\mathscr{G}(\mathscr{X} \times \mathscr{Y})$ we find that

$$\sum_{i=1}^{n} \underline{P}_\circ(f_i) - m\underline{P}_\circ(f_0) = \sum_{i=1}^{n} \underline{E}_P((f_i)_\circ) - m\underline{E}_P((f_0)_\circ)$$
$$\leq \sup_{y \in \mathscr{Y}} \left[\sum_{i=1}^{n} (f_i)_\circ(y) - m(f_0)_\circ(y) \right]$$
$$= \sup_{y \in \mathscr{Y}} \left[\sum_{i=1}^{n} \underline{P}_{\Phi(y)}(f_i(\cdot, y)) - m\underline{P}_{\Phi(y)}(f_0(\cdot, y)) \right]$$
$$\leq \sup_{y \in \mathscr{Y}} \sup_{x \in \mathscr{X}} \left[\sum_{i=1}^{n} f_i(x, y) - m f_0(x, y) \right] = \sup \left[\sum_{i=1}^{n} f_i - m f_0 \right],$$

where the first inequality follows from the coherence of the natural extension $\underline{E}_P$ [Theorem 1(i)], and the second from the coherence of the lower previsions $\underline{P}_{\Phi(y)}, y \in \mathscr{Y}$.

(ii). First, fix any P in $\mathscr{M}(\underline{P})$ and any $K \in \mathscr{K}(\Phi)$. Consider any gamble f on $\mathscr{X} \times \mathscr{Y}$. We infer from Eqs. (15) and (11) that $K(y, f) \geq f_\circ(y)$ for all $y \in \mathscr{Y}$, and therefore

$PK(f) = P(K(\cdot, f)) \geq P(f_\circ) \geq \underline{E}_P(f_\circ) = \underline{P}_\circ(f)$, where the first inequality follows from the coherence [monotonicity] of the linear prevision P, and the second from Eq. (4). This shows that $PK \in \mathcal{M}(\underline{P}_\circ)$.

Next, fix any gamble f on $\mathcal{G}(\mathcal{X} \times \mathcal{Y})$. We infer from Eqs. (15) and (3) and the coherence of the lower previsions $\underline{P}_{\Phi(y)}$, $y \in \mathcal{Y}$ that there is some $K \in \mathcal{K}(\Phi)$ such that $f_\circ = K(\cdot, f)$. Similarly, there is some $P \in \mathcal{M}(\underline{P})$ such that $\underline{E}_P(f_\circ) = P(f_\circ)$, and therefore $\underline{P}_\circ(f) = P(K(\cdot, f)) = PK(f)$.

(iii). For any gambles f and g on $\mathcal{X} \times \mathcal{Y}$, $(f \wedge g)_\circ = f_\circ \wedge g_\circ$, using Eq. (11) for the converse inequality. To see the direct one, use that for any $\varepsilon > 0, y \in Y$ there are $F_1, F_2 \in \Phi(y)$ such that $f_\circ(y) \leq \inf_{x \in F_1} f(x, y) + \varepsilon$ and $g_\circ(y) \leq \inf_{x \in F_2} g(x, y) + \varepsilon$; given $F := F_1 \cap F_2 \in \Phi(y)$, it holds that

$$\inf_{x \in F}(f(x, y) \wedge g(x, y)) = (\inf_{x \in F} f(x, y)) \wedge (\inf_{x \in F} g(x, y)) \geq (f_\circ(y) - \varepsilon) \wedge (g_\circ(y) - \varepsilon),$$

whence $(f \wedge g)_\circ(y) \geq (f_\circ(y) \wedge g_\circ(y)) - \varepsilon$. This tells us that taking the lower inverse constitutes a $\wedge$-homomorphism between $\mathcal{G}(\mathcal{X} \times \mathcal{Y})$ and $\mathcal{G}(\mathcal{Y})$. A $\wedge$-homomorphism preserves n-monotonicity [2, Lemma 6]. □

If we restrict our attention to the $\mathcal{X}$-marginal $\underline{P}_\bullet$ of the lower prevision $\underline{P}_\circ$ on $\mathcal{G}(\mathcal{X} \times \mathcal{Y})$, we can go further: the following simple proposition is a considerable generalisation of a result mentioned by Wasserman [13, Section 2.4]; see also [14, Section 2][2]. The integral in this result is the Choquet integral, see for instance Ref. [6].

Proposition 4. *Let* $n \in \mathbb{N}$ *and let* $\underline{P}$ *be a lower prevision that avoids sure loss, and is defined on a subset of* $\mathcal{G}(\mathcal{Y})$*. If* $\underline{E}_P$ *is* n*-monotone, then so is* $\underline{P}_\bullet$*, and moreover*

$$\underline{P}_\bullet(g) = C \int g \, d\underline{P}_\bullet = C \int g_\bullet \, d\underline{E}_P = \underline{E}_P(g_\bullet) \text{ for all } g \in \mathcal{G}(\mathcal{X}). \qquad (16)$$

Proof. From Proposition 3(iii), $\underline{P}_\bullet$ is n-monotone. To prove Eq. (16), it suffices to prove that the first and last equalities hold, because of Eq. (14). To this end, use that both $\underline{E}_P$ and $\underline{P}_\bullet$ are n-monotone, and apply [11, p. 56]. □

It is also useful to consider the lower prevision $\underline{P}_\circ^r$, defined on the set of gambles

$$_\circ\mathrm{dom}\underline{P} := \{f \in \mathcal{G}(\mathcal{X} \times \mathcal{Y}) : f_\circ \in \mathrm{dom}\underline{P}\}$$

as follows:

$$\underline{P}_\circ^r(f) := \underline{P}(f_\circ) \text{ for all } f \text{ such that } f_\circ \in \mathrm{dom}\underline{P}. \qquad (17)$$

If $\underline{P}$ is coherent, then of course $\underline{P}_\circ^r$ is the restriction of $\underline{P}_\circ$ to $_\circ\mathrm{dom}\underline{P}$, because then $\underline{E}_P$ and $\underline{P}$ coincide on $\mathrm{dom}\underline{P}$ [see Theorem 1(iii)]. Interestingly and perhaps surprisingly, all the 'information' present in $\underline{P}_\circ$ is then already contained in the restricted model $\underline{P}_\circ^r$.

Proposition 5. *Let* $\underline{P}$ *be a coherent lower prevision, with* $\mathrm{dom}\underline{P} \subseteq \mathcal{G}(\mathcal{Y})$*. Then:*

(i) $\underline{P}_\circ^r$ *is the restriction of* $\underline{P}_\circ$ *to the set of gambles* $_\circ\mathrm{dom}\underline{P}$*, and therefore a coherent lower prevision on* $_\circ\mathrm{dom}\underline{P}$*.*

---

[2] Wasserman considers the special case that $\underline{P}$ is a probability measure and that g satisfies appropriate measurability conditions, so the right-most Choquet integral coincides with the usual expectation of $g_\bullet$. See also [9, Theorem 14].

(ii) *The natural extension $\underline{E}_{\underline{P}_o^{pr}}$ of $\underline{P}_o^{pr}$ coincides with the induced lower prevision $\underline{P}_o$:*
$$\underline{E}_{\underline{P}_o^{pr}} = \underline{P}_o.$$

Proof. (i). It follows from Theorem 1(iii) that $\underline{E}_{\underline{P}}$ and $\underline{P}$ coincide on $\mathrm{dom}\,\underline{P}$. For any $f \in {}_o\mathrm{dom}\,\underline{P}$, we have $f_o \in \mathrm{dom}\,\underline{P}$ and therefore $\underline{P}_o(f) = \underline{E}_{\underline{P}}(f_o) = \underline{P}(f_o) = \underline{P}_o^{pr}(f)$, also using Eqs. (13) and (17).

(ii). Since $\underline{P}_o$ is coherent [Proposition 3(i)] and coincides with $\underline{P}_o^{pr}$ on ${}_o\mathrm{dom}\,\underline{P}$, we infer from Theorem 1(ii) that $\underline{E}_{\underline{P}_o^{pr}} \leq \underline{P}_o$. Conversely, consider any gamble f on $\mathscr{X} \times \mathscr{Y}$, then we must show that $\underline{E}_{\underline{P}_o^{pr}}(f) \geq \underline{P}_o(f)$.

Fix $\varepsilon > 0$. By the definition of natural extension [for $\underline{P}$] in Eq. (2), we see that there are n in $\mathbb{N}_0$, non-negative $\lambda_1, \ldots, \lambda_n$ in $\mathbb{R}$, and gambles $g_1, \ldots, g_n$ in $\mathrm{dom}\,\underline{P}$ such that

$$f_o(y) - \underline{P}_o(f) + \frac{\varepsilon}{2} \geq \sum_{k=1}^{n} \lambda_k[g_k(y) - \underline{P}(g_k)] \text{ for all } y \in \mathscr{Y}. \tag{18}$$

For each $y \in \mathscr{Y}$, there is some set $F(y) \in \Phi(y)$ such that $\inf_{x \in F(y)} f(x,y) \geq f_o(y) - \frac{\varepsilon}{2}$. Now define the corresponding gambles h_k on $\mathscr{X} \times \mathscr{Y}$, $k = 1, \ldots, n$ by

$$h_k(x,y) = \begin{cases} g_k(y) & \text{if } y \in \mathscr{Y} \text{ and } x \in F(y) \\ L & \text{if } y \in \mathscr{Y} \text{ and } x \notin F(y), \end{cases}$$

where L is some real number strictly smaller than $\min_{k=1}^{n} \inf g_k$, to be fixed shortly. Then

$$(h_k)_o(y) = \sup_{F \in \Phi(y)} \inf_{x \in F} h_k(x,y) = \sup_{F \in \Phi(y)} \inf_{x \in F} \begin{cases} g_k(y) & \text{if } x \in F(y) \\ L & \text{otherwise} \end{cases}$$

$$= \sup_{F \in \Phi(y)} \begin{cases} g_k(y) & \text{if } F \subseteq F(y) \\ L & \text{otherwise} \end{cases} = g_k(y),$$

for any $y \in \mathscr{Y}$, so $(h_k)_o = g_k \in \mathrm{dom}\,\underline{P}$ and therefore $h_k \in {}_o\mathrm{dom}\,\underline{P}$ and $\underline{P}_o^{pr}(h_k) = \underline{P}(g_k)$. This, together with Eq. (18), allows us to infer that

$$f(x,y) - \underline{P}_o(f) + \varepsilon \geq \sum_{k=1}^{n} \lambda_k[h_k(x,y) - \underline{P}_o^{pr}(h_k)] \text{ for all } y \in \mathscr{Y} \text{ and } x \in F(y).$$

Moreover, by an appropriate choice of L [small enough], we can always make sure that the inequality above holds for *all* $(x,y) \in \mathscr{X} \times \mathscr{Y}$ (note that once L is strictly smaller than $\min_{k=1}^{n} \inf g_k$ decreasing it does not affect $\underline{P}_o^{pr}(h_k) = \underline{P}(g_k)$); then the definition of natural extension [for $\underline{P}_o^{pr}$] in Eq. (2) guarantees that $\underline{E}_{\underline{P}_o^{pr}}(f) \geq \underline{P}_o(f) - \varepsilon$. Since this inequality holds for any $\varepsilon > 0$, the proof is complete. $\square$

4 Conclusion

A multi-valued map $\Gamma \colon \mathscr{Y} \to \mathscr{P}(\mathscr{X})$—associating a non-empty subset $\Gamma(y)$ of $\mathscr{X}$ with any $y \in \mathscr{Y}$—allows us to define a filter map $\Phi \colon \mathscr{Y} \to \mathbb{F}(\mathscr{X})$ as follows:

$$\Phi(y) := \{B \subseteq \mathscr{X} : \Gamma(y) \subseteq B\} \text{ for all } y \in \mathscr{Y}.$$

Lower inverses and induced lower previsions for this specific type of filter map were discussed by Walley [12, Section 4.3.5], and studied in detail by Miranda et al. [8]: Section 3 extends their results to general filter maps. The credit for taking the first steps in this domain, and for associating lower and upper probabilities and previsions—or expectations—induced using multi-valued mappings is commonly given to Dempster [4,5]. But, as Carl Wagner has pointed out to us in private communication, important work by Straßen [10] predates Dempster's by three years, was published in a well-known and widely read journal, and has many of the relevant notions and results. To give an example, Proposition 3(ii) in the marginal extension form was already present in Straßen's paper: his result holds for finite (or compact $\mathscr{X}$), multi-valued maps Φ, and linear previsions P. In those cases he goes even further than we do, because he proves equality of the sets $\mathscr{M}(P_\circ)$ and $\{PK\colon K \in \mathscr{K}(\Phi)\}$.

Acknowledgements. The research in this paper has been supported by IWT SBO project 60043 and FWO project G.0125.12 (De Cooman), and by project MTM2010-17844 (Miranda).

References

1. Choquet, G.: Theory of capacities. Annales de l'Institut Fourier 5, 131–295 (1953-1954)
2. De Cooman, G., Troffaes, M.C.M., Miranda, E.: n-Monotone exact functionals. Journal of Mathematical Analysis and Applications 347, 143–156 (2008)
3. De Groot, M.H., Schervisch, M.J.: Probability and Statistics, 4th edn. Pearson (2011)
4. Dempster, A.P.: Upper and lower probabilities generated by a random closed interval. Annals of Mathematical Statistics 39, 957–966 (1967)
5. Dempster, A.P.: Upper and lower probabilities induced by a multivalued mapping. Ann. Math. Statist. 38, 325–339 (1967)
6. Denneberg, D.: Non-additive Measure and Integral. Kluwer, Dordrecht (1994)
7. Kallenberg, O.: Foundations of Modern Probability, 2nd edn. Probability and Its Applications. Springer (2002)
8. Miranda, E., De Cooman, G., Couso, I.: Lower previsions induced by multi-valued mappings. Journal of Statistical Planning and Inference 133(1), 177–197 (2005)
9. Miranda, E., Couso, I., Gil, P.: Approximation of upper and lower probabilities by measurable selections. Information Sciences 180(8), 1407–1417 (2010)
10. Straßen, V.: Meßfehler und Information. Zeitschrift für Wahrscheinlichkeitstheorie und Verwandte Gebiete 2, 273–305 (1964)
11. Walley, P.: Coherent lower (and upper) probabilities. Statistics Research Report 22. University of Warwick, Coventry (1981)
12. Walley, P.: Statistical Reasoning with Imprecise Probabilities. Chapman and Hall, London (1991)
13. Wasserman, L.A.: Belief functions and statistical inference. The Canadian Journal of Statistics / La Revue Canadienne de Statistique 18(3), 183–196 (1990)
14. Wasserman, L.A.: Prior envelopes based on belief functions. Annals of Statistics 18(1), 454–464 (1990)

Conditioning in Evidence Theory from the Perspective of Multidimensional Models

Jiřina Vejnarová*

Institute of Information Theory and Automation of the AS CR,
Pod Vodárenskou věží 4, 182 08 Prague, Czech Republic
vejnar@utia.cas.cz

Abstract. Conditioning belongs to the most important topics of any theory dealing with uncertainty. From the viewpoint of construction of Bayesian-network-like multidimensional models it seems to be inevitable. In evidence theory, in contrary to the probabilistic framework, various rules were proposed to define conditional beliefs and/or plausibilities (or basic assignments) from joint ones. Two of them — Dempster's conditioning rule and focusing (more precisely their versions for variables) — have recently been studied in connection with the relationship between conditional independence and irrelevance and it has been shown, that for none of them conditional irrelevance is implied by conditional independence, which seems to be extremely inconvenient. Therefore we suggest a new conditioning rule for variables, which seems to be more promising from the viewpoint of conditional irrelevance, prove its correctness and also study the relationship between conditional independence and irrelevance based on this conditioning rule.

Keywords: Evidence theory, conditioning, multidimensional models, conditional independence, conditional irrelevance.

1 Introduction

The most widely used models managing uncertainty and multidimensionality are, at present, so-called *probabilistic graphical Markov models*. The problem of multidimensionality is solved in these models with the help of the notion of conditional independence, which enables factorization of a multidimensional probability distribution into small parts (marginals, conditionals or just factors).

It is easy to realize that if we need efficient methods for representation of probability distributions (requiring an exponential number of parameters), so much greater is the need of an efficient tool for representation of belief functions, which cannot be represented by a distribution (but only by a set function), and therefore the space requirements for its representation are superexponential. To solve this problem many conditional independence concepts have been proposed [3,8,11].

* The support of Grant GAČR P402/11/0378 is gratefully acknowledged.

S. Greco et al. (Eds.): IPMU 2012, Part III, CCIS 299, pp. 450–459, 2012.

However, another problem appears when one tries to construct an evidential counterpart of Bayesian network: problem of conditioning, which is not sufficiently solved in evidence theory. There exist many conditioning rules [6], but is any of them compatible with our [8] conditional independence concept? In [16] we dealt with two conditioning rules and studied the relationship between conditional irrelevance based on them and our notion of conditional independence [8], but the results were not satisfactory. Therefore, in this paper we propose a new conditioning rule which seems to be more promising.

The contribution is organized as follows. After a short overview of necessary terminology and notation (Section 2), in Section 3 we recall two conditioning rules and introduce the new one. In Section 4 the above-mentioned concept of conditional independence is recalled, a new concept of conditional irrelevance is presented and the relationship between conditional independence and conditional irrelevance is studied.

2 Basic Concepts

In this section we briefly recall basic concepts from evidence theory [12] concerning sets and set functions.

2.1 Set Projections and Extensions

For an index set $N = \{1, 2, \ldots, n\}$ let $\{X_i\}_{i \in N}$ be a system of variables, each X_i having its values in a finite set $\mathbf{X}_i$. In this paper we will deal with a *multidimensional frame of discernment*

$$\mathbf{X}_N = \mathbf{X}_1 \times \mathbf{X}_2 \times \ldots \times \mathbf{X}_n,$$

and its *subframes* (for $K \subseteq N$) $\mathbf{X}_K = \times_{i \in K} \mathbf{X}_i$.

When dealing with groups of variables on these subframes, X_K will denote a group of variables $\{X_i\}_{i \in K}$ throughout the paper.

A *projection* of $x = (x_1, x_2, \ldots, x_n) \in \mathbf{X}_N$ into $\mathbf{X}_K$ will be denoted $x^{\downarrow K}$, i.e. for $K = \{i_1, i_2, \ldots, i_k\}$

$$x^{\downarrow K} = (x_{i_1}, x_{i_2}, \ldots, x_{i_k}) \in \mathbf{X}_K.$$

Analogously, for $M \subset K \subseteq N$ and $A \subset \mathbf{X}_K$, $A^{\downarrow M}$ will denote a *projection* of A into $\mathbf{X}_M$:[1]

$$A^{\downarrow M} = \{y \in \mathbf{X}_M \mid \exists x \in A : y = x^{\downarrow M}\}.$$

In addition to the projection, in this text we will also need an inverse operation usually called cylindrical extension. The *cylindrical extension* of $A \subset \mathbf{X}_K$ to $\mathbf{X}_L$ ($K \subset L$) is the set

$$A^{\uparrow L} = \{x \in \mathbf{X}_L : x^{\downarrow K} \in A\}.$$

Clearly, $A^{\uparrow L} = A \times \mathbf{X}_{L \setminus K}$.

---

[1] Let us remark that we do not exclude situations where $M = \emptyset$. In this case $A^{\downarrow \emptyset} = \emptyset$.

A more complicated case is to make common extension of two sets, which will be called a join. By a *join*[2] of two sets $A \subseteq \mathbf{X}_K$ and $B \subseteq \mathbf{X}_L$ $(K, L \subseteq N)$ we will understand a set

$$A \bowtie B = \{x \in \mathbf{X}_{K \cup L} : x^{\downarrow K} \in A \ \& \ x^{\downarrow L} \in B\}.$$

Let us note that for any $C \subseteq \mathbf{X}_{K \cup L}$ naturally $C \subseteq C^{\downarrow K} \bowtie C^{\downarrow L}$, but generally $C \neq C^{\downarrow K} \bowtie C^{\downarrow L}$.

Let us also note that if K and L are disjoint, then the join of A and B is just their Cartesian product $A \bowtie B = A \times B$, if $K = L$ then $A \bowtie B = A \cap B$. If $K \cap L \neq \emptyset$ and $A^{\downarrow K \cap L} \cap B^{\downarrow K \cap L} = \emptyset$ then also $A \bowtie B = \emptyset$. Generally,

$$A \bowtie B = (A \times \mathbf{X}_{L \setminus K}) \cap (B \times \mathbf{X}_{K \setminus L}),$$

i.e. a join of two sets is the intersection of their cylindrical extensions.

2.2   Set Functions

In evidence theory [12] (or Dempster-Shafer theory) two dual measures are used to model uncertainty: belief and plausibility measures. Both of them can be defined with the help of another set function called a *basic (probability or belief) assignment* m on $\mathbf{X}_N$, i.e.,

$$m : \mathcal{P}(\mathbf{X}_N) \longrightarrow [0, 1],$$

where $\mathcal{P}(\mathbf{X}_N)$ is power set of $\mathbf{X}_N$ and $\sum_{A \subseteq \mathbf{X}_N} m(A) = 1$. Furthermore, we assume that $m(\emptyset) = 0$.

A set $A \in \mathcal{P}(\mathbf{X}_N)$ is a *focal element* if $m(A) > 0$. Let $\mathcal{F}$ denote the set of all focal elements, a focal element $A \in \mathcal{F}$ is called an $m-atom$ if for any $B \subseteq A$ either $B = A$ or $B \notin \mathcal{F}$. In other words, an $m-$ atom is a setwise-minimal focal element.

Belief and *plausibility measures* are defined for any $A \subseteq \mathbf{X}_N$ by the equalities

$$Bel(A) = \sum_{B \subseteq A} m(B), \qquad Pl(A) = \sum_{B \cap A \neq \emptyset} m(B),$$

respectively.

For a basic assignment m on $\mathbf{X}_K$ and $M \subset K$, a *marginal basic assignment* of m on $\mathbf{X}_M$ is defined (for each $A \subseteq \mathbf{X}_M$) by the equality

$$m^{\downarrow M}(A) = \sum_{\substack{B \subseteq \mathbf{X}_K \\ B \downarrow M = A}} m(B). \tag{1}$$

Analogously we will denote by $Bel^{\downarrow M}$ and $Pl^{\downarrow M}$ marginal belief and plausibility measures on $\mathbf{X}_M$, respectively.

---

[2] This term and notation are taken from the theory of relational databases [1].

3   Conditioning

Conditioning belongs to the most important topics of any theory dealing with uncertainty. From the viewpoint of the construction of Bayesian-network-like multidimensional models it seems to be inevitable.

3.1   Conditioning of Events

In evidence theory the "classical" conditioning rule is the so-called *Dempster's rule of conditioning* defined for any $\emptyset \neq A \subseteq \mathbf{X}_N$ and $B \subseteq \mathbf{X}_N$ such that $Pl(B) > 0$ by the formula

$$m(A|_D B) = \frac{\displaystyle\sum_{C \subseteq \mathbf{X}_N : C \cap B = A} m(C)}{Pl(B)}$$

and $m(\emptyset|_D B) = 0$.

From this formula one can immediately obtain:

$$Bel(A|_D B) = \frac{Bel(A \cup B^C) - Bel(B^C)}{1 - Bel(B^C)},$$

$$Pl(A|_D B) = \frac{Pl(A \cap B)}{Pl(B)}. \tag{2}$$

This is not the only possibility how to perform conditioning, another — in a way symmetric — conditioning rule is the following one called *focusing* defined for any $\emptyset \neq A \subseteq \mathbf{X}_N$ and $B \subseteq \mathbf{X}_N$ such that $Bel(B) > 0$ by the formula

$$m(A|_F B) = \begin{cases} \dfrac{m(A)}{Bel(B)} & \text{if } A \subseteq B, \\ 0 & \text{otherwise.} \end{cases}$$

From the following two equalities one can see, in which sense are these two conditioning rules symmetric:

$$Bel(A|_F B) = \frac{Bel(A \cap B)}{Bel(B)}, \tag{3}$$

$$Pl(A|_F B) = \frac{Pl(A \cup B^C) - Pl(B^C)}{1 - Pl(B^C)}.$$

Formulae (2) and (3) are, in a way, evidential counterparts of conditioning in probabilistic framework. Let us note that the seemingly "natural" way of conditioning

$$m(A|_P B) = \frac{m(A \cap B)}{m(B)} \tag{4}$$

is not possible, since $m(A|_P B)$ need not be a basic assignment. It is caused by a simple fact that m, in contrary to Bel and Pl is not monotonous with respect to set inclusion. A simple counterexample can be found in [16].

Nevertheless, in Bayesian-networks-like multidimensional models we need conditional basic assignments (or beliefs or plausibilities) for variables. This problem will be in the center of our attention in the next subsection.

3.2 Conditional Variables

In [16] we presented the following two definitions of conditioning by variables, based on Dempster conditioning rule and focusing.

Let X_K and X_L ($K \cap L = \emptyset$) be two groups of variables with values in $\mathbf{X}_K$ and $\mathbf{X}_L$, respectively. Then the *conditional basic assignment according to Dempster's conditioning rule* of X_K given $X_L \in B \subseteq \mathbf{X}_L$ (for B such that $Pl^{\downarrow L}(B) > 0$) is defined as follows:

$$m_{X_K|_D X_L}(A|_D B) = \frac{\displaystyle\sum_{C \subseteq \mathbf{X}_{K \cup L}:(C \cap B^{\uparrow K \cup L})^{\downarrow K}=A} m(C)}{Pl^{\downarrow L}(B)}$$

for $A \neq \emptyset$ and $m_{K|L}(\emptyset|B) = 0$. Similarly, the *conditional basic assignment according to focusing* of X_K given $X_L \in B \subseteq \mathbf{X}_L$ (for B such that $Bel^{\downarrow L}(B) > 0$) is defined by the equality

$$m_{X_K|_F X_L}(A|_F B) = \frac{\displaystyle\sum_{C \subseteq \mathbf{X}_{K \cup L}:C \subseteq B^{\uparrow K \cup L} \& C^{\downarrow K}=A} m(C)}{Bel^{\downarrow L}(B)}$$

for any $A \neq \emptyset$ and $m_{K|_F L}(\emptyset|_F B) = 0$.

In the above-mentioned paper we proved that these definitions are correct, i.e. these rules define (generally different) basic assignments. Nevertheless, their usefulness for multidimensional models is rather questionable, as we shall see in Section 4.3.

Therefore, in this paper we propose a new conditioning rule which is, in a way, a generalization of (4). Although we said above, that it makes little sense for conditioning events, it is sensible in conditioning of variables, as expressed by Theorem 1 below. The above-mentioned problem of non-monotonicity is avoided, because a marginal basic assignment is always greater (or equal) to the joint one.

Definition 1. *Let X_K and X_L ($K \cap L = \emptyset$) be two groups of variables with values in $\mathbf{X}_K$ and $\mathbf{X}_L$, respectively. Then the conditional basic assignment of X_K given $X_L \in B \subseteq \mathbf{X}_L$ (for B such that $m^{\downarrow L}(B) > 0$) is defined as follows:*

$$m_{X_K|_P X_L}(A|_P B) = \frac{\displaystyle\sum_{\substack{C \subseteq \mathbf{X}_{K \cup L}: \\ C^{\downarrow K}=A \& C^{\downarrow L}=B}} m(C)}{m^{\downarrow L}(B)} \tag{5}$$

for any $A \subseteq \mathbf{X}_K$.

Now, let us prove that this definition is makes sense.

Theorem 1. *The set function $m_{X_K|_P X_L}$ defined for any fixed $B \subseteq \mathbf{X}_L$, such that $m^{\downarrow L}(B) > 0$ by Definition 1 is a basic assignment on $\mathbf{X}_K$.*

Proof. Let $B \subseteq \mathbf{X}_L$ be such that $m^{\downarrow L}(B) > 0$. As nonnegativity of $m_{X_K|_P X_L}(A|_P B)$ for any $A \subseteq \mathbf{X}_K$ and the fact that $m_{X_K|_P X_L}(\emptyset|_P B) = 0$ follow directly from the definition, to prove that $m_{X_K|_P X_L}$ is a basic assignment it is enough to show that

$$\sum_{A \subseteq \mathbf{X}_K} m_{X_K|_P X_L}(A|_P B) = 1.$$

To check it, let us sum the values of the numerator in (5)

$$\sum_{A \subseteq \mathbf{X}_K} \sum_{\substack{C \subseteq \mathbf{X}_{K \cup L}: \\ C^{\downarrow K}=A \, \& \, C^{\downarrow L}=B}} m(C) = \sum_{\substack{C \subseteq \mathbf{X}_{K \cup L} \\ C^{\downarrow L}=B}} m(C)$$

$$= m^{\downarrow L}(B),$$

where the last equality follows directly from (1). $\qquad\Box$

4   Conditional Independence and Irrelevance

Independence and irrelevance need not be (and usually are not) distinguished in the probabilistic framework, as they are almost equivalent to each other. Similarly, in possibilistic framework adopting De Cooman's measure-theoretical approach [7] (particularly his notion of almost everywhere equality) we proved that the analogous concepts are equivalent (for more details see [13]).

4.1   Independence

In evidence theory the most common notion of independence is that of random set independence [5].[3] It has already been proven [14,15] that it is also the only sensible one, as e.g. application of strong independence to two bodies of evidence may generally lead to a model which is beyond the framework of evidence theory.

Definition 2. Let m be a basic assignment on $\mathbf{X}_N$ and $K, L \subset N$ be disjoint. We say that groups of variables X_K and X_L are *independent with respect to a basic assignment* m (in notation $K \perp\!\!\!\perp L \, [m]$) if

$$m^{\downarrow K \cup L}(A) = m^{\downarrow K}(A^{\downarrow K}) \cdot m^{\downarrow L}(A^{\downarrow L})$$

for all $A \subseteq \mathbf{X}_{K \cup L}$ for which $A = A^{\downarrow K} \times A^{\downarrow L}$, and $m(A) = 0$ otherwise.

This notion can be generalized in various ways [3,11,15]; the concept of conditional non-interactivity from [3], based on conjunction combination rule, is used for construction of directed evidential networks in [4]. In this paper we will use

---

[3] Klir [9] calls it *non-interactivity*.

the concept introduced in [8,15], as we consider it more suitable: in contrary to other conditional independence concepts [3,11] it is *consistent with marginalization*, in other words, the multidimensional model of conditionally independent variables keeps the original marginals (for more details see [15]).

Definition 3. Let m be a basic assignment on $\mathbf{X}_N$ and $K, L, M \subset N$ be disjoint, $K \neq \emptyset \neq L$. We say that groups of variables X_K and X_L are *conditionally independent given X_M with respect to m* (and denote it by $K \perp\!\!\!\perp L | M \; [m]$), if the equality

$$m^{\downarrow K \cup L \cup M}(A) \cdot m^{\downarrow M}(A^{\downarrow M}) = m^{\downarrow K \cup M}(A^{\downarrow K \cup M}) \cdot m^{\downarrow L \cup M}(A^{\downarrow L \cup M})$$

holds for any $A \subseteq \mathbf{X}_{K \cup L \cup M}$ such that $A = A^{\downarrow K \cup M} \bowtie A^{\downarrow L \cup M}$, and $m(A) = 0$ otherwise.

It has been proven in [15] that this conditional independence concept satisfies so-called the semi-graphoid properties taken as reasonable to be valid for any conditional independence concept (see e.g. [10]) and it has been shown in which sense this conditional independence concept is superior to previously introduced ones [3,11].

4.2   Irrelevance

Irrelevance is usually considered to be a weaker notion than independence (see e.g. [5]). It expresses the fact that a new piece of evidence concerning one variable cannot influence the evidence concerning the other variable, in other words is irrelevant to it.

More formally: a group of variables X_L is *irrelevant* to X_K ($K \cap L = \emptyset$) if for any $B \subseteq \mathbf{X}_L$ such that $Pl^{\downarrow L}(B) > 0$ (or $Bel^{\downarrow L}(B) > 0$ or $m^{\downarrow L}(B) > 0$)

$$m_{X_K | X_L}(A|B) = m(A) \tag{6}$$

for any $A \subseteq \mathbf{X}_K$.[4]

It follows from the definition of irrelevance that it need not be a symmetric relation. Its symmetrized version is sometimes taken as a definition of independence. Let us note, that in the framework of evidence theory neither irrelevance based on Dempster conditioning rule nor that based on focusing even in cases when the relation is symmetric, imply independence, as can be seen from examples in [16].

Generalization of this notion to conditional irrelevance may be done as follows. A group of variables X_L is *conditionally irrelevant* to X_K given X_M (K, L, M disjoint, $K \neq \emptyset \neq L$) if

$$m_{X_K | X_L X_M}(A|B) = m_{X_K | X_M}(A|B^{\downarrow M}) \tag{7}$$

is satisfied for any $A \subseteq \mathbf{X}_K$ and $B \subseteq \mathbf{X}_{L \cup M}$.

---

[4] Let us note that somewhat weaker definition of irrelevance one can found in [2], where equality is substituted by proportionality. This notion has been later generalized using conjunctive combination rule [3].

Let us note that the conditioning in equalities (6) and (7) stands for an abstract conditioning rule (any of those mentioned in the previous section or some other [6]). Nevertheless, the validity of (6) and (7) may depend on the choice of the conditioning rule, as we showed in [16] — more precisely irrelevance with respect to one conditioning rule need not imply irrelevance with respect to the other.

4.3 Relationship between Independence and Irrelevance

As mentioned at the end of preceding section, different conditioning rules lead to different irrelevance concepts. Nevertheless, when studying the relationship between (conditional) independence and irrelevance based on Dempster conditioning rule and focusing we realized that they do not differ too much from each other, as suggested by the following summary.

For both conditioning rules:

- Irrelevance is implied by independence.
- Irrelevance does not imply independence.
- Irrelevance is not symmetric, in general.
- Even in case of symmetry it does not imply independence.
- Conditional independence does not imply conditional irrelevance.

The only difference between these conditioning rules is expressed by the following theorem proven in [16]

Theorem 2. *Let X_K and X_L be conditionally independent groups of variables given X_M under joint basic assignment m on $\mathbf{X}_{K \cup L \cup M}$ (K, L, M disjoint, $K \neq \emptyset \neq L$). Then*

$$m_{X_K | _F X_L X_M}(A|_F B) = m_{X_K | _F X_M}(A|_F B^{\downarrow M}) \tag{8}$$

for any $m^{\downarrow L \cup M}$-atom $B \subseteq \mathbf{X}_{L \cup M}$ such that $B^{\downarrow M}$ is $m^{\downarrow M}$-atom and $A \subseteq \mathbf{X}_K$.

From this point of view focusing seems to be slightly superior to Dempster conditioning rule, but still it is not satisfactory.

Now, let us make an analogous investigation for irrelevance based on the new conditioning rule introduced by Definition 1.

Theorem 3. *Let K, LM be disjoint subsets of N such that $K, L \neq \emptyset$. It X_K and X_L are independent given X_M (with respect to a joint basic assignment m defined on $X_{K \cup L \cup M}$), then X_L is irrelevant to X_K given X_M under the conditioning rule given by Definition 1.*

Proof. Let X_K and X_L be conditionally independent given X_M then for any $A \subseteq \mathbf{X}_{K \cup L \cup M}$ such that $A = A^{\downarrow K \cup M} \bowtie A^{\downarrow L \cup M}$

$$m(A) \cdot m^{\downarrow M}(A^{\downarrow M}) = m^{\downarrow K \cup M}(A^{\downarrow K \cup M}) \cdot m^{\downarrow L \cup M}(A^{\downarrow L \cup M})$$

and $m(A) = 0$ otherwise. From this equality we immediately obtain that for all A such that $m^{\downarrow L}(A^{\downarrow L \cup M}) > 0$ (it implies that also $m^{\downarrow M}(A^{\downarrow M}) > 0$) equality

$$\frac{m(A)}{m^{\downarrow L \cup M}(A^{\downarrow L \cup M})} = \frac{m^{\downarrow K \cup M}(A^{\downarrow K \cup M})}{m^{\downarrow M}(A^{\downarrow M})}$$

is satisfied. Let us note that the left-hand side of the equality is equal to $m_{X_K | X_{L \cup M}}(A^{\downarrow K} | A^{\downarrow L \cup M})$, while the right-hand side equals $m_{X_K | X_M}(A^{\downarrow K} | A^{\downarrow L})$, which means, that X_L is irrelevant to X_K.   □

The reverse implication is not valid, as can be seen from the next example.

Example 1. Let X_1 and X_2 be two binary variables (with values in $\mathbf{X}_i = \{a_i, \bar{a}_i\}$) with joint basic assignment m defined as follows:

$$m(\{(a_1, a_2)\}) = \frac{1}{4},$$

$$m(\{a_1\} \times \mathbf{X}_2) = \frac{1}{4},$$

$$m(\mathbf{X}_1 \times \{a_2\}) = \frac{1}{4},$$

$$m(\mathbf{X}_1 \times \mathbf{X}_2 \setminus \{(\bar{a}_1, \bar{a}_2)\}) = \frac{1}{4}.$$

From these values one can obtain

$$m^{\downarrow 2}(\{a_2\}) = m^{\downarrow 2}(\mathbf{X}_2) = \frac{1}{2}.$$

Evidently, it is not possible to condition by $\{\bar{a}_2\}$ and we have to confine ourselves to conditioning by $\{a_2\}$:

$$m_{X_1 | _P X_2}(\{a_1\} | _P \{a_2\}) = \tfrac{1}{2} = m^{\downarrow 1}(\{a_1\}),$$
$$m_{X_1 | _P X_2}(\{\bar{a}_1\} | _P \{a_2\}) = 0 = m^{\downarrow 1}(\{\bar{a}_1\}),$$
$$m_{X_1 | _P X_2}(\mathbf{X}_1 | _P \{a_2\}) = \tfrac{1}{2} = m^{\downarrow 1}(\mathbf{X}_1),$$

i.e. X_2 is irrelevant to X_1,[5] but X_1 and X_2 are not independent, as the focal element $\mathbf{X}_1 \times \mathbf{X}_2 \setminus \{(\bar{a}_1, \bar{a}_2)\}$ is not a rectangle.   ◇

Theorem 3 and Example 1 express the expected property: conditional independence is stronger than conditional irrelevance. Nevertheless, it is evident from the example, that irrelevance (with respect to this conditioning rule) does not imply independence even in case of symmetry.

5   Conclusions

We introduced a new conditioning rule for variables in evidence theory, proved its correctness and showed that conditional irrelevance based on this conditioning rule is implied by recently introduced conditional independence. From this

---

[5] Since we can interchange X_1 and X_2, it is evident that also X_1 is irrelevant to X_2.

viewpoint, it is superior to previously suggested conditioning rules. It will enable us to decompose multidimensional models in evidential framework into conditional basic assignments in a way analogous to Bayesian networks in probabilistic framework.

References

1. Beeri, C., Fagin, R., Maier, D., Yannakakis, M.: On the desirability of acyclic database schemes. J. of the Association for Computing Machinery 30, 479–513 (1983)
2. Ben Yaghlane, B., Smets, P., Mellouli, K.: Belief functions independence: The marginal case. Int. J. Approx. Reasoning 29, 47–70 (2002)
3. Ben Yaghlane, B., Smets, P., Mellouli, K.: Belief functions independence: II. the conditional case. Int. J. Approx. Reasoning 31, 31–75 (2002)
4. Yaghlane, B.B., Smets, P., Mellouli, K.: Directed Evidential Networks with Conditional Belief Functions. In: Nielsen, T.D., Zhang, N.L. (eds.) ECSQARU 2003. LNCS (LNAI), vol. 2711, pp. 291–305. Springer, Heidelberg (2003)
5. Couso, I., Moral, S., Walley, P.: Examples of independence for imprecise probabilities. In: de Cooman, G., Cozman, F.G., Moral, S., Walley, P. (eds.) Proceedings of ISIPTA 1999, pp. 121–130 (1999)
6. Daniel, M.: Belief conditioning rules for classic belief functions. In: Kroupa, T., Vejnarová, J. (eds.) Proceedings of WUPES 2009, pp. 46–56 (2009)
7. De Cooman, G.: Possibility theory I – III. Int. J. General Systems 25, 291–371 (1997)
8. Jiroušek, R., Vejnarová, J.: Compositional models and conditional independence in Evidence Theory. Int. J. Approx. Reasoning 52, 316–334 (2011)
9. Klir, G.J.: Uncertainty and Information. Foundations of Generalized Information Theory. Wiley, Hoboken (2006)
10. Lauritzen, S.L.: Graphical Models. Oxford University Press (1996)
11. Shenoy, P.P.: Conditional independence in valuation-based systems. Int. J. Approx. Reasoning 10, 203–234 (1994)
12. Shafer, G.: A Mathematical Theory of Evidence. Princeton University Press, Princeton (1976)
13. Vejnarová, J.: Conditional independence relations in possibility theory. Int. J. Uncertainty, Fuzziness and Knowledge-Based Systems 8, 253–269 (2000)
14. Vejnarová, J.: On two notions of independence in evidence. In: Itoh, T., Shirouha, A. (eds.) Proceedings of 11th Czech-Japan Seminar on Data Analysis and Decision Making under Uncertainty, Sendai University, pp. 69–74 (2008)
15. Vejnarová, J.: On conditional independence in evidence theory. In: Augustin, T., Coolen, F.P.A., Moral, S., Troffaes, M.C.M. (eds.) Proceedings of ISIPTA 2009, Durham, UK, pp. 431–440 (2009)
16. Vejnarová, J.: Conditioning, conditional independence and irrelevance in evidence theory. In: Coolen, F., de Cooman, G., Fetz, T. (eds.) Proceedings of ISIPTA 2011, Innsbruck, Austria, pp. 381–390 (2011)

A New Method for Learning
Imprecise Hidden Markov Models

Arthur Van Camp and Gert de Cooman

Ghent University, SYSTeMS Research Group
Technologiepark–Zwijnaarde 914, 9052 Zwijnaarde, Belgium
{arthur.vancamp,gert.decooman}@UGent.be

Abstract. We present a method for learning imprecise local uncertainty models in stationary hidden Markov models. If there is enough data to justify precise local uncertainty models, then existing learning algorithms, such as the Baum–Welch algorithm, can be used. When there is not enough evidence to justify precise models, the method we suggest here has a number of interesting features.

Keywords: Hidden Markov model, learning, expected counts, imprecise Dirichlet model.

1 Introduction

In practical applications of reasoning with hidden Markov models, or HMMs, an important problem is the assessment of the local uncertainty models. In many applications, the amount of data available for learning the local models is limited. This may be due to the costs of data acquisition, lack of expert knowledge, time limitations, and so on [4,9]. In this case, we believe using precise(-probabilistic) local uncertainty models is hard to justify. This leads us to use imprecise(-probabilistic) local uncertainty models, turning the HMM into an imprecise hidden Markov model (iHMM).

Convenient imprecise probability models are coherent lower previsions, see [6] for a detailed exposition. In this paper we develop a method for learning imprecise local models, in the form of coherent lower previsions, in iHMMs.

Learning of iHMMs has been explored earlier [1,5]. However, these papers deal with learning transition models and do not consider learning emission models. In this paper, we want to extend this to learning all the local models of an iHMM.

We start with a short introduction of the relevant aspects of HMMs and iHMMs in Section 2. In Section 3, we show how to learn imprecise local models—first if the state sequence is supposed to be known, and finally for hidden state sequences. In Section 4, we recall basic aspects of the Baum–Welch algorithm, relevant to our purpose. In Section 5, we apply our method to a problem of predicting future earthquake rates.

2 Hidden Markov Models and Basic Notions

2.1 Precise Hidden Markov Models

An HMM with length n has n state variables X_t that are hidden or unobservable, and n observation variables O_t that are observable. The figure below shows a graphical

S. Greco et al. (Eds.): IPMU 2012, Part III, CCIS 299, pp. 460–469, 2012.

representation of a HMM, with the local uncertainty model (characterised by a mass function in the precise case) for each variable shown next to the corresponding node.

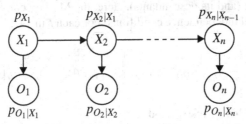

Each state variable X_t, with t in $\{1,\ldots,n\}$, takes one of the m possible values in the finite set $\mathscr{X}_t = \mathscr{X} := \{\xi_1,\ldots,\xi_m\}$. Each observation variable O_t, with t in $\{1,\ldots,n\}$, takes one of the p possible values in the finite set $\mathscr{O}_t = \mathscr{O} := \{\omega_1,\ldots,\omega_p\}$. We denote by x_t a generic value that X_t takes in $\mathscr{X}$, and by o_t a generic value that O_t takes in $\mathscr{O}$.

The local uncertainty model $p_{X_t|X_{t-1}}$ describes probabilistic knowledge about state variable X_t, conditional on the previous state variable X_{t-1}, with t in $\{2,\ldots,n\}$, and is called a *precise transition model*. The probability that state variable X_t takes value x_t, conditional on $X_{t-1} = x_{t-1}$, is written as $p_{X_t|X_{t-1}}(x_t|x_{t-1})$.

The local uncertainty model $p_{O_t|X_t}$ describes probabilistic knowledge about observation variable O_t, conditional on the corresponding state variable X_t, with t in $\{1,\ldots,n\}$, and is called a *precise emission model*. The probability that observation variable O_t takes value o_t, conditional on $X_t = x_t$, is written as $p_{O_t|X_t}(o_t|x_t)$.

The only variable we have not paid attention to so far is the first state variable X_1. The local uncertainty model p_{X_1} describes probabilistic knowledge about the first state variable X_1, and is not conditional. It is called a *precise marginal model*. The probability that state variable $X_1 = x_1$ is written as $p_{X_1}(x_1)$.

We write the state sequence as $X_{1:n} = x_{1:n}$ and the observation sequence as $O_{1:n} = o_{1:n}$. We use notations like $A_{p:n} := (A_p,\ldots,A_n)$ if $p \leq n$ and $A_{p:n} := \emptyset$ if $p > n$. For notational convenience, we also use another way of denoting state and observation sequences. There is a unique $l_{1:n} \in \times_{i=1}^{n}\mathscr{X}_i$ such that the state sequence $X_{1:n} = x_{1:n}$ can be written as $X_{1:n} = (\xi_{l_1},\ldots,\xi_{l_n})$, and a unique $h_{1:n} \in \times_{i=1}^{n}\mathscr{O}_i$ such that the observation sequence $O_{1:n} = o_{1:n}$ can be written as $O_{1:n} = (\omega_{h_1},\ldots,\omega_{h_n})$. We will use these unique letters l_i and h_i throughout.

We assume each HMM to be *stationary*, meaning that $p_{O_t|X_t} = p_{O|X}$ for all t in $\{1,\ldots,n\}$ and $p_{X_t|X_{t-1}} = p_{X_i|X_{i-1}}$ for all t,i in $\{2,\ldots,n\}$. The probability $p_{O|X}(\omega_h|\xi_l)$, with h in $\{1,\ldots,p\}$ and l in $\{1,\ldots,m\}$, of a state variable that takes value ξ_l emitting value ω_h is also denoted as E_{hl}. Furthermore, the probability $p_{X_t|X_{t-1}}(\xi_h|\xi_l)$, with l,h in $\{1,\ldots,m\}$ (this probability does not depend on t since the HMM is stationary), of a transition from a state variable taking value ξ_l to a state variable taking value ξ_h is also denoted as T_{lh}. Finally, the probability $p_{X_1}(\xi_l)$ that the first state variable X_1 assumes the value ξ_l is also denoted by p_l.

The model parameter $\boldsymbol{\theta}$ is the vector with all parameters of the marginal, transition and emission models. It has $m(p+m+1)$ elements, and is explicitly defined as:

$$\boldsymbol{\theta} := \begin{bmatrix} p_1 & \cdots & p_m & T_{11} & \cdots & T_{mm} & E_{11} & \cdots & E_{pm} \end{bmatrix}.$$

We write models that depend on (components of) $\boldsymbol{\theta}$ as models conditional on $\boldsymbol{\theta}$.

In our HMMs, we impose the usual *Markov condition* for Bayesian networks: for any variable, conditional on its mother variable, the non-parent non-descendent variables are independent of it (and its descendants). Here, the Markov condition reduces to the following conditional independence conditions. For each t in $\{1, \ldots, n\}$:

$$p_{X_t|X_{1:t-1}, O_{1:t-1}}(x_t|x_{1:t-1}, o_{1:t-1}, \boldsymbol{\theta}) = p_{X_t|X_{t-1}}(x_t|x_{t-1}),$$
$$p_{O_t|X_{1:n}, O_{1:t-1}, O_{t+1:n}}(o_t|x_{1:n}, o_{1:t-1}, o_{t+1:n}, \boldsymbol{\theta}) = p_{O_t|X_t}(o_t|x_t).$$

2.2 Imprecise Hidden Markov Models

An iHMM has the same graphical structure as an HMM, with the precise-probabilistic local models replaced by imprecise-probabilistic variants. Convenient imprecise probability models are coherent lower previsions.

A coherent lower prevision (or lower expectation functional) $\underline{P}$ is a real-valued functional defined on real-valued functions—called *gambles*—of variables. We denote the set of all gambles on the variable X by $\mathscr{L}(\mathscr{X})$. A gamble is interpreted as an uncertain award or penalty: it yields $f(x)$ if X takes value x in $\mathscr{X}$. A *coherent lower prevision* $\underline{P}$ defined on $\mathscr{L}(\mathscr{X})$ satisfies the following requirements:

C1. $\underline{P}(f) \geq \min_{x \in \mathscr{X}} f(x)$ for all f in $\mathscr{L}(\mathscr{X})$;
C2. $\underline{P}(\mu f) = \mu \underline{P}(f)$ for all real $\mu \geq 0$ and all f in $\mathscr{L}(\mathscr{X})$;
C3. $\underline{P}(f+g) \geq \underline{P}(f) + \underline{P}(g)$ for all f, g in $\mathscr{L}(\mathscr{X})$.

With a coherent lower prevision, we can associate a conjugate coherent upper prevision $\overline{P}$ as follows: $\overline{P}(f) := -\underline{P}(-f)$ for all gambles f. The interpretation of coherent lower and upper previsions is as follows. $\underline{P}(f)$ is a subject's supremum buying price for the gamble f, and consequently $\overline{P}(f)$ is his infimum selling price for f. For more information, see for instance [6].

The lower and upper probability of an event $A \subseteq \mathscr{X}$ are defined as $\underline{P}(A) := \underline{P}(\mathbb{I}_A)$ and $\overline{P}(A) := \overline{P}(\mathbb{I}_A)$, where $\mathbb{I}_A$ is the indicator (gamble) of a set A, which assumes the value 1 on A and 0 elsewhere.

We denote the *imprecise marginal model* by $\underline{Q}_1$, defined on $\mathscr{L}(\mathscr{X}_1)$. The *imprecise transition model* for state variable X_t, for t in $\{2, \ldots, n\}$, is denoted by $\underline{Q}_t(\cdot|X_{t-1})$, defined on $\mathscr{L}(\mathscr{X}_t)$ and the *imprecise emission model* for observation variable O_t, for t in $\{1, \ldots, n\}$, is denoted by $\underline{S}_t(\cdot|X_t)$, defined on $\mathscr{L}(\mathscr{O}_t)$. We assume our iHMM also to be stationary, meaning that the local models do not depend on t.

In an iHMM, the Markov condition turns into the *conditional irrelevance assessment*, meaning that, conditional on its mother variable, the non-parent non-descendant variables are assumed to be epistemically irrelevant to the variable and her descendants (see [3]). With this conditional irrelevance assessment, the following recursion relations hold for the joint lower prevision $\underline{P}_t(\cdot|X_{t-1})$ on $\mathscr{L}(\times_{i=t}^n (\mathscr{X}_i \times \mathscr{O}_i))$:

$$\underline{P}_t(\cdot|X_{t-1}) = \underline{Q}_t(\underline{E}_t(\cdot|X_t)|X_{t-1}) \qquad \text{for } t = n, \ldots, 2,$$
$$\begin{cases} \underline{E}_n(\cdot|X_n) = \underline{S}_n(\cdot|X_n) \\ \underline{E}_t(\cdot|X_t) = \underline{P}_t(\cdot|X_{t-1}) \otimes \underline{S}_{t-1}(\cdot|X_{t-1}) \qquad \text{for } t = n-1, \ldots, 1, \end{cases}$$

The joint lower prevision $\underline{P}$ defined on $\mathscr{L}(\times_{i=1}^{n}(\mathscr{X}_i \times \mathscr{O}_i))$ of all the variables is given by $\underline{P}_f(\cdot) = \underline{Q}_1(\underline{E}_t(\cdot|X_t))$.

In the next section, we start by presenting a method for learning the imprecise local uncertainty models of an iHMM, if both the observation sequence and the state sequence is given. Since the state sequence is actually unobservable, in Section 3.3 we present a method to estimate the relevant quantities from only an observation sequence.

3 Learning Imprecise Local Uncertainty Models

Since transitions between state variables and emissions of observation variables can be seen as instances of IID processes, whose behaviour is usefully summarised by multinomial processes, a convenient model to describe uncertainty about transition and emission probabilities are the conjugate Dirichlet models. One important imprecise-probabilistic variant of these is the imprecise Dirichlet model (IDM) [7].

3.1 Imprecise Dirichlet Model

Without going into too much detail, let us briefly recall the relevant ideas about the IDM. If $n(A)$ is the number of occurrences of an event A in N experiments, then the lower and upper probability of A according to an IDM are defined as

$$\underline{P}(A) = \frac{n(A)}{N+s} \text{ and } \overline{P}(A) = \frac{n(A)+s}{N+s},$$

where s is a hyperparameter called the number of pseudo-counts. This is a non-negative real number on which the imprecision $\Delta(P(A)) := \overline{P}(A) - \underline{P}(A) = s/N+s$ depends. The larger s, the more imprecise the inferences. If $s = 0$, the resulting precise model returns the relative frequency $\overline{P}(A) = \underline{P}(A) = n(A)/N$ of the occurrence of A.

Once we have chosen a value for s, we can use the IDM to infer interval estimates for the probability of A from observations. The choice of s is, however, fairly arbitrary; see also [7], where it is argued that for example $s = 2$ might be a good choice.

3.2 Known State Sequence

Our aim is to learn local models, based on a known observation sequence $O_{1:n} = (\omega_{h_1}, \ldots, \omega_{h_n})$. Assume for the time being the state sequence $X_{1:n} = x_{1:n} = (\xi_{l_1}, \ldots, \xi_{l_n})$ to be also known, then we can build imprecise estimates for the local uncertainty models as follows.

We first define for each i and g in $\{1, \ldots, m\}$ the following numbers (or rather functions of the state sequence $x_{1:n}$) n_{ξ_i} and n_{ξ_i,ξ_g} as:

$$n_{\xi_i}(x_{1:n}) := \sum_{t=1}^{n} \mathbb{I}_{\{\xi_i\}}(x_t) \text{ and } n_{\xi_i,\xi_g}(x_{1:n}) := \sum_{t=2}^{n} \mathbb{I}_{\{(\xi_i,\xi_g)\}}(x_{t-1},x_t).$$

The interpretation of these numbers is immediate: n_{ξ_i} is the number of times the value ξ_i is reached in the whole state sequence $x_{1:n}$ and n_{ξ_i,ξ_g} is the number of times that a state transition from value ξ_i to value ξ_g takes place in the whole state sequence $x_{1:n}$.

Imprecise Transition Model: The event of interest here is the transition from a state variable taking value ξ_i in $\mathscr{X}$ to the subsequent state variable taking value ξ_g in $\mathscr{X}$. This event occurs n_{ξ_i,ξ_g} times. The number of "experiments" N is the number of times $\sum_{g=1}^{m} n_{\xi_i,\xi_g}$ that a transition from value ξ_i takes place. The IDM leads to the following imprecise transition model (in terms of lower and upper transition probabilities):

$$\underline{Q}(\{\xi_g\}|\xi_i) = \frac{n_{\xi_i,\xi_g}}{s + \sum_{g=1}^{m} n_{\xi_i,\xi_g}} \quad \text{and} \quad \overline{Q}(\{\xi_g\}|\xi_i) = \frac{s + n_{\xi_i,\xi_g}}{s + \sum_{g=1}^{m} n_{\xi_i,\xi_g}}.$$

Since here and in what follows, the IDM produces a linear-vacuous model [6,7] for the probabilities, these lower and upper probabilities determine the imprecise model.

Imprecise Emission Model: The event of interest here is the emission of observation o in $\mathscr{O}$ from corresponding state variable taking value ξ_i in $\mathscr{X}$. This event occurs $\sum_{\{t:\omega_{h_t}=o\}} \mathbb{I}_{\{\xi_i\}}(x_t)$ times. The total number of times an emission from value ξ_i takes place, is n_{ξ_i}. The IDM then leads to the following imprecise emission model:

$$\underline{S}(\{o\}|\xi_i) = \frac{\sum_{\{t:\omega_{h_t}=o\}} \mathbb{I}_{\{\xi_i\}}(x_t)}{s + n_{\xi_i}} \quad \text{and} \quad \overline{S}(\{o\}|\xi_i) = \frac{s + \sum_{\{t:\omega_{h_t}=o\}} \mathbb{I}_{\{\xi_i\}}(x_t)}{s + n_{\xi_i}}.$$

Imprecise Marginal Model: The event of interest here is the state variable X_1 taking value ξ_i in $\mathscr{X}$. The number of times this event occurs is $\mathbb{I}_{\{\xi_i\}}(x_1)$. The total number of times state variable X_1 takes any value is of course 1. The IDM then leads to the following imprecise marginal model:

$$\underline{Q}_1(\{\xi_i\}) = \frac{\mathbb{I}_{\{\xi_i\}}(x_1)}{s+1} \quad \text{and} \quad \overline{Q}_1(\{\xi_i\}) = \frac{s + \mathbb{I}_{\{\xi_i\}}(x_1)}{s+1}.$$

3.3   Unknown State Sequence

Since in an HMM the state sequence $X_{1:n}$ is unobservable (hidden), the numbers n_{ξ_i} and n_{ξ_i,ξ_g} are actually random variables N_{ξ_i} and N_{ξ_i,ξ_g}: functions of the hidden state sequence $X_{1:n}$. This means we can no longer use them directly to learn the imprecise local models. Instead of using these random variables N_{ξ_i} and N_{ξ_i,ξ_g}, we will rather use their expected values, conditional on the known observation sequence $o_{1:n}$ and the model parameter $\boldsymbol{\theta}^*$. Here $\boldsymbol{\theta}^*$ is a local maximum of the likelihood, obtained by the Baum–Welch algorithm (see Section 4). We define the expected counts $\hat{n}_{\xi_i}$ an $\hat{n}_{\xi_i,\xi_g}$ as

$$\hat{n}_{\xi_i} := E\left(N_{\xi_i}|o_{1:n}, \boldsymbol{\theta}^*\right) = \sum_{t=1}^{n} E\left(\mathbb{I}_{\{\xi_i\}}(x_t)|o_{1:n}, \boldsymbol{\theta}^*\right) = \sum_{t=1}^{n} p_{X_t|O_{1:n}}(\xi_i|o_{1:n}, \boldsymbol{\theta}^*)$$

$$\hat{n}_{\xi_i,\xi_g} := E\left(N_{\xi_i,\xi_g}\Big|o_{1:n}, \boldsymbol{\theta}^*\right) = \sum_{t=2}^{n} E\left(\mathbb{I}_{\{(\xi_i,\xi_g)\}}(x_{t-1},x_t)\Big|o_{1:n}, \boldsymbol{\theta}^*\right)$$

$$= \sum_{t=2}^{n} p_{X_{t-1:t}|O_{1:n}}(\xi_i,\xi_g|o_{1:n}, \boldsymbol{\theta}^*).$$

We can calculate $\boldsymbol{\theta}^*$, and from this $p_{X_t|O_{1:n}}(\xi_i|o_{1:n},\boldsymbol{\theta}^*)$ and $p_{X_{t-1:t}|O_{1:n}}(\xi_i,\xi_g|o_{1:n},\boldsymbol{\theta}^*)$, efficiently with the Baum–Welch algorithm and forward and backward probabilities. Instead of using real counts of transitions and emissions, we use the expected number of occurrences of these events to build the imprecise local models. These expected numbers of occurrences are non-negative real numbers instead of non-negative integers. The estimated imprecise transition model is given by

$$\underline{Q}(\{\xi_g\}|\xi_i) = \frac{\hat{n}_{\xi_i,\xi_g}}{s+\sum_{g=1}^m \hat{n}_{\xi_i,\xi_g}} \quad \text{and} \quad \overline{Q}(\{\xi_g\}|\xi_i) = \frac{s+\hat{n}_{\xi_i,\xi_g}}{s+\sum_{g=1}^m \hat{n}_{\xi_i,\xi_g}},$$

the estimated imprecise emission model by

$$\underline{S}(\{o\}|\xi_i) = \frac{\sum_{\{t:\omega_{h_t}=o\}} p_{X_t|O_{1:n}}(\xi_i|o_{1:n},\boldsymbol{\theta}^*)}{s+n_{\xi_i}}$$

$$\text{and} \quad \overline{S}(\{o\}|\xi_i) = \frac{s+\sum_{\{t:\omega_{h_t}=o\}} p_{X_t|O_{1:n}}(\xi_i|o_{1:n},\boldsymbol{\theta}^*)}{s+n_{\xi_i}},$$

and the estimated imprecise marginal model by

$$\underline{Q}_1(\{\xi_i\}) = \frac{p_{X_1|O_{1:n}}(\xi_i|o_{1:n},\boldsymbol{\theta}^*)}{s+1} \quad \text{and} \quad \overline{Q}_1(\{\xi_i\}) = \frac{s+p_{X_1|O_{1:n}}(\xi_i|o_{1:n},\boldsymbol{\theta}^*)}{s+1}.$$

3.4 Imprecision of the Imprecise Local Uncertainty Models

The imprecision $\Delta(Q(\{\xi_h\}|\xi_i))$ of the imprecise transition model and the imprecision $\Delta(S(\{o\}|\xi_i))$ of the imprecise emission model satisfy interesting properties.

Proposition 1. *The harmonic mean $H_{\Delta(Q)}$ of the set $\{\Delta(Q(\{\xi_h\}|\xi_i)) : i \in \{1,\dots,m\}\}$ is given by $H_{\Delta(Q)} = ms/ms+n-1$ and the harmonic mean $H_{\Delta(S)}$ of the set $\{\Delta(S(\{o\}|\xi_i)) : i \in \{1,\dots,m\}\}$ is given by $H_{\Delta(S)} = ms/ms+n$.*

Proof. The harmonic mean $H_{\Delta(Q)}$ of $\{\Delta(Q(\{\xi_h\}|\xi_i)) : i \in \{1,\dots,m\}\}$ is given by

$$H_{\Delta(Q)} = \frac{m}{\sum_{i=1}^m \frac{1}{\Delta(Q(\{\xi_h\}|\xi_i))}} = \frac{ms}{\sum_{i=1}^m \left(s+\sum_{g=1}^m \hat{n}_{\xi_i,\xi_g}\right)}$$

$$= \frac{ms}{ms+\sum_{t=1}^{n-1}\sum_{i=1}^m E\left(\mathbb{I}_{\{\xi_i\}}(X_t)|o_{1:n},\boldsymbol{\theta}^*\right)} = \frac{ms}{ms+\sum_{t=1}^{n-1} 1} = \frac{ms}{ms+n-1}.$$

The harmonic mean $H_{\Delta(S)}$ of $\{\Delta(S(\{o\}|\xi_i)) : i \in \{1,\dots,m\}\}$ is given by

$$H_{\Delta(S)} = \frac{m}{\sum_{i=1}^m \frac{1}{\Delta(S(\{o\}|\xi_i))}} = \frac{ms}{\sum_{i=1}^m (s+n_{\xi_i})} = \frac{ms}{ms+n}. \qquad \square$$

$H_{\Delta(Q)}$ increases with m (if $n > 1$) and decreases with n, and $H_{\Delta(S)}$ increases with m and decreases with n. The IDM yields more precise estimates as the number of relevant observations (of transitions or emissions) increases: the more relevant data, the more precise the estimates. For a fixed number of data (observation sequence length n), the precision tends to decrease as the number of possible state values m increases. Notably in cases where states are useful fictions (as in the earthquake example discussed further on), there is a cost to increasing the number of states. The increase of the imprecision with increasing m is, obviously, not present in precise HMM estimation. When making inferences based on precise HMM estimation, for example using the Viterbi algorithm for state sequence estimation, all results seem equally reliable, regardless of the number of possible state values m. But when making inferences in iHMMs, based on the model estimates provided by our method, for example using the EstiHMM algorithm [2], this is not the case: for smaller m, inferences will be more precise (or decisive); and if m is fairly large, inferences about state sequences will tend to become more imprecise. Lumping states together will increase the predictive power (for a given observation sequence), refining states will reduce it: there is a certain limit on what can be inferred using an iHMM estimated from a given information sequence, which is not there if we use a precise HMM estimation. Using precise HMM estimation, the coarseness of the state space representation has no influence on the precision, irrespective of the amount of data available. We believe this is a weakness rather than a strength of precise models.

4   The Baum–Welch Algorithm

We give a brief overview of how to find the model parameter $\boldsymbol{\theta}^*$ using the Baum–Welch algorithm. It is an EM algorithm specifically for learning HMMs (see, e.g., [9]). It iteratively finds a (local) maximum $\boldsymbol{\theta}^*$ of the likelihood, which we define presently.

4.1   Likelihood in Hidden Markov Models

The complete likelihood $L_{o_{1:n},x_{1:n}}(\boldsymbol{\theta})$ in an HMM, with the observation sequence $O_{1:n} = o_{1:n}$ as data, an arbitrary state sequence $X_{1:n} = x_{1:n}$ and model parameter $\boldsymbol{\theta}$, is defined as $p_{O_{1:n},X_{1:n}}(o_{1:n},x_{1:n}|\boldsymbol{\theta})$. By the Markov condition, this can be written as $L_{o_{1:n},x_{1:n}}(\boldsymbol{\theta}) = p_{l_1}\prod_{t=2}^{n}T_{l_{t-1}l_t}\prod_{t=1}^{n}E_{h_t l_t}$. Although we are interested in the likelihood for the observation sequence $L_{o_{1:n}}(\boldsymbol{\theta}) := p_{O_{1:n}}(o_{1:n}|\boldsymbol{\theta})$, the Baum–Welch algorithm finds a maximum $\boldsymbol{\theta}^*$ for the complete likelihood. Welch proves [8] that the Baum–Welch algorithm also locally maximises the likelihood for the observations.

A $\boldsymbol{\theta}^*$ that maximises $L_{o_{1:n},x_{1:n}}(\boldsymbol{\theta})$ also maximises $\ln L_{o_{1:n},x_{1:n}}(\boldsymbol{\theta})$, given by:

$$\ln L_{o_{1:n},x_{1:n}}(\boldsymbol{\theta}) = \sum_{z=1}^{m}\mathbb{I}_{\xi_z}(x_1)\ln p_z + \sum_{i=1}^{m}\sum_{g=1}^{m}n_{\xi_i,\xi_g}\ln T_{ig} + \sum_{t=1}^{n}\sum_{z_t=1}^{m}\mathbb{I}_{\xi_{z_t}}(x_t)\ln E_{h_t z_t}. \quad (1)$$

The Baum–Welch algorithm consists in executing two steps—the *Expectation (E) step* and the *Maximisation (M) step*—iteratively until some convergence is achieved.

4.2   Expectation Step

In the E step we calculate the expectation of the complete log-likelihood conditional on the observations $o_{1:n}$ (and of course the model parameter $\boldsymbol{\theta}$). We call this expecation $\ln \hat{L}_{o_{1:n}}(\boldsymbol{\theta}) := E\left(\ln L_{o_{1:n},X_{1:n}}(\boldsymbol{\theta})|o_{1:n},\boldsymbol{\theta}\right)$. It is given by the right-hand side of (1), but with the indicators and the n_{ξ_i,ξ_g} replaced by their expectations, as in Section 3.3.

4.3 Maximisation Step

In this step we search the argument $\boldsymbol{\theta}^*$ that maximises the expectation of the complete log-likelihood.

Lemma 1. *The argument $\boldsymbol{\theta}^*$ that maximises the expected complete log-likelihood of a HMM with observation sequence $\omega_{h_1:h_n}$ is given by, for all $i, g \in \{1, \ldots, m\}$ and all $h \in \{1 \ldots, p\}$:*

$$p_i^* = p_{X_1|O_{1:n}}(\xi_i|o_{1:n}, \boldsymbol{\theta}^*), T_{ig}^* = \frac{\hat{n}_{\xi_i, \xi_g}}{\sum_{g=1}^m \hat{n}_{\xi_i, \xi_g}}, \text{ and } E_{hi}^* = \frac{\sum_{\{t:h_t=h\}} p_{X_t|O_{1:n}}(\xi_i|o_{1:n}, \boldsymbol{\theta}^*)}{\hat{n}_{\xi_i}}.$$

By repeatedly performing the E step followed by the M step (with in the E step $\boldsymbol{\theta}$ taken as $\boldsymbol{\theta}^*$), we eventually reach a stable value of $\boldsymbol{\theta}^*$, guaranteed to be also a local maximum of the likelihood for the observation sequence.

Incidentally, Lemma 1 guarantees that our method, with the choice for the pseudo-counts $s = 0$, gives local models that maximise the likelihood for the observation sequence.

5 Predicting the Earth's Earthquake Rate

5.1 Introduction

We apply our method to a problem where we are interested in using HMMs to predict earthquake rates in future years. To do this, we will see that we need to learn a transition model. To this end, we use data of counted annual numbers of major earthquakes (with magnitude 7 and higher).

We assume that the earth can be in m different seismic states $\lambda_1, \ldots, \lambda_m$ and that the occurrence of earthquakes in a year depends on the seismic state λ of the Earth in that year. We assume that the Earth, being in a seismic state λ, "emits" a number of earthquakes o governed by a Poisson distribution with parameter λ: $p_{O|X}(o|\lambda) = e^{-\lambda}\lambda^o/o!$.

The data are (yearly) earthquake counts over 107 subsequent years, from 1900 to 2006. It is freely available on http://neic.usgs.gov/neis/eqlists.

We model this problem as an iHMM of length 107, in which each observation variable O_i corresponds to one of the 107 yearly earthquake counts. The states correspond to the seismic states Earth can be in. The set of seismic states $\{\lambda_1, \ldots, \lambda_m\}$ defines the possibility space $\mathscr{X}$ of the state variables in the HMM.

5.2 Results

Imprecise Transition Model. Since there is only 107 years of data, we believe that a precise local transition model is not justified, so we decided to try an imprecise estimation for the transition model. The emission model is kept precise for simplicity, due to its relation to a Poisson process.

To show how the imprecision changes with changing number of possible state values m, we plot the learned transition model for varying m. The figure below shows, as a function of m (ranging from 3 to 10), the imprecision $\Delta(Q(\{\lambda.\}|\lambda_1))$, …, $\Delta(Q(\{\lambda.\}|\lambda_m))$ of the transition probabilities of going from state λ_i to state $\lambda.$, for $s = 2$ (this imprecision depends on the state λ_i, but not on the state $\lambda.$ the transition goes to).

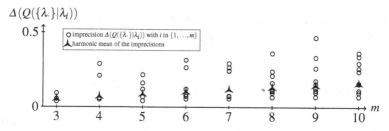

The harmonic mean of the imprecisions increases with m, as predicted by Proposition 1.

Predicting the Earthquake Rate. With the learned transition model (with $m = 3$), we make predictions of the earthquake rate in future years. We do this in order to validate our learned model. We want to make inferences about the years 2007, 2016, 2026 and 2036: we are interested in the model describing the state variables of these years, updated using the observation sequence. We can use this updated model to get some idea of the future earthquake rate. To perform such updating, we can use the MePiCTIr algorithm [3].

The figure below shows conservative approximations (the smallest hexagons with vertices parallel with the borders of the simplex) of such updated models describing future state variables. In the dark grey credal sets, we have used the transition model estimates for $s = 2$, and in the light grey ones the estimated transition models for $s = 5$.

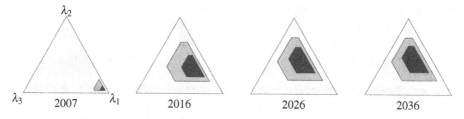

The precision of the inferences decreases as we move forward in time. For 2007, we can be fairly confident that the local seismic rate of the earth will be close to λ_1, while for 2036, we can only make very imprecise inferences about the seismic rate. This is a property that predictions with precise HMMs do not have.

6   Conclusion

We have presented a new method for learning imprecise local uncertainty models in stationary hidden Markov models. In contradistinction with the classical EM learning algorithm, our approach allows the local models to be imprecise, which is useful if there is insufficient data to warrant precision. We have studied some of the properties of our learned local models, especially with respect to their imprecision.

We conclude by proposing some avenues for further research. We have based the present discussion on the maximum likelihood approach of learning in Bayesian networks. The epistemic nature of imprecise probability theory however suggests that a Bayesian learning approach would be more appropriate, and we intend to investigate this in the near future.

Acknowledgements. Arthur Van Camp is a Ph.D. Fellow of the Ghent University Special Research Fund (BOF) and wishes to acknowledge its financial support. We are indebted to Jasper De Bock and Marco Zaffalon for suggesting and discussing the idea of using expected counts in an IDM, and for suggesting to use the Baum–Welch algorithm.

References

1. Antonucci, A., de Rosa, R., Giusti, A.: Action recognition by imprecise hidden Markov models. In: Proceedings of the 2011 International Conference on Image Processing, Computer Vision and Pattern Recognition (IPCV 2011), pp. 474–478. CSREA Press (2011)
2. De Bock, J., de Cooman, G.: State sequence prediction in imprecise hidden Markov models. In: Coolen, F., de Cooman, G., Fetz, T., Oberguggenberger, M. (eds.) ISIPTA 2011: Proceedings of the Seventh International Symposium on Imprecise Probability: Theories and Applications, Innsbruck, pp. 159–168. SIPTA (2011)
3. de Cooman, G., Hermans, F., Antonucci, A., Zaffalon, M.: Epistemic irrelevance in credal nets: The case of imprecise markov trees. International Journal of Approximate Reasoning 51(9) (2010)
4. Durbin, R., Eddy, S., Krogh, A., Mitchison, G.: Biological sequence analysis: probabilistic models of proteins and nucleic acids. Cambridge University Press (1998)
5. Van Camp, A., de Cooman, G., De Bock, J., Quaeghebeur, E., Hermans, F.: Learning imprecise hidden Markov models. Poster at ISIPTA 2011 (2011)
6. Walley, P.: Statistical Reasoning with Imprecise Probabilities. Chapman and Hall, London (1991)
7. Walley, P.: Inferences from multinomial data: learning about a bag of marbles. Journal of the Royal Statistical Society, Series B 58, 3–57 (1996) (with discussion)
8. Welch, L.: Hidden Markov models and the Baum–Welch algorithm. IEEE Information Theory Society Newsletter, 1, 10–13 (2003)
9. Zucchini, W., MacDonald, I.L.: Hidden Markov models for time series: an introduction using R. Chapman and Hall (2009)

Inference Using Compiled Product-Based Possibilistic Networks

Raouia Ayachi[1,2], Nahla Ben Amor[1], and Salem Benferhat[2]

[1] LARODEC, Institut Supérieur de Gestion Tunis, Le Bardo, Tunisie, 2000
raouia.ayachi@gmail.com, nahla.benamor@gmx.fr
[2] CRIL-CNRS, Université d'Artois, France, 62307
benferhat@cril.univ-artois.fr

Abstract. Possibilistic networks are important graphical tools for representing and reasoning under uncertain pieces of information. In possibility theory, there are two kinds of possibilistic networks depending if possibilistic conditioning is based on the minimum or on the product operator. This paper explores inference in product-based possibilistic networks using compilation. This paper also reports on a set of experimental results comparing product-based possibilistic networks and min-based possibilistic networks from a spatial point of view.

1 Introduction

Possibility theory [11,12] offers either an ordinal framework where only the plausibility ordering between information is important or a numerical one for representing uncertainty. This leads to two kinds of possibilistic networks: min-based possibilistic networks and product-based possibilistic networks. Existing works [1,2] for handling possibilistic inference through compilation only concern min-based possibilistic networks. The present paper proposes an alternative implementation of inference using product-based possibilistic networks. We will emphasize on similarities and differences between product-based possibilistic networks, min-based possibilistic networks and Bayesian networks under compilation, while using the same DAG structure. More explicitly, we will propose the *Prod-Π-DNNF* method that focuses on compiling the CNF encoding associated with the product-based possibilistic network in order to efficiently ensure inference. In the logical setting, there is an important difference in computational complexity between the inference process from product-based and min-based possibilistic logic. Indeed, the inference from product-based bases requires m calls to the SAT (satisfiability tests) with m is the number of formulas in the knowledge base. While inference in the min-based case only needs $log_2\ n$ SAT calls while n is the number of different certainty degrees used in the possibilistic knowledge base. This paper shows that, in the compilation setting, the difference in the inference process is less important. The paper unveils that the encoding differs from the ordinal to the numerical interpretation. In fact, Prod-Π-DNNF makes use of the strategy *one variable per equal parameters per Conditional Possibility Table (CPT)*, contrarily to the min-based case which offers the possibility

S. Greco et al. (Eds.): IPMU 2012, Part III, CCIS 299, pp. 470–480, 2012.

to associate *a unique variable to equal parameters per all CPTs*. We also propose an experimental study to emphasize on the differences regarding the behaviors of product-based and min-based possibilistic networks under compilation.

The paper is organized as follows: Section 2 presents a brief refresher on product-based possibilistic networks and compilation. Section 3 describes the new method Prod-Π-DNNF. Section 4 is dedicated to the experimental study.

2   Basic Backgrounds

Let $V = \{X_1, ..., X_N\}$ be a set of variables. We denote by D_{X_i} the domain associated with X_i. By x_i (resp. x_{ij}), we denote any of the instances of X_i (resp. the jth instance of X_i). When there is no confusion we use x_i to mean any instance of X_i. $D_{X_i} = \{x_{i1}, ..., x_{in}\}$ where n is the number of instances of X_i. Ω denotes the universe of discourse, which is the cartesian product of all variable domains in V. Each element $\omega \in \Omega$ is called an *interpretation* of Ω.

2.1   Possibility Theory

This subsection briefly recalls some elements of possibility theory; for more details we refer the reader to [11,12]. Possibility theory is seen as a simple and natural model for handling uncertain data. Its basic building block, i.e., the concept of a *possibility distribution*, denoted by π, is a mapping from Ω to the unit interval $[0, 1]$. The particularity of the possibilistic scale is that it can be interpreted in twofold: a *numerical* one when values have a real sense and an *ordinal* one when values only reflect a total pre-order between the different states of the world. This paper explores the numerical interpretation of possibility theory. The degree $\pi(\omega)$ represents the compatibility of ω with available pieces of information. By convention, $\pi(\omega) = 1$ means that ω is totally possible, and $\pi(\omega) = 0$ means that ω is impossible. Uncertainty of an event $\phi \subseteq \Omega$ can be expressed by the *possibility measure* $\Pi(\phi) = max_{\omega \in \phi} \pi(\omega)$ which evaluates the extent to which ϕ is consistent with the available beliefs. The *product-based conditioning* [14] consists of proportionately increasing the possibility degrees of elements in Ω consistent with ϕ. Formally,

$$\Pi(\omega \mid \phi) = \begin{cases} \frac{\pi(\omega)}{\Pi(\phi)} & \text{if } \omega \models \phi \text{ and } \Pi(\phi) \neq 0 \\ 0 & \text{otherwise} \end{cases} \tag{1}$$

2.2   Possibilistic Networks

The two interpretations of the possibilistic scale lead to two counterparts of standard Bayesian networks (BNs) [4], min-based possibilistic networks corresponding to the ordinal interpretation and product-based possibilistic networks corresponding to the numerical interpretation. It is well known that product-based possibilistic networks are close to BNs since they share the same graphical component (i.e., DAG) and also the product operator. There is however a major difference. It concerns the inference process. Indeed, the marginalisation in the probabilistic framework uses the sum operation while in possibilistic framework the marginalisation is based on the maximum operation.

A possibilistic network over a set of N variables $V = \{X_1, .., X_N\}$, denoted by $\Pi G_\otimes$, where $\otimes = \{*, min\}$ comprises:

- A *graphical component* composed of a DAG where nodes represent variables and edges encode links between variables. The parent set of any variable X_i is denoted by $U_i = \{U_{i1}, ..., U_{im}\}$ where U_{i1} is the first parent of U_i and m is the number of parents of X_i. In what follows, we use x_i, u_i, u_{ij} to denote, respectively, possible instances of X_i, U_i and U_{ij}.

- A *numerical component* that quantifies different links. Uncertainty of each node in $\Pi G_\otimes$ is represented by a local normalized possibility distribution in the context of its parents (i.e., $\forall u_i, max_{x_i} \Pi(x_i|u_i) = 1$).

The joint possibility distribution associated with $\Pi G_\otimes$ is computed using the so-called possibilistic chain rule. Formally:

Definition 1. *Let $\Pi G_\otimes$ be a possibilistic network of N variables, then the joint possibility distribution is defined by the product-based chain rule expressed by:*

$$\pi_\otimes(X_1, \ldots, X_N) = \otimes_{i=1..N} \ \Pi(X_i \mid U_i) \qquad (2)$$

where $\otimes$ corresponds to $*$ (resp. min) for ΠG_* (resp. ΠG_{min}).

In this paper, we focus on ΠG_* illustrated below.

Example 1. *Let us consider the product-based possibilistic network ΠG_* used throughout the whole paper and composed of two binary variables A and B s.t. $\Pi(A) = [a_1, a_2] = [1, 0.4]$ and $\Pi(B|A) = [b_1|a_1, b_1|a_2; b_2|a_1, b_2|a_2] = [1, 0.8; 0.8, 1]$.*

We obtain a joint possibility distribution of ΠG_* using Equation (2). For instance, $\pi_*(a_1, b_2) = \Pi(a_1) * \Pi(b_2|a_1) = 1 * 0.8 = 0.8$.

2.3   Compilation Concepts

Knowledge compilation is an artificial intelligence area related to a mapping problem from intractable logical theories into suitable target compilation languages [5]. These latters are characterized by a *succinctness* criteria and a set of *queries* and *transformations* performed in polynomial time with respect to the size of compiled bases. Within the multitude of target compilation languages [10], the *Negation Normal Form (NNF)* language represents the pivotal language from which a variety of languages give rise by imposing some conditions on it. In this paper, we focus our attention on a subset of NNF, i.e., *Decomposable Negation Normal Form (DNNF)* language that satisfies the *decomposability* property stating that conjuncts of any conjunction share no variables [8]. A subset of DNNF, called *deterministic DNNF* (d-DNNF) and less succinct than DNNF, is obtained by adding the *determinism* (d) property stating that disjuncts of any disjunction are logically contradictory [10]. DNNF supports a rich set of polynomial-time operations which can be performed simply and efficiently. From the most used ones, we can cite:

- *Conditioning*: Let α be a propositional formula and let ρ be a consistent term, then conditioning α on ρ, denoted by $\alpha|\rho$ generates a new formula in which each propositional variable $P_i \in \alpha$ is set to $\top$ if P_i is consistent with ρ^1 and $\perp$ otherwise.

- *Forgetting*: The forgetting of P_i from α is equivalent to a formula that do not mention P_i. Formally: $\exists P_i.\alpha = \alpha|P_i \vee \alpha|\neg P_i$.

In [13], authors have generalized the set of NNF languages by the *Valued Negation Normal Form (VNNF)* which offers an enriched representation of functions. Within VNNF's operations, we cite *max-variable elimination* which consists in forgetting variables using the max operator. As a special case of VNNFs, Π-DNNFs, which are the possibilistic counterpart of DNNFs, have been explored in [2]. Note that formulas can be represented, in a compact manner, as Directed Acyclic graphs (DAGs) using circuits (e.g., boolean circuits, arithmetic circuits, etc.). The size of any circuit C, denoted by $Size(C)$, corresponds to the number of edges in its DAG.

3   Compilation-Based Inference of ΠG_*

Emphasis has been recently placed on inference in BNs under compilation [7,9,15]. The main idea consists in compiling the *Conjunctive Normal Form (CNF)* encoding associated with the BN into the d-DNNF language, then compiling it to efficiently compute the effect of an evidence on a set of variables of interest X. In this section, we propose to study the possibilistic counterpart of [9] with product-based possibilistic networks. The proposed method, denoted by *Prod-Π-DNNF*, requires two major phases as depicted by Figure 1: an *encoding and compilation* phase and an *inference* one detailed below:

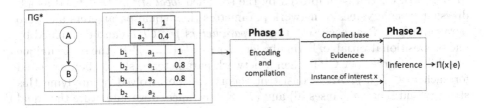

Fig. 1. Principle of Prod-Π-DNNF

3.1   Encoding and Compilation Phase

The starting point of Prod-Π-DNNF is the CNF encoding of ΠG_* as shown in Figure 1. First, we need to represent instances of variables and also parameters using a set of propositional variables dispatched into a set of *instance indicators* and a set of *parameter variables* defined as follows:

---

1 P_i is consistent with ρ if there exists an interpretation that satisfies both P_i and ρ.

- $\forall X_i \in V$, $\forall x_{ij} \in D_{X_i}$, we associate an *instance indicator* $\lambda_{x_{ij}}$. When there is no ambiguity, we use λ_{x_i} instead of $\lambda_{x_{ij}}$.
- $\forall x_{ij} \in D_{X_i}$, $\forall u_i \in D_{U_i}$ s.t. $u_i = \{u_{i1}, ..., u_{im}\}$, we associate a *parameter variable* $\theta_{x_i|u_i}$ for each network parameter $\Pi(x_i|u_i)$.

Using these propositional variables, the CNF encoding of ΠG_*, denoted by C_*, is formally defined by Definition 2.

Definition 2. *Let ΠG_* be a product-based possibilistic network. Let $\lambda_{x_{ij}}$, ($i \in \{1,..,N\}$, $j \in \{1,..,k\}$) be the set of instance indicators and $\theta_{x_i|u_i}$ be the set of parameter variables, then $\forall X_i \in V$, C_* contains the following clauses:*

− *Mutual exclusive clauses:*

$$\lambda_{x_{i1}} \vee \lambda_{x_{i2}} \vee \cdots \lambda_{x_{in}} \tag{3}$$

$$\neg \lambda_{x_{ij}} \vee \neg \lambda_{x_{ik}}, j \neq k \tag{4}$$

− *Network parameter clauses:* $\forall$ $\theta_{x_i|u_i}$, *we have:*

$$\lambda_{x_i} \wedge \lambda_{u_{i1}} \wedge \ldots \wedge \lambda_{u_{im}} \rightarrow \theta_{x_i|u_i} \tag{5}$$

$$\theta_{x_i|u_i} \rightarrow \lambda_{x_i} \tag{6}$$

$$\theta_{x_i|u_i} \rightarrow \lambda_{u_{i1}}, \cdots, \theta_{x_i|u_i} \rightarrow \lambda_{u_{im}} \tag{7}$$

The encoding C_* is a logical representation of ΠG_* using a set of clauses where clauses (3) and (4) state that indicator variables are exclusive and clauses (5), (6) and (7) simply encode the fact that the possibility degree of $x_i|u_i$ is equal to $\Pi(x_i|u_i)$. C_* can be improved by the so-called *local structure* defined as addressing specific values of network parameters (i.e., equal parameters and zero parameters). In fact, each set of *equal parameters per CPT* can be assigned by one propositional variable. Formally, let $L_{CPT} = \{v_1, ..., v_p\}$ be the set of unique possibility degrees per CPT, then a network parameter θ_i should be associated for each $v_i \in L_{CPT}$. An inconsistent theory can be involved by applying this strategy and keeping clauses (6) and (7). For instance, if we substitute the equal parameters $\theta_{a_2|b_1}$ and θ_{a_1} by a single one (i.e., θ_1), then we will obtain $\theta_1 \rightarrow \lambda_{a_1}$ and $\theta_1 \rightarrow \lambda_{a_2}$ which is inconsistent. To avoid this problem, additional clauses (6) and (7) should be dropped from C_*. Aside from equal parameters, each $\theta_{x_i|u_i}$ equal to 0, can be dropped from C_* by replacing its clauses by a shorter clause involving only indicator variables, namely: $\neg \lambda_{x_i} \vee \neg \lambda_{u_{i1}} \vee \cdots \vee \neg \lambda_{u_{im}}$. Once ΠG_* is logically represented into C_*, this latter is then compiled into the most succinct language DNNF. The compiled base is denoted by C_{DNNF}.

Example 2. *Considering ΠG_* of Example 1. Table 1 represents its CNF encoding, C_*, using Definition 2, and Figure 2 represents the compiled base of this encoding.*

3.2   Inference Phase

Given the compiled base C_{DNNF} resulting from Phase 1, an instance of interest x of some variables $X \subseteq V$ and an evidence e of some variables $E \subseteq V$, we can efficiently compute the effect of e on x, namely $\Pi_c(x|e)$. Using Equation (1), it is clear that we should compute both of $\Pi_c(x, e)$ and $\Pi_c(e)$ while following these three steps:

Table 1. CNF encoding C_* of ΠG_* of Example 1

Variable A		Variable B	
Mutual exclusive clauses		Mutual exclusive clauses	
$(\lambda_{a_1} \vee \lambda_{a_2}) \wedge (\neg\lambda_{a_1} \vee \neg\lambda_{a_2})$		$(\lambda_{b_1} \vee \lambda_{b_2}) \wedge (\neg\lambda_{b_1} \vee \neg\lambda_{b_2})$	
Parameter clauses		Parameter clauses	
$\Pi(a_1) = 1$	$(\lambda_{a_1} \to \theta_{a_1}) \wedge (\theta_{a_1} \to \lambda_{a_1})$	$\Pi(b_1|a_1) = 1$	$(\lambda_{a_1} \wedge \lambda_{b_1} \to \theta_1)$
$\Pi(a_2) = 0.4$	$(\lambda_{a_2} \to \theta_{a_2}) \wedge (\theta_{a_2} \to \lambda_{a_2})$	$\Pi(b_1|a_2) = 0.8$	$(\lambda_{a_2} \wedge \lambda_{b_1} \to \theta_2)$
-		$\Pi(b_2|a_1) = 0.8$	$(\lambda_{a_1} \wedge \lambda_{b_2} \to \theta_2)$
-		$\Pi(b_2|a_2) = 1$	$(\lambda_{a_2} \wedge \lambda_{b_2} \to \theta_1)$

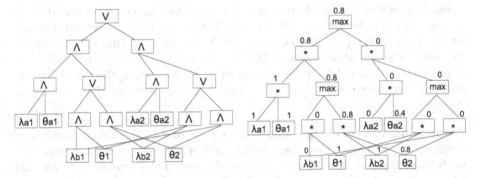

Fig. 2. Compiled base C_{DNNF} **Fig. 3.** Max-prod circuit $C^*_{\Pi-DNNF}$

3.2.1   Updating Instance Indicators

This step serves to record the instance of interest x and the evidence e into instance indicators λ_{x_i}. It corresponds to conditioning the compiled base C_{DNNF} on e and x. The conditioned compiled base is denoted by $[C_{DNNF}|x, e]$. Formally: $\forall \lambda_{x_i}$ of $X_i \in V$, λ_{x_i} is set to $\top$ if $x_i \sim e$ and $x_i \sim x$, $\bot$ otherwise where $\sim$ denotes the compatibility relation, i.e., $x_i \sim e$ refers to the fact that x_i and e agree on values.

3.2.2   Mapping Logical Representation into a Product-Based Representation

In this step, we transform the logical compiled base resulting from the previous step into a valued representation. In this step, it is important to note that the valued compiled bases, named *arithmetic circuits* and used in the probabilistic method [9] cannot be applied in our case since its operators (i.e., * and +) are different from those that should be used in the product-based case (i.e., * and max). For this reason, we propose to use a new *max-prod circuit* suitable for the product-based case. In fact, given the conditioned compiled base resulting from the previous step, we should apply the following operations: (i) replace $\vee$ and $\wedge$ by max and *, respectively, (ii) substitute each $\top$ (resp. $\perp$) by 1 (resp. 0) and (iii) associate $\Pi(x_i|u_i)$ to each $\theta_{x_i|u_i}$.

Definition 3. *A max-prod circuit of a DNNF sentence C_{DNNF}, denoted by $C^*_{\Pi-DNNF}$, is a valued sentence where $\wedge$ and $\vee$ are substituted by * and max, respectively. Leaf nodes correspond to circuit inputs (i.e., indicator and parameter variables), internal nodes correspond to max and * operators, and the root corresponds to the circuit output.*

It is obvious that the mapping from logical to numerical representation is established in a polynomial time since it corresponds to a set of trivial substitution operations. The use of *valued DNNFs* with max and * operators (i.e., max-prod circuits relative to product-based possibilistic networks) differs from the probabilistic case since inference in bayesian networks requires *valued d-DNNFs* with + and * operators (i.e., arithmetic circuits relative to Bayesian networks). This is essentially due to the fact that probabilistic computations require the determinism property (i.e., *d*) to ensure polytime model counting [10]. Following the succinctness relation between DNNF and d-DNNF stating that DNNF is more succinct than d-DNNF [8], we can give this important theoretical result, asserting that max-prod circuits are considered more compact than arithmetic circuits.

Proposition 1. *Let BN be a Bayesian network and C^+_{DNNF} be its arithmetic circuit using the probabilistic compilation method proposed in [9]. Let ΠG_* be a product-based possibilistic network sharing the same DAG structure as BN. Let $C^*_{\Pi-DNNF}$ be the max-prod circuit of ΠG_*. Then, from a theoretical point of view, we have:*

$$Size(C^*_{\Pi-DNNF}) \leq Size(C^+_{DNNF}) \tag{8}$$

3.2.3   Computation

The max-prod circuit is a special case of VNNFs where operators only restrict to max and *. In literature, max-prod circuits have been used under different notations to answer different queries. In fact, in [6], authors have explored circuits with max and *, called *maximizer circuits* to answer the *Most Probable Explanation*[2] (MPE) probabilistic query. While in [3], authors proposed *decision circuits* which add the operator + to max and * of maximizer circuits in order to

---

[2] A MPE is a complete variable instantiation with the highest probability given the current evidence.

evaluate influence diagrams. In our case, we are interested in computing $\Pi_c(x, e)$ and $\Pi_c(e)$ by evaluating $C^*_{\Pi-DNNF}$. Even we are in presence of a max-prod circuit similar to maximizer and decision circuits, we cannot use neither MPE nor evaluation of influence diagrams queries to compute $\Pi_c(x, e)$ and $\Pi_c(e)$. In fact, evaluating $C^*_{\Pi-DNNF}$ consists in applying max and * operators in a bottom-up way. The final result can be found at the root. Inference is guaranteed to be established in polytime since it corresponds to a simple propagation from leaves to root. Note that such computation corresponds to *max-variable elimination*.

It is worth pointing out that the query used for evaluating $C^*_{\Pi-DNNF}$ do not correspond to a *model counting problem* as in the probabilistic case [9]. This means that under compilation product-based possibilistic networks are not close to probabilistic ones and do not share the same features as BNs.

Example 3. *Considering the compiled base of Figure 2. Let us compute the effect of the evidence a_1 on the instance of interest b_2 (i.e., $\Pi_c(b_2|a_1)$). To compute $\Pi_c(a_1, b_2)$, we should first record a_1 and b_2 into instance indicators by setting λ_{a_1} and λ_{b_2} (resp. λ_{a_2} and λ_{b_1}) to $\top$ (resp. $\perp$). The logical compiled base arisen from Step 1 is then mapped into a max-prod circuit depicted by Figure 3. By applying max and * in a bottom-up fashion as shown in Figure 3, we can deduce that $\Pi_c(a_1, b_2)$ is equal to 0.8. Hence, $\Pi_c(b_2|a_1) = \frac{0.8}{1} = 0.8$.*

4   Prod-Π-DNNF vs Min-Π-DNNF

Proposition 1 shows that max-prod circuits are more compact than arithmetic circuits. We aim now to compare them to their qualitative counterpart in the possibilistic framework i.e. min-max circuits. In fact, in previous works [1,2], we have extended the idea of compiling BNs into min-based possibilistic networks by proposing several variants of CNF encodings especially for causal networks and binary possibilistic networks. Here, we are interested in comparing Prod-Π-DNNF to Min-Π-DNNF [2]. Roughly speaking, Min-Π-DNNF follows the same principles as Prod-Π-DNNF but one of the major differences resides in the *possibilistic local structure* since Min-Π-DNNF do not use the same encoding strategy as Prod-Π-DNNF, namely: *one variable per equal parameters per CPT*. In fact, if we consider the scale $L_{CPTs} = \{v_1, ..., v_p\}$ of possibility degrees used in all CPTs without redundancy, then Min-Π-DNNF uses *possibilistic local structure* [2] which consists in assigning a propositional variable θ_i for each $v_i \in L_{CPTs}$. This is essentially due to the *idempotency* property of the min operator.

Clearly, from a theoretical point of view, the possibilistic local structure allows the generation of more compact compiled bases. Our target through the current experimental study is to study in depth the emphasis of local structure and possibilistic local structure while encoding the network and their behaviors on compiled bases parameters. To this end, we consider randomly generated possibilistic networks by setting the number of nodes to 50, the maximum number of parents per node to 3 and the number of instances per variable to 2 and 3. We also vary possibility distributions (except for the normalization value 1) using two parameters: (EP_{CPTs} (%)): *the percent of equal parameters within all*

$CPTs$ and (EP_{CPT}): *the number of equal parameters per CPT.* For each experimentation, we generate 100 possibilistic networks by setting $\%EP_{CPTs}$ to $\{0\%, 10\%, 30\%, 50\%, 70\%, 100\%\}$. For instance, 50% means that each possibility degree v_i appears in 50% of all CPTs. The extreme case 0% (resp. 100%) states that each v_i appears in only one CPT (resp. all CPTs). For each percentage of $\%EP_{CPTs}$, we set two values to EP_{CPT}, namely: (1): *each v_i appears once in a CPT (except the degree 1 needed for normalization)* and (> 1): *each v_i appears randomly more than once.*

Table 2. Prod-Π-DNNF vs Min-Π-DNNF (better values are in bold)

		Prod-Π-DNNF				Min-Π-DNNF			
		C_*		$C^*_{\Pi-DNNF}$		C_{min}		$C^{min}_{\Pi-DNNF}$	
EP_{CPTs} (%)	EP_{CPT}	Variables	Clauses	Nodes	Edges	Variables	Clauses	Nodes	Edges
0	1	372	1298	**5716**	**13995**	180	464	466482	1050671
	>1	213	595	**3140**	**6179**	143	447	24003	58082
10	1	334	1099	**2363**	**5394**	131	429	156148	392150
	>1	206	497	**1377**	**2396**	103	392	10931	27134
30	1	323	1062	**1918**	**4148**	119	415	58840	153619
	>1	194	496	**1064**	**1801**	100	407	2879	8100
50	1	316	975	**1795**	**3731**	107	358	10395	26347
	>1	202	492	**1101**	**1870**	96	438	3241	7422
70	1	306	936	**2401**	**5475**	107	408	23310	53928
	>1	205	480	**1668**	**3244**	97	390	3827	8630
100	1	298	871	**1453**	**2965**	99	376	9526	23067
	>1	197	466	**880**	**1391**	95	413	965	2050

The experimental results are shown in Table 2 where C_{min} and $C^{min}_{\Pi-DNNF}$ denote, respectively the CNF encoding of ΠG_{min} and its min-max circuit (DNNF using min and max operators). Let us study in depth CNF parameters and compiled bases parameters of Prod-Π-DNNF and Min-Π-DNNF.

- **CNF encodings:** It is clear from columns 3, 4, 7 and 8 that Min-Π-DNNF uses less CNF variables and clauses than Prod-Π-DNNF regardless of $EP_{CPT} > 1$. In fact, the variable gain (i.e., $\frac{Vars\ C_{min}}{Vars\ C_*}$) is around 38% and the clause gain (i.e., $\frac{Cls\ C_{min}}{Cls\ C_*}$) is around 40% by considering $EP_{CPT} = 1$ for each percentage of EP_{CPTs}. Hence, we can deduce that by rising EP_{CPTs}, the number of CNF variables and clauses in Min-Π-DNNF is increasingly reduced, which proves the interest of using possibilitic local structure.

- **Compiled bases:** Compiled bases parameters do not follow the same behavior as CNF encodings. In fact, Prod-Π-DNNF is characterized by a lower number of nodes and edges comparing to those of Min-Π-DNNF even if Min-Π-DNNF outperforms Prod-Π-DNNF regarding CNF parameters. We can point out from columns 3, 4, 5 and 6 that increasing the number of equal parameters per CPT (i.e., $EP_{CPT} > 1$) for each EP_{CPTs} has a considerable impact on both CNF parameters and compiled bases parameters. More precisely, the node gain (i.e., $\frac{Nde \ C^{*}_{\Pi-DNNF}}{Nde \ C^{min}_{\Pi-DNNF}}$) is around 25% and the edge gain (i.e., $\frac{Edg \ C^{*}_{\Pi-DNNF}}{Edg \ C^{min}_{\Pi-DNNF}}$) is around 20% by considering $EP_{CPT} = \{1, > 1\}$. The question that may arise is: *Why Prod-Π-DNNF has less nodes and edges than Min-Π-DNNF even if this latter has less CNF parameters?* In fact, a possible explanation is that possibilistic local structure do not maintain the network structure which is indispensable in compilation. When a propositional variable encodes several parameters pertaining to some CPTs, in this case we cannot know neither its network variable nor its parents. Contrarily to Prod-Π-DNNF, local structure increases of course the number of CNF parameters but do not alter the network structure, which justifies why from a spatial point of view, Prod-Π-DNNF outperforms Min-Π-DNNF regarding compiled bases parameters.

5   Conclusion

This paper proposed a compilation-based inference method dedicated for product-based possibilistic networks. Interestingly enough, Prod-Π-DNNF uses *local structure* and *max-prod circuits*, which are theoretically more compact than arithmetic circuits, in order to efficiently compute the impact of evidence on variables. Our experimental study confirms the fact that having less CNF parameters do not obviously improve compiled bases parameters. Our future work consists in exploring the different variants of CNF encodings studied in [1,2] for product-based possibilistic networks.

References

1. Ayachi, R., Ben Amor, N., Benferhat, S.: Compiling Min-based Possibilistic Causal Networks: A Mutilated-Based Approach. In: Liu, W. (ed.) ECSQARU 2011. LNCS, vol. 6717, pp. 700–712. Springer, Heidelberg (2011)
2. Ayachi, R., Ben Amor, N., Benferhat, S., Haenni, R.: Compiling possibilistic networks: Alternative approaches to possibilistic inference. In: UAI, pp. 40–47 (2010)
3. Bhattacharjya, D., Shachter, R.: Evaluating influence diagrams with decision circuits. In: UAI
4. Borgelt, C., Gebhardt, J., Kruse, R.: Possibilistic graphical models. In: ISSEK
5. Cadoli, M., Donini, F.: A survey on knowledge compilation. AI Communications 10(3-4), 137–150 (1997)
6. Chan, H., Darwiche, A.: On the robustness of most probable explanations. In: UAI, pp. 63–71 (2006)
7. Chavira, M., Darwiche, A.: Compiling bayesian networks with local structure. In: IJCAI, pp. 1306–1312 (2005)
8. Darwiche, A.: Decomposable negation normal form. Journal of the ACM 48(4), 608–647 (2001)
9. Darwiche, A.: A logical approach to factoring belief networks. In: KR, pp. 409–420 (2002)
10. Darwiche, A., Marquis, P.: A knowledge compilation map. Journal of Artificial Intelligence Research 17, 229–264 (2002)

11. Dubois, D., Prade, H.: Possibility theory:An approach to computerized, Processing of uncertainty. Plenium Press (1988)

12. Dubois, D., Prade, H.: Possibility theory. In: Encyclopedia of Complexity and Systems Science. Springer (2009)

13. Fargier, H., Marquis, P.: On valued negation normal form formulas. In: IJCAI, pp. 360–365 (2007)

14. Hisdal, E.: Conditional possibilities independence and non interaction. Fuzzy Sets and Systems 1 (1978)

15. Wachter, M., Haenni, R.: Logical Compilation of Bayesian Networks with Discrete Variables. In: Mellouli, K. (ed.) ECSQARU 2007. LNCS (LNAI), vol. 4724, pp. 536–547. Springer, Heidelberg (2007)

Dynamic Directed Evidential Networks with Conditional Belief Functions: Application to System Reliability

Wafa Laâmari[1], Boutheina Ben Yaghlane[1], and Christophe Simon[2]

[1] LARODEC Laboratory - Institut Supérieur de Gestion de Tunis, Tunisia
[2] CRAN - Université de Lorraine - CNRS, UMR 7039, France

Abstract. The temporal dimension is a very important aspect which must be taken into consideration when reasoning under uncertainty.

The main purpose of this paper is to address this problem by a new evidential framework for modeling temporal changes in data. This method, allowing to model uncertainty and to manage time varying information thanks to the evidence theory, offers an alternative framework for dynamic probabilistic and dynamic possibilistic networks. It is applied to a system reliability analysis for the sake of illustration.

Keywords: Dynamic graphical models, theory of evidence, time varying information, managing uncertainty.

1 Introduction

Over the past years, available knowledge in various real-world applications has been characterized by the uncertainty which may be either aleatory or epistemic. Several network-based approaches have been developed for modeling knowledge such as probabilistic, possibilistic and evidential graphical models. These graphical models provide representational and computational aspects making them a powerful tool for representing knowledge and reasoning under uncertainty.

In modeling knowledge, there is also the problem of changes over time of the existing knowledge. A wide variety of methods have been developed to take into account time varying information with uncertainties, including those relying on network-based approaches. Murphy developed dynamic Bayesian networks (DBNs) that aimed to represent the temporal dimension under the probabilistic formalism [6]. This formalism provides tools to handle efficiently the aleatory uncertainty, but not the epistemic uncertainty. Recently, Heni et al. [3] proposed dynamic possibilistic networks (DPNs) for modeling uncertain sequential data. Weber et al. [13] also introduced dynamic evidential networks (DENs) to model the temporal evolution of uncertain knowledge. Based on an extension of the Bayes' theorem to the representation of the Dempster-Shafer's belief functions theory [10], DENs do not fully exploit the abilities of the evidential formalism.

The aim of the paper is to propose a new network-based approach considering the temporal dimension: the dynamic directed evidential network with conditional belief functions (DDEVN).

S. Greco et al. (Eds.): IPMU 2012, Part III, CCIS 299, pp. 481–490, 2012.

The paper is structured as follows. In Sect.2, we briefly recall some theoretical concepts related to static and dynamic graphical models. We sketch in Sect.3 the directed evidential network with conditional belief functions (DEVN) proposed by Ben Yaghlane [1] and we introduce the DDEVN which extends static DEVN to enable modeling changes over time. In Sect.4, we give the propagation algorithm in the DDEVN. Section 5 is devoted to an illustration of the new framework in the reliability area.

2   Static and Dynamic Directed Graphical Models

Graphical models [5], [8] combine the graph theory with any theory dealing with uncertainty to provide a general framework for an intuitive and a clear graphical representation of real-world problems. Some basic concepts related to static and dynamic directed graphical models are recalled in this section.

2.1   Static Directed Graphical Models

A static directed graphical model (DGM) consists of two distinct parts: the qualitative part and the quantitative part.

The qualitative part is represented in a DGM by a directed acyclic graph (DAG) $G = (N,E)$, where N is a non empty finite set of nodes representing the variables of the problem, and E is a set of directed edges representing the conditional independencies between the variables.

The quantitative part is expressed by a set of local functions (potentials) associated to each variable according to the uncertainty modeling framework. For each root node X, an a priori function $F(X)$ has to be defined over its states. For other nodes, a conditional function $F[Pa(X)](X)$ is specified for each possible state of X knowing the states of its parents denoted by $Pa(X)$.

Basically, DGMs do not allow to manage time varying knowledge because they do not represent the temporal dimension. Nevertheless, various dynamic networks have been proposed [2], [3], [6], [13].

2.2   Dynamic Directed Graphical Models

A dynamic directed graphical model (DDGM) is a directed graphical model providing explicitly the temporal dimension. At each time slice k $(k \geq 0)$, a variable X is represented in a DDGM by a node X_k. Thus, each time slice k is represented by a set of nodes N_k including all the variables of this time slice k.

The qualitative dependency between a node X_k and a node Y_{k+1} is represented by a directed edge linking the two nodes. This edge, denoting a transition function, is defined by a conditional value table as follows:

$$F[X_k](Y_{k+1}) = \begin{bmatrix} f[A_1^{X_k}](A_1^{Y_{k+1}}) & \dots & f[A_1^{X_k}](A_{Q_Y}^{Y_{k+1}}) \\ \dots & \dots & \dots \\ f[A_{Q_X}^{X_k}](A_1^{Y_{k+1}}) & \dots & f[A_{Q_X}^{X_k}](A_{Q_Y}^{Y_{k+1}}) \end{bmatrix}. \tag{1}$$

where $A_i^{X_k}$ is the i-th state of X_k and $A_j^{Y_{k+1}}$ is the j-th state of Y_{k+1}.

Dynamic directed graphical models used in [3], [6], [13] are supposed to be:

- Stationary: $F[X_k](Y_{k+1})$ does not depend on k.
- Markovian: $F(Y_{k+1})$ depends only on the distributions of the parent nodes of Y_{k+1}. Thus the future time slice is conditionally independent of the past ones given the present time slice [6].

As a new set of nodes N_k is introduced in the DDGM to represent each new time slice k, the major drawback of this standard DDGM representation is that with a large number of time slices, the graphical structure becomes huge, and as a result the inference process is cumbersome and time consuming. To overcome this problem, the proposed solution for DDGM is to keep the network in a compact form with only two consecutive time slices.

With the new representation, a DDGM is defined as a couple (G_0, G_k), where G_0 denotes the DGM corresponding to time slice $k = 0$ and G_k denotes a 2-time slices DGM (2-TDGM) in which only two nodes are introduced to represent a same variable at successive time steps: the first node is used to model a variable in the time slice k and the second one is used to represent this variable at the time slice $k + 1$.

The concept of the outgoing interface I_k has been defined in [6] as:
$I_k = \{X_k \in N_k \ / \ (X_k, Y_{k+1}) \in E(k, k+1) \text{ and } Y_{k+1} \in N_{k+1}\}$, where N_k is the set of nodes modeling the time slice k, N_{k+1} is the set of nodes modeling the time slice $k + 1$ and $E(k, k+1)$ is the set of edges linking two nodes X_k and Y_{k+1} belonging to the successive time slices k and $k + 1$.

In the 2-TDGM shown in Fig.1 (b), the interface $I_0 = \{V1_0, V2_0, V3_0\}$ is the set of nodes of time slice $k = 0$ which have got child nodes in time slice $k + 1 = 1$.

A 1.5 DDGM is a graph resulting from a 2-TDGM by the elimination of nodes not belonging to the outgoing interface I_k.

By the elimination of R_k and O_k (which do not belong to I_k) from the 2-TDGM of Fig.1 (b), we obtain the 1.5 DDGM shown in Fig.1 (c).

3 Static and Dynamic Directed Evidential Networks with Conditional Belief Functions

Evidential networks with conditional belief functions (ENCs) were initially proposed by Smets [12] and studied later by Xu and Smets [14]. Xu proposed the graphical representation and the inference algorithm which are exploited only with binary relations between nodes [14]. Ben Yaghlane proposed in [1] the directed evidential network with conditional belief functions (DEVN) to model the relations for any number of nodes.

3.1 Directed Evidential Networks with Conditional Belief Functions

A DEVN is a DGM based on the evidence theory with a set of belief functions M associated to each variable. For each root node X, having a frame of discernment Ω_X constituted by q mutually exhaustive and exclusive hypotheses, an a priori belief function $M(X)$ has to be defined over the 2^q focal sets A_i^X by the following equation:

$$M(X) = [m(\emptyset) \quad m(A_1^X)....m(A_i^X)....m(A_{2q-1}^X)] \ . \tag{2}$$

with

$$m(A_i^X) \geq 0 \quad \text{and} \quad \sum_{A_i^X, A_i^X \in 2^{\Omega_X}} m(A_i^X) = 1 \ . \tag{3}$$

where $m(A_i^X)$ is the belief that X verifies the focal element A_i^X's hypotheses.

For other nodes, a conditional belief function $M[Pa(X)](X)$ is specified for each possible focal set A_i^X knowing the focal sets of the parents of X. The propagation algorithm is performed in a secondary computational data structure called the modified binary join tree (MBJT) [1].

Modified Binary Join Tree. The MBJT was proposed in [1] as a refinement of the binary join tree (BJT) [11]. Contrary to the BJT, the MBJT emphasizes explicitly the conditional relations in the DEVN for using them when performing the inference process [1]. The MBJT construction process is based on the fusion algorithm [11].

The algorithm of the static MBJT construction process is described as follows:

Algorithm 1. Static MBJT Construction

Input: a DEVN, an elimination Sequence
Output: a MBJT
1. Determine the subsets that form the hypergraph H from the DEVN
2. Arrange the subsets of H in a binary join tree using the elimination sequence
3. Attach singleton subsets to the binary join tree
4. Make the join tree binary again if it becomes non-binary when attaching a singleton subset to it
5. Draw rectangles containing the conditional relations between variables instead of circles containing just the list of these variables (to obtain the MBJT)

Note that if we just perform steps 1, 2, 3 and 4, we obtain a BJT. These steps are more detailed in [11] and more details for the MBJT are given in [1].

3.2 Dynamic Directed Evidential Networks with Conditional Belief Functions (DDEVN)

DDEVNs are introduced in a way similar to other DDGMs, in the sense that the considered problems are those whose dynamics can be modeled as stochastic processes which are stationary and Markovian. DDEVN is defined as a couple (D_0, D_k), where D_0 is the DEVN representing the time slice $k = 0$ and D_k denotes a 2-time slice DEVN (2-TDEVN) with only two consecutive time slices. The temporal dependencies between variables are represented in DDEVN by transition-belief mass using (1).

4   Propagation in DDEVN

The reasoning process is made in the DDEVN through an adaptation of the exact Interface algorithm defined by Murphy for DBNs [6], [7]. With its two consecutive time slices, a 2-TDEVN allows to compute the belief mass distribution of a variable X at any time step $k = T$, starting from an observed situation at the initial time step $k = 0$ and transition distributions illustrating the temporal dependencies between two consecutive time slices.

Algorithm 2. Construction and initialization of M_0

Input: a 2-TDEVN
Output: a MBJT M_0, an outgoing interface I_0
1. Identify I_0 by selecting nodes in the outgoing interface of time slice $k = 0$
   $I_0 \leftarrow \{x \in N_0 \ / \ (x,y) \in E(0,1) \ and \ y \in N_1\}$
2. Eliminate each node belonging to N_1 from the 2-TDEVN
3. Construct the MBJT M_0 from the resulting structure using Algorithm 1
4. Let P be the set of the given potentials[1]
   For i=1 to length(P)
      If P(i) is an a priori belief function distribution
         assign P(i) to the corresponding singleton node[2]
      Else
         assign P(i) to the corresponding conditional node in M_0.
      End if
   End for

Algorithm 3. Construction and initialization of M_k

Input: a 2-TDEVN
Output: a MBJT M_k, an outgoing interface I_k
1. $I_k \leftarrow \{x \in N_k \ / \ (x,y) \in E(k,k+1) \ and \ y \in N_{k+1}\}$
2. Eliminate from the 2-TDEVN each node belonging to N_k and not to I_k (to obtain a 1.5 DDEVN)
3. Construct the MBJT M_k from the 1.5 DDEVN using Algorithm 1
4. Let P be the set of potentials relative only to variables of time slice $k + 1$
   For i=1 to length(P)
      If P(i) is an a priori belief function distribution
         assign P(i) to the corresponding singleton node in M_k.
      Else
         assign P(i) to the corresponding conditional node in M_k.
      End if
   End for

For the inference in the DDEVN, two MBJTs are created. The first MBJT, denoted M_0, represents the initial time step $k = 0$, while the second one, denoted M_k, corresponds to each time slice $k > 0$. The propagation process can be performed for computing nodes' marginals, either in MBJT M_0 or in MBJT M_k

---

[1] The potentials are the a priori and the conditional mass tables associated to variables.
[2] Singleton node is a node in a MBJT which contains just one variable in M_0.

Algorithm 4. Propagation in the DDEVN

Input: M_0 and M_k

Output: marginal distributions

1. Performing the propagation process in M_0[3]
   Let n be the number of singleton nodes in I_0
   For i=1 to n
       node=$I_0(i)$;
       Marg_distr= Marginal_distribution(node);
       Add Marg_Distr to the interface potentials IP_0;
   End for

2. **If** $k > 0$
       For i=1 to k
           For j=1 to length(IP_{i-1})
               Current_potential=$IP_{i-1}(j)$;
               Associate Current_potential to the corresponding singleton node in M_k;
           End for
           Performing the propagation process in M_k;
           Let n be the number of singleton nodes in I_i;
           For nb=1 to n
               node=$I_i(nb)$;
               Marg_Distr= Marginal_Distribution(node);
               Add Marg_Distr to IP_i;
           End for
       End for
   End if

3. **If** $k = 0$
       Compute_Marginals(M_0)[4]
   Else
       Compute_Marginals(M_k)
   End if

---

depending on the time slice k. M_0 is used for computing the nodes' marginals at time slice $k = 0$, while M_k is used when computing marginals in a time step $k \geq 1$. As when inferring in the junction tree [3], [6], the key idea is that when advancing from the past time step $k - 1$ to the current time step k, we need to store the marginals of variables in the outgoing interface I_k that will be useful as observations introduced in the corresponding nodes in the next inference.

By recursively performing the bidirectional message-passing scheme in M_k, we can compute the marginals of variables at any time step.

The construction processes of the MBJTs are given in the following algorithms:

The propagation process in the DDEVN is given by the following algorithm:

---

[3] The propagation process is performed as in the static MBJT. For details, the reader is referred to [1].

[4] To compute the marginal for a node, we combine its own initial potential with the messages received from all the neighbors during the propagation process [1].

5 Illustrative Case Study

For the sake of illustration, let us apply the DDEVN to the reliability analysis of the well known valve system [9], [13]. It consists of three valves (components). Each valve Vi has two disjoint states ($\{Up\}, \{Down\}$): Up, shortly written U, is the working state and $Down$, shortly written D, is the fail state. Thus, the frame of discernment of each valve is $\Omega = \{Up, Down\}$ and its corresponding power set is $2^\Omega = \{\emptyset, \{Up\}, \{Down\}, \{Up, Down\}\}$. The valve system has a 2-out-of-3 configuration, denoted 2oo3 which is a special configuration widely used in real applications. To ensure the ability of this system to perform its function, two valves at least must be operating to make the valve system functioning. In the classical reliability analysis, the reliability of the valve system is its probability to be in the state $\{Up\}$ during a mission time.

Figure 1 (a) shows the DAG corresponding to the valve system in which each node Vi represents the i-th valve of the system, the node O represents the logical '2oo3' gate and the node R represents the valve system reliability.

5.1 Application of the DDEVN to the Valve System Reliability

The valve system is modeled by the DDEVN shown in Fig.1 (b). Each node Vi_k represents the i-th valve in the time slice k, node O_k represents the logical 2oo3 gate in the time slice k, and node R_k represents the state of the system in the k-th time slice.

Figure 1 (c) shows the 1.5   DDEVN created from the 2-TDEVN given in Fig.1 (b) by removing all nodes in the time slice k not belonging to I_k.

The belief mass distributions of the three valves at the time step $k+1$ which depend on their distributions at the time step k are represented in Tables 1, 2 and 3. Table 5 represents the a priori mass distributions of the valves at the time step 0. The conditional mass distribution relative to node R_k is given in Table 4. The conditional belief mass distribution relative to node O_k is defined equivalent to the logical '2oo3' gate.

Tables 1 and 2. *Conditional mass tables* $M[V1_k](V1_{k+1})$ *and* $M[V2_k](V2_{k+1})$

$V1_{k+1}\backslash V1_k$	U	D	$U \cup D$
U	0.998	0	0.000
D	0.001	1	0.001
$U \cup D$	0.001	0	0.999

$V2_{k+1}\backslash V2_k$	U	D	$U \cup D$
U	0.997	0	0.000
D	0.002	1	0.002
$U \cup D$	0.001	0	0.998

Tables 3 and 4. *Conditional mass tables* $M[V3_k](V3_{k+1})$ *and* $M[O_k](R_k)$

$V3_{k+1}\backslash V3_k$	U	D	$U \cup D$
U	0.996	0	0.000
D	0.003	1	0.003
$U \cup D$	0.001	0	0.997

$R_k\backslash O_k$	U	D	$U \cup D$
U	1	0	0
D	0	1	0
$U \cup D$	0	0	1

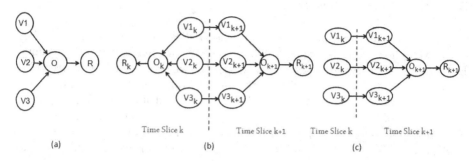

Fig. 1. The DAG (a), the 2-TDEVN (b) and the 1.5 DDEVN (c) of the Valve System

Table 5. The a priori mass tables $M(V1_0)$, $M(V2_0)$ and $M(V3_0)$

Vi_0	U	D	$U \cup D$
$m(Vi_0)$	1.0	0.0	0.0

Construction and Initialization of M_0 and M_k. Using the 2-TDEVN in Fig.1, the MBJTs M_0 and M_k shown in Fig.2 are constructed by applying the first three steps of algorithms 2 and 3. Using the a priori and the conditional mass tables, M_0 and M_k are initialized by assigning each belief function distribution to the corresponding node (the fourth step of algorithms 2 and 3).

Performing the Propagation Process in the DDEVN. Suppose now that we wish to compute the valve system reliability at time step $k = 1200$. We first

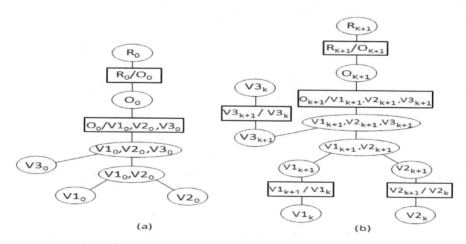

Fig. 2. The MBJTs M_0 (a) and M_k (b) for the Valve System

perform the inference process in M_0 and we compute the marginals of nodes in the outgoing interface $I_0 = \{V1_0, V2_0, V3_0\}$ (the first step of algorithm 4).

The marginal distributions of the outgoing interface I_0's nodes will be used when performing the second propagation in the MBJT M_k in the next time slice ($k = 1$). They will be respectively introduced in nodes $V1_0$, $V2_0$ and $V3_0$ of M_k. After performing the inference algorithm, M_k yields the marginals of nodes $V1_1$, $V2_1$ and $V3_1$ (forming the outgoing interface I_1) which are the sufficient information needed to continue the propagation in the following time slice $k = 2$. After carrying out the inference process in the MBJT M_k recursively for 1200 time slices, we obtain the following distribution for node R_{1200} corresponding to the reliability of the valve system $M(R_{1200}) = [m(\emptyset) = 0 \; m(\{Up\}) = 0.00314 \; m(\{Down\}) = 0.9656 \; m(\{Up, Down\}) = 0.0313]$

The lower bound $(Bel(Up))$ and the upper bound $(Pl(Up))$ of the system Reliability over 1200 time steps are depicted in Fig.3.

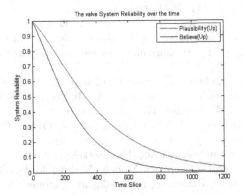

Fig. 3. The Valve System Reliability over time

5.2 DEN and DDEVN for the System Reliability Assessment

A comparison of the static evidential network (EN) and the static DEVN was proposed in [4]. It reveals that if we apply the two evidential models to assess a system reliability under the closed or the open-world assumptions, they provide the same reliability evaluation as the one given by the mathematical formula.

To show the capacity of the DDEVN to compute the system reliability over time, it is important to compare the assessment of the system reliabilities that it provides and those obtained by the dynamic evidential network (DEN). Regarding this aspect and after applying the two evidential models to the studied system, we found no essential differences between them, since they provide the same reliability evaluation of the system at each time slice k (from 0 to 1200).

6   Conclusion

Inspired by the same aims of DBNs and DPNs and also with the intent to make the DEVN able to dynamically model a problem under uncertainty, we have extended in this paper the static DEVN into the dynamic DEVN that we called DDEVN. DDEVN was applied to the reliability study of a well known system: the valve system. We have shown that this new framework allows to efficiently model the temporal evolution of this system with uncertainty. In future work, the development of new algorithms to perform the propagation process in the DDEVN will be of a great interest.

References

1. Ben Yaghlane, B., Mellouli, K.: Inference in Directed Evidential Networks Based on the Transferable Belief Model. Int. J. Approx. Reasoning 48(2), 399–418 (2008)
2. Dagum, P., Galper, A., Horwitz, E.: Dynamic Networks Models for Forecasting. In: Proc. UAI 1992, pp. 41–48 (1992)
3. Heni, A., Ben Amor, N., Benferhat, S., Alimi, A.: Dynamic Possibilistic Networks: Representation and Exact Inference. In: IEEE International Conference on Computational Intelligence for Measurement Systems and Applications (CIMSA 2007), Ostuni, Italy, pp. 1–8 (2007)
4. Laâmari, W., Ben Yaghlane, B., Simon, C.: Comparing Evidential Graphical Models for Imprecise Reliability. In: Deshpande, A., Hunter, A. (eds.) SUM 2010. LNCS, vol. 6379, pp. 191–204. Springer, Heidelberg (2010)
5. Lauritzen, S.L.: Graphical Models. Clarendon Press, Oxford (1996)
6. Murphy, K.: Dynamic Bayesian Networks: Representation, Inference and Learning. PhD thesis, Dept. Computer Science, UC, Berkeley (2002)
7. Murphy, K.: Probabilistic Graphical Models. Michael Jordan (2002)
8. Pearl, J.: Probabilistic Reasoning in Intelligent Systems: Networks of Plausible Inference. Morgan Kaufmann (1988)
9. Satoh, N., Sasaki, M., Yuge, T., Yanagi, S.: Reliability of 3-State Device Systems with Simultaneous Failures. IEEE Transactions on Reliability 42, 470–477 (1993)
10. Shafer, G.: A Mathematical Theory of Evidence. Princeton University Press, Princeton (1976)
11. Shenoy, P.P.: Binary Join Trees for Computing Marginals in the Shenoy-Shafer Architecture. Int. J. Approx. Reasoning 17(2-3), 239–263 (1997)
12. Smets, P.: Belief Function: the Disjunctive Rule of Combination and the Generalized Bayesian Theorem. Int. J. Approx. Reasoning 9, 1–35 (1993)
13. Weber, P., Simon, C.: Dynamic Evidential Networks in System Reliability Analysis: A Dempster Shafer Approach. In: 16th Mediterranean Conference on Control and Automation, France, vol. 93, pp. 262–267 (2008)
14. Xu, H., Smets, P.: Evidential Reasoning with Conditional Belief Functions. In: Heckerman, D., Poole, D., Lopez De Mantaras, R. (eds.) UAI 1994, pp. 598–606. Morgan Kaufmann, California (1994)

Likelihood-Based Robust Classification with Bayesian Networks

Alessandro Antonucci[1], Marco E.G.V. Cattaneo[2], and Giorgio Corani[1,*]

[1] Istituto Dalle Molle di Studi sull'Intelligenza Artificiale (IDSIA)
Manno-Lugano Switzerland
{alessandro,giorgio}@idsia.ch
[2] Department of Statistics, LMU Munich
München Germany
cattaneo@stat.uni-muenchen.de

Abstract. Bayesian networks are commonly used for classification: a structural learning algorithm determines the network graph, while standard approaches estimate the model parameters from data. Yet, with few data the corresponding assessments can be unreliable. To gain robustness in this phase, we consider a *likelihood-based* learning approach, which takes all the model quantifications whose likelihood exceeds a given threshold. A new classification algorithm based on this approach is presented. Notably, this is a *credal* classifier, i.e., more than a single class can be returned in output. This is the case when the Bayesian networks consistent with the threshold constraint assign different class labels to a test instance. This is the first classifier of this kind for general topologies. Experiments show how this approach provide the desired robustness.

Keywords: Classification, likelihood-based learning, Bayesian networks, credal networks, imprecise probabilities, credal classifiers.

1 Introduction

The development of classifiers, i.e., algorithms to assign *class* labels to instances described by a set of *features*, is a major problem of AI, with lots of important applications, ranging from pattern recognition to prediction to diagnosis. Probabilistic approaches to classification are particularly popular and effective. In particular, the naive Bayes (e.g., [9, Chap. 17]) assumes conditional independence for the features given the class. Despite the generally good performances of this classifier, these assumptions are often unrealistic and other models with less restrictive assumptions have been proposed. These can be expressed in the framework of *Bayesian networks* [12] by directed graphs.

Besides classifiers based on special topologies (e.g., tree-augmented [7]), *structural learning* algorithms (e.g., K2 [9, Chap. 18]) can learn the network structure

---

* The research in this paper has been partially supported by the Swiss NSF grants n. 200020-132252, the Hasler foundation grant n. 10030 and the Computational Life Sciences - Ticino in Rete project.

S. Greco et al. (Eds.): IPMU 2012, Part III, CCIS 299, pp. 491–500, 2012.

from data. Regarding the learning of the parameters, this can be either based on Bayesian (e.g., a uniform Dirichlet prior) or frequentist (maximum-likelihood) approaches. The latter is unbiased and independent from the prior specification, but generally lead to inferior classification performances, especially on data sets where the contingency tables, which contain the counts of the joint occurrences of specific values of the features and the class, are characterised by several zeros [7]. To obtain more reliable estimates for the Bayesian network parameters, a *likelihood-based* approach [4,11] can be considered. This is a generalization of the frequentist approach towards *imprecise probabilities* [13], i.e., robust models based on sets of probability distributions. Loosely speaking, the idea is to consider, instead of the single maximum-likelihood estimator, all the models whose likelihood is above a certain threshold level. When applied to classification with Bayesian networks, this approach produces a classifier based, instead of a single, on a collection of Bayesian networks (with the same topology) or, in other words, a *credal network* [6]. If different Bayesian networks associated to the classifier assign different classes on a same test instance, the classifier returns all these classes. This is an example of *credal classification*, comparable with those proposed in [5], being in fact an extension of what we proposed in [1] for the naive case. To the best of our knowledge, this is the first credal classifier for general topologies.[1] A notable feature of our classifier is that, in the likelihood evaluation, we also consider the test instance with missing value for the class. This is important to obtain more accurate classification performances when coping with zero counts. The paper is organised as follows. We review background material about classification with Bayesian networks (Sect. 2.1) and likelihood-based approaches (Sect. 2.2). Then, in Sect. 3.1, our approach is presented by means of a simple example. Discussion on how to cope with zero counts is in Sect. 3.2, while Sect. 3.3 reports the formula for the classifier. The classifier performances are empirically tested in Sect. 4. Conclusions and outlooks are finally in Sect. 5.

2   Background

2.1   Classification with Bayesian Networks

Consider a set of variables $\mathbf{X} := (X_0, X_1, \ldots, X_n)$, with X_i taking values in a finite set Ω_{X_i}, for each $i = 0, 1, \ldots, n$. Regard X_0 as the *class* and other variables as *features* of a classification task based on a data set of joint observations, i.e., $\mathcal{D} := \{(x_0^{(j)}, x_1^{(j)}, \ldots, x_n^{(j)})\}_{j=1}^N$. A *classifier* is an algorithm assigning a class label $x_0^* \in \Omega_{X_0}$ to a generic test instance $(\tilde{x}_1, \ldots, \tilde{x}_n)$ of the features. In particular, *probabilistic classifiers* learn from data a joint probability mass function $P(X_0, \ldots, X_n)$ and, with 0-1 losses, assign to the test instance the class label:

$$x_0^* := \arg \max_{x_0 \in \Omega_{X_0}} P(x_0 | \tilde{x}_1, \ldots, \tilde{x}_n). \tag{1}$$

---

[1] Other credal classifiers are based on the *imprecise Dirichlet model*, but there are no classification algorithms for general topologies [5].

The learning of a joint mass function from the data $\mathcal{D}$ can be approached within the framework of *Bayesian networks* [12]. A Bayesian network induces a compact specification of the joint based on independencies among its variables. These are depicted by directed acyclic graphs with nodes in one-to-one correspondence with the variables in $\mathbf{X}$. Markov condition gives semantics: every variable is conditionally independent of its non-descendants non-parents given its parents. *Structural learning* algorithms [9, Chap. 18] can learn the graph modeling independencies in this way. Let $\mathcal{G}$ be this graph. For each $i = 0, \ldots, n$, denote by Π_i the parents of X_i according to $\mathcal{G}$. The factorization induced by these independencies is:

$$P(x_0, x_1, \ldots, x_n) = \prod_{i=0}^{n} P(x_i | \pi_i), \tag{2}$$

where π_i is the value of Π_i consistent with $(x_0, x_1, \ldots, x_n)$. To do classification, i.e., to assign a class label as in (1) to the test instance, we check, for each $x_0', x_0'' \in \Omega_{X_0}$, whether or not:

$$\frac{P(x_0' | \tilde{x}_1, \ldots, \tilde{x}_n)}{P(x_0'' | \tilde{x}_1, \ldots, \tilde{x}_n)} = \frac{P(x_0', \tilde{x}_1, \ldots, \tilde{x}_n)}{P(x_0'', \tilde{x}_1, \ldots, \tilde{x}_n)} > 1. \tag{3}$$

This inequality can be rewritten as:

$$\frac{P(x_0' | \tilde{\pi}_0)}{P(x_0'' | \tilde{\pi}_0)} \cdot \prod_{i=1}^{n} \frac{P(\tilde{x}_i | \tilde{\pi}_i')}{P(\tilde{x}_i | \tilde{\pi}_i'')} = \frac{P(x_0' | \tilde{\pi}_0)}{P(x_0'' | \tilde{\pi}_0)} \prod_{i=1,\ldots,n : X_0 \in \Pi_i} \frac{P(\tilde{x}_i | x_0', \tilde{\pi}_i)}{P(\tilde{x}_i | x_0'', \tilde{\pi}_i)} > 1, \tag{4}$$

where $\tilde{\pi}_0$ is the value of the parents of X_0 consistent with $(\tilde{x}_1, \ldots, \tilde{x}_n)$; $\tilde{\pi}_i'$ and $\tilde{\pi}_i''$ are the values of Π_i consistent, respectively, with $(x_0', \tilde{x}_1, \ldots, \tilde{x}_n)$ and $(x_0'', \tilde{x}_1, \ldots, \tilde{x}_n)$ (for each $i = 1, \ldots, n$), and the presence of X_0 among the parents of X_i is emphasized in the second product where (with a small abuse of notation) $\tilde{\pi}_i$ denote the state of $\Pi_i \setminus \{X_0\}$ consistent with $(\tilde{x}_1, \ldots, \tilde{x}_n)$. The first derivation in (4) follows from (2), the second comes from the fact that the terms in the products associated to variables X_i which are not children of X_0 (nor X_0 itself) are one. Hence, when doing classification with Bayesian networks, we can focus on the *Markov blanket* of X_0 (Fig. 1), i.e., (i) the class X_0; (ii) the parents of X_0; (iii) the children of X_0; and (iv) the parents of the children of X_0.

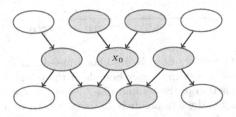

Fig. 1. A Bayesian network. The nodes of the Markov blanket of X_0 are in grey.

Regarding the quantification of the conditional probabilities in (2) (or, after the above discussion, only of those in the Markov blanket of X_0) from data, standard techniques can be adopted. For the conditional $P(X_i|\pi_i)$, a Bayesian approach with Dirichlet prior with parameter st_i, for each $x_i \in \Omega_{X_i}$, would give:

$$P(x_i|\pi_i) := \frac{n(x_i, \pi_i) + st_i}{n(\pi_i) + s}, \tag{5}$$

for each $i = 1, \ldots, n$, $x_i \in \Omega_{X_i}$, $\pi_i \in \Omega_{\Pi_i}$, where $n(\cdot)$ is a *count function* returning the counts for the data in $\mathcal{D}$ satisfying the event specified in its argument. Similarly, a frequentist (maximum-likelihood) approach would use expression (5) with $s = 0$. These approaches are known to produce potentially unreliable estimates if only few data are available, this being particularly true if zero counts occur. An extension of the frequentist approach to partially overcome these problems is presented in the next section.

2.2   Likelihood-Based Learning of Imprecise-Probabilistic Models

Likelihood-based approaches [4,11] are an extension of frequentist approaches intended to learn sets, instead of single, distributions, from data, this making the corresponding parameters estimates more robust and hence reliable. The basic idea is to start with a collection of candidate models, and then keep only those assigning to the available data a probability beyond a certain threshold. We introduce this with the following example.

Example 1. *Consider a Boolean X, for which N observations are available, and n of them report true. If $\theta \in [0, 1]$ is the chance that X is true, likelihood of data is $L(\theta) := \theta^n \cdot (1 - \theta)^{N-n}$ and its maximum $\theta^* = n/N$. For each $\alpha \in [0, 1]$, consider the values of θ such that $L(\theta) \geq \alpha L(\theta^*)$. Fig. 2 shows the behaviour of these probability intervals, which can be also regarded as confidence intervals [8], for increasing values of N.*

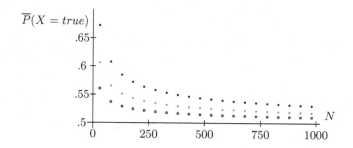

Fig. 2. Probability intervals obtained by likelihood-based learning for different values of α for Ex. 1. The plot shows the upper bounds of the interval probability that the variable is true as a function of the sample size N, when $n/N = 1/2$ (lower bounds are symmetric). Black, gray and white points refer, respectively, to $\alpha = .8, .5, .15$.

The above technique can be extended to the general case, and interpreted as a learning procedure [3,10] in the following sense. Consider a *credal set* $\mathbf{P}$, i.e., a collection of probability distributions all over the same variable. Assume the elements of $\mathbf{P}$ are indexed by parameter $\theta \in \Theta$, i.e., $\mathbf{P} := \{P_\theta\}_{\theta \in \Theta}$. Given the data $\mathcal{D}$, consider the normalised likelihood:

$$L(\theta) := \frac{P_\theta(\mathcal{D})}{\sup_{\theta' \in \Theta} P_{\theta'}(\mathcal{D})}, \tag{6}$$

likelihood-based learning consists in removing from $\mathbf{P}$ the distributions whose normalised likelihood is below a threshold. Thus, given $\alpha \in [0,1]$, we consider the (smaller) credal set:

$$\mathbf{P}_\alpha := \{P_\theta\}_{\theta \in \Theta : L(\theta) \geq \alpha}. \tag{7}$$

Note that $\mathbf{P}_{\alpha=1}$ is a "precise" credal set including only the maximum-likelihood distribution, while $\mathbf{P}_{\alpha=0} = \mathbf{P}$. Likelihood-based learning is said to be *pure*, if the credal set $\mathbf{P}$ includes all the possible distributions that can be specified over the variable under consideration.

3   Robust Likelihood-Based Classifiers

3.1   A Demonstrative Example

Consider a classification task as in Sect. 2.1 with a single feature and both variables Boolean. Assuming that $X_0 \rightarrow X_1$ is the graph obtained from the data (note that this models no independence at all), (2) rewrites as:

$$P(x_0, x_1) := P(x_1|x_0) \cdot P(x_0), \tag{8}$$

for each x_0, x_1. As a probability mass function over a Boolean variable can be specified by a single parameter, all Bayesian networks over this graph are parametrized by $\theta = (\theta_1, \theta_2, \theta_3)$ with $\theta_1 := p(x_0)$, $\theta_2 := p(x_1|x_0)$, $\theta_3 := p(x_1|\neg x_0)$. Let P_θ denote the corresponding joint distribution as in (8). A pure likelihood-based approach consists in starting from $\Theta := [0,1]^3 \subseteq \mathbb{R}^3$. The data set $\mathcal{D}$ to be used to refine this credal set can be equivalently characterized by four counts, i.e., $n_1 := n(x_0, x_1)$, $n_2 := n(x_0, \neg x_1)$, $n_3 := n(\neg x_0, x_1)$, $n_4 := (\neg x_0, \neg x_1)$. The corresponding likelihood, i.e.,

$$L(\theta) \propto (\theta_1 \cdot \theta_2)^{n_1} \cdot (\theta_1 \cdot (1-\theta_2))^{n_2} \cdot ((1-\theta_1) \cdot \theta_3)^{n_3} \cdot ((1-\theta_1) \cdot (1-\theta_3))^{n_4}, \tag{9}$$

attains its maximum when the parameters are estimated by the relative frequencies. For a more robust parameters estimation, given $\alpha \in [0,1]$, all the quantifications satisfying (7) can be considered. A collection of Bayesian networks (all over the same graph), i.e., a *credal network* [6] is therefore considered as a more robust and reliable model of the process generating the data. This model can be used for classification. Yet, when evaluating the ratio as in (3), different P_θ can produce different optimal classes.

To decide whether or not a class is dominating another one, a possible, conservative, approach consists in assuming that a probability dominates another one if and only if this is true for all the distributions. In practice we extend (3) to sets of distributions as follows:

$$\inf_{P_\theta \in \mathbf{P}_\alpha} \frac{P_\theta(x_0'|\tilde{x}_1, \ldots, \tilde{x}_n)}{P_\theta(x_0''|\tilde{x}_1, \ldots, \tilde{x}_n)} > 1. \tag{10}$$

This is a well-known decision criterion for imprecise-probabilistic models called *maximality* [13]. Unlike (3), testing dominance with (10) for each pair of classes can lead to multiple undominated classes. This produces a *credal* classifier, which can assign more than a class to test instances. To check (10), the likelihood should be evaluated as a function of ratio (3). This can be done by sampling as in Fig. 3. Yet, different models with different likelihoods can have the same ratio, i.e., the function is not single-valued. Nevertheless, to check dominance it is sufficient to determine whether or not the models (points) with ordinate (likelihood) greater than α all have a ratio (abscissa) greater than one. To do that, it is possible to focus on the left-most point (α-cut) where the likelihood upper envelope is α.

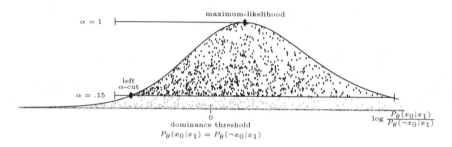

Fig. 3. Likelihood-based classification of a test instance $X_1 = x_1$ for model in Sect. 3.1 with $[n_1, n_2, n_3, n_4] = [2, 2, 1, 3]$. Black line is the upper envelope (see Sect. 3.3) and x-scale logarithmic. On this instance, (10) is not satisfied: x_0 does not dominate $\neg x_0$.

3.2   Coping with Zero Counts

In the above described procedure, likelihood was identified with the probability $P(\mathcal{D}|\theta)$ assigned by the Bayesian network associated to θ to the data. Yet, if there is an attribute $\tilde{x}_i$ in the test instance such that the relative counts are zero, the corresponding maximum-likelihood probability is zero, this preventing dominances in (10). Similar problems occur even within the Bayesian framework [12]. However, the test instance $(\tilde{x}_1, \ldots, \tilde{x}_n)$ has also been observed: it is an incomplete datum with class X_0 missing. Therefore, as in a semi-supervised setting, it could be involved in the likelihood evaluation as well, i.e.,

$$L'(\theta) \propto P(\mathcal{D}|\theta) \cdot \sum_{x_0 \in \Omega_{X_0}} P_\theta(x_0, \tilde{x}_1, \ldots, \tilde{x}_n). \tag{11}$$

Besides being more correct, this also prevents the above issue with zero counts. The maximum-likelihood estimate of θ can be calculated with the EM algorithm, which completes the test instance with fractional counts for the different values of X_0. We denote by $\hat{n}(\cdot)$ the counting function obtained by augmenting the counts about $\mathcal{D}$ with these fractional counts. Note that, while $n() = N$, $\hat{n}() = N + 1$.

3.3   Analytic Formulae for the Upper Envelope of the Likelihood

Following the approach in Sect. 3.1 we derive here an analytic expression for the upper envelope of the likelihood (11) as a function of the probability ratio (3). Each point of this upper envelope corresponds to a particular quantification P_θ of the Bayesian network. If $\theta(t)$ is a function of $t \in [a,b]$ such that there is a one-to-one correspondence between the quantifications $P_{\theta(t)}$ and the points of the upper envelope of the likelihood (when t varies in $[a,b]$), then

$$\left\{ \left(\frac{P_{\theta(t)}(x'_0, \tilde{x}_1, \ldots, \tilde{x}_n)}{P_{\theta(t)}(x''_0, \tilde{x}_1, \ldots, \tilde{x}_n)}, L'(\theta(t)) \right) : t \in [a,b] \right\} \tag{12}$$

is a parametric expression for the graph of the upper envelope.

A function $\theta(t)$ with the above property was obtained in [4] for the case without summation in (11), i.e., without considering the test instance in the likelihood. This result is not directly applicable to the likelihood (11), but we can obtain an approximation of the desired upper envelope if we use the function $\hat{\theta}(t)$ resulting from the expected likelihood delivered by the EM-algorithm, i.e., the likelihood corresponding to the augmented counts $\hat{n}(\cdot)$. Our approximation is then given by (12) with $\hat{\theta}(t)$ instead of $\theta(t)$.

To simplify the analytic formulae, we assume that the children of X_0 in the Bayesian network are denoted by $X_1, \ldots, X_k$ (with $k \leq n$). We first define:

$$a := -\min\{\hat{n}(x'_0, \tilde{\pi}_0), \hat{n}(\tilde{x}_1, x'_0, \tilde{\pi}_1), \ldots, \hat{n}(\tilde{x}_k, x'_0, \tilde{\pi}_k)\}, \tag{13}$$

$$b := \min\{\hat{n}(x''_0, \tilde{\pi}_0), \hat{n}(\tilde{x}_1, x''_0, \tilde{\pi}_1), \ldots, \hat{n}(\tilde{x}_k, x''_0, \tilde{\pi}_k)\}. \tag{14}$$

For each $t \in [a, b]$, let us consider the following functions:

$$x(t) := \frac{\hat{n}(x'_0, \tilde{\pi}_0) + t}{\hat{n}(x''_0, \tilde{\pi}_0) - t} \cdot \prod_{i=1}^{k} \frac{\frac{\hat{n}(\tilde{x}_i, x'_0, \tilde{\pi}_i) + t}{\hat{n}(x'_0, \tilde{\pi}_i) + t}}{\frac{\hat{n}(\tilde{x}_i, x''_0, \tilde{\pi}_i) - t}{\hat{n}(x''_0, \tilde{\pi}_i) - t}}, \tag{15}$$

$$y(t) := y_0(t) \cdot \left[\sum_{x_0 \in \Omega_{X_0}} k_{x_0}(t) \right], \tag{16}$$

where:

$$y_0(t) := [\hat{n}(x'_0, \tilde{\pi}_0) + t]^{n(x'_0, \tilde{\pi}_0)} \cdot [\hat{n}(x''_0, \tilde{\pi}_0) - t]^{n(x''_0, \tilde{\pi}_0)}$$
$$\cdot \prod_{i=1}^{k} \left[\frac{[\hat{n}(\tilde{x}_i, x'_0, \tilde{\pi}_i) + t]^{n(\tilde{x}_i, x'_0, \tilde{\pi}_i)}}{[\hat{n}(x'_0, \tilde{\pi}_i) + t]^{n(x'_0, \tilde{\pi}_i)}} \cdot \frac{[\hat{n}(\tilde{x}_i, x''_0, \tilde{\pi}_i) - t]^{n(\tilde{x}_i, x''_0, \tilde{\pi}_i)}}{[\hat{n}(x''_0, \tilde{\pi}_i) - t]^{n(x''_0, \tilde{\pi}_i)}} \right], \tag{17}$$

$$k_{x_0}(t) := \begin{cases} [\hat{n}(x_0, \tilde{\pi}_0) + t] \cdot \prod_{i=1}^{k} \frac{\hat{n}(\tilde{x}_i, x_0, \tilde{\pi}_i) + t}{\hat{n}(x_0, \tilde{\pi}_i) + t} & \text{if } x_0 = x_0', \\ [\hat{n}(x_0, \tilde{\pi}_0) - t] \cdot \prod_{i=1}^{k} \frac{\hat{n}(\tilde{x}_i, x_0, \tilde{\pi}_i) - t}{\hat{n}(x_0, \tilde{\pi}_i) - t} & \text{if } x_0 = x_0'', \\ \hat{n}(x_0, \tilde{\pi}_0) \quad \cdot \prod_{i=1}^{k} \frac{\hat{n}(\tilde{x}_i, x_0, \tilde{\pi}_i)}{\hat{n}(x_0, \tilde{\pi}_i)} & \text{if } x_0 \in \Omega_{X_0} \setminus \{x_0', x_0''\}. \end{cases} \tag{18}$$

Theorem 1. *If $[x(a), x(b)] = [0, +\infty]$, our approximation of the upper envelope of the normalized likelihood (11) as a function of the probability ratio (3) is parametrized by $(x(t), y(t)/y(0))$ with $t \in [a, b]$.*

Theorem 2. *If $x(a) > 0$, the parametrization in Th. 1 holds in the region $[x(a), x(b)]$, while in the region $[0, x(a)]$, a parametrization is $(\tau \cdot x(a), y'(\tau)/y(0))$ with $\tau \in [0, 1]$ and:*

$$y'(\tau) := \tau^{-a + n(x_0') - \hat{n}(x_0')} \cdot y_0(a) \cdot \left[\tau \, k_{x_0'}(a) + \sum_{x_0 \in \Omega_{X_0} \setminus \{x_0'\}} k_{x_0}(a) \right]. \tag{19}$$

The proofs of the two theorems are omitted for lack of space, but can be found in [2]. As a simple application of these results, it is straightforward to evaluate the upper envelope of the likelihood for the example in Fig. 3 when only the complete data are considered in the likelihood, i.e., only $y_0(t)$ is considered in (17). In this case, $t \in [-2, 1]$ and:

$$\begin{bmatrix} x(t) \\ y(t) \end{bmatrix} = \begin{bmatrix} (2 + t) \cdot (1 - t)^{-1} \\ (2 + t)^2 \cdot (1 - t) \end{bmatrix}. \tag{20}$$

Given the above parametrization of the likelihood upper envelope, classification can be performed by checking whether or not the left α-cut has abscissa greater than one. For the situation in Th. 1, this can be numerically done in few iteration by bracketing the (unique) zero of $g(t) := y(t) - \alpha y(0)$ in the region $t \in [a, 0]$, unless the corresponding bounds on $x(t)$ are greater (or smaller) than one (and similarly proceed for Th. 2).

4   Preliminary Results

To describe the performance of a credal classifier, multiple indicators are needed. We adopt the following:

- *determinacy*: percentage of instances classified with a single class;
- *single accuracy*: accuracy over instances classified with a single class;
- *set-accuracy*: accuracy over instances classified with more classes;
- *indeterminate output size*: average number of classes returned when the classification is indeterminate.

Table 1. Main characteristics of the data sets

Dataset		Iris	Glass	Ecoli	Breast	Haberman	Diabetes	Ionosphere
Size	N	150	214	336	699	306	768	351
Features	k	4	7	6	9	2	6	33
Classes	$|\Omega_{X_0}|$	3	7	8	2	2	2	2

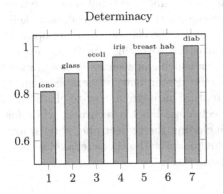

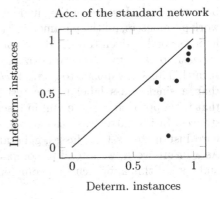

Fig. 4. Experimental results: determinacy of the likelihood-based classifier (*left*) and comparison of the accuracy achieved by the standard network on the instances classified determinately and indeterminately by the likelihood-based classifier (*right*)

Roughly speaking, a credal classifier identifies *easy* instances, over which it returns a single class, and *hard* instances, over which it returns more classes. A credal classifier is effective at recognizing hard instances if its precise counterpart undergoes a considerable drop of accuracy on them. As a precise counterpart of the likelihood-based credal classifier we consider a Bayesian network with the same graph, but whose parameters are learned precisely as in (5); this model is referred to as the *standard network* in the following. The graph is learned using the K2 score [9, Chap. 18]. The considered data sets and their main characteristics are shown in Tab. 1. We run 5 runs of 5 folds cross-validation, for a total of 25 training/test experiments on each data set.

The determinacy of the likelihood-based classifier (with $\alpha = 0.15$) is generally around 90% or higher, as shown in the left plot of Fig. 4; in general, the determinacy increases on larger data sets. The likelihood-based classifier is effective at detecting hard instances; this can be appreciated by the right plot of Fig. 4, which compares the accuracy obtained by the standard network on the instances recognized as easy and hard by the likelihood-based classifier. The accuracy of the standard network clearly drops on the instances indeterminately classified by the likelihood-based model; the drop is statistically significant (Wilcoxon signed-rank test, *p*-value < 0.01). The set-accuracy and the indeterminate output size are meaningful only on data sets with more than 2 classes. On such data sets, the likelihood-based classifier returns a number of classes which is on average 58% of the total classes, achieving on average a set-accuracy of 84%.

In future more extensive experiments should be carried out, comparing the likelihood-based model against credal classifiers already present in literature.

5   Conclusions and Outlooks

A new, likelihood-based approach, to classification with Bayesian networks has been proposed. Instead of the single maximum-likelihood estimation of the network parameters, all the parametrizations assigning to the available data a likelihood beyond a given threshold are considered. All the classes which are optimal at least for a network parametrization consistent with this constraint are returned. This corresponds to a *credal classifier* which can eventually assign more than a single class label to the test instance. Preliminary experiments show that this approach is successful in discriminating hard- from easy-to-classify instances. In the latter case the single, correct, class label is returned, while for hard instances a set of classes, generally including the correct one, is returned. As a future work, we intend to compare this model with other credal classifiers and extend this approach to incomplete data sets.

References

1. Antonucci, A., Cattaneo, M., Corani, G.: Likelihood-based naive credal classifier. In: ISIPTA 2011, pp. 21–30. SIPTA (2011)
2. Antonucci, A., Cattaneo, M., Corani, G.: Likelihood-based robust classification with Bayesian networks. Technical Report IDSIA-01-12, IDSIA (2012)
3. Cattaneo, M.: Statistical Decisions Based Directly on the Likelihood Function. PhD thesis, ETH Zurich (2007)
4. Cattaneo, M.: Likelihood-based inference for probabilistic graphical models: Some preliminary results. In: PGM 2010, pp. 57–64. HIIT Publications (2010)
5. Corani, G., Antonucci, A., Zaffalon, M.: Bayesian networks with imprecise probabilities: Theory and application to classification. In: Data Mining: Foundations and Intelligent Paradigms, pp. 49–93. Elsevier (2010)
6. Cozman, F.G.: Credal networks. Artif. Intell. 120, 199–233 (2000)
7. Friedman, N., Geiger, D., Goldszmidt, M.: Bayesian networks classifiers. Mach. Learn. 29, 131–163 (1997)
8. Hudson, D.J.: Interval estimation from the likelihood function. J. R. Stat. Soc., Ser. B 33, 256–262 (1971)
9. Koller, D., Friedman, N.: Probabilistic Graphical Models. MIT Press (2009)
10. Moral, S.: Calculating uncertainty intervals from conditional convex sets of probabilities. In: UAI 1992, pp. 199–206. Morgan Kaufmann (1992)
11. Pawitan, Y.: In All Likelihood. Oxford University Press (2001)
12. Pearl, J.: Probabilistic Reasoning in Intelligent Systems. Morgan Kaufmann (1988)
13. Walley, P.: Statistical Reasoning with Imprecise Probabilities. Chapman and Hall (1991)

Collecting Information Reported by Imperfect Information Sources

Laurence Cholvy

ONERA
2 avenue Edouard Belin
31055 Toulouse, France

Abstract. This paper studies how an agent can believe a new piece of information, not only when it is directly provided by another agent but also when it is reported through an agent who cites a third one. Two models are presented, the first one in modal logic and the other one in the Theory of Evidence. They both consider as primitive two positive properties of agents: their ability of reporting true information and their ability of reporting only true information, as well as their negative counterparts i.e, their ability of reporting false information and their ability of reported only false information.

Keywords: Beliefs, modal logic, Theory of Evidence.

1 Introduction

In a multi-agent system such as a system of surveillance and monitoring for urban, environmental, security or defense purposes, there are some agents whose function is to collect information provided by some other agents called information sources. These information sources (sensors, radars or humans) may observe the current situation or they may be themselves informed by some other agents.

As for the agent in charge of collecting information, before processing the piece of information it receives, and in particular before fusing it with other pieces of information [1], [2], has to decide how strong it accepts it. Obviously, it can accept this information if it trusts the information source for providing true information or equivalently, if it trusts the information source for not delivering false information. Thus, knowing that the source is truthful [3] will help the agent to accept the piece of information it receives as a new belief. Symmetrically, knowing that it is a liar will help it to accept its opposite as a new belief.

For instance, assume that in order to estimate the rate of a river flow I call a friend who lives in the mountains near the glacier where the river springs are. This friend tells me that the outside temperature has risen recently. If I trust this friend for telling me true information, then I can believe what he is reporting i.e I can believe that the temperature near the glacier has risen recently. From this, I will be able to deduce that the river flow will rise in few days. At the opposite, assume that instead of calling my friend, I read the weather forecast in my newspaper which reports that the temperature in the mountains has risen

S. Greco et al. (Eds.): IPMU 2012, Part III, CCIS 299, pp. 501–510, 2012.

recently. If I know that the weather forecast provided in this newspaper is always false, then I can infer that what my newspaper is reporting is false i.e I can conclude that the temperature has not risen in the mountains. Consequently, I will be able to deduce that the river flow will not rise in few days[1].

In [5], Demolombe studied several properties an information source can have, among which *validity* and *completeness* are worth pointing out. Roughly speaking, a valid agent only reports information that are true in the world and a complete agent reports any information that are true in the world. Validity and completeness are important in the question we address. Indeed, if the agent who receives a new piece of information trusts the information source for being valid, then it can believe this piece of information. At the opposite, an agent who does not receive a given piece of information from an information source assumed to be complete can believe that this piece of information is false.

Demolombe's work focuses on pieces of information provided directly by an information source. But in some cases, the information source does not provide explicitly the very information of interest but cites another source. This is the case for instance when I am informed by my neighbour that one of his friends living in the mountains told him that the temperature has risen recently there. Here, my neighbour does not tell me that the temperature has risen in the mountains but he reports that his friend reported it. Consequently, trusting my neighbour for delivering true weather report is not useful here. However, trusting my neighbour for telling me the truth and trusting my neighbour's friend for delivering true weather report will allow me to believe that indeed, the temperature has risen recently in the mountains. Notice that here, the very information which interests me is reported through two agents, my neighbour's friend and my neighbour, the second one citing the first one. The question of estimating if an agent can believe a piece of information when it is reported through several agents is the object of our current research. In previous papers [7], [8] we have investigated different models for addressing this question. Following Demolombe, these models emphasize the importance of the property of *validity*. But they also emphasize the importance of a dual property which characterizes agents who report only false information. We will call them *misinformers*[2]. The present paper extends [8] and considers the property of *completeness* as well as its negative counterpart.

This paper is organized as follows. Section 2 presents a model in modal logic and formally introduces the four properties: validity, completeness and their negative counterparts. Section 3 assumes uncertainty and presents a second model based on Theory of Evidence. We prove that this second model extends the first one. Finally, section 4 lists some concluding remarks.

2   A Logical Model

We consider an agent i who is about receiving a piece of information φ. We aim at seeing how i can use its beliefs about the information sources in order to

---

[1] Assuming that the river is only filled with the glacier water.

[2] In our previous work, the term which was used was "invalid".

accept or not accept φ as a new belief. We first examine the case when i is in direct contact with the information source. Then we study the case when there is third agent between the source and i. Due to the limitation of the paper length, the general case of any number of agents is not studied. All along this section, the question is: *(Q) Can i believe φ ?*

2.1   The Logical Framework

The work which influenced us is Demolombe's work [5] which, in particular, formalizes in modal logic the relations which exist between a piece of information, its truth and the mental attitudes of the agent which produces this piece of information. The operators of the modal logic used in this paper are: B_i ($B_i p$ means "agent i believes that p"), K_i ($K_i p$ means "agent i strongly believes that p); I_i^j ($I_i^j p$ means "agent i informs agent j that p"). Operator B_i obeys KD system which is quite usual for beliefs and operator I_i^j only obeys rule of equivalence substitutivity [6]. K_i obeys KD system plus axiom (KT) i.e $K_i(K_i p \to p)$. Furthermore we have $K_i p \to B_i p$ and also $I_i^j p \to K_j I_i^j p$ and $\neg I_i^j p \to K_j \neg I_i^j p$.

According to Demolombe, agent i is valid with regard to j for p iff, if i informs j about p, then p is true. Thus $valid(i,j,p) \equiv I_i^j p \to p$. Agent i is complete with regard to j for p iff if p is the case then i informs j about p. Thus: $complete(i,j,p) \equiv p \to I_i^j p$.

These notions are then be used to derive the beliefs of an agent who receives a piece of information. For instance, $I_f^i risen \wedge K_i valid(f,i,risen) \to K_i risen$ is a theorem in this framework. It means that if my friend tells me that the temperature has risen in the mountains and if I strongly believe that my friend is valid with regard to the weather report in the moutains, then I strongly believe that the temperature has risen there. In the same way, $\neg I_f^i risen \wedge K_i complete(f,i,risen) \to K_i \neg risen$ is a theorem. It means that if my friend did not tell me that the temperature has risen in the mountains and if I strongly believe that my friend is complete with regard to the weather report in the moutains, then I strongly believe that the temperature has not risen there.

Validity and *completeness* are positive properties since in a situation of collecting information, an information source which is valid and complete for some φ is of the utmost importance. However, not all the information sources are as perfect as this. This is why here, we introduce negative counterpart of these properties and consider *misinformers* and *falsifiers*. According to our proposal, a misinformer is an agent who only reports false information. A falsifier agent is an agent who reports false information.

For giving these properties formal definitions, we consider a modal logic which is a simpler version of the logic used in [5] with two operators, one for representing the agent beliefs and the other for representing the fact that an agent has reported a piece of information. $B_i \varphi$ means that agent i believes that φ. Modalities B_i obeys the following axiomatics: $B_i \varphi \wedge B_i(\varphi \to \psi) \to B_i \psi$, $B_i \neg \varphi \to \neg B_i \varphi$ and $\frac{\varphi}{B_i \varphi}$. $R_i \varphi$ means that the agent i reports that the proposition φ is true. The modality R obeys the following axiomatics: $R_i(\varphi \wedge \psi) \leftrightarrow R_i \varphi \wedge R_i \psi$ and $\frac{\varphi \leftrightarrow \psi}{R_j \varphi \leftrightarrow R_j \psi}$. The four properties we want to focus on are then modelled as follows:

$$\text{valid}(i, \varphi) \equiv R_i\varphi \to \varphi$$
$$\text{misinformer}(i, \varphi) \equiv R_i\varphi \to \neg\varphi$$
$$\text{complete}(i, \varphi) \equiv \varphi \to R_i\varphi$$
$$\text{falsifier}(i, \varphi) \equiv \neg\varphi \to R_i\varphi$$

2.2   Agent i Is in Direct Contact with the Source

Here we consider that agent i is in direct contact with the information source named j. There are two cases.

First case. j indeed reports φ and i is aware of it i.e we have $B_i R_j \varphi$. The following proposition answers the question Q.

Theorem 1. *The following formulas are theorems and their premisses are exclusive.*

$$B_i R_j\varphi \wedge B_i valid(j, \varphi) \to B_i\varphi$$
$$B_i R_j\varphi \wedge B_i misinformer(j, \varphi) \to B_i\neg\varphi$$

I.e., if i believes that j reported φ and if it believes that j is valid (resp, misinformer) for information φ then it can conclude that φ is true (resp, false). Furthermore, since i cannot believe j both valid and misinformer, it cannot infer both φ and $\neg\varphi$

Second case. j did not report φ and i is aware of it, i.e we have $B_i \neg R_j \varphi$. The following proposition answers the question Q.

Theorem 2. *The following formulas are theorems and their premisses are exclusive.*

$$B_i \neg R_j\varphi \wedge B_i complete(j, \varphi) \to B_i\neg\varphi$$
$$B_i \neg R_j\varphi \wedge B_i falsifier(j, \varphi) \to B_i\varphi$$

I.e., if i believes that j has not reported φ while it believes that j is complete for φ then it can conclude that φ is false. Furthemore, if i believes that j has not reported φ while it believes that j is a falsifier for φ then it can conclude that φ is true.

2.3   There Is a Third Agent between Agent i and the Source

Here we consider that agent i is not in direct contact with the agent which is supposed to provide information, named k, but there is a go-between agent, named j. There are four cases.

First Case. j reports that k reported φ and i knows it, i.e $B_i R_j R_k \varphi$. The following proposition answers the question Q.

Theorem 3. *The following formulas are theorems and the premisses are exclusive.*

$$B_i R_j R_k \varphi \wedge B_i valid(j, R_k \varphi) \wedge B_i valid(k, \varphi) \to B_i \varphi$$
$$B_i R_j R_k \varphi \wedge B_i valid(j, R_k \varphi) \wedge B_i misinformer(k, \varphi) \to B_i \neg \varphi$$
$$B_i R_j R_k \varphi \wedge B_i misinformer(j, R_k \varphi) \wedge B_i complete(k, \varphi) \to B_i \neg \varphi$$
$$B_i R_j R_k \varphi \wedge B_i misinformer(j, R_k \varphi) \wedge B_i falsifier(k, \varphi) \to B_i \varphi$$

For instance, my neighbour told me that one of his friends who lives in the moutains told him that the temperature has risen. Suppose I know that when my neighbour says such a sentence, it is false i.e, I can infer that his friend did not tell him that the temperature has risen. But suppose that I know that his friend always informs him when the temperature rises. Then, I can conclude that the temperature had not risen.

<u>Second Case.</u> j does not report that k reported φ and i knows it, i.e $B_i \neg R_j R_k \varphi$. The following proposition answers the question Q.

Theorem 4. *The following formulas are theorems and their premisses are exclusive.*

$$B_i \neg R_j R_k \varphi \wedge B_i complete(j, R_k \varphi) \wedge B_i complete(k, \varphi) \to B_i \neg \varphi$$
$$B_i \neg R_j R_k \varphi \wedge B_i complete(j, R_k \varphi) \wedge B_i falsifier(k, \varphi) \to B_i \varphi$$
$$B_i \neg R_j R_k \varphi \wedge B_i falsifier(j, R_k \varphi) \wedge B_i valid(k, \varphi) \to B_i \varphi$$
$$B_i \neg R_j R_k \varphi \wedge B_i falsifier(j, R_k \varphi) \wedge B_i misinformer(k, \varphi) \to B_i \neg \varphi$$

<u>Third Case.</u> j reports that k did not report φ and i knows it, i.e $B_i R_j \neg R_k \varphi$. The following proposition answers the question Q.

Theorem 5. *The following formulas are theorems and their premisses are exclusive.*

$$B_i R_j \neg R_k \varphi \wedge B_i valid(j, \neg R_k \varphi) \wedge B_i complete(k, \varphi) \to B_i \neg \varphi$$
$$B_i R_j \neg R_k \varphi \wedge B_i misinformer(j, \neg R_k \varphi) \wedge B_i valid(k, \varphi) \to B_i \varphi$$
$$B_i R_j \neg R_k \varphi \wedge B_i misinformer(j, \neg R_k \varphi) \wedge B_i misinformer(k, \varphi) \to B_i \neg \varphi$$
$$B_i R_j \neg R_k \varphi \wedge B_i valid(j, \neg R_k \varphi) \wedge B_i falsifier(k, \varphi) \to B_i \varphi$$

<u>Fourth Case.</u> j did not report that k did not report φ and i knows it, i.e $B_i \neg R_j \neg R_k \varphi$. The following proposition answers the question Q.

Theorem 6. *The following formulas are theorems and their premisses are exclusive.*

$$B_i \neg R_j \neg R_k \varphi \wedge B_i complete(j, \neg R_k \varphi) \wedge B_i valid(k, \varphi) \to B_i \varphi$$
$$B_i \neg R_j \neg R_k \varphi \wedge B_i complete(j, \neg R_k \varphi) \wedge B_i misinformer(k, \varphi) \to B_i \neg \varphi$$
$$B_i \neg R_j \neg R_k \varphi \wedge B_i falsifier(j, \neg R_k \varphi) \wedge B_i complete(k, \varphi) \to B_i \neg \varphi$$
$$B_i \neg R_j \neg R_k \varphi \wedge B_i falsifier(j, \neg R_k \varphi) \wedge B_i falsifier(k, \varphi) \to B_i \varphi$$

3   Taking Uncertainty into Account

The previous model allows an agent to reason in a binary way with its beliefs about the different sources being valid, misinformer, complete or falsifier. No uncertainty can be expressed. This is why, here, we consider another kind of formalism, the Theory of Evidence [9], to take uncertainty into account. Again, we consider an agent i who is about receiving a piece of information φ. The question is now: *(Q) How strong can i believe φ ?*

3.1   The Numerical Model

In order to answer question Q in an uncertainty setting, our model is based on the degrees at which i thinks that the source j is valid (resp is a misinformer, or complete,or is a falsifier). We consider a *classical* propositional language the two letters of which are: φ and $R_j\varphi$ representing respectively the facts "information φ is true" and "j reported information φ"[3].

Definition 1. *Consider two agents i and j and a piece of information φ. Let $d_j \in [0,1]$ and $d'_j \in [0,1]$ two real numbers[4] such that $0 \le d_j + d'_j \le 1$. d_j is the degree at which i thinks that j is valid for φ and d'_j is the degree at which i thinks that j is a misinformer for φ (written $VM(i,j,\varphi,d_j,d'_j)$) iff i's beliefs can be modelled by the mass assignment $m^{VM(i,j,\varphi,d_j,d'_j)}$ defined by:*

$$m^{VM(i,j,\varphi,d_j,d'_j)}(R_j\varphi \to \varphi) = d_j$$
$$m^{VM(i,j,\varphi,d_j,d'_j)}(R_j\varphi \to \neg\varphi) = d'_j$$
$$m^{VM(i,j,\varphi,d_j,d'_j)}(True) = 1 - (d_j + d'_j)$$

We have shown in [10] that exhaustive hypotheses of a frame of discernment can be considered as logical interpretations and that assigning a mass on a disjunction of exhaustive hypothesis is equivalent to assigning this mass on any propositional formula satisfied by all the interpretations in the disjunction. Consequently, here, the mass assigment is expressed on formulas and not on the eight interpretations of the language (the one in which j has reported φ and j has reported information $\neg\varphi$ and φ is true; the one in which j has reported information φ and j did not report information $\neg\varphi$ and φ is true,...) which would be much more fastidious.

According to definition 1, if i believes at degree d_j that j is valid for φ and believes at degree d'_j that j is a misinformer then its belief degree in the fact "if j reports φ then φ is true" is d_j; its belief degree in the fact "if j reports φ then φ is false" is d'_j; and its total ignorance degree is $1 - (d_j + d'_j)$.

---

[3] We insist on the fact that the language which is considered in this section is classical and not modal. Consequently, $R_j\varphi$ is not a modal formula here but a propositionnal letter.

[4] These degrees should be indexed by i but index i is omitted for readability.

Definition 2. *Consider two agents i and j and a piece of information φ. Let $c_j \in [0,1]$ and $c'_j \in [0,1]$ two real numbers[5] such that $0 \le c_j + c'_j \le 1$. c_j is the degree at which i thinks that j is complete for φ and c'_j is the degree at which i thinks that j is a falsifier for φ (written $CF(i,j,\varphi,c_j,c'_j)$) iff i's beliefs can be modelled by the mass assignment $m^{CF(i,j,\varphi,c_j,c'_j)}$ defined by:*

$$m^{CF(i,j,\varphi,c_j,c'_j)}(\varphi \to R_j\varphi) = c_j$$
$$m^{CF(i,j,\varphi,c_j,c'_j)}(\neg\varphi \to R_j\varphi) = c'_j$$
$$m^{CF(i,j,\varphi,c_j,c'_j)}(True) = 1 - (c_j + c'_j)$$

According to definition 2, if i believes at degree c_j that j is complete for φ and believes at degree c'_j that j is a falsifier then its belief degree in the fact "if φ is true then j reports φ" is c_j; its belief degree in the fact "if φ is false then j reports φ" is c'_j; and its total ignorance degree is $1 - (c_j + c'_j)$.

3.2 Agent i Is in Direct Contact with the Source

Let us first give the following preliminary definitions.

Definition 3. *m^{VMCF} denotes the mass assignment obtained by combining the two previous mass assignments. I.e,*

$$m^{VMCF} = m^{VM(i,j,\varphi,d_j,d'_j)} \oplus m^{CF(i,j,\varphi,c_j,c'_j)}.$$

This assignment represents the beliefs of i about j being valid, complete, a misinformer or a falsifier for information φ.

Definition 4. *m^ψ is the mass assignments defined by: $m^\psi(\psi) = 1$.*

In particular, if ψ is $R_j\varphi$, then $m^{R_j\varphi}$ represents the fact that agent i is certain that j has reported φ. If ψ is $\neg R_j\varphi$, then $m^{\neg R_j\varphi}$ represents the fact that agent i is certain that j did not report φ.

First case. We assume that j reported φ and that i is aware of it . In this case, i's beliefs can be modelled by the following mass assignment m:

$$m = m^{VMCF} \oplus m^{R_j\varphi}$$

Theorem 7. *Let Bel be the belief function associated with assignment m. Then, $Bel(\varphi) = d_j$ and $Bel(\neg\varphi) = d'_j$*

Consequently, when i knows that j reported φ and when $VM(i,j,\varphi,d_j,d'_j)$ and $CF(i,j,,\varphi,c_j,c'_j)$, then i believes φ more than $\neg\varphi$ if and only if $d_j > d'_j$ i.e, its belief degree in j's being valid is greater that its belief degree in j's being a misinformer. This result is not surprising.

---

[5] Again these degrees should be indexed by i but index i is omitted for readibility.

Theorem 8.

If $VM(i,j,\varphi,1,0)$ then $Bel(\varphi) = 1$ and $Bel(\neg\varphi) = 0$ i.e, i believes φ and does not believe $\neg\varphi$;

If $VM(i,j,\varphi,0,1)$ then $Bel(\varphi) = 0$ and $Bel(\neg\varphi) = 1$ i.e, i does not believe $\neg\varphi$ and believes φ.

We find again the results of theorem 1.

Second case. j did not report φ and i is aware of it. In this case, i's beliefs can be modelled by the mass assignment m:

$$m = m^{VMCF} \oplus m^{\neg R_j\varphi}$$

Theorem 9. *Let Bel be the belief function associated with assignment m. Then, $Bel(\varphi) = c'_j$ and $Bel(\neg\varphi) = c_j$*

Consequently, when i knows that j did report φ and when $VM(i,j,\varphi,d_j,d'_j)$ and $CF(i,j,,\varphi,c_j,c'_j)$ then i believes φ more than $\neg\varphi$ if and only if $c'_j > c_j$ i.e, its belief degree in j's being a falsifier is greater that its belief degree in j's being complete.

Theorem 10.

If $CF(i,j,\varphi,1,0)$, then $Bel(\varphi) = 0$ and $Bel(\neg\varphi) = 1$ i.e, i does not believes φ and believes $\neg\varphi$;

If $CF(i,j,\varphi,0,1)$, then $Bel(\varphi) = 1$ and $Bel(\neg\varphi) = 0$ i.e, i believes φ and does not believe $\neg\varphi$.

We find again the results of theorem 2.

3.3   There Is a Third Agent between i and the Source

Like in section 3.2 we consider here that i is not in direct contact with the agent k supposed to provide the information, but there is a go-between agent named j. In order to answer question Q in this case, we consider a propositional language whose letters are: φ, $R_k\varphi$, $R_jR_k\varphi$, $R_j\neg R_k\varphi$. These letters respectively represent "information φ is true, k reported information φ, j reported that k reported φ, j reported that k did not report φ.

Preliminaries. In this section, the mass assigment m^{VMCF} is defined by:

Definition 5.
$$m^{VMCF} = m^{VM(i,j,R_k\varphi,d_j,d'_j)} \oplus m^{CF(i,j,R_k\varphi,c_j,c'_j)} \oplus m^{VM(i,k,\varphi,d_k,d'_k)} \oplus m^{CF(i,k,\varphi,c_k,c'_k)}$$

This assignment represents the beliefs of i as regard to agent j being valid, complete, a misinformer or a falsifier for information $R_k\varphi$ and as regard to agent k being valid, complete, a misinformer or a falsifier for information φ.

First case. Assume that j reported that k φ and that i is aware of it . In this case, i's beliefs are modelled by the mass assignment m defined by:

$$m = m^{VMCF} \oplus m^{R_j R_k \varphi}$$

Theorem 11. *Let Bel be the belief function associated with assignment m.*
$Bel(\varphi) = d_k.ck' + d_k.d_j - d_k.ck.d_j - d_k.c'_k.d'_j + c'_k.d_j$ *and*
$Bel(\neg\varphi) = d'_k.ck + d'_k.d_j - d'_k.c_k.d_j + c_k.d'_j - d'_k.c_k.d'_j$

Theorem 12.
If $VM(i,j,R_k\varphi,1,0)$ and $VM(i,k,\varphi,1,0)$ then $Bel(\varphi) = 1$ and $Bel(\neg\varphi) = 0$.
If $VM(i,j,R_k\varphi,1,0)$ and $VM(i,k,\varphi,0,1)$ then $Bel(\varphi) = 0$ and $Bel(\neg\varphi) = 1$.
If $VM(i,j,R_k\varphi,0,1)$ and $CF(i,k,\varphi,1,0)$ then $Bel(\varphi) = 0$ and $Bel(\neg\varphi) = 1$.
If $VM(i,j,R_k\varphi,0,1)$ and $CF(i,k,\varphi,0,1)$ then $Bel(\varphi) = 1$ and $Bel(\neg\varphi) = 0$.

We find again the results of theorem 3.

Three other cases.
The three other cases are not considered here due to the limitation of the paper length but we can easily prove that we find results of theorem 4, theorem 5 and theorem 6 in particular cases.

4   Concluding Remarks

In situation of information fusion, we expect that the agents who provide information fulfill some positive properties so that the agent who is in charge of merging can believe the information it receives. However, information sources may be imperfect and fulfill negative properties. In such a case, how do they influence the believes of the agent who receives information ? This is the question which has been addressed in this paper. Not only we dealt with information provided directly by an agent but we also consider the case when there is a third agent who cites the previous one, a case which has received little attention in the litterature.

The logical model defined previously allows an user to deductively infer wether it can accept a piece of information as a new belief. But this model also offers the possibility to make abductive reasoning on the agent properties. For instance given that $B_i R_j R_k \phi$ and $B_i valid(j, R_k\phi)$ we can abductively find the epistemic properties of the agents that are required to explain $B_i\phi$. Here, one of this plausible assumption is $B_i valid(k, \phi)$. Studying this abductive reasoning in a graph of communicating agents constitutes an interesting extension of this present work, not only in the logical setting but also in the evidential framework.

Another promising extension would be to introduce more uncertainty in the model by considering that agents may be uncertain about information they deliver. This would allow us to deal with the case when an agent reports that some fact is highly certain or when an agent reports that another agent has reported that some fact was fairly certain. Modelling this kind of uncertainty and mixing it with the one which is introduced in this paper would allow us to deal with more realistic reported information.

Another work we foresee is to compare the numerical model defined here with the model expressed in possibilistic logic by [4] and also with the model of graded trust of [11] which proposes a qualitative approach to graded beliefs.

Acknowledgements. This work is supported by ONERA and by ANR (Agence Nationale de la Recherche) under project CAHORS.

References

1. Benferhat, S., Dubois, D., Kaci, S., Prade, H.: Possibilistic Merging and Distance-Based Fusion of Propositional Information. Annals of Mathematics and Artificial Intelligence 34(1-3), 217–252 (2002)
2. Konieczny, S., Pino Pérez, R.: Logic Based Merging. Journal of Philosophical Logic 40(2), 239–270 (2011)
3. Pichon, F., Dubois, D., Denoeux, T.: Relevance and Truthfulness in Information Correction and Fusion. International Journal of Approximate Reasoning 53(2), 159–175 (2012)
4. Dubois, D., Prade, H.: Valid or Complete Information in Databases. A Possibility Theory-Based Analysis. In: Tjoa, A.M. (ed.) DEXA 1997. LNCS, vol. 1308, Springer, Heidelberg (1997)
5. Demolombe, R.: Reasoning About Trust: A Formal Logical Framework. In: Jensen, C., Poslad, S., Dimitrakos, T. (eds.) iTrust 2004. LNCS, vol. 2995, pp. 291–303. Springer, Heidelberg (2004)
6. Chellas, B.F.: Modal logic: An introduction. Cambridge University Press (1980)
7. Cholvy, L.: Evaluation of Information Reported: A Model in the Theory of Evidence. In: Hüllermeier, E., Kruse, R., Hoffmann, F. (eds.) IPMU 2010, Part I. CCIS, vol. 80, pp. 258–267. Springer, Heidelberg (2010)
8. Cholvy, L.: How Strong Can an Agent Believe Reported Information? In: Liu, W. (ed.) ECSQARU 2011. LNCS, vol. 6717, pp. 386–397. Springer, Heidelberg (2011)
9. Shafer, G.: A mathematical Theory of Evidence. Princeton University Press (1976)
10. Cholvy, L.: Non-exclusive Hypothesis in Dempster-Shafer Theory. International Journal of Approximate Reasoning 53(4), 493–501 (2012)
11. Demolombe, R.: Graded trust. In: Proceedings of the Workshop on Trust in Agent Societies, Budapest (2009)

Ranking Aggregation Based on Belief Function

Andrea Argentini and Enrico Blanzieri

Dipartimento di Ingegneria e Scienza dell'informazione, Università di Trento Italy
{argentini,blanzier}@disi.unitn.it

Abstract. In this work we consider the case of the ranking aggregation problem that includes the true ranking in its formulation. The goal is to find an estimation of an unknown true ranking given a set of rankings provided by different quality experts. This is the case when bioinformatic experts provide ranked items involved in an unknown biological phenomenon regulated by its own physical reality. We devise an innovative solution called Belief Ranking Estimator (BRE), based on the belief function framework that permits to represent beliefs on the correctness of each item rank as well as uncertainty on the quality of the rankings from the subjective point of view of the expert. Moreover, weights computed using a true-ranking estimator are applied to the original belief basic assignment in order to take into account the quality of the input rankings. The results of an empirical comparison of BRE with weighting schema against competitor methods for ranking aggregation show that our method improves significantly the performance when the quality of the ranking is heterogeneous.

1 Introduction

The ranking aggregation problem faces the necessity to combine different rankings on a finite set of items, in order to produce a new ranking that satisfies specific criteria. The problem of ranking aggregation emerges when it is necessary to combine the opinion of experts with different background, such as the combination of ranked lists of differently expressed genes provided by different microarray analysis methods, or the combination of search engine results [6], or committee decision making. Most of the methods proposed for the combination of rankings aim to minimize the distance between the input rankings for a given ranking distance. This is the case of Spearman Footrule Optimal aggregator [6] and the cross-entropy method [9] to approximate the Kendall Optimal aggregator. Other aggregator methods are based on heuristics such as Markov Chain solutions [6] and the Borda Count[3] that includes the mean and the median. Despite the presence of a true ranking is overlooked in the ranking aggregation formulation, the relation between ranking aggregation methods and the true ranking has been investigated [1] and it emerges that the quality of the results is affected by the noise on the input rankings.

In this work ranking aggregation is faced assuming the existence of a true ranking of the set of items and the goal is to find a satisfying estimation of the

S. Greco et al. (Eds.): IPMU 2012, Part III, CCIS 299, pp. 511–520, 2012.
© Springer-Verlag Berlin Heidelberg 2012

unknown true ranking given a set of input rankings provided by experts with different approximation quality. The main difference with respect to ranking aggregation solutions based on minimization criteria is that we assume that the true ranking over the set of items does exist. We claim that this is the case when the rankings come from bioinformatic rankers because of the underlying physical reality of the unknown biological phenomenon at hand. The solution to the ranking aggregation problem is based on Belief Function Theory. Belief Function Theory provides a solid framework for reasoning with imprecise and uncertain data, allowing the modeling of subjective knowledge in a non Bayesian way. Belief function theory has been applied in decision making [12] and also in machine learning problems such as clustering [8] and classification [13]. The application of Belief Function to rankings gives the possibility to encode different a priori knowledge about the correctness of the ranking positions and also to weight the reliability of the experts involved in the combination. Moreover, to the best of our knowledge the use of Belief Function on the ranking aggregation problem has not been proposed yet in literature. Our solution, called Belief Ranking Estimator (BRE), estimates the true ranking in an unsupervised way given a set of input rankings. We evaluate BRE on total rankings in synthetic data, comparing our method against some ranking aggregation competitor methods. A preliminary version of this work has been presented as student poster at ECSQARU 2011 [2].

The paper is organized as follows. In the following two sections we briefly present the ranking aggregation methods and the Belief Function framework. A successive section is devoted to the presentation of our method and another to the empirical evaluation results. Finally, we draw some conclusions.

2   Ranking Aggregation Methods

The state-of-the-art methods for the ranking aggregation problem can be divided into optimization and heuristic methods. Optimization methods aim to find a ranking that minimizes the distance of the input rankings, given a ranking distance. This category includes the Footrule Optimal aggregation and Kendall optimal aggregation based respectively on the Spearman Footrule and Kendall distances [5]. Since the Kendall optimal aggregation is a NP-hard problem [6], stochastic search solution has been proposed such as the cross-entropy Monte Carlo approach [9]. The Spearman Footrule Optimal aggregation for total rankings is computable in polynomial time by reduction to the computation of the minimum cost of perfect matching on a bipartite graph [6]. On the other hand, heuristic methods, such as Borda Count[3][6] and Markov chain [6] provide more simple solutions without optimizing any criterion. Borda Count assigns to each item in a ranking a score corresponding to the position in which the item appears, for each item all the scores are summed up along all the rankings and finally the items are ranked by their total score. As particular cases, the mean and the median are simply the rankings provided by the re-ranked values of the mean and median of the input rankings.

3   Belief Functions Theory

The theory of the Belief Functions, also known as Dempster-Shafer theory, is based on the pioneering work of Dempster [4] and Shafer [10]. More recent advances of this theory has been introduced in the *Transferable Belief Model* (TBM), proposed by Smets [11]. The framework is composed of three parts: (1) Model the belief of an expert on a frame of decision, (2) combine and update the belief and (3) make decision on the frame. We define $\Theta = \{\theta_1, \ldots, \theta_k\}$, called the *frame of discernment*, as the set of propositions exclusive and exhaustive in a certain domain. A function $m : 2^\Theta \to [0, 1]$ is called *basic belief assignment* (bba) if it satisfies : $\sum_{A \subseteq \Theta} m(A) = 1$. The *bba* is a way to represent the belief held by an expert on the frame Θ. $m(A)$ represents the belief that supports the set A and it makes no additional claims to any subsets included in A. In order to combine distinct sources $m_1, \ldots, m_n$ on Θ, the framework provides several combination rules, such as conjunctive rules, disjunctive rules and cautious rules [11]. One of the most used rule is the conjunctive rule defined as:

$$m_1 \textcircled{\cap} m_2(A) = \sum_{B \cap C = A} m_1(B) m_2(C) \quad A \subseteq \Theta \tag{1}$$

The conjunctive rule is associative and it is justified when all the sources of beliefs are supposed to assert the truth and to be independent. For Belief Function theory is a generalization of probability in a Bayesian setting, homologous of the conditioning and marginalization rules are expressed in the framework. In order to make decisions dealing with belief functions, TBM [11] includes the pignistic transformation function *Betp* defined as:

$$Betp(\theta) = \sum_{A \subseteq \Theta} \frac{m(A)}{1 - m(\phi)|A|} \quad \forall \theta \in \Theta \tag{2}$$

which transforms the mass functions into a probability space.

4   Method

4.1   Notation and Definition of the Problem

Let $X = \{x_1, \ldots, x_n\}$ be a set of items to be ranked by an expert opinion. We denote as $\tau = (\tau(1), \ldots, \tau(n))$ a ranking associated to X, where $\tau(i)$ is the rank associated to the item x_i. We suppose to have $\tau^{T_{rank}} = \{\tau^{T_{rank}}(1), \ldots, \tau^{T_{rank}}(n)\}$ that is the golden true ranking on the items of X, and we denote as R_j the expert involved in the ranking, so for each expert we have a corresponding ranking $\tau^{R_j} = \{\tau^{R_j}(1), \ldots, \tau^{R_j}(n)\}$. We suppose also that the most important item for a ranker R_j receives a rank value equal to n. This assumption in the case of permutations does not lead to any loss of generality. The problem in its general form is stated as follows. Given N rankings τ^{R_j} of length n of the n items $X = \{x_1, \ldots, x_n\}$, namely permutations, that estimate with unknown quality the unknown true ranking $\tau^{T_{rank}}$ find a ranking that estimates the true ranking.

Algorithm 1. Belief Ranking Estimator

---

input I=$\tau^1,\ldots,\tau^N$ {a vector of N Rankings}
input T {Numbers of iterations}
input TE {True-ranking estimator method}
  k= 0
  BE=Belief_From_Rankings(I)
  $FinalRank_k$=Combination(BE)
  while k != T **do**
    $\bar{w}$=ComputeWeights(I,TE(I))
    BE=ApplyWeights($\bar{w}$,BE)
    $FinalRank_k$=Combination(BE)
    I[pos(max($\bar{w}$))]=$FinalRank_k$
    BE=Belief_From_Rankings(I)
    k++
  end while
output $FinalRank_k$

4.2 Belief Ranking Estimator

The Belief Ranking Estimator (BRE) method is an unsupervised algorithm that iteratively computes an estimation of an unknown true ranking, given a sample of unknown-quality permutations assumed to be approximations of the true ranking. As showed in Alg. 1 the input parameters are the rankings, the number of iterations and the true-ranking estimator method TE. The algorithm is structured in the following parts: the mapping of the item ranks into bba (*Belief_From_Ranking*), the weights computation from the true-ranking estimator used (*ComputeWeights*), the application of the weights to the current belief model of the rankers (*Apply-Weights*), finally the output ranking is produced by the combination of all the bba's of the rankings. As true-ranking estimator is possible to use any ranking aggregation method. After the first iteration, the method replaces the worst ranking according to the weights, with the combined ranking produced in the previous iteration. At each iteration, this replacement drives the method to combine rankings that are supposed to be better than the original worst ranking, and to produce as output a better estimator. With $T = 0$ the algorithm computes the combination of the initial assignment without any weighting.

BBA from the Rankings: For our problem, we consider a simple frame of discernment $\Theta = \{P, \neg P\}$, where P, $\neg P$ are the hypotheses that an item is ranked in the right position or not respectively. Given a set of N rankings $\tau^1,\ldots\tau^j,\ldots,\tau^N$ of the same n items, the bba of the j-th ranking on the i-th item is assigned as:

$$m_{ji}(P) = \frac{\tau^j(i)}{n}$$
$$m_{ji}(\neg P) = 0$$
$$m_{ji}(\Theta) = 1 - \frac{\tau^j(i)}{n} \tag{3}$$

The bba definition reflects the fact that the high-ranked items should have more belief to be in the right position from the point of view of the expert who expressed the ranking. Since the lack of external information about the correctness of the ranking we are not able to assert if an item is not in the right position ($\neg P$), the remain belief is assigned consequently to the uncertainty about the two possible hypotheses, namely to Θ. We point out that the assignment of belief in Eq. 3 is strongly related to the choice of having the high-rank values assigned to the most important items.

Weight Computation: The weights of the rankings are computed as the normalized values of the Spearman Footrule distance [5][6] between the rankings and the true-ranking estimator method as following :

$$W_j = \frac{F(\tau^j, \tau^{TE})}{\frac{1}{2}n^2} \quad \forall j \in 1..N$$

Where $F(\cdot,\cdot)$ is the Spearman Footrule distance defined over two rankings π,σ as $F(\pi,\sigma) = \Sigma_{i=1}^n \mid \pi(i) - \sigma(i) \mid$ and τ^{TE} is the ranking produced by the true-ranking estimator. Since weight values are in the interval $[0,1]$, rankings are estimated to be similar or dissimilar to the estimator when the weight values go to 0 or tend to 1 respectively. According with this, the worst rankers will have the higher weight values. By $\bar{w}$ is denoted the vector of the weights computed for all the N rankings.

Application of the Weights: The application of the weights to the correspondent mass distribution of the rankings is computed in the *ApplyWeight* routine, as follows:

$$if \quad w_j = Min(\{w_1,\ldots,w_N\}) \qquad\qquad if \quad w_j \neq Min(\{w_1,\ldots,w_N\})$$
$$m'_{ji}(P) = m_{ji}(P) + (W_j * m_{ji}(\Theta)) \qquad m'_{ji}(\Theta) = m_{ji}(\Theta) + (W_j * m_{ji}(P))$$
$$m'_{ji}(\neg P) = 0 \qquad\qquad\qquad\qquad\qquad m'_{ji}(\neg P) = 0$$
$$m'_{ji}(\Theta) = 1 - m'_{ji}(P) \qquad\qquad\qquad m'_{ji}(P) = 1 - m'_{ji}(\Theta)$$

where m_{ji} are the bba of the j-th ranking on the i-th item, $Min(\cdot)$ is the minimum function and m'_{ji} are the modified bba's. The idea is to reduce the uncertainty, proportionally to the correspondent weight for the best rankings (namely, the ranking with minimum weight), and to increase the uncertainty for all the other rankings. Note that the bba's of $\neg P$ are not modified, since there is no evidence of the items being in wrong positions.

Combination: The final step is the combination of the bba of each item among all the rankings, using the conjunctive rule as follows:

$$m_i^O(P) = \bigcirc_{j=1}^N m_{ji}(P)$$
$$m_i^O(\neg P) = \bigcirc_{j=1}^N m_{ji}(\neg P) \qquad\qquad (4)$$
$$m_i^O(\Theta) = \bigcirc_{j=1}^N m_{ji}(\Theta)$$

Eq.3

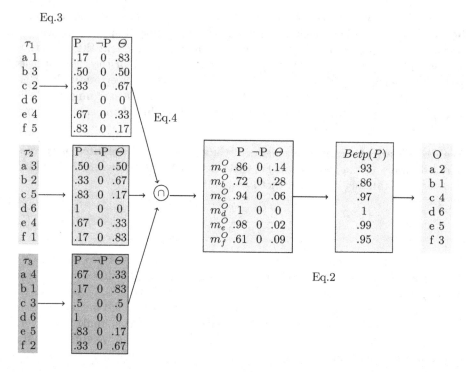

Fig. 1. Example of BRE with NW schema: bba from rankings (Eq. 3), combination (Eq. 4) and the ranking outcome (Eq. 2)

where $i \in 1, \ldots, n$ and m_i^O is the combined belief distribution for the i-th item. $m_i^O(\neg P)$ is zero since $m_{ji}(\neg P)$ is not a focal element in our frame. The conflict after the combination is equal zero since $m_{ji}(\neg P)$ are not focal elements. The use of the conjunctive rule is justified when all the sources of belief are assumed to tell the truth and to be independent. These requirements are fully satisfied here, since we suppose that the rankings are independent and totally reliable because the unsupervised context does not allow to make other assumptions on their quality. We apply the Eq. 2 on the m_i^O in order to make decisions on the frame Θ. The final ranking $O = (O(1), \ldots, O(i), \ldots, O(n))$ is produced by sorting all the items with respect to $BetP_i(P)$, that corresponds to the probability of the i-th item of being in the right position.

Although there is no theoretical constraint about the number of iterations, we propose as maximum number of iterations $MAXT = \frac{N}{2} + 1$. The rational of this rule of the thumb is that replacing more then one half of the original rankings can possibly lead to poor performance due to the replacement of some of the best rankings with information affected by the worse ones. We refer respectively to the weighting schema and the iterative version as $BRE - 1T$ and $BRE - MAXT$ version. A $BRE - NW$ version corresponding to T=0, is also evaluated in this work. $BRE - NW$ combines the belief distribution of the input rankings without the application of the weights, as showed in Fig. 1.

5   Experimental Results on Synthetic Data

To the best of our knownledge no real data on total rankings includes an available true ranking. For this reason we have decided to evaluate BRE on synthethic data that suits perfectly the problem at hand. The aim of this series of experiments is to evaluate the ranking produced by BRE against a set of competitors. The set includes the mean, the median and a competitor based on optimization, the Spearman Footrule optimal aggregation (Opt_list) [6], for we deal with total rankings and BRE uses the Spearman Footrule distance internally. As true-ranking estimator inside BRE we use the same ranking aggregation method competitors, the goal being to investigate if BRE increases the performance with respect to the methods used as true-ranking estimator. The performance is measured with the Spearman correlation coefficient ρ (defined as $\rho(\pi, \sigma) = 1 - \frac{6\sum_{i=1}^{n}(\pi(i) - \sigma(i))^2}{n(n^2 - 1)}$ [7]) and with the Spearman footrule distance (F) computed with respect to the true ranking (τ^{Trank}) and are showed in Tab. 1. We notice that ρ is a correlation coefficient, higher values up to 1 means rankings likely similar. As regard to the Spearman Footrule distance F, values around 0 means similar rankings.

For all the synthetic data experiments, the input rankings are randomly generated under the constraint to exhibit fixed values of ρ with a fixed ranking τ^{Trank} of 300 items. In order to have more reliable results we performed 10 independent replicas of the procedure using the same generation parameters and the results showed are the average over the replicas. The statistical significance of the difference of the averages between BRE and its competitors used as estimators are computed with a t-Test with $\alpha = 0.05$. We generate our data with a number of rankings to combine N equal to 3, 10, 30. For each N value, we propose different cases that correspond to different values of ρ with respect to the τ^{Trank}. With $N = 3$ we define 4 different cases: (*case 1*) 1 ranker extremely good (ρ=.80) with respect to the others (ρ=.06, .01), (*case 2*) two good rankers (ρ = .60, .40) and a very poor one (ρ=.01), (*case 3*) 3 rankers with high correlation (ρ=.80, .60, .10), (*case 4*) 3 rankers with poor correlation (ρ=.01, .06, .03). With $N = 10$ and $N = 30$, three cases *good*, *equal* and *poor* are defined. In the case *good* the 80% of the rankers are highly correlated ($\rho \in [0.95, 0.70]$) and the remaining 20% are low correlated ($\rho \in [0.30, 0.1]$). In the case *equal* the rankers are equally distributed among the three types: highly, medium ($\rho \in [0.70, 0.30]$) and low correlated. Finally, the case *poor* is similar to the *good* one, but with inverted percentages of highly and low correlated rankers. For $N = 10, 30$ ρ of the generated rankings with respect to τ^{Trank} are randomly chosen within the defined intervals.

The comparison between BRE with the mean as true-ranking estimator and mean as aggregation method, shows that BRE-1T and BRE-MAXT outperforms the mean in most of the cases for both evaluation measures (ρ and F), except for the cases 1 and 4 (N=3) where the mean shows higher results. BRE-1T shows significant performance in the majority of the evaluated cases. Regarding the poor case for N=10 and N=30, BRE-1T has shown a significant

Table 1. Spearman correlation coefficent (ρ) and Spearman Footrule distance (F) of BRE and of the competitor methods w.r.t. the true ranking. • means that BRE is significantly better than the corresponding competitor, and o means that BRE is significantly worse.

Method	T.E.	Evaluation measure ρ									
		3 Rankers Cases MAXT=3T				10 Rankers Cases MAXT=5T			30 Rankers Cases MAXT=15T		
	cases	1	2	3	4	good	equal	poor	good	equal	poor
Mean		.4781	.5419	.7958	.0782	.9621	.8760	.7793	.9856	.9543	.8802
Median		.4257	.5106	.7678	.0693	.9748	.8656	.7641	.9941	.9546	.8579
Opt_list		.4065	.4953	.7515	.0594	.9754	.8686	.7681	.9957	.9663	.8787
BRE-NW		.4888	.5254	.7799	.0804	.9383	.8453	.7723	.9409	.8941	.8074
BRE-1T	Mean	.3826	.5742	.8226•	.0722	.9763•	.9207•	.8893•	.9903•	.9742•	.9353•
BRE-MAXT	Mean	.3464	.5780	.8311•	.0666	.9782•	.9270•	.8880•	.9785•	.9714•	.9372•
BRE-1T	Median	.4305	.5865•	.8229•	.0699	.9751	.9208•	.8890•	.9904•	.9743•	.9342•
BRE-MAXT	Median	.3981	.5915•	.8319•	.0660	.9781	.9276•	.8914•	.9784o	.9709•	.9371•
BRE-1T	OptList	.4717	.5826•	.8234•	.0729	.9767	.9212•	.8856•	.9904o	.9755•	.9374•
BRE-MAXT	OptList	.4415	.5844•	.8328 •	.0692	.9783	.9276•	.8919•	.9780o	.9716•	.9391•
		Evaluation measure: F									
Mean		.4117	.4045	.2828	.5318	.1763	.2858	.3461	.1637	.2639	.3438
Median		.4160	.4057	.2575	.5687	.0673	.2186	.2927	.02290	.1359	.2813
Opt_list		.4551	.4399	.2808	.6311	.0535	.1780	.2523	.0144	.0671	.1660
BRE-NW		.4511	.4393	.2912	.6235	.1444	.2368	.3129	.1444	.1919	.2669
BRE-1T	Mean	.4938	.4132	.2578•	.6262o	.0926•	.1688	.1982o	.0592•	.0936•	.1482•
BRE-MAXT	Mean	.5079	.4108	.2475•	.6282o	.0888•	.1625•	.2014•	.0852•	.1044•	.1525•
BRE-1T	Median	.4704	.4071	.2581	.6275o	.0953o	.1687•	.1983•	.0591o	.0936•	.1493•
BRE-MAXT	Median	.4815	.4044	.2473	.6284o	.0890o	.1619•	.1977•	.0851o	.1057•	.1531•
BRE-1T	OptList	.4488	.4113•	.2576•	.6254	.0919o	.1683•	.2011•	.0590o	.0914o	.1456•
BRE-MAXT	OptList	.4569	.4098•	.2469•	.6264	.0888o	.1618•	.1967•	.0861o	.1043o	.1510•

improvement with respect to the mean in terms of F and ρ, whereas the mean is more influenced by the low-quality rankings.

Taking into account the median as true-ranking estimator, we notice that BRE-1T outperforms the median as baseline method in most of the cases evaluated for both evaluation measure, except for the good case with N=30 where the median outperforms BRE. Also for the median, BRE-1T performance shows a significant improvements in the poor cases for $N = 10, 30$ in terms of the evaluation measures.

Opt_list shows the best values of ρ and F with respect to the mean and the median in all the three cases with N=30 and N=10. BRE-1T with Opt_list as estimator outperforms significantly the Opt_list method in all poor cases($N = 10, 30$) except for the good case (N=30,10) and the equal case with N=10 where the Opt_List shows the best results among all the other competitors as F distance.

From Tab. 1, we notice that BRE-MAXT shows significant improvement w.r.t. the estimators in the same cases of the 1T version. We point out that in the good and equal cases (N=10), BRE-MAXT outperforms signicantly the 1T version even if just for small differences of ρ and F. Increasing the number of rankings (N=30), the iterative version seems to be not so effective due to the majority of good rankings. Since the 1T version outperforms signicantly the NW schema in

Table 2. Average Spearman correlation coefficent (ρ) and Spearman Footrule distance (F) of BRE and the other competitors w.r.t. true ranking for the 3 cases with N=10, 30

Methods	True.Rank.Est	Evaluation measure ρ	
		10 Rankers	30 Rankers
Mean		.8725	.940
Median		.8649	.9355
Opt_list		.8707	.9469
BRE-1T	Mean	.9288	.9666
BRE-1T	Median	.9283	.9663
BRE-1T	Opt_list	.9326	.9629
		Evaluation measure F	
Mean		.2694	.2572
Median		.1929	.1467
Opt_list		.1613	.0825
BRE-1T	Mean	.1532	.1003
BRE-1T	Median	.1541	.1007
BRE-1T	Opt_list	.1537	.0987

all the cases, the NW has been tested w.r.t. the competitors only for the cases 1 and 4 (N=3), but BRE-NW outperforms significantly median and Opt_list in terms of ρ only in the case 1. We can notice that our method with the weighting schema gives a notable contribution to increase the performance with respect to the aggregation methods used as true-ranking estimator in the cases where the quality of the rankings is heterogeneous such as the equal and the poor cases. In cases where the majority of the rankings are highly correlated as in the good case, BRE provides also interesting results even if it outperforms significantly only the mean.

Taking into account the average of the results among the three cases (N=10, 30) showed in Tab. 2, we can assert that BRE-1T outperforms the competitors for both N values in terms of ρ and F. Only for $N = 30$ Opt_list shows slightly better value F (.0825) instead of BRE-1T (.987). We point out that the high results reported by Opt_list in terms of F are also related to the fact that Opt_list optimizes the F distance. As final consideration from Tab. 2, BRE with weighting schema can be applied successfully even if the quality of the ranking is not known a priori since BRE outperforms almost all the competitors in terms of average of the three cases (good, equal and poor) for N=10, 30.

6   Conclusion

In this work we have presented the Belief Ranking Estimator (BRE), an unsupervised method that estimates a true ranking given a set of input rankings. BRE, through the use of the belief function framework, models the uncertainty of each ranking and combine them according to weights computed as distances from a true-ranking estimator that can be provided by any ranking aggregation method. From results on synthetic data, with low-quality input rankings BRE with weighting schema has provided better estimation of the true ranking with respect to the mean, median and the Footrule optimal aggregations method used as competitors. Moreover, we point out that BRE shows significantly higher performance with respect to the competitors also when an increasing of the number of rankings is involved. As future work, we plan to extend BRE to the aggregation of top-k lists.

References

1. Adali, S., Hill, B., Magdon-Ismail, M.: The Impact of Ranker Quality on Rank Aggregation Algorithms: Information vs. Robustness. In: Proceedings of the 22nd International Conference on Data Engineering, pp. 37–37 (2006)
2. Argentini, A., Blanzieri, E.: Unsupervised Learning of True Ranking Estimators using the Belief Function Framework. Technical Report DISI-11-480 (2011)
3. Borda, J.C.: Mémoire sur les Élections au Scrutin. Histoire de l' Académie Royale des Sciences (1781)
4. Dempster, A.P.: Upper and Lower Probabilities Generated by a Random Closed Intervals. The Annals of Mathematical Statistics 39, 957–966 (1968)
5. Diaconis, P., Graham, R.L.: Spearman's Footrule as a Measure of Disarray. Journal of the Royal Statistical Society. Series B (Methodological) 30(2), 262–268 (1979)
6. Dwork, C., Kumar, R., Naor, M., Sivakumar, D.: Rank Aggregation Methods for the Web. In: Proceedings of the 10th WWW Conference, pp. 613–622 (2001)
7. Kendall, M.G.: Rank Correlation Methods. Griffin (1948)
8. Masson, M., Denoeux, T.: Clustering Interval-Valued Proximity Data Using Belief Functions. Pattern Recogn. Lett. 25 (January 2004)
9. Pihur, V., Datta, S., Datta, S.: Weighted Rank Rggregation of Cluster Validation Measures: a Monte Carlo Cross-Entropy Approach. Bioinformatics 23(13), 1607–1615 (2007)
10. Shafer, G.: A Mathematical Theory of Evidence, vol. 1. Princeton University Press, Princeton (1976)
11. Smets, P., Kennes, R.: The Transferable Belief Model. Artificial Intelligence 66(2), 191–234 (1994)
12. Yager, R.: Decision Making Under Dempster-Shafer Uncertainties. International Journal of General System 20(3), 233–245 (1992)
13. Younes, Z., Abdallah, F., Denœux, T.: An Evidence-Theoretic K-Nearest Neighbor Rule for Multi-Label Classification. Scalable Uncertainty Management, 297–308 (2009)

Evaluating the Uncertainty of a Boolean Formula with Belief Functions

Christelle Jacob[1,2,*], Didier Dubois[2], and Janette Cardoso[1]

[1] Institut Supérieur de l'Aéronautique et de l'Espace (ISAE), DMIA department,
Campus Supaéro, 10 avenue Édouard Belin - Toulouse
[2] Institut de Recherche en Informatique de Toulouse (IRIT), ADRIA department,
118 Route de Narbonne 31062 Toulouse Cedex 9, France
{jacob@isae.fr,dubois@irit.fr,cardoso@isae.fr}

Abstract. In fault-tree analysis, probabilities of failure of components are often assumed to be precise and the events are assumed to be independent, but this is not always verified in practice. By giving up some of these assumptions, results can still be computed, even though it may require more expensive algorithms, or provide more imprecise results. Once compared to those obtained with the simplified model, the impact of these assumptions can be evaluated. This paper investigates the case when probability intervals of atomic propositions come from independent sources of information. In this case, the problem is solved by means of belief functions. We provide the general framework, discuss computation methods, and compare this setting with other approaches to evaluating the uncertainty of formulas.

Keywords: Fault-trees, Belief functions, Boolean satisfaction.

1 Introduction

One of the objectives of safety analysis is to evaluate the probabilities of dreadful events. In an analytical approach, this dreadful event is described as a Boolean function F of some atomic events, that represent the failures of the components of a system, or possibly some of its configuration states. This method requires that all probabilities of elementary component failures or configuration states be known and independent, in order to compute the probability of the dreadful event. But in real life scenarios, those assumptions are not always verified. This study takes place in the context of maintenance and dependability studies (Airbus project @MOST) in aviation business.

In this paper, we first investigate different approaches using interval computations in order to compute the probability of a Boolean expression in terms of the probabilities of its literals, a problem of direct relevance in fault-tree analysis. The usual assumptions that probabilities of literals are known and the corresponding events are independent are removed. We consider the situation when

---

* C. Jacob has a grant supported by the @MOST Prototype, a joint project of Airbus, IRIT, LAAS, ONERA and ISAE.

S. Greco et al. (Eds.): IPMU 2012, Part III, CCIS 299, pp. 521–531, 2012.

knowledge about probabilities is incomplete (only probability intervals are available), and envisage two assumptions about independence: first the case when no assumption is made about dependence between events represented by atoms, and then the case when the probability intervals come from independent sources of information. We more specifically investigate the use of belief functions to model the latter case, taking advantage of the fact that imprecise probabilities on a binary set are belief functions. We give results on the form of the global belief function resulting from applying Dempster rule of combination to atomic belief functions. We provide results on the computation of belief and plausibility of various kinds of propositional formulas, as found in the application to fault tree analysis. We compare the obtained results with those obtained in other scenarios (stochastic independence between atoms, and the no independence assumption).

2   Evaluation of the Probability of a Boolean Expression

Let $\mathcal{X}$ be a set of Boolean variables $x_1, \ldots, x_n$ such that $x_i \in \Omega_i = \{A_i, \neg A_i\}$; $A_1, \ldots, A_n$ denote atomic symbols associated to elementary faults or configuration states of a system. We denote by $\Omega = \prod_{i=1}^{n} \{A_i, \neg A_i\}$ the set of interpretations $\mathcal{X} \to \{0, 1\}$. An element $\omega \in \Omega$ is also called *minterm*, and it corresponds to a *stochastic elementary event*. It can also be interpreted as describing the state of the world at a given time. It can be written both as a maximal conjunction of literals or denoted by the set of its positive literals (it is *Herbrand's notation*). Let F be a Boolean formula expressed by means of the variables x_i: its models form a subset $[F]$ of Ω, the set of states of the world where F is true; also called the *set of minterms* of F. Hence, the probability of F, $P(F)$, can be written as the sum:

$$P(F) = \sum_{\omega \in [F]} p(\omega) \tag{1}$$

where $p(\omega)$ stands for $P(\{\omega\})$. When the independence of the x_i's is assumed (i.e. A_i independent of A_j, $\forall i \neq j$), this sum becomes:

$$P(F) = \sum_{\omega \in [F]} [\prod_{A_i \in \mathcal{L}_\omega^+} P(A_i) \prod_{A_i \in \mathcal{L}_\omega^-} (1 - P(A_i))] \tag{2}$$

where $\mathcal{L}_\omega^+$ is the set of positive literals of ω and $\mathcal{L}_\omega^-$ the set of its negative literals.

In the case where $P(A_i)$ is only known to lie in an interval, i.e. $P(A_i) \in [l_i, u_i], i = 1 \ldots n$, the problem is to compute the tightest range $[l_F, u_F]$ containing the probability $P(F)$. Let $\mathscr{P}$ be the convex probability family $\{P, \forall i \ P(A_i) \in [l_i, u_i]\}$ on Ω. In the following, we shall formally express this problem under various assumptions concerning independence.

2.1   Without Any Independence Hypothesis

Without knowledge about the dependency between the $x_i, i = 1 \ldots n$, finding the tightest interval for the range $[l_F, u_F]$ of $P(F)$ boils down to a *linear optimization problem under constraints.* This goal is achieved by solving the two following problems:

$$l_F = \min(\sum_{\omega \models F} p(\omega)) \text{ and } u_F = \max(\sum_{\omega \models F} p(\omega))$$

under the constraints $l_i \leq \sum_{\omega \models A_i} p(\omega) \leq u_i, i = 1 \ldots n$ and $\sum p(\omega) = 1$.

Solving each of those problems can be done by linear programming with 2^n unknown variables $p(\omega)$. It is a particular case of the probabilistic satisfiability problem studied in [3], where known probabilities are attached to *sentences* instead of just atoms.

2.2   When Variables x_i Are Stochastically Independent

In the case where the independence of the $x_i, i = 1 \ldots n$, is assumed,

$$p(\omega) = \prod_{i=1}^{n} P(x_i(\omega)) \tag{3}$$

where: $x_i(\omega) = \begin{cases} A_i \text{ if } \omega \models A_i \\ \neg A_i \text{ otherwise} \end{cases}$. The corresponding probability family $\mathscr{P}_I = $

$\{\prod_{i=1}^{n} P_i \mid P_i(\{A_i\}) \in [l_i, u_i]\}$, where P_i is a probability measure on Ω_i, is not

convex. Indeed, take two probability measures $P, P' \in \mathscr{P}_I$, $P = \prod_{i=1}^{n} P_i$ and

$P' = \prod_{i=1}^{n} P_i'$. For $\lambda \in [0,1]$, the sum $\lambda \prod_{i=1}^{n} P_i + (1-\lambda) \prod_{i=1}^{n} P_i' \neq \prod_{i=1}^{n} (\lambda P_i + (1-\lambda) P_i')$,

so it is not an element of $\mathscr{P}_I$.

This assumption introduces some non-linear constraints in the previous formulation, hence the previous methods (section 2.1) cannot be applied. Instead of a linear problem with 2^n variables, we now have a non-linear optimization problem with n variables. Interval Analysis can be used to solve it [1].

3   The Case of Independent Sources of Information

When there is no knowledge about the dependency between the x_i's, but the information about $P(A_i)$ comes from independent sources, *belief functions* can be used to solve the problem of probability evaluation. The information $P(A_i) \in [l_i, u_i]$ is totally linked to its source. l_i can be seen as the degree of belief of A_i and u_i as its plausibility: $l_i = Bel(A_i)$ and $u_i = Pl(A_i)$ in the sense of Shafer.

Proposition 1. *The interval $[l_i, u_i]$ defines a unique belief function on Ω_i.*

Proof: To see it we must find a unique mass assignment and the solution is:

- $Bel(\{A_i\}) = l_i = m^i(\{A_i\})$;
- $Pl(\{A_i\}) = 1 - Bel(\{\neg A_i\}) = u_i \implies m^i(\{\neg A_i\}) = Bel(\{\neg A_i\}) = 1 - u_i$;
- The sum of masses is $m^i(\{A_i\}) + m^i(\{\neg A_i\}) + m^i(\Omega_i) = 1$, so $m^i(\Omega_i) = u_i - l_i$.

We call such m^i *atomic mass functions*. In order to combine two independent mass functions, Dempster rule of combination should be used.

Definition 1 (Dempster-Shafer rule)
For two masses m^1 and m^2, the joint mass $m^{1,2}$ can be computed as follows:

- $m^{1,2}(\varnothing) = 0$

- $m^{1,2}(S) = \dfrac{\displaystyle\sum_{B \cap C = S} m^1(B) m^2(C)}{1 - \displaystyle\sum_{B \cap C = \varnothing} m^1(B) m^2(C)}, \forall S \subseteq \Omega$

In our problem, each source gives an atomic mass function, and there are n sources, so the mass function over all Ω is : $m_\Omega = m^1 \oplus \cdots \oplus m^n$. To find this m_Ω for n atomic mass functions, we can use the associativity of Dempster rule of combination. Here, $A_i, i = 1, \ldots, n$ are atomic symbols, they are always compatible, i.e. $A_i \wedge A_j \neq \varnothing$ for all $A_i, A_j, i \neq j$. So the denominator is one in the above equation.

A focal element of m^Ω is made of a conjunction of terms of the form $A_i, \neg A_j$ and Ω_k (which is the tautology), for $i \neq j \neq k$. Hence it is a *partial model*. Let $\mathcal{P}(F)$ bet the set of partial models ϕ of a Boolean formula F, that are under the form of conjunction of elements $\lambda_i \in \{A_i, \neg A_i, \Omega_i\}$: $\phi = \underset{i=1,\ldots,n}{\wedge} \lambda_i$. Then, $\mathcal{P}(F) = \{\phi = \underset{A_i \in \mathcal{L}_\phi^+}{\wedge} A_i \underset{\neg A_i \in \mathcal{L}_\phi^-}{\wedge} \neg A_i \models F\}$, with $\mathcal{L}_\phi^+$ (resp. $\mathcal{L}_\phi^-$) the set of positive (resp. negative) literals of ϕ.

Proposition 2 (Combination of n atomic mass functions)
For n atomic masses $m^i, i = 1, \ldots, n$ on Ω_i, the joint mass m^Ω on Ω can be computed as follows for any partial model ϕ:

$$m^\Omega(\phi) = \prod_{i \in \mathcal{L}_\phi^+} l_i \prod_{i \in \mathcal{L}_\phi^-} (1 - u_i) \prod_{i \notin \mathcal{L}_\phi} (u_i - l_i) \qquad (4)$$

This modeling framework differs from the usual one when atomic variables are supposed to be stochastically independent. Here, the independence assumption pertains to the sources of information, not the physical variables.

4   The Belief and Plausibility of a Boolean Formula

The belief of a Boolean formula F, of the form $Bel(F) = \sum_{\phi \models F} m_\Omega(\phi)$, theoretically requires 3^n computations due to the necessity of enumerating the partial models for n atomic variables. Indeed, all conjunctions $\phi = \underset{i=1,\ldots,n}{\wedge} \lambda_i$ must be checked for each $\lambda_i \in \{A_i, \neg A_i, \Omega_i\}$. Verifying that a partial model implies F also requires 2^n computations. Plausibility computation, given by the equation $Pl(F) = \sum_{S \wedge \phi \neq \varnothing} m_\Omega(\phi)$ requires to determine partial models not incompatible with F. From the partial models, it will need at most 2^n computation. But it can also be computed by using the duality of belief and plausibility given by:

$$Pl(F) = 1 - Bel(\neg F) \qquad (5)$$

Example 1. **Belief functions of the disjunction** $F = A_1 \vee A_2$

	A_1	$\neg A_1$	Ω_1
A_2	$A_1 \wedge A_2$ $l_1 l_2$	$\neg A_1 \wedge A_2$ $(1 - u_1)l_2$	A_2 $(u_1 - l_1)l_2$
$\neg A_2$	$A_1 \wedge \neg A_2$ $l_1(1 - u_2)$	$\neg A_1 \wedge \neg A_2$ $(1 - u_1)(1 - u_2)$	$\neg A_2$ $(u_1 - l_1)(1 - u_2)$
Ω_2	A_1 $l_1(u_2 - l_2)$	$\neg A_1$ $(1 - u_1)(u_2 - l_2)$	Ω $(u_1 - l_1)(u_2 - l_2)$

Partial models that imply F are $\{A_1, A_2, A_1 \wedge \neg A_2, A_2 \wedge \neg A_1, A_1 \wedge A_2\}$, so: $Bel(F) = (u_1 - l_1)l_2 + l_1(u_2 - l_2) + l_1 l_2 + l_1(1 - u_2) + l_2(1 - u_1) = l_1 + l_2 - l_1 l_2$, that also reads $1 - (1 - l_1)(1 - l_2)$. Likewise, partial models that are compatible with F are $\{A_1 \wedge A_2, \Omega, A_1, A_2, \neg A_1, \neg A_2, A_1 \wedge \neg A_2, A_2 \wedge \neg A_1\}$, hence $Pl(F) = u_1 + u_2 - u_1 u_2 = 1 - (1 - u_1)(1 - u_2)$.

4.1   Conjunctions and Disjunctions of Literals

In the more general case, we can compute the belief and plausibility of conjunctions and disjunctions of literals indexed by $K \subseteq \{1, \ldots, n\}$.

Proposition 3. *The belief of a conjunction C, and that of a disjunction D of literals $x_i, i \in K$ are respectively given by:*

$$Bel(C) = \prod_{i \in \mathcal{L}_C^+} l_i \prod_{i \in \mathcal{L}_C^-} (1 - u_i); \quad Bel(D) = 1 - \prod_{i \in \mathcal{L}_D^+} (1 - l_i) \prod_{i \in \mathcal{L}_D^-} u_i.$$

We can deduce the plausibility of conjunctions and disjunctions of literals, noticing that

$$Bel(\vee_{i \in \mathcal{L}^+} A_i \vee \vee_{i \in \mathcal{L}^-} \neg A_i) = 1 - Pl(\wedge_{i \in \mathcal{L}^+} \neg A_i \wedge \wedge_{i \in \mathcal{L}^-} A_i)$$

Proposition 4. *The plausibility of a conjunction C, and that of a disjunction D of literals $x_i, i \in K$ are respectively given by:*

$$Pl(C) = \prod_{i \in \mathcal{L}_C^+} (1 - l_i) \prod_{i \in \mathcal{L}_C^-} u_i; \quad Pl(D) = 1 - \prod_{i \in \mathcal{L}_D^+} l_i \prod_{i \in \mathcal{L}_D^-} (1 - u_i)$$

4.2   Application to Fault-Trees

Definition 2 (Fault-tree). *A fault-tree is a graphical representation of chains of events leading to a dreadful event (failure).*

Classical fault-trees are a graphical representation dedicated to Boolean functions that are representable by means of two operators $\vee$(OR) and $\wedge$(AND).

Only few applications of Dempster-Shafer theory to fault-Tree Analysis are reported in literature. Limbourg et al. [2] created a Matlab toolbox where each probability is modeled by a random interval on [0,1]. Instead of Dempster rule, they use Weighted average [4] for the aggregation of the belief functions of different variables. Murtha [5] uses the same method in an application to small unmanned aerial vehicles. Another method using 3-valued logic proposed by Guth [6] is compared by Cheng to interval computation, over small examples of Fault-trees [7]. The above results can be specialized to fault trees.

A path in a fault tree links the top (dreadful) event to the leaves of the tree: it is called a *cut*. When this path has a minimal number of steps, it is said to be a *minimal cut*. Each cut is a *conjunction of atoms*. As a consequence of the above results we can compute the belief and plausibility of conjunctions and disjunction of k atoms $A_1, \ldots A_k$:

$$Bel(C) = \prod_{i=1}^{k} l_i, \qquad\qquad Pl(C) = \prod_{i=1}^{k} u_i \qquad (6)$$

$$Bel(D) = 1 - \prod_{i=1}^{k}(1 - l_i), \qquad\qquad Pl(D) = 1 - \prod_{i=1}^{k}(1 - u_i). \qquad (7)$$

From a Fault-tree F, an approximation can be obtained by means of minimal cuts. For a given *order* (maximal number of atoms in conjunctions), appropriate software can find the set of all Minimal Cuts that lead to the top event. The disjunction of all those Minimal Cuts will give us a partial Fault-tree which will be an approximation of F. Fig. 1 is an example of such a Partial Fault-tree.

The Boolean formula F' represented by this tree will always be under the form of a disjunction of conjunctions of atoms $C_1 \vee \ldots \vee C_m$. The formula written in this form will be referred to as a Disjunctive Atomic Normal Form (DANF) (excluding

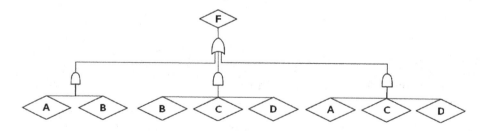

Fig. 1. Example of Partial Fault Tree

negative literals). In order to compute the Belief function of such a formula, we should generalize the computation of the belief of a disjunction of k atoms.

Proposition 5. *[Belief of a disjunctive atomic normal form (DANF)]*

$$Bel(C_1 \vee ... \vee C_m) = \sum_{i=1}^{m} Bel(C_i) - \sum_{i=1}^{m-1} \sum_{j=i+1}^{m} Bel(C_i \wedge C_j)$$

$$+ \sum_{i=1}^{m-2} \sum_{j=i+1}^{m-1} \sum_{k=j+1}^{m} Bel(C_i \wedge C_j \wedge C_k) - ... + (-1)^{m+1} Bel(C_1 \wedge ... \wedge C_m),$$

where C_i are conjunctions of atoms.

During the computation, the conjunctions of conjunctions, such as $C_i \wedge C_j \wedge C_k$ must be simplified, deleting redundant atoms. Note that this apparent additivity of a generally non-additive function is due to the specific shape of focal elements (partial models). In general, for S and T Boolean formulas, we cannot write $Bel(S \vee T) = Bel(S) + Bel(T) - Bel(S \wedge T)$, because there are focal elements in $S \vee T$ that are subsets of neither S nor T nor $S \wedge T$. Here due to the DANF form, all partial models of $C_1 \vee ... \vee C_m$ are conjunctions of literals appearing in the conjunctions.

A similar result holds for computing the plausibility of a DNF.

Proposition 6 (Pl of a disjunctive atomic normal form (DANF)).

$$Pl(C_1 \vee ... \vee C_m) = \sum_{i=1}^{m} Pl(C_i) - \sum_{i=1}^{m-1} \sum_{j=i+1}^{m} Pl(C_i \wedge C_j)$$

$$+ \sum_{i=1}^{m-2} \sum_{j=i+1}^{m-1} \sum_{k=j+1}^{m} Pl(C_i \wedge C_j \wedge C_k) - ... + (-1)^{m+1} Pl(C_1 \wedge ... \wedge C_m),$$

where C_i are conjunctions of literals.

Thanks to the duality between Belief and Plausibility, both computations are quite similar, hence the time complexity does not increase. It is also much less time consuming than an exhaustive computation as presented in section 3.

4.3   General Case

The general case of a Boolean formula with positive and negative literals is more tricky. Such a formula can appear, for example, in fault-trees representing different modes in a system, or representing exclusive failures [1]. Of course we can assume the formula is in DNF format. But it will be a conjunction of literals, and it is no longer possible to apply the two previous propositions. Indeed when conjunctions contain opposite literals, they have disjoint sets of models but their disjunctions may be implied by partial models (focal elements) that imply none of the conjuncts. For instance consider $A \vee (\neg A \wedge B)$ (which is just the disjunction $A \vee B$ we know how to deal with). It does not hold that $Bel(A \vee (\neg A \wedge B)) = Bel(A) + Bel(\neg A \wedge B)$, since the latter sum neglects $m(B)$, where B is a focal element that implies neither A nor $\neg A \wedge B$. However if $C_1 \vee ... \vee C_m$ are pairwise mutually inconsistent partial models such that no disjunction of C_i and C_j contains a partial model implying neither C_i nor C_j, the computation can be simplified since then $Bel(C_1 \vee ... \vee C_m) = \sum_{i=1}^{m} Bel(C_i)$. For instance, the belief in an exclusive OR $Bel((A_1 \wedge \neg A_2) \vee (A_2 \wedge \neg A_1))$ is of this form. More work is needed in the general case.

5 Comparison between Interval Analysis and Dempster-Shafer Theory

Table 1 summarizes the results obtained using the two methods seen in section 2.2 and 3 applied to Boolean formulas: (i) the belief functions method with the assumption that the probability values come from independent sources of information, and (ii) the full-fledged interval analysis method under the assumption that all atomic events are independent [1]. These two assumptions do not reflect the same kind of situations. In particular the independence between sources of information may be justified if elementary components in the device under study are different from one another, which often implies that the sources of information about them will be distinct. However the fact that such elementary components interact within a device tends to go against the statistical independence of their respective behaviors.

Those results are given for the basic Boolean operators with variables A, B, C and D. The probability interval used for those computations are: $P(A) \in [0.3, 0.8]$, $P(B) \in [0.4, 0.6]$, $P(C) \in [0.2, 0.4]$, and $P(D) \in [0.1, 0.5]$.

Table 1. Comparison between Interval Analysis and Dempster-Shafer Theory

Connective	Formula	Belief Functions (i)	Interval Analysis (ii)
OR	$A \vee B$	$l_F = l_A + l_B - l_A l_B = 0.58$	$l_F = l_A + l_B - l_A l_B = 0.58$
		$u_F = u_A + u_B - u_A u_B = 0.92$	$u_F = u_A + u_B - u_A u_B = 0.92$
AND	$A \wedge B$	$l_F = l_A l_B = 0.12$	$l_F = l_A l_B = 0.12$
		$u_F = u_A u_B = 0.48$	$u_F = u_A u_B = 0.48$
IMPLIES	$A \Rightarrow B$	$l_F = l_A + (1 - u_A)(1 - u_B) = 0.48$	$l_F = 1 - u_A + l_B u_A = 0.52$
		$u_F = 1 - l_A(u_B - l_A) = 0.94$	$u_F = 1 - l_A + u_B l_A = 0.88$
ExOR	$A \triangle B$	$l_F = l_A(1 - u_B) + l_B(1 - u_A)$	$[0.44, 0.56]$
		$u_F = u_A + u_B - l_A l_B - u_A u_B$	
		$[l_F, u_F] = [0.2, 0.8]$	
Fault-tree (Fig. 1)	F	$l_F = l_A l_B + l_B l_C l_D + l_A l_C l_D - 2 l_A l_B l_C l_D$	$l_F = l_A l_B + (1 - l_A) l_B l_C l_D + (1 - l_B) l_A l_C l_D$
		$u_F = u_A u_B + u_B u_C u_D + u_A u_C u_D - 2 u_A u_B u_C u_D$	$l_F = u_A u_B + (1 - u_A) u_B u_C u_D + (1 - u_B) u_A u_C u_D$
		$[l_F, u_F] = [0.1292, 0.568]$	$[l_F, u_F] = [0.1292, 0.568]$

In Interval Analysis, knowing the monotonicity of a formula makes the determination of its range straightforward. A Boolean formula is *monotonic* with respect to a variable when we can find an expression of the formula where this variable appears only in a positive or negative way. It is the case for the formulas *And*, *Or*, and *Implies*.

But when the monotonicity is not easy to study, an exhaustive computation for all intervals boundaries must be carried out, like for the *Equivalence* and the *Exclusive Or* [1].

The difference between the results varies a lot with the formula under study. Sometimes, using the Dempster-Shafer theory give the same results as interval analysis, hence, in those cases, the dependency assumption does not have a big influence on the output value; e.g in case of conjunction and disjunction of literals, but also disjunction of conjunctions of atoms (as shown in table 1). This is not surprising as focal elements also take the form of conjunctions of literals, and their masses are products of marginals. The fact that in such cases the same results are obtained does not make the belief function analysis redundant: it shows that the results induced by the stochastic independence assumption are valid even when this assumption is relaxed, for some kinds of Boolean formulas. For more general kinds of Boolean formulas, the intervals computed by using belief functions are in contrast wider than when stochastic independence is assumed.

In general, the probability family induced by the stochastic independence assumption will be included in the probability family induced by the belief functions. This proposition can be proved using the results of Fetz [9] and Couso and Moral [10]. Any probability measure in $\mathcal{P}(m) = \{P \geq Bel\}$ dominating a belief function induced by a mass function m can be written in the form:

$$P = \sum_{E \subseteq \Omega} m(E) \cdot P_E$$ where P_E is a probability measure such that $P_E(E) = 1$

that shares the mass $m(E)$ among elements of E. For a function of two Boolean variables x_1 and x_2, with two ill-known probability values $P_1(A_1) = p_1$ and $P_1(A_2) = p_2$, p_1 is of the form $l_1 + \alpha(u_1 - l_1)$ for some $\alpha \in [0, 1]$ and p_2 is of the form $l_2 + \beta(u_2 - l_2)$ for some $\beta \in [0, 1]$. The explicit sharing, among interpretations, of the masses $m(E)$, induced by probability intervals $[l_1, u_1]$ and $[l_2, u_2]$, that enables $P = P_1 P_2$ to be recovered is:

1. The masses on interpretations bear on singletons, hence do not need to be shared.

2. The masses on partial models are shared as follows
   - $m(A_1)\beta$ is assigned to $A_1 A_2$, $m(A_1)(1 - \beta)$ to $A_1 \neg A_2$.
   - $m(A_2)\alpha$ is assigned to $A_1 A_2$, $m(A_2)(1 - \alpha)$ to $\neg A_1 A_2$.
   - $m(\neg A_1)\beta$ is assigned to $\neg A_1 A_2$, $m(\neg A_1)(1 - \beta)$ to $\neg A_1 \neg A_2$.
   - $m(\neg A_2)\alpha$ is assigned to $A_1 \neg A_2$, $m(A_2)(1 - \alpha)$ to $\neg A_1 \neg A_2$.

3. $m(\Omega)$ is shared as follows: $\alpha\beta m(\Omega)$ to $A_1 A_2$, $(1 - \alpha)\beta m(\Omega)$ to $\neg A_1 A_2$, $\alpha(1 - \beta)m(\top)$ to $A_1 \neg A_2$, $(1 - \alpha)(1 - \beta)m(\top)$ to $A_1 A_2$.

It can be checked that the joint probability $P_1 P_2$ is the form $\sum_{E \subseteq \Omega} m(E) \cdot P_E$ using this sharing of masses. This result can be extended to more than 2 variables. It indicates that the assumptions of source independence is weaker than the one of stochastic independence, and is of course stronger than no independence assumption at all. So the belief function approach offers a useful and tractable approach to evaluate the impact of stochastic independence assumptions on the knowledge of the probability of dreadful events in fault-tree analysis.

6   Conclusion

The more faithful models are to the actual world, the more their complexity increases. When assumptions are made to simplify the model, then it is important to know how far the results stand away from reality in order to use them as appropriately as possible. Having a means to compare different kinds of models and different kinds of assumptions can be a good asset in order to make best decisions out of the models. In this paper, we have laid bare three kinds of assumptions for the calculation of the probability of some risky event in terms of probability of basic atomic formulas. We have focused on the belief function approach that assumes independence between sources of information proving imprecise probabilistic information. We did also gave a formal solution for an application to fault-tree analysis based on a DNF conversion. A practical scalable solution for handling general Boolean formulas is a topic for further research.

References

1. Jacob, C., Dubois, D., Cardoso, J.: Uncertainty Handling in Quantitative BDD-Based Fault-Tree Analysis by Interval Computation. In: Benferhat, S., Grant, J. (eds.) SUM 2011. LNCS, vol. 6929, pp. 205–218. Springer, Heidelberg (2011)
2. Limbourg, P., Savić, R., Petersen, J., Kochs, H.-D.: Fault Tree Analysis in an Early Design Stage using the Dempster-Shafer Theory of Evidence. In: European Safety and Reliability Conference, ESREL 2007, pp. 713–722. Taylor & Francis Group, Stavanger (2007)
3. Hansen, P., Jaumard, B., Poggi de Aragão, M., Chauny, F., Perron, S.: Probabilistic satisfiability with imprecise probabilities. International Journal of Approximate Reasoning 24(2-3), 171–189 (2000)
4. Ferson, S., Kreinovich, V., Ginzburg, L., Myers, D.S., Sentz, K.: Constructing Probability Boxes and Dempster-Shafer Structures. Sandia Nat. Lab., Albuquerque (2003)
5. Murtha, J.F.: Evidence Theory and Fault-tree Analysis to Cost-effectively improve Reliability in Small UAV Design. Virginia Polytechnic Inst. & State University
6. Guth, M.A.: A Probability foundation for Vagueness and Imprecision in Fault-tree Analysis. IEEE Trans. Reliability 40(5), 563–570 (1991)

7. Cheng, Y.-L.: Uncertainties in Fault Tree Analysis. TamKang Journal of Science and Engineering 3(1), 23–29 (2000)
8. Brualdi, R.: Introductory combinatorics, 4th edn., Lavoisier (2004)
9. Fezt, T.: Sets of Joint Probability Measures Generated by Weighted Marginal Focal Sets. In: 2nd Int. Symp. on Imp. Probabilities & Their Applications, New York (2001)
10. Couso, I., Moral, S.: Independence concepts in evidence theory. International Journal of Approximate Reasoning 51, 748–758 (2010)

Introduction to an Algebra of Belief Functions on Three-Element Frame of Discernment — A Quasi Bayesian Case

Milan Daniel*

Institute of Computer Science,
Academy of Sciences of the Czech Republic
Pod Vodárenskou věží 2, CZ – 182 07 Prague 8, Czech Republic
milan.daniel@cs.cas.cz

Abstract. The study presents an introduction to algebraic structures related to belief functions (BFs) on 3-element frame of discernment.

Method by Hájek & Valdés for BFs on 2-element frames [15,16,20] is generalized to larger frame of discernment. Due to complexity of the algebraic structure, the study is divided into 2 parts, the present one is devoted to the case of quasi Bayesian BFs.

Dempster's semigroup of BFs on 2-element frame of discernment by Hájek-Valdés is recalled. A new definition of Dempster's semigroup (an algebraic structure) of BFs on 3-element frame is introduced; and its subalgebras in general, subalgebras of Bayesian BFs and of quasi Bayesian BFs are described and analysed. Ideas and open problems for future research are presented.

Keywords: belief function, Dempster-Shafer theory, Dempster's semigroup, homomorphisms, conflict between belief functions, uncertainty.

1 Introduction

Belief functions (BFs) are one of the widely used formalisms for uncertainty representation and processing that enable representation of incomplete and uncertain knowledge, belief updating, and combination of evidence [18].

A need of algebraic analysis of belief functions (BFs) on frames of discernment with more then two elements arised in our previous study of conflicting belief functions (a decomposition of BFs into their non-conflicting and conflicting parts requires a generalization of Hájek-Valdés operation "minus") [12] motivated by series of papers on conflicting belief functions [1,6,9,17,19]. Inspired by this demand we start with algebraic analysis of BFs on 3-element frame in this study.

Here we generalize the method by Hájek & Valdés for BFs on 2-element frame [15,16,20] to larger frame of discernment. Due to complexity of the algebraic structure, the study is divided into 2 parts; the present one is devoted to the

* This research is supported by the grant P202/10/1826 of the Grant Agency of the Czech Republic. Partial support by the Institutional Research Plan AV0Z10300504 "Computer Science for the Information Society: Models, Algorithms, Applications" is also acknowledged.

S. Greco et al. (Eds.): IPMU 2012, Part III, CCIS 299, pp. 532–542, 2012.
© Springer-Verlag Berlin Heidelberg 2012

special case of quasi Bayesian BFs (i.e., to the case of very simple BFs), the second part devoted to general BFs is under preparation [13].

The study starts with belief functions and algebraic preliminaries, including Hájek-Valdés method in Section 2. A Definition of Dempster's semigroup (an algebraic structure) of BFs on 3-element frame (Section 3) is followed by a study of its subalgebras in general, of Bayesian BFs and of quasi Bayesian BFs (Section 4). Ideas and open problems for future research are presented in Section 5.

2   Preliminaries

2.1   General Primer on Belief Functions

We assume classic definitions of basic notions from theory of *belief functions* [18] on finite frames of discernment $\Omega_n = \{\omega_1, \omega_2, ..., \omega_n\}$, see also [4–9]. A *basic belief assignment (bba)* is a mapping $m : \mathcal{P}(\Omega) \longrightarrow [0,1]$ such that $\sum_{A \subseteq \Omega} m(A) = 1$; the values of the bba are called *basic belief masses (bbm)*. $m(\emptyset) = 0$ is usually assumed. A *belief function (BF)* is a mapping $Bel : \mathcal{P}(\Omega) \longrightarrow [0,1]$, $Bel(A) = \sum_{\emptyset \neq X \subseteq A} m(X)$. A *plausibility function* $Pl(A) = \sum_{\emptyset \neq A \cap X} m(X)$. There is a unique correspondence among m and corresponding Bel and Pl thus we often speak about m as of belief function.

A *focal element* is a subset X of the frame of discernment, such that $m(X) > 0$. If all the focal elements are *singletons* (i.e. one-element subsets of Ω), then we speak about a *Bayesian belief function* (BBF); in fact, it is a probability distribution on Ω. If all the focal elements are either singletons or whole Ω (i.e. $|X| = 1$ or $|X| = |\Omega|$), then we speak about a *quasi-Bayesian belief function* (qBBF), that is something like 'un-normalized probability distribution', but with a different interpretation. If all focal elements are nested, we speak about *consonant belief function*.

Dempster's (conjunctive) rule of combination $\oplus$ is given as $(m_1 \oplus m_2)(A) = \sum_{X \cap Y = A} K m_1(X) m_2(Y)$ for $A \neq \emptyset$, where $K = \frac{1}{1-\kappa}$, $\kappa = \sum_{X \cap Y = \emptyset} m_1(X) m_2(Y)$, and $(m_1 \oplus m_2)(\emptyset) = 0$, see [18]. Let us recall U_n the *uniform Bayesian belief function*[1] [9], i.e., the uniform probability distribution on Ω_n, and *normalized plausibility of singletons*[2] of Bel: the BBF $Pl\_P(Bel)$ such, that $(Pl\_P(Bel))(\omega_i) = \frac{Pl(\{\omega_i\})}{\sum_{\omega \in \Omega} Pl(\{\omega\})}$ [2,8].

An *indecisive BF* is a BF, which does not prefer any $\omega_i \in \Omega_n$, i.e., BF which gives no decisional support for any ω_i, i.e., BF such that $h(Bel) = Bel \oplus U_n = U_n$, i.e., $Pl(\{\omega_i\}) = const.$, i.e., $(Pl\_P(Bel))(\{\omega_i\}) = \frac{1}{n}$, [10].

Let us define *Exclusive BF* as a BF such that $Pl(X) = 0$ for some $\emptyset \neq X \subset \Omega$; BF is non-exclusive otherwise, thus for non-exclusive BFs it holds true that, $Pl(\{\omega_i\}) \neq 0$ for all $\omega_i \in \Omega$. *(Simple) complementary BF* has up to two focal

---

[1] U_n which is idempotent w.r.t. Dempster's rule $\oplus$, and moreover neutral on the set of all BBFs, is denoted as $_{nD}0'$ in [8], $0'$ comes from studies by Hájek & Valdés.

[2] Plausibility of singletons is called *contour function* by Shafer in [18], thus $Pl\_P(Bel)$ is a normalization of contour function in fact.

elements $\emptyset \neq X \subset \Omega$ and $\Omega \setminus X$. *(Simple) quasi complementary BF* has up to 3 focal elements $\emptyset \neq X \subset \Omega$, $\Omega \setminus X$ and Ω.

2.2   Belief Functions on 2-Element Frame of Discernment; Dempster's Semigroup

Let us suppose, that the reader is slightly familiar with basic algebraic notions like *a semigroup* (an algebraic structure with an associative binary operation), *a group* (a structure with an associative binary operation, with a unary operation of inverse, and with a neutral element), *a neutral element* n ($n * x = x$), an *absorbing element* a ($a * x = a$), *an idempotent* i ($i * i = i$), *a homomorphism* f ($f(x * y) = f(x) * f(y)$), etc. (Otherwise, see e.g., [4,7,15,16].)

We assume $\Omega_2 = \{\omega_1, \omega_2\}$, in this subsection. There are only three possible focal elements $\{\omega_1\}, \{\omega_2\}, \{\omega_1, \omega_2\}$ and any normalized *basic belief assignment (bba)* m is defined by a pair $(a, b) = (m(\{\omega_1\}), m(\{\omega_2\}))$ as $m(\{\omega_1, \omega_2\}) = 1 - a - b$; this is called *Dempster's pair* or simply *d-pair* in [4,7,15,16] (it is a pair of reals such that $0 \leq a, b \leq 1, a + b \leq 1$).

Extremal d-pairs are pairs corresponding to BFs for which either $m(\{\omega_1\}) = 1$ or $m(\{\omega_2\}) = 1$, i.e., $\bot = (0, 1)$ and $\top = (1, 0)$. The set of all non-extremal d-pairs is denoted as D_0; the set of all non-extremal *Bayesian d-pairs* (i.e. d-pairs corresponding to Bayesian BFs, where $a + b = 1$) is denoted as G; the set of d-pairs such that $a = b$ is denoted as S (set of indecisive[3] d-pairs), the set where $b = 0$ as S_1, and analogically, the set where $a = 0$ as S_2 (simple support BFs). Vacuous BF is denoted as $0 = (0, 0)$ and there is a special BF (d-pair) $0' = (\frac{1}{2}, \frac{1}{2})$, see Fig. 1.

The *(conjunctive) Dempster's semigroup* $\mathbf{D_0} = (D_0, \oplus, 0, 0')$ is the set D_0 endowed with the binary operation $\oplus$ (i.e. with the Dempster's rule) and two distinguished elements 0 and 0'. Dempster's rule can be expressed by the formula $(a, b) \oplus (c, d) = (1 - \frac{(1-a)(1-c)}{1-(ad+bc)}, 1 - \frac{(1-b)(1-d)}{1-(ad+bc)})$ for *d-pairs* [15]. In D_0 it is defined further: $-(a, b) = (b, a)$, $h(a, b) = (a, b) \oplus 0' = (\frac{1-b}{2-a-b}, \frac{1-a}{2-a-b})$, $h_1(a, b) = \frac{1-b}{2-a-b}$, $f(a, b) = (a, b) \oplus (b, a) = (\frac{a+b-a^2-b^2-ab}{1-a^2-b^2}, \frac{a+b-a^2-b^2-ab}{1-a^2-b^2})$; $(a, b) \leq (c, d)$ iff $[h_1(a, b) < h_1(c, d)$ or $h_1(a, b) = h_1(c, d)$ and $a \leq c]$[4].

The principal properties of $\mathbf{D_0}$ are summarized by the following theorem:

Theorem 1. *(i)   The Dempster's semigroup* $\mathbf{D_0}$ *with the relation* $\leq$ *is an ordered commutative (Abelian) semigroup with the neutral element* 0; 0' *is the only non-zero idempotent of* $\mathbf{D_0}$.
(ii) $\mathbf{G} = (G, \oplus, -, 0', \leq)$ *is an ordered Abelian group, isomorphic to the additive group of reals with the usual ordering. Let us denote its negative and positive cones as* $G^{\leq 0'}$ *and* $G^{\geq 0'}$.
(iii)   The sets S, S_1, S_2 *with the operation* $\oplus$ *and the ordering* $\leq$ *form ordered commutative semigroups with neutral element* 0; *they are all isomorphic to the positive cone of the additive group of reals.*

---

[3]   BFs (a, a) from S are called *indifferent* BFs by Haenni [14].
[4]   Note, that $h(a, b)$ is an abbreviation for $h((a, b))$, similarly for $h_1(a, b)$ and $f(a, b)$.

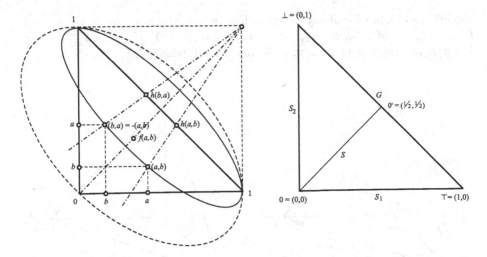

Fig. 1. Dempster's semigroup D_0. Homomorphism h is in this representation a projection to group G along the straight lines running through the point $(1,1)$. All the Dempster's pairs lying on the same ellipse are mapped by homomorphism f to the same d-pair in semigroup S.

(iv)   h is an ordered homomorphism: $(D_0, \oplus, -, 0, 0', \leq) \longrightarrow (G, \oplus, -, 0', \leq)$; $h(Bel) = Bel \oplus 0' = Pl\_P(Bel)$, i.e., the normalized plausibility of singletons probabilistic transformation.
(v)   f is a homomorphism: $(D_0, \oplus, -, 0, 0') \longrightarrow (S, \oplus, -, 0)$; (but, not an ordered one).

For proofs see [15,16,20].

2.3   BFs on n-Element Frames of Discernment

Analogically to the case of Ω_2, we can represent a BF on any n-element frame of discernment Ω_n by an enumeration of its m values (bbms), i.e., by a (2^n-2)-tuple $(a_1, a_2, ..., a_{2^n-2})$, or as a (2^n-1)-tuple $(a_1, a_2, ..., a_{2^n-2}; a_{2^n-1})$ when we want to explicitly mention also the redundant value $m(\Omega) = a_{2^n-1} = 1 - \sum_{i=1}^{2^n-2} a_i$. For BFs on Ω_3 we use $(a_1, a_2, ..., a_6; a_7) = (m(\{\omega_1\}), m(\{\omega_2\}), m(\{\omega_3\}), m(\{\omega_1, \omega_2\})$ $m(\{\omega_1, \omega_3\}), m(\{\omega_2, \omega_3\}); m(\{\Omega_3\}))$.

3   Dempster's Semigroup of Belief Functions on 3-Element Frame of Discernment Ω_3

3.1   Basics

Let us sketch the basics of Dempster's semigroup of BFs on 3-element frame of discernment Ω_3 in this subsection. Following the subsection 2.3 and Hájek & Valdés' idea of the classic (conjunctive) Dempster's semigroup [15,16,20], we have a unique representation of any BF on 3-element frame by *Dempster's 6-tuple* or *d-6-tuple*[5] $(d_1, d_2, d_3, d_{12}, d_{13}, d_{23})$, such that $0 \leq d_i, d_{ij} \leq 1$, $\sum_{i=1}^{3} d_i + \sum_{ij=12}^{23} d_{ij} \leq 1$. These can be presented them in 6-dimensional 'triangle', Fig. 2.

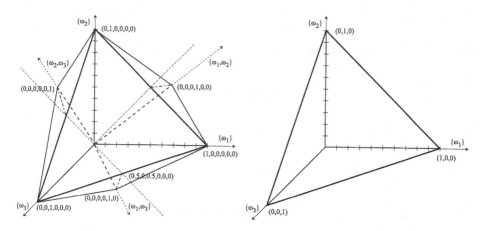

Fig. 2. General BFs on 3-element frame Ω_3

Fig. 3. Quasi Bayesian BFs on 3-element frame Ω_3

Generalizing the Hájek – Valdés terminology we obtain two special Dempster's 6-tuples $0 = (0, 0, ..., 0)$ representing the vacuous belief function (VBF) and $0' = U_3 = (\frac{1}{3}, \frac{1}{3}, \frac{1}{3}, 0, 0, 0)$ corresponding to the uniform distribution of bbms to all singletons. Generalization of extremal d-pairs are *categorical d-6-tuples* $(1, 0, ..., 0)$, $(0, 1, 0, ..., 0)$, $(0, 0, 1, 0, 0, 0)$, $(0, 0, 0, 1, 0, 0)$, $(0, ..., 0, 1, 0)$, $(0, ..., 0, 1)$ which represent categorical BFs on Ω_3. Further generalization of extremal (i.e. categorical) d-pairs are *exclusive d-6-tuples* $(a, b, 0, 1-a-b, 0, 0)$, $(a, 0, b, 0, 1-a-b, 0)$, $(0, a, b, 0, 0, 1-a-b)$, we can see, that the categorical 6-tuples are the special cases of exclusive 6-tuples, the most special case are categorical singletons.

There are *simple d-6-tuples* $(a, 0, ..., 0)$, $(0, a, 0, ..., 0)$, $(0, 0, a, 0, 0, 0)$, $(0, 0, 0, a, 0, 0)$, $(0, ..., 0, a, 0)$, $(0, ..., 0, a)$ corresponding to simple (support) BFs and 6 *consonant d-6-tuples* $(a, 0, 0, b, 0, 0)$, $(a, 0, 0, 0, b, 0)$, etc. corresponding to consonant BFs. We can note, that simple 6-tuples are special cases of consonant ones.

It is possible to prove that Dempster's combination $\oplus$ is defined for any pair of non-exclusive BFs (d-6-tuples) and that the set of all non-exclusive BFs is closed under $\oplus$, thus we can introduce the following version of the definition:

Definition 1. *The (conjunctive) Dempster's semigroup* $\mathbf{D}_3 = (D_3, \oplus, 0, 0')$ *is the set* D_3 *of all non-exclusive Dempster's 6-tuples, endowed with the binary operation* $\oplus$ *(i.e. with the Dempster's rule) and two distinguished elements* 0 *and* $0' = U_3$, *where* $0 = 0_3 = (0, 0, ..., 0)$ *and* $0' = 0'_3 = U_3 = (\frac{1}{3}, \frac{1}{3}, \frac{1}{3}, 0, 0, 0)$.

There is a homomorphism $h : \mathbf{D}_3 \longrightarrow \mathcal{BBF}_3 = \{Bel \in D_3 \mid Bel \text{ is BBF}\}$ defined by $h(Bel) = Bel \oplus U_3$; it holds true that $h(Bel) = Pl\_P(Bel)$ [10].

---

[5] For simplicity of expressions, we speak often simply on 6-tuples only.

3.2   The Extended Dempster's Semigroup

There are only single 2 extremal (categorical, exclusive) d-pairs on Ω_2, thus the extension of $\mathbf{D}_0$ to $\mathbf{D}_0^+$, (where $D_0^+ = D_0 \cup \{\bot, \top\}$ and $\bot \oplus \top$ is undefined) is important for applications, but it is not interesting from the theoretical point of view.

There are 6 categorical (exclusive) d-6-tuples in $\mathbf{D}_3^+$ (in the set of BFs defined over Ω_3) and many general exclusive 6-tuples (BFs) in $\mathbf{D}_3^+$, thus the issue of extension of Dempster's semigroup to all BFs is more interesting and also more important, because a complex structure of exclusive BFs is omitted in Dempster's semigroup of non-exclusive BFs, in the case of Ω_3. Nevertheless, due to the extent of this text we are concentrating only on the non-extended case in this study.

4   Subalgebras of Dempster's Semigroup

4.1   Subalgebras of $\mathbf{D}_0$ and Ideas of Subalgebras of $\mathbf{D}_3$

There are the following subalgebras of $\mathbf{D}_0$: subgroup of (non-extremal) BBFs $G = (\{BBFs\}, \oplus, -, 0')$, two trivial subgroups $0 = (\{0\}, \oplus, -, 0)$ and $0' = (\{0'\}, \oplus, -, 0')$, (other two trivial groups $\bot = (0, 1)$ and $\top = (1, 0)$ are subalgebras of $\mathbf{D}_0^+$); there are 3 important subsemigroups $S = (\{(s, s) \in D_0\}, \oplus)$, $S_1 = (\{(a, 0) \in D_0\}, \oplus)$, $S_2 = (\{(0, b) \in D_0\}, \oplus)$, further there are many subsemigroups which are endomorphic images of S_1 and S_2 by endomorphisms of $\mathbf{D}_0$, for endomorhpisms of $\mathbf{D}_0$ see [3,5] and [10]. Note that there are also other semigroups that are derived from the already mentioned subalgebras: $\mathbf{D}_0^{\geq 0}$ and $\mathbf{D}_0^{\leq 0'}$, positive and negative cones of G (i.e. $G^{\geq 0'}, G^{\leq 0'}$) with or without $0'$, versions of S, S_1, S_2 with or without absorbing elements $0', (1, 0), (0, 1)$, versions of S, S_1, S_2 without 0, and further $S \cup G, S_1 \cup G, S_2 \cup G, S \cup G..., S_1 \cup G..., S \cup G..., S_2 \cup G..., 0 \cup G, 0 \cup G..., 0 \cup G..., 0 \cup 0' = (\{0, 0'\}, \oplus)$, some of these subsemigroups given by union have variants without 0 and/or $0'$ with or without extremal elements $\bot$ or $\top$ (note that subalgebras with $\bot$ or $\top$ are subalgebras of extended Dempster's semigroup $\mathbf{D}_0^+$ in fact). Altogether there are many subalgebras, but there are only 4 non-trivial and really important ones: subgroup G and 3 subsemigroups S, S_1, and S_2.

From [4,15,16] we know that 0 is neutral element of $\mathbf{D}_0$, thus 0 is also neutral element of all subsemigroups of $\mathbf{D}_0$ containing 0, hence $\mathbf{D}_0$ and its subsemigroups containing 0 are monoids, i.e. we have the following observation.

Observation 1. *Dempster's semigroup $\mathbf{D}_0$ and its subsemigroups S, S_1 and S_2 are monoids.*

The 3-element case is much more complex. In accordance with a number of possible focal elements and a representation of BFs by d-6-tuples we cannot display general BFs on 3-element case by 3-dimensional but by 6-dimensional triangle, see Fig. 2. Also the generalization of Dempster's semigroup and its subalgebras is much more complicated, as there is a significantly greater amount of structurally more complex subalgebras. Subsequently the issue of homomorphisms

of corresponding structures is more complex. Nevertheless, there is a simplified special case of quasi Bayesian BFs, which are representable by "triples"
$(d_1, d_2, d_3, 0, 0, 0)$, as $d_{12} = d_{13} = d_{23} = 0$ for qBBFs, see Fig. 3. -

4.2   The Subgroups/Subalgebras of Bayesian Belief Functions

Before studying the simplified case of quasi Bayesian BFs we will utilize the
results on their special case of BBFs from [10].

Following [10] we have "−" for any BBF $(d_1, d_2, d_3, 0, 0, 0)$, such that $d_i >$
0, and neutrality of $0' = 0'_3$, in the following sense: $-(d_1, d_2, d_3, 0, 0, 0; 0) =$
$(x_1, x_2, x_3, 0, 0, 0; 0) = (x_1, \frac{d_1}{d_2}x_1, \frac{d_1}{d_3}x_1, 0, 0, 0; 0)$, where $x_1 = 1/(1 + \sum_{i=2}^{3} \frac{d_i}{d_i}) =$
$1/(1 + \frac{d_1}{d_2} + \frac{d_1}{d_3})$, such that, $(d_1, d_2, d_3, 0, 0, 0) \oplus -(d_1, d_2, d_3, 0, 0, 0) = U_3 = 0'_3$.
We can prove equality of BBFs $(d_1, d_2, d_3, 0, 0, 0)$, such that $d_i > 0$ with non-
exclusive BBFs, further we have definition of $\oplus$, consequently we can prove
closeness of non-exclusive BBFs w.r.t. $\oplus$, hence $G_3 = (\{(d_1, d_2, d_3, 0, 0, 0) \mid d_i >$
$0, \sum_{i=1}^{3} d_i = 1\}, \oplus, -, 0'_3)$ is a group, i.e. subgroup of $\mathbf{D}_{3-0}$. As we have 3 different
non-ordered elements, without any priority, we do not have any linear ordering
of G_3 in general, thus neither any isomorphism to additive group of reals in
general. This is the difference of G_3 subgroup of $\mathbf{D}_{3-0}$ from G subgroup of $\mathbf{D}_0$.

There are several subalgebras of special BBFs (subalgebras both of G_3 and
of $\mathbf{D}_{3-0}$). Let us start with subalgebras of BBFs $(d_1, d_2, d_2, 0, 0, 0; 0)$ where
$d_2 = m(\omega_2) = m(\omega_3)$. The set of these BBFs is closed w.r.t. $\oplus$. There is
$minus_{2=3}(d_1, d_2, d_2, 0, 0, 0; 0) = (\frac{d_2}{d_2+2d_1}, \frac{d_1}{d_2+2d_1}, \frac{d_1}{d_2+2d_1}, 0, 0, 0; 0) = (\frac{1-d_1}{1+3d_1}, \frac{2d_1}{1+3d_1},$
$\frac{2d_1}{1+3d_1}, 0, 0, 0; 0)$, for any $0 \le d_1 \le 1, d_2 = \frac{1}{2}(1-d_1)$, such that $(d_1, \frac{1}{2}(1-d_1), \frac{1}{2}(1-$
$d_1), 0, 0, 0; 0) \oplus minus_{2=3}(d_1, \frac{1}{2}(1 - d_1), \frac{1}{2}(1 - d_1), 0, 0, 0; 0) = (\frac{1}{3}, \frac{1}{3}, \frac{1}{3})$, hence
$minus_{2=3}$[6] is inverse w.r.t. $\oplus$ on the set. Thus $G_{2=3} = (\{(d_1, d_2, d_2, 0, 0, 0; 0)\}, \oplus,$
$minus_{2=3}, 0'_3)$ is subgroup of G_3 and of $\mathbf{D}_{3-0}$. As there is a natural linear order
of d_1's from 0 to 1, consequently, there is also a linear order of $G_{2=3}$, thus $G_{2=3}$
is an ordered group of BBFs. Analogically there are ordered subgroups $G_{1=3}$ and
$G_{1=2}$. Based on these facts and on analogy of $G_{2=3}$, $G_{1=3}$, and $G_{1=2}$ with G,
there is the following hypothesis. Unfortunately, isomorphisms of the subgroups
to $(Re, +, -, 0)$ have not been observed till now.

Hypothesis 1. *$G_{2=3}$, $G_{1=3}$, and $G_{1=2}$ are subgroups of $\mathbf{D}_{3-0}$ isomorphic to
the additive group of reals.*

Positive and negative cones $G_{1=2}^{\ge 0'}, G_{1=3}^{\ge 0'}, G_{2=3}^{\ge 0'}, G_{1=2}^{\le 0'}, G_{1=3}^{\le 0'}, G_{2=3}^{\le 0'}, (G_{1=2}^{> 0'}, G_{1=3}^{> 0'},$
$G_{2=3}^{> 0'}, G_{1=2}^{< 0'}, G_{1=3}^{< 0'}, G_{2=3}^{< 0'})$ of $G_{1=2}, G_{1=3}, G_{2=3}$ with and without $0'$ are subsemigroups of G_3 and consequently also subsemigroups of $\mathbf{D}_{3-0}$.

4.3   The Subsemigroup of Quasi-bayesian Belief Functions

Let us turn our attention to the set of all non-exclusive quasi-Bayesian belief
functions $\mathbf{D}_{3-0} = \{(a, b, c, 0, 0, 0); 0 \le a + b + c \le 1, 0 \le a, b, c\}$. This includes

---

[6] The name $minus_{2=3}$ reflects the fact, that the operation is a generalization of Hájek-
Valdés operation "minus" $(-(a, b) = (b, a))$ to $G_{2=3}$.

neutral element 0 and idempotent $0' = U_3$. Considering only non-exclusive qBBFs, $\oplus$ is always defined, closeness w.r.t. $\oplus$ is obvious, hence we have a subsemigroup (with neutral element, thus monoid) $\mathbf{D}_{3-0}$.

Subgroup G_3 of $\mathbf{D}_3$ and its subalgebras are also subalgebras of $\mathbf{D}_{3-0}$. Analogously to subsemigroups S and S_i of $\mathbf{D}_0$, there are subsemigroups $S_1 = (\{(d_1, 0, 0, 0, 0, 0) \in D_{3-0}\}, \oplus)$, $S_2 = (\{(0, d_2, 0, 0, 0, 0) \in D_{3-0}\}, \oplus)$, $S_3 = (\{(0, 0, d_3, 0, 0, 0) \in D_{3-0}\}, \oplus)$ and $S_0 = (\{(s, s, s, 0, 0, 0) \in D_{3-0}\}, \oplus)$ are subsemigroups of $\mathbf{D}_{3-0}$. and similarly also $S_{1-2} = (\{(s, s, 0, 0, 0, 0) \in D_{3-0}\}, \oplus)$ (without $(\frac{1}{2}, \frac{1}{2}, 0, 0, 0, 0)$), S_{1-3}, and S_{2-3} of $\mathbf{D}_{3-0}$. All of them are isomorphic to the positive cone of the additive group of reals $\mathbf{Re}_{\geq 0}$. Using isomorphicity of S_1 (subsemigroup of D_0), there are simple isomorphisms $z_i : S_i \subset D_3 \longrightarrow S_1 \subset D_0$: $z_1(d_1, 0, 0, 0, 0, 0) = (d_1, 0)$, $z_2(0, d_2, 0, 0, 0, 0) = (d_2, 0)$, $z_3(0, 0, d_3, 0, 0, 0) = (d_3, 0)$. Analogously there is $z_{1-2} : S_{1-2} \subset D_3 \longrightarrow S \subset D_0$: $z_{1=2}(s, s, 0, 0, 0, 0) = (s, s)$, where S is already isomorphic to S_1 (and $\mathbf{Re}_{\geq 0}$) using Valdes' isomorphism $\varphi : S_1 \to S$ given by $\varphi(x_1, 0) = (\frac{x_1}{1+x_1}, \frac{x_1}{1+x_1})$, see [20].

For subsemigroup S_0 in $\mathbf{D}_3$ we can use isomorphicity of S_1 verified in the previous paragraph, further we have to define new isomorphism $\varphi_3 : S_1 \to S$ given by $\varphi_3(d_1, 0, 0, 0, 0, 0) = (\frac{d_1}{1+2d_1}, \frac{d_1}{1+2d_1}, \frac{d_1}{1+2d_1}, 0, 0, 0)$ for $0 \leq d_1 \leq 1$, where $\varphi_3^{-1}(s, s, s, 0, 0, 0) = (\frac{s}{1-2s}, 0, 0, 0, 0, 0)$ for $0 \leq s \leq \frac{1}{3}$. Let us verify the homomorphic properties: we have to verify $\varphi_3((a, 0, 0, 0, 0, 0) \oplus (b, 0, 0, 0, 0, 0)) \stackrel{?}{=} \varphi_3(a, 0, 0, 0, 0, 0) \oplus \varphi_3(b, 0, 0, 0, 0, 0)$: $\varphi_3((a, 0, 0, 0, 0, 0) \oplus (b, 0, 0, 0, 0, 0)) = \varphi_3(a + b - ab, 0, 0, 0, 0, 0) = (c, c, c, 0, 0, 0)$, where $c = \frac{a+b-ab}{1+2a+2b-2ab}$; $(u, u, u, 0, 0, 0) \oplus (v, v, v, 0, 0, 0) = (w, w, w, 0, 0, 0)$, where $w = \frac{u+v-5uv}{1-6uv}$, thus $\varphi_3(a, 0, 0, 0, 0, 0) \oplus \varphi_3(b, 0, 0, 0, 0, 0) = (\frac{a}{1+2a}, \frac{a}{1+2a}, \frac{a}{1+2a}, 0, 0, 0) \oplus (\frac{b}{1+2b}, \frac{b}{1+2b}, \frac{b}{1+2b}, 0, 0, 0) = (s, s, s, 0, 0, 0)$, where $s = \frac{\frac{a}{1+2a} + \frac{b}{1+2b} - 5\frac{a}{1+2a}\frac{b}{1+2b}}{1 - 6\frac{a}{1+2a}\frac{b}{1+2b}} = \frac{a+b+ab}{1+2a+2b-2ab} = c$.

Hence φ_3 is really a homomorphism, i.e. we have the following lemma:

Lemma 1. S_0 *is subsemigroup of* $\mathbf{D}_{3-0}$ *isomorphic to the positive cone of the additive group of reals extended with* ∞.

Let us consider subsemigroup $\mathbf{D}_{1-2=3} = (\{(d_1, d_2, d_2, 0, 0, 0\}, \oplus)$ now. Analogously to $G_{2=3}$, $d_2 = d_3$, but $d_1 + 2d_2 \leq 1$ here. Thus $G_{2=3}$ is proper subalgebra of $\mathbf{D}_{1-2=3}$. There are subsemigroups $S_1, S_{2=3} = (\{(0, d_2, d_2)\}, \oplus)$ and S_0, we have already seen that S_1 and S_0 are isomorphic to $\mathbf{Re}_{\geq 0}$ and $\mathbf{Re}_{\geq 0}^+$, the same holds also for $S_{2=3}$ using simple isomorphism $z : S_{2=3} \longrightarrow S \subset D_0$, such that $z(0, d_2, d_2) = (d_2, d_2)$. A structure of the subsemigroup $\mathbf{D}_{1-2=3}$ is very similar to that of $\mathbf{D}_0$, we can even extend the operation $minus_{2=3}$ from $G_{2=3}$ to the entire $\mathbf{D}_{1-2=3}$, where $minus_{2=3}(d_1, d_2, d_2, 0, 0, 0) = (x_1, x_2, x_2)$, such that $x_1 = d_1 + 2d_2 - 2\frac{2d_1 + d_2 - d_1^2 - 2d_2^2 - 3d_1 d_2}{3 - d_1 - 5d_2}$, $x_2 = \frac{2d_1 + d_2 - d_1^2 - 2d_2^2 - 3d_1 d_2}{3 - d_1 - 5d_2}$. Assuming validity of Hypothesis 1, the subsemigroup $\mathbf{D}_{1-2=3} = (\{(d_1, d_2, d_2, 0, 0, 0\}, \oplus, minus_{2=3}, 0, U_3)$ is isomorphic to Dempster's semigroup $\mathbf{D}_0$. The same for $\mathbf{D}_{2-1=3}$ and $\mathbf{D}_{3-1=2}$.

We can observe that subsemigroups $\mathbf{D}_{1-2} = (\{(d_1, d_2, 0, 0, 0\}, \oplus)$, $\mathbf{D}_{1-3}$, $\mathbf{D}_{2-3}, S_{1-2}, S_{1-3}, S_{2-3}$ are not included $\mathbf{D}_{3-0}$ (due to exclusive BBFs, e.g. $(d_1, 1 - d_1, 0, 0, 0, 0)$ for $\mathbf{D}_{1-2}$), thus they are subalgebras of $\mathbf{D}_{3-0}^+$ only.

We can summarize the properties of subsemigroup $\mathbf{D}_{3-0}$ of qBBFs as:

Theorem 2. *(i) Monoid* $\mathbf{D}_{3-0} = (D_{3-0}, \oplus, 0, U_3)$ *is a subsemigroup of* $\mathbf{D}_3$ *with neutral element* $0 = (0,0,0,0,0,0)$ *and with the only other idempotent* $0' = U_3 = (\frac{1}{3}, \frac{1}{3}, \frac{1}{3}, 0, 0, 0)$.

(ii) Subgroup of non-exclusive BBFs $G_3 = (\{(a, b, c, 0, 0, 0) \mid a + b + c = 1, 0 < a, b, c\}, \oplus, " - ", U_3)$ *and its subalgebras are subalgebras of* $\mathbf{D}_{3-0}$.

(iii) The sets of non-exclusive BFs $S_0, S_1, S_2, S_3, S_{1-2}, S_{1-3}, S_{2-3}$ *with the operation* $\oplus$ *and VBF* 0 *form commutative semigroups with neutral element* 0 *(monoids); they all are isomorphic*[7] *to the positive cone of the additive group of reals* $\mathbf{Re}_{\geq 0}$ *(to* $\mathbf{Re}_{\geq 0}^{+}$ *extended with* ∞ *in the case of* S*).*

(iv) Subsemigroups $\mathbf{D}_{1-2=3}$, $\mathbf{D}_{2-1=3}$ *and* $\mathbf{D}_{3-1=2}$ *(with their subalgebras* S_i*'s,* $G_{2=3}, G_{1=3}$ *and* $G_{1=2}$*) are subsemigroups (resp. subgroups in the case of* G_i*'s) of* $\mathbf{D}_{3-0}$ *(hence also of* $\mathbf{D}_3$*). Assuming validity of Hypothesis 1,* $\mathbf{D}_{1-2=3}$, $\mathbf{D}_{2-1=3}$ *and* $\mathbf{D}_{3-1=2}$ *are isomorphic to Dempster's semigroup* $\mathbf{D}_0$.

(v) Semigroups of non-exclusive BFs $(\{(a, b, 0, 0, 0, 0) \mid a+b < 1\}, \oplus)$, $(\{(a, 0, c, 0, 0, 0) \mid a + c < 1\}, \oplus)$, $(\{(0, b, c, 0, 0, 0) \mid b + c < 1\}, \oplus)$, *are subsemigroups of* $\mathbf{D}_{3-0}$ *and all three are isomorphic to* $\mathbf{D}_0$ *without set of BBFs* G.

(vi) h is homomorphism: $(D_{3-0}, \oplus, 0, U_3) \longrightarrow (G_3, \oplus, " - ", U_3)$; $h(Bel) = Bel \oplus 0' = Pl_-P(Bel)$, *i.e., the normalized plausibility of singletons probabilistic transformation.*

A generalization of the Hájek-Valdés operation "minus" $-$ and of homomorphism f from $\mathbf{D}_0$ to D_{3-0} is still under development.

5   Ideas for Future Research and Open Problems

The presented introductive study opens many interesting problems related to algebraic properties of belief functions on 3-element frame of discernment.

- Elaboration of the properties of D_{3-0} and related substructures required by investigation of conflicting BFs [12]:
  - a generalization of operation $-$ to D_{3-0} analogously to the operation $minus_{2=3}$ from $\mathbf{D}_{1-2=3}$;
  - and related issue: a generalization of the homomorphism f to D_{3-0}.
- The basic study of qBBFs should be supplemented by description of the extension D_{3-0} to D_{3-0}^{+} containing all quasi Bayesian BFs.
- Study of properties of general BFs, i.e. the semigroup $\mathbf{D}_3 = (D_3, \oplus, 0, U_3)$.

6   Conclusion

Dempster's semigroup of belief functions on 3-element frame of discernment was defined. Its substructures related to Bayesian and to quasi Bayesian belief functions were described and analyzed.

---

[7] o-isomorphic as in the case of $\mathbf{D}_0$ in fact, see Theorem 1. There is no ordering of elements of Ω_3, thus we are not interested in ordering of algebras S_i in this text.

A basis for a solution of the questions coming from research of conflicting belief functions (e.g. an existence of a generalisation of Hájek-Valdés operation "minus") was established.

References

1. Ayoun, A., Smets, P.: Data association in multi-target detection using the transferable belief model. Int. Journal of Intelligent Systems 16, 1167–1182 (2001)
2. Cobb, B.R., Shenoy, P.P.: A Comparison of Methods for Transforming Belief Function Models to Probability Models. In: Nielsen, T.D., Zhang, N.L. (eds.) ECSQARU 2003. LNCS (LNAI), vol. 2711, pp. 255–266. Springer, Heidelberg (2003)
3. Daniel, M.: More on Automorphisms of Dempster's Semigroup. In: Proceedings of the 3rd Workshop in Uncertainty in Expert Systems; WUPES 1994, pp. 54–69. University of Economics, Prague (1994)
4. Daniel, M.: Algebraic Structures Related to Dempster-Shafer Theory. In: Bouchon-Meunier, B., Yager, R.R., Zadeh, L.A. (eds.) IPMU 1994. LNCS, vol. 945, pp. 51–61. Springer, Heidelberg (1995)
5. Daniel, M.: Algebraic Properties of Structures Related to Dempster-Shafer Theory. In: Bouchon-Meunier, B., Yager, R.R., Zadeh, L.A. (eds.) Proceedings IPMU 1996, pp. 441–446. Universidad de Granada, Granada (1996)
6. Daniel, M.: Distribution of Contradictive Belief Masses in Combination of Belief Functions. In: Bouchon-Meunier, B., Yager, R.R., Zadeh, L.A. (eds.) Information, Uncertainty and Fusion, pp. 431–446. Kluwer Acad. Publ., Boston (2000)
7. Daniel, M.: Algebraic Structures Related to the Combination of Belief Functions. Scientiae Mathematicae Japonicae 60, 245–255 (2004); Sci. Math. Jap. Online 10
8. Daniel, M.: Probabilistic Transformations of Belief Functions. In: Godo, L. (ed.) ECSQARU 2005. LNCS (LNAI), vol. 3571, pp. 539–551. Springer, Heidelberg (2005)
9. Daniel, M.: Conflicts within and between Belief Functions. In: Hüllermeier, E., Kruse, R., Hoffmann, F. (eds.) IPMU 2010. LNCS (LNAI), vol. 6178, pp. 696–705. Springer, Heidelberg (2010)
10. Daniel, M.: Non-conflicting and Conflicting Parts of Belief Functions. In: Coolen, F., de Cooman, G., Fetz, T., Oberguggenberger, M. (eds.) ISIPTA 2011; Proceedings of the 7th ISIPTA, pp. 149–158. Studia Universitätsverlag, Innsbruck (2011)
11. Daniel, M.: Conflicts of Belief Functions. Technical report V-1108, ICS AS CR, Prague (2011)
12. Daniel, M.: Morphisms of Dempster's Semigroup: A Revision and Interpretation. In: Barták, R. (ed.) Proc. of 14th Czech-Japan Seminar on Data Analysis and Decision Making under Uncertainty CJS 2011, pp. 26–34. Matfyzpress, Prague (2011)
13. Daniel, M.: Introduction to an Algebra of Belief Functions on Three-element Frame of Discernment — a General Case (in preparation)
14. Haenni, R.: Aggregating Referee Scores: an Algebraic Approach. In: COMSOC 2008, 2nd International Workshop on Computational Social Choice, Liverpool, UK (2008)
15. Hájek, P., Havránek, T., Jiroušek, R.: Uncertain Information Processing in Expert Systems. CRC Press, Boca Raton (1992)
16. Hájek, P., Valdés, J.J.: Generalized algebraic foundations of uncertainty processing in rule-based expert systems (dempsteroids). Computers and Artificial Intelligence 10, 29–42 (1991)

17. Liu, W.: Analysing the degree of conflict among belief functions. Artificial Intelligence 170, 909–924 (2006)
18. Shafer, G.: A Mathematical Theory of Evidence. Princeton University Press, New Jersey (1976)
19. Smets, P.: Analyzing the combination of conflicting belief functions. Information Fusion 8, 387–412 (2007)
20. Valdés, J.J.: Algebraic and logical foundations of uncertainty processing in rule-based expert systems of Artificial Intelligence. PhD Thesis, Czechoslovak Academy of Sciences, Prague (1987)

Application of Evidence Theory and Discounting Techniques to Aerospace Design

Fiona Browne[1], David Bell[1], Weiru Liu[1], Yan Jin[1], Colm Higgins[1],
Niall Rooney[2], Hui Wang[2], and Jann Müller[3]

[1] School of Mechanical and Aerospace Engineering, School of Electronics,
Electrical Engineering and Computer Science, Queen's University Belfast
{f.browne,da.bell,w.liu,y.jin,c.j.higgins}@qub.ac.uk
[2] Artificial Intelligence & Applications Research Group,
School of Computing & Mathematics, University of Ulster
{nf.rooney,h.wang}@ulster.ac.uk
[3] SAP Research Belfast, The Concourse, Queen's Road, Belfast BT3 9DT
{jann.mueller}@sap.com

Abstract. Critical decisions are made by decision-makers throughout the life-cycle of large-scale projects. These decisions are crucial as they have a direct impact upon the outcome and the success of projects. To aid decision-makers in the decision making process we present an evidential reasoning framework. This approach utilizes the Dezert-Smarandache theory to fuse heterogeneous evidence sources that suffer from levels of uncertainty, imprecision and conflicts to provide beliefs for decision options. To analyze the impact of source reliability and priority upon the decision making process, a reliability discounting technique and a priority discounting technique, are applied. A maximal consistent subset is constructed to aid in defining where discounting should be applied. Application of the evidential reasoning framework is illustrated using a case study based in the Aerospace domain.

Keywords: evidential reasoning, information fusion, Dezert-Smarandache theory, Dempster-Shafer theory, discounting techniques.

1 Introduction

Decision making in large-scale projects are often sophisticated and complex processes where selections have an impact on diverse stages of the project life-cycle and ultimately the outcome of the project. Evidence supporting/opposing the various design options can be extracted from diverse heterogeneous information sources. However, evidence items vary in terms of reliability, completeness, precision and may contain conflicting information. Aerospace is a highly competitive field with constant demands on aircraft production to improve safety, performance, speed, reliability and cost effectiveness [10]. Design decisions made throughout an aircraft life-cycle are critical as they directly effect the factors above. Decision making in Aerospace involves the evaluation of multiple decision options against criteria such as detailed requirement specifications and International Aviation Standards. To address these limitations we propose an

S. Greco et al. (Eds.): IPMU 2012, Part III, CCIS 299, pp. 543–553, 2012.

evidential reasoning framework to support decision analysis using information fusion techniques based on Belief Function theory to manage uncertainty and conflict in evidence sources. The novelty of this paper lies in the application of these techniques to decision-making in the Aerospace domain.

This research is an element of a larger collaborative project, DEEPFLOW, which encompasses the areas of natural language processing, high performance computing, computational semantics, and reasoning with uncertainty. The project aims to develop a framework to identify, extract and reason with information contained within large complex interrelated documents which can be applied to many diverse problem domains. Information extracted from these data are used as input to the evidential reasoning framework.

Investigations have been performed in the Aerospace domain where various approaches have been applied to reason with data which are incomplete and uncertain. Such approaches include Bayesian theory, Dempster-Shafer theory (DS) and Dezert-Smarandache theory (DSm) which have been used to fuse uncertain and unreliable information in areas involving sensor information fusion [1] and target identification [4] where systems are required to deal with imprecise information and conflicts which may arise among sensors. A study by Xiaoqing et al. [5] provides an example of how argumentation and reasoning can be applied to handle uncertainty and conflicts in decision making.

As summarized above, Bayesian methods and Evidence theories such as DS [6] have commonly been used to handle uncertainty. As a generalized probability approach, DS has some distinct features compared with Bayesian theory. DS can represent ignorance caused by lack of information and can aggregate beliefs when new evidence is accumulated. DSm can be considered as a generalization of DS whereby the rule of combination takes into account both uncertain and paradoxical information [3]. In this paper we apply DSm to fuse pieces of evidence for decision making purposes.

Evidence sources involved in the fusion process may not always have equal reliability or priority. Reliability can be viewed as an objective property of an evidence source whereas priority is viewed as a subjective property expressed by an expert [7]. Counter-intuitive results could be obtained if unequal sources are fused and these factors are not taken into consideration. To highlight the importance of all this in the decision making process we apply two discounting techniques: reliability discounting using Shafer's classical discounting approach and priority discounting based on the importance discounting technique [7]. We construct a maximal consistent subset to aid in defining where discounting should be applied. To evaluate the proposed framework we present a scenario detailing a decision making process in which a design engineer selects a material to construct a wing spar of an aircraft. A spar is an integral structural member of the wing which carries the flight loads and the weight of the wings.

The paper is organized as follows: in section 2 the basics of Evidence theory and combination rules are introduced. In section 3 the reliability discounting and priority discounting techniques are detailed. A case study in section 4 presents an applied scenario based in the Aerospace domain comparing DS and DSm approaches and the impact of discounting factors on decision analysis. Conclusions are provided in section 5.

2   Theory of Belief Functions

DS Theory. DS (evidential theory) is a generalization of traditional probability. This theory provides a mathematical formalism to model our belief and uncertainty on possible decision options for a given decision making process. In DS the frame of discernment denoted by $\Theta = \{\theta_1, ..., \theta_n\}$ contains a finite set of n exclusive and exhaustive hypotheses. The set of subsets of Θ is denoted by the power set 2^Θ. For instance, $\{A, C, W\}$ is the frame for materials (aluminium, composite, wood) from which an engineer selects one to construct a wing spar.

DSm. DSm proposes new models for the frame of discernment and new rules of combination that take into account both paradoxical and uncertain information. In DSm, the free DSm model, $\Theta = \{\theta_1, ..., \theta_n\}$ is assumed to be exhaustive but not necessarily exclusive due to the intrinsic nature of its elements, the set of subsets are denoted by the hyper power-set D^Θ (Dedekind's lattice) described in detail in [8] which is created with $\cup$ and $\cap$ operators. Using the hybrid DSm (hDSm) model integrity constraints can be set on elements of Θ reducing cardinality and computation time compared to the free model. When Shafer's model holds i.e. all exclusivity constraints on elements are included the D^Θ reduces to the power set 2^Θ. We denote G^Θ the general set on which will be defined the basic belief assignments, i.e. $G^\Theta = 2^\Theta$ when DS is adopted or $G^\Theta = D^\Theta$ when DSm is preferred depending on the nature of the problem.

A basic belief assignment (bba) expressing belief assigned to the elements of G^Θ provided by an evidential source is a mapping function $m : G^\Theta \rightarrow [0, 1]$ representing the distribution of belief satisfying the conditions:

$$m(\emptyset) = 0 \ \text{ and } \ \sum_{A \in G^\Theta} m(A) = 1 \tag{1}$$

In evidence theory, a probability range is used to represent uncertainty. The lower bounds of this probability is called **Belief(Bel)** and the upper bounds **Plausibility(Pl)**. The generalized Bl and the Pl for any proposition $A \in G^\Theta$ can be obtained by:

$$Bel(A) = \sum_{\substack{B \subseteq A \\ B \in G^\Theta}} m(B) \ \text{ and } \ Pl(A) = \sum_{\substack{B \cap A \neq 0 \\ B \in G^\Theta}} m(B) \tag{2}$$

In DSm the Proportional Conflict Redistribution Rule no. 5 (PCR5) has been proposed as an alternative to Dempster's rule for combining highly conflicting sources of evidence. Below Dempster's combination rule and PCR5 are briefly detailed, a complete presentation of DSm can be found in [8].

Dempster's Rule of Combination. In DS, Dempster's rule of combination is symbolized by the operator $\oplus$ and used to fuse two distinct sources of evidence B_1 and B_2 over the same frame Θ. Let Bel_1 and Bel_2 represent two belief functions over the same frame Θ and m_1 and m_2 their respective bbas. The combined belief function $Bel = Bel_1 \oplus Bel_2$ is obtained by the combination of m_1 and m_2 as: $m(\emptyset) = 0$ and $\forall C \neq \emptyset \subseteq \Theta$

$$m(C) \equiv [m_1 \oplus m_2](C) = \frac{\sum_{A \cap B = C} m_1(A) m_2(B)}{1 - \sum_{A \cap B = \emptyset} m_1(A) m_2(B)} \qquad (3)$$

Dempster's rule of combination is associative ($[m_1 \oplus m_2] \oplus m_3 = m_1 \oplus [m_2 \oplus m_3]$) and commutative ($m_1 \oplus m_2 = m_2 \oplus m_1$).

PCR5 Rule of Combination. The PCR5 rule can be used in DSm to combine bbas. PCR5 transfers the conflicting mass only to those elements that are involved in the conflict and proportionally to their individual masses. This preserves the specificity of the information in the fusion process [3]. For two independent bbas m_1 and m_2 the PCR5 rule defined by [8] is as follows: $m_{PCR5}(\emptyset) = 0$ and $\forall (X \neq \emptyset) \in G^\Theta$

$$m_{PCR5}(A) =$$

$$\sum_{\substack{X_1, X_2 \in G^\Theta \\ X_1 \cap X_2 = A}} m_1(X_1) m_2(X_2) + \sum_{\substack{X \in G^\Theta \\ X \cap A = \emptyset}} \left[\frac{m_1(A)^2 m_2(X)}{m_1(A) + m_2(X)} + \frac{m_2(A)^2 m_1(X)}{m_2(A) + m_1(X)} \right] \qquad (4)$$

All fractions in (4) which have a denominator of zero are discarded. All propositions/sets in the formula are in canonical form. PCR5 is commutative and not associative but quasi-associative.

Probabilistic Transformation. We need to obtain pignistic probabilities for decision making purposes for this study. Fused beliefs are mapped to a probability measure using the generalized pignistic transformation approach $DSmP$ [2], an alternative to the familiar approach $BetP$ proposed by Smets et al [9]. $DSmP$ is advantageous as it can be applied to all models (DS, DSm, hDSm) and can work on both refined and non-refined frames. $DSmP$ is defined by $DSmP_\epsilon(\emptyset) = 0$ and $\forall X \in G^\Theta$ by

$$DSmP_\epsilon(X) = \sum_{Y \in G^\Theta} \frac{\sum_{\substack{Z \subseteq X \cap Y \\ C(Z) = 1}} m(Z) + \epsilon \cdot C(X \cap Y)}{\sum_{\substack{Z \subseteq Y \\ C(Z) = 1}} m(Z) + \epsilon \cdot C(X \cap Y)} m(Y) \qquad (5)$$

where G^Θ corresponds to the hyper power set; $C(X \cap Y)$ and $C(Y)$ denote the cardinals of the sets $X \cap Y$ and Y respectively; $\epsilon \geq 0$ is a tuning parameter which allows the value to reach the maximum Probabilistic Information Content (PIC) of the approximation of m into a subjective probability measure [2]. The PIC value is applied to measure distribution quality for decision-making.

The PIC of a probability measure denoted P associated with a probabilistic source over a discrete finite set $\Theta = \{\theta_1, ..., \theta_n\}$ is defined by:

$$PIC(P) = 1 + \frac{1}{H_{max}} \cdot \sum_{i=1}^{n} P\{\theta_i\}log_2(P\{\theta_i\}) \tag{6}$$

where H_{max} is the maximum entropy value. A PIC value of 1 indicates the total knowledge to make a correct decision is available whereas zero indicates the knowledge to make a correct decision does not exist [2].

3   Evidential Operations

Evidence to support or refute design options in a decision making process can be extracted from numerous information sources including reports, journals and magazine articles. Some sources may be regarded as being reliable or have a higher priority than others. It is important to manage these factors in the fusion process to reduce errors in reporting beliefs for decision options. Prior knowledge is applied to estimate both the reliability and priority discounting values.

To aid with determining which sources should be discounted before fusion, we can construct a *maximal consistent subset*. This involves constructing a subset of sources that are consistent with each other. Discounting could be applied to sources deemed dissimilar or non-coherent. To measure the coherence between evidence sources the Euclidean similarity measure based on distance is applied, other distance measure are also applicable. This measure is commutative. Let $\Theta = \{\theta_1, ..., \theta_n\}$ where $n > 1$ and m_1 and m_2 are defined over G^Θ, X_i is the ith element of G^Θ and $|G^\Theta|$ the cardinality of G^Θ, the function can be defined by:

$$S(m_1, m_2) = 1 - \frac{1}{\sqrt{2}}\sqrt{\sum_{i=1}^{|G^\Theta|}(m_1(X_i) - m_2(X_i))^2} \tag{7}$$

Application of other similarity approaches could also have been applied, however, Euclidean distance was selected for simplicity.

Reliability Discounting Techniques. In reliability discounting a discounting factor α in $[0, 1]$ can be applied to characterize the quality of an evidence source [7]. For instance, evidence extracted from an aviation journal is considered higher quality than a blog post. The reliability factor transforms the belief of each source to reflect credibility. Shafer's discounting technique [6] has been proposed for the combination of unreliable evidence sources. Incorporation of the reliability factor $1 - \alpha \in [0, 1]$ in the decision making process is defined as:

$$\begin{cases} m_\alpha(X) = \alpha \cdot m(X), \forall X \subset \Theta \\ m_\alpha(\Theta) = \alpha \cdot m(\Theta) + (1 - \alpha) \end{cases} \tag{8}$$

whereby $\alpha = 0$ represents a fully reliable source and $\alpha = 1$ an unreliable source. The discounted mass is committed to $m(\Theta)$. Using prior knowledge, we set reliability factors whereby evidence extracted from a journal, magazine and blog post are represented by the factors $\alpha = 0.1$, $\alpha = 0.3$, $\alpha = 0.7$ respectively.

Priority Discounting Technique. Source priority can be viewed as a subjective attribute whereby an expert can assign a priority value to an individual source [3]. We characterize priority using a factor denoted β in $[0, 1]$, representative of a priority weight assigned by an expert to a source. The highest priority assigned to a source is characterized by $\beta = 1$ and minimum $\beta = 0$. In this research, pieces of evidence have been ranked in accordance to priority; for instance, it is essential that the material selected to construct a wing spar is verified to be *safe*. Therefore a piece of evidence supporting the material safety is set with a priority factor of 1. Priority discounting is defined with respect to $\emptyset$ and not Θ as in the Shafer reliability approach. The discounting of a source having a priority factor β can be defined as:

$$\begin{cases} m_\beta(X) = \beta \cdot m(X), \text{ for } X \neq \emptyset \\ m_\beta(\emptyset) = \beta \cdot m(\emptyset) + (1 - \beta) \end{cases} \tag{9}$$

which allows $m(\emptyset) \geq 0$, thereby preserving specificity of the primary information as all focal elements are discounted with same priority factor [7]. When full priority is selected by the expert i.e. $\beta = 1$, the source will retain its full importance in the fusion process. Therefore the original mass of the bba is not changed. PCR5 is applied to demonstrate the fusion process when priority discounting is used as Dempster's rule of combination does not respond to the discounting of sources towards the empty set [7]

4   Case Study

This study is intended to illustrate how heterogeneous information from disparate sources can be fused to aid engineers when deciding upon material for a wing spar. The PCR5 rule of combination has been selected to fuse pieces of evidence. Dempster's rule of combination is used for comparative purposes as this rule may generate errors in decision making when the level of conflict between evidence sources is high. Furthermore, priority discounting cannot be illustrated using the DS approach. Before fusion, a maximal consistent subset (i.e. sets of consistent evidential sources) is determined. Obtaining the maximum consistent subset will aid in identifying sources to be discounted. Either reliability or priority discounting can be applied. The aim of applying these approaches is to improve the correctness of fusion results. Decision making is based on pignistic probabilities where results are presented using both *DSmP* and *BetP* transformation methods for comparative purposes.

Standards, Requirements and Evidence. The material selected to construct a wing spar must fulfill specified design requirements. It is assumed that an aviation expert has assigned priory and reliability values. To determine if materials adhere to these requirements we have extracted evidence from a total of 50 heterogeneous sources including: 18 journal articles, 6 technical white papers,

9 books, 7 aviation magazines and 10 blogs (argumentation mining is being applied in DEEPFLOW to automatically extract these information). These sources varied in terms of certainty and consistency, and the resulting knowledge base could contain some conflicting evidence. Using this information, an input evidence vector was constructed by mapping the evidence for the design options to relevant design requirements fulfilled or otherwise. A sample vector is presented in Table 1.

Table 1. Sample Evidence Vector

	Aluminium	Composite	Wood
Evidence	Tolerant material	Damage resistance	Limited availability
Reliability	Journal (0.1)	Magazine (0.3)	Blog (0.7)
Requirement	Safety	Damage Tolerance	Availability
Priority	High priority (1)	High priority (1)	Low priority (0.2)

4.1 Implementation of Scenario

An engineer has the task of selecting a material from the set: aluminum (A), composites (C) and wood (W) to construct a wing spar. The frame of discernment $\Theta = \{A, C, W\}$, is used in the fusion. For simplification, we assume that the selected material needs to fulfill just four requirements: safety, damage tolerance, ease of fabrication and availability of supply. We use four different evidence sources that assign belief to the hypotheses. The estimated respective bbas: m_1, m_2, m_3 and m_4 are given in Table 2. These are estimated using information from the digital knowledge base along with expert knowledge.

Table 2. Basic Belief Assignments for Evidence Sources

	A	C	W	Θ
m_1	0.4	0.5	0	0.1
m_2	0.7	0	0.3	0
m_3	0.2	0.8	0	0
m_4	0.4	0.4	0.1	0.1

Maximal Consistent Subset. It is known that conflict between evidence sources can have a detrimental impact upon the fusion process. To address this, we present a methodology to determine a maximal consistent subset. Before fusion is performed, priority or reliability discounting factors can be applied to those bbas which are considered dissimilar. An outline of this methodology is presented in Algorithm 1. The first step is to rank the evidential sources represented by bbas (m_1, m_2, m_3, m_4) based on their information content. Information content values were obtained using the PIC formula detailed in Equation 6. m_4

Algorithm 1. Calculation of Maximal Consistent Subset

FORALL bbas calculate information content using PIC approach
SELECT bba with highest information content, add to maximal consistent subset.
If more than one bba have the same PIC value, choose one arbitrarily
REPEAT
    FIND most similar bbas using distance measure to those bbas in maximal consistent subset
    IF similarity value > threshold then join bba to maximal consistent subset
    UNTIL similarity values for all remaining bbas not in maximal consistent subset obtain value < threshold or no bbas remain

---

was identified as obtaining the highest PIC value and this is the first member of a potential maximal consistent subset. In the next step, m_4 is joined by other bbas considered most similar to m_4. The similarity (S) for the subsets: $\{m_4, m_1\}$, $\{m_4, m_2\}$ and $\{m_4, m_3\}$ was calculated. A threshold parameter (tuned by the system designer) was set at 0.65 which was judged an acceptable threshold similarity value. The highest similarity value of 0.86 was obtained for $\{m_4, m_1\}$. Therefore the maximal consistent subset now consists of m_1 and m_4. We measure the similarity between the bbas in the current maximal consistent subset and m_2 and m_3, respectively. It was observed that $S(m_2, m_{1,4})$ and $S(m_3, m_{1,4})$ were both low 0.27 and 0.52, respectively (where $m_{1,4}$ represents the both subsets m_1 and m_4). Both these values fall below the threshold parameter, therefore m_2 and m_3 are not considered members of the maximal consistent subset.

To highlight the importance of considering conflict in the decision making process we present a number of examples where evidence sources are fused using PCR5 and Dempster's rule of combination. In the first example evidence sources are considered equal; in the second and third, we use reliability and priority discounting, respectively.

Example 1: No Discounting. We present the case where evidence was fused using the PCR5 and Demspter's rule of combination based on the assumption that all sources are equal in terms of reliability and priority. Furthermore, the maximal consistent subset and identification of dissimilar sources were not considered. The results obtained for this scenario are shown in Table 3. Pignistic values are presented for both combination rules, $m_{12}..., m_{1234}$ corresponds to the sequential fusion of the sources $m_1..., m_4$. The PIC criterion was applied to obtain information content values for the probability distributions generated by *DSm* and *BetP*.

Based on the results in Table 3 it can be seen that PCR5 and Dempster's rule of combination assigned different probability values to the hypotheses. Dempster's rule of combination distributes uniformly over all focal elements of 2^Θ the total conflicting mass resulting in a potentially imprecise and incorrect result. In comparison, PCR5 obtains more realistic probabilistic values transferring conflicting masses proportionally to non-empty sets.

Table 3. Dempster's Rule of Combination and PCR5 Rule No Discounting

| | PCR5 | | | | | | Dempster's Rule of Combination | | | | | |
| | Generalized BetP | | | $DSmP_{\epsilon=0}$ | | | BetP | | | $DSmP_{\epsilon=0}$ | | |
	m_{12}	m_{123}	m_{1234}	m_{12}	m_{123}	m_{1234}	m_{12}	m_{123}	m_{1234}	m_{12}	m_{123}	m_{1234}
A	0.62	0.38	0.40	0.62	0.38	0.40	0.92	1.00	**1.00**	0.92	1.00	**1.00**
C	0.24	0.59	**0.58**	0.24	0.59	**0.58**	0.00	0.00	0.00	0.00	0.00	0.00
W	0.14	0.03	0.02	0.14	0.03	0.02	0.08	0.00	0.00	0.08	0.00	0.00
Θ	0.00	0.00	0.00	0.00	0.00	0.00	0.00	0.00	0.00	0.00	0.00	0.00
PIC			0.30			0.30			1.00			1.00

Example 2: Reliability Discounting. Reliability weightings for the pieces of evidence represented by bbas depend on the source from which the information was extracted (where α_1 =journal, α_2 =magazine, α_3 =blog and α_4 =magazine). This results in the discounting factors $\alpha_1 = 0, \alpha_2 = 0.3, \alpha_3 = 0.7, \alpha_4 = 0.3$. Taking into consideration the maximal consistent subset, reliability discounting factors are applied to the dissimilar sources m_2 and m_3. As m_4 is a member of the maximal consistent subset it is not discounted. Table 4 presents results where reliability discounting is applied and evidence sources fused using Dempster's rule of combination and PCR5 respectively. Dempster's rule of combination and PCR5 rule assign the highest belief to hypothesis C followed by A when reliability factors and consistent subsets are considered. By applying reliability discounting factors the degree of conflict between m_2 and m_3 was reduced. The discounted mass was committed to Θ resulting in Dempster's combination rule assigning similar probabilities to the PCR5 approach. This highlights the effect that conflict can have on the fusion process when compared to the results without discounting in Table 3.

Table 4. Dempster's and PCR5 Rule of Combination Results Reliability Discounting

| | PCR5 | | | | | | Dempster's Rule of Combination | | | | | |
| | Generalized BetP | | | $DSmP_{\epsilon=0}$ | | | BetP | | | $DSmP_{\epsilon=0}$ | | |
	m_{12}	m_{123}	m_{1234}	m_{12}	m_{123}	m_{1234}	m_{12}	m_{123}	m_{1234}	m_{12}	m_{123}	m_{1234}
A	0.469	0.341	0.364	0.479	0.341	0.364	0.502	0.502	0.351	0.517	0.351	0.351
C	0.485	0.644	**0.615**	0.497	0.651	**0.616**	0.459	0.459	**0.637**	0.470	0.637	**0.639**
W	0.046	0.015	0.021	0.024	0.008	0.020	0.040	0.040	0.012	0.012	0.012	0.009
Θ	0.000	0.000	0.000	0.000	0.000	0.000	0.000	0.000	0.000	0.000	0.000	0.000
PIC			0.32			0.32			0.36			0.37

Example 3: Priority Discounting. Pieces of evidence represented by bbas were ranked in order of priority based on the expert opinion of a design engineer (where β_1 =safety, β_2 =availability of supply, β_3 =ease of fabrication and β_4 =damage resistance). The priority factors for the respective four bbas are: $\beta_1 = 1, \beta_2 = 0.2, \beta_3 = 0.6, \beta_4 = 1$. The impact of this approach is demonstrated

using the PCR5 rule of combination. m_1 and m_4 were identified as the highest priority bbas and both are members of the maximal consistent subset. By applying priority discounting to m_2 and m_3 we can view the impact on the decision making process in Table 5 where hypothesis C obtains the highest pignistic value followed by A. Marginal higher PIC values (i.e. the probability of making a precise/correct decision is increased) were obtained compared to the PCR5 fusion in Table 3 where no discounting was performed. These results demon-

Table 5. PCR5 Rule of Combination with Priority Discounting

	Generalized BetP			$DSmP_{\epsilon=0}$		
	m_{12}	m_{123}	m_{1234}	m_{12}	m_{123}	m_{1234}
A	0.453	0.351	0.372	0.463	0.352	0.372
C	0.508	0.633	**0.606**	0.523	0.643	**0.607**
W	0.039	0.016	0.022	0.013	0.005	0.021
Θ	0.000	0.000	0.000	0.000	0.000	0.000
PIC			0.31			0.32

strate how consistency measuring and discounting techniques may be beneficial within decision support systems. Furthermore, the examples reflect the difficulty in decision making within Aerospace. For example, the metal Aluminium has commonly been applied to construct wing spars with advantageous properties including ease of manufacture and repair. In comparison, the use of composites in aircraft is more recent than aluminum resulting in less knowledge on its safety. However, composites are light weight and cost effective. The use of DEEPFLOW offers benefits here. For instance, in the cases of conflicts or inconclusive decisions, DEEPFLOW could further examine and obtain additional evidence from unstructured documents to strengthen or weaken the arguments.

5   Conclusion

This paper provides an overview of our proposed evidential reasoning framework which is applied in the DEEPFLOW project. Furthermore, we detail a novel application of this framework to decision analysis in the Aerospace domain. A case study was used to illustrate the importance of selecting a valid combination rule to analyze critical design decisions when information is conflicting and uncertain. Furthermore, it highlighted the importance of taking into account discounting factors obtained from prior knowledge and measuring consistency between evidence sources before making design decisions. In future work we will further investigate the complexity of the algorithm to obtain the maximal consistent subset and the impact this has on the fusion process. As part of this research we will also compare and contrast different distance measures to measure similarity. This evidential framework can be applied to aid decision-making in other problem domains where information may be incomplete and unreliable.

Acknowledgments. The DEEPFLOW project is funded by Invest NI ref: RD1208002 and SAP (AG).

References

1. Basir, O., Yuan, X.: Engine fault diagnosis based on multi-sensor information fusion using Dempster-Shafer evidence theory. Information Fusion 8(4), 379–386 (2007)
2. Dezert, J., Smarandache, F.: A new probabilistic transformation of belief mass assignment. In: 2008 11th International Conference on Information Fusion, pp. 1–8. IEEE (2008)
3. Dezert, J., Tacnet, J.M., Batton-Hubert, M., Smarandache, F.: Multi-criteria decision making based on DSmT-AHP. In: 1st Workshop on the Theory of Belief Functions (2010)
4. Leung, H., Wu, J.: Bayesian and Dempster-Shafer target identification for radar surveillance. IEEE Transactions on Aerospace and Electronic Systems 36(2), 432–447 (2000)
5. Liu, X., Khudkhudia, E., Leu, M.: Incorporation of evidences into an intelligent computational argumentation network for a web-based collaborative engineering design system. In: CTS 2008, pp. 376–382 (2008)
6. Shafer, G.: A mathematical theory of evidence, vol. 1. Princeton university press, Princeton (1976)
7. Smarandache, F., Dezert, J., Tacnet, J.: Fusion of sources of evidence with different importances and reliabilities. In: 2010 13th Conference on Information Fusion (FUSION), pp. 1–8. IEEE (2010)
8. Smarandache, F., Dezert, J. (eds.): Advances and Applications of DSmT for Information Fusion, vol. 1-3. American Research Press, Rehoboth (2009)
9. Smets, P., Kennes, R.: The transferable belief model. Artificial intelligence 66(2), 191–234 (1994)
10. Yao, W., Chen, X., Luo, W., van Tooren, M., Guo, J.: Review of uncertainty-based multidisciplinary design optimization methods for aerospace vehicles. Progress in Aerospace Sciences 47(6), 450–479 (2011)

Constructing Rule-Based Models
Using the Belief Functions Framework

Rui Jorge Almeida[1], Thierry Denoeux[2], and Uzay Kaymak[3]

[1] Erasmus University Rotterdam, Erasmus School of Economics,
P.O. Box 1738, 3000 DR Rotterdam, The Netherlands
rjalmeida@ese.eur.nl
[2] Université de Technologie de Compiègne, U.M.R. C.N.R.S. 6599 Heudiasyc
B.P. 20529 F-60205 Compiègne, France
thierry.denoeux@hds.utc.fr
[3] School of Industrial Engineering, Eindhoven University of Technology,
P.O. Box 513, 5600 MB Eindhoven, The Netherlands
u.kaymak@ieee.org

Abstract. We study a new approach to regression analysis. We propose a new rule-based regression model using the theoretical framework of belief functions. For this purpose we use the recently proposed Evidential c-means (ECM) to derive rule-based models solely from data. ECM allocates, for each object, a mass of belief to any subsets of possible clusters, which allows to gain a deeper insight on the data while being robust with respect to outliers. The proposed rule-based models convey this added information as the examples illustrate.

1 Introduction

Dempster-Shafer theory of evidence is a theoretical framework for reasoning with partial and unreliable information [1]. It provides a very powerful tool to deal with epistemic uncertainty, by allowing experts to express partial beliefs, such as partial or even total ignorance in a very flexible way, and can be easily extended to deal with objective probabilities. It provides tools to combine several pieces of evidence, such as the conjunctive and the disjunctive rules of combination. Furthermore, using for instance the pignistic transformation, it is possible to solve decision making problems.

Real-world problems can be solved using the Dempster-Shafer theory of evidence by modeling information pieces using a belief function on a specific domain, and manipulating the resulting belief functions using available operations of this framework. The two conventional sources of partial or unreliable knowledge are human experts and observation data. In this work, we consider the latter. Observation data often contain partial and unreliable information. The framework of belief functions is well suited to deal with such data.

Rule-based models are simple, yet powerful tools that can be used for a great variety of problems, such as regression, classification, decision making and control. An example of such a model, defined in the framework of fuzzy sets, is the

S. Greco et al. (Eds.): IPMU 2012, Part III, CCIS 299, pp. 554–563, 2012.
© Springer-Verlag Berlin Heidelberg 2012

Takagi-Sugeno fuzzy model [2]. Usually these types of models translate the domain knowledge and relation between the variables defined for the system model in the form of if-then rules. The if-then rules provide a transparent description of the system, which may reflect the possible nonlinearity of the system. One way of obtaining rule-based models from data is using product-space clustering. A clustering algorithm finds a partition matrix which best explains and represents the unknown structure of the data with respect to the model that defines it [3]. Different clustering algorithms can be used, which will yield different information and insights about the underlying structure of the data.

In this paper we study how to construct, within the framework of belief functions, as understood in the transferable belief model [4], a rule-based model, by means of product-space clustering for regression analysis. We use the Evidential c-means (ECM) algorithm [5] to derive rule-based models solely from data.

Regression analysis is a technique for modeling and analyzing relationships between variables. More specifically, regression analysis helps to ascertain the causal effect of one variable upon another. In classical statistics, it is assumed that the variables are measured in a precise and certain manner. In reality, observation data often contain partial and unreliable information both on the dependent and independent variables. Several approaches have been proposed to deal with different origins of uncertainty in the data, such as fuzzy linear regression [6,7], fuzzy rule-base models [2], fuzzy rule-base models with a belief structure as output [8], nonparametric belief functions [9] and function regression using neural network with adaptive weights [10]. The approach proposed in this work combines the formalism to handle imprecise and partially conflicting data, given by the belief function theory, with a transparent description of the system in the form of if-then rules.

This paper is organized as follows. Section 2 reviews briefly the main concepts underlying the theory of belief functions, and explains the clustering algorithm used for deriving a credal partition from object data. Section 3 proposes a rule-based model for regression analysis and the identification of the model parameters. An example is shown in Section 4 and finally the conclusions and future work are given in Section 5.

2 Belief Functions

2.1 Basic Concepts

Dempster-Shafer theory of evidence is a theoretical framework for reasoning with partial and unreliable information. In the following, we briefly recall some of the basics of the belief function theory. More details can be found in [1,4,11]. In this work, we adopt the subjectivist, nonprobabilistic view of Smet's transferable belief model (TBM) [4,11]

Let Ω be a finite set of elementary values ω called the frame of discernment. A basic belief assignment (bba)[1] is defined as a function m from 2^{Ω} to $[0, 1]$, satisfying:

$$\sum_{A \subseteq \Omega} m(A) = 1 , \tag{1}$$

which represents the partial knowledge regarding the actual value taken by ω. The subsets A of $\Omega = \{\omega_1, \ldots, \omega_c\}$ such that $m(A) > 0$ are the focal sets of m. Each focal set A is a set of possible values for ω and the value $m(A)$ can be interpreted as the part of belief supporting exactly that the actual event belongs to A. Perfect knowledge of the value of ω is represented by the allocation of the whole mass of belief to a unique singleton of Ω and m is called a certain bba. Complete ignorance corresponds to $m(\Omega) = 1$, and is represented by the vacuous belief function [1]. When all focal sets of m are singletons, m is equivalent to a probability function and is called a Bayesian bba.

A bba m such that $m(\emptyset) = 0$ is said to be normal [1]. This condition may be relaxed by assuming that ω might take its value outside Ω, which means that Ω might be incomplete [12]. The quantity $m(\emptyset)$ is then interpreted as a mass of belief given to the hypothesis that ω might not lie in Ω.

The information provided by a bba m can be represented by a belief function $bel : 2^\omega \mapsto [0, 1]$, defined as

$$\text{bel}(A) = \sum_{\emptyset \neq B \subseteq A} m(B) \quad \forall A \subseteq \Omega. \tag{2}$$

The quantity bel(A) represents the amount of support given to A. A bba m can be equivalently represented by a plausibility function $pl : 2^\Omega \mapsto [0, 1]$, defined as

$$\text{pl}(A) = \sum_{B \cap A \neq \emptyset} m(B) \quad \forall A, B \subseteq \Omega. \tag{3}$$

The plausibility pl(A) represents the potential amount of support given to A.

Given two bba's m_1 and m_2 defined over the same frame of discernment Ω and induced by two distinct pieces of evidence, we can combine them using a binary set operation $\triangledown$, which can be defined as [11]:

$$m_1 \textcircled{\triangledown} m_2(A) = \sum_{B \triangledown C = A} m_1(B) m_2(C), \quad \forall A \in \Omega. \tag{4}$$

The conjunctive and disjunctive rule can be obtained by choosing $\triangledown = \cap$, and $\triangledown = \cup$, respectively. For the case of the conjunctive rule $\textcircled{\cap}$, the normality condition $m(\emptyset) = 0$ may be recovered, by using the Dempster normalization procedure, by converting the subnormal BBA $(m_1 \textcircled{\cap} m_2)$ into a normal one $(m_1 \oplus m_2)^*(A)$, defined as follows:

$$(m_1 \oplus m_2)^*(A) = \frac{(m_1 \textcircled{\cap} m_2)(A)}{1 - (m_1 \textcircled{\cap} m_2)(\emptyset)}, \quad \forall A \neq \emptyset, (m_1 \oplus m_2)^*(\emptyset) = 0. \tag{5}$$

The Dempster's rule of combination [1], noted as $\oplus$ corresponds to the conjunctive sum combined by the Dempster's normalization. The choice of the combination rule depends on the reliability of the two sources. The conjunctive rule should be used when all sources of information are fully reliable and distinct. Otherwise, if there are doubts over the reliability of at least one sources then the disjunctive rule of combination should be chosen.

The decision making problem regarding the selection of one single hypothesis in Ω, is solved in the transferable belief model framework, by using a pignistic probability, BetP, defined, for a normal bba, by [11]:

$$\text{BetP}(\omega) \triangleq \sum_{\omega \in A} \frac{m(A)}{|A|} \quad \forall \omega \in \Omega, \tag{6}$$

where $|A|$ denotes the cardinality of $A \subseteq \Omega$. It is shown, that this is the only transformation between belief function and a probability function satisfying elementary rationality requirements, in which each mass of belief $m(A)$ is equally distributed among the elements of A [13].

2.2   Evidential c-Means Algorithm

In [5], the Evidential c-Means (ECM) algorithm was proposed to derive a credal partition from object data. In this algorithm the partial knowledge regarding the class membership of an object i is represented by a bba m_i on the set Ω. This representation makes it possible to model all situations ranging from complete ignorance to full certainty concerning the class label of the object. This idea was also applied to proximity data [14].

A credal partition is defined as the n-tuple $M = (m_1, m_2, \ldots, m_n)$. It can be seen as a general model of partitioning, where:

- when each m_i is a certain bba, then M defines a conventional, crisp partition of the set of objects; this corresponds to a situation of complete knowledge;
- when each m_i is a Bayesian bba, then M specifies a fuzzy partition, as defined by Bezdek [15];

Determining a credal partition M from object data, using ECM, implies determining, for each object i, the quantities $m_{ij} = m_i(A_j)$, $A_j \neq \emptyset, A_j \subseteq \Omega$) in such a way that the mass of belief m_{ij} is low (high) when the distance d_{ij} between i and the focal set A_j is high (low). The distance between an object and any non empty subset of Ω is defined by associating to each subset A_j of Ω the barycenter $\bar{\mathbf{v}}$ of the centers associated to the classes composing A_j. Each cluster ω_k is represented by a center $\mathbf{v}_k \in \mathbb{R}^p$. Specifically,

$$s_{kj} = \begin{cases} 1, & \text{if } \omega_k \in A_j \\ 0 & \text{otherwise} \end{cases}. \tag{7}$$

The barycenter $\bar{\mathbf{v}}_j$ associated to A_j is:

$$\mathbf{v}_j = \frac{1}{|A_j|} \sum_{k=1}^{c} s_{kj} \mathbf{v}_k, \tag{8}$$

The distance d_{ij} is then defined as $d_{ij}^2 \triangleq ||\mathbf{x}_i - \bar{\mathbf{v}}_j||$. The proposed objective function for ECM, used to derive the credal partition M and the matrix V containing the cluster centers, is given by:

$$J_{ECM}(M, V, A) = \sum_{i=1}^{n} \sum_{\{j/A_j \subseteq \Omega, A_j \neq \emptyset\}} \tau_j^\alpha m_{ij}^\beta d_{ij}^2 + \sum_{i=1}^{n} \delta^2 m_{i\emptyset}^\beta, \tag{9}$$

subject to

$$\sum_{\{j/A_j \subseteq \Omega, A_j \neq \emptyset\}} m_{ij} + m_{i\emptyset} = 1, \; \forall i = 1, \ldots, n, \tag{10}$$

where $\beta > 1$ is a weighting exponent that controls the fuzziness of the partition, δ controls the amount of data considered as outliers and $m_{i\emptyset}$ denotes $m_i(\emptyset)$, the amount of evidence that the class of object i does not lie in Ω. The weighting coefficient τ_j^α was introduced to penalize the subsets in Ω of high cardinality and the exponent α allows to control the degree of penalization. The second term of (10) is used to give a separate treatment term for the empty set. This focal element is in fact associated to a noise cluster, which allows to detect atypical data. The minimization of (10) can be done using the Lagrangian method, with the following update equation for the credal partition:

$$m_{ij} = \frac{c_j^{-\alpha/(\beta-1)} d_{ij}^{-2/(\beta-1)}}{\sum\limits_{A_j \neq \emptyset} c_j^{-\alpha/(\beta-1)} d_{ij}^{-2/(\beta-1)} + \delta^{-2/(\beta-1)}}, \; \forall i = 1, \ldots, n, \; \forall j/A_j \subseteq \Omega, A_j \neq \emptyset, \tag{11}$$

and

$$m_{i\emptyset} = 1 - \sum_{A_j \subseteq \Omega, A_j \neq \emptyset} m_{ij}, \; \forall i = 1, \ldots, n. \tag{12}$$

The credal partition provides different structures, which can give different types of information about the data. A possibilistic partition could be obtained by computing from each bba m_i the plausibilities $\mathrm{pl}_i(\{\omega_k\})$ of the different clusters, using (3). The value $\mathrm{pl}_i(\{\omega_k\})$ represents the plausibility that object i belongs to cluster k. In the same way, a probabilistic fuzzy partition may be obtained by calculating the pignistic probability $\mathrm{BetP}_i(\{\omega_k\})$, using (6) induced by each bba m_i. Furthermore, other approximations such as a hard credal partition and lower and upper approximations of each cluster can be retrieved from the credal partition [5]. The information obtained from the credal partition and its approximations can be considered intuitive and simple to interpret. In this work, we try to incorporate the additional degrees of freedom and information obtained from the credal partition, in the rule-based classification systems.

3   Rule-Based Model

3.1   Regression Problem

Supervised learning is concerned with the prediction of an quantitative measure of the output variable y, based on a vector $\mathbf{x} = (x_1, \ldots, x_p)$ of n observed input variables. Let $\mathbf{x}$ be an arbitrary vector, and y the corresponding unknown output. In classical regression literature, the objective is to determine the best mathematical expression describing the functional relationship between one response and one or more independent variables. Following the nomenclature used, the problem is to obtain some information on y from the training set $\mathcal{L} = \{(\mathbf{x}_i, y_i)\}_{i=1}^n$ of n observations of the input and output variables. Classically, it is assumed that the variables are measured in a precise and certain manner. In reality, observation data often contain partial and unreliable information both on the dependent and independent variables. For this case, it necessary to use a formalism to handle such imprecise and partially conflicting data, such as the belief function framework.

3.2 Model Structure

Given a data set with n data samples, given by $X = \{\mathbf{x}_1, \mathbf{x}_2, \ldots, \mathbf{x}_n\}$, $\mathbf{y} = \{y_1, y_2, \ldots, y_n\}$ where each data sample has a dimension of p $(n \gg p)$, following a structure similar to a Takagi-Sugeno fuzzy model [2], the objective is to obtain, directly from the data, rule-based models according to

$$R_j : \text{If } x_1 \text{ is } M_{j1} \text{and } x_2 \text{ is } M_{j2} \text{ and } \ldots \text{ and } x_p \text{ is } M_{jp} \text{ then } y_j = f_j(\mathbf{x}), \quad (13)$$

where R_j denotes the j-th rule, $j = 1, 2, \ldots, K$ is the number of rules, $\mathbf{x} \in \mathbb{R}^p$ is the antecedent variable, M_j is the (multidimensional) antecedent set M_{jq} of the j-th rule for $q = 1, \ldots, p$. Each rule j has a different function f_j yielding a different value y_j for the output. This type of system consists of a set of if-then rules combined with an inference mechanism and logical connectives to establish relations between the variables defined for the model of the system. This type of model can be identified, by product space clustering. A possibility for the output function, is to use an affine function for the output function as:

$$y_j = \mathbf{a}_j^T \mathbf{x} + b_j.$$

The sets M_j are ill-known regions of $\mathbb{R}^p$. For a given $\mathbf{x}$ it is not possible to define exactly to which region M_j belongs, but instead, it is possible to compute a mass function based on the credal partition M. From this mass function it is possible to compute the pignistic expectation of y given by:

$$y_{bet}(\mathbf{x}) = \sum_{A_j \subseteq \Omega, A_j \neq \emptyset} m^\Omega(A_j) \frac{1}{|A_j|} y_j \qquad (14)$$

where

$$m^\Omega(A_j) = \frac{\beta_j(\mathbf{x})}{\sum_{B_j \subseteq \Theta, B_j \neq \emptyset} \beta_j(\mathbf{x})}, \qquad (15)$$

$\beta_j(\mathbf{x})$ is the degree of activation, and $|A_j|$ is the cardinality of $A_j \subseteq \Omega$.

3.3   Model Parameters

To form the rule-base model from the available learning set $\mathcal{L}$, the structure of the model is first determined and afterward the parameters of the structure are identified. Clustering is applied to the learning set $\mathcal{L}$, using ECM. The number of rules characterizes the structure of a rule-based system and in our case corresponds to the number of non-empty subsets of partitions obtained from the clustering algorithm.

In this work, we use ECM to partition the space using the framework of belief function. The Evidential c-Means algorithm was proposed to derive a credal partition from object data. In this algorithm the partial knowledge regarding the observation data of an object is represented by a basic belief assignment on the finite set of frame of discernment. This representation makes it possible to model all situations ranging from complete ignorance to full certainty. Using the credal partition it is possible to highlight the points that unambiguously belong to one cluster, and the points that lie at the boundary of two or more clusters. For this research we try to incorporate the added degrees of freedom and information obtained from the credal partition, in the rule-based systems. This type of model will provide a rich description of the data and its underlying structure, while making it robust to partial and unreliable data.

Antecedent Belief Functions. The antecedent functions can be obtained by projecting the credal partition onto the antecedent variables. The principle of generating antecedent functions by projection is to project the multidimensional sets defined point wise in the rows of the credal partition matrix $M = (m_1, \ldots, m_n)$ onto the individual antecedent variables of the rules. This method projects the credal partition matrix onto the axes of the antecedent variables x_q, $1 \leq q \leq p$.

In order to obtain the mass of belief functions for the antecedent sets M_{jq}, the multidimensional set defined pointwise in the j-th row of the partition matrix M are projected onto the axes of the antecedent variables x_q, by:

$$m_{M_{jq}}(x_{qi}) = \mathrm{proj}_q(m_{ij}). \tag{16}$$

where m_{ij} is given by (11), defined on frame of discernment Ω. In order to obtain a model, the point-wise defined sets M_{jq} can be approximated by appropriate parametric functions. Several types of functions such as triangular, gaussian or trapezoidal, can be used. In this work we choose a combination of gaussian functions of the form

$$M_{jq} \approx f(x_q; \sigma_{1jq}, c_{1jq}, \sigma_{2jq}, c_{2jq}) = e^{\left(\frac{-(x_q - c_{1jq})^2}{2\sigma_{1jq}^2} + \frac{-(x_q - c_{2jq})^2}{2\sigma_{2jq}^2} \right)}. \tag{17}$$

When computing the degree of activation $\beta_j(\mathbf{x})$ of the j-th rule, the original cluster in the antecedent product space is reconstructed by applying the intersection operator in the cartesian product space of the antecedent variables:

$$\beta_j(\mathbf{x}) = m_{Mj1}(x_1) \wedge m_{Mj2}(x_2) \wedge \ldots \wedge m_{Mjp}(x_p), \tag{18}$$

where $\wedge$ denotes a t-norm. Suitable possible t-norms are the product or the minimum operator. In this work, we consider the p features to be uncorrelated, hence we use the product operator. Other possibilities [16] include combination operators which generalize Dempster rule and the cautious rule [17], based on a generalized discounting process or alternatively a parameterized family of t-norms containing both the product and the minimum as special cases, such as Frank's family of t-norms [18]

Consequents Parameters. The consequent parameters for each rule can be estimated by the least-squares method. A set of optimal parameters with respect to the model output can be estimated from the identification data set by ordinary least-squares methods. This approach is formulated as a minimization of the total prediction error of the model. Let $V_j^T = [a_j^T, b_j]$ be the vector of consequent parameters, let X_e denote the regressor matrix $[X; 1]$ and let W_j denote a diagonal matrix with the normalized degree of activation $\beta_j(\mathbf{x})$ in its i-th diagonal element. Denote $X' = [W_1 X_e, \ldots, W_K X_e]$. Assuming that the columns of X_e are linearly independent, the resulting solution of the least-squares problem $y = X'V + \varepsilon$ becomes

$$V = [X'^T X']^{-1} X'^T \mathbf{y}. \tag{19}$$

The determination of the consequent parameters concludes the identification of the rule-based system.

4 Examples

In this section, two examples are presented to verify the validity of the proposed strategy. One is a univariate function, while the other is the gas furnace data of Box and Jenkins [19]. To assess model performance, the mean squares error (MSE) will be used. We compare the results obtained using belief rule–base models proposed in this paper to Takagi–Sugeno fuzzy rule–base models and also to the results presented in [8]. The Takagi–Sugeno fuzzy rule–base models antecedent membership functions are obtained using Fuzzy C-Means [15] while the consequent parameters are obtained using by least-square estimation.

For the first example, let us consider the approximation of a nonlinear static univariate function:

$$y(x) = 3 \exp^{-x^2} \sin(\pi x) + \eta \tag{20}$$

where η is a normal distribution with zero mean and variance 0.15 and x is an input random sample vector of size $n = 30$, uniformly distributed in the domain $[-3, 3]$.

The Box and Jenkins gas furnace data is a well known and frequently used benchmark data for modeling and identification. The data consist of 296 measurements. The input $u(t)$ is the gas flow rate and the output is CO_2 concentration in outlet gas $y(t)$. A possible way of modeling this process is to consider that the output $y(t)$ is a function of the input variables $x = [y(t-1), u(t-4)]^T$.

For both examples a belief rule–base model was derived with $c = 3$ clusters. The resulting model will have $K = 2^c - 1$ rules, as we do not consider a rule for the empty–set. This model was compared to a FCM T–S fuzzy model with $c = 3, 7$ clusters, resulting in a model with 3 or 7 rules. The results for this model can be found in Table 1.

Table 1. MSE for the univariate static function and the gas furnace example

Model	Univariate	Gas furnace
Ramdani [8]	0.018	0.045
FCM $c = 3$	0.432	0.070
FCM $c = 7$	0.013	0.064
ECM $c = 3$	0.017	0.063

Table 1 shows that the MSE obtained with the belief rule–base model proposed in this paper are in line with previous studies. Notice that both FCM and ECM use Euclidean distance as the inner product norm. A more suitable choice for modeling this type of systems is to employ an adaptive distance norm, such as the Mahalanobis distance, to detect clusters of different shape and orientation [20]. This explains the poor results in the univariate case for the fuzzy–rule base models with $c = 3$ clusters. Notice that in the case of the belief rule–base models, a rule is derived for each possible subset of clusters. Thus local models are identified for objects which are clearly identified as belonging to one cluster, but also to objects in overlapping cluster regions. This is an advantage of the proposed method as it helps to improve the results using a low number of clusters. Adding more clusters may increase the number of overlapping cluster regions and consequently the number of rules. This may result in a system which will overfit the data. Furthermore, we note that the proposed model is developed in an automated manner solely from data. This model combines the capability to handle imprecise and partially conflicting data, given by the belief function theory, with a transparent description of the system in the form of if-then rules.

5 Conclusions and Future Work

This paper proposes the use of the credal partition obtained from the Evidential C-Means based on the theoretical framework of belief functions, to derive rule-based models. This type of model provides a rich description of the data and its underlying structure, which can be successfully translated into rules, while making it robust to partial and unreliable data. Future research will focus on assessing properties and characteristics of the proposed model.

Acknowledgments. This work was supported by the European Science Foundation through COST Action IC0702, under the grant ECOST-STSM-IC0702-180411-006041.

References

1. Shafer, G.: A mathematical theory of evidence. Princeton university press (1976)
2. Takagi, T., Sugeno, M.: Fuzzy identification of systems and its aplication to modeling and control. IEEE Transactions on Systems, Man and Cybernetics 15, 116–132 (1985)
3. Hartigan, J.A.: Clustering Algorithms. Wiley Interscience, New York (1974)
4. Smets, P., Kennes, R.: The transferable belief model. Artif. Intell. 66, 191–234 (1994)
5. Masson, M.H., Denoeux, T.: ECM: An evidential version of the fuzzy c-means algorithm. Pattern Recognition 41, 1384–1397 (2008)
6. Tanaka, H., Uejima, S., Asai, K.: Linear regression analysis with fuzzy model. IEEE Transactions on Systems, Man and Cybernetics 12, 903–907 (1982)
7. Chang, Y.H.O., Ayyub, B.M.: Fuzzy regression methods - a comparative assessment. Fuzzy Sets and Systems 119, 187–203 (2001)
8. Ramdani, M., Mourot, G., Ragot, J.: A multi-modeling strategy based on belief function theory. In: 44th IEEE Conference on Decision and Control 2005 and 2005 European Control Conference, CDC-ECC 2005, pp. 3261–3266 (2005)
9. Petit-Renaud, S., Denoeux, T.: Nonparametric regression analysis of uncertain and imprecise data using belief functions. International Journal of Approximate Reasoning 35, 1–28 (2004)
10. Denoeux, T.: Function approximation in the framework of evidence theory: A connectionist approach. In: Proceedings of the 1997 International Conference on Neural Networks, Houston, USA (1997)
11. Smets, P.: The transferable belief model for quantified belief representation. In: Gabbay, D., Smets, P. (eds.) Handbook of Defeasible Reasoning and Uncertainty Management Systems. Kluwer, Dordrecht (1998)
12. Smets, P.: The combination of evidence in the transferable belief model. IEEE Trans. Pattern Anal. Mach. Intell. 12, 447–458 (1990)
13. Smets, P.: Decision making in the TBM: the necessity of the pignistic transformation. Int. J. Approx. Reasoning 38, 133–147 (2005)
14. Masson, M.H., Denux, T.: RECM: Relational evidential c-means algorithm. Pattern Recogn. Lett. 30, 1015–1026 (2009)
15. Bezdek, J.C.: Pattern Recognition with Fuzzy Objective Function Algorithms. Plenum Press, New York (1981)
16. Quost, B., Masson, M.H., Denoeux, T.: Classifier fusion in the dempster-shafer framework using optimized t-norm based combination rules. International Journal of Approximate Reasoning 52, 353–374 (2011); Dependence Issues in Knowledge-Based Systems
17. Kallel, A., Hégarat-Mascle, S.L.: Combination of partially non-distinct beliefs: The cautious-adaptive rule. International Journal of Approximate Reasoning 50, 1000–1021 (2009); Special Section on Graphical Models and Information Retrieval
18. Klement, E., Mesiar, R., Pap, E.: Triangular Norms. Kluwer Academic Publishers, Dordrecht (2000)
19. Box, G.E.P., Jenkins, G.M.: Time Series Analysis, Forecasting, and Control. Holden-Day, San Francisco (1976)
20. Gustfson, D., Kessel, W.: Fuzzy clustering with a fuzzy covariance matrix. In: Proceedings of IEEE Conference on Decision and Control, CDC, San Diego, CA, USA, pp. 761–766 (1979)

An Evidential Framework for Associating Sensors to Activities for Activity Recognition in Smart Homes

Yaxin Bi, Chris Nugent, and Jing Liao

School of Computing and Mathematics, University of Ulster
Newtownabbey, Co. Antrim, BT37 0QB, UK
{y.bi,cd.nugent}@ulster.ac.uk, liao-j1@email.ulster.ac.uk

Abstract. Activity recognition under instances of uncertainty is currently recognised as being a challenge within the application domain of Smart Homes. In such environments, uncertainty can be derived from the reliability of sensor networks, the interaction between human and physical objects and the variability of human activities. Nevertheless, it is a difficult process to quantify these sources of uncertainty within the context of an effective reasoning model in order to accurately recognize activities of daily living (ADL). In this paper we propose an evidential framework, where a sensor network is modelled as an evidence space and a collection of ADLs is subsequently modelled as an activity space. The relation between the two spaces is modelled as a multi-valued probabilistic mapping. We identify two sources of uncertainty in terms of sensor uncertainty and relation uncertainty that is reflected in the interaction between sensors and ADLs. Estimations of the respective types of uncertainty were achieved through manufacture statistics for the sensor technology and by learning statistics from sensor data. A preliminary experimental analysis has been carried out to illustrate the advantage of the proposed approach.

Keywords: Belief functions, Sensor fusion, activity recognition, smart homes.

1 Introduction

Activity recognition with uncertain, incomplete and sometimes inaccurate information is necessary whenever any system interacts in an intelligent way with its environment. This follows directly from the fact that understanding the world is possible only by perceiving interactions with the environment through sensing networks which provide partially processed sensory information, i.e. knowledge and evidence sources about the environment. Due to the limited capability of any single sensor unit in addition to the possibility of faults within the sensor networks such as malfunctioning of sensors, transmission errors between sensors and receivers, the sensed information is inherently uncertain and incomplete [1] [2].

S. Greco et al. (Eds.): IPMU 2012, Part III, CCIS 299, pp. 564–574, 2012.
© Springer-Verlag Berlin Heidelberg 2012

Perceptual information is not readily captured in terms of simple truths and falsities even though binary sensors are deployed within the environment. Therefore when there is a general lack of sample sensor data and appropriate statistics are not in place, neither logical nor standard probabilistic reasoning techniques are uniformly applicable to such a recognition problem.

This is exactly the case which has commonly been recognised for Smart Home systems deploying a range of sensor networks. A Smart Home is a residential environment that is equipped with different types of sensors and computing technologies. In such an environment, sensors are unobtrusively embedded in familiar physical devices and appliances. Sensors, together with computational intelligence as a whole, provide the ability to perceive the states of devices and inhabitants' interactions with the surroundings of the environment and can also record events or actions which occur in real living, and react accordingly to the dynamic changes of the environment itself. Such a seamless integration makes the conventional interaction paradigm to shift from human-to-computer to human-to-surrounding interaction and link intelligence to home environments, leading to an emerging personal healthcare and assistive living paradigm. With this paradigm, ADLs can be automatically monitored, and the risks and declines in health and behavioural of residents can be monitored, assessed and accurately altered. As a result, functional services and assistance of caregivers can be provided as required, which enable ageing inhabitants to stay at homes independently as long as possible. Nevertheless, the precise assessment and recognition process has to be carried out with inherently uncertain or incomplete sensory information. Therefore it is fundamental to have a viable mechanism in place for appropriately handling uncertainty existing within Smart Homes.

In recent years a number of reasoning with uncertainty techniques have been proposed for Smart Homes in an effort to address the challenges associated with uncertainty present in the data gleaned from the sensor networks. In [7], Tapia used a probabilistic method to learn activity patterns and then applied the learned knowledge to reason about activities. In [8], the authors developed an uncertainty model based on a predicate representation of contexts and associated confidence values. The model proposed forms a basis for reasoning about uncertainty using various mechanisms such as probabilistic logic, Bayesian networks and fuzzy logic, each of which is useful in handling uncertainty in different contexts. Although the proposed model has the ability to handle uncertainty to some extent, it remains unclear how inhabitants' contexts of interest can be automatically identified and how confidence values for predicates defined for contexts can be effectively estimated.

Of particular interest to our study here are those studies which were developed on the basis of the DS theory, as it is capable of handling and managing a range of uncertainty tasks. In [3] Hong et al. proposed a general ontology for ADLs and presented an evidential model for reasoning about the activities, which could be tailored to general scenarios. Hyun in [4] illustrated that the DS theory could provide an efficient way to incorporate and reduce the impact of uncertainty in an inference process. Nevertheless in these studies, the authors have not clearly quantified the extent of the uncertainty involved in the reasoning procedure and have not considered the role of activity patterns obtained from historical sensor data. In our previous work [5], an analysis has been undertaken to investigate two types of uncertainty, namely hardware uncertainty and context uncertainty, which may exist in Smart Homes along with an improved approach of calculating discounting values. In [6] a revised lattice structure and the weighting factor methods were developed for quantifying connections between different layers within a lattice designed for the overall purpose of activity recognition. With the statistical weight factor method presented in [6], the lattice based evidential model can incorporate statistical activity patterns into the activity recognition process.

In this study, we build upon the previous work and propose an evidential framework for associating sensors to activities for the purposes of activity recognition. In this approach we define a formal approach to represent sensors and activities, i.e. to consider sensor networks as an evidence space and ADLs as a hypothesis space, and to formulate the relation between the two spaces by a mechanism of multi-valued mapping. Nevertheless, a problem with this formulation is that the multi-valued mapping has difficulty in expressing the uncertainty which is inherent in the relation between the sensed information and the activities [9]. In order to deal with this issue, we initially propose to define the multi-valued mapping in the DS theory as a probabilistic approach where the extents of uncertainty can be represented in the form of conditional probabilities. Following this, we describe sensor uncertainty by a means of manufacture statistics in terms of prior probabilities and then formulate the product of the conditional probabilities and the prior probabilities as basic probability assignments (*bpa*). In this way, *bpas* are defined over all subsets of an activity space, which satisfy the conditions of evidential functions in the DS theory and can be further combined by Dempster's rule of combination for the purposes of inferring activities.

2 Activities and Uncertainty in Smart Homes

Designing smart homes is a goal that appeals to researchers in a variety of disciplines, including pervasive and mobile computing, artificial intelligence, sensor technology, multimedia computing and agent-based software. Many researchers have used typical activity scenarios as in [10] or descriptions of activities in [11] to help illustrate the possible behaviours of inhabitants and the approaches of monitoring activities within a smart environment. Figure 1 depicts a general relationship structure between sensors and activities, where sensors are attached to physical devices or appliances − objects − with which inhabitants interact whilst conducting ADLs within smart homes, such as toileting, bathing, preparing meals, etc. From Figure 1, it can be viewed that an activity can be detected by an inhabitant's location along with the objects involved in the activity. For example, a toileting activity consists of going to the bathroom, flushing the toilet, turning on the tap and washing hands. All these sequences, the objects involved and the activity structure can be abstractly explained by Figure 1.

There are different levels of uncertainty which may exist in smart homes and the inference process when recognizing activities. In order to incorporate the uncertainty into an activity recognition process, the sources of uncertainty may be characterized into two categories. The first is related to the reliability of sensors, which is referred to as sensor uncertainty. This type of uncertainty originates from the sensors themselves or within the sensor networks, such as the sensors being broken, the sensors' battery exhausted, the transmission errors between the receiver and the transmitter, etc [12]. The sensor uncertainty is unavoidable and unpredictable, however, this type of uncertainty can be estimated through hundreds of thousands of lab based tests when the sensors are examined performing typical operations. The second category of uncertainty is related to the interaction between the sensors and the activities of inhabitants and is referred to as relation uncertainty. In general the sensed information about the environment provided by the sensors is not sufficient to be able to identify an activity with total certainty. For instance, the activity of going to the bathroom does not mean that the inhabitant has used the toilet. This level of information merely only implies the possibility that a toilet activity may have taken place. Hence, it is crucial to know how likely an activity would occur given the condition of sensors activated in order to recognize activities more precisely.

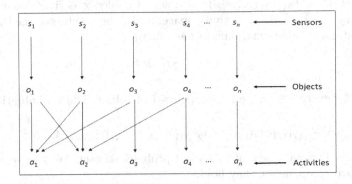

Fig. 1. Relation of Sensors − Objects − Activities

3 Basics of the Dempster-Shafer (DS) Theory of Evidence

The DS theory of evidence remedies the limitations of the traditional Bayesian belief model to allow the explicit representation of uncertainty and management of conflict information involved in the decision making process [13]. It formulates a proposition set as a frame of discernment, denoted by Θ and its power set 2^Θ is all the subsets of Θ.

Definition 1. Let Θ be a frame of discernment. Let m be a mass function, which is defined as a assignment function assigning a numeric value in $[0, 1]$ to $X \in 2^\Theta$ with two conditions as specified below.

$$1)\ m(\emptyset) = 0,\quad 2)\ \sum_{X \subseteq \Theta} m(X) = 1$$

where X is called a focal element, focus or singleton if X is one element subset with $m(X) > 0$.

Definition 2. Let Θ be a frame of discernment. Let m_1 and m_2 be two mass functions defined for $X, Y \subseteq \Theta$. Dempster's rule of combination (or Dempster's rule) is, denoted by $\oplus$, defined as

$$(m_1 \oplus m_2)(A) = \frac{\sum_{X \cap Y = A} m_1(X) m_2(Y)}{\sum_{X \cap Y \neq \emptyset} m_1(X) m_2(Y)} \tag{1}$$

where the operator $\oplus$ is also called the *orthogonal sum*. $N = \sum_{X \cap Y \neq \emptyset} m_1(X) m_2(Y)$ is the *normalization constant*. $E = 1 - N$ is called the *conflict factor*. This rule strongly emphasizes the agreement between multiple independent sources and ignores all the conflicting evidence through a normalization factor.

Definition 3. Let $\mathcal{A} = \langle \Omega, \Theta, \psi \rangle$ express the relation between sensors and activities. Let $\Omega = \{s_1, s_2, \ldots, s_{|\Omega|}\}$ be a set of evidence derived from sensors, $\Theta = \{a_1, a_2, \ldots, a_{|\Theta|}\}$ be an activity space, and ψ be a subset-valued mapping (also called multi-valued mapping [9]) as follows:

$$\psi : \Omega \to 2^{2^{\Theta} \times [0,1]}$$

such that for every $s \in \Omega$, we have a pair set of subsets and probabilities,

$$\psi(s) = \{(A_1, p_s(A_1|s)), (A_2, p_s(A_2|s)), \ldots, (A_n, p_s(A_n|s))\}. \tag{2}$$

$\psi(s)$ is named as an image of s, a focal probabilistic set. We can separate an image to two components, they hold,

$$A_1, A_2, \ldots A_n \in 2^{\Theta}, \text{ and } p_s(A_1|s), p_s(A_2|s), \ldots, p_s(A_n|s) \in [0,1].$$

For the convenience of our discussion, we introduce a term for an activity space and a multi-valued mapping, called a granule set, denoted by $G(s)$ and $G(p)$ respectively. A granule set of activities is then denoted by $G(s) = \{A_1, A_2, \ldots A_n\}$; and the granule set of relation with a sensor s under the subset-valued mapping is denoted by:

$$G(p) = \{\ p_s(A_1|s), p_s(A_2|s), \ldots, p_s(A_n|s)\}. \tag{3}$$

Equation (3) precisely describes a formal association between sensors and activities, quantifying the uncertainty being inherent in their relation by means of conditional probabilities. It can be noted that the focal probabilistic set ψ of a sensor source $s \in \Omega$ satisfies the following conditions:

(1) $A_i \neq \emptyset$ for $i = 1, \ldots, n$;
(2) $p_s(A_i|s) \geq 0$ for $i = 1, \ldots, n$;
(3) $\sum_{i=1}^{n} p_s(A_i|s) = 1$.

The above conditions are slightly different than those presented in [9]. Here we remove the constraint of $A_i \cap A_j = \emptyset$ $(i \neq j)$ as it is likely that there is overlap between two complex activities.

4 Formulation of Association between Sensors and Activities

In the case of applying the previous formulation into the process of activity recognition, it is necessary to look at a generalization of this formulation. Suppose we have a group of activities to be involved as presented below:

$$A_1, A_2, \ldots, A_{2^{|\Theta|}-1} \subseteq \Theta.$$

which is supported by a collection of possible sensors Ξ_i, denoted by,

$$S_{i1}, S_{i2}, \ldots, S_{i,2^{|\Xi_i|}-1} \subseteq \Xi_i, \text{where } \Xi_i \subseteq \Omega$$

For every $A \subseteq \Theta$, by applying the subset-value mapping function ψ, Ξ_i can be associated to A, we thus obtain a granule set of conditional probabilistic relation below:

$$G(p) = \{p_{i1}(A|S_{i1}), p_{i2}(A|S_{i2}), \ldots, p_{i,2^{|\Xi_i|}-1}(A|S_{i,2^{|\Xi_i|}-1})\},$$

Consider all activity subsets in 2^{Θ}, we can preset all respective conditional probabilistic mappings in the form of a matrix.

$$
\begin{bmatrix} G(p_{i1}) \\ G(p_{i2}) \\ \vdots \\ G(p_{i2^{|\Xi_i|}-1}) \end{bmatrix} = \begin{bmatrix} p_{i1}(A_1|S_{i1}) & \cdots & p_{i1}(A_j|S_{i1}) & \cdots & p_{i1}(\Theta|\Xi_{i1}) \\ p_{i2}(A_1|S_{i2}) & \cdots & p_{i2}(A_j|S_{i2}) & \cdots & p_{i2}(\Theta|\Xi_{i2}) \\ \vdots & \vdots & \vdots & \vdots & \vdots \\ p_{i2^{|\Xi_i|}-1}(A_1|\Xi_i) & \cdots & p_{i2^{|\Xi_i|}-1}(A_j|S_{i2^{|\Xi_i|}-1}) & \cdots & p_{i2^{|\Xi_i|}-1}(\Theta|\Xi_i) \end{bmatrix} \quad (4)
$$

For each row, the conditions given in Definition 3 hold, which forms a basis for defining a mass function. Once we have the mass functions, it is straightforward to determine an activity of interest through a maximum selection.

5 Uncertainty with Sensor Sources

Given the formulation in Section 4, now we consider the formulation of the uncertainty associated with the sensor sources. As previously mentioned, there are a number of factors affecting the reliability of sensors, their reliability can normally be estimated by manufacturer statistics. Such quantities can be directly adapted to represent the degrees of sensor reliability. Thus for a group of sensors, namely Ξ_i, we can define prior probabilities for them, denoted by r_i such that $r_i : 2^{\Xi_i} \to [0,1]$ over all subsets of Ξ_i.

$$r_i = \{r_i(S_{i1}), r_i(S_{i2}), \ldots, r_i(S_{i,2^{|\Xi_i|-1}})\}. \tag{5}$$

In relation to the above the representation of uncertainty, it is necessary to consider how two categories of uncertainty expressed in Equations (4) and (5) can be aggregated to represent the degrees of uncertainty for the activities involved. We can write Equation (5) as a transposed one dimensional matrix and multiply it with Equation (4), hence we have:

$$\begin{bmatrix} r_i(S_{i1}) \\ r_i(S_{i2}) \\ \vdots \\ r_i(S_{i,2^{|\Xi_i|-1}}) \end{bmatrix}^T \times \begin{bmatrix} G(p_{i1}) \\ G(p_{i2}) \\ \vdots \\ G(p_{i2^{|\Xi_i|-1}}) \end{bmatrix} \tag{6}$$

$$= [\, p_{i1}(A_1|S_{i1})r_i(S_{i1}) + p_{i2}(A_1|S_{i2})r_i(S_{i2}) + \ldots + + p_{i,2^{|\Xi_i|-1}}(A_1|\Xi_i)r_i(\Xi_i)$$

$$p_{i1}(A_2|S_{i1})r_i(S_{i1}) + p_{i2}(A_2|S_{i2})r_i(S_{i2}) + \ldots + p_{i,2^{|\Xi_i|-1}}(A_2|\Xi_i)r_i(\Xi_i)$$

$$\vdots \qquad \qquad \vdots \qquad \qquad \vdots$$

$$p_{i1}(\Theta|S_{i1})r_i(S_{i1}) + s_{i2}(\Theta|S_{i2})r_i(E_{i2}) + \ldots + p_{i,2^{|\Xi_i|-1}}(\Theta|\Xi_i)r_i(\Xi_i)\,].$$

For any $A \subseteq \Theta$ we can write the above expression as a uniform formula as presented in Equation (7).

$$p_{i1}(A|S_{i1})r_i(S_{i1}) + p_{i2}(A|S_{i2})r_i(S_{i2}) + \ldots + p_{i,2^{|\Xi_i|-1}}(A|\Xi_i)r_i(\Xi_i) \tag{7}$$

Equation (7) can be used to define a mass function $2^{\Theta} \to [0,1]$, since if $A = \emptyset$, it results in zero, otherwise we have

$$\sum_{A \subseteq \Theta} \sum_{j=1}^{2^{|\Xi_i|-1}} p_{ij}(A|S_{ij})r_i(S_{ij}) = \sum_j \sum_A p_{ij}(A|S_{ij})r_i(S_{ij})$$

$$= \sum_j (r_i(S_{ij})(\sum_A p_{ij}(A|S_{ij}))) = \sum_j (r_i(S_{ij}) \times (1)) = \sum_j r_i(S_{ij}) = 1.$$

which satisfy the condition given in Definition 1.

Given different groups of sensors, denoted by $\Xi_1, \Xi_2, \ldots$, in the same way, we can obtain all respective mass functions. Through the use of Dempster's rule of combination we can combine pieces of sensor evidence together to recognize the most likely activity. In an effort to convey these concepts we present a simple tolieting scenario in the following Section to help illustrate how the underlying concept and formulation can be used for the purpose of activity recognition.

6 A Preliminary Evaluation

An example: consider the scenario where the bathroom door sensor and motion sensor are activated, and then 3 sensors in the bathroom the light, flush and hot tap are activated. There are many kinds of activities which may be related to these sensors within the bathroom, such as "Toileting", "Personal hygiene", and "Washing hands". In this scenario we use "Toileting" as an example to illustrate the reasoning process for activity recognition through calculating mass probabilities.

First we consider a frame of discernment with two activities of toileting and non-toileting, denoted by $\Theta = \{a, \bar{a}\}$. A group of sensors considered here include s_1 for "flush" and s_2 for "hot tap", denoted by $\Xi_1 = \{s_1, s_2\}$. When these sensors are activated, they indicate strongly to support $\{a\}$ and refute $\{\bar{a}\}$, whereas when they are deactivated, their support should be distributed over $\{\bar{a}\}$ and Θ. With the above notations, we can define an evidence space $\Xi_1 = \{s_1, s_2\}$ and multi-valued mapping functions $p_{11}, p_{12}, p_{13} : 2^\Theta \to [0, 1]$ such that

$$p_{11}(\{a\}|\{s_1\})=0.8, p_{11}(\{\bar{a}\}|\{s_1\})=0, p_{11}(\Theta|\{s_1\})=0.2;$$

$$p_{12}(\{a\}|\{s_2\})=0, p_{12}(\{\bar{a}\}|\{s_2\})=0.5, p_{12}(\Theta|\{s_2\})=0.5;$$

$$p_{13}(\{a\}|\Xi_1)=0.40, p_{13}(\{\bar{a}\}|\Xi_1)=0.25, p_{13}(\Theta|\Xi_1)=0.35.$$

The conditional probabilities above can be estimated from sensor data by statistical learning. An example for sensors of tap(hot)(ID: 68), tap(cold)(ID: 88), flush(ID: 100), and light(ID: 101) is shown in Figure 2, which are used to derive these mass probabilities.

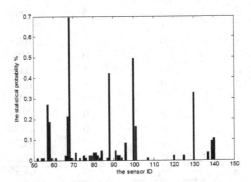

Fig. 2. Statistical Probabilities of Sensors

The support for the activities from the different sensors may not be equally important due to the difference of the sensor reliability. Consider that the signal from sensor s_1 is very weak and based on the degree of its estimated reliability, we can assign 0.2 to s_1, denoted by $r_1(\{s_1\}) = 0.2$, 0.5 to s_2, denoted by $r_1(\{s_2\}) = 0.5$ and 0.3 to Ξ_1, denoted by $r_1(\Xi_1) = 0.3$. By using formula

(6), we can obtain the mass values for the tolieting and non-toileting activities: $m(\{a\}) = 0.28, m(\{\bar{a}\}) = 0.325, m(\Theta) = 0.395$. From this group of the mass values, it is possible to select an activity based on the maximum selection. Moreover, for each group of sensors Ξ_i, we can derive a mass function supported for an activity hypothesis, and by using Equation (1) all mass functions can be combined to constrain a single or a set of activities.

Experiment: In the previous Sections, we have presented an evidential framework for activity recognition for Smart Homes. To assess its effectiveness we have carried out an experiment using the dataset collected by the MIT laboratory [7]. In their experiments, 77 switch sensors were installed in a single-person apartment to collect data about a resident's activity over a period of two weeks. These sensors were attached to daily objects such as drawers, refrigerators and containers to record activation-deactivation events when the subject carried out daily activities. In our experiment, we choose the data collected for one person, namely subject 1, and used a leave-one-out cross-validation as an evaluation method where 13 days of data were used for training and one day of data was used for testing, and the final result is an average of all the folds. The estimated performance is measured by Precision and Recall, respectively. A partial conceptual comparison with the results reported in [7] is also performed. The experimental results are shown in Table 1.

Table 1. Results from two weeks of sensor data [7]

Date	True Positive	False Positive	False Negative	Precision	Recall
27/3	3	0	0	100%	100%
28/3	3	0	1	100%	75%
29/3	8	1	0	88.9%	100%
30/3	3	0	4	100%	42.9%
31/3	3	1	0	75%	100%
1/04	4	0	1	100%	80%
2/04	5	5	0	50%	100%
3/04	2	0	1	100%	66.7%
4/04	3	0	1	100%	75%
5/04	5	3	0	62.5	100%
6/04	9	9	0	50%	100%
7/04	6	0	0	100%	100%
8/04	5	1	0	83.3%	100%
9/04	9	10	1	47.3%	90%
total	68	30	9	69.4%	88.3%

From the results presented in Table 1 we can view that the proposed method correctly recognize 69.4% of the toileting activities in precision, and 88.3% in recall. In particular on the 27th March there are no false positive and false negative values at all. In comparison with the results of 62% in precision and 83.5% in recall for the toileting activity recognition reported in [7], our method outperforms their method in this sense.

7 Summary and Future Work

In this paper we have introduced an evidential framework for associating sensors to activities by means of a multi-valued probabilistic mapping for recognizing activities in Smart Homes. We have identified two categories of uncertainty in terms of sensor uncertainty and relation uncertainty, and formulated how to use the framework to represent and aggregate them. A viable statistical approach has been proposed to learn multi-valued probabilistic mappings for estimating the degree of relation uncertainty. On the basis of the established formalism, we have developed computational methods for inferring activities by aggregating multi-valued probabilities committed to sensor-activity relation with the prior probabilities committed to the reliability of sensor sources, both of which are expressed by matrices. A preliminary experiment has been performed on a toileting activity using the MIT dataset [7], the results attained have demonstrated the advantage of the proposed method. Plans for future work involve the notion to scale up our experiments involving a broad range of sensor data encompassing a variety of ADLs and to apply the proposed method in a real world environment, such as that in a personal healthcare home environment.

References

1. Elouedi, Z., Mellouli, K., Smets, P.: Assessing sensor reliability for multisensor data fusion within the transferable belief model. IEEE Trans. on SMC-Part B 34(1), 782–787 (2004)
2. Strat, T.M.: The generation of explanations within evidential reasoning. In: Proceedings of International Joint Conference of Artificial Intelligence, pp. 1097–1104 (1987)
3. Hong, X., Nugent, C., Mulvenna, M., McClean, S., Scotney, B., Devlin, S.: Evidential fusion of sensor data for activity recognition in smart homes. Pervasive and Mobile Computing 5, 236–252 (2009)
4. Lee, H., Choi, J.S., Elmasri, R.: Sensor Data Fusion Using DSm Theory for Activity Recognition under Uncertainty in Home-Based Care. In: Conf. 2009 Int. on Advanced Information Networking and Applications, USA, pp. 517–524 (2009)
5. Liao, J., Bi, Y., Nugent, C.D.: Using the Dempster-Shafer Theory of Evidence With a Revised Lattice Structure for Activity Recognition. IEEE Transactions on Information Technology in Biomedicine 15(1), 74–82 (2011)
6. Liao, J., Bi, Y., Nugent, C.D.: Weight Factor Algorithms for Activity Recognition in Lattice-Based Sensor Fusion. In: Proceedings of Knowledge Science, Engineering and Management, pp. 365–376 (2011)
7. Tapia, E.M.: Activity recognition in the home setting using simple and ubiquitous sensors. M.S. thesis, School of Architecture and Planning; Massachusetts Institute of Technology, USA (2003)
8. Ranganathan, A., Al-Muhtadi, J., Campbell, R.H.: Reasoning about uncertain contexts in pervasive computing environments. In: IEEE Pervasive Computing, pp. 62–70 (April-June 2004)
9. Yen, J.: GERTIS: A Dempster-Shafer Approach to Diagnosing Hierarchical Hypotheses. Communications of the ACM 32(5), 573–585 (1989)

10. Nugent, C.D., Davies, R.J., Hallberg, J., Donnelly, M.P., Synnes, K., Poland, M., Wallace, J., Finlay, D., Mulvenna, M., Craig, D.: HomeCI - A visual editor for healthcare professionals in the design of home based care. In: Conf. EMBS. 2007 IEEE Int. Conf. Engineering in Medicine and Biology Society, pp. 2787–2790 (2007)
11. Philipose, M., Fishkin, K., Perkowitz, M.: Inferring activities from interactions with objects. In: IEEE CS and IEEE Comsoc, vol. 1536-1268, pp. 50–57 (April 2004)
12. Tapia, E.M., Intille, S.S., Larson, K.: Activity Recognition in the Home Using Simple and Ubiquitous Sensors. In: Ferscha, A., Mattern, F. (eds.) PERVASIVE 2004. LNCS, vol. 3001, pp. 158–175. Springer, Heidelberg (2004)
13. Shafer, G.: A Mathematical theory of evidence. Princeton Univ. Press, Princeton (1976)

Positive and Negative Dependence for Evidential Database Enrichment

Mouna Chebbah[1,2], Arnaud Martin[2], and Boutheina Ben Yaghlane[3]

[1] LARODEC Laboratory, University of Tunis, ISG Tunis, Tunisia
[2] IRISA, Université de Rennes1, Lannion, France
[3] LARODEC Laboratory, University of Carthage, IHEC Carthage, Tunisia

Abstract. Uncertain databases are used in some fields to store both certain and uncertain data. When uncertainty is represented with the theory of belief functions, uncertain databases are assumed to be evidential. In this paper, we suggest a new method to quantify the source degree of dependence in order to enrich its evidential database by adding this dependence information. Enriching evidential databases with its sources degree of dependence can help user when making his decision. We used some generated mass functions to test the proposed method.

Keywords: Theory of belief functions, combination, dependence, belief clustering, evidential databases.

1 Introduction

Databases are used to store a high quantity of structured data which are usually perfect. Most of the time, available data are imperfect, thus the use of uncertain databases in order to store both certain and uncertain data. Many theories manage uncertainty such as the *theory of probabilities*, the *theory of fuzzy sets*, the *theory of possibilities* and the *theory of belief functions*. The theory of belief functions introduced by [4,11] is used to model imperfect (imprecise and/or uncertain) data and also to combine them. In evidential databases, uncertainty is handled with the theory of belief functions.

In many fields such as target recognition the number of evidential databases is great, and they store most of the time the same information provided by different sources. Therefore, integrating evidential databases reduces the quantity of data to be stored and also helps decision makers when handling all available information. Decision makers will use only an integrated evidential database rather than many separated ones.

To combine uncertain information from different evidential databases many combination rules can be used. Integrating evidential databases is useful when sources are cognitively independent. A source is assumed to be cognitively independent towards another one when the knowledge of that source does not affect the knowledge of the first one. Enriching evidential databases with information about its source dependence informs the user about the interaction between sources. In some cases, like when a source is completely dependent on another one, the user can decide to discard the dependent source and its evidential database is not integrated. Thus, we suggest a method to estimate the dependence between sources and to analyze the type of dependence when

S. Greco et al. (Eds.): IPMU 2012, Part III, CCIS 299, pp. 575–584, 2012.

sources are dependent, thus a source may be dependent towards another one by saying the same thing (positive dependence) or saying the opposite (negative dependence).

In the following, we introduce preliminaries of Dempster-Shafer theory as well as evidential databases in the second section. In the third section, a belief clustering method is presented and its classification result is used to estimate the sources degree of independence. If sources seem to be dependent, it is interesting to investigate whether this dependency is positive or negative in the fourth section. This method is tested on random mass functions in the fifth section. Finally, conclusions are drawn.

2   Theory of Belief Functions

The theory of belief functions [4,11] is used to model imperfect data.

In the theory of belief functions, the *frame of discernment* also called *universe of discourse* $\Omega = \{\omega_1, \omega_2, \ldots, \omega_n\}$ is a set of n elementary and mutually exclusive and exhaustive hypotheses. These hypotheses are all the possible and eventual solutions of the problem under study.

The *power set* 2^Ω is the set of all subsets made up of hypotheses and union of hypotheses from Ω.

The *basic belief function (bba)* also called *mass function* is a function defined on the power set 2^Ω and affects a value from $[0,1]$ to each subset. A mass function m is a function:

$$m : 2^\Omega \mapsto [0,1] \tag{1}$$

such that:

$$\sum_{A \subseteq \Omega} m(A) = 1 \tag{2}$$

One or many subsets may have a non null mass, this mass is the source's belief that the solution of the problem under study is in that subset.

The *belief function (bel)* is the minimal belief allocated to a subset A justified by available information on B ($B \subseteq A$):

$$\begin{aligned} bel : 2^\Omega &\to [0,1] \\ A &\mapsto \sum_{B \subseteq A, B \neq \emptyset} m(B) \end{aligned} \tag{3}$$

The implicability function b is proposed to simplify computations:

$$\begin{aligned} b : 2^\Omega &\to [0,1] \\ A &\mapsto \sum_{B \subseteq A} m(B) = bel(A) + m(\emptyset) \end{aligned} \tag{4}$$

The theory of belief functions is used to model uncertain information and also to combine them. A great number of combination rules are proposed such as *Dempster's rule of combination* [4] which is used to combine two different mass functions m_1 and m_2 provided by two different sources as follows:

$$m_{1 \oplus 2}(A) = (m_1 \oplus m_2)(A) = \begin{cases} \dfrac{\sum\limits_{B \cap C = A} m_1(B) \times m_2(C)}{1 - \sum\limits_{B \cap C = \emptyset} m_1(B) \times m_2(C)} & \forall A \subseteq \Omega, A \neq \emptyset \\ 0 & \text{if } A = \emptyset \end{cases} \tag{5}$$

The pignistic transformation is used to compute pignistic probabilities from masses in the purpose of making a decision. The pignistic probability of a singleton X is given by:

$$BetP(X) = \sum_{Y \in 2^{\Theta}, Y \neq \emptyset} \frac{|X \cap Y|}{|Y|} \frac{m(Y)}{1 - m(\emptyset)}. \tag{6}$$

2.1 Conditioning

When handling a mass function, a new evidence can arise confirming that a proposition A is true. Therefore, the mass affected to each focal element C has to be reallocated in order to take consideration of this new evidence. This is achieved by the conditioning operator. Conditioning a mass function m over a subset $A \subseteq \Omega$ consists on restricting the frame of possible propositions 2^{Ω} to the set of subsets having a non empty intersection with A. Therefore the mass allocated to $C \subseteq \Omega$ is transferred to $\{C \cap A\}$. The obtained mass function, result of the conditioning, is noted $m_{[A]} : 2^{\Omega} \to [0, 1]$ such that [10]:

$$m_{[A]}(C) = \begin{cases} 0 & \text{for } C \not\subseteq A \\ \sum_{X \subseteq \bar{A}} m(C \cup X) & \text{for } C \subseteq A \end{cases} \tag{7}$$

where $\bar{A}$ is the complementary of A.

2.2 Generalized Bayesian Theorem and Disjunctive Rule of Combination

The *generalized bayesian theorem (GBT)*, proposed by Smets [9], is a generalization of the bayesian theorem where the joint belief function replaces the conditional probabilities. Let X and Y be two dependent variables defined on the frames of discernment Ω_X and Ω_Y. Suppose that the conditional belief function $bel_{[X]}(Y)$ represents the conditional belief on Y according to X.

The aim is to compute the belief on X conditioned on Y. Thus, the GBT is used to build $bel_{[Y]}(X)$:

$$bel_{[Y]}(X) = b_{[Y]}(X) - b_{[Y]}(\emptyset)$$
$$bel_{[Y]}(X) = \prod_{x_i \in X} b_{[x_i]}(\bar{Y}) \tag{8}$$

The conditional belief function $bel_{[X]}(Y)$ can be extended to the joint frame of discernment $\Omega_X \times \Omega_Y$, then conditioned on $y_i \subseteq \Omega_Y$ and the result is then marginalized on X, the corresponding operator is the disjunctive rule of combination:

$$bel_{[X]}(Y) = b_{[X]}(Y) - b_{[X]}(\emptyset)$$
$$bel_{[X]}(Y) = \prod_{x_i \in X} b_{[x_i]}(Y) \tag{9}$$

2.3 Evidential Database

Classic databases are used to store certain data, whereas data are not always certain but can sometimes be uncertain and even incomplete. The use of *evidential database*

(*EDB*), also called *D-S database*, for storing data from different levels of uncertainty. Evidential databases proposed by [1] and [6] are databases containing both certain and/or uncertain data. Uncertainty and incompleteness in evidential databases are modeled with the theory of belief functions previously introduced.

An evidential database is a database having n records and p attributes such that every attribute a ($1 \leq a \leq p$) has an exhaustive domain Ω_a containing all its possible values: its *frame of discernment* [6].

An EDB has at least one *evidential attribute*. Values of this attribute can be uncertain, thus these values are mass functions and named *evidential values*. An *evidential value* V_{ia} for the ith record and the ath attribute is a mass function such that:

$$m_{ia} : 2^{\Omega_a} \rightarrow [0,1] \text{ with:}$$
$$m_{ia}(\emptyset) = 0 \text{ and } \sum_{X \subseteq \Omega_a} m_{ia}(X) = 1 \qquad (10)$$

Table 1 is an example of an evidential database having 2 evidential attributes namely *road condition* and *weather*. Records of this evidential database are road condition and weather predictions for the five coming days according to one source. The domain $\Omega_{weather} = \{Sunny\ S,\ Rainy\ R,\ Windy\ W\}$ is the frame of discernment of the evidential attribute *weather* and the domain $\Omega_{RC} = \{Safe\ S,\ Perilous\ P,\ Dangerous\ D\}$ is the frame of discernment of the evidential attribute *road condition*.

Table 1. Example of an EDB

Day	Road condition	Weather
d_1	$\{P \cup D\}(1)$	$S(0.3)$ $R(0.7)$
d_2	$S(1)$	$S(0.2)$ $\{S \cup W\}(0.6)$ $\{S \cup R \cup W\}(0.2)$
d_3	$\{S \cup P \cup D\}(1)$	$\{S \cup R \cup W\}(1)$
d_4	$S(0.6)$ $\{S \cup P\}(0.4)$	$S(0.4)$ $\{S \cup R \cup W\}(0.6)$
d_5	$S(1)$	$S(1)$

3   Independence

Evidential databases previously described store a great number of records (objects). Similar objects may be stored in that type of databases meaning that similar situations can be redundant. Clustering techniques are used to group several similar objects into the same cluster. When having n objects, the most similar ones are affected to the same group. Applying a clustering technique to evidential database records (*i.e.* to mass functions) is useful in order to group redundant cases. Some evidential clustering techniques are already proposed such as [5,2,8]. A method of sources independence estimating is presented in [3] and recalled in the following. In this paper we suggest to specify the type of dependence when sources are dependent and also to use this information for evidential database enrichment.

3.1 Clustering

We use here a clustering technique using a distance on belief functions given by [7] such as in [2]. The number of clusters C have to be known, a set T contains n objects $o_i : 1 \leq i \leq n$ which values m_{ij} are belief functions defined on the frame of discernment Ω_a. Ω_a is the frame of discernment of the evidential attribute.

This set T is a table of an evidential database having at least one evidential attribute and at most p evidential attributes. m_{ia} is a mass function value of the ath attribute for the ith object (record), this mass function is defined on the frame of discernment Ω_a (Ω_a is the domain of the ath attribute). A dissimilarity measure is used to quantify the dissimilarity of an object o_i having $\{m_{i1}, \ldots, m_{ij}, \ldots, m_{ip}\}$ as its attributes values towards a cluster Cl_k containing n_k objects o_j. The dissimilarity D of the object o_i and the cluster Cl_k is as follows:

$$D(o_i, Cl_k) = \frac{1}{n_k} \sum_{j=1}^{n_k} \frac{1}{p} \sum_{l=1}^{p} d(m_{il}^{\Omega_a}, m_{jl}^{\Omega_a}) \tag{11}$$

and

$$d(m_1^{\Omega_a}, m_2^{\Omega_a}) = \sqrt{\frac{1}{2}(m_1^{\Omega_a} - m_2^{\Omega_a})^t \underline{D}(m_1^{\Omega_a} - m_2^{\Omega_a})} \tag{12}$$

with:

$$\underline{D}(A, B) = \begin{cases} 1 & \text{if } A = B = \emptyset \\ \frac{|A \cap B|}{|A \cup B|} & \forall A, B \in 2^{\Omega_a} \end{cases} \tag{13}$$

We note that $\frac{1}{p} \sum_{l=1}^{p} d(m_{il}^{\Omega_a}, m_{jl}^{\Omega_a})$ is the dissimilarity between two objects o_i and o_j. The dissimilarity between two objects is the mean of the distances between belief functions values of evidential attributes (evidential values). Each object is affected to the closest cluster (having the minimal dissimilarity value) in an iterative way until reaching the stability of the cluster repartition.

3.2 Independence Measure

Definition 1. *Two sources are considered to be independent when the knowledge of one source does not affect the knowledge of the other one.*

The aim is to study mass functions provided by two sources in order to reveal any dependence between these sources. Provided mass functions are stored in evidential databases, thus each evidential database stores objects having evidential values for some evidential attributes. Suppose having two evidential databases EDB_1 and EDB_2 provided by two distinct sources s_1 and s_2. Each evidential database contains about n records (objects) and p evidential attributes. Each mass function stored in that EDB can be a classification result according to each source. The aim is to find dependence between sources if it exists. In other words, two sources s_1 and s_2 classifying each one n objects. m_{ia} (a^{th} attribute's value for the ith object) provided by s_1 and that provided by s_2 are referred to the same object i. If s_1 and s_2 are dependent, there will be a relation between their belief functions. Thus, we suggest to classify mass functions of each source in order to verify if clusters are independent or not. The proposed method is in two steps, in the first step mass functions of each source are classified then in the second step the weight of the linked clusters is quantified.

1. Step 1: Clustering
   Clustering technique, presented in section 3.1, is used in order to classify mass functions provided by both s_1 and s_2, the number of clusters can be the cardinality of the frame of discernment. After the classification, objects stored in EDB_1 and provided by s_1 are distributed on C clusters and objects of s_2 stored in EDB_2 are also distributed on C clusters. The output of this step are C clusters of s_1, noted Cl_{k_1} and C different clusters of s_2, noted Cl_{k_2}, with $1 \leq k_1, k_2 \leq C$.

2. Step 2: Cluster independence
   Once cluster repartition is obtained, the degree of independence and dependence between sources are quantified in this step. The most similar clusters have to be linked, a cluster matching is performed for both clusters of s_1 and that of s_2. The dissimilarity between two clusters Cl_{k_1} of s_1 and Cl_{k_2} of s_2 is the mean of distances between objects o_i contained in Cl_{k_1} and all the objects o_j contained on Cl_{k_2}:

$$\delta^1(Cl_{k_1}, Cl_{k_2}) = \frac{1}{n_{k_1}} \sum_{l=1}^{n_{k_1}} D(o_l, Cl_{k_2}) \tag{14}$$

We note that n_{k_1} is the number of objects on the cluster Cl_{k_1} and δ^1 is the dissimilarity towards the source s_1.

Dissimilarity matrix M_1 and M_2 containing respectively dissimilarities between clusters of s_1 according to clusters of s_2 and dissimilarities between clusters of s_2 according to clusters of s_1, are defined as follows:

$$M_1 = \begin{pmatrix} \delta^1_{11} & \delta^1_{12} & \cdots & \delta^1_{1C} \\ \cdots & \cdots & \cdots & \cdots \\ \delta^1_{k1} & \delta^1_{k2} & \cdots & \delta^1_{kC} \\ \cdots & \cdots & \cdots & \cdots \\ \delta^1_{C1} & \delta^1_{C2} & \cdots & \delta^1_{CC} \end{pmatrix} \quad \text{and} \quad M_2 = \begin{pmatrix} \delta^2_{11} & \delta^2_{12} & \cdots & \delta^2_{1C} \\ \cdots & \cdots & \cdots & \cdots \\ \delta^2_{k1} & \delta^2_{k2} & \cdots & \delta^2_{kC} \\ \cdots & \cdots & \cdots & \cdots \\ \delta^2_{C1} & \delta^2_{C2} & \cdots & \delta^2_{CC} \end{pmatrix} \tag{15}$$

We note that $\delta^1_{k_1 k_2}$ is the dissimilarity between Cl_{k_1} of s_1 and Cl_{k_2} of s_2 and $\delta^2_{k_1 k_2}$ is the dissimilarity between Cl_{k_2} of s_2 and Cl_{k_1} of s_1 and $\delta^1_{k_1 k_2} = \delta^2_{k_2 k_1}$. M_2 the dissimilarity matrix of s_2 is the transpose of M_1 the dissimilarity matrix of s_1. Clusters of s_1 are matched to the most similar clusters of s_2 and clusters of s_2 are linked to the most similar clusters of s_1. Two clusters of s_1 can be linked to the same cluster of s_2. A different matching of clusters is obtained according to s_1 and s_2. A set of matched clusters is obtained for both sources and a mass function can be used to quantify the independence between each couple of matched clusters. Suppose that the cluster Cl_{k_1} of s_1 is matched to Cl_{k_2} of s_2, a mass function m defined on the frame of discernment $\Omega_I = \{Dependent \ \bar{I}, Independent \ I\}$ describes how much this couple of clusters is independent or dependent as follows:

$$\begin{cases} m^{\Omega_I}_{k_1 k_2}(\bar{I}) = \alpha(1 - \delta^1_{k_1 k_2}) \\ m^{\Omega_I}_{k_1 k_2}(I) = \alpha \delta^1_{k_1 k_2} \\ m^{\Omega_I}_{k_1 k_2}(\bar{I} \cup I) = 1 - \alpha \end{cases} \tag{16}$$

where α is a discounting factor. When $\alpha = 1$, the obtained mass function is a probabilistic mass function which quantifies the dependence of each matched clusters according to each source. A mass function is obtained for each matched clusters Cl_{k_1} and Cl_{k_2}, thus C mass functions are obtained for each source. The combination of that C mass functions $m_{k_1 k_2}^{\Omega_I}$ using Dempster's rule of combination is a mass function m^{Ω_I} reflecting the overall dependence of one source towards the other one:

$$m^{\Omega_I} = \oplus m_{k_1 k_2}^{\Omega_I} \tag{17}$$

After the combination, two mass functions describing the dependence of s_1 towards s_2 and that of s_2 towards s_1 are obtained. Pignistic probabilities are derived from mass functions using the pignistic transformation in a purpose of making decision about the dependence of sources. A source s_1 is dependent on the source s_2 if $BetP(\bar{I}) \geq 0.5$ otherwise it is independent. $BetP(\bar{I})$ is the pignistic probability of $\bar{I}$ computed from $m_{s_1}^{\Omega_I}(\bar{I})$.

4   Negative and Positive Dependence

A mass function describing the independence of one source towards another one can inform about the degree of dependence but does not inform if this dependence is positive or negative. In the case of dependent sources, this dependence can be positive meaning that the belief of one source is directly affected by the belief of the other one, thus both sources have the same knowledge. In the case of negative dependence, the knowledge of one source is the opposite of the other one.

Definition 2. *A source is positively dependent on another source when the belief of the first one is affected by the knowledge of the belief of the second one and both beliefs are similar.*
    If a source s_1 is negatively dependent on s_2, s_1 is always saying the opposite of what said s_2.

Definition 3. *A source is negatively dependent on another source when their beliefs are different although the belief of the first one is affect by the knowledge of the belief of the second one.*
    If matched clusters contain the same objects thus these clusters are positively dependent. It means that both sources are almost classifying objects in the same way. If matched clusters contain different objects thus one source is negatively dependent on the other because it is classifying differently the same objects. A mass function defined on the frame of discernment $\Omega_P = \{Positive\ Dependent\ P,\ Negative\ Dependent\ \bar{P}\}$ can be built in order to quantify the positivity or negativity of the dependence of a cluster Cl_{k_1} of s_1 and a cluster Cl_{k_2} of s_2 such that Cl_{k_1} and Cl_{k_2} are matched according to s_1 as follows:

$$\begin{cases} m_{k_1 k_2}^{\Omega_P}(P|\bar{I}) = 1 - \dfrac{|Cl_{k_1} \cap Cl_{k_2}|}{|Cl_{k_1}|} \\ m_{k_1 k_2}^{\Omega_P}(\bar{P}|\bar{I}) = \dfrac{|Cl_{k_1} \cap Cl_{k_2}|}{|Cl_{k_1}|} \\ m_{k_1 k_2}^{\Omega_P}(P \cup \bar{P}|\bar{I}) = 0 \end{cases} \tag{18}$$

We note that these mass functions are conditional mass functions because they do not exist if sources are independent, thus these mass functions are dependent on the dependency of sources. These mass functions are also probabilistic. In order to have the marginal mass functions, the Disjunctive Rule of Combination proposed by Smets [9] in section 2.2 can be used in order to compute the marginal mass functions defined on the frame of discernment Ω_P. Marginal mass functions are combined using Dempster's rule of combination presented in equation (5), then the pignistic transformation is used to compute pignistic probabilities which are used to decide about the type of dependence and also to enrich the corresponding evidential databases.

5   Example

The method described above is tested on generated mass functions. Mass functions are generated randomly using the following algorithm:

Algorithm 1. Mass generating

Require: $|\Omega|, n$: number of mass functions
1: **for** $i = 1$ to n **do**
2:    Choose randomly F, the number of focal elements on $[1, |2^{\Omega}|]$.
3:    Divide the interval $[0, 1]$ into F continuous sub intervals.
4:    Choose randomly a mass from each sub interval and attribute it to focal elements.
5:    Attribute these masses to focal elements previously chosen.
6:    The complement to 1 of the attributed masses sum is affected to the total ignorance $m(\Omega)$.
7: **end for**
8: **return** n mass functions

This algorithm is used to generate n random mass functions which decisions (using the pignistic transformation) are not known, whereas in the case of positive or negative dependence decision classes have to be checked.

1. Positive dependence:
   When sources are positively dependent, the decided class (using the pignistic transformation) of one is directly affected by that of the other one. To test this case, we generated 100 mass functions on a frame of discernment of cardinality 5. Both sources are classifying objects in the same way because one of the sources is positively dependent on the other as follows:
   Applying the method described above, we obtained this mass function defined on the frame $\Omega_P = \{P, \ \bar{P}\}$ and describing the positive and negative dependence of s_1 towards s_2:
   $m(P) = 0.679, m(\bar{P}) = 0.297, m(\bar{P} \cup P) = 0.024$
   Using the pignistic transformation $BetP(P) = 0.691$ and $BetP(\bar{P}) = 0.309$, meaning that s_1 is positively dependent on s_2. The marginal mass function of the positive and negative dependence of s_2 according to s_1:
   $m(P) = 0.6459, m(\bar{P}) = 0.3272, m(\bar{P} \cup P) = 0.0269$
   Using the pignistic transformation $BetP(P) = 0.6593$ and $BetP(\bar{P}) = 0.3407$, meaning that s_2 is positively dependent on s_1.

Algorithm 2. Positive dependent Mass function generating

Require: n mass functions generated using algorithm 1, Decided classes
1: **for** $i = 1$ to n **do**
2:    Find the m focal elements of the ith mass function
3:    **for** $j = 1$ to m **do**
4:       The mass affected to the jth focal element is transferred to its union with the decided class.
5:    **end for**
6: **end for**
7: **return** n mass functions

---

2. Negative dependence:

   When sources are negatively dependent, one of the sources is saying the opposite of the other one. In other words, when the classification result of the first source is a class A, the second source may classify this object in any other class but not A. Negative dependent mass functions are generated in the same way as positive dependent mass functions but the mass of each focal element is transferred to focal elements having a null intersection with the decided class. In that case, we obtain this mass function of the dependence of s_1 according to s_2:

   $m(P) = 0.0015$, $m(\bar{P}) = 0.9909$, $m(\bar{P} \cup P) = 0.0076$

   Using the pignistic transformation $BetP(P) = 0.0053$ and $BetP(\bar{P}) = 0.9947$, meaning that s_1 is negatively dependent on s_2. The marginal mass function of the dependence of s_2 according to s_1:

   $m(P) = 0.0011$, $m(\bar{P}) = 0.9822$, $m(\bar{P} \cup P) = 0.0167$

   Using the pignistic transformation $BetP(P) = 0.00945$ and $BetP(\bar{P}) = 0.99055$, meaning that s_2 is negatively dependent on s_1. These mass functions are added to the corresponding evidential databases to enrich them. $m_{k_1 k_2}^{\Omega_I}$ are not certain mass functions, thus some degree of total ignorance appears in $m(\bar{P} \cup P)$ when using the DRC.

6 Conclusion

Enriching evidential databases with dependence information can inform users about the degree of interaction between their sources. In some cases where one source is completely dependent on an another one, the evidential database of that source can be discarded when making a decision. In this paper, we suggested a method estimating the dependence degree of one source towards another one. As a future work, we may try to estimate the dependence of one source according to many other sources and not only one source.

References

1. Bach Tobji, M.-A., Ben Yaghlane, B., Mellouli, K.: A New Algorithm for Mining Frequent Itemsets from Evidential Databases. In: Information Processing and Management of Uncertainty (IPMU 2008), Malaga, Spain, pp. 1535–1542 (2008)

2. Ben Hariz, S., Elouedi, Z., Mellouli, K.: Clustering Approach Using Belief Function Theory. In: Euzenat, J., Domingue, J. (eds.) AIMSA 2006. LNCS (LNAI), vol. 4183, pp. 162–171. Springer, Heidelberg (2006)
3. Chebbah, M., Martin, A., Ben Yaghlane, B.: About sources dependence in the theory of belief functions. In: The 2nd International Conference on Belief Functions (BELIEF 2012), Compiègne, France (2012)
4. Dempster, A.P.: Upper and Lower probabilities induced by a multivalued mapping. Annals of Mathematical Statistics 38, 325–339 (1967)
5. Denoeux, T.: A k-nearest neighbor classification rule based on Dempster-Shafer theory. IEEE Transactions on Systems, Man and Cybernetics 25(5), 804–813 (1995)
6. Hewawasam, K.K.R.G.K., Premaratne, K., Subasingha, S.P., Shyu, M.-L.: Rule Mining and Classification in Imperfect Databases. In: Int. Conf. on Information Fusion, Philadelphia, USA, pp. 661–668 (2005)
7. Jousselme, A.-L., Grenier, D., Bossé, E.: A new distance between two bodies of evidence. Information Fusion 2, 91–101 (2001)
8. Masson, M.-H., Denoeux, T.: ECM: an evidential version of the fuzzy c-means algorithm. Pattern Recognition 41, 1384–1397 (2008)
9. Smets, P.: Belief Functions: the Disjunctive Rule of Combination and the Generalized Bayesian Theorem. International Journal of Approximate Reasoning 9, 1–35 (1993)
10. Smets, P., Kruse, R.: The transferable belief model for belief representation. In: Uncertainty in Information Systems: From Needs to Solutions, pp. 343–368 (1997)
11. Shafer, G.: A mathematical theory of evidence. Princeton University Press (1976)

Handling Interventions with Uncertain Consequences in Belief Causal Networks

Imen Boukhris[1,2], Zied Elouedi[1], and Salem Benferhat[2]

[1] LARODEC, Université de Tunis, ISG de Tunis, Tunisia
[2] CRIL, Université d'Artois, Faculté Jean Perrin, France
imen.boukhris@hotmail.com, zied.elouedi@gmx.fr,
benferhat@cril.univ-artois.fr

Abstract. Interventions are tools used to distinguish between mere correlations and causal relationships. These standard interventions are assumed to have certain consequences, i.e. they succeed to put their target into one specific state. In this paper, we propose to handle interventions with uncertain consequences. The uncertainty is formalized with the belief function theory which is known to be a general framework allowing the representation of several kinds of imperfect data. Graphically, we investigate the use of belief function causal networks to model the results of passively observed events and also the results of interventions with uncertain consequences. To compute the effect of these interventions, altered structures namely, belief mutilated graphs and belief augmented graphs with uncertain effects are used.

1 Introduction

Causality is an important issue used in significant applications in several areas. Bayesian networks [6,16] which are directed acyclic graphs have long been considered as tools to model causation. However, different networks can be equivalent if they describe exactly the same conditional independence relation and induce the same joint distributions. Only one of these networks follows the causal process, the so-called causal network.

Upon observations, beliefs have to be revised. On a Bayesian network, two main methods can be used for revising the beliefs when the input information is uncertain: virtual evidence method [15] and Jeffrey's rule [12]. On one hand, virtual evidence uses a likelihood ratio to represent the strength of the confidence towards the observed event. On the other hand, Jeffrey's rule is an extension of Bayesian conditioning. It is based on probability kinematics whose principle is to minimize belief change. Even if these methods differ according to the way the uncertain evidence is specified, in [5] the authors prove that they are equivalent and that one can translate between them.

Pearl [16] has proposed to use the concept of intervention as a tool to distinguish between mere correlations and causal links. Interventions consist in external actions that allow to test if setting the value of a variable causally affects the value of another. A correlation without causation is therefore a symmetric

S. Greco et al. (Eds.): IPMU 2012, Part III, CCIS 299, pp. 585–595, 2012.
© Springer-Verlag Berlin Heidelberg 2012

relation that involves the observation of events simultaneously but an action on one of them does not have an impact on the occurrence of the other ones. The "do" operator was introduced by Pearl (e.g. [16]) to represent interventions in the setting of probabilistic graphical models. It is used to distinguish between observed states of variables and state of variables generated by interventions. Alternative causal networks were proposed in other uncertainty frameworks. In fact, possibilistic causal networks were proposed to handle cases requiring pure qualitative and ordinal handling [2] and belief function causal networks [4] are ideal tools in situations where data are missing.

However, acting on a variable and setting it into one specific value is not always possible to achieve. Therefore, handling interventions whose consequences are uncertain is required. Despite its need in real world applications, only few works in the probabilistic setting addressed this issue (e.g. [9,13,22]). Besides in these works, imperfect interventions are different from what is considered in the scope of this paper. In fact, they are considered as external actions that change the local probability distribution of the target variable.

The belief function theory offers natural tools to represent interventions with uncertain consequences. It is considered as a general framework for reasoning with uncertainty. Indeed, it has connections to other uncertainty frameworks such as probability and possibility theories. Therefore, it is appropriate to manage imperfect data. However, no works have been proposed to deal with interventions that fail to put their targets into one specific state under the belief function framework.

This paper presents a causal model able to represent the results of observations that may be uncertain and also interventions with uncertain consequences. We propose to handle these interventions on altered belief function causal networks, namely mutilated graph and augmented graphs with uncertain effects.

The rest of the paper is organized as follows: In Section 2, we briefly recall the basics of belief function theory and belief function causal networks. In Section 3, we introduce the Jeffrey-Dempster's rule of conditioning [14]. Then in Section 4, we investigate its relations with the concept of belief function observations and stress on the differences between observations and interventions for belief causation. In Section 5, we detail how interventions with uncertain consequences can be represented in the belief function framework. Section 6 concludes the paper.

2   Belief Function Theory and Causal Networks

2.1   Basics of Belief Function Theory

In this section, we briefly sketch the basic concepts of belief function theory. For more details see [17,19]. The basic belief assignment (bba), denoted by m^{Θ} (or m), is a mapping from 2^{Θ} to $[0,1]$ such that:

$$\sum_{A \subseteq \Theta} m^{\Theta}(A) = 1. \tag{1}$$

For each subset A of Θ, $m(A)$ is called the basic belief mass (bbm). It represents the part of belief *exactly committed to the event* A of Θ. Subsets of Θ such that $m(A) > 0$ are called focal elements and denoted by $\mathcal{F}_\Theta$. We denote the set of focal elements belonging to a subset A of the frame of discernment as $\mathcal{F}_A$. When the emptyset is not a focal element, the bba is called *normalized*. Total ignorance corresponds to $m(\Theta) = 1$ and certainty is represented by the allocation of the whole mass to a unique singleton of Θ.

The plausibility function $Pl : 2^\Theta \to [0,1]$ is defined as:

$$Pl(A) = \sum_{B \cap A \neq \emptyset} m(B). \tag{2}$$

Two bba's m_1 and m_2 provided by two distinct and reliable sources, may be aggregated using Dempster's rule of combination, denoted by $\oplus$, as follows:

$$m_1 \oplus m_2(A) = \begin{cases} K \cdot \sum_{B \cap C = A} m_1(B) \cdot m_2(C), & \forall B, C \subseteq \Theta \quad \text{if } A \neq \emptyset \\ 0 & \text{otherwise.} \end{cases} \tag{3}$$

where $K^{-1} = 1 - \sum_{B \cap C = \emptyset} m_1(B) \cdot m_2(C)$ is the normalization factor.

Conditioning allows to change the knowledge the agent had, update masses originally defined on $A \subseteq \Theta$, following the information that an event $B \subseteq \Theta$ is true. With Dempster's rule of conditioning, all non vacuous events implying $\overline{B}$ will be transferred to the part of A compatible with the evidence namely, $A \cap B$ [19]. In the case, where $A \cap B = \emptyset$, several methods exist for transferring the remaining evidence [20]. $m(A|B)$ denotes the degree of belief of A in the context where B holds with $A, B \subseteq \Theta$. It is computed by:

$$m(A|B) = \frac{\sum_{C, C \cap B = A} m(C)}{Pl(B)} \tag{4}$$

Specialization is an extension of set inclusion. A mass function m is a specialization of m', denoted $m \sqsubseteq m'$, iff there is a square matrix Σ with a general term $\sigma(A,B)$, $A, B \subseteq \Theta$ where: $\sum_{A \subseteq W} \sigma(A, B) = 1$, $\forall B \subseteq \Theta$, $\sigma(A, B) > 0 \implies A \subseteq B$, $A, B \subseteq \Theta$ and $m(A) = \sum_{B \subseteq W} \sigma(A, B) m'(B)$, $\forall A \subseteq \Theta$.

A vacuous extension is changing the referential by adding new variables, a mass function m^X defined on Θ_X will be expressed on $\Theta_X \times \Theta_Y$ as follows:

$$\forall x \subseteq \Theta_X, \forall y \subseteq \Theta_Y; m^{X \uparrow XY}(x, y) = \begin{cases} m^X(x) & \text{if } y = \Theta_Y \\ 0 & \text{otherwise} \end{cases} \tag{5}$$

Let $m^X(x|y)$ be defined on Θ_X for $y \subseteq \Theta_Y$. To get rid of conditioning, we have to compute its ballooning extension. It is the least committed belief function defined on $\Theta_X \times \Theta_Y$. If this deconditionalized subset has to be conditionalized on x, it yields $m^X(x|y)$. It is defined as:

$$m_y^{X \uparrow XY}(\theta) = \begin{cases} m^X(x|y) & \text{if } \theta = (x, y) \cup (\Theta_X, \overline{y}) \\ 0 & \text{otherwise.} \end{cases} \tag{6}$$

2.2   Belief Function Causal Networks

A belief causal network [4] is a particular case of a belief function network [1,23]. In this graphical model denoted G, arcs describe causal relationships instead of dependence relations. It is defined on two levels:

- Qualitative level: represented by a directed acyclic graph (DAG), $\mathcal{G} = (V,E)$ where V is a set of variables and E is a set of arcs encoding causal links among variables. A variable A_j is called a parent of a variable A_i if there is an edge from A_j to A_i. A subset from the set of the parents of A_i, $PA(A_i)$, is denoted by $Pa(A_i)$. A subset from one parent node, $PA_j(A_i)$, is denoted by $Pa_j(A_i)$.

- Quantitative level: represented by the set of bba's associated to each node in the graph. For each root node A_i (i.e. $Pa(A_i) = \emptyset$) having a frame of discernment Θ_{A_i}, an a priori mass $m^{A_i}(a)$ is defined on the powerset $2^{\Theta_{A_i}}$ (i.e. $a \subseteq \Theta_{A_i}$). For other nodes, a conditional bba $m^{A_i}(a|Pa(A_i))$ is specified for each value of A_i knowing each instance of $Pa(A)$ such that $\sum_{a \subseteq \Theta_{A_i}} m^{A_i}(a \mid Pa(A_i)) = 1$ and $m^{A_i}(\emptyset \mid Pa(A_i)) = 0$.

With belief function networks, it is possible to deal with ill-known or ill-defined a priori knowledge including conditional ones to compute a posteriori distribution and therefore solving the problem of choosing an appropriate a priori. The definition of the joint distribution under a belief function framework is different from the construction made in Bayesien networks. In fact, it is obtained by combining the local distribution of each node (for more details see [3]):

$$m^{V=A_1,\ldots,A_n} = \oplus_{A_i \in V}(\oplus_{Pa_j(A_i)} m^{A_i}(a_i|Pa_j(A_i))^{\uparrow A_i \times PA_j(A_i)})^{\uparrow V}. \tag{7}$$

3   Jeffrey Rule of Conditioning

3.1   Jeffrey's Rule in a Probabilistic Framework

An a prior probability P_E is revised into a posterior distribution $P_{E*_r I}$ in the presence of new uncertain information denoted by I, and $P_I(I_i) = p_i$. The coefficients p_i's are seen as imposed constraints. Two natural properties have been proposed:

- *Success* where the input information imposed the belief change operation as a constraint. It means that after the revision operation, the input evidence should be retained. The probability of each event I_i must be equal to p_i: $P_{E*_r I} = p_i$.

- *Minimal change* which means that $P_{E*_r I}$ should minimize relative entropy with respect to the original distribution under the probabilistic constraints defined by the input I. In fact, the conditional probability degree of any event A given any event I_i should remain the same in the original and the revised distributions: $\forall I_i, \forall A, P_{E*_r I}(A|I_i) = P_E(A|I_i)$.

Jeffrey's rule is an extension of probabilistic conditioning defined as [12]:

$$P_{E*_r I}(A) = \sum_{1,\ldots,n} p_i \frac{P_E(A \cap I_i)}{P_E(I_i)}. \tag{8}$$

It is a unique solution that satisfies both success and minimal change properties.

3.2   Extension of Jeffrey's Rule to the Belief Function Framework

Several proposals have been suggested as counterparts of Jeffrey's rule under the belief function framework. Actually, in [18] the author considers that Jeffrey's generalization can be found using Dempster's rule of combination. However, in [21] it was pointed out that Dempster's rule of combination is symmetric while one characteristic of Jeffrey's rule is its asymmetry [7]. Three extensions of Jeffrey's rule were proposed in [11]: plausible, credible and possible conditioning. In [21], the author explains that the drawback of these rules is that they do not satisfy the success properties and thus cannot be considered as true extensions of it to belief functions. Therefore, he proposed another rule satisfying the success and the minimal change constraints. However, like the rule proposed in [10], he first assumes that the input evidence is defined on a partition of Θ and not on 2^{Θ}. Then to be applied, the new evidence should be consistent with the agent's beliefs. Besides, it fails to extend Dempster's rule of conditioning.

Recently, in [14] a revision rule was proposed, so-called the Jeffrey-Dempster's rule. It generalizes Jeffrey's rule from probability to mass functions. It also succeeds to extend Dempster's rule of conditioning. Accordingly, we adopt this rule in this paper. The idea of this rule is to share proportionally the input masses m_I among a family of focal subsets of m_E in conformity with the idea of minimal change. A minimal requirement of minimal change is formalized as $m(E *_r I)$ is a specialization of m which can be seen as a generalization of implication in propositional logic. This revision rule can be written in an extensive way as:

$$m(E *_r I)(C) = \sum_{E,I,E\cap I=C,Pl_k(I)>0} \frac{m_E(E)m_I(I)}{Pl_E(I)} + 1_{\{Pl_k(C)=0\}}m_I(C) \quad (9)$$

where $1_{\{Pl_k(C)=0\}} = 1$ if $Pl_E(C) > 0$ and 0 otherwise.

In [8], it was shown that this revision rule coincides with Dempster's rule of combination when the input is strongly consistent with the prior mass function which satisfies the minimal change constraint. The two properties like the one proposed by Jeffrey still holds for $m_{E*_r I}$ with a restricted form of input data:

- *Success* the revision result $m_{E*_r I}$ is a specialization of m_I, $m_{E*_r I} \sqsubseteq m_I$.
- *Minimal change* If $I \in \mathcal{F}_I$ is such that $A \in \mathcal{F}_E$, either $A \subseteq I$ or $A \subseteq I^c$, and $\forall F \neq I \in \mathcal{F}_I$, $F \cap I = \emptyset$, then $\forall A \subseteq I$, $m_{E*_r I}(A|I) = m_E(A|I)$.

4   Observations vs Interventions

4.1   Observations

Passively seeing the spontaneous behavior of the system tells us if some events are statistically related to other ones. An observation may be certain or uncertain. The effect of a certain observation is computed using Dempster's rule of conditioning (Eq. 4). In the case of an uncertain observation, beliefs have to be revised using Jeffrey-Dempster's rule of conditioning (Eq. 9). As mentioned in Section 3, this rule is a generalization of Dempster's rule of conditioning when

m_I is a certain bba. However, correlated events identified with observations are not necessarily causally related.

Example 1. Let us represent beliefs about the presence of sugar in a cup of coffee and the sweetness of the coffee with two variables S ($\Theta_S = \{s_1, s_2\}$ where s_1 is yes and s_2 is no) and C ($\Theta_C = \{c_1, c_2\}$ where c_1 is sweet and c_2 is bitter). Let us suppose that the prior beliefs are defined as $m_E(\{s_1\})=0.1$, $m_E(\{s_2\})=0.7$, $m_E(\Theta_S)=0.2$. If $m_I(\{s_1\})=0.9$, $m_I(\{s_2\})=0.05$ and $m_I(\Theta_S)=0.05$ then beliefs are revised by computing $m_{E*_r I}$ using Equation 9 (see Table 1). We find that $m_{E*_r I}(\{s_1\})= 0.905$, $m_{E*_r I}(\{s_2\}) = 0.085$, $m_{E*_r I}(\Theta_S)= 0.01$. As you notice, $m_{E*_r I}(\{s_1\}) > m_I(\{s_1\})$ which reflects the confirmation effect of this rule.

Table 1. $m_{E*_r I}$

m_E \ m_I	$m_I(\{s_1\})$=**0.9**	$m_I(\{s_2\})$=**0.05**	$m_I(\Theta_S)$=**0.05**
$m_E(\{s_1\})$=**0.1**	$\{s_1\} = 0.9 * 0.1/0.3 = $ **0.3**	$\emptyset$=**0**	$\{s_1\} = 0.05 * 0.1/1 = $ **0.005**
$m_E(\{s_2\})$=**0.7**	$\emptyset = 0$	$\{s_2\} = 0.05 * 0.7/0.9 = $ **0.04**	$\{s_2\} = 0.05 * 0.7/1 = $ **0.035**
$m_E(\Theta_S)$=**0.2**	$\{s_1\} = 0.9 * 0.2/0.3 = $ **0.6**	$\{s_2\} = 0.05 * 0.2/0.9 = $**0.01**	$\Theta_S = 0.05 * 0.2/1 = $ **0.01**

4.2   Interventions

An intervention is an exterior action made in order to observe the behavior of other variables after this manipulation. It is usually defined as succeeding to force the target variable to take one specific value and makes its original causes no more responsible of its state. Following the notation introduced by Pearl [16], we use the do-operator, $do(a_{ij})$, to denote the fact of setting the value a_{ij} on the variable A_i and $(.|do(a_{ij}))$ is used to compute the effect of an intervention.

Example 2. Assume that your friend has added all the quantity of the sugar in the container into your cup. It is obvious that this action has an impact on the sweetness of the coffee. It forces it to take the value "sweet", i.e. do(sweet). Note that this intervention does not affect your initial beliefs regarding the initial use of sugar.

Motivated by the fact that in real world applications forcing a variable to take one certain specific value is not generally feasible and that eventually like for observations, the consequences of interventions may be uncertain, we propose to qualify interventions as:

- *standard* interventions: External actions that succeed to force a variable to take a specific fixed and known value. A certain bba is specified for the target variable. It is the kind of interventions we presented above.

- interventions with *uncertain consequences*: Manipulations that may fail to put their targets into exactly one state. Therefore, a new bba expressing the uncertainty is specified for the target variables. This bba is defined either (1) from only the effect of the intervention which means that it is the only responsible of its current state. The manipulated variable becomes independent from its original causes. (2) from the interaction between the effect of the intervention and the initial causes of the target variable.

5 Graphical Representation of Interventions

In [4], we have presented how to graphically represent standard interventions under the belief function framework. In this section, we detail how to model interventions with uncertain consequences. Altered belief function causal networks, namely belief graph mutilation and belief graph augmentation with uncertain effects are introduced: mutilated graphs are used to represent the effect of an intervention that makes the manipulated variable independent from its original causes and augmented graphs for interventions interacting with the initial causes.

5.1 Belief Graph Mutilation for Interventions Controlling the State of the Variable

Since only the intervention specifies the value of the manipulated variable, graphically it amounts to cut the event off from its initial causes by deleting the causal links pointing towards the event. By mutilating the graph, all the other causes than the one of the intervention will be excluded. No changes affect other nodes. Let $\mathcal{G}$ be a belief function network on which we *attempt* to make an intervention on a variable $A_i \in V$ to allow it take the value $a_{ij} \in \Theta_{A_i}$ $(do(a_{ij}))$, where V is the set of all the nodes. Let us denote by $\mathcal{F}_I$, the set of the focal elements representing the uncertain consequences of the intervention where a bbm α_j is allocated to each focal element. We define mutilation on two steps:

1. Arcs pointing to A_i in $\mathcal{G}$ will be deleted. The obtained mutilated graph is denoted $\mathcal{G}_{mut}$. Its associated belief distribution is denoted $m_{\mathcal{G}_{mut}}$. This intervention affects the computation of the joint distribution $m_{\mathcal{G}}$ by transforming it into $m_{\mathcal{G}}(.|do(a_{ij}))$.
2. The intervention, $do(a_{ij})$, leads to a change of the local bba of the variable A_i such as:

$$\forall a \subseteq A_i, m^{A_i}(a) = \begin{cases} \alpha_j & \text{if } a \in \mathcal{F}_I \\ 0 & \text{otherwise} \end{cases} \tag{10}$$

Proposition 1. *The global joint distribution upon attempting to force a variable A_i to take the value a_{ij} is given by:*
$m_{\mathcal{G}}^V(.|do(a_{ij})) =$

$$\begin{cases} (\oplus_{A_i \neq A_j \in V}(\oplus_{Pa_j(A_j)} m^{A_j}(.|Pa_j(A_j))^{\uparrow A_j \times PA_j(A_j)})^{\uparrow V}) \oplus m^{A_i}(a) & \text{if } A_i = a, a \in \mathcal{F}_I. \\ 0 & \text{otherwise}. \end{cases} \tag{11}$$

Note that a standard intervention corresponds to observing $A_i = a_{ij}$ i.e. applying the definition of conditioning (Eq. 4, Eq. 9) after mutilating the graph (Eq. 10). However, an intervention with uncertain consequences does not correspond to an uncertain observation on the mutilated graph (i.e. revision with Jeffrey-Dempster's rule of conditioning (Eq. 9)).

$$m_{\mathcal{G}_{mut}}^V(.|\mathcal{F}_I) \neq m_{\mathcal{G}}^V(.|do(a_{ij})). \tag{12}$$

Example 3. Suppose that your friend puts few drops of lactose into the cup of coffee. However it is known that unlike sugar, lactose is poorly soluble. Adding lactose will affect the sweetness of the coffee but without certainty. It is considered an external intervention on the variable C that attempts to force it to take the value "sweet" (i.e. $C = c_1$). Accordingly, $\mathcal{F}_I = \{c_1, \Theta_C\}$. Graphically this action will lead to the disconnection of C from its original cause as shown in Figure 1. Therefore, beliefs about the occurrence of S remain unchanged. The joint belief distribution $m_{\mathcal{G}_{mut}}^{SC}$ associated to the mutilated graph represents the effect of the intervention $do(c_1)$ on the joint distribution $m_{\mathcal{G}}^{SC}$.

In Table 2, we present the bba $m_{\mathcal{G}_{mut}}^{SC}$. As S and C become independent, their combination can be computed by making the pointwise product of their masses. $m_{\mathcal{G}_{mut}}^{SC} = m^S(s) \cdot m^C(c)$ if $c \in \mathcal{F}_I$ and 0 otherwise. The bba conditioned by the uncertain inputs on the mutilated graph is revised using Jeffrey-Dempster's rule as shown in the left row of Table 2 which is as you notice different from $m_{\mathcal{G}_{mut}}^{SC}$.

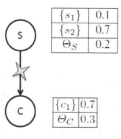

$\{s_1\}$	0.1
$\{s_2\}$	0.7
Θ_S	0.2

$\{c_1\}$	0.7
Θ_C	0.3

Fig. 1. Mutilated graph

Table 2. $m_{\mathcal{G}_{mut}}^{SC}$

	$m_{\mathcal{G}_{mut}}^{SC}$	revised $m_{\mathcal{G}_{mut}}^{SC}$
$\{(s_1, c_1)\}$	=0.07	0.091
$\{(s_2, c_1)\}$	=0.49	0.637
$\{(s_1, c_1),(s_2, c_1)\}$	=0.14	0.182
$\{(s_1, c_1),(s_1, c_2)\}$	=0.03	0.009
$\{(s_2, c_1),(s_2, c_2)\}$	=0.21	0.063
$\Theta_S \times \Theta_C$	=0.06	0.018

5.2   Belief Graph Augmentation for Interventions Interacting with Initial Causes

An extra node in the system, called "DO", is added to the set of parents of the node concerned by the intervention. The resulting augmented graph is denoted G_{aug} and its associated belief distribution is denoted m_{Gaug}.

This variable can take the values in $do(A_i = a_{ij})$, $\forall a_{ij} \in \Theta_{A_i}$ and $do_{nothing}$. $do_{nothing}$ means that there is no action on the variable A_i, which corresponds to the case of observations; $do(A_i = a_{ij})$ means that we attempt to force the variable A_i to take the value a_{ij}. The new conditional joint distribution is then computed from the node DO and the original causes.

Belief function graphical models present natural tools to model such causes since conditionals can be defined per each edge.

If there are no interventions, then the bba of the DO node is defined by:

$$m^{DO}(do) = \begin{cases} 1 & \text{if } do = do_{nothing} \\ 0 & \text{otherwise} \end{cases} \tag{13}$$

In this case:

$$m^{A_i}(a|do_{nothing}) = \begin{cases} 1 & \text{if } a = \Theta_{A_i} \\ 0 & \text{otherwise} \end{cases} \tag{14}$$

Proposition 2. *An augmented belief causal graph where the DO node is set to the value nothing encodes the same distribution that an original causal graph.*

$$m^V_{\mathcal{G}_{aug}}(.|DO = do_{nothing}) = m^V_{\mathcal{G}} \qquad (15)$$

An intervention that attempts to set the variable A_i to the value a_{ij} is a certain action, then the bba relative to the DO node is a certain bba defined by:

$$m^{DO}(do) = \begin{cases} 1 & \text{if } do = do(a_{ij}) \\ 0 & \text{otherwise} \end{cases} \qquad (16)$$

Even thought it is a certain intervention, its consequences are uncertain. We denote by $\mathcal{F}_I$ the set of the focal elements representing the uncertain consequences of the intervention. In this case, we have:

$$\forall a \subseteq \Theta_{A_i}, m^{A_i}(a|do(a_{ij})) = \begin{cases} \alpha_j & \text{if } a \in \mathcal{F}_I \\ 0 & \text{otherwise} \end{cases} \qquad (17)$$

It is a generalization of the certain case where $\mathcal{F}_I = \{a_{ij}\}$ and $\alpha_j = 1$.

Proposition 3. *The new distribution of the target variable is computed from the combined effect of the intervention with the original causes.*

$$m^{A_i}(a|Pa_j(A_i), do) = \begin{cases} m^{A_i}(.|Pa_j(A_i)) \oplus m^{A_i}(.|do(a_{ij}))) & \text{if } do = do(a_{ij}). \\ m^{A_i}(a_{ij}|Pa_j(A_i)) & \text{if } do = do_{nothing}. \\ 0 & \text{otherwise}. \end{cases} \qquad (18)$$

Example 4. Some restaurants use salt to remove the bitter taste of the coffee. However this action may react with the initial causes (here the presence of sugar) to determine the sweetness of the coffee. The new joint distribution is therefore computed as shown in Table 3.

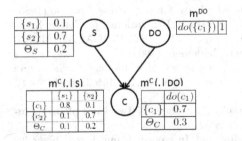

s_1	0.1
s_2	0.7
Θ_S	0.2

$m^C(.|s)$

	$\{s_1\}$	$\{s_2\}$
$\{c_1\}$	0.8	0.1
$\{c_2\}$	0.1	0.7
Θ_C	0.1	0.2

m^{DO}

$do(\{c_1\})$	1

$m^C(.|DO)$

	$do(c_1)$
$\{c_1\}$	0.7
Θ_C	0.3

Fig. 2. Augmented graph

Table 3. $m^C(.|s, do)$

	$\{(s_1, do(c_1))\}$	$\{(s_2, do(c_1))\}$
$\{c_1\}$	0.94	0.47
$\{c_2\}$	0.03	0.41
Θ_C	0.03	0.12

6   Conclusion

This paper provided a causal graphical model to deal with interventions under the belief function framework. We explained that interventions generally have uncertain consequences and should be well modeled. We showed that uncertain interventions have a natural encoding under the belief function framework and may be graphically modeled using belief causal networks. The effect of interventions are computed on altered networks, namely mutilated and augmented belief graphs with uncertain effects.

As future works, we intend to deal with interventions whose occurrences are uncertain. We also plan to explore the relationships between interventions and the belief changes using Jeffrey-Dempster's rule.

References

1. Ben Yaghlane, B., Mellouli, K.: Inference in directed evidential networks based on the transferable belief model. Int. J. Approx. Reasoning 48(2), 399–418 (2008)
2. Benferhat, S., Smaoui, S.: Possibilistic causal networks for handling interventions: A new propagation algorithm. In: AAAI, pp. 373–378 (2007)
3. Boukhris, I., Benferhat, S., Elouedi, Z.: Representing Belief Function Knowledge with Graphical Models. In: Xiong, H., Lee, W.B. (eds.) KSEM 2011. LNCS, vol. 7091, pp. 233–245. Springer, Heidelberg (2011)
4. Boukhris, I., Elouedi, Z., Benferhat, S.: Modeling interventions using belief causal networks. In: FLAIRS 2011, pp. 602–607 (2011)
5. Chan, H., Darwiche, A.: On the revision of probabilistic beliefs using uncertain evidence. Artif. Intell. 163(1), 67–90 (2005)
6. Darwiche, A.: Modeling and Reasoning with Bayesian Networks. Cambridge University Press (2009)
7. Dubois, D., Prade, H.: On the unicity of Dempster rule of combination. Int. J. Intell. System 1, 133–142 (1986)
8. Dubois, D.: Information Fusion and Revision in Qualitative and Quantitative Settings. In: Liu, W. (ed.) ECSQARU 2011. LNCS, vol. 6717, pp. 1–18. Springer, Heidelberg (2011)
9. Eberhardt, F., Scheines, R.: Interventions and causal inference. Philos. Sci. 74, 981–995 (2007)
10. Halpern, J.Y.: Reasoning about Uncertainty. The MIT Press (2003)
11. Ichihashi, H., Tanaka, H.: Jeffrey-like rules of conditioning for the Dempster-Shafer theory of evidence. Inter. J. Approx. Reasoning 3, 143–156 (1989)
12. Jeffrey, R.C.: The Logic of Decision, 2nd edn. Univ. Chicago Press, Chicago (1983)
13. Korb, K.B., Hope, L.R., Nicholson, A.E., Axnick, K.: Varieties of Causal Intervention. In: Zhang, C., W. Guesgen, H., Yeap, W.-K. (eds.) PRICAI 2004. LNCS (LNAI), vol. 3157, pp. 322–331. Springer, Heidelberg (2004)
14. Ma, J., Liu, W., Dubois, D., Prade, H.: Bridging jeffrey's rule, agm revision and dempster conditioning in the theory of evidence. Int. J. Art. Intell. Tools 20(4), 691–720 (2011)
15. Pearl, J.: Probabilistic reasoning in intelligent systems: Networks of plausible inference. Morgan Kaufmann Publishers (1988)
16. Pearl, J.: Causality: Models, Reasonning and Inference. Cambridge University Press (2000)

17. Shafer, G.: A Mathematical Theory of Evidence. Princeton Univ. Press, Princeton (1976)
18. Shafer, G.: Jeffrey's rule of conditioning. Philisophy of Sciences 48, 337–362 (1981)
19. Smets, P.: The combination of evidence in the transferable belief model. IEEE Trans. Pattern Anal. Mach. Intell. 12(5), 447–458 (1990)
20. Smets, P.: About updating. In: UAI 1991, pp. 378–385 (1991)
21. Smets, P.: Jeffrey's rule of conditioning generalized to belief functions. In: UAI 1993, pp. 500–505 (1993)
22. Teng, C.M.: Applications of causal inference. In: ISAIM (2012)
23. Xu, H., Smets, P.: Evidential reasoning with conditional belief functions. In: UAI 1994, pp. 598–606 (1994)

K-Modes Clustering Using Possibilistic Membership

Asma Ammar[1], Zied Elouedi[1], and Pawan Lingras[2]

[1] LARODEC, Institut Supérieur de Gestion de Tunis, Université de Tunis
41 Avenue de la Liberté, 2000 Le Bardo, Tunisie
asma.ammar@voila.fr, zied.elouedi@gmx.fr
[2] Department of Mathematics and Computing Science, Saint Marys University
Halifax, Nova Scotia, B3H 3C3, Canada
pawan@cs.smu.ca

Abstract. This paper describes an extension of the standard k-modes method (SKM) to cluster categorical objects under uncertain framework. Our proposed approach combines the SKM with possibility theory in order to obtain the so-called k-modes method based on possibilistic membership (KM-PM). This latter makes it possible to deal with uncertainty in the assignment of the objects to different clusters using possibilistic membership degrees. Besides, it facilitates the detection of boundary objects by taking into account of the similarity of each object to all clusters. The KM-PM also overcomes the numeric limitation of the existing possibilistic clustering approaches (i.e. the dealing only with numeric values) and easily handles the extreme cases of knowledge, namely the complete knowledge and the total ignorance. Simulations on real-world databases show that the proposed KM-PM algorithm gives more meaningful results.

1 Introduction

Clustering is a well known unsupervised technique from the machine learning area. Clustering methods aim to partition objects into subsets called clusters where objects of the same cluster share common characteristics, and objects from different clusters are dissimilar to each other.

Clustering methods can be divided into two categories according to the structure of the clusters obtained. They consist of crisp (or hard) clustering and soft clustering. In the crisp clustering, if an object is an element of a particular cluster it cannot be a member of any other cluster i.e. each object is forced to belong to exactly one cluster. However, in some cases, an object can share some similarities with other objects belonging to different clusters. As a result, it is more correct to take into account of these real-world situations and to adapt a soft partitioning where an object can be associated to multiple clusters. In this case, a membership degree is defined and it indicates the degree of belongingness of objects to more than one cluster.

In fact, using soft clustering conveys more information than crisp clustering by taking into account of different dependency and similarities between all objects (in same or in different clusters).

S. Greco et al. (Eds.): IPMU 2012, Part III, CCIS 299, pp. 596–605, 2012.

Among the well-known crisp clustering approaches, we can mention the k-means method [2][12] which provides interesting results when it clusters data with numeric attributes. This method has been improved by several researchers to deal with uncertainty in the belonging of objects to different clusters. Different soft clustering methods based on the k-means have been proposed namely the fuzzy c-means [4], the evidential c-means [13] and the possibilistic c-means [11] providing interesting results respectively in fuzzy, evidential and possibilistic frameworks.

Nevertheless, working only with numeric values limits the use of these approaches especially in data mining field where there are large databases containing categorical values. In order to overcome this limitation, Huang [8][10] has proposed the k-modes method, a version of the k-means approach dealing easily with categorical databases. The standard version of the k-modes method has been improved and combined by uncertainty theories namely the belief function and the possibility theories in order to handle uncertain framework especially in data mining field. We can mention the belief k-modes [3] and the possibilistic k-modes [1] which are two crisp approaches giving interesting results to cluster real-world uncertain databases with categorical attributes characterized by imperfect values.

As soft clustering can be of great practical interest, in this paper, we develop a new method under possibilistic environment in order to cluster categorical objects into soft partitions. In other words, our proposed method adapts the possibility theory to the k-modes approach in order to express the uncertainty in the belonging of objects to all clusters. The choice of this non-classical theory i.e. the possibility theory is due to its interesting clustering results in several works [11][15][16][18] and its aptitude to easily handle extreme cases of knowledge. In our method, we define a possibility distribution to each object reflecting the degree of belongingness of the training instances to different clusters.

An important motivation for using the possibilistic membership values is their ability to correctly interpret the degree of belongingness of each object to different clusters. Moreover, they offer the possibility to help the user to determine the final clusters and to identify the boundary objects.

This paper is organized as follows: Section 2 and Section 3 provide respectively an overview of the k-modes method and the possibility theory; Section 4 focuses on our proposed approach by explaining its main parameters. Section 5 details experimental results using real-world databases.

2   The K-Modes Method

The k-means method [2][12] is a well known approach that has shown spectacular performance for clustering objects with numeric attributes. Unfortunately, there are many databases containing only categorical training instances in data mining field and the k-means method is unable to cluster this type of attributes. To solve this problem, the k-modes method has been developed in [8][10] and has been improved in order to overcome the numeric limitation of the k-means approach and to cluster categorical data.

Generally, the k-modes algorithm uses the same principle as the k-means; but removes some of its limitations and keeps its performance. Comparison of the k-means the k-modes is described in Table 1.

Table 1. K-means vs. k-modes

	K-means (MacQueen 1967)	K-modes (Huang 1997)
Data	Continuous	Categorical
Cluster representative	Mean (centroid)	Mode
Distance measure	Numeric data measure	Simple matching
Update centroid/mode	Average of the attribute values of objects belonging to the same cluster	Frequency-based method
Clustering process	Same process	

Assume that we have of two categorical objects $X_1 = (x_{11}, x_{12}, ..., x_{1m})$ and $Y_1 = (y_{11}, y_{12}, ..., y_{1m})$ with m attributes. The simple matching dissimilarity measure d $(0 \leq d \leq m)$ is computed using Equation (1):

$$d(X_1, Y_1) = \sum_{t=1}^{m} \delta(x_{1t}, y_{1t}) \ . \tag{1}$$

$$\delta(x_{1t}, y_{1t}) = \begin{cases} 0 \text{ if } x_{1t} = y_{1t} \\ 1 \text{ if } x_{1t} \neq y_{1t} \ . \end{cases} \tag{2}$$

The objective function corresponding to the k-modes method for clustering a set of n categorical objects $S = \{X_1, X_2, ..., X_n\}$ into k clusters with $k \leq n$ is detailed in Equation (3):

$$\min \ D(W, Q) = \sum_{j=1}^{k} \sum_{i=1}^{n} \omega_{ij} d(X_i, Q_j) \ . \tag{3}$$

With $Q = (Q_1, Q_2, ..., Q_k)$ k-modes of S, where Q_j corresponds to a cluster C_j. $W = [\omega_{ij}]$ is an $n \times k$ matrix, $\sum_{j=1}^{k} \omega_{ij} = 1$ and $\omega_{ij} \in \{0, 1\}$ is the membership degree of the object X_i in the cluster C_j.

$$\omega_{ij} = \begin{cases} 0 \text{ if } X_i \notin C_j \\ 1 \text{ if } X_i \in C_j \ . \end{cases} \tag{4}$$

3 Possibility Theory

Possibility theory is an uncertainty theory proposed first by Zadeh in [17] then, developed by several researchers including Dubois and Prade [5][6][7]. In this section, we briefly review this theory by focusing on some of the basic concepts then we examine some possibilistic clustering approaches.

3.1   Possibility Distribution

Assume that $\Omega = \{\varpi_1, \varpi_2, ..., \varpi_i\}$ is the universe of discourse as defined in [17] by Zadeh. The possibility distribution function denoted by π is a fundamental concept in possibility theory and it associates to each element ϖ_i from Ω a value from the interval $L=[0, 1]$. L presents the possibilistic scale and it can be defined under qualitative case where only the order is important by $(L, <)$ or in the quantitative case by $[0, 1]$ (numerical possibility degrees). If $\pi(\varpi_i) = 1$ it means that it is fully possible that ϖ_i is achieved. However, if $\pi(\varpi_i) = 0$; ϖ_i can be interpreted as an impossible event.

It is also important to mention the extreme cases of knowledge in possibility theory which are the complete knowledge and the total ignorance defined respectively as follows:

- $\exists \varpi_0, \pi(\varpi_0) = 1$ and $\pi(\varpi) = 0$ otherwise,
- $\forall \varpi \in \Omega, \pi(\varpi) = 1$.

Moreover, a possibility distribution is normalized when it satisfies Equation (5):

$$max_i \{\pi(\varpi_i)\} = 1 . \tag{5}$$

3.2   Possibilistic Clustering

Several possibilistic clustering approaches are based on the fuzzy clustering concept. This latter has proved its performance to detect clusters with different forms i.e. volume and thin clusters (curves or surfaces).

The fuzzy c-means method (FCM) [4] is a well known fuzzy clustering approach that has shown interesting results. It is a soft clustering approach where each object is assigned to all the clusters with various degrees of membership. However, the FCM has a trouble in noisy environment and uses a probabilistic constraint leading to the misinterpretation of the compatibility degree of an object to different clusters.

Despite its limitations, the FCM approach has been considered as the basis of most fuzzy clustering approaches and even some possibilistic clustering methods mainly the possibilistic c-means denoted by PCM [11] which overcomes the FCM drawbacks.

Several works have dealt with the belonging of objects to different clusters and have shown interesting results through the use of the possibility theory. However, they are unable to work with categorical objects. They perform only with quantitative attributes, which limits their use especially in the data mining field where there is a large number of categorical databases.

4   The K-Modes Method with Possibilistic Membership

The use of an appropriate objective function is a primary task allowing the success of clustering methods and guarantees interesting results. To this end, we have followed these requirements to set the objective function of our method (i.e. KM-PM):

1. Adapt an appropriate dissimilarity measure to calculate the dissimilarity between modes and objects.
2. Set membership degrees in order to specify the degree of belongingness of each object to all clusters.
3. Represent the membership values through possibilistic degrees defined in possibility theory for dealing with uncertainty.

The KM-PM method is based on the minimization of the following objective function (O.F.) described and compared to the fuzzy k-modes (FKM) [9] and the possibilistic c-means (PCM) [11] objective functions in Table 2.

Table 2. The O.F. of the KM-PM, the FKM and the PCM

Fuzzy k-modes	Possibilistic c-means	
$\sum_{j=1}^{k} \sum_{i=1}^{n} \omega_{ij}^{\alpha} d(X_i, Q_j)$	$\sum_{j=1}^{k} \sum_{i=1}^{n} \omega_{ij}^{\alpha} d_{ij}^{2} + \sum_{j=1}^{k} \eta_j \sum_{i=1}^{n} (1 - \omega_{ij})^{\alpha}$	
$\alpha > 1,\ 0 \leq \omega_{ij} \leq 1$ and $\sum_{j=1}^{k} \omega_{ij} = 1$	η is the penalty term and α the fuzziness degree	
d is the simple matching measure	d_{ij}^{2} is squared Euclidean distance	
KM-PM		
$\sum_{j=1}^{k} \sum_{i=1}^{n} \omega_{ij} d(X_i, Q_j)$		
$\max_j \omega_{ij} = 1$ for all i and $0 \leq \omega_{ij} \leq 1$		
d is the simple matching measure and ω_{ij} the possibilistic membership degree		

The O.F. of the KM-PM has a close link with the fuzzy k-modes O.F. since, both of them use the same dissimilarity measure d and a membership degree ω describing the uncertainty in the belonging of the object to different clusters. However, the possibilistic c-means O.F. differs from the O.F. of our method by using the Euclidean distance applied to numeric attributes and the penalty term to avoid the misinterpretation of the object [11].

Our proposed possibilistic method uses different parameters described in detail as follows:

1. **The simple matching dissimilarity measure:** allowing the computation of the dissimilarity between the objects and the modes. It compares each attribute value relative to the mode to the attribute value of all objects using Equation (1).
2. **The possibilistic membership degree:** $\omega_{ij} \in [0, 1]$ is obtained as follows: We compute the dissimilarity values between each object and modes using Equation (1). After that, we transform the dissimilarity (dis) to a similarity degree (sim) by applying this formula: $sim = A - dis$, where A is the total number of attributes. Then, we divide the obtained value by A in order to normalize it and to obtain ω_{ij} between 0 and 1. This latter will refer to the degree of belongingness of the object i to the cluster j.
   We can mention two extreme cases:

   − $\omega_{ij}=0$, it means that the object i does not belong to the cluster j i.e. there is no similarity between the object and the mode.

- $\omega_{ij}=1$, in this case we are sure that the object i belongs to the cluster j and we can conclude that it is similar to its mode.

Note that if $\omega_{ij} > \omega_{i(j+1)}$ (respectively $\omega_{ij} < \omega_{i(j+1)}$) it means that the object i belongs to the cluster j more (respectively less) than to the cluster $j+1$.

3. **A new method to update clusters' modes:** we need a method that takes into account of the possibilistic membership degrees ω of each object to different clusters when it updates the modes. So, the updating of the clusters' modes will depend on the possibilistic membership degrees.

   The following steps are followed to update the modes:
   - First, we compute the dissimilarities between modes and objects then we determine ω_{ij} of the object i to the cluster j as described above.
   - After that, for each value v of the attribute t, we sum the degree ω_{ijtv} relative to the object i in the cluster j.
   - Finally, the value v that achieves the maximum of the summation will represent the new value in the mode.

   Therefore, the update of the cluster modes is described by the Equation (6):

$$\forall j \in k, t \in A, Mode_{jt} = \max_v \sum_{i=1}^n \omega_{ijtv} \ . \tag{6}$$

with

$$\forall i \in n, \max_j (\omega_{ij}) = 1 \ . \tag{7}$$

Equation (7) guarantees the normalization.

By using these parameters, it is expected that the KM-PM gives us more accurate and exact results since our method avoids the SKM drawbacks and keeps its effectiveness.

The KM-PM algorithm, described as follows, takes as input a categorical data set and the number of clusters to form (k). It provides as a result the objects assigned to k clusters with possibilistic membership. As the KM-PM algorithm is an extension of the SKM algorithm, it guarantees the minimization of the objective function described in Table 2 by using the parameters defined above.

Algorithm. KM-PM

Begin

1. *Select randomly the k initial modes, one mode for each cluster.*
2. *Allocate each object to all clusters based on possibilistic membership degrees after computing the distance measure using Equation (1).*
3. *Update the cluster mode using Equation (6).*
4. *Retest the similarity between objects and modes. Reallocate objects to clusters using possibilistic membership degrees then update the modes.*
5. *Repeat (4) until all objects are stable.*

End.

---

5 Experiments

5.1 The Framework

In order to test our proposed method and obtain correct results, we carry out eight runs on different categorical real-world databases from UCI: Machine Learning Repository [14]. The used data sets are illustrated in Table 3 where #Classes presents the number of clusters to form.

Table 3. Description of the used data sets

Datatbases	#Instances	#Attributes	#Classes	Notations
Shuttle Landing Control	15	6	2	SLC
Balloons	20	4	2	Bal
Post-Operative Patient	90	8	3	POP
Congressional Voting Records	435	16	2	CVR
Balance Scale	625	4	3	BS
Tic-Tac-Toe Endgame	958	9	2	TE
Solar-Flare	1389	10	3	SF
Car Evaluation	1728	6	4	CE

5.2 Evaluation Criteria

To evaluate the performance of our method, we emphasize on three evaluation criteria namely the accuracy, the number of iterations and the execution time.

1. The accuracy (AC) [8] is defined by this formula $AC=\frac{\sum_{j=1}^{k} a_j}{n}$ with $k \leq n$, n presents the total number of objects and a_j is the number of correctly classified objects.
2. The number of iterations (IN) presents the iterations number needed to obtain the final partitions. They are relative to the main program.
3. The execution time (ET) is the time taken to execute the whole algorithm.

5.3 Experimental Results

The main aim of this section is to illustrate the experimental results given by the new possibilistic method that uses possibilistic membership degrees. Thus, we cross validate by dividing observations randomly into a training set and a test set. We focus on the accuracy, the number of iterations and the execution times. We apply our possibilistic algorithm to eight different categorical data sets from UCI: Machine Learning Repository [14].

All results are analyzed and detailed in Table 4.

Through Table 4, we can observe that the KM-PM gives more accurate results for most databases than the standard method (SKM). For example for the Solar-Flare data set, we obtain an accuracy of 0.91 by applying the KM-PM and 0.87 by using the SKM.

Table 4. The evaluation criteria of the proposed method vs. SKM

Data sets	SLC	Bal	POP	CVR	BS	TE	SF	CE
SKM								
AC	0.61	0.52	0.684	0.825	0.785	0.513	0.87	0.795
IN	8	9	11	12	13	12	14	11
ET/second	12.431	14.551	17.238	29.662	37.819	128.989	2661.634	3248.613
KM-PM								
AC	0.63	0.65	0.74	0.79	0.82	0.59	0.91	0.87
IN	4	4	8	6	2	10	12	12
ET/second	10.28	12.56	15.23	28.09	31.41	60.87	87.39	197.63

Moreover, the KM-PM algorithm guarantees interesting results obtained only after few number of iterations and execution time. For the Balance scale data set for example, only two iterations (corresponding to 31.41 seconds) are needed for the KM-PM to obtain the final results. However, the SKM needs 13 iterations (corresponding to 37.819 seconds) to get final partitions.

Besides, we observe that the ET (calculated per second) increases proportionally with the number of instances in the training set. However, the ET corresponding to the KM-PM is always lower than the standard approach especially for the Solar-flare and the Car evaluation data sets.

Figure 1 explains graphically the AC of the KM-PM compared to the SKM.

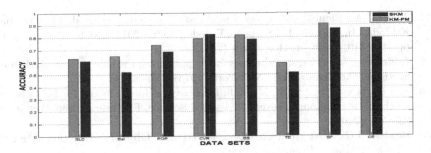

Fig. 1. The AC of the KM-PM vs. SKM

It is obvious that Figure 1 emphasizes on the results of the KM-PM based on the first evaluation criterion. It shows again that the KM-PM has the highest AC.

The improvement of the SKM results through the KM-PM is due to the ability of the new method to provide more precise assignment of each object to the corresponding clusters. In fact, there are some objects in the training set that cannot be classified to exactly one cluster due to their similarities to more than one set. They have common characteristics. As a result, considering these objects as parts of different clusters based on the possibilistic membership degrees translates their similarities to several sets and does not force any instance to belong to just one cluster. Generally, we can conclude based on the AC, the IN and the ET that the KM-PM improves the quality of clustering results. It assigns the degree of belongingness of each object to all clusters in order to detect boundary objects and to give precise membership.

6   Conclusion

In this paper, we have developed a new method combining possibility theory and k-modes method in order to deal with categorical values and handle uncertainty in the belonging of the objects to different clusters by using possibilistic membership degrees.

In order to adapt appropriate parameters to our proposed approach, we have analysed some existing methods mainly the PCM [11] and the FKM [9]. After that, we have set some requirements to fix the objective function of our algorithm. Finally, we have tested the KM-PM on several real-world databases [14] and the results indicate the performance gain from this new possibilistic method.

As future work, other aspects of uncertainty in possibilistic framework will be studied. Moreover, our proposed approach can be extended to develop other methods such as the dynamic possiblistic k-modes.

References

1. Ammar, A., Elouedi, Z.: A New Possibilistic Clustering Method: The Possibilistic K-Modes. In: Pirrone, R., Sorbello, F. (eds.) AI*IA 2011. LNCS (LNAI), vol. 6934, pp. 413–419. Springer, Heidelberg (2011)
2. Anderberg, M.R.: Cluster Analysis for Applications. Probability and Mathematical Statistics. Academic Press, New York (1973)
3. Ben Hariz, S., Elouedi, Z., Mellouli, K.: Selection Initial modes for Belief K-modes Method. International Journal of Applied Science, Engineering and Technology 4, 233–242 (2007)
4. Bezdek, J.C.: Pattern Recognition with Fuzzy Objective Function Algorithms. Kluwer Academic Publishers (1981)
5. Dubois, D., Prade, H.: Possibility theory: An approach to computerized processing of uncertainty. Plenium Press, New York (1988)
6. Dubois, D., Prade, H.: Possibility theory and data fusion in poorly informed environments. Control Engineering Practice 25, 811–823 (1994)
7. Dubois, D., Prade, H.: Possibility theory: Qualitative and quantitative aspects. In: Gabbay, D.M., Smets, P. (eds.) Handbook of Defeasible Reasoning and Uncertainty Management Systems, vol. I, pp. 169–226. Kluwer Academic Publishers, Netherlands (1998)
8. Huang, Z.: Extensions to the k-means algorithm for clustering large data sets with categorical values. Data Mining Knowl. Discov. 2, 283–304 (1998)
9. Huang, Z., Ng, M.K.: A Fuzzy k-Modes Algorithm for Clustering Categorical Data. IEEE Transactions on Fuzzy Systems 7, 446–452 (1999)
10. Huang, Z., Ng, M.K.: A note on k-modes clustering. Journal of Classification 20, 257–261 (2003)

11. Krishnapuram, R., Keller, J.M.: A possibilistic approach to clustering. IEEE Trans. Fuzzy System 1, 98–110 (1993)
12. MacQueen, J.B.: Some methods for classification and analysis of multivariate observations. In: The 5th Berkeley Symposium on Mathematical Statistics and Probability, pp. 281–297 (1967)
13. Masson, M.H., Denoeux, T.: ECM: An evidential version of the fuzzy c-means algorithm. Pattern Recognition 41, 1384–1397 (2008)
14. Murphy, M.P., Aha, D.W.: Uci repository databases (1996), http://www.ics.uci.edu/mlearn
15. Pal, N.R., Pal, K., Keller, J.M., Bezdek, J.C.: A possibilistic fuzzy c-means clustering algorithm. IEEE Transactions on Fuzzy Systems, 517–530 (2005)
16. Yang, M.S., Wu, K.L.: Unsupervised possibilistic clustering. Pattern Recognition 39, 5–21 (2006)
17. Zadeh, L.A.: Fuzzy sets as a basis for a theory of possibility. Fuzzy Sets and Systems 1, 3–28 (1978)
18. Zhang, J.S., Leung, Y.W.: Improved possibilistic c-means clustering algorithms. IEEE Transactions on Fuzzy Systems 23 (2004)

Author Index